Abney, Abner, Abna, Abnee

Who Were You?

Great Grandfather,
I love you.
Who were you?
I wish I could bounce on your knee,
Like I did with your son.
But before my time began,
Your time on Earth was done.

Great Grandmother,
I love you.
Who were you?
I wish you could hug me dearly,
Like you did with your daughter.
And teach me about Jesus,
The way you taught her.

Ancestors, all
I love you.
Who were you?
On parchment and stone,
Much more than a name.
For parts of what you were
Are all that I became.

R. Robert Abney Jr.
(I woke from a dream and wrote this at 3:00 a.m.)
Monday, the 5th of October, 2020
Chalmette, Louisiana

Earlier Works by the Author

- *The Historian* (official magazine of the *Society of United Genealogists, International*) (early 1990's)
- *The Art of Ancestral Chart Drawing "The Abney Method"* (published by *the Society of United Genealogists, International 1992*)
- *The History of the Noble de Saint-Germain Family (1st edition, self-published 1993)*
- *The Abney Family Researcher* (official newsletter of the *Centralized Abney Archives*) (1996-2003)
- *Abney: Ancestry and Genealogy of Dr. Abraham Abney of Virginia* (1st edition, 1st printing soft cover)
  - *ISBN: 978-0-999-3282-1-7; LCCN: 2018941901* (published May 28, 2018)
- *Abney: Ancestry and Genealogy of Dr. Abraham Abney of Virginia* (1st edition, 1st printing hard cover)
  - *ISBN: 978-0-999-3282-1-7; LCCN: 2018941901* (published May 28, 2018)
- *Abney: Ancestry and Genealogy of Dr. Abraham Abney of Virginia* (1st edition, 2nd printing hard cover)
  - *ISBN: 978-0-999-3282-0-0; LCCN: 2017915356* (second [perpetual] printing June 2018)
- *Abney: Ancestry and Genealogy of Dr. Abraham Abney of Virginia* (2nd edition, hard cover only)
  - *ISBN: 978-0-9993282-2-4; LCCN: 2018952526* (published September 3, 2018, perpetual printing)
- *Don't Fear the Past* (article) published in *the Historian*; reprinted in the newsletter of the Ottawa Branch of the Ontario Genealogical Society, *Ontario Ancestors*
- a variety of poems (some of which are included in his books), songs, and news articles…
- also, creator of the cartoon: *Gene E. Ologist* and his wife, *Jeanie Ologist*

~ Abney, Abner, Abna, Abnee ~
Ancestry and Genealogy of
Abner Abney of Virginia
First Edition

Raymond Robert "Bobby" Abney Jr., author

including the independent research of
Morgan F. Abney, John M. Abney, Sandy Abner Cook, Judy Lewis Vietri & Grace Crouch Prater

Chalmette, St. Bernard Parish, Louisiana
2020

Printed in the United States of America by:

IngramSpark

Published November 22, 2020 on the birthday of the author's grandfather:
Robert Ralph Abney
(22 Nov 1889-15 Apr 1964) by:

Raymond Robert Abney Jr.
1213 Indiana St.
Chalmette, LA 70043

Additional copies of this book may be ordered from rrabneyjr@hotmail.com
(see order form near the back of the book)

Book Cover created by Stacie Kyomi Arai Abney

ISBN: 978-0-9993282-3-1

Library of Congress Control Number: 2020918505

About the Author

Raymond Robert "RR" Abney Jr. "the Historian"

The youngest of two children, and only son of Raymond Robert Abney Sr. and Clothilde Anysia Hingle, Raymond Robert "Bobby" Abney Jr. was born in Touro Infirmary, New Orleans, Orleans Parish, Louisiana, on 16 January 1958. The author is a 6th great-grandnephew of Abner Abney, the subject of this book. "RR" sired six children before he married Mary Grace Lazo Mercader on 8 Apr 2018 in Manila, Philippines. They had two children: Antoine-Robert Mercader "Merc" Abney (17 Nov 2018) who died in infancy in Chalmette, LA; and Marae Mercedes "Mercy" Abney (7 Jul 2019) who was stillborn in Slidell, LA. Should the reader be interested in discovering more about the author, he/she is encouraged to obtain the **Abney Family History Series, Volume I**, titled **Abney**, subtitled **Ancestry and Genealogy of Dr. Abraham Abney of Virginia**.

The Author's Tribute to Genealogists of Yore

Instead of a traditional "About the Author", I'd like to memorialize, with honor, a few of those Abney researchers who came before me. The earlier days of genealogical research are nearly lost. Back then, one had to be a serious sleuth, studying thousands of documents looking for the one that might prove one more generation or one more spouse. Younger family historians, new to the "hobby" (obsession) will scant know the pleasure of walking through muddy cemeteries, reading through delicate, centuries-old documents in dusty courthouses, and going through sheet-after-sheet of microfiche and reel-after-reel of microfilm in quiet archives and libraries. It is almost a religious experience touching a document which was signed by one's ancestor. As concerns the electronic transfer of data, as I said (after receiving a letter from the esteemed Cousin Douglas Overton Blue), "It is a shame the beauty of handwritten letters is lost to this generation". There was a feeling a person received from a handwritten letter that is absent in typewritten letters. The old, archaic ways, although inefficient, were fun and exciting! But out with the old and in with the new, as the adage goes. The good news is, with the advent of computers and the Internet, old documents, many of which were lost to the ravages of the Earth's whims (as mine was in Hurricane Katrina), can now be saved forever. A computer image is not a beautiful document. Yet, it is better to have an image of a document in perpetuity, than to risk losing it as we've lost so many treasured documents.

Having worked with many of the notable genealogists from the older generations, I stand in awe of those earlier researchers, who laid the very foundation of this current author's works. Yes, those earlier researchers had many flaws in their conclusions. But any work attempting to cover such a large period of history will, inevitably, have errors and omissions, my own included.

I therefore think it only fitting to honor a few of the genealogists who pioneered the study of the Abney family.

From the *Greatest Generation* *(the G.I. Generation)* (born 1901-1927) with whom I've personally corresponded:

John Robert Hensell, author 1910-2000		Charlotte Abney Metzger, author 1912-2003		Jennie Helen Abney Gant, beloved cousin 1927-2020
Blanche Shivers Abna 1903-1988	Wilda Smith Brent 1908-1991	Lois Gracie Abna Duckett 1908-1984	Edward W. Reed 1913-1997	John Kennedy Brown Sr. 1914-1995
Annie Sherard Jeter 1916-1998	Maj. Henry Kibby Thayer Jr. 1916-2006	William Gilder Godsey Sr. 1917-2002	Miriam Korff York 1918-2006	Frederick Sherwood Abney 1919-2004
Mary Collie Cooper 1921-2003	James Marion Chaney Abney 1922-1998	Desma Clarkson Johnson 1922-2018	Earl Edward Tipton 1929-2013	Kathryn Hamilton Willis born 1923
DeLoris Strohm Fellars born 1923	Louis Oswell Abney 1923-2014	Joe Herbert Baker Jr. 1924-2001	Hazel Dean Overstreet 1920-2003	Marjorie Johnson Diamond 1923-2011
John Abney Kirkpatrick 1925-2007	Mary Jo Priddy Powell 1925-1919	Virginia Abney Downs 1926-2015	Grace Fisher Deupree 1927-2017	Colleen Moore Kenyon 1927-2020

...and those in the *Silent Generation* *(the Lucky Few)* (born 1928-1945) with whom I've personally corresponded:

Morgan Floyd Abney, contributor born 1937		Margaret Griffey Harlow, mentor born 1929-2019		
Ella Rogers Abney born 1928	Capt. James Irvin Johnston 1929-2012	Douglas Overton Blue born 1929	Nona Edwards McPherson born 1929	Carolyn Berry Bishop Becker 1930-2015
Donald Elson Abney born 1930	Carrie Scales Evans born 1931	Richard Lee Abney 1932-2013	Roy Edward Addicks Sr. born 1933	Geraldine Coffman Edwards born 1933
Mary Blain Pruitt 1936-2006	Luther "Brabham" Dukes born 1936	Huston "Earl" Abney 1937-2019	Myrna Holcomb Lazenby born 1937	Barbara Lear Holland born 1937
Glee Newman Burgher born 1937	James Kenneth Abney Jr. born 1939	Robert Hal Abney born 1939	Mary Kendall Abney 1939-2003	William G. Kennerly Sr. born 1940
Joseph Clair Myers born 1940	Lucy Hardy Bryan born 1941	Cora Weaver East born 1941	Ira Charles Franklin 1942-2019	Lynda Greene Allen born 1942
Fred Gordon Abney born 1943	Ruth Ackerman Dunham born 1944	Sandra Abney Eastwood born 1944	Janice Batte Craven born 1945	John Bentley Mays born 1941

...and let's memorialize those Abney researchers born in the *Nineteenth Century* who truly pioneered Abney genealogy:

Hon. John Rutledge Abney 1850-1927	John Abney Chapman 1826-1906	John Pym Yeatman 1830-1910	James Addison Abney Sr 1846-1947	Isham Goss Abney 1857-1945
Agatha Abney Woodson 1859-1952	Samuel Edward Mays 1864-1932	Martin Jackson Abney 1872-1948	Howard Teasley Abney 1894-1956	Ted Butler Bernard 1899-1988

...and a man born in the *Eighteenth Century* who loved his family genealogy:

Thomas Hamilton Abney 1793-1870
...who on Aug. 30, 1859 wrote, in a letter to his son, Alexander Abney: *I was under the impression that I had given you chronological account of our genealogy, and I know that I have, but you have paid so little attention to it, and it ought to be the most cherished reminiscence of our lives to remember our genealogy, especially when we can trace it back for centuries with so much gratitude to God and satisfaction to ourselves.*

Of course, there are countless others, some I never knew, some whose work has been lost. But these are some of those genealogists I most recognize as the great pioneers of Abney family research. Thank you, one and all, for your wonderful work with the Abney family; And God bless you!

Your appreciative *Baby Boomer* cousin,

Raymond Robert "Bobby" Abney Jr.
Fortiter et Honeste

Dedications

(First Dedication)

for my beloved wife…

Mary Grace Lazo Mercader Abney

of Calbayog, Samar, Philippines

Your patience has eased my mind and your love has filled my heart.
You are my forever girl.

(Second Dedication)

for my beloved son…

Antoine-Robert Mercader "Merc" Abney

of Chalmette, St. Bernard Parish, Louisiana
17th November 2018
aged 35 minutes

Thank you for saying "hello" before joining our family in Heaven.
Born in my hands, I was the first to hold you and kiss you.
You will always be missed and remembered and loved.

(Third Dedication)

for my beloved daughter…

Marae Mercedes "Mercy" Abney

of Slidell, St. Tammany Parish, Louisiana
7th July 2019
stillborn

I miss singing "Daddy's Little Girl" to you.
You have my undying love.

About the Contributors

Morgan Floyd Abney (descendant of Abner Abney via Hezekiah Abney)

Morgan Floyd Abney is a descendant of Dannett Abney Sr. through his son, Abner Abney (the subject of this book). This second volume of the **Abney Family History Series** was his brainchild. Morgan was born in 1937 in Giles Holler, Lee County, Virginia. In 1950 he joined the U. S. Marine Corps and later transferred to the United States Army in 1955. He served a total of 30 years retiring in 1980. His service included four tours in Vietnam. After retiring from the military, he started his own auto repair business, *Morgan's Automotive* and kept it until his health required giving it up in 2013. At about the same time he became interested in genealogy and has been pursuing his family history ever since and helping out many other Abney descendants along the way. One of his unfinished tasks is to find the burial location of his great-grandfather, and Confederate veteran, Pinkney Floyd Abney. Morgan Abney resides with his wife, Janet in Georgetown, Williamson County, Texas. Because of Cousin Morgan, much research on the line of Abner Abney which has helped the author to solidify the position of Abner's grandson and namesake, Pvt. Abner Abney as a son of Elisha Abney Sr. Moreover, Cousin Morgan is a great patriot who loves his country and his family.

Sandrea Kay "Sandy" Abner Cook (descendant of Abner Abney via Menan Abner)

Sandy Abner Cook is descendant of Abner Abney, the subject of this book. Sandy's interest in family history was nurtured as a child by her paternal grandmother, Amanda Cobb Abner aka Mom Abner. Pop Abner, her grandfather, whose birth name was Robert "Boyd" Abner and her grandmother grew up in the mountains of Knox County, in Eastern Kentucky. Sandy, a retired elementary teacher, and her husband Fred live in Southern Indiana. They love to travel, at times stopping along the way to research family. Sandy's wonderful knowledge of the family of Menan Abner has helped this author to more properly report this family group and their descendants.

Judy May Lewis Vietri (descendant of Abner Abney via John Abney Sr.)

Judy Lewis Vietri is 81 years young, and has been enjoying genealogy since she was in her 40's. Her grandmother mentioned to her that her family was related to the outlaw gang known as the Dalton Boys (and several other gangs, as well). She loved having outlaws for relatives and began working on her family history. Judy's work, especially her census work, proved invaluable to connecting Menan Abner to his children. Sandy Abner Cook continues that work, but rightfully credits Judy for the initial breakthrough. Judy is still living in the same house they purchased in 1966.

John Michael Abney (descendant of George Abney)

John Michael Abney is a descendant of Dannett Abney Sr., though his son George Abney (ca.1697 - 1766). John has been involved in genealogy since the bug bit him in the fall of 1992. He has attended multiple courses at the Institute of Genealogy and Historical Research, then at Samford University and has taught beginning genealogy classes for his local genealogy society and community college. He is an active member of a number of state and local genealogy and historical societies and is a past Board member of the Missouri State Genealogical Association. He currently serves as the Newsletter Editor and Recording Secretary for the Iron County (MO) Historical Society. He resides in Farmington, MO with his wife Karen and their granddaughter Samantha. John's expertise on the line of Elisha Abney Sr., wonderful ability to discover documentation and especially proofreading has been a great blessing to the author.

Grace Lynette Crouch Prater (descendant of Paul Abney)

Grace Lynette Crouch Prater was born August 18, 1967 to Virginia Mae Abney and Eugene Thomas Crouch, in Lexington, Ky. She got started in genealogy in high school for a homework assignment. That was all it took to get her hooked on this wonderful hobby. She began working on the Abney line in 1983. Grace has three children and ten grandchildren. She graduated college with a Graphic Arts degree and later went on to get degrees in Mechanical Drafting, Crime Scene Photography and Criminal Justice.

Genealogists of Abner Abney's Line

I would like to recognize the following family researchers/genealogists whom, as far as we can determine, are descended from Abner **Abney**, and have researched the Abney family and related families. I have been pleased to personally work with these fine researchers:

Lois Grace Dell "Gracie" Abna Duckett, Carrie Abner Ford*, Christopher Abner, Geraldine Abner*, Jerimy Sean Abner, Ronald Ray Abner*, Sandrea "Sandy" Abner Cook (contributor), Steve Tyson Abner, Anita Abney (wife of Daniel Abney), Cathy Lynn Abney Burden, Charlotte Ann Abney Metzger (author), Deborah Abney Blus, Huston "Earl" Abney, James Marion Chaney Abney, Jeffery Earl "Jeff" Abney, Jerrell Wayne Abney, Morgan Floyd Abney (originator, contributor), Omar "William" Abney, Patsy Ruth Abney Dyke, Sherry Baker (cousin to the Kentucky Abners), Barbara Kristen Bailey Abney, Barbara Bailey, Regina Barnes*, Carolyn Berry Bishop Becker (see addenda, page 266), Deborah "Rachel" Bishop (see addenda, page 266), Janie Bishop Campbell, Owen Blevins*, Penny Brewer Blankinship, Penny Brown, Wanda Conley*, Cindy Crane*, Delores Darlene Dixon Renfroe, Doris Dorf*, Martin C. Finch, Frankie "Jeanine" Fraley Wiley, Mary Elizabeth Greear South, Tony Hammock, Cynthia Ann Hillis McBride, Billy "Christopher" Hunt, Kirk Christopher Jenkins, Kimberly Johnson, Marjorie K. Johnson Diamond, Mary Louise Kendall Abney, William Glenn "Billy" Kinsolving Jr., Laura Marie Knoll Lamb, Judy Lewis Vietri (contributor), Laura E. Metcalf Johnson, Janice Katherine "Jan" Miller Elliott, Lecia Gayle Moore House, Joseph Clair Myers Jr., Edward Nove "Eddie" Renfroe, Ruth Ann Robinson Ruesing, Jonathan Logan Smith, Penny Whitaker Brown, others.

* indicates that the information on this genealogist's line was lost in the author's collection to Hurricane Katrina.

I, who bring you the *Abney Family History Series, Vol. II*, would like to thank each of these genealogists for their time and efforts spent on researching the **Abney** family. Their work went neither unrecognized nor unappreciated. If I've missed anyone, please accept my apology. Through the many difficult times in life, it is often easy to forget those who help you most. Computer crashes and hurricanes notwithstanding, I bring you this book on our wonderful family, variously named: Abney, Abner, Abna and Abnee.

your cousin,

Raymond Robert "Bobby" Abney Jr.
Fortiter et Honeste

As mentioned in volume I, there are, no doubt, many others. However, a consequence of a computer crash in the 1990's caused the loss of some 60 or more lines of data from genealogists. To these unnamed genealogists, I apologize.

Please see each individual genealogist's entry (indexed) for their contribution to this work.

Abbreviations & Symbols
Used in this Book

Abbreviations & symbols used in this book…

The date format used in this book is dd-mmm-yyyy (i.e. 16 Jan 1958) or d-mmm-yyyy (i.e. 5 Feb 1992)

The months of the year shall be written as follows:
Jan   Feb   Mar   Apr   May   Jun   Jul   Aug   Sep   Oct   Nov   Dec

The days of the week shall be written as follows:
Sun   Mon   Tue   Wed   Thu   Fri   Sat

Standard two-letter USA state abbreviations and two-letter Canadian province abbreviations will be used.

Some Abbreviations used in this book and on documents

Abbreviation	Meaning	Abbreviation	Meaning
"Symbols" and "Numbers"		**"H"**	
1h, 2h…	1st husband, 2nd husband…	h/o	husband of
1w, 2w, 3w…	1st wife, 2nd wife, 3rd wife…	Hosp.	Hospital
&c.	etc. (and others)	**"I"**	
£	British Pound Sterling		
[#]£ [#]s. [#] p.	[#] pounds [#] shillings [#] pence	Iss.	Issue (progeny, children)
† or d.	died		
=, m., marr.	married	**"J"**	
≠	unmarried, never married	Jr. or Junr. (sometimes son of Sr.)	Junior (used to differentiate two persons of the same name)
ſ	"Long s" (Old English)		
(1812)	War of 1812 (1812-1815)	**"K"**	
		(Korea)	Korean War (1950-1953)
"A"			
a. or ac.	acre of land	**"L"**	
Accot. or Acct.	Account	lbs.	pounds (measure of weight)
ae.	age (in years)		
aft.	after	**"M"**	
Am.	American (U.S.A.)	m/o	mother of
ARW, Am. Rev.	American Rev. War 1765-1783	m., marr., =	married
		Mem.	Memorial (in cemetery names)
"B"		Meth.	Methodist
b/o	brother of	MOB&S	Mil. Order of the Bars & Stars
b.	born	MW	Mexican-Am. War 1846-1848
bapt. or bp.	baptized		
bef.	before	**"N"**	
Bib.	Bible (usually a family Bible)	Nam	Viet Nam War soldier (1955-75)
br., adj.	boardering (adjacent to)	(n.n.)	Nomen nescio (*I do not know [the name, or the surname]*)
BNO	Battle of New Orleans (1815)	**"O"**	
bur.	buried	obit	obituary
"C"		orig., originator	originator for the writing of this book, Morgan F. Abney (#1156)
(c)	Companion of William I		
ca.	circa (about, approximately)	**"P"**	
CA	Continental Army (Am. Rev.)	p	"by" (in Old English)
Cem.	Cemetery	Par.	parish (in LA - in lieu of county)
Cen.	Census record	Plt., Plts.	plaintiff, plaintiffs in court
Ch.	Church		
Co.	County	**"R"**	
Cr. or Crk.	Creek	r. or Riv. or R.	river
(CSA)	Confederate Soldier 1860-5	RD	Revolutionary War Doctor
CSA, C.S.A.	Confederate States of America	RS	Revolutionary War Soldier
Currt.	Current (as in Current Money)		

"D"		"S"	
d/o	daughter of	/s/	signed
d. or †	died	s/o	son of
DAR	Daughters of the Am. Rev.	SAR	Sons of the Am. Rev.
DCV	Daughters of Confederate Vets.	SCV	Sons of Confederate Veterans
dau. or dau	daughter	Sd.	said (previously mentioned)
decd. or deced.	deceased	Sr. or Senr. (Sometimes father of Jr.)	Senior (used to differentiate two persons of the same name.)
Defendt.	defendant (in a court case)	St.	Saint, sometimes street
Depy. Sherf.	Deputy Sheriff	"T"	
Dist.	District (div. of colony or state)	Terr.	Territory (before statehood)
dt.	date	th.	thrived (was living)
		tobo.	tobacco
"E"		Twp	township within a county
Esq.	Esquire		
est.	estimated (less accurate than ca.)	"U"	
Exrs.	Executors (will)	UA	Union Soldier (1860-1865)
		UMC	United Methodist Church
"F"			
f/o	father of	"V"	
FCMC	1st Congregational Meth. Ch.	Viz. or Vizt.	videlicet (that is to say…)
FIW	French & Indian War 1754-1763		
FW	Florida War 1835-1842	"W"	
		/w/	witness signature
"G"		w/o	wife of
Gen. or gen'l	General (highest ranking officer)	wdo	widower, widow
Gent. or Gentn.	Gentleman (nobleman)	WWI	World War I soldier (1914-18)
(gen.)	genealogist	WWII	World War II soldier (1939-45)
(gen-DAR)	DAR person and/or genealogist	"Y"	
(Gen.#)	Generation Number	ye	plural form of thou (your)
		yt.	abbreviation of "that"

Some Given Name Abbreviations and Nicknames

Abbreviation	Name	Nickname
Abra., Abram., Abrm., Abe.	Abraham	Abe
Artr.	Arthur	Art
Benj.	Benjamin	Benny
Casan., Casana	Cassandra	
Cathn., Kathn.	Catherine, Katherine	Cathy, Katie, Kate
Chas.	Charles	Charlie, Chuck
Dant.	Dannett, Dannitt, Danite, &c.	
Davd., Dd.	David	Dave, Davy
Edw.	Edward	Ed, Eddie
Edm.	Edmund	Ed, Eddie
Eliz.	Elizabeth	Liz, Lizzie
	Dorothy	Dolly
Geo.	George (Fr. Georges)	
Hy., Heny.	Henry	Hank
Jas.	James	Jim, Jimmy
Jn.	John	Johnny
Jno., Jon.	Jonathan	Johnny
Jos.	Joseph	Joe, Joey
Margt.	Margaret	Marge, Margie, Maggie
	Martha	Patsy
	Mary	Molly
Michl.	Michael	Mike
Nathl., Nat.	Nathaniel	Nathan, Nate
Rayd.	Raymond	Ray
Richd.	Richard	Dick, Rich, Rick, Richy, Ricky
Robt.	Robert	Bob, Bobby, Robbie
Saml.	Samuel	Sam, Sammy
	Susannah	Susan, Susie
Thos.	Thomas	Tom, Tommy
Wm.	William (Fr. Guillaume)	Bill, Billy, Willy

Corrigenda to the
Abney Family History Series, Vol. I

Corrected family of Elisha Abney (Abner) Sr.

Not previously having researched this branch of the family until requested to write this book, the author was forced to heavily rely on the research of others. Having now researched this family extensively, the author is certain of the account given here in the right side of this table:

Erroneous Family of Elisha Abney/Abner Sr. Vol. I, 2nd Ed., pg.90	birth	Updated and Corrected Family of Elisha Abney/Abner Sr.	birth
Abner Abney (?) m. Alyda Russell	-	**Joshua Abney m. Pattie Phelps**	**ca.1771**
Joshua Abney (Abner) m. Patsy Phelps	ca.1774	**(daughter [Jerusha "Shrew"?])**	**ca.1773**
Jerusha "Shrew" Abney (Abner)	ca.1776	**(daughter [Ann?])**	**ca.1775**
Hezekiah Abney m. (n.n. Calloway?)	ca.1780	**(daughter [n.n.])**	**ca.1777**
Ann Abney (Abner)	ca.1782	**Pvt. Abner Abney m. Alyda Russell**	**ca.1779**
Elisha Abney Jr. m. Nancy Loving	ca.1783	**Hezekiah Abney m. ([n.n.] [Calloway?])**	**ca.1781**
Dorcas Abney (Abner) m. John Wood	ca.1786	**Dorcas "Tabitha" Abney/Abner m. John Wood**	**ca.1784**
Menan Abner m1. Agnes "Aggy" Bowling; m2. Lucinda Benge; m3. Elizabeth Lucas Wells	ca.1790	**Elisha Abner Jr. m. Nancy "Lucy" Loving**	**ca.1787**
Mary Abney (Abner) m. Samuel Bishop	ca.1792	**Menan Abner m1. Agnes Bowling; m2. Lucinda Benge; m3. Elizabeth Lucas (widow Wells)**	**ca.1790**
John Abner (Abney) m1. n.n.; m2. Millie Noble	ca.1794	**John Abney Sr. m1. Pamelia Watts; m2. Millie Noble**	**ca.1794**
Rebecca Abney (Abner)	09 Dec 1796	**Mary Abner (b.1794-1800) m. Samuel Bishop**	**ca.1795**
Margaret Larken Abner (Abney) m. Isham Smith	ca.1800	**Margaret Larken Abner m. Isham O. Smith**	**1798**
Enoch Abner (Abney)	ca.1793	**Enoch Abney m1. Anna Price; m2. Eliz. Thomas**	**ca.1803**
William Abner (Abney)	1807		

Evolution of a Family Group Sheet

As an unfortunate side effect of creating, as the author has ventured, such an extensive genealogy, there will be errors. Let's look at the evolution of the family of Elisha Abney Sr. since Cousin John Hensell first published this family in 1988 to this book in 2020:

Hensell Supplement: 1988	Abney, 1st edition: 2018	Abney, 2nd edition: 2018	Abney, Abner, Abna, Abnee: 2020
Shrew (Jerusha) ca.1776	Abner (?)	Abner (?)	**Joshua Abney, ca.1771**
Joshua, ca.1778	Joshua, ca.1774	Joshua, ca.1774	**(daughter [Jerusha "Shrew"?]) ca.1773**
Hezekiah, ca.1780	Jerusha "Shrew", c.1776	Jerusha "Shrew", ca.1776	**(daughter [Ann?]), ca.1775**
Ann, ca.1782	Hezekiah, ca.1780	Hezekiah, ca.1780	**(daughter [n.n.]), ca.1777**
Elisha, ca.1784	Ann, ca.1782	Ann, ca.1782	**Pvt. Abner Abney, ca.1779**
Dorcas, ca.1786	Elisha Jr., ca.1783	Elisha Jr., ca.1783	**Hezekiah Abney, ca.1781**
Monroe, ca.1788	Dorcas, ca.1786	Dorcas, ca.1786	**Dorcas "Tabitha" Abney. ca.1784**
Mennen, ca.1790	Monroe, ca.1788	Menan, ca.1790	**Elisha Abner Jr., ca.1787**
Mary "Polly", ca.1792	Menan, ca.1790	Mary, ca.1792	**Menan Abner, ca.1790**
John, ca.1794	Mary "Polly", ca.1792	John, ca.1794	**John Abney Sr., ca.1794**
Rebecca, Dec. 9, 1796	John, ca.1794	Rebecca, 1796	**Mary Abner, ca.1795**
Margaret Laken, ca.1798	Rebecca, 1796	Margaret Larken, ca.1800	**Margaret Larken, 1798**
Enoch, ca.1803	Margaret Larken, ca.1800	Enoch, ca.1793	**Enoch Abner, ca.1803**
William, 1807	Enoch, ca.1803	William, 1807	
	William, 1807		

1.   Joshua Abney, born ca.1771 – Joshua has been one of the constants of this family. The only thing the author was forced to change was to move his birth year up to correctly match the census records. Joshua's birth year has been a mystery to family historians. When Contributor John M. Abney discovered the military service of Joshua's brother, Abner, the author realized that Abner was almost certainly born in 1779. Since (on average), children were born about two years apart in the 18th century (about three years apart for an

older woman), the author retreated the ages of Joshua and his three mystery sisters one year to make them born on odd years. This had the effect of making Joshua's age correct in every census (see Appendix B). Joshua married 1795 Martha "Pattie" Phelps and had issue.

2. Jerusha "Shrew" Abney (?), born est.1773– To my knowledge, only Cousin John Hensell knows his source for the daughter he called "Shrew (Jerusha)". Although the author has found no evidence of her name, he has found undeniable evidence of her existence. Since it is very possible Cousin John had proof of her name, the author has, in great respect to Cousin John Hensell, chosen to keep the name in this pedigree. The author also had the choice of keeping her as the eldest daughter (as Cousin John had) or keeping her birth year the same as Cousin John's. Since it is easier to confuse a birth year than a birth order, in the author's opinion, the author has chosen to keep Shrew as the alleged eldest daughter. Marriage and children are unknown at this writing.

3. Ann Abney (?), born est.1775 – Like Shrew, only Cousin John Hensell knew his source for her name. The author has chosen to keep her as the second daughter with a different birth year. Marriage and children are unknown at this writing.

4. (daughter) Abney, born est.1777 – Due to another female present in both the 1787 tax record of Elisha Abney Sr. and the 1790 census record, the author is compelled to place another daughter in this position. Marriage and children are unknown at this writing.

5. Pvt. Abner Abney (War of 1812), born ca.1779 – The author had worked on this Abner Abney decades ago. However, he was never quite able to place him. With the information given by Contributor John M. Abney that "his" Isaac Abney never made it to Carter Co., Tennessee, the only choice for placement was in Elisha Abney Sr.'s family. Calculating his marrying age at 21 in 1803, Abner fit perfectly into this family throughout each tax and census record. Contributor John M. Abney also discovered the only known record (Road Orders in 1804) in which Abner Abney appears with Elisha Abney [Sr or Jr. not identified]. Moreover, Contributor Morgan Abney learned of an Abner Abney who died in 1838 in Texas. Given that, Contributor John M. Abney did more research and discovered Pvt. Abner Abney's military record in the War of 1812 and the Battle of New Orleans. That record, which gave Abner's enlistment age as 34 in January 1814, almost certainly gives us a birth year of 1779, born in Contributor John M. Abney also discovered Pvt. Abner Abney's enlistment record which gives him as age 34 born in Amherst Co., Virginia, solidifying Pvt. Abner Abney's rightful place in the Elisha Abney Sr. family. With that, the birth years of his older siblings and Hezekiah Abney were corrected, all of which match the tax and census records (see Appendix B) Abner Abney married 1803 Alyda Russell. Whether or not they had issue remains a mystery.

6. Hezekiah Abney, born ca.1781 – Another constant in this family, Hezekiah is firmly entrenched. Moreover, the author has determined that Hezekiah knew not only the correct spelling of his surname, but his age as well. With his birth year at 1781, his age is correct in every census (including the 1760, IF his birthdate was AFTER the census was taken). His wife is said to be a Calloway and had issue.

7. Dorcas "Tabitha" Abner, born ca.1784 – Dorcas was another constant in this family. The author needed only adjust her birth year to match census records. By the way, the names "Dorcas" and "Tabitha" are identical in the Holy Bible (From Acts 9:36 *Now there was at Joppa a disciple named Tabitha, which means Dorcas or Gazelle. She was full of good works and acts of charity*). Dorcas "Tabitha" Abner married John Woods and had issue.

8. Elisha Abner Jr., born ca.1787 – Elisha was another constant in this family. Again, the author was only forced to adjust his birth year to match census records. He married ca.1806 Nancy "Lucy" Loving.

9. Menan Abner, born ca.1790 – Menan (which spelling is Biblically correct in the King James Version) is also a constant in this family. Like his brothers, Abner, Hezekiah and John, Menan was aware of his correct age. The family of Menan was a mess, as reported in earlier works. Due in great part to the work of Contributor Judy Lewis Vietri, and the continuation of her work by Contributor Sandrea Abner Cook, this family has come together quite nicely. Menan married thrice, leaving issue with each wife. He firstly married 1813 to Agnes "Aggy" Bowling; secondly 1829 to Lucinda Benge; and thirdly 1836 to Elizabeth Lucas (widow Wells).

10. John Abney Sr., born ca.1794 – John is another, like his elder brothers, Abner and Hezekiah, who knew his proper surname and age. Aside from his marriage license and the 1850 Kentucky census-taker (both of whom used *Abner*), the fact that *Abney* was used in each census prior to 1850, and further that his eldest son Lincoln used the phonetically spelled *Abnee*, bears out the author's conclusion. John married twice: firstly ca.1825 to Pamelia Watts and had issue; secondly 1829 to Millie Noble and had issue.

11. Mary "Polly" Abney, born ca.1795 – Another daughter firmly established in this family. Her birth year was adjusted to agree with census records. She married 1811 to Samuel "Sam" Bishop and had issue.

12. Margaret Larken Abner, born 14 Feb 1798 – She is the only child for which we have a full birthdate and a full death date. She married 1819 to Isham O. Smith and had issue.

13. Enoch Abney Jr., born ca.1803 – He is firmly established in this family, although there may be some doubt about his birth year. Although the 1850 and 1820 censuses agree, the 1830 and 1840 censuses disagree, having him born between 1791 and 1800. Enoch also knew his last name was *Abney*. Despite the fact that both names *Abney* and *Abner* were used in Kentucky, his descendants outside of Kentucky used *Abney*. Enoch married Anna Price and had issue.

What happened to Rebecca, Monroe and William?

- Elisha Abney Sr. was Rebecca C. Abney's grandfather, not father. She was a daughter of Joshua Abney & Marth Phelps, born 09 Feb 1796. With such large families, it is very easy to mistake one's grandchild for one's child.

- There was no Monroe Abney. Of the three marriage records of Menan Abney, one was believed to read "Monroe". It does not. Upon closer inspection it is obvious all three marriages were of Menan Abney.

- Like the situation with Rebecca, Elisha Abney Sr. was William "Buck" Abney's grandfather. Again, when people have such large families, the grandchildren are of similar age, even older than the children. This is also the case in the author's immediate family. The difficulty is compounded when records are sparse, and information on those records is scant. Nonetheless, William "Buck" Abner (born 04 Aug 1807) was a son of Elisha Abner Jr. (NOT Sr.) and Nancy "Lucy" Loving.

Family of Isaac Abney (son of Sgt. George Abney and Sarah "Sally" Griffith)

Another family line that gets corrected is in the George Abney branch (which was published with errors in the first Abney volume: Abney, Ancestry and Genealogy of Dr. Abraham Abney of Virginia). It was reported by earlier researchers that one Isaac Abney (son of Sgt. George Abney and Sarah "Sally" Griffith) married Dicy *Russell* in Carter County, Tennessee. Descendant and contributor, John M. Abney, has now confirmed that, while Cousin John Hensell assigned the surname *Russell* to Isaac's wife, Dicy (as well as an alleged county of marriage – Carter Co., TN), Dicy's surname is still unknown. There is no doubt a certain Russell family was tied to the Abney family in Carter County, Tennessee. However, Isaac

Abney never lived in Carter County, Tennessee, and his wife's surname is, again, unknown. This error snowballed into an additional error of placing Leonard Jasper Abney Sr. into the family of Isaac Abney and Dicy (as shown in Vol. I of Abney). This, then, needs to be corrected. Not having, heretofore, studied the family of Sgt. George Abney and Sally Griffith with the attention it deserves, the author was only able to report the work of other genealogists. Now, however, the facts must be shared.

By request of the author, Contributor John Michael Abney (descendant of Isaac Abney) has graciously provided the following:

Numerous family histories have Isaac [Abney] marrying Dicy Russell in Carter County, Tennessee. This is in error as: (1) The referenced Carter County marriage record was between Abner Abney and Aldya Russell; (2) Isaac never went by the name Abner in any record where he has been found; (3) Isaac, to the best of our knowledge, never lived in Carter County. Upon leaving South Carolina, he is found in records with his father in Warren County, Tennessee (1805 tax records) and with his own family in the 1820 federal census. Upon leaving Warren County he moved to Jackson County, Tennessee and is believed to have spent the rest of his life there appearing in the federal census for Jackson County in 1830, 1840, and 1850 (showing his age as 79).

Author's note: Even by today's standards, Carter County (in West Tennessee) is very far from Jackson County (in Middle Tennessee).

For this next paragraph, the reader is encouraged to review Volume III, Issue III (May 1999) of *the Abney Family Researcher* newsletter by this current author. For clarification, the author has shown by a greater weight or preponderance of the evidence, that Dannett Abney (son of George Abney) married his cousin, Cassandra Abney (daughter of Dr. Abraham Abney), a very common occurrence in the eighteenth century. This was a very interesting discovery and corrected decades old beliefs. Earlier researchers believed that since Edward Dean, in his will, called Dannett Abney his brother-in-law, then Edward's wife, Rebecca must be Dannett Abney's sister. In fact, Edward Dean's and Dannett Abney's wives were sisters, making the two men brothers-in-law. This discovery, then brought Rebecca Abney (wife of Edward Dean) and Cassandra Abney (wife of Dannett Abney) into their rightful place in the family of Dr. Abraham Abney and his wife Cassandra (Meredith?). Since Cassandra Abney was Dr. Abraham Abney's daughter, and Dannett was George Abney's son, descendants of these two have a double connection to the Abney family, through George Abney in the paternal line, and through Dr. Abraham Abney in the maternal line. This is why this branch of the family was covered so extensively in the descendants of Dr. Abraham Abney. The same branch would be rightfully covered as descendants of George Abney.

The author held hope that by the printing of this second volume of the Abney Family History Series these relationships would be firm. However, that proof is still wanting, and Leonard Jasper Abney Sr.'s ancestry is still very much in abeyance.

Possible Parentage of Leonard Jasper Abney Sr.
(but see Secundo Addendum, page 266 for updated information)

Due in part to the statement (by Hensell in *Abney Supplement*) that Isaac Abney Sr. (son of Sgt. George Abney, RS and Sarah "Sally" Griffith) married Dicy Russell in Carter County, Tennessee (which is now known to be a completely erroneous statement), and lacking a qualified candidate, the author surmised that Isaac sired Leonard Jasper Abney Sr. (born 15 May 1806 in Tennessee). Being informed (by Contributor John M. Abney) that Isaac Abney never went to Carter County, Tennessee, and his wife, Dicy was NOT proven to have been a RUSSELL, it is obvious this assumption was incorrect.

Therefore, the parentage of Leonard Jasper Abney Sr. is, as it has been, still unknown. Even if we eliminate the "known" possibilities, we are still left with the possibility of unknown lines.

Ruling out the families who could have sired a son in 1806 and who migrated to Tennessee and/or Illinois:

- Paul Collins Abney m. Dorothy "Dolly" Rutherford were still in Spartanburg Co., South Carolina in 1808.
- Pvt. Paul Abney/Abner m. Rhoda Norman had a daughter, Delilah born on 18 May 1806 so they could not have also had a son born three days earlier.
- None of the sons of Pvt. Paul Abney/Abner and Rhoda Norman sired children before 1807.
- Nathaniel Abney m. Sarah Canada were still in Union Co., South Carolina in 1810.

This leaves only (that we are aware of) Elisha Abney/Abner Sr. and his sons, and the sons of Sgt. George Abney and his wife, Sarah Griffith.

By 1810, Elisha Abney/Abner Sr. had moved on to Kentucky, as did most of his children. However, Abner Abney did NOT appear in the Kentucky census or court records. If, as the author believes, Abner and his wife Alyda remained in Carter County, Tennessee, he could have appeared on the 1810 census. However, the 1810 Census of Carter County, Tennessee was destroyed (along with the 1800 and 1820 censuses) in a courthouse fire in November, 1932. Therefore, if, again, as the author believes, Abner was still in Carter County, Tennessee, he and Alyda could have been Leonard J. Abney's parents, since Leonard was born on 15 May 1806 in Tennessee.

Elisha Sr.'s last son was Enoch, born in Carter County, Tennessee in 1803. Elisha Sr. was age 62. More importantly, his wife was probably at the end of her child-bearing years. So that would rule him out. His sons are of great interest.

- Joshua Abney married Martha Phelps in Green Co., Kentucky by 1795. None of his children were born in Tennessee.
- **Abner Abney married Alyda Russell in Carter Co., Tennessee on 26 Aug 1803! While all his younger brothers (and father) migrated to Kentucky, Abner Abney is unaccounted for. He is last seen in Carter County, Tennessee on 13 Feb 1804 in a court record concerning Road Orders. Moreover, unlike the majority of his younger brothers, Abner is only seen using the surname, Abney. He joined the U.S. Army out of Gallatin, Tennessee on 22 Jan 1814 (although he may have been living in Kentucky). Now we know he was still alive in 1814. Moreover, if he was the unidentified male enumerated in the census of his brother, Joshua Abney, he was still alive in 1820, as well. He has not been proved to be the Abner Abney who died in Texas in 1838.**
- Hezekiah Abney was in Jackson Co., Georgia by 1804. None of his children were born in Tennessee.

Addenda et Corrigenda to Abney, Vol. I

- Elisha Abney Jr. married Nancy Loving in Kentucky ca.1806. There are two sons on his 1810 census enumerations. Those sons are William (age 3) and Lacy (newborn). There is no room for another son; and none of his family was born in Tennessee.
- Menan Abney: His first marriage was to Aggy Bowling in Clay Co., Kentucky in 1813. He sired so children in Tennessee.
- John Abney Sr.: Albeit not physically, John was too young to have sired Leonard. He was 12 years of age when Leonard was born. John married (as his first wife) Pamelia Watts in Clay Co., Kentucky ca.1825. He sired no children in Tennessee.
- Enoch Abney Sr. was three years old in 1806 and too young to be Leonard's father.

That leaves us with only one interesting prospect in this line: **Abner Abney m. Alyda Russell**. It is most unfortunate that the census record of 1810 in Carter County, Tennessee was destroyed. If Abner Abney appeared on that record with a son under age 10, we would have what we need. Barring that, we are at an impasse at this time.

As to the sons of Sgt. George Abney m. Sarah "Sally" Griffith:

Isaac Abney Sr. (b.ca.1771) and Dicy are still prospects.
George Abney (b.ca.1773) and Maacah Bailey are still prospects.
William Abney (unknown)
Samuel Abney is still a possibility.
Joshua Abney, b.1784 married in 1806 and is not considered a prospect.

That would give us five known possibilities. But…how many other Abney men migrated to Tennessee by 1806?

Therefore, after all the hours, days, weeks, months and years working on this line, much to the chagrin of the author of descendants of Leonard Jasper Abney Sr., we are still stuck on this line. However…

Due to DNA matches, we are 99% certain Leonard Jasper Abney Sr. was born in Carter County, TN…and was probably a son of Pvt. Abner Abney. There was too much new information to make changes here. Read the Secundo Addendum on page 266 for the latest update.

For research purposes, herewith we include a timeline of Leonard Jasper Abney Sr.:

15 May 1806	born in Tennessee
ca.1829	married Ellen "Gincy" Crenshaw
1830	living in Hancock Co., IL
27 Oct 1830	birth of L. Francis Abney
ca.1832	birth of daughter (n.n.)
09 Nov 1834	birth of Mary N. Abney
26 Dec 1834	living in Des Moines Co., IA Territory
1836	Des Moines Co., IA Territory Census
27 Jun 1837	birth of Elizabeth Abney in Iowa
30 Mar 1840	birth of Franklin M. Abney in Iowa
19 Dec 1842	birth of Leonard Jasper Abney Jr. in Iowa
22 Aug 1846	birth of Gincy "Virginia" Abney in Iowa
19 Jul 1864	died in Des Moines Co., IA; buried in Ridge Park Cemetery, Marshall, Saline Co., MO

That written, as this book is nearing publication, it is becoming clearer that Pvt. Abner Abney and Alyda Russell may be Leonard's parents. (See Addenda, page 266 for further information.)

Addenda et Corrigenda to Abney, Vol. I

Table of Contents

Abney: Ancestry and Genealogy of Abner Abney of Virginia

Table of the Pedigrees

Table of Maps, Documents and Pictures

Prologue

The Abner Abney Family

"…it ought to be the most cherished reminiscence of our lives to remember our genealogy…"
Thomas Hamilton Abney (1793-1870)

This branch of the Noble Abney Family has had some information published on it previously, in books, manuscripts and newsletters. Cousin John Hensell had attempted to assemble the Abney's of the first generation and carry on their prodigy as best as he could. Much of his work was from other researchers and there were, of course, many errors. Although this current author was able to put together a factual first generation, some of the errors in the second and third generations have continued to creep into subsequent publications, including the first book in this series. Much of the information passed to this author, and further to the reader, has been shown to be inaccurate in part.

The best book on Abner Abney's family, to date, seems to have been *In Search of Kate*, by Charlotte Ann Abney Metzger, but it is very limited in its scope. Her direct line was from John Abney *the Hatter*, son of Abner Abney. John is one of only three children mentioned in his father's will; and John's line is proved throughout. Metzger commits the majority of her book, not to all the descendants of Abner Abney, but to his son John Abney's descendants. Therefore, the family of Elisha Abney/Abner is in large part, ignored. Although an excellent book, *In Search of Kate* does not cover the whole of Abner Abney's descendants, the majority of which stem from Elisha Abney/Abner.

There was a Milly Abney also mentioned in the will of Abner Abney. This daughter is largely a mystery in the family. To this author's knowledge, no researcher has ever discovered whether she married and/or had children. She was mentioned under guardianship of Sam Taliaferro, believed to have been her step-father (second husband of Anne [Key?], widow of Abner Abney). The second marriage of the widow Anne is unproved.

As to the very prolific Elisha Abney/Abner, we will, in this volume, correct many of the previous errors, and bring new information to light. (Besides correcting some of the information published on this family, we will also correct information on another family line [George Abney, *see Corrigenda to Vol. I*, in this book, on page xviii-xix under the heading "Family of Isaac Abney"]). The earlier generation of the Elisha Abney Sr. line has been very difficult to document, although the author and contributors have made their most valiant efforts so to do. In this volume, we will be forced to report what we know on this line, and give opinions and best estimates on information which cannot definitively be proven. That written, the author is 99% positive of the account of the immediate family of Elisha Abney Sr., given here.

Genealogy is a never-ending study. It stands to reason, if we cannot prove the entire line by now, perhaps we must be satisfied with what we can prove, and publish that. If we wait until more information surfaces, we will never publish a book because there is always something else waiting to be found. Hopefully, this book (as is hoped with all the published works of the author), will serve as a guideline to one's personal genealogical research; and those descendants will learn more about their own particular branch of the family and share it with others.

As this current author wrote on the Abner Abney family (see **Abney Family Series, Vol.I**, 2nd Edition, page 90): *Elisha Abney/Abner's family… All of the issue given him in this record is not absolutely proved, but the work of other genealogists.* That section went on to list the possible children of Elisha Abney Sr., son of Abner Abney, as follows: 1. Abner, 2. Joshua, 3. Jerusha "Shrew", 4. Hezekiah, 5. Ann, 6. Elisha Jr., 7. Dorcas "Tabitha", 8. Menan, 9. Mary, 10. John, 11. Rebecca, 12. Margaret Larken, 13. Enoch and 14. William. While that account is erroneous, it is not without merit, especially including the mysterious Abner (whom we now know to be Pvt. Abner Abney from the War of 1812).

For this current book, the author has worked out this more accurate, and quite nearly perfect account of the family of Elisha Abney Sr.:

> **Elisha Abney (Abner) Sr., b.est.1741 Goochland Co., VA; d.aft.1820 Clay Co., KY**
> **+ (n.n.), m.est.1770 in Albemarle Co., VA**
>> **1. Joshua Abney, b.ca.1771 Albemarle Co., VA; d.1845 Jefferson Co., IL; m. Martha Pattie Phelps & had issue**
>> **2. (daughter [Jerusha "Shrew"?]) Abney, b.est.1773 Albemarle Co., VA of whom nothing further**
>> **3. (daughter [Ann?]) Abney, b.est.1775 Albemarle Co., VA of whom nothing further**
>> **4. (daughter?), (n.n.) Abney, b.est.1777 Amherst Co., VA of whom nothing further**
>> **5. Pvt. Abner Abney, b.ca.1779 in Amherst Co., VA; m.1803 Carter Co., TN to Alyda Russell. Issue unknown.**
>> **6. Hezekiah Abney, b.ca.1781 Amherst Co., VA; d.ca.1861 Cleburne Co., AL; m. (n.n.) Calloway?] & had issue**
>> **7. Dorcas "Tabitha" Abney, b.ca.1784 Amherst Co., VA; m. John Woods & had issue**
>> **8. Elisha Abney Jr, b.ca.1787 Wilkes Co., NC; d.ca.1855 Owsley Co., KY; m. Nancy "Lucy" Loving & had issue**
>> **9. Menan Abner, b.ca.1790 Wilkes Co., NC; d.ca.1853 Clay Co., KY; m1. Agnes "Aggy" Bowling & had issue;**
>>   **m2. Lucinda Benge & had issue; m3. Elizabeth Lucas (widow Wells) & had issue**
>> **10. John Abney Sr., b.1794 Wash. Co., Southwest Territory (later Carter Co., TN); d.aft.1860 Owsley Co., KY;**
>>   **m1. Pamelia Watts & had issue; m2. Millie Noble & had issue**
>> **11. Mary "Polly" Abner, b.ca.1795 Wash. Co., Southwest Terr. (later Carter Co., TN); d.1881 Clay Co., KY;**
>>   **m. Samuel "Sam" Bishop & had issue**
>> **12. Margaret Larken Abner (Abney), b.14 Feb1798 Carter Co., TN; d.18 Oct 1870 Henry Co., KY;**
>>   **m. Isham O. Smith & had issue**
>> **13. Enoch Abney Sr., b.ca.1803 Carter Co., TN; d.1854 Stone Co., MO; m1. Anna Price & had issue;**
>>   **m2. Elizabeth Thomas, but no issue**

Note the "preferred" surnames which the author utilizes in this record. These surnames will be used consistently, more or less, throughout this volume. The reason for this is simple, The author has determined the surname actually used by the individual. Therefore, instead of lumping everyone into the antiquated Abney/Abner appellation, the author will use the following surnames (See Appendix A: Etymology, page 257):

Elisha Abney Sr. – He knew his surname. It doesn't matter what the record-keeper wrote. When Elisha signed his name, he signed *Abney*.
Joshua Abney – Although his marriage license reads *Abner*, his children went by *Abney* indicating he knew his surname.
Jerusha "Shrew", Ann & (n.n.) [daughters] –There is no reason to believe they would have gone by a different surname than *Abney*.
Hezekiah Abney – He knew his name as the vast majority of his descendants to this day are still called *Abney*.
Abner Abney – He went by *Abney* in all records discovered on him. If Leonard Jasper Abney Sr. was his son…then all his descendants did as well.
Dorcas "Tabitha" Abney – On her marriage license, her surname is spelled *Abny* and her father signed *Abney*.
Elisha Abner Jr. – All records and descendants indicate he used the surname *Abner*
Menan Abner – All records and descendants indicate he used the surname *Abner*
John Abney Sr. – Although most of his descendants went by *Abner*, his eldest son went by *Abnee*, indicating he knew the correct pronunciation.
Mary "Polly" Abner – The author believes she was married as an *Abner*
Margaret Larken Abner – married as an *Abner*
Enoch Abney Sr. – Most of his descendants went by the surname *Abney*, indicating they knew their proper surname.

The reader will notice that the alleged William Abney (#14 in the erroneous family) has been omitted from this record. William was a grandson of Elisha Abney/Abner Sr., not a son (see *Corrigenda,* page xviii). Similarly, Rebecca Abney (#11 in the erroneous family) was determined to have been a granddaughter (not a daughter) of Elisha Sr. (see *Corrigenda,* page xviii). With that in mind, even some of the possible daughters (enumerated in this present record, on page 1: nos. 2, 3, and 4) may not have been daughters at all. In the early census and tax records, only the Head of Household (Elisha in this case) was named and identified. The remaining members of his household were only enumerated as members of his household (divided into males and females); and not even not identified as family, much less as his children. An additional possibility is these females could have been in-laws, borders, servants or any other female living in the household. There is just no way of knowing. **However, the females listed above are most probably daughters, since the tax record and census record are in agreement and the children were not yet married in 1787 and 1790.** The eldest, Joshua was married in 1795, a full five years after the 1790 census. Given the age of the family at the time of the early tax and census records, it is very probable that they were daughters. As for the alleged names (Jerusha "Shrew" and Ann), only Cousin John Hensell (*Abney Supplement* [1988], page 7) would know his source, but he has passed away on June 9, 2000 (God rest his soul).

One very exciting addition to this family (since the early days of research) is Pvt. Abner Abney. Discovered decades ago, by the author, it is only recently we have been able to firmly place him into this family. Believing Abner belonged in this family (prosopography, nomenclature), the author placed him there in Volume I of the **Abney Family History Series**. With the additional research on this family, the author believed him to have been born ca.1782 in Amherst County, Virginia. However, since Contributor John M. Abney discovered his military record, we know absolutely that he was born in Amherst County, and moreover, that he was age 34 when he enlisted on Jan. 22, 1814. This gives us a high probability that he was born in 1779, hence would have been 34 years of age in January 1814. It is very exciting to have Pvt. Abner Abney in his rightful position in the Abney family. Thanks to Contributors Morgan F. Abney and John M. Abney for their excellent discoveries of Pvt. Abner Abney's records.

One very important change is the birth year of Elisha Abner Jr. (given here as ca.1787 instead of 1784). While it is true, the 1850 census gives Elisha's age as 67, and every census record concurs back through 1820, it is also true the 1810 census disagrees with his age, and he is not accounted for on the 1787 Wilkes County Tax Record. Although some believe he is accounted for on the 1787 tax record, the author is quite certain that the male accounted for on that tax record is the *heretofore unrecognized* Pvt. Abner Abney. If, as the author believes, Elisha Abner Jr. was born circa 1787, the age on every census record agrees (save the 1850 census, which, again, the author believes gives his age incorrectly). One thing is for certain in genealogy, the facts closer to the event are *most* often the more accurate (although this is not always the case). In 1810, Elisha would probably have had a better idea of his age than in 1850. Ages often "changed" more or less than the expected 10 years from census-to-census. And the author believes the age of Elisha Jr. was correct in every census from 1790-1840, and misgiven in 1850. There will be more on this later. Also see the chart in Appendix B, page 259 (*When & Where Were the Children of Elisha Abney Sr. Born?*)

Finally, be certain to read *Appendix A* showing the etymology of Abner, Abna and Abnee in this branch of the Abney family.

As in the first volume, the author will close this prologue with the words of his mentor, Margaret Louise Griffey Harlow:

"Be happy if someone can prove you wrong...
because then you'll have proof, and that's
what you are searching for in the first place."

Let us then conclude this prologue and begin to unravel the descendants of:

Abner Abney of Virginia.

fortiter et honeste

(Bravely and Honorably)
Abney Family Motto

Margaret Louise Griffey Harlow
        (1929-2019)
(Rest in Peace, my dear friend and mentor)

Chapter I

Ancestry of Abner Abney of Virginia
The Noble Abney Family

Pedigree of yᵉ d'Abney Lords of Belvoir

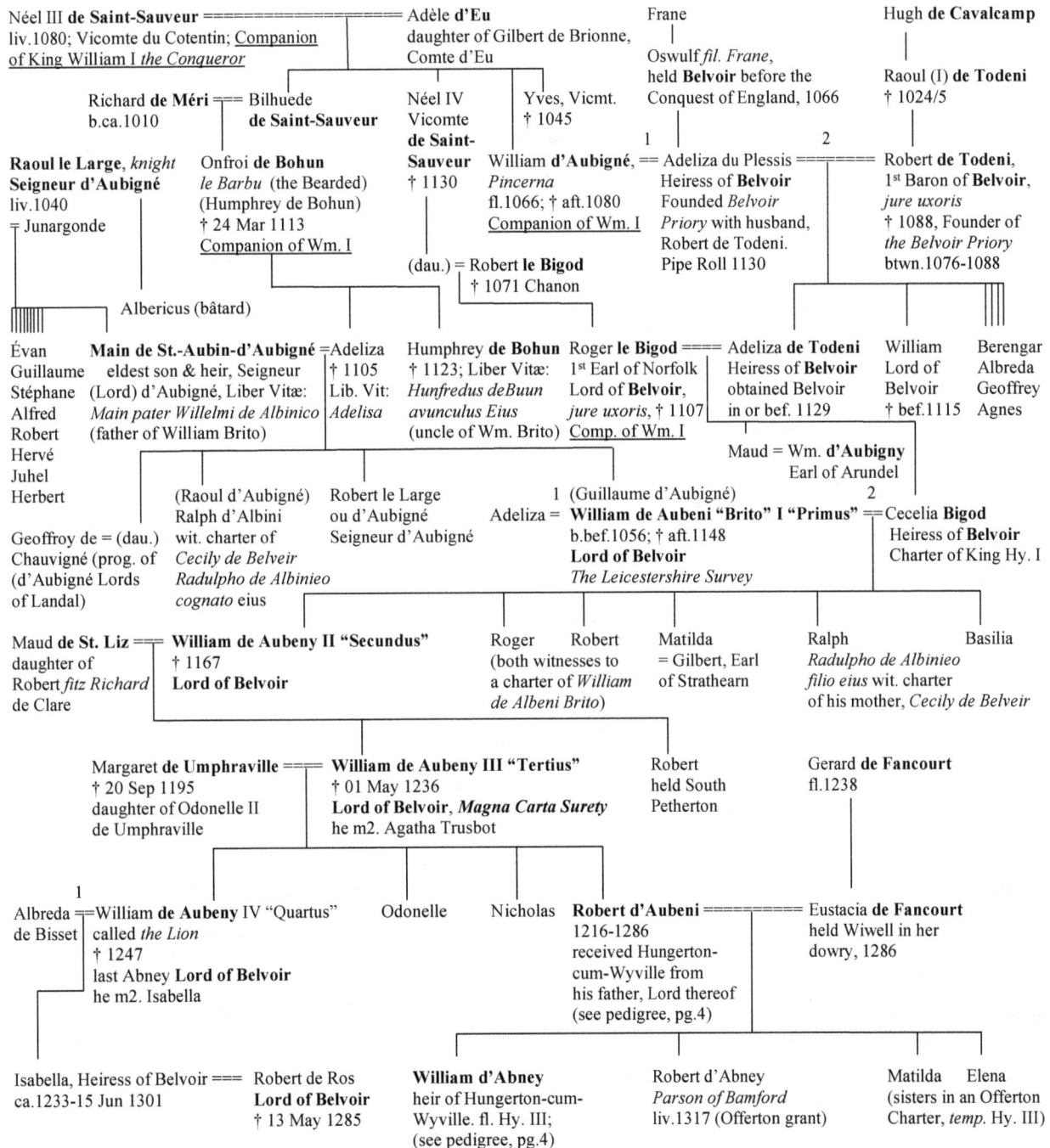

Néel III de Saint-Sauveur ================== **Adèle d'Eu**
liv.1080; Vicomte du Cotentin; Companion   daughter of Gilbert de Brionne,
of King William I *the Conqueror*   Comte d'Eu

Frane
|
Oswulf *fil. Frane*,
held **Belvoir** before the
Conquest of England, 1066

Hugh **de Cavalcamp**
|
Raoul (I) **de Todeni**
† 1024/5

Richard de Méri === Bilhuede
b.ca.1010   **de Saint-Sauveur**

Néel IV   Yves, Vicmt.
Vicomte   † 1045
de Saint-

1 ============ **2**

Raoul le Large, *knight*   Onfroi **de Bohun**
Seigneur d'Aubigné   *le Barbu* (the Bearded)
liv.1040   (Humphrey de Bohun)
╤ Junargonde   † 24 Mar 1113
    Companion of Wm. I

Sauveur   William **d'Aubigné,** == Adeliza du Plessis ======== Robert **de Todeni,**
† 1130   *Pincerna*   Heiress of **Belvoir**   1ˢᵗ Baron of **Belvoir,**
    fl.1066; † aft.1080   Founded *Belvoir*   *jure uxoris*
    Companion of Wm. I   *Priory* with husband,   † 1088, Founder of
        Robert de Todeni.   *the Belvoir Priory*
        Pipe Roll 1130   btwn.1076-1088

(dau.) = Robert **le Bigod**
    † 1071 Chanon

Albericus (bâtard)

Évan   **Main de St.-Aubin-d'Aubigné** =Adeliza   Humphrey **de Bohun**   Roger **le Bigod** ==== Adeliza **de Todeni**   William   Berengar
Guillaume   eldest son & heir, Seigneur   † 1105   † 1123; Liber Vitæ: 1ˢᵗ Earl of Norfolk   Heiress of **Belvoir**   Lord of   Albreda
Stéphane   (Lord) d'Aubigné, Liber Vitæ: Lib. Vit: *Hunfredus deBuun*   Lord of **Belvoir,**   obtained Belvoir   **Belvoir**   Geoffrey
Alfred   *Main pater Willelmi de Albinico*   Adelisa   *avunculus Eius*   *jure uxoris,* † 1107   in or bef. 1129   † bef.1115   Agnes
Robert   (father of William Brito)   (uncle of Wm. Brito)   Comp. of Wm. I
Hervé
Juhel   Maud = Wm. **d'Aubigny**
Herbert   Earl of Arundel

Geoffroy de = (dau.)   (Raoul d'Aubigné)   Robert le Large   **1** (Guillaume d'Aubigné)   **2** =Cecelia **Bigod**
Chauvigné (prog. of   Ralph d'Albini   ou d'Aubigné   Adeliza = **William de Aubeni "Brito" I "Primus"** ==   Heiress of **Belvoir**
(d'Aubigné Lords   wit. charter of   Seigneur d'Aubigné   b.bef.1056; † aft.1148   Charter of King Hy. I
of Landal)   *Cecily de Belveir*   **Lord of Belvoir**
    Radulpho de Albinieo   *The Leicestershire Survey*
    cognato eius

Maud **de St. Liz** === **William de Aubeny II "Secundus"**   Roger   Robert   Matilda   Ralph   Basilia
daughter of   † 1167   (both witnesses to   = Gilbert, Earl   *Radulpho de Albinieo*
Robert *fitz Richard*   **Lord of Belvoir**   a charter of *William*   of Strathearn   *filio eius* wit. charter
de Clare   *de Albeni Brito*)   of his mother, *Cecily de Belveir*

Margaret **de Umphraville** === **William de Aubeny III "Tertius"**   Robert   Gerard **de Fancourt**
† 20 Sep 1195   † 01 May 1236   held South   fl.1238
daughter of Odonelle II   **Lord of Belvoir,** *Magna Carta Surety*   Petherton
de Umphraville   he m2. Agatha Trusbot

1
Albreda ╤William **de Aubeny** IV "Quartus"   Odonelle   Nicholas   Robert **d'Aubeni** ========= Eustacia **de Fancourt**
de Bisset │ called *the Lion*   1216-1286   held Wiwell in her
    │ † 1247   received Hungerton-   dowry, 1286
    │ last Abney **Lord of Belvoir**   cum-Wyville from
    │ he m2. Isabella   his father, Lord thereof
        (see pedigree, pg.4)

Isabella, Heiress of Belvoir === Robert de Ros   **William d'Abney**   Robert d'Abney   Matilda   Elena
ca.1233-15 Jun 1301   **Lord of Belvoir**   heir of Hungerton-cum-   *Parson of Bamford*   (sisters in an Offerton
    † 13 May 1285   Wyville. fl. Hy. III;   liv.1317 (Offerton grant)   Charter, *temp.* Hy. III)
        (see pedigree, pg.4)

Pedigree of yᵉ d'Abney Family of Derbyshire

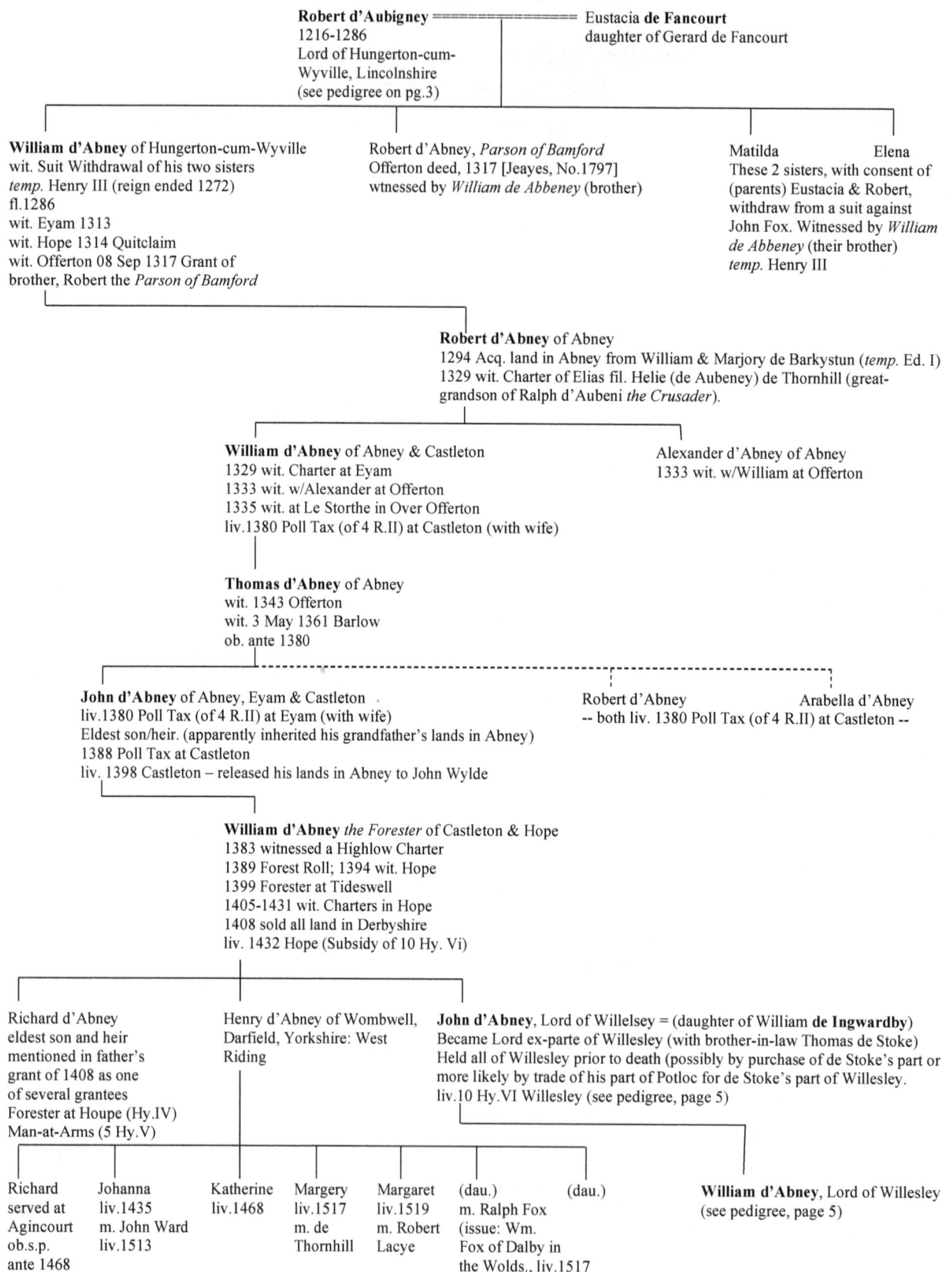

Robert d'Aubigney ================ Eustacia **de Fancourt**
1216-1286   daughter of Gerard de Fancourt
Lord of Hungerton-cum-
Wyville, Lincolnshire
(see pedigree on pg.3)

William d'Abney of Hungerton-cum-Wyville
wit. Suit Withdrawal of his two sisters
temp. Henry III (reign ended 1272)
fl.1286
wit. Eyam 1313
wit. Hope 1314 Quitclaim
wit. Offerton 08 Sep 1317 Grant of
brother, Robert the *Parson of Bamford*

Robert d'Abney, *Parson of Bamford*
Offerton deed, 1317 [Jeayes, No.1797]
wtnessed by *William de Abbeney* (brother)

Matilda   Elena
These 2 sisters, with consent of
(parents) Eustacia & Robert,
withdraw from a suit against
John Fox. Witnessed by *William
de Abbeney* (their brother)
temp. Henry III

Robert d'Abney of Abney
1294 Acq. land in Abney from William & Marjory de Barkystun (*temp.* Ed. I)
1329 wit. Charter of Elias fil. Helie (de Aubeney) de Thornhill (great-
grandson of Ralph d'Aubeni *the Crusader*).

William d'Abney of Abney & Castleton
1329 wit. Charter at Eyam
1333 wit. w/Alexander at Offerton
1335 wit. at Le Storthe in Over Offerton
liv.1380 Poll Tax (of 4 R.II) at Castleton (with wife)

Alexander d'Abney of Abney
1333 wit. w/William at Offerton

Thomas d'Abney of Abney
wit. 1343 Offerton
wit. 3 May 1361 Barlow
ob. ante 1380

John d'Abney of Abney, Eyam & Castleton
liv.1380 Poll Tax (of 4 R.II) at Eyam (with wife)
Eldest son/heir. (apparently inherited his grandfather's lands in Abney)
1388 Poll Tax at Castleton
liv. 1398 Castleton – released his lands in Abney to John Wylde

Robert d'Abney   Arabella d'Abney
-- both liv. 1380 Poll Tax (of 4 R.II) at Castleton --

William d'Abney the *Forester* of Castleton & Hope
1383 witnessed a Highlow Charter
1389 Forest Roll; 1394 wit. Hope
1399 Forester at Tideswell
1405-1431 wit. Charters in Hope
1408 sold all land in Derbyshire
liv. 1432 Hope (Subsidy of 10 Hy. Vi)

Richard d'Abney
eldest son and heir
mentioned in father's
grant of 1408 as one
of several grantees
Forester at Houpe (Hy.IV)
Man-at-Arms (5 Hy.V)

Henry d'Abney of Wombwell,
Darfield, Yorkshire: West
Riding

John d'Abney, Lord of Willelsey = (daughter of William **de Ingwardby**)
Became Lord ex-parte of Willesley (with brother-in-law Thomas de Stoke)
Held all of Willesley prior to death (possibly by purchase of de Stoke's part or
more likely by trade of his part of Potloc for de Stoke's part of Willesley.
liv.10 Hy.VI Willesley (see pedigree, page 5)

Richard	Johanna	Katherine	Margery	Margaret	(dau.)	(dau.)	**William d'Abney**, Lord of Willesley
served at	liv.1435	liv.1468	liv.1517	liv.1519	m. Ralph Fox		(see pedigree, page 5)
Agincourt	m. John Ward		m. de	m. Robert	(issue: Wm.		
ob.s.p.	liv.1513		Thornhill	Lacye	Fox of Dalby in		
ante 1468					the Wolds., liv.1517		

Pedigree of yᵉ Abney Lords of Willesley (Derbyshire)

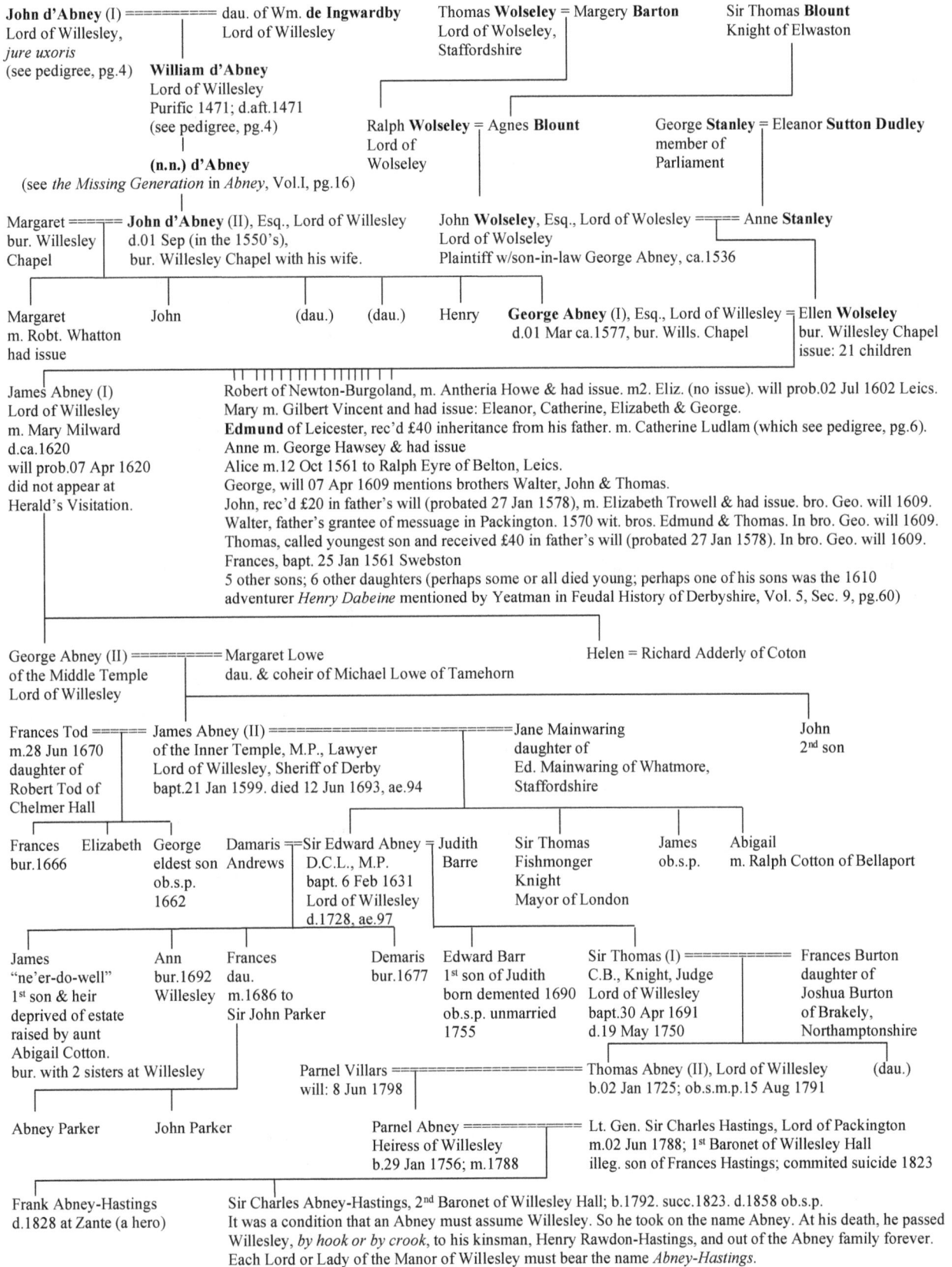

John d'Abney (I) ========= dau. of Wm. **de Ingwardby**
Lord of Willesley,   Lord of Willesley
jure uxoris
(see pedigree, pg.4)   **William d'Abney**
     Lord of Willesley
     Purific 1471; d.aft.1471
     (see pedigree, pg.4)

Thomas **Wolseley** = Margery **Barton**   Sir Thomas **Blount**
Lord of Wolseley,   Knight of Elwaston
Staffordshire

     (n.n.) d'Abney
(see *the Missing Generation* in *Abney*, Vol.I, pg.16)

Ralph **Wolseley** = Agnes **Blount**   George **Stanley** = Eleanor **Sutton Dudley**
Lord of   member of
Wolseley   Parliament

Margaret ===== **John d'Abney** (II), Esq., Lord of Willesley   John **Wolseley**, Esq., Lord of Wolesley ===== Anne **Stanley**
bur. Willesley   d.01 Sep (in the 1550's),   Lord of Wolseley
Chapel   bur. Willesley Chapel with his wife.   Plaintiff w/son-in-law George Abney, ca.1536

Margaret   John   (dau.)   (dau.)   Henry   **George Abney** (I), Esq., Lord of Willesley = Ellen **Wolseley**
m. Robt. Whatton   d.01 Mar ca.1577, bur. Wills. Chapel   bur. Willesley Chapel
had issue   issue: 21 children

James Abney (I)   Robert of Newton-Burgoland, m. Antheria Howe & had issue. m2. Eliz. (no issue). will prob.02 Jul 1602 Leics.
Lord of Willesley   Mary m. Gilbert Vincent and had issue: Eleanor, Catherine, Elizabeth & George.
m. Mary Milward   **Edmund** of Leicester, rec'd £40 inheritance from his father. m. Catherine Ludlam (which see pedigree, pg.6).
d.ca.1620   Anne m. George Hawsey & had issue
will prob.07 Apr 1620   Alice m.12 Oct 1561 to Ralph Eyre of Belton, Leics.
did not appear at   George, will 07 Apr 1609 mentions brothers Walter, John & Thomas.
Herald's Visitation.   John, rec'd £20 in father's will (probated 27 Jan 1578), m. Elizabeth Trowell & had issue. bro. Geo. will 1609.
     Walter, father's grantee of messuage in Packington. 1570 wit. bros. Edmund & Thomas. In bro. Geo. will 1609.
     Thomas, called youngest son and received £40 in father's will (probated 27 Jan 1578). In bro. Geo. will 1609.
     Frances, bapt. 25 Jan 1561 Swebston
     5 other sons; 6 other daughters (perhaps some or all died young; perhaps one of his sons was the 1610
     adventurer *Henry Dabeine* mentioned by Yeatman in Feudal History of Derbyshire, Vol. 5, Sec. 9, pg.60)

George Abney (II) ========= Margaret Lowe   Helen = Richard Adderly of Coton
of the Middle Temple   dau. & coheir of Michael Lowe of Tamehorn
Lord of Willesley

Frances Tod ===== **James Abney** (II) ======================= Jane Mainwaring   John
m.28 Jun 1670   of the Inner Temple, M.P., Lawyer   daughter of   2ⁿᵈ son
daughter of   Lord of Willesley, Sheriff of Derby   Ed. Mainwaring of Whatmore,
Robert Tod of   bapt.21 Jan 1599. died 12 Jun 1693, ae.94   Staffordshire
Chelmer Hall

Frances   Elizabeth   George   Damaris === Sir Edward Abney = Judith   Sir Thomas   James   Abigail
bur.1666   eldest son   Andrews   D.C.L., M.P.   Barre   Fishmonger   ob.s.p.   m. Ralph Cotton of Bellaport
     ob.s.p.   bapt. 6 Feb 1631   Knight
     1662   Lord of Willesley   Mayor of London
         d.1728, ae.97

James   Ann   Frances   Demaris   Edward Barr   Sir Thomas (I) ========== Frances Burton
"ne'er-do-well"   bur.1692   dau.   bur.1677   1ˢᵗ son of Judith   C.B., Knight, Judge   daughter of
1ˢᵗ son & heir   Willesley   m.1686 to   born demented 1690   Lord of Willesley   Joshua Burton
deprived of estate   Sir John Parker   ob.s.p. unmarried   bapt.30 Apr 1691   of Brakely,
raised by aunt   1755   d.19 May 1750   Northamptonshire
Abigail Cotton.
bur. with 2 sisters at Willesley   Parnel Villars =================== Thomas Abney (II), Lord of Willesley   (dau.)
     will: 8 Jun 1798   b.02 Jan 1725; ob.s.m.p.15 Aug 1791

Abney Parker   John Parker   Parnel Abney ============ Lt. Gen. Sir Charles Hastings, Lord of Packington
     Heiress of Willesley   m.02 Jun 1788; 1ˢᵗ Baronet of Willesley Hall
     b.29 Jan 1756; m.1788   illeg. son of Frances Hastings; commited suicide 1823

Frank Abney-Hastings   Sir Charles Abney-Hastings, 2ⁿᵈ Baronet of Willesley Hall; b.1792. succ.1823. d.1858 ob.s.p.
d.1828 at Zante (a hero)   It was a condition that an Abney must assume Willesley. So he took on the name Abney. At his death, he passed
     Willesley, *by hook or by crook*, to his kinsman, Henry Rawdon-Hastings, and out of the Abney family forever.
     Each Lord or Lady of the Manor of Willesley must bear the name *Abney-Hastings*.

Pedigree of yᵉ Abney Family of Leicester

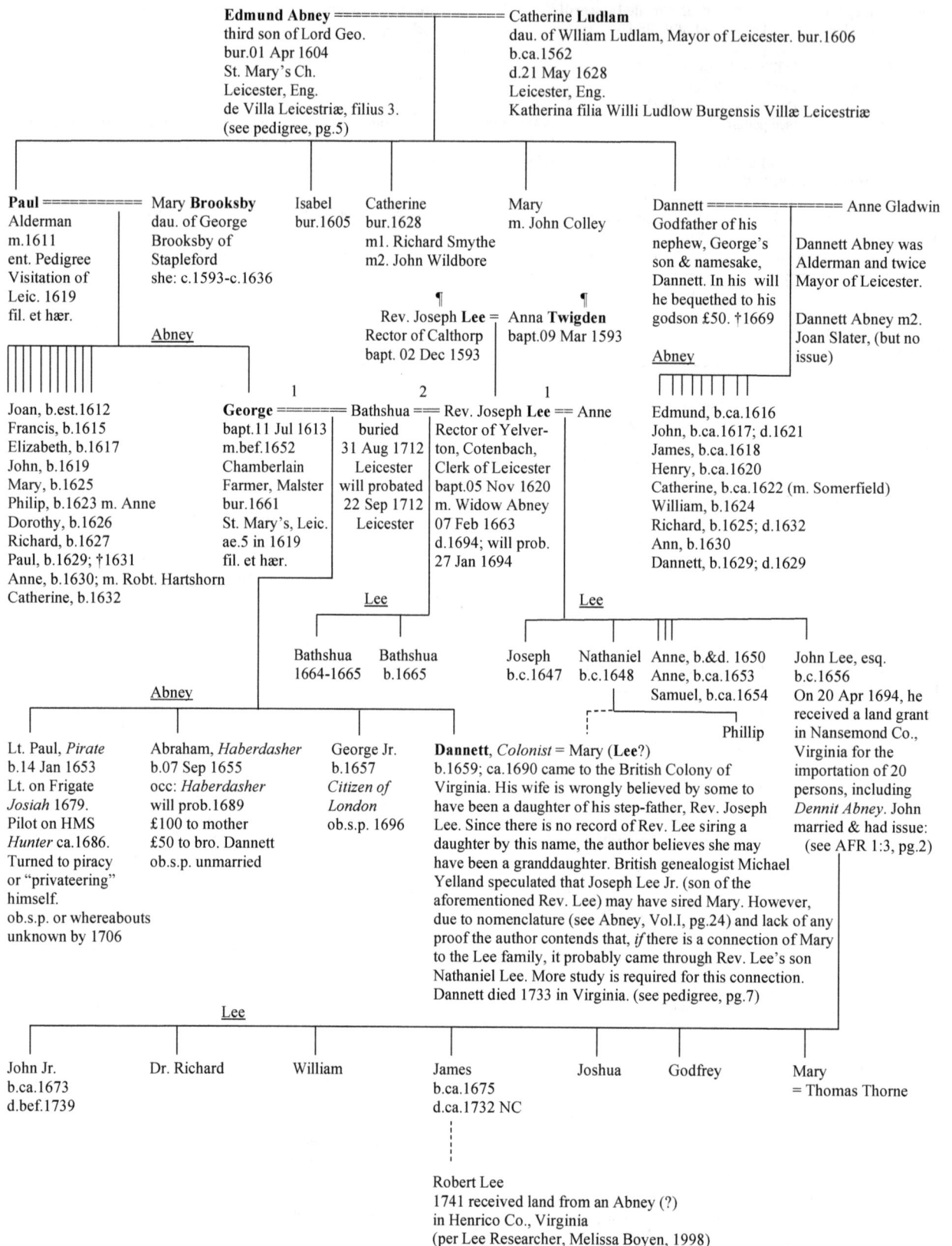

Edmund Abney ================= **Catherine Ludlam**
third son of Lord Geo.   dau. of Wlliam Ludlam, Mayor of Leicester. bur.1606
bur.01 Apr 1604   b.ca.1562
St. Mary's Ch.   d.21 May 1628
Leicester, Eng.   Leicester, Eng.
de Villa Leicestriæ, filius 3.   Katherina filia Willi Ludlow Burgensis Villæ Leicestriæ
(see pedigree, pg.5)

Paul =========== Mary **Brooksby**   Isabel   Catherine   Mary   Dannett =============== Anne Gladwin
Alderman   dau. of George   bur.1605   bur.1628   m. John Colley   Godfather of his   Dannett Abney was
m.1611   Brooksby of   m1. Richard Smythe   nephew, George's   Alderman and twice
ent. Pedigree   Stapleford   m2. John Wildbore   son & namesake,   Mayor of Leicester.
Visitation of   she: c.1593-c.1636   ¶   ¶   Dannett. In his will
Leic. 1619   Rev. Joseph **Lee** = Anna **Twigden**   he bequethed to his   Dannett Abney m2.
fil. et hær.   Rector of Calthorp   bapt.09 Mar 1593   godson £50. †1669   Joan Slater, (but no
        Abney   bapt. 02 Dec 1593   Abney   issue)

                              1   2   1

Joan, b.est.1612   **George** ======= Bathshua === Rev. Joseph **Lee** == Anne   Edmund, b.ca.1616
Francis, b.1615   bapt.11 Jul 1613   buried   Rector of Yelver-   John, b.ca.1617; d.1621
Elizabeth, b.1617   m.bef.1652   31 Aug 1712   ton, Cotenbach,   James, b.ca.1618
John, b.1619   Chamberlain   Leicester   Clerk of Leicester   Henry, b.ca.1620
Mary, b.1625   Farmer, Malster   will probated   bapt.05 Nov 1620   Catherine, b.ca.1622 (m. Somerfield)
Philip, b.1623 m. Anne   bur.1661   22 Sep 1712   m. Widow Abney   William, b.1624
Dorothy, b.1626   St. Mary's, Leic.   Leicester   07 Feb 1663   Richard, b.1625; d.1632
Richard, b.1627   ae.5 in 1619   d.1694; will prob.   Ann, b.1630
Paul, b.1629; †1631   fil. et hær.   27 Jan 1694   Dannett, b.1629; d.1629
Anne, b.1630; m. Robt. Hartshorn
Catherine, b.1632   Lee   Lee

                      Bathshua   Bathshua   Joseph   Nathaniel   Anne, b.&d. 1650   John Lee, esq.
                      1664-1665   b.1665   b.c.1647   b.c.1648   Anne, b.ca.1653   b.c.1656
                                                   Samuel, b.ca.1654   On 20 Apr 1694, he
                  Abney   received a land grant
                                            Phillip   in Nansemond Co.,

Lt. Paul, *Pirate*   Abraham, *Haberdasher*   George Jr.   **Dannett**, *Colonist* = Mary (**Lee**?)   Virginia for the
b.14 Jan 1653   b.07 Sep 1655   b.1657   b.1659; ca.1690 came to the British Colony of   importation of 20
Lt. on Frigate   occ: *Haberdasher*   *Citizen of*   Virginia. His wife is wrongly believed by some to   persons, including
Josiah 1679.   will prob.1689   *London*   have been a daughter of his step-father, Rev. Joseph   *Dennit Abney*. John
Pilot on HMS   £100 to mother   ob.s.p. 1696   Lee. Since there is no record of Rev. Lee siring a   married & had issue:
Hunter ca.1686.   £50 to bro. Dannett   daughter by this name, the author believes she may   (see AFR 1:3, pg.2)
Turned to piracy   ob.s.p. unmarried   have been a granddaughter. British genealogist Michael
or "privateering"   Yelland speculated that Joseph Lee Jr. (son of the
himself.   aforementioned Rev. Lee) may have sired Mary. However,
ob.s.p. or whereabouts   due to nomenclature (see Abney, Vol.I, pg.24) and lack of any
unknown by 1706   proof the author contends that, *if* there is a connection of Mary
                                     to the Lee family, it probably came through Rev. Lee's son
                                     Nathaniel Lee. More study is required for this connection.
                                     Dannett died 1733 in Virginia. (see pedigree, pg.7)

        Lee

John Jr.   Dr. Richard   William   James   Joshua   Godfrey   Mary
b.ca.1673   b.ca.1675   = Thomas Thorne
d.bef.1739   d.ca.1732 NC

                                  Robert Lee
                                  1741 received land from an Abney (?)
                                  in Henrico Co., Virginia
                                  (per Lee Researcher, Melissa Boyen, 1998)

Pedigree of yᵉ Abney Family of yᵉ British Colonies and the United States of America

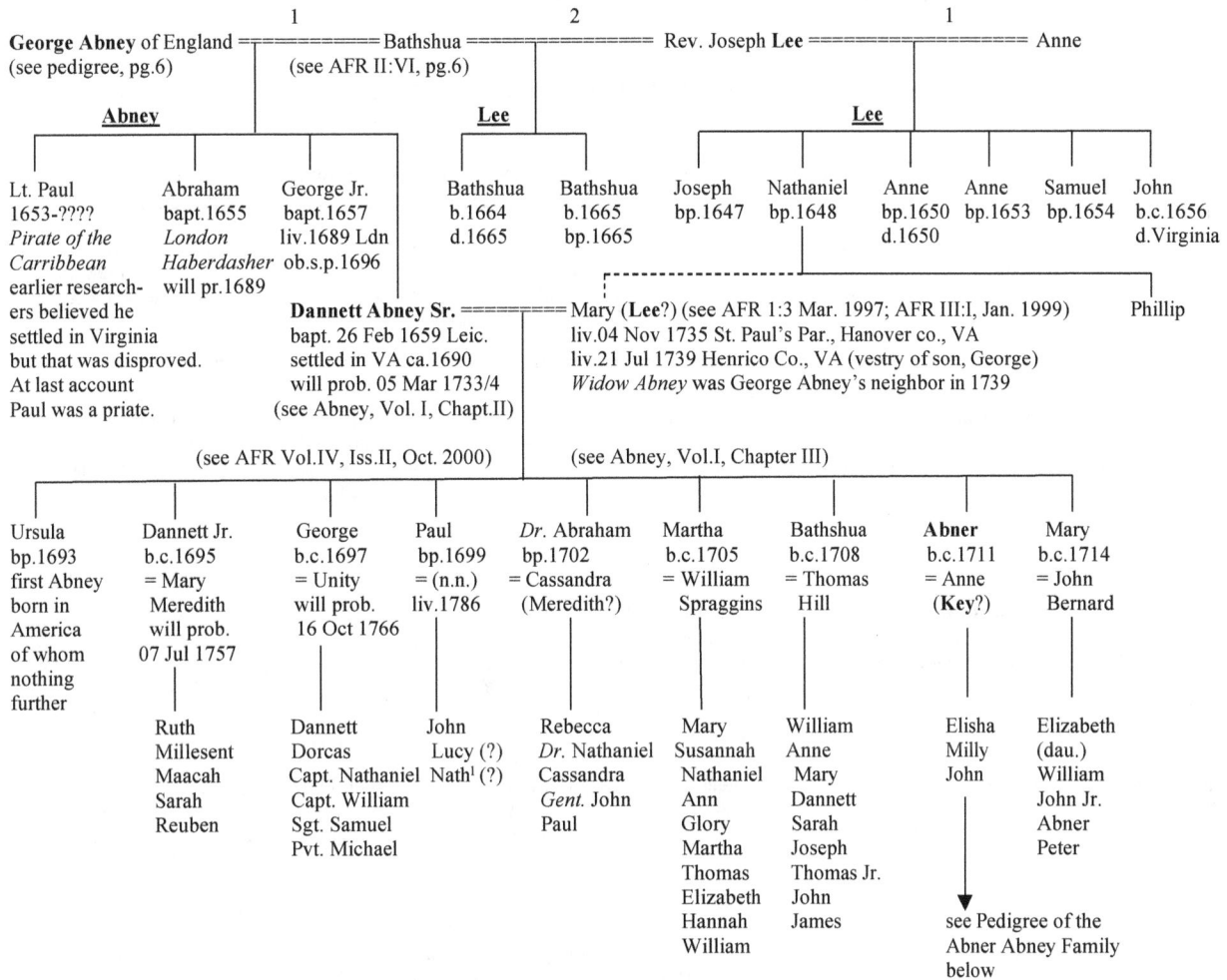

	1		2		1	

George Abney of England ========= Bathshua ============== Rev. Joseph **Lee** ================= Anne
(see pedigree, pg.6)   (see AFR II:VI, pg.6)

Abney   **Lee**   **Lee**

Lt. Paul	Abraham	George Jr.	Bathshua	Bathshua	Joseph	Nathaniel	Anne	Anne	Samuel	John
1653-????	bapt.1655	bapt.1657	b.1664	b.1665	bp.1647	bp.1648	bp.1650	bp.1653	bp.1654	b.c.1656
Pirate of the	*London*	liv.1689 Ldn	d.1665	bp.1665			d.1650			d.Virginia
Carribbean	*Haberdasher*	ob.s.p.1696								
earlier research-	will pr.1689									
ers believed he										
settled in Virginia		**Dannett Abney Sr.** ======== Mary (**Lee**?) (see AFR 1:3 Mar. 1997; AFR III:I, Jan. 1999)							Phillip
but that was disproved.		bapt. 26 Feb 1659 Leic. liv.04 Nov 1735 St. Paul's Par., Hanover co., VA							
At last account		settled in VA ca.1690 liv.21 Jul 1739 Henrico Co., VA (vestry of son, George)							
Paul was a priate.		will prob. 05 Mar 1733/4 *Widow Abney* was George Abney's neighbor in 1739							
		(see Abney, Vol. I, Chapt.II)							

(see AFR Vol.IV, Iss.II, Oct. 2000)   (see Abney, Vol.I, Chapter III)

Ursula	Dannett Jr.	George	Paul	*Dr.* Abraham	Martha	Bathshua	**Abner**	Mary
bp.1693	b.c.1695	b.c.1697	bp.1699	bp.1702	b.c.1705	b.c.1708	b.c.1711	b.c.1714
first Abney	= Mary	= Unity	= (n.n.)	= Cassandra	= William	= Thomas	= Anne	= John
born in	Meredith	will prob.	liv.1786	(Meredith?)	Spraggins	Hill	(**Key**?)	Bernard
America	will prob.	16 Oct 1766						
of whom	07 Jul 1757							
nothing								
further								

	Ruth	Dannett	John	Rebecca	Mary	William	Elisha	Elizabeth
	Millesent	Dorcas	Lucy (?)	*Dr.* Nathaniel	Susannah	Anne	Milly	(dau.)
	Maacah	Capt. Nathaniel	Nath¹ (?)	Cassandra	Nathaniel	Mary	John	William
	Sarah	Capt. William		*Gent.* John	Ann	Dannett		John Jr.
	Reuben	Sgt. Samuel		Paul	Glory	Sarah		Abner
		Pvt. Michael			Martha	Joseph		Peter
					Thomas	Thomas Jr.		
					Elizabeth	John	see Pedigree of the	
					Hannah	James	Abner Abney Family	
					William		below	

Pedigree of the Abner Abney Family

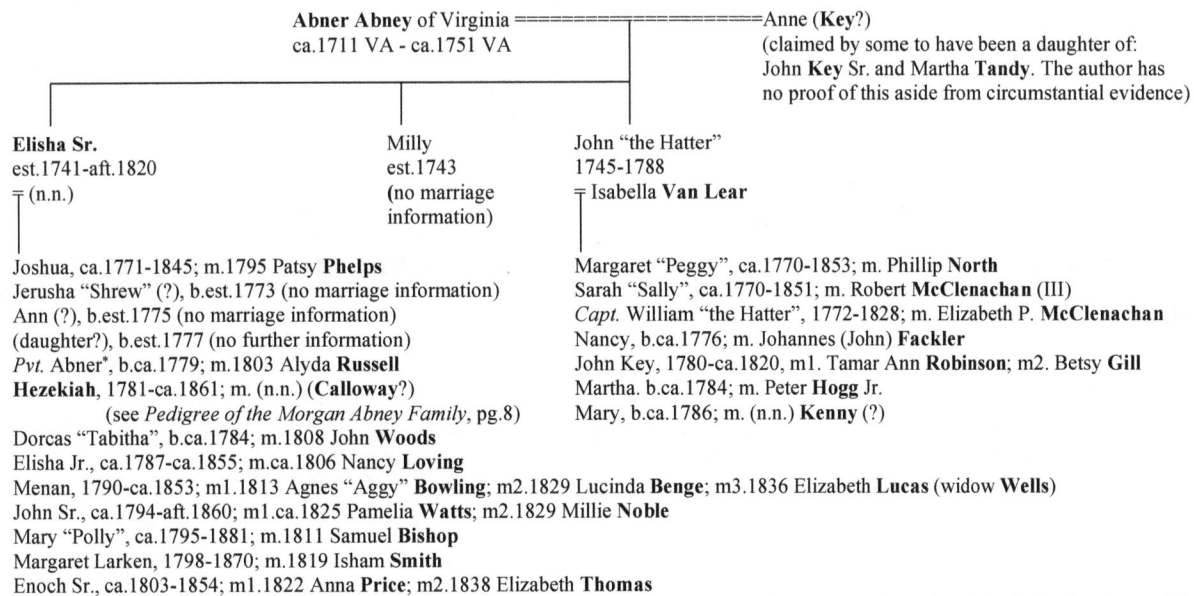

Abner Abney of Virginia ======================= Anne (**Key**?)
ca.1711 VA - ca.1751 VA   (claimed by some to have been a daughter of:
       John **Key** Sr. and Martha **Tandy**. The author has
       no proof of this aside from circumstantial evidence)

Elisha Sr.	Milly	John "the Hatter"
est.1741-aft.1820	est.1743	1745-1788
⊤ (n.n.)	(no marriage	⊤ Isabella **Van Lear**
	information)	

Joshua, ca.1771-1845; m.1795 Patsy **Phelps**   Margaret "Peggy", ca.1770-1853; m. Phillip **North**
Jerusha "Shrew" (?), b.est.1773 (no marriage information)   Sarah "Sally", ca.1770-1851; m. Robert **McClenachan** (III)
Ann (?), b.est.1775 (no marriage information)   *Capt.* William "the Hatter", 1772-1828; m. Elizabeth P. **McClenachan**
(daughter?), b.est.1777 (no further information)   Nancy, b.ca.1776; m. Johannes (John) **Fackler**
Pvt. Abner*, b.ca.1779; m.1803 Alyda **Russell**   John Key, 1780-ca.1820, m1. Tamar Ann **Robinson**; m2. Betsy **Gill**
Hezekiah, 1781-ca.1861; m. (n.n.) (**Calloway**?)   Martha. b.ca.1784; m. Peter **Hogg** Jr.
     (see *Pedigree of the Morgan Abney Family*, pg.8)   Mary, b.ca.1786; m. (n.n.) **Kenny** (?)
Dorcas "Tabitha", b.ca.1784; m.1808 John **Woods**
Elisha Jr., ca.1787-ca.1855; m.ca.1806 Nancy **Loving**
Menan, 1790-ca.1853; m1.1813 Agnes "Aggy" **Bowling**; m2.1829 Lucinda **Benge**; m3.1836 Elizabeth **Lucas** (widow **Wells**)
John Sr., ca.1794-aft.1860; m1.ca.1825 Pamelia **Watts**; m2.1829 Millie **Noble**
Mary "Polly", ca.1795-1881; m.1811 Samuel **Bishop**
Margaret Larken, 1798-1870; m.1819 Isham **Smith**
Enoch Sr., ca.1803-1854; m1.1822 Anna **Price**; m2.1838 Elizabeth **Thomas**

           *Pvt. Abner Abney fought in the Battle of New Orleans

Due to the fact that Cousin Morgan Floyd Abney is the inspiration for this book (and will receive the very first copy), we will follow his lineage from Hezekiah Abney.

Pedigree of the Morgan Floyd Abney Family

Hezekiah Abney of Virginia ===================== (n.n.) (**Calloway?**)

John	Benjamin Hezekiah	Elizabeth	Delilah	**Wiley**		Andrew	James	Presley	Joel
c.1802-bef.1840	1804-1878	b.c.1806	b.c.1808	c.1811-c.1895		b.c.1813	1815-1890	b.c.1825	c.1828-aft.1880
= (n.n.)	=1 E. Hogan	= Yarborough	= Yarborough	=1 Eliz. **Brumbelow**		= S. Collins	=1 D. Daniel	= C. Hollingsworth	= Delila A. (N.N.)
	=2 S.A. Harper			=2 Mary Black			=2 S. Miller		

Pinkney Floyd, CSA	Pvt. Thomas "Jackson", CSA	Martha Jane	James Allen	Elmira	Sarah E.
1842-1870	1846-1907	c.1847-1931	1850-1910	1852-1932	c.1854-????
= Sarah Graham	= Dorothy C. Cleveland	= Wm. Wilkerson	=1 Margt. Wilkerson	=1 Jn Silas Carver	=1 J.W. Wilkerson
			=2 Margt. Johnson	=2 Chas Bushnell	(=2 Dick Jones?)

Laura E.	John "Roscoe"	Sarah Ann "Sally"
1862-1939	1865-1908	1870-bef.1906
= Frank Dobbins	= Sarah Ruth **Ramsey**	= George Mac Inman

Ethel Winaforde	Carrie Olivie	Loretta	Elizabeth E.	John Floyd
1892-1966	1896-1974	1898-1987	1902-1978	1904-1988
= John L. Marcum	= Lincoln L. Marcum	= Dewey Lee	= Dennis J. Evans	=1 Martha Ann Farris
				=2 Sarah Delilah McCurry

Delores Lee	Joy	Dora	Margaret Marie	John Roscoe	**Morgan Floyd (contributor,**
1928-2009	c.1930	ca.1933	1934-1990	1936-1937	b.1937 originator)
= (n.n.) Rank			=1 Geo. Rice Lyerly		=1 Nellie J. Williams
			=2 Eugene Albert Dixon		=2 Janet M. Kiser

			Delores Dixon		Gary Wayne
			= Edward Renfroe		b.1959

Note: The pedigrees on pages 1-7, excluding the pedigree for Abner Abney, are reprinted from Chapter I of the **Abney Family History Series, Volume I,** *Abney: Ancestry and Genealogy of Dr. Abraham Abney of Virginia*, second edition (ISBN: 978-0-9993282-2-4, LCCN: 2018952526), published 3 Sep 2018 by this current author.

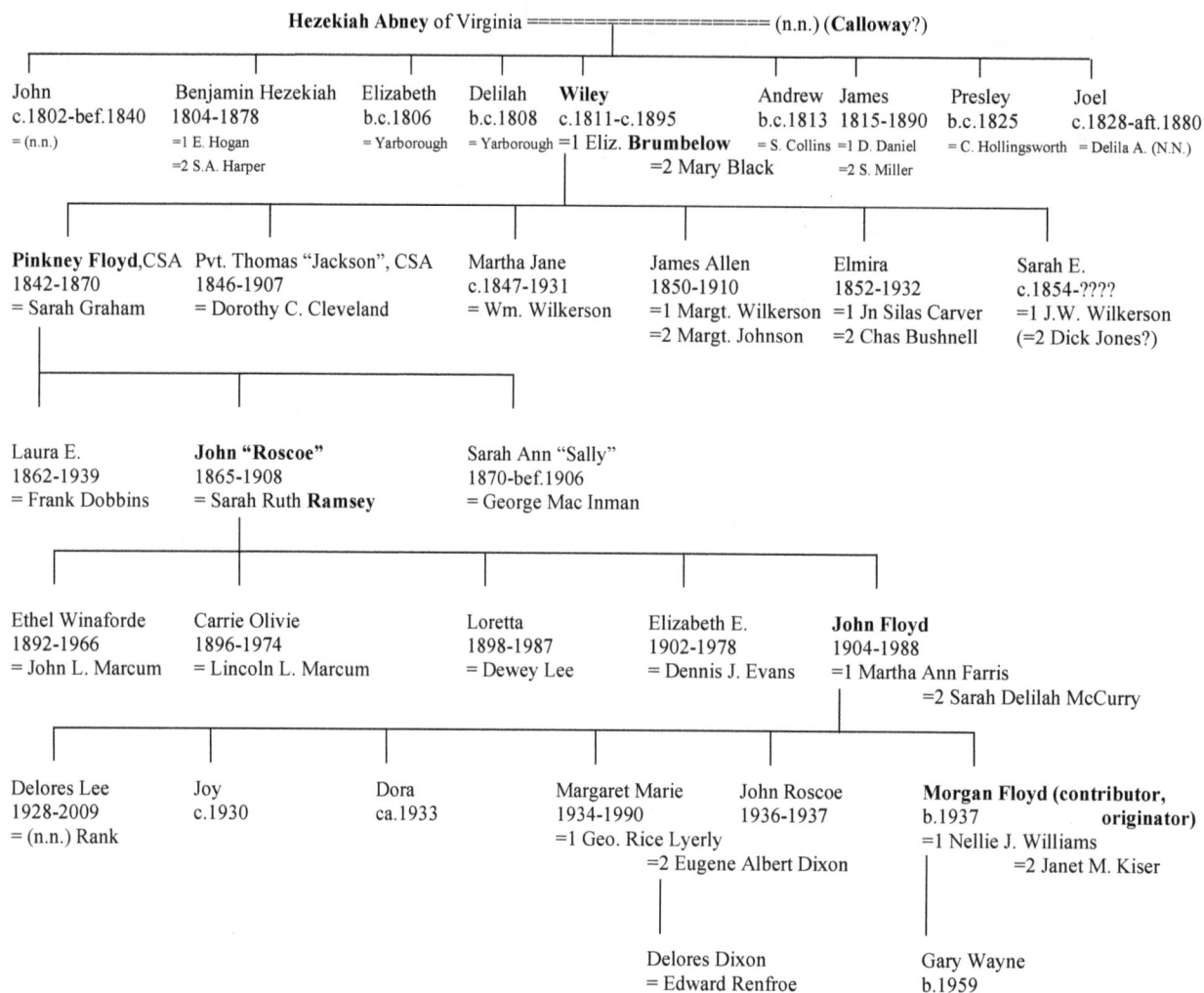

Authors and Contributors

Pedigree of Contributors and the Author not Descended from Abner Abney of Virginia

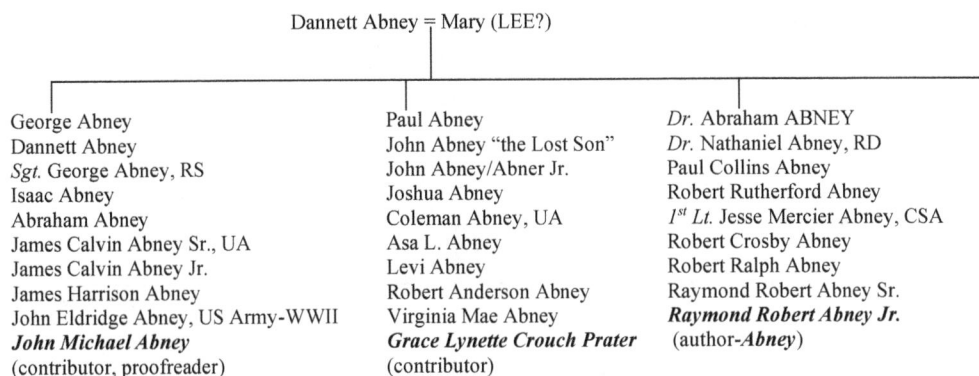

Dannett Abney = Mary (LEE?)

George Abney	Paul Abney	*Dr.* Abraham ABNEY
Dannett Abney	John Abney "the Lost Son"	*Dr.* Nathaniel Abney, RD
Sgt. George Abney, RS	John Abney/Abner Jr.	Paul Collins Abney
Isaac Abney	Joshua Abney	Robert Rutherford Abney
Abraham Abney	Coleman Abney, UA	*1st Lt.* Jesse Mercier Abney, CSA
James Calvin Abney Sr., UA	Asa L. Abney	Robert Crosby Abney
James Calvin Abney Jr.	Levi Abney	Robert Ralph Abney
James Harrison Abney	Robert Anderson Abney	Raymond Robert Abney Sr.
John Eldridge Abney, US Army-WWII	Virginia Mae Abney	***Raymond Robert Abney Jr.***
John Michael Abney	***Grace Lynette Crouch Prater***	(author-***Abney***)
(contributor, proofreader)	(contributor)	

Pedigree of Contributors and an Author Descended from Abner Abney of Virginia

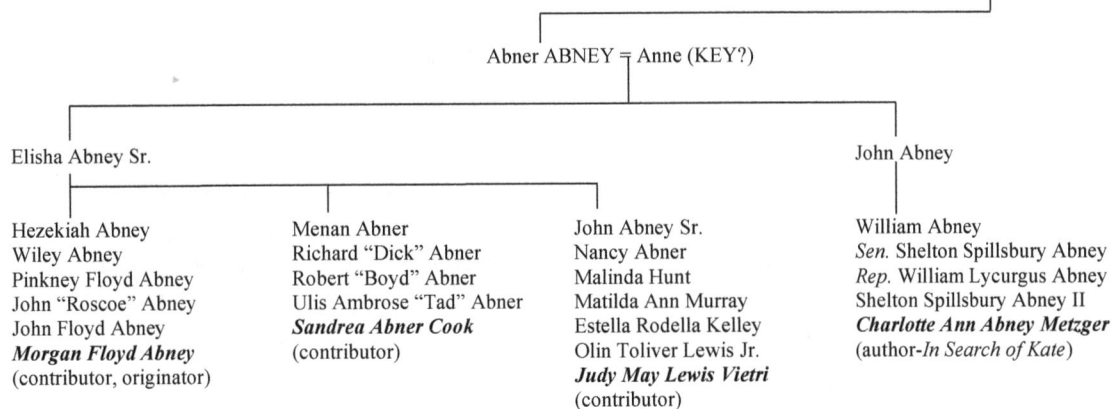

Abner ABNEY = Anne (KEY?)

Elisha Abney Sr.   John Abney

Hezekiah Abney	Menan Abner	John Abney Sr.	William Abney
Wiley Abney	Richard "Dick" Abner	Nancy Abner	*Sen.* Shelton Spillsbury Abney
Pinkney Floyd Abney	Robert "Boyd" Abner	Malinda Hunt	*Rep.* William Lycurgus Abney
John "Roscoe" Abney	Ulis Ambrose "Tad" Abner	Matilda Ann Murray	Shelton Spillsbury Abney II
John Floyd Abney	***Sandrea Abner Cook***	Estella Rodella Kelley	***Charlotte Ann Abney Metzger***
Morgan Floyd Abney	(contributor)	Olin Toliver Lewis Jr.	(author-*In Search of Kate*)
(contributor, originator)		***Judy May Lewis Vietri***	
		(contributor)	

It is amazing the diversity of the family lines involved in the research of this book. The author of this book, author Charlotte Ann Abney Metzger, and the five contributors descend from four of the five sons of Dannett Abney Sr., which is amazing in itself. But add to that the fact that author Metzger and three contributors descend from both sons of this volume's subject, Abner Abney! This was truly an amazingly coordinated effort.

"Genealogists truly improve the work of other genealogists!"
…Raymond Robert "RR" Abney Jr.

Pedigree of Willie Sandlin, World War I *Congressional Medal of Honor* Recipient

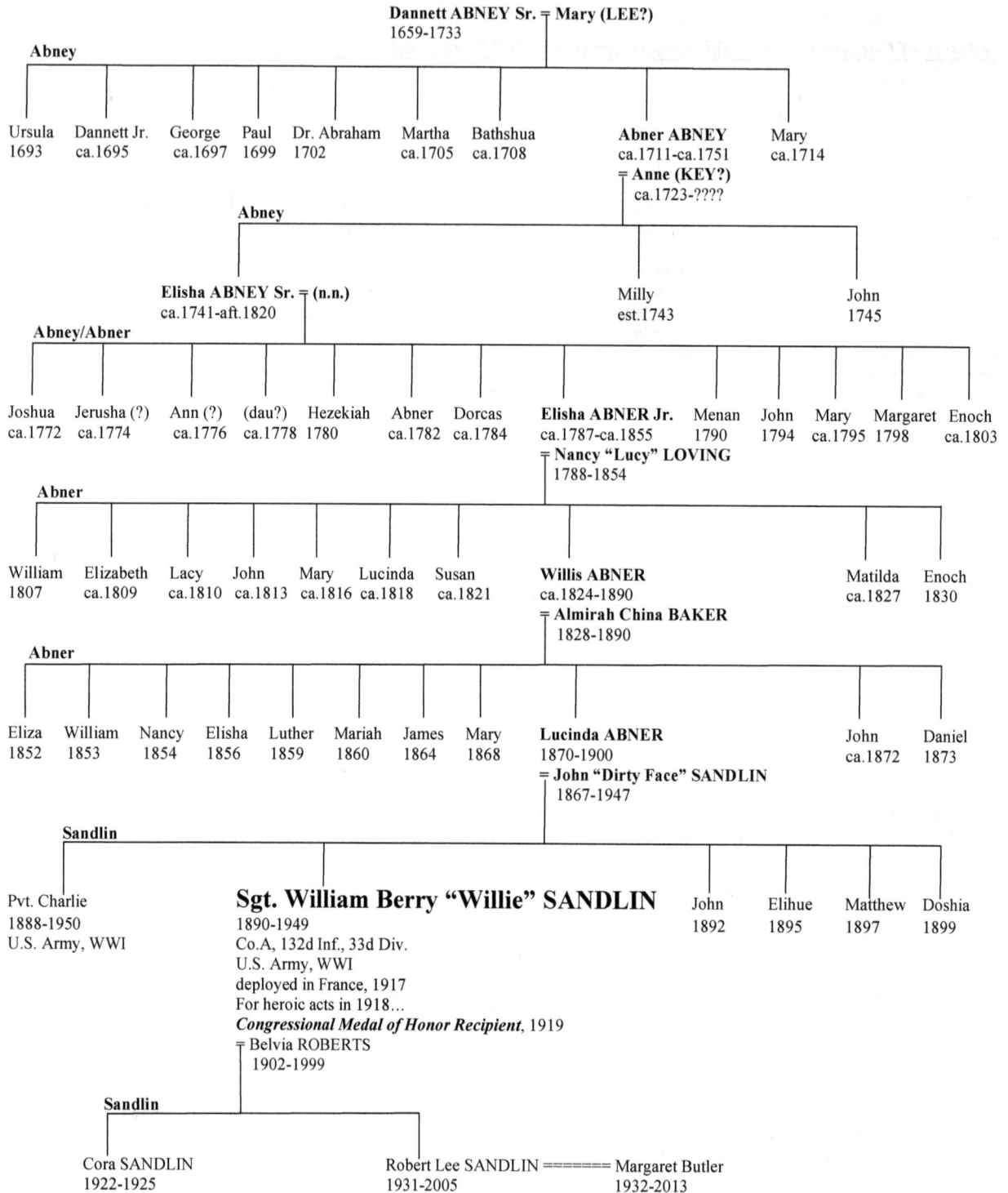

Dannett ABNEY Sr. ᵵ **Mary (LEE?)**
1659-1733

Abney

| Ursula 1693 | Dannett Jr. ca.1695 | George ca.1697 | Paul 1699 | Dr. Abraham 1702 | Martha ca.1705 | Bathshua ca.1708 | **Abner ABNEY** ca.1711-ca.1751 | Mary ca.1714 |

Abner ABNEY
ca.1711-ca.1751
ᵵ **Anne (KEY?)**
ca.1723-????

Abney

| **Elisha ABNEY Sr.** ᵵ **(n.n.)** ca.1741-aft.1820 | Milly est.1743 | John 1745 |

Abney/Abner

| Joshua ca.1772 | Jerusha (?) ca.1774 | Ann (?) ca.1776 | (dau?) ca.1778 | Hezekiah 1780 | Abner ca.1782 | Dorcas ca.1784 | **Elisha ABNER Jr.** ca.1787-ca.1855 | Menan 1790 | John 1794 | Mary ca.1795 | Margaret 1798 | Enoch ca.1803 |

Elisha ABNER Jr.
ca.1787-ca.1855
ᵵ **Nancy "Lucy" LOVING**
1788-1854

Abner

| William 1807 | Elizabeth ca.1809 | Lacy ca.1810 | John ca.1813 | Mary ca.1816 | Lucinda ca.1818 | Susan ca.1821 | **Willis ABNER** ca.1824-1890 | Matilda ca.1827 | Enoch 1830 |

Willis ABNER
ca.1824-1890
ᵵ **Almirah China BAKER**
1828-1890

Abner

| Eliza 1852 | William 1853 | Nancy 1854 | Elisha 1856 | Luther 1859 | Mariah 1860 | James 1864 | Mary 1868 | **Lucinda ABNER** 1870-1900 | John ca.1872 | Daniel 1873 |

Lucinda ABNER
1870-1900
= **John "Dirty Face" SANDLIN**
1867-1947

Sandlin

| Pvt. Charlie 1888-1950 U.S. Army, WWI | **Sgt. William Berry "Willie" SANDLIN** 1890-1949 | John 1892 | Elihue 1895 | Matthew 1897 | Doshia 1899 |

Sgt. William Berry "Willie" SANDLIN
1890-1949
Co.A, 132d Inf., 33d Div.
U.S. Army, WWI
deployed in France, 1917
For heroic acts in 1918...
Congressional Medal of Honor Recipient, 1919
ᵵ Belvia ROBERTS
1902-1999

Sandlin

| Cora SANDLIN 1922-1925 | Robert Lee SANDLIN 1931-2005 | ======= | Margaret Butler 1932-2013 |

Sgt. Willie Sandlin and his wife are the first two people buried in the
Kentucky Veterans Cemetery South East in Hyden, Leslie County, Kentucky.

Chapter II

Abner Abney of the British Colony of Virginia
Youngest Son of Dannett Abney Sr. & Mary (Lee?)

Abner Abney was born in King William County in the British Colony of Virginia, around 1711 (by the author's estimate).[1] Virginia had been a Royal Colony since 1624 and was now well established.[2] Abner's father, Dannett Abney (Sr.) arrived in the colony around 1690 or so. Dannett Abney Sr. & his wife, Mary (Lee?) had nine known children, to wit: Ursula (bapt.1693); Dannett Jr. (eldest son and heir-at-law, b.ca.1695); George (b.ca.1697); Paul (bapt.1699); Abraham (bapt.1702 [see Volume I of the Abney Family History Series: *Abney – Ancestry and Genealogy of Dr. Abraham Abney of Virginia*]); Martha (b.ca.1705); Bathshua (b.ca.1708); Abner (our subject, b.ca.1711); and Mary (b.ca.1714).[3]

As with the majority of his siblings, Abner was given a Biblical name. In the Bible, Abner (son of Ner) was a cousin of King Saul (first king of Israel and Judah), and commander-in-chief of King Saul's army.[4]

Probably due to the destruction of documents by war and natural disasters, no record of Abner's birth or baptism have ever been located. At least three of his siblings (Ursula, Paul and Abraham) were baptized in the Abingdon Parish Church in Gloucester County, Virginia.[5] The baptismal records of the other siblings (Dannett Abney Jr., George Abney and Martha) have not been discovered and feared lost forever.

Bathshua, Abner and Mary may still have been baptized in Abingdon Parish if that was the closest church to their home in King William County, Virginia. There was a church in New Kent County, Virginia (St. Peter's Parish Church) established in 1702.[6] This church may have been closer to the Abney family than the Abingdon church. Still, no such baptismal records have been discovered heretofore. The author has not given up hope.

Unfortunately, very little information has surfaced on Abner Abney since the publishing of *Abney*, Vol. I.[7] By 1704, Dannett Abney Sr. and Mary (Lee?) had purchased land in King William County, Virginia.[8] It is suspected this is where they were living when Abner Abney was born.

About Abner Abney's childhood, nothing is known. His paternal grandfather, George Abney predeceased him in England by five decades;[9] and his paternal grandmother died in England when Abner was but a year old.[10] Of his maternal grandparents, nothing definitively is known. The author theorizes the maternal grandfather was Nathaniel Lee of Leicester, England. However, proof is lacking. If correct, Abner's maternal grandparents were either in England or deceased when he was born. Still, he certainly grew up without the doting of any of his grandparents.

Abner's father was a cooper (barrel-maker) and land owner.[11, 12] The boys (sons of Dannett Abney Sr.), no doubt, worked the land; and Abner would have been taught the value of a good day's work. Yet, again, of his childhood nothing is known and we are left only to speculate.

The first mention of Abner Abney in any Virginia record heretofore discovered is when he appears as a devisee of his father, Dannett Abney Sr.[13] Abner, along with his brother, Paul Abney, were the favored sons of their father, Dannett Sr. (in the last will and testament of the latter). The reason for this is unknown, but the author has posited a theory:

Dannett Abney Jr., George Abney and Dr. Abraham Abney were very successful land owners in old Virginia.[14] On the other hand, Paul Abney does not seem to have been as prosperous, as there is little to indicate he had any valuable real estate. The first discovered record of Paul purchasing land was in 1742, ten years after his father's death.[15] Subsequently, there are additional records of Paul purchasing and selling land. He was a planter in old Virginia. However, by 1776, Paul was a pauper. We find him and his wife receiving living assistance in a series of vestries (over some five years), to wit:[16]

- 09 May 1776   *Order'd that the wardens provide coarse linen for Two Sheets & 2 pr. Breeches for Paul Abney*
- 17 Dec 1777   *At the Poor House this day: To Paul Abney 1 year to commence from 1st Jany. 1778 5.*
- 15 Feb 1779   *At Stephen James's Feby 15th 1779: To Paul Abney for 1 year comm'g from 1st Jany last   20.*
- 08 Sep 1780   *At the Widow Fargusons Sept. 8th 1780: To Paul Abney & wife for their support to the 1st Jany. next   100.*
- 25 Feb 1781   *The 26th of Feby. 1781 at Charlottesville... To Paul Abner & wife do (support pr. Year)   600.*

As to why Abner Abney was a favored son of his father, it appears from all indications he was the youngest son and his father desired to give him a start in his adult life.

Returning to the Last Will and Testament of Dannett Abney Sr. (Abner Abney's father), we read (verbatim transcription by the author from a copy of the will donated by Cousin Lisa Franklin):[17]

> **In the Name of God amen i Dannitt Abney of Spotsilvana**
> **County being in Good health of Body and perfect mind and ~**
> **memory prais bee Given to Almighty God do make and ordain**
> **this my last will and Testament in manner and form as foloethe**
> **First and prinsably I Comend my Sole into the hands of Almighty**
> **God hoping threw the meritt Death and passion of my Savior**
> **Jesus Crist to have full and free pardon of my Sins and To**
> **inherit Ever lasting Life and my body committed To the Earth to bee**
> **Decantly Buried at the Discretion of my Executrix hearafter ~**
> **Named and touching ye Disposal of all such temporal Estate**
> **as it hath pleased Almighty God to bestow upon mee I Give &**
> **Dispose thereof as followeth item i make my Loving Wife**
> **Mary Abney my Sole Exectrix and i Give to my wyfe Mary**
> **Abney all my Estate Reall and personall and to hir disposal**
> **it is my Desire that if ye plantation whear i now Live is not**
> **Sold before my Wyfes Death that Shee wold give ye plantati:**
> **son and land belonging to to it to my tow Sons paul Abney**
> **and Abner Abney and for the rest of my Estate that Shee is**
> **pofsefsed with at hir death I Desire that my wyfe wold give**
> **it to ye Children that are most Dutifull to hir in Witnefs**
> **Whereof i have put my hand and Seal this fifth day of february**
> **one thousand and Seven hundred thirty Tow ~**

> **Signned and in ye**   **Dannitt Abney (Seal)**
> **presants of ~**
> **Paul Abney**
> **Abner abney**
> **William trusty**
> **Mary Abney**

> **Will Book A. page 210**
> **At a Court held for Spotsylvania County on Tuesday, March the**
> **5th 1733/4 ~**
> **This Will being exhibitted and Sworn To p Mary**
> **Abney Executrix therein Named was proved p the Oathes of**
> **Abner Abney Mary Abney** the younger **and William Trusty and Admitted**
> **To Record ~**
> **Test:**
> **John Waller Ct Clrk**

This is where we have definitive proof that Abner was a son of Dannett Abney Sr. Note that Abner also witnessed the will, and proved the will in court on 05 Mar 1733. (Note: at the time Dannett Abney's will was written, the *New Year* began on March 25th. For this reason, many records keepers and clerks wrote dates in March as double years. In this case, the County Clerk, John Waller, wrote March the 5th 1733/4. Do not be confused. The correct year was 1733. In twenty days, the year was to become 1734, therefore the month of March was in both years, 1733 and 1734 (but the record was NOT). If the will had been proved on March 25th, Waller would have written March the 25th 1733/4 and it would have been 1734.[18] This, then is absolutely proof the will was proved in 1733 at the very end of the year…the year in which Dannett Abney Sr. died.

It appears neither Abner Abney nor his brother, Paul Abney received the land in which they were devised in their father's will. On 04 Nov 1735, Mary Abney sold the Spotsylvania County land to Edwin Hickman.[19]

Between 1733 and 1752, Abner Abney's life is somewhat of a mystery. From his will (plate C), we know he owned land in Albemarle County, Virginia (which county was formed from Goochland County). But when and how he came to own this land is unknown, at least by this author.

Goochland County, Virginia (Home of Founding Father and third President of the United States of America, Thomas Jefferson) was created in 1728 from the original Henrico Shire. It seems that Abner Abney was living in Spotsylvania County, Virginia when his father died…and probably living on his father's estate. But later, it is suspected he moved to Goochland County before his land fell into Albemarle County, Virginia.

Establishing the birth years of Abner's immediately family, we are left with but few facts. According to Metzger, Abner's son, John, was born in 1745.[20] Since John and Milly were to share 100 acres and Elisha was to receive a full 100 acres, the author estimates Elisha was the eldest child (although this reasoning is not conclusive). Using John Abney's birthdate as our starting point, we can estimate Milly was born around 1743 and Elisha Abney/Abner was born around 1741; making Abner's marriage to Anne (Key?) around 1740 or so. The author also suspects this marriage was in Goochland County, Virginia. There are those who believe that Abner Abney's wife, Anne was a daughter of John Key Sr. and Martha Tandy. Although this author has no proof of this relationship, the fact that his grandson was named *John Key Abney* and one *John Key* witnessed his will are definitely nomenclatural clues.

Since, as the author believes, Abner Abney and his wife, Anne were probably living in Goochland County, Virginia, it stands to reason at least the first two of their children were born there. Again, this is speculation. If Elisha was born around 1741 and Milly around 1743, they would have been born in Goochland County.

In 1744, the western part of Goochland County became Albemarle County.[21] Since Abner's will was written and filed in this latter county, we surmise his land in the former county must have fallen into Albemarle County in 1744.

If this suspicion is correct, we can also surmise that John Abney, apparently the youngest child of Abner Abney, was born in 1745 in Albemarle County, Virginia.[22]

From here, the life of Abner Abney is, once again, a mystery. We know he obtained at least a couple of hundred acres of land in Albemarle County, Virginia. In addition to his homestead, he also had what he referred to as his "Parsil Estate". Still, these are meager holdings for an eighteenth-century man. Now, his life was going to be cut short due to a very serious illness, the exact illness being unknown to researchers, but alluded to in his will.[23]

On 25 Sep 1751, Abner Abney, being sick in body, wrote his will in Albemarle County, Virginia.[24] For an Abney of the first generation born in Virginia, Abner was very young to be at death's door.

According to this author, the approximate ages at their deaths of the sons of Dannett Abney Sr. were as follows:[25]

Dannett Abney Jr.	age 62
George Abney	age 69
Paul Abney (bapt. 1699)	age 87+
Abraham Abney (bapt. 1702)	age 83
Abner Abney	age 41

This illness Abner Abney contracted in his middle-age also explains his small family. If, as the author believes, Abner married about 1740, he had barely a decade to sire children before the onset of his serious illness.[26]

Within the next nine months after Abner wrote his will, he passed away, probably in 1751. We surmise this because his will was presented to court on 11 Jun 1752.[27] At this time, June was <u>not</u> the sixth month of the year. Note that Abner Abney's will was presented in the same year (1752) that Great Britain, including the British Colony of Virginia, changed their calendar to match the Gregorian (Catholic) Calendar. If the reader studied the author's article *Great Britain Calendar Act of 1751* published in 1998 and reprinted in *Abney, Vol. I*, (p.xix, Ed.1; p.xxiii, Ed.2.) the reader will be able to fully understand this calendar change. Understanding the manner in which the calendar was rendered in 1751/2, we can see that there is a 67% (6/9) chance he died in 1751; and a 33% (3/9) chance that he died in 1752.

This is how the months ran after Abner Abney wrote his will:

- 25 Sept. 1751 Abner Abney wrote his will
1. October 1751
2. November 1751
3. December 1751
4. January 1751
5. February 1751
6. March 1751

- 25 March 1752 (*New Year's Day* 1752)
7. April 1752
8. May 1752
9. June 1752
- 11 June 1752 Anne (Key?) Abney presented Abner Abney's will to the court in Albemarle County for probation.

Because Abner Abney was *very sick and weak* when he wrote his will, this author will go with the 67% chance and conclude Abner Abney died ca.1751 (sometime between September 1751 and March 1751). Do not be confused! January, February and most of March came <u>after</u> September in 1751.

On 11 Jun 1752, Abner's widow, Anne presented his will in court in Albemarle County, Virginia (see Plate C):[28]

Last Will and Testament of Abner Abney

**In the name of God & in Gods name & So forth in the first place
I leave my Soul to God that gave it which am now in my perfect
Senses & memory but very Sick & weak hoping that the Lord will
be merciful to me now as followeth, To wit; I give unto my Dear beloved
Wife the hack of Land which now I live on unto her not to be
mislisted During her Life or Widow hood & afterwards the Entry [Entirety?] of
the hundred acres joining I leave it to be Equally Divided between
my Son John Abney & my Daughter Milley Abney To them & their
heirs forever after their mothers Life or widowhood I leave unto
my Son Elish Abney one hundred acres of Land lying on Mechems
River to him & his heirs forever I leave my Dearly beloved wife my
Parsil Estate & hole & Sole Exectory which is my last Will & Testament**

**Given under my hand & Seal this twenty fifth of September in the Year
of our Lord 1751
Abner Abney (Seal)**

**Test p us,
John Key, Robert (his R mark) foster, Dorathy foster**

**At a Court held for Albemarle County the 11th Day of June 1752
This last Will & Testament of Abner Abney deced was presented into
Court by Anne Abney Widow Exx. therein named was proved by the
Oaths of John Key Robert Foster & Dorathy Foster the witnefses thereof
& ordered to be recorded & on the motion of the said Executrix who made Oath
according to Law Certificate is granted her for obtaining a Probat she
in due form giving Security on which she with John Key her Security
entered into & acknowledged their bond for the said Anne's due & faithful
performance of the said will.**

So, we know from Abner Abney's will, he absolutely had at least three surviving children (probably no more), to wit: John Abney, Milley [Milly] Abney and Elish[a] Abney. The lives of these children will be discussed in Chapter III.

As concerns the witnesses (John Key, Robert Foster, and Dorathy *[sic]* Foster), the author surmises that this *John Key* was actually John Key Jr., son of John Key Sr. and Martha Tandy. The author is unaware of the identities of Robert and Dorothy Foster, although Dorothy could have been Dorothy Key, sister of Anne. But again, this is conjecture.

The fact that one *John Key* witnessed Abner Abney's will, and Abner's son, John Abney named a son *John Key Abney*, certainly lends credence to the belief that Anne who married Abner Abney was indeed a *Key*, and a daughter of John Key. [note: Some claim Abner's son was named John Key Abney, but the author has seen no proof of this.]

Abner Abney lived a relatively short life and never amassed a fortune. As Charlotte Ann Abney Metzger stated it (in her book *In Search of Kate*, privately published 1978), *based on the inventory of his estate, his assets were modest.*[29] His total estate totaled £20.19s.8p (20 English pounds sterling, 19 shillings, 8 pence) (see Plate D).

Considering the fact that he owned at least 200 acres of land, not counting his "Persil Estate", there were certainly some records of land transactions for Abner Abney. These records may have been lost or, hopefully, exist and are waiting to be discovered.

Abner Abney was, no doubt, buried in Albemarle County, Virginia. However, his grave has not been located.

To finalize this chapter, let us visit **two mysteries** we have on the Abner Abney line:

Firstly, it was brought to the author's attention by Contributor John M. Abney, that there was a land grant dated 10 Sep 1755 in Albemarle Co., Virginia to one Abner Abney.[30] Because of the name of the grantee (Abner Abney) and place (Albemarle Co., Virginia), it seems obvious that this land was granted to the subject or our book. However, our Abner Abney died ca.1751, some four years prior to this land grant. The grantee, Abner Abney allegedly received, in this grant, 100 acres on the branches of Meadow Creek.

We know Abner Abney mentioned, in his will, land as follows:
1. I give unto my Dear beloved Wife the hack of land which now I live on...
2. ...the hundred acres joining to be equally divided between my son John...& my daughter Milley Abney...
3. ...unto my son Elish Abney one hundred acres of Land lying on Mechems *(sic)* River...
4. I leave my Dearly beloved wife my Parsil Estate...

Are these four different parcels of land (the hack on which he lived, the 100 acres adjoining, the 100 acres on Mechums River and the *Parsil Estate*)? Is one of these 100-acre parcels the land that was granted (albeit posthumously) by the 1755 grant? Was there another Abner Abney who was an adult in 1755? Did Paul Abney (brother of Abner Abney) name a son Abner, after his brother?

This grant raises many questions for which the author is unable to supply definitive answers. At this time, the author believes this grant was to Abner Abney, son of Dannett Abney Sr., but he died prior to finalizing the grant. If that is the case, and he had already paid the necessary monies, did his estate get the grant in 1755? This is probable.

Secondly, there was a Samuel Abner who married Mary Parks.[31] They had a son, William M. Abner who (according to FindaGrave.com) was born 20 Jan 1849 in Kentucky and died 08 Jul 1917 in Clark Co., Kentucky. He married twice, firstly on 21 Dec 1869 to Isabelle Kidd and secondly ca.1880 to Isabel B. Maupin. According to William's Death Certificate, his parents were Samuel Abner and Mary Parks. The author has been unable to locate this couple.

On the 1860 census, there is one William Abner (age 12, born in Kentucky) living in Madison County, Kentucky with the family of one William P. Roberts (age 70, born in North Carolina) and Susan Roberts (age 28), Frass Roberts (age 6), Robert Roberts (age 5) and Mary Roberts (age 2), the final four persons born in Kentucky.[32] The author is unsure if this William Abner is the same as the William M. Abner for whom he searches, but it seems rather likely. Due to research by Contributor Sandrea Abner Cook, the author believes this Samuel may not be part of the Clay County Abner's. In fact, he may not be an "Abney" descendant at all. He is probably from an immigrant Abner family.

Reiteration of the first generation born in America show Abner Abney with his siblings:[33]

Generation One
(the first ABNEY's born in America)

Dannett ABNEY Sr. m. Mary (LEE?) and had issue:

1. *Ursula ABNEY (1693 - ????) baptized 1693 of whom nothing further*
2. *Dannett ABNEY Jr. (est. 1695 - ca. 1757) married Mary MEREDITH (liv.01 Mar 1764)*
3. *George ABNEY (est. 1697 - 01 Oct 1766) married Unity (n.n.) (liv.20 Jul 1769)*
4. *Paul ABNEY (1699 - liv. 30 Sep 1786) married (n.n.) of whom nothing is known*
5. *Dr. Abraham ABNEY (1702 - liv. 04 Jun 1783) married Cassandra (MEREDITH?) (liv.01 Jan 1787)*
6. *Martha ABNEY (est. 1705 - liv. 15 Mar 1759) married William SPRAGGINS (prob.15 Mar 1759)*
7. *Bathshua ABNEY (est. 1708 - liv. 25 Oct 1773) married Thomas HILL (prob.25 Oct 1773)*
8. *Abner ABNEY (est. 1711 - ca. 1751) married Anne (KEY?) (liv.11 Jun 1752)*
9. *Mary ABNEY (est. 1714 - liv. Jan 1761) married John BERNARD (liv. Jan 1761)*

End Notes:

1. See the **Abney Family History Series, Volume I,** *Abney: Ancestry and Genealogy of Dr. Abraham Abney of Virginia*, second edition (ISBN: 978-0-9993282-2-4, LCCN: 2018952526), published 3 Sep 2018 by this current author.
2. https://www.ducksters.com/geography/us_states/virginia_history.php
3. See the **Abney Family History Series, Volume I,** *Abney: Ancestry and Genealogy of Dr. Abraham Abney of Virginia*, second edition (ISBN: 978-0-9993282-2-4, LCCN: 2018952526), published 3 Sep 2018 by this current author.
4. The Holy Bible (1 Samuel 14:50, et al) *Abiner* (the long form of Abner) means *Son of Ner*. In the Holy Bible, also see: 1 Sam 17:55, 26:5; 2 Sam 2:12, 2:18, et al; also see Josephus' *Antiquities*, Book 7, Chapter 1.
5. The Register of Abingdon Parish, Gloucester County, Virginia, 1677-1780, by Robert W. Robins (1981)
6. http://www.brutonparish.org/article298315.htm
7. See the **Abney Family History Series, Volume I,** *Abney: Ancestry and Genealogy of Dr. Abraham Abney of Virginia*, second edition (ISBN: 978-0-9993282-2-4, LCCN: 2018952526), published 3 Sep 2018 by this current author.
8. Deed of King William County, Virginia from James and Margaret Honey 600 acres to Isaac Hill; and 400 acres to Matthew Lea and *Dannett Abney*, dated 15 April 1704 and recorded 20 May 1704.
9. The Register of St. Mary, Leicester, Co. Leicester, First Volume (1909), Transcribed by Henry Hartopp
10. P.R., Leicester – A copy of the Last Will and Testament of Bathshua Lee is in the author's possession
11. Spotsylvania County, Virginia, Deed Book A, a deed dated 07 Jul 1724 shows *Dannett Abney Senr. of St. Margaretts Parish, King Wm Co., cooper* purchasing land with his son, Dannett Abney Junr. from Jn Wilkins of St. Geo. Par., Spotsylvania Co., Virginia.
12. That Dannett Abney Sr. was a land owner is attested to by the many Virginia deeds in which he appears buying and selling
13. Last Will and Testament of Dannett Abney Sr.
14. That these sons of Dannett Abney Sr. were successful is attested to by the many Virginia deeds in which they appear as buyers
15. Deed of Goochland County, Virginia dated 02 Mar 1742, from Anthony Pounay to Paul Abney, 100 acres in Goochland County
16. Fredericksville Parish Vestry Book 1742-1787 by Rosalie Edith Davis (1981)
17. Last Will and Testament of Dannett Abney, 1732, Spotsylvania County Will Book A, page 209
18. See *The Great Britain Calendar Act of 1751 (How Calendar Changes affect history)* in *Abney, Vol. I*, page xix, by this author
19. Spotsylvania County, Virginia deed dated 01 Oct 1745 wherein Edwin Hickman sold land *in Spotsylvania, conveyed to Hickman by Mary Abney, as by deeds, Nov. 4, 1735,* to Giles Tompkins. The 1735 deed has not been located by the author.
20. In Search of Kate, by Charlotte Ann Abney Metzger (1978)
21. Wikipedia – Goochland County, Virginia https://en.wikipedia.org/wiki/Goochland_County,_Virginia
22. Since Metzger claims John was born in 1745, and Albemarle County was created in 1744, it is obvious John was born in that county
23. In his will, Abner Abney claimed he was "in my perfect senses & memory but very sick and weak hoping that the Lord will be merciful"
24. Last Will and Testament of Abner Abney "Given under my hand & Seal this twenty fifth of September in the Year of our Lord 1751
25. See the **Abney Family History Series, Volume I,** *Abney: Ancestry and Genealogy of Dr. Abraham Abney of Virginia*, second edition (ISBN: 978-0-9993282-2-4, LCCN: 2018952526), published 3 Sep 2018 by this current author.
26. Abner Abney named only three children in his will, and it is believed these were the only three children he sired
27. Last Will and Testament of Abner Abney – Albemarle County Will Book A, page 38
28. *ibid.*
29. In Search of Kate, by Charlotte Ann Abney Metzger (1978)
30. Land Office Patents No.31, 1751-1756 (v.1 & 2 p.1-751, p.671 (Reel 29) Colonial Land Office Patents, 1623-1774, Library of Virginia Archives.
31. Findagrave.com for William M. Abner
32. Eighth Census of the United States of America (1860 Federal Census) taken in Madison County, Virginia.
33. See the **Abney Family History Series, Volume I,** *Abney: Ancestry and Genealogy of Dr. Abraham Abney of Virginia*, second edition (ISBN: 978-0-9993282-2-4, LCCN: 2018952526), published 3 Sep 2018 by this current author.

Chapter III

The Children of Abner Abney
The Virginians

In the Last Will and Testament of Abner Abney, three children are named, to wit: John, Milley <sp> and Elish <sp>.[1] In the author's opinion, these are the only children (or only surviving children) of Abner Abney and his wife, Anne.

As the author has revealed in the previous chapter (see page 13), Elisha is believed to be the eldest (born est.1741), followed by Milly (born est.1743) and finally the youngest, John (born 1745)[2].

Based on the estimated birth years, we can now, also determine, with some degree of accuracy, where each was born.

Goochland County, Virginia was formed in 1728 from the original Henrico Shire.[3] Later, in 1744, Albemarle County was formed from the northern part of Goochland County.[4] Since we can be certain Abner Abney died in Albemarle County around 1751 (where his will was both written and presented to court), and his Albemarle County land was in the north (Mechum's River, mentioned in his will is in the north of the county), we can also assume he was in Goochland County prior to the formation of Albemarle. Therefore, if he married circa 1740, the wedding was probably in Goochland County. It then stands to reason his first two (known) children were born in Goochland County. Since Albemarle County was formed in 1744, and John was born in 1745, we can surmise John was born in Albemarle County. Therefore, unless and until new information is discovered, we will conclude that the children of Abner Abney and Anne (Key?) were born as follows:

1. Elisha Abney Sr. (a.k.a. Elisha Abner) was born circa 1741 in Goochland Co., Virginia
2. Milly Abney was born circa 1743 in Goochland Co., Virginia
3. John Abney was born in 1745 in Albemarle Co., Virginia

For the remnant of this chapter, the author will make every attempt to estimate years and places of births, marriages, migrations and deaths as accurately as possible. The author will advise the reader what logic was used in making these estimations. Please understand, due to a general lack of early records-keeping coupled with the loss of so many precious records, providing exact dates and locations is simply impossible.

There is no doubt some readers, researchers and genealogists will disagree, at least in part, with the conclusions of the author. But that is perfectly okay. All of the author's published works are meant to be guidelines for one's own research. If you are able to prove these conclusions wrong, please do so in order that we may more correctly document the history of the great Abney family.

Elisha Abney (a.k.a. Elisha Abner) Sr.
Virginia Pioneer

Elisha Abney (Sr.), believed to have been the eldest son/child of Abner Abney and Anne (Key?) was also known, at certain periods in time, as Elisha Abner. This was, no doubt, due to the way he pronounced his surname and the unfamiliarity of the recorder. It appears the surname spelled *Abner* (in lieu of Abney; but at times both spellings were used in different records for the same locations) began to be used when Elisha was in North Carolina;[5] and the surname stuck with certain members of his family when they came of age in Kentucky. Other children, however, continued to use the correct spelling, *Abney*. Elisha Abney Sr. had, as we will see, quite a pioneering spirit.

Elisha Abney Sr. was born, by the author's estimate, around 1741 in Albemarle County, Virginia. When he was about ten years old (more or less), his father died in that same county.[6] As revealed in the previous chapter, Elisha Abney was to receive 100 acres of land in Albemarle County from his father's estate. This author believes he did, in fact, receive that parcel of land.

Elisha seems to have gotten a late start in his adult life, at least as a family man. He appears to have been about 30 years of age when he married around 1770.[7] At the time of his marriage, he was probably still living in Albemarle County, Virginia on the land he inherited from his father. The author has found no proof of the name or names of Elisha's wife or wives. One rather ridiculous genealogy gives Mary Unity Polly "Nancy" Calloway (daughter of Thomas S. Calloway and Mary Baker).[8] This record goes as far as giving full birth and death dates (8 Jan 1741 VA – 14 Oct 1827 Oldham, KY). Firstly, it is rather doubtful a person born in 18th century colonial America will have so many names. (one very common mistake made by family researchers is to assign another name to an ancestor when they think another record is about their ancestor, but the names are different.) Secondly, the genealogy cannot give so little as one source for this rather creative name. As far as the author knows, no proof exists of any name for Elisha's wife or wives.

In 1761, the southern half of Albemarle County became Amherst County.[9] However, Elisha's land was not in the southern half. Mechum's River, on which river Elisha's inherited land lay, was in the northern part of Albemarle County, ergo Elisha's land did not fall into Amherst County.[10]

Therefore, the author believes that Elisha Abney Sr. and his wife began their family in Albemarle County, Virginia, probably having three children there, to wit: Joshua, born circa 1771; Jerusha, nicknamed *Shrew* (?); born estimated 1773; and Ann (?), born estimated 1775.[11]

ELISHA ABNEY MOVES HIS FAMILY TO AMHERST COUNTY, VIRGINIA

The author believes, however, that Elisha Abney's first move out of Albemarle County was to Amherst County, Virginia. This probably occurred around 1777 or so. The reason for this belief is that on 29 Mar 1779 in Amherst County, Virginia, Elisha Abney witnessed a deed of Jonathan Witt Jr. to Littleberry Witt and Jonathan Witt Sr.[12] The author believes these Witt men were kinsmen of Elisha Abney, being descended from Paul Abney (Elisha's uncle).[13] Of course the witnessing of this deed does not mean Elisha lived in Amherst County at the time. However, it was a family deed, and it is doubtful Elisha would have travelled from his home in northern Albemarle County to witness a deed in Amherst County. Moreover, on 02 Oct 1780, Elisha Abney *of Amherst County, Virginia* purchased 150 acres of land from Samuel Ayres and wife, Rachel for £250.[14] The land was in Amherst County on a branch of Stoney Creek off of Rockfish River. Since Elisha was described as being *of Amherst County,* we can be certain he had already been established in Amherst County prior to purchasing this the land.

From this point on, we must remember there are many inaccuracies in the information contained in the census records. Birthdates, birth years and birth places were often forgotten by the person, or guessed at by the census informant (who ofttimes simply did not know the answer to the census-taker question and guessed). The census-taker may also have recorded information erroneously, the informant relying on the census-takers literacy to spell names and estimate birth years. Moreover, many of these individuals of the 17th through 19th centuries were illiterate. This caused many errors, not only in dates and places but in nomenclature, as well. The pronunciation of the surname, "Abney" (as "Abner" and "Abna") coupled with illiteracy is probably what caused the surname variations "Abner" and "Abna" to be created. Below are some examples of erroneous information recorded in the 1850 census records in this family alone.

As examples: Seven Records with Erroneous Information

- In the 1850 census, Elisha Abney Sr. was enumerated as *Enoch Abner Sr.*[15] The only person living in the household with Elisha Sr. was obviously his son, Enoch (age 17). It is likely the census-taker made the mistake here.
- In the 1860 census Hezekiah Abney (son of Elisha Abney Sr.) is reportedly born in South Carolina.[16] The simple fact that the family was living in Amherst County, Virginia makes this claim impossible. Neither was he born in Wilkes County, North Carolina as most believe. Since he grew up in the Carolinas (from about age five to about age 13, the mistake is understandable.

- Elisha Abner [Jr.] (son of Elisha Abney Sr.), in the 1850 census is listed at age 67 born in Virginia.[17] However, if he was age 67 and born ca.1784, we have two problems: a) one son is missing from the 1787 Tax Record of his father, *Elisha Abner*; b) his age in the 1810 census record is wrong. This author believes Elisha Jr. was born ca.1787 in Wilkes County, North Carolina.
- According to the 1850 census, Dorcas "Tabitha" Abney (daughter of Elisha Sr.), by now married and known as *Tabithey Woods* was born in Tennessee.[18] The problem is, Dorcas was born (about 1784) some eight years before Tennessee was created. Tennessee was granted statehood in 1796 (see Appendix C, page 261). Tabitha grew up in Tennessee, making this error understandable.
- John Abney (son of Elisha Sr.) was reportedly born in Tennessee.[19] There is no doubt John grew up in Tennessee. However, Carter County, Tennessee did not exist when John was born (1794). At the time he was born, the area was known as Southwest Territory. (See Appendix C, page 261)
- Mary Bishop (née Abney/Abner), according to the 1850 census, is 75 years of age born in Tennessee.[20] This information is almost too erroneous to visit. IF she was 75 years of age, she would have been born in 1775 and Tennessee didn't exist until 1796. Additionally, her age would have been wrong in <u>every</u> other census. No doubt her alleged age of 75 should have been properly recorded as age 55.
- Margaret Larken Abney, listed as *Margaret L. Smith* in the 1850 census, was given as age 52 born in Virginia.[21] In 1860 she was given as age 62 born in Virginia.[22] However, when she was born (1798), her family had not been in Virginia for over a decade. No. She was actually born in Tennessee.

Let the seven examples given above serve to inform the reader that the census records cannot always be trusted. The researcher must make every attempt to deduce which information is correct, and which is erroneous. It is ludicrous to contend that a person was born in a place that didn't exist, or at a time which is obviously incorrect. The information contained in this book is the author's best estimation based on documentation, prosopography and nomenclature. The author believes this information may <u>not</u> be 100% accurate, but simply the most accurate heretofore published.

Returning to our chronology, while in Amherst County, Virginia, it appears Elisha Abney Sr. and his wife had four more children, to wit: a daughter, (n.n.) whose name is not known, born estimated 1777;[23] Abner, born in 1779;[24] Hezekiah, born in 1781;[25] and Dorcas (also known as *Tabitha*), born circa 1784.[26]

Now the reader well-versed in the genealogy of this family will immediately see multiple differences from previously published works and "accepted" information. Before you write to the author, study the reasoning given here and perhaps you will agree. If not, by all means write and give your opinions, ideas, and proofs.

ELISHA ABNEY MOVES HIS FAMILY TO WILKES COUNTY, NORTH CAROLINA

While his brother John Abney remained in Virginia, as opportunities began to open up in the newly formed United States of America, Elisha Abney found it desirable to move on from his old Virginia home. Although we know from a tax record of 1787 that Elisha Abney had certainly migrated (from Amherst County, Virginia) to Wilkes County, North Carolina, without additional documentation, we cannot ascertain exactly *when* he made this move. For the sake of argument, we will consider this move happened shortly after the birth of Dorcas Abney in 1784. North Carolina is the first place where we find Elisha's surname given as ***Abner*** instead of ***Abney***.

In 1787, we have a Tax Record of ***Elisha Abner*** in Wilkes County, North Carolina.[27] The author identifies the Elisha Abner household as follows:

	enumeration	identity	approximate age
•	White Male 21 – 60	Elisha Abney Sr.	46
•	White Male <21 or >60	Joshua Abney	16
•	White Male <21 or >60	Abner Abney	8
•	White Male <21 or >60	Hezekiah Abney	6
•	Female (no age given)	(wife of Elisha Sr.)	unknown
•	Female (no age given)	Jerusha "Shrew" (?)	14
•	Female (no age given)	Ann (?)	12
•	Female (no age given)	(daughter?)	10
•	Female (no age given)	Dorcas "Tabitha"	3

While in Wilkes County, Elisha Abney Sr. and his wife seem to have had two children, both boys, to wit: Elisha Jr., born circa 1787 (and just after the tax record);[28] and Menan, born in 1790.[29]

The reader is herewith advised that the author is not "forcing" Elisha Abner Jr. into that birth order. If we had only the census records of 1790-1840, plus the 1787 Tax Record previously mentioned, the 1787 birth year fits perfectly. If the 1850 census is correct, then the 1810 census is not correct! Simply put, placing Elisha Abner Jr. in the 1787 position (born after the tax record), not only does the 1810 census work, but every other census and tax record save the 1850 census. So, to the author, it is a very easy solution: choose the 1810 census (which was closest to the birth event), or the 1850 census (in which the informant probably was not even Elisha Jr., but his wife who would have no firsthand knowledge of Elisha's birth details). In choosing ca.1787, every census is correct. (See Appendix B, pg.259).

Of all the middle census records located on the children of Elisha Abney Sr. (1850, 1860), the only enumeration which provided no serious errors was the Menan census of 1850. It gives *Menen Abner* age 60 born in North Carolina.[30]

ELISHA ABNEY SR. MOVES HIS FAMILY TO GREENVILLE COUNTY, SOUTH CAROLINA

Sometime before the First United States Census taken (Census Day was 2 Aug 1790), Elisha Abney Sr. moved his growing family to South Carolina where he settled in Greenville County in the old Ninety-Six District.[31] His stay in South Carolina was very brief, and it does not appear that he and his wife had any children there.

He was living in Greenville County when the First Census of the United States was taken in 1790. He, as *Elisha Abner* was "Head of Household" of eleven people. The author identifies the Elisha Abner household as follows:

enumeration	identity	approximate age
• Male 16+	Elisha Abney Sr.	49
• Male 16+	Joshua Abney	19
• Male <16	Abner Abney	11
• Male <16	Hezekiah Abney	9
• Male <16	Elisha Abner Jr.	3
• Male <16	Menan Abner	newborn
• Female (no age given)	(wife of Elisha Sr.)	unknown
• Female (no age given)	Jerusha "Shrew" (?)	17
• Female (no age given)	Ann (?)	15
• Female (no age given)	(daughter?)	13
• Female (no age given)	Dorcas "Tabitha"	6

When we compare Elisha Abney Sr.'s family group of the 1787 tax record to the 1790 census record, it is amazing how perfectly they agree:

1787 Tax List, Wilkes Co., NC		1790 Census, Greenville Co., 96 Dist., SC		
enumeration	approximate age	identity	approximate age	enumeration
male 21–60	46	Elisha Sr.	49	male 16+
female (no age)	(unknown)	(Elisha's wife)	(unknown)	female (no age)
male <21	16	Joshua	19	male 16+
female (no age)	14	Jerusha "Shrew" (?)	17	female (no age)
female (no age)	12	Ann (?)	15	female (no age)
female (no age)	10	(daughter?)	13	female (no age)
male <21	8	Abner	11	male <10
male <21	6	Hezekiah	9	male <10
female (no age)	3	Dorcas "Tabitha"	6	female (no age)
-	not yet born	Elisha Jr.	3	male <10
-	not yet born	Menan	newborn	male <10

Again, the author has no proof of the daughters previously identified as Jerusha and Ann, and has no proof that the unnamed female is a daughter. But they fit perfectly into the family as shown above, and in both records.

ELISHA ABNEY SR. MOVES HIS FAMILY TO THE SOUTHWEST TERRITORY

There was a group of settlers from Virginia who created the Watauga Association and settled in a certain area (in the far northeastern area of today's state of Tennessee) in 1769.[32] They applied to be united with Virginia but were refused. In turn, they applied to be united with North Carolina and were approved in 1776. North Carolina named the area Washington District.[33] This area was only officially Washington District for one year (November 1776-November 1777). After that time, it was considered an informal district. In 1784 the district was transferred to an extra-legal state, known as the **State of Franklin** (see Plate G).[34] The State of Franklin submitted a petition for statehood on 16 May 1785. Although a simple majority of seven states voted to admit the new state as **Frankland**, constitutionally, a two-thirds majority is required and Frankland never became a U.S. State. Instead, it became a *de facto* independent republic. Eight counties were named, to wit: Blount, Sevier, Caswell, Greene, Spencer, Washington, Sullivan and Wayne. Most notable for our purposes is Wayne County which area would much later become Carter County, Tennessee. Eventually, the government of the State of Franklin collapsed and the territory returned to the control of North Carolina in 1789 (although this now-defunct state would remain functional until 1791). North Carolina ceded the area to the United States in 1790. The United States formed an area called the **United States Territory South of the River Ohio** or simply, **Southwest Territory**.[35] **Southwest Territory** remained so until the State of Tennessee was admitted to the union on 1 Jun 1796.[36]

Returning to our narrative, shortly after the 1790 census was taken, a new opportunity was opening up in the Southwest Territory, and Elisha Abney Sr. (for some reason) received a grant there from the State of North Carolina. He moved his family (ca.1793) to Southwest Territory and settled in the area of the old Wayne County, Franklin, now called Washington County, Southwest Territory. It is unknown why Elisha Abney Sr. received a land grant to this area from the State of North Carolina; however, it is possible it was for service (military or civil) to the Continental Army during the American Revolution. This grant has not been discovered; but he mentioned the grant when he sold the land in Carter County, Tennessee in a deed dated 4 Oct 1805 which states that *Elisha Abner* is selling *part of a tract of land granted by the State of North Carolina to the said Elisha Abner.*[37] Although many grants were received for military service, no record of Elisha Abney Sr. serving in the American Revolution has been located as of yet.

Elisha Abney Sr. and wife seem to have had their remaining children in this area, although the name (of the area) would change. Since their son, John was born in 1794, he would have been born in Washington County, Southwest Territory. Later, he might have said he was born in Tennessee (which state the county eventually fell into). We know he claimed to have been from Tennessee, and he was, more or less, correct. He was actually born in that part of Southwest Territory, which would later become Carter County, Tennessee. Mary (nicknamed "Polly") could make the same claim. Being born circa 1795, she, too would have been born in Washington County, Southwest Territory.

It is not known whether Joshua (eldest son of Elisha Abney Sr.) ever moved to Southwest Territory. When the Commonwealth of Kentucky was granted statehood on 1 Jun 1792, Joshua was about age 20. He may have seen adventure in the newly admitted state as quite desirable. To be certain, he appears in Green County, Kentucky by 1795 when he married (at about age 24) to Martha "Pattie" Phelps (about age 20), on 6 May.[38] Perhaps he separated from his father's home prior to the move to Southwest Territory.

Of the eldest daughters, or alleged daughters, even less is known. In the 18th century, it was legal for a girl to marry at age 12 (with consent of her parent or guardian).[39] By the author's calculations:
- Jerusha *Shrew* (?) may have attained that age by 1783, but she was still accounted for on the 1790 census.
- Ann (?) may have attained that age by 1785, but she, too was still accounted for on the 1790 census.
- The unknown daughter may have attained that age by 1787, but likewise, was accounted for in 1790.

Therefore, the three eldest sisters and their brother, Joshua Abney could all possibly have left their father's home prior to his move to Southwest Territory. The 1800 census of Carter County, Tennessee was lost in a courthouse fire in 1933,[40] eliminating our opportunity to learn who was in Elisha Abney Sr.'s household at that time. This tragic disaster is devastating to descendants of this family hoping to learn more about their ancestors.

By the 1810 census, no child older than Menan Abner (b.1790) resides in their father, Elisha Abney Sr.'s household.[41]

From 1796, and without a move necessary, Elisha was now living in Carter County, Tennessee, for Tennessee was admitted to the union on 1 Jun 1796, and the northern part of Washington County became Carter County.[42] Here, the remaining two Elisha Abney Sr. children were born, to wit: Margaret Larken, born 1798; and Enoch, born ca.1803.

An in-depth study (see Appendix B) of records from 1787-1860 provided a very solid basis for this family group: [43]

| Name of the child of: | Birth Information | | |
Elisha Abney Sr.	year	county	state
Joshua Abney	ca.1771	Albemarle Co.	Virginia
(Jerusha *Shrew*?) Abney	est.1773	Albemarle Co.	Virginia
(Ann?) Abney	est.1775	Albemarle Co.	Virginia
(daughter, n.n.) Abney	est.1777	Amherst Co.	Virginia
Pvt. Abner Abney	ca.1779	Amherst Co.	Virginia
Hezekiah Abney	ca.1781	Amherst Co.	Virginia
Dorcas "Tabitha Abney	ca.1784	Amherst Co.	Virginia
Elisha Abner Jr.	ca.1787	Wilkes Co.	North Carolina
Menan Abner	ca.1790	Wilkes Co.	North Carolina
John Abney Sr.	ca.1794	Washington Co.	Southwest Territory
Mary "Polly" Abner	ca.1795	Washington Co.	Southwest Territory
Margaret Larken Abner	1798	Carter Co.	Tennessee
Enoch Abney Sr.	ca.1803	Carter Co.	Tennessee

It is interesting to note that of the seven children whose 1850 census records have been located, five of them children knew their age, to wit: Hezekiah, Menan, John, Margaret and Enoch. Elisha Jr. was only four years off. Mary's age being a full 20 years off is obviously a communication error between the informant and the census taker.

On 9 Aug 1796, *Elisha Abner* purchased land in Carter County, Tennessee from Abel Simpkins via his attorney-in-fact, Thomas Gourley:[44]

This Indenture made this ninth day of August in the year of our Lord one thousand seven hundred and ninety six Between Thomas Gourley Attorney in fact for Abel Simpkins of the County of Carter and the State of Tennessee of the one part and Elisha Abner of the County and State aforesaid of the other part. Witnesseth that the said Thomas Gourley for and in consideration of the sum of Five hundred Dollars to him the said Simpkins in hand paid by the said Elisha Abner the receipt whereof I do hereby acknowledge...do grant and sell...unto the said Elisha Abner his Heirs & assigns forever all that tract or parcel of land situate lying & being in the County & State aforesaid on the East side of Doe River a branch of Watauga it being part of a tract of land granted by the State of North Carolina to the said Abel Simpkins, Beginning at a stake in said Doe River eight poles due East due East from said Simpkins corner on a large Spanish Oak...thereunto belonging to the said Elisha Abner & him the Said Abel Simpkins doth covenant and agree to & with the said Elisha Abner that he said Elisha Abner his Heirs & assigns... ...Abel Simpkins On Witness whereof I have hereunto set my hand & seal the day and year first above written. Signed sealed & delivered in the presence of Tho. Gourley {seal} Atto in fact for Abel Simpkkins

(witnesses)
Thomas Russell
James Russell Jurat

Carter County February Term 1799. This deed was legally administered to record let it be registered
Registered March the 15th 1799.   *Test Geo Williams C.C.*

Note that Elisha Abney Sr. had already been living in Carter County when he purchased this land, as he was designated in the deed as being "of the County [Carter] and State [Tennessee] aforesaid". This is proof that Elisha Abney Sr. received his North Carolina land grant prior to this indenture.

Elisha Abney Sr., as *Elisha Abner* appeared on tax lists in Carter Co., Tennessee in 1796, 1797, 1799.[45] Elisha Abney Sr., as *Elisha Abney* appeared on a tax list in Carter Co., Tennessee in 1800.[46]

Around 1801 or so, another son of Elisha, namely Hezekiah Abney married. The author has been unable to find any proof of the wife outside of the references in *Abney Supplement* by Cousin John Hensell (pages 7 and 16):[47]
3-11c. Hezekiah Abney, ca. 1780 Wilkes Co., N.C.; living in Cleburne Co., Ala. after 18670; married _____ Callaway ca. 1800 and had issue.
(page 16)
3-11c. Heziah Abney and _____ Callaway had:
4-26a. John Abney, ca. 1802 Ky. – Jackson Co., Ga.; married ca.1824.

If Hensell is correct, this author has speculated that, perhaps, Hezekiah Abney may have joined his brother, Joshua Abney in Green County, Kentucky. If he did, it was only for a brief period of time, as, according to his son Benjamin Hezekiah Abney, Hezekiah was in Georgia by about 1804.[48] This scenario puts Hezekiah Abney marrying in Kentucky, possibly even Green County. More research is needed on Hezekiah; and maybe in Green County, Kentucky.

Abner Abney married on 26 Aug 1803 to Alyda Russell in Carter County, Tennessee.[49]

Contributor John M. Abney discovered a record dated 13 Feb 1804 in the *Court of Pleas and Quarter Sessions* which helps support the author's belief that Abner Abney (who married Alyda Russell)) was a son of Elisha Abney Sr.:[50]

*(P. 11) Ordered by the Court that Joseph Fisher be appointed overseer of the public Road in the room of Thomas Anderson, and that hands formerly Under Anderson be his hands, to wit, **Abner Abney**, Joseph Campbell, Jeremiah Campbell, Phillip Mulkey, Thomas Linvill, Joseph Bridges, Jacob Fisher, **Elisha Abney**, Thomas Russell and Samuel Bishop.*

Since Elisha Abney Sr. was about 63 years of age, and Elisha Abner Jr. was about 17 years of age, Elisha Jr. was probably the *Elisha Abney* mentioned in the court record. The only problem is that if both Elisha's were in the public records, the suffix Sr. or Jr. would probably have been used (i.e. in the 1820 census, Elisha Abner Junr. lives next to Elisha Abner). Either way, it puts Abner Abney in close association with the Elisha Abney Sr. family.

On 13 May 1805, Elisha Abney was appointed to serve as a juror for the May 1805 session of the Court of Pleas and Quarter Sessions:[51]

*Ordered by the Court that David Waggoner, John Poland, Lenard Shown, Christian Snider, Garland Wilson, Benj[a] Tompkins, George Crosswhite, Andrew Baker, W[m] Bunton, John Fletcher, Robert Parsons, Ja[s] Shuffield, Isaiah Stephens, Tho Elliott, **Elisha Abner**, W[m] Bridges, John Fisher, John Smith sen[r] Henry Nave, James Moore Jun[r], Jon[a] Buck, Solomon Hendrix, John Lusk, Brewer McKechen, John Macay, Tho. Rowe, Garret Reasoner, Samuel Smawlin, Francis Mofall sen[r], John Love, Isaac Taylor, Thomas Tipton, Gawin Patterson, Michael Hyder, David Cunningham and James Lacy be jurors to may session 1805.*

Elisha Abney Sr. and family were apparently planning a mass exodus from Tennessee to Kentucky (everyone except those who had already married).

In the final record of Carter Co., Tennessee discovered thus far, we find Elisha Abner Sr. selling the land he received by grant from North Carolina:[52]

This Indenture made this fourth day of October in the year of our Lord one thousand Eight hundred and five Between Elisha Abner of the County of Carter and State of Tennessee of the one part and Isaac Lincoln... of the other part. Witnesseth that the said Elisha Abner for and in consideration of the sum of four hundred Dollars to him in hand paid by the said Isaac Lincoln... all that tract or parcel of land situate lying & being in the County and State aforesaid on the East side of Doe River a branch of Watauga it being part of a tract of land granted by the State of North Carolina to the said Elisha Abner... one hundred and fifty acres and three quarters and sixteen poles... unto the said Isaac Lincoln... I have hereunto set my hand and seal the day and date above written
Signed Sealed & Delivered in   Elisha Abney {Seal}
presence of James (his x mark) Peters and
Thomas C. Patton Jurat

This deed was entered into record on 10 Nov 1805,[53] and registered at the Carter County court on 15 Feb 1806.[54]

It is interesting to note, that although throughout the deed, Elisha is referred to as *Elisha Abner*, he correctly signs the deed, *Elisha Abney*.

This still leaves us with a question: What happened to the land he purchased from Abel Simpkins (via his attorney-in-fact, Thomas Gourley)? Was this land given or sold to his son, Abner Abney? No other Abner or Abney deed has been located to date, and no deed of Abner Abney purchasing or selling land has ever been located.

Since it appears Elisha Abney Sr. was headed to the Commonwealth of Kentucky, we must assume he settled in a county which, in large part "became" Clay County (for Clay County did not yet exist).[55] Ergo, the author believes Elisha Abney Sr. settled his family in Madison County, Kentucky ca.1805/6.

In 1806, plans were in the works to create Clay County, Kentucky, largely out of Madison County with smaller parts of Floyd and Knox Counties.

Elisha Abner Jr. was the next to marry, ca.1806 in Kentucky.[56] Again, since Clay County did not yet exist (as it was still pending), it is likely Elisha and Abner Jr. married Nancy "Lucy" Loving in Madison County, Kentucky.

In 1807, Clay County was carved out of Madison County, Kentucky, including smaller parts of Floyd and Knox Counties. The majority of the Clay County land was from Madison County (and the northern part of Clay County would, in 1843 become Owsley County).[57] Since much of the Abner land would later fall into Owsley County, this helped the author determine where their Clay County land lie. At this time, in 1807, the Abner land fell into Clay Co.

Dorcas "Tabitha" was the next of Elisha's children to marry. We find their marriage license in Clay County, Kentucky dated 12 Dec 1808:[58]

> *John Wood & Darkey Abny.* The marriage bond was signed by *Elisha Abney.*

To this author, it is obvious Elisha Abney Sr. knew his surname was *Abney, just as he signed it.* It was the fault of the records-keepers and illiteracy that subsequent generations changed the spelling to *Abner.*

The Third Federal Census (Census Day was 4 Aug 1810) finds *Elisha Abner* [Sr.] in Clay County, Kentucky. The census enumeration accounts for Elisha's wife and unmarried children, to wit:[59]

Gender/Age	Identification by the author
m 45+	(Elisha Abney Sr., ae.69)
f 45+	(wife, name/age unknown)
m 16-25	(Menan, b.1790, ae.20)
m 10-15	(John, b.1794, ae.16)
f 10-15	(Mary, b.ca.1795, ae.15)
f <10	(Margaret Larken, b.1798, ae.12)
m <10	(Enoch., b.c.1803, ae.7)

Next door to Elisha Abney Sr. was his son, *Elisha Abner Junr.:*[60]

Gender/Age	Identification by the author
m.16<25	(Elisha Jr., ae.23)
f.26<44	(Nancy "Lucy" Loving, ae.26)
m.<10	(William, ae.3)
f.<10	(Elizabeth, ae.1)
m.<10	(Lacy, newborn)

Census records have not been located for other children: Joshua (who may have been en route to the newly created Butler Co., Kentucky); Hezekiah (who should have been located in Jackson Co., Georgia); Abner (who would join the U.S. Army as a private in the Infantry on 22 Jan 1814); and the mostly unidentified daughters; Dorcas may have been with one of the many Wood(s) families in Kentucky, but the author has not identified which Wood(s) family might contain Dorcas and her husband, John.

The next of Elisha Abney Sr.'s children to marry was Mary "Polly" Abner. She married Samuel "Sam" Bishop, and the author wonders if this was the same Samuel Bishop who was on the Road Crew in Carter County, Tennessee in 1804 (see this chapter, page 23, 4th paragraph). According Hensell, et al, they were married in Clay County, Kentucky, which seems correct. Hensell gives the wedding date as 15 Nov 1811, to wit:[61]

Samuel Bishop, died 182/30; married Mary "Polly" Abner/Abney (3-10i) – see ABNER/ABNEY – Nov. 15, 1811 Clay Co., Ky. and had: 2-00a. William Bishop [and two other unnamed children].

Other researchers give 11 Nov 1811 as the marriage license date.[62] The author has been unable to locate the marriage license. These three sources could all be correct as it is possible that they obtained the marriage license on Monday, 11-11-11 and married four days later, on Friday, 15 Nov 1811.

Next to marry was Menan Abner. He married the first of his three wives, namely Agnes "Aggy" Bowling on 22 Mar 1813 in Clay County, Kentucky:[63]

We, Menan Abner, William Bowling and Christopher Bowling...authorize a marriage...between the s^d. Menan Abner and Aggy Bowling... /s/ Menan (his x mark) Abner /s/ William (his x mark) Bowling

The General Index to Marriages misinterpreted the name *Menan* to be *Monroe*.[64] But a reading of the actually marriage license makes it evident the name was *Menan Abner*. Due to this error, this author followed the lead of Hensell and other earlier genealogists who believed Elisha Abney Sr. had a son named *Monroe Abney*.[65] Thanks to Contributor Sandy Abner Cook for providing copies of the actual marriage record.

On 22 Jan 1814, Abner Abney enlisted in the U.S. Army out of Gallatin (Sumner Co.), Tennessee as a private in the 44 U.S. Infantry. He was recruited by Capt. Butler, company commander. Regimental commanders were Cols. Anderson and Ross. This record was discovered by Contributor John M. Abney. The record proves the author's belief that he was born in Amherst County, Virginia. Pvt. Abner Abney was age 34, 5'8", hazel eyes, black hair, and dark complexion. It is obvious that, after a four-day unauthorized leave of absence, Pvt. Abner Abney returned to his unit and, doubtlessly, fought in the Battle of New Orleans (8 Jan 1815). He was still present on a roll dated in 1815: [66]

22 Jan 1814	Enlisted at Gallatin, Tennessee for the duration of the war
30 Jan 1814	RR (Recruiting Return) Gallatin, Tenn.
14 Feb 1814	RR no Capt. New Orleans
25 Jul 1814	Deserted – probably enjoying a rowdy time in New Orleans! The author knows New Orleans!
29 Jul 1814	Apprehended
08 Jan 1815	Battle of New Orleans
15 Apr 1815	DR (Descriptive Roll) Capt. Isaac L. Baker's Co.

On 15 Nov 1819, Elisha Sr.'s youngest daughter, Margaret Larken Abner married Isham O. Smith in Clay Co.[67]

The final record in which we find Elisha Abney Sr. is the Fourth Federal Census of 1820 (Census Day was 7 Aug 1820), in which the author was forced to re-identify this household. The census enumeration (under the mistaken name of *Enoch Abner fr.*) accounts for Elisha (his wife apparently had passed away) and his youngest child, Enoch, to wit:[68]

Gender/Age	Identification by the author
m 45+	Elisha Sr. (b.ca.1741, ae.79)
m 16-25	Enoch (b.ca.1803, ae.17)

The census-taker used a "long s" (i.e. *ʃ*) for the suffix of the name *Enoch Abner*. Do not be confused: it is *ʃr.* (Senior), not Jr. The neighbor of the alleged *Enoch Abner fr.* was none other than *Eliʃha Abner* [Elisha Abner Jr., son of Elisha Abney Sr.]. The name Elisha is also spelled using a "long s". Preceding the entry of Elisha Abner Jr. is *Menan Abner* [his brother]. In combination with these three families next to each other, the accents, and the illiteracy, the census-taker appears so thoroughly confused about the identity of the head of household., that without knowing this family group, it would be difficult to understand this census enumeration. This census-taker error has caused many to give Elisha Abney Sr. a middle name of "Enoch". Nevertheless, there is absolutely no reason to believe Elisha Abney Sr. had a middle name, and every reason to believe he did not. There is not one record wherein Elisha Abney Sr. uses a middle name or middle initial.

In the meantime, known 1820 census enumerations for Elisha Abney Sr.'s children are as follows:
Joshua Abney (Morgantown, Butler County, Kentucky)[69]

Gender/Age	Identification by the author
m 45+	Joshua, b.ca.1772, ae. abt. 48)
f 45+	Pattie, b.ca.1775, ae. abt. 45)
m 26<45	*Pvt.* Abner Abney (?), ae.41 – Morgantown is 70 miles due north of Gallatin where he enlisted.)
m 16<26	Paul, b.1801, ae. abt. 19
m 10<16	Wm., b.1805, ae. abt. 15
f 10<16	(dau?), b.ca.1807, ae. abt. 13
m 10<16	Silas, b.c.1810, ae. abt. 10
m <10	Jesse, b.ca.1812, ae. abt. 8

Elisha Abner (Clay County, Kentucky)[70]

Gender/Age	Identification by the author
m.26<45	Elisha Jr., b.ca.1787, ae. abt. 33
f.26<45	Nancy "Lucy" Loving, b.1788, ae. abt. 32
m.10<16	William, b.1807, ae. abt. 13
f.10<16	Elizabeth, b.ca.1809 ae. abt. 11
m.<10	Lacy, b.ca.1810, ae. abt. 10
m.<10	John, b.ca.1813, ae. abt.7
f.<10	Mary, b.ca.1816, ae. abt. 4
f.<10	Lucinda, b.ca.1818, ae. abt. 2
f.<10	Susannah, newborn

Menan Abner (Clay County, Kentucky)[71]

Gender/Age	Identification by the author
m.26<45	Menan, b.1790, ae. abt. 29 if his birthday was after the census was taken
f.16<26	Agnes "Aggy" Bowling, b.ca.1795, ae. abt. 25
m.26<45	(probably his brother, John Abney, b.1794, ae. abt. 26)[72]
m.<10	Elisha, b.est.1814, ae. abt. 6
m.<10	James Monroe, b.1816, ae. abt. 4
m.<10	Richard, b.ca.1818, ae. abt. 1 if his birthday was after the census was taken
m.<10	(Samuel?) newborn son – born in the census year

Saml Bishop (Clay County, Kentucky)[73]

Gender/Age	Identification by the author
m.26<45	Samuel Bishop, b.ca.1785, ae. abt. 35
f.26<45	Mary "Polly" Abner, b.ca.1795, ae. abt.26 if her birthday was before the census was taken
m.<5	Elisha, b.ca.1813, ae. abt. 7
f.<5	Nancy, b.ca.1815, ae. abt. 5
m.<5	William, b.ca.1818, ae. abt. 4

[Author's note: This enumeration seems to be missing one male age 5<10 as their eldest son, Abel, was ae.8. None of these three sons died young; all married and had issue. It seems to be a simple case of omission by the census-taker.]

Isham Smith (Clay County, Kentucky)[74]

Gender/Age	Identification by the author
m.26<45	(Isham Smith, ae.28)
f.16<26	(Margt. Larken Abner, ae.22)
m.<5	(n.n.)
m.<5	(n.n.)

[Author's note: The author is unable to identify the two young boys in this record. The first son of record appears to be Charles Smith, born 1822, and would not appear in this record. Since census day in 1820 was August 7, and Isham Smith married Margaret Abner on November the previous year, it is possible they had twins born in the census year. This is the only explanation for these two boys, unless they were not part of their immediate family.]

Elisha Abney Sr. disappears from the records at this point in our narrative. He was about 79 years old when the 1820 census was taken. There is no way to know how much longer he lived, but he cannot be accounted for on any 1830 census heretofore discovered, neither under his own name nor accounted for in a household of any of his children.

Still, Elisha Abney Sr. lived a long and interesting life. He managed live in two countries (Virginia was a British Colony when he lived there; and the United States of America), five states (Virginia, North Carolina, South Carolina, Tennessee and Kentucky), and one U.S. territory (Southwest Territory, before it became Tennessee). He seems to have sired a baker's dozen children, all of whom were very prolific in their own right.

Elisha Abney Sr. was certainly buried in Clay County, Kentucky, either on his own land, or in one of the Abner Cemeteries found in the area. Hopefully, in time, continued research will bring new documents to light and we can learn more about this very interesting man.

Milly Abney (a.k.a. Milley Abney)
Girl of Mystery

Milly Abney is the one child of Abner Abney & Anne of whom researchers have been able to find so little information. We know absolutely that she was a minor when her father passed away around 1751; and even a full nine years later.[75]

By the author's estimate, Milly was the second child. However, the author is not resolute in this belief.

Milly was devised land by her father, Abner Abney in his will, to wit She and her brother, John were to receive an equal share of land, to wit:[76]

...I give unto my Dear beloved Wife the hack of land which now I live on unto her not to be mislisted During her Life or Widow hood & afterwards the Entry of the hundred acres joining I leave it to be Equally Divided between my Son John Abney & my Daughter Milley Abney To them & their heirs forever after their mothers Life or widowhood...

The author was aware of a guardianship record for Milly Abney, but that source was lost in Hurricane Katrina. In his newsletter, *the Abney Family Researcher* of October, 2000, this author wrote:[77]

After Abner Abney's death, it appears his widow, Anne (Key) remarried ca.1760 to Samuel Taliaferro (who was granted guardianship to Milly Abney, daughter of Abner and Anne).

In 1860 (some say 1862), one Samuel Taliaferro was named as Milly's guardian. By the author's estimates, Milly would have been about 17 (or 19) years of age.

This year 1762 also marked the appearance of a wife for Samuel Taliaferro Jr. - possibly the widowed Ann Abney of Moore's Creek, for whose child Samuel Taliaferro served as guardian.[78]

Why would she take a guardian now, nine years after the death of her father? Perhaps because she wanted to marry. By Virginia law, she would still require a parent or guardian to marry as she had not yet attained the age of consent.[79]

Sometime past, there was a Findagrave.com entry for this Milly Abney, but it has since been removed, probably due to inaccurate information. It read:[80]

Milly Abney McCarty 1743-1837

Visiting the URL listed in the end notes, one only finds a screen, *This memorial has been removed.* The obvious conclusion is that the information therein was erroneous.

To spend more time on Milly would be a disservice to this book, as when all is said and done, we are left only with conjecture.

John Abney
The Hatter

John Abney "the Hatter" was born in 1745 in Albemarle County, Virginia.[81] Due to his eventual employ as a haberdasher, the author, many decades ago, gave him the appellation "the Hatter" to differentiate him from so many other John Abney's.

Some give John the middle name, *Key*, however, the author has seen no indication that John had a middle name.[82] To be certain, he named a son, *John Key Abney.* However, this does not in any way translate to his name being the same. By all indications, none of Abner Abney's children bore a middle name.
John and his sister, Milly were devised an equal share of land in their father's will:[82]

...I give unto my Dear beloved Wife the hack of land which now I live on unto her not to be mislisted During her Life or Widow hood & afterwards the Entry of the hundred acres joining I leave it to be Equally Divided between my Son John Abney & my Daughter Milley Abney To them & their heirs forever after their mothers Life or widowhood...

Whether or not John and his sister ever claimed that land is unknown. What is known is that John married Isabella Van Lear on 10 Jul 1769 in Augusta County, Virginia.[83] Whether John had already left Albemarle County for Augusta County is not known for certain. What is known for certain is that from the time of this marriage (if not before) he remained in Augusta County the rest of his life.[84]

There are, in fact, numerous extant records for John Abney "the Hatter". Since there is no need to "find" or "follow" John through the various colonies, states and territories, we will be content, herewith to include a few records about John and his family from *Chronicles of the Scotch-Irish Settlement in Virginia* by Lyman Chalkley:[85]

vol. 1

- *November 22, 1769 (61) Called Court on James Denniston, for breaking into shop of John Abney and stealing silver coin – 39 lashes.*
- *November 20, 1776 (132) John Abney appointed Constable.*
- *September 17, 1777 (230) Jacob Peck, vice John Abney - Constable.*
- *May, 1783 (B). John Abney vs. John Campbell and John Henderson. – Petition, 29th July, 1783. Henderson dead.*
- John is witness to a deed of Thomas Thackum of Henrico County.
- *June 16, 1789. (95) Isabella Abney, executrix of John Abney, deceased, who was one of the executors of John McDonagh, deceased.*
- *May 21, 1790 (261) Death of John Abney and Thomas Smith, executors of John McDonagh abates suit.*
- *June 21, 1791 (472) James Kirk, orphan of James Kirk, aged 18 years, appears and consents to serve William Abney as apprentice until seven months after he is of age.*
- *March 25, 1793 (259) ...Robert Gratton as Captain of a Company of Cavalry to be raised in Staunton – recommended. David Perry as First Lieutenant of said Company; William Abney as Second Lieutenant of said Company...*
- *April 16, 1794 (78-79) William Abney qualified Second Lieutenant of a troop of Cavalry in Staunton, and in 3d Division.*
- *January 19, 1795 (504) James Keith, aged 8 years the 18th of next month, to be bound to William Abney to learn mystery of a hatter.*
- *William Abney vs. Robert Garland. Robert Christian, apprentice to plaintiff, went to Amherst Court, where he lost money and hats of plaintiff, which he was there to sell for plaintiff, at cards to defendant. Christian was afterwards a soldier in United States Army.*

vol.2

- *Marriage Licenses in Augusta County...1769 – July 10, John Abney...*
- *1792 – January 17th – By Rev. John McCune (Cue): March 29th, Philip North and Margaret Abney...*
- *1792 – March 29, Phillip North and Margaret Abney (spinster), daughter of John Abney, deceased; surety, David Parry.*
- *1794 – December 23, Wm. Abney and John McDowell, surety. Wm. Abney and Elizabeth McClenachan, daughter of Alex. McClenachan (consent). Teste: John McDowell.*
- *Humphrey's administrator vs. McClenachan's administrator – O. S. 281; N. S. 99 – Bill, June, 1798, by Alexr. Humphreys, that on 3d October, 1795, Alexr. McClenachan contracted to sell orator 6,666 2/3 acres in Kentucky, due McClenachan for military service in late war, and 4,000 acres as assignee of William Long, also entitled for military service. McClenachan died, intestate, leaving a son John and two daughters, Elizabeth, wife of William Abney, and Letitia, wife of Morris Austin.*
- *1797 – July 4, Robert McClenachan and Jno. McDowell, surety. Robert McClenachan and Sally Abney, daughter of John Abney, deceased, Isabella Abney (consent). Teste: Wm. Abney.*
- *1798 – July 17, John Fackler and Robert McClenachan, surety. John Fackler and Nancy Abney, daughter of John Abney, deceased.*
- *1798 – September 18, Peter Hog and Robt. McClenachan, surety. Peter Hog and Patsy Abney, daughter of John Abney, deceased, Isabella Abney (consent). Teste: James Hog.*
- *Patrick vs. Abney – O.S. 300; N.S. 107 – Bill, 3d April, 1815. In – 1788, John Abney of Staunton died, testate (he was a hatter) leaving wife Isabella and 7 children, viz: William; Margaret, who married Philip North, now deceased; John; Nancy, who married John Hicklin, now deceased; Sarah, who married Robert McClenachan; Patsey, who married Peter Hogg, and Polly. John Abney lives in Kentucky. Hog and wife live in Mason County. John Gunn was a hatter in Staunton in 1789. Jacob Peck was a butcher. William Abney was 8th August and was in 23d year when married. He was 16 at father's death. Mrs. Robertson was William's aunt. William went to Pittsburg in 1794 against the insurgents. William went to Parson Chambers' school.*

vol. 3

- *8th July, 1772. John Frogg and Agatha to John Abney, £300, lots 11, No. 16 and another joining No. 11; also 120 acres in Beverley Manor. Delivered: John Abney, May Court, 1774*
- *26th February, 1774. James Hartgrove's estate appraised by John Griffen, Thos. Smith, John Abney.*
- *13th December, 1774. Thomas Dunbarr's estate appraised by James Hill, Valentine Cloninger, John Abney.*
- *17th August, 1776. Doctor William McClenachan's estate appraised by Thomas Smith, John Abney, Alex. Gibson. Above valued by Doctor John Jackson 20th February, 1776,*
- *16th August, 1783. William Burk's estate appraised by John Abney, Peter Hanger, Thos. Scott.*
- *29th July, 1783. Jacob Van Lear's will – To wife, Margaret; to son, Jacob, all lands; to son, John, £15; to daughter, Gartry Robinson, 50 shillings; to daughter, Isabel Abney, 50 shillings. Executors, Jacob Van Lear and John Christians. Teste: Patrick and John Christian. Proved, 18th November, 1783, by the witnesses. Jacob qualifies.*
- *Jno. McDonough's estate in account with Jno. Abney, continued from 18th July, 1786 – Paid Braxton Eastham; 1787, received from Geo. Huddle for rent; Geo. Woland, ditto.*

- *John McDonough's estate in account with estate of John Abney, executor, deceased.*
- *26ᵗʰ January, 1815. Elizabeth Heizer's will... Teste: Wm. Abney, Mathias Swink. 2d May, 1815. Codicil – She is widow of Samuel Heizer, deceased. Proved, 26ᵗʰ February, 1816. Executors qualify.*
- *21ˢᵗ October, 1772. Robert, John and William Christian to Gilbert Christian. Teste: William Anderson, Jacob Van Lear, John Abney. Delivered: Wm. Anderson, 9ᵗʰ April, 1774.*
- *4ᵗʰ October, 1786. Deed... to Thomas Thackum, of Henrico County... Teste: ...John Abney...*
- *9ᵗʰ January, 1790. Organization of Staunton Fire company. ...Wm. Abney...*
- *29ᵗʰ April, 1783. Jonathan Dunbarr's estate appraised by Thos. Smith. John Abney, Wm. Blear.*
- *29ᵗʰ April, 1783. John McDonough's will (sadler)... Executors, Thos. Smith, John Abney, Richard Madison...*

John Abney "the Hatter" wrote his will on 14 Jun 1788 in Augusta County, Virginia:[86]

Staunton   June 14ᵗʰ 1788.
      The Last Will & Testament of John Abney

In the name of God Amin.–
        Being in an imperfect State of Health but of a Sound and Sinses do Settle my worldly affairs in the following manner. ——
1ˢᵗ my body to be buried in a decent manner–
2ⁿᵈ All my lawful debts to be paid as loans on money may be collected–
3ʳᵈ I give and bequeath to my beloved wife Isabella during her widowhood my houses & lotts commonly known by the Number 11 & 16 with the other lots and lands adjoining these over the Creek, containing five acres, also 120 acres of Woodland and an Entry joining the same of a 100 acres the former land joining Robert Ruds land and if she marry then to have the one half during life- Also one negro girl named Annie to be hers during life and at her death to be divided between my children her and her increase if any at her discretion. Likewise the rest of the negroes and all the hous hold furniture in like manner–
4ᵗʰ I give and bequeath to my son William at his mothers death the house and lot I now live on in consequence of his assisting to [-?-] and school the rest of the children and if he should die without issue, the said house and lott to be the property of my son John and his heirs also it is my desire that my son William should carry on the hatting trade for the support of my family and if he should marry he may live on the remaining one half of my lot when he thinks most convenient and at the death of his mother when he becomes possessed of her house and lot to relinquish his right to the other lotts–
5ᵗʰ I have also 250 acres of land adjoining Tumber and the plantation that Donnely now lives on also my plantation in Albemarl County near Charlottsville I allow to be sold for the support of my family if necessity require, & all my lands in the Western Country to be equally divided between my children, except my right to my lands on Green River, which I allow for my son John as his part of the Western Lands. – 6ᵗʰ My bond Book debts, & publick papers when collected to be for the Support of my wife & Children–
        I appoint my wife Isabella my Sole Executrix of this my last Will & Testiment revoking & making void all and every Will or Wills before this date, and this only to be my last Will & Testament As witness my hand and Seal the day & date first above written
                John Abney {Seal}
Test
W. Chambers
Alexʳ. Humphrey
        At a Court held for Augusta County September 16ᵗʰ 1788
        This Last Will and Testiment of John Abney Decᵈ. was presented in Court by Isabella Abney the Executrix therein named and proved by the oaths of William Chambers & Alexander Humphreys Witnesses thereto & is ordered to be recorded, on the motion of the said...

Like his father, John seems to have died in his middle age (about age 43). His will was proved by the witnesses and his widow, Isabella qualified as executrix.

John was, no doubt, buried in Staunton, Augusta County, Virginia. Still, to the author's knowledge, the location of the grave is unknown.

It is also noteworthy that the *Daughters of the American Revolution* accepts applications for descendants of John Abney due to his civil service. A biography edited by Janne (Shoults) Gorman on WikiTree reads as follows:[87]

John Abney was born circa 1745, in Virginia and during the time of the American Revolutionary War, he and his wife, Isabella Van Lear were living in Staunton, Augusta county, Virginia, where he paid supply tax, in 1783. This tax was in support of the new government of the United States in an attempt to decrease the deficit acquired during the Revolutionary War and in support of the War that continued with the British until the end of the War of 1812. (Source: Library of Virginia, Augusta County, Va., Personal Property Tax, 1782-1795, Reel #23)

John is honored for his Patriotic Service by the Society of the Daughters of the American Revolution, as DAR Ancestor #A000250. DAR records indicate that John died before June 14, 1788, in Staunton, Augusta county, Virginia. Applications for membership in the Society of the DAR have been made by the descendants of John and Isabella Abney by their son, William Abney, who married Elizabeth McClanahan; and their daughters, Martha "Patsy" Abney, who married Peter Earl Hogg; and Sarah Abney, who married Robert McClanahan. (Source: DAR Ancestor #A000250

Therefore, descendants of John Abney "the Hatter" are encouraged to join the various Daughters, Sons and Children of the American Revolution.

End Notes:

1. Last Will and Testament of Abner Abney – Albemarle County Will Book A, page 38
2. In Search of Kate, by Charlotte Ann Abney Metzger (1978)
3. Goochland County, Virginia Genealogy and History (http://genealogytrails.com/vir/goochland/)
4. Albemarle County, Virginia Genealogy and History (http://genealogytrails.com/vir/albemarle/)
5. 1787 Tax List, Wilkes County, North Carolina, Isbels District, page 001 – *Elisha Abner*
6. For the explanation on the year of Abner Abney's death (ca.1751), see Chapter II, page 14, beginning at the first paragraph.
7. The author's calculations here are based on the marriage of Joshua Abney (Elisha's eldest son). Joshua was married 06 May 1795. If he was 21 years of age, he could have been born no later than, say 1774. However, the author believes a daughter fit into that time frame. Therefore, backing up two years (the average span between births), we have circa 1772 and the marriage a year earlier, say 1771.
8. *https://www.familysearch.org/tree/pedigree/landscape/L5DC-GV3.* The author has never been able to locate a name for Elisha's wife or wives. There are speculations, as the example given from FamilySearch.org. Other examples show that Elisha married a Mary Calloway or a Nancy Calloway, daughter of Revolutionary War Officer, Col. William Calloway. The author also believes these claims are only creative guesses (and wishful thinking) because Hezekiah Abney (son of Elisha) had a grandson Wilburn Callaway Abney. However, if, as has been asserted, Hezekiah's wife was Frances Anne Calloway, that would eliminate for the search for a namesake for his grandson. The author has no proof that Hezekiah's wife was Frances Anne Calloway, either. In short, the author believes all alleged names give for Elisha Abney Sr.'s wife are creative guesses…and the contributors to this book are unanimous in the belief that Elisha's wife or wives are unknown.
9. Virginia Genealogy Trails! Amherst County Virginia Genealogy and History (http://genealogytrails.com/vir/amherst/)
10. The location of the land (Mechems <*sic*> River) inherited by Elisha Abney from his father, Abner is given in the Last Will and Testament of the latter (see end note #1 above). The location of Mechum River is from a Rand McNally Atlas, an Albemarle County, Virginia (1911).
11. The *name* Joshua Abney is documented. However, the other two names come from *Abney Supplement* by John R. Hensell (self-published 1988), pg.7. The author has not been able to confirm these two daughters, given by Hensell as *Shrew (Jerusha) and Ann*. This current author does not know where these names come from, however, "Shrew" could be an obvious nickname for "Jerusha". Moreover, the Tax Record of 1787 for Elisha Abner in Wilkes County, North Carolina shows five females, which the author interprets as possibly being Elisha's wife and four daughters: Jerusha, Ann, (n.n.) and Dorcas). The 1790 Federal Census also shows five females, which the author identifies as Elisha's wife; and four daughters, to wit: Jerusha "Shrew" (?), Ann (?), (n.n.) and Dorcas. The birth years given by Hensell are different than the birth years given here. Based on every available tax and census record, this current author believes these birth years are closer to facts. (See Appendix B on pages 259-260 establishing Elisha Abney Sr.'s children)
12. Amherst County, Virginia Deed dated 29 Mar 1779 of Jonathan Witt Jr. of Amherst County to Littleberry Witt and Jonathan Witt Sr. was witnessed by Elisha Abney. The author first posited the theory of the Abney-Witt connection many years ago and reported it in the previous Abney book. See the **Abney Family History Series, Volume I,** ***Abney: Ancestry and Genealogy of Dr. Abraham Abney of Virginia***, second edition (ISBN: 978-0-9993282-2-4, LCCN: 2018952526), published 3 Sep 2018 by this current author.
13. See the **Abney Family History Series, Volume I,** ***Abney: Ancestry and Genealogy of Dr. Abraham Abney of Virginia***, second edition (ISBN: 978-0-9993282-2-4, LCCN: 2018952526), published 3 Sep 2018 by this current author., ppg.84-85
14. Amherst County, Virginia Deed dated 02 Oct 1780 of Samuel Ayres and wife Rachel to Elisha Abney *of Amherst County* for £250, 150 acres on a branch of Stoney Creek of Rockfish River. Note here that Elisha Abney was already "of Amherst County" meaning he was living in this county even prior to purchasing this land.
15. Seventh Census of the United States of the household of *Enoch Abner Sr.* in Kentucky
16. Eighth Census of the United States of the household of *Joel Abna* in Alabama wherein Hezekiah is named as *Hesaciah Abney*
17. Seventh Census of the United States of the household of *Elisha Abner* [Jr.] in Kentucky
18. Seventh Census of the United States of the household of *John Woods* [Jr.] in Kentucky wherein Dorcas is named as *Tabithey Woods*
19. Seventh Census of the United States of the household of *John Abner Sr.* in Kentucky
20. Seventh Census of the United States of the household of *William Bishop* in Kentucky wherein Mary is named as *Mary Bishop*
21. Seventh Census of the United States of the household of *Isham Smith* in Kentucky wherein Margaret is named as *Margaret L. Smith*
22. Eighth Census of the United States of the household of *Isham Smith* in Kentucky wherein Margaret is named as *Margrett L. Smith*
23. The unknown female whom the author believes to have been a daughter is established in the 1787 Tax Record of Wilkes County, NC as well as the 1790 Federal Census in Greenville Co., Ninety-Six District, SC. (See Appendix B establishing Elisha Abney Sr.'s children)
24. Abner Abney is established in this family by prosopography and nomenclature. He was a mystery to the author in the past, and even a main subject in the author's newsletter (see the *Abney Family Researcher*, Vol.III, Issue II [March 1999]). The author, at that time, believed that Abner Abney was nearer kin to Pvt. Paul Abney/Abner, but that was never conclusive. Firstly, we can take his name. It is quite obvious and easy to believe that Elisha would name a son *Abner* after his own father. Secondly, this Abner Abney married in

Carter County, Tennessee in 1803. We know, unambiguously that Elisha Abney Sr. was in Carter County, Tennessee. He purchased 150 acres of land there in 1796. He also appears on the Tax Records in Carter County in 1796, 1798, 1799 and 1800. Then we have Elisha selling land a mere two years after Abner's wedding on 04 Oct 1805 in Carter County, Tennessee (Elisha Abner to Isaac Lincoln, $400 for 150 acres). There is little doubt in the author's mind, that Abner Abney belongs in this family group. He is also accounted for in the 1787 Tax Record of Wilkes County, North Carolina (although other researchers erroneously believe this is Elisha Abner Jr.); and on the 1790 census of Greenville County, Ninety-Six District, South Carolina. The author believes that researchers have Elisha Abner Jr.'s birth year wrong. Yes, on the 1850 census it was claimed his age was 67. But the author believes his age was 63. In the 1840 census, Elisha Jr. is listed as age over 16 and under 25. If he was 67 in 1850, he would have had to have been 27 in 1810, but he was not. It is more likely he knew his age as a young man, and forgot it as he grew older. Every census agrees with him born in 1787 (except the 1850) just as every census agrees with him born in 1784 (except the 1810). Moreover, born in 1787 he does not need to be accounted for in the 1787 Tax Record, because he was not alive. Yet, he and Abner Abney are both accounted for in the 1790 Census Record. Since Abner Abney married before Elisha Jr., we can safely assume Abner was the elder of the two, hence the male given on the 1787 record. An additional clue discovered by Contributor John M. Abney has Abner Abney and Elisha Abney as workers on a Road Crew in a Carter County Tennessee court record dated 13 Feb 1804. After this was written, Contributor John M. Abney discovered a military record of this Abner Abney. He was 34 years of age in Jan 1814, born in Amherst County, Virginia. This is positively in agreement with the author's conclusions. The major change is Abner will be listed as an older brother of Hezekiah in the birth order. (See Appendix B establishing Elisha Abney Sr.'s children)

25. Hezekiah is well-established; however, it has been believed for decades that he was born in Wilkes County, North Carolina. The author absolutely and unequivocally takes issue with this belief. In the 1860 census, Hezekiah was listed as being from South Carolina. While he spent some of his childhood in South Carolina, this still does not prove those researchers who believe he was born in *North* Carolina. Since the author has shown Elisha Abney had purchased land in Amherst County, Virginia in 1780, he had already been living there as he was referred to as *of Amherst County* (see end notes 12 and 14 above). It is highly doubtful that Elisha was purchasing land in Amherst County (the same year Hezekiah was born) only to be migrating within no more than two months to North Carolina. No, Hezekiah Abney was born in Amherst County, Virginia ca.1781. (See Appendix B establishing Elisha Abney Sr.'s children)

26. Dorcas Abney is well-established as a daughter of Elisha Abney Sr. and is accounted for in both the 1787 Wilkes County, NC Tax Record and the 1790 Federal Census in Greenville Co., Ninety-Six District, SC. (See Appendix B for Elisha Abney Sr.'s children)

27. 1787 Census, North Carolina, State Census, 1784-1787 provided to the author by Contributor John M. Abney

28. Although many believe Elisha Abner Jr. was born ca.1784 in Virginia as per the 1850 census, the author does not concur. As pointed out, the 1810 census shows Elisha Abner Jr. age 25 or younger. The 1787 Tax List of Elisha Abney Sr. shows three boys. If Elisha Jr. was born in 1784, it would show four boys. See *Seven Records with Erroneous Information* on page 18 and 19. As the reader will see, the 1790 census accounts for all the three boys in the 1787 Tax Record plus the additional two boys born in Wilkes County, North Carolina. (See Appendix B establishing Elisha Abney Sr.'s children)

29. Menan is well-established as a son of Elisha Abney Jr. In the past, he was confused with a fictitious Monroe Abner. Many thanks to Contributor Sandrea Abner Cook for sending the marriage documents to the author, proving once and for all that there was no Monroe Abner, but he was Menan Abner who married: 1) Agnes "Aggy" Bowling; 2) Lucinda Benge; and 3) Elizabeth Lucas (widow Wells). (See Appendix B establishing Elisha Abney Sr.'s children)

30. Seventh Census of the United States (1850) – household of *Menen Abner* (Clay Co., Kentucky)

31. First Census of the United States of the household of *Elisha Abner* in South Carolina

32. https://en.wikipedia.org/wiki/Watauga_Association

33. https://en.wikipedia.org/wiki/Washington_District,_North_Carolina#History

34. *The True Story of the Short-Lived State of Franklin* (article in the Smithsonian Magazine), by Kat Eschner, dated August 23, 2017 (https://www.smithsonianmag.com/smart-news/true-story-short-lived-state-franklin-180964541/)

35. https://en.wikipedia.org/wiki/Southwest_Territory

36. https://en.wikipedia.org/wiki/Tennessee

37. Carter County, Tennessee deed from Elisha Abner to Isaac Lincoln dated 4 Oct 1805.

38. Marriage Bond of Joshua Abner and Will Phelps dated 6 May 1795 for the marriage of Joshua Abner and Pattie Phelps, Green Co., KY.

39. https://en.wikipedia.org/wiki/Marriageable_age#Americas

40. https://en.wikipedia.org/wiki/Carter_County,_Tennessee

41. Third Census of the United States (1810) – household of Elisha Abner (Clay Co., Kentucky)

42. https://mapgeeks.org/tennessee/#Map_of_Tennessee_County_Formations_1777-1985

43. Tax Record of 1787 in Wilkes County, North Carolina; Federal Census Records of South Carolina (1790), Kentucky (1810, 1820, 1830, 1840, 1850) Georgia (1830, 1840) and Alabama (1860).

44. Carter County, Tennessee deed from Abel Simpkins to Elisha Abner dated 09 Aug 1796

45. Tax Lists from Carter County, Tennessee for the years 1796, 1797, 1799:
     a. Entry for Elisha Abner (1796), *Tennessee, Early Tax List Records, 1783-1895*, Digital image *Ancestry.com* (http//www.ancestry.com : accessed 18 September 2000).
     b. Entry for Elisha Abner (1797), *Tennessee, Early Tax List Records, 1783-1895*, Digital image *Ancestry.com* (http//www.ancestry.com : accessed 18 September 2000).
     c. Entry for Elisha Abner (1799), *Tennessee, Early Tax List Records, 1783-1895*, Digital image *Ancestry.com* (http//www.ancestry.com : accessed 18 September 2000).

46. Tax List from Carter County, Tennessee for the years 1800: Entry for Elisha Abney (1800), *Tennessee, Early Tax List Records, 1783-1895*, Digital image *Ancestry.com* (http//www.ancestry.com : accessed 18 September 2000).

47. *Abney Supplement* by John R. Hensell (self-published 1988), ppg.7 and 16

48. Federal Census Records of 1850 (Cobb Co., Georgia: *Benjamin Abney*, ae.46); 1860 (Calhoun Co., Alabama: *Benjamin Abna*, ae.53); and 1870 (Cleburne Co., Alabama: *Benjamin Abny*, ae.66) all claim Benjamin Hezekiah Abney was born in Georgia.

49. Marriage Bond of Abner Abney and Benjamin Russell dated 26 Aug 1803 for the marriage of Abner Abney and Alyda Russell, Carter County, Tennessee: Abner Abney marriage bond, *Carter County Marriage Records 1796-1950*, , digital image (FHL Film 007718484) *Family Search* (http://www.familysearch.org : accessed 19 September 2020).

50. Entry for Elisha & Abner Abney (13 Feb 1804), County Court minutes, 1804-1826, Carter County, Tennessee (transcribed by Historical Records Survey (WPA), digital image *Family Search* (http://www.familysearch.org : accessed 18 September 2020) original page 11 (left margin of document).

51. Entry for Elisha Abner (13 May 1805), County Court minutes, 1804-1826, Carter County, Tennessee (transcribed by Historical Records Survey (WPA), digital image *Family Search* (http://www.familysearch.org : accessed 18 September 2020) original page 158 (left margin of document).

52. Carter County [Tennessee] *Register of Deeds, Deed Book Volume A*; 544 -545, Elisha Abney to Isaac Lincoln, digital image *Family Search* (http://www.familysearch.org : accessed 17 September 2020).

53. Entry for Elisha Abner (10 Nov 1805), County Court minutes, 1804-1826, Carter County, Tennessee (transcribed by Historical Records Survey (WPA), digital image *Family Search* (http://www.familysearch.org : accessed 18 September 2020) original page 247 (left margin of document).

54. Carter County [Tennessee] *Register of Deeds, Deed Book Volume A*; 544 -545, Elisha Abney to Isaac Lincoln, digital image *Family Search* (http://www.familysearch.org : accessed 17 September 2020).

55. https://en.wikipedia.org/wiki/Clay_County,_Kentucky

56. based on the 04 Aug 1807 birthdate of the eldest child of Elisha Abner Jr., namely William "Buck" Abner.

57. https://mapgeeks.org/kentucky/#Map_of_Kentucky_County_Formations_1776-1939

58. Clay County, Kentucky marriage license: *James Wood to Darkey Abner.*

59. Third Census of the United States (1810) – household of *Elisha Abner* (page 160) (Clay Co., Kentucky)

60. Third Census of the United States (1810) – household of *Elisha Abner Junr.* (page 160) (Clay Co., Kentucky)

61. *Abney Supplement* John R. Hensell (self-published 1988), pg.45

62. Family researchers, Mary Collie Cooper and Owen Blevins both give the marriage license date as 11 Nov 1811.

63. Clay County, Kentucky Marriage License *Menan Abner to Aggy Bowling*

64. Clay County, Kentucky General Index to Marriages

65. *Abney Supplement* John R. Hensell (self-published 1988), pg.7

66. Register of Enlistments in the U.S. Army, 1798-1914; (National Archives Microfilm Publication M233, 81 rolls); Records of the Adjutant General's Office, 1780's-1917, Record Group 94; National Archives, Washington, D.C. discovered by Contributor John M. Abney.

67. *Abney Supplement* John R. Hensell (self-published 1988), pg.7 (which claims the marriage was 29 Nov 1819. According to family researcher, Marjorie Johnson Diamond, the marriage was 15 Nov 1819. Owen Blevins corroborates Cousin Marjorie's information.

68. Fourth Federal Census of the United States (1820) – household of *Enoch Abner (S?)r.* (Clay Co., Kentucky, pg.117)

69. Fourth Federal Census of the United States (1820) – household of *Joshua Abney* (Morgantown, Butler Co., Kentucky, pg.318)

70. Fourth Federal Census of the United States (1820) – household of *Elisha Abner* (Clay Co., Kentucky, pg.117)

71. Fourth Federal Census of the United States (1820) – household of *Menan Abner* (Clay Co., Kentucky, pg.117)

72. Since John Abney has not been located in the 1820 census, and we know him to have married a few years later, and further that Menan and John are near siblings (in age), it is logical John was living with his brother Menan when this census was taken.

73. Fourth Federal Census of the United States (1820) – household of *Saml Bishop* (Clay Co., Kentucky, pg.117)

74. Fourth Federal Census of the United States (1820) – household of *Isham Smith* (Clay Co., Kentucky, pg.117)

75. based on a record of guardianship ca.1760/2. Source lost in Hurricane Katrina

76. Last Will and Testament of Abner Abney – Albemarle County Will Book A, page 38

77. *The Abney Family Researcher* Newsletter, Volume IV, Issue II (October, 2000), page 3, by this current author

78. from *National Genealogical Society Quarterly*, pg. 238 as reported in *Old Pendleton District Newsletter*, Vol.19 No.5 May 2005

79. From *Library of Virginia Research Notes Number 26 – Early Virginia Marriage Records... Consents: According to Virginia law, individuals under the age of twenty-one needed the consent of a parent or guardian to marry. In the seventeenth and eighteenth centuries, officials were especially concerned about females under the age of sixteen marrying without consent. County clerks were not authorized to issue a marriage license without certificate (permission) from the parent, master, or guardian. In the nineteenth century, a parent or guardian could give consent verbally to the clerk of the court, or provide written consent in front of one to two witnesses; the consent was then delivered to the county clerk.*

80. https://www.findagrave.com/memorial/183543046/_

81. In Search of Kate, by Charlotte Ann Abney Metzger (1978)

82. Last Will and Testament of Abner Abney – Albemarle County Will Book A, page 38

83. Augusta County Marriages 1748-1850 by John Vogt and T. William Kethley Jr. (1986)

84. The statement that John Abney lived the rest of his life in Augusta County, Virginia is validated by the fact that each record subsequent to and including his marriage through to the administration of his estate is in Augusta County, Virginia.

85. Chronicles of the Scotch-Irish Settlement in Virginia, Vol. 1, 2 and 3, by Lyman Chalkley

86. Will of John Abney, Staunton, Virginia 14 Jun 1788 (Green County Kentucky Will Book #1, 1794-1816, p.80) (much thanks to Contributor Grace Lynette Crouch Prater for sharing the copy of this will)

87. https://www.wikitree.com/wiki/Abney-140

Chapter IV

Migrations of Abner Abney's Grandchildren
Where did they go?

Following are the known or implied migrations of the grandchildren of **Abner Abney**:

The Children of Elisha Abney/Abner Sr.

- *Joshua Abney*
  - ca.1771   born, probably in Albemarle Co., VA
  - ca.1777   migrated with his parents to Amherst Co., VA
  - 1787   accounted for on the tax list of his father in Wilkes Co., NC
  - 1790   accounted for on the census of his father in Greenville Co., 96 Dist., SC
  - 1792   Commonwealth of Kentucky admitted to the union. formation of Green Co.
  - ca.1793   migrated to the Southwest Territory with his parents (?) or to Kentucky (?)
  - 1795   married in Green Co., KY to Martha "Pattie" Phelps
  - 1810   formation of Butler Co., KY – Joshua not located in census
  - 1820   census enumeration in Morgantown, Butler Co., KY
  - 1830   census enumeration in Clark Co., IL
  - 1845   died in Jefferson Co., IL. Buried there in Abner Cemetery

- *Jerusha "Shrew" (?) Abney*
  - est.1773   born, probably in Albemarle Co., VA
  - ca.1777   migrated with her parents to Amherst Co., VA
  - 1787   accounted for on the tax list of her father in Wilkes Co., NC
  - 1790   accounted for on the census of her father in Greenville Co., 96 Dist., SC
  - (no further information on this daughter)

- *Ann (?) Abney*
  - est.1775   born, probably in Albemarle Co., VA
  - ca.1777   migrated with her parents to Amherst Co., VA
  - 1787   accounted for on the tax list of her father in Wilkes Co., NC
  - 1790   accounted for on the census of her father in Greenville Co., 96 Dist., SC
  - (no further information on this daughter)

- *(n.n.) Abney*
  - est.1777   born, probably in Amherst Co., VA
  - 1787   accounted for on the tax list of her father in Wilkes Co., NC
  - 1790   accounted for on the census of her father in Greenville Co., 96 Dist., SC
  - (no further information on this daughter)

(continued on next page)

The Children of Elisha Abney/Abner Sr. (continued)

- *Pvt. Abner Abney*
  - ca.1779   born in Amherst Co., VA
  - 1787   accounted for on the tax list of his father in Wilkes Co., NC
  - 1790   accounted for on the census of his father in Greenville Co., 96 Dist., SC
  - ca.1793   migrated to the Southwest Territory with his parents
  - 1796   lived in Carter Co., TN (which was created from Southwest Territory)
  - 1800   probably living in Carter Co., TN with his parents (that census is lost)
  - 26 Aug 1803   married in Carter Co., TN to Alyda Russell
  - 13 Feb 1804   Carter Co., TN court record for Road Orders *Abner Abney...Elisha Abney...*
  - 22 Jan 1814   Abner Abney enlisted in the U.S. Army out of Gallatin (Sumner Co.), TN
  - 30 Jan 1814   RR (Recruiting Return) Gallatin, Tenn.
  - 14 Feb 1814   RR no Capt. New Orleans
  - 25 Jul 1814   Deserted – probably enjoying a rowdy time in New Orleans!
  - 29 Jul 1814   Apprehended
  - 08 Jan 1815   Battle of New Orleans
  - 15 Apr 1815   DR (Descriptive Roll) Capt. Isaac L. Baker's Co.
  - 1820   It is probable he was the unidentified man living with his brother, Joshua in KY

[Author's note: Contributor Morgan F. Abney discovered an Abner Abney who died in Clarksville, Red River Co., TX. It is possible, but not proven, that his could be the same Pvt. Abner Abney. More research is needed.]

- *Hezekiah Abney*
  - ca.1781   born in Amherst Co., VA
  - 1787   accounted for on the tax list of his father in Wilkes Co., NC
  - 1790   accounted for on the census of his father in Greenville Co., 96 Dist., SC
  - ca.1793   migrated to the Southwest Territory with his parents
  - 1796   State of Tennessee admitted to the union. Carter County formed
  - 1796   lived in Carter Co., TN (which was created from Southwest Territory)
  - 1800   probably living in Carter Co., TN with his parents (that census is lost)
  - ca.1800   May have joined his brother, Joshua in Green Co., KY (?)
  - ca.1802   According to Hensell, Hezekiah had a son (John) born in KY. no proof.
  - ca.1804   living in Jackson Co., GA where his son, Benjamin H. was born
  - 1830   census enumeration in Jackson Co., GA
  - 1832   formation of Cobb Co., GA from Cherokee Nation
  - 1840   census enumeration in Cobb Co., GA
  - 26 Jun 1860   living with his son, Joel Abney in Calhoun Co., AL
  - 1861   died in Cleburne Co., AL. Buried there in Shoal Creek Cemetery

- *Dorcas "Tabitha" Abney*
  - ca.1784   born, probably in Amherst Co., VA
  - 1787   accounted for on the tax list of her father in Wilkes Co., NC
  - 1790   accounted for on the census of her father in Greenville Co., 96 Dist., SC
  - ca.1793   migrated to the Southwest Territory with her parents
  - 1796   lived in Carter Co., TN (which was created from Southwest Territory)
  - 1800   probably living in Carter Co., TN with her parents (that census is lost)
  - ca.1806   may have migrated to Madison Co., KY with her father
  - 1807   formation of Clay Co., KY from Madison Co., et al
  - 12 Dec 1808   married John Woods in Clay Co., KY
  - 1840   accounted for on the census of her husband, John Woods (sic) in Clay CO., KY
  - 1843   formation of Owsley Co. from part of Clay Co. Woods' land fell into Owsley Co.
  - 04 Sep 1850   with her husband on the census in Owsley Co., KY as "Tabithey" Woods
  - (no further information on this daughter – there is a claim she is buried in Clay Co., KY)

(continued on next page)

The Children of Elisha Abney/Abner Sr. (continued)

- ***Elisha Abney/Abner Jr.***
  - o ca.1787 born, probably in Wilkes Co., NC <u>after</u> his father's tax list entry
  - o 1790 accounted for on the census of his father in Greenville Co., 96 Dist., SC
  - o ca.1793 migrated to the Southwest Territory with his parents
  - o 1796 lived in Carter Co., TN (which was created from Southwest Territory)
  - o 1800 probably living in Carter Co., TN with his parents (that census is lost)
  - o ca.1806 may have migrated to Madison Co., KY with his father
  - o ca.1806 married (probably in Madison Co., KY) to Nancy "Lucy" Loving
  - o 1807 formation of Clay Co., KY from Madison Co., et al
  - o 1810 Head of Household on census in Clay Co., KY
  - o 1820 Head of Household on census in Clay Co., KY
  - o 1830 Head of Household on census in Clay Co., KY
  - o 1840 Head of Household on census in Clay Co., KY
  - o 1843 formation of Owsley Co. from part of Clay Co. Elisha's land fell into Owsley Co.
  - o 16 Aug 1850 Head of Household on census in Owsley Co., KY
  - o ca.1855 died in Owsley Co., KY. Buried in Teges Cemetery, Clay Co., KY

- ***Menan Abney/Abner***
  - o ca.1790 born, probably in Wilkes Co., NC <u>before</u> his father's census enumeration
  - o 1790 accounted for on the census of his father in Greenville Co., 96 Dist., SC
  - o ca.1793 migrated to the Southwest Territory with his parents
  - o 1796 lived in Carter Co., TN (which was created from Southwest Territory)
  - o 1800 probably living in Carter Co., TN with his parents (that census is lost)
  - o ca.1806 may have migrated to Madison Co., KY with his father
  - o 1807 formation of Clay Co., KY from Madison Co., et al
  - o 1810 accounted for on the census of his father in Clay Co., KY
  - o 22 Mar 1813 married in Clay Co., KY to Agnes "Aggy" Bowling
  - o 1820 Head of Household on census in Clay Co., KY
  - o 07 Oct 1829 married in Clay Co., KY to Lucinda Benge
  - o 1830 Head of Household on census in Clay Co., KY
  - o 11 Oct 1836 married in Clay Co., KY to Elizabeth Lucas (widow Wells)
  - o 14 Sep 1850 Head of Household on census in Clay Co., KY
  - o ca.1853 died in Clay Co., KY. Buried in Cortland Cemetery, Cow Creek, Clay Co., KY
  - o 04 Aug 1853 Administration of his estate in Clay Co., KY

- ***John Abney Sr.***
  - o ca.1794 born in Washington Co., Southwest Territory (later Carter Co., TN)
  - o 1796 lived in Carter Co., TN (which was created from Southwest Territory)
  - o 1800 probably living in Carter Co., TN with his parents (that census is lost)
  - o ca.1806 may have migrated to Madison Co., KY with his father
  - o 1807 formation of Clay Co., KY from Madison Co., et al
  - o 1810 accounted for on the census of his father in Clay Co., KY
  - o 1820 Head of Household on census in Clay Co., KY
  - o ca.1825 (According to gen. Judy Vietri) married (in Clay Co., KY?) to Pamelia Watts
  - o 07 Oct 1829 married in Clay Co., KY to Millie Noble
  - o 1830 Head of Household on census in Clay Co., KY
  - o 1840 Head of Household on census in Clay Co., KY
  - o 1843 formation of Owsley Co. from part of Clay Co. John's land fell into Owsley Co.
  - o 25 Sep 1850 Head of Household on census in Owsley Co., KY
  - o 01 Aug 1860 living with his nephew, Enoch Abner (son of Elisha Jr.) in Owsley Co., KY
  - o (no further information on this son)

(continued on next page)

The Children of Elisha Abney/Abner Sr. (continued)

- *Mary "Polly" Abney/Abner*
    - ca. 1795 — born in Washington Co., Southwest Territory (later Carter Co., TN)
    - 1796 — lived in Carter Co., TN (which was created from Southwest Territory)
    - 1800 — probably living in Carter Co., TN with her parents (that census is lost)
    - ca.1806 — may have migrated to Madison Co., KY with her father
    - 1807 — formation of Clay Co., KY from Madison Co., et al
    - 1810 — accounted for on the census of her father in Clay Co., KY
    - 15 Nov 1811 — married in Clay Co., KY to Samuel "Sam" Bishop
    - 1830 — Head of Household on census in Clay Co., KY
    - 1840 — Head of Household on census in Clay Co., KY
    - 29 Aug 1850 — Living with her son, William Bishop in Clay Co., KY in the census
    - 20 Apr 1881 — died in Clay Co., KY. buried in Laurel Point Cemetery, Clay Co., KY

- *Margaret Larken Abney/Abner*
    - 14 Feb 1798 — born in Carter Co., TN
    - 1800 — probably living in Carter Co., TN with her parents (that census is lost)
    - ca.1806 — may have migrated to Madison Co., KY with her father
    - 1807 — formation of Clay Co., KY from Madison Co., et al
    - 1810 — accounted for on the census of her father in Clay Co., KY
    - 15 Nov 1819 — married in Clay Co., KY to Isham O. Smith
    - 1830 — accounted for on the census of her husband in Clay Co., KY
    - 1840 — accounted for on the census of her husband in Clay Co., KY
    - 28 Aug 1850 — enumerated with her husband, Isham Smith in Henry Co., KY
    - 25 Jun 1860 — enumerated with her husband, Isham Smith in Henry Co., KY
    - 18 Oct 1870 — died in Henry Co., KY. buried in Eminence Cemetery, Henry Co., KY

- *Enoch Abney Sr.*
    - ca.1803 — born in Carter Co., TN
    - ca.1806 — may have migrated to Madison Co., KY with his father
    - 1807 — formation of Clay Co., KY from Madison Co., et al
    - 1810 — accounted for on the census of his father in Clay Co., KY
    - 1820 — accounted for on the census of his father, Enoch Abner Sr. (sic)
    - 1830 — Head of Household on census in Clay Co., KY
    - 1840 — Head of Household on census in Clay Co., KY
    - 28 Sep 1850 — Head of Household on census in Taney Co., MO
    - 1854 — died in Stone Co., MO.

The Children of Milly Abney
- At this time there are no known children of Milly Abney

The Children of John Abney "the Hatter"

- *Sarah "Sally" Abney*
  - ca.1769 — born in Augusta Co., VA
  - 04 Jul 1797 — married in Augusta Co., VA to Robert McClenachan
  - 1810 — accounted for on the census of her husband, Robert McClenachan
  - 11 Sep 1853 — died in Barren Co., KY

- *Margaret "Peggy" Abney*
  - ca.1770 — born in Augusta Co., VA
  - 04 Jul 1797 — married in Augusta Co., VA to Philip North
  - 1820 — Head of Household on census in Staunton, Augusta Co., VA
  - 23 Aug 1850 — enumerated in the household of her son, John A. North in Greenbrier Co., VA
  - 31 Mar 1851 — died in VA. Buried in Lewisburg, Greenbrier, VA (now in WV)

- *Capt. William Abney "the Hatter"*
  - 08 Aug 1772 — born in Staunton, Augusta Co., VA
  - 23 Dec 1794 — married in Augusta Co., VA to Elizabeth Parks McClenachan
  - 1810 — Head of Household on census in Augusta Co., VA
  - 1812 — Ran for Virginia House of Delegates in Augusta Co., VA
  - 1820 — Head of Household on census in Augusta Co., VA
  - 20 Jun 1824 — died in Augusta Co., VA (death date according to family Bible)
  - 25 Aug 1828 — Estate administered in Augusta Co., VA

- *Nancy Abney*
  - ca.1776 — born in Staunton, Augusta Co., VA
  - 17 Jul 1798 — married in Augusta Co., VA to Johannes "John" Fackler
  - (unknown) — married to (n.n.) Gardner
  - (unknown) — married to John Hicklin
  - 24 Nov 1828 — still living
  - (no further information on this daughter)

- *John Key Abney*
  - 20 Mar 1780 — born in Augusta Co., VA
  - 1799 — acquired land in Green Co., KY
  - 01 May 1800 — married in Green Co., KY to Betsy Gill
  - 04 Apr 1803 — married in Fincastle, Montgomery Co., VA to Tamar Ann Robinson
  - 1810 — Head of Household on census in Greensburg, Green Co., VA
  - 1820 — Head of Household on census in Greensburg, Green Co., VA
  - bef.1828 — died in Green Co., KY

- *Martha Abney*
  - ca.1784 — born in Augusta Co., VA
  - 18 Sep 1798 — married in Augusta Co., VA to Peter Hogg Jr.
  - 1820 — accounted for on the census of her husband, Peter Hogg in Mason Co., VA
  - 1830 — Head of Household in Mason Co., VA
  - 24 Mar 1846 — died in Mason Co., VA. Buried in Mason Co., VA (now in WV)

- *Mary Abney*
  - ca.1786 — born in Augusta Co., VA
  - ???? — (According to Hensell, married a KENNY)
  - (no further information on this daughter)

Photographs, Maps and Documents

King William County, Virginia about the time Abner Abney was born (circa 1711).	Spotsylvania County, Virginia at the time Abner Abney proved his father's will in court.
King William Co., VA 1703-1719	**Spotsylvania Co., VA** 1732-1733

maps from Map Geeks (https://mapgeeks.org), edited by R.R. Abney Jr.

← Last Will and Testament of Dannett Abney Sr. was written 5 Feb 1732 in Spotsylvania County, Virginia. Witnessed by:
Paul Abney [son]
Abner Abney [son]
William Trusty
Mary Abney *the Younger* **[daughter-in-law])**

The Last Will and Testament of Dannett Abney Sr. was probated 5 Mar 1733 by the oaths:
Abner Abney
Mary Abney *the Younger*
William Trusty
↓

Last Will & Testament of Dannett Abney Sr. and probate thereof provided by genealogist, Lisa Renae Franklin

Abner Abney's first two children are apparently born 1741-3 in Goochland Co., VA.	By 1745, Abner Abney's land fell into Albemarle Co., VA, where his son, John was born.

Goochland Co., VA

1739-1742

Albemarle Co., VA

1745

	Albemarle County, Virginia 1751-2 when Abner Abney's Last Will & Testament was written and probated.

There is no proof of the birth years, much less the birthdates of Abner Abney's three children. We only know they were all young (i.e. minors) when Abner Abney died. Since Elisha Abney received the lion's share of the inheritance, the author believes he was the eldest child. Milly is loosely considered the second child. Since she chose a guardian in 1760, she was still underage (i.e. under 18). Therefore a 1743 birth year estimate would be feasible. As for John's birth year, it was given by Metzger *In Search of Kate* as well as DAR records which claim circa 1745.

Albemarle Co., VA

1750-1752

maps from Map Geeks (https://mapgeeks.org), edited by R.R. Abney Jr.

Last Will & Testament of
Abner Abney
written 5 Sep 1751
Witnesses: John Key, Robert R. Foster and Dorathy (sic) Foster

Last Will and Testament of Abner Abney provided by Contributor Morgan Floyd Abney

Inventory of Abner Abney, appraised and presented to Albemarle Court 14 Dec 1752

3

Abney's Apprisal

W[e] Suant to an order a Court wee y[e] Subsc[ribers] have met & first being sworn have appraisd y[e] Estate of Abner Abney Dec[eas]t as P[er] Inventory

	£	s	d
One Horse	4	0	0
6 Head Cattle & 1 Bell	5	12	6
7 Head of Hoggs	2	1	0
1 p[ai]r Stillards	0	7	6
1 p[ai]r Wedges	0	4	0
Old Iron	0	6	0
1 Hilling Hoe	0	2	0
1 Box Iron	0	4	0
1 Parcel of Carpent[er]s Tools	0	9	0
1 Old Saddle & Housen	0	10	0
1 Weaver Loom &c	0	10	0
1 Bed & furniture	3	5	0
A parcel of Bottles	0	2	6
The old pewter	0	8	2
1 Case of Knives & forks	0	4	0
2 Basons & 1 Dish	0	8	6
1 Gun Barrel & lock	0	6	0
1 Flax wheel	0	12	0
1 Trunk	0	4	0
1 Chest	0	1	6
a parcel of Old Lumber	0	8	0
2 Potts & a Frying Pan	0	5	6
1 old Pigin & Pale	0	2	0
3 old Tubs	0	3	0
Saspan Candle mold & Cup &c	0	3	6
	£20	19	8

Tho[mas] Smith
John Clark and
John Grills

This Inventory & Appraisment of the Estate of Abner Abney dec[eas]d was returned into Albemarle County Court the 14th Day of December 1752 and ordered to be recorded

Test

John Nicholas Clk

John Abney (son of Abner Abney) married Isabella Van Lear 10 Jul 1769 in Augusta County, Virginia and had issue: Sarah (ca.1770), Margaret (ca.1771), William (1772), Nancy (1776), John Key (1780), Martha (1781) and Mary (ca.1786). John lived the remainder of his lifetime in Augusta County, Virginia.

Elisha Abney Sr. (son of Abner Abney) married an unknown woman ca.1770 in Albemarle County, Virginia. They had three children in Albemarle County, to wit: Joshua (ca.1771), and daughters, (Jerusha "Shrew"?) (ca.1773), and (Ann?) (ca.1775). Elisha Abney Sr. would not remain in Virginia, however. By 1787 he and his family are found in Wilkes County, North Carolina.

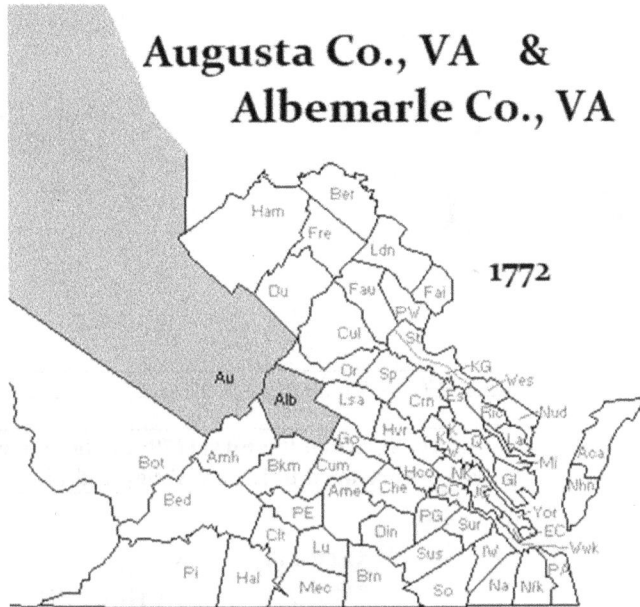

From about 1777 to 1784, Elisha Abney Sr. was living in Amherst County, Virginia. Here, it appears, four children are born to Elisha and his wife, to wit: a daughter, (n.n.) (ca.1777), Abner (ca.1779), Hezekiah (ca.1781) and Dorcas (ca.1784). Amherst County boundaries did not change during these years.

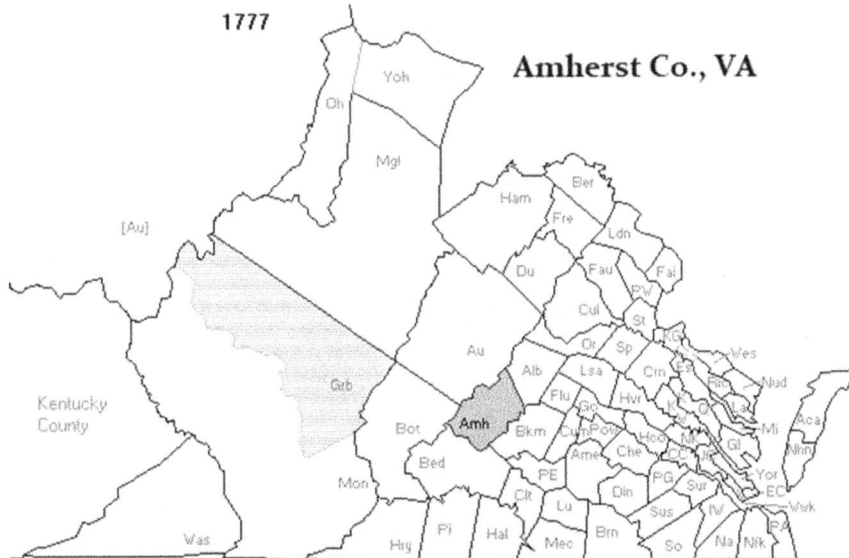

maps from Map Geeks, edited by R.R. Abney Jr.

By 1787, Elisha Abney found his way to North Carolina where he appeared in a tax list in Wilkes County. He seems to have sired two sons in Wilkes County, to wit: Elisha Jr. (ca.1787) and Menan (ca.1790).

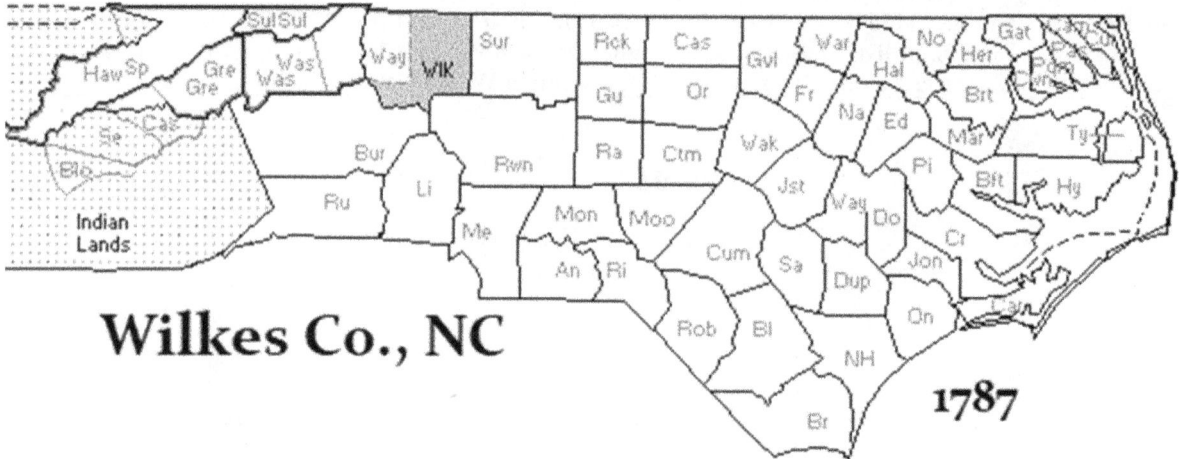

Wilkes Co., NC

1787

map from Map Geeks, edited by R.R. Abney Jr.

Elisha Abney was living in Greenville County, SC when the First (1790) Federal Census was taken. It does not appear that any children were born to Elisha Abney and his wife here.

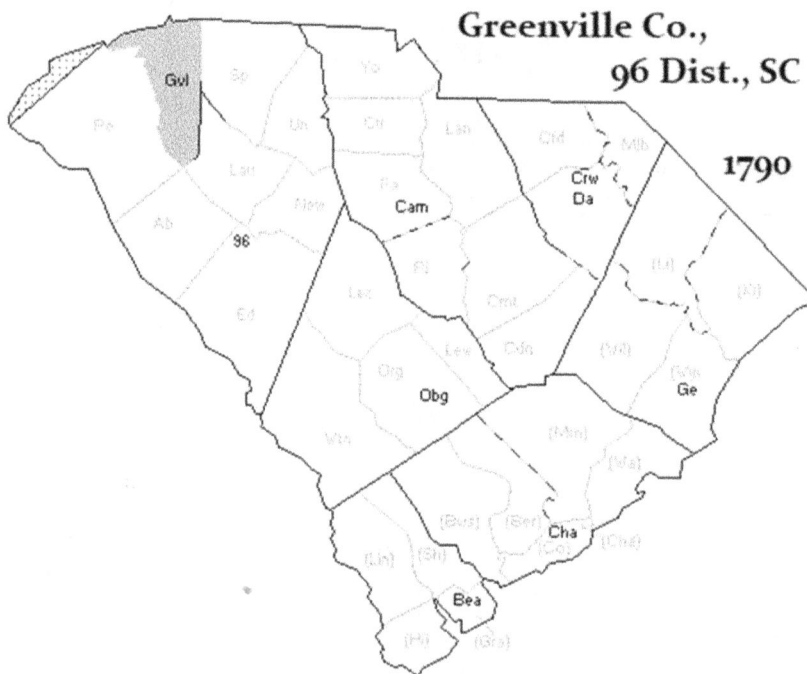

Greenville Co., 96 Dist., SC

1790

map from Map Geeks, edited by R.R. Abney Jr.

The little-known State of Franklin became known as Southwest Territory

The State of Franklin was formed in 1784 in a location owned by North Carolina. The government of the State of Franklin attempted to become a new state of the United States. Although they won a simple majority, they needed two thirds of the states, therefore, never succeeded in becoming a state of the United States. In 1789 the State of Franklin was dissolved. On 2 Apr 1790, North Carolina ceded the *Southwest Territory*, as it became known, to the Federal Government. The county, known as Wayne County in the State of Franklin, was part of Washington County in the state of North Carolina. This is the area in which Elisha Abney settled.

from https://sparkplaza.com/2016/06/22/the-lost-state-of-franklin/

THE EIGHT COUNTIES OF THE STATE OF FRANKLIN, CIRCA 1786 (Today in Northeast Tennessee)

map by https://en.wikipedia.org/wiki/User:Iamvered

Southwest Territory

The Southwest Ordinance was adopted on 26 May 1790 which made all the territory *south-west of the Ohio River* one district. That district became known as *Southwest Territory*. In 1791, the population of Southwest Territory was 35,691. Sometime after the First (1790) Federal Census was taken Elisha Abney left South Carolina and headed for the Southwest Territory. He lived in Washington County (part of the old Wayne County part of the now-defunct State of Franklin). Here, it appears two of his children were born, to wit: John Abney Sr. (1794) and Mary "Polly" Abney (ca.1795). By 1795, the population of Southwest Territory had grown to 77,262. Elisha Abney Sr. settled in the northeast part of the Southwest Territory, a part of Wayne County (see plate E).

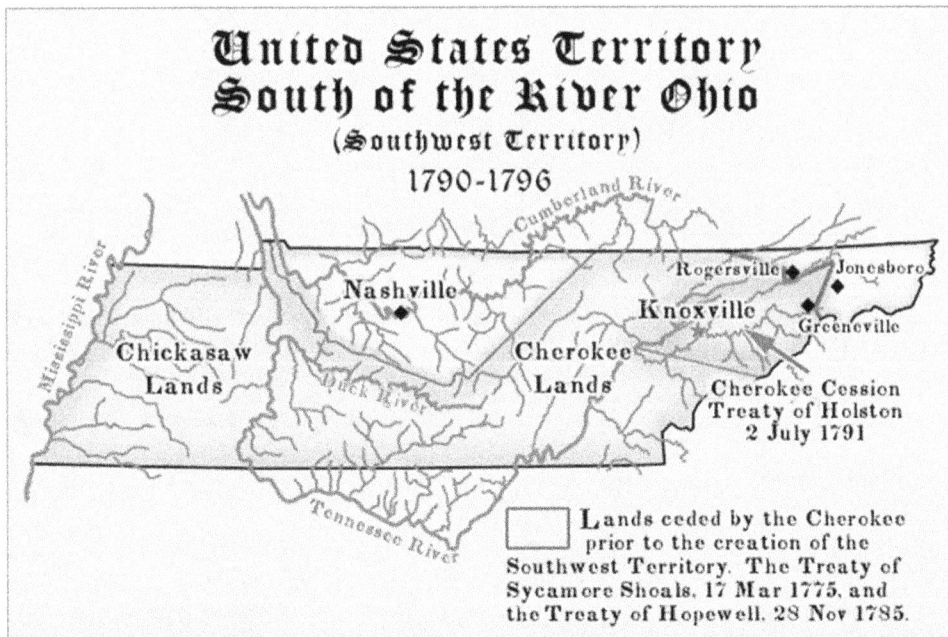

map by https://en.wikipedia.org/wiki/User:Iamvered, CC BY-SA 3.0, https://commons.wikimedia.org/w/index.php?curid=3868073

Elisha Abney Sr. migrated from South Carolina to Southwest Territory, probably because he received a grant there from the State of North Carolina. When John Abney (ca.1794) and his sister, Mary "Polly" Abney (ca.1795) were born to Elisha Abney Sr. and his wife, the area they lived in was known as Washington County, Southwest Territory. Washington County's borders remained the same during these years. Although John and Mary would later claim to have been born in Tennessee, Tennessee did not yet exist as a state until 1796. Therefore, they were born in Washington County, Southwest Territory which became Carter County, Tennessee in 1796.

Washington Co., Southwest Territory

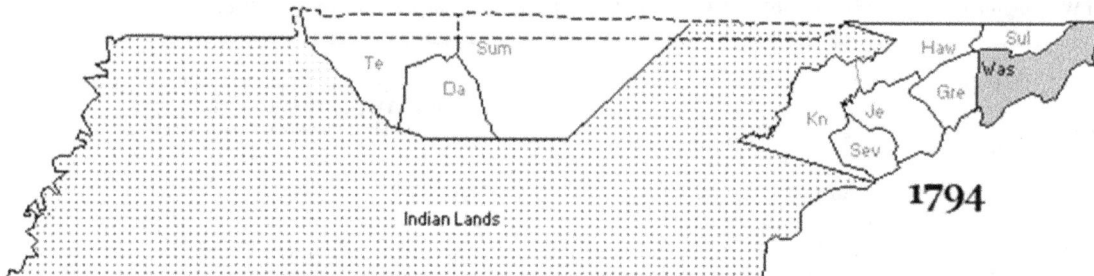

1794

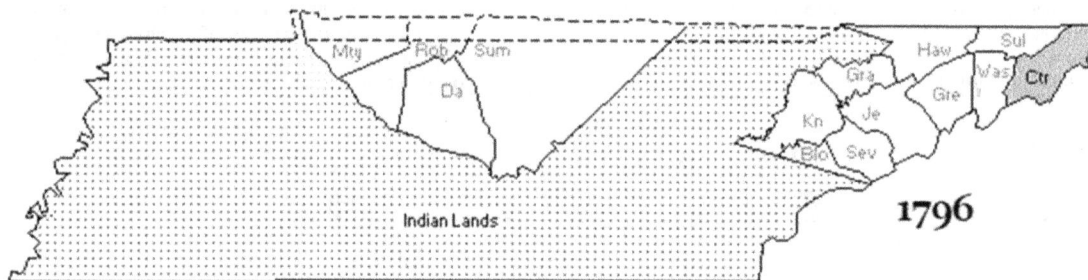

map from Map Geeks, edited by R.R. Abney Jr.

Tennessee became the 16th state when it was admitted to the union in 1796; and Carter County was carved out of the old Washington County, Southwest Territory. Here, in Carter County, Tennessee, the remaining children of Elisha Abney Sr. were born, to wit: Margaret Larken (1798) & Enoch (ca.1803).

Carter Co., TN

1796

map from Map Geeks, edited by R.R. Abney Jr.

The children of Elisha Abney Sr. were growing to adulthood. They were still living in Carter County, Tennessee as late as 1805 and probably a little later. All except for Joshua, who had migrated to Kentucky.

Carter Co., TN

1801

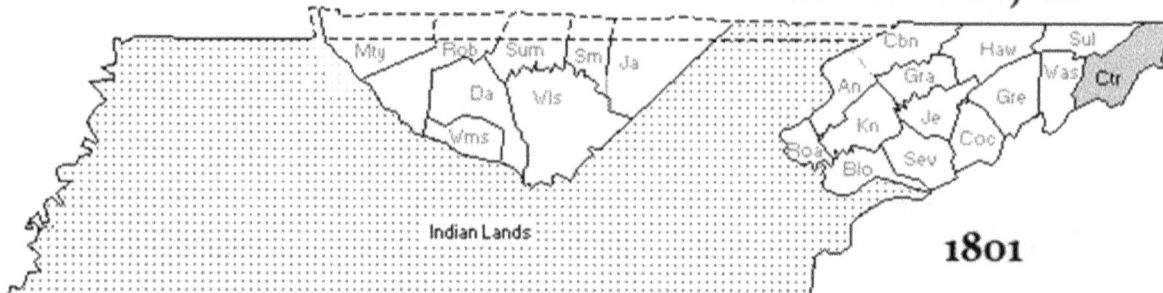

maps from Map Geeks, edited by R.R. Abney Jr.

The Commonwealth of Kentucky was admitted to the union as the 15th state in 1792. For the majority of the grandchildren of Abner Abney (as well as his son, Elisha), Kentucky became quite irresistible.	
Joshua Abney, eldest son of Elisha Abney Sr., migrated to Green County. There he married on 6 May 1795 to Martha "Pattie" Phelps. Their first child was born there in 1796.	John Key Abney (youngest son of John Abney *the Hatter*; and first cousin of Joshua Abney) also migrated to Green County. It is unknown at this time if they were neighbors. John secured land in Green County, Kentucky in 1799; and married there in 1800 to Betsy Gill.

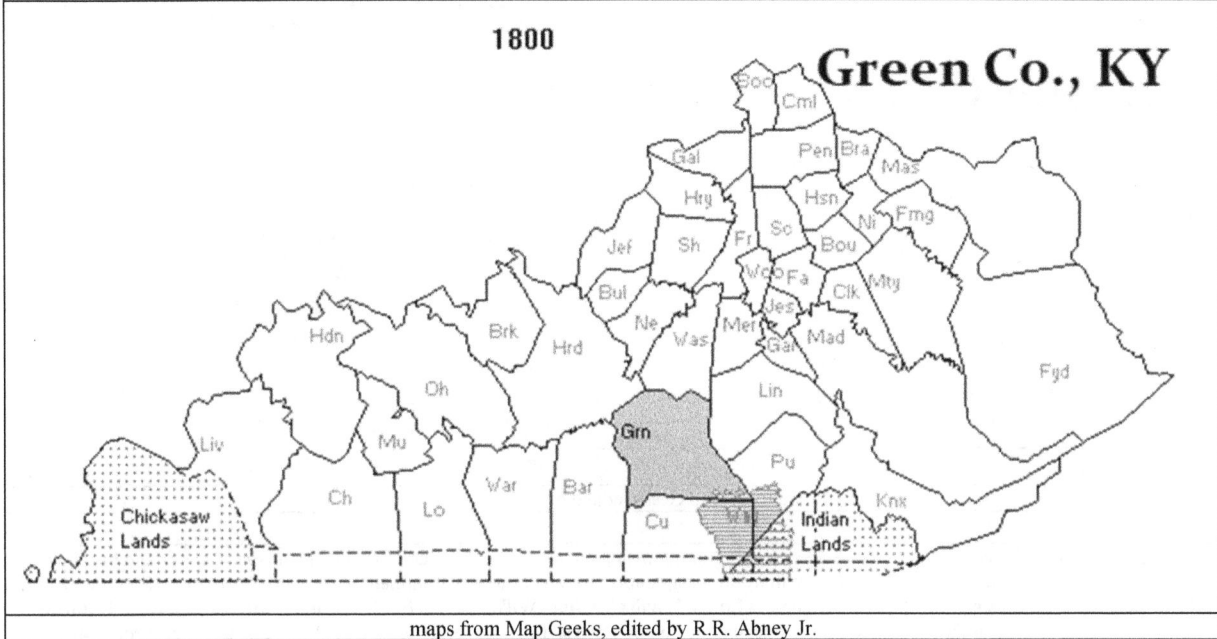

1800

Green Co., KY

maps from Map Geeks, edited by R.R. Abney Jr.

Elisha Abney Sr. sold his Carter County, Tennessee land and migrated to Kentucky. Since Clay County was not yet formed, it is suspected Elisha lived in Madison County, Kentucky. As can be seen from this map, Clay County was taken mostly from the southern portion of Madison County, with additional parts of Floyd and Knox Counties. Although the county boundaries were pending in 1806, they were permanent in 1807.

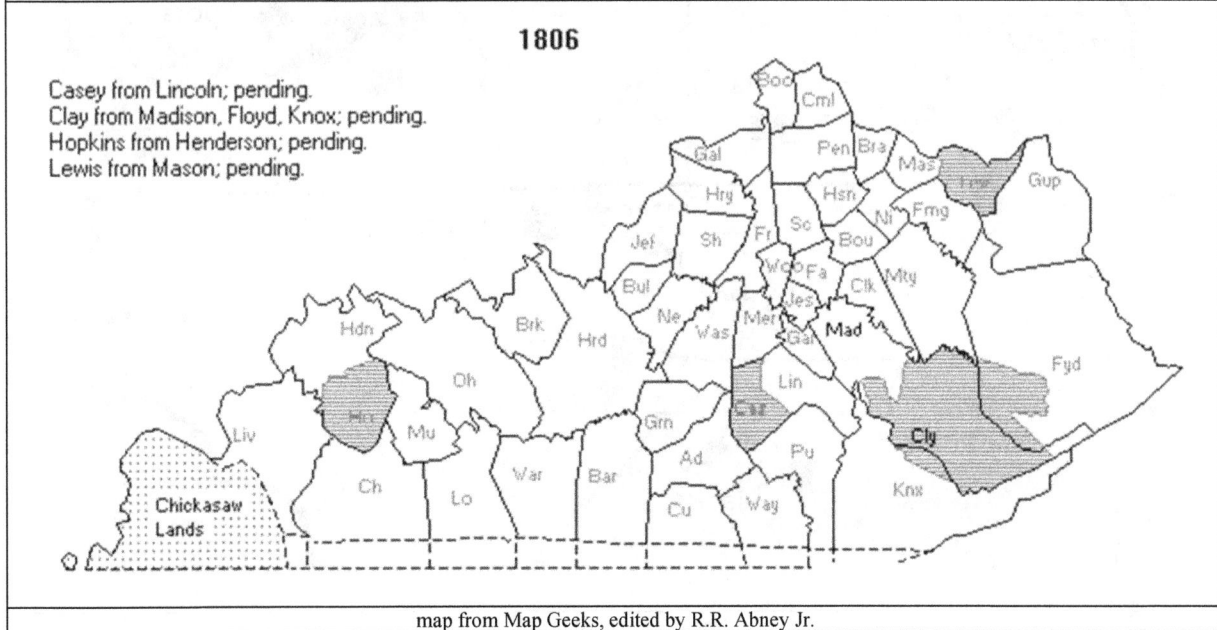

1806

Casey from Lincoln; pending.
Clay from Madison, Floyd, Knox; pending.
Hopkins from Henderson; pending.
Lewis from Mason; pending.

map from Map Geeks, edited by R.R. Abney Jr.

By 1810, Elisha Abney Sr. and what appears to be the majority of his children had migrated to Kentucky, a state where the surname spelling *Abner* became the norm instead of the spelling error. Elisha and family appear to have settled in Madison County (see Plate I), which part later fell into Clay County. Kentucky is also the state where the surname spelling *Abnee* became normalized.

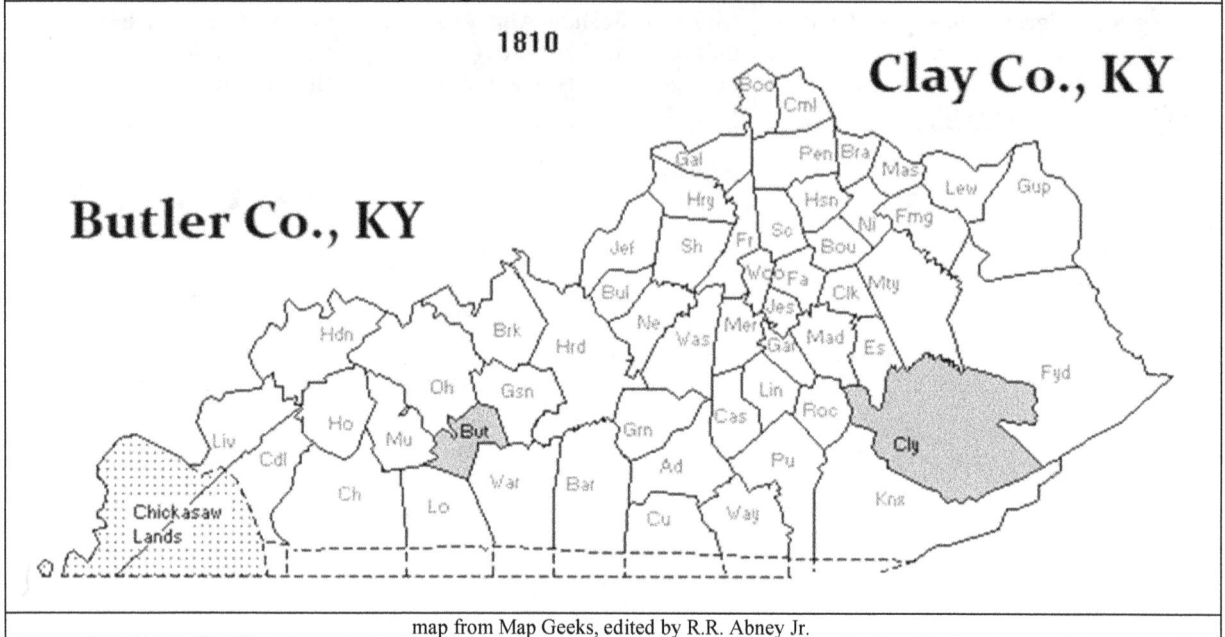

map from Map Geeks, edited by R.R. Abney Jr.

Below is a section of a modern-day United States County Map, showing the locations of the counties in which Abner Abney and his children and grandchildren migrated to and lived, in proximity to each county. In **Virginia**: King William Co., Spotsylvania Co., Goochland Co., Fluvanna Co., Albemarle Co., Amherst Co. and Augusta Co.; In **North Carolina**: Wilkes Co.; In **South Carolina**: Greenville Co.; In **Tennessee**: Carter County (note: This is the same location as Washington Co., Southwest Territory) and Sumner Co. (where Pvt. Abner Abney enlisted); In **Kentucky**: Green Co., Butler Co. and Clay Co.; In **Georgia**: Jackson Co. and Cobb Co.; In **Alabama**: Calhoun Co.

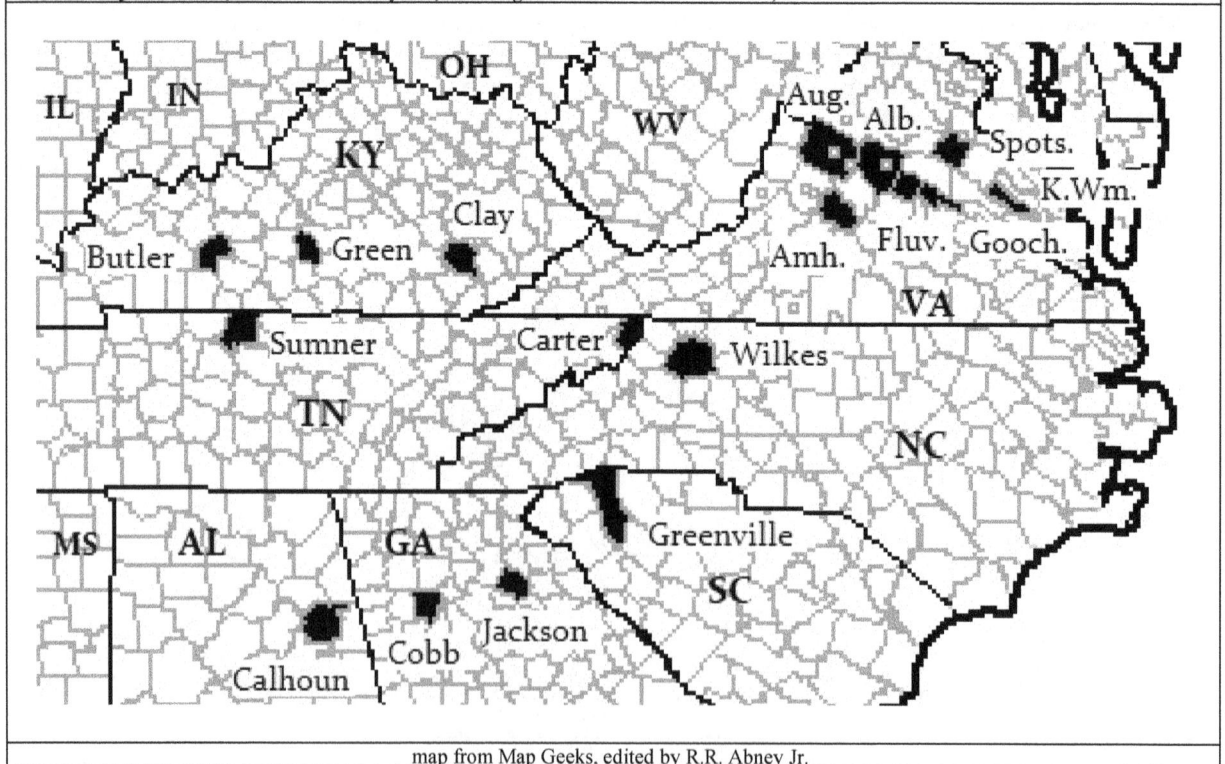

map from Map Geeks, edited by R.R. Abney Jr.

All-American Hero

The Abney family has many patriots who fought in the various wars throughout history. Many received prestigious decorations, some did not. But all were and still are great American heroes. The contributors to this book were unanimous, however, (and the author agreed) in their desire to recognize and honor the only World War I *Congressional Medal of Honor* recipient from the entire state of Kentucky, Sgt. William Berry "Willie" Sandlin, son of John "Dirty Face" Sandlin and Lucinda Abner (See pedigree page 10. See family page 75 and issue pages 124-125)

Congressional Medal of Honor Recipient

Sgt. William Berry "Willie" Sandlin
1890-1949

← *WWI Medal of Honor recipient Willie Sandlin. He wears the Medal of Honor, the French Médaille militaire, the French Croix de guerre with bronze palm and the Italian Croce al Merito di Guerra*

Willie Sandlin was born in Breathitt County. He was the only Kentuckian to receive the Medal of Honor in World War I. Of all the American servicemen who fought during the Great War, only Sergeant Alvin C. York received more decorations for valor than Sandlin. Born of humble parents, he had the misfortune to lose his mother when he was a small boy. He grew to manhood with few advantages. At an early age, he enlisted in the United States Regular Army. The hardships of youth had taught him well the lesson of taking care of himself. Straight as an arrow, with keen, alert, but steady black eyes, black hair, powerfully muscular, but not heavy built, he was a splendid type of the sturdy men who come from the Kentucky mountain counties. He was not assertive, but almost timid. But his mother was an Abner, and the Abners were among the sturdiest, most reliant stock of the old time families in Perry County. His quick black eyes and muscular frame came from his mother.

He enlisted in the army in 1912 and served on the Mexican border. In 1917, he was sent to France with the 132d Infantry. Promoted to sergeant, Sandlin single-handedly destroyed three German machine gun emplacements and killed twenty-four of the enemy on September 26, 1918, at Bois de Forges. For that action, he was awarded the Medal of Honor on February 9, 1919.

He showed conspicuous gallantry in action by advancing alone directly on a machinegun nest which was holding up the line with its fire. He killed the crew with a grenade and enabled the line to advance. Later in the day he attacked alone and put out of action 2 other machinegun nests, setting a splendid example of bravery and coolness to his men.

Officers and Men Being Presented with Medal of Honor at Chaumont, February 9, 1919
Left to right: Captains Edward C. Allworth, George H. Mallon, George G. McMurtry, 1st Lieutenants Samuel Woodfill, Harold A. Furlong, 2d Lieutenant Donald M. Call, 1st Sergeants Johannes S. Anderson, Sydney G. Gumpertz, Sergeants Willie Sandlin, Archie A. Peck, Harold I. Johnston, Corporals Frank J. Bart, Jesse N. Funk, Berger H. Loman, Private 1st Class Charles D. Barger, Privates Thomas C. Neibaur, Clayton K. Slack

Information on Sgt. Willie Sandlin from Wikipedia (https://en.wikipedia.org/wiki/Willie_Sandlin)

Prelude to Chapter V

Descendants of Abner Abney of Virginia
Abney, Abner, Abna, Abnee

This brings us to the descendants of Abner Abney of Virginia. The majority of the information on the following pages has been taken from public records (census, marriage, death, Bible entries, obituaries, headstones, books, newspapers, court records, &c.). Much of it was donated by other family genealogists, most of whom are mentioned on pages ????, and pg.??? – genealogists of Abner Abney's Line. The major contributors were Morgan Floyd Abney (#???), who first suggested a volume on Abner Abney; John Michael Abney (of the George Abney line), proofreader for this volume; Sandy Abner Cook (#???), who was a tremendous help to the author, Grace Lynette Crouch Prater (of the Paul Abney line); and Judy Vietri (#???), whom the author worked with beginning in 2002, and whose work was invaluable in setting the family of Menan Abner in proper order.

The reader is encouraged to review the abbreviations (ppg. ??? & ??? in this book) in order to fully understand these entries.

Some interesting notes to look out for in the entries of certain persons:

Service in the military is greatly appreciated and honored by the author. When military service is known, that will be indicated in parentheses after the name, for example:

- (RS, RD, ARW) American Revolutionary War (1765-1783) [Rev. Soldier; Rev. Doctor; CS-Civil Service]
- (War of 1812) War of 1812 (1812-1815)
- (BNO) Battle of New Orleans (Jan 8-18, 1815 specific, celebrated battle of the War of 1812)
- (FW) Florida War (Second Seminole War 1835-1842)
- (MW) Mexican-American War (1846-1848)
- (CSA) Confederate Army (War for Southern Independence 1860-1865)
- (UA) Union Army (War for Southern Independence 1860-1865)
- (WWI) World War I (1914-1918)
- (WWII) World War II (1939-1945)
- (Korea) Korean War (1950-1953)
- (Nam) Vietnam War (1955-1975)

et cetera…

There may be others not listed above. Additionally, if the type of service is known (rank, medical, civil, &c.), that will also be indicated. Finally, if known, the branch of service will be listed:

- USArmy United States Army
- USAAF United States Army Air Force
- USAF United States Air Force
- USN United States Navy
- USMC United States Marine Corps
- USCG United States Coast Guard

et cetera… we apologize for all the wonderful service men and women we missed. To these and others…
THANK YOU FOR YOUR MILITARY SERVICE!

Other notations might be

- Rev. Christian Minister
- Fr. Catholic Priest
- Judge elected Judge
- Dr. doctor
- Rep. Representative
- Sen. Senator

Also, the suffix (gen.) after one's name means this person was a known genealogist, many with whom the author has personally worked.

For the non-genealogist, an explanation of the United States Census system is in order. In addition to state, territorial & local censuses, the United States commissions Federal Censuses, taken every ten years. Although they contain wonderful information, they are somewhat unreliable since:

- many families purposely avoided the census taker
- many families were accidentally missed by the census taker
- many informants lied to the census taker
- many informants simply did not know the answer to the questions, and gave a best guess
- many informants were illiterate

- some census records have been lost or destroyed, included nearly the entire 1890 census, and unfortunately for this work, the 1800 Carter County, Tennessee census.
- it is not known if the people in the household are members of the family, as relationships are not given in the censuses from 1790–1870.

The First Federal Census was taken in 1790. It named only the *Head of Household* and gave scant additional information such as the number of: males 16 and over, males under 16, females, other free persons and slaves. This leaves the reader to guess who is recorded in the house. Many times, members of the household were NOT immediate family and often not family at all. These included servants, boarders, lodgers, etc.

The census from 1800 to 1840 recorded the name of the *Head of Household*, and numbers of males and females in different age categories, and little else, including numbers of slaves. These censuses were still lacking the names of the other members of the household.

In the 1850 and 1860 census all members of the household were named. Unfortunately, relationships were not given.

Finally, in 1880 the census taker was required to record the relationships of the household members to the *Head of Household*.

The 1890 census was almost completely destroyed. The very small surviving part of that census is useless to this volume. 1900 – 1940 give excellent information, the latter being the last census published heretofore. By law, a census cannot be published until 72 years after it was taken. The 1950 Census will be available for public viewing on 01 Apr 2022. This will be an exciting time in genealogical circles.

There is much conflicting information out there, partly due to the fact that many people simply either did not know or did not remember their birthdays. It is interesting to see the estimated birth year of a person change from census to census. A person might give age 42 in the 1850 census, and age 45 on the 1860 census (aging only three years in ten)!

Likewise, Death Certificates are only as reliable as the person giving the information, which is often someone less emotional and less knowledgeable than a nearer family member. Headstone inscriptions are often wrong due to bad information and monumental mason errors. If you see a headstone with one date (est.1844) and this book records another date (est. March 1840), as in the case of Nancy Abner (daughter of Lacy Abner & Cynthia Combs), wife of James Eversole, it is because the author has relied on more accurate information than the stone mason had available. Since Nancy was accounted for on the 1840 census (female under five years of age), age ten in the 1850 census, and gave "March 1840" as her birth month & year in the 1900 census, it is obvious she was NOT born in 1844 as her headstone purports. She was born in March, 1840. Another great example is the 1900 census enumeration of Leander Abner and his wife "Iba". The author, for the sake of argument, will assume, on this particular Friday, that the informant was the wife (as the husband, in this case a Farmer, was probably out working the fields). The informant knew neither the birth month nor year of the housewife, but "guessed" she was 35 years of age. The informant knew that "Iba" had lost two children, so she was intimately connected with this family. However, the informant was also unable to come up with two of her children's birth months.

In short, one must use logic in determining what information is most correct. If, for example, a person was born in 1899, the 1900 census (which information was given, probably by the mother and nearer to the event) will be more accurate, say, than a death certificate. Just because someone says they are a hundred years old, for example does not mean they are. The best example of this was given in volume I in the Prologue in the case of Samuel P. Albin who believed he was born in 1875 when he was actually born in 1884. The 1900 census was certainly more accurate than his memory. Had he been born in 1875, he would have appeared with his parents on the 1880 census.

Finally, copyist and typographical errors creep into family histories. A glance at the copyist entries given on *Findagrave.com* as compared to the actual headstones are amazing. Typographical errors in books like *Abney* (Hensell, 1974) and *Abney Supplement* (Hensell, 1988) are astounding. There are literally hundreds of dates that are off by a day or two, a month, or years. Any typographical errors in this volume can be blamed solely on the author, who is also the typist.

Finally, in this chapter is given the author's account of the Abney family as descended from Abner Abney of the British Colony of Virginia. This record is accurate to the best of the author's knowledge. However, the author knows that there is much more information to be had. The author did not read every census record, although many were studied, as indicated in each individual's biography.

With that in mind, this chapter is not the *be-all-end-all* of the family. Some examples:

- An entry may give a number of children to a certain couple. Yet, they may have had more children unknown to the author.
- An entry may read that a certain couple had no children. But they did! Perhaps they had no children known to the author or contributor.
- Some children may be erroneously assigned to the wrong father, or mother, this often occurs when obituaries are unclear.
- An entry may read that a certain person married their spouse firstly (1)…when that person actually married that spouse secondly (2) or so. Multiple marriages without wedding dates are often confusing. The author relied, sometimes, on death dates of former spouses.
- There are conflicts as to which cemeteries some persons are buried in.
- There are instances where the birthdates of individuals are unknown. Therefore, the birth order will be incorrect.

There are many other problems the author had to weed through to arrive at this very lengthy chapter. The author has tried to be brief, but thorough.

The author is certain this book will serve as the most accurate guide ever published on the Abner Abney branch of the Noble Abney Family, although, admittedly, the book *In Search of Kate* offered a highly accurate, albeit miniscule account of one son of Abner Abney. However, do not believe everything you read in any family history. Prove your family history for yourself. It is fun, educating and rewarding. Strive to prove every generation!

Searching for one's forebears (ancestors) is called hunting…hence the term "hunting for bears" (hunting forebears).

Happy hunting!

Chapter V

Descendants of Abner Abney of Virginia

Generation One

1. Abner^1 Abney, b. ca.1711 King William Co., VA. He m. Anne (Key?). He left a will on 25 Sep 1751 in Albemarle Co., VA and d. and was bur. in Albemarle Co., VA ca.1751. His will was proved in Albemarle County court 11 Jun 1752. (Abner Abney's ancestry is delineated in Chapter I. For a detailed analysis of Abner's ancestry, see **Volume I** of the **Abney Family History Series**: **Abney: Ancestors and Descendants of Dr. Abraham Abney** © 2018 by this author, Raymond Robert Abney Jr.) Abner Abney's life is chronicled in Chapter II (page 11) of this current book.

  Anne (Key?), b. ca.1723 VA. Some claim she was a daughter of John Key Sr. and Martha Tandy, although the author has been unable to verify this connection. Anne was executrix for her husband Abner's will. She may have m2. Samuel Taliaferro ca.1760, but this is just speculation.
Known children of Abner^1 Abney and Anne (Key?):

    2   i.   Elisha^2, b. est.1741 Goochland Co., VA; m. (n.n.)
         ii.   Milly, b. est.1743 Goochland Co., VA, VA. (Her life is chronicled in Chapter III, page 27)
    3   iii.   John, b. 1745 Albemarle Co., VA; m. Isabella Van Lear.

Generation Two

2. Elisha^2 Abney Sr. (Abner^1). b. est.1741 Goochland Co., VA. He m. (n.n.) est.1770 Albemarle Co., VA. (His life is chronicled in Chapter III.)

  Nothing is known by this author of Elisha's wife except that she was born in or before 1755. Names have been assigned to her (Mary Unity Calloway, for one), but there is no proof. If, as is claimed, that Mary Unity Calloway was Elisha Abney Sr.'s wife, then it must be explained (which it cannot), why she was married to two men and having their babies at the same time. (See the Primum Addendum on page 265.)
Known children of Elisha^2 Abney Sr. and (n.n.):

    4   i.   Joshua^3, b. ca.1771 Albemarle Co., VA; m. Martha "Pattie" Phelps.
         ii.   Jerusha "Shrew" (?), b. est.1773 Albemarle Co., VA., of whom nothing further. (See Chapter IV, page 33)
         iii.   Ann (?), b. est.1775 Albemarle Co., VA., of whom nothing further. (See Chapter IV, page 33)
         iv.   (dau.) (?), b. est.1777 Amherst Co., VA., of whom nothing further. (See Chapter IV, page 33)
         v.   *Pvt.* Abner, b. ca.1779 Amherst Co., VA. He m. Alyda Russell on 26 Aug 1803 Carter Co., TN. (See Chapter III, page 25. Also see Chapter IV, page 34; Also see the *Secundo Addendum*, page 266 for his possible descendants.)
    5   vi.   Hezekiah, b. ca.1781 Amherst Co., VA; m. (n.n.) (Calloway?).
    6   vii.   Dorcas "Tabitha," b. ca.1784 Amherst Co., VA; m. John Wood(s).
    7   viii.   Elisha Jr., b. ca.1787 Wilkes Co., NC; m. Nancy "Lucy" Loving.
    8   ix.   Menan, b. 1790 Wilkes Co., NC; m1 Agnes "Aggy" Bowling; m2 Lucinda Benge; m3 Elizabeth Lucas (widow Wells).
    9   x.   John Sr., b. 1794 Washington Co., Southwest Territory; m. Pamelia Watts; m. Millie Noble.
    10   xi.   Mary "Polly," b. ca.1795 Washington Co., Southwest Territory; m. Samuel "Sam" Bishop.
    11   xii.   Margaret Larken, b. 14 Feb 1798 Carter Co., TN; m. Isham O. Smith.
    12   xiii.   Enoch, b. ca.1803 Carter Co., TN; m1. Anna Price; m2. Elizabeth W. Thomas.

3. John^2 Abney "the Hatter" (Abner^1). b.1745 Albemarle Co., VA. He m. Isabella Van Lear, daughter of Jacob Van Lear and Margaret Gorrissen, on 10 Jul 1769 Augusta Co., VA. He appeared on the census of 1787 Augusta Co., VA. He wrote his will on 14 Jun 1788, Staunton, Augusta Co., VA and He d. and bur. there in 1788; His estate was probated on 16 Sep 1788 Staunton, Augusta Co., VA. (His life is chronicled in Chapter III)

  Isabella Van Lear, b. ca.1751 Augusta Co., VA. In 1783, Isabella (written as Isabel in her father's will) inherited 50 shillings from her father, Jacob. On 16 Jun 1789, Isabella was in Court in Augusta County, Virginia to represent her deceased husband as executrix, to wit: *Isabella Abney, executrix of John Abney, deceased, who was one of the executors of John McDonagh, deceased.* Isabella also gave consent for the marriages of her daughters, Patsy and Sally. In 1810, she is Head of Household on the 1810 & 1820 Censuses in Augusta Co., VA. She d.5 Feb 1828 Augusta Co., VA. Her estate was administered on 24 Nov 1828 Augusta Co., VA.
Known children of John^2 Abney "the Hatter" and Isabella Van Lear:

    13   i.   Sarah "Sally"^{3}, b. ca.1770 Augusta Co., VA; m. Robert McClenachan [III].
    14   ii.   Margaret "Peggy," b. ca.1771 Augusta Co., VA; m. Philip North.
    15   iii.   William, b. 8 Aug 1772 Staunton, Augusta Co., VA; m. Elizabeth Parks McClenachan.
    16   iv.   Nancy, b. 1776 Augusta Co., VA; m1. Johannes "John" Fackler; m2. (n.n.) Gardner; m3. John Hicklin.
    17   v.   John Key, b. 20 Mar 1780 Augusta Co., VA; m. Betsy Gill; m. Tamar Ann Robinson.
    18   vi.   Martha "Patsy," b. 1781 Augusta Co., VA; m. Peter Earl Hogg Jr.
         vii.   Mary "Polly", b. ca.1786 Augusta Co., VA. She m. (n.n.) Kenny. (See Chapter IV, page 37.)

Generation Three

4. Joshua^3 Abney (Elisha^2, Abner^1), b. ca.1771 Albemarle Co., VA. He m. Martha "Pattie" Phelps, daughter of William Phelps Sr., RS and Nancy Nail, on 6 May 1795 Green Co., KY. He appeared as Head of Household on the census of 1820 Morgantown, Butler Co., KY. He appeared as Head of Household on the censuses of 1830 Clark Co., IL and 1840 Jefferson Co., IL. He d.1845 Jefferson Co., IL and was bur. Abner Cem., Nason, Jefferson Co., IL. (see Chapter IV, page 33.)

  Martha "Pattie" Phelps, b. ca.1775 VA. She was liv. 68 after 1795 Butler Co., KY. She d.10 Jul 1857 Butler Co., KY and was bur. Peyton Phelps Cem., Jetson, Butler Co., KY.
Known children of Joshua^3 Abney and Martha "Pattie" Phelps:

    19   i.   Rebecca C.^{4}, b. 9 Feb 1796 Green Co., KY; m. John Chancellor.
    20   ii.   Paul Colby, b. 7 Sep 1801 Green Co., KY; m1. Mary G. Beasley; m2. Nancy Little.
    21   iii.   William, b. 1 Oct 1802 Green Co., KY; m1. Tabitha Jones; m2. Lucinda "Lucy" Robinson.
    22   iv.   Silas, b. ca.1810 Butler Co., KY; m. Aseneth "Martha" Moore.
    23   v.   Jesse, b. ca.1812 Butler Co., KY; m. (n.n.).

5. Hezekiah³ Abney (Elisha², Abner¹), b. ca.1781 Amherst Co., VA. He m. (n.n.) (Calloway?) ca.1801. He was in Georgia by about 1804, the approximate year a son was born. He appeared as Head of Household on the censuses of 1830 Jackson Co., GA and 1840 Cobb Co., GA. He was liv. on 26 Jun 1860 with son, Joel Abney, Calhoun Co., AL. He d.1861 Cleburne Co., AL and was bur. Shoal Creek Cem., Cleburne Co., AL. (See Chapter IV, page 34.)

(n.n.) (Calloway?), b. btwn. 1780-1789. Due to the fact that her son, Benjamin Hezekiah Abney named a son, Wilburn "Callaway" Abney, it is believed her surname was Calloway. The author has been unable to independently verify neither this nor any other possible given name(s). Known children of Hezekiah³ Abney and (n.n.) (Calloway?):

24	i.	John⁴, b. ca.1802 KY; m. (n.n.). (According to *Abney Supplement* by John R. Hensell [1988], page 16.)
25	ii.	Benjamin Hezekiah, b. 1804 Jackson Co., GA; m. Elizabeth Hogan; m. Sarah Ann "Frances" Harper.
	iii.	Elizabeth b. ca.1806 Jackson Co., GA. She m. John Yarborough on 8 Jan 1828 Jackson Co., GA. John Yarborough appeared as Head of Household on the censuses of 1830 Jackson Co., GA and 1840 Cobb Co., GA.
26	iv.	Delilah, b. ca.1808 Jackson Co., GA; m. Jonathan Yarborough.
27	v.	Wiley, b. ca.1810 Jackson Co., GA; m. Elizabeth Brumbelow; m. Mary Black.
	vi.	Stephen, b. ca.1811 Jackson Co., GA. He d.1865.
28	vii.	Andrew, b. ca.1813 Jackson Co., GA; m. Susan Collins.
29	viii.	James M., b. 8 Jul 1815 Jackson Co., GA; m1. Dulcina "Cenie" Daniel; m2. Sarah Miller.
30	ix.	Jeff Pressley "Pres," b. ca.1825 Jackson Co., GA; m. Charlotte Hollingsworth.
31	x.	Joel Jonathan, b. ca.1828 Jackson Co., GA; m. Delila Dillian Ann "Dilly" Smith.

6. Dorcas "Tabitha"³ Abney (Elisha², Abner¹) b. ca.1784 Amherst Co., VA. The names Dorcas and Tabitha are identical in the Holy Bible (See Acts 9:36). She m. John Woods, son of Samuel Woods Sr. and Elizabeth Wilson, on 12 Dec 1808 Clay Co., KY. She and John Woods appeared on the census of 4 Sep 1850 Owsley Co., KY and was bur. Clay Co., KY. (See Chapter IV, page 34.)

John Woods, b.1785 SC. He appeared as Head of Household on the censuses of 1830 and 1840 Clay Co., KY. He d.1855 Owsley Co., KY and was bur. Old Richard Reynolds Cem., Cow Creek, Owsley Co., KY. Known children of Dorcas "Tabitha"³ Abney and John Woods:

	i.	John Jr.⁴, b.27 Nov 1808 Clay Co., KY. He m. Viney (n.n.).
32	ii.	Henry, b. 1809 Clay Co., KY; m. (n.n.).
33	iii.	William, b. ca.1814 KY; m1. Nancy Morris; m2. Nancy Sizemore.
34	iv.	Lilburn, b. ca.1816 Clay Co., KY; m. Mahalia Sizemore.
	v.	Susan, b.1817 KY.
35	vi.	Elizabeth, b. 1819 Clay Co., KY; m. James Adgar McGuire.
36	vii.	Joseph, b. 20 Mar 1820; m. Martha "Patsy" (n.n.).
37	viii.	Samuel, b. 1825 Clay Co., KY; m. Sarah "Sally" Tucker.
	ix.	Theresa "Theresy", b.2 Jun 1833 Clay Co., KY. She d.21 Feb 1912 Rockcastle Co., KY, at age 78.

7. Elisha³ Abner Jr. (Elisha² Abney, Abner¹), b. ca.1787 Wilkes Co., NC. He was the first of this line to assume the surname, *Abner* (See Etymology in Appendix A, page 257). He m. Nancy "Lucy" Loving, daughter of William Loving and Patsy Hargrove, ca.1806 Madison Co., KY. He appeared as Head of Household on the censuses of 1810, 1820, 1830 and 1840 Clay Co., KY. He and Nancy "Lucy" Loving appeared on the census of 16 Aug 1850 Owsley Co., KY. He d. ca.1855 Owsley Co., KY and was bur. Teges Cem., Clay Co., KY. (See Chapter IV, page 35.)

Nancy "Lucy" Loving, b.1788 Greenbriar, Chesterfield Co., VA. She d.14 Oct 1854 Clay Co., KY. Known children of Elisha³ Abner Jr. and Nancy "Lucy" Loving:

38	i.	William "Buck"⁴, b. 4 Aug 1807 Clay Co., KY; m. Jane Virginia "Jennie" Baker.
	ii.	Elizabeth, b. ca.1809 Clay Co., KY.
39	iii.	Lacy, b. ca.1810 Clay Co., KY; m. Cynthia Combs.
40	iv.	John A., b. ca.1813 Clay Co., KY; m1. Nancy Jane "Chesney" McJunkin; m2. Mary Courtney.
41	v.	Mary Lucinda "Polly," b. ca.1816 Clay Co., KY; m. Andrew "Andy" Baker.
42	vi.	Lucinda, b. ca.1818 Clay Co., KY; m. James Williams.
43	vii.	Susannah "Susan," b. ca.1820 Clay Co., KY; m. Wilson "Willis" Gabbard Sr.
44	viii.	Nancy Ann, b. ca.1822 Clay Co., KY; m. Lewis Sandlin.
45	ix.	Willis, b. ca.1824 Clay Co., KY; m. Almirah China Baker.
46	x.	Matilda, b. ca.1827 Clay Co., KY; m1. William Baker; m2. Ira Baker.
47	xi.	Enoch, b. 2 Jul 1830 Manchester, Clay Co., KY; m. Martha Jane Gilbert.

8. Menan³ Abner (Elisha² Abney, Abner¹), b.1790 Wilkes Co., NC. The Biblical name "Menan" is found in Luke 3:31. Like his brother, Elisha Jr., Menan also assumed the surname *Abner* (See Etymology in Appendix A, page 257). He m1. Agnes "Aggy" Bowling, daughter of William Bolling and Sarah Fugate, on 22 Mar 1813 Clay Co., KY. He appeared as Head of Household on the census of 1820 Clay Co., KY. He m2. Lucinda Benge on 7 Oct 1829 Clay Co., KY. He appeared as Head of Household on the census of 1830 Clay Co., KY. He m3. Elizabeth Lucas (widow of James Wells) on 11 Oct 1836 Clay Co., KY. He and Elizabeth Lucas appeared on the census of 14 Sep 1850 Clay Co., KY. He d. ca.1853 Clay Co., KY and was bur. Cortland Cem., Cow Creek, Owsley Co., KY. His estate was administered on 4 Aug 1853 Clay Co., KY. (See Chapter IV, page 35.)

Agnes "Aggy" Bowling, b. ca.1795. She d. ca.1829 and was bur. Cortland Cem., Cow Creek, Owsley Co., KY. Known children of Menan³ Abner and Agnes "Aggy" Bowling all b. Clay Co., KY:

	i.	Elisha⁴, b. est.1814. He m. Mary Wells, daughter of John Wells and Elizabeth Lucas, in 1839.
48	ii.	James Monroe, b. 1816; m. Sythia "Almira" McGill.
49	iii.	Richard "Dick," b. ca.1818; m. Lucinda "Lucy" Wells.
	iv.	(son?), b. ca.1820.
50	v.	Mary "Polly," b. ca.1821; m. David Benge Jr.
	vi.	Nancy, b. est.1825. She and James M. "Jim" Swafford obtained a marriage license on New Year's Eve, 31 Dec 1842 Clay Co., KY. She m. James M. "Jim" Swafford on 3 Jan 1843 Clay Co., KY. She d. ca.1844.

James M. "Jim" Swafford b. Jan. 15, 1822 Lawrence Co. Tn. His father's family was in Lawrence Co. TN. in the 1820's and his mother, Polly Smith, is believed to have d. there. *"He and his* [half?] *brother, William Riley, were back in Clay Co. Ky by 1840 where he m. Nancy Abner Aug. 3, 1842. William Riley gave consent. Nancy d. shortly afterward and he recalled that loss to his grandson, Madison E. Swofford many years later.* [Jim m2. Malinda Gregory on 25 Jul 1846 Clay Co., KY.] *After his marriage to Malinda Gregory, they moved to Davies Co. Mo. in 1854 along with his brother John and Sister Anna Lipps and their families. There he suffered another loss when Malinda d. at the birth of their son Isaac. Shortly afterwards he m3. Susan Tippet* [Jim m. Susan E. Tippet on 3 May 1863 Daviess Co., MO.] *who also had a son, Charley M., about 6 months old, Charley was given the Swofford name. The name Swafford was spelled Swofford from the time they moved to Missouri."* From **Families of the Ozarks** by Melanie Easterly. James d.18 Oct 1896 AR at age 74.

      vii.   (dau. of Menan?), b. est.1827.

Lucinda Benge, b. ca.1811.
Known children of Menan[3] Abner and Lucinda Benge both b. Clay Co., KY:

      i.   (dau.?)[4], b. ca.1830.
      ii.   Susan, b. ca.1832.

Elizabeth Lucas, b. ca.1802 PA. She m1. John Wells on 11 Dec 1817 Clay Co., KY. She was liv. on 12 Jul 1870 with step-son, Richard Abner, Clay Co., KY.
Known children of Menan[3] Abner and Elizabeth Lucas both b. Clay Co., KY:

51   i.   John[4], b. ca.1837; m. Matilda Robertson.
52   ii.   Alabama, b. ca.1842; m. Charles Robertson.

9. John[3] Abney Sr. (Elisha[2], Abner[1]), b.1794 Washington Co., Southwest Territory. He might be accounted for on the census enumeration of his brother, Menan in 1820 Clay Co., KY. He m1. Pamelia Watts ca.1825 Clay Co., KY. He m2. Millie Noble on 7 Oct 1829 Clay Co., KY. He appeared as Head of Household on the censuses of 1830 and 1840 Clay Co., KY. From Wikipedia: *The first settlers in Owsley County were John Renty Baker and John Abner. They settled there in about 1780* [author's note: John was born ca.1794. How could he settle in the county 16 years before he was born?] *near the present Clay County line at Courtland. A gravestone in a cemetery on Upper Buffalo Creek reads, "Milly, wife of John Abner, d. March 1846"* in 1843. The part of Clay Co. where John lived became Owsley Co., KY in 1843. He appeared on the census of 25 Sep 1850 Owsley Co., KY. He was liv. on 1 Aug 1860 with nephew, Enoch Abner (son of Elisha), Owsley Co., KY. John d. ca.1862 Owsley Co., KY and was bur. John Baker Cem., Owsley Co., KY. (See Chapter IV, page 35.)

Pamelia Watts, b. Perry Co., KY. She d. before Oct 1829 Clay Co., KY.
Known children of John[3] Abney Sr. and Pamelia Watts both b. Clay Co., KY:

53   i.   Lincoln "Link"[4], b. 10 May 1826; m. Sarah "Margaret" Evans.
54   ii.   Nancy Caroline, b. 27 Dec 1836; m1. James B. Hunt; m2. James Lafayette Scroggins.

Millie Noble, b. before 1811. She d.Mar 1846 Owsley Co., KY and was bur. John Baker Cem., Owsley Co., KY.
Known children of John[3] Abney Sr. and Millie Noble:

55   i.   Malinda[4], b. ca.1830 Clay Co., KY; m. Enos Bartlett.
56   ii.   Lewis, b. 10 Mar 1831 Clay Co., KY; m. Amelia Ann "Milly" Gum.
      iii.   William, b.10 Jan 1835 Clay Co., KY. He appears to have assumed the surname *Abner* (See Etymology in Appendix A, page 257). He appeared as Head of Household on the censuses of 8 Jul 1870 and 11 Jun 1880 Lee Co., KY. He was liv. on 9 Jun 1900 as a boarder with the George Cundiff family, Lee Co., KY. He d.11 Mar 1908 Lee Co., KY, at age 73 and was bur. Lutes Abner Cem., Primrose, Lee Co., KY. Neither wife nor issue has been located for William.
      iv.   Pvt. Elisha (UA), b.1837 Clay Co., KY. He also assumed the surname *Abner* (See Etymology in Appendix A, page 257). He was liv. as a boarder with Levi Bowman on 7 Jul 1860 Owsley Co., KY. He joined the Union Army on 24 Sep 1861 Co.D, 8th KY Inf. He d. in battle 12 Mar 1863 in Tennessee.
57   v.   Mary J. "Polly," b. May 1840 Clay Co., KY; m. Enos Bartlett.
58   vi.   John, b. 14 Dec 1844 Owsley Co., KY; m. Sarah "Ellen" Lutes.

10. Mary "Polly"[3] Abner (Elisha[2] Abney, Abner[1]), b. ca.1795 Washington Co., Southwest Territory. Like her brothers, Elisha Jr. and Menan, she also seems to have assumed the surname *Abner* (See Etymology in Appendix A, page 257). She m. Samuel "Sam" Bishop on 15 Nov 1811 Clay Co., KY. She appeared as Head of Household on the censuses of 1830 and 1840 Clay Co., KY. She was liv. on 29 Aug 1850 with son, William Bishop, Clay Co., KY. She d.20 Apr 1881 Clay Co., KY and was bur. Laurel Point Cem., Clay Co., KY. (See Chapter IV, page 36.)

Samuel "Sam" Bishop, b. ca.1785 Clay Co., KY. He appeared as Head of Household on the census of 1820 Clay Co., KY. He d.13 Feb 1826 Clay Co., KY.
Known children of Mary "Polly"[3] Abner and Samuel "Sam" Bishop all b. Clay Co., KY:

59   i.   Abraham "Abel"[4], b. 20 Apr 1812; m. Nancy Robinson.
60   ii.   Elisha Monroe, b. 1813; m. Amy Johnson.
      iii.   Nancy, b. ca.1815.
61   iv.   William S, b. 1818; m. Susan Barrett.
62   v.   Bryson "Brice," b. 1822; m. Eliza "Lizie" Allen.
      vi.   Elsie, b. ca.1824.
      vii.   Rachel, b. ca.1825.
      viii.   Samuel Jr., b.1827.
      ix.   Alice, b. ca.1829.

11. Margaret Larken[3] Abner (Elisha[2] Abney, Abner[1]), b.14 Feb 1798 Carter Co., TN. Like her older brothers, Elisha Jr. and Menan, and older sister, Mary, she also seems to have assumed the surname *Abner* (See Etymology in Appendix A, page 257). She m. Isham O. Smith on 15 Nov 1819 Clay Co., KY. She and Isham O. Smith appeared on the censuses of 28 Aug 1850 Henry Co., KY and 25 Jun 1860 Pleasureville, Henry Co., KY. She d.18 Oct 1870 Henry Co., KY, at age 72 and was bur. Eminence Cem., Eminence, Henry Co., KY. (See Chapter IV, page 36.)

Isham O. Smith, b.5 Nov 1792 VA. He appeared as Head of Household on the censuses of 1820, 1830 and 1840 Clay Co., KY. He d.12 Apr 1873 Henry Co., KY, at age 80 and was bur. Eminence Cem., Eminence, Henry Co., KY.

Known children of Margaret Larken*3* Abner and Isham O. Smith all b. Clay Co., KY:
        63   i.   Charles*4*, b. 1822; m. Margaret Anglin.
             ii.   Thomas W., b. ca.1824. In 1860, he was a Stock Trader. He was listed as a resident in Thomas W. Smith's household in the census report on 25 Jun 1860 with his father, Isham Smith, Pleasureville, Henry Co., KY.
             iii. Cuthbert, b. ca.1835.
             iv. Lycurgus, b. ca.1835.
             v.   Abner Green, b.12 Feb 1836. He m. Elizabeth Kephart. He d.9 Jul 1916 Eminence, Henry Co., KY, at age 80 and was bur. Eminence Cem., Eminence, Henry Co., KY.
                   Elizabeth Kephart, b.1839. She d.1907.
             vi. Sarah I., b. ca.1838.

12. Enoch*3* Abney Sr. (Elisha*2*, Abner*1*), b. ca.1803 Carter Co., TN. He m1. Anna Price on 23 Jan 1822 Clay Co., KY. He appeared as Head of Household on the census of 1830 Clay Co., KY. He m2. Elizabeth W. Thomas on 27 Aug 1838 Clay Co., KY, but no issue. He appeared as Head of Household on the census of 1840 Clay Co. He was a cooper and migrated to Missouri ca.1846. He and Elizabeth W. Thomas appeared on the census of 29 Sep 1850 Taney Co., MO. He d.1854 Stone Co., MO. (See Chapter IV, page 36.)
    Anna Price d. ca.1837 KY.
Known children of Enoch*3* Abney Sr. and Anna Price all b. Clay Co., KY:
        64   i.   Enoch*4*, b. ca.1823; m. Catherine Lucas.
        65   ii.   Hila Ann "Hiley," (some say *Holly Ann*) b. ca.1825; m. James Wells.
        66   iii. Andrew "Jackson," b. 4 Mar 1826; m. Mary "Margaret" Moody; m. L.A. Holley.
             iv. Lewis, b. ca.1829. Lewis assumed the surname *Abner* (See Etymology in Appendix A, page 257). He was liv. 29 Jul 1850 with bro., Enoch Abner, Clay Co., KY.
             v.   T.C (son), b. ca.1831 of whom nothing further.
        67   vi. Nancy E., b. 4 Apr 1833; m. Pvt. Benjamin Wood (CSA).
             vii. James C., b. ca.1836. Liv. on 3 Jul 1860 with brother, Jackson Abney, Savannah, Andrew Co., MO. Ca. 1866, James and his brother, Andrew "Jackson" Abney were in business of stock-raising, together in Pine Bluffs, Laramie Co., WY.
        68   viii. Martha Jane, b. ca.1837; m. William Garner.
    Elizabeth W. Thomas, b. ca.1810 NC.

13. Sarah "Sally"*3* Abney (John*2*, Abner*1*), b. ca.1770 Augusta Co., VA. She m. Robert McClenachan [III], son of Dr. Robert McClenachan Jr. (Doctor in the Continental Army during the American Revolutionary War) and Catherine Madison, on Independence Day, 4 Jul 1797 Augusta Co., VA. She d.11 Sep 1853 Barren Co., KY. (See Chapter IV, page 37.)
    Robert McClenachan [III] was bapt.19 Apr 1770 Augusta Co., VA. After the death of his parents, Robert Jr. went to court in Augusta County, Virginia and chose his guardian, to wit: *"Robert McClenachan, orphan of Robert McClenachan, chose Alexander McClenachan his guardian."* Alexander was Robert Jr.'s paternal uncle. He appeared as Head of Household on the census of 1810 Greensburg, Green Co., KY. He d.1824 Barren Co., KY.
Known children of Sarah "Sally"*3* Abney and Robert McClenachan [III] all b. Barren Co., KY:
        69   i.   Isabelle*4*, b. 4 May 1801; m. David W. Merry.
             ii.   Madison, b. ca.1802. He m. Lourany (Sarah) Melton on 27 Oct 1823 Barren Co., KY.
        70   iii. Jane Ann, b. Christmas Eve, 24 Dec 1804; m. Johnson Monroe Jr.
             iv. James, b. est.1806. He m. America T. Byrd on 13 Jan 1834 Barren Co., KY.
                 America T. Byrd. Her father, John Byrd gave his written permission for her to marry James McClanahan.
             v.   Elizabeth, b. ca.1808. She m. John Green on 20 Oct 1836 Barren Co., KY.
        71   vi. Tamar, b. 1810; m. David Gerald McKinney Sr; m. William Campbell Rhea Jr.
        72   vii. Mary Elizabeth "Beth," b. 1812; m. James Owen.
             viii. Susan, b. ca.1816. She m. William Tennison on New Year's Day, 1 Jan 1842 Barren Co., KY.

14. Margaret "Peggy"*3* Abney (John*2*, Abner*1*), b. ca.1771 Augusta Co., VA. She m. Philip North on 29 Mar 1792 Augusta Co., VA. They were m. by the Rev. John McCue (author's note: The same Rev. McCue also presided over the marriage of Margaret's brother, William Abney and William's bride, Elizabeth). The marriage record reads, *"1792-March 29, Phillip North and Margaret Abney (spinster), a daughter of John Abney, deceased; surety, David Parry.* She appeared as Head of Household on the census of 1820 Staunton, Augusta Co., VA. She was liv. on 23 Aug 1850 with son, John A. North, Greenbrier Co., VA. She d.31 Mar 1851 VA and was bur. Old Stone Presbyterian Ch. Cem., Lewisburg, Greenbrier Co., WV. (She died in that part of Virginia which in 1863 became West Virginia). (See Chapter IV, page 37.)
    Philip North, b. ca.1771. He d. before 3 Apr 1815 and is bur. Old Stone Presbyterian Ch. Cem., Lewisburg, Greenbrier Co., WV.
Known child of Margaret "Peggy"*3* Abney and Philip North:
        73   i.   John Abney*4*, b. 15 Dec 1794 Staunton, Augusta Co., VA; m. Charlotte Blain.

15. *Capt.* William*3* Abney "the Hatter" (Militia) (John*2*, Abner*1*), b.8 Aug 1772 Staunton, Augusta Co., VA. The author also gave William (like his father, John), the appellation *the Hatter* to differentiate him from the myriad William Abney's in the family. William attended Parson Chamber's School. He was 16 years old when his father died. His father bequeathed his hatting trade to him in his will. William became involved in the affairs of the county (Augusta) and the militia. He was a member of the Staunton Fire Co. (org. 09 Jan 1790). On 25 Mar 1793, he was named Second Lieutenant of a Company of Cavalry to be raised in Staunton. On 16 Apr 1794, he qualified Second Lieutenant of that troop of Cavalry in Staunton, and in 3rd Division. In 1794, he was with the company which went to Pittsburgh against the insurgents. William finally achieved the rank of Captain. William m. Elizabeth Parks McClenachan, daughter of Alexander McClenachan Sr., RS and Eleanor "Sallie" Shelton, on 23 Dec 1794 in the Wilson Presbyterian Church, Old Stone, Augusta Co., VA. They were married by the Rev. John McCue on 23 Dec 1794: *"1794-December 23, Wm. Abney and John McDowell, surety. Wm. Abney and Elizabeth McClenachan, daughter of Alex. McClenachan (consent). Teste: John McDowell".* Just over two years later, Capt. William was appointed administrator for the estate of Alexander McClanachan, his father-in-law. His wife, Elizabeth McClanachan, was first cousin to his sister, Sarah's husband, Robert McClanachan. William's bond, as administrator of Alex. McClenachan is dated 5th April, 1797. On 27 Mar 1804, William Abney was also the administrator of John Fackler, the latter being William's brother-in-law. He appeared as Head of Household on the census of 1810 Augusta Co., VA. In 1812, William ran for Virginia House of Delegates

from Augusta County as a Democrat running against three Federalists. He finished in third with 299 votes. The victor in that race was Col. Andrew Anderson, a Federalist. Anderson had received 535 votes to Abney's 299 votes. William was a witness to the will of Elizabeth Heizer on 26 Jan 1815. He appeared as Head of Household on the census of 1820 Augusta Co., VA. William d.20 Jun 1824 Augusta Co., VA, at age 51. Although his estate was probated on 25 Aug 1828 Augusta Co., VA., the Family Bible records his death some four years earlier as 20 Jun 1824. Not having seen the Bible record, the author is resigned to the report given by author, Charlotte Abney Metzger (*In Search of Kate*). Although a handwritten "4" may be mistaken for an "8", sometimes estate settlements were dragged out many years. For this reason, we record his death as Metzger. William is said to have had an aunt called "Mrs. Robertson". This was his mother's sister, Gartry Van Lear Robinson. (See Chapter IV, page 37.)

Elizabeth Parks McClenachan, b.27 Jun 1774 Augusta Co., VA. She d.7 Jul 1854 Mint Spring, Augusta Co., VA, at age 80 and was bur. Tinkling Spring Presb. Ch. Cem., Fishersville, Augusta Co., VA.

Known children of Capt. William[3] Abney "the Hatter" (Militia) and Elizabeth Parks McClenachan all born in Augusta Co., VA:

	i.	Alexander M.[4]. Alexander, b.27 Sep 1795 Augusta Co., VA. He d.10 Aug 1796 Augusta Co., VA. in infancy.
	ii.	Sally, b.27 Jan 1797. She d.2 Mar 1797 Augusta Co., VA. in infancy.
74	iii.	Elizabeth "Betsy," b. 31 Mar 1798 Augusta Co., VA; m. Byrd S. Grills.
	iv.	Nancy, b.9 May 1800. She d. unmarried 27 Aug 1879 Augusta Co., VA at age 79. Her obituary read: *"ABNEY - At her home, near Mint Spring, in this county, on the 27th ult., Miss Nancy Abney, aged seventy odd years."*
75	v.	Letticia, b. 17 Jan 1802 Augusta Co., VA; m. Adam Swink.
76	vi.	Mary Jane, b. 21 Dec 1803 Augusta Co., VA; m. Jefferson Burr Kinsolving.
77	vii.	William Austine, b. 21 May 1806 Augusta Co., VA; m. Virginia Lewis Kinsolving.
	viii.	John K., b.24 Sep 1808 Augusta Co., VA. He d.3 Oct 1808 Augusta Co., VA in infancy.
78	ix.	Isabella, b. 21 Nov 1809 Augusta Co., VA; m. Charles T. Grills.
79	x.	Shelton Spillsbury, b. 26 Jun 1813 Staunton, Augusta Co., VA; m. Martha Jane Davis.
	xi.	Lycurgus, b.6 Dec 1816 Augusta Co., VA. He d.24 Oct 1845 at age 28.

16. Nancy[3] Abney (John[2], Abner[1]), b.1776 Augusta Co., VA. She m1. Johannes "John" Fackler on 17 Jul 1797 Staunton, Augusta Co., VA. Their marriage reads: *"1798-July 17, John Fackler and Robert McClenachan, surety. John Fackler and Nancy Abney, daughter of John Abney, deceased."* She m2. (n.n.) Gardner, but no issue. She m3. John Hicklin (who d. before 1815), but no issue. She was liv. on 24 Nov 1828. (See Chapt.IV, pg.37)

Johannes "John" Fackler, b.10 Nov 1772 Hagerstown, Washington Co., MD. He d.16 Feb 1807 Staunton, Augusta Co., VA, at age 34.

Known children of Nancy[3] Abney and Johannes "John" Fackler all born in Staunton, Augusta Co., VA:

	i.	William G.[4], b.1799. He m. Bessie (n.n.). He d.1828 Madison Co., AL and was bur. Maple Hill Cem., Huntsville, Madison Co., AL.
		Bessie (n.n.) d.1 May 1932 and was bur. Maple Hill Cem., Huntsville, Madison Co., AL.
80	ii.	John Jacob, b. 1801 Staunton, Augusta Co., VA; m. Elizabeth Melvina Turner.
	iii.	Abney M., b. est.1803 VA. He appeared on the census of 1830 Lynchburg, Campbell Co., VA.

17. John Key[3] Abney (John[2], Abner[1]), b.20 Mar 1780 Augusta Co., VA. He secured a land grant in Green County, Kentucky, and moved there in 1799. He m1. Betsy Gill on 1 May 1800 Green Co., KY. She died shortly thereafter. He m2. Tamar Ann Robinson, daughter of John Robinson and Gertrude Van Lear, on 4 Apr 1803 Fincastle, Montgomery Co., VA. He appeared as Head of Household on the censuses of 1810 and 1820 Greensburg, Green Co., KY. He d. between 1820 and 1828 Green Co., KY. (See Chapter IV, page 37.)

Betsy Gill, b. before 1784. She d. before 4 Apr 1803 Green Co., KY.
There were no known children of John Key[3] Abney and Betsy Gill.

Tamar Ann Robinson, b.14 Jun 1785 Montgomery Co., VA. She appeared as Head of Household on the census of 1830 Green Co., KY. She d. ca.1841.

Known children of John Key[3] Abney and Tamar Ann Robinson all born in Green Co., KY:

81	i.	Isabella[4], b. ca.1805; m. William Campbell Rhea Jr.
82	ii.	John R.K., b. ca.1806; m. Ann Kenney.
83	iii.	Robert Milton, b. 5 Jan 1808 (said to have been born at Abney's Ferry, Green Co., KY); m. Catherine Powell Smith.
84	iv.	Gertrude Robinson, b. ca.1810; m. Samuel P. Lasley.
	v.	Cynthia P., b. ca.1812; She m. Joseph Day on 21 Jan 1830 Greensburg, Green Co., KY.
		Joseph Day, b. ca.1805 Green Co., KY.
85	vi.	Mary B., b. ca.1816; m. Isaac Faulkner.
	vii.	(dau.), b. ca.1816.
86	viii.	Letitia P., b. 19 Apr 1818; m. John Fauchee Cash.

18. Martha "Patsy"[3] Abney (John[2], Abner[1]), b.1781 Augusta Co., VA. She m. Peter Earl Hogg Jr., son of Capt. Peter Earl Hogg Sr. and Elizabeth (n.n.), on 18 Sep 1798 Augusta Co., VA. Their marriage record reads: *"1798-September 18, Peter Hog and Robt. McClenachan, surety. Peter Hog and Patsy Abney, daughter of John Abney, deceased, Isabella Abney (consent). Teste: James Hog"*. They were m. by the Rev. Jno. Montgomery. Patsy and her husband, Peter were liv. in Mason County, Virginia in 1815. She appeared as Head of Household on the census of 1830 Mason Co., VA. She d.24 Mar 1846 Mason Co., VA and was bur. Lone Oak Cem., Point Pleasant, Mason Co., WV. (Mason County, VA became Mason County, WV in 1863) (See Chapter IV, page 37.)

Peter Earl Hogg Jr appeared as Head of Household on the census of 1820 Mason Co., VA. He d. before 1830.

Known children of Martha "Patsy"[3] Abney and Peter Earl Hogg Jr.:

87	i.	Thomas Gory[4], b. 12 Aug 1800 Kanawha Co., VA; m. Lucy Ball.
88	ii.	Julia Ann, b. 10 Aug 1808 VA; m. Thomas Ball.
89	iii.	Mary Margaret, b. 20 Aug 1811 VA; m. Henry Capehart.
	iv.	Abney W., b.2 May 1818 Mason Co., VA; m. Mary "Polly" Skeen in 1842. He d.12 Jan 1873 Mason Co., WV, age 54.
		Mary "Polly" Skeen d.10 Jan 1867 Mason Co., WV.

Generation Four

19. Rebecca C.*⁴* Abney (Joshua*³*, Elisha*²*, Abner*¹*), b.9 Feb 1796 Green Co., KY. She m. John Chancellor, son of David Chancellor and Margaret Phelps, on 5 Aug 1812 Butler Co., KY. She and John Chancellor appeared on the census of 10 Oct 1850 Clark Co., IL. She d.26 Sep 1855 Martinsville, Clark Co., IL, at age 59 and was bur. Martinsville City Cem., Martinsville, Clark Co., IL.

    John Chancellor was, b.17 Jun 1793 (Mason Co. or Green Co.?), KY. He appeared as Head of Household on the censuses of 1840, 1850, 1860 and 1870 Clark Co., IL. He d.24 Aug 1879 Martinsville, Clark Co., IL, at age 86 and was bur. Martinsville City Cem.
Known children of Rebecca C.*⁴* Abney and John Chancellor:

90	i.	David*⁵*, b. 17 Apr 1813 KY; m. Eleanor K. "Ellen" Auld.
91	ii.	Ewing, b. 14 Oct 1813 Morgantown, Butler Co., KY; m. Huldah Lee.
92	iii.	Joshua, b. 5 Jan 1816 KY; m. Phebe Moore.
	iv.	Polly Ann, b. ca.1818. She d.12 May 1831.
93	v.	Levi, b. 15 Feb 1820 Morgantown, Butler Co., KY; m. Elizabeth "Eliza" Auld.
94	vi.	Martha Ann, b. 19 Jan 1823 KY; m. John Montgomery.
95	vii.	William M., b. 29 Jan 1827; m. Mary Ann Peters.
96	viii.	John M., b. 9 Jan 1833; m. E. (n.n.).
	ix.	Polly Ann, b.4 May 1834 Martinsville, Clark Co., IL. She d.12 May 1834 Martinsville, Clark Co., IL and was bur. Martinsville City Cem., Martinsville, Clark Co., IL.

20. Rev. Paul Colby*⁴* Abney (Joshua*³*, Elisha*²*, Abner*¹*), b.7 Sep 1801 Green Co., KY. He was Baptist Minister. He m1. Mary G. Beasley, daughter of William E. Beasley, RS and Elizabeth Taylor, on 7 Sep 1821 Butler Co., KY. He appeared as Head of Household on the census of 1830 Butler Co., KY. He m2. Nancy Little on 24 Feb 1846 Butler Co., KY. He and Nancy Little appeared on the censuses of 16 Sep 1850 and 29 Jun 1860 Butler Co., KY. He d. ca.1867 Butler Co., KY and was bur. Mount Vernon Cem., Dexterville, Butler Co., KY.

    Mary G. Beasley, b.1797 Warren Co., KY. She d. bef.1846 Butler Co., KY and was bur. Mount Vernon Cem., Dexterville, Butler Co., KY.
Known children of Rev. Paul Colby*⁴* Abney and Mary G. Beasley all born in Butler Co., KY:

	i.	Albert*⁵*, b. ca.1823.
97	ii.	John William, b. 1826; m. Keziah Daugherty.
98	iii.	Mary Ann, b. 6 Nov 1827; m. Thomas W. Moore.
99	iv.	Nicey G., b. Jun 1829; m. Jesse G. Deweese Jr.
	v.	Patsy J., b. ca.1842.

    Nancy Little, b. ca.1827 KY. She m1. ca.1840 John J. Embry. (They had a daughter named Martha Jane Embry who married Pvt. John William Abney Jr., son of John William Abney Sr. and Keziah Daugherty.) She appeared as Head of Household on the census of 1 Aug 1870 Butler Co., KY. She d.1897 and was bur. Mount Vernon Cem., Dexterville, Butler Co., KY.
Known children of Rev. Paul Colby*⁴* Abney and Nancy Little:

100	i.	Hannah Curtis*⁵*, b. 1848 Butler Co., KY; m. Alfred Wayne Daugherty.
101	ii.	Isaac Newton, b. 24 Oct 1849 Butler Co., KY; m. Sylvia Embry.
102	iii.	Silas Curtis, b. 1851 KY; m. Calista "Calesty" Barton.

21. William*⁴* Abney (Joshua*³*, Elisha*²*, Abner*¹*), b.1 Oct 1802 Green Co., KY. He m. Tabitha Jones on 21 Dec 1833 Edwards Co., IL. He was liv. ca.1837 Posey Co., IN. He m. Lucinda "Lucy" Robinson on 15 Apr 1846 Jefferson Co., IL. He and Lucinda "Lucy" Robinson appeared on the census of 10 Aug 1850 Jefferson Co., IL. He d.26 Oct 1858 Nason, Jefferson Co., IL, at age 56 and was bur. Abner Cem., Nason, Jeff. Co., IL.

    Tabitha Jones, b.1810 KY. She d.1844 Jefferson Co., IL.
Known children of William*⁴* Abney and Tabitha Jones all born in Jefferson Co., IL:

103	i.	Francis Marion*⁵*, b. 15 Feb 1838; m1. Felicia A. (n.n.); m2. Elizabeth A. Huston; m3. Louisa Catherine Trout.
	ii.	Oliver H. "Perry", b. ca.1843.
	iii.	Joshua, b.1844. He d. before 1850 Jefferson Co., IL.

    Lucinda "Lucy" Robinson, b. ca.1827 IL.
Known children of William*⁴* Abney and Lucinda "Lucy" Robinson were all born in Jefferson Co., IL as follows:

104	i.	Louis Frank*⁵*, b. 11 Apr 1850; m. Lequincey J. "Lory" Melton.
	ii.	Evaline, b. ca.1853.
	iii.	William N, b. ca.1855.
	iv.	Martha C, b. ca.1858.

22. Silas*⁴* Abney (Joshua*³*, Elisha*²*, Abner*¹*), b. ca.1810 Butler Co., KY. He m. Aseneth "Martha" Moore ca.1834 Martinsville, Clark Co., IL. He appeared as Head of Household on the census of 1840 Jefferson Co., IL. He and Aseneth "Martha" Moore appeared on the census of 2 Sep 1850 Jefferson Co., IL. He d. after 1850 IL and was bur. Abner Cem., Nason, Jefferson Co., IL.

    Aseneth "Martha" Moore, b. ca.1817 VA.
Known children of Silas*⁴* Abney and Aseneth "Martha" Moore:

	i.	Martha J.*⁵*, b.1835 IL.
	ii.	Jesse, b.1837 IL.
	iii.	William P., b.3 Dec 1838 and d.12 Feb 1851 Martinsville, Clark Co., IL, at age 12 and was bur. Martinsville City Cem., Martinsville, Clark Co., IL.
	iv.	Mary Ann, b.28 Feb 1840 and d.12 Feb 1851 Martinsville, Clark Co., IL, at age 10 and was bur. Martinsville City Cem., Martinsville, Clark Co., IL.
	v.	Rosetta, b.1844.

23. Jesse*⁴* Abney (Joshua*³*, Elisha*²*, Abner*¹*), b. ca.1812 Butler Co., KY. He m. (n.n.) ca.1835. He appeared as Head of Household on the census of 1840 Jefferson Co., IL.

Known children of Jesse[4] Abney and (n.n.) both b. KY:
>   i.   (dau)[5], b. ca.1836.
>   ii. (dau), b. ca.1838.

24. **John[4] Abney** (Hezekiah[3], Elisha[2], Abner[1]), b. ca.1802 KY (according to John Hensell (*Abney Supplement* 1988). He m. (n.n.) ca.1824. He appeared as Head of Household on the census of 1830 Jackson Co., GA. He d. before 1840 Jackson Co., GA.
Known children of John[4] Abney and (n.n.):
>   i.   (dau.?)[5], b. ca.1825. She appeared on the census of 1830 Jackson Co., GA.
>   ii. (son?), b. ca.1827 GA. He was liv. in 1830 Jackson Co., GA.

25. **Benjamin Hezekiah[4] Abney** (Hezekiah[3], Elisha[2], Abner[1]), b.1804 Jackson Co., GA. He m1. Elizabeth Hogan on 30 Jan 1827 Jackson Co., GA. He appeared as Head of Household on the censuses of 1830 Jackson Co., GA and 1840 Cobb Co., GA. He and Elizabeth Hogan appeared on the censuses of 12 Nov 1850 Cobb Co., GA and 20 Jun 1860 Calhoun Co., AL. He m2. Sarah Ann "Frances" Harper on 22 Oct 1868 Cleburne Co., AL. He and Sarah Ann "Frances" Harper appeared on the census of 9 Jul 1870 Cleburne Co., AL. He d.1878 Cleburne Co., AL and was bur. Shoal Creek Cem., Cleburne Co., AL.
Elizabeth Hogan, b. ca.1802 GA. She d.1866 AL and was bur. Shoal Creek Cem., Cleburne Co., AL.
Known children of Benjamin Hezekiah[4] Abney and Elizabeth Hogan:
105	i.	Wilburn Callaway "Cal"[5], b. 4 Jan 1828 Jackson Co., GA; m1. Rebecca Martha Shipp; m2. Martha E. "Jane" Hogan.
106	ii.	Benjamin D. "Ben," b. Aug 1828 Jackson Co., GA; m1. Sarah E. Greene; m2. Mary A. "Molly" Prisket.
	iii.	Eliza, b. ca.1829 Jackson Co., GA.
107	iv.	Andrew "Jackson," b. 25 Jan 1833 GA; m. Mary A. (n.n.).
108	v.	Hezekiah "Van Buren," b. 29 May 1834 GA; m. Margaret Emeline "Emmie" Shipp.
	vi.	Elizabeth, b. ca.1835 Jackson Co., GA. She d.1849 and was bur. Liberty Hill Cem., Acworth, Cobb Co., GA.
	vii.	Amanda Carol, b. ca.1836 Jackson Co., GA. She d.1850 and was bur. Liberty Hill Cem., Acworth, Jackson Co., GA.
109	viii.	Pvt. George Washington (CSA), b. 10 Mar 1837 GA; m. Elizabeth Jane Chandler.
110	ix.	William Thomas, b. Sep 1838 GA; m. Martha W. Perry.
	x.	Mary Jane, b. ca.1839 Powder Springs, GA.
	xi.	John (CSA), b.11 Nov 1846. He began military service on 4 Mar 1862 enlisted in 45th GA, Co.D, Monroe Co., GA. He was wounded in action on 30 Jul 1864 at Petersburg, VA. John was captured on 25 Mar 1865 Petersburg, VA. He d.7 Apr 1865 Washington, DC, at age 18 and was bur. Arlington National Cem., Arlington, Arlington Co., VA.
111	xii.	Eli Newton "Bish," b. 1 Aug 1848 GA; m. Sarah Adaline Busbey.
112	xiii.	James Alfred "Alf," b. 20 Aug 1850 Cobb Co., GA; m. Nancy J. Grubbs.
113	xiv.	Joseph Calloway, b. 11 Dec 1853 Oak Level, Benton, Cleburne Co., AL; m1. Georgiane Bowen; m2. Josephine L.B. "Jossie" Butler.

Sarah Ann "Frances" Harper , b. ca.1840 GA. She appeared as Head of Household on the census of 5 Jun 1880 Cleburne Co., AL.
Known children of Benjamin Hezekiah[4] Abney and Sarah Ann "Frances" Harper all born in Oak Level, Cleburne Co., AL:
	i.	Martha M.[5], b. ca.1866; She m. William T. Jackson on 30 Nov 1892 Cleburne Co., AL.
	ii.	Luella, b. ca.1869.
114	iii.	Charles Robert "Bob," b. Jul 1872; m. Sarah Ann "Annie" Stephenson.
115	iv.	John J., b. 13 Sep 1873; m. Louisa "Francis" Dollar.
	v.	Elizabeth, b. ca.1878.

26. **Delilah[4] Abney** (Hezekiah[3], Elisha[2], Abner[1]), b. ca.1808 Jackson Co., GA. She m. Jonathan Yarborough on 13 Dec 1830 Jackson Co., GA. She and Jonathan Yarborough appeared on the censuses of 31 Oct 1850 Jackson Co., GA and 8 Aug 1860 Cutoff Dist., Jackson Co., GA. She d.1880 Jackson Co., GA. (Is this the same man as "John Yarborough" who married Delilah's sister, Elizabeth?)
Jonathan Yarborough, b. ca.1800 GA. He appeared as Head of Household on the census of 1840 Cobb Co., GA.
Known children of Delilah[4] Abney and Jonathan Yarborough all b. GA:
	i.	Dyer[5], b. ca.1832.
116	ii.	Hezekiah M., b. ca.1834; m. Rebecca A. (n.n.).
	iii.	Wiley, b. ca.1839.
	iv.	Joseph, b. ca.1841.
	v.	Joel, b. ca.1843.
	vi.	Eliza J., b. ca.Apr 1850.

27. **Wiley[4] Abney** (Hezekiah[3], Elisha[2], Abner[1]), b. ca.1810 Jackson Co., GA. He m1. Elizabeth Brumbelow ca.1840 Cobb Co., GA. He appeared as Head of Household on the census of 1840 Cobb Co., GA. He and Elizabeth Brumbelow appeared on the censused of 15 Oct 1850 Cobb Co., GA and 22 Jun 1860 Paulding Co., GA. He was living with his son-in-law, John Silas Carver on 12 Jul 1870 Floyd Co., GA. He m2. Mary Black on 20 Nov 1870 Floyd Co., GA. In 1892 we read: *"On 27 Nov. ult.* [1892] *in Paulding Co., Jackson Abner* [Abney], *Wiley Abney, and J.P. Davis assaulted and stabbed J.L. Williams, who has since died. Issued 29 Dec. 1892 on 27 Nov 1892 Paulding Co., GA.* No further information on the outcome of this alleged assault. Wiley d.1895 Burnt Hickory, Paulding Co., GA and was bur. Friendship PBC Cem., Paulding Co., GA.
Elizabeth Brumbelow, b. ca.1814 TN. She d.1865.
Known children of Wiley[4] Abney and Elizabeth Brumbelow all b. Cobb Co., GA:
117	i.	Pinkney Floyd[5], b. Jan 1842; m. Sarah Graham.
118	ii.	Thomas "Jackson," b. 22 Jul 1846; m. Dorothy C. Cleveland.
119	iii.	Martha Jane, b. Feb 1848; m. William Shedrick Harrison Wilkerson.
120	iv.	James Allen, b. 27 May 1850; m1. Margaret E. Wilkerson; m2. Margaret Jane "Maggie" Johnson.
121	v.	Nancy Elmira "Elmiry," b. 1 May 1852; m. John Silas Carver.
122	vi.	Sarah E., b. ca.1854; m. T.W. Wilkerson.

There were no known children of Wiley[4] Abney and Mary Black.

28. Andrew⁴ Abney (Hezekiah³, Elisha², Abner¹), b. ca.1813 Jackson Co., GA. He m. Susan Collins ca.1837 Cobb Co., GA. He appeared as Head of Household on the census of 1840 Cobb Co., GA. He and Susan Collins appeared on the census of 8 Nov 1850 Cobb Co., GA. He d. bef.1860 and was bur. Liberty Hill Cem., Acworth, Cobb Co., GA.
   Susan Collins, b. ca.1810 GA.
Known children of Andrew⁴ Abney and Susan Collins all b. Cobb Co., GA:
       123   i.   James Franklin⁵, b. 29 Nov 1838; m. Elisabeth Key "Eliza" Brooks.
              ii.   Phebe, b. ca.1840.
       124   iii. John, b. ca.1842; m. Martha "Jane" Brown.
              iv.   Elizabeth, b. ca.1844.
              v.   Mary, b. ca.1846.

29. James M.⁴ Abney (CSA) (Hezekiah³, Elisha², Abner¹), b.8 Jul 1815 Jackson Co., GA. He m1. Dulcina "Cenie" Daniel ca.1845. He m2. Sarah Miller before 1870 GA. He and Sarah Miller appeared on the census of 13 Jun 1870 Meriwether Co., GA. He d.16 Jan 1890 at age 74 and was bur. Friendship PBC Cem., Paulding Co., GA.
   Dulcina "Cenie" Daniel, b. ca.1818 GA (?). She appeared as Head of Household on the censuses of 28 Aug 1860, 19 Jul 1870 and 11 Jun 1880 Heard Co., GA. She d.7 Nov 1893 and was bur. Franklin City Cem., Franklin, Heard Co., GA.
Known children of James M.⁴ Abney (CSA) and Dulcina "Cenie" Daniel:
       125   i.   William Duncan "Bill"⁵, b. Sep 1846 GA; m. Julia A.F. Pike.
              ii.   Mary "Josaphine", b. ca.1850 GA. She was liv. on 28 Aug 1860 Franklin, Heard Co., GA.
       126   iii. James Andrew "Jim," b. 30 Nov 1855 Franklin, Heard Co., GA; m. Mary Ann Elizabeth Thornton.
              iv.   Benjamin, b. ca.1859 GA.

   Sarah Miller, b.23 Feb 1818. She m1. William Turner. She d.30 Sep 1880 at age 62 and was bur. Friendship PBC Cem., Paulding Co., GA. There were no known children of James M.⁴ Abney (CSA) and Sarah Miller.

30. Jeff Pressley "Pres"⁴ Abney (Hezekiah³, Elisha², Abner¹), b. ca.1825 Jackson Co., GA. He m. Charlotte Hollingsworth on 23 Oct 1845 DeKalb Co., GA. He d.1855.
   Charlotte Hollingsworth, b. ca.1828 SC. She appeared as Head of Household on the censuses of 10 Aug 1860 Barnes Dist., DeKalb Co., GA and 2 Sep 1870 Newton Co., GA. She was liv. on 9 Jun 1880 with son-in-law, *George Haners*, Rockdale Co., GA and on 7 Jun 1900 with daughter, *Julia Hanners*, Fort Payne, DeKalb Co., AL. She d. after 1900.
Known children of Jeff Pressley "Pres"⁴ Abney and Charlotte Hollingsworth:
       127   i.   Julia A.R.⁵, b. ca.1848 AL; m. George Wesley Hanners.
       128   ii.   John Newton Nathan, b. 9 Feb 1851 DeKalb Co., GA; m. Martha Cynthia Maddox.
              iii. Martha E., b. ca.1852.

31. Joel Jonathan⁴ Abney (Hezekiah³, Elisha², Abner¹), b. ca.1828 Jackson Co., GA. He m. Delila Ann "Dilly" Smith ca.1852. He and Dilly Smith appeared on the censuses of 26 Jun 1860 Calhoun Co., AL and 7 Jun 1880 Cleburne Co., AL. He d.Jul 1891 Cleburne Co., AL and was bur. Shoal Creek Cem., Cleburne Co., AL.
   Delila Ann "Dilly" Smith, b.5 Jul 1833 GA. She was liv. with her son-in-law, Willie J. Jackson on the census of 22 Jun 1900 Piedmont, Calhoun Co., AL. She d.20 Apr 1910 at age 76 and was bur. Shoal Creek Cem., Cleburne Co., AL.
Known children of Joel Jonathan⁴ Abney and Delila Ann "Dilly" Smith:
       129   i.   Elizabeth⁵, b. 19 Mar 1854 GA; m. William A. Johnson.
              ii.   Mary, b. ca.1857 GA.
       130   iii. Sarah Jane "Janie," b. 29 Jun 1859 AL; m. John Wiley Johnson.
       131   iv.   John William, b. 9 Apr 1861 Cleburne Co., AL; m. Sidney Varjulia Crews.
       132   v.   Rebecca Bethena, b. 2 Sep 1865 Cleburne Co., AL; m. Hirram Franklin "Frank" Waddle.
       133   vi.   Martha "Mattie," b. 16 Nov 1873 Cleburne Co., AL.

32. Henry⁴ Woods (Dorcas³ Abney, Elisha², Abner¹), b.1809 Clay Co., KY. He m. (n.n.) est.1827. He appeared as Head of Household on the census of 1840 Jessamine Co., KY.
   (n.n.), b. between 1810 and 1819.
Known children of Henry⁴ Woods and (n.n.):
              i.   (dau.?)⁵, b. est.1828.
              ii.   (dau.?), b. est.1830.
              iii. (son?), b. est.1835.
              iv.   (dau.?), b. est.1838.
              v.   (dau.?), b. est.1840.

33. William⁴ Woods (Dorcas³ Abney, Elisha², Abner¹), b. ca.1814 KY. He m1. Nancy Morris est.1840. He appeared as Head of Household on the census of 1840 Clay Co., KY. He appeared on the census of 1 Aug 1850 with his brother, Lelbon Woods, Clay Co., KY. He and Nancy Sizemore obtained a marriage license on 25 Apr 1853 Clay Co., KY. He m2. Nancy Sizemore.
   Nancy Morris, b.1825 KY.
Known children of William⁴ Woods and Nancy Morris both b. Clay Co., KY:
       134   i.   Theophilus⁵, b. 1844; m. Juda n.n. (according to genealogist, Mary Elizabeth Greear South, Theophilus was *possibly a son of William Woods and Nancy Morris*. This connection, to the knowledge of the author, has not been proved.
              ii.   Viney, b.1848.
   Nancy Sizemore, b. ca.1832 Clay Co., KY. She appeared on the census of 1860 Clay Co., KY.

Known children of William⁴ Woods and Nancy Sizemore all b. Clay Co., KY:
    i.   Louticia⁵, b. ca.1855.
    ii. Abijah, b. ca.1857.
    iii. Creasey, b. ca.1858.
    iv. Elizabeth, b. ca.1863.
    v. Lilburn., b. ca.1865.

34. Lilburn⁴ Woods (Dorcas³ Abney, Elisha² Abner¹), b. ca.1816 Clay Co., KY. He and Mahalia Sizemore obtained a marriage license on 7 Jul 1846 Clay Co., KY. He and Mahalia Sizemore appeared on the census of 1 Aug 1850 Clay Co., KY. He d.1871 Leslie Co., KY and was bur. Woods Cem., Thousandsticks, Leslie Co., KY.
   Mahalia Sizemore, b. ca.1826 KY. She d.1908 and was bur. Woods Cem., Thousandsticks, Leslie Co., KY.
Known children of Lilburn⁴ Woods and Mahalia Sizemore all b. Clay Co., KY:
    i.   Lucinda⁵, b. ca.1847.
    ii. Wade, b. ca.1849.
    iii. Felix "Taylor", b.8 Jun 1850. He d.15 Aug 1934 at age 84 and was bur. Woods Keen Cem., Dryhill, Leslie Co., KY.
    iv. Ann, b. ca.1853.
    v. Sally, b. ca.1855.
    vi. Mary, b. ca.1857.
    vii. Joseph, b. ca.1858.
    viii. John, b. ca.1860.
    ix. Pleasant, b. ca.1861.
    x. Charity, b. ca.1865.
    xi. Lucas, b. ca.1867.
    xii. Russell, b. Apr 1870.

35. Elizabeth⁴ Woods (Dorcas³ Abney, Elisha² Abner¹), b.1819 Clay Co., KY. She m. James "Adger" McGuire on 24 Aug 1839 Owsley Co., KY. She and J. Adger McGuire appeared on the census of 6 Sep 1850 Owsley Co., KY and was bur. Merritt Cem., Wildie, Rockcastle Co., KY.
   James "Adger" McGuire, b.23 Feb 1805 Proctor, Owsley Co., KY.
Known children of Elizabeth⁴ Woods and James Adgar McGuire:
    i.   John⁵, b.1840 Owsley Co., KY. He m. Martha A. Griffin in 1866. (She was liv. Audrain Co., MO)
135 ii. Margaret, b. Jun 1841 Mount Vernon, Rockcastle Co., KY; m1. Speed Steele; m2. Solomon Childress.
    iii. Archibald, b.16 Jan 1842 Rockcastle Co., KY. He d.1848.
136 iv. Christina, b. 5 Feb 1844 KY; m1. Cpl. James B. Dooley (UA); m2. George M. Johnson.
    v. Tabitha, b.1848 KY. She d.1862.
    vi. Elvilla (Everly), b.18 Mar 1850 Owsley Co., KY.
    vii. James W., b.1854 Rockcastle Co., KY.

36. Joseph⁴ Woods (Dorcas³ Abney, Elisha² Abner¹), b.20 Mar 1820. He m. Martha "Patsy" (n.n.). He d.28 Apr 1886 at age 66 and was bur. Merritt Cem., Wildie, Rockcastle Co., KY.
   Martha "Patsy" (n.n.), b.29 Dec 1825. She d.6 Jan 1894 at age 68 and was bur. Merritt Cem., Wildie, Rockcastle Co., KY.
Known children of Joseph⁴ Woods and Martha "Patsy" (n.n.) all b. KY:
    i.   Cynthia⁵, b. ca.1846.
    ii. Catherine, b. ca.1848.
    iii. William, b. ca.1849.

37. Samuel⁴ Woods (Dorcas³ Abney, Elisha² Abner¹), b.1825 Clay Co., KY. He m. Sarah "Sally" Tucker ca.1847.
   Sarah "Sally" Tucker, b. ca.1829 VA.
Known child of Samuel⁴ Woods and Sarah "Sally" Tucker:
    i.   Joseph⁵, b. ca.1848 KY.

38. William "Buck"⁴ Abner (Elisha³, Elisha² Abney, Abner¹), b.4 Aug 1807 Clay Co., KY. He m. Jane Virginia "Jennie" Baker, daughter of Robert Julius "Bob" Baker and Elizabeth "Liddy" Hammond, on 2 Jun 1827 Clay Co., KY. He appeared as Head of Household on the censuses of 1830 and 1840 Clay Co., KY. He and Jane Virginia "Jennie" Baker appeared on the census of 16 Aug 1850 Owsley Co., KY. He appeared as Head of Household on the censuses of 9 Jun 1860, 27 Jul 1870 and 28 Jun 1880 Owsley Co., KY. He d.11 Aug 1883 Owsley Co., KY, at age 76 and was bur. William Abner Cem., Southfork, Owsley Co., KY.
   Jane Virginia "Jennie" Baker, b. ca.1808. She d.1885 Owsley Co., KY and was bur. William Abner Cem., Southfork, Owsley Co., KY.
Known children of William "Buck"⁴ Abner and Jane Virginia "Jennie" Baker:
    i.   Lucinda⁵ m. (n.n.) Lynch, b.1828 Clay Co., KY. She d.1888.
137 ii. Susan Florence, b. 1832 Clay Co., KY; m. Robert Allen; m. William Parker.
138 iii. David, b. 24 Jan 1834 Clay Co., KY; m. Mary "Polly" Parker.
    iv. Mary "Polly", b. ca.1836 Clay Co., KY. She was liv. on 28 Jun 1880 with bro., Robert Abner, Owsley Co., KY.
139 v. Easter, b. ca.1838 Clay Co., KY; m. Adoniram "Niram" Allen.
    vi. Nancy, b. ca.1840 Clay Co., KY.
140 vii. Lewis "Levi," b. 22 Jun 1842 Clay Co., KY; m. Rachel Allen.
    viii. Elizabeth, b. ca.1844 Owsley, KY. She m. Robert L. Abner (Robert's parentage is unknown).
    ix. William O., b. Aug 1847 Owsley Co., KY. He was liv. on 28 Jun 1880 with bro., Robert Abner, Owsley Co., KY. [author's note: A genealogy by Owen Blevins shows William O. Abner's wife as Nancy Eversole. However, the same genealogy also shows another William "Bill" Abner's wife as the same, and with the same marriage date.]
141 x. Sophia, b. Apr 1850 Owsley Co., KY; m. James Deaton.
142 xi. Robert "Robin," b. 2 Mar 1851 Owsley Co., KY; m. Sarah Ann Deaton.

39. Lacy*⁴* Abner (Elisha*³*, Elisha*²* Abney, Abner*¹*), b. ca.1810 Clay Co., KY. He m. Cynthia Combs on 30 Mar 1837 Clay Co., KY. He appeared as Head of Household on the census of 1840 Clay Co., KY. He and Cynthia Combs appeared on the censuses of 16 Aug 1850, 31 Jul 1860 and 11 Jun 1880 Owsley Co., KY. He d.11 Aug 1883 Owsley Co., KY and was bur. Cortland Cem., Owsley Co., KY.
    Cynthia Combs, b. ca.1819.
Known children of Lacy*⁴* Abner and Cynthia Combs:
              i.   Maria*⁵*, b. ca.1838 KY.
143   ii.   Nancy, b. Mar 1840 Clay Co., KY; m. James Eversole.
144   iii.   Mary "Polly," b. ca.1841 Clay Co., KY.
145   iv.   John W., b. Mar 1844 Owsley Co., KY; m. Joice "Joicy" Burns.
146   v.   Minerva, b. 1846 Owsley Co., KY; m. Brison Barrett.
             vi.   Catherine, b. ca.1847 Owsley Co., KY. She was liv. on 16 Aug 1870 with brother-in-law, Bricen Barrrett, Buffalo, Owsley Co., KY.
            vii.   Elizabeth, b. ca.Jun 1850 Owsley Co., KY. She d.1880 KY.
147   viii.   Leander A. "Lee," b. 18 Apr 1852 Owsley Co., KY; m. Elizabeth Cynthia "Ibbie" Bishop.
148   ix.   Harvey, b. 3 Mar 1856 Owsley Co., KY; m. Mary Jane Dean.
149   x.   Amanda Jane, b. ca.1858 Owsley Co., KY; m. Irvine Bishop.
150   xi.   Samuel, b. 10 Aug 1863 Owsley Co., KY; m. Mariah Bishop.

40. John A.*⁴* Abner (Elisha*³*, Elisha*²* Abney, Abner*¹*), b. ca.1813 Clay Co., KY. He m1. Nancy Jane "Chesney" McJunkin, d/o William Chesney McJunkin and Mary Bailey, 2 Jul 1838 Clay Co., KY. He appeared as Head of Household on the census of 1840 Clay Co., KY. He and Nancy Jane "Chesney" McJunkin appeared on the census of 8 Sep 1850 Owsley Co., KY. He m2. Mary Courtney on 29 Jan 1860 Grant Co., KY. He and Mary Courtney appeared on the census of 15 Jun 1860 Grant Co., KY. He d.Dec 1890 and was bur. White-Deaton Cem., Barwick, Breathitt Co., KY.
    Nancy Jane "Chesney" McJunkin, b. ca.1825 Owsley Co., KY. She d. ca.1859 Grant Co., KY and was bur. Owsley Co., KY.
Known children of John A.*⁴* Abner and Nancy Jane "Chesney" McJunkin:
              i.   Mary*⁵*, b. ca.1840 Clay Co., KY.
             ii.   Elisha, b. Christmas Day, 25 Dec 1841 Clay Co., KY. He m1. Elizabeth C. "Lizzie" McCann on 10 Dec 1867 Pendleton Co., KY. He and Elizabeth C. "Lizzie" McCann appeared on the censuses of 9 Jun 1870 and 1 Jun 1880 Cordova, Grant Co., KY. He m2. Malinda Whitson on 30 Sep 1890 Scott Co., KY. He and Malinda Whitson appeared on the census of 2 Jun 1900 Harrison Co., KY. He d.10 Aug 1925 Stonewall, Scott Co., KY, at age 83 and was bur. Raven Creek Cem., Hinton, Harrison Co., KY.
                      Malinda Whitson, b.7 Jun 1848 Harrison Co., KY. She m1. (n.n.) Wright. She d.13 Apr 1937 Stonewall, Scott Co., KY, at age 88 and was bur. Raven Creek Cem., Hinton, Harrison Co., KY.
151   iii.   William M., b. 26 Jul 1844 Owsley Co., KY; m. Nancy Ann Phillips.

There were no known children of John A.*⁴* Abner and Mary Courtney.

41. Mary Lucinda "Polly"*⁴* Abner (Elisha*³*, Elisha*²* Abney, Abner*¹*), b. ca.1816 Clay Co., KY. She m. Andrew "Andy" Baker, son of Robert Julius "Bob" Baker and Elizabeth "Liddy" Hammond, on 5 Oct 1833 Clay Co., KY. She and Andrew "Andy" Baker appeared on the census of 16 Aug 1850 Owsley Co., KY. She d.15 Aug 1887 Owsley Co., KY and was bur. Cortland Cem., Cow Creek, Owsley Co., KY.
    Andrew "Andy" Baker, b.28 Jan 1810 Clay Co., KY. He m. Rachel Wilson in 1827. He appeared as Head of Household on the census of 1840 Clay Co., KY. He was shot to death 15 Sep 1854, Owsley Co., KY, at age 44 and was bur. Cortland Cem., Cow Creek, Owsley Co., KY.
Known children of Mary Lucinda "Polly"*⁴* Abner and Andrew "Andy" Baker:
152   i.   John "Red John"*⁵*, b. ca.1835 KY; m. (n.n.).
             ii.   Nancy, b. ca.1837 Clay Co., KY. She m. William Perry "Budhead" Bishop. She d.1884 KY and was bur. Cortland Cem., Cow Creek, Owsley Co., KY.
                      William Perry "Budhead" Bishop, b.1836. He d.1920.
            iii.   Robert "Red Bob", b. May 1839 Clay Co., KY. *Red Bob* was an infamous Moonshiner. He was captured by a Revenue Agent. He m. Margaret Ethel Gabbard He d.1910 and was bur. Cortland Cem., Cow Creek, Owsley Co., KY.
                      Margaret Ethel Gabbard, b.1844. She d.1899.
            iv.   Louisa, b. ca.1842 Clay Co., KY.
             v.   Andrew "Jackson", b. ca.1844 Owsley Co., KY.
            vi.   Martha, b. ca.1847 Owsley Co., KY.
           vii.   Lydia, b. ca.1849 Owsley Co., KY.
          viii.   Perlina, b.9 Jan 1852 Owsley Co., KY. She m. Michael Lee "Bundy Mike" Gabbard est.1873. She d.1917 Owsley Co., KY and was bur. Cortland Cem., Cow Creek, Owsley Co., KY.
                      Michael Lee "Bundy Mike" Gabbard, b.1852. He d.1940.
            ix.   Julius S, b. ca.1854 KY.

42. Lucinda*⁴* Abner (Elisha*³*, Elisha*²* Abney, Abner*¹*), b. ca.1818 Clay Co., KY. She m. James Williams ca.1842. She and James Williams appeared on the census of 17 Aug 1850 Owsley Co., KY. She d.8 Aug 1900 and was bur. Laurel Point Cem., Buckhorn, Perry Co., KY.
    James Williams, b. ca.1818.
Known children of Lucinda*⁴* Abner and James Williams:
              i.   Matilda*⁵*, b. ca.1843 KY.
             ii.   Mary "Polly", b. ca.1845 KY.
            iii.   Eliza, b. ca.1846 KY.
            iv.   Nancy, b. ca.1849 KY.
             v.   Lewis, b. ca.1850 KY.
            vi.   John, b. ca.1854 KY.
           vii.   Enoch, b. ca.1855 KY.

43. Susannah "Susan"[4] Abner (Elisha[3], Elisha[2] Abney, Abner[1]), b. ca.1820 Clay Co., KY. She m. Wilson "Willis" Gabbard Sr. on 13 Sep 1838 Clay Co., KY. She and Wilson "Willis" Gabbard Sr. appeared on the censuses of 17 Aug 1850 and 15 Jun 1860 Owsley Co., KY. She d.1906.
   Wilson "Willis" Gabbard Sr, b. ca.1820. He appeared as Head of Household on the census of 1840 Breathitt Co., KY. He d.1870 Owsley Co., KY and was bur. John Baker Cem., Owsley Co., KY.
Known children of Susannah "Susan"[4] Abner and Wilson "Willis" Gabbard Sr.:
   i.   Jackson[5], b. ca.1840 Clay Co., KY.
   ii. Wilson "Willis" Jr., b. ca.1843 Owsley Co., KY.
   iii. Mary "Polly", b. ca.1845 Owsley Co., KY.
   iv. Elisha, b. ca.1848 Owsley Co., KY.
   v.   Michael L., b. ca.1851 Owsley Co., KY.
   vi. William, b. ca.1855 Owsley Co., KY.

44. Nancy Ann[4] Abner (Elisha[3], Elisha[2] Abney, Abner[1]), b. ca.1822 Clay Co., KY. She m. Lewis Sandlin ca.1845 Owsley Co., KY. She and Lewis Sandlin appeared on the censuses of 17 Aug 1850, 9 Jun 1860 and 10 Aug 1870 Owsley Co., KY. She d. after 1880.
   Lewis Sandlin, b. ca.1824 Clay Co., KY. He d.1911.
Known children of Nancy Ann[4] Abner and Lewis Sandlin all b. Owsley Co., KY:
153   i.   Willis[5], b. ca.1846; m. Eliza Jane Abner.
      ii.   Mary J., b. ca.1847.
      iii. Zilpha "Zilphey", b. ca.1849.
154   iv.   James Franklin "Red Jim," b. 1853; m. Eliza Jane Gross.
      v.   Sophia, b. ca.1856.
      vi.   John C.B., b. ca.1858.
      vii. William J., b. ca.1860.
      viii. Robert, b. ca.1867.

45. Willis[4] Abner (Elisha[3], Elisha[2] Abney, Abner[1]), b. ca.1824 Clay Co., KY. He m. Almirah China Baker, daughter of John Hammond Baker and Lucinda Amis, ca.1850 Owsley Co., KY. He and Almirah China Baker appeared on the censuses of 6 Aug 1860 Owsley Co., KY and 24 Jun 1880 Breathitt Co., KY. He d.1 Dec 1890 Owsley Co., KY and was bur. Cortland Cem., Cow Creek, Owsley Co., KY.
   Almirah China Baker, b.8 Sep 1828 Clay Co., KY. She d.2 May 1890 Owsley Co., KY, at age 61 and was bur. Cortland Cem., Cow Creek.
Known children of Willis[4] Abner and Almirah China Baker all b. Owsley Co., KY:
155   i.   Eliza[5], b. 28 Mar 1852; m. James M. Todd Baker.
156   ii.   William "Bill," b. 7 Dec 1853; m. Nancy Ann Eversole.
      iii. Nancy, b.20 Sep 1854. She m. (n.n.) Bowling. She d. Independence Day, 4 Jul 1931 Clay Co., KY, at age 76 and was bur. Teges Cem., Clay Co., KY.
157   iv.   Elisha B., b. 22 Jul 1856; m. Nancy Ann Begley.
      v.   Luther, b.Jun 1859. He m. Elizabeth Morris on 28 Oct 1890 Perry Co., KY.
158   vi.   Mariah, b. 1 May 1860; m. William M. Harris.
      vii. James, b.1864.
159   viii. Mary "Polly," b. 23 Sep 1868; m1. George Washington Terry; m2. Joseph Estep.
160   ix.   Lucinda, b. Dec 1870; m. John "Dirty Face" Sandlin.
161   x.   John Wesley, b. ca.May 1872; m1. Lucy White; m2. Cassie Andrews; m3. Mattie Belle Slaughter.
162   xi.   Daniel Boone, b. 21 Mar 1873; m. Catherine Morris.

46. Matilda[4] Abner (Elisha[3], Elisha[2] Abney, Abner[1]), b. ca.1827 Clay Co., KY. She m1. William Baker ca.1848 Owsley Co., KY. She appeared on the census of 16 Aug 1850 with her father, Elisha Abner Jr., Owsley Co., KY. She m2. Ira Baker ca.1851 Owsley Co., KY. She and Ira Baker appeared on the census of 15 Jun 1860 Owsley Co., KY.
   There were no known children of Matilda[4] Abner and William Baker.
Known children of Matilda[4] Abner and Ira Baker all b. Owsley Co., KY:
   i.   Mary J.[5], b. ca.1852.
   ii. Susan C., b. ca.1854.
   iii. Elijah W., b. ca.1857.
   iv. Sarah E., b.May 1859.

47. Pvt. Enoch[4] Abner (UA) (Elisha[3], Elisha[2] Abney, Abner[1]), b.2 Jul 1830 Manchester, Clay Co., KY. He m. Martha Jane Gilbert, daughter of Jackson Gilbert and Lydia Fox, in Feb 1857 Owsley Co., KY. He and Martha Jane Gilbert appeared on the censuses of 1 Aug 1860 Booneville, Owsley Co., KY, 11 Jul 1870 Perry Co., KY, 25 Jun 1880 Hilburn, Madison Co., AR and 20 Jun 1900 Baldwin, Madison Co., AR. He d.11 Jan 1917 Clay Co., KY, at age 86 and was bur. Teges Cem., Clay Co., KY.
   Martha Jane Gilbert, b.Mar 1838 Breathitt Co., KY. She d.1921 St. Paul, Madison Co., AR.
Known children of Pvt. Enoch[4] Abner (UA) and Martha Jane Gilbert:
163   i.   Lacy[5], b. 8 Dec 1857 Booneville, Owsley Co., KY; m. Sarah Hammonds.
164   ii.   Andrew Jackson "Jack," b. 27 May 1859 Booneville, Owsley Co., KY; m. Nancy Jane Sayler.
      iii. Elisha B., b.1 Oct 1861 Owsley Co., KY. He m. Ellen Herndon Madison Co., AR. He d.30 Dec 1941 Madison Co., AR, at age 80 and was bur. Kilgore Cem., Madison Co., AR.
               Ellen Herndon, b.12 Jan 1857. She d.8 Sep 1921 at age 64 and was bur. Kilgore Cem., Madison Co., AR.
      iv.   Lucinda "Cindy" m. Arch Gipson, b.20 Jul 1864 Booneville, Owsley Co., KY. She was liv. AR. She d.15 Jan 1959 Spiro, Le Flore Co., OK, at age 94 and was bur. New Hope Garden of Memories, Spiro, Le Flore Co., OK.
165   v.   Kenas "Keene," b. 13 Jan 1869 London, Laurel Co., KY; m. Mary Ann Tuttle.
166   vi.   Nancy Jane, b. Jan 1873 Madison Co., AR; m. William J. Justice.
167   vii. Lydia, b. 9 Jun 1876 AR; m. Robert Marshall Morris.
168   viii. Leona "Margaret," b. Oct 1879 AR; m1. (n.n.) Fisher; m2. Abraham M. Meredith.

48. James Monroe[4] Abner (Menan[3], Elisha[2] Abney, Abner[1]), b.1816 Clay Co., KY. He m. Sythia "Almira" McGill, daughter of James McGill and Mary Burns, on 21 Aug 1852 Clay Co., KY. He and Sythia "Almira" McGill appeared on the census of 25 Jul 1860 Clay Co., KY. He d. ca.1866 Clay Co., KY.

    Sythia "Almira" McGill, b.22 Mar 1833 Hancock Co., TN. She m2. Benjamin Franklin Young on 22 Nov 1866 Clay Co., KY. She and Benjamin Franklin Young appeared on the census of 8 Jun 1880 Pond Creek, Jackson Co., KY. She d.4 Mar 1914 Knox Co., KY, at age 80.
Known children of James Monroe[4] Abner and Sythia "Almira" McGill:
169	i.	John[5], b. Jun 1853 Knox Co., KY; m. Sarah Jane Noe.
170	ii.	Mary C, b. 1854 Clay Co., KY; m. Taylor Hignite.
171	iii.	Pierce, b. 15 May 1861 Clay Co., KY; m1. Sophia "Sofie" Smith; m2. Ellen Harvey Roberts.
172	iv.	Daniel Isaac, b. 1865 Clay Co., KY; m1. (n.n.); m2. Mary Elizabeth Cole; m3. Rosanna R "Rosie" Smith.

49. Richard "Dick"[4] Abner (Menan[3], Elisha[2] Abney, Abner[1]), b. ca.1818 Clay Co., KY. He m. Lucinda "Lucy" Wells, daughter of John Wells and Elizabeth Lucas, on 1 Jul 1837 Clay Co., KY. He appeared as Head of Household on the census of 1840 Clay Co., KY. He witnessed the marriage license of [his sister] Nancy Abner and James M. "Jim" Swafford on New Year's Eve, 31 Dec 1842 Clay Co., KY. He and Lucinda "Lucy" Wells appeared on the censuses of 10 Sep 1850, 17 Jul 1860 and 12 Jul 1870 Clay Co., KY and 17 Jun 1880 Knox Co., KY (where he was a cooper). He d. before 28 May 1897 Clay Co., KY and was bur. H.W. Childers Cem., Sprule, Knox Co., KY. (The wonderful work of contributors, Judy Lewis Vietri and Sandrea Abner Cook brought the knowledge that Richard Abner belonged to this family group. A process of elimination, along with nomenclature and prosopography, has confirmed their work. With Richard's close association with the Menan Abner family, he is rightfully placed here, as his Menan's son.

    Lucinda "Lucy" Wells, b.Feb 1822 Clay Co., KY. She was liv. on 21 Jun 1900 with her daughter, Susan Smith, Knox Co., KY.
Known children of Richard "Dick"[4] Abner and Lucinda "Lucy" Wells:
173	i.	Elizabeth "Lizzie"[5], b. ca.1838 KY; m. Elisha Robinson.
174	ii.	Susan E., b. Jan 1844 Knox Co., KY; m. Henry Clay Smith.
	iii.	Emily, b. Apr 1846 Clay Co., KY. She was liv. on 14 Jun 1880 with brother-in-law, H.C. Smith, Knox Co., KY. She was liv. on 21 Jun 1900 with sister, Susan Smith, Knox Co., KY. She m. Carter Helton on 21 Dec 1908 KY. She d. Independence Day, 4 Jul 1914 Clay Co., KY, at age 68 and was bur. H.W. Childers Cem., Sprule, Knox Co., KY.
175	iv.	Julia, b. 22 Apr 1847 Clay Co., KY; m. William P. Hammons.
	v.	Menan, b. ca.1851 Clay Co., KY.
176	vi.	James "Jim," b. 25 Nov 1852 Clay Co., KY; m. Amelia Jane "Jennie" Cobb.
177	vii.	Elisha, b. 2 Apr 1855 Clay Co., KY; m. Mary Jane Jarvis.
178	viii.	Charles Madison "Charley," b. 2 Aug 1857 Clay Co., KY; m. Susan Ann Cobb.
	ix.	Mary M., b.23 Mar 1861 Clay Co., KY. She m. Joseph R. Cobb on 23 Dec 1880 at Richard Abner's home, Knox Co., KY. She d.6 Nov 1936 Clay Co., KY, at age 75 and was bur. Cobb Cem., Fox, Estill Co., KY.
179	x.	Joseph "Joel," b. ca.1864 Clay Co., KY; m. Mary E. Clouse.

50. Mary "Polly"[4] Abner (Menan[3], Elisha[2] Abney, Abner[1]), b. ca.1821 Clay Co., KY. She m. David Benge Jr., son of David Benge Sr. and Elizabeth (n.n.), on 29 Jun 1839 Clay Co., KY. She and David Benge Jr. appeared on the censuses of 14 Sep 1850, 2 Jul 1860 and 1 Jul 1870 Clay Co., KY. She d. before 15 Jun 1880 Clay Co., KY.

    David Benge Jr, b.1815 KY. He appeared as Head of Household on the census of 15 Jun 1880 Clay Co., KY.
Known children of Mary "Polly"[4] Abner and David Benge Jr. all b. Clay Co., KY:
i.	Elizabeth "Betsy"[5], b. ca.1840.
ii.	Eliza, b. ca.1842.
iii.	Richard, b. ca.1843.
iv.	Franklin, b. ca.1844.
v.	Lucinda, b. ca.1845.
vi.	Mary, b.17 Aug 1853.
vii.	Henry, b.25 May 1856.
viii.	Lyon S., b.4 Feb 1859.
ix.	Theophilus G., b.23 Oct 1861.
x.	Margaret, b. ca.1865.
xi.	George "Madison", b. ca.1868.

51. John[4] Abner (Menan[3], Elisha[2] Abney, Abner[1]), b. ca.1837 Clay Co., KY. He m. Matilda Robertson on 9 Jul 1857 Clay Co., KY. He and Matilda Robertson appeared on the census of 28 Jul 1860 Clay Co., KY. He d. before 29 Jul 1870 Manchester, Clay Co., KY.

    Matilda Robertson, b. ca.1844 Clay Co., KY. She appeared as Head of Household on the census of 29 Jul 1870 Manchester, Clay Co., KY. She m2. John Turner est.1873.
Known children of John[4] Abner and Matilda Robertson all b. Clay Co., KY:
180	i.	Martha Ann[5], b. ca.1859; m. Richard Allen Abner.
181	ii.	James Daniel, b. 16 Jul 1863; m. Minerva Jane Hensley.
	iii.	William, b. ca.1868.

52. Alabama[4] Abner (Menan[3], Elisha[2] Abney, Abner[1]), b. ca.1842 Clay Co., KY. She m. Charles Robertson on 3 Oct 1857 Clay Co., KY.
    Charles Robertson, b. ca.1834 NC.
Known child of Alabama[4] Abner and Charles Robertson:
i.	Elisha[5], b. ca.1859 Clay Co., KY.

53. Lincoln "Link"[4] Abnee (John[3] Abney, Elisha[2], Abner[1]), b.10 May 1826 Clay Co., KY. Lincoln was the first to assume the surname *Abnee* (see Etymology in Appendix A, page 257). He was liv. on 28 Aug 1850 with the Samuel Bartlett family, Nicholas Co., KY. He m. Sarah "Margaret" Evans, daughter of Ralph "Rafe" Evans and Mahala "Mahaley" Bartlett, on 1 Oct 1851 Fleming Co., KY. He and Sarah "Margaret" Evans appeared on the censuses of 14 Jun 1860 Fleming Co., KY and 17 Aug 1870 and 1 Jun 1880 Lower Blue Lick, Nicholas Co., KY. Lincoln Abnee was a

farmer, miller and millwright, postmaster and he was magistrate of Lower Blue Licks Precinct. He built and ran a mill on Licking River. He and his sons also ran a store ca.1882 Blue Licks, Nicholas Co., KY. He d.16 Sep 1899 Nicholas Co., KY, at age 73 and was bur. Mount Pisgah Cem., Fairview, Fleming Co., KY. From: *The Post Offices of Nicholas County*: *"Where Elk Creek joins the Licking River, about two miles above Blue Lick Springs (and thirteen miles north of Carlisle), Lincoln Abnee (ne 1826) built a water-powered grist and sawmill. Soon a community called Abners Mill grew up around it and two other mills, a distlllery, tobacco prizing house, store, and school. A post office called Abner was established here on June 14, 1888, with John w. Gill, postmaster, (Lincoln Abnee was the second postmaster), and operated through September 1903. Nothing marks the site today. Why and how Abner was corrupted from Abnee is not known. The Abnees are still an important Nicholas County family."* This current author finds it so interesting (if not humorous) that the author of that quote thinks *Abnee* was corrupted from *Abner*, not realizing that *Abnee* is more phonetically correct than *Abner*. This is the reason the author believes Lincoln Abnee knew the correct pronunciation of his surname; and that it was taught to him by his father, John Abney Sr.

Sarah "Margaret" Evans, b.19 Sep 1836 Fleming Co., KY. She appeared on the census of 5 Jun 1900 Nicholas Co., KY. She d. before 1911 Nicholas Co., KY.

Known children of Lincoln "Link"[4] Abnee and Sarah "Margaret" Evans:

182   i.   Serilda[5], b. 3 Feb 1852 Nicholas Co., KY; m. William Thomas Shy.

183   ii.   Robert S., b. 9 May 1854 Nicholas Co., KY; m. Emma J. Brooks.

      iii.   John "Milton", b.15 Sep 1855 Nicholas Co., KY. He was liv. on 7 Jun 1880 Lower Blue Lick, Nicholas Co., KY. He was liv. on 15 Apr 1910 as a boarder with Mrs. Anna Berry, Lexington, Fayette Co., KY. He d.23 Jan 1918 St. Joseph's Hosp., Lexington, Fayette Co., KY, at age 62 and was bur. Paris Cem., Paris, Bourbon Co., KY. John "Milton" was co-owner of *Abnee & Mussinon* [Tobacco] *Company*.

      iv.   Mary Frances "Fannie" m. (n.n.) Hildreth. , b.8 Dec 1857 and d.26 Feb 1929 Fleming Co., KY, at age 71.

184   v.   William Henry, b. 22 Mar 1859 Fleming Co., KY; m. Mary H. "Mollie" Lincks.

185   vi.   Effie D., b. Jun 1861 Nicholas Co., KY; m. Hiram B. Marlow.

      vii.   James C., b.19 Mar 1864 Nicholas Co., KY. He was assassinated 21 Feb 1889 at age 24 and was bur. Mount Pisgah Cem., Fairview, Fleming Co., KY.

      viii.   Lee, b.Aug 1867 Fleming Co., KY. He d. ca.1871.

      ix.   Charles R. "Charlie", b.16 Mar 1870 Nicholas Co., KY. He was liv. on 5 Jun 1900 with his mother, *Margaret Abner*, Nicholas Co., KY. He m. Tabitha Lillian Boggess, daughter of Lorenzo D. Boggess and Mary Elizabeth Bailey, ca.1909. He and Tabitha Lillian Boggess appeared on the census of 23 Apr 1910 Nicholas Co., KY. He appeared on the census of 6 Jun 1920 Rafferty, Nicholas Co., KY. He d.24 May 1931 Nicholas Co., KY, at age 61 and was bur. Sunnyside Cem., Ewing, Nicholas Co., KY.

           Tabitha Lillian Boggess, b.28 Oct 1886 Robertson Co., KY. She d.6 Sep 1919 Nicholas Co., KY, at age 32.

186   x.   Clarence Thomas, b. 26 May 1871 Nicholas Co., KY; m1. Mary J. Boggess; m2. Hattie Swartz; m3. Ellie (n.n.).

54. Nancy Caroline[4] Abner (John[3] Abney, Elisha[2], Abner[1]), b.27 Dec 1836 Clay Co., KY. She m. James B. Hunt on 3 Sep 1846 Owsley Co., KY. She and James B. Hunt appeared on the census of 25 Sep 1850 Owsley Co., KY. She m. James Lafayette Scroggins on 30 Sep 1855 Barry Co., MO. She and James Lafayette Scroggins appeared on the census of 22 Jun 1860 Sugar Creek, Barry Co., MO. She d.4 Jan 1899 MO at age 62 and was bur. Keytesville City Cem., Keytesville, Chariton Co., MO.

James B. Hunt, b.18 Apr 1828 Monroe Co., TN. He d. ca.1855 Barry Co., MO.

Known children of Nancy Caroline[4] Abner and James B. Hunt:

187   i.   Malinda[5], b. 11 Sep 1847 Owsley Co., KY; m. William E. Murray.

      ii.   Mary Jane, b. ca. Jan 1850 Owsley Co., KY.

      iii.   Eliza Marie, b.15 Oct 1852 Clay Co., KY. She d. Christmas Eve, 24 Dec 1925 Stella, McDonald Co., MO, at age 73 and was bur. on 27 Dec 1925 Lowell Cem., Lowell, Cherokee Co., KS.

James Lafayette Scroggins, b. ca.1795 VA. He d. before 16 Jan 1867 Barry Co., MO.

Known children of Nancy Caroline[4] Abner and James Lafayette Scroggins:

      i.   Alfonzo[5], b. ca.1860 MO. He d.1921.

      ii.   Mary Lafetta, b.1865. She d.1919.

55. Malinda[4] Abner (John[3] Abney, Elisha[2], Abner[1]), b. ca.1830 Clay Co., KY. She m. Enos Bartlett, son of Samuel Bartlett and Margaret Tulley, on 24 Sep 1848 Owsley Co., KY. She d.1860 Nicholas Co., KY and was bur. Standiford Cem., Nicholas Co., KY.

Enos Bartlett, b.1813 Nicholas Co., KY. He m2. Mary J. "Polly" Abner (see #57 on page 54), daughter of John Abney Sr. and Millie Noble, ca.1862 KY. He d.12 Jun 1874 Neosho Twp., Cherokee Co., KS and was bur. Oak Hill Cem., Chetopa, Labette Co., KS.

Known children of Malinda[4] Abner and Enos Bartlett:

      i.   Nancy[5], b.26 Aug 1850 Clay Co., KY.

      ii.   John, b.21 Mar 1852 Blue Licks, Nicholas Co., KY. She d. Mar 1936 Lee Co., KY.

      iii.   William, b.24 Jan 1853 Nicholas Co., KY. He d.1878 Cherokee Co., KS.

      iv.   Jasper, b.28 Jan 1856 Nicholas Co., KY. He d.17 Jan 1885 Cherokee Co., KS, at age 28.

56. Lewis[4] Abner (John[3] Abney, Elisha[2], Abner[1]), b.10 Mar 1831 Clay Co., KY. Lewis and his younger brothers assumed the surname *Abner* (see Etymology in Appendix A, page 257). He m. Amelia Ann "Milly" Gum, daughter of William Gum and Lucinda Benton, on 11 Jul 1859 Clay Co., KY. He and Amelia Ann "Milly" Gum appeared on the censuses of 19 Jul 1860 Proctor, Owsley Co., KY, 8 Jul 1870 Lee Co., KY and 11 Jun 1880 Lee Co., KY. Lewis filed a petition on 1 Jul 1909, Lee Co., KY to have [his brother] William Abner's lands divided between his heirs, to wit:

O   Lewis Abner & John Abner, brothers of William Abner, 1/6 interest each.

O   2.-7. Robert Abnee, Milton Abnee, Fannie Hildreth (née Abnee), Effie D. Marlow (née Abnee), Charlie Abnee, Clarence Abnee, children of his deceased brother, Link Abner.

O   8. Sim Shy, son of Surilda Shy, deceased, who was a daughter of said Link Abner.

O   9.-11. Rowena H. Jefferson, Ora Lee Abner, Arris V. Abner, grandchildren of said Link Abner and children of William Abner, deceased, who was the son of Link Abner. Heirs #2-11 1/6 interest jointly.

○   12. Mollie Abner, widow of William Abner, deceased son of Link Abner. No real interest.

○   13.-14. John Bartlett & Charlie Bartlett, child and grandchild of Malinda Bartlett, 1/6 interest jointly (wife of Enos Bartlett)

○   15.-17. Perry Bartlett, Milton Bartlett and Laura Lutes, children and only heirs at law of Mary Bartlett, deceased sister of William Abner, 1/6 interest jointly (2nd wife of Enos Bartlett)

○   18.-19. Malinda Murray and Louisa Gay (later her name was corrected to Eliza), only children and only heirs at law of Nancy Hunt, deceased sister of said William Abner. 1/6 interest jointly. (wife of James Hunt).

Lewis appeared on the census of 27 Apr 1910 St. Helens, Lee Co., KY. He d.5 Nov 1911 Lee Co., KY, at age 80 and was bur. on 6 Nov 1911 Lutes Abner Cem., Primrose, Lee Co., KY.

  Amelia Ann "Milly" Gum, b.24 Nov 1839 KY. She d.19 Jul 1902 at age 62 and was bur. Lutes Abner Cem., Primrose, Lee Co., KY.
Known children of Lewis⁴ Abner and Amelia Ann "Milly" Gum:

	i.	Jesse B.⁵, b.1864 Owsley Co., KY. He d.Apr 1907 Fincastle, Lee Co., KY and was bur. Lutes Abner Cem., Primrose.
	ii.	Laura Frances, b.14 Sep 1865 Owsley Co., KY. She m. William P. Jones in 1887. She d.1 Apr 1919 at age 53 and was bur. Riverview Cem., Beattyville, Lee Co., KY.
188	iii.	John W., b. 25 May 1867 Owsley Co., KY; m. Georgia A. "Georgie" Ketchum.
189	iv.	Lucinda, b. 18 Dec 1869 Owsley Co., KY; m. Russell Scott.
190	v.	Malinda A, b. 3 Sep 1871 Lee Co., KY; m. Niniven Martin Quillen.
	vi.	Polly J., b. ca.1873 Lee Co., KY.
	vii.	Alcy E., b. ca.1875 Lee Co., KY.
	viii.	Phebe E., b.17 Apr 1876 Lee Co., KY. She d.18 Jul 1876 Lee Co., KY and was bur. Lutes Abner Cem., Primrose, KY.
191	ix.	Lewis A., b. 20 Feb 1879 Primrose, Lee Co., KY; m. Louchester "Chester" Cockerham; m. Sarah "Sallie" Taulbee.
192	x.	Nannie Emma, b. 22 Jan 1881 Lee Co., KY; m. Charles Henderson Bailey.
	xi.	Breckinridge "Breck", b.3 May 1882 Lee Co., KY. He m. Ulelar "Lelar" Davis on 6 Jul 1904 Lee Co., KY. He and Ulelar "Lelar" Davis were liv. on 27 Apr 1910 with his father, Lewis Abner Sr., St. Helens, Lee Co., KY. He and Ulelar "Lelar" Davis appeared on the census of 22 Jan 1920 Saint Helens, Lee Co., KY. He d.11 Oct 1935 KY at age 53.

  Ulelar "Lelar" Davis, b.15 Feb 1885 KY. She d.31 Mar 1964 KY at age 79 and was bur. Davis Cem., Monica, Lee Co., KY.

57. Mary J. "Polly"⁴ Abner (John³ Abney, Elisha², Abner¹), b. May 1840 Clay Co., KY. She m. Enos Bartlett, son of Samuel Bartlett and Margaret Tulley, ca.1862 KY. She d.14 Jun 1905 Cherokee Co., KS, at age 65 and was bur. Oak Hill Cem., Chetopa, Labette Co., KS.

  Enos Bartlett, b.1813 Nicholas Co., KY. He m1. Malinda Abner (see #55 on page 53), daughter of John Abney Sr. and Millie Noble, on 24 Sep 1848 Owsley Co., KY. He d.12 Jun 1874 Neosho Twp., Cherokee Co., KS and was bur. Oak Hill Cem., Chetopa, Labette Co., KS.
Known children of Mary J. "Polly"⁴ Abner and Enos Bartlett:

	i.	Perry⁵, b.5 Dec 1863 IN.
	ii.	Milton, b.27 Mar 1866 Platte Co., MO. He d.11 Oct 1922 Miami, Ottawa Co., OK, at age 56.
	iii.	Laura, b.9 Jun 1874 Neosho Twp., Cherokee Co., KS. She d.15 Mar 1966 Fayette Co., KY, at age 91.

58. John⁴ Abner Jr. (John³ Abney, Elisha², Abner¹), b.14 Dec 1844 Owsley Co., KY. He assumed the surname *Abner* (see Etymology in Appendix A, page 257). He was liv. on 17 Aug 1870 with brother, Lincoln Abnee, Lower Blue Lick, Nicholas Co., KY. He m. Sarah "Ellen" Lutes, daughter of Charles Lutes and Lucinda Plumber, on 8 Dec 1878 Lee Co., KY. He and Sarah "Ellen" Lutes appeared on the censuses of 11 Jun 1880 and 4 Jun 1900 Lee Co., KY; and 7 Jan 1920 Fincastle, Lee Co., KY. He d.14 Aug 1924 at age 79; bur. Lutes Abner Cem., Primrose, Lee Co., KY.

  Sarah "Ellen" Lutes, b.10 Apr 1855 Owsley Co., KY. She d.23 Jun 1927 KY at age 72 and was bur. Lutes Abner Cem., Primrose, KY.
Known children of John⁴ Abner Jr. and Sarah "Ellen" Lutes:

	i.	Callie⁵, b. Oct 1879 Lee Co., KY. She was a teacher.
	ii.	Pearl, b. Dec 1880 Lee Co., KY. She was a teacher.
	iii.	Nancy A., b.9 Sep 1882 Lee Co., KY. She d.7 Mar 1967 Fayette Co., KY, at age 84.
193	iv.	Grover "Cleveland," b. Christmas Eve, 24 Dec 1884 Lee Co., KY; m. Edna Mae Davis.
194	v.	John Henry, b. 14 Nov 1886 Fincastle, Lee Co., KY; m. Doll "Dolly" Drake.
195	vi.	William, b. 26 Nov 1890 Lee Co., KY; m. Oma Marshall.
196	vii.	Arthur "Doc," b. 3 Dec 1896 Lee Co., KY; m. Carrie Kincaid.

59. Abraham "Abel"⁴ Bishop (Mary³ Abner, Elisha² Abney, Abner¹), b.20 Apr 1812 Clay Co., KY. He m. Nancy Robinson on 8 Oct 1833 Madison Co., KY. He and Nancy Robinson appeared on the censuses of 30 Aug 1850, Jun 1860 and 17 Aug 1870 Clay Co., KY. He d.26 Apr 1887 Clay Co., KY, at age 75 and was bur. Bishop Bend Cem., Trixie, Clay Co., KY.

  Nancy Robinson, b.27 Apr 1812 KY. She d.28 Apr 1895 at age 83 and was bur. Bishop Bend Cem., Trixie, Clay Co., KY.
Known children of Abraham "Abel"⁴ Bishop and Nancy Robinson all b. Clay Co., KY:

197	i.	David G.⁵, b. 1835; m. Mary "Polly" Bishop.
	ii.	Elizabeth, b. ca.1838.
	iii.	Mary Ann, b. ca.1842.
	iv.	Samuel, b. ca.1845.
198	v.	John, b. Christmas Eve, 24 Dec 1848; m. Lucy "Catherine" Cole.
	vi.	Columbus, b. ca.1849.
	vii.	James A., b.20 Jan 1851. He d.23 Mar 1928 Clay Co., KY, at age 77.
	viii.	Sally, b. ca.1853.
	ix.	Drucilla, b. ca.Nov 1859.

60. Elisha Monroe⁴ Bishop (Mary³ Abner, Elisha² Abney, Abner¹), b.1813 Clay Co., KY. He m. Amy Johnson. He appeared as Head of Household on the census of 1840 Clay Co., KY. He and Amy Johnson appeared on the census of 29 Aug 1850 Clay Co., KY. He d.1888.

  Amy Johnson, b.1816. She d.1880.

Known children of Elisha Monroe[4] Bishop and Amy Johnson:

199	i.	Mary "Polly"[5], b. 22 Sep 1835 Clay Co., KY; m. Pvt. David G. Bishop (UA).
	ii.	John, b. ca.1840 KY.
	iii.	Christena, b. ca.1841 KY.
200	iv.	Alexander "Alex," b. 22 Aug 1842 Teges, Clay Co., KY; m. (n.n.).
	v.	James, b. ca.1847 KY.
201	vi.	Nancy, b. ca.1849 KY; m. Abijah Gabbard.
	vii.	Elisha Monroe Jr., b.9 Jun 1859 Clay Co., KY. He d.15 Oct 1947 Clay Co., KY, at age 88 and was bur. Bishop Cem., Trixie, Clay Co., KY.

61. **William S.[4] Bishop** (Mary[3] Abner, Elisha[2] Abney, Abner[1]), b.1818 Clay Co., KY. He m. Susan Barrett ca.1839. He appeared as Head of Household on the census of 1840 Clay Co., KY. He and Susan Barrett appeared on the census of 29 Aug 1850 Clay Co., KY. He d.30 Apr 1888 Clay Co., KY and was bur. Laurel Point Cem., Clay Co., KY.

Susan Barrett, b.1826. She d.1902.
Known children of William S.[4] Bishop and Susan Barrett all b. KY:

i.	Theophilus[5], b. ca.1841.
ii.	William, b. ca.1843.
iii.	Richard, b. ca.1845.
iv.	Mary, b. ca.1847.
v.	Squire, b. ca.1850.
vi.	James, b. ca.Jul 1850.

62. **Bryson "Brice"[4] Bishop** (Mary[3] Abner, Elisha[2] Abney, Abner[1]), b.1822 Clay Co., KY. He m. Eliza "Lizie" Allen. He appeared on the census of 29 Aug 1850 Clay Co., KY. He d.1870.

Eliza "Lizie" Allen, b.1825. She was liv. on 15 Jun 1900 with son-in-law, Robert Abner, Clay Co., KY.
Known children of Bryson "Brice"[4] Bishop and Eliza "Lizie" Allen:

	i.	William[5], b. ca.1842 KY.
	ii.	Sally, b. ca.1845 KY.
	iii.	Nancy, b. ca.1847 KY.
202	iv.	Esther, b. 1 Oct 1862 Clay Co., KY; m. Robert Abner.

63. **Charles[4] Smith** (Margaret[3] Abner, Elisha[2] Abney, Abner[1]), b.1822 Clay Co., KY. He m. Margaret Anglin, daughter of Rev. James Anglin and Jane Barrett, on 12 Jan 1842 Clay Co., KY.

Margaret Anglin, b.1822 Clay Co., KY.
Known children of Charles[4] Smith and Margaret Anglin:

	i.	James[5], b. ca.1843 KY.
	ii.	Isham, b. ca.1845 KY.
	iii.	Jane, b. ca.1847 KY.
	iv.	Susan, b. ca.1848 KY.
	v.	Nancy Ann, b.Feb 1850 KY.
203	vi.	Mary Ann "Polly," b. 7 Jul 1859 Jackson Co., KY; m. Newton Johnson.

64. **Enoch[4] Abner Jr.** (Enoch[3] Abney, Elisha[2], Abner[1]), b. ca.1823 Clay Co., KY. He m. Catherine Lucas on 13 Jan 1842. He and Catherine Lucas appeared on the censuses of 29 Jul 1850, 21 Jun 1860, 1 Aug 1870 and 11 Jun 1880 Clay Co., KY and d. sometime after the 1880 census and was bur. Abner-Stewart Cem., Bluehole, Clay Co., KY. (Catherine Lucas d.1912.)
Known children of Enoch[4] Abner Jr. and Catherine Lucas all born in Clay Co., KY:

205	i.	William Squire[5], b. 4 Dec 1842 Clay Co., KY; m. Julia Elizabeth Cottongim.
	ii.	John, b.ca.1844 and d.1917 Clay Co., KY and was bur. Esau-Gabbard Cem., Ricetown, Owsley Co., KY.
206	iii.	Richard Allen, b. 9 Jun 1848 Clay Co., KY; m1. M. Murray; m2. Martha Ann Abner; m3. S. Stewart; m4. Nancy France.
207	iv.	Mary, b. 7 Sep 1849 Clay Co., KY.
208	v.	Susan, b. 7 Sep 1852 Clay Co., KY; m1. Jarvis Pinner; m2. Theophilus T. Collett.
209	vi.	Milton, b. ca.10 Oct 1854 Clay Co., KY; m. Mariah Stewart.
210	vii.	Lucy, b. ca.1857 Clay Co., KY; m. John E. Roberts.
211	viii.	Theophilus General "Theo," b. 27 Aug 1861 Clay Co., KY; m. Mary "Isabella" Stewart.
	ix.	Sarah C, b.1865. She m1. John B. Hayes on 8 Jun 1882 Clay Co., KY. She m2. William Toulman Garrard. She d.1932 and was bur. Winchester Cem., Winchester, Clark Co., KY. (John B. Hayes, b. ca. 1850.) William Toulman Garrard, b.1871. He d.1928 and was bur. Winchester Cem., Winchester, Clark Co., KY.

65. **Hila Ann "Hiley"[4] Abner** (Enoch[3] Abney, Elisha[2], Abner[1]), b. ca.1825 Clay Co., KY. She m. James Wells on 2 Oct 1841 Clay Co., KY. She and James Wells appeared on the censuses of 14 Sep 1850, 17 Jul 1860, 12 Jul 1870 and 23 Jun 1880 Clay Co., KY.

James Wells, b. ca.1827 KY.
Known children of Hila Ann "Hiley"[4] Abner and James Wells all b. Clay Co., KY:

i.	Sarah "Sally"[5], b. ca.1843.
ii.	Eliza "Lizie", b. ca.1851.
iii.	Alabama, b.5 Feb 1852.
iv.	Lucinda, b.19 Jul 1855.
v.	America, b. ca.1858.
vi.	Matilda, b. ca.1862.
vii.	Jane, b. ca.1864.
viii.	John, b. ca.1866.

66. Andrew "Jackson"[4] Abney (Enoch[3], Elisha[2], Abner[1]), b.4 Mar 1826 Clay Co., KY. He lived ca.1846 Savannah, Andrew Co., MO. He m1. Mary "Margaret" Moody on 14 Sep 1847 Andrew Co., MO. He and Mary "Margaret" Moody appeared on the censuses of 4 Oct 1850 Andrew Co., MO (where he was a blacksmith); 3 Jul 1860 Savannah, Andrew Co., MO. He lived in 1863 Denver, Denver Co., CO. He lived in 1864 NE. He and his brother, James C. Abney were in the stock-raising business ca.1866, Pine Bluffs, Laramie Co., WY. He lived in 1866 Cheyenne, Laramie Co., WY. He and Mary "Margaret" Moody appeared on the census of 16 Jun 1870 Cheyenne, Laramie Co., WY. He appeared on the census of 28 Jun 1880 Weld Co., CO. He m2. L.A. Holley on 28 Sep 1889 Denver, Denver Co., CO. He d.16 Mar 1896 Denver, Denver Co., CO, at age 70 and was bur. Lakeview Cem., Cheyenne, Laramie Co., WY. From Wyoming Tribune no. 89 March 17, 1896 page 4:

The death of Jackson Abney in Denver on Saturday evening brings to the memory of many old timers in Cheyenne recollections of early experiences in the new West. More than thirty years ago Jackson Abney was an active contractor, freighter and Indian fighter over those stretches of country now occupied by railroads, ranches and irrigated homes.

The Denver Republican prints the following interesting sketch of his life both before he came west in 1863, and after his arrival upon the plains, which were populated by buffalo and coyotes and terrorized by savages.

Few westerners have had a more thrilling and interesting life experience than Jackson Abney. He was a Kentuckian, being b.Lexington on March 4, 1826. For nineteen years he resided there and received the best education that Lexington could afford and this was very good. When 20 he moved to Missouri to engage in the dry goods business and afterward in stock raising. In the course of his migrations he arrived at St. Joseph, where he carried on the same business but he lived in Savannah, some miles down the Missouri river, where he conducted a large plantation, employing 150 slaves. Those were the times of the abolitionists.

Nowhere did they fight with more zeal in and about Kansas. Owning so many slaves naturally made Mr. Abney a mark for abolitionists and he had great difficulty in keeping them. The abolitionists would make frequent raids on his plantation and haul away the slaves to Kansas. By and by he had none left. In all that border warfare he took little part, having no inclination to fight his fellow men in such a cause. When matters became even more serious after the civil war broke out and his family was unsafe when he was away - as he was frequently absent on western expeditions - he moved to Denver with his wife and six children in 1863.

The emigration to Denver in '63 was not Mr. Abney's first appearance here: he had been on several visits before that. His business had latterly become that of a "freighter" and many were the long caravans he led across the plains. At least sixteen times he crossed them and almost each time at the peril of his life from Indians.

Mr. Abney built a residence on Arapahoe street where the Cooper-Hagus store now is and maintained an extensive corral and outfitting place at Blake and Fifteenth street. He was a conspicuous figure in the great Cherry creek flood in 1864 and was especially daring in the rescue of four negroes out of a tree. In all the city's Indian troubles he took a leading part and there was no more valiant defender of women and children and property than he.

In 1864 he was for a brief time in Nebraska, he became a contractor of the Union Pacific railway and followed the road as far as Cheyenne. After that he went into the business of stock raising in Wyoming conducting it with his brother, James C. Abney, and he was at one time offered $150,000 for his interest in it. His ranch was in the Pine Bluffs region. He built one of the first houses in Cheyenne.

He was m. twice. In 1847 he m. Miss May(Margaret) Moody and in 1889 Mrs. L.A. Lawley of Denver. He had in all ten children, seven girls and three boys. Mrs. Florence Small of New Mexico, Mrs. Dr. Anna Grace Corey of Denver, James Abney, Mrs. C.B. Clay and Miss Margaret Abney survive him, and also his second wife.

Mr. Abney died of an acute attack of stomach trouble at the age of 70 years.

Mary "Margaret" Moody, b.1 Jun 1828 Richland Co., OH. She d.26 Jun 1879 Cheyenne, Laramie Co., WY, at age 51.
Known children of Andrew "Jackson"[4] Abney and Mary "Margaret" Moody:

        i.   Charles[5], b. ca.1848 Savannah, Andrew Co., MO; He m. (n.n.). He d.20 Apr 1849 MO.
212   ii. Martha Alice, b. ca.Mar 1850 Savannah, Andrew Co., MO; m. Charles H. Lamkin.
      iii. Julia Emmeline, b.Dec 1851 Savannah, Andrew Co., MO. She d.16 Sep 1852 Savannah, Andrew Co., MO and was bur. Savannah Cem., Savannah, Andrew Co., MO.
      iv. Frances E., b. ca.1854 Savannah, Andrew Co., MO.
      v. Anna Grace "Annie", b.1856 Andrew Co., MO. She m1. John C. Burns (of Texas) on 6 Mar 1872 Laramie Co., WY. She m2. Dr. George Washington Corey in 1885 Cheyenne, Laramie Co., WY. She d.20 Apr 1897 Sheridan Hotel, Telluride, San Miguel Co., CO and was bur. Lone Tree Cem., San Miguel Co., CO.
            Dr. George Washington Corey, b.1833. He d.1913.
213   vi. Mary Agnes, b. New Year's Eve, 31 Dec 1858 Savannah, Andrew Co., MO; m. Charles Edward Clay.
214   vii. James M., b. 20 Jan 1860 Savannah, Andrew Co., MO; m1. Frances Margaret "Fannie" Gill; m2. Opal Margaret Houser.
     viii. Fannie "Margaret", b. Oct 1872 WY. She was liv. on 3 Jun 1880 with brother-in-law, Chas. E. Clay, Cheyenne, Laramie Co., WY. She m. James Carragher in 1899. She and James Carragher appeared on the census of 17 Jun 1900 Albany Co., WY. She d.1912 and was bur. Douglas Park Cem., Douglas, Converse Co., WY.
            James Carragher, b.12 Jun 1854 Livingston Co., NY. He d.28 Dec 1904 Douglas, Converse Co., WY, at age 50 and was bur. Douglas Park Cem., Douglas, Converse Co., WY.

There were no known children of Andrew "Jackson"[4] Abney and L.A. Holley.

67. Nancy E.[4] Abner (Enoch[3] Abney, Elisha[2], Abner[1]), b.4 Apr 1833 Clay Co., KY. She m. Pvt. Benjamin Wood (CSA) ca.1847. She and Pvt. Benjamin Wood (CSA) appeared on the census of 15 Nov 1850 Marion Co., AR. She d.26 Nov 1930 Kansas City, Jackson Co., MO, at age 97 and was bur. Wade Chapel Cem., Republic, Greene Co., MO.
Pvt. Benjamin Wood (CSA), b.25 Aug 1830 AR. He was captured on 1 Oct 1864 Jefferson City, MO. He d.24 Jan 1865 (pneumonia), Madison Co., IL, at age 34 and was bur. Confederate Cem., Alton, Madison Co., IL.
Known children of Nancy E.[4] Abner and Pvt. Benjamin Wood (CSA):

      i. Berry Jackson[5], b.5 Nov 1848 AR. He d.10 Nov 1930 Greene Co., MO, at age 82 and was bur. Wade Chapel Cem., Republic, Greene Co., MO.
      ii. Benjamin "Benny."
     iii. Mary.
     iv. Sarah Alice, b.1857. She d.1928.
     v. Caroline Charity, b.1859. She d.1944.
     vi. Martha A., b.1862. She d.1933.

68. Martha Jane*4* Abney (Enoch*3*, Elisha*2*, Abner*1*), b. ca.1837 Clay Co., KY. She m. William Garner on 20 Oct 1853 Stone Co., MO. She d. Jul 1879 Alpine, Clark Co., AR.

William Garner, b. ca.1834 McNary Co., IA. He d. ca.1884 Alpine, Clark Co., AR.

Known children of Martha Jane*4* Abney and William Garner:

      i.   Susanna H.*5*, b. ca.1856. She was liv. in 1870 Alpine, Clark Co., AR.

215   ii. James L., b. 11 Mar 1857 Alpine, Clark Co., AR; m1. Sarah Chapman; m2. Julia Elizabeth Fox.

69. Isabelle*4* McClenachan (Sarah*3* Abney, John*2*, Abner*1*), b.4 May 1801 Barren Co., KY. She m. David W. Merry on 29 Apr 1822 Barren Co., KY and was bur. Old Nebo Cem., Greenville, Bond Co., IL. She d. New Year's Eve, 31 Jan 1873 Bond Co., IL, at age 71.

David W. Merry, b.6 Mar 1801 VA. He d.22 Jan 1857 Bond Co., IL, at age 55 and was bur. Old Nebo Cem., Greenville, Bond Co., IL.

Known children of Isabelle*4* McClenachan and David W. Merry:

      i.   William*5*, b.28 Jan 1824 KY. He m. Charlotte Ann Rodgers. and had issue. He d.29 Nov 1902 WI at age 78 and was bur. Greenwood Cem., Platteville, Grant Co., WI.

           Charlotte Ann Rodgers, b.29 Aug 1831 IL. She d.20 Jan 1911 IL at age 79 and was bur. Greenwood Cem.

     ii. Thomas O., b.29 Apr 1826 (calculated birth date), KY. He d.13 Mar 1844 Bond Co., IL, at age 17.

    iii. Robert, b.8 Feb 1829. He m. Mary E. Clouse in 1849 and had issue. He d.26 May 1885 Greenville, Bond Co., IL, at age 56 and was bur. Hazel Dell Cem., Greenville, Bond Co., IL.

           Mary E. Clouse, b.28 Oct 1834 and d.5 Aug 1897 Bond Co., IL, at age 62 and was bur. Hazel Dell Cem.

    iv. James Crawford, b.1830. He d.1899.

     v. Anne Watt, b.1832. She d.1911.

    vi. Samuel, b.1834. He d.1898.

   vii. Frederick K., b.1836. He d.1883.

  viii. Rachel E., b.1838. She d.1869.

    ix. Andrew B., b.1840. He d.1906.

     x. David W., b.1843. He d.1892.

    xi. Charles, b.1872. He d.1872.

   xii. Leona Mary, b.1874. She d.1875.

70. Jane Ann*4* McClenachan (Sarah*3* Abney, John*2*, Abner*1*), b. Christmas Eve, 24 Dec 1804 Barren Co., KY. She m. Johnson Monroe Jr., son of Johnson Monroe Sr. and Amelia Hooper, on 21 May 1823 Barren Co., KY. She d.28 Oct 1880 Wayne Co., IL, at age 75.

Johnson Monroe Jr., b. ca.1790 Lunenburg Co., VA. He migrated from Lunenburg County to Greenville Co., SC and followed his father to Barren County, Virginia. Johnson died ca.1838 while on a trip from Barren County, VA to Wayne County, IL. His estate was probated on 15 Oct 1838 Barren Co., KY.

Known children of Jane Ann*4* McClenachan and Johnson Monroe Jr.:

      i.   Ester*5* m. (n.n.) Cook.

216   ii. Martha C., b. 23 Mar 1826 Barren Co., KY; m. Absalom G. Owen.

217   iii. Elizabeth, b. 19 Jul 1829 Barren Co., KY; m. David Baker.

218   iv. Emily, b. 30 Dec 1833 Barren Co., KY; m1. Jacob Baker; m2. John Wesley Cissna.

     v. James C., b.21 Dec 1835. He m. Elizabeth Stevens. He d.23 Jun 1919 Wayne Co., IL, at age 83 and was bur. Hopewell Cem., Wayne City, Wayne Co., IL.

           Elizabeth Stevens, b.14 Apr 1838. She d.20 Nov 1920 Wayne Co., IL, at age 82.

    vi. Sarah, b.1836. She m. John I. Farmer. She d.1897 Wayne Co., IL and was bur. Ebenezer Cem., Wayne Co., IL.

   vii. David Crockett, b. New Year's Day, 1 Jan 1839. He m. Margaret R. Duke on 22 Mar 1861. He d.16 Mar 1920 Wayne Co., IL, at age 81 and was bur. Ebenezer Cem., Wayne Co., IL.

           Margaret R. Duke, b.19 Feb 1841. She d.12 Sep 1912 at age 71.

71. Tamar*4* McClenachan (Sarah*3* Abney, John*2*, Abner*1*), b.1810 Barren Co., KY. She m1. David Gerald McKinney Sr. on 13 Jan 1834. She m2. William Campbell Rhea Jr. (widower of her first cousin, Isabella Abney, see #81), son of William Campbell Rhea Sr. and Elizabeth Brownlee, on 6 Sep 1845 Barren Co., KY. She and William Campbell Rhea Jr. appeared on the censuses of 23 Jul 1850 and 28 Aug 1860 Barren Co., KY. She d.1899 Barren Co., KY.

David Gerald McKinney Sr, b.1809 VA. He d.1845 Barren Co., KY.

Known children of Tamar*4* McClenachan and David Gerald McKinney Sr.:

      i.   William J.*5*, b.1835 KY.

     ii. Mary Evans, b. ca.1837 KY.

    iii. John R., b. ca.1839 KY.

219   iv. David Gerald, b. Oct 1841 Barren Co., KY; m. Sallie Ann Evans.

William Campbell Rhea Jr, b.1790 Rockbridge Co., VA. He m1. Isabella Abney and had issue (see #81 on page 60), daughter of John Key Abney and Tamar Ann Robinson, on 30 Mar 1824 Green Co., KY. He appeared as Head of Household on the census of 1840 Green Co., KY. He d.1861 Glasgow, Barren Co., KY.

Known children of Tamar*4* McClenachan and William Campbell Rhea Jr. all b. Barren Co., KY:

220   i.   William Zachariah Taylor "Zack"*5*, b. 1849; m. Matilda Margaret Roach.

     ii. J.C., b.1850.

    iii. N.C., b.1853.

72. Mary Elizabeth "Beth"*4* McClenachan (Sarah*3* Abney, John*2*, Abner*1*), b.1812 Barren Co., KY. She m. James Owen on 20 Oct 1840 Barren Co., KY. She d.11 Mar 1852 Hart Co., KY.

Known child of Mary Elizabeth "Beth"*4* McClenachan and James Owen:

      i.   Martha Jane*5*, b.1849. She d.1886.

73. John Abney⁴ North (Margaret³ Abney, John², Abner¹), b.15 Dec 1794 Staunton, Augusta Co., VA. He m. Charlotte Blain, daughter of Rev. Daniel Blain & Mary Hanna, on 15 Jul 1819 Rockbridge Co., VA. He and Charlotte Blain appeared on the census of 23 Aug 1850 Greenbrier Co., VA. He d.26 Sep 1857 Lewisburg, Greenbrier Co., WV, at age 62 and was bur. Old Stone Presbyterian Ch. Cem., Lewisburg, Greenbrier Co., WV.
     Charlotte Blain, b.23 Apr 1800 Lexington, Rockbridge Co., VA. She d.22 Apr 1883 Caldwell, Greenbrier Co., WV, at age 82 and was bur. Old Stone Presbyterian Ch. Cem., Lewisburg, Greenbrier Co., WV.
Known children of John Abney⁴ North and Charlotte Blain:
        i.   Margaret A.⁵, b. Aug 1820. She m. Robert Johnston in 1845. She d.Jun 1851 at age 30 and was bur. on 4 Jun 1851 Shockoe Hill Cem., Richmond, VA.
             Rep. Robert Johnston (CSA), b.1818. Judge (1880-1885), Robert served in the Virginia Legislature. At the division, he represented Virginia's 15ᵗʰ District in the provisional, first and second Confederate Congress. He m2. Laura Ellen Criss. He died of Tuberculosis at Harrisonburg, VA in 1885 and was buried in Woodbine Cem., Harrisonburg, VA.
        ii.   Mary E., b.16 May 1822 Lewisburg, Greenbrier Co., WV. She m. Thomas Flournoy Hamner. She d.16 Jul 1855 at age 33 and was bur. Old Stone Presbyterian Ch. Cem., Lewisburg, Greenbrier Co., WV.
        iii.   Isabella Abney, b.21 Jun 1824 Lewisburg, Greenbrier Co., WV. She m. James Robinson Caldwell on 17 Nov 1851. She d.7 May 1897 at age 72 and was bur. Old Stone Presbyterian Ch. Cem., Lewisburg, Greenbrier Co., WV.
             James Robinson Caldwell, b.17 Aug 1820 Augusta Co., VA. He d.1 Feb 1904 at age 83 and was bur. Old Stone.
        iv.   Martha Jane, b.7 Jul 1828 Lewisburg, Greenbrier Co., WV. She m. Robert Flournoy Dennis. She d.27 Sep 1895 at age 67 and was bur. Old Stone Presbyterian Ch. Cem., Lewisburg, Greenbrier Co., WV.
             Robert Flournoy Dennis, b.28 Sep 1823 Charlotte Co., VA. He d.8 Oct 1897 at age 74 and was bur. Old Stone.

74. Elizabeth "Betsy"⁴ Abney (William³, John², Abner¹), b.31 Mar 1798 Augusta Co., VA. She m. Byrd S. Grills, son of John Grills Sr, on 5 Jan 1820. She and Byrd S. Grills appeared on the census of 30 Nov 1850 Montgomery Co., VA. She d.3 Jun 1854 at age 56.
     Byrd S. Grills, b. ca.1795 VA. He appeared as Head of Household on the census of 1820 Newbern, Montgomery Co., VA, 1830 Christiansburg, Montgomery Co., VA. and 1840 Newbern, Pulaski Co., VA.
Known children of Elizabeth "Betsy"⁴ Abney and Byrd S. Grills all b. VA:
        i.   (son)⁵, b. ca.1820.
        ii.   (dau), b. ca.1823.
        iii.   (dau), b. ca.1826.
        iv.   (dau), b. ca.1830.
        v.   (son), b. ca.1836.

75. Letticia⁴ Abney (William³, John², Abner¹), b.17 Jan 1802 Augusta Co., VA. She m. Adam Swink on 4 Jan 1838 Augusta Co., VA. She and Adam Swink appeared on the census of 20 Sep 1850 Augusta Co., VA. She d.22 Jun 1856 at age 54 and was bur. Bethel Presbyterian Ch. Cem., Middlebrook, Augusta Co., VA.
     Adam Swink, b.1 Oct 1786 VA. He m. Margaret Wilson in 1812. He d.8 Dec 1862 at age 76 and was bur. Bethel Presbyterian Ch. Cem.
Known children of Letticia⁴ Abney and Adam Swink:
        i.   Elizabeth A.⁵, b. ca.1838. She d.1914.
        ii.   Lavlet Ella, b.1840. She d.1894.
        iii.   Calvin Lycurgus, b.1843. He d.1930.

76. Mary Jane⁴ Abney (William³, John², Abner¹), b.21 Dec 1803 Augusta Co., VA. She m. Jefferson Burr Kinsolving, son of James M. Kinsolving Sr., RS and Elizabeth Leigh, on 21 Dec 1826. She and Jefferson Burr Kinsolving appeared on the census of 12 Sep 1850 Caldwell Co., KY. She, appeared as Head of Household on the census of 12 Jun 1860 Princeton, Caldwell Co., KY (where she was referred to as *Family Governess.* She d.14 Feb 1863 KY at age 59.
     Jefferson Burr Kinsolving, b.4 Jun 1801 VA. He appeared as Head of Household on the census of 1830 Albemarle Co., VA and 1840 Newbern, Dyer Co., TN. He d.15 Sep 1854 at age 53.
Known children of Mary Jane⁴ Abney and Jefferson Burr Kinsolving all b. VA:
        i.   Elizabeth M.⁵, b. ca.1827. She d. before 1840.
   221 ii.   William Abney "Will," b. 23 Oct 1829; m. Sorilda Elizabeth Glenn.
        iii.   Xistera V., b. ca.1832.
        iv.   George Washington, b. ca.1834.
        v.   Andrew Jackson, b. ca.1837.
        vi.   Virginia Anne, b. ca.1841. She m. John Prince ca.1859. She and John Prince were living with her mother, *M. Kinsolving* on the census of 12 Jun 1860, Princeton, Caldwell Co., KY.
             John Prince, b. ca.1841 GA.

77. William Austine⁴ Abney (William³, John², Abner¹)., b.21 May 1806 Augusta Co., VA. In his father's will, William was given a negro boy named "Benjamin." William m. Virginia Lewis Kinsolving, daughter of George Washington Kinsolving and Ann Rogers Barksdale, on 20 Feb 1830 Albermarle Co., VA. He appeared as Head of Household on the census of 1840 Augusta Co., VA. He and Virginia Lewis Kinsolving appeared on the censuses of 20 Sep 1850 Augusta Co., VA, 26 Jul 1860 Staunton, Augusta Co., VA and 23 Aug 1870 South River, Augusta Co., VA. He d.12 Mar 1877 Mint Spring, Augusta Co., VA, at age 70 and was bur. Abney Family Cem., Mint Spring, Augusta Co., VA.
     Virginia Lewis Kinsolving, b.Mar 1807 Albemarle Co., VA. She d.12 Mar 1871 Augusta Co., VA and was bur. Abney Family Cem.
Known children of William Austine⁴ Abney and Virginia Lewis Kinsolving:
   222 i.   Cornelia Ann⁵, b. Oct 1831 Staunton, Augusta Co., VA; m. John Grills.
        ii.   Celestine W., b.13 Sep 1833 VA. d.23 Dec 1893 VA at age 60 and was bur. Thornrose Cem., City of Staunton, VA.
   223 iii.   Ulysses Van Buren, b. 1836 Staunton, Augusta Co., VA; m. Melissa Bledsoe.
        iv.   Virginia Louise, b.Oct 1838 VA. She was liv. on 9 Jul 1900 with brother, Wm. G. Abney, South River, Augusta Co., VA. She was liv. on 2 May 1910 with brother, William G. Abney, South River, Augusta Co., VA. She d.30 Dec 1913 City of Staunton, VA, at age 75 and was bur. Thornrose Cem., City of Staunton, VA. Her obituary read:

> *Miss Virginia Abney died at the Augusta Sanatorium yesterday at 10:30 o' clock, and her remains were taken to her home near Brookwood. Miss Abney, was a member of Emmanuel Episcopal church, was 75 years of age, and well known and had many friends in both city and county. She was a sister of W. G. Abney, a prominent county man, and a former member of the vestry of Emmanuel church. Mr. Abney and two sisters, Misses Ella and Belle, both at home, survive her. The funeral will be held at one o'clock Wednesday at the home near Brookwood, and burial will be in Thornrose cemetery at 3:30 o'clock.*

    v.   *Pvt.* William George (CSA), b.31 Aug 1840 Brookwood, Augusta Co., VA. He began military service on 18 Apr 1861 private, Co. E, 5th VA Inf., Greenville, Augusta Co., VA. On 15 Feb 1862 he re-enlisted. He was wounded in his side on 27 Jun 1862 at Gaines' Mill, VA. He was wounded again on 3 May 1863 at Chancellorsville, VA. He was wounded again, this time in the ear on 5 May 1864 at Wilderness, VA. He was present at Lee's Surrender at Appomattox Court House, VA on 9 Apr 1865. He was a Member of the Stonewall Jackson Camp #25, Confederate Veterans in 1893. He, appeared as Head of Household on the census of 9 Jul 1900 South River, Augusta Co., VA and 2 May 1910 South River, Augusta Co., VA. He d.3 Sep 1917 Mint Spring, Augusta Co., VA, at age 77 and was bur. Thornrose Cem., City of Staunton, VA.

    vi.   Ella Parks, b. 23 Aug 1842 Augusta Co., VA. She was living on 9 Jul 1900 and 2 May 1910 with her brother, William G. Abney. South River, Augusta Co., VA. She died 9 Sep 1922 in Brookwood, Augusta Co., VA and was buried in Thornrose Cem., City of Staunton, VA. Her obituary read: *Miss Ella P. Abney, 80 years old, died at the home of her grand-nephew, J. Abney Clarkson, this morning at 1:20 o'clock following an illness of nine years. Death was not unexpected. Services will be held from the Clarkson home Sunday afternoon at three o'clock, conducted by the Rev. J. J. Gravatt Jr., rector of Trinity church. Miss Abney had been a member of Emmanuel church since it was founded. Burial will be in Thornrose cemetery. Miss Abney leaves one sister, Miss Isabel K. Abney; one nephew, W. O. Abney, and one niece, Miss Virginia Grills. She was a daughter of the late William A. and Virginia Abney. Miss Abney was paralyzed nine years ago. She was a native of Augusta county, having been born that same place where she died.*

    vii.   Ovid L. (CSA), b.1844. He began military service on 10 Nov 1862 Co. E, 5th VA Inf. Reg., VA. He d.11 Nov 1862 in his father's home, Augusta Co., VA and was bur. Abney Family Cem., Mint Spring, Augusta Co., VA.

    viii.   Isabelle Kinsolving, b.14 Aug 1845 Augusta Co., VA. She was liv. on 9 Jul 1900 and 2 May 1910 with brother, William G. Abney, South River, Augusta Co., VA. She d.6 Oct 1922 Augusta Co., VA, at age 77 and was bur. Thornrose Cem., City of Staunton, VA. Her obituary read: *Miss Isabelle Kinsolving Abney, died at "Solitude," her home near Brookwood, at ten o'clock Friday night. She had been in decling <sic> health for a number of years, and during the last two months her condition was critical practically all the time. Miss Abney was seventy-six years old and was born and spent her entire life where she died. She was the last of the Abney family. Miss Ella Parks Abney, a sister, died at "Solitude," four weeks ago. Funeral services will be held from the house this afternoon at three o'clock, conducted by the Rev. J. Lewis Gibbs, rector of Emmanuel Episcopal church, of which Miss Abney had been a member since it was founded. Bearers will be: active, G. S. Cecil, W. N. Danner, J. S. Cochran, Dr. W. F. Deekens, R. S. Black, R. S. Moffett; honorary, Lacy Black, Alexander F. Robertson, Jos. B. Woodward, Jos. A. Glasgow. Miss Abney is survived by a nephew, W. O. Abney, of Charleston, W. Va., andn a niece, Miss Virginia Grills. J. Abney Clarkson is a great nephew of the deceased.*

78. Isabella[4] Abney (William[3], John[2], Abner[1]), b.21 Nov 1809 Augusta Co., VA. She m. Charles T. Grills, son of John Grills Sr, on 24 Nov 1829 Augusta Co., VA. She d.26 Dec 1845 Barren Co., KY, at age 36.

    Charles T. Grills, b. ca.1800 VA. He appeared as Head of Household on the census of 1830 Christianburg, Montgomery Co., VA.
Known children of Isabella[4] Abney and Charles T. Grills both b. Montgomery Co., VA:

  224   i.   John[5], b. ca.1832; m. Cornelia Ann Abney.

          ii.   Byrd, b.23 Oct 1834. He m. Sarah Minerva "Minnie" Abney, daughter of *Sen.* Shelton S. Abney and Martha Davis, on 2 Oct 1859. He and Sarah Minerva "Minnie" Abney were liv. on 19 Jun 1860 with father-in-law, S.S. Abney, Hawcreek Twp., Augusta Co., VA. He d.17 Sep 1861 Typhoid Fever, Warsaw, MO, at age 26 and was bur. Saline Co., MO.

               Sarah Minerva "Minnie" Abney, b.4 Oct 1836 Greenville, Augusta Co., VA. She m2. *Judge* John C. Thompson on 17 Jun 1866. She m3. George Alexander Murrell on 2 Jan 1879. She d.25 Jan 1888 Saline Co., MO, at age 51.

79. *Sen.* Shelton Spillsbury[4] Abney (US Senator) (William[3], John[2], Abner[1]), b.26 Jun 1813 Staunton, Augusta Co., VA. In his father's will, he was given a negro boy named "Alexander". Shelton was a farmer and merchant who became a U.S. Senator. He m. Martha Jane Davis, daughter of William Caldwell Davis and Sarah Van Lear, on 5 Dec 1835 Staunton, Augusta Co., VA. He appeared as Head of Household on the census of 1840 Augusta Co., VA. He and Martha Jane Davis appeared on the census of 13 Sep 1850 Augusta Co., VA. He was made postmaster on 1 Jun 1853 Staunton, Augusta Co., VA. He migrated in 1855 Saline Co., MO. He was elected 1858 U.S. Representative out of Morgan Co., MO. He and Martha Jane Davis appeared on the census of 19 Jun 1860 and 21 Jul 1870 Haw Creek Twp., Augusta Co., VA. He was elected U.S. Senator for the 28th District in Missouri in 1872 and served until 1876. He and Martha Jane Davis appeared on the census of 28 Jun 1880 Haw Creek, Augusta Co., VA. In 1885 he moved to Saline Co., MO and in 1886 was living near Versailles, Morgan Co., MO. He d.11 Mar 1887 Morgan Co., MO, at age 73 and was bur. (in a field) in Stover, Morgan Co., MO. His estate was probated on 1 Apr 1887.

    Martha Jane Davis, b.19 Mar 1819 Augusta Co., VA. She d.8 Sep 1893 Morgan Co., MO, at age 74 and was bur. (in a field) in Stover.
Known children of Sen. Shelton Spillsbury[4] Abney (US Senator) and Martha Jane Davis:

  225   i.   Sarah Minerva "Minnie"[5], b. 4 Oct 1836 Greenville, Augusta Co., VA; m1. Byrd Grills (CSA); m2. *Judge* John C. Thompson; m3. George Alexander Murrell.

  226   ii.   Elizabeth McClenachan "Lizzie," b. 3 Feb 1839 Augusta Co., VA; m. John P. Ingram Sr.

          iii.   John Hanger, b.18 Jan 1843 Augusta Co., VA. He d.13 Sep 1863 from Diphtheria, Saline Co., MO, at age 20.

  227   iv.   William Lycurgus, b. 9 Feb 1846 Augusta Co., VA; m. Mary Frances "Fanny" Geisinger.

  228   v.   Margaret Letticia "Maggie," b. 10 Oct 1849 Augusta Co., VA; m. John Huston Wilhelm.

80. John Jacob[4] Fackler (Nancy[3] Abney, John[2], Abner[1]), b.1801 Staunton, Augusta Co., VA. He m. Elizabeth Melvina Turner on 17 Jan 1826 Madison Co., AL. He appeared as Head of Household on the census of 1830 Huntsville, Madison Co., AL. He and Elizabeth Melvina Turner appeared on the census of 17 Dec 1850 Huntsville, Marion Co., AL. He d.30 Jul 1874 Huntsville, Madison Co., AL and was bur. Maple Hill Cem., Huntsville, Madison Co., AL.

    Elizabeth Melvina Turner, b.1804 VA. She d.14 Dec 1871 Madison Co., AL.

Known children of John Jacob[4] Fackler and Elizabeth Melvina Turner all b. AL:
    i.   Calvin Morgan[5], b. ca.1827. He d.1864.
    ii.   John Turner, b. ca.1828. He d.1910.
    iii. Charles William, b. ca.1834.
    iv.   Sally Morgan, b. ca.1837. She m. Lewis Charlton Pynchon. She d.Jul 1924 and was bur. Maple Hill Cem., Huntsville,
          Madison Co., AL.
             Lewis Charlton Pynchon, b.1830. He d.1897.
    v.   Elvira Turner "Ella", b. ca.1839. She m. William Lytle Nichol in 1864. She d.Jun 1869 and was bur. Maple Hill Cem.
             William Lytle Nichol, b.1828. He d.1901.
    vi.   Mary Franklin, b. ca.1842. She d.23 Aug 1910 and was bur. Maple Hill Cem., Huntsville, Madison Co., AL.

81. Isabella[4] Abney (John[3], John[2], Abner[1]), b. ca.1805 Green Co., KY. She m. William Campbell Rhea Jr., son of William Campbell Rhea Sr. and
Elizabeth Brownlee, on 30 Mar 1824 Green Co., KY. She d. between 1840 and 1845 KY.
    William Campbell Rhea Jr., b.1790 Rockbridge Co., VA. He appeared as Head of Household on the census of 1840 Green Co., KY. He m2.
Tamar McClenachan (1st cousin of Isabella Abney), dau. of Robert McClenachan [III] and Sarah "Sally" Abney, on 6 Sep 1845 Barren Co., KY.
He and Tamar McClenachan appeared on the censuses of 23 Jul 1850 and 28 Aug 1860 Barren Co., KY. He d.1861 Glasgow, Barren Co., KY.
Known children of Isabella[4] Abney and William Campbell Rhea Jr.:
    229   i.   Tamar Ann[5], b. 24 May 1826 Green Co., KY; m. John Hugh Montgomery.
    230   ii.   Elizabeth Cynthia, b. 24 Oct 1828 Greensburg, Green Co., KY; m. James Madison Barnett.
    231   iii. Narcissa M., b. 26 Jul 1832 Green Co., KY; m. Joseph D. Williams.
    232   iv.   Isabella Vasser, b. 1835 Green Co., KY; m. William H. Middleton.

82. John R.K.[4] Abney (John[3], John[2], Abner[1]), b. ca.1806 Green Co., KY. He m. Ann Kenney on 22 Dec 1835 Muhlenberg Co., KY. He appeared
as Head of Household on the census of 1840 Muhlenberg Co., KY.
    Ann Kenney, b. ca.1820 KY. She appeared as Head of Household on the census of 1850 Daviess Co., KY.
Known children of John R.K.[4] Abney and Ann Kenney:
    i.   Cynthia[5], b. ca.1837. She appeared on the census of 1850 Davis Co., MO.
    ii.   (dau), b. ca.1839 Muhlenberg Co., KY.
    iii. John, b. ca.1843. He appeared on the census of 1850 MO.
    iv.   Isabella, b. ca.1845. She appeared on the census of 1850 Davies Co., MO.
    v.   Albert, b. ca.1849. He appeared on the census of 1850 Davies Co., MO.

83. Robert Milton[4] Abney (John[3], John[2], Abner[1]), b.5 Jan 1808 Abney's Ferry, Green Co., KY. He m. Catherine Powell Smith, daughter of Aaron
Smith and Rebecca Frey, on 14 Nov 1831 Hardin Co., KY. He appeared as Head of Household on the census of 1840 Hardin Co., KY. He and
Catherine Powell Smith appeared on the censuses of 26 Aug 1850 Hamilton, LaRue Co., KY, 25 Jul 1860 LaRue Co., KY; and 2 Aug 1870 and 7
Jun 1880 Magnolia, LaRue Co., KY. He d.6 Nov 1880 Magnolia, LaRue Co., KY, at age 72 and was bur. Magnolia Presbyterian Ch. Cem., Magnolia, LaRue
Co., KY. Three of his sons served in Co. F, 15th KY Reg. Two of his sons died at the Battle of Perryville and another at Atlanta, Georgia.
    Catherine Powell Smith, b.9 Jul 1815 Lexington, Fayette Co., KY. She d.13 Apr 1885 Magnolia, LaRue Co., KY, at age 69.
Known children of Robert Milton[4] Abney and Catherine Powell Smith:
    233   i.   James Carydon[5], b. 25 Aug 1832 Hardin Co., KY; m. Sophia Weston Slaughter.
          ii.   John Key, b.21 Apr 1835 Hardin Co., KY. He appeared on the census of 3 Aug 1860 LaRue Co., KY. He d.5 Aug 1864
                Atlanta, Fulton Co., GA, at age 29.
          iii. William R., b.4 Feb 1837 Hardin Co., KY. He m1. Sarah "Caroline" Read on 25 Mar 1858. He and Sarah "Caroline" Read
                were liv. on 3 Aug 1860 in Jas. P. Smith household, LaRue Co., KY. He m2. Dorcas A. Walters on 4 Feb 1868. He and
                Dorcas A. Walters appeared on the censuses of 1 Aug 1870 Magnolia, LaRue Co., KY and 25 Jun 1880 LaRue Co., KY.
                He d.16 Apr 1894 at age 57.
                   Sarah "Caroline" Read, b.26 Feb 1835 LaRue Co., KY. She d.16 Feb 1866 KY at age 30.
                   Dorcas A. Walters, b.3 Apr 1847 KY. She d.5 Jul 1930 Louisville, Jefferson Co., KY, at age 83.
          iv.   Elbert Preston, b.18 Feb 1840 Hardin Co., KY. He was killed in action 8 Oct 1862, Perryville, Boyle Co., KY, age 22.
    234   v.   Milton Anderson, b. New Year's Eve, 31 Jan 1842 LaRue Co., KY; m. Ellina Frances Slaughter.
          vi.   Aaron Fry, b.26 Jun 1844 LaRue Co., KY. He was killed in action 8 Oct 1862, Perryville, Boyle Co., KY, at age 18 and
                was bur. Magnolia Presbyterian Ch. Cem., Magnolia, LaRue Co., KY.
    235   vii. Charles "Thomas," b. 2 Apr 1847 LaRue Co., KY; m. Eleaseph Vittitow; m. Mary C. "Molly" Miller.
    236   viii. Joshua Bayne "Josh," b. 31 Jul 1849 LaRue Co., KY; m. Nancy Carpenter "Nannie" Miller.
    237   ix.   Elizabeth Ann, b. 6 Sep 1851 LaRue Co., KY; m. John T. Howell (UA).
          x.   Mary Lou, b.7 Aug 1857 LaRue Co., KY. She m. David F. Ragland. She d.1 Nov 1884 at age 27 and was bur. Magnolia
                Presbyterian Ch. Cem., Magnolia, LaRue Co., KY.
                   David F. Ragland, b.1851. He m2. Kate Jones. He d.1940 and was bur. Magnolia Presbyterian Ch. Cem.

84. Gertrude Robinson[4] Abney (John[3], John[2], Abner[1]), b. ca.1810 Green Co., KY. She m. Samuel P. Lasley, son of James Lasley and Susanna
Smith, on 18 Dec 1827 Green Co., KY. She d. before 29 Aug 1850 KY.
    Samuel P. Lasley, b.30 Sep 1800 Green Co., KY. He appeared on the census of 1830 Green Co., KY. He appeared as Head of Household on
the census of 1840 Hardin Co., KY. He m2. Mary (n.n.). He and Mary (n.n.) appeared on the censuses of 29 Aug 1850 Hamilton, LaRue Co., and
8 Aug 1870 Magnolia, LaRue Co., KY. He d.8 Sep 1890 Green Co., KY, at age 89 and was bur. on 10 Sep 1890 Our Lady of Mercy Catholic Ch.
Cem., Hodgenville, LaRue Co., KY.
Known children of Gertrude Robinson[4] Abney and Samuel P. Lasley:
    i.   M.E. (son) Terrance[5], b. ca.1830 Green Co., KY.
    238   ii.   Mary Jane, b. 24 May 1832 Green Co., KY; m. John Reason Burch.
          iii. John Smith, b.1834. He m. Harriett Williamson in 1855. He d.1905 and was bur. Red Hill Cem., Hodgenville, LaRue Co.,
                KY.

Harriett Williamson, b.1837. She d.1908 and was bur. Red Hill Cem., Hodgenville, LaRue Co., KY.
239   iv.   Margaret Nancy, b. 1838 LaRue Co., KY; m. Capt. Aaron Smith Bayne (UA).
      v.   Menoah Smith, b.20 Dec 1839 Green Co., KY. He m. Jane Hills. He d.23 Feb 1880 Hardin Co., KY, at age 40 and was bur. on 26 Feb 1880 Elizabethtown, Hardin Co., KY.
            Jane Hills, b.23 Oct 1840. She d.16 Nov 1923 at age 83 and was bur. Elizabethtown City Cem., Elizabethtown.
     vi.   N. (son), b.1841 Green Co., KY.

85. Mary B.⁴ Abney (John³, John², Abner¹), b. ca.1816 Green Co., KY. She m. Isaac Faulkner on 21 Jan 1834 Greensburg, Green Co., KY. She and Isaac Faulkner appeared on the census of 20 Aug 1850 Green Co., KY. She d.10 Jun 1855 Green Co., KY and was bur. Greensburg City Cem., Greensburg, Green Co., KY.
    Isaac Faulkner, b.1808 Green Co., KY. He m. Nancy Jane Crail in 1856. He and Nancy Jane Crail appeared on the census of 19 Jul 1860 Green Co., KY. He d.1882 and was bur. Crail Cem., Crailhope, Green Co., KY.
Known children of Mary B.⁴ Abney and Isaac Faulkner all b. Green Co., KY:
      i.   Cynthia Emma "Sinthy"⁵, b.17 Jun 1836. She m. Miles H. Houk. She d.18 Dec 1901 Green Co., KY, at age 65 and was bur. Crail Cem., Crailhope, Green Co., KY.
            Miles H. Houk, b.20 Sep 1812. He bur. Crail Cem., Crailhope, Green Co., KY.
     ii.   Sarah Amanda, b. ca.1838.
    iii.   Samuel A., b. ca.1840.
    iv.   John M., b. ca.1842.
     v.   Mary J., b. ca.1844.
    vi.   Narcissa H., b. ca.1845.
   vii.   Aletha L., b. ca.1848.
  viii.   Baby, b. ca.May 1850.
    ix.   Levi, b. ca.1851.
     x.   James, b. ca.1853.
    xi.   Hugh K., b. ca.1854.

86. Letitia P.⁴ Abney (John³, John², Abner¹), b.19 Apr 1818 Green Co., KY. She m. John Fauchee Cash ca.1835. She and John Fauchee Cash appeared on the censuses of 4 Sep 1850 and Jun 1860 Hardin Co., KY. She d.12 Jul 1864 at age 46 and was bur. Gilead Bapt. Ch. Cem., Glendale.
    John Fauchee Cash, b.16 Aug 1807 Hardin Co., KY. He appeared as Head of Household on the census of 1840 Hardin Co., KY. He m2. Margaret (n.n.). He and Margaret (n.n.) appeared on the census of 20 Jun 1870 Wallingford, Hardin Co., KY. He d.17 Jul 1885 Hardin Co., KY, at age 77 and was bur. Gilead Bapt. Ch. Cem., Glendale, Hardin Co., KY.
Known children of Letitia P.⁴ Abney and John Fauchee Cash:
      i.   Sarah A.⁵, b. ca.1837 KY.
     ii.   Josiah B., b. ca.1839 KY. He d.16 Dec 1857 Hardin Co., KY.
    iii.   Andrew S., b. ca.1841 KY.
    iv.   William H., b. ca.1843 KY.
     v.   Warren T., b. ca.1845 KY.
    vi.   Robert A., b. ca.1848 KY.
   vii.   Samuel W., b. ca.1852 Hardin Co., KY.
  viii.   Cyntha M.A.F., b.16 Apr 1855 Hardin Co., KY.
    ix.   Thomas D., b. ca.1858 Hardin Co., KY.
     x.   Florence, b. ca.1861 Hardin Co., KY.

87. Thomas Gory⁴ Hogg (Martha³ Abney, John², Abner¹), b.12 Aug 1800 Kanawha Co., VA. He m. Lucy Ball in 1827. He d.19 Oct 1873 Mason Co., WV, at age 73 and was bur. Somerville Cem., Mason Co., WV. [author's note: Mason Co., VA became Mason Co., WV in 1863]
    Lucy Ball, b.16 Nov 1810 Mason Co., WV. She d.20 Sep 1872 Mason Co., WV, at age 61 and was bur. Somerville Cem., Mason Co., WV.
Known child of Thomas Gory⁴ Hogg and Lucy Ball:
      i.   James Abney⁵, b.23 Jul 1828 Mason Co., VA. He m. Susan Knight. He d.20 Dec 1894 Mason Co., WV, at age 66 and was bur. Lone Oak Cem., Point Pleasant, Mason Co., WV.
            Susan Knight, b.5 Jul 1831. She d.12 Apr 1926 at age 94 and was bur. Lone Oak Cem., Point Pleasant.

88. Julia Ann⁴ Hogg (Martha³ Abney, John², Abner¹), b.10 Aug 1808 VA. She m. Thomas Ball. She d.24 Aug 1880 at age 72 and was bur. Ball Cem., Mason Co., WV. [author's note: Mason Co., VA became Mason Co., WV in 1863]
    Thomas Ball, b.10 Feb 1802. He d.8 Oct 1869 at age 67 and was bur. Ball Cem., Mason Co., WV.
Known children of Julia Ann⁴ Hogg and Thomas Ball:
      i.   Lewis P.⁵, b.1829. He d.1854.
     ii.   Robert Harding, b.1831. He d.1891.
    iii.   Eliza Ann, b.1835. She d.1838.
    iv.   Martha Jane, b.1843. She d.1925.
     v.   Arabella R., b.1845. She d.1923.
    vi.   Maria S., b.1851. She d.1917.

89. Mary Margaret⁴ Hogg (Martha³ Abney, John², Abner¹), b.20 Aug 1811 VA. She m. Henry Capehart ca.1829 Mason Co., VA. She and Henry Capehart appeared on the census of 21 Aug 1850 Mason Co., VA. She d.9 Mar 1890 New Haven, Mason Co., WV, at age 78 and was bur. Capehart Cem., Mason Co., WV. [author's note: Mason Co., VA became Mason Co., WV in 1863]
    Henry Capehart, b.1800 Mason Co., VA. He d.10 Oct 1881 New Haven, Mason Co., WV and was bur. Capehart Cem., Mason Co., WV.
Known children of Mary Margaret⁴ Hogg and Henry Capehart:
      i.   Elizabeth Matilda⁵, b.1836. She d.1894.
     ii.   George P., b.1839. He d.1886.

         iii.   James Henry, b.1842. He d.1880.

         iv.   Olevia Jane, b.1844. She d.1923.

240   v.   William H., b. 30 Jul 1846 New Haven, Mason Co., VA; m. Sarah Jane Gilpin.

         vi.   Abney W., b.1849 VA. He m. Caroline (n.n.) ca.1870 VA. He and Caroline (n.n.) appeared on the censuses of 29 Jul 1870 New Haven, Mason Co., WV. and 20 Jun 1900 Towanda, Phillips Co., KS. He d.1921 and was bur. in 1922 Hill City Cem., Hill City, Graham Co., KS.

               Caroline (n.n.), b.1847 VA. She d.1917 and was bur. Hill City Cem., Hill City, Graham Co., KS.

         vii.   Thomas Gory, b.1853. He d.1931.

Generation Five

90. David[5] Chancellor (Rebecca[4] Abney, Joshua[3], Elisha[2], Abner[1]), b.17 Apr 1813 KY. He m. Eleanor K. "Ellen" Auld on 11 Sep 1841 Martinsville, Clark Co., IL He d.17 Mar 1848 Martinsville, Clark Co., IL, age 34 and was bur. Martinsville City Cem., Martinsville, Clark Co., IL.

     Eleanor K. "Ellen" Auld, b.31 Oct 1818 OH. She appeared as Head of Household on the census of 13 Oct 1850 Martinsville, Clark Co., IL. She m. Floyd E. Ferris in 1860. She and Floyd E. Ferris appeared on the census of 7 Aug 1860 Clark Co., IL. She appeared as Head of Household on the census of 14 Jul 1870 Clark Co., IL. She was liv. on 24 Jun 1880 and 5 Jun 1900 with son-in-law, Pike Crabtree, Casey Twp., Clark Co., IL. She d.3 Nov 1903 Martinsville, Clark Co., IL, at age 85 and was bur. Martinsville City Cem., Martinsville, Clark Co., IL.

Known children of David[5] Chancellor and Eleanor K. "Ellen" Auld:

241   i.   Polly Anna[6], b. 14 Jun 1842 Martinsville, Clark Co., IL; m. Pike Crabtree.

242   ii.   Mary Ellen, b. 20 Mar 1844; m. James Nelson Griffith.

243   iii.   Rebecca Eleanora, b. 25 Feb 1847; m. James Gaston Gillilan.

        iv.   David F., b.1848. He d.1848.

91. Ewing[5] Chancellor (Rebecca[4] Abney, Joshua[3], Elisha[2], Abner[1]), b.14 Oct 1813 Morgantown, Butler Co., KY. He m. Huldah Lee in 1832 IL. He appeared as Head of Household on the census of 1840 Clark Co., IL. He d.10 Feb 1852 (at home), Casey, Clark Co., IL, at age 38 and was bur. Martinsville City Cem., Martinsville, Clark Co., IL.

     Huldah Lee, b.24 Jan 1817 Grayson Co., KY. She m2. A.J. Haskins. She and A.J. Haskins appeared on the census of 4 Jun 1860 Cumberland, Clark Co., IL. She was liv. on 26 Jul 1870 with her son, Henry C. Chancellor, Lincoln, Crawford Co., KS and on 9 Jun 1880 with her son, Ewing Chancellor, Lincoln, Crawford Co., KS. She d.9 Feb 1884 Arcadia, Crawford Co., KS, age 67; bur. Old Arcadia Cem., Arcadia, Crawford Co., KS.

Known children of Ewing[5] Chancellor and Huldah Lee:

        i.   Nancy[6], b.1834 IL.

        ii.   John, b.1837 IL.

        iii.   Levi, b.8 Dec 1839 Clark Co., IL. He d.15 Dec 1839 Clark Co., IL and was bur. Martinsville City Cem., Martinsville.

244   iv.   Mary "Isabelle," b. 26 Dec 1839 Casey, Clark Co., IL; m. Henry Oscar "Mac" McKay.

        v.   Thomas J., b. ca.1842 IL. He was a school teacher. He was liv. on 26 Jul 1870 with his brother, Henry C. Chancellor, Lincoln, Crawford Co., KS.

        vi.   Elizabeth, b.1844. She d.13 Sep 1844 and was bur. Martinsville City Cem., Martinsville, Clark Co., IL.

245   vii.   Henry Columbus, b. May 1846 IL; m. Sarah Jane Hoberry.

        viii.   William Henry, b.5 May 1846 Martinsville, Clark Co., IL. He d.2 Jun 1846 Martinsville, Clark Co., IL and was bur. Martinsville City Cem., Martinsville, Clark Co., IL.

        ix.   Ewing (Jr.), b.1850 IL. He m. Rachel Elizabeth (n.n.). He and Rachel Elizabeth (n.n.) appeared on the census of 9 Jun 1880 Lincoln, Crawford Co., KS. He d.1931 and was bur. Washington Street Cem., Casey, Clark Co., IL.

             Rachel Elizabeth (n.n.), b.1856. She d.1935 and was bur. Washington Street Cem., Casey, Clark Co., IL.

        x.   Huldah C., b.29 Jun 1852. She d.17 Mar 1866 Martinsville, Clark Co., IL, at age 13 and was bur. Martinsville City Cem.

92. Joshua[5] Chancellor (Rebecca[4] Abney, Joshua[3], Elisha[2], Abner[1]), b.5 Jan 1816 KY. He m. Phebe Moore on 5 Mar 1837. He appeared as Head of Household on the census of 1840 Clark Co., IL. He and Phebe Moore appeared on the censuses of 15 Oct 1850, 1 Jun 1860 and 22 Jul 1870 Cumberland, Clark Co., IL. He d.28 Oct 1903 at age 87 and was bur. Washington Street Cem., Casey, Clark Co., IL.

     Phebe Moore, b.4 Dec 1816 OH. She d.7 Mar 1898 at age 81 and was bur. Washington Street Cem., Casey, Clark Co., IL.

Known children of Joshua[5] Chancellor and Phebe Moore:

        i.   Rebecca J.[6], b. ca.1855 IL.

        ii.   Savana, b. ca.1867.

93. Levi[5] Chancellor (Rebecca[4] Abney, Joshua[3], Elisha[2], Abner[1]), b.15 Feb 1820 Morgantown, Butler Co., KY. He m. Elizabeth "Eliza" Auld ca.1840. He and Elizabeth "Eliza" Auld appeared on the census of 13 Oct 1850 Martinsville, Clark Co., IL. He d.8 Dec 1857 Clark Co., IL, at age 37 and was bur. Martinsville City Cem., Martinsville, Clark Co., IL.

     Elizabeth "Eliza" Auld, b.20 Oct 1822 Harrison Co., OH. She appeared as Head of Household on the census of 11 Jun 1860 Clark Co., IL. She d.6 Feb 1865 Martinsville, Clark Co., IL, at age 42 and was bur. Martinsville City Cem., Martinsville, Clark Co., IL.

Known children of Levi[5] Chancellor and Elizabeth "Eliza" Auld all b. IL:

246   i.   William Henry[6], b. ca.1841; m. Sophia (n.n.).

        ii.   Mary Jane, b. ca.1844.

247   iii.   John Wesley, b. ca.1846; m. Louisa (n.n.).

        iv.   Martha Ann, b. ca.1848.

        v.   Rebecca E., b. ca.1848.

        vi.   David E., b. ca.1857. He was living with on 6 Aug 1870 with the Joseph Dole family, Mattoon, Coles Co., IL.

        vii.   Joshua N., b. ca.1857.

94. Martha Ann[5] Chancellor (Rebecca[4] Abney, Joshua[3], Elisha[2], Abner[1]), b.19 Jan 1823 KY. She m. John Montgomery on 21 Nov 1838. She d.20 Feb 1901 at age 78 and was bur. Martinsville City Cem., Martinsville, Clark Co., KY.

     John Montgomery, b.5 Sep 1813 KY. He d.30 Sep 1863 at age 50 and was bur. Martinsville City Cem., Martinsville, Clark Co., KY.

Known children of Martha Ann[5] Chancellor and John Montgomery:
       i.   (dau.)[6], b. ca.1839. She d.9 Oct 1840.
      ii.   John Jr., b. ca.1841 IL.
     iii.   Joshua, b.12 Feb 1844 IL. He d.18 Aug 1925 Martinsville, Clark Co., KY, at age 81; was bur. Martinsville City Cem.
248   iv.   Henry Clay, b. 6 Oct 1846 Clark Co., IL; m1. Mary Abagill Watts; m2. Florence (n.n.).
      v.   Elizabeth, b. ca.1849 IL.
     vi.   Polly Ann, b. ca.1851 IL.
    vii.   Cinderella, b. ca.1853 IL.
   viii.   David, b. ca.1856 IL.
     ix.   Alice, b. ca.1858 IL.
      x.   Louisa, b.6 Jan 1861. She d.17 Feb 1878 at age 17.
     xi.   Louella, b.6 Jan 1861. She d.3 May 1880 at age 19.

95. William M.[5] Chancellor (UA) (Rebecca[4] Abney, Joshua[3], Elisha[2], Abner[1]), b.29 Jan 1827. He m. Mary Ann Peters. He and Mary Ann Peters appeared on the census of 11 Jun 1860 Martinsville, Clark Co., IL. He d.18 Jan 1862 at age 34 and was bur. Mount City Cem., Johnson Township, Clark Co., IL.
   Mary Ann Peters, b.31 Jul 1826 MD. She appeared as Head of Household on the censuses of 28 Jun 1870 and 23 Jun 1880 Martinsville, Clark Co., IL. She d.2 Aug 1880 at age 54 and was bur. Mount Cem., Johnson Township, Clark Co., IL.
Known children of William M.[5] Chancellor (UA) and Mary Ann Peters:
249   i.   John W.[6], b. ca.1846 IL; m. Sarah (n.n.).
     ii.   Mary M., b.3 Jul 1849 IL. She d.26 Sep 1854 at age 5 and bur. Martinsville City Cem., Martinsville, Clark Co., IL.
    iii.   Paragon D. "Perry", b. ca.1852 IL.
    iv.   Joshua G., b. ca.1855 IL.
250   v.   Catherine Josephine, b. 3 Jan 1858 Martinsville, Clark Co., IL; m. Oliver Hazard Harmeson.
    vi.   Amanda, b. ca.1860 IL.

96. John M.[5] Chancellor (Sr.) (Rebecca[4] Abney, Joshua[3], Elisha[2], Abner[1]), b.9 Jan 1833. He m. E. (n.n.). He d.20 Jan 1857 at age 24 and was bur. Martinsville City Cem., Martinsville, Clark Co., IL.
Known child of John M.[5] Chancellor (Sr.) and E. (n.n.):
      i.   John M. (Jr.)[6], b.6 Mar 1857 IL. He was liv. on 1 Jun 1860 with uncle, Joshua Chancellor, Cumberland, Clark Co., IL. He d.26 Aug 1864 at age 7 and was bur. Martinsville City Cem., Martinsville, Clark Co., IL.

97. John William[5] Abney Sr. (Paul[4], Joshua[3], Elisha[2], Abner[1]), b.1826 Butler Co., KY. He m. Keziah Daugherty, daughter of Moses Daugherty and (n.n., a Cherokee Indian), on 4 Mar 1844 Springfield, Roberson Co., TN. He and Keziah Daugherty appeared on the census of 16 Sep 1850 Butler Co., KY. He d.1870 Butler Co., KY and was bur. Embry Cem., Welchs Creek, Butler Co., KY.
   Keziah Daugherty, b.1827 KY. She appeared on the census of 1850 Butler Co., KY. She d.1860 Butler Co., KY.
Known children of John William[5] Abney Sr. and Keziah Daugherty:
251   i.   John William Jr.[6], b. 1845 Butler Co., KY; m. Martha Jane "Pattie" Embry.
252   ii.   Pheoby Jane, b. 8 Nov 1846 KY; m. Rev. John Thomas Daugherty.
253   iii.   Jasper N., b. 24 Sep 1848 KY; m1. and div. Mary Ann "Polly" Snodgrass; m2. Jennie Etherton.
254   iv.   James "Lewis," b. 11 Oct 1850 Butler Co., KY; m. Mary M. Kizer.
255   v.   Mary Ann, b. 7 Dec 1852 Butler Co., KY; m. Francis Marion Daugherty.
256   vi.   Martha Barbara "Patsy," b. Feb 1854; m. Joseph P. Hunter.
257   vii.   Jesse G., b. 29 Apr 1857 Butler Co., KY; m. Mahala Persilla Daugherty.
258   viii.   Daniel M., b. Oct 1858 Butler Co., KY; m. Mary Francis Moore.

98. Mary Ann[5] Abney (Paul[4], Joshua[3], Elisha[2], Abner[1]), b.6 Nov 1827 KY. She m. Thomas W. Moore on 11 Oct 1847 Butler Co., KY. She and Thomas W. Moore appeared on the census of 14 Sep 1850 Butler Co., KY. She d.Oct 1905 Butler Co., KY, at age 77 and was bur. Mount Vernon Cem., Dexterville, Butler Co., KY.
   Thomas W. Moore, b.28 Dec 1815 KY. He d.30 Aug 1908 Butler Co., KY, at age 92 and was bur. Mount Vernon Cem., Dexterville, KY.
Known children of Mary Ann[5] Abney and Thomas W. Moore:
      i.   Nicey E.[6], b.18 Dec 1848 Butler Co., KY, She d.22 Feb 1918 Butler Co., KY, at age 69, bur. Mount Vernon Cem.
     ii.   Alfred .J, b. ca.1850 KY.
    iii.   Martha A., b. ca.1853 KY.
259   iv.   Calvin P., b. 16 Dec 1853 Butler Co., KY; m. Mary M. Howard.
     v.   Curran T., b.16 Dec 1853 Butler Co., KY. He m. Mary Felty. He d.5 Nov 1930 Ohio Co., KY, at age 76.
           Mary Felty, b.7 May 1859. She d.14 Jun 1910 at age 51 and was bur. Mount Vernon Cem., Dexterville, KY.
260   vi.   Paul Abney, b. 23 Nov 1857 Morgantown, Butler Co., KY; m. Katherine Jane "Katie" Moore.
261   vii.   Finis A., b. 24 Sep 1858 Butler Co., KY; m. Louiza J. Howard; m. Lenora J. Heath.
   viii.   John, b. ca.1861 KY.
262   ix.   Mary C., b. 26 Oct 1862 KY; m. Rev. Silas V. Baize.
263   x.   Thomas, b. 29 Apr 1866 KY; m. Delia White Barton.

99. Nicey G.[5] Abney (Paul[4], Joshua[3], Elisha[2], Abner[1]), b.Jun 1829 Butler Co., KY. She m. Jesse G. Deweese Jr., son of Jesse G. Deweese Sr. and Polly Ann Sowder, on 22 Jun 1853 Butler Co., KY. She d.25 Feb 1916 Hopkinsville, Christian Co., KY, at age 86 and was bur. Mount Vernon Cem., Dexterville, Butler Co., KY.
   Jesse G. Deweese Jr, b.1818 Cumberland Co., KY. He m1. Malinda Pitman on 29 Aug 1837 Warren Co., KY. He d. ca.1862 Butler Co., KY and was bur. Pearson Miller Deweese Cem., Jetson, Butler Co., KY.

Known children of Nicey G.⁵ Abney and Jesse G. Deweese Jr.:
    i. Louisa Ann⁶, b.4 Nov 1854 Butler Co., KY. She d.15 Aug 1874 Butler Co., KY, at age 19.
  264 ii. Lucinda Bartholomew, b. 21 Jul 1856; m. Commodore J. Flener.
    iii. Paul A., b.28 Jun 1858 Butler Co., KY. He m. Antha W. Flener, daughter of Moses Flener, on 6 Dec 1880 Butler Co.,
     KY. He d.19 Jun 1902 Butler Co., KY, at age 43 and was bur. Morgan-Smith Cem., Butler Co., KY.
      Antha W. Flener, b.1861. She d.10 Oct 1903.
  265 iv. Elijah Covington, b. 1860 Butler Co., KY; m. Melissa Ingram; m. Elizabeth Whitaker.
    v. Jesse G., b. ca.1862 Butler Co., KY. He d. before 1900.

100. Hannah Curtis⁵ Abney (Paul⁴, Joshua³, Elisha², Abner¹), b.1848 Butler Co., KY. She appeared on the census of 1850 Butler Co., KY. She m.
Alfred Wayne Daugherty on New Year's Eve, 31 Jan 1867. She d.1880 and was bur. Mount Vernon Cem., Dexterville, Butler Co., KY.
 Alfred Wayne Daugherty, b.1844 Ohio Co., KY. He d.1904.
Known children of Hannah Curtis⁵ Abney and Alfred Wayne Daugherty:
    i. Nancy⁶.
  266 ii. Armedia W., b. 28 Feb 1871 KY; m. Perry Monroe Evans.
  267 iii. Hannah Curtis, b. 7 Dec 1879; m. Samuel Thomas Evans.

101. Isaac Newton⁵ Abney (Paul⁴, Joshua³, Elisha², Abner¹), b.24 Oct 1849 Butler Co., KY. He m. Sylvia Embry on 26 Sep 1867. He and Sylvia
Embry were on the census of 9 Jan 1920 Butler Co., KY. He and Sylvia Embry were living on 12 Apr 1930 with son, Cletus Abner, Butler Co.,
KY. He d.22 Jun 1933 Butler Co., KY, at age 83 and was bur. Mount Vernon Cem., Dexterville, Butler Co., KY.
 Sylvia Embry, b.1864 KY. She d.1936 Butler Co., KY and was bur. Mount Vernon Cem., Dexterville, Butler Co., KY.
Known children of Isaac Newton⁵ Abney and Sylvia Embry:
  268 i. Harrison⁶, b. 10 Jul 1887; m. Louella F. Flener.
    ii. Cletus, b.25 Feb 1890 Butler Co., KY. He was liv. on 9 Jan 1920 with his father, Isaac N. Abner, Butler Co., KY. He
     appeared on the census of 12 Apr 1930 Butler Co., KY. He was liv. on 1 May 1940 with brother, Harrison Abner, Butler
     Co., KY. He d.26 Feb 1963 Hopkinsville, Christian Co., KY, at age 73 and was bur. Mount Vernon Cem., Dexterville.
  269 iii. Ada, b. 24 Jun 1892 KY; m. Isaac Morten Snodgrass.

102. Silas Curtis⁵ Abney (Paul⁴, Joshua³, Elisha², Abner¹), b.1851 KY. He m. Calista "Calesty" Barton on 10 Jan 1871 Butler Co., KY. He appeared
on the census of 10 May 1910 as a boarder with Dunaway family, Estill Co., KY. He d.1911.
 Calista "Calesty" Barton, b.Feb 1854 KY. She appeared as Head of Household on the census of 8 Jun 1900, Livermore, McLean Co., KY.
Known children of Silas Curtis⁵ Abney and Calista "Calesty" Barton:
  270 i. Rena Ann "Renie"⁶, b. 28 Oct 1875 KY; m1. Robert Weekley Goff; m2. Felix Matthew "Pheak" Loyd.
  271 ii. Homer, b. 18 Apr 1877 Butler Co., KY; m. Nicey J. Moore.
  272 iii. George W, b. 18 Apr 1880 KY; m. Katie May McManaway.

103. Francis Marion⁵ Abney (William⁴, Joshua³, Elisha², Abner¹), b.15 Feb 1838 Jefferson Co., IL. He m1. Felicia A. (n.n.). He m2. Elizabeth A.
Huston in 1879. He m3. Louisa Catherine Trout, daughter of James Trout and Amanda Arnold, ca.1882. He d.10 Apr 1916 Dexter, Stoddard Co.,
MO, at age 78 and was bur. Hagy Cem., Dexter, Stoddard Co., MO.
 Felicia A. (n.n.), b. ca.1842 IL.
Known children of Francis Marion⁵ Abney and Felicia A. (n.n.):
    i. James "Monroe"⁶, b.24 Aug 1860 Harrisburg, Saline Co., IL. He d.13 Feb 1936 Dexter, Stoddard Co., MO, at age 75 and
     was bur. Hagy Cem., Dexter, Stoddard Co., MO.
    ii. Francis, b.1862 IL.
    iii. Sarah "Almeda", b.27 Apr 1868 IL. She m. John Bedford Dooley in 1887. She d.2 Sep 1932 Pontiac, Oakland Co., MI, at
     age 64 and was bur. Sunset Hill Cem., Harrisburg, Saline Co., IL.
      John Bedford Dooley, b.8 Dec 1864. He d.13 Mar 1920 at age 55 and was bur. Sunset Hill Cem., Harrisburg.
    iv. Pruella J., b. ca.1871.
    v. Adeline, b. ca.1872.
  273 vi. Effie, b. Jul 1874 Harrisburg, Saline Co., IL; m. Hamilton "Mack" McCoy.
    vii. Dartheda, b. ca.1878 IL.
 Elizabeth A. Huston, b.1857 IL.
Known child of Francis Marion⁵ Abney and Elizabeth A. Huston:
    i. Delpha A.⁶, b.Jan 1880 IL.
 Louisa Catherine Trout, b.1 Dec 1858 IL. She d.18 Aug 1939 Dexter, Stoddard Co., IL, at age 80 and was bur. Bankston Cem., Harrisburg.
Known children of Francis Marion⁵ Abney and Louisa Catherine Trout:
  274 i. Cora A.⁶, b. 1884; m. Edward H. Robertson.
    ii. Evertt Leroy, b.13 Oct 1888. He d.9 Sep 1942 at age 53 and was bur. Dexter Cem., Dexter, Stoddard Co., MO.
  275 iii. Myrtha Juanita, b. 7 Feb 1898; m. Sgt. Calvin Shepard Crozier (USA-WWI); m. Harry S. Boyles.
    iv. Lovette Frances, b.26 Oct 1902. She d.25 Oct 1980 at age 77 and was bur. Dexter Cem., Dexter, Stoddard Co., MO.

104. Louis Frank⁵ Abner (William⁴ Abney, Joshua³, Elisha², Abner¹), b.11 Apr 1850 Jefferson Co., IL. He m. Lequincey J. "Lory" Melton ca.1883.
He appeared as Head of Household on the census of 9 Jun 1900 Independence Twp., Baxter Co., AR. He d.21 Apr 1904 at age 54 and was bur.
Wesley Chapel Cem., Baxter Co., AR.
 Lequincey J. "Lory" Melton, b.Jun 1850 TN.
Known children of Louis Frank⁵ Abner and Lequincey J. "Lory" Melton:
    i. Nora B.⁶, b.1 May 1884. She m. (n.n.) Davis. She d.22 May 1904 at age 20 and was bur. Wesley Chapel Cem., Baxter.
  276 ii. William T., b. 8 Mar 1886 AR; m. Ella Mable Ward.
  277 iii. Roy E., b. 12 May 1888; m. Leona Hattie Stone.
  278 iv. Mary Roxie, b. 25 Sep 1890; m. Arch Dearmore.

105. Wilburn Callaway "Cal"*⁵* Abney (Benjamin*⁴*, Hezekiah*³*, Elisha*²*, Abner*¹*), b.4 Jan 1828 Jackson Co., GA. He m1. Rebecca Martha Shipp on 20 Mar 1851. He and Rebecca Martha Shipp appeared on the census of 22 Jun 1860 Paulding Co., GA. He m2. Martha E. "Jane" Hogan. He and Martha E. "Jane" Hogan appeared on the censuses of 30 Jun 1870, 2 Jun 1880 and 8 Jun 1900 Paulding Co., GA. He d.4 Jan 1910 Catoosa Co., GA, at age 82 and was bur. Wood Station Cem., Ringgold, Catoosa Co., GA.

Rebecca Martha Shipp, b.17 Dec 1832 GA. She d.16 Mar 1867 at age 34.

Known children of Wilburn Callaway "Cal"*⁵* Abney and Rebecca Martha Shipp:

    279   i.   Elizabeth Parethena*⁶*, b. 16 May 1852 GA; m. Dr. George Washington Wills.

            ii.   James, b. ca.1854.

    280   iii.   Washington "Andrew," b. 29 Oct 1856 Floyd Co., GA; m. Ella Charlotte Bohannan.

    281   iv.   Lula "Nancy," b. May 1860 Paulding Co., GA; m. Turner B. Brown.

Martha E. "Jane" Hogan, b.29 Jan 1837 SC. She m1. Elijah Christopher Columbus O'Dell in 1856. She lived on 26 Apr 1910 with daughter, Datha Blalock, DeKalb Co., AL. She d.23 Aug 1915 DeKalb Co., AL, at age 78; bur. Town Creek Bapt. Ch. Cem., Chavies, DeKalb Co., AL.

Known children of Wilburn Callaway "Cal"*⁵* Abney and Martha E. "Jane" Hogan:

    282   i.   Vera "Datha"*⁶*, b. 16 Jun 1869 GA; m. William R. Blalock.

    283   ii.   Robert E., b. 13 Aug 1871 GA; m1. Mary C. Abney; m2. Vastie C. "Vassie" Wells.

    284   iii.   Corrin Frances, b. 18 May 1873 Paulding Co., GA; m. John Hennaly Camp.

    285   iv.   Benjamin F. "Ben," b. 1876 GA; m1. (n.n.); m2. Margaret E. "Maggie" McRae.

106. Benjamin D. "Ben"*⁵* Abney (Benjamin*⁴*, Hezekiah*³*, Elisha*²*, Abner*¹*), b. Aug 1828 Jackson Co., GA. . Ben received a land grant in Martlin, Marshall County, Alabama. He m1. Sarah E. Greene. He and Sarah E. Greene appeared on the census of 9 Jul 1860 Guntersville, Marshall Co., AL. He m2. Mary A. "Molly" Prisket on 16 Sep 1862 Marshall Co., AL. He and Mary A. "Molly" Prisket appeared on the censuses of 16 Jul 1870, 14 Jun 1880 and 20 Jun 1900 Marshall Co., AL. He d.27 Feb 1907 Martling, Marshall Co., AL, at age 78 and was bur. Martling Community Cem., Martling, Marshall Co., AL.

Sarah E. Greene, b. ca.1838 AL. She d. ca.1861 Marshall Co., AL.

Known children of Benjamin D. "Ben"*⁵* Abney and Sarah E. Greene:

    286   i.   George Washington*⁶*, b. 4 Aug 1855 Marietta, Cobb Co., GA; m1. & div. Olivia Josephine Hill; m2. Ida Cowen.

    287   ii.   Mary Ann C., b. 15 Feb 1857 AL; m. John Washington Moore.

    288   iii.   James Alfred, b. Nov 1859 Marshall Co., AL; m. Lucinda "Lucindy" Martin.

    289   iv.   William "Henry," b. 10 Jun 1860 Guntersville, Marshall Co., AL; m1. Martha Elizabeth Hodgins; m2. Willie E. Kent; m3. Ida Jane Fortson.

    290   v.   David, b. 10 Jun 1861 AL; m. Mariah King.

Mary A. "Molly" Prisket, b.Oct 1847 AL. She d.13 Dec 1922 at age 75 and was bur. Martling Community Cem., Martling, AL.

Known children of Benjamin D. "Ben"*⁵* Abney and Mary A. "Molly" Prisket:

            i.   John*⁶*, b. ca.1866 AL.

            ii.   Molley, b. ca.1867 AL.

            iii.   Phoebe Parthena "Thena", b.Sep 1869 Marshall Co., AL. She m. Lemuel W. Roden on 16 Sep 1872. She and Lemuel W. Roden appeared on the censuses of 8 Jun 1900, 21 Apr 1910 and 15 Jan 1920 Marshall Co., AL. She d.30 Aug 1935 at age 65 and was bur. Martling Community Cem., Martling, Marshall Co., AL.

                     Lemuel W. Roden, b.Sep 1861.

            iv.   Manda, b. ca.1871 AL. She appeared on the census of 1880 Marshall Co., AL.

    291   v.   David "Dee," b. 20 Apr 1874 AL; m. Annie Critcher.

            vi.   Albert, b. ca.May 1880 Marshall Co., AL.

    292   vii.   Eva L., b. 19 Sep 1883 Marshall Co., AL; m. John Richard Rooks.

107. Andrew "Jackson"*⁵* Abney (Benjamin*⁴*, Hezekiah*³*, Elisha*²*, Abner*¹*), b.25 Jan 1833 GA. He m. Mary A. (n.n.) ca.1851. He and Mary A. (n.n.) appeared on the censuses of 4 Jul 1860 Calhoun Co., AL; 13 Jun 1870 Cleburne Co., AL and 24 Jun 1880 Marshall Co., AL. He was liv. on 13 Jun 1900 with his daughter, Drucilla Weemes, Goodwin, St. Francis Co., AR. He d.8 Nov 1900 AR at age 67 and was bur. Goodwin Mem. Cem., Goodwin, St. Francis Co., AR.

Mary A. (n.n.), b. ca.1831 GA. She d. before 13 Jun 1900.

Known children of Andrew "Jackson"*⁵* Abney and Mary A. (n.n.):

    293   i.   Sarah Emily*⁶*, b. 22 Aug 1854 Calhoun Co., AL; m. Francis "Marion" Reeves.

    294   ii.   Amanda Catherine "Mandy," b. 6 Sep 1855 GA; m. William B. Sargent.

            iii.   Mary Jo, b. ca.1857 GA.

            iv.   Thomas E.H., b. ca.1859 AL.

            v.   Frances "Elizabeth", b. ca.1861 AL.

            vi.   John Trucksom, b.2 Nov 1864 AL. He d. before 1870 (?).

            vii.   Ada Duet "Edie", b.7 Jun 1866 AL.

            viii.   Clementine, b. ca.Apr 1870 AL.

    295   ix.   Drucilla Parker, b. 15 Apr 1871 AL; m. James M. Weemes.

108. Hezekiah "Van Buren"*⁵* Abney (Benjamin*⁴*, Hezekiah*³*, Elisha*²*, Abner*¹*), b.29 May 1834 GA. He m. Margaret Emeline "Emmie" Shipp ca.1856. He and Margaret Emeline "Emmie" Shipp appeared on the censuses of 28 Jun 1860 Calhoun Co., AL; 30 Jun 1870 California, Paulding Co., GA; 8 Jun 1880 Cobb Co., GA and 4 Jun 1900 Bartow Co., GA. He d.23 Mar 1906 Bartow Co., GA, at age 71 and was bur. Libery Hill Cem., Acworth, Cobb Co., GA. One of the daughters of Hezekiah Van Buren and Margaret Emeline Shipp Abney m. a McCrary and probably d. before 1900. In the 1900 census, there is a granddaughter Mary McCrary (age3) liv. with them.

Margaret Emeline "Emmie" Shipp, b.3 Sep 1838 GA. She appeared as Head of Household on the censuses of 5 May 1910 and 20 Jan 1920 Bartow Co., GA. She d.29 Jul 1924 GA at age 85 and was bur. Liberty Hill Cem., Acworth, Cobb Co., GA. ; and in the 1910 census, the granddaughter, Mary McCrary (age 13) is liv. with the widow Margaret Shipp Abney.

Known children of Hezekiah "Van Buren"[5] Abney and Margaret Emeline "Emmie" Shipp:

	i.	Margaret E.[6], b. ca.1857 Cobb Co., GA.
296	ii.	Sarah Elizabeth, b. Christmas Day, 25 Dec 1857 Calhoun Co., AL; m. Richard Thompson Ellison.
	iii.	Mary J., b. ca. Dec 1859 Calhoun Co., AL.
	iv.	Luada "Ludy", b. ca.1868 Calhoun Co., AL.
	v.	Elijah, b. ca. Dec 1869 GA. He d. before 8 Jun 1880.
297	vi.	Hezekiah Van Buren "Bud," b. 23 May 1872 Cobb Co., GA; m. Sarah S. "Sallie" Earwood.
	vii.	Juliar, b. Sep 1874 Cobb Co., GA.; d.27 Mar 1944 at age 69 and was bur. Liberty Hill Cem., Acworth, Cobb Co., GA.
298	viii.	George Washington "Dodge," b. 17 Feb 1878 Cobb Co., GA; m. Mary Fountain.
	ix.	Hattie Isabelle "Bell," b. Sep 1879 Cobb Co., GA. She d.5 Jun 1944 at age 64 and was bur. Liberty Hill Cem., Acworth.

109. Pvt. George Washington[5] Abney Sr. (CSA) (Benjamin[4], Hezekiah[3], Elisha[2], Abner[1]), b.10 Mar 1837 GA. He m. Elizabeth Jane Chandler on 22 Feb 1860 Cleburne Co., AL. He and Elizabeth Jane Chandler appeared on the censuses of 20 Jun 1860 Calhoun Co., GA; 8 Jun 1880 St. Clair Co., AL; and 28 Jun 1900 and 30 Apr 1910 Jefferson Co., AL. He d.23 Apr 1914 at age 77 and was bur. Friendship UMC Cem. (on top of Horse Branch Hill), Gardendale, Jefferson Co., AL.

Elizabeth Jane Chandler, b.27 Sep 1842 AL. She appeared on the census of 20 Jun 1860 Calhoun Co., AL. She d.29 Apr 1911 at age 68 and was bur. Friendship UMC Cem. (on top of Horse Branch Hill), Gardendale, Jefferson Co., AL.

Known children of Pvt. George Washington[5] Abney Sr. (CSA) and Elizabeth Jane Chandler:

	i.	Mary E.[6], b. ca.1862 St. Clair Co., AL.
299	ii.	George Washington, b. Apr 1863 St. Clair Co., AL; m. Lou "Ellen" Cheek.
	iii.	Samuel N., b. ca.1865 St. Clair Co., AL.
	iv.	Louisa M., b. ca.1867 AL.
300	v.	John F. b. 1869 St. Clair Co., AL; m. Sarah Ann Fortenberry.
301	vi.	William Callaway, b. 25 Nov 1870 St. Clair Co., AL; m. Sarah Ann "Annie" Kelsoe.
302	vii.	Alex Franklin "Frank," b. 1872 St. Clair Co., AL; m1. Nancy Ava "Avie" Sullivan; m2. Mattie Milstead.
303	viii.	Marion "Thomas," b. 6 Feb 1874 St. Clair Co., AL; m. Ophelia Barron.
	ix.	Mattie Samantha, b.21 Sep 1875 St. Clair Co., AL. She m. John Alexander Hodges ca.1900. She and John Alexander Hodges appeared on the censuses of 30 Apr 1910 Jefferson Co., AL and 21 Jan 1920 Coalburg, Jefferson Co., AL. She d.29 Mar 1954 Birmingham, Jefferson Co., AL, at age 78; bur. Friendship UMC Cem., Gardendale, Jefferson Co., AL.
		John Alexander Hodges, b.3 Sep 1872. He d.4 Aug 1924 at age 51 and was bur. Friendship UMC Cem.
304	x.	Peter Columbus "Pete," b. 18 Jan 1878 St. Clair Co., AL; m. Alice Miranda Billingsley.
305	xi.	James Madison "Jim," b. 14 Jan 1880 St. Clair Co., AL; m. Nettie Nancy Brooks.
306	xii.	Isa Jane "Icie," b. 14 Feb 1881 AL; m. Rev. William D. Stewart.

110. William Thomas[5] Abney (Benjamin[4], Hezekiah[3], Elisha[2], Abner[1]), b. Sep 1838 GA. He m. Martha W. Perry ca.1867 Cleburne Co., AL. He and Martha W. Perry appeared on the census of 12 Jun 1880 Cleburne Co., AL. He appeared on the census of 5 Jun 1900 Tallapoosa, Haralson Co., GA. He d.3 Jul 1900 at age 61 and was bur. Ebenezer Ch. Cem., Haralson Co., GA.

Martha W. Perry, b.Mar 1843 AL. She d.1908 and was bur. Ebenezer Ch. Cem., Haralson Co., GA.

Known children of William Thomas[5] Abney and Martha W. Perry all b. AL:

	i.	Henry C.[6], b. Jun 1868; m. Ellen C. "Ella" Vaughn.
	ii.	Elizabeth, b. ca.1871.
308	iii.	Mary C., b. 30 Jan 1873.
	iv.	Emma, b.Apr 1874.
309	v.	William Talton, b. 3 May 1876; m. Narcissus Shipp.
	vi.	James "Thomas", b.10 Apr 1879. He d.29 May 1907 at age 28; bur. Ebenezer Church Cem., Haralson Co., GA.
	vii.	Andrew J., b.Feb 1887.

111. Eli Newton "Bish"[5] Abney (Benjamin[4], Hezekiah[3], Elisha[2], Abner[1]), b.1 Aug 1848 GA. He m. Sarah Adaline Busbey on 21 Dec 1868 Cleburne Co., AL. He and Sarah Adaline Busbey appeared on the censuses of 17 Jun 1880, 2 Jun 1900 and 30 Apr 1910 Oak Level, Cleburne Co., AL. He d. before 1920 and was bur. Camp Creek Bapt. Ch. Cem., Oak Level, Cleburne Co., AL.

Sarah Adaline Busbey, b.Jul 1848 SC. She was liv. on 3 Jan 1920 with her son, John Abney, Oak Level, Cleburne Co., AL. She d.16 Oct 1923 Cleburne Co., AL, at age 75 and was bur. Camp Creek Bapt. Ch. Cem., Oak Level, Cleburne Co., AL.

Known children of Eli Newton "Bish"[5] Abney and Sarah Adaline Busbey:

	i.	(n.n.)[6], b. ca.1869 AL; d. before 1880.
	ii.	(n.n.), b. ca.1871 AL; d. before 1880.
	iii.	(n.n.), b. ca.1873 AL; d. before 1880.
310	iv.	Leticia Cathren, b. 29 Dec 1875 Oak Level, Cleburne Co., AL; m. William Aaron Lorren.
311	v.	Eli Franklin, b. 26 Nov 1876 Oak Level, Cleburne Co., AL; m. Anna "Leanna" Potts.
312	vi.	Posey Osiciro, b. 18 Jun 1878 Oak Level, Cleburne Co., AL; m. Rosie P. Waites.
	vii.	Noel R., b.May 1881 Oak Level, Cleburne Co., AL. He d.1900 and was bur. Camp Creek Bapt. Ch. Cem., Oak Level
313	viii.	Rosa Lee, b. 14 Mar 1883 AL; m. Isaac C. Crawford.
	ix.	R.H. (dau.), b.Mar 1885 AL.
314	x.	Sarah Elizabeth, b. 10 Mar 1887 AL; m. Walter Pickens McWhorter.
315	xi.	John Andrew "Andy," b. 13 May 1889 Cleburne Co., AL; m. Berta Ruth "Bert" Farmer.
316	xii.	Benjamin Earl "Ben," b. 3 Mar 1891 AL; m. Winnie Ellen Little.
	xiii.	Pearlie M., b.27 Mar 1893 AL; m. (n.n.) Combs; Liv. on 3 Jan 1920 with her brother, John Abney, Oak Level, Cleburne Co., AL. She d.New Year's Eve, 31 Jan 1970 at age 76 and was bur. Holly Pond Cem., Holly Pond, Cullman Co., AL.

112. James Alfred "Alf"*⁵* Abney (Benjamin*⁴*, Hezekiah*³*, Elisha*²*, Abner*¹*), b.20 Aug 1850 Cobb Co., GA. He m. Nancy J. Grubbs on 14 Feb 1869 Cleburne Co., AL. He and Nancy J. Grubbs appeared on the census of 8 Jun 1880 Davisville, Calhoun Co., AL. He d. New Year's Day, 1 Jan 1898 GA at age 47 and was bur. Pleasant Hope Cem., Rome, Floyd Co., GA.
        Nancy J. Grubbs, b. ca.1849 AL. She d.23 May 1928 Lindale, Floyd Co., GA and was bur. Pleasant Hope Cem., Rome, Floyd Co., GA.
Known children of James Alfred "Alf"*⁵* Abney and Nancy J. Grubbs:
    317   i.   Martha Elizabeth*⁶*, b. 3 Nov 1869 Cleburne Co., AL; m. James Samuel Burkhalter.
    318   ii.   Marion Matthew, b. 29 Apr 1871 Calhoun Co., AL; m. Sarah "Alice" Morris.
    319   iii. Melissa Cordelia "Delia," b. 10 Sep 1873 AL; m. Thomas Seals Burkhalter.
    320   iv.   Geretie M., b. 24 May 1876 AL; m. Adolphus Dempsey "Dolf" Miller.
    321   v.   William "Taylor," b. 29 Apr 1879 AL; m. Emma F. "Emmie" Cashion.
    322   vi.   Lillie, b. 31 Jul 1883; m. Forrest Ranger Reynolds.
    323   vii. Lottie Zefro, b. 21 Apr 1885 Polk Co., GA; m. Robert Sidney "Bob" Broadaway.
    324   viii. Sylvester B. "Vester," b. 9 Feb 1887 GA; m. Mamie Lee Bradshaw.

113. Joseph Calloway*⁵* Abney (Benjamin*⁴*, Hezekiah*³*, Elisha*²*, Abner*¹*), b.11 Dec 1853 Oak Level, Benton, Cleburne Co., AL. He m1. Georgiane Bowen on 28 Jan 1877 Paulding Co., GA, but no issue. He m2. Josephine L.B. "Jossie" Butler on 1 Dec 1878 Paulding Co., GA. He and Josephine L.B. "Jossie" Butler appeared on the census of 9 Jun 1880 Paulding Co., GA. He d.29 Sep 1888 Paulding Co., GA, at age 34 and was bur. New Hope Cem., Dallas, Paulding Co., GA.
        Josephine L.B. "Jossie" Butler, b.11 Aug 1859. She m2. George Washington McMichen in 1889. She d.28 Jun 1933 Paulding Co., GA, at age 73 and was bur. New Hope Cem., Dallas, Paulding Co., GA.
Known children of Joseph Calloway*⁵* Abney and Josephine L.B. "Jossie" Butler:
    325   i.   Robert Andrew "Andy"*⁶*, b. 18 Aug 1880 Paulding Co., GA; m. Henrietta "Etta" Barnett.
           ii.   Charlotte "Lottie" m. Zollie A. Prewett. , b.3 Jan 1882 Paulding Co., GA and was bur. New Hope Cem., Dallas, Paulding Co., GA. She d.22 Jun 1959 Atlanta, Fulton Co., GA, at age 77.
                 Zollie A. Prewett, b.23 Oct 1878. He d.27 Jun 1955 at age 76 and was bur. New Hope Cem., Dallas, GA.
    326   iii. Minnie Beatrice, b. 1884; m. John Franklin Prewett.
    327   iv.   Alonzo Calloway "Lon," b. 18 May 1886 Paulding Co., GA; m. Ruth Gravett.

114. Charles Robert "Bob"*⁵* Abney (Benjamin*⁴*, Hezekiah*³*, Elisha*²*, Abner*¹*), b. Jul 1872 Cleburne Co., AL. He m. Sarah Ann "Annie" Stephenson on 7 Sep 1894 Cleburne Co., AL. He and Sarah Ann "Annie" Stephenson appeared on the censuses of 11 Jun 1900, 26 Apr 1910, 19 Jan 1920, 17 Apr 1930 and 10 Apr 1940 Cleburne Co., AL. He d.13 Apr 1941 Edwardsville, Cleburne Co., AL, at age 68 and was bur. Camp Creek Bapt. Ch. Cem., Oak Level, Cleburne Co., AL.
        Sarah Ann "Annie" Stephenson, b.23 Dec 1869 AL; d.21 Aug 1955 Fruithurst, Cleburne Co., AL, ae.85; bur. Camp Creek Bapt. Ch. Cem.
Known children of Charles Robert "Bob"*⁵* Abney and Sarah Ann "Annie" Stephenson:
           i.   Jesse B.*⁶*, b.23 Jul 1896 AL. He d.28 May 1981 at age 84; bur. Upper Cane Creek Cem., Fruithurst, Cleburne Co., AL.
    328   ii.   John Robert, b. 26 Sep 1899 Cleburne Co., AL; m. Mahala "Gertrude" Price.
           iii. (baby), b. after 1900 AL. He d. before 1910 AL.
    329   iv.   William Thomas "Bill," b. 19 Jun 1903 Fruithurst, Cleburne Co., AL; m. Essie Mae "Leona" Williams.

115. John J.*⁵* Abney (Benjamin*⁴*, Hezekiah*³*, Elisha*²*, Abner*¹*), b.13 Sep 1873 Cleburne Co., AL. He m. Louisa "Francis" Dollar ca.1894. He and Louisa "Francis" Dollar appeared on the censuses of 22 Jun 1900 St. Clair Co., AL; 27 Apr 1910 Coal City, St. Clair Co., AL and 18 Jan 1920 Friendship, St. Clair Co., AL. He d.19 Jul 1926 at age 52 and was bur. Friendship Bapt. Ch. Cem., Odenville, St. Clair Co., AL.
        Louisa "Francis" Dollar, b.6 Sep 1871 AL. She was liv. on 3 Apr 1940 with her son, Jasper Abney, St. Clair Co., AL. She d.22 Apr 1951 Ashville, St. Clair Co., AL, at age 79 and was bur. Friendship Bapt. Ch. Cem., Odenville, St. Clair Co., AL.
Known children of John J.*⁵* Abney and Louisa "Francis" Dollar all b. AL:
           i.   (baby)*⁶*, b. ca.1895. He/she d. before 1900 AL.
           ii.   Annie R. "Bertie", b.Feb 1897.
           iii. Jasper W., b.1904. He appeared on the census of 18 Apr 1930 Moffett State Farm Prison, Jack Springs, Escambia Co., AL. He appeared on the census of 3 Apr 1940 St. Clair Co., AL. He d.22 Mar 1951 Ashville, St. Clair Co., AL.
           iv.   Orbie M., b.27 Nov 1909. m. Ozella J. (n.n.). He appeared on the census of 8 Apr 1930 South St. Clair (County) Jail, Pell City, St. Clair Co., AL. He was liv. on 3 Apr 1940 with brother, Jasper Abney, St. Clair Co., AL. He d.2 Apr 1986 at age 76 and was bur. Piney Grove Bapt. Ch. Cem., Ashville, St. Clair Co., AL.
                 Ozella J. (n.n.), b.6 Jan 1916. She d.15 Apr 2008 at age 92 and was bur. Piney Grove Bapt. Ch. Cem.

116. Hezekiah M.*⁵* Yarborough (Delilah*⁴* Abney, Hezekiah*³*, Elisha*²*, Abner*¹*), b. ca.1834 GA. He m. Rebecca A. (n.n.). He and Rebecca A. (n.n.) appeared on the census of 8 Aug 1860 Cutoff Dist., Jackson Co., GA. (Rebecca A., b. ca.1837 GA.)
Known child of Hezekiah M.*⁵* Yarborough and Rebecca A. (n.n.):
           i.   William H.*⁶*, b. ca.1859 GA.

117. Pvt. Pinkney Floyd*⁵* Abney (CSA) (Wiley*⁴*, Hezekiah*³*, Elisha*²*, Abner*¹*), b. Jan 1842 Cobb Co., GA. He m. Sarah Graham ca.1861. Pinkney fought in the War for Southern Independence for the Confederate Army. He enlisted at Dalton, GA in Capt. Matthew's Co., Co. B, 41st Infantry Reg. He was captured near Marietta, GA in 1864 and transferred to Nashville, and later onto Louisville Military Prison. He was transferred to Camp Morton in Marion Co., IN on 01 Jul 1864 and transferred in a prisoner exchange on 15 Mar 1865. Pinckney was admitted to Jackson Hospital in Richmond, VA on 24 Mar 1865. He d.1870 GA and was bur. Abney Cem., Lee Co., VA.
        Sarah Graham, b. ca.1840 GA. She appeared as Head of Household on the census of 25 Aug 1870 Floyd Co., GA. She m. John Carmichael on 13 Jan 1874 Washington Co., TN. She and John Carmichael appeared on the census of 3 Jun 1880 Greene Co., TN.
Known children of Pvt. Pinkney Floyd*⁵* Abney (CSA) and Sarah Graham:
    330   i.   Laura E.*⁶*, b. Nov 1864 GA; m. Franklin "Frank" Dobbins.
    331   ii.   John "Roscoe," b. 9 Jun 1865 Rome, Floyd Co., GA; m. Sarah Ruth Ramsey; m. Laura Johnson.
    332   iii. Sarah Ann "Sally," b. 1870 GA; m. George Mac Inman.

118. Pvt. Thomas "Jackson"⁵ Abney (CSA) (Wiley⁴, Hezekiah³, Elisha², Abner¹), b.22 Jul 1846 Cobb Co., GA. He m. Dorothy C. Cleveland on 8 Dec 1867 Paulding Co., GA. He and Dorothy C. Cleveland appeared on the censuses of 11 Jun 1870 Polk Co., GA; 10 Jun 1880 Fish Creek, Polk Co., GA and 21 Jun 1900 Burnt Hickory, Paulding Co., GA. He d.6 Apr 1907 Burnt Hickory, Paulding Co., GA, at age 60 and was bur. Floyd Creek Baptist Church Cem., Polk Co., GA.
    Dorothy C. Cleveland, b.Jul 1847 GA. She d. after 1900.
Known children of Pvt. Thomas "Jackson"⁵ Abney (CSA) and Dorothy C. Cleveland all b. Fish Creek, Polk Co., GA:
    333   i.   James Henry⁶, b. 20 Nov 1869; m. Sarah Elizabeth "Sallie" Dodd.
           ii.   John W., b. ca.1871.
           iii. George W., b. ca.1874.
           iv.   M.A.E., b. ca.1876.
           v.   Sarah Lou Ellen, b. ca.1878.

119. Martha Jane⁵ Abney (Wiley⁴, Hezekiah³, Elisha², Abner¹), b.Feb 1848 Cobb Co., GA. She m. William Shedrick H. Wilkerson in 1865. She and William Shedrick Harrison Wilkerson appeared on the census of 21 Jun 1900 Burnt Hickory, Paulding Co., GA. She d.1931 Hall Co., GA.
    William Shedrick Harrison Wilkerson, b.Oct 1844 AL.
Known children of Martha Jane⁵ Abney and William Shedrick Harrison Wilkerson:
           i.   John⁶, b.1872.
           ii.   Thomas H., b.1873.
           iii. Lucy, b.1874.
           iv.   Clark E., b.1878.

120. James Allen⁵ Abney (Wiley⁴, Hezekiah³, Elisha², Abner¹), b.27 May 1850 Cobb Co., GA. He was liv. on 6 Aug 1871 Calhoun Co., AL. He m1. Margaret E. Wilkerson on 6 Aug 1871 Calhoun Co., AL. He and Margaret E. Wilkerson appeared on the census of 12 Jun 1880 Calhoun Co., AL. He m2. Margaret Jane "Maggie" Johnson on 3 Feb 1885 Calhoun Co., AL. He and Margaret Johnson appeared on the census of 19 Jun 1900 Polk Co., GA. He d.3 Mar 1910 at age 59 and was bur. Hills Creek Baptist Church Cem., Rockmart, Polk Co., GA.
    Margaret E. Wilkerson, b.1857 Calhoun Co., AL. She d.1880 Calhoun Co., AL.
Known children of James Allen⁵ Abney and Margaret E. Wilkerson all b. Calhoun Co., AL:
           i.   Sarah⁶, b. ca.1873. She m. John n.n. (Higgins/Gagen) in 1889.
           ii.   Mary "Minnie", b.21 Jan 1875; d.25 Jan 1938 Stilesboro, Bartow Co., GA, age 63; bur. in 1938 Floyd Creek Baptist Cem.
           iii. Viola, b. ca.1877. She m. Joe H. Adams.
           iv.   Maud M., b.Jun 1880. She m. Martin Beesby.
           v.   Thomas "Tommy", b.13 Sep 1883. He d.13 Sep 1883 Calhoun Co., AL.

    Margaret Jane "Maggie" Johnson, b.1865. She m2. Frank Williams in 1918. She was bur. Comers Cem., Sylacauga, Talladega Co., AL.
Known children of James Allen⁵ Abney and Margaret Jane "Maggie" Johnson:
    334   i.   Emily Elmira⁶, b. 13 Sep 1885 Calhoun Co., AL; m. Robert Lee Gray; m. J.L. Newton.
           ii.   Lottie Rebecca Anna Lee, b.25 Sep 1886 Bartow Co., GA. She m. Samuel Goodman Siniard. She d.16 Apr 1964 Floyd Co., GA, at age 77.
    335   iii. John Allen, b. 7 Apr 1888 GA; m. Hazzle N. Denton.
           iv.   Oran Biago "Van", b.6 Aug 1890 GA. He m. Anna Lee Liniard on 28 Oct 1906 Bartow Co., GA. He d.4 Sep 1961 Pell City, St. Clair Co., GA, at age 71.
           v.   Fannie Alice, b.26 Jun 1892 GA. She m. James Orville Barnett on 26 Dec 1909.
           vi.   Martha Jane, b.7 Jul 1894 Stilesboro, Bartow Co., GA. She m. Obie Dower Haines on 17 Apr 1912 Sylacuaga, AL. She d.19 Jul 1981 Sylacuaga, Talladega Co., AL, at age 87 and was bur. in 1981 Evergreen Cem.
           vii. Mark Adkinson, b.6 Nov 1896 GA. He m. Nellie (n.n.) Tarpon Springs, FL. He d. AR
           viii. Katie May, b.28 May 1899 GA. She m. Robert Cain on 2 Dec 1915.
           ix.   Jesse Ben, b.20 Apr 1902 GA. He m. Ora Jones on 12 Mar 1928. He d.28 May 1930 GA at age 28.

121. Nancy Elmira "Elmiry"⁵ Abney (Wiley⁴, Hezekiah³, Elisha², Abner¹), b.1 May 1852 Cobb Co., GA. She m. John Silas Carver on 17 Apr 1869 Floyd Co., GA. She and John Silas Carver appeared on the censuses of 12 Jul 1870 Floyd Co., GA; 12 Jun 1880 Burnt Hickory, Paulding Co., GA and 14 Jun 1900 Talladega Co., AL. She d.13 Apr 1932 Talladega Co., AL, ae.79; bur. Marble City Cem., Sylacauga, Talladega Co., AL.
    John Silas Carver, b.3 Aug 1845. He d.2 Sep 1901 at age 56 and was bur. Lanier Cem., Grasmere, Talladega Co., AL.
Known children of Nancy Elmira "Elmiry"⁵ Abney and John Silas Carver:
           i.   James "Frank"⁶, b. ca.Apr 1870 GA.
           ii.   William "Willie", b. ca.1872 GA.
           iii. Sarah, b. ca.1875 GA.
           iv.   Joe Ella, b. ca.1877 GA.
           v.   Henry, b. ca.1880 GA.
           vi.   Archie, b. ca.1885 GA.
           vii. Renie, b. ca.1887 GA.
           viii. Maggie, b. ca.1888 GA.
           ix.   Walter, b. ca.1891 AL.
           x.   Mellie, b. ca.1892 AL.

122. Sarah E.⁵ Abney (Wiley⁴, Hezekiah³, Elisha², Abner¹), b. ca.1854 Cobb Co., GA. She m. T.W. Wilkerson on 12 Mar 1875 Calhoun Co., AL. She and T.W. Wilkerson appeared on the census of 17 Jun 1880 Calhoun Co., AL. She m2. Dick Jones (per Hensell).
    T.W. Wilkerson, b. ca.1850 GA.
Known children of Sarah E.⁵ Abney and T.W. Wilkerson both b. AL:
           i.   James A.⁶, b. ca.1877.
           ii.   Charles R., b. ca.1879.

123. Pvt. James Franklin⁵ Abney (CSA) (Andrew⁴, Hezekiah³, Elisha², Abner¹), b.29 Nov 1838 Cobb Co., GA. He joined the Confederate Army in May 1861. He m. Elisabeth Brooks on 9 Nov 1865 Troup Co., GA. He and "Eliza" Brooks appeared on the census of 1880 Carroll Co., GA.
   Elisabeth Key "Eliza" Brooks, b.1836 GA. She m. John Towles in 1855. She d.1913; bur. Forest Hill Cem., Birmingham, Jefferson Co., AL.
Known child of Pvt. James Franklin⁵ Abney (CSA) and Elisabeth Key "Eliza" Brooks:
   336   i.   Jesse Brooks⁶, b. 28 Sep 1867; m1. Wilhelmina "Mina" Abel; m2. Olive Adele Brockert.

124. John⁵ Abney (Andrew⁴, Hezekiah³, Elisha², Abner¹), b. ca.1842 Cobb Co., GA. He m. Martha "Jane" Brown. He d.13 Nov 1922 Attalla, Etowah Co., AL and was bur. Carnes Chapel Cem., Ivalee, Etowah Co., AL.
   Martha "Jane" Brown, b.30 Oct 1874 GA. She d.25 Mar 1920 Etowah Co., AL, at age 45 and was bur. Carnes Chapel Cem., Ivalee, AL.
Known child of John⁵ Abney and Martha "Jane" Brown:
       i.   Willie Tead⁶ , b.14 Sep 1901. She m. Willie E. Aderholt. She d.4 Aug 1969 at age 67 and was bur. Noble Hill Cem., Attalla, Etowah Co., AL.
            Willie E. Aderholt, b.23 Jan 1901. He d.4 Apr 1967 at age 66 and was bur. Noble Hill Cem., Attalla, AL.

125. William Duncan "Bill"⁵ Abner (James⁴ Abney, Hezekiah³, Elisha², Abner¹), b.Sep 1846 GA. He was liv. on 19 Jul 1870 with his mother, *Senia Abner*, Heard Co., GA. He is the first in his family to have assumed the surname spelling *Abner* (see Etymology in Appendix A, page 257). He m.ca.1870 Julia A.F. Pike, daughter of Thomas Pike and Vina Adams, ca.1875. He and Julia A.F. Pike appeared on the censuses of 8 Jun 1880 and 4 Jun 1900 Franklin, Heard Co., GA.
   Julia A.F. Pike, b.Mar 1851 GA. She was liv. on 23 Jul 1870 with her mother, *Viney Pike*, Heard Co., GA. She d.1900 GA.
Known children of William Duncan "Bill"⁵ Abner and Julia A.F. Pike:
       i.   Ida Lue⁶, b.18 Sep 1871 Heard Co., GA. She m. J.W. Griffith. She d.3 Feb 1919 at age 47 and was bur. Holly Creek Cem., Broken Bow, McCurtain Co., OK.
            J.W. Griffith, b.12 Jun 1872. He d.27 Sep 1954 at age 82; bur. Lexington Cem., Lexington, Cleveland Co., OK.
   337   ii. Charlie M., b. ca.1872 Heard Co., GA; m. (n.n.).
   338   iii. James R. "Jim," b. 10 Mar 1874 Heard Co., GA; m. Thuella Bernetie "Ella" Craven.
   339   iv. Wyatt Joel Heflin "Heff," b. 26 Aug 1876 Heard Co., GA; m. Tommie Lee Hannah.
   340   v.   Josaphine "Jossie," b. 8 Oct 1878 Heard Co., GA; m. Earnest W. Purgason.
   341   vi. Rufus Cook, b. 15 Oct 1882 Heard Co., GA; m. Cora Pauline West.
   342   vii. Carrie Dell, b. 11 Jun 1885 Franklin, Heard Co., GA; m. Merritt D. Daniel.
   343   viii. Wiley "Frank," b. Aug 1890 Heard Co., GA; m. Odessa Bell "Dessie" White.

126. James Andrew "Jim"⁵ Abna (James⁴ Abney, Hezekiah³, Elisha², Abner¹), b.30 Nov 1855 Franklin, Heard Co., GA. He is the first in his family to have assumed the surname spelling *Abna* (see Etymology in Appendix A, page 257). He m. Mary Ann Elizabeth Thornton. He and Mary Ann Elizabeth Thornton appeared on the census of 7 Jun 1880 Heard Co., GA. He d.18 Jul 1945 College Park, Fulton Co., GA, at age 89 and was bur. Hillview East Cem., LaGrange, Troup Co., GA.
   Mary Ann Elizabeth Thornton, b.10 May 1859 Franklin, Heard Co., GA. She d.26 Aug 1939 West Point, Troup Co., GA, at age 80 and was bur. Hillview East Cem., LaGrange, Troup Co., GA.
Known children of James Andrew "Jim"⁵ Abna and Mary Ann Elizabeth Thornton all b. Franklin, Heard Co., GA:
   344   i.   Callie Eugenia⁶, b. 16 Sep 1877; m. Calvin Strickland.
       ii. Detie "Annie", b.16 Aug 1879. She m. George Mitchell. She lived in 1910 Justice, Brazoria Co., TX. She d.21 Feb 1951 Fulton Co., GA, at age 71.
   345   iii. Robert James, b. 2 Feb 1882; m. Frances Sarah Jones.
   346   iv. Molly Lee, b. 7 Jan 1885; m. Jonathan Britton Hill.
   347   v.   Emily Ophelia, b. 13 May 1887; m. John Bogus Gable.
   348   vi. Lina, b. 24 Feb 1890; m. Wesley Green Renfroe.
   349   vii. Katie Dell, b. 9 Aug 1892; m. Fred M. Montgomery.
   350   viii. Minnie Elizabeth, b. 17 Apr 1895; m. Walter Thomas Sheets.
   351   ix. Ales Ridley "Abe," b. 11 Jan 1898; m. Nell L. "Nellie" Harry.

127. Julia A.R.⁵ Abney (Jeff⁴, Hezekiah³, Elisha², Abner¹), b. ca.1848 AL. She m. George Wesley Hanners ca.1876. She and George Wesley Hanners appeared on the census of 9 Jun 1880 Rockdale Co., GA. She appeared on the census of 7 Jun 1900 Fort Payne, DeKalb Co., AL.
   George Wesley Hanners, b.26 Dec 1857 Fulton Co., GA. He d.7 Jan 1926 Taylor, Williamson Co., TX, at age 68.
Known children of Julia A.R.⁵ Abney and George Wesley Hanners:
       i.   Thomas P.⁶, b. ca.1877 GA.
       ii. Georgie, b. ca.1879 GA.
       iii. Ida, b.Feb 1882 AL.

128. John Newton Nathan⁵ Abney (Jeff⁴, Hezekiah³, Elisha², Abner¹), b.9 Feb 1851 DeKalb Co., GA. He m. Martha Cynthia Maddox on 18 Dec 1878. He and Martha Cynthia Maddox appeared on the censuses of 9 Jun 1880 Rockdale Co., GA; 5 Jun 1900 San Francisco, San Francisco Co., CA and 19 Apr 1910 Honey Creek Dist., Rockdale Co., GA. He and Martha Cynthia Maddox were liv. on 2 Jan 1920 with their son-in-law, Gus Bocakis, San Francisco, San Francisco Co., CA and 18 Apr 1930 with thei son-in-law, Gus Bocakis, San Mateo, San Mateo Co., CA. He d.10 Sep 1934 San Francisco, San Francisco Co., CA, at age 83 and was bur. Sunset Maus. and Columbarium, El Cerrito, Contra Costa Co., CA.
   Martha Cynthia Maddox m. John Lynch Pyle. , b.25 Jul 1847 GA. She d.19 Nov 1939 CA at age 92 and was bur. Sunset Maus.
Known children of John Newton Nathan⁵ Abney and Martha Cynthia Maddox:
   352   i.   James "Chalmers"⁶, b. 14 Oct 1879 Conyers, Rockdale Co., GA; m. Jennie Cochran.
   353   ii. Jacob Kearney "Jake," b. 26 Oct 1881 Honey Creek, Rockdale Co., GA; m. Eugénie Adélaïde Argoud.
   354   iii. Arizona "Elizabeth," b. 10 May 1884 GA; m1. William F. Riley; m2. Louis Angelo Chiappella.
       iv. Charles Lealand Presley, b. Jan 1886 GA. He m. Lizzie Cooper. He and Lizzie Cooper appeared on the census of 19 Apr 1910 Honey Creek Dist., Rockdale Co., GA. He appeared on the census of 20 Apr 1940 San Francisco, San Francisco Co., CA. He d.1957. (Lizzie Cooper, b. ca.1887 GA.)

v. Livy Turner Quigg "Bill", b.14 Jun 1888 CA. He was liv. on 23 Apr 1910 with brother-in-law, Wm. F. Riley, San Francisco, San Francisco Co., CA. He m. Eugenia E. Swanson in 1923. He and Eugenia E. Swanson appeared on the census of 4 Apr 1930 Seattle, King Co., WA. He d.23 Jun 1974 Seattle, King Co., WA, at age 86 and was bur. Evergreen-Washelli Mem. Park, Seattle, King Co., WA.

Eugenia E. Swanson, b.15 Jul 1891 WA. She was liv. on 3 Apr 1940 with brother, Oscar C. Swanson, Pierce Co., WA. She d.12 Apr 1969 Puyallup, Pierce Co., WA, at age 77.

vi. Harvey Linton, b.22 Jul 1890. He m. Frances W. (n.n.). He d.10 Feb 1965 at age 74 and was bur. Forest Hill Cem., Birmingham, Jefferson Co., AL.

Frances W. (n.n.), b.24 Aug 1903. She d.20 Jan 2000 at age 96 and was bur. Forest Hill Cem., Birmingham.

vii. Frances Lucinda "Fanny", b.19 Jun 1891 Conyers, Rockdale Co., GA. She m. Constantinos N. "Gus" Bovakis in 1918. She and Constantinos N. "Gus" Bovakis appeared on the censuses of 2 Jan 1920 San Francisco, San Francisco Co., CA and 18 Apr 1930 San Mateo, San Mateo Co., CA. She d.8 Aug 1983 San Mateo Co., CA, at age 92 and was bur. Sunset Maus. and Columbarium, El Cerrito, Contra Costa Co., CA.

Constantinos N. "Gus" Bovakis, b.21 May 1892 Greece. He immigrated in 1909. He was naturalized in 1918. He d.2 Nov 1961 San Francisco, San Francisco Co., CA, at age 69 and was bur. Sunset Maus. and Columbarium, El Cerrito.

129. **Elizabeth⁵ Abney** (Joel⁴, Hezekiah³, Elisha², Abner¹), b.19 Mar 1854 GA. She m. William A. Johnson ca.1877. She and William A. Johnson appeared on the census of 4 Jun 1900 Cedartown, Polk Co., GA. She d.30 Jul 1935 Polk Co., GA, at age 81 and was bur. Roberts Funeral Home Cem., Polk Co., GA.

William A. Johnson, b.20 Jun 1857 Cherokee Co., GA; d.7 Dec 1927 Rome, Floyd Co., GA, age 70 and was bur. Roberts Funeral Home Cem.
Known children of Elizabeth⁵ Abney and William A. Johnson:

355   i.   Florence⁶, b. Oct 1877 AL; m. (n.n.).
      ii. James, b.Jan 1880.
      iii. Annie, b.May 1881.
      iv. Ola, b.21 Apr 1892. She m. Nim W. Sorrells. She d.24 Oct 1918 at age 26 and was bur. New Harmony Cem., Cedartown, Polk Co., GA.

Nim W. Sorrells, b.7 Nov 1890. He m. Nettie Belle Youngblood. He d.2 Dec 1984 at age 94 and was bur. Roberts Funeral Home Cem., Polk Co., GA.

130. **Sarah Jane "Janie"⁵ Abney** (Joel⁴, Hezekiah³, Elisha², Abner¹), b.29 Jun 1859 AL. She m. John Wiley Johnson ca.1879. She d.5 Jan 1936 Beckville, Panola Co., TX, at age 76 and was bur. Martin Cem., Tatum, Rusk Co., TX.

John Wiley Johnson, b.3 Apr 1860 Buchanan, Haralson Co., GA; d.10 Sep 1932 Beckville, Panola Co., TX, age 72 and was bur. Martin Cem.
Known children of Sarah Jane "Janie"⁵ Abney and John Wiley Johnson:

356   i.   Viola M.⁶, b. 25 Mar 1880 Oak Level, Cleburne Co., AL; m. Burrell Peoples "Burl" Bailey.
357   ii. Levia Jane, b. 2 Jul 1882 GA; m1. Asa Hightower; m2. James Thomas; m3. Charley Clemons; m4. John Brincefield.
358   iii. Lou Etta, b. 25 Feb 1885 GA; m. Henry Mack Pittman.
359   iv. George B., b. 14 Mar 1888 Cleburne Co., AL; m. Lena Estelle Pittman.
360   v.   John Thomas, b. 17 Oct 1894 Jackson Co., AL; m. Flora Edith "Eddie" Williamson.

131. **John William⁵ Abney** (Joel⁴, Hezekiah³, Elisha², Abner¹), b.9 Apr 1861 Cleburne Co., AL. He m. Sidney Varjulia Crews on 18 Dec 1887 Cleburne Co., AL. He and Sidney Varjulia Crews appeared on the censuses of 3 May 1910 Jackson Co., AL; 6 Jan 1920 Stevenson, Jackson Co., AL & 17 Apr 1930 Lupton City, Hamilton Co., AL. He d.11 Oct 1932 Hamilton Co., TN, ae.71; Jackson Chapel Cem., Hixson, Hamilton Co., TN.

Sidney Varjulia Crews, b.30 Jul 1870 LaGrange, Troup Co., GA. She was liv. on 3 Apr 1940 with son-in-law, William Bean, Lupton City, Hamilton Co., AL. She d.23 Aug 1961 Hamilton Co., TN, at age 91 and was bur. Jackson Chapel Cem., Hixson, Hamilton Co., TN.
Known children of John William⁵ Abney and Sidney Varjulia Crews:

361   i.   Minnie Lou⁶, b. 4 Jan 1889 Cleburne Co., AL; m1. Samuel Benton Wininger; m2. John Alfred DeBerry.
362   ii.   Essie L., b. 23 Dec 1889 AL; m. William "Robert" Bean.
363   iii. William A., b. 19 Jun 1892 Cleburne Co., AL; m1. Martha Jane "Janie" Roberts; m2. Nancy Wise.
364   iv.   Louis David, b. 23 Dec 1893 Cleburne Co., AL; m1. (n.n.); m2. Clara E. Tidwell.
365   v.   Alonzo, b. 24 Nov 1896 AL; m. Elsie L. Spence.
      vi.   John "Wesley", b.29 Apr 1900. He m. Faithia (n.n.) He d.8 Jun 1969 Akron, Summit Co., OH, at age 69 and was bur. Jackson Chapel Cem., Hixson, Hamilton Co., TN.
      vii. Arthur C., b.9 Jun 1902 AL. He m. Madge P. (n.n.) ca.1922. He and Madge P. (n.n.) were liv. on 16 Apr 1930 with his niece, Eva M. Penney, Lupton City, Hamilton Co., TN. He d.5 Dec 1979 Chattanooga, Hamilton Co., TN, at age 77 and was bur. Chattanooga Mem. Park, Chattanooga, Hamilton Co., TN.

Madge P. (n.n.), b.Christmas Day, 25 Dec 1907 AL; d.12 Feb 1994 at age 86 and was bur. Chattanooga Mem. Park.
      viii. Mae Ellen, b.29 May 1904 AL. She m. Marvin Weaver (USN-WWII). She d.18 Aug 1981 New Boston, Wayne Co., MI, at age 77 and was bur. Michigan Mem. Park, Flat Rock, Wayne Co., MI.

Marvin Weaver (USN-WWII), b.1 Jun 1908. He d.7 Mar 1981 at age 72 and was bur. Michigan Mem. Park.
      ix.   Janus, b.8 Jan 1907 AL. He d.2 May 1971 Hamilton Co., TN, at age 64 and was bur. Jackson Chapel Cem., Hixson, Hamilton Co., TN.

132. **Rebecca Bethena⁵ Abney** (Joel⁴, Hezekiah³, Elisha², Abner¹), b.2 Sep 1865 Cleburne Co., AL. She m. Hirram Franklin "Frank" Waddle on 21 Jan 1886 Cleburne Co., AL. She d.22 Jan 1919 Hokes Bluff, Etowah Co., AL, at age 53; bur. Pine Grove Cem., Glencoe, Etowah Co., AL.

Hiram Franklin "Frank" Waddle, b.20 Jul 1861. He d.30 Jan 1949 at age 87 and was bur. Riverside Mem. Park, Jacksonville, Duval Co., FL.
Known children of Rebecca Bethena⁵ Abney and Hirram Franklin "Frank" Waddle:

366   i.   Nancy Annie⁶, b. 4 Feb 1888 Hokes Bluff, Etowah Co., AL; m. John Dossie Lee.
367   ii.   Lawson Lee, b. Christmas Day, 25 Dec 1890; m. Mabel Lowery.
368   iii. Lelius Johnson, b. New Year's Day, 1 Jan 1894; m. Winifred Oveda Cannon.
369   iv.   Elsie Bethena, b. 17 Dec 1897; m. Lonnie Lee Walden.

v. Hershell Clab. "Bud", b.16 Jul 1901. He m. Grace V. (n.n.). Bud d.29 Dec 1974 at age 73 and was bur. Riverside Mem. Park, Jacksonville, Duval Co., FL.
      Grace V. (n.n.), b.10 Oct 1916. She d.1 Aug 1990 at age 73 and was bur. Riverside Mem. Park, Jacksonville.

133. Martha "Mattie"[5] Abney (Joel[4], Hezekiah[3], Elisha[2], Abner[1]), b.16 Nov 1873 Cleburne Co., AL. She m. William G. "Will" Jackson in 1892 Cleburne Co., AL. She d.29 Jul 1927 Floyd Co., GA, at age 53.
   William G. "Will" Jackson, b.9 Mar 1873 GA. He d.13 Apr 1926 at age 53 and was bur. McFry Cem., Piedmont, Calhoun Co., AL.
Known children of Martha "Mattie"[5] Abney and William G. "Will" Jackson:
      i. Oscar M.[6], b. Dec 1893; He m. Lillie E. Lawler 12 Aug 1919 Calhoun Co., AL; bur. McFry Cem., Piedmont, AL.
            Lillie E. Lawler, b.1889. She m. (n.n.) Martin. She d.1961 and was bur. McFry Cem., Piedmont, Calhoun Co., AL.
      ii. Lettie Pearl, b.1896. She m. Marshal Monroe Simpson. She d.1968; bur. Oaknoll Mem. Gardens Cem., Rome, GA.
            Marshal Monroe Simpson, b.1893 Piedmont, Calhoun Co., AL. He m1. Tessie C. "Dowdy" Kilgo in 1914. He d.19 Mar 1978 Cedartown, Polk Co., GA and was bur. Oaknoll Mem. Gardens Cem., Rome, Floyd Co., GA.
  370 iii. Marvin, b. 1 Jun 1900; m. Rochelle Chastain.
      iv. Johnny, b.1904. He d.2 Aug 1971 Oxford, Calhoun Co., AL and was bur. McFry Cem., Piedmont, Calhoun Co., AL.
      v. Charnell R., b.1914. He m. Eva Brown, He d.1980 GA and was bur. Oaknoll Mem. Gardens Cem., Rome, Floyd Co., GA.
            Eva Brown, b.13 Jul 1914. She d.23 Oct 2001 Rome, Floyd Co., GA, at age 87 and was bur. Oaknoll Mem. Gardens.

134. Theophilus[5] Wood (?) (William[4] Woods, Dorcas[3] Abney, Elisha[2], Abner[1]), b.1844 Clay Co., KY. He m. Juda (n.n.) He and Juda (n.n.) appeared on the census of 1870 Clay Co., KY. (Juda was b.ca.1847)
   Juda (n.n.) b. ca.1847.
Known children of Theophilus[5] Wood (?) and Juda n.n. all b. Clay Co., KY:
      i. Mary J.[6], b. ca.1837
      ii. Bettie, b. ca.1865
      iii. Wade, b. ca.1869

135. Margaret[5] McGuire (Elizabeth[4] Woods, Dorcas[3] Abney, Elisha[2], Abner[1]), b.Jun 1841 Mount Vernon, Rockcastle Co., KY. She m. Speed Steele ca.1862. She m. Solomon Childress on 14 Jan 1887. She d.1919 Mount Vernon, Rockcastle Co., KY and was bur. Merritt Cem., Wildie, Rockcastle Co., KY.
Known children of Margaret[5] McGuire and Speed Steele:
      i. Nancy[6], b.1863.
  371 ii. George Thomas, b. 1874; m. Emma Catherine "Kate" May.
      iii. Lucy, b.1878. She d.1965.
      iv. Lula Belle, b.1883. She d.1924.

   Solomon Childress, b.1823 NC. He d. Rockcastle Co., KY and was bur. Flatrock Cem., Orlando, Rockcastle Co., KY.
There were no known children of Margaret[5] McGuire and Solomon Childress.

136. Christina[5] McGuire (Elizabeth[4] Woods, Dorcas[3] Abney, Elisha[2], Abner[1]), b.5 Feb 1844 KY. She m. Cpl. James B. Dooley (UA) ca.1865. She m. George M. Johnson ca.1871. She d.1 Dec 1902 at age 58 and was bur. Merritt Cem., Wildie, Rockcastle Co., KY.
   Cpl. James B. Dooley (UA), b.14 Apr 1842 Rockcastle Co., KY. He d.22 Mar 1868 Rockcastle Co., KY, at age 25 and was bur. Old McGuire Family Cem. His body was exhumed and reinterred in 2005 Phillips Cem., Goochland, Rockcastle Co., KY.
Known children of Christina[5] McGuire and Cpl. James B. Dooley (UA):
      i. William Isaac[6], b.1866. He d.1952.
      ii. James Franklin, b.1868. He d.1952.
   George M. Johnson, b.3 Mar 1833. He d.30 Sep 1906 at age 73 and was bur. Merritt Cem., Wildie, Rockcastle Co., KY.
Known children of Christina[5] McGuire and George M. Johnson:
      i. George T.[6], b.1872. He d.1949.
      ii. Willis C., b.1876. He d.1977.
      iii. Grover Cleveland, b.1884. He d.1952.
      iv. Theresa Jane, b.1889. She d.1982.

137. Susan Florence[5] Abner (William[4], Elisha[3], Elisha[2] Abney, Abner[1]), b.1832 Clay Co., KY. She m. Robert Allen in 1851 Clay Co., KY. She and Robert Allen appeared on the census of 30 Jun 1860 Clay Co., KY. She m. William Parker in 1869 Owsley Co., KY. She d. Owsley Co., KY and was bur. Owsley Co., KY.
   Robert Allen, b. ca.1823 Clay Co., KY. He was a Merchant.
Known children of Susan Florence[5] Abner and Robert Allen:
      i. William[6].
      ii. Benjamin, b. ca.1852 Clay Co., KY.
  372 iii. Nancy Baker, b. 8 Jul 1854 Clay Co., KY; m. Archibald "Taylor" Abney.
      iv. Josephine, b. Feb 1856 Clay Co., KY. She was liv. on 4 Jun 1880 with bro.-in-law, Taylor Abney, Rockcastle Co., KY. She was liv. on 20 Jun 1900 with bro.-in-law, J.T. Abney, Rockcastle Co., KY.
      v. America, b. ca.1857 Clay Co., KY.
      vi. Breck, b. ca.1860 Clay Co., KY.
      vii. Lucinda, b. ca.1862 Clay Co., KY.
      viii. Daniel, b. ca.1868 Clay Co., KY.

Known child of Susan Florence[5] Abner and William Parker:
  373 i. William Jr.[6], b. 18 Oct 1872 KY; m. Nannie A. Gay.

138. David[5] Abner (William[4], Elisha[3], Elisha[2] Abney, Abner[1]), b.24 Jan 1834 Clay Co., KY. He was a Constable. He was liv. on 30 Jun 1860 with brother-in-law, Robert Allen, Clay Co., KY. He m. Mary "Polly" Parker on 7 Jan 1861 Clay Co., KY. He and Mary "Polly" Parker appeared on the censuses of 7 Jun 1880 and 15 Jun 1900 Clay Co., KY. He d.23 Dec 1908 Clay Co., KY, at age 74 and was bur. Teges Cem., Clay Co., KY.
　　Mary "Polly" Parker, b. New Year's Day, 1 Jan 1830 KY. She appeared as Head of Household on the census of 18 Apr 1910 Clay Co., KY. She d.18 Apr 1919 Clay Co., KY, at age 89 and was bur. Teges Cem., Clay Co., KY.
Known children of David[5] Abner and Mary "Polly" Parker:
374　i.　Robert[6], b. 11 Mar 1861 Clay Co., KY; m. Esther Bishop.
　　ii.　Susan, b. ca.1863 Clay Co., KY.
　　iii.　Mary E., b.23 Dec 1864 Clay Co., KY. She m. James M. Wilson. She d.22 Oct 1944 London, Laurel Co., KY, at age 79 and was bur. A.R. Dyche Mem. Park, London, Laurel Co., KY.
　　　　James M. Wilson, b.1 Oct 1863. He d.21 Nov 1948 at age 85 and was bur. A.R. Dyche Mem. Park, London, KY.
375　iv.　William W., b. 25 Nov 1867 Owsley Co., KY; m. Margaret E. (n.n.).
　　v.　Kate, b. ca.1872 Clay Co., KY. She m. William Moberly. She and William were liv. on 18 Apr 1910 with her mother, *Polly Abner*, Clay Co., KY. (William Moberly, b. ca.1873 KY.)

139. Easter[5] Abner (William[4], Elisha[3], Elisha[2] Abney, Abner[1]), b. ca.1838 Clay Co., KY. She m. Adoniram "Niram" Allen on 15 Sep 1855 Clay Co., KY. She and Adoniram "Niram" Allen appeared on the censuses of 30 Jun 1860, 13 Jul 1870 and 10 Jun 1880 Clay Co., KY.
　　Adoniram "Niram" Allen, b. ca.1830 KY.
Known children of Easter[5] Abner and Adoniram "Niram" Allen all b. Clay Co., KY:
　　i.　Permulia[6], b. ca.1857.
　　ii.　Edmond H., b. ca.1858.
　　iii.　Simon K., b. ca.1860.
　　iv.　Levi, b. ca.1863.
　　v.　Sophy, b. ca.1865.
　　vi.　Elizabeth "Betty", b. ca.1867.
376　vii.　Sarah Jane, b. ca.Nov 1869.
　　viii.　Robert, b. ca.1872.
　　ix.　Emily, b. ca.1875.
　　x.　William, b. ca.1879.

140. Lewis "Levi"[5] Abner (William[4], Elisha[3], Elisha[2] Abney, Abner[1]), b.22 Jun 1842 Clay Co., KY. He m. Rachel Allen on 21 Jan 1867 Clay Co., KY. He and Rachel Allen appeared on the census of 21 Jun 1900 Allen, Clay Co., KY. He d.4 Dec 1924 at age 82 and was bur. Patsy Allen Cem.
　　Rachel Allen, b.Apr 1848 KY. She d.1910 and was bur. Patsy Allen Cem., Teges, Clay Co., KY.
Known children of Lewis "Levi"[5] Abner and Rachel Allen:
　　i.　Ellen[6], b. ca.1871 Clay Co., KY.
　　ii.　Beverly P., b.23 Aug 1872 Clay Co., KY. He m1. Georgia O. Allen on 7 May 1898 Manchester, Clay Co., KY. He and Georgia O. Allen were divorced before 1900. He m2. Edna Ketchum on 17 Aug 1906 Lee Co., KY. He m3. Delilah Coldiron on 26 Jan 1914 Clay Co., KY. He d.25 Mar 1938 Clay Co., KY, at age 65 and was bur. Patsy Allen Cem., Teges (Georgia O. Allen was b. ca.1874 Clay Co., KY. Edna Ketchum was b. ca.1890. Delilah Coldiron, was b. New Year's Day, 1 Jan 1892 Manchester, Clay Co., KY. She d.2 Jun 1964 Oneida, Clay Co.)
377　iii.　Letta May "Lettie," b. 18 Mar 1876 Clay Co., KY; She m. and div. J.E. Stanfield.
　　iv.　Millard F., b.28 Jan 1878 Clay Co., KY. He d.17 Apr 1942 KY at age 64 and was bur. Patsy Allen Cem., Teges, Clay Co.
378　v.　Martha B., b. Apr 1880 Clay Co., KY; m. Beverly Baker.
379　vi.　Shelby C., b. 29 Apr 1883 Teges, Clay Co., KY; m. Carrie Bell McDaniel.
380　vii.　George W., b. 14 Oct 1885 Clay Co., KY; m. Malinda "Linda" Lewis; m. May B. Rogers.
381　viii.　Walter Gray, b. 1 May 1889 Clay Co., KY; m. Nora Campbell.

141. Sophia[5] Abner (William[4], Elisha[3], Elisha[2] Abney, Abner[1]), b. Apr 1850 Owsley Co., KY. She m. James Deaton. She and James Deaton appeared on the census of 28 Jun 1880 Owsley Co., KY. She d.1920.
Known child of Sophia[5] Abner and James Deaton:
　　i.　Isaac[6], b. ca.1878 KY.

142. Robert "Robin"[5] Abner (William[4], Elisha[3], Elisha[2] Abney, Abner[1]), b.2 Mar 1851 Owsley Co., KY. He m. Sarah Ann Deaton ca.1871. He and Sarah Ann Deaton appeared on the censuses of 28 Jun 1880 Owsley Co., KY; 21 Jun 1900 Clay Co., KY and 14 May 1910 Oneida, Clay Co., KY. He d.19 Oct 1923 Hamilton, Butler Co., OH, at age 72 and was bur. Greenwood Cem., Hamilton, Butler Co., OH.
　　Sarah Ann Deaton, b.1856 KY. She d.20 Aug 1924 Hamilton, Butler Co., OH and was bur. Greenwood Cem., Hamilton, Butler Co., OH.
Known children of Robert "Robin"[5] Abner and Sarah Ann Deaton:
382　i.　Charles Benjamin "Ben"[6], b. 17 Sep 1873 Owsley Co., KY; m. Rachel Allen.
383　ii.　Mary Alice, b. 28 Apr 1875 Owsley Co., KY; m. Thomas Taylor.
384　iii.　Nancy Geneva "Jennie," b. 28 Oct 1878 Owsley Co., KY; m. Robert Allen.
385　iv.　Jack Robert, b. 30 Mar 1880 Owsley Co., KY; m1. Laura B. Darrell; m2. Sallie Hall.
　　v.　(n.n.), b. ca.1883 Owsley Co., KY; d. before 1900 Owsley Co., KY.
386　vi.　Cleveland "Cleve," b. 4 Mar 1885 Owsley Co., KY; m. Lillie Burns.
387　vii.　Susan "Susie," b. 24 Mar 1888; m. Benjamin Harrison Gabbard.
388　viii.　Daniel Boone, b. 17 May 1890 Owsley Co., KY; m. Fannie Pearl Evans.
　　ix.　(n.n.), b. ca.1892 Owsley Co., KY; d. before 1900 Owsley Co., KY.
　　x.　William, b.20 Aug 1894 Owsley Co., KY. He d.6 Apr 1949 Jefferson, Montgomery Co., OH, at age 54 and was bur. Greenwood Cem., Hamilton, Butler Co., OH.
　　xi.　(n.n.), b. ca.1896 Owsley Co., KY; d. before 1900 Owsley Co., KY.
　　xii.　Pearl, b.1898 KY. She d. before 1910 Clay Co., KY.

143. Nancy[5] Abner (Lacy[4], Elisha[3], Elisha[2] Abney, Abner[1]), b. Mar 1840 Clay Co., KY. She m. James Eversole in 1860. She was liv. on 22 Jun 1900 with son-in-law, Dudley Barger, Clay Co., KY. She d.1907 and was bur. Samuel Hacker Cem., Panco, Clay Co., KY.
    James Eversole, b.12 Apr 1834. He d.12 Apr 1916 at age 82 and was bur. Tanksley Cem., Tanksley, Clay Co., KY.
Known children of Nancy[5] Abner and James Eversole:
     i. Margaret[6], b.1861. She d.1914.
     ii. Abner, b.1864. He d.1949.
     iii. William, b.1866. He d.1950.
     iv. Samuel, b.1874. He d.1895.

144. Mary "Polly"[5] Abner (Lacy[4], Elisha[3], Elisha[2] Abney, Abner[1]), b. ca.1841 Clay Co., KY. She and her daughter, Eliza J. Abner were liv. on 11 Jun 1880 with father, Lacy Abner, Owsley Co., KY.
Known child of Mary "Polly"[5] Abner:
     i. Eliza J.[6], b. ca.1878 KY. She and Mary "Polly" Abner were liv. on 11 Jun 1880 with father, Lacy Abner, Owsley Co., KY.

145. John W.[5] Abner (Lacy[4], Elisha[3], Elisha[2] Abney, Abner[1]), b. Mar 1844 Owsley Co., KY. He m. Joice "Joicy" Burns in 1867 Butler Co., KY. He and Joice "Joicy" Burns appeared on the census of 2 Jun 1900 Buffalo, Owsley Co., KY. He d.1910 and was bur. John Abner Cem., Booneville, Owsley Co., KY.
    Joice "Joicy" Burns, b.16 Feb 1846 Buffalo, Clay Co., KY. She appeared as Head of Household on the census of 12 Feb 1920 Bullskin, Clay Co., KY. She d.4 May 1925 Clay Co., KY, at age 79 and was bur. Barger Cem., Clay Co., KY.
Known children of John W.[5] Abner and Joice "Joicy" Burns all b. Owsley Co., KY:
 389 i. Leander F. "Lee"[6], b. 5 Aug 1868.
     ii. Cyntha A., b.Mar 1872.
 390 iii. Wiley Burns, b. 12 Jun 1874; m. Leathan McIntosh.

146. Minerva[5] Abner (Lacy[4], Elisha[3], Elisha[2] Abney, Abner[1]), b.1846 Owsley Co., KY. She m. Brison Barrett in 1867. She and Brison Barrett appeared on the censuses of 16 Aug 1870 and 11 Jun 1880 Buffalo, Owsley Co., KY; d.16 Nov 1891; bur. Job Allen Cem., Oneida, Clay Co., KY.
Known children of Minerva[5] Abner and Brison Barrett all b. Owsley Co., KY:
     i. Mary J.[6], b. ca.1868.
     ii. Susan, b. ca.1870.
     iii. Kizzie, b. ca.1874.
     iv. Edward, b. ca.1879.

147. Leander A. "Lee"[5] Abner (Lacy[4], Elisha[3], Elisha[2] Abney, Abner[1]), b.18 Apr 1852 Owsley Co., KY. He m. Elizabeth Cynthia "Ibbie" Bishop ca.1880 KY. He and Elizabeth Cynthia "Ibbie" Bishop appeared on the censuses of 8 Jun 1900 Allen, Clay Co., KY; 18 Apr 1910 and 16 Jan 1920 Burning Springs, Clay Co., KY; and 23 Apr 1930 Jackson Co., KY. He d.1936 Jackson Co., KY; bur. Liberty Cem., Egypt, Jackson Co., KY.
    Elizabeth Cynthia "Ibbie" Bishop, b.1864 Booneville, Owsley Co., KY. She d.Jul 1936 Egypt, Jackson Co., KY and was bur. Liberty Cem.
Known children of Leander A. "Lee"[5] Abner and Elizabeth Cynthia "Ibbie" Bishop all b. Clay Co., KY:
     i. (n.n.)[6], b. ca.1881. He/she d. before 1900 Clay Co., KY.
     ii. McHenry, b.Jan 1883.
 391 iii. Manerva, b. 20 Apr 1885; m. Hugh White Robertson.
     iv. Lula "Luly", b.1887.
     v. (n.n.), b. ca.1889. He/she d. before 1900 Clay Co., KY.
     vi. Willie, b.Jun 1892.
     vii. Martha Jane, b.1894. She m. Robert Hardin on 12 Jul 1913 Butler Co., OH.
        Robert Hardin, b.12 Oct 1891 Rockcastle Co., KY.
     viii. Gilbert, b. Oct 1896.
     ix. Isaac, b. Jun 1899.
     x. Colby, b. ca.1905.
     xi. Fielding, b. ca.1907.
     xii. Nancy M., b. ca.1909.

148. Harvey[5] Abner (Lacy[4], Elisha[3], Elisha[2] Abney, Abner[1]), b.3 Mar 1856 Owsley Co., KY. He m. Mary Jane Dean ca.1884. He and Mary Jane Dean appeared on the censuses of 11 Jun 1900, 22 Apr 1910, 28 Jan 1920 and 9 Apr 1930 Allen, Clay Co., KY. He d.16 Jan 1932 Clay Co., KY, at age 75 and was bur. Job Allen Cem., Oneida, Clay Co., KY.
    Mary Jane Dean, b.17 May 1865 Island City, Owsley Co., KY. She d.17 Feb 1935 Clay Co., KY, at age 69 and was bur. Job Allen Cem.
Known children of Harvey[5] Abner and Mary Jane Dean:
     i. Ezekiel[6], b.10 Feb 1886 Doorway, Perry Co., KY; d.11 Oct 1918 Oneida, Clay Co., KY, age 32; bur. Job Allen Cem.
 392 ii. Elsey Ann "Annie," b. 8 May 1888 Owsley Co., KY; m. James F. Jackson.
 393 iii. James B., b. 12 May 1890 Owsley Co., KY; m. Verna E. "Vernie" Felty.
 394 iv. Bryson "Brice," b. 18 Apr 1892 Owsley Co., KY; m. Ida A. Byrd.
 395 v. Lucy, b. Mar 1894 Clay Co., KY; m. Harrison Singleton.
 396 vi. John "Johnie," b. 8 Feb 1896 Owsley Co., KY; m1. Sophia Combs; m2. (n.n.); m3. Mae Bishop.
     vii. (n.n.), b. ca.1898. He/she d. before 1900.

149. Amanda Jane[5] Abner (Lacy[4], Elisha[3], Elisha[2] Abney, Abner[1]), b. ca.1858 Owsley Co., KY. She m. Irvine Bishop on 31 Oct 1874 Owsley Co., KY. She d. ca.1920.
    Irvine Bishop, b.20 Aug 1856 Clay Co., KY. He d.6 Apr 1913 Owsley Co., KY, at age 56.
Known children of Amanda Jane[5] Abner and Irvine Bishop:
     i. Susan F.[6], b.1879. She d.1950.
     ii. James H., b.1885. He d.1960.

        iii.   Mariah, b.1887. She d.1960.
        iv.   Rhoda, b.1899.
        v.   Mattie, b.1900.

150. Samuel⁵ Abner (Lacy⁴, Elisha³, Elisha² Abney, Abner¹), b.10 Aug 1863 Owsley Co., KY. Samuel did not on appear on his father's 1870 census...but he did appear on his father's 1880 census! Was he missed in the first census, living elsewhere or adopted? He m. Mariah Bishop in 1886 Owsley Co., KY. He and Mariah Bishop appeared on the census of 1 Jun 1900 Buffalo, Owsley Co., KY. He d.12 Jan 1940 Lawrenceburg, Dearb. Co., IN, at age 76 and was bur. Greendale Cem., Greendale, Dearb. Co., IN.
    Mariah Bishop, b.23 Feb 1870 Owsley Co., KY. She d.23 Sep 1930 Lawrenceburg, Dearb. Co., IN, at age 60 and was bur. Greendale Cem
Known children of Samuel⁵ Abner and Mariah Bishop all b. Owsley Co., KY:
        i.   Amanda "Mandy"⁶, b.Nov 1887.
        ii.   Arch, b.15 May 1891. He m. Della Mae Woods on 3 May 1925. He d.27 Sep 1952 at age 61 and was bur. Greendale Cem.
        iii.   Mary E., b. Apr 1892. She m. (n.n.) Daniel ca.1912 Owsley Co., KY. She d. ca.1970. (Mr. Daniel was b. ca. 1890 KY)
    397   iv.   John, b. 20 Feb 1895; m. Mary Elizabeth "Lizzie" Hill.

151. William M.⁵ Abner (CSA) (John⁴, Elisha³, Elisha² Abney, Abner¹), b.26 Jul 1844 Owsley Co., KY. He m. Nancy Ann Phillips on 28 Feb 1868 Pendleton Co., KY. He and Nancy Ann Phillips appeared on the censuses of 5 Jul 1870 Pendleton Co., KY; 2 Jun 1880 Cordova, Grant Co., KY; and 23 Jun 1900 Callenville, Pendleton Co., KY. He d.12 Feb 1917 at age 72 and was bur. Gumlick Church Cem., Falmouth, Pendleton Co., KY.
    Nancy Ann Phillips, b.Nov 1846 KY. She d.1910 and was bur. Gumlick Church Cem., Falmouth, Pendleton Co., KY.
Known child of William M.⁵ Abner (CSA) and Nancy Ann Phillips:
    398   i.   Mollie Elizabeth⁶, b. 3 Jan 1871 Pendleton Co., KY; m. William Joseph Wells.

152. John "Red John"⁵ Baker (Mary⁴ Abner, Elisha³, Elisha² Abney, Abner¹), b. ca.1835 KY. He m. (N.N.).

Known child of John "Red John"⁵ Baker and (N.N.):
        i.   Garrett⁶, b.1856. He d.1879.

153. Willis⁵ Sandlin (Nancy⁴ Abner, Elisha³, Elisha² Abney, Abner¹), b. ca.1846 Owsley Co., KY. He m. Eliza Jane Abner on 25 Mar 1900 Perry Co., KY. Eliza Jane is believed to have been a cousin of Willis. However, her parentage is unknown to the author at this time.
    Eliza Jane Abner, b.7 Jun 1874 Owsley Co., KY. She d.15 Dec 1944 Owsley Co., KY, at age 70.
Known children of Willis⁵ Sandlin and Eliza Jane Abner:
        i.   Martha⁶.
        ii.   Ballard.
        iii.   Susan.

154. James Franklin "Red Jim"⁵ Sandlin (Nancy⁴ Abner, Elisha³, Elisha² Abney, Abner¹), b.1853 Owsley Co., KY. He m. Eliza Gross. He d.1923.
    Eliza Jane Gross, b.1853. She d.1934.
Known child of James Franklin "Red Jim"⁵ Sandlin and Eliza Jane Gross:
    399   i.   Isabel Gross⁶, b. 1878; m. Orville Baker Riley.

155. Eliza⁵ Abner (Willis⁴, Elisha³, Elisha² Abney, Abner¹), b.28 Mar 1852 Owsley Co., KY. She m. James M. Todd Baker on 29 Dec 1874 Breathitt Co., KY. She and James M. Todd Baker appeared on the census of 11 Jun 1880 Owsley Co., KY. She, appeared as Head of Household on the census of 2 May 1910 Crockettsville, Breathitt Co., KY. She d.28 Sep 1916 Owsley Co., KY, at age 64 and was bur. Cortland Cem., Cow Creek, Owsley Co., KY.
    James M. Todd Baker, b.15 May 1854 Owsley Co., KY. He d.20 Jul 1907 Owsley Co., KY, at age 53 and was bur. Cortland Cem., Cow Creek.
Known children of Eliza⁵ Abner and James M. Todd Baker:
        i.   Alfred⁶, b. ca.1876 KY.
        ii.   William, b. ca.1878 KY.
    400   iii.   Robert H. "Fox," b. 12 Oct 1880 Owsley Co., KY; m. Mary Alice Baker.
    401   iv.   Bryson "Bryce," b. 31 Oct 1882 Breathitt Co., KY; m. Lucretia "Crettie" Burns.
    402   v.   Elisha, b. 22 Jun 1885 Owsley Co., KY; m. America Daniel.
    403   vi.   Charles "Charlie," b. 10 Aug 1887 Owsley Co., KY; m. Isabelle "Belle" Bowling.
        vii.   Levi, b.Apr 1890 KY. He d.7 Dec 1953 Lexington, Fayette Co., KY, at age 63 and was bur. Highland Cem., Owsley Co.
        viii.   Grover C., b.12 Aug 1894 Owsley Co., KY. He m. Emma (n.n.). He d.17 Oct 1918 Owsley Co., KY, at age 24 and was bur. Cortland Cem., Cow Creek, Owsley Co., KY.

156. William "Bill"⁵ Abner (Willis⁴, Elisha³, Elisha² Abney, Abner¹). He, b.7 Dec 1853 Owsley Co., KY. He m. Nancy Ann Eversole on 15 Aug 1877 Breathitt Co., KY. He and Nancy Ann Eversole appeared on the census of 3 May 1910 Bowling, Perry Co., KY. He d.14 Nov 1913 Perry Co., KY, at age 59 and was bur. Abner-Napier Family Cem., Gays Creek, Perry Co., KY.
    Nancy Ann Eversole, b.28 Nov 1858 Buckhorn, Perry Co., KY. She d.23 Oct 1927 Perry Co., KY, at age 68.
Known children of William "Bill"⁵ Abner and Nancy Ann Eversole:
        i.   Izah⁶, b.1877. He d.1880 and was bur. Abner-Napier Family Cem., Gays Creek, Perry Co., KY.
    404   ii.   Robert F, b. 7 Jun 1878 Perry Co., KY; m. Alaphair F. "Alley" Barger.
    405   iii.   Mary Rachel, b. 12 Apr 1880 Bowlington, Perry Co., KY; m. Abraham Napier.
    406   iv.   Justus Tucker, b. 11 Feb 1882 Perry Co., KY; m. Emmer Langdon.
    407   v.   Nancy "Nannie," b. 22 Jan 1884; m. Finley F. Bowling Sr.
    408   vi.   Elmira, b. 8 Feb 1886; m. Daniel "Little Dan" Barger.
    409   vii.   Hannah, b. 29 Dec 1888 Buckhorn, Perry Co., KY; m. Henry Napier.
    410   viii.   Elizabeth "Lizzie," b. 21 Oct 1890; m. Robert Sandlin Bowling.

411   ix.   Willis E., b. 21 Oct 1890; m. Sattie Barger.
412   x.   Lucy, b. Feb 1893; m. Andrew Gay.
413   xi.   Rebecca, b. 15 Jun 1895; m. John B. Smith.
414   xii.   Anderson "Ance," b. 8 Apr 1899 Perry Co., KY; m. Leatha Dixon.
415   xiii.   Rachel, b. 8 Apr 1899; m. Rufus Barger.

157. **Elisha B.⁵ Abner** (Willis⁴, Elisha³, Elisha² Abney, Abner¹), b.22 Jul 1856 Owsley Co., KY. He was liv. on 25 Jun 1880 liv. with uncle, Enoch Abner, Hilburn, Madison Co., KY. He m. Nancy Ann Begley in 1889. He, appeared as Head of Household on the census of 6 Jun 1900 Bowling, Perry Co., KY. He d.21 Oct 1908 Perry Co., KY, at age 52 and was bur. Laurel Point Cem., Buckhorn, Perry Co., KY.

Nancy Ann Begley, b.15 Jun 1871 Perry Co., KY. She m2. Tilford Felty Barger in 1912. She d.26 Nov 1946 Perry Co., KY, at age 75 and was bur. Abner Family Cem., Buckhorn, Perry Co., KY.
Known children of Elisha B.⁵ Abner and Nancy Ann Begley:
       i.   Jesse⁶, b. Sep 1890 KY.
       ii.   Salley, b. Oct 1892 KY.
       iii.   Willis, b. Sep 1894 KY.
416   iv.   Edward "Ned," b. 17 Jul 1896 Perry Co., KY; m. Cory Begley.
       v.   Almira, b. Apr 1898 KY.

158. **Mariah⁵ Abner** (Willis⁴, Elisha³, Elisha² Abney, Abner¹) m. William M. Harris. , b.1 May 1860 Owsley Co., KY. She d.10 Jun 1940 Jackson Co., KY, at age 80 and was bur. Harris Cem., Jackson Co., KY.

William M. Harris, b.10 Mar 1865 Owsley Co., KY. He d.11 Nov 1938 Owsley Co., KY, at age 73 and was bur. Harris Cem., Jackson Co.
Known child of Mariah⁵ Abner and William M. Harris:
       i.   Gilbert⁶, b.6 Jun 1883 Breathitt Co., KY. He m1. Mattie Rice on 13 Jan 1904. He m2. Lillie Belle Riley ca.1910. He appeared as Head of Household on the census of 3 May 1910 Crockettsville, Breathitt Co., KY. He was shot in the face and chest in Owsley Co., KY and d.2 Aug 1913, at age 30. He was bur. Cortland Cem., Cow Creek, Owsley Co., KY.
          Lillie Belle Riley, b. ca.1894 KY.

159. **Mary "Polly"⁵ Abner** (Willis⁴, Elisha³, Elisha² Abney, Abner¹), b.23 Sep 1868 Owsley Co., KY. She m1. George Washington Terry in 1887. She m2. Joseph Estep in 1897. She d.1922 Beattyville, Lee Co., KY and was bur. Proctor-Arch Farm Cem., Beattyville, Lee Co., KY.

George Washington Terry, b.1843 Breathitt Co., KY. He d.1895 Owsley Co., KY and was bur. Cortland Cem., Cow Creek, Owsley Co., KY.
Known children of Mary "Polly"⁵ Abner and George Washington Terry:
417   i.   Brownlow "Brown"⁶, b. 9 Jan 1889 Breathitt Co., KY; m. America Bryant.
418   ii.   Mattie, b. 7 Feb 1892; m. Green B. Woods.
       iii.   Oscar, b.Sep 1894 Perry Co., KY. He d.1905 Lee Co., KY; bur. Proctor-Arch Farm Cem., Beattyville, Lee Co., KY.
Joseph Estep, b.20 Jan 1870 Cincinnati, Hamilton Co., OH. He d.23 Jun 1942 Beattyville, Lee Co., KY, age 72; bur. Proctor-Arch Farm Cem.
Known child of Mary "Polly"⁵ Abner and Joseph Estep:
419   i.   Isabella⁶, b. 11 Nov 1911 Beattyville, Lee Co., KY; m. Felix M. Barnard.

160. **Lucinda⁵ Abner** (Willis⁴, Elisha³, Elisha² Abney, Abner¹), b.Dec 1870 Owsley Co., KY. She m. John "Dirty Face" Sandlin ca.1887. She appeared as Head of Household on the census of 5 Jun 1900 Leslie Co., KY (as a widow). She d.8 Aug 1900 Leslie Co., KY, at age 29 and was bur. Cortland Cem., Cow Creek, Owsley Co., KY.

John "Dirty Face" Sandlin, b.17 Mar 1867 Perry Co., KY. He d.3 Feb 1947 Benton Co., AR, at age 79 and was bur. Mount Pleasant Cem., Hiwasse, Benton Co., AR.
Known children of Lucinda⁵ Abner and John "Dirty Face" Sandlin:
       i.   *Pvt.* Charlie (USArmy-WWI)⁶, b.25 Nov 1888 KY. He was stationed on 19 Apr 1910 at Fort Wayne, Detroit, Wayne Co., MI. He d.19 Oct 1950 at age 61 and was bur. Sandlin Cem., Confluence, Leslie Co., KY.
420   ii.   *Sgt.* William Berry "Willie" (USArmy-WWI) He, b. New Year's Day, 1 Jan 1890 Breathitt Co., KY. He was the only World War I Medal of Honor recipient from Kentucky. (See page 10 and plate K.) He m. Belvia Roberts.
       iii.   John "Johnny", b.11 Aug 1892 Breathitt Co., KY. He m. Hallie Wooton. He d.29 Nov 1972 at age 80 and was bur. Sandlin Cem., Confluence, Leslie Co., KY.
          Hallie Wooton, b.16 Mar 1895. She d.9 Sep 1985 at age 90 and was bur. Sandlin Cem., Confluence, Leslie Co., KY.
       iv.   Elihue "Sonny", b.14 Feb 1895 Breathitt Co., KY. He was liv. on 2 May 1910 with the Baker family (hired hand), Crockettsville, Breathitt Co., KY. He m. Laura Riley. He d.25 Mar 1928 Owsley Co., KY, at age 33 and was bur. Cortland Cem., Cow Creek, Owsley Co., KY.
          Laura Riley, b.8 Feb 1901 Dalesburg, Fleming Co., KY. She d.25 Oct 1993 Scottsburg, Scott Co., IN, at age 92 and was bur. Scottsburg Cem., Scottsburg, Scott Co., IN.
       v.   Matthew "Matha", b.Mar 1897 Breathitt Co., KY.
       vi.   Doshia, b.Oct 1899 KY.

161. **John Wesley⁵ Abner** (Willis⁴, Elisha³, Elisha² Abney, Abner¹), b. ca.May 1872 Owsley Co., KY. He m1. Lucy White on 30 Mar 1893 Perry Co., KY. He m2. Cassie Andrews ca.1901. He m3. Mattie Belle Slaughter. He d.9 Mar 1949 Muhlenberg Co., KY and was bur. Pleasant Hill Cem., Greenville, Muhlenberg Co., KY.

Lucy White, b.12 Nov 1868 KY. She d.20 Mar 1918 Breathitt Co., KY, at age 49; bur. White-Deaton Cem., Barwick, Breathitt Co., KY.
Known children of John Wesley⁵ Abner and Lucy White:
421   i.   Lula⁶, b. 28 Jun 1896; m. Samuel Strong.
       ii.   Clara E., b.3 Nov 1903 IN. She m. Howard W. Hill on 29 Dec 1923. She d.May 1995 OH at age 91 and was bur. Green Mound Cem., New Madison, Darke Co., OH.
          Howard W. Hill, b.14 Mar 1904 IN. He d.19 Sep 1984 OH at age 80 and was bur. Green Mound Cem., New Madison.
422   iii.   Lillie, b. 1909; m. William Clay Willoughby.
Cassie Andrews, b.4 Jun 1865. She d.7 Nov 1924 at age 59 and was bur. Eaves Cem., Powderly, Muhlenberg Co., KY.

There were no known children of John Wesley⁵ Abner and Cassie Andrews.
    Mattie Belle Slaughter, b.13 Oct 1882 KY. She d.28 Aug 1959 Greenville, Muhlenberg Co., KY, at age 76.
There were no known children of John Wesley⁵ Abner and Mattie Belle Slaughter.

162. Daniel Boone⁵ Abner (Willis⁴, Elisha³, Elisha² Abney, Abner¹), b.21 Mar 1873 Owsley Co., KY. He m. Catherine Morris. He d.8 Oct 1955 Middletown, Butler Co., OH, at age 82 and was bur. Woodside Cem., Middletown, Butler Co., OH.
    Catherine Morris, b.8 May 1876 Perry Co., KY. She d.7 May 1946 Middletown, Butler Co., OH, at age 69 and was bur. Woodside Cem.
Known children of Daniel Boone⁵ Abner and Catherine Morris:
    423   i.   Elisha Morris⁶, b. 14 Jun 1894 KY; m. Gertrude Williams.
    424   ii.   Jerry, b. 4 Jun 1898 Perry Co., KY; m. Nola Watson.
    425   iii. Dora Lee, b. 23 Apr 1910 Wolfe Co., KY; m. Cpl. Vernon Carroll (USArmy).
           iv.   Naomi "Oma", b.13 Jun 1913 Butler Co., OH. She d.3 Jun 1931 Middleton, Butler Co., OH, age 17; bur. Woodside Cem.

163. Lacy⁵ Abner (Enoch⁴, Elisha³, Elisha² Abney, Abner¹), b.8 Dec 1857 Booneville, Owsley Co., KY. He m. Sarah Hammonds on 29 Nov 1882 Franklin Co., AR. He d.1945 Madison Co., AR and was bur. Kilgore Cem., Madison Co., AR.
    Sarah Hammonds, b.May 1863 KY. She d.31 Mar 1886 Johnson Co., AR, age 22 and was bur. Richard W. Dick Hill Cem., Franklin Co., AR.
Known child of Lacy⁵ Abner and Sarah Hammonds:
           i.   Lucy A.⁶, b.1884. She m. (n.n.) Watkins. She d.1965 and was bur. Hillcrest Burial Park, Kent, King Co., WA.

164. Andrew Jackson "Jack"⁵ Abner (Enoch⁴, Elisha³, Elisha² Abney, Abner¹), b.27 May 1859 Booneville, Owsley Co., KY. He m. Nancy Jane Sayler in 1884 Madison Co., AR. He and Nancy Jane Sayler appeared on the census of 20 Jun 1900 Baldwin, Madison Co., AR. He d.26 Mar 1936 Madison Co., AR, at age 76 and was bur. Riverside Cem., St. Paul, Madison Co., AR.
    Nancy Jane Sayler, b.14 Dec 1866 Madison Co., AR. She d.2 Nov 1937 at age 70 and was bur. Riverside Cem., St. Paul, Madison Co., AR.
Known children of Andrew Jackson "Jack"⁵ Abner and Nancy Jane Sayler:
           i.   Eli Cleveland⁶, b.29 Mar 1885 Madison Co., AR. He d.28 Aug 1938 at age 53 and was bur. Farmington Cem., Farmington, Washington Co., AR.
           ii.   Floyd, b.13 Sep 1887 Madison Co., AR. He d.13 Sep 1887 Madison Co., AR and was bur. Riverside Cem., St. Paul.
    426   iii. John Preston, b. 28 Jul 1889 Madison Co., AR; m. Julia Hibbard.
    427   iv.   Walter S., b. 21 Sep 1891 Madison Co., AR; m. Joy Jane Davidson.
    428   v.   Fred, b. 25 Mar 1895 St. Paul, Madison Co., AR; m. Cora Mae Long.
    429   vi.   Emily Frances, b. 29 Mar 1897 St. Paul, Madison Co., AR; m. George Watkins.
    430   vii. Hugh Dinsmore, b. 28 Jan 1900 St. Paul, Madison Co., AR; m. Lucy Landers.
           viii. Rachel Velma, b.25 Mar 1903 Madison Co., AR. She m. Dailey B. Baker ca.1918. She d.4 May 1983 at age 80 and was bur. Mountain View Cem., Ozark, Franklin Co., AR.
                 Dailey B. Baker, b.23 Jun 1893. He m. Etta D. Byrd in 1914. He d.4 Oct 1987 at age 94; bur. Mountain View Cem.
    431   ix.   Jefferson Davis "Jeff," b. 2 Feb 1906 Madison Co., AR; m. Gladys P. Stephens.

165. Kenas "Keene"⁵ Abner (Enoch⁴, Elisha³, Elisha² Abney, Abner¹), b.13 Jan 1869 London, Laurel Co., KY. He m. Mary Ann Tuttle in Madison Co., AR. He d.2 May 1945 Gage Co., NE, at age 76 and was bur. Evergreen Home Cem., Beatrice, Gage Co., NE.
    Mary Ann Tuttle, b.5 Jun 1874 London, Laurel Co., KY. She d.15 Nov 1946 Beatrice, Gage Co., NE, at age 72; bur. Evergreen Home Cem.
Known children of Kenas "Keene"⁵ Abner and Mary Ann Tuttle:
    432   i.   Robert L.⁶, b. 27 Feb 1906; m. Verda Edna Imes.
           ii.   Joseph V., b.27 May 1908. He d.3 Mar 1921 at age 12 and was bur. Evergreen Home Cem., Beatrice, Gage Co., NE.
    433   iii. Roy Vernon, b. 8 Jan 1911; m. Maude E. Linscott.

166. Nancy Jane⁵ Abner (Enoch⁴, Elisha³, Elisha² Abney, Abner¹), b. Jan 1873 Madison Co., AR. She m. William J. Justice ca.1887. She and William J. Justice appeared on the censuses of 26 Jun 1900 and 25 Apr 1910 Newcomb, Laurel Co., KY; and 15 Jan 1920 Morgan Co., TN. She d.12 Mar 1940 Morgan Co., TN, at age 67.
    William J. Justice, b.Mar 1853 TN.
Known children of Nancy Jane⁵ Abner and William J. Justice:
           i.   William "Harvey"⁶, b. Mar 1890 AR. He d.1956.
           ii.   Riley, b. Apr 1893 AR.
           iii. Lee, b. May 1895 AR.
           iv.   Walter "McKinley", b.Apr 1896 AR. He d.1963.
           v.   Martha Ellen, b.May 1899 KY. She d.1987.
           vi.   Rachel M., b.1901 KY. She d.1976.
           vii. Lydia M., b.1907 KY.
           viii. Maggie, b.1908.
           ix.   Pearlie "Minnie", b.1910 KY.
           x.   Alice, b.1912 KY.
           xi.   Cara, b. ca. Dec 1919 TN.

167. Lydia⁵ Abner (Enoch⁴, Elisha³, Elisha² Abney, Abner¹), b.9 Jun 1876 AR. She m. Robert Marshall Morris. She d.19 Feb 1947 Placer Co., CA, at age 70 and was bur. Roseville Public Cem. Dist., Roseville, Placer Co., CA.
    Robert Marshall Morris, b.15 Jun 1870. He d.12 Nov 1948 Madera Co., CA, at age 78 and was bur. Roseville Public Cem. Dist., Roseville.
Known children of Lydia⁵ Abner and Robert Marshall Morris:
           i.   Noah⁶, b.1905. He d.1958.
           ii.   Emily Dessie, b.1906. She d.1981.
           iii. Robert, b.1917. He d.1943.

168. Leona "Margaret"⁵ Abner (Enoch⁴, Elisha³, Elisha² Abney, Abner¹), b. Oct 1879 AR. She m1. (n.n.) Fisher ca.1896. She m2. Abraham M. Meredith in 1903. She and Abraham M. Meredith appeared on the census of 27 Apr 1910 Galena, Jasper Co., MO.
Known child of Leona "Margaret"⁵ Abner and (n.n.) Fisher:
    i.   (baby)⁶, b. ca.1897 AR; d. before 1900.
   Abraham M. Meredith d.22 Oct 1923 and was bur. City of Mesa Cem., Mesa, Maricopa Co., AZ.
Known child of Leona "Margaret"⁵ Abner and Abraham M. Meredith:
    i.   Clyde M.⁶, b. ca. Jun 1908 WA.

169. John⁵ Abner (James⁴, Menan³, Elisha² Abney, Abner¹), b. Jun 1853 Knox Co., KY. He was liv. on 12 Jul 1870 with uncle, Richard Abner, Clay Co., KY. He m. Sarah Jane Noe ca.1875. He and Sarah Jane Noe appeared on the census of 23 May 1910 Israel, Preble Co., OH. He d.Jan 1919 at age 65 and was bur. Salem Friends Cem., Salem, Union Co., IN.
   Sarah Jane Noe, b.13 Jun 1858 Clay Co., KY. She d.22 Jun 1939 Liberty, Union Co., IN, at age 81 and was bur. Salem Friends Cem., Salem
Known children of John⁵ Abner and Sarah Jane Noe:
         i.   Hannah Jane⁶, b. Apr 1876 Union Co., IN.
434   ii.   Roscoe C., b. 7 Jul 1877 Union Co., IN; m1. Adelaid May Tolliver; m2. Mary Frances Waltz.
       iii.   Alphonsas, b.1880 IN.
435   iv.   Smith Lowell, b. 22 Jun 1881 Liberty, Union Co., IN; m. Goldie Maude Bruce.
        v.   Hollis Glencoe, b.12 Sep 1882 IN. He m. Emily Jane Freeman. He d.27 Mar 1936 Laurel, Franklin Co., IN, at age 53 and was bur. Reily Cem., Reily, Butler Co., OH.
           Emily Jane Freeman, b.New Year's Day, 1 Jan 1870 KY. She d.18 May 1940 Franklin Co., IN, at age 70.
       vi.   Minnie, b.Jun 1886 Union Co., IN.
436   vii.   Bessie P., b. 26 Jun 1889 Union Co., IN; m. and div. (n.n.) Robinson.
      viii.   Winfield Scott, b.12 Dec 1892 Union Co., IN. He d.7 Dec 1917 Oxford, Butler Co., OH, at age 24; Salem Friends Cem.
       ix.   Ruby Lena, b.15 Jan 1901 Union Co., IN. She m. Chauncey J. Lowe. She d.2 Dec 1983 Richmond, Wayne Co., IN, at age 82 and was bur. Riverside Cem., Cambridge City, Wayne Co., IN.
           Chauncey J. Lowe, b.1898. He d.1993 and was bur. Riverside Cem., Cambridge City, Wayne Co., IN.

170. Mary C.⁵ Abner (James⁴, Menan³, Elisha² Abney, Abner¹), b.1854 Clay Co., KY. She m. Taylor Hignite in 1876. She d.1919.
   Taylor Hignite, b.18 Feb 1855 Clay Co., KY. He d.28 Apr 1916 Garrard Co., KY, at age 61.
Known children of Mary C.⁵ Abner and Taylor Hignite:
         i.   Fannie⁶, b.22 Aug 1880. She m. Sol A. Hammons. She d.12 Dec 1964 at age 84.
           Sol A. Hammons, b.9 Nov 1868. He d.17 Aug 1936 at age 67.
       ii.   Hugh Louis, b.1882. He d.1966.

171. Pierce⁵ Abner (James⁴, Menan³, Elisha² Abney, Abner¹), b.15 May 1861 Clay Co., KY. He m1. Sophia "Sofie" Smith, daughter of William Smith and Mary Abner, on 5 Feb 1885 KY. He m2. Ellen Harvey Roberts on 3 Sep 1891 Clinton, DeWitt Co., IL. He and Ellen Harvey Roberts appeared on the censuses of 2 Jun 1900 Mount Hope, McLean Co., IL; and 16 Apr 1910 Illini, Macon Co., IL. He d.1 Jun 1931 Hammond, Lake Co., IN, at age 70 and was bur. Elmwood Cem., Hammond, Lake Co., IN.
   Sophia "Sofie" Smith, b. ca.1869 Clay Co., KY. She was liv. on 14 Jun 1900 with grandfather, William Smith, Otter Creek, Clay Co., KY. She d.29 Dec 1941 Knox Co., KY.
Known child of Pierce⁵ Abner and Sophia "Sofie" Smith:
437   i.   Joseph L. "Joe"⁶, b. 22 Jan 1889 KY; m1. Rosana Frederick; m2. Effie Jane Stewart.
   Ellen Harvey Roberts, b. ca.1852 Madison Co., KY.
There were no known children of Pierce⁵ Abner and Ellen Harvey Roberts.

172. Daniel Isaac⁵ Abner (James⁴, Menan³, Elisha² Abney, Abner¹), b. between 1861 and 1865 Clay Co., KY. Daniel's birthdate is somewhat of a mystery. In the 1900 census, he gives May 1861 (which was his brother, Pierce's birthdate). In 1910 he gives age 45 (i.e. ca.1865). His headstone also gives 1865. Either he was a twin of his brother, Pierce, or born some 4 years later. He m1. (n.n.) est.1883 KY. He m2. Mary Elizabeth Cole ca.1885. He m3. Rosanna R "Rosie" Smith on 27 Sep 1897 Manchester, Clay Co., KY. He and Rosanna R "Rosie" Smith appeared on the censuses of 2 Jul 1900 Clay Co., KY; and 22 Apr 1910 Harrison, Union Co., IN. He d.1924 IN and was bur. Boston Cem., Boston, Wayne Co., IN. In addition to his eight children, Daniel also raised two stepchildren, *William Smith* and *Cordelia Smith*. By the 1920 Census, these two were named as *William Abner* and *Cordelia Abner*, but were still listed as stepchildren.
   There were no known children of Daniel Isaac⁵ Abner and (n.n.).
   Mary Elizabeth Cole, b. ca.1863 KY. She d. ca.1895 KY.
Known children of Daniel Isaac⁵ Abner and Mary Elizabeth Cole all b. Clay Co., KY:
438   i.   Taylor⁶, b. 18 Feb 1886; m. Lola Catherine Cheek; m. Myra F. White.
       ii.   Roxy, b.Dec 1890.
      iii.   Calvin Daniel, b.Apr 1894.
   Rosanna R. "Rosie" Smith, b.1871 Clay Co., KY. She m1. (n.n.) Smith. She d.14 Dec 1914 IN; bur. Boston Cem., Boston, Wayne Co., IN.
Known children of Daniel Isaac⁵ Abner and Rosanna R "Rosie" Smith:
         i.   Priscilla⁶, b.5 Mar 1899 Manchester, Clay Co., KY. She m1. George Everett Carman on 30 Sep 1897 Wayne Co., IN; She m2. Wilbur Haisley ca. Sep 1922 Wayne Co., IN. She d.16 Jun 1972 Richmond, Wayne Co., IN, at age 73.
           George Everett Carman, b.30 Sep 1897.
           Wilbur Haisley, b.28 Jul 1888 Lynn, Randolph Co., IN.
439   ii.   Martha Helen, b. 9 Apr 1901 Clay Co., KY; m. Forest O. Hill.
440   iii.   Clara Eva, b. 2 Nov 1903 Union Co., IN; m. Howard W. Hill.
441   iv.   James Monroe, b. 28 May 1907 Union Co., IN; m. Wanda Catherine Wise.
        v.   Marietta, b.20 Nov 1908 Randolph Co., IN. She m. Morris Clyde Chenoweth on Christmas Eve, 24 Dec 1929 Wayne, Co., IN. She d.20 Jan 1997 Dayton, Montgomery Co., OH, at age 88.
           Morris Clyde Chenoweth, b.1906. He d.1975.

173. Elizabeth "Lizzie"⁵ Abner (Richard⁴, Menan³, Elisha² Abney, Abner¹), b. ca.1838 KY. She m. Elisha Robinson on 26 Aug 1858 Clay Co., KY. She and Elisha Robinson appeared on the censuses of 12 Jul 1870 Clay Co., KY; and 14 Jun 1880 Knox Co., KY. She d.1910 and was bur. H.W. Childers Cem., Sprule, Knox Co., KY.
    Elisha Robinson, b.1837 Clay Co., KY. He d.13 Oct 1892 Knox Co., KY and was bur. H.W. Childers Cem., Sprule, Knox Co., KY.
Known children of Elizabeth "Lizzie"⁵ Abner and Elisha Robinson:
      i.   Louise America⁶, b.1859. She m. James Smith ca.1879. She d.1936.
           James Smith, b. ca.1861 KY.
      ii. Susan M., b.1861. She d.1910.
      iii. Nancy, b.1865. She d.1926.
      iv. Zelpha "Zelphy", b.1867. She d.1903.
      v. (baby girl), b/d.1874.
      vi. Henry, b. ca.1876 Knox Co., KY. He d.1956.
      vii. Nathan Fidilla, b.1878. He d.1948.
      viii. Daniel, b..Sep 1881 Knox Co., KY. He was liv. on 21 Jun 1900 with aunt, Susan Smith, Knox Co., KY. He d.1914.

174. Susan E.⁵ Abner (Richard⁴, Menan³, Elisha² Abney, Abner¹), b.Jan 1844 Knox Co., KY. She m. Henry Clay Smith. She and Henry Clay Smith appeared on the census of 14 Jun 1880 Knox Co., KY. She appeared as Head of Household on the census of 21 Jun 1900 Knox Co., KY. She d.1 May 1919 Knox Co., KY, at age 75 and was bur. H.W. Childers Cem., Sprule, Knox Co., KY.
    Henry Clay Smith, b.1844 Clay Co., KY.
Known children of Susan E.⁵ Abner and Henry Clay Smith all b. KY:
      i.   Mary E.⁶, b. ca.1868.
      ii. Lucy, b. ca.1871.
      iii. John, b. ca.1876.
      iv. Richard, b. ca.1878.
      v. Jabe, b. Feb 1880.
      vi. Campbell, b. ca.1883.

175. Julia⁵ Abner (Richard⁴, Menan³, Elisha² Abney, Abner¹), b.22 Apr 1847 Clay Co., KY. She m. William P. Hammons on 24 Apr 1879 Knox Co., KY. She d.15 Feb 1913 Knox Co., KY, at age 65.
Known children of Julia⁵ Abner and William P. Hammons:
      i.   Martha⁶, b.1883. She d.1975.
      ii. James "Jim", b.1885. He d.1966.
      iii. Lura, b.1887.
      iv. Lucy, b.1889. She d.1968.

176. James "Jim"⁵ Abner (Richard⁴, Menan³, Elisha² Abney, Abner¹), b.25 Nov 1852 Clay Co., KY. He m. Amelia Jane "Jennie" Cobb on 1 Feb 1881 Knox Co., KY. He and Amelia Jane "Jennie" Cobb appeared on the census of 1 Jun 1900 Knox Co., KY. He d.1905 and was bur. H.W. Childers Cem., Sprule, Knox Co., KY.
    Amelia Jane "Jennie" Cobb, b.May 1861 KY. She d.15 Sep 1915 at age 54 and was bur. H.W. Childers Cem., Sprule, Knox Co., KY.
Known children of James "Jim"⁵ Abner and Amelia Jane "Jennie" Cobb all b. Knox Co., KY:
  442 i.   Elisha⁶, b. Mar 1882; m. Margret "Maggie" Smith.
  443 ii. Maggie Mae, b. 6 Oct 1883; m. Henry Robinson.
  444 iii. Robert "Boyd," b. 22 Aug 1885.
  445 iv. Dora Mae, b. New Year's Day, 1 Jan 1888; m. Elisha Vaughn Jr.
         v. (n.n.) d. before 1900 Knox Co., KY.
  446 vi. Chester Garfield, b. 11 May 1896; m. Susanna Cox.

177. Elisha⁵ Abner (Richard⁴, Menan³, Elisha² Abney, Abner¹), b.2 Apr 1855 Clay Co., KY. He m. Mary Jane Jarvis on 27 Sep 1878 Knox Co., KY. He and Mary Jane Jarvis appeared on the census of 17 Jun 1880 Knox Co., KY. He d. New Year's Day, 1 Jan 1910 Knox Co., KY, at age 54 and was bur. H.W. Childers Cem., Sprule, Knox Co., KY.
    Mary Jane Jarvis, b.16 Jul 1860 Knox Co., KY. She d.24 Oct 1910 Knox Co., KY, at age 50 and was bur. H.W. Childers Cem., Sprule.
Known children of Elisha⁵ Abner and Mary Jane Jarvis all b. Knox Co., KY:
      i.   James R.⁶, b.Feb 1880.
      ii. Millard, b.10 Apr 1893. He d.5 Oct 1913 (nm.), Knox Co., KY, at age 20 and was bur. H.W. Childers Cem., Sprule.
  447 iii. Lloyd W., b. 26 Jul 1895; m. Julia Ethel Helton.

178. Charles Madison "Charley"⁵ Abner (Richard⁴, Menan³, Elisha² Abney, Abner¹), b.2 Aug 1857 Clay Co., KY. He m. Susan Ann Cobb on 30 Mar 1882 Knox Co., KY. He d.22 Sep 1925 Knox Co., KY, at age 68 and was bur. Cobb Cem., Tedders, Knox Co., KY.
    Susan Ann Cobb, b.30 Oct 1863 Knox Co., KY. She d.27 Aug 1959 Knox Co., KY, at age 95; bur. Cobb Cem., Tedders, Knox Co., KY.
Known children of Charles Madison "Charley"⁵ Abner and Susan Ann Cobb:
      i.   Mariah June⁶, b.14 Feb 1883 Knox Co., KY. She d.13 Sep 1944 Knox Co., KY, at age 61 and was bur. Cobb Cem.
      ii. Julie m. Peter Cox KY. , b.10 Oct 1885 Knox Co., KY. She d.16 Apr 1917 Knox Co., KY, at age 31; bur. Cobb Cem.
  448 iii. Gilbert G., b. 14 Oct 1886 Knox Co., KY; m. Ada Trent.
  449 iv. Sarah, b. 18 Dec 1888 KY; m. Robert Tuttle; m. John R. Smith.
  450 v. Robert "Bob," b. 8 Jun 1891; m. Mary "Jennie" Smith.
  451 vi. Sam, b. 2 Dec 1893; m1. Martha Cobb; m2. Tennie Cottongim.
  452 vii. Finley L., b. 25 Sep 1896; m. Cordie H. Trent.
  453 viii. Maggie, b. 20 Feb 1899; m. Ace Hatfield Sr.
      ix. John H., b.2 Aug 1901. He m. Rella Mills in 1935. He d.20 Jan 1977, age 75; bur. Fisher Cem., Heidrick, Knox Co., KY.
           Rella Mills, b.10 May 1915 KY. She d.3 Apr 1984 Knox Co., KY, at age 68 and was bur. Fisher Cem., Heidrick.

179. Joseph "Joel"⁵ Abner (Richard⁴, Menan³, Elisha² Abney, Abner¹), b. ca.1864 Clay Co., KY. He m. Mary E. Clouse on 6 May 1886 at the home of Rachel Clouse, Knox Co., KY. He d. before 28 May 1897 Gray, Knox Co., KY.
  Mary E. Clouse m. James Smith on 28 May 1897 at the home of Lucy Abner, Knox Co., KY.
Known child of Joseph "Joel"⁵ Abner and Mary E. Clouse:
    454   i.   Theodore⁶, b. 29 Jul 1891; m. Stella Cole.

180. Martha Ann⁵ Abner (John⁴, Menan³, Elisha² Abney, Abner¹), b. ca.1859 Clay Co., KY. She m. Richard Allen Abner, son of Enoch Abner Jr. and Catherine Lucas, on 15 Jul 1871 Clay Co., KY. She d. before 1879 Clay Co., KY.
  Richard Allen Abner, b.9 Jun 1848 Clay Co., KY. He m1. Martha Murray on Christmas Day, 25 Dec 1867 Clay Co., KY. He was liv. on 1 Aug 1870 with father, Enoch Abner, Clay Co., KY. He m3. Sarah Stewart on 18 Jan 1879 Clay Co., KY. He and Sarah Stewart appeared on the census of 9 Jun 1880 Clay Co., IL. He m4. Nancy "Nannie" France on 8 Jul 1898 Clay Co., KY. He and Nancy appeared on the censuses of 29 Jun 1900 and 29 Apr 1910 Clay Co., KY. He d.30 May 1916 Clay Co., KY, at age 67; bur. John C. White Homestead Cem., Cottongim, Clay Co., KY.
Known children of Martha Ann⁵ Abner and Richard Allen Abner:
    455   i.   Nancy⁶, b. ca.1872; m. Stephen Burnett.
           ii. Lucy C., b. ca.1877 Clay Co., KY. She d.1949 IL.

181. James Daniel⁵ Abner (John⁴, Menan³, Elisha² Abney, Abner¹), b.16 Jul 1863 Clay Co., KY. He m. Minerva Jane Hensley on 23 Aug 1889 Clay Co., KY. He and Minerva Jane Hensley appeared on the census of 11 Jun 1900 Kavanaugh, Jackson Co., KY. He d.31 Mar 1921 Madison Co., KY, at age 57 and was bur. Abner Family Cem., Jackson Co., KY.
  Minerva Jane Hensley, b.10 Apr 1869 Jackson Co., KY. She d.17 Dec 1950 Hamilton, Butler Co., OH, at age 81; bur. Abner Family Cem.
Known children of James Daniel⁵ Abner and Minerva Jane Hensley:
    456   i.   Rosa Lee⁶, b. 25 May 1885 Clay Co., KY; m. Abijah Morgan Lyttle.
    457   ii. Emma A., b. 2 Oct 1890 Clay Co., KY; m. Gentry Cox.
           iii. Ella, b. Aug 1893 Jackson Co., KY.
           iv. William Robert, b.29 Dec 1894 Breathitt Co., KY; d. KY.
    458   v.   Della "Dellie," b. 1 Dec 1895 Jackson Co., KY; m. Thomas P. Cox.
           vi. Minnie, b. Mar 1898 Jackson Co., KY.
           vii. James Clark, b.2 Mar 1900 Jackson Co., KY. He m. Hester Roark. He d.New Year's Eve, 31 Dec 1936 Jackson Co., KY, at age 36 and was bur. Bales-Roark Cem., Jackson Co., KY.
                  Hester Roark, b.1902. She d.1992.
           viii. Turner, b.26 May 1900 Jackson Co., KY. He m. Lola (n.n.). He d.21 Dec 1981 Jackson Co., KY, at age 81 and was bur. Russell Flat Cem., Sand Springs, Jackson Co., KY.
                  Lola (n.n.), b.3 Feb 1910. She d.10 Feb 1988 at age 78 and was bur. Russell Flat Cem., Sand Springs.
    459   ix. Lewis Marshall, b. 24 May 1905 Jackson Co., KY; m. Retha Becky Webb.
    460   x.   Dow L., b. 1907 Jackson Co., KY; m. Osa Ison.
           xi. Lula Florence, b.5 Feb 1910 Jackson Co., KY. She d.9 Sep 1912 Jackson Co., KY, at age 2.

182. Serilda⁵ Abnee (Lincoln⁴, John³ Abney, Elisha², Abner¹), b.3 Feb 1852 Nicholas Co., KY. She m. William Thomas Shy ca.1875 Nicholas Co., KY. She d.8 Sep 1900 KY at age 48 and was bur. Frankfort Cem., Frankfort, Frankfort Co., KY.
  William Thomas Shy, b.10 Jun 1849 Nicholas Co., KY. He d.4 Aug 1899 KY at age 50 and was bur. Frankfort Cem., Frankfort.
Known child of Serilda⁵ Abnee and William Thomas Shy:
           i.   Sim L.⁶, b.1877 KY. He was liv. on 23 Apr 1910 with uncle Charles R. Abnee, Nicholas Co., KY. He d.1945 and was bur. Sunnyside Cem., Ewing, Fleming Co., KY.

183. Robert S.⁵ Abnee (Lincoln⁴, John³ Abney, Elisha², Abner¹), b.9 May 1854 Nicholas Co., KY. He m. Emma J. Brooks, daughter of Adolphus Brooks and Mary E. (n.n.), on 18 Apr 1878 Nicholas Co., KY. He and Emma were liv. on 8 Jun 1880 with his father-in-law, Adolphus Brooks, Lower Blue Lick, Nicholas Co., KY. He and Emma appeared on the censuses of 4 Jun 1900 Nicholas Co., KY; 23 Apr 1910, 8 Jan 1920 and 2 Apr 1930 Burika, Robertson Co., KY. He d.15 Feb 1937 Mt. Olivet, Robertson Co., KY, at age 82; bur. Carlisle Cem., Carlisle, Nicholas Co., KY.
  Emma J. Brooks, b.21 Jan 1857 Lewis Co., KY. She d.8 Dec 1939 Fleming Co., KY, at age 82 and was bur. Carlisle Cem., Carlisle.
Known children of Robert S.⁵ Abnee and Emma J. Brooks:
           i.   Homer⁶, b. ca.Mar 1880 Lower Blue Lick, Nicholas Co., KY. He was liv. on 11 Jun 1900 boarder with William Ekley family, Rumsey, McLean Co., KY.
           ii. Herman, b.16 Jun 1881 Nicholas Co., KY. He d. Independence Day, 4 Jul 1926 Nicholas Co., KY, at age 45 and was bur. Carlisle Cem., Carlisle, Nicholas Co., KY.
           iii. Russell, b.5 Mar 1883 Nicholas Co., KY. He was liv. on 28 Apr 1910 with grandmother, Mary E. Brooks, Nicholas Co., KY. He m. Margaret E. "Maggie" Pryor ca.1924. He and Margaret E. "Maggie" Pryor appeared on the censuses of 9 Apr 1930 and 25 Apr 1940 Nicholas Co., KY. He d. New Year's Eve, 31 Dec 1970 Carlisle, Nicholas Co., KY, at age 87 and was bur. Carlisle Cem., Carlisle, Nicholas Co., KY.
                  Margaret E. "Maggie" Pryor, b.16 Sep 1899. She d.28 Sep 1975 Nicholas Co., KY, at age 76; bur. Carlisle Cem.
           iv. Ennis, b.29 May 1885 Nicholas Co., KY. He d.28 Dec 1970 Nicholas Co., KY, at age 85 and was bur. Sunnyside Cem., Ewing, Fleming Co., KY.
    461   v.   Bessie, b. 30 Dec 1887 Nicholas Co., KY; m. William Dorsey Rogers.
           vi. Nona, b. Apr 1889 Nicholas Co., KY. She m. Thornton Morris Sellers. d.14 Apr 1983 Robertson Co., KY.
                  Thornton Morris Sellers, b.1884. He d.1965.

   vii. Malcolm, b.23 Aug 1891 Nicholas Co., KY. He m1. Catherine L. (n.n.). He and Catherine L. (n.n.) appeared on the census of 16 Jan 1920 Detroit, Wayne Co., MI. He was liv. on 10 Apr 1940 as a boarder with the Dotson family, Burika, Robertson Co., KY. He m2. Ruth Dotson. He d.10 Sep 1956 Lexington, Fayette Co., KY, at age 65 and was bur. Sunnyside Cem., Ewing, Fleming Co., KY.

     Catherine L. (n.n.), b. ca.1881 OH. She m1. (n.n.) Underwood ca.1904 OH. She appeared as Head of Household on the census of 12 Apr 1930 Detroit, Wayne Co., GA.

     Ruth Dotson, b.1910.

   viii. Edward "Eddie", b.Jan 1894 Nicholas Co., KY. He d.14 Mar 1926 Nicholas Co., KY, at age 32; Carlisle Cem., Carlisle.

184. William Henry⁵ Abnee (Lincoln⁴, John³ Abney, Elisha², Abner¹), b.22 Mar 1859 Fleming Co., KY. He m. Mary H. "Mollie" Lincks ca.1885. He d.1898 Nicholas Co., KY and was bur. Carlisle Cem., Carlisle, Nicholas Co., KY.

  Mary H. "Mollie" Lincks, b.1865 KY. She appeared as Head of Household on the census of 20 Apr 1910 Lexington, Fayette Co., KY. She appeared as Head of Household on the census of 2 Jan 1920, 7 Apr 1930 and 20 Apr 1940 Lexington, Fayette Co., KY. She d.1941.

Known children of William Henry⁵ Abnee and Mary H. "Mollie" Lincks all b. Carlisle, Nicholas Co., KY:

   i. Rowena H.⁶, b.Apr 1887. She d.15 Aug 1961 Fayette Co., KY, at age 74.

   ii. John Lincoln, b.27 Sep 1891. He d.7 Oct 1895 Carlisle, Nicholas Co., KY, at age 4 and was bur. Carlisle Cem., Carlisle.

   iii. Ora Lee "Orie", b.21 Jul 1893. She d.23 Jun 1985 Fayette Co., KY, at age 91 and was bur. Carlisle Cem., Carlisle.

  462 iv. Airis "Victor," b. 18 Jun 1897; m. Sarah "Irene" Brogle.

185. Effie D.⁵ Abnee (Lincoln⁴, John³ Abney, Elisha², Abner¹), b. Jun 1861 Nicholas Co., KY. She m. Hiram B. Marlow on 3 Aug 1886 same.

  Hiram B. Marlow, b.1861. He d.1943.

Known children of Effie D.⁵ Abnee and Hiram B. Marlow:

   i. Thomas A.⁶, b.1889. He d.1960.

   ii. Joe E., b.1901.

186. Clarence Thomas⁵ Abnee (Lincoln⁴, John³ Abney, Elisha², Abner¹), b.26 May 1871 Nicholas Co., KY. He m1. Mary J. Boggess, daughter of Lorenzo D. Boggess and Mary Elizabeth Bailey, ca.1899. He and Mary J. Boggess were liv. on 5 Jun 1900 with his mother, *Margaret Abner*, Nicholas Co., KY. He and Mary J. Boggess appeared on the census of 23 Apr 1910 Nicholas Co., KY. He m2. Hattie Swartz ca.1915. He and Hattie Swartz appeared on the census of 6 Jun 1920 Rafferty, Nicholas Co., KY. He m3. Ellie (n.n.) before 1930. He and Ellie (n.n.) appeared on the census of 16 Apr 1930 Nicholas Co., KY. He d.22 Apr 1936 Carlisle, Nicholas Co., KY, at age 64; bur. Sunnyside Cem., Ewing, Fleming Co., KY.

  Mary J. Boggess, b.29 Sep 1872 Mt. Olive, Robertson Co., KY. She d.1 May 1914 Carlisle, Nicholas Co., KY, age 41; bur. Sunnyside Cem.

Known children of Clarence Thomas⁵ Abnee and Mary J. Boggess:

   i. Opal⁶, b. ca.1902 KY. She d.1919 and was bur. Sunnyside Cem., Ewing, Fleming Co., KY.

  463 ii. Claude, b. Independence Day, 4 Jul 1904 Carlisle, Nicholas Co., KY; m1. Gladys Maybrier; m2. Audrey "Mabel" Mitchell.

  Hattie Swartz, b.1881 Nicholas Co., KY. She d.10 Dec 1922 Fayette Co., KY and was bur. Sunnyside Cem., Ewing, Fleming Co., KY.

Known child of Clarence Thomas⁵ Abnee and Hattie Swartz:

  464 i. Shy Conley⁶, b. 26 Apr 1921 Nicholas Co., KY; m. Betty Jane Dollins.

  Ellie (n.n.), b. ca.1884 KY. She m1. (n.n.) Letcher ca.1900.

There were no known children of Clarence Thomas⁵ Abnee and Ellie (n.n.).

187. Malinda⁵ Hunt (Nancy⁴ Abner, John³ Abney, Elisha², Abner¹), b.11 Sep 1847 Owsley Co., KY. She m. William E. Murray on 18 Sep 1865 Boone Co., AR. She and William E. Murray appeared on the census of 23 Jun 1870 Sugar Creek, Barry Co., MO. She d.23 Nov 1926 Afton, Ottowa Co., OK, at age 79 and was bur. Rolston Cem., Bernice, Delaware Co., OK.

  William E. Murray, b.31 Aug 1842 (west) TN. He d.14 Feb 1924 Needmore, Delaware Co., OK, at age 81 and was bur. Rolston Cem., Bernice.

Known children of Malinda⁵ Hunt and William E. Murray:

  465 i. Matilda Ann⁶, b. 11 May 1867 Seligman, Barry Co., MO; m. William Riley Kelley.

   ii. Susan J., b.6 Sep 1869 Barry Co., MO. She d.23 Aug 1875 Barry Co., MO, at age 5.

   iii. Mary Edna, b.23 Oct 1871 Seligman, Barry Co., MO. She m. John P. Thomas Skelton ca.1888. She d.23 Jan 1925 Centralia, Lewis Co., WA, at age 53.

     John P. Thomas Skelton, b.25 Mar 1870 Seligman, Barry Co., MO; d.14 Oct 1940 Centralia, Lewis Co., WA, age 70.

   iv. Richard, b.19 Sep 1873 Barry Co., MO. He d.18 Apr 1875 Barry Co., MO, at age 1.

   v. Nancy C, b.11 Feb 1875 Seligman, Barry Co., MO; d.24 Aug 1895 Needmore, Delaware Co., Indian Terr. (OK), age 20.

   vi. Viola Bell, b.Sep 1877 Barry Co., MO. She m. Dillard Ozrow Weston on 24 Mar 1907 Cherokee Co., KS. She d. Independence Day, 4 Jul 1963 Miami, Ottawa Co., OK, at age 85.

     Dillard Ozrow Weston, b.May 1880 Sugar Creek, Barry Co., MO. He d.2 Oct 1930 Joplin, Jasper Co., MO, age 50.

   vii. Dula Melinda, b.17 Dec 1879 Seligman, Barry Co., MO. She m. Moses Monroe "Mose" Garrison on 10 Nov 1901 Miami, Ottawa Co., Indian Territory (OK). She d.2 Feb 1956 Modesto, Stanislaus Co., CA, at age 76.

     Moses Monroe "Mose" Garrison, b.22 Aug 1874 MO. He d.18 Jan 1947 Madera, Madera Co., CA, at age 72.

   viii. William "Buck", b.21 Mar 1882 Seligman, Barry Co., MO. He m. Edna F. Vaughan on 1 Nov 1903 Needmore, Delaware Co., Indiana Territory (OK). He d.21 May 1963 Chehalis, Lewis Co., WA, at age 81.

     Edna F. Vaughan, b.Nov 1881 AR. She d.28 Oct 1962 Chehalis, Lewis Co., WA, at age 80.

   ix. Iva M, b.27 Feb 1884 Seligman, Barry Co., MO; m. John "Frank" Horton. d.16 Feb 1937 Miami, Ottawa Co., OK, ae.52.

     John "Frank" Horton, b.22 Jun 1874. He d.2 Sep 1943 Tulsa, Tulsa Co., OK, at age 69.

188. John W.⁵ Abner (Lewis⁴, John³ Abney, Elisha², Abner¹), b.25 May 1867 Owsley Co., KY. He m. Georgia A. "Georgie" Ketchum on 27 Oct 1895 Lee Co., KY. He and Georgia A. "Georgie" Ketchum appeared on the census of 2 Jun 1900 Lee Co., KY. He d.12 Dec 1905 Lee Co., KY, at age 38 and was bur. Lutes Abner Cem., Primrose, Lee Co., KY.

  Georgia A. "Georgie" Ketchum, b.22 Jan 1876 KY. She m. Andrew Sears ca.1909. She and Andrew Sears appeared on the census of 29 Apr 1910 Hamilton, Warren Co., OH. She d.24 Jul 1921 Lemon, Butler Co., OH, at age 45.

Known children of John W.⁵ Abner and Georgia A. "Georgie" Ketchum all b. Lee Co., KY:
  i. Bernice⁶, b.4 Mar 1897. She m1. William Raider on 15 Feb 1913 Butler Co., OH. They were divorced ca.1916. She m2. Monroe Browning on 16 Mar 1917 Butler Co., OH. She m3. Clifford Bailey on 11 Aug 1924 Butler Co., OH.
    William Raider, b.8 Apr 1888 Irvin, Estill Co., KY.
    Monroe Browning, b. Jellico, Campbell Co., TN. He d. before 11 Aug 1924.
    Clifford Bailey, b.Mar 1887 KY and was bur. on 24 Sep 1941.
  ii. Frances, b.17 Mar 1898. She m. Roy Selby on 26 Dec 1922 Wayne Co., IN.
    Roy Selby, b.1 Oct 1899 OH.
  iii. Arthur G, b.Jan 1900. He was liv. on 22 Apr 1910 with his uncle, Charlie Bailey family, St. Helens, Lee Co., KY. He was liv. on 18 Apr 1930 Dayton, Montgomery Co., OH. He was liv. on 1 Apr 1935 Longview State Hosp., Cincinnati, Hamilton Co., OH. He was liv. on 4 Apr 1940 Longview State Hosp., Cincinnati, Hamilton Co., OH.

189. Lucinda⁵ Abner (Lewis⁴, John³ Abney, Elisha², Abner¹), b.18 Dec 1869 Owsley Co., KY. She m. Russell Scott ca.1890. She d.14 Mar 1917 at age 47 and was bur. Lutes Abner Cem., Primrose, Lee Co., KY.
  Russell Scott, b.6 Nov 1868 Nicholas Co., KY. He d.12 Aug 1936 KY at age 67.
Known children of Lucinda⁵ Abner and Russell Scott:
  i. Robert L.⁶, b. ca.1891.
  ii. Mary A, b. ca.1899.

190. Malinda A.⁵ Abner (Lewis⁴, John³ Abney, Elisha², Abner¹), b.3 Sep 1871 Lee Co., KY. She m. Niniven Martin Quillen ca.1901. She d.20 Mar 1952 Lexington, Fayette Co., KY, at age 80 and was bur. Quillen Cem., Lee Co., KY.
  Niniven Martin Quillen, b.15 Oct 1873 Heidelberg, Lee Co., KY. He d.27 Jan 1951 Lexington, Fayette Co., KY, at age 77; bur. Quillen Cem.
Known children of Malinda A.⁵ Abner and Niniven Martin Quillen all b. Lee Co., KY:
  i. Rowena⁶, b. ca.1904.
  ii. Eva, b.1904. She d.2002.
  iii. Sophia, b. ca.1906.
  iv. Viola, b. ca.1908.
  v. Floyd A., b.1909. He d.1982.

191. Lewis A.⁵ Abner (Lewis⁴, John³ Abney, Elisha², Abner¹), b.20 Feb 1879 Primrose, Lee Co., KY. He m1. Louchester "Chester" Cockerham ca.1902 Lee Co., KY. He and Louchester "Chester" Cockerham appeared on the census of 28 Apr 1910 Saint Helens, Lee Co., KY. He m2. Sarah "Sallie" Taulbee ca.1916 Lee Co., KY. He and Sarah "Sallie" Taulbee appeared on the censuses of 12 Jan 1920, 11 Apr 1930 and 29 Apr 1940 Saint Helens, Lee Co., KY. He d.23 Dec 1945 Primrose, Lee Co., KY, at age 66 and was bur. Abner Cem., Primrose, Lee Co., KY.
  Louchester "Chester" Cockerham, b.3 Mar 1881 Lee Co., KY; d.10 Apr 1916 Saint Helens, Lee Co., KY, age 35; bur. Abner Cem., Primrose.
Known children of Lewis A.⁵ Abner and Louchester "Chester" Cockerham:
  466 i. Robert Lewis⁶, b. 26 Jan 1903 Lee Co., KY; m. Sallie Drake.
       ii. William "Willie", b.15 Jul 1905 Lee Co., KY. He m. Lillie Arnold. He d.30 Jun 1938 at age 32 and was bur. Abner Cem., Primrose, Lee Co., KY.
         Lillie Arnold, b.30 Apr 1910 KY. She d.25 Jul 1957 at age 47.
  467 iii. James "Bethel," b. 2 Jul 1908 Lee Co., KY; m. Geneva F. Lucas.
  468 iv. Gerald, b. 16 Oct 1912 Lee Co., KY; m. Beatrice C. (n.n.).
       v. Ila Gay, b.24 Mar 1915 Primrose, Lee Co., KY. She d.9 Oct 1915 Primrose, Lee Co., KY and was bur. Abner Cem., Primrose, Lee Co., KY.

  Sarah "Sallie" Taulbee, b.18 Sep 1893 KY. She d.28 Feb 1978 at age 84 and was bur. Abner Cem., Primrose, Lee Co., KY.
Known children of Lewis A.⁵ Abner and Sarah "Sallie" Taulbee:
  i. F. Coleman⁶, b.2 Sep 1917 Lee Co., KY. He d.11 Jun 1967 at age 49.
  ii. Ernest C., b. ca.1921 Lee Co., KY.
  iii. Z. Sam, b.3 Nov 1922 Lee Co., KY. He d.8 Mar 1984 at age 61.
  iv. Emma Jo m. PFC Charles Raymond Marshall (USArmy-WWII). , b.13 Mar 1926. She d.2 Oct 1989 at age 63 and was bur. Abner Cem., Primrose, Lee Co., KY.
    PFC Charles Raymond Marshall (USArmy-WWII), b.7 Apr 1922. He d.2 Dec 1966 at age 44 and was bur. Lucas Cem., Monica, Lee Co., KY.
  469 v. Frank Cardine "Boose," b. 18 Jul 1928 Primrose, Lee Co., KY; m. Elmer Spencer.
       vi. Lorena "Susie", b.27 Sep 1931. She m. S.Sgt. Silas E. Marshall. She d. Christmas Day, 25 Dec 2004 at age 73 and was bur. Abner Cem., Primrose, Lee Co., KY.
         S.Sgt. Silas E. Marshall, b.21 Oct 1924. He d.12 May 1989 at age 64 and was bur. Marshall Cem., Lee Co., KY.

192. Nannie Emma⁵ Abner (Lewis⁴, John³ Abney, Elisha², Abner¹), b.22 Jan 1881 Lee Co., KY. She m. Charles Henderson Bailey on 18 May 1904 Lee Co., KY. She and Charles Henderson Bailey appeared on the census of 22 Apr 1910 St. Helens, Lee Co., KY. She d.3 Feb 1932 Lee Co., KY, at age 51 and was bur. Lutes Abner Cem., Primrose, Lee Co., KY.
  Charles Henderson Bailey, b.9 May 1882 Wolfe Co., KY. He d.16 Jun 1947 Primrose, Lee Co., KY, at age 65.
Known children of Nannie Emma⁵ Abner and Charles Henderson Bailey:
  i. Cord Wayne "Cordy"⁶, b.1905. He d.1950.
  ii. Eunice, b.1907. She d.1961.
  iii. Geneva Lee, b.1913. She d.2000.
  iv. James Russell, b.1916. He d.1942.
  v. Edgar Ray, b.1923. He d.1958.

193. Grover "Cleveland"⁵ Abner (John⁴, John³ Abney, Elisha², Abner¹), b.Christmas Eve, 24 Dec 1884 Lee Co., KY. He m. Edna Mae Davis on 27 Dec 1909 Lee Co., KY. He and Edna Mae Davis appeared on the census of 27 Apr 1910 St. Helens, Lee Co., KY. He d.10 Jul 1917 Lee Co., KY, at age 32 and was bur. Davis Cem., Monica, Lee Co., KY.
    Edna Mae Davis, b.14 Feb 1895 KY. She m2. James Marion Palmer. She d.16 Jun 1971 at age 76 and was bur. Davis Cem., Monica.
Known children of Grover "Cleveland"⁵ Abner and Edna Mae Davis:
> i.   Churchill Cornelius⁶, b.29 Dec 1910 Stanford, Lincoln Co., KY. He m. Hettie Pearl Beard on 4 Jun 1929 Lebanon, Marion Co., KY. He and Hettie Pearl Beard appeared on the census of 25 Apr 1930 Saint Helens, Lee Co., KY. He d.9 Aug 1930 Beattyville, Lee Co., KY, at age 19 and was bur. Davis Cem., Monica, Lee Co., KY.
> > Hettie Pearl Beard, b.25 Sep 1913. She m2. Kenneth King McGinnis on 3 Mar 1938. She d.31 Jul 2006 at age 92.
> 470   ii.   Nancy Pearl, b. 9 Feb 1917 Primrose, Lee Co., KY; m1. Carlie Daili Durbin; m2. Joe Heving; m3. Paul M. Burgan.

194. John Henry⁵ Abner (John⁴, John³ Abney, Elisha², Abner¹), b.14 Nov 1886 Fincastle, Lee Co., KY. He m. Doll "Dolly" Drake ca.1914. He and Doll "Dolly" Drake appeared on the censuses of 9 Jan 1920, 9 Apr 1930 and 8 May 1940 Saint Helens, Lee Co., KY. He d.16 Nov 1947 Vada, Lee Co., KY, at age 61 and was bur. Lutes Abner Cem., Primrose, Lee Co., KY.
    Doll "Dolly" Drake, b.25 Aug 1893. She d.7 Sep 1988 at age 95 and was bur. Lutes Abner Cem., Primrose, Lee Co., KY.
Known children of John Henry⁵ Abner and Doll "Dolly" Drake:
> i.   Charles "Kenneth"⁶, b.2 Dec 1915 Vada, Lee Co., KY. He appeared on the census of 12 Apr 1940 Saint Helens, Lee Co., KY. He m. Nola (n.n.). He d.8 Mar 1949 Lexington, Fayette Co., KY, at age 33 and was bur. Lutes Abner Cem., Primrose.
> ii.   Ishmael Drake, b.11 Aug 1917 Lee Co., KY. He d.19 Nov 1918 Lee Co., KY, at age 1 and was bur. Lutes Abner Cem.
> iii.   Ila "Rae", b. ca.Jun 1919 Lee Co., KY.
> iv.   Nola Thomas, b.22 Jun 1925 Lee Co., KY. He m. Vergie A. Powell. He d.10 Apr 2007 at age 81 and was bur. Calvary Assembly of God Cem., Morganton, Burke Co., NC.
> > Vergie A. Powell, b.12 Apr 1920. She d.27 Nov 1997 at age 77; bur. Calvary Assembly of God Cem., Morganton.
> v.   Milanesne V. "Mila", b. ca.1927 Lee Co., KY.
> vi.   Arthur Vaughn, b.11 Oct 1927 Lee Co., KY. He m. Anna Lee Davis. He d.13 Jul 2007 at age 79; bur. Lutes Abner Cem.
> > Anna Lee Davis, b.5 May 1929 Beattyville, Lee Co., KY. She d.20 Feb 2011 at age 81; bur. Lutes Abner Cem.

195. Pvt. William⁵ Abner Sr. (USArmy-WWI) (John⁴, John³ Abney, Elisha², Abner¹), b.26 Nov 1890 Lee Co., KY. He m. Oma Marshall ca.1918. He and Oma Marshall were liv. on 7 Jan 1920 with his father, John Abner, Fincastle, Lee Co., KY. He and Oma Marshall appeared on the censuses of 5 Apr 1930 and 10 May 1940 Lee Co., KY. He d.9 Feb 1978 Fayette Co., KY, at age 87.
    Oma Marshall, b.28 Nov 1898 KY. She d.18 Jun 1969 at age 70 and was bur. Riverview Cem., Beattyville, Lee Co., KY.
Known children of Pvt. William⁵ Abner Sr. (USArmy-WWI) and Oma Marshall both b. Lee Co., KY:
> i.   Geneva Maxine⁶, b.25 Jul 1920. She m. Clyde M. Caddell (USArmy-WWII) on 14 Nov 1945. She d.1 Mar 2008 Louisville, Jefferson Co., KY, at age 87 and was bur. Resthaven Mem. Cem., Louisville, Jefferson Co., KY.
> > Clyde M. Caddell (USArmy-WWII), b.4 Jun 1917 Lancing, Morgan Co., TN. He d.3 Oct 2018 Louisville, Jefferson Co., KY, at age 101 and was bur. Resthaven Mem. Cem., Louisville, Jefferson Co., KY.
> ii.   William "Bill" Jr., b. ca.1923.

196. Arthur "Doc"⁵ Abner (John⁴, John³ Abney, Elisha², Abner¹), b.3 Dec 1896 Lee Co., KY. He m. Carrie Kincaid ca.1923. He and Carrie Kincaid appeared on the censuses of 11 Apr 1930 Lee Co., KY and of 20 Apr 1940 Lee Co., KY. He d.Jan 1971 Flora, Clay Co., IL, at age 74 and was bur. Floral Garden of Memories Cem., Flora, Clay Co., IL.
    Carrie Kincaid, b.6 Mar 1902 KY. She d.Nov 1986 at age 84 and was bur. Floral Garden of Memories Cem., Flora, Clay Co., IL.
Known children of Arthur "Doc"⁵ Abner and Carrie Kincaid:
> i.   Willis Harold⁶, b.3 Feb 1929 Lee Co., KY; d.11 Feb 1929 Lee Co., KY; bur. Lutes Abner Cem., Primrose, Lee Co., KY.
> ii.   Mitzi Jean, b.21 Dec 1935 Beattyville, Lee Co., KY. She m. Richard Arthur Goldstein on 22 Mar 1957. She d.15 Jun 2017 Effingham, Effingham Co., IL, at age 81 and was bur. Elmwood Cem., Flora, Clay Co., IL.
> > Richard Arthur Goldstein, b.12 Apr 1936. He d.3 May 2005 at age 69; bur. Elmwood Cem., Flora, Clay Co., IL.
> 471   iii.   Arthur Thomas "Tom," b. 22 Nov 1938 Beattyville, Lee Co., KY; m. Carolyn Sue Erwin.

197. Pvt. David G.⁵ Bishop (UA) (Abraham⁴, Mary³ Abner, Elisha² Abney, Abner¹), b.1835 Clay Co., KY. He m. Mary "Polly" Bishop, daughter of Elisha Monroe Bishop and Amy Johnson, on 17 Jan 1867 Clay Co., KY. He and Mary "Polly" Bishop appeared on the censuses of 11 Aug 1870 and of 21 Jun 1880 Clay Co., KY. He d.28 May 1889 and was bur. Bishop Bend Cem., Trixie, Clay Co., KY.
    Mary "Polly" Bishop, b.22 Sep 1835 Clay Co., KY. She d.15 May 1927 Clay Co., KY, at age 91 and was bur. Bishop Bend Cem., Trixie.
Known children of Pvt. David G.⁵ Bishop (UA) and Mary "Polly" Bishop all b. Clay Co., KY:
> i.   Abel⁶, b. ca.1868.
> ii.   Elisha A., b. ca.Feb 1869. He d.1930.
> iii.   John, b. ca.1871.
> iv.   Nancy, b. ca.1873.
> 472   v.   James David, b. 23 Oct 1875; m. Lucy Katherine Nuckols.
> vi.   Charles "Alexander", b. ca.1876. He d.1937.
> vii.   Amanda "Amy", b. ca.1878.
> viii.   Charity, b.1883. She d.1954.

198. John⁵ Bishop (UA) (Abraham⁴, Mary³ Abner, Elisha² Abney, Abner¹), b.Christmas Eve, 24 Dec 1848 Clay Co., KY. He m. Lucy "Catherine" Cole on 6 Mar 1869 Clay Co., KY. He and Lucy "Catherine" Cole appeared on the censuses of 8 Jun 1880 Owsley Co., KY; and 1 Jun 1900 Buffalo, Owsley Co., KY. He d.12 Oct 1911 Conkling, Owsley Co., KY, at age 62 and was bur. Bishop Bend Cem., Trixie, Clay Co., KY.
Known children of John⁵ Bishop (UA) and Lucy "Catherine" Cole:
> i.   Mary Jane⁶, b.1878. She d.1953.
> 473   ii.   Robert Grant, b. 16 Apr 1881 Owsley Co., KY; m. Delphia Gabbard.
> iii.   David C., b.1884. He d.1968.

199. Mary "Polly"⁵ Bishop (Elisha⁴, Mary³ Abner, Elisha² Abney, Abner¹), b.22 Sep 1835 Clay Co., KY. She m. Pvt. David G. Bishop (UA), son of Abraham "Abel" Bishop and Nancy Robinson, on 17 Jan 1867 Clay Co., KY. She and Pvt. David G. Bishop (UA) appeared on the census of 11 Aug 1870 Clay Co., KY. She and Pvt. David G. Bishop (UA) appeared on the census of 21 Jun 1880 Clay Co., KY. She d.15 May 1927 Clay Co., KY, at age 91 and was bur. Bishop Bend Cem., Trixie, Clay Co., KY.

Pvt. David G. Bishop (UA), b.1835 Clay Co., KY. He d.28 May 1889 and was bur. Bishop Bend Cem., Trixie, Clay Co., KY.

Known children of Mary "Polly"⁵ Bishop and Pvt. David G. Bishop (UA) all b. Clay Co., KY:

      i.   Abel⁶, b. ca.1868. (see page 82).
      ii.   Elisha A., b. ca.Feb 1869. (see page 82).
      iii. John, b. ca.1871. (see page 82).
      iv. Nancy, b. ca.1873. (see page 82).
      v.   James David, b. 23 Oct 1875; m. Lucy Katherine Nuckols. (see # 472 on page 133).
      vi. Charles "Alexander," b. ca.1876. (see page 82).
      vii. Amanda "Amy," b. ca.1878. (see page 82).
      viii. Charity, b. 1883. (see page 82).

200. Alexander "Alex"⁵ Bishop (Elisha⁴, Mary³ Abner, Elisha² Abney, Abner¹), b.22 Aug 1842 Teges, Clay Co., KY. He m. (n.n.). He d.11 Sep 1924 Clay Co., KY, at age 82 and was bur. Laurel Point Cem., Clay Co., KY.

Known child of Alexander "Alex"⁵ Bishop and (n.n.):

      i.   Charity⁶ m. Sidney Gabbard, son of Elisha Gabbard & Mary Peters. She d.21 Jul 1954 and was bur. Henry Gabbard Cem. Sidney Gabbard d.8 Nov 1938.

201. Nancy⁵ Bishop (Elisha⁴, Mary³ Abner, Elisha² Abney, Abner¹) m. Abijah Gabbard, son of Isaac H. Gabbard and Jane Isaacs. , b. ca.1849 KY. Abijah Gabbard, b.21 Jun 1843. He d.1927.

Known children of Nancy⁵ Bishop and Abijah Gabbard:

      i.   Amanda⁶.
      ii.   George Washington.

202. Esther⁵ Bishop (Bryson⁴, Mary³ Abner, Elisha² Abney, Abner¹), b.1 Oct 1862 Clay Co., KY. She m. Robert Abner, son of David Abner and Mary "Polly" Parker, ca.1880. She and Robert Abner were liv. on 7 Jun 1880 with father, David Abner, Clay Co., KY. She and Robert Abner appeared on the censuses of 15 Jun 1900 and 18 Apr 1910 Clay Co., KY. She and Robert Abner were liv. on 6 May 1930 with son-in-law, Henry Wood, Sturgeon, Jackson Co., KY; and 25 Apr 1940 with son, John B. Abney, Sturgeon, Jackson Co., KY. She d.20 Dec 1949 Union Co., IN, at age 87 and was bur. Liberty Cem., Egypt, Jackson Co., KY.

Robert Abner, b.11 Mar 1861 Clay Co., KY. He d.14 Apr 1941 Fayette Co., IN, at age 80 and was bur. Liberty Cem., Egypt, Jackson Co., KY.

Known children of Esther⁵ Bishop and Robert Abner all b. Clay Co., KY:

             i.   Dory⁶, b.May 1881.
             ii.   Mary, b.Oct 1882. She d.1975.
  474   iii. William D., b. Jun 1884; m. Ella Allen; div. Ella Allen.
  475   iv. Lillie, b. May 1885; m. Henry Wood.
  476   v.   John B., b. Apr 1886; m. Nannie J. Wood.
  477   vi. Daniel P. "Dan," b. 20 Jun 1889; m. Lucy Noe.
  478   vii. Shelby, b. Feb 1891; m. Eva Bowman.
  479   viii. Ida, b. 22 Jun 1894; m. Lucian S. Byrd Sr.
             ix. Robert Jr., b. Feb 1896.
             x.   Taylor, b.Aug 1899. He d.1990.

203. Mary Ann "Polly"⁵ Smith (Charles⁴, Margaret³ Abner, Elisha² Abney, Abner¹), b.7 Jul 1859 Jackson Co., KY. She m. Newton Johnson, son of Elisha Johnson and Eleanor Fortner, on 18 May 1876 Montgomery Co., KY. She d.31 Mar 1927 Midway, Woodford Co., KY, at age 67 and was bur. Midway Cem., Midway, Woodford Co., KY.

Newton Johnson, b.22 Dec 1857 Morgan Co., KY. He d.17 Dec 1917 Wiboux, MT, at age 59 and was bur. Wiboux, MT.

Known child of Mary Ann "Polly"⁵ Smith and Newton Johnson:

  480   i.   James Kelter⁶, b. 1 Jun 1902 Clark Co., KY; m. Katie Clark.

204. (Numbered in error. See #211 on page 85)

205. William Squire⁵ Abner (Enoch⁴, Enoch³ Abney, Elisha², Abner¹), b.4 Dec 1842 Clay Co., KY. He m. Julia Elizabeth Cottongim on New Year's Day, 1 Jan 1870. He and Julia Elizabeth Cottongim appeared on the censuses of 11 Jun 1880 and 6 Jun 1900 Clay Co., KY. He d.7 Feb 1917 Clay Co., KY, at age 74 and was bur. Paces Creek Cem., Garrard, Clay Co., KY.

Julia Elizabeth Cottongim, b.7 Feb 1855 Clay Co., KY. She d.12 Jul 1932 Clay Co., KY, at age 77.

Known children of William Squire⁵ Abner and Julia Elizabeth Cottongim all b. Clay Co., KY (see Quarto Addendum for more issue):

             i.   Mary Jane "Jenny"⁶, b. ca.1870.
  482   ii.   Lucy "Catherine," b. 18 Jan 1873; m. James Henry "Jim" Henson.
             iii. Nancy, b.10 Aug 1876. She d.3 Jan 1953 at age 76 and was bur. Paces Creek Cem., Garrard, Clay Co., KY.
  483   iv. John, b. May 1878; m. Bettie Lee "Betsie" Harris.

206. Richard Allen⁵ Abner (Enoch⁴, Enoch³ Abney, Elisha², Abner¹), b.9 Jun 1848 Clay Co., KY. He m1. Martha Murray on Christmas Day, 25 Dec 1867 Clay Co., KY. He was liv. on 1 Aug 1870 with father, Enoch Abner, Clay Co., KY. He m2. Martha Ann Abner, daughter of John Abner and Matilda Robertson, on 15 Jul 1871 Clay Co., KY. He m3. Sarah Stewart on 18 Jan 1879 Clay Co., KY. He and Sarah Stewart appeared on the census of 9 Jun 1880 Clay Co., IL. He m4. Nancy "Nannie" France on 8 Jul 1898 Clay Co., KY. He appeared on the census of 29 Jun 1900 Clay Co., KY. He and Nancy "Nannie" France appeared on the census of 29 Apr 1910 Clay Co., KY. He d.30 May 1916 Clay Co., KY, at age 67 and was bur. John C. White Homestead Cem., Cottongim, Clay Co., KY.

Martha Murray d. before 1870 Clay Co., KY.
There were no known children of Richard Allen[5] Abner and Martha Murray.
    Martha Ann Abner, b. ca.1859 Clay Co., KY. She d. before 1879 Clay Co., KY.
Known children of Richard Allen[5] Abner and Martha Ann Abner:
> i.   Nancy[6], b. ca.1872; m. Stephen Burnett. (see page 79 and #455 on page 130).
> ii. Lucy C., b. ca.1877 Clay Co., KY. (see page 79).

    Sarah Stewart, b. ca.1854 KY.
Known children of Richard Allen[5] Abner and Sarah Stewart all b. Clay Co., KY:
> i.   Lizzie B.[6], b.Mar 1887. She m. Luther Frederick on 22 Dec 1909 Manchester, Clay Co., KY.
>   Luther Frederick, b. ca.1884.
> ii. Mary B, b.7 Mar 1887. She d.28 May 1958 Clay Co., KY, at age 71.
> iii. John, b.Feb 1889.
> 484   iv. Alabama, b. Oct 1891; m. Martin J. "Mart" Fisher Sr.

    Nancy "Nannie" France m2. Taylor Henson. , b. Nov 1882 KY. She and Taylor Henson appeared on the census of 7 Jan 1920 White Branch, Clay Co., KY. She m3. (n.n.) White before 1930. She appeared as Head of Household on the census of 19 Apr 1930 Wallins Creek, Harlan Co., KY. She d.6 Mar 1966 Harlan Co., KY, at age 83.
Known children of Richard Allen[5] Abner and Nancy "Nannie" France:
> i.   Maggie[6], b.Apr 1899.
> 485   ii. Theo, b. 26 Dec 1902 Clay Co., KY; m. Artie "Elise" Kinder.
> iii. Roy, b.25 Apr 1904 Clay Co., KY. He m. Fannie Caldwell on 4 Jun 1932 Wallins Creek, Harlan Co., KY. He d.14 Dec 1989 Chicago, Cook Co., IL, at age 85.
>   Fannie Caldwell, b. ca.1908.
> iv. Stella Lillian "Lillie" m. Matt Morgan. , b. ca.1906 Clay Co., KY. She d.7 May 1964 Wallins Creek, Harlan Co., KY. Matt Morgan, b.1898. He d.1966.
> v.   Leonard, b.15 Mar 1908 Clay Co., KY. He d.10 Mar 1971 Wallins Creek, Harlan Co., KY, at age 62.
> vi. Lydia m. James Wyrick. , b. ca.1911 Clay Co., KY. She d.11 Oct 1944 Twila, Harlan Co., KY and was bur. Banner Fork Cem.#01, Wallins Creek, Harlan Co., KY.
> vii. Pearl, b. ca.1913 Clay Co., KY.
> viii. Sudie, b. ca. Jul 1916 Clay Co., KY.

207. Mary[5] Abner (Enoch[4], Enoch[3] Abney, Elisha[2], Abner[1]), b.7 Sep 1849 Clay Co., KY. She m. William Smith on 1 Oct 1867 Clay Co., KY. She and William Smith appeared on the census of 5 Jun 1880 Manchester, Clay Co., KY; and 14 Jun 1900 Otter Creek, Clay Co., KY. She d.3 Feb 1929 Knox Co., KY, at age 79.
    William Smith, b.May 1850 Clay Co., KY. He d. ca.1905 Otter Creek, Clay Co., KY.
Known children of Mary[5] Abner and William Smith all b. Clay Co., KY:
> 486   i.   Sophia "Sofie"[6], b. ca.1869; m. Pierce Abner.
> ii. Richard G., b. ca.1870. He d.1943.
> iii. Martha, b. ca.1873.
> iv. Susan, b. ca.1875.
> v.   Jabel, b. ca.1876.
> vi. Rosa, b. ca.1876.
> vii. John, b. ca.Mar 1880.
> viii. Beverly, b. ca.1883.
> ix. David, b. ca.1886.
> x.   Ella, b. ca.1888.
> xi. Prudie, b. ca.1890.
> xii. Nellie, b. ca.1892.

208. Susan[5] Abner (Enoch[4], Enoch[3] Abney, Elisha[2], Abner[1]), b.7 Sep 1852 Clay Co., KY. She m1. Jarvis Pinner on 7 Jun 1869 Clay Co., KY. She and Jarvis Pinner appeared on the census of 28 Jun 1870 Clay Co., KY. She m2. Theophilus T. Collett ca.1892. She and Theophilus T. Collett appeared on the census of 30 Apr 1910 Manchester, Clay Co., KY.
There were no known children of Susan[5] Abner and Jarvis Pinner.
    Theophilus T. Collett, b. ca.1856 KY.
Known child of Susan[5] Abner and Theophilus T. Collett:
> i.   Nellie[6], b. ca.1893 Clay Co., KY.

209. Milton[5] Abner Sr. (Enoch[4], Enoch[3] Abney, Elisha[2], Abner[1]), b. ca.10 Oct 1854 Clay Co., KY. He m. Mariah Stewart on 3 Aug 1878 Clay Co., KY. He and Mariah Stewart appeared on the census of 30 Jun 1900 Clay Co., KY. He and Mariah Stewart appeared on the census of 28 Apr 1910 Whites Branch, Clay Co., KY. He d.23 Jan 1918. He and Mariah Stewart appeared on the census of 10 Jan 1920 Whites Branch, Clay Co., KY.
    Mariah Stewart, b.May 1859 KY. She d.23 Apr 1939 at age 79.
Known children of Milton[5] Abner Sr. and Mariah Stewart all b. Clay Co., KY:
> i.   Mary B.[6], b. ca.1879.
> 487   ii. Dora E., b. 22 Apr 1882; m. John C. Lawson.
> iii. Flora, b.Aug 1883.

    488   iv.   Emma, b. Sep 1885; m. Carlo Lyttle Lewis.

            v.   Ida, b.18 Sep 1886. She m1. Lucian S. Byrd on 28 Dec 1910 Clay Co., KY. She m2. Hiram Valentine. and Hiram Valentine appeared on the census of 8 Apr 1940 Cottongim, Clay Co., KY. She d.7 Feb 1965 at age 78 and was bur. Engine Cem., Bluehole, Clay Co., KY.

                    Lucian S. Byrd, b.1882. He d.1955.

                    Hiram Valentine, b.25 Oct 1899. He d.25 Oct 1964 at age 65 and was bur. Engine Cem., Bluehole, Clay Co., KY.

            vi.   Ella, b.18 Sep 1887. She was liv. on 8 Apr 1940 with brother-in-law, Hiram Valentine, Clay Co., KY.

    489   vii.   Taylor, b. Mar 1890; m. Minnie Herd.

    490   viii.   Ollie, b. 8 Jun 1893; m. Sawyers R. Smith.

            ix.   Eva F., b.15 Dec 1895. She d.16 Apr 1920 Clay Co., KY, at age 24 and was bur. Orchild Hill Cem., Urban, Clay Co., KY.

    491   x.   John "Johnny Beerfield," b. 18 Feb 1899; m. Mallie Bundy.

    492   xi.   Harvey, b. 3 Mar 1901; m. Ida "Belle" Herd.

            xii.   Anderson, b. ca.1904. He d.28 Jan 1972.

210. Lucy[5] Abner (Enoch[4], Enoch[3] Abney, Elisha[2], Abner[1]), b. ca.1857 Clay Co., KY. She m. John E. Roberts on 15 Jun 1876. She and John E. Roberts appeared on the census of 9 Jun 1880 Clay Co., KY.
Known child of Lucy[5] Abner and John E. Roberts:

            i.   Abijah[6], b. ca.1878 Clay Co., KY.

211. Theophilus General "Theo"[5] Abner Sr. (Enoch[4], Enoch[3] Abney, Elisha[2], Abner[1]), b.27 Aug 1861 Clay Co., KY. He m. Mary "Isabella" Stewart on 18 Nov 1881 Clay Co., KY. He and Mary "Isabella" Stewart appeared on the censuses of 28 Jun 1900 Clay Co., KY; 5 May 1910 and 16 Jan 1920 Whites Branch, Clay Co., KY; and 15 Apr 1930 Lincoln, Clay Co., KY. He d.20 Sep 1933 at age 72.

    Mary "Isabella" Stewart, b.Dec 1866 KY. , b. before 1930 KY.
Known children of Theophilus General "Theo"[5] Abner Sr. and Mary "Isabella" Stewart:

    493   i.   Amelia May "Mealie"[6], b. May 1883 Clay Co., KY.

    494   ii.   Thomas "Tommy," b. 23 Apr 1885 Clay Co., KY; m. Isabelle "Belle" Smith.

    495   iii.   Steven "Steve," b. 6 Jun 1889 Clay Co., KY; m. Susan Lewis.

            iv.   Beverly "Beve", b. ca.1892. He d.22 Jan 1955.

    496   v.   Eva Mae "Evie," b. 22 Oct 1893 Clay Co., KY; m. Elbert Sams.

            vi.   Maude, b. ca.1895. She d. before 1900.

            vii.   Amanda, b. ca.1899 Clay Co., KY. She m. William A. Jackson on 29 May 1921 Clay Co., KY.

                    William A. Jackson, b.1890.

    497   viii.   Theophilus "General," b. 11 Apr 1904 Clay Co., KY; m. Hester Broughton.

    498   ix.   Cora, b. 12 Apr 1906 Clay Co., KY; m. Lawrence Swafford.

212. Martha Alice[5] Abney (Andrew[4], Enoch[3], Elisha[2], Abner[1]), b. ca. Mar 1850 Savannah, Andrew Co., MO. She m. Charles H. Lamkin on 17 Jun 1866 Otoe Co., NE. She d.30 Jan 1879 Pueblo, Pueblo Co., CO.

    Charles H. Lamkin, b.1844 AR. He d.11 Apr 1919 CO.
Known children of Martha Alice[5] Abney and Charles H. Lamkin:

            i.   Richard H.[6], b.1869.

            ii.   Jennie, b. ca.1872.

            iii.   Addison Jackson, b.1876. He d.1921.

213. Mary Agnes[5] Abney (Andrew[4], Enoch[3], Elisha[2], Abner[1]), b.New Year's Eve, 31 Dec 1858 Savannah, Andrew Co., MO. She m. Charles Edward Clay on 19 Oct 1876 Cheyenne, Laramie Co., WY. She and Charles Edward Clay appeared on the census of 3 Jun 1880 Cheyenne, Laramie Co., WY. She d.22 Aug 1904 Elma, Chehalis Co., WA, at age 45 and was bur. Masonic Cem., Elma, Grays Harbor Co., WA.

    Charles Edward Clay, b.18 Nov 1838 Bedford Co., VA. He d.18 Aug 1905 Elma, Grays Harbor Co., WA, at age 66; bur. Masonic Cem., Elma.
Known children of Mary Agnes[5] Abney and Charles Edward Clay:

            i.   Mary E.[6], b. ca. Apr 1877; d.23 Aug 1881 Cheyenne, Laramie Co., WY; bur. Lakeview Cem., Cheyenne, WY.

214. James M.[5] Abney (Andrew[4], Enoch[3], Elisha[2], Abner[1]), b.20 Jan 1860 Savannah, Andrew Co., MO. He m1. Frances Margaret "Fannie" Gill on 19 Nov 1886 Albany Co., WY. He and Frances Margaret "Fannie" Gill appeared on the censuses of 14 Jun 1900 and 29 Apr 1910 Inez, Converse Co., WY; and 17 Jan 1920 Careyhurst, Converse Co., WY. He m2. Opal Margaret Houser on 20 Oct 1929 Harrison, Sioux Co., NE. He and Opal Margaret Houser appeared on the census of 11 Apr 1930 Careyhurst, Converse Co., WY. He d.9 Jun 1930 home, Boxelder, Converse Co., WY, at age 70 and was bur. Douglas Park Cem., Douglas, Converse Co., WY. From his obituary:
James Abney early in life became identified with the cattle business. He was only about 12 years of age when he began as a rider on the range and his whole life was spent in the cattle and ranch business. In the eighties he came to central Wyoming, which had been his home until his death. On November 19, 1886 he was married in Douglas to Frances Margaret Gill, this being the first marriage celebrated in what is now Converse County (then a part of Albany County). Mrs. Abney d. July 20, 1927. On October 20, 1929 he was m. at Harrison, Nebraska to Mrs. Opal Entaminger, who survives him. No children were born to Mr. Abney, but a niece of the first Mrs. Abney, Mrs. Percy Brockway, was adopted and raised by them. A sister, Mrs. Florence Small, lives in New Mexico.

    Frances Margaret "Fannie" Gill, b.17 Oct 1859 Pittsburgh, Allegheny Co., PA. She d.20 Jul 1927 Douglas, Converse Co., WY, at age 67 and was bur. Douglas Park Cem., Douglas, Converse Co., WY.
Adopted child of James M.[5] Abney and Frances Margaret "Fannie" Gill:

            i.   Eula[6], b. Aug 1880 NE. Eula was a niece of James and Frances on the Gill side of the family. According to James M. Abney's obituary, she was adopted by them.

    Opal Margaret Houser, b. ca.1887. She m1. Jacob Entzminger in 1906. She m3. Francis C. Sorensen in 1944.
There were no known children of James M.[5] Abney and Opal Margaret Houser.

215. James L.⁵ Garner (Martha⁴ Abney, Enoch³, Elisha², Abner¹), b.11 Mar 1857 Alpine, Clark Co., AR. He m1. Sarah Chapman on 13 Feb 1877 Clark Co., AR. He m2. Julia Elizabeth Fox, d/o of Richard C. Fox and Nancy A. Deaton, on 2 Jun 1901; d.4 Aug 1928 Alpine, Clark Co., age 71.
    Sarah Chapman, b. ca.1854. She d. before 1900.
Known children of James L.⁵ Garner and Sarah Chapman:
       i.   William⁶, b. ca.1879 Clark Co., AR. He d. after 1880 Clark Co., AR.
      ii.   Seaborn D., b. ca.1887. He m1. Dena Bell Partridge on 20 Dec 1903. He m2. Caroline Fox.
     iii.   Ada, b. May 1889. She m. Calvin Howell on 12 Apr 1902.
     iv.   Alfred, b. Apr 1891. He m. Alice Dickson on 25 Oct 1908.

    Julia Elizabeth Fox, b.20 Aug 1875 Clark Co., AR. She d.18 Jul 1947 Clark Co., AR, at age 71.
Known children of James L.⁵ Garner and Julia Elizabeth Fox all b. Clark Co., AR:
       i.   Ernest Goodin⁶, b.31 Mar 1902; m. Jessie Bates on 19 Apr 1926. He d.24 Oct 1958 at age 56.
499   ii.   Jasper Lafayette, b. 28 Mar 1903; m. Bertha Ann Craig.
     iii.   Docia, b.12 May 1905.
     iv.   Ola May, b.13 Nov 1906; m. James R. Thomason on 15 Sep 1926. She d.Sep 1968 at age 61.
      v.   Oshia Lee, b.13 Nov 1906; m. Charlie Hughes on 15 May 1926. She d. ca.1969.
     vi.   Flora Edith, b.4 Mar 1908; m. Harmon H. Hewett on 13 May 1926. She d.26 Nov 1985 at age 77.
    vii.   France Monroe, b.10 May 1910; m. Mary R. McJunkin on 17 Jun 1939. He d.Nov 1981 at age 71.
   viii.   Hattie Bell, b.9 May 1912; m. Fletcher Webb on 28 Nov 1933. She m. Archie McJunkin on 20 Jun 1938.
     ix.   Effie Cleone, b.11 Oct 1914; m. Lee Watkins on 23 Oct 1933.
      x.   Jessie Evert, b.17 Jul 1917; d.28 Sep 1948 at age 31.
     xi.   Luin Austin, b.21 May 1920; m. Mary E. Billingsley on 20 Aug 1938. He d.1978.

216. Martha C.⁵ Monroe (Jane⁴ McClenachan, Sarah³ Abney, John², Abner¹), b.23 Mar 1826 Barren Co., KY. She m. Absalom G. Owen. She d.29 Mar 1901 Wayne Co., IL, at age 75 and was bur. Ebenezer Cem., Wayne Co., IL.
    Absalom G. Owen, b.19 Jun 1816. He d.6 May 1887 Wayne Co., IL, at age 70.
Known children of Martha C.⁵ Monroe and Absalom G. Owen:
       i.   Nancy Jane⁶, b.1849. She d.1886.
      ii.   Martha Ellen, b.1853. She d.1924.
     iii.   David Curtis, b.1858. He d.1927.

217. Elizabeth⁵ Monroe (Jane⁴ McClenachan, Sarah³ Abney, John², Abner¹), b.19 Jul 1829 Barren Co., KY. She m. David Baker in 1857. She d.10 Nov 1913 Chicago, Cook Co., IL, at age 84 and was bur. Maple Hill Cem., Fairfield, Wayne Co., IL.
    David Baker, b.1828. He d.1912 and was bur. Maple Hill Cem., Fairfield, Wayne Co., IL.
Known children of Elizabeth⁵ Monroe and David Baker:
       i.   Miriam⁶, b.1853. She d.1917.
      ii.   Marion Osmond, b.1859. He d.1914.
     iii.   Ira Cloyd, b.1863. He d.1928.
     iv.   Sherman D., b.1867. He d.1939.

218. Emily⁵ Monroe (Jane⁴ McClenachan, Sarah³ Abney, John², Abner¹), b.30 Dec 1833 Barren Co., KY. She m. Jacob Baker on 1 Dec 1848 Wayne Co., IL. She m. John Wesley Cissna, son of James Cissna and Catherine Ewing, on 6 Dec 1868 Arrington Twp, Mayes Co., IL. She d.28 Dec 1908 Wayne Co., IL, at age 74.
    Jacob Baker, b.1824. He d.1864 Vicksburg, MS.
Known children of Emily⁵ Monroe and Jacob Baker:
       i.   Emma⁶, b. IL. She d. age 6, Wayne Co., IL.
      ii.   Loretta Louella "Etta", b.4 Feb 1859 Arrington Twp., Wayne Co., IL; d.18 Aug 1918 Fairfield, Wayne Co., IL, age 59.

    John Wesley Cissna was bur. Maple Hill Cem. He, b.11 Nov 1822 London, Madison Co., OH. He d.19 May 1896 Fairfield at age 73.
Known children of Emily⁵ Monroe and John Wesley Cissna:
       i.   Mary Chloe⁶, b.1 Nov 1869 Wayne Co., IL. She m. Orin C. Fogle on 2 Mar 1893 Fairfield, Wayne Co., IL. She d.23 Oct 1949 Holdenville, Hughes Co., OK, at age 79 and was bur. Maple Hill Cem., Fairfield, Wayne Co., IL.
      ii.   John Alexis, b.30 Jul 1872 Wayne Co., IL. He m1. Lass Roberts on 1 Oct 1896 Lawrenceville, IL. He m2. Gertrude (n.n.). He m3. Annie Shaw San Antonio, Bexar Co., TX. He d.2 May 1937 San Antonio, Bexas Co., TX, at age 64 and was bur. San Fernando Cem. #3, San Antonio, Bexas Co., TX.
     iii.   Bess Emily "Bessie", b.4 Sep 1873 Wayne Co., IL. She m. Joseph Benjamin Handley on 28 Nov 1901. She d.5 Dec 1969 Champagne, IL, at age 96.

219. David Gerald⁵ McKinney Jr. (Tamar⁴ McClenachan, Sarah³ Abney, John², Abner¹) m. Sallie Ann Evans. He, b.Oct 1841 Barren Co., KY. He d.17 Sep 1919 Barren Co., KY, at age 77.
    Sallie Ann Evans, b.1839 Barren Co., KY.
Known child of David Gerald⁵ McKinney Jr. and Sallie Ann Evans:
    500   i.   Melford Evans "Meil"⁶, b. 21 Feb 1874 Cave City, Barren Co., KY; m. Lula Jane Anderson.

220. William Zachariah Taylor "Zack"⁵ Rhea (Tamar⁴ McClenachan, Sarah³ Abney, John², Abner¹), b.1849 Barren Co., KY. He m. Matilda Margaret Roach in 1869. He d.7 Apr 1884 South Bend, Young Co., TX and was bur. Tonk Valley Cem., Young Co., TX.
    Matilda Margaret Roach, b.20 Jul 1854. She m. James Augustus Brock on 12 Mar 1885 Navarro Co., TX. She d.27 Oct 1919 at age 65.
Known children of William Zachariah Taylor "Zack"⁵ Rhea and Matilda Margaret Roach:
       i.   Wilbert Smiley⁶.

ii.   Jeanett Bell, b.14 Apr 1878 China Spring, McLennan Co., TX. She d.18 Aug 1959 TX at age 81 and was bur. Sunset Mem. Park, San Antonio, Bexar Co., TX.

501   iii. Ada Lee, b. 3 Apr 1880 Little Rock, Saline Co., AR; m. Aron Samuel "Sam" Barton.

221. Rev. William Abney "Will"[5] Kinsolving (Mary[4] Abney, William[3], John[2], Abner[1]), b.23 Oct 1829 VA. He m. Sorilda Elizabeth Glenn on 25 Mar 1852 Caldwell Co., KY. He and Sorilda Elizabeth Glenn appeared on the censuses of 8 Jun 1860, 19 Jul 1870, 22 Jun 1880 and 26 Jun 1900 Lyon Co., KY. He d.7 Sep 1903 Lyon Co., KY, at age 73 and was bur. Glenns Chapel Meth. Ch. Cem., Eddyville, Lyon Co., KY.
   Sorilda Elizabeth Glenn, b.7 Feb 1832 KY. She d.18 Jun 1894 KY at age 62 and was bur. Glenns Chapel Meth. Ch. Cem., Eddyville.
Known children of Rev. William Abney "Will"[5] Kinsolving and Sorilda Elizabeth Glenn:
         i.   Mary Verona[6], b.1853. She d.1933.
         ii.   Thomas Jefferson, b.1855. He d.1856.
         iii. William Glenn, b.1858. He d.1933.
502   iv.   Finis Ewing, b. 18 Sep 1859 Lyon Co., KY; m. Pearl E. Lamb.
         v.   Floyd, b.1862.
         vi.   Giles Clark, b.1865. He d.1897.
         vii. Lula, b.1869. She d.1925.
         viii. Martin Luther, b.1874. He d.1954.

222. Cornelia Ann[5] Abney (William[4], William[3], John[2], Abner[1]), b.Oct 1831 Staunton, Augusta Co., VA. She m. John Grills, son of Charles T. Grills and Isabella Abney, on 16 Sep 1858 Augusta Co., VA. She and John Grills were liv. on 26 Jul 1860 with father-in-law, William A. Abney, Staunton, Augusta Co., VA. She d.1909 WV and was bur. Spring Hill Cem., Huntington, Cabell Co., WV.
   John Grills was liv. Prov. Springs. He was liv. MO. He, b. ca.1832 Montgomery Co., VA.
Known children of Cornelia Ann[5] Abney and John Grills:
         i.   Virginia Isabella[6], b.1860. She d.1943.
         ii.   Charles Lycurges, b.1866. He m. Nannie Catherine Comp on 9 Jan 1892 OK Terr. He d.1899.
               Nannie Catherine Comp, b.1873. She d.1958.

223. Ulysses Van Buren[5] Abney (William[4], William[3], John[2], Abner[1]), b.1836 Staunton, Augusta Co., VA. He m. Melissa Bledsoe on 20 Oct 1869 Staunton, Augusta Co., VA. He was liv. on 23 Aug 1870 and children with father, William A. Abney, Augusta Co., VA. He was liv. on 9 Jul 1900 with brother, Wm. G. Abney, South River, Augusta Co., VA. He d.Sep 1909 Augusta Co., VA; bur. Thornrose Cem., City of Staunton, VA.
   Melissa Bledsoe, b.1848 Augusta Co., VA. She d. Augusta Co., VA and was bur. Thornrose Cem., City of Staunton, VA.
Known children of Ulysses Van Buren[5] Abney and Melissa Bledsoe:
503   i.   Mary Bledsoe "Minnie"[6], b. 29 Jul 1861; m. Joseph Nelson "Josi" Clarkson.
         ii.   William Ovid, b.4 May 1863 Richmond, VA. He was liv. on 14 Jun 1900 with cousin, Frank M. Abney, Charleston, Kanawha Co., WV. He appeared on the census of 5 May 1910 Charleston, Kanawha Co., WV. He was president of *Union Trust Co.* from 1913-1929. He m. Florence Jeroloman. He appeared on the census of 4 Apr 1930 Charleston, Kanawha Co., WV. He was also vice president of *Charleston National Bank* and co-owner of *Abney Barnes Co.* in Charleston. He d.4 Aug 1949 Charleston, Kanawha Co., WV, at age 86 and was bur. Spring Hill Cem., Charleston, Kanawha Co., WV.
               Florence Jeroloman, b.26 Dec 1876 NY; m1. Capt. Addison M. Scott in 1907. She d.2 Jun 1961 Charleston, age 84.

224. John[5] Grills (Isabella[4] Abney, William[3], John[2], Abner[1]), b. ca.1832 Montgomery Co., VA. He m. Cornelia Ann Abney, daughter of William Austine Abney and Virginia Lewis Kinsolving, on 16 Sep 1858 Augusta Co., VA. He and Cornelia Ann Abney were liv. on 26 Jul 1860 with father-in-law, William A. Abney, Staunton, Augusta Co., VA. He liv. Providence Springs, Charlotte, Kanawha Co., WV.
   Cornelia Ann Abney, b.Oct 1831 Staunton, Augusta Co., VA. She d.1909 WV and was bur. Spring Hill Cem., Huntington, Cabell Co., WV.
Known children of John[5] Grills and Cornelia Ann Abney:
         i.   Virginia Isabella[6], b. 1860. (see above under #222 Cornelia Ann Abney).
         ii.   Charles Lycurges, b. 1866. (see above under #222 Cornelia Ann Abney); m. Nannie Catherine Comp.

225. Sarah Minerva "Minnie"[5] Abney (Shelton[4], William[3], John[2], Abner[1]), b.4 Oct 1836 Greenville, Augusta Co., VA. She m. Byrd Grills (CSA), son of Charles T. Grills and Isabella Abney, on 2 Oct 1859. She and Byrd Grills (CSA) were liv. on 19 Jun 1860 with father-in-law, S.S. Abney, Hawcreek Twp., Augusta Co., VA. She m. Judge John C. Thompson on 17 Jun 1866. She m. George Alexander Murrell on 2 Jan 1879. She d.25 Jan 1888 Saline Co., MO, at age 51.
   Byrd Grills (CSA), b.23 Oct 1834 Montgomery Co., VA. He d.17 Sep 1861 Typhoid Fever, Warsaw, MO, at age 26; bur. Saline Co., MO.
There were no known children of Sarah Minerva "Minnie"[5] Abney and Byrd Grills (CSA).

   Judge John C. Thompson was Judge. He lived Arrow Rock, MO. He d.17 Feb 1878.
There were no known children of Sarah Minerva "Minnie"[5] Abney and Judge John C. Thompson.

George Alexander Murrell, b.8 Feb 1826. He was a wealthy land owner. He m. Sophia McMahan. He d.7 Dec 1911 at age 85.
Known children of Sarah Minerva "Minnie"[5] Abney and George Alexander Murrell:
         i.   Minnie Sophie[6], b.19 Sep 1880. She m. Alfredo Scotti ca.1912. She and Alfredo Scotti appeared on the censuses of 3 Feb 1920 Whittier, Los Angeles Co., CA, 2 Apr 1930 Whittier and 2 Apr 1940 Whittier, Los Angeles Co., CA. She d.7 Dec 1969 at age 89 and was bur. Ridge Park Cem., Marshall, Saline Co., MO.
               Alfredo Scotti, b. ca.1875 Naples, Italy. He m. (n.n.) in 1902. He was naturalized in 1913.

226. Elizabeth McClenachan "Lizzie"[5] Abney (Shelton[4], William[3], John[2], Abner[1]), b.3 Feb 1839 Augusta Co., VA. She m. John P. Ingram Sr. on 23 Feb 1860.
   John P. Ingram Sr, b. ca.1813. He m. (n.n.). He d.2 Oct 1875.
Known children of Elizabeth McClenachan "Lizzie"[5] Abney and John P. Ingram Sr.:
         i.   Bettie L.[6], b.13 Feb 1861.

     ii.   Willie Hanger, b.8 Jul 1864. He d.17 Oct 1906 at age 42; bur. Walker-Wright Cem., Cross Timbers, Hickory Co., MO.

    iii.   Martha Jane "Mattie" m. Andrew Jackson Hodges. , b.4 Jun 1867 MO. She d.6 May 1940 Fristoe, Benton Co., MO, at age 72 and was bur. Walker-Wright Cem., Cross Timbers, Hickory Co., MO.

          Andrew Jackson Hodges, b.1866. He d.1932.

    iv.   Sadie, b.7 Oct 1870.

     v.   Margaret Abney "Maggie", b.11 Jan 1874 Benton Co., MO. She m. Matt Bishop Mitchener. She d.28 Oct 1947 Saline Co., MO, at age 73 and was bur. Malta Bend Cem., Malta Bend, Saline Co., MO.

          Matt Bishop Mitchener, b.2 Mar 1872. He d.20 Mar 1948 at age 76 and was bur. Malta Bend Cem., Malta Bend.

227. *Rep.* William Lycurgus[5] Abney Sr. (CSA) (Shelton[4], William[3], John[2], Abner[1]), b.9 Feb 1846 Augusta Co., VA. He m. Mary Frances "Fanny" Geisinger, daughter of *Capt.* Samuel Levi Geisinger and Elizabeth Julius, on 28 Oct 1875 Arrow Rock, Saline Co., MO. He and Mary Frances "Fanny" Geisinger were liv. on 28 Jun 1880 with his father, Shelton Abney, Haw Creek, Augusta Co., VA. He was elected to the House of Representatives in 1888 to represent MO. He and Mary Frances "Fanny" Geisinger appeared on the censuses of 8 Jun 1900 and 5 May 1910 Salt Fork Twp., Saline Co., MO. He was liv. on 9 Jan 1920 with son, Hood Abney, Marshall, Saline Co., MO. He d.17 Feb 1933 Napton, Saline Co., MO, at age 87 and was bur. Mem. Presbyterian Ch. Cem., Napton, Saline Co., MO.

    Mary Frances "Fanny" Geisinger, b.22 Oct 1847 Middletown, Frederick Co., MD. She d.12 Mar 1913 Napton, Saline Co., MO, at age 65 and was bur. Mem. Presbyterian Ch. Cem., Napton, Saline Co., MO.

Known children of Rep. William Lycurgus[5] Abney Sr. (CSA) and Mary Frances "Fanny" Geisinger:

     i.   Samuel Levi Geisinger "Guy"[6], b.4 Jun 1877 Morgan Co., MO. He appeared on the census of 28 Jan 1920 Salt Fork, Saline Co., MO. He m1. Bess Lee "Bessie" Thorpe on 26 Dec 1927. He was elected to the House of Representatives out of Saline Co., MO in 1930. He and Bess appeared on the census of 9 Apr 1930 Salt Fork, Saline Co., MO. Guy was reelected to the House of Representatives and served from 1936-1940. He m2. Anna (n.n.) on 28 Dec 1937 Marshall, MO. He and Anna appeared on the census of 15 Apr 1940 Marshall, Saline Co., MO. He was reelected on 5 Nov 1940. He d. in office 17 Jan 1942, Marshall, Saline Co., MO, at age 64. His wife, as *Mrs. Guy Abney* was elected to replace him on 04 Aug 1942. Guy was bur. Mem. Presbyterian Ch. Cem., Napton, Saline Co., MO.

          Bess Lee "Bessie" Thorpe, b.3 Mar 1887. She m1. Marvin Sprigg ca.1908. She and Marvin Sprigg appeared on the census of 28 Jan 1920 Salt Fork, Saline Co., MO. She d.17 Jun 1933 Sali Fork, Saline Co., MO, at age 46.

          Rep. Anna (n.n.) m1. (n.n.) Huggins. She m2. Guy Abney. After her second husband died in office, she was elected to replace him on 04 Aug 1942 as U.S. Representative.

504   ii.   Shelton Spillsbury, b. 5 Dec 1879 (near Versailles), Morgan Co., MO; m. Virginia Katherine Smith.

505   iii.   William Lycurgus "Will," b. 26 Sep 1883 Morgan Co., MO; m. Mary "Rowena" McMahan.

506   iv.   Harry Fox "Hood," b. 23 Mar 1890 Morgan Co., MO; m. Mary Berry Smith; m. Elizabeth Rachel Hawkins.

228. Margaret Letticia "Maggie"[5] Abney (Shelton[4], William[3], John[2], Abner[1]), b.10 Oct 1849 Augusta Co., VA. She m. John Huston Wilhelm on 26 Feb 1871 Saline Co., MO. She d.16 May 1913 Marshall, Saline Co., MO, at age 63 and was bur. Ridge Park Cem., Marshall, Saline Co., MO.

    John Huston Wilhelm, b.17 Jul 1851 MO. He d.12 Aug 1918 Marshall, Saline Co., MO, at age 67 and was bur. Ridge Park Cem., Marshall.

Known children of Margaret Letticia "Maggie"[5] Abney and John Huston Wilhelm:

     i.   Harry A.[6], b.4 Feb 1872 MO. He m1. Pearl Belle Sphar. He m2. Lucy McClure. He d.24 Feb 1927 Kansas City, Jackson Co., MO, at age 55 and was bur. Ridge Park Cem., Marshall, Saline Co., MO.

          Pearl Belle Sphar, b.1871. She d.1919.

          Lucy McClure, b.1869. She d.1953.

    ii.   William Byrd "Willie" m. Rebecca Elizabeth Hess. He, b.7 Apr 1873 Versailles, Morgan Co., MO. He d.22 Jun 1955 Marshall, Saline Co., MO, at age 82 and was bur. Ridge Park Cem., Marshall, Saline Co., MO.

          Rebecca Elizabeth Hess, b.1858. She d.1944.

229. Tamar Ann[5] Rhea (Isabella[4] Abney, John[3], John[2], Abner[1]), b.24 May 1826 Green Co., KY. She m. John Hugh Montgomery on 24 Oct 1842 Sumner Co., TN. She d.20 Mar 1865 Green Co., KY, at age 38.

    John Hugh Montgomery, b.16 Apr 1823 Green Co., KY. He d.18 Aug 1899 Bell Co., TX, at age 76.

Known children of Tamar Ann[5] Rhea and John Hugh Montgomery:

     i.   Elizabeth Ann[6], b.1843 1920.

    ii.   William David, b.1845. He d.1894.

    iii.   Tabitha Isabella, b.1847. She d.1894.

    iv.   Joshua Thomas, b.1850. He d.1928.

     v.   Richard Moore, b.1852. He d.1920.

    vi.   Robert Alexander, b.1854. He d.1920.

    vii.   Narcissa Frances, b.1857. She d.1939.

    viii.   John Albert, b.1860. He d.1924.

    ix.   Sarah Lou, b.1862. She d.1928.

230. Elizabeth Cynthia[5] Rhea (Isabella[4] Abney, John[3], John[2], Abner[1]), b.24 Oct 1828 Greensburg, Green Co., KY. She m. James Madison Barnett on 19 Dec 1847 Barren Co., KY. She d.16 Aug 1895 Upton, Hardin Co., KY, at age 66.

    James Madison Barnett, b.27 Dec 1817 Barren Co., KY. He d.4 Feb 1875 Hart Co., KY, at age 57.

Known children of Elizabeth Cynthia[5] Rhea and James Madison Barnett:

     i.   William Green[6], b.1848. He d.1892.

    ii.   Robert Edgar, b.1850. He d.1851.

    iii.   Narcissa Ophelia, b.1852. She d.1916.

    iv.   Buena Vista, b.1854. She d.1888.

     v.   Edwin Ruthvine, b.1856. He d.1882.

    vi.   Anna Rebecca Phillips, b.1859. She d.1900.

    vii.   Milton Elbert Vanlier, b.1863. He d.1939.

---

       viii. Sarah Josephine Isabella, b.1865. She d.1919.
        ix. Bazzil Duke, b.1868. He d.1913.

231. Narcissa M.[5] Rhea (Isabella[4] Abney, John[3], John[2], Abner[1]), b.26 Jul 1832 Green Co., KY. She m. Joseph D. Williams on 5 Jun 1860 Adair Co., KY. She d.27 May 1866 at age 33.
    Joseph D. Williams, b.1822 KY. He d.6 Dec 1904.
Known children of Narcissa M.[5] Rhea and Joseph D. Williams:
         i. Jennie Dorothy[6], b.1861. She m. John James Moore on 3 Feb 1885 Green Co., KY. She d.1944.
             John James Moore, b.1859. He d.1942.
        ii. Isabella, b.1862. She m. John Robert Wilson on 14 Dec 1880 Green Co., KY. She d.1935.
             John Robert Wilson, b.1858. He d.1911.

232. Isabella Vasser[5] Rhea (Isabella[4] Abney, John[3], John[2], Abner[1]), b.1835 Green Co., KY; m. William H. Middleton May 1852 Barren Co., KY.
    William H. Middleton, b.5 Aug 1824 Hardin Co., KY. He d.17 May 1899 Hodgenville, LaRue Co., KY, at age 74.
Known children of Isabella Vasser[5] Rhea and William H. Middleton:
         i. Mary Elizabeth[6], b. ca.1853.
        ii. Elliott L.F., b.1855. He d.1880.
       iii. Syntha, b.1857.
       iv. Sarah Margaret, b.1858.

233. James Carydon[5] Abney (Robert[4], John[3], John[2], Abner[1]), b.25 Aug 1832 Hardin Co., KY. He m. Sophia Weston Slaughter, daughter of John Slaughter of Harden and Mildred Cash, on 13 Nov 1856 Hardin Co., KY. He and Sophia Weston Slaughter were liv. on 3 Aug 1860 with his brother, John Abney, LaRue Co., KY. He and Sophia Weston Slaughter appeared on the censuses of 1 Aug 1870, 9 Jun 1880 and 1 Jun 1900 Magnolia, LaRue Co., KY. He d.28 Jun 1901 Magnolia, LaRue Co., KY, age 68; bur. Magnolia Presbyterian Ch. Cem., Magnolia, LaRue Co., KY.
    Sophia Weston Slaughter, b.6 Jul 1834 KY. She was liv. on 25 Apr 1910 with son-in-law, Henry Gardner, Magnolia, LaRue Co., KY. She d.14 Apr 1914 Magnolia, LaRue Co., KY, at age 79 and was bur. Magnolia Presbyterian Ch. Cem., Magnolia, LaRue Co., KY.
Known children of James Carydon[5] Abney and Sophia Weston Slaughter all b. LaRue Co., KY:
         i. J.R.[6], b. ca.1858. He d. before 1870 LaRue Co., KY.
        ii. William Elbert, b.1 Sep 1860. He d.15 Jun 1862 LaRue Co., KY, at age 1 and was bur. Magnolia Presbyterian Ch. Cem.
507   iii. Josie Adah, b. 27 Sep 1862; m. Henry Gardner.
508   iv. Charles Milton "Charlie," b. 2 Aug 1864; m1. Lenora "Nora" Beavers; m2. Mary West.
        v. John Robert (William's twin), b.21 Feb 1872. He d.21 Feb 1872 LaRue Co., KY.
       vi. William A. (John's twin), b.21 Feb 1872. He d.21 Feb 1872 LaRue Co., KY.

234. Milton Anderson[5] Abney (Robert[4], John[3], John[2], Abner[1]), b.31 Jan 1842 LaRue Co., KY. He m. Ellina Frances Slaughter on 10 Mar 1864. He and Ellina Frances Slaughter appeared on the census of 3 Jun 1880 Magnolia, LaRue Co., KY. He d.17 Oct 1912 Lowder, Sangamon Co., IL, at age 70 and was bur. Virden Cem., Virden, Macoupin Co., IL.
    Ellina Frances Slaughter, b.26 Feb 1844 Barren Co., KY. She d.21 Jan 1923 Sangamon Co., IL, at age 78 and was bur. Virden Cem., Virden.
Known children of Milton Anderson[5] Abney and Ellina Frances Slaughter:
         i. William[6].
        ii. Homer. He m. Minnie West.
509   iii. Mildred Antoinette "Nettie," b. 7 Dec 1864 LaRue Co., KY; m. David S. Lewis.
510   iv. Joseph Gillian, b. 14 Sep 1866 LaRue Co., KY; m. Lula "Lulie" Friend.
        v. Edwin Lively, b.3 Oct 1868 Magnolia, LaRue Co., KY. He m. Daisy D. Conner on 8 Feb 1879 KY. He d.14 Dec 1953 Springfield, Sangamon Co., IL, at age 85 and was bur. Oak Ridge Cem., Springfield, Sangamon Co., IL.
             Daisy D. Conner, b.8 Feb 1879 KY; d.10 Apr 1952 Springfield, Sangamon Co., IL, at age 73; bur. Oak Ridge Cem.
       vi. Sarah Doris, b.1877 LaRue Co., KY. She m. Harry Boggs on 7 Apr 1915.
      vii. Sophia Ella, b.13 Feb 1879.
     viii. Cora Mae, b.Aug 1886 KY. She d.12 Feb 1906 Talkington, Sangamon Co., IL, at age 19.

235. Charles "Thomas"[5] Abney (Robert[4], John[3], John[2], Abner[1]), b.2 Apr 1847 LaRue Co., KY. He m. Eleaseph Vittitow on 19 Dec 1870 LaRue Co., KY. He appeared on the census of 8 Jun 1880 Magnolia, LaRue Co., KY. He m. Mary C. "Molly" Miller on 29 Jun 1885. He and Mary C. "Molly" Miller appeared on the censuses of 2 Jun 1900 Magnolia, LaRue Co., KY and 20 Jan 1920 Hardin Co., KY. He d.29 Apr 1920 Elizabethtown, Hardin Co., KY, at age 73 and was bur. Gilead Bapt. Ch. Cem., Glendale, Hardin Co., KY.
    Eleaseph Vittitow, b.29 Jul 1848. She d.20 Mar 1880 KY at age 31 and was bur. Magnolia Presbyterian Ch. Cem., Magnolia, LaRue Co., KY.
Known children of Charles "Thomas"[5] Abney and Eleaseph Vittitow:
         i. Elmer "James"[6], b.27 Dec 1872 LaRue Co., KY. He m. Melvina Rowena "Mellie" Shipp on 20 Feb 1905 London, Laurel Co., KY. He and Melvina Rowena "Mellie" Shipp appeared on the census of 28 Apr 1910 and 17 Jan 1920 Talkington, Sangamon Co., IL. He d. New Year's Eve, 31 Dec 1948 LaRue Co., KY, at age 76 and was bur. Magnolia Presbyterian Ch. Cem., Magnolia, LaRue Co., KY.
             Melvina Rowena "Mellie" Shipp, b.26 Mar 1881; d.15 Oct 1964 KY, age 83; bur. Magnolia Presbyterian Ch. Cem.

    Mary C. "Molly" Miller, b.Apr 1850 Hardin Co., KY. She appeared as Head of Household on the census of 11 Apr 1930 Hardin Co., KY. She d.24 Oct 1933 Hardin Co., KY, at age 83 and was bur. Gilead Bapt. Ch. Cem., Glendale, Hardin Co., KY.
Known children of Charles "Thomas"[5] Abney and Mary C. "Molly" Miller:
         i. Marvin S.[6], b.16 Oct 1887 LaRue Co., KY. He d.6 Jan 1889 LaRue Co., KY, age 1; bur. Magnolia Presbyterian Ch. Cem.
        ii. Mallie Rose m. Calvin A. Cartwright. , b.15 Feb 1892 Magnolia, LaRue Co., KY. She d.26 Oct 1957 Louisville, Jefferson Co., KY, at age 65 and was bur. Floydsburg Cem., Crestwood, Oldham Co., KY.
             Calvin A. Cartwright, b.10 Oct 1898. He d.14 Jun 1979 at age 80 and was bur. Floydsburg Cem., Crestwood.

---

236. Joshua Bayne "Josh"⁵ Abney (Robert⁴, John³, John², Abner¹), b.31 Jul 1849 LaRue Co., KY. He m. Nancy Carpenter "Nannie" Miller on 3 Nov 1882 Hodgenville, LaRue Co., KY. He and Nancy Carpenter "Nannie" Miller appeared on the censuses of 8 Jun 1900 and 26 Jan 1920 Magnolia, LaRue Co., KY. He d.3 Oct 1928 IL at age 79 and was bur. Magnolia Presbyterian Ch. Cem., Magnolia, LaRue Co., KY.
    Nancy Carpenter "Nannie" Miller, b.23 Jul 1854 LaRue Co., KY; d.9 Feb 1920 LaRue Co., KY, age 65; bur. Magnolia Presbyterian Ch. Cem.
Known children of Joshua Bayne "Josh"⁵ Abney and Nancy Carpenter "Nannie" Miller both b. LaRue Co., KY:
    511   i.   Ada⁶, b. 20 Dec 1883; m. John Thomas Hines.
           ii.   Curtis M, b.12 Aug 1885. He d.4 Feb 1923 LaRue Co., KY, at age 37 and was bur. Magnolia Presbyterian Ch. Cem.

237. Elizabeth Ann⁵ Abney (Robert⁴, John³, John², Abner¹) m. John T. Howell (UA). , b.6 Sep 1851 LaRue Co., KY. She and John T. Howell (UA) appeared on the census of 17 Jun 1880 LaRue Co., KY. She d.12 Jun 1886 at age 34 and was bur. Riverview Cem., New Haven, Nelson Co., KY.
    John T. Howell (UA), b.18 Jun 1844 LaRue Co., KY. He d.24 Oct 1927 KY at age 83.
Known children of Elizabeth Ann⁵ Abney and John T. Howell (UA) all b. LaRue Co., KY:
           i.   James Robert⁶, b.1870. He m. Jessie Elizabeth Waters on 2 Oct 1893 Nelson Co., KY. He d.12 Dec 1955.
                 Jessie Elizabeth Waters, b.7 Mar 1873 KY. She d.11 Apr 1924 Louisville, Jefferson Co., KY, at age 51.
           ii.   Mary C., b. ca.1873.
           iii. Nannie Alice, b.4 Oct 1874. She m. Michael David Lawless on 3 May 1899 Louisville, Jefferson Co., KY. She d.16 Mar 1962 at age 87.
                 Michael David Lawless, b.18 May 1864 Winchester, Scott Co., IL. He d.30 Jan 1938 Scott Co., IL, at age 73.

238. Mary Jane⁵ Lasley (Gertrude⁴ Abney, John³, John², Abner¹), b.24 May 1832 Green Co., KY. She m. John Reason Burch on 8 Apr 1854 LaRue Co., KY. She d..
    John Reason Burch, b.24 Mar 1829 LaRue Co., KY. He d.27 Jun 1903 at age 74 and was bur. Holy Cross Cem., Holy Cross, Marion Co., KY.
Known children of Mary Jane⁵ Lasley and John Reason Burch:
           i.   John Emmett Hanson⁶, b.1858. He d.1949.
           ii.   William K., b.1862. He d.1892.
           iii. Harry Hays, b.1864. He d.1867.
           iv.   Nannie Lucy, b.1866.
           v.   Mollie, b.1868.
           vi.   Henry Lyman, b.1869. He d.1940.
           vii. Mary Belle, b.1872. She d.1962.

239. Margaret Nancy⁵ Lasley (Gertrude⁴ Abney, John³, John², Abner¹), b.1838 LaRue Co., KY. She m. Capt. Aaron Smith Bayne (UA) on 21 Jan 1858 New Haven, LaRue Co., KY. She and Capt. Aaron Smith Bayne (UA) appeared on the census of 16 Jul 1860 LaRue Co., KY. She d.3 Sep 1866 KY and was bur. Bacon Creek Bapt. Cem., Hammondsville, Hart Co., KY.
    Capt. Aaron Smith Bayne (UA), b.22 Nov 1833 Elizabethtown, Hardin Co., KY. He was killed in action on New Year's Eve, 31 Dec 1862 in Murfreesboro, Rutherford Co., TN, at age 29 and was bur. Bacon Creek Cem., Hammondsville, Hart Co., KY.
Known children of Margaret Nancy⁵ Lasley and Capt. Aaron Smith Bayne (UA):
    512   i.   Wilhelmina Loretta "Lura"⁶, b. 20 Oct 1858 Centerpoint, LaRue Co., KY; m. Dr. Charles Zachary Aud.
           ii.   Girtie A., b. ca.1862 LaRue Co., KY; liv. 24 Jun 1880 with brother-in-law, Charles Aud, Elizabethtown, Hardin Co., KY.

240. William H.⁵ Capehart (Mary⁴ Hogg, Martha³ Abney, John², Abner¹), b.30 Jul 1846 New Haven, Mason Co., VA. He m. Sarah Jane Gilpin in 1865. He and Sarah Jane Gilpin appeared on the censuses of 29 Jul 1870 New Haven, Mason Co., WV and 23 Jun 1880 Sutton, Meigs Co., OH. He d.15 Jul 1928 Syracuse, Meigs Co., OH, at age 81 and was bur. Carleton Cem., Syracuse, Meigs Co., OH.
    Sarah Jane Gilpin, b.1848 WV. She d.1926 Meigs Co., WV and was bur. Carleton Cem., Syracuse, Meigs Co., WV.
Known children of William H.⁵ Capehart and Sarah Jane Gilpin:
           i.   Abney Winfield⁶, b.5 Jun 1866 Fayette Co., WV; m. Edna Almeda Seals; d.10 Feb 1937 Syracuse, Meigs Co., OH, ae.70.
                 Edna Almeda Seals, b.5 Feb 1870 Belpre, Washington Co., OH. She d.10 Mar 1913 Syracuse, Meigs Co., OH, at age 43 and was bur. Carleton Cem., Syracuse, Meigs Co., OH.
           ii.   John W., b.8 Jul 1873 OH. He m. Anna James. He d.28 Jan 1952 Columbus, Franklin Co., OH, at age 78 and was bur. Green Lawn Cem., Columbus, Franklin Co., OH.
                 Anna James, b.31 Oct 1878. She d.17 Jul 1964 at age 85 and was bur. Green Lawn Cem., Columbus.

Generation Six

241. Polly Anna⁶ Chancellor (David⁵, Rebecca⁴ Abney, Joshua³, Elisha², Abner¹), b.14 Jun 1842 Martinsville, Clark Co., IL. She m. Pike Crabtree on 2 Feb 1866. She and Pike Crabtree appeared on the censuses of 14 Jul 1870 Orange Twp., Clark Co., IL; 24 Jun 1880 and 5 Jun 1900 Casey Twp., Clark Co., IL; and 30 Apr 1910 Rock Twp., Ellis Co., OK. She d.9 Sep 1915 OK at age 73; bur. Gage Mem. Cem., Gage, Ellis Co., OK.
    Pike Crabtree, b.22 Mar 1842 Clark Co., OH. He was liv. on 6 Jan 1920 with son, John Thomas Crabtree, Justice Twp., Ellis Co., OK. He was liv. on 18 Apr 1930 with daughter, *Eva Closson*, Rock Twp., Ellis Co., OK. He d.27 Feb 1934 Gage, Ellis Co., OK, age 91; bur. Gage Mem. Cem.
Known children of Polly Anna⁶ Chancellor and Pike Crabtree:
    513   i.   John Thomas⁷, b. 27 May 1876 Clark Co., IL; m. Ica Ellen McFarland.
    514   ii.   Effie Iva (Eva's twin), b. 7 Oct 1879 Martinsville, Clark Co., IL; m. William J. "Will" McFarland.
           iii. Eva (Effie's twin), b.7 Oct 1879 Martinsville, Clark Co., IL. She was liv. on 6 Jan 1920 with brother, J.T. Crabtree, Justice Twp., Ellis Co., OK. She m. Murry E. Closson ca.1929. She and Murry Closson appeared on the censuses of 18 Apr 1930 Rock Twp., Ellis Co., OK and 14 May 1940 Austin Twp., Ellis Co., OK; d.19 Nov 1959, ae.80; bur. Gage Mem. Cem. Murry E. Closson, b. ca.1881 MN. In 1930 he was proprietor of an Amusement Park.

242. Mary Ellen⁶ Chancellor (David⁵, Rebecca⁴ Abney, Joshua³, Elisha², Abner¹), b.20 Mar 1844. She m. James Nelson Griffith. She and James Nelson Griffith appeared on the census of 22 Jun 1880 Casey Twp., Clark Co., IL. She appeared as Head of Household on the census of 5 Jun 1900 Casey Twp., Clark Co., IL. She d.4 Feb 1911 at age 66 and was bur. Gage Cem., Gage, Ellis Co., OK.

James Nelson Griffith, b.1 Feb 1838 OH; d.21 Dec 1881 Martinsville, Clark Co., IL, at age 43; bur. Baird Cem., Martinsville, Clark Co., IL.
Known children of Mary Ellen⁶ Chancellor and James Nelson Griffith:

- 515   i.   David Floyd⁷, b. 2 Feb 1862 IL; m. Lydia C. Weir; m. Roxie Ray.
-     ii.   Simeon A., b. ca.1864 IL.
-     iii.   Eliza Ellen, b. ca.1866 IL.
-     iv.   Orpha E., b. ca.1868 IL.
- 516   v.   Euphame Rachel, b. 25 Feb 1870 IL; m. Charles Solman Simmons.
- 517   vi.   Hezekiah, b. 8 Oct 1873 Casey, Clark Co., IL; m. Cora E. Bryant.
-     vii.   John W., b. ca.1874 IL.
-     viii.   Sophia, b. ca.1879 IL.
-     ix.   James "Edward", b.Jun 1882 Cook Co., IL. He d.20 Mar 1957 at age 74; bur. Harmon Cem., Harmon, Ellis Co., OK.

243. Rebecca Eleanora⁶ Chancellor (David⁵, Rebecca⁴ Abney, Joshua³, Elisha², Abner¹), b.25 Feb 1847. She m. James Gaston Gillilan on 12 Feb 1872 Clark Co., IL.

James Gaston Gillilan, b.12 Feb 1845 OH.
Known children of Rebecca Eleanora⁶ Chancellor and James Gaston Gillilan all b. Clark Co., IL:

-     i.   Linnie Bell⁷, b.5 Jan 1873. She m. Sam Shoemaker on 23 Jul 1889 Cumberland Co., IL. She and Sam Shoemaker liv. Raton, Colfax Co., NM. and Los Angeles, Los Angeles Co., CA.
    -        Sam Shoemaker, b. Red Oaks, IA.
-     ii.   Minnie May, b.1 Aug 1875; m1. (n.n.) Trent. She m2. Carvil Godfrey.
-     iii.   Jane, b.1 Aug 1875. She d. ca.1880.
-     iv.   Horace Warren. He, b. New Year's Day, 1 Jan 1878. He m. Ova Smith in 1900.
-     v.   Lavina Pearl, b.27 Mar 1883. m. Otha Hardy.
- 518   vi.   Florence Ann, b. 24 Mar 1886; m. Joseph Myers .

244. Mary "Isabelle"⁶ Chancellor (Ewing⁵, Rebecca⁴ Abney, Joshua³, Elisha², Abner¹), b.26 Dec 1839 Casey, Clark Co., IL. She m. Henry Oscar "Mac" McKay, son of Robert McKay and Winifred H. (n.n.). She d.22 Mar 1920 Humphreys, Sullivan Co., MO, at age 80 and was bur. Humphreys Cem., Humphreys, Sullivan Co., MO.

Henry Oscar "Mac" McKay, b.28 Mar 1837 Shelby Co., IN. He d.30 May 1919 Humphreys, Sullivan Co., MO, age 82; bur. Humphreys Cem.
Known children of Mary "Isabelle"⁶ Chancellor and Henry Oscar "Mac" McKay:

- 519   i.   Henry Columbus "Clum"⁷, b. 27 Dec 1859 IN; m. Sarah M. Palmer.
- 520   ii.   Robert Leroy, b. 3 Dec 1862 IL; m. Altha Lewis; m. Martha "Mattie" Swank.
- 521   iii.   Arminta Jane, b. 18 May 1865; m. F.L. Pickett.
- 522   iv.   Walter Delbert, b. 19 Jun 1872 Sullivan Co., MO; m. Hattie Grace Williams.

245. Henry Columbus⁶ Chancellor Sr. (Ewing⁵, Rebecca⁴ Abney, Joshua³, Elisha², Abner¹), b.May 1846 IL; m. Sarah Jane Hoberry ca.1867. He and Sarah appeared on the census of 26 Jul 1870 Lincoln, Crawford Co., KS. He d.1922; bur. Rosebank Cem., Mulberry, Crawford Co., KS.

Sarah Jane Hoberry, b.Jun 1848 KY. She d.1911 and was bur. Rosebank Cem., Mulberry, Crawford Co., KS.
Known children of Henry Columbus⁶ Chancellor Sr. and Sarah Jane Hoberry:

- 523   i.   Henry Columbus⁷, b. 2 Jan 1868 Arcadia, Crawford Co., KS; m1. Irma C. (n.n.); m2. Pearl Victoria Freeman.
- 524   ii.   John "William," b. Feb 1870 KS; m. Mary (n.n.).
-     iii.   Albert, b.Mar 1872 KS. He d.1904 and was bur. Rosebank Cem., Mulberry, Crawford Co., KS.
-     iv.   Elbert, b.Mar 1872 KS. He d.1915 and was bur. Rosebank Cem., Mulberry, Crawford Co., KS.
-     v.   Louis, b. ca.1874 KS.
- 525   vi.   Lottie I, b. 8 Oct 1876 Arcadia, Crawford Co., KS; m. Adolphos Marion "Dolly" Moore.
-     vii.   Frederick, b.Nov 1878 KS.
-     viii.   Maggie, b.Oct 1881 KS.
-     ix.   Ada, b.Dec 1883 KS. She d.1904 and was bur. in 1904 Rosebank Cem., Mulberry, Crawford Co., KS.
-     x.   Grace Leona "Gracie", b.Jun 1889 KS. She d.1977 and was bur. Rosebank Cem., Mulberry, Crawford Co., KS.
- 526   xi.   Chester Arthur "Art," b. 17 Jul 1891 KS; m. Alla "Allie" Slate.

246. William Henry⁶ Chancellor (Levi⁵, Rebecca⁴ Abney, Joshua³, Elisha², Abner¹), b. ca.1841 IL. He m. Sophia (n.n.). He and Sophia (n.n.) appeared on the census of 29 Jul 1870 Mattoon, Coles Co., IL.

Sophia (n.n.), b. ca.1846 OH.
Known children of William Henry⁶ Chancellor and Sophia (n.n.) all b. IL:

-     i.   Charles G.⁷, b. ca.1864.
-     ii.   John E., b. ca.1865.
-     iii.   Louisa, b. ca.1867.
-     iv.   Effie E., b. ca.1869.
-     v.   Minnie E., b. ca.1875.
-     vi.   Sue E., b.Aug 1879.

247. John Wesley⁶ Chancellor (Levi⁵, Rebecca⁴ Abney, Joshua³, Elisha², Abner¹), b. ca.1846 IL. He m. Louisa (n.n.) in Apr 1870 IL.

Louisa (n.n.), b. ca.1849 OH.
Known child of John Wesley⁶ Chancellor and Louisa (n.n.):

-     i.   Clara⁷, b. ca.1871 IL.

248. Henry Clay⁶ Montgomery (UA) (Martha⁵ Chancellor, Rebecca⁴ Abney, Joshua³, Elisha², Abner¹), b.6 Oct 1846 Clark Co., IL; m1. Mary Watts on 11 Mar 1866 Clark Co., IL. He and Mary appeared on the censuses of 22 Jul 1870 Cumberland, Clark Co., IL; and 10 Jun 1880 Casey, Clark Co., IL; m2. Florence (n.n.) ca.1918 Clark Co., IL. He d.22 Aug 1938 Clark Co., IL, age 91; bur. Washington Street Cem., Casey, Clark Co., IL.

Mary Abagill Watts, b.7 Jan 1848 IN. She d.23 Jan 1916 Clark Co., IL, at age 68 and was bur. Washington Street Cem., Casey, Clark Co., IL.
Known children of Henry Clay⁶ Montgomery (UA) and Mary Abagill Watts:

      i.   Martha Jane "Mat"⁷, b.17 Jul 1866 Clark Co., IL. She m. Charles "Samuel" Hillard, son of James Henry Hillard and Julia
             Ann Hudlemier, in 1886. She d.17 May 1963 Clark Co., IL, age 96; bur. Washington Street Cem., Casey, Clark Co., IL.
             Charles "Samuel" Hillard, b.25 Nov 1860 Montgomery Co., MD. He d.10 Apr 1938 Clark Co., IL, at age 77 and was
             bur. Washington Street Cem., Casey, Clark Co., IL.
      ii.   Sherman, b.Jul 1870 Clark Co., IL. He m. Zona Kite. He d.1950 Clark Co., IL.
             Zona Kite, b.7 Feb 1880 Casey, Clark Co., IL; d.23 Jan 1938 Casey, Clark Co., IL, age 57; bur. Washington St. Cem.
      iii. David "Eddie" m. Viola V. (n.n.). He, b.Oct 1872 Clark Co., IL. He d.1926 Clark Co., IL; bur. Washington St. Cem.
             Viola V. (n.n.), b.1873. She d.1955 IL and was bur. Washington Street Cem., Casey, Clark Co., IL.
      iv. Otto, b.18 Aug 1875 Clark Co., IL. He d.New Year's Eve, 31 Dec 1875 Clark Co., IL.
      v.   Minnie, b. ca.1877 Clark Co., IL.
527   vi. Cora A., b. Oct 1879 IL; m. William D. Howe.
      vii. Henry Sheldon, b.24 Apr 1882 Clark Co., IL. He m. Myrtle Swim. He d.14 Mar 1964 Vigo Co., IN, at age 81 and was
             bur. Washington Street Cem., Casey, Clark Co., IL.
             Myrtle Swim, b.1882. She d.1970.
      viii. John, b.11 May 1883 Clark Co., IL. He d.22 Jul 1883 Clark Co., IL; bur. Washington Street Cem., Casey, Clark Co., IL.
      ix. Harrison, b.13 Oct 1884 Clark Co., IL. He d.14 Jun 1905 Clark Co., IL, at age 20 and was bur. Washington Street Cem.
      x.   (infant son), b.1888 Clark Co., IL. He d.26 Mar 1888 Clark Co., IL and was bur. Washington Street Cem.
      xi. (infant son), b.1889 Clark Co., IL. He d.27 Sep 1889 Clark Co., IL.

There were no known children of Henry Clay⁶ Montgomery (UA) and Florence (n.n.).

249. John W.⁶ Chancellor (William⁵, Rebecca⁴ Abney, Joshua³, Elisha², Abner¹), b. ca.1846 IL. He m. Sarah (n.n.).
    Sarah (n.n.), b. ca.1850 IL.
Known children of John W.⁶ Chancellor and Sarah (n.n.) all b. IL:
      i.   Clara⁷, b. ca.1871.
      ii.   Harrison, b. ca.1877.
      iii. William, b. ca.1879.

250. Catherine Josephine⁶ Chancellor (William⁵, Rebecca⁴ Abney, Joshua³, Elisha², Abner¹), b.3 Jan 1858 Martinsville, Clark Co., IL. She m.
Oliver Hazard Harmeson on 24 Oct 1879. She and Oliver Hazard Harmeson liv. 23 Jun 1880 with her mother, *widow* Mary A. Chancellor,
Martinsville, Clark Co., IL. She d.21 Apr 1942 at home, Mattoon, Coles Co., IL, at age 84. was bur. Casey, Clark Co., IL.
    Oliver Hazard Harmeson, b.6 Nov 1855 Olivet, Vermilion Co., IL. He d.10 Apr 1927 Mattoon, Coles Co., IL, at age 71 and was bur. Casey.
Known children of Catherine Josephine⁶ Chancellor and Oliver Hazard Harmeson:
      i.   George C.⁷.
528   ii.   Norma Agnes, b. 15 Sep 1883; m. Ivory Albert Burmmett.

251. Pvt. John William⁶ Abney Jr. (UA) (John⁵, Paul⁴, Joshua³, Elisha², Abner¹), b.1845 Butler Co., KY. He m. Martha Jane "Pattie" Embry,
daughter of John J. Embry and Nancy Little, on 19 Dec 1861 Butler Co., KY. He d.16 May 1862 Davidson Co., TN; bur. (as *John W. Abner*)
Nashville National Cem., Madison, Davidson Co., TN.
    Martha Jane "Pattie" Embry, b.14 Feb 1841 Butler Co., KY. She appeared on the census of 1 Aug 1870 Butler Co., KY. She d.12 Dec 1920
Butler Co., KY, at age 79 and was bur. Mount Vernon Cem., Dexterville, Butler Co., KY.
Known child of Pvt. John William⁶ Abney Jr. and Martha Jane "Pattie" Embry:
529   i.   Nancy Little⁷, b. 15 Oct 1862 Butler Co., KY.

252. Pheoby Jane⁶ Abney (John⁵, Paul⁴, Joshua³, Elisha², Abner¹), b.8 Nov 1846 KY. She m. Rev. John Thomas Daugherty, son of William B.
Daugherty and Abigail White, ca.1866. She d.16 Jan 1882 at age 35 and was bur. Elder-Anderson Cem., Caneyville, Grayson Co., KY.
    Rev. John Thomas Daugherty, b.25 Aug 1844. He d.26 Dec 1890 at age 46 and was bur. Elder-Anderson Cem., Caneyville, Grayson Co., KY.
Known children of Pheoby Jane⁶ Abney and Rev. John Thomas Daugherty:
      i.   Wiley V.⁷, b.1866. He d.29 Aug 1950.
      ii.   William B., b.1866. He d.29 Aug 1950.
      iii. Austin Columbus, b.1868 Butler Co., KY. He d.15 Nov 1955 Caneyville, Grayson Co., KY.
      iv. Marcus D., b.1870. He d.1947.
530   v.   Silavnus, b. 29 Jan 1873 Caneyville, Grayson Co., KY; m. Ruthia Taylor.
      vi. Barbara, b. ca.1875.
531   vii. Samuel J., b. 30 Aug 1878; m. Pollie Woosley.
      viii. Roxanna, b. after 1880.

253. Jasper N.⁶ Abney (John⁵, Paul⁴, Joshua³, Elisha², Abner¹), b.24 Sep 1848 KY. He m1. Mary Ann "Polly" Snodgrass, daughter of Christopher
Columbus Snodgrass and Hannah Embry, on 14 Jan 1867 Butler Co., KY. He and Mary appeared on the census of 1 Aug 1870 Butler Co., KY. He
and Mary Ann "Polly" Snodgrass were divorced in Apr 1901 Rockport, Spencer Co., IN. He m2. Jennie Etherton on 14 Feb 1910 Spencer Co., IN.
He d.3 Oct 1914 Rockport, Ohio Co., KY, at age 66 and was bur. Sunset Hill Cem., Rockport, Spencer Co., IN.
    Mary Ann "Polly" Snodgrass, b.27 Feb 1848 KY. She d.20 Nov 1911 Spencer Co., IN, at age 63 and was bur. Sunset Hill Cem., Rockport.
Known children of Jasper N.⁶ Abney and Mary Ann "Polly" Snodgrass:
      i.   Lucy⁷. She m. James Bartley on 15 Aug 1898 Spencer Co., IN.
      ii.   Hallie. She m. Willie Cook on 29 Dec 1896 Spencer Co., IN.
      iii. Edward, b.10 Nov 1867. He d.22 Mar 1886 at age 18.
      iv. Hue E., b.1868.
      v.   Hannah Belle, b.14 Dec 1869. She d.14 Dec 1887 Rockport, Spencer Co., IN, age 18 and was bur. Sunset Hill Cem.

532 vi. Keziah, b. 23 Jan 1872 Butler Co., KY; m. Daniel V. Axton ; m. William Caldwell Perry.
533 vii. Commodore Perry, b. 7 Jan 1873 KY; m. Amelia M. Freschly.
viii. Elias, b.7 Apr 1876 Butler Co., KY. He m. Gertrude Wesley on 27 Jun 1901. He m. Bessie Wilmot. He d.4 Jan 1920 Spencer Co., IN, at age 43 and was bur. Sunset Hill Cem., Rockport, Spencer Co., IN.
ix. Ellis, b.30 Apr 1878 KY. He m. Bertha V. Ellison, daughter of George W. Ellison and Minerva Abshire, on 15 Sep 1908 Spencer Co., IN. He d.17 Feb 1912 Rockport, Spencer Co., IN, at age 33 and was bur. Sunset Hill Cem., Rockport.
    Bertha V. Ellison, b.21 Jul 1888 Warrick Co., IN. She m2. John Lewis Wallace in 1919. She d.6 Jan 1984 Newburgh, Warrick Co., IN, at age 95 and was bur. Park Lawn Cem. and Mausoleum, Evansville, Vanderburgh Co., IN.
x. Fred "Freddie", b.4 Apr 1880. He d.15 Aug 1885 at age 5.
534 xi. Elijah "Dige," b. 1 Jul 1882 Rockport, Spencer Co., IN; m. Francis Carter.
xii. Clyde, b.24 Aug 1888. He d.16 Jun 1889 and was bur. on 22 Jun 1889 Sunset Hill Cem., Rockport, Spencer Co., IN.

There were no known children of Jasper N.[6] Abney and Jennie Etherton.

254. James "Lewis"[6] Abney (John[5], Paul[4], Joshua[3], Elisha[2], Abner[1]), b.11 Oct 1850 Butler Co., KY. He m. Mary M. Kizer on 18 Jul 1867 Sumner Co., TN. He and Mary M. Kizer appeared on the census of 11 May 1910 McLean Co., KY. He d.27 Jul 1932 McLean Co., KY, at age 81 and was bur. Mount Vernon Baptist Church Cem., Calhoun, McLean Co., KY.
    Mary M. Kizer, b.1841 TN. She m2. (n.n.) Wilson. She d.22 Aug 1927 McLean Co., KY and was bur. Mount Vernon Baptist Church Cem.
Known children of James "Lewis"[6] Abney and Mary M. Kizer:
535 i. John William[7], b. 25 Jul 1868 KY; m1. Mary Sarah Fleenor; m2. Bessie Kizer.
536 ii. Mary Angieline "Angie," b. 14 Dec 1871 KY; m. George Wilson.
537 iii. James Wesley, b. 20 May 1874; m. Minnie Daugherty.
iv. Nancy Jane, b.1875 KY. She m. Abraham Kinney on 29 Jan 1896 McLean Co., KY. She d.1958.
v. Sarah L., b.1878 KY. She d.1891 KY.
538 vi. George Washington, b. 2 Jun 1880 KY; m. Betty Nolin.
539 vii. William M., b. 6 Jun 1882 McLean Co., KY; m. Lula "Lou" Kessinger.
540 viii. Charles Newton "Charlie," b. 1883 KY; m. Agnes (n.n.).

255. Mary Ann[6] Abney (John[5], Paul[4], Joshua[3], Elisha[2], Abner[1]), b.7 Dec 1852 Butler Co., KY. She m. Francis Marion Daugherty, son of William B. Daugherty and Abigail White, on 27 Nov 1866 Butler Co., KY. She and Francis Marion Daugherty appeared on the census of 1 Aug 1870 Butler Co., KY. She d.6 Jun 1944 Hartford, Ohio Co., KY, at age 91 and was bur. Green Brier Cem., Utica, Daviess Co., KY.
    Francis Marion Daugherty, b.24 Jun 1850 Butler Co., KY.
Known children of Mary Ann[6] Abney and Francis Marion Daugherty all b. Butler Co., KY:
i. Hermina[7], b. ca.1868.
ii. Montreville, b. ca.Jun 1870.
iii. Abigail.
541 iv. Naoma, b. 3 May 1875; m. Dr. Elonzo Snodgrass.

256. Martha Barbara "Patsy"[6] Abney (John[5], Paul[4], Joshua[3], Elisha[2], Abner[1]), b. Feb 1854. She m. Joseph P. Hunter. She d.5 Dec 1918 Ohio Co., KY, at age 64 and was bur. Rosine Cem., Rosien, Ohio Co., KY.
    Joseph P. Hunter, b.20 May 1834 KY. He m. Maria (n.n.) est.1859. He d.16 Nov 1907 Ohio Co., KY, at age 73.
Known children of Martha Barbara "Patsy"[6] Abney and Joseph P. Hunter:
542 i. Fannie Cates[7], b. 29 Apr 1883 KY; m. Pinkney B. Hart.
543 ii. Mollie Tichenor, b. 30 Jun 1885; m. Lee Jones.
544 iii. Carey, b. 7 Nov 1894 McLean Co., KY; m. Myrtle Abney.

257. Jesse G.[6] Abney (John[5], Paul[4], Joshua[3], Elisha[2], Abner[1]), b.29 Apr 1857 Butler Co., KY. He m. Mahala Persilla Daugherty on 14 Oct 1875 McLean Co., KY. He and Mahala appeared censuses of 22 Jun 1880 and 28 Jun 1900 McLean Co., KY. He d.1910 and was bur. Mount Zion Presbyterian Ch. Cem., Central City, Muhlenberg Co., KY.
    Mahala Persilla Daugherty, b.May 1853 KY. She appeared as Head of Household on the censuses of 25 Apr 1910 and 30 Jan 1920 Central City, Muhlenberg Co., KY and was bur. Mount Zion Presbyterian Ch. Cem., Central City, Muhlenberg Co., KY. She d.1937.
Known children of Jesse G.[6] Abney and Mahala Persilla Daugherty:
545 i. Lucy Jane[7], b. 19 Aug 1878; m1. (n.n.) Bartley; m2. (n.n.) Wells.
546 ii. Walter Green, b. 28 Aug 1879 Butler Co., KY; m. Laura Riggs.
iii. Martha L., b. ca.Feb 1880 McLean Co., KY.
iv. Susan Ann, b.25 Feb 1882 McLean Co., KY; d.7 Mar 1915 Muhlenberg Co., KY, age 33; bur. Mt. Zion Presby. Ch. Cem.
v. Charles H., b.Jul 1887 McLean Co., KY.

258. Daniel M.[6] Abney (John[5], Paul[4], Joshua[3], Elisha[2], Abner[1]), b.Oct 1858 Butler Co., KY. He m. Mary Francis Moore, daughter of John Moore and Ellen Kiser. He d.1892.
    Mary Francis Moore, b.1863. She d.17 Apr 1911 McLean Co., KY; bur. Mount Liberty Baptist Church Cem., Wyman, McLean Co., KY.
Known children of Daniel M.[6] Abney and Mary Francis Moore:
547 i. Lon J. "Lonnie"[7], b. 29 May 1880 Daviess Co., KY; m. Mittie L. Pinkston.
ii. Nancy Jane, b.4 May 1882. She m. William "Will" Evans on New Year's Day, 1 Jan 1899. She d.18 Sep 1929 at age 47 and was bur. Mount Liberty Bapt. Ch. Cem., Wyman, McLean Co., KY.
iii. John, b. KY.
iv. Bessie, b. KY.
v. Lulu, b. KY.
vi. Katie, b. KY.
548 vii. Sallie Barbara, b. 24 Aug 1891; m. Ernest Deno.

259. Calvin P.⁶ Moore (Curran's twin) (Mary⁵ Abney, Paul⁴, Joshua³, Elisha², Abner¹), b.16 Dec 1853 Butler Co., KY. He m. Mary M. Howard. He and Mary M. Howard appeared on the census of 11 Jun 1880 Burdens, Butler Co., KY. He d.29 Apr 1915 Butler Co., KY, at age 61 and was bur. Mount Vernon Cem., Dexterville, Butler Co., KY.
      Mary M. Howard, b.1859. She d. between 1886 and 1893.
Known children of Calvin P.⁶ Moore (Curran's twin) and Mary M. Howard:
      549   i.   Newell⁷, b. 12 Feb 1875 KY; m. Lula E. Taylor.
      550   ii. Lafayette, b. 8 Feb 1877 Butler Co., KY; m. Elmeda (n.n.).
      551   iii. John W., b. 22 Aug 1879 Butler Co., KY; m. Etty Roxie Howard.
               iv. Howard, b.23 Sep 1886 KY. He m. Julia Kessinger ca.1909. He and Julia Kessinger appeared on the census of 15 Apr 1930 Ohio Co., KY. He d.2 Nov 1933 at age 47 and was bur. Green River Cem., Ohio Co., KY.
                    Julia Kessinger, b.2 Mar 1890. She d.3 Jan 1974 at age 83 and was bur. Green River Cem., Ohio Co., KY.

260. Paul Abney⁶ Moore (Mary⁵ Abney, Paul⁴, Joshua³, Elisha², Abner¹), b.23 Nov 1857 Morgantown, Butler Co., KY. He m. Katherine Jane "Katie" Moore on 5 Nov 1878 Butler Co., KY. He d.1897 Butler Co., KY and was bur. Mount Vernon Cem., Dexterville, Butler Co., KY.
      Katherine Jane "Katie" Moore, b.24 Aug 1862 Dexterville, Butler Co., KY. She d.23 Jul 1945 Hopkinsville, Christian Co., KY, at age 82 and was bur. Mount Vernon Cem., Dexterville, Butler Co., KY.
Known children of Paul Abney⁶ Moore and Katherine Jane "Katie" Moore:
               i.   Mary A.⁷, b. ca.1879.
               ii. Elsie Ann, b.4 Jan 1880 Morgantown, Butler Co., KY. She d.23 May 1933 Saybrook, McLean Co., IL, at age 53.
               iii. Thomas S., b.13 Jan 1883 KY. He d.29 Jul 1921 at age 38.
      552   iv. Nicey J., b. 30 Sep 1883; m. Homer Abner, son of Silas Curtis Abney (#102) and Calista Barton (see page 64)
      553   v.   Veachel Loven, b. 1 Jul 1885 KY; m. Clodia Phelps.
               vi. Lelia Brown, b.5 Dec 1889 KY. She d.10 Sep 1943 Butler Co., KY, at age 53.
               vii. Nellie, b.23 Nov 1891 Welcome, Butler Co., KY. She d.20 Apr 1923 Ohio Co., KY, at age 31.
               viii. Frank Pierson, b.19 Nov 1893 KY. He d.26 Aug 1971 Cromwell, Ohio Co., KY, at age 77.
               ix. Paul "Alice", b.20 May 1897 Butler Co., KY. She m. Nathan T. Moore. She d.16 Feb 1923 Ohio Co., KY, at age 25.
                    Nathan T. Moore (#555), b.1889. He d.1975. (Nathan and Alice had issue: Lucy (b. ca.1915) and Lawson (b. ca.1918).

261. Finis A.⁶ Moore (Mary⁵ Abney, Paul⁴, Joshua³, Elisha², Abner¹), b.24 Sep 1858 Butler Co., KY. He m1. Louiza J. Howard ca.1880. He m2. Lenora J. Heath. He and Lenora J. Heath appeared on the census of 21 Apr 1910 Butler Co., KY. He d.24 Nov 1939 McHenry, Ohio Co., KY, at age 81 and was bur. Render Cem., McHenry, Ohio Co., KY.
      Louiza J. Howard, b.6 Oct 1853. She d.12 Sep 1884 at age 30.
Known children of Finis A.⁶ Moore and Louiza J. Howard both b. Butler Co., KY:
      554   i.   Finis⁷, b. ca.1882; m. Mary (n.n.).
               ii. Angeline, b.19 May 1883. She m. Perry L. Snodgrass, son of Isaac E. Snodgrass and Frances Jane Gilstrap, ca.1901. She and Perry L. Snodgrass appeared on the censuses of 14 May 1910 and 22 Jan 1920 Butler Co., KY. She d.17 Oct 1963 Ohio Co., KY, at age 80 and was bur. Mount Vernon Cem., Dexterville, Butler Co., KY.
                    Perry L. Snodgrass, b.9 May 1878 Butler Co., KY. He d.3 Jan 1956 Butler Co., KY, at age 77.

      Lenora J. Heath, b.10 Mar 1869 Woodbury, Butler Co., KY. She d.8 Jul 1948 McHenry, Ohio Co., KY, at age 79.
Known children of Finis A.⁶ Moore and Lenora J. Heath:
      555   i.   Nathan T.⁷, b. 3 Sep 1889; m. Paul "Alice" Moore (d/o Paul Abney Moore and Katherine Moore); m. Lelia Jane Burden.
               ii. Viola A. "Ola", b.11 Feb 1891. She d.6 Sep 1980 at age 89 and was bur. Render Cem., McHenry, Ohio Co., KY.
      556   iii. Daniel Lee "Dan," b. 15 May 1896; m. Delia Ann Burden.
      557   iv. Thomas Shofta "Tom," b. 7 Feb 1900 Ohio Co., KY; m. Effie Marie Trail.
      558   v.   Nola Jane, b. 16 Feb 1903 Butler Co., KY; m. Myrtle Hurt (WWI).
      559   vi. Bessie, b. 28 May 1909 Butler Co., KY; m. Audra Embry.
      560   vii. Jessie, b. 28 May 1909; m. Wilma Lois Bishop.

262. Mary C.⁶ Moore (Mary⁵ Abney, Paul⁴, Joshua³, Elisha², Abner¹), b.26 Oct 1862 KY. She m. Rev. Silas V. Baize, son of John Henry Baize and Martha Ann Watson, ca.1891. She and Rev. Silas V. Baize appeared on the census of 12 Jun 1900 Butler Co., KY. She d.23 Feb 1943 Lawrence Co., TN, at age 80 and was bur. John Lay Cem., Ethridge, Lawrence Co., TN.
      Rev. Silas V. Baize, b.20 Sep 1864 Ohio Co., KY. He d.28 May 1948 TN at age 83 and was bur. John Lay Cem., Ethridge, Lawrence Co., TN.
Known children of Mary C.⁶ Moore and Rev. Silas V. Baize both b. KY:
      561   i.   Estella "Stella"⁷, b. New Year's Eve, 31 Dec 1892; m. Charlie Baker; m. Adam B. Fain.
               ii. Ellda, b.Dec 1893.

263. Thomas⁶ Moore (Mary⁵ Abney, Paul⁴, Joshua³, Elisha², Abner¹), b.29 Apr 1866 KY. He m. Delia White Barton ca.1892. He d.11 Mar 1937 Butler Co., KY, at age 70 and was bur. Mount Vernon Cem., Dexterville, Butler Co., KY.
      Delia White Barton, b.18 Feb 1872 KY. She d.5 Feb 1917 Butler Co., KY, at age 44.
Known children of Thomas⁶ Moore and Delia White Barton:
      562   i.   Brankley B.⁷, b. 13 Apr 1893 Butler Co., KY; m. Alice L. Embry.
               ii. Mary Bell, b.10 Aug 1896 Butler Co., KY. She d.10 Mar 1976 Hartford, Ohio Co., KY, at age 79 and was bur. Sunnyside Cem., Beaver Dam, Ohio Co., KY.
               iii. Nicy Jane, b.24 Mar 1904 Butler Co., KY. She d.23 Sep 1956 Ohio Co., KY, at age 52 and was bur. Sunnyside Cem.
               iv. Lulia, b.15 Aug 1906 Butler Co., KY. She d.15 Aug 1906 Butler Co., KY and was bur. Mount Vernon Cem., Dexterville.
               v.   Katie Altha, b.17 Feb 1908 Butler Co., KY. She d.13 Feb 1995 Muhlenberg Co., KY, at age 86; bur. Sunnyside Cem.
               vi. Charlie T., b.27 Feb 1911 Ohio Co., KY. He d.3 Aug 1985 Ohio Co., KY, at age 74 and was bur. Sunnyside Cem.

264. Lucinda Bartholomew⁶ Deweese (Nicey⁵ Abney, Paul⁴, Joshua³, Elisha², Abner¹), b.21 Jul 1856. She m. Commodore J. Flener ca.1885. She d.23 Feb 1923 at age 66 and was bur. Mount Vernon Cem., Dexterville, Butler Co., KY.

Commodore J. Flener, b.10 Apr 1858. He d.20 Jun 1924 at age 66 and was bur. Mount Vernon Cem., Dexterville, Butler Co., KY.
Known children of Lucinda Bartholomew⁶ Deweese and Commodore J. Flener:
> 563   i.   Louella F.⁷, b. 8 Apr 1886 Butler Co., KY; m. Harrison Abner.
> 564   ii.   Perry Hines, b. 22 Dec 1887 Flener, Butler Co., KY; m. Hallie B. Howard.

265. Elijah Covington⁶ De Weese (Nicey⁵ Abney, Paul⁴, Joshua³, Elisha², Abner¹), b.1860 Butler Co., KY. He m. Melissa Ingram ca.1886. He m. Elizabeth Whitaker in 1919.

Melissa Ingram, b.1868. She d.1914.
Known children of Elijah Covington⁶ De Weese and Melissa Ingram:
> 565   i.   Dexter⁷, b. 1899 KY; m. Emma Klumple.
>   ii.   Brodie C., b.14 Feb 1909. He m. Ruth (n.n.) on 27 Jan 1927. He d.28 Sep 1976 at age 67 and was bur. Rose Hill Cem., Central City, Muhlenberg Co., KY.
>   Ruth (n.n.), b.24 Sep 1904. She d.24 Nov 2004 at age 100.

There were no known children of Elijah Covington⁶ De Weese and Elizabeth Whitaker.

266. Armedia W.⁶ Daugherty (Hannah⁵ Abney, Paul⁴, Joshua³, Elisha², Abner¹), b.28 Feb 1871 KY. She m. Perry Monroe Evans, son of William T. Evans and Elizabeth Burden. She d.3 Nov 1947 Burnham, Howell Co., MO, at age 76 and was bur. Burnham Cem., Burnham, Howell Co., MO.

Perry Monroe Evans, b.Jul 1864 KY; d.3 Sep 1927 Okfuskee, Okfuskee Co., OK, age 63; bur. Highland Cem., Okemah, Okfuskee Co., OK.
Known children of Armedia W.⁶ Daugherty and Perry Monroe Evans:
> 566   i.   May⁷, b. 19 May 1894 Willow Springs, Howell Co., MO; m1. William Conn; m2. Wallice Downes; m3. Alvin Monroe Whitehead; m4. William McKinley.
>   ii.   Maude, b.1898. She d.May 1917 Okemah, Okfuskee Co., OK and was bur. Highland Cem., Okemah, Okfuskee Co., OK.
>   iii.   Willie, b.3 Jun 1909 Okemah, Okfuskee Co., OK.; d.2 Apr 1936 Norman, Cleveland Co., OK, ae. 26; bur. Highland Cem.

267. Hannah Curtis⁶ Daugherty (Hannah⁵ Abney, Paul⁴, Joshua³, Elisha², Abner¹), b.7 Dec 1879. She m. Samuel Thomas Evans, son of Harrison Evans and Elizabeth (n.n.), in 1897. She d.12 Nov 1916 at age 36 and was bur. Robertson Cem., Glen Dean, Breckinridge Co., KY.

Samuel Thomas Evans, b.13 Feb 1878 KY. He m. Mattie Smith in 1919. He d.5 May 1967 Bloomington, McLean Co., IL, at age 89.
Known children of Hannah Curtis⁶ Daugherty and Samuel Thomas Evans:
>   i.   Garnett⁷, b.1898. He d.1989.
>   ii.   Easter, b.1900. She d.1992.
>   iii.   Mae, b.1902. She d.1984.
>   iv.   Emmett, b.1905. He d.2001.
>   v.   Hallie, b.1907. She d.2004.
>   vi.   Vida, b.1908. She d.1968.
>   vii.   Dumpet, b.1911. He d.1913.
>   viii.   Vena, b.1913. She d.2007.
>   ix.   Joe, b.1914. He d.2000.
>   x.   Paul, b.1916. He d.1986.

268. Harrison⁶ Abner (Isaac⁵ Abney, Paul⁴, Joshua³, Elisha², Abner¹), b.10 Jul 1887. He m. Louella F. Flener (#563), daughter of Commodore J. Flener and Lucinda Bartholomew Deweese He and Louella F. Flener appeared on the census of 1 May 1940 Butler Co., KY. He d.13 Oct 1959 at age 72 and was bur. Mount Vernon Cem., Dexterville, Butler Co., KY.

Louella F. Flener, b.8 Apr 1886 Butler Co., KY. She d.27 Jul 1958 Bowling Green, Warren Co., KY, at age 72; bur. Mount Vernon Cem.
Known children of Harrison⁶ Abner and Louella F. Flener:
>   i.   Erdie Lee⁷, b.4 Feb 1925. She m. Cpl. Paul John Stopka (USAAF-WWII). She d.8 Sep 2011 at age 86 and was bur. Fort Snelling National Cem., Minneapolis, Hennepin Co., MN.
>   Cpl. Paul John Stopka (USAAF-WWII), b.13 Feb 1919. He d.28 Jan 2000 at age 80; bur. Fort Snelling National Cem.
>   ii.   Orvel, b.11 Jul 1909. He d.Oct 1912 at age 3 and was bur. Mount Vernon Cem., Dexterville, Butler Co., KY.
> 567   iii.   Ora V., b. 22 Sep 1910; m. James Doolin"Jim" Evans Sr.
> 568   iv.   Senora, b. 29 Jun 1912; m. Obie Coots.
> 569   v.   Louie, b. 26 May 1914 Butler Co., KY; m. Carl Evans.
> 570   vi.   Lester C., b. 16 May 1915; m. Elsie (n.n.).
>   vii.   Eulalia, b.2 Sep 1916. She m. Waller D. Spencer on 28 Aug 1932. She d.8 Oct 1976 at age 60 and was bur. Crescent Hill Cem., Scottsville, Allen Co., KY.
>   Waller D. Spencer, b.19 Sep 1891. He d.12 Nov 1973 at age 82 and was bur. Crescent Hill Cem., Scottsville
>   viii.   Lester B., b.3 Oct 1919. He m. Bonnie L. (n.n.) on 31 Oct 1947. He d.21 Jan 2006 at age 86 and was bur. on 23 Jan 2006 Sunnyside Cem., Beaver Dam, Ohio Co., KY.
>   Bonnie L. (n.n.), b.9 Nov 1929.
> 571   ix.   Verline T., b. 31 May 1921 Butler Co., KY; m. Roy Lee Hudson.
>   x.   Carolyn Faye m. Bobby D. Kelley. , b.8 Nov 1945 Butler Co., KY. She d.3 Jan 2016 Bowling Green, Warren Co., KY, at age 70 and was bur. Leach Cem., Horse Branch, Ohio Co., KY.
>   Bobby D. Kelley, b. Christmas Day, 25 Dec 1943.

269. Ada⁶ Abney (Isaac⁵, Paul⁴, Joshua³, Elisha², Abner¹), b.24 Jun 1892 KY. She m. Isaac Morten Snodgrass, son of Isaac E. Snodgrass and Margaret Smith, in 1911. She d.23 Nov 1915 Butler Co., KY, at age 23 and was bur. Isiah Evans Cem., Morgantown, Butler Co., KY.

Isaac Morten Snodgrass m2. Lilly Eathel Alford est.1918. He, b.20 Apr 1889 KY. He d.16 Oct 1969 at age 80 and was bur. Isiah Evans Cem., Morgantown, Butler Co., KY.

Known child of Ada[6] Abney and Isaac Morten Snodgrass:
   i. Zorah "Hazie"[7], b.3 Oct 1915 Butler Co., KY. She d.3 Oct 1915 Butler Co., KY and was bur. Isiah Evans Cem.

270. Rena Ann "Renie"[6] Abner (Silas[5] Abney, Paul[4], Joshua[3], Elisha[2], Abner[1]), b.28 Oct 1875 KY. She m1. Robert Weekley Goff, son of Isaac Jackson Goff, on 12 Sep 1890 Butler Co., KY. She m2. Felix Matthew "Pheak" Loyd, son of Kennett Marion Loyd and Martha Jane Allen, in 1898. She d.11 Nov 1925 Owensboro, Daviess Co., KY, at age 50 and was bur. Rosehill Elmwood Cem., Owensboro, Daviess Co., KY.
  Robert Weekley Goff, b.3 Nov 1874 Butler Co., KY. He d.20 Feb 1939 Rosine, Ohio Co., KY, at age 64 and was bur. Mount Vernon Cem., Dexterville, Butler Co., KY.
Known child of Rena Ann "Renie"[6] Abner and Robert Weekley Goff:
  572 i. Flora Inez[7], b. 12 Mar 1892 Butler Co., KY; m. Counce Turner.

Felix Matthew "Pheak" Loyd, b.6 Nov 1874. He d.4 Apr 1958 at age 83 and was bur. Rosehill Elmwood Cem., Owensboro, Daviess Co., KY.
Known children of Rena Ann "Renie"[6] Abner and Felix Matthew "Pheak" Loyd:
  573 i. Aubrey[7], b. 30 Jan 1906 Ohio Co., KY; m. Catherine Anastasia Marian Soeder.
    ii. Corbie, b.7 Dec 1908 Ohio Co., KY. He d.6 Nov 1988 Louisville, Jefferson Co., KY, at age 79 and was bur. Resthaven Mem. Cem., Louisville, Jefferson Co., KY.
  574 iii. Ray, b. 5 Feb 1917 McHenry, Ohio Co., KY; m. Gertrude "Alene" Gilpin.

271. Homer[6] Abner (Silas[5] Abney, Paul[4], Joshua[3], Elisha[2], Abner[1]), b.18 Apr 1877 Butler Co., KY. He m. Nicey J. Moore, daughter of Paul Abney Moore and Katherine Jane "Katie" Moore, on 1 Feb 1904 Butler Co., KY. He and Nicey J. Moore appeared on the censuses of 18 Apr 1910 Central City, Muhlenberg Co., KY; and 18 Apr 1930 and 13 Apr 1940 Centertown, Ohio Co., KY. He d.28 Mar 1963 Centertown, Ohio Co., KY, at age 85 and was bur. Mount Vernon Cem., Dexterville, Butler Co., KY.
  Nicey J. Moore, b.30 Sep 1883. She d.3 Jan 1970 at age 86 and was bur. Mount Vernon Cem., Dexterville, Butler Co., KY.
Known children of Homer[6] Abner and Nicey J. Moore:
  575 i. Carl "Carlie"[7], b. 11 Jun 1906; m. Nellie Irene Barrett.
  576 ii. Oakie Pearl, b. 20 Apr 1909; m. Robert Elson Hoskins.
  577 iii. Charlie, b. 17 Feb 1913 Ohio Co., KY; m. Cornelia B. Doyal.
  578 iv. Tom, b. 5 Nov 1914 Butler, Pendleton Co., KY; m. Lois "Lee" Smith.
  579 v. Hubert B., b. 20 Apr 1917 Butler Co., KY; m. Stella J. Sheffield.
    vi. Troy "Willie", b.29 Oct 1919 KY. He m. Justine Sheffield, daughter of William Dean Sheffield and Mable Frances Smith, on 26 Sep 1952. He d.12 May 1972 Proviso, Cook Co., IL, at age 52 and was bur. Calvary Cem., Portage, Porter Co., IN.
     Justine Sheffield, b.2 Feb 1931. She d.13 Feb 1984 at age 53 and was bur. Calvary Cem., Portage, Porter Co., IN.
    vii. Jack, b.4 Oct 1921 KY. He m. Wilda Katheryn Patterson, daughter of Cortis Owen Patterson and Eva Gertrude Patterson, on 30 Aug 1944. He d.4 Jan 2004 at age 82 and was bur. Oakwood Cem., Hartford, Ohio Co., KY.
     Wilda Katheryn Patterson, b.10 Sep 1927. She d.30 Nov 2010 at age 83 and was bur. Oakwood Cem., Hartford.
    viii. (infant son), b.21 Feb 1926 Centertown, Ohio Co., KY. He d.21 Feb 1926 Centertown, Ohio Co., KY.
    ix. Everette, b.18 Apr 1929 KY; m. Ritta Jane Coffman, d/o of Claude Reynolds Coffman and Eunice Bishop, on 6 Aug 1956 Robertson Co., TN; d.Aug 1981 Dyer, Lake Co., IN, age 52; bur. Memory Lane Mem. Cem., Schererville, Lake Co., IN.
     Ritta Jane Coffman, b.7 Jul 1933. She d.27 Dec 1969 at age 36 and was bur. Memory Lane Mem. Cem., Schererville.

272. George W.[6] Abner (Silas[5] Abney, Paul[4], Joshua[3], Elisha[2], Abner[1]), b.18 Apr 1880 KY. He m. Katie May McManaway ca.1913. He d.8 Aug 1943 Somerville, Morgan Co., AL, at age 63 and was bur. New Friendship Bapt. Ch. Cem., Somerville, Morgan Co., AL.
  Katie May McManaway, b.6 Jul 1881 KY. She d.14 Mar 1978 Somerville, Morgan Co., KY, at age 96.
Known children of George W.[6] Abner and Katie May McManaway:
  580 i. Sally "Sadie"[7], b. 6 Mar 1914 Morgan Co., AL; m. James Elsworth Sowers.
  581 ii. Newt, b. 16 Apr 1916 TN; m. Audie Macie Dunaway.
  582 iii. Bertha Lee "Berthie," b. 19 Jan 1919 Priceville, Morgan Co., AL; m. Claude Aleen Davis.
  583 iv. Arrie, b. 10 Nov 1921 Morgan Co., AL; m. Lois "Myrtle" Murphree.
  584 v. Clistie, b. 4 Apr 1922 Priceville, Morgan Co., AL; m. PFC Carl Thomas Bradley (USArmy-WWI, Korea).
  585 vi. Hobert P, b. 15 Feb 1925 Morgan Co., AL; m. Flora Elizabeth Anders; m. Carol (n.n.).
    vii. Marie, b.5 Jan 1928 Morgan Co., AL. She m. Revis Joree Stone (USArmy). She d.19 Dec 2010 Moulton, Lawrence Co., AL, at age 82 and was bur. New Friendship Bapt. Church Cem., Somerville, Morgan Co., AL.
     Revis Joree Stone (USArmy), b.29 Jan 1936. He d.4 May 1989 at age 53; bur. New Friendship Bapt. Ch. Cem.
  586 viii. James "Owen," b. 30 Jun 1929 Morgan Co., AL.
  587 ix. Maudie, b. 12 Sep 1932 Morgan Co., AL; m. James Olan Reeves (USArmy-WWII).
    x. Florence m. LeRoy Nelson. , b.15 Oct 1936 Morgan Co., AL. She d.24 Feb 2002 Moulton, Lawrence Co., AL, at age 65 and was bur. New Friendship Bapt. Church Cem., Somerville, Morgan Co., AL.
     LeRoy Nelson, b.28 Jul 1928. He d.10 Apr 1980 at age 51.

273. Effie[6] Abney (Francis[5], William[4], Joshua[3], Elisha[2], Abner[1]), b. Jul 1874 Harrisburg, Saline Co., IL. She m. Hamilton "Mack" McCoy. She d.25 Feb 1958 Galveston, Galveston Co., TX, at age 83 and was bur. Old Bear Creek Cem., Linden, Cass Co., TX.
  Hamilton "Mack" McCoy, b.10 Jun 1865 Linden, Cass Co., TX. He d.19 Dec 1950 Linden, Cass Co., TX, at age 85 and was bur. Old Bear Creek Cem., Linden, Cass Co., TX.
Known child of Effie[6] Abney and Hamilton "Mack" McCoy:
   i. Eldon[7], b.1894. He d.1939.

274. Cora A.[6] Abney (Francis[5], William[4], Joshua[3], Elisha[2], Abner[1]), b.1884. She m. Edward H. Robertson, son of William A. Robertson and Margaret Willard. She d.1977 and was bur. Oak Forest Cem., Birch Tree, Shannon Co., MO.
  Edward H. Robertson, b.19 Sep 1870 IL. He d.19 Mar 1917 Bartlett, Shannon Co., MO, at age 46.

Known children of Cora A.[6] Abney and Edward H. Robertson:
    i.   Catherine M.[7], b.4 Apr 1909; m. (n.n.) Hug; d.13 Aug 2000 age 91; bur. Lakewood Park Cem., Affton, St. Louis Co., MO.
    ii. William M., b.20 Oct 1915. He m. Marie (n.n.). He d.24 Mar 1994 at age 78 and was bur. Sullivan IOOF Cem., Sullivan, Franklin Co., MO.

275. Myrtha Juanita[6] Abney (Francis[5], William[4], Joshua[3], Elisha[2], Abner[1]), b.7 Feb 1898. She m1. Sgt. Calvin Shepard Crozier (USArmy-WWI) in 1919. She m2. Harry S. Boyles in 1927. She d.21 Apr 1988 at age 90 and was bur. Dexter Cem., Dexter, Stoddard Co., MO.
    Sgt. Calvin Shepard Crozier (USArmy-WWI), b.15 Apr 1892 TX; d.22 Jul 1953 NM, age 61; bur. Fort Bayard Nat'l Cem., Fort Bayard, NM.
Known child of Myrtha Juanita[6] Abney and Sgt. Calvin Shepard Crozier (USA-WWI):
    i.   Vesta Ruth[7], b.1920. She d.1939.

    Harry S. Boyles, b.30 Mar 1888. He d.26 Oct 1974 at age 86 and was bur. Dexter Cem., Dexter, Stoddard Co., MO.
Known child of Myrtha Juanita[6] Abney and Harry S. Boyles:
    i.   Charles[7], b.1931. He d.2018.

276. William T.[6] Abner (Louis[5], William[4] Abney, Joshua[3], Elisha[2], Abner[1]), b.8 Mar 1886 AR; m. Ella Mable Ward, dau. of Willard Harvey Ward and Mary Etta Glasgow. He d.Apr 1964 Wichita, Sedgwick Co., KS, age 78; bur. Resthaven Gardens of Memory, Wichita, Sedgwick Co., KS.
    Ella Mable Ward, b.1893 MO. She d.1969 KS and was bur. Resthaven Gardens of Memory, Wichita, Sedgwick Co., KS.
Known child of William T.[6] Abner and Ella Mable Ward:
    588   i.   Henry Dale[7], b. 3 May 1928; m. Ruby Faye Moore.

277. Pvt. Roy E.[6] Abner (WWI) (Louis[5], William[4] Abney, Joshua[3], Elisha[2], Abner[1]), b.12 May 1888; m. Leona Hattie Stone, d/o William Spencer Stone and Almedia Walton. He d.27 Mar 1971 Lodi, San Joaquin Co., CA, at age 82; bur. Baxter Mem. Gardens, Mountain Home, Baxter Co., AR.
    Leona Hattie Stone, b.23 Dec 1909 Clarkridge, Baxter Co., AR. She d.7 Dec 1981 Dallas, Dallas Co., TX, at age 71; bur. Baxter Mem. Gardens.
Known children of Pvt. Roy E.[6] Abner (WWI) and Leona Hattie Stone:
    i.   Ray T.[7].
    ii. Arvilla m. (n.n.) Barrett.

278. Mary Roxie[6] Abner (Louis[5], William[4] Abney, Joshua[3], Elisha[2], Abner[1]), b.25 Sep 1890. She m. Arch Dearmore, son of Leodonas Dearmore and Elizabeth Gray. She d.23 Feb 1965 at age 74 and was bur. Gassville Cem., Gassville, Baxter Co., AR.
    Arch Dearmore, b.9 Jun 1884. He d.4 Jun 1951 at age 66 and was bur. Gassville Cem., Gassville, Baxter Co., AR.
Known children of Mary Roxie[6] Abner and Arch Dearmore both b. Gassville, Baxter Co., AR:
    i.   Clovis Henry[7], b.3 Mar 1918. He m. Dula Marie Mooney, daughter of Ernest W. Mooney and Rilla Dell Reed. He d.24 Aug 1998 Brookfield, Cook Co., IL, at age 80; bur. Chapel Hill Gardens West, Oakbrook Terrace, DuPage Co., IL.
            Dula Marie Mooney, b.12 Nov 1919 Wetumka, Hughes Co., OK. She d.22 Jan 1986 Brookfield, Cook Co., IL, at age 66 and was bur. Chapel Hill Gardens West, Oakbrook Terrace, DuPage Co., IL.
    589   ii. Estalena, b. 2 Sep 1929; m. Robert Megee.

279. Elizabeth Parethena[6] Abney (Wilburn[5], Benjamin[4], Hezekiah[3], Elisha[2], Abner[1]), b.16 May 1852 GA. She m. Dr. George Washington Wills in 1871. She and Dr. George Washington Wills appeared on the censuses of 9 Jun 1880 Cobb Co., GA; 7 Jun 1900 DeKalb Co., AL and 22 Apr 1910 Walker Co., GA. She d.1 Sep 1916 Hamilton Co., TN, at age 64 and was bur. Rocky Springs, Walker Co., GA.
    Dr. George Washington Wills, b.3 Feb 1851 Paulding Co., GA. He d.19 Feb 1912 Coosa Co., AL, at age 61 and was bur. Mount Olive Cem., Mount Olive, Coosa Co., AL.
Known children of Elizabeth Parethena[6] Abney and Dr. George Washington Wills:
    590   i.   Ida Irene[7], b. 2 Oct 1872 Paulding Co., GA; m. Anselm Abel Ashcraft.
    591   ii.   Etta, b. 29 Oct 1874; m. William M. Brock.
    592   iii. Minnie M., b. 8 Sep 1877; m. Robert Edward Downs.
          iv.   Oscar C., b.Sep 1880 GA.
          v.   Lula D., b.Jan 1884 AL.
          vi.   Daisy E., b.Jan 1887 AL.
          vii. Georgia D., b.Sep 1889 GA.
          viii. Walter, b.Feb 1892 GA.

280. Washington "Andrew"[6] Abney (Wilburn[5], Benjamin[4], Hezekiah[3], Elisha[2], Abner[1]), b.29 Oct 1856 Floyd Co., GA. He m. Ella Charlotte Bohannan on Christmas Eve, 24 Dec 1880. He and Ella Charlotte Bohannan appeared on the censuses of 4 Jun 1900 Walker Co., GA; 21 Apr 1910 Catoosa Co., GA. and 13 Jan 1920 LaFayette, Walker Co., GA. He appeared on the census of 4 Apr 1930 LaFayette, Walker Co., GA. He d.7 Jan 1940 Walker Co., GA, at age 83 and was bur. LaFayette Cem., LaFayette, Walker Co., GA.
    Ella Charlotte Bohannan, b.22 Oct 1866 Paulding Co., GA. She d.3 May 1921 Walker Co., GA, at age 54 and was bur. LaFayette Cem.
Known children of Washington "Andrew"[6] Abney and Ella Charlotte Bohannan:
    593   i.   John Calloway[7], b. 22 Aug 1881 West Armuchee, Walker Co., GA; m. Grace V. Mize.
    594   ii.   Grover Cleveland, b. 3 Jul 1885 West Amurchee, Walker Co., GA; m. Lillian "Lillie" Black.
    595   iii. Mollie, b. 15 Apr 1888 West Amurchee, Walker Co., GA; m. Lloyd Williams.
    596   iv.   William Luther "Luke," b. 10 May 1889 West Amurchee, Walker Co., GA; m. Maude Victoria Williams.
          v.   Bennie, b.10 Mar 1891. She d.21 Aug 1892 at age 1 and was bur. McWilliams Cem., Villanow, Walker Co., GA.
    597   vi.   Stella "Lee," b. 23 Dec 1892 GA.
    598   vii. Luvena "Myrtis," b. 15 Jun 1895 GA; m. John E. Edge.
    599   viii. James Mack "Jim," b. 15 May 1898 GA; m. Mary Bulah Evitt.
          ix.   Eunice Rebecca, b.29 Apr 1902 GA. She m. George McLafferty. She lived Anniston, AL and in 1984 LaFayette, GA.
                George McLafferty d. Anniston, AL.
    600   x.   Jesse Andrew "Jess," b. 27 Oct 1904 West Armuchee, Walker Co., GA; m. Martha Camp Shaw.

281. Lula "Nancy"[6] Abney (Wilburn[5], Benjamin[4], Hezekiah[3], Elisha[2], Abner[1]), b.May 1860 Paulding Co., GA. She m. Turner B. Brown ca.1881. She and Turner B. Brown appeared on the censuses of 18 Jun 1900, 15 Apr 1910, 8 Jan 1920 and Apr 1930 Red Rock, Cobb Co., GA. She was liv. on 7 Apr 1940 with her daughter, Nora Brown, Cobb Co., GA. She d.1944 and was bur. New Hope Cem., Dallas, Paulding Co., GA.
    Turner B. Brown (an unknown value) HS b.dt. wrong. He, b.May 1854 GA. He d.1936; bur. New Hope Cem., Dallas, Paulding Co., GA.
Known children of Lula "Nancy"[6] Abney and Turner B. Brown:
        i.   John[7], b.1882. He d.1884 and was bur. New Hope Cem., Dallas, Paulding Co., GA.
        ii.   Alice, b.1884. She d.1884 and was bur. New Hope Cem., Dallas, Paulding Co., GA.
        iii. Calloway, b.1886. He d.1887 and was bur. New Hope Cem., Dallas, Paulding Co., GA.
601   iv.   Nora May, b. Jul 1888 GA; m. John "Oscar" Hall.

282. Vera "Datha"[6] Abney (Wilburn[5], Benjamin[4], Hezekiah[3], Elisha[2], Abner[1]), b.16 Jun 1869 GA. She m. William R. Blalock ca.1894. She and William R. Blalock appeared on the censuses of 26 Apr 1910, 8 Jan 1920 and 3 Apr 1930 DeKalb Co., AL. She d.1 Feb 1950 at age 80 and was bur. Town Creek Bapt. Ch. Cem., Chavies, DeKalb Co., AL.
    William R. Blalock, b.13 Feb 1848. He d.6 Sep 1924 at age 76 and was bur. Town Creek Bapt. Ch. Cem., Chavies, DeKalb Co., AL.
Known children of Vera "Datha"[6] Abney and William R. Blalock:
        i.   Huston[7], b. ca.1904.
        ii.   Ernest, b. ca.1906.

283. Robert E.[6] Abney (Wilburn[5], Benjamin[4], Hezekiah[3], Elisha[2], Abner[1]), b.13 Aug 1871 GA. He m1. Mary C. Abney, daughter of William Thomas Abney and Martha W. Perry, ca.1884. He and Mary C. Abney appeared on the censuses of 11 Jun 1900 Tallapoosa, Haralson Co., GA; 2 May 1910 and 9 Jan 1920 Buchanan, Haralson Co., GA. He m2. Vastie C. "Vassie" Wells on 18 Apr 1926 Haralson Co., GA. He and Vastie C. "Vassie" Wells appeared on the censuses of 18 Apr 1930 Polk Co., GA and 29 Apr 1940 Buchanan, Haralson Co., GA. He d.17 Jul 1948 at age 76 and was bur. Buchanan City Cem., Buchanan, Haralson Co., GA.
    Mary C. Abney, b.30 Jan 1873 AL. She d.9 Mar 1924 Buchanan, Haralson Co., GA, at age 51 and was bur. Buchanan City Cem., Buchanan.
Known children of Robert E.[6] Abney and Mary C. Abney:
602   i.   Lillie Mae[7], b. 18 May 1896 Paulding Co., GA; m. Henry Charles Pope; m. (n.n.) Camp.
        ii.   Martha, b.Feb 1898 GA.
603   iii. Minnie L, b. 22 May 1902 Buchanan, Haralson Co., GA; m. Harvey Jackson "Jack" Perry Sr.
        iv.   Dora, b.1907 GA. She d.1927 and was bur. Buchanan City Cem., Buchanan, Haralson Co., GA.
        v.   Robert, b.1910 GA. He d.1933 and was bur. Buchanan City Cem., Buchanan, Haralson Co., GA.
604   vi.   Marvin "Doc," b. 12 Oct 1913 GA; m. Lucille Elizabeth Williams.
        vii. Datha, b. ca.Oct 1916 GA.

    Vastie C. "Vassie" Wells, b.19 Feb 1881 GA. She lived in 1935 Haralson Co., GA. She d.29 Jun 1956 at age 75 and was bur. Tallapoosa E. Bapt. Ch. Cem., Tallapoosa, Haralson Co., GA.
There were no known children of Robert E.[6] Abney and Vastie C. "Vassie" Wells.

284. Corrin Frances[6] Abney (Wilburn[5], Benjamin[4], Hezekiah[3], Elisha[2], Abner[1]), b.18 May 1873 Paulding Co., GA. She m. John Hennaly Camp on 17 Dec 1896. She and John Hennaly Camp appeared on the censuses of 11 Jun 1900 Acorntree, Paulding Co., GA; 13 Jan 1920 and 16 Apr 1930 California, Paulding Co., GA. She d.2 Jan 1952 New Hope, Paulding Co., GA, at age 78 and was bur. New Hope Cem., Dallas, Paulding Co., GA.
    John Hennaly Camp was bur. New Hope Cem., Dallas, Paulding Co., GA. He, b. Christmas Eve, 24 Dec 1872 Paulding Co., GA. He d.29 Nov 1941 New Hope, Paulding Co., GA, at age 68 and was bur. New Hope Cem., Dallas, Paulding Co., GA.
Known children of Corrin Frances[6] Abney and John Hennaly Camp:
        i.   Bertha L.[7], b.12 Dec 1897 Paulding Co., GA. She m. Houston Blalock. d.20 Aug 1973 GA at age 75; New Hope Cem.
                Houston Blalock, b.3 Jan 1903. He d.13 Sep 1973 at age 70 and was bur. New Hope Cem., Dallas, Paulding Co., GA.
605   ii.   Alice "Mae," b. 10 Jan 1899 Paulding Co., GA; m. Willie Arthur Davis.
        iii. Isabel, b. ca.1902 GA.
        iv.   Lizzie, b. ca.1905 GA.
606   v.   Emma Lou, b. 5 Oct 1908 Cobb Co., GA; m. Pvt. Marcus Pritchett (USArmy).
        vi.   Hennaly Nathan, b.16 Jan 1911 GA. He m. Louise G. Garrett ca.1935. He and Louise Garrett appeared on the census of 16 Apr 1940 California, Paulding Co., GA. He d.2 Oct 1994, age 83; bur. Kennesaw Mem. Park, Marietta, Cobb Co., GA.
                Louise G. Garrett, b.6 Jun 1915. She d.1 Feb 1985 at age 69; bur. Kennesaw Mem. Park, Marietta, Cobb Co., GA.
607   vii. Altha Magdelia, b. 7 Jan 1913 New Hope, Paulding Co., GA; m. Raymond Woodrow "Ray" Finch.
608   viii. Gordon Lee, b. 17 Oct 1915 GA; m. Hazel Evelyn Henson.

285. Benjamin F. "Ben"[6] Abney (Wilburn[5], Benjamin[4], Hezekiah[3], Elisha[2], Abner[1]), b.1876 GA. He m1. (n.n.) ca.1897. He was liv. on 3 May 1910 with Crawford family, Haralson Co., GA. He m2. Margaret E. "Maggie" McRae ca.1909. He and Margaret E. "Maggie" McRae appeared on the censuses of 21 Jan 1920 Buchanan, Haralson Co., GA; and 30 Apr 1930 and 26 Apr 1940 Tallapoosa, Haralson Co., GA. He d.1957 and was bur. Buchanan City Cem., Buchanan, Haralson Co., GA.
There were no known children of Benjamin F. "Ben"[6] Abney and his first wife.

    Margaret E. "Maggie" McRae, b.1887 GA. She d.1981 and was bur. Buchanan City Cem., Buchanan, Haralson Co., GA.
Known children of Benjamin F. "Ben"[6] Abney and Margaret E. "Maggie" McRae:
        i.   Joseph "Dewey"[7], b.26 May 1912 Haralson Co., GA. He lived on 1 Apr 1935 Tallapoosa, Haralson Co., GA. He was liv. on 26 Apr 1940 lodger with Barrister family, Fulton Co., GA. He m. Oudia Cook. He d.27 Mar 1997 GA at age 84 and was bur. Georgia Mem. Park, Marietta, Cobb Co., GA.
                Oudia Cook, b.11 Dec 1907. She d.30 Aug 2000 at age 92 and was bur. Georgia Mem. Park, Marietta, Cobb Co., GA.
        ii.   Gladys D., b.23 Jun 1916 Tallapoosa, Haralson Co., GA. She d.8 Aug 2015 Cleveland, White Co., GA, at age 99 and was bur. Buchanan City Cem., Buchanan, Haralson Co., GA.

    iii.   Lois, b. ca.Jul 1918 GA.
    iv.   Louise, b.21 Jan 1920 on the day her family was enumerated in the census in Haralson Co., GA! She d.17 Feb 1986 at age
            66 and was bur. Buchanan City Cem., Buchanan, Haralson Co., GA.
    v.   O. Frank, b.3 Sep 1922 Haralson Co., GA; d.16 Feb 1968, age 45; bur. College Park Cem., College Park, Fulton Co., GA.
    vi.   Earl, b. ca.1926 GA.
    vii.   Mary Nell, b. ca.1927 GA.

286. George Washington⁶ Abney (Benjamin⁵, Benjamin⁴, Hezekiah³, Elisha², Abner¹), b.4 Aug 1855 Marietta, Cobb Co., GA. He m1. Olivia
Josephine Hill on 4 Jan 1877 Marshall Co., AL. He and Olivia Josephine Hill appeared on the censuses of 24 Jun 1880 and 9 Jun 1900 Marshall
Co., AL; and 4 May 1910 Upshur Co., TX. He and Olivia Josephine Hill were divorced ca.1918. He m2. Ida Cowen in 1927. He d.15 Sep 1937
Gilmer, Upshur Co., TX, at age 82 and was bur. Gilmer City Cem., Gilmer, Upshur Co., TX.
        Olivia Josephine Hill, b.10 Jul 1854 AL. She appeared as Head of Household on the census of 19 Apr 1930 Upshur Co., TX. She d.3 Jan 1939
Gilmer, Upshur Co., TX, at age 84 and was bur. on 17 Sep 1939 Gilmer City Cem., Gilmer, Upshur Co., TX.
Known children of George Washington⁶ Abney and Olivia Josephine Hill:
        609   i.   Mary Frances⁷, b. 4 Feb 1878 AL; m. John Francis Machen.
        610   ii.   Mattie William, b. 5 Sep 1881 AL; m. James "Martin" Hall.
        611   iii.   Christopher Columbus "CC," b. 14 Jul 1884 AL; m. Mary Josephine "Josie" Aycock.
                iv.   (n.n.), b. ca.1887. She d. before 1900.
        612   v.   Perino "Frank," b. 12 Nov 1889 Marshall Co., AL; m. Gladys Susanna Mitchell; m. Annie Elizabeth Willis.

        Ida Cowen, b.20 Oct 1876 AL; m1. Robert Young Lang 1893; d.16 Mar 1939 AL; bur. Clear Springs Bapt. Ch. Cem., Sidney, AL.
There were no known children of George Washington⁶ Abney and Ida Cowen.

287. Mary Ann C.⁶ Abney (Benjamin⁵, Benjamin⁴, Hezekiah³, Elisha², Abner¹), b.15 Feb 1857 AL. She m. John Washington Moore on 9 Apr
1876. She d.30 Aug 1935 Marshall Co., Al, at age 78 and was bur. Martling Community Cem., Martling, Marshall Co., Al.
        John Washington Moore, b.22 Jul 1852 GA. He d.3 Apr 1935 Marshall Co., AL, at age 82 and was bur. Martling Community Cem., Martling.
Known children of Mary Ann C.⁶ Abney and John Washington Moore:
        613   i.   Falecia Roseline Mae "Rossie"⁷, b. 7 Mar 1877; m. Jasper Ruben Rowan.
        614   ii.   Henry Osborn, b. 18 Dec 1878; m. Della Lucendie Burt.
        615   iii.   Mary Leeoma "Oma," b. 4 May 1882; m. Edward Culbert.
                iv.   James Walter, b.1 Mar 1884. He m. Teomer E. Hodgens. He d.25 Nov 1918 DeKalb Co., AL, at age 34 and was bur. New
                        Harmony Missionary Bapt. Ch. Cem., Geraldine, DeKalb Co., AL.
                        Teomer E. Hodgens, b.25 Jul 1888. She d.28 Nov 1918 DeKalb Co., AL, at age 30; bur. New Harmony MBCC.
        616   v.   John Luther, b. 2 Sep 1886; m. Noma Mae Lee.
                vi.   Joel Oliver, b.4 Oct 1888; m. Minnie A. Johnson. He d.3 Oct 1958, age 69; bur. Eason-Johnson Cem., Marshall Co., AL.
                        Minnie A. Johnson, b.17 Feb 1891. She d.28 Dec 1948 at age 57; bur. Eason-Johnson Cem., Marshall Co., AL.
        617   vii.   Grover S., b. 21 Nov 1890; m. Eula Hays.
                viii.   Benjamin D., b.20 Feb 1894 Marshall Co., AL. He m. Frances M. (n.n.). He d.13 Jan 1969 at age 74 and was bur. Oakmont
                        Mem. Park, Lafayette, Contra Costa Co., CA.
                        Frances M. (n.n.), b.27 Dec 1894 OR. She d.27 Dec 1973 Contra Costa Co., CA, at age 79; bur. Oakmont Mem. Park.
        618   ix.   Dewey Hobson "Hob," b. 12 Dec 1898; m. Cecile Belle Carter.

288. James Alfred⁶ Abney (Benjamin⁵, Benjamin⁴, Hezekiah³, Elisha², Abner¹), b.Nov 1859 Marshall Co., AL. He m. Lucinda "Lucindy" Martin
on 20 Jan 1890 at the home of W.D. Martin, Guntersville, Marshall Co., AL. He lived ca.1893 TX. He liv. ca.1897 OK. He and Lucinda "Lucindy"
Martin appeared on the censuses of 26 Jun 1900 and 3 May 1910 Libscomb Co., TX. He d.1919; bur. Texline Cem., Texline, Dallam Co., TX.
        Lucinda "Lucindy" Martin, b.Sep 1866 AL. She appeared as Head of Household on the censuses of 20 Jan 1920 and 18 Apr 1930 Dallam Co.,
TX; and 1 May 1940 Texline, Dallam Co., TX. She d.1959 and was bur. Texline Cem., Texline, Dallam Co., TX.
Known children of James Alfred⁶ Abney and Lucinda "Lucindy" Martin:
                i.   Claire "Clevie"⁷, b.7 Jan 1891 AL. She m. John " Herman" Hohlaus. She and John " Herman" Hohlaus were liv. in 1935
                        Floyd Co., TX. She and John " Herman" Hohlaus appeared on the census of 17 Apr 1940 Springer, Colfax Co., NM. She
                        d.3 Jan 1967 at age 75 and was bur. Higgins Cem., Higgins, Lipscomb Co., TX.
                        John " Herman" Hohlaus, b.27 Oct 1888 Agate, Elbert Co., CO. He d.25 Nov 1969 Canadian, Hemphill Co., TX, at
                        age 81 and was bur. Higgins Cem., Higgins, Lipscomb Co., TX.
        619   ii.   Hattie, b. Mar 1892 AL; m. Guy Calvin Bateman.
                iii.   Bill "Willie", b.Oct 1893 TX. She was liv. on 18 Apr 1930 and 1 May 1940 with her widowed mother, Lucinda, Texline,
                        Dallam Co., TX. She d.1983 and was bur. Texline Cem., Texline, Dallam Co., TX.
                iv.   Talmage, b.Oct 1894 TX. He m. Esther Leafy Downey ca.1917. He and Esther Leafy Downey appeared on the censuses
                        of 16 Jan 1920, 5 Apr 1930 and 1 May 1940 Texline, Dallam Co., TX. He d.17 Oct 1975 and was bur. Texline Cem.
                        Esther Leafy Downey, b.13 Dec 1896 Baker City, Baker Co., OR; d.19 Oct 1991 Amarillo, Randall Co., TX, age 94.
        620   v.   Margaret B. "Maggie Bob," b. Feb 1896 TX; m. Robert Fulton Hefley.
                vi.   (n.n.), b. and d. ca.1898.
                vii.   Anna "Annie", b.Feb 1900 OK. She was liv. on 18 Apr 1930 and on 1 May 1940 with her widowed mother, Lucinda,
                        Texline, Dallam Co., TX. She d.1978 and was bur. Texline Cem., Texline, Dallam Co., TX.
        621   viii.   Earnestteen, b. Christmas Eve, 24 Dec 1901 TX; m. Smith "Edward" Temple.
        622   ix.   Temple H. "Tempie," b. 15 Feb 1904 TX; m. Pauline Beatty.

289. William "Henry"⁶ Abney (Benjamin⁵, Benjamin⁴, Hezekiah³, Elisha², Abner¹), b.10 Jun 1860 Guntersville, Marshall Co., AL. He m1. Martha
Elizabeth Hodgins ca.1879. He and Martha Elizabeth Hodgins appeared on the censuses of 17 Jun 1880 Marshall Co., AL; and 5 Jun 1900 and 21
Apr 1910 Thompson, Marshall Co., AL. He m2. Willie E. Kent in 1918. He and Willie E. Kent appeared on the censuses of 2 Jan 1920 and 14 Apr

1930 Boaz, Marshall Co., AL. He m3. Ida Jane Fortson in 1935. He and Ida Jane Fortson appeared on the census of 12 Apr 1940 Marshall Co., AL. He d.7 Dec 1942 at age 82 and was bur. New Harmony Missionary Bapt. Ch. Cem., Geraldine, DeKalb Co., AL.

Martha Elizabeth Hodgins, b.15 May 1856 AL. She d.24 Feb 1916 at age 59 and was bur. New Harmony Missionary Bapt. Ch. Cem., Geraldine. Known children of William "Henry"[6] Abney and Martha Elizabeth Hodgins:

                   i.   William "Walter"[7], b.9 Aug 1880 Marshall Co., AL. He m1. (n.n.) ca.1901. He appeared as a lodger on the censuses of 12 May 1910, Birmingham, Jefferson Co., AL and of 2 Jan 1920, Chicago, Cook Co., IL. He m2. Bertha L. (n.n.). He and Bertha L. (n.n.) appeared on the census of 11 Apr 1930 Seattle, King Co., WA. He m3. Mabel (n.n.). He and Mabel (n.n.) appeared on the census of 10 Apr 1940 Seattle, King Co., WA. He d.4 May 1967 New London, Kandiyohi Co., MN, at age 86 and was bur. Lebanon Cem., New London, Kandiyohi Co., MN.

                             Bertha L. (n.n.), b. ca.1877 Norway. She m. (n.n.) Hanson ca.1897.

                             Mabel (n.n.), b.1897 MN. She d.1976 and was bur. Redmond Cem., Redmond, King Co., WA.

623   ii.   Lillie Ann, b. 9 Dec 1881 Marhsall Co., AL; m. John "Craton" Guest.
624   iii. Jasper Emmett, b. 26 Feb 1884 Marhsall Co., AL; m. Ella M. Clements.
625   iv. James G., b. 29 Nov 1886 Marhsall Co., AL; m. Ina Bell Kent.
626   v.   Cora Lee, b. 14 Jan 1890 Marhsall Co., AL; m. Amos W. "AW" Chiles.
627   vi. Homer, b. 8 Sep 1892 Marhsall Co., AL; m. Sarah Ann Orr.
        vii. John "Bunyan", b.2 Aug 1894 Marhsall Co., AL. He m. Alice Eugenia Elrod in 1915. He and Alice Eugenia Elrod appeared on the censuses of 19 Jan 1920 Albertville, Marshall Co., AL and 3 Apr 1930 Marshall Co., AL. He and Alice Eugenia Elrod appeared on the census of 11 Apr 1940 Arab, Marshall Co., AL (where he was owner of a *Western Auto Store*). He d.21 May 1973 at age 78 and was bur. Marshall Mem. Gardens, Albertville, Marshall Co., AL.

                             Alice Eugenia Elrod, b.19 Jan 1897 Whiton, DeKalb Co., AL. She d.2 Feb 1984 Arab, Marshall Co., AL, at age 87.
628   viii. Joseph "Vernon," b. 2 Aug 1894 Marhsall Co., AL; m. Comilla Pearl Rains.
629   ix. Wilson Gordon, b. 20 Dec 1897 Marhsall Co., AL; m. Marion A. (n.n.); m. Violet Gregg.

Willie E. Kent, b.8 Jul 1865 GA. She m. J.H. Wright on 13 Oct 1882 Etowah Co., AL. She d.2 May 1934 Boaz, Marshall Co., AL, at age 68 and was bur. Red Apple Bapt. Ch. Cem., Boaz, Marshall Co., AL.
There were no known children of William "Henry"[6] Abney and Willie E. Kent.

Ida Jane Fortson, b.13 Jul 1875. She d.8 Aug 1946 at age 71 and was bur. Beulah Bapt. Ch. Cem., Boaz, Marshall Co., AL.
There were no known children of William "Henry"[6] Abney and Ida Jane Fortson.

290. David[6] Abney (Benjamin[5], Benjamin[4], Hezekiah[3], Elisha[2], Abner[1]), b.10 Jun 1861 AL. He m. Mariah King, daughter of Thomas Jefferson King and Caroline C. Johnson, on 13 Dec 1885. He d.7 Dec 1942 AL at age 81 and was bur. King's Chapel Cem., Marshall Co., AL.
    Mariah King, b.1865. She d.1900 and was bur. King's Chapel Cem., Gadsden, Marshall Co., AL.
Known child of David[6] Abney and Mariah King:
     630   i.   Vellie D.[7], b. 17 Nov 1887 AL; m. Herman Emil Vogel.

291. David "Dee"[6] Abney (Benjamin[5], Benjamin[4], Hezekiah[3], Elisha[2], Abner[1]), b.20 Apr 1874 AL. He m. Annie Critcher. He d.14 Apr 1908 at age 33 and was bur. Martling Community Cem., Martling, Marshall Co., AL.
    Annie Critcher, b.11 Feb 1870. She d.14 Dec 1948 at age 78 and was bur. Martling Community Cem., Martling, Marshall Co., AL.
Known child of David "Dee"[6] Abney and Annie Critcher:
     631   i.   James Holliway "Tiney"[7], b. 8 Aug 1905; m. Mary "Lillian" Simmons.

292. Eva L.[6] Abney (Benjamin[5], Benjamin[4], Hezekiah[3], Elisha[2], Abner[1]), b.19 Sep 1883 Marshall Co., AL. She m. John Richard Rooks on 15 Oct 1899 Marshall Co., AL. She and John Richard Rooks appeared on the censuses of 20 Jun 1900 and 30 Apr 1910 Marshall Co., AL. She d.20 Apr 1911 Marshall Co., AL, at age 27 and was bur. Martling Community Cem., Martling, Marshall Co., AL.
    John Richard Rooks, b.22 Mar 1876 GA. He appeared on the census of 14 Apr 1930 Winston Co., AL; d.4 Sep 1962 DeKalb Co., AL, age 86.
Known children of Eva L.[6] Abney and John Richard Rooks:
     632   i.   Mary "Lillian"[7], b. 10 Apr 1902 AL; m. James Mathew Huffstutler.
     633   ii. John Richard "Jack," b. 20 May 1904 Marshall Co., AL; m. Minnie Hilda "Nana" Bacon.
         iii. Otis Lamuel, b.23 Jul 1906. He m. Desser "Mae" (n.n.) in 1929. He and Desser "Mae" (n.n.) were liv. on 14 Apr 1930 with father, John Rooks, Winston Co., AL. He d.11 Jun 1979, age 72; bur. Sulligent City Cem., Sulligent, Lamar Co., AL.
                   Desser "Mae" (n.n.), b.22 Nov 1905. She d.25 Jul 1985 at age 79; bur. Sulligent City Cem., Sulligent.
         iv. Edney Forrest "Edd", b.17 Aug 1908 Marshall Co., AL. He m. Della Geneva Henson in 1937. He d.24 Nov 1939 Marshall Co., AL, at age 31 and was bur. New Friendship Cem., Union Grove, Marshall Co., AL.
                   Della Geneva Henson m. 4 times. , b.16 Feb 1922 Arab, Marshall Co., AL. She m2. Joseph A. Cama in 1969. She d. Independence Day, 4 Jul 2003 Crossville, DeKalb Co., AL, at age 81.
         v.   Lola, b.8 Aug 1910 AL. She m. Arlie Mason Courington. She d.2 Nov 1995 Jasper, Walker Co., AL, at age 85 and was bur. Bennett Cem., Thach, Walker Co., AL.
                   Arlie Mason Courington, b.23 Jun 1906. He d.20 Feb 1973 at age 66 and was bur. Bennett Cem., Thach.

293. Sarah Emily[6] Abney (Andrew[5], Benjamin[4], Hezekiah[3], Elisha[2], Abner[1]), b.22 Aug 1854 Calhoun Co., AL. She m. Francis "Marion" Reeves in 1877. She and Francis "Marion" Reeves appeared on the census of 24 Jun 1880 Marshall Co., AL. She d.20 Jul 1920 Upshur Co., TX, at age 65 and was bur. Morris Cem., Pritchett, Upshur Co., TX.
    Francis "Marion" Reeves, b.6 Apr 1857 Marshall Co., AL. He d.2 Jun 1942 Gilmer, Upshur Co., TX, at age 85; bur. Morris Cem., Pritchett.
Known children of Sarah Emily[6] Abney and Francis "Marion" Reeves:
     634   i.   Ezey Lee[7], b. 21 Dec 1878 AL; m. John Thomas "Tom" Pettit.
     635   ii. Dultsenia Catherine "Seaney," b. 21 Feb 1880 GA; m. William Thomas Foster.
         iii. Frank M., b.11 May 1882 AL. She d. 19 Jan 1959 Rusk, Cherokee Co., TX, at age 76 and was bur. Morris Cem., Pritchett.

    iv.   George William, b.2 May 1884 Fort Payne, DeKalb Co., AL. He m. Mellie Lavina Youngblood. He d.17 Oct 1964 San Diego, San Diego Co., CA, at age 80 and was bur. Glade Creek Cem., Gilmer, Upshur Co., TX.

         Mellie Lavina Youngblood, b.7 Jun 1891 GA. She d.17 May 1957 Marshall, Harrison Co., TX, at age 65 and was bur. Glade Creek Cem., Gilmer, Upshur Co., TX.

    v.   Lilburn Virgil, b.4 Sep 1887 AL. He m. Elizabeth "Lizzie" Craig. He d.14 May 1964 Gilmer, Upshur Co., TX, at age 76 and was bur. Morris Cem., Pritchett, Upshur Co., TX.

         Elizabeth "Lizzie" Craig, b.8 Mar 1894. She d.9 Mar 1974 at age 80 and was bur. Morris Cem., Pritchett.

294. Amanda Catherine "Mandy"[6] Abney (Andrew[5], Benjamin[4], Hezekiah[3], Elisha[2], Abner[1]), b.6 Sep 1855 GA. She m. William B. Sargent ca.1877. She and William B. Sargent appeared on the census of 12 Jun 1900 Titus Co., TX. She d.24 Nov 1916 at age 61 and was bur. Concord Cem., Omaha, Morris Co., TX.

     William B. Sargent, b.29 May 1855 Cherokee Co., GA. He d.12 Jan 1918 Titus Co., TX, at age 62 and was bur. Concord Cem., Omaha.

Known children of Amanda Catherine "Mandy"[6] Abney and William B. Sargent:

  636   i.   Mary "Erminta"[7], b. 30 Jan 1878 AL; m1. Thomas Sherman Bynum; m2. Cleo Carson Burton.

        ii.   James B.L., b.2 Sep 1881 AL. He d.13 Oct 1901 at age 20 and was bur. Concord Cem., Omaha, Morris Co., TX.

  637 iii.   Sarah Jane, b. 7 May 1884 AL; m1. Samuel Wesley Van Zandt; m2. Samuel Monroe Stevens; m3. Cleo Carson Burton.

  638 iv.   William Zillman, b. 27 May 1886 AL; m1. Mary Missouri Landrum; m2. Esta Mae (n.n.).

  639   v.   John Franklin, b. 9 Dec 1889 TX; m. Ocie Mae Lunsford.

  640 vi.   George Lee, b. 9 Feb 1892; m. Ollie May Moore.

  641 vii.   Albert Thadous, b. 10 Oct 1895 Morris Co., TX; m. Julia Elvia Hardin.

295. Drucilla Parker[6] Abney (Andrew[5], Benjamin[4], Hezekiah[3], Elisha[2], Abner[1]), b.15 Apr 1871 AL. She m. James M. Weemes ca.1894. She and James M. Weemes appeared on the census of 13 Jun 1900 Goodwin, St. Francis Co., AR.

     James M. Weemes, b.Apr 1872.

Known child of Drucilla Parker[6] Abney and James M. Weemes:

        i.   Ora E.[7], b.Apr 1896 TX.

296. Sarah Elizabeth[6] Abney (Hezekiah[5], Benjamin[4], Hezekiah[3], Elisha[2], Abner[1]), b. Christmas Day, 25 Dec 1857 Calhoun Co., AL. She m. Richard Thompson Ellison on 17 Mar 1876. She d.17 Apr 1890 at age 32 and was bur. Liberty Hill Cem., Acworth, Cobb Co., GA.

     Richard Thompson Ellison, b.7 Jul 1856 GA. He m2. Mattie Helen Lyle on 15 Nov 1890 Calhoun Co., AL. He d.19 Oct 1944 Birmingham, Jefferson Co., AL, at age 88 and was bur. Forest Hill Cem., Birmingham, Jefferson Co., AL.

Known children of Sarah Elizabeth[6] Abney and Richard Thompson Ellison:

  642   i.   Haze "Anna"[7], b. 4 May 1878 Acworth, Cobb Co., AR; m. John Franklin Pelfrey.

        ii.   Minnie Lee, b. est.1882 GA. She m. Edward Martin "Ed" Sprayberry. d.20 Apr 1945 Birmingham, Jefferson Co., AL.

           Edward Martin "Ed" Sprayberry, b.6 Nov 1890 GA. He d.8 Oct 1928 Columbus, Muscogee Co., GA, at age 37.

  643 iii.   Richard Lawrence, b. 20 Feb 1887 Cartersville, Bartow Co., GA; m. Alma May Newman.

        iv.   Vuron, b.Sep 1889 GA. He was liv. on 4 Jun 1900 with grandfather, Hezekiah Abney, Bartow Co., GA.

297. Hezekiah Van Buren "Bud"[6] Abney (Hezekiah[5], Benjamin[4], Hezekiah[3], Elisha[2], Abner[1]), b.23 May 1872 Cobb Co., GA. He m. Sarah S. "Sallie" Earwood ca.1894. He and Sarah S. "Sallie" Earwood appeared on the censuses of 13 Jun 1900 Bartow Co., GA; and 22 Jan 1920, 8 Apr 1930 and 18 Apr 1940 Jeter, Choctaw Co., OK. He d.11 Jul 1955 OK at age 83 and was bur. Goodland Cem., Choctaw Co., OK.

     Sarah S. "Sallie" Earwood, b.23 Mar 1877 Bartow Co., GA. She d.24 Aug 1968 OK at age 91 and was bur. Goodland Cem., Choctaw Co., OK.

Known children of Hezekiah Van Buren "Bud"[6] Abney and Sarah S. "Sallie" Earwood:

        i.   Edward L. "Eddie"[7], b.9 Nov 1895 Bartow Co., GA; d.15 Aug 1913 OK; bur. Roebuck Cem., Hugo, Choctaw Co., OK.

  644 ii.   DeWitt Talmage "Dee," b. 18 Nov 1897 Cartersville, Bartow Co., GA; m. Lela Mae Barnes.

  645 iii.   George Washington, b. 10 Jul 1899 Bartow Co., GA; m. Dovie Lee Kelly.

  646 iv.   William "Grady," b. 22 Sep 1901 GA; m. Ora Bell Barnes.

  647   v.   Paul Leonard, b. 4 Jan 1904 Choctaw Co., OK; m. Orpha Mae Pasley; m. Betty Jean Warren.

  648 vi.   Lucy "Irena," b. 3 Aug 1908 Marshall Co., AL; m. George Austin Merrick.

  649 vii.   Ephus Louis, b. 16 Sep 1910 AL; m. Minnie Delilah Swagger; m. Opal J. Tarrant.

        viii.   Earnest, b.16 Feb 1913 Choctaw Co., OK. He d.25 Aug 1975 at age 62; bur. Roebuck Cem., Hugo, Choctaw Co., OK.

        ix.   Emmett m. Lois A. Williams. He, b.27 May 1915 Choctaw Co., OK. He d.11 Dec 1989 OK at age 74 and was bur. Goodland Cem., Choctaw Co., OK.

           Lois A. Williams, b.1925. She d.1993 and was bur. Goodland Cem., Choctaw Co., OK.

        x.   Sallie Mae "Lois", b. ca.Sep 1918 Choctaw Co., OK.

  650 xi.   Hezekiah Karr, b. 29 Apr 1921; m. Agnes Johnson.

298. George Washington "Dodge"[6] Abney (Hezekiah[5], Benjamin[4], Hezekiah[3], Elisha[2], Abner[1]), b.17 Feb 1878 Cobb Co., GA. He m. Mary Fountain ca.1904. He d.14 Dec 1908 at age 30 and was bur. Liberty Hill Cem., Acworth, Cobb Co., GA.

     Mary Fountain, b.22 Apr 1880 GA. She appeared on the census of 5 May 1910 Bartow Co., GA. She appeared on the census of 9 Jan 1920 Bartow Co., GA. She d.21 Jun 1922 at age 42 and was bur. Liberty Hill Cem., Acworth, Cobb Co., GA.

Known children of George Washington "Dodge"[6] Abney and Mary Fountain all b. Floyd Co., GA:

  651   i.   Georgia Rosina[7], b. 12 Dec 1905; m. PFC Columbus Alexander Tidwell (USArmy-WWI).

        ii.   Clarence, b. Independence Day, 4 Jul 1907. He and Clifton Abney were liv. on 8 Apr 1930 boarders with Houwse family, Rome, Floyd Co., GA. He m1. Frances Armaretta Tillery. He m2. Rita (n.n.). He and Rita (n.n.) appeared on the census of 29 Apr 1940 Rome, Floyd Co., GA. He d.1 Apr 1961 at age 53 and was bur. East View Cem., Rome, Floyd Co., GA.

           Frances Armaretta Tillery, b.15 Sep 1921. She d.11 Feb 2004 at age 82; bur. East View Cem., Rome, Floyd Co., GA. Rita (n.n.), b. ca.1922 GA.

  652 iii.   Clifton, b. 2 Nov 1908; m. Beatrice Tatum.

299. George Washington[6] Abney Jr. (George[5], Benjamin[4], Hezekiah[3], Elisha[2], Abner[1]), b.Apr 1863 St. Clair Co., AL. He m. Lou "Ellen" Cheek on 22 Feb 1885 St. Clair Co., AL. He and Lou "Ellen" Cheek appeared on the censuses of 28 Jun 1900, 30 Apr 1910, 9 Jan 1920 and 4 Apr 1930 Jefferson Co., AL. He d.1934 and was bur. Friendship UMC Cem., Gardendale, Jefferson Co., AL.
     Lou "Ellen" Cheek, b.Mar 1868 Floyd Co., GA. She d.1923 and was bur. Friendship UMC Cem., Gardendale, Jefferson Co., AL.
Known children of George Washington[6] Abney Jr. and Lou "Ellen" Cheek all b. AL:
     653   i.   Samantha Jane "Janie"[7], b. 6 Aug 1887; m. William Henry Jarvis Sr.
     654   ii.   John W., b. 5 Oct 1889; m. Aslie M. (n.n.).
     655   iii. King David "Dave," b. 13 Sep 1892; m. Bessie Vita Sparks.
            iv.   Flora, b.Jun 1894.
            v.   Grace "Gracie", b. Aug 1899. She m. Charlie F. Long. She d.18 Oct 1918 Jefferson Co., AL, at age 19 and was bur. Friendship UMC Cem., Gardendale, Jefferson Co., AL.
                       Charlie F. Long, b.22 Jun 1893. He m2. Nettie M. (n.n.). He d.17 Nov 1975 at age 82 and was bur. Bivens Chapel Cem., Brookside, Jefferson Co., AL.
     656   vi.   Daisy, b. 7 Jun 1904; m. Fred Cleveland Fuller.
     657   vii. Elbert "Arnold," b. 1908; m. Linnie (n.n.).

300. John F.[6] Abney (George[5], Benjamin[4], Hezekiah[3], Elisha[2], Abner[1]), b.1869 St. Clair Co., AL. He m. Sarah Ann Fortenberry on 23 Jan 1889 home of G.W. Abney, Blount Co., AL. He and Sarah Ann Fortenberry appeared on the censuses of 12 Jun 1900 McLennan Co., TX; 16 Apr 1910 Jones Co., TX; and 19 Feb 1920 Dallas Co., TX and 17 Apr 1930 Dallas Co., TX. He d.1938 and was bur. McCree Cem., Dallas, Dallas Co., TX.
     Sarah Ann Fortenberry, b.Sep 1869 AL; liv. on 9 Apr 1940 with daughter, Virgie Young, Dallas, TX. She d.1942 TX; bur. McCree Cem.
Known children of John F.[6] Abney and Sarah Ann Fortenberry:
     658   i.   Homer Garton[7], b. 18 Sep 1890 AL; m. Lela Mae Gault.
     659   ii.   Mattie Bell, b. Jul 1893; m. Frank Alexander DeMoss.
     660   iii. Vergia Mae "Vergie," b. 4 Aug 1896 Dallas Co., TX; m. Benjamin Franklin "Frank" Young Sr.
            iv.   John A, b.2 Nov 1898 TX. He d.19 Oct 1903 at age 4 and was bur. McCree Cem., Dallas, Dallas Co., TX.
            v.   Janie Myerl, b.20 Dec 1901 TX. She d.15 Oct 1905 at age 3 and was bur. McCree Cem., Dallas, Dallas Co., TX.
            vi.   Albert Columbus, b.14 Mar 1904 TX. He d.10 Oct 1972 Garland, Dallas Co., TX, at age 68 and was bur. McCree Cem.
     661   vii. Opal Augusta, b. 30 Jun 1906; m. Fred Gus Bryant.
     662   viii. Mina Faye, b. 5 Oct 1913 TX; m. Howard Ernest Carrigan.

301. William Callaway[6] Abney (George[5], Benjamin[4], Hezekiah[3], Elisha[2], Abner[1]), b.25 Nov 1870 St. Clair Co., AL; m. Sarah Ann "Annie" Kelsoe on 6 Jul 1890 Blount Co., AL. He and Sarah Ann "Annie" Kelsoe appeared on the censuses of 12 Jun 1900, 20 Apr 1910 and 30 Jan 1920 McLennan Co., TX; and 10 Apr 1930 and 2 Apr 1940 Dallas Co., TX. He d.14 Jun 1956 McGregor, McLennan Co., TX, at age 85.
     Sarah Ann "Annie" Kelsoe, b.16 Jan 1871 Marshall Co., AL. She d.22 Sep 1968 Dallas, Dallas Co., TX, at age 97 and was bur. Crawford Cem., Crawford, McLennan Co., TX.
Known children of William Callaway[6] Abney and Sarah Ann "Annie" Kelsoe:
     663   i.   William Houston "Will"[7], b. 13 Nov 1891 AL; m. Elizabeth "Lizzie" Payne.
            ii.   Julius B., b.2 May 1894 Birmingham, Jefferson Co., AL; d.30 Oct 1925 McLennan Co., TX, age 31; bur. Crawford Cem.
            iii. (Infant Son), b.30 Nov 1896 McLennan Co., TX. He d.30 Nov 1896 McLennan Co., TX and was bur. Crawford Cem.
     664   iv.   John "Philip," b. 29 Oct 1898 Crawford, McLennan Co., TX; m. Mable Clara McAdams.
            v.   (infant son), b.13 Apr 1901 TX. He d.27 Apr 1901 McLennan Co., TX and was bur. Crawford Cem.
     665   vi.   Rosa E., b. 18 Jan 1903 TX; m. George William "Guy" Griffith.
            vii. (infant dau.), b.14 Jul 1905 TX. She d.23 Jul 1905 TX and was bur. Crawford Cem.
     666   viii. Ann May "Annie," b. ca.1907 TX; m. James "Owen" Brashear.
     667   ix.   Mammie "Alyce," b. ca.Oct 1909 TX; m. Truman Phifer.
            x.   Lourea, b. ca.1914 TX. She m. Ernest Kelly.
            xi.   Robert L., b.26 Jul 1916 McLennan Co., TX. He d.14 Feb 1973 Weatherford, Parker Co., TX, age 56; bur. Crawford Cem.
            xii. Emily "Maria" m. Odeil Lindop. , b. ca.Dec 1919 TX.

302. Alex Franklin "Frank"[6] Abney (George[5], Benjamin[4], Hezekiah[3], Elisha[2], Abner[1]), b.1872 St. Clair Co., AL. He m1. Nancy Ava "Avie" Sullivan on 15 May 1892 Cullman Co., AL. He and Nancy Ava "Avie" Sullivan appeared on the censuses of 3 Jan 1920 Jefferson Co., AL and 8 Apr 1930 Sayreton, Jefferson Co., AL. He m2. Mattie Milstead on 18 May 1935 Jefferson Co., AL. He d.9 Aug 1939 Jefferson Co., AL and was bur. Friendship UMC Cem., Gardendale, Jefferson Co., AL.
     Nancy Ava "Avie" Sullivan, b.1872. She d.7 May 1932 Sayreton, Jefferson Co., AL and was bur. Friendship UMC Cem., Gardendale
Known children of Alex Franklin "Frank"[6] Abney and Nancy Ava "Avie" Sullivan:
     668   i.   Ludie Mae[7], b. 1893; m. Frank O. "Foree" Myers; m. Robert "Frank" Clowdus; div. Robert "Frank" Clowdus.
     669   ii.   Gordon W., b. 29 Apr 1895 AL; m. Geneva M. (n.n.).
     670   iii. James William "Will," b. 8 Mar 1898 AL; m. Agnes Cox.
     671   iv.   Jesse Clinton "Clint," b. 7 Nov 1902 AL; m. Willine Wright.
     672   v.   Albert Franklin, b. 12 Oct 1905 AL; m. Clara Bell Lamons.
     673   vi.   John David, b. 14 Jan 1907 AL; m. May Belle Peffer.
     674   vii. Horace Junior "June," b. 8 Jun 1910 AL; m. Stella Mae Roberts.
     675   viii. Edith M, b. 27 Mar 1918 AL; m. Joseph Peter Giamportone (USN-WWII).

There were no known children of Alex Franklin "Frank"[6] Abney and Mattie Milstead.

303. Marion "Thomas"[6] Abney (George[5], Benjamin[4], Hezekiah[3], Elisha[2], Abner[1]), b.6 Feb 1874 St. Clair Co., AL. He m. Ophelia Barron on Christmas Eve, 24 Dec 1895 Jefferson Co., AL. He and Ophelia Barron appeared on the census of 8 Jun 1900 Jefferson Co., AL. He d.1 Oct 1910 at age 36 and was bur. Friendship UMC Cem., Gardendale, Jefferson Co., AL.
     Ophelia Barron, b.27 Jul 1877 AL. She d.13 Dec 1921 at age 44 and was bur. Friendship UMC Cem., Gardendale, Jefferson Co., AL.

Known children of Marion "Thomas"[6] Abney and Ophelia Barron:
    676   i.   Isa Belle "Icie"[7], b. 13 Oct 1896 AL; m. R.H. Myers; m. Charles Curtis Clowdus.
           ii.   Mary S., b.Mar 1900 AL.
           iii. Thomas Charles "Charlie", b. ca.1902; liv. on 9 Jan 1920 with uncle, George Abney, Jefferson Co., AL. He d.14 Jul 1955.
           iv. William "Belton", b.27 Jan 1908 AL; liv. on 9 Apr 1930 as a boarder with the Sanders family, Sayreton, Jefferson Co., AL. He m1. Hazel L. Wood in 1950. He m2. Hazel Loraine Jones on 7 Jan 1950 Jefferson Co., AL. He d.27 Jan 1982 at age 74 and was bur. Midway United Methodist Cem., Adamsville, Jefferson Co., AL.
                  Hazel L. Wood, b.21 Jun 1910 AL. She d.8 Mar 1994 AL at age 83 and was bur. Midway United Methodist Cem.
                  Hazel Loraine Jones, b. ca.1911.

304. Peter Columbus "Pete"[6] Abney (George[5], Benjamin[4], Hezekiah[3], Elisha[2], Abner[1]), b.18 Jan 1878 St. Clair Co., AL. He m. Alice Miranda Billingsley ca.1899. He and Alice Miranda Billingsley appeared on the censuses of 28 Jun 1900 St. Clair Co., AL; of 30 Apr 1910 Jefferson Co., AL; 22 Jan 1920 Coalburg, Jefferson Co., AL; 22 Apr 1930 Fairmont, Jefferson Co., AL; and 24 Apr 1940 Sayreton, Jefferson Co., AL. He d.1 Apr 1954 at age 76 and was bur. Friendship UMC Cem., Gardendale, Jefferson Co., AL.
    Alice Miranda Billingsley, b.8 Aug 1879 AL. She d.9 Sep 1947 at age 68 and was bur. Friendship UMC Cem., Gardendale, Jefferson Co., AL.
Known children of Peter Columbus "Pete"[6] Abney and Alice Miranda Billingsley:
    677   i.   George Washington[7], b. 4 Aug 1901 AL; m. Vera Hodges.
    678   ii. Julius "Vernie," b. 13 Feb 1904 AL; m. Nancy Lula Brown.
           iii. William " Clarence", b.16 Sep 1905. He d.14 Oct 1963 at age 58 and was bur. Friendship UMC Cem., Gardendale.
    679   iv. Elsie Ruby, b. 8 Apr 1908; m. Raymond Daniel Rockett Sr.
    680   v.   Hubert, b. 16 Jun 1910 AL; m. Gillian R. (n.n.).
    681   vi. Lillie Mae, b. 9 Jul 1913; m. Franklin "Floyd" Green.
           vii. (infant son), b. ca.1915 AL. He d. ca.1915 AL.

305. James Madison "Jim"[6] Abney (George[5], Benjamin[4], Hezekiah[3], Elisha[2], Abner[1]), b.14 Jan 1880 St. Clair Co., AL. He m. Nettie Nancy Brooks ca.1913. He and Nettie Nancy Brooks appeared on the censuses of 21 Jan 1920 and 25 Apr 1930 Coalburg, Jefferson Co., AL; and 23 Apr 1940 Mineral Springs, Jefferson Co., AL. He d.13 Jul 1955 at age 75 and was bur. Friendship UMC Cem., Gardendale, Jefferson Co., AL.
Known children of James Madison "Jim"[6] Abney and Nettie Nancy Brooks:
    682   i.   Elizabeth Jane "Lizzie"[7], b. 10 Mar 1914 AL; m. William Harry Madden.
    683   ii. Roy, b. 13 Aug 1915 AL; m. Magdalene Gibson.
    684   iii. Raymond Jackson, b. 13 Sep 1917 AL; m. Dorothy E. Little.
           iv. Van "Buren", b.15 Aug 1920. He d.26 Jan 1976 at age 55; bur. Friendship UMC Cem., Gardendale, Jefferson Co., AL.
           v.   William Rowland "Bill", b.7 Mar 1922; m. Pauline Estelle Tyler. He d.28 May 1954, age 32; bur. Friendship UMC Cem.
                  Pauline Estelle Tyler, b.23 Aug 1916. She d.10 Dec 2009 at age 93 and was bur. West Jeff. Freewill Bapt. Ch. Cem., West Jefferson, Jefferson Co., AL.
    685   vi. Emma Estelle, b. 2 Oct 1924; m. Edwin Grey Tate.
           vii. Doris Evelyn m. James E. Jones. , b.12 Sep 1926. She d.4 Apr 2011 at age 84 and was bur. Phillips Chapel Cem., Tuscaloosa Co., AL.
                  James E. Jones, b.28 Nov 1922. He d.25 Mar 2013 at age 90 and was bur. Phillips Chapel Cem., Tuscaloosa Co., AL.
    686 viii. Thomas Floyd "Tom," b. 14 Jul 1928 AL; m. Mary Ann "Doll" Arbuckle.
           ix. Martha "Pearl" m. (n.n.) Herring. , b.2 Aug 1933. She d.9 Feb 1995 at age 61 and was bur. Friendship UMC Cem.

306. Isa Jane "Icie"[6] Abney (George[5], Benjamin[4], Hezekiah[3], Elisha[2], Abner[1]), b.14 Feb 1881 AL. She m. Rev. William D. Stewart on 27 Nov 1898. She and Rev. William D. Stewart appeared on the censuses of 2 Jul 1900 Marcumville, Tuscaloosa Co., AL; and 7 Jan 1920 and 10 Apr 1930 Jefferson Co., AL. She d.15 Jan 1956 at age 74 and was bur. Cahaba Heights UMC Cem., Cahaba Heights, Jefferson Co., AL.
    Rev. William D. Stewart, b.11 May 1859 AL. He m. Martha Patmon ca.1880. He d.20 Dec 1930 at age 71; bur. Cahaba Heights UMC Cem.
Known children of Isa Jane "Icie"[6] Abney and Rev. William D. Stewart both b. AL:
           i.   Jewel[7], b. ca.1905.
           ii. Ruby W., b. ca.1907.

307. Henry C.[6] Abney (William[5], Benjamin[4], Hezekiah[3], Elisha[2], Abner[1]), b. Jun 1868 AL. He m. Ellen C. "Ella" Vaughn on 30 Aug 1888. He and Ellen C. "Ella" Vaughn appeared on the censuses of 19 Jun 1900 and 25 Apr 1910 Wedowee, Randolph Co., AL.
    Ellen C. "Ella" Vaughn, b.Nov 1869 SC. She appeared as Head of Household on the census of 30 Jan 1920 Randolph Co., AL. She was liv. on 23 Apr 1940 with son, James Abney, Lawrence Co., TN.
Known children of Henry C.[6] Abney and Ellen C. "Ella" Vaughn:
           i.   John F.[7], b.Jul 1889 AL.
           ii. George W., b.May 1891 AL. He appeared on the census of 1900 Randolph Co., AL.
           iii. (n.n.), b. ca.1893; d. before 1900.
           iv. Martha M., b.Jun 1895 AL. She appeared on the census of 1900 Randolph Co., AL.
           v.   James F. "Jim" m. Homa (n.n.). He, b.Jul 1897 AL. He and Homa (n.n.) appeared on the census of 23 Apr 1940 Lawrence Co., TN. He d.1962. [Homa (n.n.), b. ca.1905 AL.]
           vi. (n.n.), b. ca.1899. He/she d. before 1900.
    687   vii. Luther E., b. ca.1901 AL; m. Vanna "Estelle" Kilpatrick.
    688 viii. Emma Lee, b. 3 Dec 1903 AL; m. Albert Madison Story.

308. Mary C.[6] Abney (William[5], Benjamin[4], Hezekiah[3], Elisha[2], Abner[1]), b.30 Jan 1873 AL. She m. Robert E. Abney, son of Wilburn Callaway "Cal" Abney and Martha E. "Jane" Hogan, ca.1884. She and Robert E. Abney appeared on the censuses of 11 Jun 1900 Tallapoosa, Haralson Co., GA; and 2 May 1910 and 9 Jan 1920 Buchanan, Haralson Co., GA. She d.9 Mar 1924 Buchanan, Haralson Co., GA, at age 51 and was bur. Buchanan City Cem., Buchanan, Haralson Co., GA.

Robert E. Abney, b.13 Aug 1871 GA. He m2. Vastie C. "Vassie" Wells on 18 Apr 1926 Haralson Co., GA. He and Vastie C. "Vassie" Wells appeared on the censuses of 18 Apr 1930 Polk Co., GA and 29 Apr 1940 Buchanan, Haralson Co., GA. He d.17 Jul 1948 at age 76 and was bur. Buchanan City Cem., Buchanan, Haralson Co., GA.
Known children of Mary C.⁶ Abney and Robert E. Abney:

        i.   Lillie Mae⁷, b. 18 May 1896 Paulding Co., GA; m. Henry Charles Pope; m. (n.n.) Camp. (see # 602, page 154
       ii.   Martha, b. Feb 1898 GA. (see page 98).
      iii. Minnie L, b. 22 May 1902 Buchanan, Haralson Co., GA; m. Harvey Jackson "Jack" Perry Sr. (see # 603, pages 154-155)
      iv. Dora, b. 1907 GA. (see page 98).
       v.   Robert, b. 1910 GA. (see page 98).
      vi. Marvin "Doc," b. 12 Oct 1913 GA; m. Lucille Elizabeth Williams. (see # 604, page 155)
     vii. Datha, b. ca.Oct 1916 GA. (see page 98).

309. William Talton⁶ Abney (William⁵, Benjamin⁴, Hezekiah³, Elisha², Abner¹), b.3 May 1876 AL. He m. Narcissus Shipp ca.1897. He and Narcissus Shipp appeared on the censuses of 5 Jun 1900 Tallapoosa, Haralson Co., AL; and 6 Jan 1920 and 2 Apr 1930 Red Rock, Cobb Co., GA. He d.16 Jun 1938 at age 62 and was bur. County Line Cem., Acworth Beach, Cobb Co., GA.
    Narcissus Shipp, b.30 Mar 1874. She d.22 Jun 1932 at age 58 and was bur. County Line Cem., Acworth Beach, Cobb Co., GA.
Known children of William Talton⁶ Abney and Narcissus Shipp:

        i.   John W. (USMC)⁷, b.16 Jan 1898 GA. He m. Oneita (n.n.). He appeared on the census of 15 Mar 1920 Marine Barracks Fort Ozama, Santo Domingo, Dominican Republic. He and Oneita (n.n.) appeared on the census of 13 Apr 1940 Cass, Dubois Co., IN. He d.2 Feb 1971 at age 73 and was bur. County Line Cem., Acworth Beach, Cobb Co., GA.
             Oneita (n.n.), b.25 Feb 1896 Cuba. She was liv. on 6 Jan 1920 with father-in-law, William T. Abney, Red Rock, Cobb Co., GA. She d.12 Aug 1979 at age 83.
       ii.   Elmer, b.7 Jun 1899 GA. He d.7 Sep 1899 GA and was bur. Antioch Cem., Paulding Co., GA.
      iii. Dewey M., b.14 Mar 1901 GA. He d.19 Apr 1901 GA and was bur. Antioch Cem., Paulding Co., GA.
      iv. Virgil Lee, b.16 Apr 1903 Dallas, Paulding Co., GA. He m. Hattie Slaton in 1938. He and Hattie Slaton appeared on the census of 10 May 1940 Floyd Co., GA. He d.19 Apr 1958 Rome, Floyd Co., GA, at age 55 and was bur. Myrtle Hill Cem., Rome, Floyd Co., GA.
             Hattie Slaton, b.3 Dec 1884 Whitfield Co., GA. She d.30 Dec 1965 Rome, Floyd Co., GA, at age 81.
689   v.   Zora "Bell," b. 16 Feb 1904 GA; m. Pink W. Turley Sr.
690   vi. Elizabeth Ovelle "Lizzie," b. 19 Jan 1908 GA; m. Paul R. Colbert.
691 vii. Paul Revere, b. 19 Dec 1910 GA; m. Bessie "Granny" Adair.
     viii. Idell, b.19 Apr 1914 GA. She m. James H. "Jack" Parker. She d.5 Jun 1986 at age 72 and was bur. New Hope Cem., Dallas, Paulding Co., GA.
             James H. "Jack" Parker, b.23 Oct 1907. He d.17 Jan 1992 at age 84 and was bur. New Hope Cem.
      ix. Emma Lee, b.1916. She m. (n.n.) Turpin. She d.1984; bur. Forest Lawn Mem. Cem., Anderson, Anderson Co., SC.
692   x.   Joe Wheeler, b. 11 Nov 1917 Cobb Co., GA; m. Sophiann Anntoinette Stagliano.

310. Leticia Cathren⁶ Abney (Eli⁵, Benjamin⁴, Hezekiah³, Elisha², Abner¹), b.29 Dec 1875 Oak Level, Cleburne Co., AL. She m. William Aaron Lorren ca.1893. She and William Aaron Lorren appeared on the censuses of 5 May 1910 Cleburne Co., AL; 13 Jan 1920 Calhoun Co., AL; and 18 Apr 1930 Borden Springs, Cleburne Co., AL. She d.28 Apr 1956, age 80 and was bur. Church of Christ Cem., Borden Springs, Cleburne Co., AL.
    William Aaron Lorren, b.1 Sep 1870. He appeared on the census of 9 Apr 1940 Borden Springs, Cleburne Co., AL. He d.22 Apr 1947 at age 76 and was bur. Church of Christ Cem., Borden Springs, Cleburne Co., AL.
Known children of Leticia Cathren⁶ Abney and William Aaron Lorren:

693   i.   Emil "Newton"⁷, b. 2 Nov 1894 AL; m. Ruby Florence Warmack.
694   ii.   John Luther, b. 6 Jul 1896 Cleburne Co., AL; m. Mary Anna "May" Gilley.
      iii. W.B.L., b.21 Jun 1898 Cleburne Co., AL. He d.21 Jun 1898 and was bur. Church of Christ Cem., Borden Springs, AL.
      iv. Ora A., b.27 Oct 1899 Cleburne, AL. She d.5 Feb 1921 Cleburne, AL, at age 21.
       v.   William I, b.14 Aug 1901 Cleburne, AL. He d.15 May 1935 Anniston, Calhoun Co., AL, at age 33.
695   vi. Theresa B. "Lizzie," b. 19 Jul 1904 Cleburne, AL; m. Robert C. Dyer.
696 vii. Agee Virgil, b. ca.1906 Cleburne, AL; m. Alma M. (n.n.).
697 viii. Pearl Lena, b. 16 Apr 1908 Cleburne Co., AL; m. Floyd William Baswell.
698   ix. Jessie Carrmon, b. 14 Jul 1910 Cleburne, AL; m. Annette (n.n.).
       x.   Woodrow, b. ca.1913 Calhoun Co., AL. He m. Frances (n.n.). He and Frances (n.n.) appeared on the census of 5 Apr 1940 Calhoun, Gordon Co., AL. He d.2008. (Frances was b. ca. 1917 AL)
      xi. Shellie Lou "Tishie", b.8 Apr 1915 Cleburne Co., AL; m. Tellus Lee Hamby. She and Tellus Lee Hamby (b.NC) appeared on the census of 8 Apr 1940 Borden Springs, Cleburne Co., AL. She d.16 Nov 1994 Piedmont, Calhoun Co., AL, age 79.

311. Eli Franklin⁶ Abney (Eli⁵, Benjamin⁴, Hezekiah³, Elisha², Abner¹), b.26 Nov 1876 Oak Level, Cleburne Co., AL. He m. Anna "Leanna" Potts ca.1899. He and Anna "Leanna" Potts appeared on the censuses of 2 Jun 1900, 27 Apr 1910 and 10 Jan 1920 Cleburne Co., AL; 19 Apr 1930 Friendship, Marshall Co., AL and 10 Apr 1940 DeKalb Co., AL. He d.25 Feb 1965 Gadsden, Etowah Co., AL, at age 88.
    Anna "Leanna" Potts, b. Jul 1879 GA.
Known children of Eli Franklin⁶ Abney and Anna "Leanna" Potts all b. AL:

699   i.   John "Wesley"⁷, b. 28 Feb 1900; m. Myrtle Lucille Roberts.
       ii.   Ruth "Ruthie", b. ca.1902.
      iii. Myrtle "Myrtie", b. ca.1904.
      iv. Benjamin Franklin "Frank", b.19 Feb 1906. He d.31 Jul 1931, age 25; bur. Camp Creek Bapt. Ch. Cem., Oak Level, AL.
       v.   Pearl, b. ca.Jul 1909.
      vi. Minnie, b. ca.Aug 1916.
     vii. J.T., b. ca.1921.
    viii. William "Carl", b. ca.1924.

312. Posey Osiciro[6] Abney (Eli[5], Benjamin[4], Hezekiah[3], Elisha[2], Abner[1]), b.18 Jun 1878 Oak Level, Cleburne Co., AL. He was liv. on 16 Jun 1900 with 1st cousin, Marion M. Abney, Lake Creek, Polk Co., GA. He m. Rosie P. Waites ca.1901. He and Rosie appeared on the censuses of 30 Apr 1910 and 6 Jan 1920 Oak Level, Cleburne Co., AL. He d.30 Nov 1923, age 45; bur. Camp Creek Bapt. Ch. Cem., Oak Level, Cleburne Co., AL.
    Rosie P. Waites, b. ca.1883 AL. She d.1920 Borden Springs, Cleburne Co., AL.
Known children of Posey Osiciro[6] Abney and Rosie P. Waites all b. AL:
    700   i.   William McKinley "Mac"[7], b. 16 Sep 1902; m. Ruby Mae Smith.
           ii.   Winnie J., b. ca.1908.
    701   iii.   Jessie "Pauline," b. 23 Mar 1917; m. Lamar Brock Overstreet.

313. Rosa Lee[6] Abney (Eli[5], Benjamin[4], Hezekiah[3], Elisha[2], Abner[1]), b.14 Mar 1883 AL. She m. Isaac C. Crawford on 13 Jan 1901 Oak Level, Cleburne Co., AL. She d.13 Jul 1964 at age 81.
    Isaac C. Crawford, b.19 May 1878 AL. He d.21 May 1952 Cullman Co., AL, at age 74.
Known children of Rosa Lee[6] Abney and Isaac C. Crawford:
    702   i.   Martin Luther[7], b. 1902; m. Dallie Harris.
           ii.   Henry M., b.1903. He d.1933.
           iii.   Elmer Leonard, b.1904. He d.1972.
           iv.   William G., b.1911.
           v.   Roy L., b.1914.
           vi.   Louis A., b.1917.

314. Sarah Elizabeth[6] Abney (Eli[5], Benjamin[4], Hezekiah[3], Elisha[2], Abner[1]) m. Walter Pickens McWhorter. , b.10 Mar 1887 AL. She d. New Year's Day, 1 Jan 1962 at age 74 and was bur. Heflin Cem., Heflin, Cleburne Co., AL.
    Walter Pickens McWhorter, b.12 Nov 1882. He was arrested for moonshining on 21 Aug 1926 Oak Level, Cleburne Co., AL. He d.23 Jun 1970 Heflin, Cleburne Co., AL, at age 87 and was bur. Heflin Cem., Heflin, Cleburne Co., AL.
Known children of Sarah Elizabeth[6] Abney and Walter Pickens McWhorter:
    703   i.   Jessie P.[7], b. 24 Oct 1909; m. Mary Lee Champion.
    704   ii.   Grace N., b. 16 Oct 1913; m. Thomas C. Cochran.
           iii.   Alex N., b.16 May 1915 AL; m. Sydna S. (n.n.); d.14 Mar 1980, ae.64; bur. Hillcrest Cem., West Blocton, Bibb Co., AL.
                  Sydna S. (n.n.), b.21 Mar 1921. She d.15 Aug 2002 at age 81; bur. Hillcrest Cem., West Blocton, Bibb Co., AL.
    705   iv.   Johnnie, b. 12 Aug 1918; m. PFC Willie C. Flemons (USArmy-WWII); m. Calvin Edmund Hanks.
           v.   Lorraine, b.15 Feb 1923 Heflin, Cleburne Co., AL. She m. Clement Leroy Leiter (USArmy-WWII, Korea) in 1955. She d.20 Jul 2011 Joplin, Jasper Co., MO, at age 88 and was bur. Ozark Mem. Park Cem., Joplin, Jasper Co., MO.
                  Clement Leroy Leiter (USArmy-WWII, Korea), b.7 Feb 1920. He m1. Jessie Mary Kennedy in 1940. He d.15 Sep 2000 at age 80 and was bur. Ozark Mem. Park Cem., Joplin, Jasper Co., MO.

315. Pvt. John Andrew "Andy"[6] Abney (USArmy-WWI) (Eli[5], Benjamin[4], Hezekiah[3], Elisha[2], Abner[1]), b.13 May 1889 Cleburne Co., AL. He appeared on the census of 3 Jan 1920 Oak Level, Cleburne Co., AL. He m. Berta Ruth "Bert" Farmer ca.1920. He and Berta Ruth "Bert" Farmer appeared on the censuses of 3 Apr 1930 Fairview, Cullman Co., AL; and 28 Apr 1940 Simcoe, Cullman Co., AL. He d.13 Jan 1961 Cullman, Cullman Co., AL, at age 71 and was bur. Simcoe United Methodist Cem., Simcoe, Cullman Co., AL.
    Berta Ruth "Bert" Farmer, b.10 May 1902 GA. She d.5 May 1976 Cullman, Cullman Co., AL, at age 73.
Known children of Pvt. John Andrew "Andy"[6] Abney (USArmy-WWI) and Berta Ruth "Bert" Farmer:
    706   i.   Ruby Lee[7], b. 15 Nov 1920 Carroll Co., GA; m. Sgt. Arthur "Austin" Payne (USN-WWII).
    707   ii.   Carl Horace, b. 2 Apr 1923 Cullman, Cullman Co., AL; m. Nellie Znobia Frost; m. Margie Sue Caldwell.
    708   iii.   Mazelle, b. 27 Jul 1925 AL; m. Rev. Pless "Ivon" Echols (USArmy-WWII).
    709   iv.   Bobbie Dean, b. 3 Jul 1930; m. Cecil "Ray" Adams.
    710   v.   James Edward "Jim," b. 5 Aug 1933 AL; m. Arnita Oaks.

316. Benjamin Earl "Ben"[6] Abney (Eli[5], Benjamin[4], Hezekiah[3], Elisha[2], Abner[1]), b.3 Mar 1891 AL. He m. Winnie Ellen Little on 10 Dec 1916 Cleburne Co., AL. He and Winnie Ellen Little were liv. on 3 Jan 1920 with his brother, John Abney, Oak Level, Cleburne Co., AL. He and Winnie Ellen Little appeared on the census of 5 Apr 1930 Albertville, Marshall Co., AL. He d.4 Nov 1960 at age 69 and was bur. Simcoe United Methodist Cem., Simcoe, Cullman Co., AL.
    Winnie Ellen Little, b.29 Aug 1897. She d.8 Jan 1985 at age 87 and was bur. Simcoe United Methodist Cem., Simcoe, Cullman Co., AL.
Known children of Benjamin Earl "Ben"[6] Abney and Winnie Ellen Little:
           i.   Homer "Bill"[7] m. Geneva (n.n.). He, b.22 May 1920 GA. He d.9 May 1987 at age 66 and was bur. Crestwood Mem. Cem., East Gadsden, Etowah Co., AL.
                  Geneva (n.n.), b.1925. She d.1978 and was bur. Crestwood Mem. Cem., East Gadsden, Etowah Co., AL.
           ii.   Annie M., b. ca.1922 GA.
           iii.   Andy Edward, b.15 Jan 1924 Cleburne Co., AL. He d.15 Jan 1924 Cleburne Co., AL.
           iv.   Louise "Lemma", b.16 Jun 1925 AL. She d.27 Oct 2003 at age 78 and was bur. Bourland Cem., Keller, Tarrant Co., TX.
           v.   Armenda, b. ca.1927 AL.
           vi.   Fred Henry, b.10 Jul 1930. He d.9 Nov 1951 auto accident near Trussville, Jefferson Co., AL, at age 21 and was bur. Simcoe United Methodist Cem., Simcoe, Cullman Co., AL.

317. Martha Elizabeth[6] Abney (James[5], Benjamin[4], Hezekiah[3], Elisha[2], Abner[1]), b.3 Nov 1869 Cleburne Co., AL. She m. James Samuel Burkhalter ca.1893. She d.29 May 1958 Cedartown, Polk Co., GA, at age 88 and was bur. Pleasant Hope Cem., Rome, Floyd Co., GA.
    James Samuel Burkhalter, b.4 Mar 1866 and was bur. Pleasant Hope Cem., Rome, Floyd Co., GA. He d.21 Feb 1949 at age 82.
Known children of Martha Elizabeth[6] Abney and James Samuel Burkhalter:
           i.   Bennie C.[7], b.27 Jun 1894 Floyd Co., GA. He d.29 Aug 1894 Floyd Co., GA; bur. New Bethel Cem., Floyd Co., GA.
    711   ii.   Adele, b. 17 Aug 1895; m. Walter J. Garrard.
    712   iii.   James Othel, b. 26 Jul 1897; m. Elsie Hollis.

iv.   Roy Freemon, b.9 May 1901 GA; m. Helen West; d.12 Sep 1933, ae.32; bur. Pleasant Hope Cem., Rome, Floyd Co., GA.
      Helen West, b.21 Feb 1909 Polk Co., GA. She d.24 Sep 1989 GA at age 80 and was bur. Pleasant Hope Cem., Rome.
v.   Willard, b.15 Sep 1903 GA. He d.14 Jun 1919 GA at age 15 and was bur. Pleasant Hope Cem., Rome, Floyd Co., GA.
713   vi. Early Prentice, b. 14 Sep 1908 GA; m. Mary Evelyn Wilkerson.
714   vii. Mary Jane, b. 3 Oct 1911 Cedartown, Polk Co., GA; m. Edward Bennie Weaver Sr.

318. Marion Matthew[6] Abney (James[5], Benjamin[4], Hezekiah[3], Elisha[2], Abner[1]), b.29 Apr 1871 Calhoun Co., AL. He m. Sarah "Alice" Morris ca.1891. He and Sarah "Alice" Morris appeared on the censuses of 16 Jun 1900; 19 Apr 1910 and 20 Jan 1920 Floyd Co., GA; and 3 Apr 1930 and 2 Apr 1940 Lindale, Floyd Co., GA. He d.11 Feb 1963 at age 91 and was bur. Pleasant Hope Cem., Rome, Floyd Co., GA.
      Sarah "Alice" Morris, b.18 Dec 1873. She d.1 Dec 1950 at age 76 and was bur. Pleasant Hope Cem., Rome, Floyd Co., GA.
Known children of Marion Matthew[6] Abney and Sarah "Alice" Morris:
715   i.   James "Everett"[7], b. 25 Jul 1892 Floyd Co., GA; m. Bessie Jewell Chafin.
      ii.   Mamie L., b.30 Mar 1894 Floyd Co., GA. She m. Thomas Luther Beard. She d.22 Jun 1977 Rome, Floyd Co., GA, at age 83 and was bur. Pleasant Hope Cem., Rome, Floyd Co., GA.
            Thomas Luther Beard, b.16 Jul 1889 Floyd Co., GA; m1. Mollie B. (n.n.); d.9 Mar 1967 Rome, Floyd Co., GA.
716   iii. Henry "Curtis," b. 22 Jan 1896; m. Connie Mae Compton.
      iv.   Mary "Mollie", b.Mar 1898 GA.
717   v.   William "Bryant," b. 25 Apr 1900 AL; m. Julia "Alice" Mathis.
      vi.   Maude, b.20 Dec 1902 Polk Co., GA. She d.8 Nov 1924 Lindale, Floyd Co., GA, at age 21; bur. Pleasant Hope Cem.
718   vii. Myrtle Beatrice, b. 6 Jun 1906; m. Nolan Smith.
719   viii. Gordon Lee "Joe," b. 10 Jul 1908 Floyd Co., GA; m. Lucile Carney.
      ix.   Grady, b.6 Dec 1910 GA. He m. Maudell Smith. He and Maudell Smith appeared on the census of 11 Apr 1940 Lindale, Floyd Co., GA. He d.6 Mar 1999 Lindale, Floyd Co., GA, at age 88 and was bur. East View Cem., Rome, Floyd Co., GA.
            Maudell Smith, b.17 Nov 1913 St. Clair Co., AL; d.15 Jul 1984 Rome, Floyd Co., GA, age 70; bur. East View Cem.

319. Melissa Cordelia "Delia"[6] Abney (James[5], Benjamin[4], Hezekiah[3], Elisha[2], Abner[1]) m. Thomas Seals Burkhalter. , b.10 Sep 1873 AL. She d.16 Dec 1965 Bibb Co., GA, at age 92 and was bur. New Bethel Cem., Floyd Co., GA.
      Thomas Seals Burkhalter, b.14 Aug 1867 Floyd Co., GA. He d.16 Jul 1934 Lindale, Floyd Co., GA, age 66; bur. New Bethel Cem.
Known children of Melissa Cordelia "Delia"[6] Abney and Thomas Seals Burkhalter:
720   i.   Lenora "Mae Bell"[7], b. 24 May 1891 Floyd Co., GA; m. (n.n.) Washington.
721   ii.   Dallas Grady, b. 30 Jan 1893 GA; m. Cora Myrtle Bruce.
722   iii. Erma Gertrude, b. 11 Sep 1895; m. John Ellis Caldwell.
723   iv.   John Austin, b. 15 Dec 1897 GA; m. Minnie Lee Winkle.
724   v.   William Garvin, b. 5 Jun 1900; m. Opal Lemming.
725   vi.   Ethel Elvada, b. 24 Nov 1902 Floyd Co., GA; m. Homer Lee Brackett.
726   vii. Malory David, b. 9 Sep 1905; m. Ruby Wallace.
727   viii. Elsie Cloe, b. 27 Dec 1907; m. James Gus Cargle.
      ix.   Audrey, b.17 Aug 1911. She m. Berry "Hester" Kizziah. She d.6 Jul 1945 Floyd Co., GA, age 33; bur. New Bethel Cem.
            Berry "Hester" Kizziah, b.28 Aug 1901. He m2. Katie Watkins. He d.16 Aug 1969 at age 67; bur. East View Cem.
      x.   Zethel Rosebud m. Albert Woodrow Jones. , b.Christmas Day, 25 Dec 1915. She d.24 Aug 2004 at age 88 and was bur. Magnolia Park Cem. and Maus., Warner Robins, Houston Co., GA.

320. Geretie M.[6] Abney (James[5], Benjamin[4], Hezekiah[3], Elisha[2], Abner[1]) m. Adolphus Dempsey "Dolf" Miller. , b.24 May 1876 AL. She d.3 Feb 1966 Rome, Floyd Co., GA, at age 89 and was bur. Pleasant Hope Cem., Rome, Floyd Co., GA.
      Adolphus Dempsey "Dolf" Miller, b.17 Jan 1874 GA. He d.9 Sep 1942 Floyd Co., GA, at age 68 and was bur. Pleasant Hope Cem., Rome.
Known children of Geretie M.[6] Abney and Adolphus Dempsey "Dolf" Miller:
728   i.   Dovie Mae[7], b. Christmas Eve, 24 Dec 1893; m. Jesse Lee Cox.
      ii.   Grover Cleveland, b.14 Jul 1895. He m1. Connie Washington. He m2. Cleo E. Hobgood in 1950. He d.13 Mar 1956 at age 60 and was bur. Pleasant Hope Cem., Rome, Floyd Co., GA.
            Connie Washington, b.28 Oct 1895. She d.11 Oct 1949 at age 53 and was bur. Pleasant Hope Cem., Rome.
            Cleo E. Hobgood, b.22 Sep 1901; m1. Joseph Turner Davidson in 1920; d.3 Aug 1987, age 85; bur. East View Cem.
729   iii. Gertrude, b. 28 Jun 1897; m. Othel Blair Scoggins.
      iv.   Ruby, b.11 Jan 1902. She m1. Paul Woodfin Shiflett (USArmy-WWII) in 1919. She m2. Lloyd N. Vanderkolk (USArmy-WWII). She d.24 Aug 1999 at age 97 and was bur. Pleasant Hope Cem., Rome, Floyd Co., GA.
            Paul Woodfin Shiflett (USArmy-WWII), b.23 Oct 1886. He d.22 Aug 1964 at age 77; bur. Pleasant Hope Cem.
            Lloyd N. Vanderkolk (USArmy-WWII), b.26 May 1924. He d.3 Feb 1993 at age 68; bur. Pleasant Hope Cem.
      v.   Vera, b.23 Aug 1903 Floyd Co., GA. She d.7 Nov 1906 Floyd Co., GA, at age 3 and was bur. Pleasant Hope Cem.
      vi.   Gladys Bera, b.25 Apr 1907 Floyd Co., GA. She d.20 Jul 1968 Rome, Floyd Co., GA, at age 61.
      vii. Opal, b.4 Apr 1909 Floyd Co., GA. She d.12 Oct 1990 Rome, Floyd Co., GA, at age 81 and was bur. Pleasant Hope Cem.
      viii. Nancy Pearl, b.24 Mar 1910; m. Robert Benj. Mount (USArmy-WWII). d.13 Feb 2003, age 92; bur. Pleasant Hope Cem.
            Robert Benjamin Mount (USArmy-WWII), b.13 Mar 1919. He d.24 Mar 1960 at age 41 and was bur. Pleasant Hope Cem.

321. William "Taylor"[6] Abney (James[5], Benjamin[4], Hezekiah[3], Elisha[2], Abner[1]), b.29 Apr 1879 AL; liv. on 16 Jun 1900 with bro., Marion M. Abney, Lake Creek, Polk Co., GA; m. Emma F. "Emmie" Cashion ca.1902; d.29 Jun 1909, ae.30; bur. Pleasant Hope Cem., Rome, Floyd Co., GA.
      Emma F. "Emmie" Cashion, b.1885 GA. She and the children were liv. on 22 Apr 1910 with her father, Robert W. Cashion, Lake Creek, Polk Co., GA. She was liv. on 5 Jan 1920 she and children with mother, Nancy J. Cashion, Lake Creek, Polk Co., GA. She appeared on the census of 8 Apr 1930 Howells Dist., Floyd Co., GA. She d.1940 and was bur. Pleasant Hope Cem., Rome, Floyd Co., GA.
Known children of William "Taylor"[6] Abney and Emma F. "Emmie" Cashion:
      i.   Raymond Ollie[7], b. ca.1903 GA. He d.15 Feb 1969.
      ii.   Craton Millard, b.21 Feb 1904 GA. He d.28 Dec 1950 at age 46 and was bur. Pleasant Hope Cem., Rome, Floyd Co., GA.

730   iii.   Emma Viola, b. 21 Nov 1905 Polk Co., GA; m. Amos Gentry.

         iv.   Raleigh Claud "Taylor", b. ca.1908 GA.

322.   Lillie[6] Abney (James[5], Benjamin[4], Hezekiah[3], Elisha[2], Abner[1]) m. Forrest Ranger Reynolds. , b.31 Jul 1883. She d.7 Jul 1918 at age 34 and was bur. Pleasant Hope Cem., Rome, Floyd Co., GA.

     Forrest Ranger Reynolds, b.10 Feb 1878. He d. New Year's Eve, 31 Jan 1939 at age 60; bur. Pleasant Hope Cem., Rome, Floyd Co., GA.

Known children of Lillie[6] Abney and Forrest Ranger Reynolds:

731   i.   Gertha Estelle[7], b. 15 Jul 1902 Floyd Co., GA; m. Thomas Preston Mull.

         ii.   Jewel D., b.13 Dec 1903. He m. Mary W. (n.n.). He d.3 Jul 1985 at age 81; bur. Rose Hill Cem., Rockmart, Polk Co., GA.

             Mary W. (n.n.), b.31 Jul 1950. She d.14 Aug 1988 at age 38 and was bur. Rose Hill Cem., Rockmart, Polk Co., GA.

732   iii.   Bernice Irene, b. 26 Apr 1906 GA; m. George W. Manis.

323.   Lottie Zefro[6] Abney (James[5], Benjamin[4], Hezekiah[3], Elisha[2], Abner[1]), b.21 Apr 1885 Polk Co., GA. She m. Robert Sidney "Bob" Broadaway in 1959. She d.3 Apr 1981 Rome, Floyd Co., GA, at age 95 and was bur. Pleasant Hope Cem., Rome, Floyd Co., GA.

     Robert Sidney "Bob" Broadaway, b.13 Apr 1879 Lindale, Floyd Co., GA; d.28 Sep 1959 Rome, Floyd Co., GA; bur. Pleasant Hope Cem.

Known children of Lottie Zefro[6] Abney and Robert Sidney "Bob" Broadaway:

         i.   Buford Ceo[7], b.31 Oct 1902 Lake Creek, Polk Co., GA. He m. Myrtle Elizabeth Kenyon. He d.19 Sep 1972 Rome, Floyd Co., GA, at age 69 and was bur. Pleasant Valley North Cem., Rome, Floyd Co., GA.

             Myrtle Elizabeth Kenyon, b.13 Dec 1903 TN. She d.21 Oct 1989 Baldwin Co., GA; bur. Pleasant Valley North Cem.

         ii.   Grover O'Neal, b.30 Jun 1907 Polk Co., GA. He d.11 Jul 1964 Rome, Floyd Co., GA, at age 57; bur. Pleasant Hope Cem.

         iii.   (infant son), b.25 Jul 1910 Floyd Co., GA. He d.25 Jul 1910 Floyd Co., GA and was bur. Pleasant Hope Cem.

         iv.   James D. "Bill", b.2 Apr 1912 Floyd Co., GA. He d.6 Sep 1980 Rome, Floyd Co., GA, age 68; bur. Pleasant Hope Cem.

         v.   Nancy Erselle, b.2 Apr 1912; m. James B. Garrett on 17 Jun 1940. She d.29 May 1994 age 82; bur. Pleasant Hope Cem.

             James B. Garrett, b.15 Jul 1915. He d.30 Aug 1988 at age 73; bur. Pleasant Hope Cem., Rome, Floyd Co., GA.

         vi.   Cliff M., b.11 Apr 1918 Floyd Co., GA. He d.1 Mar 1973 Portsmouth City, VA, at age 54.

324.   Sylvester B. "Vester"[6] Abney (James[5], Benjamin[4], Hezekiah[3], Elisha[2], Abner[1]), b.9 Feb 1887 GA. He m. Mamie Lee Bradshaw ca.1910. He and Mamie Lee Bradshaw appeared on the censuses of 2 Apr 1930 Barkers Dist., Floyd Co., GA and 26 Aug 1940 Kathleen, Polk Co., FL. He d.6 Sep 1961 Rome, Floyd Co., GA, at age 74 and was bur. Pleasant Hope Cem., Rome, Floyd Co., GA.

     Mamie Lee Bradshaw, b.15 Aug 1893. She d.Christmas Day, 25 Dec 1993 at age 100 and was bur. East View Cem., Rome, Floyd Co., GA.

Known children of Sylvester B. "Vester"[6] Abney and Mamie Lee Bradshaw:

         i.   Claud Taylor[7], b.1912. He d.1940 and was bur. Pleasant Hope Cem., Rome, Floyd Co., GA.

         ii.   Dornice Ruth, b.30 Dec 1913 Floyd Co., GA. She d.22 Mar 1935 Rome, Floyd Co., GA, age 21; bur. Pleasant Hope Cem.

         iii.   Agnes, b. ca.1916.

733   iv.   Frances Marion, b. 4 Aug 1918 Floyd Co., GA; m. PFC Harry O. Stone (USArmy).

         v.   Bonnie Marie, b.7 Mar 1921. She d.11 Dec 1999 at age 78 and was bur. East View Cem., Rome, Floyd Co., GA.

734   vi.   Calvin Vester, b. 15 Dec 1925; m. Doris Juanita Bell.

735   vii.   Rayford Martin, b. 30 Mar 1928; m. Dorothy Fay "Dot" Moore.

         viii.   Nora Jane "Midgie" m. Herman L. Evans (USN-WWII). , b.10 May 1930. She d.29 Aug 1986 at age 56 and was bur. East View Cem., Rome, Floyd Co., GA.

             Herman L. Evans (USN-WWII), b.1 Dec 1925 Floyd Co., GA. He d.30 Jun 2002 Rome, Floyd Co., GA, at age 76.

325.   Robert Andrew "Andy"[6] Abney (Joseph[5], Benjamin[4], Hezekiah[3], Elisha[2], Abner[1]), b.18 Aug 1880 Paulding Co., GA. He m. Henrietta "Etta" Barnett in 1903. He and Henrietta "Etta" Barnett appeared on the censuses of 15 Apr 1910 Borden Springs, Cleburne Co., AL; and 13 Jan 1920 Raccoon Dist., Paulding Co., GA. He d.26 Mar 1924 GA at age 43 and was bur. Crossroads Bapt. Ch. Cem., Dallas, Paulding Co., GA.

     Henrietta "Etta" Barnett, b.3 Mar 1889 GA. She d.24 Mar 1959 at age 70 and was bur. Riverdale Cem., Columbus, Muscogee Co., GA.

Known children of Robert Andrew "Andy"[6] Abney and Henrietta "Etta" Barnett:

736   i.   Eunice Josephine[7], b. 13 Oct 1904 Paulding Co., GA; m. Homer Edward Hunt.

         ii.   Garl James "Jim", b.1907. He m. Jessie T. Barnes. He d.1978 and was bur. Parkhill Cem., Columbus, Muscogee Co., GA.

         iii.   Tinnie T., b.7 Jul 1908. She m. William Henry White. d.30 Oct 1982 at age 74 and was bur. Parkhill Cem., Columbus.

             William Henry White, b.10 Apr 1902. He d.6 Jun 1964 at age 62 and was bur. Parkhill Cem., Columbus.

737   iv.   Grace Pauline "Gracie," b. 20 Jul 1910; m. W. Hosey McMichen; m. Charlie Martin Culpepper.

         v.   Clyde "Walter", b.1912. He d.1929 and was bur. Crossroads Bapt. Ch. Cem., Dallas, Paulding Co., GA.

         vi.   Johnnie Lee, b.1914. He d.1914 and was bur. Crossroads Bapt. Ch. Cem., Dallas, Paulding Co., GA.

         vii.   Bertha Lea, b.9 May 1916 Paulding Co., GA. She m. Bartow Frank Downing; d.14 Nov 1994, age 78; bur. Parkhill Cem.

             Bartow Frank Downing, b.1907. He d.1983.

         viii.   Clara Ezekiel, b. ca.Sep 1919 GA. She m. Finis Ewing Drennon in 1993. She d.9 Jun 2012.

             Finis Ewing Drennon, b.1916. He d.2005.

         ix.   Dora Idell, b.9 Jun 1921. She d.23 Mar 1935 at age 13 and was bur. Riverdale Cem., Columbus, Muscogee Co., GA.

738   x.   Roberta Etta, b. 15 Nov 1923 Muscogee Co., GA; m. Ralph Thomas Murray (USNR-WWII).

         xi.   Robert E (USN-WWII), b.8 May 1924. He d.15 Jul 1980 at age 56; bur. LaFayette Cem., LaFayette, Walker Co., GA.

326.   Minnie Beatrice[6] Abney (Joseph[5], Benjamin[4], Hezekiah[3], Elisha[2], Abner[1]) m. John Franklin Prewett. , b.1884. She d.1951 and was bur. Town Creek Bapt. Ch. Cem., Chavies, DeKalb Co., AL.

     John Franklin Prewett, b.31 Mar 1875 Douglas Co., GA; d.13 Jan 1946 Fort Payne, DeKalb Co., AL, age 70; bur. Town Creek Bapt. Ch. Cem.

Known child of Minnie Beatrice[6] Abney and John Franklin Prewett:

739   i.   Alpha[7], b. 18 Nov 1900; m. Homer Carnes.

327. Alonzo Calloway "Lon"[6] Abney (Joseph[5], Benjamin[4], Hezekiah[3], Elisha[2], Abner[1]), b.18 May 1886 Paulding Co., GA. He m. Ruth Gravett ca.1913. He and Ruth Gravett appeared on the censuses of 8 Apr 1930 and 23 Apr 1940 Acorntree Dist., Paulding Co., GA. He d.22 Apr 1950 Dallas, Paulding Co., GA, at age 63 and was bur. New Hope Cem., Dallas, Paulding Co., GA.
    Ruth Gravett, b.26 Jun 1893 GA. She d.14 Sep 1990 at age 97 and was bur. New Hope Cem., Dallas, Paulding Co., GA.
Known children of Alonzo Calloway "Lon"[6] Abney and Ruth Gravett all b. GA:
        i.   Walter Cleamons[7], b.21 Jun 1914; m. Pearl Harris; He d.12 Dec 1976, age 62; bur. New Hope Cem.
            Pearl Harris, b.26 Mar 1916. She d.10 Jan 2000 at age 83 and was bur. New Hope Cem., Dallas, Paulding Co., GA.
        ii.   Lyone Cleveland, b.12 Feb 1917. He m. Mary Evelyn Bowman. He d.23 Dec 1978 at age 61; bur. New Hope Cem.
            Mary Evelyn Bowman, b.24 Mar 1927. She d.16 Feb 2017 Dallas, Paulding Co., GA, at age 89; bur. New Hope Cem.
   740   iii. Howell Herman, b. 1922; m. Katherine Louise Duncan.

328. John Robert[6] Abney (Charles[5], Benjamin[4], Hezekiah[3], Elisha[2], Abner[1]) m. Mahala "Gertrude" Price. He, b.26 Sep 1899 Cleburne Co., AL. He and Mahala "Gertrude" Price appeared on the census of 17 Apr 1930 Edwardsville, Cleburne Co., AL. He and Mahala "Gertrude" Price were liv. on 10 Apr 1940 with his father, *C. Robert Abney*, Edwardsville, Cleburne Co., AL. He d.16 Jun 1981 Heflin, Cleburne Co., AL, at age 81 and was bur. Camp Creek Bapt. Ch. Cem., Fruithurst, Cleburne Co., AL.
    Mahala "Gertrude" Price, b.16 Dec 1906 Cleburne Co., AL; d.13 Nov 1985 Anniston, Calhoun Co., AL, age 78; bur. Upper Cane Creek Cem.
Known children of John Robert[6] Abney and Mahala "Gertrude" Price:
        i.   Elizabeth "Lizzie"[7], b.21 Aug 1925 Cleburne Co., AL. She d.12 Dec 1993 at age 68 and was bur. Upper Cane Creek Cem.
   741   ii.   William "Robert," b. 15 May 1931 Edwardsville, Cleburne Co., AL; m. Verna J. Latham.
   742   iii. Jessie "Allen," b. 17 May 1935 Edwardsville, Cleburne Co., AL; m. Ruth Vertell Connell; m. Joy (n.n.).
   743   iv. Benjamin Franklin "Benny," b. 21 Oct 1938 Fruithurst, Cleburne Co., AL; m. Connie Lenell Hulsey.

329. William Thomas "Bill"[6] Abney (Charles[5], Benjamin[4], Hezekiah[3], Elisha[2], Abner[1]), b.19 Jun 1903 Fruithurst, Cleburne Co., AL. He m. Essie Mae "Leona" Williams ca.1924. He and Essie Mae "Leona" Williams appeared on the census of 17 Apr 1930 Edwardsville, Cleburne Co., AL. He and Essie Mae "Leona" Williams appeared on the census of 10 Apr 1940 Edwardsville, Cleburne Co., AL. He d.3 Jul 2002 Heflin, Cleburne Co., AL, at age 99 and was bur. Upper Cane Creek Cem., Fruithurst, Cleburne Co., AL.
    Essie Mae "Leona" Williams, b.24 Aug 1901 Cleburne Co., AL; d.13 Nov 1991 Fort Oglethorpe, Catoosa Co., GA, age 90; bur. Upper Cane Creek Cem., Fruithurst, Cleburne Co., AL.
Known children of William Thomas "Bill"[6] Abney and Essie Mae "Leona" Williams all b. Cleburne Co., AL:
        i.   Sarah "Frances"[7] m. PFC Talmadge J. Harris (USArmy). , b.1 Sep 1926. She d.30 Sep 2017 Richmond Co., GA, at age 91 and was bur. Harlem Mem. Cem., Harlem, Columbia Co., GA.
            PFC Talmadge J. Harris (USArmy), b.13 Aug 1925; d.16 Aug 1995 at age 70; bur. Harlem Mem. Cem., Harlem.
   744   ii.   Rachel Edna, b. 27 Feb 1929; m. James Hurshel Furgerson.
        iii. Annie Lou, b. ca.1931; m. (n.n.) Harris.
        iv. Ruth, b. ca.1936; m. (n.n.) Furgerson.

330. Laura E.[6] Abney (Pinkney[5], Wiley[4], Hezekiah[3], Elisha[2], Abner[1]), b.Nov 1864 GA. She m. Franklin "Frank" Dobbins ca.1884. She and Franklin "Frank" Dobbins appeared on the censuses of 16 Jun 1900, 13 May 1910 and 3 Apr 1930 Greene Co., TN. She d.1939 and was bur. Dixon Chapel Church of God Cem., Greene Co., TN.
    Franklin "Frank" Dobbins, b.Aug 1865 TN. He d.1927 and was bur. Dixon Chapel Church of God Cem., Greene Co., TN.
Known children of Laura E.[6] Abney and Franklin "Frank" Dobbins all b. TN:
   745   i.   Fannie "Ethel"[7], b. 31 Aug 1885; m. Charles Sylvester "Charley" McMackin Sr.
        ii.   Florence, b.Apr 1888.
   746   iii. Thomas "Buford," b. Jun 1891; m. Mary A. (n.n.).

331. John "Roscoe"[6] Abney (Pinkney[5], Wiley[4], Hezekiah[3], Elisha[2], Abner[1]), b.9 Jun 1865 Rome, Floyd Co., GA. He m1. Sarah Ruth Ramsey, daughter of John Ramsey and Winifred Minerva Hobbs, ca.1891. He m2. Laura Johnson ca.1895. He Roscoe returned to his first wife ca.1900. He d.20 Jul 1908 Rose Hill, Lee Co., VA, at age 43 and was bur. Abney Cem., Lee Co., VA.
    Sarah Ruth Ramsey, b.11 Sep 1868 VA. She liv. on 29 Apr 1910 liv. with her son-in-law, John Marcum, Rose Hill, Lee Co., VA. She appeared as Head of Household on the censuses of 18 Apr 1930 and 9 May 1940 Rose Hill, Lee Co., VA. She d.19 May 1949 at age 80; bur. Abney Cem.
Known children of John "Roscoe"[6] Abney and Sarah Ruth Ramsey:
   747   i.   Ethel Winaforde[7], b. 1892 VA; m. John L. Marcum.
   748   ii.   Elizabeth E. "Lizzy," b. 27 Jul 1902 VA; m. Dennis J. Evans.
   749   iii. John "Floyd," b. 15 Feb 1904 Rose Hill, Lee Co., VA; m1. Martha Ann "Annie" Farris; m. Sarah Delilah McCurry.

Known children of John "Roscoe"[6] Abney and Laura Johnson:
   750   i.   Carrie Olivia[7], b. 1896 VA; m. Lincoln L. "Link" Marcum.
        ii.   Loretta, b. Christmas Eve, 24 Dec 1898. She lived on 13 May 1910 with Unc. Frank Dobbins, Greene Co., TN. She m. Dewey Lee. She d.20 Mar 1987 at age 88 and was bur. Abney Cem., Lee Co., VA.
            Dewey Lee, b.14 Feb 1899. He d.14 Feb 1958 at age 59 and was bur. Abney Cem., Lee Co., VA.

332. Sarah Ann "Sally"[6] Abney (Pinkney[5], Wiley[4], Hezekiah[3], Elisha[2], Abner[1]), b.1870 GA. She m. George Mac Inman in 1896 Greene Co., TN. She and George Mac Inman appeared on the census of 9 Jun 1900 Greene Co., TN. She d. before 1906 Greene Co., TN and was bur. Dixon Chapel Church of God Cem., Greene Co., TN.
    George Mac Inman, b.4 Aug 1876 NC. He m. Nancy Creekmore in 1906. He d.28 Jun 1937 at age 60.
Known children of Sarah Ann "Sally"[6] Abney and George Mac Inman all b. Greene Co., TN:
        i.   (infant)[7], b. ca.1897; d. ca.1897 Greene Co., TN.
        ii.   (infant), b. ca.1898; d. ca.1898 Greene Co., TN.
        iii. (infant), b. ca.1899; d. ca.1899 Greene Co., TN.

333. James Henry⁶ Abner (Thomas⁵ Abney, Wiley⁴, Hezekiah³, Elisha², Abner¹), b.20 Nov 1869 Fish Creek, Polk Co., GA. He m. Sarah Elizabeth Dodd. He and Sarah appeared on the census of 1900 Bartow Co., GA. He d.27 Sep 1951, age 81; bur. Rose Hill Cem., Rockmart, Polk Co., GA.
     Sarah Elizabeth "Sallie" Dodd, b.6 Dec 1870 GA. She d.18 Jun 1923 at age 52 and was bur. Rose Hill Cem., Rockmart, Polk Co., GA.
Known children of James Henry⁶ Abner and Sarah Elizabeth "Sallie" Dodd:
         i.   Cecil H.⁷, b.Nov 1896 GA.
        ii.   Electer I., b.Apr 1900 Bartow Co., GA.

334. Emily Elmira⁶ Abney (James⁵, Wiley⁴, Hezekiah³, Elisha², Abner¹), b.13 Sep 1885 Calhoun Co., AL. She m1. Robert Lee Gray on 2 Feb 1902 Calhoun Co., AL. She m2. J.L. Newton. She d.30 Apr 1970 Pell City, St. Clair Co., AL, at age 84 and was bur. on 2 May 1970 Mt. Zion Cem.
     Robert Lee Gray, b.1 Feb 1878 Buckhorn Valley, Talladega Co., AL; d.25 Feb 1948 Pell City, St. Clair Co., AL; bur. Mt. Zion Church Cem.
Known children of Emily Elmira⁶ Abney and Robert Lee Gray:
         i.   Clarence Lee⁷, b.14 Nov 1902 Mt. Pizgah, St. Clair Co., AL. He m1. Dorothy Helen Benton on Christmas Eve, 24 Dec 1925. He m2. Avery Nadine Newton.
        ii.   Jessie Marie, b.5 Apr 1904 Mt. Pizgah, St. Clair Co., AL. She m. Henry Pittsford Boswell on 7 Dec 1931 Anniston, AL.
       iii.   James Abney, b.15 Mar 1906 Mt. Pizgah, St. Clair Co., AL; m. Ruth Prince; d.4 Feb 1975 Oxford, MS; bur. Oxford Cem.
       iv.   Nellie, b.20 Sep 1908 Mt. Pizgah, St. Clair Co., AL. She d.15 Apr 1979 Oxford, MS, at age 70; bur. St. Clair Cem.
        v.   Serena Mae, b. ca.1910 Mt. Pizgah, St. Clair Co., AL. She m. Frank Lee. She d.1 Sep 1960; bur. Mt. Pizgah Cem.
       vi.   Edna, b.31 May 1911 Talladega, AL. She m. Joseph Edgar Dorough on 2 Oct 1928.
      vii.   Aurell, b.24 Oct 1912 Mt. Pizgah, St. Clair Co., AL. She m. Forney Joseph Haynes on Christmas Day, 25 Dec 1931.
    viii.   Jeanette, b.13 Oct 1916 Mt. Pizgah, St. Clair Co., AL. She d.10 May 1943 Mt. Pizgah, St. Clair Co., AL, at age 26; bur. Mt. Pizgah Cem., Mt. Pizgah, St. Clair Co., AL.
       ix.   Ruby, b.23 Jul 1918 Mt. Pizgah, St. Clair Co., AL; m. Woodrow Woods Dorough 13 Apr 1940 Vincent, Shelby Co., AL.
        x.   Lois Dimple, b.13 Apr 1922 Mt. Pizgah, St. Clair Co., AL; m. William Henry Warren 22 Dec 1936 Vincent, Shelby Co.
       xi.   Dolly Dimple, b.11 Apr 1924 Mt. Pizgah, St. Clair Co., AL. She m. Homer Paul Selby on 1 Sep 1940.
      xii.   Ralph Howell, b.18 Apr 1926 Mt. Pizgah, St. Clair Co., AL; m. Mary Elizabeth Mize 20 Jul 1946 Eden, St. Clair Co., AL.

There were no known children of Emily Elmira⁶ Abney and J.L. Newton.

335. John Allen⁶ Abney (James⁵, Wiley⁴, Hezekiah³, Elisha², Abner¹), b.7 Apr 1888 GA. He m. Hazzle N. "Buzzie" Denton in 1907. He d.11 May 1967 at age 79 and was bur. in Okeechobee, FL.
Known child of John Allen⁶ Abney and Hazzle N. "Buzzie" Denton:
    751   i.   Benjamin Parker⁷, b. 27 Aug 1912.

336. Jesse Brooks⁶ Abney Sr. (James⁵, Andrew⁴, Hezekiah³, Elisha², Abner¹), b.28 Sep 1867. He m. Wilhelmina "Mina" Abel in 1896. He m. Olive Adele Brockert. He d.7 Feb 1947 at age 79 and was bur. Rose Hills Mem. Park, Whittier, Los Angeles Co., CA.
     Wilhelmina "Mina" Abel, b.26 May 1873. She d.25 Aug 1919 at age 46 and was bur. Forest Hill Cem., Birmingham, Jefferson Co., AL.
Known children of Jesse Brooks⁶ Abney Sr. and Wilhelmina "Mina" Abel both b. AL:
    752   i.   Jesse Brooks⁷, b. 18 Aug 1897; m1. Ola Estelle Gillespie; m2. Inga Kamrud.
        ii.   Ruth Aline, b.8 Feb 1904; m. Frank J. Hull; d. Burbank, Los Angeles Co., CA; bur. Valhalla Mem. Park, North Hollywood.
           Frank J. Hull, b.1889. He d.1948 and was bur. Valhalla Mem. Park, North Hollywood, Los Angeles Co., CA.
     Olive Adele Brockert, b.17 Aug 1872 IL. She d.20 Dec 1955 Los Angeles Co., CA, at age 83 and was bur. Rose Hills Mem. Park, Whittier
There were no known children of Jesse Brooks⁶ Abney Sr. and Olive Adele Brockert.

337. Charlie M.⁶ Abner (William⁵, James⁴ Abney, Hezekiah³, Elisha², Abner¹), b. ca.1872 Heard Co., GA. He m. (n.n.) ca.1898. He d. before 1900.
Known child of Charlie M.⁶ Abner and (n.n.):
         i.   Nellie L.⁷, b. Oct 1899 Heard Co., GA; liv. on 4 Jun 1900 with grandfather, William Abner, Franklin, Heard Co., GA.

338. James R. "Jim"⁶ Abner (William⁵, James⁴ Abney, Hezekiah³, Elisha², Abner¹), b.10 Mar 1874 Heard Co., GA. He m. Thuella Bernetie "Ella" Craven on 27 Feb 1904 Heard Co., GA. He and Thuella Bernetie "Ella" Craven appeared on the censuses of 28 Apr 1910 and 15 Apr 1930 Franklin, Heard Co., GA. He d.11 Feb 1952 Atlanta, Fulton Co., GA, at age 77 and was bur. Elim Bapt. Ch. Cem., Handy, Coweta Co., GA.
     Thuella Bernetie "Ella" Craven, b.19 Jan 1874 Carroll Co., GA. She d.6 Nov 1915 Heard Co., GA, at age 41 and was bur. Franklin City Cem., Franklin, Heard Co., GA.
Known children of James R. "Jim"⁶ Abner and Thuella Bernetie "Ella" Craven all b. Heard Co., GA:
         i.   Katie "Velma"⁷, b.1904. She was liv. on 22 Jan 1920 with her sisters, Orphan's Home of the North Georgia Methodist Conference, Decatur, DeKalb Co., GA. She d.18 May 1930 Heard Co., GA.
        ii.   Ethel "Willie", b.18 Aug 1906. She was liv. on 22 Jan 1920 with her sisters, Orphan's Home of the North Georgia Methodist Conference, Decatur, DeKalb Co., GA. She m. Floyd Newton Harmon. She and Floyd Newton Harmon appeared on the census of 4 Apr 1940 Atlanta, Fulton Co., GA. She d.23 Sep 1986 Newton Co., GA, at age 80.
           Floyd Newton Harmon, b.30 Dec 1903 GA. He d.1 Apr 1986 DeKalb Co., GA, at age 82.
       iii.   Allie C., b. ca.1909. She was liv. on 22 Jan 1920 with her sisters, Orphan's Home of the North Georgia Methodist Conference, Decatur, DeKalb Co., GA.

339. Wyatt Joel Heflin "Heff"⁶ Abner (William⁵, James⁴ Abney, Hezekiah³, Elisha², Abner¹), b.26 Aug 1876 Heard Co., GA. He m. Tommie Lee Hannah ca.1900. He and Tommie Lee Hannah appeared on the censuses of 4 Jun 1900 Franklin, Heard Co., GA; 28 Apr 1910 Centralhatchee, Heard Co., GA; 17 Apr 1920 Franklin, Heard Co., Ga; and 9 Apr 1930 and 2 Apr 1940 Heard Co., GA. He d.13 Apr 1952 at age 75 and was bur. Franklin City Cem., Franklin, Heard Co., GA.
     Tommie Lee Hannah, b.8 Apr 1883 GA. She d.21 Mar 1962 at age 78 and was bur. Franklin City Cem., Franklin, Heard Co., GA.

Known children of Wyatt Joel Heflin "Heff"⁶ Abner and Tommie Lee Hannah:
    753   i.   Lotice⁷, b. 21 May 1901; m. Pvt. John A. Pike (USArmy-WWI).
            ii.   Benjamin Heflin Hill "Ben", b.24 Jan 1903. He d.5 Mar 1944 at age 41 and was bur. Franklin City Cem.
    754   iii.   Richard Lee, b. 18 Mar 1905; m. Annie Mae Abner.
    755   iv.   Ludie G., b. 14 Nov 1906 Spalding Co., GA; m. John Fletcher Eady.
    756   v.   Samuel B. "Sam," b. 30 Aug 1908 GA; m. Myrtice Costley.
            vi.   Hefflin Hortense m. Walter L. Pike. , b.17 Oct 1910. She d.27 Apr 1963 at age 52.
                    Walter L. Pike, b.1905 GA. He d.4 Jun 1966 Troup Co., GA.
            vii.   Millard, b.9 Sep 1913 Heard Co., GA.
    757   viii.   Mildred Woodall, b. 9 Sep 1913 Heard Co., GA; m. James Archer Strickland.
    758   ix.   Lizzie Lou, b. 26 Mar 1915; m. George Bluford Pike; m. Robert Lee Hickey.
            x.   Julia, b. ca.1917 GA.
            xi.   Charlie Frank, b.26 May 1920. He m. Helen Jewell Pike. He d.21 Feb 1976 at age 55 and was bur. Franklin City Cem.
                    Helen Jewell Pike, b.2 Aug 1919. She d.20 Mar 1971 at age 51 and was bur. Franklin City Cem.

340. Josaphine "Jossie"⁶ Abner (William⁵, James⁴ Abney, Hezekiah³, Elisha², Abner¹), b.8 Oct 1878 Heard Co., GA. She m. Earnest W. Purgason ca.1905. She and Earnest W. Purgason appeared on the censuses of 28 Apr 1910 and 21 Apr 1930 Franklin, Heard Co., GA. She d.18 Feb 1955 at age 76 and was bur. Franklin City Cem., Franklin, Heard Co., GA.
    Earnest W. Purgason, b.10 Feb 1873. He d.22 Jan 1953 at age 79 and was bur. Franklin City Cem., Franklin, Heard Co., GA.
Known children of Josaphine "Jossie"⁶ Abner and Earnest W. Purgason:
            i.   Myra Lou⁷, b.1905. She d.1995.
            ii.   Curtis, b.1906. He d.1973.
            iii.   Harvey Hill, b.1909. He d.1972.
            iv.   Jennie M.. b.1912.
            v.   Sallie K., b.1916.
            vi.   Kate, b.11 Aug 1916. She m. Otis Oscar Williamson Jr. on 10 Apr 1946 Phenix City, Russell Co., AL.
                    Otis Oscar Williamson Jr, b.29 Sep 1925 Columbus, Muscogee Co., GA; d.25 Oct 1986 Muscogee Co., GA, age 61.
            vii.   Blueford, b.1917.
            viii.   Carrie D., b.1920.

341. Rufus Cook⁶ Abner Sr. (William⁵, James⁴ Abney, Hezekiah³, Elisha², Abner¹), b.15 Oct 1882 Heard Co., GA. He m. Cora Pauline West on Christmas Eve, 24 Dec 1905 Heard Co., GA. He and Cora Pauline West appeared on the censuses of 27 Apr 1910, 21 Jan 1920 Heard Co., GA, and 21 Apr 1930 Franklin, Heard Co., GA; and 8 Apr 1940 Pike Co., GA. He d.3 Feb 1962 Heard Co., GA, at age 79 and was bur. Corinth Cem., Corinth, Heard Co., GA.
    Cora Pauline West, b.17 Jun 1882. She d.14 Nov 1936 Troup Co., GA, at age 54 and was bur. Corinth Cem., Corinth, Heard Co., GA.
Known children of Rufus Cook⁶ Abner Sr. and Cora Pauline West all b. GA:
    759   i.   Luta⁷, b.21 Dec 1906 GA; m. Pierce Oliver Davis.
            ii.   Jimmy May C, b. ca.1908.
            iii.   Maggie R., b. ca.Feb 1910.
            iv.   Renetta, b. ca.1914.
            v.   Ora Lee, b. ca.Aug 1915.
            vi.   Rufus Cook Jr., b. ca.May 1918.
            vii.   Ambros, b. ca.1923.

342. Carrie Dell⁶ Abner (William⁵, James⁴ Abney, Hezekiah³, Elisha², Abner¹), b.11 Jun 1885 Franklin, Heard Co., GA. She m. Merritt D. Daniel on 22 Jan 1905 Heard Co., GA. She d.28 Feb 1979 LaGrange, Troup Co., GA, at age 93; bur. Shadowlawn Cem., LaGrange, Troup Co., GA.
    Merritt D. Daniel, b.2 Mar 1879 Heard Co., GA; d. New Year's Eve, 31 Dec 1961 Troup Co., GA, age 82; bur. Harmony UMC Cem., Franklin, Heard Co., GA.
Known children of Carrie Dell⁶ Abner and Merritt D. Daniel:
            i.   Jep⁷, b.18 Sep 1907. He d.9 Jul 1955 at age 47 and was bur. East Vernon Bapt. Ch. Cem., LaGrange, Troup Co., GA.
            ii.   Mildred, b.21 Jul 1910. She d.13 Aug 1910 and was bur. Harmony UMC Cem., Franklin, Heard Co., GA.
            iii.   Wilbur W., b.31 Oct 1910. He m. Carrie A. (n.n.). He d.12 Nov 1963 at age 53 and was bur. Shadowlawn Cem., LaGrange.
                    Carrie A. (n.n.), b.11 Jun 1885. She d.28 Feb 1979 at age 93 and was bur. Shadowlawn Cem., LaGrange.
    760   iv.   Rufus B., b. 11 Aug 1911; m. Edna Francis Bass.
            v.   Mary Kay, b.12 Nov 1915 Heard Co., GA. She m. Jesse Franklin Kelton. d.31 Mar 2007 Valley, Chambers Co., AL, at age 91 and was bur. Resthaven Mem. Gardens, Huguley, Chambers Co., AL.
                    Jesse Franklin Kelton, b.29 Oct 1907 Elmo, Kaufman Co., TX; d. May 1981 Chambers Co., AL, age 73 and was bur. Resthaven Mem. Gardens, Huguley, Chambers Co., AL.
            vi.   Herman, b.29 Apr 1918. He d.15 Feb 1979 at age 60 and was bur. Shadowlawn Cem., LaGrange, Troup Co., GA.
            vii.   Ralph L. b.7 Jun 1919 Heard Co., GA. He d.2 Jan 1957 Troup Co., GA, at age 37 and was bur. Shadowlawn Cem.
            viii.   Ruthie Jewell, b.25 Sep 1921 Heard Co., GA. She m. (n.n.) Bright. d.11 Feb 2001 Troup Co., GA, at age 79 and was bur. Shadowlawn Cem., LaGrange, Troup Co., GA.

343. Wiley "Frank"⁶ Abner (William⁵, James⁴ Abney, Hezekiah³, Elisha², Abner¹), b.Aug 1890 Heard Co., GA. He was liv. on 27 Apr 1910 with brother, Rufus Abner, Franklin, Heard Co., GA. He m. Odessa Bell "Dessie" White in May 1910 Heard Co., GA. He and Odessa Bell "Dessie" White appeared on the censuses of 17 Apr 1920, 22 Apr 1930 and 4 Apr 1940 Franklin, Heard Co., GA. He d.8 Aug 1977 Heard Co., GA and was bur. Franklin City Cem., Franklin, Heard Co., GA.
Known children of Wiley "Frank"⁶ Abner and Odessa Bell "Dessie" White:
            i.   Eula Mae⁷, b.29 Apr 1911; m. Hertchel Pike 1930; d.30 Jun 1990, age 79; bur. Oak Hill Cem., Newnan, Coweta Co., GA.
                    Hertchel Pike, b.28 Dec 1908. He d.12 Aug 1949 at age 40 and was bur. Wesley Chapel Cem., Heard Co., GA.

761   ii.   Annie Mae, b. 20 Feb 1913 Heard Co., GA; m1. Richard Lee Abner; m2. (n.n.) Rogers.
762   iii. Ruby Inez, b. 23 May 1916; m. Rufus Lance Arrington Sr.
       iv. Odessa R., b. ca.1918 GA.
763   v.   Frank "Amos," b. 16 Apr 1922; m. Grace Inez Pike.
       vi. Horace Lee, b.23 May 1924 Franklin, Heard Co., GA. He m. Agnes Abercrombie. He d.1 Dec 2006 Carrollton, Carroll Co., GA, at age 82 and was bur. Carroll Memory Gardens, Carrollton, Carroll Co., GA.

          Agnes Abercrombie, b.20 Oct 1922 Coweta Co., GA; d.4 Aug 1999 Carrollton, Carroll Co., GA, age 76; bur. Carroll Memory Gardens, Carrollton, Carroll Co., GA.

344. Callie Eugenia[6] Abna (James[5], James[4] Abney, Hezekiah[3], Elisha[2], Abner[1]), b.16 Sep 1877 Franklin, Heard Co., GA. She m. Calvin Strickland. d.8 Jul 1921 Carrollton, Carroll Co., GA, at age 43 and was bur. Old Camp UMC Cem., Carroll Co., GA.
    Calvin Strickland, b.15 Jul 1868 Heard Co., GA. He d.12 May 1924 LaGrange, Troup Co., GA, at age 55 and was bur. Old Camp UMC Cem.
Known child of Callie Eugenia[6] Abna and Calvin Strickland:
       i.   Arthur Amos[7], b.2 Jun 1896 Heard Co., GA. He m. Lillian Katherine Springer. He d.10 Apr 1973 Tuscaloosa, Tuscaloosa Co., AL, at age 76 and was bur. Corinth Cem., Elrod, Tuscaloosa Co., AL.
          Lillian Katherine Springer, b.22 Sep 1896 Tuscaloosa Co., AL. She d.19 Mar 1982 Northport, Tuscaloosa Co., AL, at age 85 and was bur. Corinth Cem., Elrod, Tuscaloosa Co., AL.

345. Robert James[6] Abna (James[5], James[4] Abney, Hezekiah[3], Elisha[2], Abner[1]), b.2 Feb 1882 Franklin, Heard Co., GA. He m. Frances Sarah Jones on 15 Sep 1901 Carrollton, Carroll Co., GA. He d.20 Oct 1957 Atlanta, Fulton Co., GA, at age 75; bur. Starrville Cem., Starrville, Smith Co., TX.
    Frances Sarah Jones, b.2 Oct 1879 Carrollton, Carroll Co., GA. She d.20 Jun 1961 Tyler, Smith Co., TX, at age 81; bur. Starrville Cem.
Known children of Robert James[6] Abna and Frances Sarah Jones:
764   i.   Lula[7], b. 2 Jun 1902 Franklin, Heard Co., GA; m. Terrell Jackson.
765   ii.   Eula Mae, b. 12 Mar 1904 GA; m. Benjamin Franklin "Ben" Hewitt.
766   iii. Alice, b. 25 Mar 1906 Judson, Gregg Co., TX; m. Walter Rex Smallwood Sr.
       iv. Lois Grace Dell "Gracie", b.30 Jul 1908 Cullman, Cullman Co., AL. She m. Allen Moore Duckett on 16 Apr 1937. She d.8 Jun 1984 Tyler, Smith Co., TX, at age 75 and was bur. Starrville Cem., Starrville, Smith Co., TX.
          Allen Moore Duckett, b.22 Mar 1913 Nacogdoches Co., TX; d.2 Mar 1982 Tyler, Smith Co., TX, age 68; bur. Starrville Cem., Starrville, Smith Co., TX.
767   v.   Joseph Elmer "Joe," b. 11 Aug 1910 Coleman, Perry Co., AL; m. Dessie Mae Nolan; m. Willie Frances Griffin.
       vi. Oline, b.8 Oct 1912 Judson, Gregg Co., TX. She m. Pvt. Dalton Magee (USArmy-WWII). d.New Year's Eve, 31 Jan 1990 Tyler, Smith Co., TX, at age 77 and was bur. Starrville Cem., Starrville, Smith Co., TX.
          Pvt. Dalton Magee (USArmy-WWII), b.13 Nov 1912 Henderson Co., TX. He d.5 Apr 1990 Tyler, Smith Co., TX, at age 77 and was bur. Starrville Cem., Starrville, Smith Co., TX.
768   vii. Bernice, b. 20 Mar 1916 Fisher Farm, Winona, Smith Co., TX; m. Marvin Royce Roberts.

346. Molly Lee[6] Abna (James[5], James[4] Abney, Hezekiah[3], Elisha[2], Abner[1]), b.7 Jan 1885 Franklin, Heard Co., GA. She m. Jonathan Britton Hill. She d.20 Jan 1947 GA at age 62.
Known child of Molly Lee[6] Abna and Jonathan Britton Hill:
       i.   Laura[7].

347. Emily Ophelia[6] Abna (James[5], James[4] Abney, Hezekiah[3], Elisha[2], Abner[1]), b.13 May 1887 Franklin, Heard Co., GA. She m. John Bogus Gable on 9 Mar 1902. She d.14 Apr 1960 Longview, Gregg Co., TX, at age 72 and was bur. Grace Hill Cem., Longview, Gregg Co., TX.
    John Bogus Gable, b.27 Apr 1880 GA. He d.9 Mar 1958 Longview, Gregg Co., TX, at age 77 and was bur. Grace Hill Cem., Longview.
Known children of Emily Ophelia[6] Abna and John Bogus Gable:
       i.   Clifford[7].
       ii. J.B.
       iii. Myrtle.
       iv. Alta.
       v.   Troy.
       vi. Fred.

348. Lina[6] Abna (James[5], James[4] Abney, Hezekiah[3], Elisha[2], Abner[1]), b.24 Feb 1890 Franklin, Heard Co., GA. She m. Wesley Green Renfroe on 23 Feb 1908. She d.17 Sep 1985 Houston, Harris Co., TX, at age 95 and was bur. Greenwood Cem., Longview, Gregg Co., TX.
    Wesley Green Renfroe, b.7 Sep 1876 TX. He d.27 Nov 1934 Gregg Co., TX, at age 58 and was bur. Greenwood Cem., Longview.
Known child of Lina[6] Abna and Wesley Green Renfroe:
       i.   Gaines Cody[7], b.26 Jul 1909 Gregg Co., TX. He d.22 Jan 1991 Walker Co., TX, at age 81 and was bur. Greenwood Cem.

349. Katie Dell[6] Abna (James[5], James[4] Abney, Hezekiah[3], Elisha[2], Abner[1]), b.9 Aug 1892 Franklin, Heard Co., GA. She m. Fred M. Montgomery in 1909. She d.11 May 1935 Sweetwater, Nolan Co., TX, at age 42 and was bur. Sweetwater Cem., Sweetwater, Nolan Co., TX.
    Fred M. Montgomery, b.31 Aug 1880 Nolan Co., TX. He m. Della Mae McElroy in 1902. He d.1 Aug 1930 Abilene, Taylor Co., TX, at age 49 and was bur. Sweetwater Cem., Sweetwater, Nolan Co., TX.
Known children of Katie Dell[6] Abna and Fred M. Montgomery:
       i.   Travis J.[7], b.26 Nov 1909. He d.30 Jan 1984 Nolan Co., TX, at age 74 and was bur. Sweetwater Cem., Sweetwater.
       ii. Robert Lee "Bob" m. Ida Mae Baker. He, b.12 Jul 1911 Sweetwater, Nolan Co., TX. He d.8 Dec 1975 Sweetwater, Nolan Co., TX, at age 64 and was bur. Sweetwater Cem., Sweetwater, Nolan Co., TX.
          Ida Mae Baker, b.7 Dec 1914 Mitchell Co., TX; d.5 Apr 1968 Sweetwater, Nolan Co., TX; bur. Sweetwater Cem.

350. Minnie Elizabeth[6] Abna (James[5], James[4] Abney, Hezekiah[3], Elisha[2], Abner[1]) m. Walter Thomas Sheets. , b.17 Apr 1895 Franklin, Heard Co., GA. She d.10 Sep 1972 GA at age 77 and was bur. Hillview East Cem., LaGrange, Troup Co., GA.

Walter Thomas Sheets, b.23 Nov 1892. He d.22 Mar 1962 at age 69 and was bur. Hillview East Cem., LaGrange, Troup Co., GA.
Known children of Minnie Elizabeth[6] Abna and Walter Thomas Sheets:
- i.   James Hugh Dorsey[7], b.9 Jul 1915 Heard Co., GA. He d.17 Dec 1920 Troup Co., GA, at age 5; bur. Hillview East Cem.
- ii. Joe Ales, b.10 May 1918. He d.6 Oct 1982 at age 64 and was bur. Hillview East Cem., LaGrange, Troup Co., GA.
- iii. Robert O., b.2 Apr 1921 LaGrange, Troup Co., GA. He m. Laverne Gauntt. He d.28 Apr 2008 Valley, Chambers Co., AL, at age 87 and was bur. Oakwood Cem., Lanett, Chambers Co., AL.
      Laverne Gauntt, b.6 Mar 1926.
- iv. Walter Thomas "Dub", b.27 Nov 1924. He m. Alice Marcelle Waldrop. He d.12 Feb 2002 Villa Rica, Carroll Co., GA, at age 77 and was bur. Meadowbrook Memory Gardens, Villa Rica, Carroll Co., GA.
      Alice Marcelle Waldrop, b.20 Jul 1926 Roswell, Fulton Co., GA. She d.15 Oct 2007 GA at age 81 and was bur. Meadowbrook Memory Gardens, Villa Rica, Carroll Co., GA.

351. Ales Ridley "Abe"[6] Abna Sr. (James[5], James[4] Abney, Hezekiah[3], Elisha[2], Abner[1]), b.11 Jan 1898 Franklin, Heard Co., GA. He m. Nell L. "Nellie" Harry. He d.14 Feb 1970 Fulton Co., GA, at age 72 and was bur. College Park Cem., College Park, Fulton Co., GA.
    Nell L. "Nellie" Harry, b.10 Apr 1906 GA. She d.25 Oct 1986 Fulton Co., GA, at age 80 and was bur. College Park Cem., College Park
Known children of Ales Ridley "Abe"[6] Abna Sr. and Nell L. "Nellie" Harry all b. Eagan, East Point, Fulton Co., GA:
- i.   Ales Ridley "Abe" Jr.[7], b.29 Dec 1922. He m. Katheryn Bradley. Abe was a Fire Captain. He d.10 Jun 1986 Fulton Co., GA, at age 63 and was bur. Sherwood Mem. Park and Maus., Jonesboro, Clayton Co., GA.
      Katheryn Bradley, b.1928 TX. She d.18 Feb 2005 Atlanta, Fulton Co., GA ; bur. Sherwood Mem. Park and Maus.
- ii. Harry Vernon, b.20 Mar 1925. He d.18 Dec 1990 Fulton Co., GA, at age 65 and was bur. College Park Cem.
- 769 iii. William James, b. 28 Mar 1927; m. Tommie Lee Mitchell.
- 770 iv. Donald Eugene, b. 2 Sep 1928; m. Mary Ann Smith.

352. James "Chalmers"[6] Abney (John[5], Jeff[4], Hezekiah[3], Elisha[2], Abner[1]), b.14 Oct 1879 Conyers, Rockdale Co., GA. He m. Jennie Cochran in 1905. He and Jennie were liv. on 23 Apr 1910 with brother-in-law, Wm. F. Riley, San Francisco, San Francisco Co., CA. He and Jennie Cochran appeared on the censuses of 15 Jan 1920 San Francisco, San Francisco Co., CA and 22 Apr 1930 Santa Cruz, Santa Cruz Co., CA. He and Jennie Cochran were liv. on 15 Apr 1940 with son-in-law, Henry Day, San Francisco, San Francisco Co., CA. He d.3 Jan 1946 San Francisco, San Francisco Co., CA, at age 66 and was bur. Cypress Lawn Mem. Park, Colma, San Mateo Co., CA.
    Jennie Cochran, b.24 Jun 1883 San Francisco, San Francisco Co., CA. She d.11 Aug 1955 San Francisco, San Francisco Co., CA, at age 72 and was bur. Cypress Lawn Mem. Park, Colma, San Mateo Co., CA.
Known children of James "Chalmers"[6] Abney and Jennie Cochran:
- i.   Martha "Georgia"[7], b.31 Mar 1906 CA. She m. Henry J. Day on 30 Jun 1939. She and Henry J. Day appeared on the census of 15 Apr 1940 San Francisco, San Francisco Co., CA. She d. ca.2002 Reed City, Osceola Co., MI.
      Henry J. Day, b.1896. He d.1964.
- ii. John "Percy", b.New Year's Eve, 31 Dec 1907 Rockdale Co., GA. He was liv. on 15 Apr 1940 with brother-in-law, Henry Day, San Francisco, San Francisco Co., CA. He m. Rosalie Lillian "Lillie" Lauricella. He d.14 Jul 1989 CA at age 81 and was bur. Skylawn Mem. Park, San Mateo, San Mateo Co., CA.
      Rosalie Lillian "Lillie" Lauricella, b.2 Nov 1907 CA. She m1. Robert Fred "Bert" Abney, son of James "Chalmers" Abney and Jennie Cochran, on New Year's Eve, 31 Dec 1930 Alameda, Alameda Co., CA. She and Robert Fred "Bert" Abney appeared on the census of 13 Apr 1940 San Francisco, San Francisco Co., CA. She d.26 Sep 1991 CA at age 83.
- iii. Robert Fred "Bert", b.20 Jun 1909 Rockdale Co., GA. He m. Rosalie Lillian "Lillie" Lauricella on New Year's Eve, 31 Dec 1930 Alameda, Alameda Co., CA. He and Rosalie Lillian "Lillie" Lauricella appeared on the census of 13 Apr 1940 San Francisco, San Francisco Co., CA. He d.6 Oct 1987 CA at age 78 and was bur. Skylawn Mem. Park, San Mateo.
      Rosalie Lillian "Lillie" Lauricella, b.2 Nov 1907 CA. She m2. John "Percy" Abney, son of James "Chalmers" Abney and Jennie Cochran. She d.26 Sep 1991 CA at age 83.
- iv. William, b.6 Feb 1910. He d.1 Dec 1947 at age 37; bur. Golden Gate National Cem., San Bruno, San Mateo Co., CA.
- v.   Frances Nellie, b.6 Nov 1911 CA; m1. Gavin Pes Sr. in 1934. She m2. Abner Shull in 1962; d.25 Oct 1995 SC age 83.
- vi. Thomas "Wilson" m. Gertrude Mathilda Thomford. He, b.25 May 1914 San Francisco, San Francisco Co., CA. He was liv. on 15 Apr 1940 as a boarder with Gertrude Handman, Colma, San Mateo Co., CA. He d.20 Nov 1965 San Francisco, San Francisco Co., CA, at age 51 and was bur. Golden Gate National Cem., San Francisco, San Francisco Co., CA.
      Gertrude Mathilda Thomford, b.12 Jul 1899 Hayward, Alameda Co., CA. She d.25 Sep 1956 Bayshore, San Mateo Co., CA, at age 57 and was bur. Golden Gate National Cem., San Francisco, San Francisco Co., CA.

353. Jacob Kearney "Jake"[6] Abney (John[5], Jeff[4], Hezekiah[3], Elisha[2], Abner[1]), b.26 Oct 1881 Honey Creek, Rockdale Co., GA. He was liv. on 23 Apr 1910 with his brother-in-law, Wm. F. Riley, San Francisco, San Francisco Co., CA. He m. Eugénie Adélaïde Argoud on 15 Jul 1913 San Francisco, San Francisco Co., CA. He and Eugénie Adélaïde Argoud appeared on the censuses of 6 Jan 1920, 9 Apr 1930 and 13 Apr 1940 San Francisco, San Francisco Co., CA. He d.29 Jul 1971 Contra Costa Co., CA, at age 89 and was bur. Sunset Maus. and Columbarium, El Cerrito, Contra Costa Co., CA.
    Eugénie Adélaïde Argoud, b. ca.1892 CA.
Known children of Jacob Kearney "Jake"[6] Abney and Eugénie Adélaïde Argoud:
- i.   Earl H.[7], b.24 Nov 1916.
- ii. Ernest L., b. ca.1921 CA. He m. Muriel Elaine Madieros.

354. Arizona "Elizabeth"[6] Abney (John[5], Jeff[4], Hezekiah[3], Elisha[2], Abner[1]), b.10 May 1884 GA. She m1. William F. Riley in 1906. She and William F. Riley appeared on the censuses of 23 Apr 1910, 5 Jan 1920, and 5 Apr 1930 San Francisco, San Francisco Co., CA. She m2. Louis Angelo Chiappella in 1937. She and Louis Angelo Chiappella appeared on the census of 15 Apr 1940 San Francisco, San Francisco Co., CA. She d.29 Oct 1969 San Rafael, Marin Co., CA, at age 85 and was bur. Sunset View Cem., El Cerrito, Contra Costa Co., CA.
    William F. Riley, b.1 Aug 1882 San Francisco Co., CA. He d.18 Feb 1931 San Francisco Co., CA, at age 48.

Known children of Arizona "Elizabeth"[6] Abney and William F. Riley:

      i.   Hazel Elsie[7], b.3 Nov 1907 San Francisco, San Francisco Co., CA. She m. Joseph Petrucci. She and Joseph Petrucci appeared on the census of 15 Apr 1940 San Francisco, San Francisco Co., CA. She d.22 Aug 1990 San Francisco, San Francisco Co., CA, at age 82.

            Joseph Petrucci, b.1903 Italy. He d.1995.

     ii. Grace F., b. ca.Aug 1909 CA.

    Louis Angelo Chiappella, b.27 Sep 1888 Cavour, Piedmont, Turin, Italy and was bur. Sunset Maus. and Columbarium, El Cerrito, Contra Costa Co., CA. He d.22 Mar 1976 San Mateo Co., CA, at age 87.

Known children of Arizona "Elizabeth"[6] Abney and Louis Angelo Chiappella:

      i.   Frank[7], b. ca.1935 CA.

355. Florence[6] Johnson (Elizabeth[5] Abney, Joel[4], Hezekiah[3], Elisha[2], Abner[1]), b.Oct 1877 AL. She m. (n.n.) ca.1896 and had issue.

356. Viola M.[6] Johnson (Sarah[5] Abney, Joel[4], Hezekiah[3], Elisha[2], Abner[1]), b.25 Mar 1880 Oak Level, Cleburne Co., AL. She m. Burrell Peoples "Burl" Bailey ca.1900. She d.2 Jun 1965 Beckville, Panola Co., TX, at age 85 and was bur. Martin Cem., Tatum, Rusk Co., TX.

    Burrell Peoples "Burl" Bailey, b.14 Feb 1877 Jasper Co., GA. He m1. Mary Jane Holbrook. He d.22 Jun 1958 Rusk, Cherokee Co., TX, at age 81 and was bur. Martin Cem., Tatum, Rusk Co., TX.

Known children of Viola M.[6] Johnson and Burrell Peoples "Burl" Bailey:

      i.   Sam B.[7], b.5 Apr 1901 AL. He m. Maggie Mae Grimes in 1950. He d.7 Oct 1979 Dayton, Liberty Co., TX, at age 78 and was bur. Martin Cem., Tatum, Rusk Co., TX.

            Maggie Mae Grimes, b.22 Jan 1908 Shepherd, San Jacinto Co., TX. She d.26 Apr 1976 Liberty, Liberty Co., TX, at age 68 and was bur. Ryan Cem., Tarkington Prairie, Liberty Co., TX.

     ii. Bertha Mae, b.25 Jan 1904 AL. She m. William Frank Lane. She d.22 Aug 1955 Beckville, Panola Co., TX, at age 51 and was bur. Martin Cem., Tatum, Rusk Co., TX.

            William Frank Lane, b.5 Feb 1901; d.23 Aug 1941, age 40; bur. Forest Lawn Mem. Park, Glendale, L.A. Co., CA.

    iii. Jessie, b.20 Aug 1907 Gladstone, Madison Co., AL. He m. Katie Dee Vice in 1929. He d.30 Jan 1991 Nacogdoches, Nacogdoches Co., TX, at age 83 and was bur. Langley Cem., Beckville, Panola Co., TX.

            Katie Dee Vice, b.10 Feb 1907 Beckville, Panola Co., TX; d.7 Jan 1990 Nacogdoches, Nacogdoches Co., TX, ae.82.

771   iv. Jack Allen, b. 31 Oct 1909 Jackson Co., AL; m. Gracie Magdalena Cheatwood.

      v. Annie Odessa, b.20 Nov 1914. She m. E.I. "Buck" Grimes (USArmy-WWII). She d.1 Apr 2001 at age 86 and was bur. Restland Mem. Park, Carthage, Panola Co., TX.

            E.I. "Buck" Grimes (USArmy-WWII), b.1 May 1916 Panola Co., TX. He d.26 Sep 1999 Carthage, Panola Co., TX, at age 83 and was bur. Restland Mem. Park, Carthage, Panola Co., TX.

     vi. Minnie Lou, b.28 May 1918 TX. She d.13 Aug 1975 Henderson, Rusk Co., TX, at age 57 and was bur. Tatum Cem., Tatum, Rusk Co., TX.

357. Levia Jane[6] Johnson (Sarah[5] Abney, Joel[4], Hezekiah[3], Elisha[2], Abner[1]), b.2 Jul 1882 GA. She m. Asa Hightower ca.1899. She m1. James Alford Thomas ca.1910. She m2. Charley Clemons ca.1922. She m3. John William Brincefield. She d.31 Jul 1971 Coal Co., OK, at age 89 and was bur. McCarty Cem., Coal Co., OK.

Known child of Levia Jane[6] Johnson and Asa Hightower:

772   i.   Lonie Mae[7], b. 20 Sep 1900 Jackson Co., AL; m. George Washington Brincefield.

    James Alford Thomas, b.6 Dec 1882. He d.21 Jan 1969 at age 86 and was bur. White Cem., Longview, Gregg Co., TX.

Known child of Levia Jane[6] Johnson and James Alford Thomas:

      i.   Ambro[7], b.14 Nov 1911 Sand Mountain, Bibb Co., AL. He d.1 Sep 1990 Caddo Par., LA, at age 78 and was bur. Lakeview Mem. Gardens, Oil City, Caddo Par., LA.

    Charley Clemons, b.29 Apr 1879 OK. He d.29 May 1937 OK at age 58 and was bur. McCarty Cem., Coal Co., OK.

Known child of Levia Jane[6] Johnson and Charley Clemons:

      i.   Edward Daniel "Eddie"[7] m. Bonnie Bell Waters. He, b.4 Nov 1923 Coalgate, Coal Co., OK. He d.21 Jan 1979 Pasadena, Harris Co., TX, at age 55 and was bur. Oakwood Cem., Corsicana, Navarro Co., TX.

            Bonnie Bell Waters, b.23 Sep 1927 Corsicana, Navarro Co., TX. She d.3 Dec 1983 Pasadena, Harris Co., TX, at age 56 and was bur. Oakwood Cem., Corsicana, Navarro Co., TX.

    John William Brincefield m1. Maggie Evelena Vandever. He, b.1869. He d.1965.

There were no known children of Levia Jane[6] Johnson and John William Brincefield.

358. Lou Etta[6] Johnson (Sarah[5] Abney, Joel[4], Hezekiah[3], Elisha[2], Abner[1]), b.25 Feb 1885 GA. She m. Henry Mack Pittman. She d.2 Sep 1952 Longview, Gregg Co., TX, at age 67 and was bur. Youngblood Cem., Beckville, Panola Co., TX.

    Henry Mack Pittman, b.5 Apr 1883 AL. He d.5 Jan 1974 Beckville, Panola Co., TX, at age 90 and was bur. Youngblood Cem., Beckville.

Known child of Lou Etta[6] Johnson and Henry Mack Pittman:

773   i.   Delos Harrison[7], b. 6 May 1910 Scottsboro, Jackson Co., AL; m. Daisy Lee Curry.

359. George B.[6] Johnson (Sarah[5] Abney, Joel[4], Hezekiah[3], Elisha[2], Abner[1]), b.14 Mar 1888 Cleburne Co., AL. He m. Lena Estelle Pittman. He d.13 Apr 1919 Pottawatomie Co., OK, at age 31 and was bur. Youngblood Cem., Beckville, Panola Co., TX.

    Lena Estelle Pittman, b.23 Mar 1892 AL. She d.New Year's Eve, 31 Jan 1920 Beckville, Panola Co., TX, at age 27.

Known child of George B.[6] Johnson and Lena Estelle Pittman:

774   i.   Zoda Lewis[7], b. 5 May 1908 Scottsboro, Jackson Co., AL; m. Gladys Ovelle Holt.

360. John Thomas⁶ Johnson (Sarah⁵ Abney, Joel⁴, Hezekiah³, Elisha², Abner¹), b.17 Oct 1894 Jackson Co., AL. He m. Flora Edith "Eddie" Williamson. He d.23 Oct 1962 Beckville, Panola Co., TX, at age 68 and was bur. Martin Cem., Tatum, Rusk Co., TX.
      Flora Edith "Eddie" Williamson, b.13 Dec 1891 Beckville, Panola Co., TX; d.28 Aug 1970 Tatum, Rusk Co., TX, age 78; bur. Martin Cem.
Known children of John Thomas⁶ Johnson and Flora Edith "Eddie" Williamson:
        i.   Claudine⁷, b.14 Dec 1917. She d.20 Dec 1917 and was bur. Martin Cem., Tatum, Rusk Co., TX.
        ii. Oman, b.18 Apr 1922. He d.14 Mar 1930 at age 7 and was bur. Martin Cem., Tatum, Rusk Co., TX.
        iii. Felix, b.8 May 1932. He d.13 Jun 1932 and was bur. Martin Cem., Tatum, Rusk Co., TX.

361. Minnie Lou⁶ Abney (John⁵, Joel⁴, Hezekiah³, Elisha², Abner¹), b.4 Jan 1889 Cleburne Co., AL. She m. Samuel Benton Wininger on 8 Jun 1905 Hytop, Jackson Co., AL. She m. John Alfred DeBerry in 1945. She d.26 Feb 1971 Pisgah, Jackson Co., AL, at age 82 and was bur. Pisgah Cem., Pisgah, Jackson Co., AL.
      Samuel Benton Wininger, b.7 May 1875. He d.21 Mar 1935 at age 59 and was bur. Pisgah Cem., Pisgah, Jackson Co., AL.
Known children of Minnie Lou⁶ Abney and Samuel Benton Wininger:
   775   i.   Nellie Faye⁷, b. 18 Jul 1908 Hytop, Jackson Co., AL; m. Francis "Marion" R. Liles.
   776   ii. Lucinda Katherine "Katie," b. 18 Aug 1909 Hytop, Jackson Co., AL; m. Doris Sanford Hodnett.
   777   iii. Nathan Allen, b. 30 Mar 1911 Jackson Co., AL; m. Judy E. Metcalf.
        iv. Mamie Irene, b.5 Jun 1912. She d.Nov 1912 Hytop, Jackson Co., AL.
        v.   Thomas Ethan, b.29 Oct 1913. He m. Elizabeth Ruth Hall on 24 Sep 1932 Pisgah, Jackson Co., AL. He d.28 May 1988 Chattanooga, Hamilton Co., TN, at age 74; bur. Lakewood Memory Gardens East, Chattanooga, Hamilton Co., TN.
                 Elizabeth Ruth Hall, b.1914. She d.1996; bur. Lakewood Memory Gardens East, Chattanooga, Hamilton Co., TN.
   778   vi. Oscar Dan, b. 15 Aug 1915; m. Maureen Owen.
        vii. Edith, b.22 Jul 1917. She d.1 Feb 1970 Pisgah, Jackson Co., AL, at age 52; bur. Pisgah Cem., Pisgah, Jackson Co., AL.
   779   viii. Elsie May, b. 20 Mar 1919; m. James Sanford DeBerry.

      John Alfred DeBerry, b.18 Jul 1877. He m1. Samantha Caldonia Hodnett in 1897. He d.25 Feb 1960 at age 82 and was bur. Mount Pisgah Cem., Sylvester, Worth Co., GA.
There were no known children of Minnie Lou⁶ Abney and John Alfred DeBerry.

362. Essie L.⁶ Abney (John⁵, Joel⁴, Hezekiah³, Elisha², Abner¹), b.23 Dec 1889 AL. She m. William "Robert" Bean on Christmas Day, 25 Dec 1907 Jackson Co., AL. She and William "Robert" Bean appeared on the censuses of 20 Apr 1910 Allison, Jackson Co., AL; 6 Jan 1920 Stevenson, Jackson Co., AL;. and 16 Apr 1930 and 3 Apr 1940 Lupton City, Hamilton Co., TN. She d.20 Nov 1981 Hamilton Co., TN, at age 91 and was bur. Hamilton Mem. Gardens, Hixson, Hamilton Co., TN.
      William "Robert" Bean, b.29 Oct 1888 Allison, Jackson Co., AL; d.3 Feb 1968 Hixson, Hamilton Co., TN, age 79; Hamilton Mem. Gardens.
Known children of Essie L.⁶ Abney and William "Robert" Bean:
   780   i.   Eva M. "Evie"⁷, b. ca.Mar 1909 Jackson Co., AL; m. (n.n.) Penny.
        ii. George W, b.1913 Jackson Co., AL. He d.31 Aug 1913 Hytop, Jackson Co., AL.
        iii. Nannie Bagett, b.27 Feb 1915 Maxwell, Jackson Co., AL. She d.14 Apr 2005 Flintstone, Walker Co., GA, at age 90.
        iv. Emmett, b.1916. He, b. before 1920.
   781   v.   Grace Julie "Gracie," b. 28 Apr 1917 Maxwell, Jackson Co., AL; m. (n.n.) Smith.
        vi. Addie Ruth, b.18 Oct 1922 Hamilton Co., TN. She m. Capt. James McClure Richard Jr. (USAF-WWII) in 1942. She d.12 Dec 1956 Chattanooga, Hamilton Co., TN, at age 34; bur. Chattanooga Mem. Park, Chattanooga, Hamilton Co., TN.
                 Capt. James McClure Richard Jr. (USAF-WWII), b.10 May 1913. He d.7 Jul 1963 at age 50 and was bur. Chattanooga National Cem., Chattanooga, Hamilton Co., TN.

363. William A.⁶ Abney (John⁵, Joel⁴, Hezekiah³, Elisha², Abner¹), b.19 Jun 1892 Cleburne Co., AL. He m1. Martha Jane "Janie" Roberts in 1912. He and Martha Jane "Janie" Roberts appeared on the censuses of 5 Jan 1920, 5 Apr 1930 and 17 Apr 1940 Jackson Co., AL. He m2. Nancy Wise. He d.16 May 1977 Stevenson, Jackson Co., AL, at age 84 and was bur. Stevenson City Cem., Stevenson, Jackson Co., AL.
      Martha Jane "Janie" Roberts, b.19 Jun 1891 Jackson Co., AL. She d.19 Oct 1944 Chattanooga, Hamilton Co., TN, at age 53 and was bur. Allen Cem., Jackson Co., AL.
Known children of William A.⁶ Abney and Martha Jane "Janie" Roberts:
   782   i.   William "Harvey"⁷, b. 4 Jun 1913 Jackson Co., AL; m. Johnnie Cross.
        ii. Bessie Lee "Lucy," b.16 Jan 1915 Scottsboro, Jackson Co., AL. She m. Ernest Jackson Teas. She d.3 Mar 2011 Cloud Springs, Catoosa Co., GA, at age 96 and was bur. Lakewood Memory Gardens South, Lakeview, Catoosa Co., GA.
                 Ernest Jackson Teas, b.13 Jul 1912 Stevenson, Jackson Co., GA. He d.15 Nov 1994 Fort Oglethorpe, Catoosa Co., GA, at age 82 and was bur. Lakewood Memory Gardens South, Lakeview, Catoosa Co., GA.
        iii. Sylvester, b.25 Nov 1916 Jackson Co., AL. She m. Pvt. Roy C. Shrader (USArmy). She d.30 Apr 2011 Hollywood, Jackson Co., AL, at age 94 and was bur. Pinehaven Mem. Gardens, Hollywood, Jackson Co., AL.
                 Pvt. Roy C. Shrader (USArmy), b.23 Sep 1921 AL. He d.23 Jun 1974 Jackson Co., AL, at age 52 and was bur. Pinehaven Mem. Gardens, Hollywood, Jackson Co., AL.
        iv. Delmus, b.19 Nov 1918 Jackson Co., AL. He d.25 Nov 1920 Jackson Co., AL, age 2; bur. Allen Cem., Jackson Co., AL.
        v.   Edna, b.17 Feb 1921 Jackson Co., AL. She d.Leap Day, 29 Feb 1968 CA at age 47.
        vi. Betty Jane, b. ca.1922 Jackson Co., AL.
        vii. Louise, b.1922 Jackson Co., AL.
        viii. Lorraine, b.1925 Jackson Co., AL.
   783   ix. John, b. 16 Jun 1927 Stevenson, Jackson Co., AL; m. Mary Lee Owens.
        x.   Bethel Fay, b. ca.1928 Jackson Co., AL.
        xi. Billy F., b.20 Oct 1929 Jackson Co., AL. He d.3 May 2004 Pisgah, Jackson Co., AL, at age 74.

      Nancy Wise, b.5 Dec 1910. She d.1 May 2000 at age 89 and was bur. Stevenson City Cem., Stevenson, Jackson Co., AL.
There were no known children of William A.⁶ Abney and Nancy Wise.

364. Louis David⁶ Abney (John⁵, Joel⁴, Hezekiah³, Elisha², Abner¹), b.23 Dec 1893 Cleburne Co., AL. He m1. (n.n.) ca.1913. He m2. Clara E. Tidwell in 1924. He and Clara E. Tidwell appeared on the censuses of 17 Apr 1930 Lupton City, Hamilton Co., TN and 16 Apr 1940 Hamilton Co., TN. He d.20 Dec 1978 Huntsville, Madison Co., AL, at age 84 and was bur. Hamilton Mem. Gardens, Hixson, Hamilton Co., TN.
Known children of Louis David⁶ Abney and (n.n.):
- 784   i.   Ethel⁷, b. 10 Jun 1914; m. Leonard Levee Rainey.
-       ii. Lottie T., b. ca.1916 AL.
-       iii. Bertie A., b. ca.1919 AL.

Clara E. Tidwell, b.1906 MO. She d.1965 and was bur. Hamilton Mem. Gardens, Hixson, Hamilton Co., TN.
Known child of Louis David⁶ Abney and Clara E. Tidwell:
-       i.   Thomas W.⁷, b. ca.1928 AL.

365. Alonzo⁶ Abney (John⁵, Joel⁴, Hezekiah³, Elisha², Abner¹), b.24 Nov 1896 AL. He m. Elsie L. Spence ca.1922. He and his sons were liv. on 4 May 1940 as boarders in the Treadway household, Red Bank, Hamilton Co., TN. He d.15 Mar 1968 at age 71 and was bur. Jackson Chapel Cem., Hixson, Hamilton Co., TN.
Known children of Alonzo⁶ Abney and Elsie L. Spence:
-       i.   (infant)⁷, b.19 Aug 1923 TN. He d.22 Aug 1923 Dickson, Dickson Co., TN.
-       ii. Raymond D., b.8 Sep 1930. He d.24 Feb 1979, age 48; bur. Chattanooga National Cem., Chattanooga, Hamilton Co., TN.
- 785   iii. Alvin Ray, b. 4 Dec 1932 Hixson, Hamilton Co., TN; m. Joyce (n.n.).

366. Nancy Annie⁶ Waddle (Rebecca⁵ Abney, Joel⁴, Hezekiah³, Elisha², Abner¹), b.4 Feb 1888 Hokes Bluff, Etowah Co., AL. She m. John Dossie Lee. She d.15 Aug 1978 Seminary, Covington Co., MS, at age 90 and was bur. Providence Bapt. Cem., Hattiesburg, Forrest Co., MS.
John Dossie Lee, b.2 Feb 1884 Bowdon, Carroll Co., GA; d.24 Mar 1956 Seminary, Covington Co., MS, age 72; bur. Providence Bapt. Cem.
Known children of Nancy Annie⁶ Waddle and John Dossie Lee:
-       i.   Vivian Vashti⁷, b.24 Jun 1917 Hokes Bluff, Etowah Co., AL. She d.19 Dec 2003 Hattiesburg, Forrest Co., MS, at age 86 and was bur. Providence Bapt. Cem., Hattiesburg, Forrest Co., MS.
-       ii. Tom Ed, b.5 Dec 1918. He m. Annie Pearl Ford. He d.21 Aug 1978 at age 59 and was bur. Union Bapt. Ch. Cem., Union (Seminary), Covington Co., MS.
        Annie Pearl Ford, b.11 Apr 1925 Blountville, Sullivan Co., TN. She d.19 Nov 1983 Seminary, Covington Co., MS, at age 58 and was bur. Union Bapt. Ch. Cem., Union (Seminary), Covington Co., MS.
-       iii. Robert Edward, b.25 Jul 1921 Seminary, Covington Co., MS and was bur. Providence Bapt. Cem., Hattiesburg, Forrest Co., MS. He d.15 Jul 1922 Seminary, Covington Co., MS.
-       iv. Kathelene Rebecca, b.26 Oct 1923. She d.15 Mar 1924; bur. Providence Bapt. Cem., Hattiesburg, Forrest Co., MS.
-       v.   John Dorsey, b.8 Jun 1925 Seminary, Covington Co., MS. He m. Lila Irell on 4 Sep 1954. He d.18 May 1993 Seminary, Covington Co., MS, at age 67 and was bur. Union Bapt. Ch. Cem., Union (Seminary), Covington Co., MS.
        Lila Irell, b.21 Feb 1935.

367. Pvt. Lawson Lee⁶ Waddle (USArmy-WWI) (Rebecca⁵ Abney, Joel⁴, Hezekiah³, Elisha², Abner¹) m. Mabel Lowery. He, b.Christmas Day, 25 Dec 1890. He d.21 Jul 1960 at age 69 and was bur. Long Branch Cem., Clay Co., FL.
Mabel Lowery, b.9 Sep 1897. She d.9 May 1981 at age 83 and was bur. Long Branch Cem., Clay Co., FL.
Known children of Pvt. Lawson Lee⁶ Waddle (USArmy-WWI) and Mabel Lowery:
-       i.   Yvonne⁷, b.20 Jan 1934 Hattiesburg, Forrest Co., MS. She d.13 Sep 2018 Mayo, Lafayette Co., FL, at age 84 and was bur. Pineview Mem. Gardens, Perry, Taylor Co., FL.

368. Lelius Johnson⁶ Waddle (Rebecca⁵ Abney, Joel⁴, Hezekiah³, Elisha², Abner¹) m. Winifred Oveda Cannon. He, b. New Year's Day, 1 Jan 1894. He d.9 Jun 1983 at age 89 and was bur. Long Branch Cem., Clay Co., FL.
Winifred Oveda Cannon, b.6 Sep 1900. She d.30 Jan 2000 at age 99 and was bur. Long Branch Cem., Clay Co., FL.
Known children of Lelius Johnson⁶ Waddle and Winifred Oveda Cannon:
- 786   i.   Lee Alvin⁷, b. 17 Dec 1920; m. Versie Ree Wooten.
-       ii. Joyce, b. Independence Day, 4 Jul 1925. She m. Comer Knight Suggs on 1 Nov 1943. She d.20 Oct 2010 at age 85 and was bur. Santa Fe Cem., Jacksonville, Bradford Co., FL.
        Comer Knight Suggs, b.29 Aug 1922. He d.9 Aug 2013 at age 90 and was bur. Santa Fe Cem., Jacksonville.

369. Elsie Bethena⁶ Waddle (Rebecca⁵ Abney, Joel⁴, Hezekiah³, Elisha², Abner¹), b.17 Dec 1897. She m. Lonnie Lee Walden. She d.8 Oct 1966 Jacksonville, Duval Co., FL, at age 68 and was bur. Riverside Mem. Park, Jacksonville, Duval Co., FL.
Lonnie Lee Walden, b.13 May 1898. He d.13 Nov 1977 Jacksonville, Duval Co., FL, at age 79 and was bur. Riverside Mem. Park, Jacksonville.
Known children of Elsie Bethena⁶ Waddle and Lonnie Lee Walden:
- 787   i.   Gladys Rebecca⁷, b. 2 Sep 1923 Wellington, Calhoun Co., AL; m. Albert Wright.
- 788   ii. Grovene, b. 12 Feb 1926 Calhoun Co., AL; m. Ephrain Thomas.
- 789   iii. James Edward, b. 25 Jul 1929 Rock Springs, Blount Co., AL; m. Janie (n.n.).
-       iv. Eloise, b.30 Mar 1932 AL; m. George Dewey Roberson Jr.; d.4 Apr 2003 age 71; bur. Long Branch Cem., Rock Springs, Clay Co., FL.
        George Dewey Roberson Jr, b.6 Mar 1933. He d.22 Jun 1997 at age 64 and was bur. Long Branch Cem., Rock Springs.
-       v.   Flora Mae "Flirt", b.1935. She m. Roy Lee Fowler in 1962. She d.2001 and was bur. Sawnee View Gardens and Maus., Cumming, Forsyth Co., GA.
        Roy Lee Fowler, b.1925. He d.1985 and was bur. Sawnee View Gardens and Maus., Cumming, Forsyth Co., GA.
-       vi. Alma Lee "Pal" m. Bruce T. Blair. , b.6 Sep 1936. She d.11 Mar 1996 at age 59 and was bur. Greenlawn Cem., Jacksonville, Duval Co., FL.
        Bruce T. Blair, b.23 Feb 1961. He d.18 Nov 1992 at age 31; bur. Greenlawn Cem., Jacksonville, Duval Co., FL.

370. Marvin⁶ Jackson (Martha⁵ Abney, Joel⁴, Hezekiah³, Elisha², Abner¹), b.1 Jun 1900. He m. Rochelle Chastain. He d.12 May 1962 at age 61 and was bur. Oakland Cem., Rome, Floyd Co., GA.
    Rochelle Chastain, b.25 Jul 1900. She d.25 Jun 1993 at age 92 and was bur. Oakland Cem., Rome, Floyd Co., GA.
Known children of Marvin⁶ Jackson and Rochelle Chastain:
        i.   (infant son)⁷, b.10 Nov 1921. He d.10 Nov 1921 and was bur. Friendship Bapt. Ch. Cem., Rome, Floyd Co., GA.
        ii. Stella, b.9 Jan 1923. She m. James Peter Kelley. She d.14 Oct 2006 at age 83; bur. Oakland Cem., Rome, Floyd Co., GA.
           James Peter Kelley, b.15 Nov 1922 Floyd Co., GA. He d.17 May 1990 Rome, Floyd Co., GA, at age 67 and was bur. Morning View Cem., Rome, Floyd Co., GA.
        iii. Ethel, b.10 Dec 1924 Piedmont, Calhoun Co., AL. She m. (n.n.) Miller. She d.27 May 1943 Chattanooga, Hamilton Co., TN, at age 18 and was bur. Friendship Bapt. Ch. Cem., Rome, Floyd Co., GA.
        iv. Irene, b.27 Feb 1927. She d.28 Jan 1931 at age 3 and was bur. Friendship Bapt. Ch. Cem., Rome, Floyd Co., GA.
        v. Leomia "Jackie", b.12 Aug 1929 Floyd Co., GA. She m. Vernon Dillard Wallace. She d.2 Aug 2015 Rome, Floyd Co., GA, at age 85 and was bur. Floyd Memory Gardens, Rome, Floyd Co., GA.
           Vernon Dillard Wallace, b.16 Jul 1926 Floyd Co., GA. He d.Independence Day, 4 Jul 2015 Rome, Floyd Co., GA, at age 88 and was bur. Floyd Memory Gardens, Rome, Floyd Co., GA.
        vi. Fain B., b.27 Jul 1932. He d.9 Jul 1997 at age 64 and was bur. Riverside Cem., Riverside, Riverside Co., CA.
        vii. Frank, b.27 Jul 1932. He m. Opal Elder. He d.10 Aug 2013 at age 81; bur. Northview Cem., Cedartown, Polk Co., GA.
           Opal Elder, b.27 Apr 1935 Felton, Haralson Co., GA. She d.11 Dec 2009 Cedartown, Polk Co., GA, at age 74 and was bur. Northview Cem., Cedartown, Polk Co., GA.

371. George Thomas⁶ Steele (Margaret⁵ McGuire, Elizabeth⁴ Woods, Dorcas³ Abney, Elisha², Abner¹), b.1874. He m. Emma Catherine "Kate" May. He d.1948.
    Emma Catherine "Kate" May, b. ca.1877.
Known children of George Thomas⁶ Steele and Emma Catherine "Kate" May:
        i.   James Frank⁷, b.1893. He d.1973.
        ii. Lona Elizabeth "Loney", b.1895. She d.1971.
        iii. Ernest "Victor", b.1898. He d.1965.
        iv. John Roscoe, b.1901. He d.1970.

372. Nancy Baker⁶ Allen (Susan⁵ Abner, William⁴, Elisha³, Elisha² Abney, Abner¹), b.8 Jul 1854 Clay Co., KY. She m. Archibald "Taylor" Abney, son of Jonathan Abney and Ollie Jane Sexton, ca.1868. She and Archibald "Taylor" Abney appeared on the censuses of 4 Jun 1880 and 20 Jun 1900 Rockcastle Co., KY. She d.10 Dec 1919 Rockcastle Co., KY, at age 65 and was bur. A.T. Abney Mem. Garden, Rockcastle Co., KY.
    Archibald "Taylor" Abney, b.6 Jan 1847 Disputanta, Rockcastle Co., KY. He was a son of Jonathan Abney and Ollie Jane Sexton. Jonathan was son of Pvt. William Abney, RS and Judith Graves. William was a son of John Abney, whom the author has dubbed *"the Lost Son"* (son of Paul Abney [bapt.1699], son of Dannett Abney Sr. [Colonist Ancestor]). Archibald Taylor Abney was 4th cousin, once removed of his wife, Nancy Baker Allen, and to be honest, it is doubtful if they ever knew they were related. Archibald's family never went by *Abney*, ergo it is doubtful if they would have made the familial connection between Abney and Abner. He appeared as a widower Head of Household on the census of 14 Jan 1920 Scaffold Cane, Rockcastle Co., KY; d.8 Feb 1935 Mount Vernon, Rockcastle Co., KY, ae.88; bur. A.T. Abney Mem. Garden, Rockcastle Co., KY.
Known children of Nancy Baker⁶ Allen and Archibald "Taylor" Abney:
             i.   (n.n.)⁷, b. ca.1870; d. before 1880 Rockcastle Co., KY.
  790 ii. Sarah Bluford "Blufie," b. 3 Apr 1872; m. J.E. McGuire.
  791 iii. Martha Jane, b. Jan 1874 Rockcastle Co., KY; m. Olmstead Mitchell Payne.
             iv. Mary J., b. ca.1877.
  792 v. Ollie Jane, b. 25 Apr 1879 Rockcastle Co., KY; m. Thomas Clinton Holt.
             vi. Parrie Lee, b.Mar 1885 Rockcastle Co., KY. She m. William H. Stephens. She d.19 Feb 1960 Rockcastle Co., KY, at age 74 and was bur. A.T. Abney Mem. Garden, Rockcastle Co., KY.
  793 vii. Robert T., b. 6 Nov 1890 Rockcastle Co., KY; m. Bess M. "Bessie" McWhorter.
  794 viii. Reuben J., b. 2 Jul 1894 Rockcastle Co., KY; m. Edith Ann Linville.

373. William⁶ Parker (Susan⁵ Abner, William⁴, Elisha³, Elisha² Abney, Abner¹), b.18 Oct 1872 KY. He m. Nannie A. Gay. He d.25 Mar 1942 at age 69 and was bur. Parker Cem., Island City, Owsley Co., KY.
    Nannie A. Gay, b.4 Nov 1873 KY. She d.10 Dec 1954 Conkling, Owsley Co., KY, at age 81 and was bur. Parker Cem., Island City.
Known children of William⁶ Parker and Nannie A. Gay:
        i.   Dessie⁷, b.1894. She d.1963.
        ii. Della, b.1897. She d.1968.
        iii. Kate, b.1901. She d.1966.
        iv. Minnie Lou, b.1906. She d.1968.

374. Robert⁶ Abner (David⁵, William⁴, Elisha³, Elisha² Abney, Abner¹), b.11 Mar 1861 Clay Co., KY. He m. Esther Bishop, daughter of Bryson "Brice" Bishop and Eliza "Lizie" Allen, ca.1880. He and Esther Bishop were liv. on 7 Jun 1880 with his father, David Abner, Clay Co., KY. He and Esther Bishop appeared on the censuses of 15 Jun 1900 and 18 Apr 1910 Clay Co., KY. He and Esther Bishop were liv. on 6 May 1930 with their son-in-law, Henry Wood, Sturgeon, Jackson Co., KY; and on 25 Apr 1940 with their son, John B. Abney, Sturgeon, Jackson Co., KY. He d.14 Apr 1941 Fayette Co., IN, at age 80 and was bur. Liberty Cem., Egypt, Jackson Co., KY.
    Esther Bishop, b.1 Oct 1862 Clay Co., KY. She d.20 Dec 1949 Union Co., IN, at age 87 and was bur. Liberty Cem., Egypt, Jackson Co., KY.
Known children of Robert⁶ Abner and Esther Bishop all b. Clay Co., KY:
        i.   Dory⁷, b. May 1881. (see page 83).
        ii. Mary, b. Oct 1882. (see page 83).
        iii. William D., b. Jun 1884; m. Ella Allen; div. Ella Allen. (see # 474 on page 133).
        iv. Lillie, b. May 1885; m. Henry Wood. (see # 475 on page 133).
        v. John B., b. Apr 1886; m. Nannie J. Wood. (see # 476 on page 134).

vi.   Daniel P. "Dan," b. 20 Jun 1889; m. Lucy Noe. (see # 477 on page 134).
vii.   Shelby, b. Feb 1891; m. Eva Bowman. (see # 478 on page 134).
viii.   Ida, b. 22 Jun 1894; m. Lucian S. Byrd Sr. (see # 479 on page 134).
ix.   Robert, b. Feb 1896. (see page 83).
x.   Taylor, b. Aug 1899. (see page 83).

375. William W.⁶ Abner (David⁵, William⁴, Elisha³, Elisha² Abney, Abner¹), b.25 Nov 1867 Owsley Co., KY. He m. Margaret E. (n.n.). He d.11 Jan 1951 Lancaster, Garrard Co., KY, at age 83 and was bur. Lancaster Cem., Lancaster, Garrard Co., KY.
      Margaret E. (n.n.), b.1868. She d.1947 and was bur. Lancaster Cem., Lancaster, Garrard Co., KY.
Known child of William W.⁶ Abner and Margaret E. (n.n.):
      795   i.   Gilbert Taylor⁷, b. 31 Jul 1890 KY; m. Eva Davis.

376. Sarah Jane⁶ Allen (Easter⁵ Abner, William⁴, Elisha³, Elisha² Abney, Abner¹), b. ca.Nov 1869 Clay Co., KY.
Know child of Sarah Jane⁶ Allen (out of wedlock):
      796   i.   Armilda "Mildred" (surname: Allen)⁷, b. 4 Mar 1896 KY; She m. Anderson Eversole.

377. Letta May "Lettie"⁶ Abner (Lewis⁵, William⁴, Elisha³, Elisha² Abney, Abner¹), b.18 Mar 1876 Clay Co., KY. She m. J.E. Stanfield on 7 Aug 1891. She and J.E. Stanfield were divorced before 1900.
Known children of Letta May "Lettie"⁶ Abner and J.E. Stanfield both b. KY:
      i.   Thoma⁷, (daughter) b. Mar 1892.
      ii.   Docia, b. Aug 1893.

378. Martha B.⁶ Abner (Lewis⁵, William⁴, Elisha³, Elisha² Abney, Abner¹), b. Apr 1880 Clay Co., KY; m. Bev. Baker on 30 May 1895 Clay Co.
      Beverly Baker, b.5 Mar 1878. He d.15 Mar 1939 at age 61 and was bur. Englewood Cem., Christopher, Perry Co., KY.
Known children of Martha B.⁶ Abner and Beverly Baker:
      i.   Hoak⁷.
      ii.   Helen.
      iii.   Florence.
      iv.   Blanche.
      v.   Sadie.

379. Shelby C.⁶ Abner (Lewis⁵, William⁴, Elisha³, Elisha² Abney, Abner¹), b.29 Apr 1883 Teges, Clay Co., KY. He m. Carrie Bell McDaniel ca.1924. He and Carrie Bell McDaniel appeared on the censuses of 15 Apr 1930 and 18 Apr 1940 Teges, Clay Co., KY. He d.27 May 1950 Teges, Clay Co., KY, at age 67 and was bur. Patsy Allen Cem., Teges, Clay Co., KY.
      Carrie Bell McDaniel, b.1 Sep 1903. She d.19 Jul 1984 at age 80 and was bur. Patsy Allen Cem., Teges, Clay Co., KY.
Known children of Shelby C.⁶ Abner and Carrie Bell McDaniel:
      797   i.   David Francis⁷, b. New Year's Eve, 31 Jan 1925 Teges, Clay Co., KY; m. Rozella Marie Littlefield.
      ii.   Paul H., b. ca.Dec 1926 Clay Co., KY.
      iii.   Sarah "Rose", b.22 Sep 1928 Clay Co., KY. She d.13 Feb 2013 Lexington, Fayette Co., KY, at age 84.
      iv.   Juanita, b.3 Sep 1932 Teges, Clay Co., KY. She d.28 Jun 1935 Oneida, Clay Co., KY, at age 2; bur. Patsy Allen Cem.

380. George W.⁶ Abner (Lewis⁵, William⁴, Elisha³, Elisha² Abney, Abner¹), b.14 Oct 1885 Clay Co., KY; m1. Malinda "Linda" Lewis on 26 Oct 1906 Clay Co., KY. He m2. May B. Rogers ca.1922. He d.3 Apr 1959 Oneida, Clay Co., KY, age 73; bur. Patsy Allen Cem., Teges, Clay Co., KY.
      Malinda "Linda" Lewis, b.1899. She d.1955 Clay Co., KY and was bur. Patsy Allen Cem., Teges, Clay Co., KY.
Known children of George W.⁶ Abner and Malinda "Linda" Lewis:
      i.   Ray B.⁷, b.1909. He d.1960 and was bur. Patsy Allen Cem., Teges, Clay Co., KY.
      798   ii.   Walter Clyde, b. 29 Mar 1912 Clay Co., KY; m. Chloe Sizemore.

      May B. Rogers, b.3 Oct 1900 MO. She d.19 Jan 1987 Connersville, Fayette Co., IN, age 86; bur. Laurel North Cem., Laurel, Franklin Co., IN.
Known children of George W.⁶ Abner and May B. Rogers:
      i.   Docie⁷, b.1 May 1923 Manchester, Clay Co., KY. She m. Henry Clay Osborne in 1956. She d.9 Mar 1986 Middletown, Butler Co., OH, at age 62 and was bur. Woodside Cem., Middletown, Butler Co., OH.
                  Henry Clay Osborne, b.22 Dec 1926 North Middletown, Bourbon Co., KY. He d.15 Nov 2001 OH at age 74 and was bur. Miltonville Cem., Miltonville, Butler Co., OH.
      ii.   Mildred B., b.24 Oct 1926 Clay Co., KY. She m. Paul Vincent Moster in 1950. She d.19 Feb 2010 Richmond, Wayne Co., IN, at age 83 and was bur. Laurel North Cem., Laurel, Franklin Co., IN.
                  Paul Vincent Moster, b.5 Apr 1918 IN. He d.19 Jul 2002 at age 84; bur. Laurel North Cem., Laurel, Franklin Co., IN.
      iii.   Lois E., b.3 May 1935 Clay Co., KY. She d.22 Nov 1984 Laurel, Franklin Co., IN, at age 49.

381. Cpl. Walter Gray⁶ Abner (USArmy) (Lewis⁵, William⁴, Elisha³, Elisha² Abney, Abner¹), b.1 May 1889 Clay Co., KY. He m. Nora Campbell ca.1910. He began military service on 20 Aug 1910 OH. He was honorably discharged on 19 Aug 1913. He d.24 Sep 1947 at age 58 and was bur. Patsy Allen Cem., Teges, Clay Co., KY.
      Nora Campbell, b.18 Jun 1892 Clay Co., KY. She d.21 Jul 1964 Clay Co., KY, at age 72 and was bur. Patsy Allen Cem., Teges, Clay Co., KY.
Known children of Cpl. Walter Gray⁶ Abner (USArmy) and Nora Campbell all b. KY:
      i.   Ray⁷, b. ca.1911.
      ii.   Clyde, b. ca.1913.
      iii.   Thelma Belle, b.20 Jul 1915. She m. George M. Felty (USArmy-WWII) on 20 Feb 1933. She d.25 Mar 1985 Manchester, Clay Co., KY, at age 69 and was bur. Patsy Allen Cem., Teges, Clay Co., KY.
                  George M. Felty (USArmy-WWII), b.20 Feb 1912; d.9 Dec 1999, age 87; bur. Patsy Allen Cem., Teges.

382. Charles Benjamin "Ben"⁶ Abner (Robert⁵, William⁴, Elisha³, Elisha² Abney, Abner¹), b.17 Sep 1873 Owsley Co., KY. He m. Rachel Allen ca.1898. He and Rachel Allen appeared on the censuses of 16 Jun 1900 Clay Co., KY; 15 Jan 1920 Hamilton, Butler Co., OH; 4 Apr 1930 Posey, Franklin Co., IN; and 29 Apr 1940 back in Hamilton. He d.16 Jan 1955 Hamilton, Butler Co., OH, age 81; bur. Greenwood Cem., Hamilton, OH.
    Rachel Allen, b.18 Feb 1881 Clay Co., KY. She d.8 Mar 1970 Butler Co., OH, at age 89 and was bur. Greenwood Cem., Hamilton.
Known children of Charles Benjamin "Ben"⁶ Abner and Rachel Allen:
799   i.   Ethel Mae⁷, b. 28 May 1899 Clay Co., KY; m. Herbert Baker; m. Howard Kenneth Crawley.
       ii.   (infant son), b. est.1903 Clay Co., KY. He d. est.1903.
       iii. Ellen, b. ca.1905 Clay Co., KY. She m. (n.n.) Miley.
       iv.   Nannie, b.1907 Clay Co., KY. She m1. Clinton Baker ca.1929. They were liv. on 25 Apr 1930 with his father, John A. Baker, Butler Co., OH. She m2. Fred B. Wood. She d.1985 and was bur. Glen Haven Cem., Harrison, Hamilton Co., OH.
             Clinton Baker, b. ca.1909 OH.
             Fred B. Wood, b.1907. He d.1997 and was bur. Glen Haven Cem., Harrison, Hamilton Co., OH.
       v.   Minnie, b.17 Aug 1910 Butler Co., OH. She m. Roscoe D. Sexton. She d.28 Apr 1983 Hamilton, Butler Co., OH, at age 72 and was bur. Greenwood Cem., Hamilton, Butler Co., OH.
             Roscoe D. Sexton, b.26 Mar 1914 London, Laurel Co., KY; d.24 May 1990 Hamilton,OH; bur. Greenwood Cem.
       vi.   Georgiana "Georgie", b.1913 Clay Co., KY; m. (n.n.) Million; d.23 Aug 1962 Middletown, Butler Co., OH; bur. Greenwood Cem., Hamilton, Butler Co., OH.
800   vii. Daniel "Dan," b. 17 Aug 1917 Franklin Co., IN; m. Beryle R. Kelly.
       viii. Willa E. "Willie" m. Clifford Forrester. , b. ca.1921 Butler Co., OH.
       ix.   Raymond, b.11 Dec 1922 Laurel, Franklin Co., IN; d.14 Dec 1999 Hamilton, Butler Co., OH, at age 77. He was cremated.
801   x.   Herbert, b. 11 Jun 1926 Hamilton, Butler Co., OH; m. Goldie Clark.

383. Mary Alice⁶ Abner (Robert⁵, William⁴, Elisha³, Elisha² Abney, Abner¹), b.28 Apr 1875 Owsley Co., KY. She m. Thomas Taylor in 1891 Owsley Co., KY. She d.27 Nov 1938 Trenton, Butler Co., OH, at age 63 and was bur. Greenwood Cem., Hamilton, Butler Co., OH.
    Thomas Taylor, b.1867 Claiborne Co., TN. He d.10 Oct 1951 Hamilton, Butler Co., OH and was bur. Greenwood Cem., Hamilton.
Known children of Mary Alice⁶ Abner and Thomas Taylor:
       i.   Henry⁷, b.1894. He d.1972.
       ii.   Clay, b.1896. He d.1963.
       iii. Volentine, b.1898. She d.1929.
       iv.   Zack, b.1900. He d.1953.
       v.   Martha, b.1902. She d.1984.
       vi.   J. Penn, b.1904. He d.1987.
       vii. Mary Ellis, b.1906. She d.1959.
       viii. William, b.1908. He d.1970.
       ix.   Mae Ellen, b.1911. She d.1990.
       x.   Louise P., b.1915. She d.1971.

384. Nancy Geneva "Jennie"⁶ Abner (Robert⁵, William⁴, Elisha³, Elisha² Abney, Abner¹), b.28 Oct 1878 Owsley Co., KY. She m. Robert Allen. She d.1931 and was bur. Greenwood Cem., Hamilton, Butler Co., OH.
    Robert Allen, b.1873. He d.Apr 1928 and was bur. Greenwood Cem., Hamilton, Butler Co., OH.
Known children of Nancy Geneva "Jennie"⁶ Abner and Robert Allen:
       i.   Gertrude⁷, b.1897. She d.1973.
       ii.   Ruth, b.1900. She d.1978.
       iii. Hobart, b.1902. He d.1976.
       iv.   Hazel, b.1905. She d.1982.
       v.   Daisy, b.1907. She d.1978.
       vi.   Homer, b.1910. He d.1969.
       vii. Sarah Bernice, b.1924. She d.1925.

385. Jack Robert⁶ Abner (Robert⁵, William⁴, Elisha³, Elisha² Abney, Abner¹), b.30 Mar 1880 Owsley Co., KY. He m1. Laura B. Darrell ca.1901. He and Laura B. Darrell appeared on the censuses of 5 May 1910; 9 Apr 1930; and 29 Apr 1940 Oneida, Clay Co., KY. He m2. Sallie Hall. He d.20 Feb 1957 Madison Co., KY, at age 76 and was bur. Maxaline Baker Cem., Oneida, Clay Co., KY.
    Laura B. Darrell, b.13 Jan 1881 KY. She appeared as Head of Household on the census of 14 Jan 1920 London, Laurel Co., KY. She d.27 Jul 1946 KY at age 65 and was bur. Maxaline Baker Cem., Oneida, Clay Co., KY.
Known children of Jack Robert⁶ Abner and Laura B. Darrell:
       i.   Addie⁷, b.1903 Clay Co., KY. She m. Troy Sid Cole in 1921 London, Laurel Co., KY. She d.2 May 1995 and was bur. Johnson Cem., Greeley, Lee Co., KY.
             Troy Sid Cole, b.1902. He d.1987 Madison Co., KY and was bur. Johnson Cem., Greeley, Madison Co., KY.
802   ii.   Elizabeth "Lizzie," b. 23 Sep 1904 Clay Co., KY; m1. Ezra Kelton; m2. Robert Hay; m3. Charles L. Ashton.
       iii. Pvt. Robert D. (USArmy-WWII), b.23 Nov 1908 Clay Co., KY. He d.4 Nov 1957 Hamilton, Butler Co., OH, at age 48 and was bur. World War II Field of Honor, Greenwood Cem., Hamilton, Butler Co., OH.
803   iv.   Preston Innominatus, b. 10 Apr 1910 Clay Co., KY; m1. Thelma L. Henderson; m2. Thelma L. Henderson.
804   v.   Mary, b. Christmas Day, 25 Dec 1911; m. William Edward Allen.
       vi.   Asbury, b.6 Feb 1915 Clay Co., KY. He d.29 Apr 1981 at age 66; bur. Richmond Cem., Richmond, Madison Co., KY.
       vii. Clarence, b.1917 Clay Co., KY. He d.1930 Clay Co., KY and was bur. Maxaline Baker Cem., Oneida, Clay Co., KY.
       viii. Gladys Marie m. Charles Ray Marcum. , b.1919. She d.1991 and was bur. Richmond Cem., Richmond, Madison Co., KY.
             Charles Ray Marcum, b.17 Sep 1919. He d.15 Sep 1994, age 74; bur. Richmond Cem., Richmond, Madison Co., KY.

There were no known children of Jack Robert⁶ Abner and Sallie Hall.

386. Cleveland "Cleve"[6] Abner (Robert[5], William[4], Elisha[3], Elisha[2] Abney, Abner[1]), b.4 Mar 1885 Owsley Co., KY. He m. Lillie Burns on 7 May 1911 Clay Co., KY. He d.21 Jun 1961 Hamilton, Butler Co., OH, at age 76 and was bur. Greenwood Cem., Hamilton, Butler Co., OH.

Lillie Burns, b.1891 Oneida, Clay Co., KY. She d.1 May 1969 Hamilton, Butler Co., OH and was bur. Greenwood Cem., Hamilton.
Known children of Cleveland "Cleve"[6] Abner and Lillie Burns:
  i.   Pearl C.[7], b.2 Apr 1912 Jackson Co., KY. He d.7 May 1912 Teges, Clay Co., KY and was bur. Patsy Allen Cem., Teges, Clay Co., KY.
  ii.   Ruth, b.1913. She m. (n.n.) Williamson. She d.29 Dec 1973 and was bur. Greenwood Cem., Hamilton, Butler Co., OH.

387. Susan "Susie"[6] Abner (Robert[5], William[4], Elisha[3], Elisha[2] Abney, Abner[1]) m. Benjamin Harrison Gabbard. , b.24 Mar 1888. She d.12 Jul 1966 at age 78 and was bur. Greenwood Cem., Hamilton, Butler Co., OH.

Benjamin Harrison Gabbard, b.26 May 1889. He d.8 Jan 1961 at age 71 and was bur. Greenwood Cem., Hamilton, Butler Co., OH.
Known children of Susan "Susie"[6] Abner and Benjamin Harrison Gabbard:
  i.   Audrey Jane[7], b.1918. She d.2003.
  ii.   Gladys, b.1920. She d.1991.
  iii. Clyde E., b.1924. He d.2020.

388. Daniel Boone[6] Abner (USArmy-WWI) (Robert[5], William[4], Elisha[3], Elisha[2] Abney, Abner[1]), b.17 May 1890 Owsley Co., KY. He m1. Fannie Pearl Evans on 22 Aug 1913. Div. aft. 1820. He m2. Ethel Ruby Hurst in 1924. He and Ethel Ruby Hurst appeared on the census of 14 Apr 1930 Hamilton, Butler Co., OH. He d.7 Mar 1932 Hamilton, Butler Co., OH, at age 41 and was bur. Greenwood Cem., Hamilton, Butler Co., OH.

Fannie Pearl Evans, b.1 Dec 1890 Owsley Co., KY.. She d.Nov 1980 Hamilton Co., TN, at age 89.
There were no known children of Daniel Boone[6] Abner (USArmy-WWI) and Fannie Pearl Evans.

Ethel Ruby Hurst, b.9 Aug 1903 McKee, Jackson Co., KY. She appeared as Head of Household on the census of 1940 Hamilton, Butler Co., OH. She d.22 Aug 1981 Oxford, Butler Co., OH, at age 78 and was bur. Rose Hill Burial Park, Hamilton, Butler Co., OH.
Known children of Daniel Boone[6] Abner (USArmy-WWI) and Ethel Ruby Hurst all b. Hamilton, Butler Co., OH:
  805   i.   Zetta Pearl[7], b. 6 Dec 1923; m. John A. Russo.
        ii.   Roy F., b.9 Jun 1926; d.8 Jul 1981 Hamilton, Butler Co., OH, age 55; bur. Greenwood Cem., Hamilton, Butler Co., OH.
  806   iii. Harold D., b. 12 Nov 1931; m. Jewel Dean South.

389. Leander F. "Lee"[6] Abner (John[5], Lacy[4], Elisha[3], Elisha[2] Abney, Abner[1]), b.5 Aug 1868 Owsley Co., KY. He m1. Nancy Ann Daniel. He appeared on the census of 11 Jun 1900 Clay Co., KY. He m2. Nancy Jane Bishop on 14 Apr 1902 Manchester, Clay Co., KY. He & Nancy appeared on the censuses of 22 Apr 1910, 28 Jan 1920, 14 Apr 1930 and 23 Apr 1940 Allen, Clay Co., KY; d.18 Jun 1944 Clay Co., KY, at age 75.

Nancy Ann Daniel, b.1875 Clay Co., KY. She d. before 1900.
Known child of Leander F. "Lee"[6] Abner and Nancy Ann Daniel:
  i.   Hugh[7], b. Christmas Day, 25 Dec 1895 Owsley Co., KY. He d.11 Dec 1942, Deerfield, Warren Co., OH, at age 46.
Nancy Jane Bishop, b.1877 Owsley Co., KY. She d.7 Oct 1954 Trixie, Clay Co., KY.
There were no known children of Leander F. "Lee"[6] Abner and Nancy Jane Bishop.

390. Wiley Burns[6] Abner (John[5], Lacy[4], Elisha[3], Elisha[2] Abney, Abner[1]), b.12 Jun 1874 Owsley Co., KY. He m. Leathan McIntosh ca.1895. He appeared on the census of 12 Feb 1920 Bullskin, Clay Co., KY. He and Leathan McIntosh appeared on the censuses of 8 Apr 1930 Panco, Clay Co., KY; and 1 May 1940 Clay Co., KY. He d.7 Jun 1947 Clay Co., KY, at age 72 and was bur. Fairview Cem., Panco, Clay Co., KY.

Leathan McIntosh, b.13 Mar 1876 Perry Co., KY. She d.10 Jul 1946 Lexington, Fayette Co., KY, at age 70 and was bur. Fairview Cem., Panco.
Known children of Wiley Burns[6] Abner and Leathan McIntosh:
  807   i.   Emaline[7], b. 3 Mar 1896 Owsley Co., KY; m. Jacob Carmack Jr.
  808   ii.   Isabelle, b. ca.1903 Owsley Co., KY; m. William Fugate.
  809   iii. John "Johnny," b. 3 Jun 1905 Owsley Co., KY; m. Eva Cornett; m. Frances Barger.
        iv.   Loretta, b. ca.1910 Owsley Co., KY. She m. (n.n.) White. She d.16 Apr 1958 Brutus, Clay Co., KY.
        v.   Sam, b. ca.1913 Clay Co., KY. He m. Mary Belle Barger on 30 Jun 1932 Manchester, Clay Co., KY.
              Mary Belle Barger, b. ca.1912.
        vi.   Della, b. ca.1914 Clay Co., KY. She m. Seth Baker on 14 Aug 1932 Panco, Clay Co., KY.
              Seth Baker, b. ca.1911.
  810   vii. Mattie, b. ca.Jul 1916 Clay Co., KY; m. Ray Barger.

391. Manerva[6] Abner (Leander[5], Lacy[4], Elisha[3], Elisha[2] Abney, Abner[1]), b.20 Apr 1885 Clay Co., KY. She m. Hugh White Robertson ca.1904. She and Hugh White Robertson appeared on the censuses of 29 Jan 1920 Allen, Clay Co., KY and 15 Apr 1930 Teges, Clay Co., KY. She d.13 Aug 1958 Manchester, Clay Co., KY, at age 73 and was bur. Patsy Allen Cem., Teges, Clay Co., KY.

Hugh White Robertson, b.Feb 1881 KY. He d.25 Mar 1961 Hamilton, Butler Co., OH, at age 80 and was bur. Patsy Allen Cem., Teges.
Known children of Manerva[6] Abner and Hugh White Robertson:
  i.   Lula[7], b. ca.1905 Clay Co., KY.
  ii.   John, b. ca.1908 Clay Co., KY.
  iii. Preston, b. ca.1911 Clay Co., KY.
  iv.   Rose, b.16 Mar 1913 Manchester, Clay Co., KY. She d.17 Aug 1991 Manchester, Clay Co., KY, at age 78.
  v.   Gilbert, b. ca.1916 Clay Co., KY.

392. Elsey Ann "Annie"[6] Abner (Harvey[5], Lacy[4], Elisha[3], Elisha[2] Abney, Abner[1]), b.8 May 1888 Owsley Co., KY. She m. James F. Jackson on 1 Aug 1906 Clay Co., KY. She d.27 Oct 1916 Clay Co., KY, at age 28 and was bur. Job Allen Cem., Oneida, Clay Co., KY.

James F. Jackson, b. Dec 1877 Owsley Co., KY. He d.23 Aug 1918 Clay Co., KY, at age 40 and was bur. Job Allen Cem., Oneida.
Known children of Elsey Ann "Annie"[6] Abner and James F. Jackson:
  i.   Clay[7], b. ca.1911. He was liv. ca.1911 and on 9 Apr 1930 with grandfather, Harvey Abner, Allen, Clay Co., KY.
  ii.   Opha, b.1913. She d.1916.
  iii. Brice, b.1915. He d.1916.

393. James B.[6] Abner (Harvey[5], Lacy[4], Elisha[3], Elisha[2] Abney, Abner[1]), b.12 May 1890 Owsley Co., KY. He m. Verna E. "Vernie" Felty on 9 Jan 1919 Clay Co., KY. He and Verna E. "Vernie" Felty appeared on the censuses of 30 Jan 1920 Allen, Clay Co., KY; 23 Apr 1930 Sexton Creek, Clay Co., KY; and 26 Apr 1940 Clay Co., KY. He d.8 Aug 1954 KY at age 64 and was bur. Baker Hill Cem., Portersburg, Clay Co., KY.
     Verna E. "Vernie" Felty, b. Leap Day, 29 Feb 1904 Clay Co., KY; d.30 Mar 1977 Orlando, Orange Co., FL, age 73; Job Allen Cem., Oneida.
Known children of James B.[6] Abner and Verna E. "Vernie" Felty all b. Clay Co., KY:
         i.   Virgie[7] d. Orlando, Orange Co., FL. , b. ca.Aug 1919.
         ii.   Chester, b.3 Nov 1921. He m. Eula B. Davidson on 13 Oct 1951 Manchester, Clay Co., KY. He d.25 Jul 1983 Clay Co., KY, at age 61 and was bur. Job Allen Cem., Oneida, Clay Co., KY.
                   Eula B. Davidson, b.18 Feb 1926; d.27 Nov 2000, age 74; bur. Hensley Holiness Ch. Cem., Hensley, Clay Co., KY.
  811 iii.   Robert "Pearl," b. 7 Oct 1923; m. Mary Childs.
         iv.   Martha Jane, b. ca.1925. She d.8 Sep 1925 Clay Co., KY and was bur. Teges Cem., Clay Co., KY.
         v.   Johnny, b. ca.Nov 1926. He d. before 2012 Clay Co., KY.
         vi.   Melvin, b. ca.1933.
  812 vii.   Billy Gene, b. 19 May 1937; m. Ruby L. Huggins.
  813 viii. Raleigh Alben, b. 19 Oct 1939; m. (n.n.).
         ix.   Fred d. TX.
         x.   Woodrow "Woody."

394. Bryson "Brice"[6] Abner (Harvey[5], Lacy[4], Elisha[3], Elisha[2] Abney, Abner[1]), b.18 Apr 1892 Owsley Co., KY. He m. Ida A. Byrd on 4 Jan 1922 Teges, Clay Co., KY. He and Ida A. Byrd appeared on the censuses of 2 Apr 1930 Allen, Clay Co., KY and 25 Apr 1940 Clay Co., KY. He d.24 Nov 1959 Oneida, Clay Co., KY, at age 67 and was bur. Job Allen Cem., Oneida, Clay Co., KY.
     Ida A. Byrd, b.13 Oct 1904 Clay Co., KY; d.10 Mar 2007 Indianapolis, Marion Co., IN, age 102; bur. Mem. Park Cem., Indianapolis, IN.
Known children of Bryson "Brice"[6] Abner and Ida A. Byrd all b. Clay Co., KY:
  814 i.   Preston[7], b. 14 Apr 1923; m. Bernice (n.n.).
         ii.   Pauline, b. ca.Sep 1925. She m. Charles C. Campbell on 27 Mar 1946 Manchester, Clay Co., KY.
                   Charles C. Campbell, b. ca.1920.
         iii. Conrad W, b.25 Nov 1935. He d.1 Jun 1994 Beech Grove, Marion Co., IN, at age 58 and was bur. Mem. Park Cem.

395. Lucy[6] Abner (Harvey[5], Lacy[4], Elisha[3], Elisha[2] Abney, Abner[1]), b.Mar 1894 Clay Co., KY. She m. Harrison Singleton on 17 Jul 1912 Clay Co., KY. She d.1 Jun 1999 Indianapolis, Marion Co., IN, at age 105.
     Harrison Singleton, b.20 Jan 1889 KY. He d.12 Mar 1936 Laurel, Franklin Co., IN, at age 47.
Known children of Lucy[6] Abner and Harrison Singleton:
         i.   Pearl[7], b.1913. She d.1977.
         ii.   Ida, b.1914. She d.1914.
         iii. Delora, b.1915. She d.1988.
         iv.   Mae, b.1918. She d.1989.
         v.   Brice, b.1920. He d.1987.
         vi.   Johnie, b.1924. He d.1971.
         vii. Calvin, b.1925. He d.1928.
         viii. Edgar W., b.1932.
         ix.   Davis Wayne, b.1935.

396. John "Johnie"[6] Abner (USArmy-WWII) (Harvey[5], Lacy[4], Elisha[3], Elisha[2] Abney, Abner[1]), b.8 Feb 1896 Owsley Co., KY. He began military service on 24 May 1918 Co.C, 51st Inf., 6th Army Div. and was honorably discharged on 23 Jun 1919. He m1. Sophia Combs on 9 Jan 1922 Clay Co., KY. He m2. (n.n.). He and his son, Manford Abner were liv. on 9 Apr 1930 with his father, Harvey Abner, Allen, Clay Co., KY. He m3. Mae Bishop on 17 Mar 1931 Trixie, Clay Co., KY. He and Mae Bishop appeared on the census of 26 Apr 1940 Clay Co., KY. He d.10 Nov 1949 Clay Co., KY, at age 53 and was bur. Abner Cem., Lincoln, Clay Co., KY.
     Sophia Combs, b.1891. She m. (n.n.) Bowles. She d.1926 and was bur. Patsy Allen Cem., Teges, Clay Co., KY.
Known child of John "Johnie"[6] Abner (USArmy-WWII) and Sophia Combs:
         i.   Manford[7], b.19 Mar 1925 Clay Co., KY. He d.28 Jan 1934 Teges, Clay Co., KY, at age 8 and was bur. Patsy Allen Cem..
There were no known children of John "Johnie"[6] Abner (USArmy-WWII) and (n.n.).
     Mae Bishop, b. ca.1907.
There were no known children of John "Johnie"[6] Abner (USArmy-WWII) and Mae Bishop.

397. John[6] Abner (Samuel[5], Lacy[4], Elisha[3], Elisha[2] Abney, Abner[1]) m. Mary Elizabeth "Lizzie" Hill, daughter of Samuel Hill and Jane "Jennie" Gabbard. He, b.20 Feb 1895 Owsley Co., KY. He d.9 Mar 1917 Owsley Co., KY, at age 22.
     Mary Elizabeth "Lizzie" Hill, b.1900 Owsley Co., KY; d.25 Mar 1931 Perry Co., KY; bur. Esau-Gabbard Cem., Ricetown, Owsley Co., KY.
Known children of John[6] Abner and Mary Elizabeth "Lizzie" Hill:
  815 i.   Isaac[7], b. 28 Feb 1914 Owsley Co., KY; m. Myrtle Gabbard.

398. Mollie Elizabeth[6] Abner (William[5], John[4], Elisha[3], Elisha[2] Abney, Abner[1]), b.3 Jan 1871 Pendleton Co., KY. She m. William Joseph Wells on 20 Oct 1887 Pendleton Co., KY. She d.6 Jun 1928 Pendleton Co., KY, at age 57.
     William Joseph Wells, b.1862. He d.1937.
Known children of Mollie Elizabeth[6] Abner and William Joseph Wells:
         i.   William Chester[7], b.1889. He d.1971.
         ii.   Nannie A., b.1893. She d.1969.
         iii. Abner, b.1896. He d.1977.
         iv.   Emma Mable, b.1896.
         v.   Zada L., b.1897. She d.1985.

399. Isabel Gross[6] Sandlin (James[5], Nancy[4] Abner, Elisha[3], Elisha[2] Abney, Abner[1]) m. Orville Baker Riley. , b.1878. She d.1947. Orville Baker Riley, b.1875. He d.1949.
Known child of Isabel Gross[6] Sandlin and Orville Baker Riley:
      816   i.   Elizabeth[7], b. 1903; m. Nathan Ellington Greear Sr.

400. Robert H. "Fox"[6] Baker (Eliza[5] Abner, Willis[4], Elisha[3], Elisha[2] Abney, Abner[1]), b.12 Oct 1880 Owsley Co., KY. He m. Mary Alice Baker, daughter of Robert R. Baker and Mary Gabbard, ca.1903. He, 39, appeared as Head of Household on the census of 17 Jan 1920 Crockettsville, Breathitt Co., KY. He d.13 Mar 1960 Breathitt Co., KY, at age 79 and was bur. Cortland Cem., Cow Creek, Owsley Co., KY.
    Mary Alice Baker, b.8 Apr 1880 Owsley Co., KY. She m1. Price McIntosh ca.1895. She d.13 Apr 1969 Owsley Co., KY, at age 89 and was bur. Cortland Cem., Cow Creek, Owsley Co., KY.
Known children of Robert H. "Fox"[6] Baker and Mary Alice Baker:
            i.   Shelby[7], b.26 Dec 1904 Breathitt Co., KY; m. Marie H. (n.n.); d.16 Jul 1976 Breathitt Co., KY, at age 71 and was bur. Cortland Cem., Cow Creek, Owsley Co., KY.
                 Marie H. (n.n.), b.1910.
           ii.   Cash, b.25 Feb 1907 Owsley Co., KY. He d.18 Jun 1954 Owsley Co., KY, at age 47; bur. Cortland Cem., Cow Creek.
          iii.   Stella, b.22 Jun 1914 Crockettsville, Breathitt Co., KY. She m. James Clell Neace in 1943. She d.14 Jun 2006 SC at age 91 and was bur. Cortland Cem., Cow Creek, Owsley Co., KY.
                 James Clell Neace, b.1 Jun 1920 Middletown, Butler Co., OH. He d.29 Nov 2005 Blackville, Barnwell Co., SC, at age 85 and was bur. Cortland Cem., Cow Creek, Owsley Co., KY.
          iv.   Earl, b.5 Nov 1917 Breathitt Co., KY. He d.2 Oct 1970 Jackson, Breathitt Co., KY, at age 52 and was bur. Cortland Cem., Cow Creek, Owsley Co., KY.

401. Bryson "Bryce"[6] Baker (Eliza[5] Abner, Willis[4], Elisha[3], Elisha[2] Abney, Abner[1]), b.31 Oct 1882 Breathitt Co., KY. He m. Lucretia "Crettie" Burns, daughter of John S. Burns and Arminia Allen, ca.1908. He and Lucretia appeared on the censuses of 2 May 1910; 17 Jan 1920; and 5 Apr 1930 Crockettsville, Breathitt Co., KY. He d.10 Feb 1943 Owsley Co., KY, at age 60 and was bur. Cortland Cem., Cow Creek, Owsley Co., KY.
    Lucretia "Crettie" Burns, b.20 Oct 1886 Owsley Co., KY. She d.15 Oct 1967 Owsley Co., KY, at age 80; bur. Cortland Cem., Cow Creek.
Known children of Bryson "Bryce"[6] Baker and Lucretia "Crettie" Burns:
      817   i.   Emma[7], b. 1 Jul 1909 Breathitt Co., KY; m. Owens Brewer.
           ii.   Tressie, b. ca.1911 KY. She d.1952.
      818   iii.   Rosco, b. 17 Jul 1912; m. Edna (n.n.).
          iv.   Luther, b.1914. He d.1978.
           v.   Delbert, b. ca.1917 KY.
          vi.   Morley, b.27 Jun 1918 Owsley Co., KY. He d.Nov 1918 Owsley Co., KY and was bur. Cortland Cem., Cow Creek, Owsley Co., KY.
         vii.   Mollie, b.27 Jun 1918 Owsley Co., KY. She d.9 Nov 1919 Owsley Co., KY, at age 1 and was bur. Cortland Cem., Cow Creek, Owsley Co., KY.
        viii.   Ollie, b. ca.1919. She m. (n.n.) Dean. She d.2001.
          ix.   Arnold, b.1921. He d.1998.

402. Elisha[6] Baker (Eliza[5] Abner, Willis[4], Elisha[3], Elisha[2] Abney, Abner[1]), b.22 Jun 1885 Owsley Co., KY; m. America Daniel, daughter of George Washington Daniel and Lucinda Jane Allen; d.13 Mar 1964 Buffalo, LaRue Co., KY, age 78; bur. Cortland Cem., Cow Creek, Owsley Co., KY.
    America Daniel, b.1889.
Known children of Elisha[6] Baker and America Daniel:
            i.   Delia[7], b.1911.
           ii.   Moody, b.1913.
          iii.   Oscar, b.1915.
          iv.   Mimia, b.1920.
           v.   William, b.1923.
          vi.   Samuel, b.1926.
         vii.   David, b.1928.
        viii.   Flossie, b.1930.

403. Charles "Charlie"[6] Baker (Eliza[5] Abner, Willis[4], Elisha[3], Elisha[2] Abney, Abner[1]), b.10 Aug 1887 Owsley Co., KY. He m. Isabelle "Belle" Bowling ca.1907. He and Isabelle appeared on the censuses of 2 May 1910; 17 Jan 1920; and 5 Apr 1930 Crockettsville, Breathitt Co., KY. He d.5 Apr 1975 Perry Co., KY, at age 87 and was bur. Cortland Cem., Cow Creek, Owsley Co., KY.
    Isabelle "Belle" Bowling, b.2 May 1889 KY. She d.5 Jun 1967 Owsley Co., KY, at age 78 and was bur. Cortland Cem., Cow Creek.
Known children of Charles "Charlie"[6] Baker and Isabelle "Belle" Bowling:
            i.   Euna "Uny"[7], b.4 Sep 1909 Owsley Co., KY. She m. Willie Morris. She d.1 Jul 1937 Owsley Co., KY, at age 27 and was bur. Cortland Cem., Cow Creek, Owsley Co., KY.
           ii.   Alfa, b. ca.1912 KY.
          iii.   Roberta "Berdie", b.1914 KY.
          iv.   Dosha "Doshie", b.1915. She d.1975.
           v.   Custer, b. ca.1919 KY.
          vi.   Flora "Flossie", b.1921. She d.1978.
         vii.   Alfred "Russell", b.1923. He d.2005.
        viii.   Clyde, b.1925. He d.1945.
          ix.   Nola, b. ca.1927 KY.
           x.   Wallace, b.1930. He d.1967.
          xi.   Mary Helen, b.1932. She d.1989.

404. Robert F.[6] **Abner** (William[5], Willis[4], Elisha[3], Elisha[2] Abney, Abner[1]), b.7 Jun 1878 Perry Co., KY. He m. Alaphair F. "Alley" Barger, daughter of Justice Barger and Nancy Burns, in 1905. He and Alaphair F. "Alley" Barger appeared on the censuses of 3 May 1910 Perry Co., KY; and 12 Feb 1920 Bullskin, Clay Co., KY. He d.1 May 1962 Brown Co., OH, at age 83 and was bur. Laurel Cem., Laurel, Clermont Co., OH.

Alaphair F. "Alley" Barger, b.17 Jun 1885 Perry Co., KY. She d.5 Dec 1965 Brown Co., OH, at age 80 and was bur. Laurel Cem., Laurel.
Known children of Robert F.[6] Abner and Alaphair F. "Alley" Barger:

<ul>
<li>819   i.   Mamie[7], b. 11 Nov 1905 KY; m. Clarence Barger Sr.</li>
<li>820   ii.   Elbert, b. 26 Feb 1907 KY; m. Maude Combs.</li>
<li>iii.   Eva, b. ca.Dec 1908 KY and was bur. Buckhorn Cem., Buckhorn, Perry Co., KY.</li>
<li>iv.   Walter m. Hazel I. (n.n.). He, b.4 Nov 1911. He d.13 Feb 1983 at age 71; bur. Laurel Cem., Laurel, Clermont Co., OH.
Hazel I. (n.n.), b.1922. She d.2018 and was bur. Laurel Cem., Laurel, Clermont Co., OH.</li>
<li>v.   Billie, b.11 Mar 1913 and d.27 Nov 1914 Perry Co., KY, at age 1; bur. Buckhorn Cem., Buckhorn, Perry Co., KY.</li>
<li>vi.   Elmer m. Nancy J. (n.n.). He, b.26 Feb 1915. He d.18 Sep 1980 at age 65 and was bur. Laurel Cem., Laurel.
Nancy J. (n.n.), b.1928. She d.2000 and was bur. Laurel Cem., Laurel, Clermont Co., OH.</li>
<li>821   vii.   Willis, b. 8 May 1917; m. Betty M. McClaskie; m. Marcella "Marty" Decknadel.</li>
<li>822   viii.   Homer, b. 24 Jan 1921; m. Lena Combs.</li>
<li>ix.   Carter L., b.12 Feb 1924. He d.22 Sep 1994 at age 70 and was bur. Laurel Cem., Laurel, Clermont Co., OH.</li>
</ul>

405. Mary Rachel[6] **Abner** (William[5], Willis[4], Elisha[3], Elisha[2] Abney, Abner[1]), b.12 Apr 1880 Bowlington, Perry Co., KY. She m. Abraham Napier, son of John Couch Napier and Elizabeth Barger, ca.1904. She and Abraham Napier appeared on the census of 3 May 1910 Bowling, Perry Co., KY. She appeared as Head of Household on the census of 4 Feb 1920 Bowling, Perry Co., KY. She d.2 Nov 1954 Bowlington, Perry Co., KY, at age 74 and was bur. Abney-Napier Family Cem., Gays Creek, Perry Co., KY.

Abraham Napier, b.25 Nov 1885 Perry Co., KY; killed in a coal mine on 5 Sep 1917 at age 31; bur. Clara Barger Cem., Saul, Perry Co., KY.
Known children of Mary Rachel[6] Abner and Abraham Napier:

<ul>
<li>i.   Lula "Luly"[7], b.9 Oct 1904. She m. Cpl. Malchus Bowling (USArmy-WWI). She d.2 Jan 1985 at age 80 and was bur. Moberly Graveyard, Estill Co., KY.
Cpl. Malchus Bowling (USArmy-WWI), b.3 Sep 1894. He d.13 Dec 1962 at age 68 and was bur. Moberly Graveyard.</li>
<li>823   ii.   Florence "Flossie," b. 20 Apr 1906; m. Jessie Bowling.</li>
<li>iii.   Edmond, b.9 Nov 1908. He d.12 Feb 1998 at age 89.</li>
<li>iv.   John William, b.14 Jun 1912 KY. He m. Oma Louise Abner, daughter of Robert Abner and Maude Miller, in 1978. He d.31 Aug 1992 KY at age 80 and was bur. Moberly Graveyard, Estill Co., KY.
Oma Louise Abner, b.25 Jan 1930 OH. She m1. John Ginter. She d.2 Jul 2013 Lutheran Community Home, Seymour, Jackson Co., IN, at age 83 and was bur. Fairview Cem., Brownstown, Jackson Co., IN.</li>
<li>v.   Elmira N., b.3 Jan 1915 Perry Co., KY. She m1. Landrum L. Barger, son of Jessie G. Barger and Susan Baker. She and Landrum L. Barger appeared on the census of 8 Apr 1940 Dayton, Montgomery Co., OH. She m2. Richard E. Cornelison. She d.29 Jun 1995 Estill Co., KY, at age 80 and was bur. Moberly Graveyard, Estill Co., KY.
Landrum L. Barger, b.1908. He d.26 Feb 1941 Dayton, Montgomery Co., OH.
Richard E. Cornelison, b.31 Aug 1909. He d.30 Apr 1977 at age 67 and was bur. Moberly Graveyard, Estill Co., KY.</li>
<li>vi.   Elizabeth "Bess" m. Henry Hacker. She m. (n.n.) Ledford. , b.30 Dec 1917 KY. She d.14 Sep OH. She was cremated.</li>
<li>vii.   Nancy Ann, b.30 Dec 1917. She d.1940 and was bur. Abner-Napier Family Cem., Gays Creek, Perry Co., KY.</li>
</ul>

406. Justus Tucker[6] **Abner** (William[5], Willis[4], Elisha[3], Elisha[2] Abney, Abner[1]), b.11 Feb 1882 Perry Co., KY. He m. Emmer Langdon, daughter of Samuel P. Langdon and Rebecca Stidham, ca.1913. He d.9 Oct 1918 Perry Co., KY, at age 36.

Emmer Langdon, b.23 Feb 1897. She m2. John Dixon Sr. ca.1919. She d.27 May 1987 at age 90; bur. Riverside Cem., Hazard, Perry Co., KY.
Known children of Justus Tucker[6] Abner and Emmer Langdon:

<ul>
<li>i.   Britton L. "Brit"[7], b.16 Sep 1914 Hazard, Perry Co., KY. He d.17 Feb 2003 Winchester, Clark Co., KY, at age 88 and was bur. Parlor Grove Cem., Waynesburg, Lincoln Co., KY.</li>
<li>ii.   Daniel Langdon "Dan", b.22 Feb 1916 Perry Co., KY. He m. Nella Barger on 11 Jan 1943 Cumberland Co., NC. He d.30 Sep 1944 killed in action, Netherlands, at age 28 and was bur. Bowling Cem., Bowlington, Perry Co., KY.
Nella Barger, b.30 Apr 1911.</li>
<li>iii.   Anderson, b.21 Nov 1917 KY. He d.1 Oct 1921 Bowlington, Perry Co., KY, at age 3 and was bur. Bowling Cem., Bowlington, Perry Co., KY.</li>
</ul>

407. Nancy "Nannie"[6] **Abner** (William[5], Willis[4], Elisha[3], Elisha[2] Abney, Abner[1]), b.22 Jan 1884. She m. Finley F. Bowling Sr., son of Elisha Bowling and Salley (n.n.), ca.1908. She and Finley F. Bowling Sr. appeared on the censuses of 3 May 1910 and 6 Feb 1920 Bowling, Perry Co., KY; 17 Apr 1930 Harrison Co., KY; and 24 Apr 1940 Bowling, Perry Co., KY. She d.18 Feb 1950 at age 66 and was bur. Bowling Cem., Bowlington, Perry Co., KY.

Finley F. Bowling Sr, b.1882 KY. He d. Boone Co., KY and was bur. Richwood Presbyterian Cem., Walton, Boone Co., KY.
Known children of Nancy "Nannie"[6] Abner and Finley F. Bowling Sr. all b. Perry Co., KY,:

<ul>
<li>i.   Ethel A.[7], b. ca.1909.</li>
<li>ii.   Walter A., b. ca.1912.</li>
<li>iii.   Finley F., b. ca.1925.</li>
</ul>

408. Elmira[6] **Abner** (William[5], Willis[4], Elisha[3], Elisha[2] Abney, Abner[1]), b.8 Feb 1886. She m. Daniel "Little Dan" Barger ca.1923. She d.13 Dec 1962 at age 76 and was bur. Buckhorn Cem., Buckhorn, Perry Co., KY.

Daniel "Little Dan" Barger, b.15 May 1885. He d.19 Feb 1959 at age 73 and was bur. Buckhorn Cem., Buckhorn, Perry Co., KY.
Known children of Elmira[6] Abner and Daniel "Little Dan" Barger:

<ul>
<li>i.   Rufus[7] m. Ida (n.n.). He, b.26 Sep 1924. He d.27 Oct 1967 at age 43 and was bur. Buckhorn Cem., Buckhorn.
Ida (n.n.), b.10 Mar 1935. She d.19 Mar 1995 at age 60 and was bur. Buckhorn Cem., Buckhorn, Perry Co., KY.</li>
<li>ii.   Ruth m. Cpl. Vernon McIntosh (USArmy-Korea). , b.2 Mar 1928. She d.26 May 2008 at age 80; bur. Buckhorn Cem.
Cpl. Vernon McIntosh (USArmy-Korea), b.14 May 1931. He d.30 Apr 1987 at age 55 and was bur. Buckhorn Cem.</li>
</ul>

iii.   Ella, b.26 Apr 1930 Cincinnati, Hamilton Co., OH. She d.5 Mar 2010 Hamilton, Butler Co., OH, at age 79 and was bur. Greenwood Cem., Hamilton, Butler Co., OH.

409. Hannah[6] Abner (William[5], Willis[4], Elisha[3], Elisha[2] Abney, Abner[1]), b.29 Dec 1888 Buckhorn, Perry Co., KY. She m. Henry Napier, son of John Couch Napier and Elizabeth Barger, in 1913. She d.1 Apr 1970 Scott Co., IN, at age 81; bur. Tunnel Hill Cem., Dunraven, Perry Co., KY.
    Henry Napier, b.17 Mar 1896 Perry Co., KY. He m. Hazel Burris. He d.17 Dec 1976 Lawrenceburg, Dearb. Co., IN, at age 80 and was bur. Greendale Cem., Greendale, Dearb. Co., IN.
Known children of Hannah[6] Abner and Henry Napier:
        824   i.   Eldren[7], b. 23 Apr 1914 Perry Co., KY; m. Orpha Julie Gross.

410. Elizabeth "Lizzie"[6] Abner (Willis' twin) (William[5], Willis[4], Elisha[3], Elisha[2] Abney, Abner[1]), b.21 Oct 1890. She m. Robert Sandlin Bowling, son of John Bowling. She and Robert Sandlin Bowling appeared on the census of 3 May 1910 Bowling, Perry Co., KY. She d.13 Dec 1962 at age 72 and was bur. Abner Family Cem., Buckhorn, Perry Co., KY.
    Robert Sandlin Bowling, b.2 Jul 1890 Bowlington, Perry Co., KY. He d.3 Oct 1964 Brockton, Plymouth Co., MA, at age 74 and was bur. on 5 Oct 1964 Nemasket Hill Cem., Middleborough, Plymouth Co., MA.
Known children of Elizabeth "Lizzie"[6] Abner (Willis' twin) and Robert Sandlin Bowling:
        825   i.   Nancy Ann[7], b. 9 Jan 1926 Bowlington, Perry Co., KY; m. PFC Letcher Smith (USArmy-WWII).
        826   ii.   Bill, b. 20 Sep 1927 Bowlington, Perry Co., KY; m. Tilda Marie (n.n.).
        827   iii. Elmira, b. 6 Nov 1934 Louisville, Jefferson Co., KY; m. Herbert "Gerald" Payne.

411. Willis E.[6] Abner (USArmy; Elizabeth's twin) (William[5], Willis[4], Elisha[3], Elisha[2] Abney, Abner[1]), b.21 Oct 1890 Lillian, Perry Co., KY. He appeared in the census of 3 May 1910 Bowling, Perry Co., KY as *brother-in-law* liv. with Robert Bowling. He associated with (but never married) Elizabeth Bowling, d/o of Elisha Bowling and Ann Napier. He m. Sattie Barger, d/o of Henry D. Barger and Newark "Arkey" Gilbert, on 3 Jun 1918 Perry Co., KY. Willis d.7 Jun 1971 Hamilton, Butler Co., OH, age 80; bur. Rose Hill Burial Park, Hamilton, OH. (see Addenda, page 268).
    Elizabeth Bowling, b.30 Mar 1890 KY. She m. Justice Tucker Begley and had issue: Sally Begley and Justus Begley. She d.2 May 1983 Cincinnati, Hamilton Co., OH, at age 93 and was bur. Spring Grove Cem., Cincinnati, Hamilton Co., OH.
Known child of Willis E.[6] Abner (USArmy; Elizabeth's twin) and Elizabeth Bowling.
        827.5   i.   Cpl. Gordon Willis (USArmy-WWII)[7], b.13 Apr 1918 Bowlington, Perry Co., KY; d.24 Apr 1972 Cincinnati, Hamilton Co., OH, age 54; He was a grandfather of Jerimy Sean Abner (gen.) (see Tertio Addendum, page 268).
    Sattie Barger, b.Jun 1893 Perry Co., KY. She d.12 Sep 1959 Hamilton Co., OH, age 66; bur. Rose Hill Burial Park, Hamilton, Butler Co., OH.
Known children of Willis E.[6] Abner (USArmy; Elizabeth's twin) and Sattie Barger:
               i.   Denver, b.6 Oct 1921. He d.6 Sep 1983 at age 61 and was bur. Rose Hill Burial Park, Hamilton, Butler Co., OH.
               ii.   Billie, b.5 Dec 1927 OH. He m. Mattie Velma Callahan, daughter of David John Callahan and Hazel Dell Allen, in 1948. He d. in Still, Dept. du Bas-Rhin, Alsace, France and was bur. Rose Hill Burial Park, Hamilton, Butler Co., OH.
                        Mattie Velma Callahan, b.8 May 1924. She d.10 Oct 2008 at age 84 and was bur. Desert View Mem. Park, Victorville, San Bernardino Co., CA.
        828   iii. Pearl, b. 20 Feb 1931 Hamilton, Butler Co., OH; m. Donald Retherford.
               iv.   Merlie, b.1935. d.1971
               v.   Rufus, b.17 Apr 1938 Butler Co., OH. He d.17 Oct 1968 El Paso, El Paso Co., TN, at age 30 and was bur. Rose Hill Burial Park, Hamilton, Butler Co., OH.

412. Lucy[6] Abner (William[5], Willis[4], Elisha[3], Elisha[2] Abney, Abner[1]), b.Feb 1893. She m. Andrew Gay. She d.Apr 1970 at age 77.
Known child of Lucy[6] Abner and Andrew Gay:
               i.   Gentry[7], b.16 Jun 1927 KY. He d.8 May 1954 OH at age 26 and was bur. Bowling Cem., Bowlington, Perry Co., KY.

413. Rebecca[6] Abner (William[5], Willis[4], Elisha[3], Elisha[2] Abney, Abner[1]), b.15 Jun 1895. She m. John B. Smith on 23 May 1919. She d.10 Nov 1962 Perry Co., KY, at age 67.
Known children of Rebecca[6] Abner and John B. Smith:
               i.   Wilmer James[7], b.24 Mar 1920 Buckhorn, Perry Co., KY. He d.15 Oct 1990 Cincinnati, Hamilton Co., OH, at age 70 and was bur. Vine Street Hill Cem., Cincinnati, Hamilton Co., OH.
               ii.   Joseph J., b.4 Dec 1927. He d.27 Jan 1998 at age 70 and was bur. Spring Grove Cem., Cincinnati, Hamilton Co., OH.

414. Anderson "Ance"[6] Abner (William[5], Willis[4], Elisha[3], Elisha[2] Abney, Abner[1]) m. Leatha Dixon. He, b.8 Apr 1899 Perry Co., KY. He d.28 Jan 1972 Fayette Co., KY, at age 72 and was bur. Abner Family Cem., Jackson Co., KY.
    Leatha Dixon, b.15 Jul 1903 KY. She d.2 Jul 2002 Jackson, Breathitt Co., KY, at age 98.
Known child of Anderson "Ance"[6] Abner and Leatha Dixon:
        829   i.   Adolph[7], b. 5 Mar 1927; m. Lavonne Rosalean "Bonnie" Rickard.

415. Rachel[6] Abner (William[5], Willis[4], Elisha[3], Elisha[2] Abney, Abner[1]), b.8 Apr 1899. She m. Rufus Barger, son of Henry D. Barger and Newark "Arkey" Gilbert, ca.1920. She and Rufus Barger appeared on the censuses of 25 Apr 1930 Hamilton, Butler Co., OH; and 10 May 1940 Hanover, Butler Co., OH. She d.8 Dec 1975 at age 76 and was bur. Abner-Napier Family Cem., Gays Creek, Perry Co., KY.
    Rufus Barger, b.1898 KY; m2. Margaret Baker; d.20 Feb 1973 Oakland Park, Broward Co., FL; bur. Greenwood Cem., Hamilton, OH.
Known children of Rachel[6] Abner and Rufus Barger:
               i.   Marjorie[7] m. Roy Osborne. , b.17 Dec 1924 Hamilton, Butler Co., OH. She d.12 Oct 1941 Hamilton, Butler Co., OH, at age 16 and was bur. Greenwood Cem., Hamilton, Butler Co., OH.
               ii.   Thomas M. "Tommie", b.26 Feb 1936. He d.5 Nov 1999 Butler Co., OH, at age 63. He was cremated.

416. Edward "Ned"[6] Abner (Elisha[5], Willis[4], Elisha[3], Elisha[2] Abney, Abner[1]), b.17 Jul 1896 Perry Co., KY. He m. Cory Begley in 1915. He d.1958 Perry Co., KY and was bur. Abner Family Cem., Buckhorn, Perry Co., KY.
    Cory Begley, b.12 Dec 1896 Perry Co., KY; d.25 Oct 1975 Buckhorn, Perry Co., KY, ae.78; bur. Lucy Angel Cem., Buckhorn, Perry Co., KY.

Known children of Edward "Ned"*⁶* Abner and Cory Begley:

             i.   Sally*⁷*, b.1917 Perry Co., KY. She d.Mar 1996 Perry Co., KY; bur. Abner Family Cem., Buckhorn, Perry Co., KY.

830   ii.   Elizabeth, b. 30 Apr 1920 Perry Co., KY; m. PFC Hargis Oliver Sr. (USArmy-WWII).

831   iii.   Daniel B. "Dan," b. 20 Jan 1922 Buckhorn, Perry Co., KY; m. Ruby Daniel.

          iv.   Nancy Jane m. Gilbert "Gib" Hibbard. , b.25 Oct 1923 Perry Co., KY. She d.24 Aug 1993 Manchester, Clay Co., KY, at age 69 and was bur. Hibbard Cem., Barcreek, Clay Co., KY.

                    Gilbert "Gib" Hibbard, b.17 Apr 1916. He d.7 Mar 1995 at age 78; bur. Hibbard Cem., Barcreek, Clay Co., KY.

832   v.   Taulbee, b. 16 Aug 1925 Hazard, Perry Co., KY; m. Dorothy M. Stroud.

          vi.   Alice m. Amerida Adams. , b.11 Nov 1928 Hazard, Perry Co., KY. She d.14 May 1993 Perry Co., KY, at age 64.

833   vii.   Edward "Ed," b. 19 May 1929 Perry Co., KY; m. Jeanette McKnight.

834 viii.   Charlie, b. 23 Oct 1933 Perry Co., KY; m. Hazel Susan Rice.

835   ix.   Dorothy, b. 11 Nov 1935 Buckhorn, Perry Co., KY; m. Green Berry Adams.

836   x.   Willis, b. 27 Dec 1938 Buckhorn, Perry Co., KY; m. Janice Kay Brooks.

417. Brownlow "Brown"*⁶* Terry (Mary*⁵* Abner, Willis*⁴*, Elisha*³*, Elisha*²* Abney, Abner*¹*), b.9 Jan 1889 Breathitt Co., KY. He m. America Bryant ca.1911. He d.1 Apr 1967 Jackson, Breathitt Co., KY, at age 78 and was bur. Hugh Bryant Cem., Copebranch, Breathitt Co., KY.

    America Bryant, b.1896 Breathitt Co., KY. She d.1964 Breathitt Co., KY and was bur. Hugh Bryant Cem., Copebranch, Breathitt Co., KY.

Known children of Brownlow "Brown"*⁶* Terry and America Bryant:

837   i.   Hugh*⁷*, b. 8 Jan 1912 Athol, Lee Co., KY; m. Laura Barrett.

          ii.   Ralph, b.27 Dec 1913 Breathitt Co., KY. He m. Dorothy Lawson. He d.21 Dec 1971 Warren Co., OH, at age 57 and was bur. Deerfield Cem., South Lebanon, Warren Co., OH.

                    Dorothy Lawson, b.11 May 1921 Lee Co., KY. She d.2 Jul 1993 Warren Co., OH, at age 72; bur. Deerfield Cem.

         iii.   John Terry, b.16 Mar 1916. He m. Laura Jean Gilbert. He d.6 Jul 1992 KY at age 76 and was bur. Deerfield Cem.

                    Laura Jean Gilbert, b.1 Apr 1928 KY. She d.6 Aug 1992 OH at age 64 and was bur. Deerfield Cem.

         iv.   Gladys Francis, b.24 Jul 1918 KY. She m. PFC James L. Strong (USArmy-WWII) in 1936. She d.7 Jun 1991 Mount Orab, Brown Co., OH, at age 72 and was bur. Rose Hill Cem., Mason, Warren Co., OH.

                    PFC James L. Strong (USArmy-WWII), b.5 Jun 1918 Athol, Lee Co., KY. He d.29 Jan 1994 Mount Orab, Brown Co., OH, at age 75 and was bur. Rose Hill Cem., Mason, Warren Co., OH.

         v.   Beulah m. Robert Brandenburg (USArmy-WWII). , b.13 Oct 1920 Athol, Lee Co., KY. She d.5 Jun 1996 Kettering, Montgomery Co., OH, at age 75 and was bur. Miami Valley Memory Gardens, Springboro, Warren Co., OH.

                    Robert Brandenburg (USArmy-WWII), b.10 Nov 1918 Beattyville, Lee Co., KY. He d.6 May 2002 Dayton, Montgomery Co., OH, at age 83 and was bur. Miami Valley Memory Gardens, Springboro, Warren Co., OH.

         vi.   Virgil Oscar m. Pearlie (n.n.). He, b.11 Mar 1923 Breathitt Co., KY. He d.3 Apr 1953 Breathitt Co., KY, at age 30 and was bur. Hugh Bryant Cem., Copebranch, Breathitt Co., KY.

                    Pearlie (n.n.), b.11 Jul 1923. She d.1 Sep 1975 at age 52; bur. Hugh Bryant Cem., Copebranch, Breathitt Co., KY.

        vii.   George m. Avis Hensley. He, b.8 Apr 1926 Breathitt Co., KY. He d.10 Aug 2004 Breathitt Co., KY, at age 78 and was bur. Hugh Bryant Cem., Copebranch, Breathitt Co., KY.

                    Avis Hensley, b.18 Feb 1934 Breathitt Co., KY. She d.25 Jan 2020 Lexington, Fayette Co., KY, at age 85 and was bur. Hugh Bryant Cem., Copebranch, Breathitt Co., KY.

      viii.   Franklin B., b.28 Aug 1928 KY. He d.8 Nov 1978 KY at age 50.

         ix.   Mary Joyce "Bug" m. Ambrose Hall. , b.10 Sep 1930 KY. She d.11 Sep 2003 KY at age 73 and was bur. Jackson Cem., Jackson, Breathitt Co., KY.

                    Ambrose Hall, b.22 Apr 1924 KY. He d.4 Nov 2002 KY at age 78 and was bur. Jackson Cem., Jackson.

         x.   Scerilda Mae m. Pvt. Burchell Hensley (USArmy-Korea). , b.9 Apr 1933 Breathitt Co., KY. She d.23 Jun 1957 Dayton, Montgomery Co., OH, at age 24 and was bur. Hugh Bryant Cem., Copebranch, Breathitt Co., KY.

                    Pvt. Burchell Hensley (USArmy-Korea), b.28 Jun 1928. He d.24 Oct 1970 at age 42 and was bur. Hugh Bryant Cem., Copebranch, Breathitt Co., KY.

         xi.   Ina Pearl, b.9 Sep 1935 Breathitt Co., KY. She m1. Eugene Gabbard Sr. She m2. Howard Noble. She d.2 Jun 2004 Breathitt Co., KY, at age 68 and was bur. Hugh Bryant Cem., Copebranch, Breathitt Co., KY.

                    Eugene Gabbard Sr, b.7 Mar 1930. He d.1 Sep 1982 at age 52; bur. Gabbard Cem., Jetts Creek, Breathitt Co., KY.

418. Mattie*⁶* Terry (Mary*⁵* Abner, Willis*⁴*, Elisha*³*, Elisha*²* Abney, Abner*¹*) m. Green B. Woods. , b.7 Feb 1892. She d.1 Oct 1988 at age 96 and was bur. Shepherd Cem., Booneville, Owsley Co., KY.

    Green B. Woods, b.22 Jun 1897 Breathitt Co., KY. He d.17 Jan 1981 Clay City, Powell Co., KY, at age 83 and was bur. Clay City Eaton Cem.

Known child of Mattie*⁶* Terry and Green B. Woods:

838   i.   Gracie E.*⁷*, b. 25 Sep 1913 Breathitt Co., KY; m. Wesley Durbin.

419. Isabella*⁶* Estep (Mary*⁵* Abner, Willis*⁴*, Elisha*³*, Elisha*²* Abney, Abner*¹*), b.11 Nov 1911 Beattyville, Lee Co., KY. She m. Felix M. Barnard. She d.14 May 1995 Indianapolis, Marion Co., IN, at age 83 and was bur. Crothersville Cem., Crothersville, Jackson Co., IN.

    Felix M. Barnard, b.15 Feb 1904. He d.23 Jan 1977 at age 72 and was bur. Crothersville Cem., Crothersville, Jackson Co., IN.

Known children of Isabella*⁶* Estep and Felix M. Barnard:

             i.   Virgil*⁷*, b.18 Mar 1931 Laurel Co., KY. He d.28 Nov 1965 Indianapolis, Marion Co., IN, at age 34 and was bur. Crothersville Cem., Crothersville, Jackson Co., IN.

          ii.   Nellie Sue, b.26 Jan 1950. She d.19 Dec 1972 at age 22 and was bur. Crothersville Cem., Crothersville, Jackson Co., IN.

420. Sgt. William Berry "Willie" *⁶* Sandlin (USArmy-WWI) (Lucinda*⁵* Abner, Willis*⁴*, Elisha*³*, Elisha*²* Abney, Abner*¹*) was b. New Year's Day, 1 Jan 1890 Breathitt Co., KY. He joined the U.S. Army in 1912. In 1917 he was deployed with Co. A, 132d Infantry, 33d Division in France. On 26 Sep 1918 during the *Battle of Argonne Forest* (the last battle of World War I) on 26 Sep 1918 at Bois de Forges, Meuse, Grand Est, France Sgt. Sandlin single-handedly destroyed three German machine gun emplacements and killed 24 enemies. He was awarded the ***Congressional Medal of Honor***, and is the only Kentuckian in World War I to have received this prestigious honor. (see plate K and pedigree, pg.10). He d.29 May 1949 at age 59 as a result of complications from a poison gas attack on his company by the Germans in the heroic battle. He was bur. Hurricane Cem. in Leslie Co., KY (near Hyden); In Sep 1990, his remains were exhumed and reinterred in the Zachary Taylor National Cem., Louisville, Jefferson Co., KY. In 2016 a new bridge crossing the Middle Fork Kentucky River (on Hwy. 30) was named the *Sergeant Willie Sandlin Memorial Bridge* in his honor. (The bridge coordinates from googlemaps.com: 37.487274,-83.480391.) Sgt. Sandlin's pistol, medal of honor and bronze star were donated by his family to the Kentucky Historical Society in Frankfort, Franklin Co., KY in 2018. On 3 May 2018, his body was reinterred once again, this time to the Kentucky Veterans Cem. Southeast), Hyden, Leslie Co., KY. He and his wife, Belvia were the first burials in the cemetery. Sgt. Willie Sandlin's artifacts are available for viewing at the *Kentucky Historical Society*, or on the Internet at:

https://kyhistory.pastperfectonline.com/search?utf8=%E2%9C%93&search_criteria=%22Willie+Sandlin+Collection%22

Belvia Roberts, b.16 Jun 1902. She d.5 Feb 1999, age 96. She was also reinterred Kentucky Veterans Cem. Southeast, Hyden, Leslie Co., KY.
Known children of Sgt. Willie[6] Sandlin (USArmy-WWI) and Belvia Roberts:
      i.   Cora[7], b.15 Dec 1922 Leslie Co., KY; d.2 Sep 1925 Leslie Co., KY, age 2; bur. Owls Nest Cem., Hyden, Leslie Co., KY.
      ii. Robert Lee, b.2 Nov 1931 Hyden, Leslie Co., KY. He m. Margaret Butler. He d.22 Jun 2005 Louisville, Jefferson Co., KY, at age 73 and was bur. Cave Hill Cem., Louisville, Jefferson Co., KY.
          Margaret Butler, b.30 Jun 1932. She d.17 Sep 2013 Louisville, Jefferson Co., KY, at age 81; bur. Cave Hill Cem.

421. Lula[6] Abner (John[5], Willis[4], Elisha[3], Elisha[2] Abney, Abner[1]), b.28 Jun 1896. She m. Samuel Strong in 1920. She d.11 Jun 1961 at age 64 and was bur. White-Deaton Cem., Barwick, Breathitt Co., KY.
    Samuel Strong, b.1 Oct 1896. He d.26 Aug 1974 Shelbyville, Shelby Co., IN, at age 77 and was bur. White-Deaton Cem., Barwick.
Known child of Lula[6] Abner and Samuel Strong:
      i.   Marvin M.[7], b.21 Sep 1936 Hazard, Perry Co., KY. He d.12 Mar 2016 Annville, Jackson Co., KY, at age 79.

422. Lillie[6] Abner (John[5], Willis[4], Elisha[3], Elisha[2] Abney, Abner[1]) m. William Clay Willoughby. , b.1909. She d.1985 and was bur. Willoughby Cem., Jeffersonville, Montgomery Co., KY.
    William Clay Willoughby, b.1901. He d.1975 and was bur. Willoughby Cem., Jeffersonville, Montgomery Co., KY.
Known child of Lillie[6] Abner and William Clay Willoughby:
   839   i.   Albert[7], b. 12 Apr 1927 Mount Sterling, Montgomery Co., KY; m. Clarene McCarty.

423. Elisha Morris[6] Abner Sr. (Daniel[5], Willis[4], Elisha[3], Elisha[2] Abney, Abner[1]) m. Gertrude Williams. He, b.14 Jun 1894 KY. He d.11 Oct 1962 Middletown, Butler Co., OH, at age 68 and was bur. Woodside Cem., Middletown, Butler Co., OH.
    Gertrude Williams, b.11 May 1901 Morgan Co., KY. She d.17 Dec 1973 Middletown, Butler Co., OH, at age 72 and was bur. Woodside Cem.
Known children of Elisha Morris[6] Abner Sr. and Gertrude Williams:
   840   i.   Beulah Lenora[7], b. 9 Aug 1919 KY; m. Clyde Keeton.
   841   ii. Bernice M., b. 14 Jan 1922; m. Pvt. Emmett A. Curry Jr. (USArmy-WWII).
         iii. Easter, b.2 Nov 1924 Boyd Co., KY; d.9 Nov 1924 Boyd Co., KY; bur. Woodside Cem., Middletown, Butler Co., OH.
         iv. Inez Beatrice, b.1925; m. M. Pat Salyers. d.1995; bur. Woodland Cem. and Arboretum, Dayton, Montgomery Co., OH.
   842   v. Naomi Faye, b. 27 Oct 1930 Ashland, Boyd Co., KY; m. Ivor Roberts.
         vi. Elisha Morris, b.7 Mar 1933; m. Barbara Lloyd; d.26 Jun 1994, ae.61; bur. Ridgeview Mem. Park, Allen, Collin Co., TX.
            Barbara Jean Lloyd, b.1 Mar 1935 OH; d.19 Nov 2014 Plano, Collin Co., TX, age 79; bur. Ridgeview Mem. Park
   843 vii. James Larry, b. 21 Oct 1936 Ashland, Boyd Co., KY; m. Carolyn R. Taylor.
   844 viii. Gary Wayne, b. 18 Sep 1939 Ashland, Boyd Co., KY; m. Mable E. Dean.

424. Jerry[6] Abner (Daniel[5], Willis[4], Elisha[3], Elisha[2] Abney, Abner[1]), b.4 Jun 1898 Perry Co., KY. He m. Nola Watson on Christmas Day, 25 Dec 1918. He d.26 Nov 1981 Middleton, Butler Co., OH, at age 83 and was bur. Woodside Cem., Middleton, Butler Co., OH.
    Nola Watson, b.4 Apr 1900 KY. She d.23 Jun 1967 Middleton, Butler Co., OH, at age 67 and was bur. Woodside Cem., Middleton.
Known children of Jerry[6] Abner and Nola Watson:
      i.   Ruby[7] m. (n.n.) Raleigh.
      ii. Dorothy m. (n.n.) Kash.
      iii. Ruth E, b.20 Oct 1919 Middleton, Butler Co., OH; m. Jesse McIntosh; d.28 Jan 2003 KY, age 83; bur. Woodside Cem.
          Jesse McIntosh, b.21 Mar 1914 Buckhorn, Perry Co., KY. He d.6 Sep 2013 Lexington, Fayette Co., KY, at age 99 and was bur. Woodside Cem., Middleton, Butler Co., OH.
   845   iv. Dan B. "Bo," b. 26 Mar 1928 Middleton, Butler Co., OH; m. Juanita Lovely.
        v. Willie, b.25 Sep 1930 Jackson Co., KY. He m. Deloras June Gay. He d.7 Apr 2008 Sandgap, Jackson Co., KY, at age 77 and was bur. Steele Cem., Foxtown, Jackson Co., KY.
          Deloras June Gay, b.14 Jul 1933 Jackson Co., KY; d.17 May 2006 Berea, Madison Co., KY, age 72; bur. Steele Cem.
      vi. Ninnie, b.26 Mar 1941 KY; m. Albert Russell. She d.18 Jul 1986 Connersville, Fayette Co., IN, at age 45 and was bur. Dale Cem., Connersville, Fayette Co., IN.
          Albert Russell, b.21 Jun 1933 Jackson Co., KY. He d.3 Nov 1999 McKee, Jackson Co., KY, age 66; bur. Dale Cem.

425. Dora Lee[6] Abner (Daniel[5], Willis[4], Elisha[3], Elisha[2] Abney, Abner[1]) m. Cpl. Vernon Carroll (USArmy). , b.23 Apr 1910 Wolfe Co., KY. She d.26 Jul 1996 Middleton, Butler Co., OH, at age 86 and was bur. Woodside Cem., Middleton, Butler Co., OH.
    Cpl. Vernon Carroll (USArmy), b.18 May 1905 KY. He d.24 May 1961 Middleton, Butler Co., OH, at age 56 and was bur. Woodside Cem.
Known children of Dora Lee[6] Abner and Cpl. Vernon Carroll (USArmy):
      i.   Dave[7].
      ii. Darrell Gene, b.28 Oct 1945. He m. Marie Reescy. He d.7 Jul 2020 Middleton, Butler Co., OH, at age 74.

426. John Preston[6] Abner (Andrew[5], Enoch[4], Elisha[3], Elisha[2] Abney, Abner[1]), b.28 Jul 1889 Madison Co., AR. He m. Julia Hibbard, daughter of Hiram Hibbard and Elizabeth Maples, on 13 Jun 1909 St. Paul, Madison Co., AR. He d.17 Mar 1948 Orange Co., CA, at age 58 and was bur. Olive Grove Cem., Whittier, Los Angeles Co., CA.
    Julia Hibbard, b.New Year's Day, 1 Jan 1888 London, Laurel Co., KY. She d.1973 ON, Canada and was bur. Olive Grove Cem., Whittier.

Known children of John Preston[6] Abner and Julia Hibbard:

  i. Gracie Cleo[7], b.10 Aug 1910 Madison Co., AR. She d.Independence Day, 4 Jul 2002 at age 91 and was bur. Memory Garden Mem. Park, Brea, Orange Co., CA.

  ii. Maysel, b.1 Mar 1912 Huntsville, Madison Co., AR. She m. Paul Olive Ferguson. She d.5 Jul 2004 Fayetteville, Washington Co., AR, at age 92 and was bur. Tuttle Cem., Tuttle, Washington Co., AR.

    Paul Olive Ferguson, b.14 Feb 1912 Madison Co., AR. He d.31 Aug 1975 Madison Co., AR, age 63; bur. Tuttle Cem.

846 iii. William Cleveland "Bill," b. 21 Jun 1914 Madison Co., AR; m. Geneva Cornett; m. Lewise Miles; m. Nora Bethel Moore.

  iv. Edith, b.19 Apr 1917 Madison Co., AR.

  v. Opal "Betty", b.9 Jul 1919 Madison Co., AR. She d.Jul 1993.

  vi. Faye, b.10 Jul 1921 Madison Co., AR. She d.1974 CA.

  vii. Geneva Gail "Jean", b.22 Jul 1925 St. Paul, Madison Co., AR. She m. Albert Felan Harrison Jr. on 5 Mar 1944 CA. She d.19 Apr 2013 Upland, San Bernardino Co., CA, at age 87; bur. Memory Garden Mem. Park, Brea, Orange Co., CA.

    Albert Felan Harrison Jr, b. New Year's Eve, 31 Dec 1925 Drakes Creek, Madison Co., AR. He d.23 Mar 1982 Los Angeles Co., CA, at age 56.

  viii. Frankie, b.19 Feb 1929 Madison Co., AR.

427. Pvt. Walter S.[6] Abner (USArmy) (Andrew[5], Enoch[4], Elisha[3], Elisha[2] Abney, Abner[1]), b.21 Sep 1891 Madison Co., AR. He m. Joy Davidson ca.1916. He and Joy Jane Davidson appeared on the census of 24 Apr 1930 Bristow, Creek Co., OK. He d.5 Jul 1961 at age 69; bur. Bristow Cem.
 Joy Jane Davidson, b.1899. She d.1969 and was bur. Bristow Cem., Bristow, Creek Co., OK.
Known child of Pvt. Walter S.[6] Abner (USArmy) and Joy Jane Davidson:

  i. Cloe D.[7], b.25 Jul 1924. He d.14 Jun 1974 at age 49 and was bur. Bristow Cem., Bristow, Creek Co., OK.

428. PFC Fred[6] Abner (USArmy-WWI) (Andrew[5], Enoch[4], Elisha[3], Elisha[2] Abney, Abner[1]), b.25 Mar 1895 St. Paul, Madison Co., AR. He m. Cora Mae Long on 26 Jan 1919 Dutton, Madison Co., AR. He d.21 Aug 1971 Chelan, Chelan Co., WA, at age 76 and was bur. Chelan Fraternal Cem., Chelan, Chelan Co., WA.
 Cora Mae Long, b.7 May 1901 Aurora, Madison Co., AR. She d.16 Nov 1995 Brewster, Chelan Co., WA, at age 94.
Known children of PFC Fred[6] Abner (USArmy-WWI) and Cora Mae Long:

  i. Ruth R.[7], b.2 Dec 1923 Aurora, Madison Co., AR. She m. PFC Wayne Robinson (USArmy-WWII) in 1942. She d.1 Mar 2019 Wentachee, Chelan Co., WA, at age 95 and was bur. Chelan Fraternal Cem., Chelan, Chelan Co., WA.

    PFC Wayne Robinson (USArmy-WWII), b.27 Sep 1924 St. Paul, Madison Co., AR. He d.29 Sep 2008 Magazine, Logan Co., AR, at age 84.

  ii. Georgia Alice, b.22 Jan 1926 St. Paul, Madison Co., AR. She m. Silvanus "Perk" Easley on Christmas Eve, 24 Dec 1943 Delaney, Madison Co., AR. She d.22 Feb 1975 Wentachee, Chelan Co., WA, at age 49 and was bur. Chelan Fraternal Cem., Wentachee, Chelan Co., WA.

    Silvanus "Perk" Easley, b.4 Oct 1921 Crosses, Madison Co., AR. He d.30 Jan 2009 Chelan, Chelan Co., WA, age 87.

  iii. Unice Verda "Babe" m. Ronald A. Medley (USN). , b.18 Dec 1928. She d.16 Aug 1999 at age 70 and was bur. Riverside National Cem., Riverside, Riverside Co., CA.

    Ronald A. Medley (USN), b.5 Mar 1926. He d.16 May 1993 at age 67 and was bur. Riverside National Cem.

  iv. Wilma June, b.20 Mar 1935 St. Paul, Madison Co., AR. She m. George William Conley in 1950. She d.19 Aug 2011 Wentachee, Chelan Co., WA, at age 76 and was bur. Cashmere Cem., Cashmere, Chelan Co., WA.

    George William Conley, b.14 Mar 1931 Cass, Franklin Co., AR. He d.2 Oct 2013 East Wenatchee, Douglas Co., WA, at age 82 and was bur. Cashmere Cem., Cashmere, Chelan Co., WA.

429. Emily Frances[6] Abner (Andrew[5], Enoch[4], Elisha[3], Elisha[2] Abney, Abner[1]), b.29 Mar 1897 St. Paul, Madison Co., AR. She m. George Watkins in 1913. She d.14 Sep 1968 CA at age 71 and was bur. Arroyo Grande Cem., Arroyo Grande, San Luis Obispo Co., CA.
 George Watkins, b.5 Apr 1885 St. Paul, Madison Co., AR. He d.8 Apr 1963 Phoenix, Maricopa Co., AZ, at age 78 and was bur. Resthaven Park West Cem., Glendale, Maricopa Co., AZ.
Known child of Emily Frances[6] Abner and George Watkins:

  i. Marcus Dane "Mark"[7], b.20 Dec 1914 St. Paul, Madison Co., AR. He m. Edith Marie Patrick. He d.27 May 1985 Ceres, Stanislaus Co., CA, at age 70 and was bur. Ceres Mem. Park, Ceres, Stanislaus Co., CA.

    Edith Marie Patrick, b.13 Feb 1920 Madison Co., AR. She d.5 Dec 1983 Pettigrew, Madison Co., AR, at age 63 and was bur. Pine Grove Cem., Pettigrew, Madison Co., AR.

430. Hugh Dinsmore[6] Abner (Andrew[5], Enoch[4], Elisha[3], Elisha[2] Abney, Abner[1]), b.28 Jan 1900 St. Paul, Madison Co., AR. He m. Lucy Landers. He d.6 Sep 1964 Chelan Falls, Chelan Co., WA, at age 64 and was bur. Chelan Fraternal Cem., Chelan, Chelan Co., WA.
Known children of Hugh Dinsmore[6] Abner and Lucy Landers:

  i. (dau.)[7] m. Marvin Langley.

  ii. (dau.) m. Joyce Byrd.

  iii. Oleta "Fern", b.19 Feb 1934 St. Paul, Madison Co., AR. She m. Cpl. Troy Arthur Parker (USArmy-Korea) on 28 Jan 1950 Japton, Madison Co., AR. She m. David Harper. She d.15 Sep 2002 Brewster, Okanogan Co., WA, at age 68 and was bur. Omak Mem. Cem., Okanogan, Okanogan Co., WA.

    Cpl. Troy Arthur Parker (USArmy-Korea), b.16 Mar 1931 Fayetteville, Washington Co., AR. He d.2 Sep 1978 Omak, Okanogan Co., WA, at age 47 and was bur. Omak Mem. Cem., Okanogan, Okanogan Co., WA.

431. Jefferson Davis "Jeff"[6] Abner (Andrew[5], Enoch[4], Elisha[3], Elisha[2] Abney, Abner[1]), b.2 Feb 1906 Madison Co., AR. He m. Gladys P. Stephens. He d.3 Aug 1976 at age 70 and was bur. Walnut Grove Cem., Crosses, Madison Co., AR.
 Gladys P. Stephens, b.25 Aug 1913. She d.18 Nov 1989 at age 76 and was bur. Walnut Grove Cem., Crosses, Madison Co., AR.
Known children of Jefferson Davis "Jeff"[6] Abner and Gladys P. Stephens:

847 i. Emily "Mavis"[7], b. 28 Mar 1934 St. Paul, Madison Co., AR; m. Waldon Dewey Powell; m. William Clifford Long.

848 ii. Loraine, b. 2 Nov 1936 AR; m. Floyd Leon Hull.

432. Robert L.⁶ Abner (Kenas⁵, Enoch⁴, Elisha³, Elisha² Abney, Abner¹), b.27 Feb 1906. He m. Verda Edna Imes. He d.5 Apr 1992 at age 86 and was bur. Evergreen Home Cem., Beatrice, Gage Co., NE.
    Verda Edna Imes, b.15 Jan 1908. She d.27 May 1996 at age 88 and was bur. Evergreen Home Cem., Beatrice, Gage Co., NE.
Known child of Robert L.⁶ Abner and Verda Edna Imes:
        i.   Shirley Ann⁷, b.16 Jul 1932. She d.16 Jul 1932 and was bur. Evergreen Home Cem., Beatrice, Gage Co., NE.

433. Roy Vernon⁶ Abner (Kenas⁵, Enoch⁴, Elisha³, Elisha² Abney, Abner¹), b.8 Jan 1911. He m. Maude E. Linscott. He d.13 Sep 1995 Gage Co., NE, at age 84 and was bur. Blue Springs Cem., Blue Springs, Gage Co., NE.
    Maude E. Linscott, b.28 Sep 1917 Holmesville, Gage Co., NE. She d.11 Sep 2006 Bayard, Morrill Co., NE, at age 88; bur. Blue Springs Cem.
Known children of Roy Vernon⁶ Abner and Maude E. Linscott:
        i.   R. Roger⁷, b.9 Dec 1941 Scottsbluff, Scotts Bluff Co., NE. He d.30 Apr 2007 Scottsbluff, Scotts Bluff Co., NE, at age 65 and was bur. Blue Springs Cem., Blue Springs, Gage Co., NE.
      ii.   Susan, b. est.1943 NE.
     iii.   Mary Ann, b. NE.

434. Roscoe C.⁶ Abner (John⁵, James⁴, Menan³, Elisha² Abney, Abner¹), b.7 Jul 1877 Union Co., IN. He m1. Adelaid May Tolliver in 1898. He m2. Mary Frances Waltz on 26 Jan 1918. He d.Jan 1944 Madison Co., IN, at age 66 and was bur. Elwood Cem., Elwood, Madison Co., IN.
    Adelaid May Tolliver, b.23 Feb 1883 IN. She d.10 Apr 1914 Center, Union Co., IN, age 31; bur. Silver Creek Cem., Liberty, Union Co., IN.
Known children of Roscoe C.⁶ Abner and Adelaid May Tolliver:
849   i.   Bert Hollis⁷, b. 21 Nov 1900 Liberty, Union Co., IN; m1. Dorothy M. Stalnaker; m2. Rowena E. Hinds; m3. Eva Hopper.
      ii.   Grace Mildred, b.16 Jul 1905 and d.4 Aug 1905 Union, Union Co., IN; bur. Salem Friends Cem., Salem, Union Co., IN.
850 iii.   Harold Merle, b. 19 Aug 1906 IN; m. Ruth Louise Zahrt.
     iv.   (infant daughter), b.8 Mar 1914 and d.9 Mar 1914 Center, Union Co., IN; bur. West Point Cem., Liberty, Union Co., IN.
851   v.   Florence May, b. 17 Nov 1917 Union Co., IN; m. Clarence Verle Creamer.
There were no known children of Roscoe C.⁶ Abner and Mary Frances Waltz.

435. Smith Lowell⁶ Abner (John⁵, James⁴, Menan³, Elisha² Abney, Abner¹), b.22 Jun 1881 Liberty, Union Co., IN. He m. Goldie Maude Bruce. He d.9 Dec 1967 Connersville, Fayette Co., IN, at age 86 and was bur. Dunlapsville Cem., Dunlapsville, Union Co., IN.
    Goldie Maude Bruce, b.9 May 1880 Union Co., IN. She d.6 Feb 1962 Connersville, Fayette Co., IN, at age 81 and was bur. Dunlapsville Cem.
Known children of Smith Lowell⁶ Abner and Goldie Maude Bruce:
852   i.   Esther Leotta⁷, b. 6 Oct 1901 Liberty, Union Co., IN; m. Robert Clifford Worster.
      ii.   Roy Irving, b.23 Jan 1904 IN. He m. Ethel Swango in 1926. He d.18 Dec 1986 Fairfield, Butler Co., OH, at age 82 and was bur. Arlington Mem. Gardens, Mount Healthy, Hamilton Co., OH.
           Ethel Swango, b.19 Jan 1908 Jeffersonville, Montgomery Co., KY. She d.8 Mar 1999 Fairfield, Butler Co., OH, at age 91 and was bur. Arlington Mem. Gardens, Mount Healthy, Hamilton Co., OH.
853 iii.   Mary E., b. 10 May 1907 Union Co., IN; m. Herbert Riley Eastin; m. Lloyd Russell Behymer.
     iv.   Wilber Loren, b.2 Jul 1909 Union Co., IN. He d.Aug 1984 Henry Co., IN, at age 75 and was bur. Glen Cove Cem., Knightstown, Henry Co., IN.
      v.   Clinton Dale, b.14 Jul 1912 Dunlapsville, Union Co., IN. He d.27 Jan 1938 Connersville, Fayette Co., IN, at age 25 and was bur. Salem Friends Cem., Salem, Union Co., IN.
     vi.   Hazel Marie, b.13 Jun 1915 Union Co., IN. She m. (n.n.) Hughes. d.23 Feb 2002 Richmond, Wayne Co., IN, at age 86 and was bur. Dunlapsville Cem., Dunlapsville, Union Co., IN.
   vii.   Cecil G., b.19 Jul 1917. He d.5 Aug 2002 at age 85 and was bur. Dunlapsville Cem., Dunlapsville, Union Co., IN.
  viii.   Lowell Eugene, b.21 Mar 1923 Fayette Co., IN. He m. Leona Marie Butler in 1963. He d.8 Feb 1989 Indianapolis, Marion Co., IN, at age 65. He was cremated.
           Leona Marie Butler, b.27 Jan 1923 Paris, Edgar Co., IL. She d.New Year's Eve, 31 Jan 2014 Indianapolis, Marion Co., IN, at age 91 and was bur. Washington Park East Cem., Indianapolis, Marion Co., IN.

436. Bessie P.⁶ Abner (John⁵, James⁴, Menan³, Elisha² Abney, Abner¹), b.26 Jun 1889 Union Co., IN. She m. (n.n.) Robinson ca.1906. She and (n.n.) Robinson were divorced before 1910.
Known child of Bessie P.⁶ Abner and (n.n.) Robinson:
        i.   Opal F.⁷, b. ca.1907 IN.

437. Joseph L. "Joe"⁶ Abner (Pierce⁵, James⁴, Menan³, Elisha² Abney, Abner¹), b.22 Jan 1889 KY. [Author's note: His headstone (18 Feb 1889-19 Jul 1952) and Death Certificate (22 Jan 1889-02 Jul 1952) are in disagreement on both the birth date and the date of death. Obviously the certificate must be correct, at least as concerns his date of death. To further complicate matters, the 1900 Census (wherein he is enumerated with his grandfather, William Smith, give his birth month and year as Mar 1890. He was liv. on 14 Jun 1900 with his grandfather, William Smith, Clay Co., KY. He m1. Rosana Frederick on 2 Mar 1912 Clay Co., KY. He and Rosana Frederick appeared on the census of 15 Jan 1920 Goose Rock, Clay Co., KY. He appeared on the census of 25 Apr 1930 Auburn, Barrow Co., GA. He m2. Effie Jane Stewart ca.1933. He and Effie Jane Stewart appeared on the census of 6 Apr 1940 Blue Hole, Clay Co., KY. He d.2 Jul 1952 Pineville, Bell Co., KY, at age 63.
    Rosana Frederick, b. ca.1893 Clay Co., KY. She appeared on the census of 7 Apr 1930 with brother, Bardley Frederick, Laurel Co., KY.
Known children of Joseph L. "Joe"⁶ Abner and Rosana Frederick both b. Clay Co., KY:
        i.   William⁷, b.7 Dec 1912. He d.10 Dec 1912 Clay Co., KY.
854   ii.   Sophie, b. 29 Jan 1915; m. Thomas "Tommy" Smith.
    Effie Jane Stewart, b.1897 KY. She d.1957 Knox Co., KY and was bur. Calvin Jordan Cem., Woollum, Knox Co., KY.
Known children of Joseph L. "Joe"⁶ Abner and Effie Jane Stewart:
855   i.   Thea⁷, b. 6 Jul 1934 Knox Co., KY; m. Wanda Gibson.
856   ii.   Boone, b. 19 Jun 1936 Hammond, Knox Co., KY; m. (n.n.).
857 iii.   John N., b. 22 Feb 1940 Knox Co., KY; m. Lydia Ann Smith.

438. Taylor⁶ Abner (Daniel⁵, James⁴, Menan³, Elisha² Abney, Abner¹), b.18 Feb 1886 Clay Co., KY. He m1. Lola Catherine Cheek, daughter of James Cheek and Araminta Kisling, on 25 Aug 1909 Union Co., IN. He and Lola Catherine Cheek were liv. on 21 Apr 1910 her father, James Cheek, Harrison, Union Co., IN. He and Lola Cheek appeared on the census of 9 Jan 1920 Richmond, Wayne Co., IN. He was liv. on 20 Apr 1940 as a boarder with W.M. Mitchel, Garrard Co., KY. He lived in 1949 Chicago, Cook Co., IL. He m2. Myra F. White ca.Jun 1949 Wayne Co., IN.
    Lola Catherine Cheek, b.23 Nov 1889 Preble Co., OH. She m2. Harry S. Cordell before 1930. She and Harry S. Cordell appeared on the census of 4 Apr 1930 Richmond, Wayne Co., IN. She d.21 Jan 1963 Richmond, Wayne Co., IN, at age 73.
Known children of Taylor⁶ Abner and Lola Catherine Cheek:
    i.   Elsie Maxine⁷, b. ca.1912. She d.20 Dec 1927.
    ii.   Ruth Katherine, b.16 May 1914 Richmond, Wayne Co., IN. She m1. Richard William Louis Essenmacher on 18 Jan 1933 Wayne Co., IN. She m2. George Ellsworth Godsey on 13 Sep 1936 Wayne Co., IN. She m3. Benjamin Weaver on 21 Oct 1939 Richmond, IN. She d.10 Sep 1994 Orange Co., FL, at age 80.
                Richard William Louis Essenmacher, b.1910. He d.1969.
                George Ellsworth Godsey, b.1915. He d.1987.
858 iii. Wilson Taylor, b. 5 Sep 1915 Richmond, Wayne Co., IN; m. Zola Ethel Bane.
    iv.   Arthur J., b. ca.Aug 1918 Richmond, Wayne Co., IN. He d.18 Apr 1920 Richmond, Wayne Co., IN.
    v.   Beatrice Mary, b.10 Aug 1921 Richmond, Wayne Co., IN. She m. (n.n.) Skaggs. She m. Bert Lambert on 5 Jan 1946 Wayne Co., IN. She d.26 Mar 1996 Henderson, Rusk Co., TX, at age 74.
There were no known children of Taylor⁶ Abner and Myra F. White.

439. Martha Helen⁶ Abner (Daniel⁵, James⁴, Menan³, Elisha² Abney, Abner¹), b.9 Apr 1901 Clay Co., KY. She m. Forest O. Hill on 25 May 1918 Wayne Co., IN. She d.Jun 1981 Lynn, Randolph Co., IN, at age 80.
    Forest O. Hill, b.1896. He d.1985.
Known children of Martha Helen⁶ Abner and Forest O. Hill:
    i.   Janet⁷, b.1920.
    ii.   Gerald, b.1923. He d.1974.

440. Clara Eva⁶ Abner (Daniel⁵, James⁴, Menan³, Elisha² Abney, Abner¹), b.2 Nov 1903 Union Co., IN. She m. Howard W. Hill on 29 Dec 1923 Wayne Co., IN. She d.2 May 1995 Darke Co., OH, at age 91.
    Howard W. Hill, b.1904. He d.1984.
Known children of Clara Eva⁶ Abner and Howard W. Hill:
    i.   Richard Dean⁷, b.1925. He d.2006.
    ii.   James Elwood, b.1927.

441. James Monroe⁶ Abner Sr. (Daniel⁵, James⁴, Menan³, Elisha² Abney, Abner¹) m. Wanda Catherine Wise. He, b.28 May 1907 Union Co., IN. He d.14 Mar 1972 Darke Co., OH, at age 64.
    Wanda Catherine Wise, b.1905. She d.1979.
Known children of James Monroe⁶ Abner Sr. and Wanda Catherine Wise:
859 i.   James Monroe⁷, b. 28 May 1929 Greensfork, Randolph Co., IN; m. Glenna Mae Skinner.
    ii.   William Daniel, b.27 Feb 1931. He m. Donna Joan Snyder (b.1934). He d.31 Oct 1995 at age 64.
    iii. Amarallis Rose, b.19 Dec 1934 Crete, Greensfork, Randolph Co., IN. m. Lester Duane Arnett (1932-2002).
    iv.   Dale Landis, b.6 Dec 1937. He d.10 Apr 1986 at age 48.

442. Elisha⁶ Abner (James⁵, Richard⁴, Menan³, Elisha² Abney, Abner¹), b.Mar 1882 Knox Co., KY. He m. Margret "Maggie" Smith, daughter of Milton Smith, on 5 May 1902 Knox Co., KY. He d.1903 Knox Co., KY and was bur. H.W. Childers Cem., Sprule, Knox Co., KY.
    Margret "Maggie" Smith, b.9 Sep 1883; m2. James S. Jones in 1906; d.18 Feb 1980; bur. Walnut Grove Cem., Clinton, Vermillion Co., IN.
Known children of Elisha⁶ Abner and Margret "Maggie" Smith:
    i.   Ballinger⁷, b.25 Mar 1903 Hopper, Knox Co., KY. He was liv. on 5 May 1910 with grandfather, Milton Smith, Whites Branch, Clay Co., KY. He d.1 May 1913 Hopper, Knox Co., KY, age 10; bur. Nan Riley Cem., Woollum, Knox Co., KY.

443. Maggie Mae⁶ Abner (James⁵, Richard⁴, Menan³, Elisha² Abney, Abner¹), b.6 Oct 1883 Knox Co., KY. She m. Henry Robinson on 30 Nov 1900 Campbell Co., TN. She d.17 Oct 1936 Knox Co., KY, at age 53 and was bur. H.W. Childers Cem., Sprule, Knox Co., KY.
    Henry Robinson, b.9 Jun 1880. He d.9 Sep 1956 Knox Co., KY, at age 76 and was bur. H.W. Childers Cem., Sprule, Knox Co., KY.
Known children of Maggie Mae⁶ Abner and Henry Robinson:
    i.   Bertha⁷, b.21 Aug 1903 Fayette Co., KY. She d.22 Jul 1977 Bell Co., KY, at age 73.
    ii.   Walter, b.16 May 1905 Knox Co., KY. He m. Alta Messer on 13 Dec 1934 Girdler, Knox Co., KY. He d.13 Mar 1982 Lexington, Fayette Co., KY, at age 76.
    iii. Bessie, b.7 Jul 1907 Knox Co., KY. She m. Charlie Chillders on 6 Feb 1931 Knox Co., KY. She d.10 Aug 1964 Barbourville, Knox Co., KY, at age 57.
    iv.   Lizzie, b.1909 Knox Co., KY. She m. Hobert L. "Hobie" Sharp on 3 Oct 1925 Cranes Nest, Knox Co., KY.
    v.   Robert "Boyd", b.15 Jan 1911 Knox Co., KY. He m. Lula Warren on 12 Jan 1933 Sprule, Knox Co., KY. He d.13 Jul 1992 Columbus, Bartholomew Co., IN, at age 81.
    vi.   Allie Myrtle, b.1 Nov 1912 Knox Co., KY. She m. James "Henry" Warren on 10 Jun 1923 Knox Co., KY. She d.4 Feb 1988 Barbourville, Knox Co., KY, at age 75.
    vii. Mitchell, b.11 Apr 1915 Knox Co., KY; m. Edna Derosette. He d.27 Mar 2005 Girdler, Knox Co., KY, age 89.
    viii. Harvie m. Pollie Smallwood. He, b.20 Jul 1917 Knox Co., KY. He d.13 Apr 1984 Barbourville, Knox Co., KY, at age 66.
    ix.   Dorothy E., b.28 Nov 1920 Knox Co., KY. She d.1921. She d.1 Aug 1921 Knox Co., KY.
    x.   Dora "Chelcea", b.11 Aug 1922 Knox Co., KY; m. Dewey Dan Parker bef.1940. She d.1 Oct 1982 Bell Co., KY, age 60.

444. Robert "Boyd"[6] Abner (James[5], Richard[4], Menan[3], Elisha[2] Abney, Abner[1]), b.22 Aug 1885 Knox Co., KY. He m. Amanda May "Mandy" Cobb on 1 Mar 1906 Knox Co., KY. He and Amanda appeared on the censuses of 15 Apr 1910 Girdler, Knox Co., KY; and 14 Apr 1930 and 15 Apr 1940 Clinton, Vermillion Co., IN; d.6 Apr 1964 Clinton, Vermillion Co., IN, age 78; bur. Walnut Grove Cem., Clinton, Vermillion Co., IN.

    Amanda May "Mandy" Cobb, b.7 Aug 1887 Knox Co., KY. She d.4 Feb 1988 Clinton, Vermillion Co., IN, age 100; bur. Walnut Grove Cem.
Known children of Robert "Boyd"[6] Abner and Amanda May "Mandy" Cobb:

860	i.	Jennie Nancy "Nannie"[7], b. 11 Dec 1906 Knox Co., KY; m1. Huram Clyde "Hutie" Delph; m2. James H. Martin; m3. William "Darald" Aldridge; m4. George Dewey Mitchell.
	ii.	Lula Ann "Lulie", b.3 Feb 1909 Knox Co., KY. She d.9 Aug 1918 Clinton, Vermillion Co., IL, at age 9 and was bur. H.W. Childers Cem., Sprule, Knox Co., KY.
	iii.	(baby dau.) was stillborn 1911 Hopper, Knox Co., KY.
	iv.	Arnold Thomas, b.26 Oct 1912 Knox Co., KY. He was liv. in 1940 as a boarder with Joe Abner, North, Lake Co., IN. He and his brother, Joseph Homer "Chip" Abner were liv. on 10 Apr 1940 as lodgers with the William Aldridge family, North, Lake Co., IN. He m. Mary Ann Smith. He d.29 Nov 1984 Terre Haute, Vigo Co., IN, at age 72.
		Mary Ann Smith, b.30 Oct 1966.
	v.	(baby dau.) was stillborn 1915 Clinton, Vermillion Co., IL.
	vi.	(baby) was stillborn 1916 Clinton, Vermillion Co., IL.
861	vii.	Ulis Ambrose "Tad," b. 5 Apr 1918 Clinton, Vermillion Co., IN; m. Goldie Ione Payton
862	viii.	Joseph Homer "Chip," b. 20 May 1920 Clinton, Vermillion Co., IN; m. Mary Frances D'Angelo.
863	ix.	James "Elmer," b. 4 Nov 1922 Clinton, Vermillion Co., IN; m. Betty R. Gray.
864	x.	Beulah Irene "Boots," b. 1 May 1926 Clinton, Vermillion Co., IN; m. Earl Leon Guinn.

445. Dora Mae[6] Abner (James[5], Richard[4], Menan[3], Elisha[2] Abney, Abner[1]), b. New Year's Day, 1 Jan 1888 Knox Co., KY; m. Elisha Vaughn Jr. on 13 Sep 1905 at her mother's home, Knox Co., KY; d.9 Sep 1924 Knox Co., KY, at age 36; bur. H.W. Childers Cem., Sprule, Knox Co., KY.

    Elisha Vaughn Jr, b.7 Jun 1883 Knox Co., KY. He d.22 Aug 1972 Heidrick, Knox Co., KY, at age 89 and was bur. H.W. Childers Cem.
Known children of Dora Mae[6] Abner and Elisha Vaughn Jr. all b. Knox Co., KY:

i.	Irene[7], b.19 Oct 1905. She m. Walter C. Hopkins on 15 Nov 1923 Knox Co., KY. She d.18 Apr 1984 Evansville, Vanderburgh Co., IN, at age 78.
ii.	William "Henry", b.3 Oct 1908; m. Lucy Ann Stewart on 2 Jul 1928 Knox Co., KY; d.2 Sep 1988 Knox Co., KY, age 79.
iii.	John, b.3 Oct 1910. He d.19 Feb 1934 Caleb Creek, Knox Co., KY, at age 23.
iv.	James Arthur, b.13 Feb 1913. He d.23 Dec 1913 Hopper, Knox Co., KY.
v.	Garrett G., b.24 Oct 1915. He m. Helen Jean Allen. He d.18 Jan 1990 Knox Co., KY, at age 74.
vi.	Amanda Jane, b.9 Aug 1917. She m. Taylor E. Sharp on 18 Jul 1931 Knox Co., KY. She d.21 Mar 2005 Keavy, Laurel Co., KY, at age 87.
vii.	Ethel Grace m. James Warren. , b.3 Nov 1919. She d.15 Sep 2002 Girdler, Knox Co., KY, at age 82.
viii.	Maggie Lucy m. John W. Nelson. , b.2 Jan 1922. She d.30 May 1983 Barbourville, Knox Co., KY, at age 61.
ix.	Chester P., b.22 Jun 1923. He d.25 Aug 1923 Knox Co., KY.

446. Chester Garfield[6] Abner (James[5], Richard[4], Menan[3], Elisha[2] Abney, Abner[1]), b.11 May 1896 Knox Co., KY. He m. Susanna Cox on 15 Sep 1917 Corbin, Knox Co., KY. He d.4 Dec 1925 Barbourville, Knox Co., KY, at age 29.
Known children of Chester Garfield[6] Abner and Susanna Cox:

i.	Lula Ethel[7], b.12 Aug 1918 Knox Co., KY; m. Connie Mack Mabry; d.11 Jan 2007 Spartanburg, Spart. Co., SC, ae.88.
ii.	Laura Ellen m. Heinar Tamme Spartanburg, Spartanburg Co., SC. , b.23 Jun 1920 Gray, Knox Co., KY. She d.9 Nov 1999 Port Townsend, Jefferson Co., WA, at age 79.
iii.	Justice Boyd, b.1 Sep 1922 Knox Co., KY. He d.10 Jun 1938 Paintsville, Johnson Co., KY, at age 15.

447. Lloyd W.[6] Abner (Elisha[5], Richard[4], Menan[3], Elisha[2] Abney, Abner[1]), b.26 Jul 1895 Knox Co., KY. He m. Julia Ethel Helton. He d.17 Feb 1951 Laurel Co., KY, at age 55 and was bur. Rest Haven Cem., Corbin, Knox Co., KY.

    Julia Ethel Helton, b.14 Sep 1899 Harlan Co., KY. She d.28 Jan 1986 Corbin, Knox Co., KY, at age 86 and was bur. Rest Haven Cem., Corbin.
Known children of Lloyd W.[6] Abner and Julia Ethel Helton all b. Knox Co., KY:

865	i.	Verna Bruce[7], b. 18 Jul 1926; m1. S.Sgt. Leon Arthur Pittman; m2. (n.n.) Wyatt.
866	ii.	Cholista Maxine, b. 12 Jun 1929; m. George R. Ledford (USN-WWII).
867	iii.	Glenna Ester, b. 31 Mar 1932; m. Eugene Smith; m. (n.n.) Morgan.

448. Gilbert G.[6] Abner (Charles[5], Richard[4], Menan[3], Elisha[2] Abney, Abner[1]), b.14 Oct 1886 Knox Co., KY. He m. Ada Trent. He d.18 Dec 1953 Knox Co., KY, at age 67 and was bur. Nan Riley Cem., Woollum, Knox Co., KY.

    Ada Trent, b.10 May 1894 KY. She d.15 Nov 1984 at age 90 and was bur. Nan Riley Cem., Woollum, Knox Co., KY.
Known children of Gilbert G.[6] Abner and Ada Trent all b. Knox Co., KY:

868	i.	Walter[7], b. 30 Jan 1912; m. Axie Grubb.
	ii.	Minnie, b.6 Nov 1913. She d.6 Nov 1918 Knox Co., KY, at age 5 and was bur. Cobb Cem., Tedders, Knox Co., KY.
	iii.	McKinley, b.Dec 1915. He d.23 Oct 1918 Knox Co., KY, at age 2 and was bur. Cobb Cem., Tedders, Knox Co., KY.
	iv.	Georgia, b.1 Jun 1935; She m. Clyde Mills on 21 Dec 1950. She d.19 Apr 2017 Lexington, Fayette Co., KY, at age 81 and was bur. Nicholson Cem. #1, Brock, Laurel Co., KY.
		Clyde Mills, b.6 May 1930. He d.14 Nov 2002 at age 72 and was bur. Nicholson Cem. #1, Brock, Laurel Co., KY.

449. Sarah[6] Abner (Charles[5], Richard[4], Menan[3], Elisha[2] Abney, Abner[1]), b.18 Dec 1888 KY. She m1. Robert Tuttle on 8 Apr 1914. She m2. John R. Smith on 24 Sep 1920. She d.11 Mar 1978 Knox Co., KY, at age 89 and was bur. Fisher Cem., Heidrick, Knox Co., KY.

    Robert Tuttle, b.1892 KY.
Known children of Sarah[6] Abner and Robert Tuttle:

i.	Dewey[7], b.1914. He d.1989.
ii.	John A., b.1920. He d.1923.

John R. Smith, b.7 Mar 1890 KY. He d.12 Nov 1955 KY at age 65 and was bur. Calvin Jordan Cem., Woollum, Knox Co., KY.
Known children of Sarah⁶ Abner and John R. Smith:
  i.   Ellen⁷, b.1921. She d.1926.
  ii. Tip, b.1924. He d.1993.
  iii. Floyd, b.1928. He d.2004.
  iv. Willie M., b.1930. He d.1982.

450. Robert "Bob"⁶ Abner (Charles⁵, Richard⁴, Menan³, Elisha² Abney, Abner¹), b.8 Jun 1891. He m. Mary "Jennie" Smith on 15 Feb 1912. He d.7 Oct 1985 at age 94 and was bur. Fisher Cem., Heidrick, Knox Co., KY.
  Mary "Jennie" Smith, b.22 Apr 1892. She d.2 Jun 1975 at age 83 and was bur. Fisher Cem., Heidrick, Knox Co., KY.
Known child of Robert "Bob"⁶ Abner and Mary "Jennie" Smith:
  869 i.   Tommy⁷, b. 9 Sep 1912; m. Hilda Fisher.

451. Sam⁶ Abner (Charles⁵, Richard⁴, Menan³, Elisha² Abney, Abner¹), b.2 Dec 1893. He m1. Martha Cobb. He m2. Tennie Cottongim. He d.16 Dec 1977 at age 84 and was bur. Fisher Cem., Heidrick, Knox Co., KY.
  Martha Cobb, b.24 Sep 1898. She d.13 Nov 1972 at age 74 and was bur. Cobb Cem., Sprule, Knox Co., KY.
There were no known children of Sam⁶ Abner and Martha Cobb.
  Tennie Cottongim, b.19 Dec 1894. She d.3 Sep 1936 at age 41 and was bur. Fisher Cem., Heidrick, Knox Co., KY.
Known children of Sam⁶ Abner and Tennie Cottongim:
  i.   Mary Bernice⁷ m. Ralph Sterling Doolin. , b.22 Aug 1933 Knox Co., KY. She d.9 Jan 2017 Barbourville, Knox Co., KY, at age 83 and was bur. Tuggle-Doolin Cem., Heidrick, Knox Co., KY.
       Ralph Sterling Doolin, b.21 Jun 1932 Knox Co., KY. He d.19 Jun 2012 Barbourville, Knox Co., KY, at age 79 and was bur. Tuggle-Doolin Cem., Heidrick, Knox Co., KY.

452. Finley L.⁶ Abner (Charles⁵, Richard⁴, Menan³, Elisha² Abney, Abner¹) m. Cordie H. Trent. He, b.25 Sep 1896. He d.3 Aug 1989 at age 92 and was bur. Fisher Cem., Heidrick, Knox Co., KY.
  Cordie H. Trent, b.5 Feb 1903. She d.22 Dec 1987 at age 84 and was bur. Fisher Cem., Heidrick, Knox Co., KY.
Known children of Finley L.⁶ Abner and Cordie H. Trent:
  i.   Randall⁷, b.27 Feb 1921 Knox Co., KY. He d.27 Aug 1921 Knox Co., KY; bur. Cobb Cem., Tedders, Knox Co., KY.
  870 ii. John "David," b. 22 Aug 1924; m. Beaulah Jackson; m. Myrtle Henson.
  iii. Hazel Ernestine m. SFC James W. Davis (USArmy-WWII, Korea). , b.5 Feb 1927. She d.5 May 1999 at age 72 and was bur. Fort Sam Houston National Cem., San Antonio, Bexar Co., TX.
       SFC James W. Davis (USArmy-WWII, Korea), b.25 Nov 1926; d.27 Jan 2000; bur. Fort Sam Houston Nat'l Cem.
  iv. Claud, b.17 Apr 1930 Knox Co., KY. He d.23 Jan 1931 Knox Co., KY and was bur. Cobb Cem., Tedders, Knox Co., KY.
  871 v.   Charles Franklin, b. 21 Jan 1937 KY; m. Judith Mina Daley.

453. Maggie⁶ Abner (Charles⁵, Richard⁴, Menan³, Elisha² Abney, Abner¹), b.20 Feb 1899. She m. Ace Hatfield Sr. in 1919. She d.10 Jul 1982 Kalamazoo Co., MI, at age 83 and was bur. Fisher Cem., Heidrick, Knox Co., KY.
  Ace Hatfield Sr, b.31 Aug 1899. He d.16 Oct 1971 at age 72 and was bur. Fisher Cem., Heidrick, Knox Co., KY.
Known children of Maggie⁶ Abner and Ace Hatfield Sr.:
  i.   Bertha⁷, b.1920. She d.1994.
  ii.   Leonard James, b.1922. He d.1985.
  iii. Charles F., b.1924. He d.1924.
  iv.   John Henry, b.1926. He d.1994.
  v.   Elmer, b.1931. He d.1991.
  vi.   Bonnie, b.1934. She d.2013.
  vii. James A., b.1936. He d.2011.
  viii. Ace, b.1938. He d.2000.
  ix.   Pattie Sue, b.1941. She d.1941.

454. Theodore⁶ Abner (Joseph⁵, Richard⁴, Menan³, Elisha² Abney, Abner¹), b.29 Jul 1891. He m. Stella Cole ca.1921. He d.16 Jun 1940 at age 48 and was bur. Barbourville Cem., Barbourville, Knox Co., KY.
  Stella Cole, b.14 Oct 1903 Clay Co., KY. She d.14 Jan 1994 Knox Co., KY, at age 90; bur. Barbourville Cem., Barbourville, Knox Co., KY.
Known children of Theodore⁶ Abner and Stella Cole:
  i.   Dorothy⁷, b.30 Mar 1922 Barbourville, Knox Co., KY. She m. Otis F. Melton on 16 Oct 1941. She d.31 Jul 2008 Corbin, Knox Co., KY, at age 86 and was bur. Faulkner Chapel Cem., Swanond, Knox Co., KY.
  872 ii. George Arthur, b. 26 Jan 1925; m. Rose Marie "Rosie" Lax.
  iii. Louis Edward, b.3 Feb 1929 Knox Co., KY. He d.28 Nov 1997 Richmond Co., GA, at age 68 and was bur. Hillcrest Mem. Park Cem., Augusta, Richmond Co., GA.
  iv. Wilma Audell "Dell", b.25 Oct 1930. She m. (n.n.) Botkins. d.9 Apr 1988 at age 57 and was bur. North Thompson Bapt. Ch. Cem., Vidalia, Toombs Co., GA.

455. Nancy⁶ Abner (Martha⁵, John⁴, Menan³, Elisha² Abney, Abner¹), b. ca.1872; m. Stephen Burnett on 31 May 1894 Knox Co., KY. She d.1922.
  Stephen Burnett, b.1868. He d.1947.
Known children of Nancy⁶ Abner and Stephen Burnett:
  i.   William⁷, b.1896.
  ii. Henry, b.1898. He d.1965.
  iii. Mollie, b.1902.
  iv. Lizzie, b.1907.
  v.   Walter, b.1909. He d.1975.
  vi. Tom, b.1912.

456. Rosa Lee⁶ Abner (James⁵, John⁴, Menan³, Elisha² Abney, Abner¹), b.25 May 1885 Clay Co., KY. She m. Abijah Morgan Lyttle ca.1901. She d.16 Feb 1936 Witt, Estill Co., KY, at age 50.
    Abijah Morgan Lyttle, b.1859. He d.1944.
Known children of Rosa Lee⁶ Abner and Abijah Morgan Lyttle:
      i.   Lillian⁷, b.1902. She d.1986.
      ii.   Jessie Viola, b.1904. She d.2002.
      iii.   Arthur C, b.1906. He d.1980.
      iv.   Bidy, b.1912. She d.1920.
      v.   Edward F., b.1915. He d.1968.
      vi.   Harold Eugene, b.1918. He d.1949.
      vii.   Charles Everett, b.1922. He d.1986.
      viii.   James P., b.1928. He d.1975.

457. Emma A.⁶ Abner (James⁵, John⁴, Menan³, Elisha² Abney, Abner¹), b.2 Oct 1890 Clay Co., KY. She m. Gentry Cox on 9 Oct 1905 Estill Co., KY. She d.18 Mar 1973 Estill Co., KY, at age 82 and was bur. Russell Flat Cem., Sand Springs, Jackson Co., KY.
    Gentry Cox, b.13 Jun 1880. He d.17 Aug 1925 at age 45 and was bur. Russell Flat Cem., Sand Springs, Jackson Co., KY.
Known children of Emma A.⁶ Abner and Gentry Cox:
      i.   Myrtle M.⁷, b.1906. She d.1978.
      ii.   Rosa Ethel, b.1908. She d.1995.
      iii.   Sylvia J., b.1910. She d.1979.
      iv.   Mary Ella, b.1912. She d.1912.
      v.   Minerva Mae, b.1913. She d.1991.
      vi.   Daniel Preston, b.1914. He d.2004.
      vii.   Hazel Minnie, b.1918. She d.2002.
      viii.   Delbert, b.1919. He d.1981.
      ix.   Gracy, b. ca.1921.
      x.   William W., b.1921. He d.1997.
      xi.   Lola Florence, b.1924. She d.2006.
      xii.   Clarence G, b.1926. He d.1999.

458. Della "Dellie"⁶ Abner (James⁵, John⁴, Menan³, Elisha² Abney, Abner¹) m. Thomas P. Cox. , b.1 Dec 1895 Jackson Co., KY. She d.6 Jul 1990 Hamilton, Butler Co., OH, at age 94 and was bur. Rose Hill Burial Park, Hamilton, Butler Co., OH.
    Thomas P. Cox, b.27 Jul 1888 Jackson Co., KY. He d.11 Nov 1966 Hamilton, Butler Co., OH, at age 78.
Known children of Della "Dellie"⁶ Abner and Thomas P. Cox:
      i.   James D.⁷, b.1912. He d.1988.
      ii.   Charley, b.1914. He d.1985.
      iii.   Willie, b.1921. He d.1997.

459. Lewis Marshall⁶ Abner (James⁵, John⁴, Menan³, Elisha² Abney, Abner¹), b.24 May 1905 Jackson Co., KY. He m. Retha Becky Webb on 4 Nov 1931. He d.22 Oct 1982 McKee, Jackson Co., KY, at age 77 and was bur. Abner Family Cem., Jackson Co., KY.
    Retha Becky Webb, b.21 Jun 1909 Jackson Co., KY She d.28 Dec 1979 Jackson Co., KY, at age 70 and was bur. Abner Family Cem.
Known children of Lewis Marshall⁶ Abner and Retha Becky Webb both b. Jackson Co., KY:
      i.   Ray Lewis⁷, b.1 Jul 1932. He d.17 Jun 2005 Jackson Co., KY, at age 72; bur. Abner Family Cem., Jackson Co., KY.
  873 ii.   Carmel, b. 25 Jan 1942; m. Norma Whicker.

460. Dow L.⁶ Abner (James⁵, John⁴, Menan³, Elisha² Abney, Abner¹), b.1907 Jackson Co., KY. He m. Osa Ison on 20 Jan 1931 Irvine, Estill Co., KY. He d.1993 McKee, Jackson Co., KY and was bur. Bales-Roark Cem., Jackson Co., KY.
    Osa Ison, b.1909. She d.2005 and was bur. Bales-Roark Cem., Jackson Co., KY.
Known children of Dow L.⁶ Abner and Osa Ison:
      i.   Dan L.⁷, b.1 Nov 1934 McKee, Jackson Co., KY. He m. Mildred J. Smith on 30 Jul 1955. He d.7 Jun 2010 Middletown, Butler Co., OH, at age 75 and was bur. Butler County Mem. Park, Trenton, Butler Co., OH.
          Mildred J. Smith, b.11 Sep 1934 Knott Co., KY. She d.27 Oct 2019 Middletown, Butler Co., OH, at age 85 and was bur. Butler County Mem. Park, Trenton, Butler Co., OH.

461. Bessie⁶ Abnee (Robert⁵, Lincoln⁴, John³ Abney, Elisha², Abner¹), b.30 Dec 1887 Nicholas Co., KY. She m. William Dorsey Rogers on 24 Aug 1907 Robertson Co., KY. She d.15 Jun 1949 Burika, Robertson Co., KY, at age 61.
    William Dorsey Rogers, b.17 Jul 1886 Donaldson, Hot Spring Co., AR. He d.3 Aug 1951 Robertson Co., KY, at age 65.
Known children of Bessie⁶ Abnee and William Dorsey Rogers:
      i.   Bernice⁷, b.1909 Robertson Co., KY; m. Gilbert Cooper (b.1902) on 14 Oct 1925 Mason Co., KY. She d.16 Mar 1948.
      ii.   Ruth, b.1910. He d.1981.
      iii.   John Robert, b.1911. He d.1958.
      iv.   William Clinton, b.1916. He d.1963.

462. Airis "Victor"⁶ Abnee Sr. (William⁵, Lincoln⁴, John³ Abney, Elisha², Abner¹), b.18 Jun 1897 Carlisle, Nicholas Co., KY. He was Composing Room Foreman for the *Lexington Herald*, Lexington, Fayette Co., KY. He m. Sarah "Irene" Brogle ca.1921 KY. He and Sarah "Irene" Brogle appeared on the censuses of 16 Apr 1930 and 2 Apr 1940 Cincinnati, Hamilton Co., OH. He d.11 Oct 1984 Cook Co., IL, at age 87 and was bur. Spring Grove Cem., Cincinnati, Hamilton Co., OH.
    Sarah "Irene" Brogle, b.24 Oct 1896 Garrard, Clay Co., KY. She d.1 Apr 1977 Cincinnati, Hamilton Co., OH, age 80; bur. Spring Grove Cem.
Known child of Airis "Victor"⁶ Abnee Sr. and Sarah "Irene" Brogle:
  874 i.   Airis "Victor" Jr.⁷, b. 1923 KY; m. Doris Heuck.

463. Claude[6] Abnee (Clarence[5], Lincoln[4], John[3] Abney, Elisha[2], Abner[1]), b. Independence Day, 4 Jul 1904 Carlisle, Nicholas Co., KY. He m1. Gladys Maybrier ca.1925. He m2. Audrey "Mabel" Mitchell ca.1934. He and Audrey "Mabel" Mitchell appeared on the census of 23 Apr 1940 Mays Lick, Mason Co., KY. He d.12 Mar 1964 Carlisle, Nicholas Co., KY, at age 59 and was bur. Carlisle Cem., Carlisle, Nicholas Co., KY.
Known child of Claude[6] Abnee and Gladys Maybrier:
      i.   Myrtle[7], b. ca.1926 Nicholas Co., KY.
    Audrey "Mabel" Mitchell, b. ca.1898 Nicholas Co., KY. She m1. (n.n.) Williams.
Known children of Claude[6] Abnee and Audrey "Mabel" Mitchell:
      i.   Mary J. "Tootsie"[7], b. ca.1938 Mason Co., KY. She m1. Dennis Duane Kelley in 1965 Nicholas Co., KY. She and Dennis Duane Kelley were divorced. She m2. (n.n.) Bush.
          Dennis Duane Kelley, b.17 Oct 1942 Carlisle, Nicholas Co., KY.
875   ii.   Wanda Claudia "C," b. 6 Sep 1939 Nicholas Co., KY; m. Gerald Richard Jefferson.
876   iii.   Dorothy Belle, b. 10 Nov 1940 Carlisle, Nicholas Co., KY; m. William Lee "Bill" Earlywine.
877   iv.   Jerry Wayne, b. 24 Jul 1947 Carlisle, Nicholas Co., KY; m. Lydia Vice.

464. Shy Conley[6] Abnee (Clarence[5], Lincoln[4], John[3] Abney, Elisha[2], Abner[1]), b.26 Apr 1921 Nicholas Co., KY. He m. Betty Jane Dollins 15 Nov 1946 Nicholas Co., KY. He d.24 Apr 2010 at home, Upper Blue Licks, Nicholas Co., KY, age 88; bur. Carlisle Cem., Carlisle, Nicholas Co., KY.
    Betty Jane Dollins, b.13 Feb 1925 Carlisle, Nicholas Co., KY. She d.2 Feb 2005 Carlisle, Nicholas Co., KY, at age 79; bur. Carlisle Cem.
Known child of Shy Conley[6] Abnee and Betty Jane Dollins:
878   i.   William Conley "Conn"[7], m. Barbara (n.n.).

465. Matilda Ann[6] Murray (Malinda[5] Hunt, Nancy[4] Abner, John[3] Abney, Elisha[2], Abner[1]), b.11 May 1867 Seligman, Barry Co., MO. She m. William Riley Kelley on 28 Feb 1886 Barry Co., MO; d.25 Apr 1941 Dawson, Tulsa Co., OK, age 73; bur. Oaklawn Cem., Tulsa, Tulsa Co., OK.
    William Riley Kelley, b.2 Feb 1865 MO. He d.31 Oct 1930 Dawson, Tulsa Co., MO, at age 65 and was bur. Oaklawn Cem., Tulsa.
Known children of Matilda Ann[6] Murray and William Riley Kelley:
879   i.   Estella Rodella "Stella"[7], b. 2 Feb 1887 Seligman, Barry Co., MO; m. Olin Toliver Lewis Sr; m. Clarence Edward Watts.
      ii.   Dessie Delvie Eveline, b.14 Feb 1889 Seligman, Barry Co., MO. She m. Mack D. Green on 14 Mar 1907 Dawson, Tulsa Co., OK. She d.3 Nov 1979 Tulsa, Tulsa Co., OK, at age 90.
          Mack D. Green, b.15 Dec 1886 Peace Valley, Howell Co., MO. He d. ca.2 Aug 1965 Dawson, Tulsa Co., OK.
    iii.   Orson, b.27 Jun 1891. He d.4 Feb 1895 Indian Territory (OK) at age 3.
    iv.   Golda "Goldie", b.21 Oct 1899 Indian Territory (OK). She d.3 Nov 1906 Dawson, Tulsa Co., OK, at age 7.

466. Robert Lewis[6] Abner (Lewis[5], Lewis[4], John[3] Abney, Elisha[2], Abner[1]), b.26 Jan 1903 Lee Co., KY. He m. Sallie Drake ca.1927. He and Sallie Drake appeared on the censuses of 11 Apr 1930 and 30 Apr 1940 Saint Helens, Lee Co., KY. He d.1 Sep 1966 Lexington, Fayette Co., KY, at age 63 and was bur. Abner Cem., Primrose, Lee Co., KY.
    Sallie Drake, b.15 Feb 1908 Wolfe Co., KY. She d.26 Apr 1991 at age 83 and was bur. Abner Cem., Primrose, Lee Co., KY.
Known children of Robert Lewis[6] Abner and Sallie Drake:
      i.   Thomas Martin[7], b.23 Aug 1929 KY. He d.4 Dec 1951 KY at age 22 and was bur. Abner Cem., Primrose, Lee Co., KY.
      ii.   Bobby, b. ca.1933 Saint Helens, Lee Co., KY.

467. James "Bethel"[6] Abner (Lewis[5], Lewis[4], John[3] Abney, Elisha[2], Abner[1]), b.2 Jul 1908 Lee Co., KY. He m. Geneva F. Lucas on 18 Nov 1933. He and Geneva F. Lucas appeared on the census of 29 Apr 1940 Saint Helens, Lee Co., KY. He d.25 Apr 1997 Bronston, Pulaski Co., KY, at age 88 and was bur. Abner Cem., Primrose, Lee Co., KY.
    Geneva F. Lucas, b.8 Oct 1912 Lee Co., KY. She d.12 Apr 1999 Bronston, Pulaski Co., KY, at age 86 and was bur. Abner Cem., Primrose.
Known child of James "Bethel"[6] Abner and Geneva F. Lucas:
      i.   Joyce Irene[7], b.15 Aug 1934 Lee Co., KY. She d.15 Aug 1934 Lee Co., KY and was bur. Abner Cem., Primrose.

468. Gerald[6] Abner (Lewis[5], Lewis[4], John[3] Abney, Elisha[2], Abner[1]), b.16 Oct 1912 Lee Co., KY. He m. Beatrice C. (n.n.). He d.25 Feb 1993 at age 80 and was bur. Abner Cem., Primrose, Lee Co., KY.
    Beatrice C. (n.n.), b.6 Dec 1914. She d.21 Oct 1992 at age 77 and was bur. Abner Cem., Primrose, Lee Co., KY.
Known child of Gerald[6] Abner and Beatrice C. (n.n.):
      i.   Larry Ray[7], b.23 Jan 1943 Primrose, Lee Co., KY. He d.23 Jan 1943 Primrose, Lee Co., KY; bur. Abner Cem., Primrose.

469. Frank Cardine "Boose"[6] Abner (USArmy-Korea) (Lewis[5], Lewis[4], John[3] Abney, Elisha[2], Abner[1]), b.18 Jul 1928 Primrose, Lee Co., KY. He m. Elmer Spencer. He d.28 Mar 2016 Hazard, Perry Co., KY, at age 87 and was bur. Abner Cem., Primrose, Lee Co., KY.
Known children of Frank Cardine "Boose"[6] Abner (USArmy-Korea) and Elmer Spencer:
      i.   Arvin[7] m. Pauline (n.n.).
      ii.   Forest.

470. Nancy Pearl[6] Abner (Grover[5], John[4], John[3] Abney, Elisha[2], Abner[1]), b.9 Feb 1917 Primrose, Lee Co., KY. She m1. Carlie Daili Durbin in 1934. She m2. Joe Heving in 1940. She m3. Paul M. Burgan in 1979. She d.20 May 1998 Covington, Kenton Co., KY, at age 81 and was bur. Saint Mary's Cemetery, Fort Mitchell, Kenton Co., KY.
    Carlie Daili Durbin, b.1909. He d.1970.
Known child of Nancy Pearl[6] Abner and Carlie Daili Durbin:
      i.   James Raymond "Jim"[7], b.1935. He d.2013.
    Joe Heving, b.2 Sep 1900 Covington, Kenton Co., KY. From FindaGrave.com: *Major League Baseball Player. The right-hander pitched 13 years from 1930-45 with the New York Giants, Chicago White Sox, Cleveland Indians, Boston Red Sox and Boston Braves, compiling a 76-48 record and 3.90 earned run average. He was 60-35 in relief appearances. When he was 11-3 with the Red Sox in 1939, all his victories came in relief. He made 40 career starts, completing 17 of them.* He d.11 Apr 1970 at age 69; bur. Saint Mary's Cemetery, Fort Mitchell, Kenton Co., KY. There were no known children of Nancy Pearl[6] Abner and Joe Heving.
    Paul M. Burgan, b.1938. He d.2001. (There were no known children of Nancy Pearl[6] Abner and Paul M. Burgan.)

471. Arthur Thomas "Tom"[6] Abner (Arthur[5], John[4], John[3] Abney, Elisha[2], Abner[1]), b.22 Nov 1938 Beattyville, Lee Co., KY. He m. Carolyn Sue Erwin 25 Jun 1965 Flora, Clay Co., IL. He d.6 May 2020 Flora, Clay Co., IL, age 81; bur. Floral Garden of Memories Cem., Flora, Clay Co., IL.

Carolyn Sue Erwin, b.19 Feb 1944 Clay Co., IL. She d.7 Nov 2013 Flora, Clay Co., IL, at age 69; bur. Floral Garden of Memories Cem., Flora.
Known children of Arthur Thomas "Tom"[6] Abner and Carolyn Sue Erwin:
      i.   Randy[7] m. Erica (n.n.).
      ii.   Michelle m. Kenny Pietz.
      iii.   Jason m. Patti (n.n.).

472. James David[6] Bishop (David[5], Abraham[4], Mary[3] Abner, Elisha[2] Abney, Abner[1]), b.23 Oct 1875 Clay Co., KY. He m. Lucy Katherine Nuckols in Apr 1895 KY. He and Lucy Katherine Nuckols appeared on the censuses of 1 Jun 1900 Owsley Co., KY; 18 Apr 1910 Island Creek, Owsley Co., KY; and 27 Jan 1920 and 8 Apr 1930 Clay Co., KY. He d.6 Dec 1954 at age 79 and was bur. Coldiron Cem., Laurel Creek, Clay Co., KY.

Lucy Katherine Nuckols, b.3 Jun 1883 Clay Co., KY. She d.28 Dec 1963 KY at age 80 and was bur. Coldiron Cem., Laurel Creek.
Known children of James David[6] Bishop and Lucy Katherine Nuckols:
      i.   Oscar[7], b.1897 KY. He d.1986.
      ii.   (infant), b. ca.1898 KY. He d. before 1900 KY.
      iii.   (infant), b. ca.1899 KY. She d. before 1900 KY.
880   iv.   Walter I, b. 30 Aug 1900 KY; m. Mollie Gay; m. Dora Carmack.
      v.   Roy Abel, b.1903 KY. He d.1945.
      vi.   Estelle, b. ca.1906 KY.
      vii.   Roscoe, b. ca.1908 KY.
      viii.   Addie "Mae", b.1910 KY. She d.1988.
      ix.   Mary, b.1912. She d.2007.
      x.   Marigold, b. ca.1913 KY.
      xi.   McKinley Kevin, b.1915. He d.2004.
      xii.   June "Thelma", b.1917. She d.1983.
      xiii.   Gordon "Pershing", b.1919. He d.2004.
      xiv.   Alice, b.1920. She d.2016.

473. Robert Grant[6] Bishop (John[5], Abraham[4], Mary[3] Abner, Elisha[2] Abney, Abner[1]), b.16 Apr 1881 Owsley Co., KY. He m. Delphia Gabbard in 1897. He and Delphia Gabbard appeared on the censuses of 1 Jun 1900 Buffalo, Owsley Co., KY; and 22 Apr 1910 and 31 Jan 1920 Allen, Clay Co., KY. He d.9 Dec 1963 Clay Co., KY, at age 82 and was bur. Bishop Bend Cem., Trixie, Clay Co., KY.

Delphia Gabbard, b.3 Feb 1883 Owsley Co., KY. She d.20 Jun 1946 Clay Co., KY, at age 63 and was bur. Bishop Bend Cem., Trixie.
Known children of Robert Grant[6] Bishop and Delphia Gabbard all b. KY:
      i.   Mary E.[7], b.Sep 1898.
      ii.   Lydia K., b.Oct 1899.
      iii.   John "Johnny", b. ca.1901.
      iv.   Alex, b. ca.1903.
      v.   Drucilla "Drucie" d.1907 KY. , b.1907.
      vi.   Ida May, b.1907. She d.1908 KY.
      vii.   George, b. ca.1909.
      viii.   Virgil, b.1910. He d.1985.
      ix.   Pinie, b.1912. She d.2008.
      x.   Saytha, b. ca.1915.
      xi.   Clay, b. ca.1916.
881   xii.   Rosa Belle, b. 27 Jun 1918; m. Oakie Johnson.
      xiii.   Nellie, b.1921. She d.1921 KY.
      xiv.   Ella, b.1921. She d.1921 KY.
      xv.   Orval, b. ca.1922.
      xvi.   Arlie, b.1924. He d.1943.

474. William D.[6] Abner (Esther[5] Bishop, Bryson[4], Mary[3] Abner, Elisha[2] Abney, Abner[1]), b.Jun 1884 Clay Co., KY. He m. Ella Allen on 25 Jul 1905 Clay Co., KY. He and Ella Allen appeared on the census of 11 May 1910 Oneida, Clay Co., KY. They were divorced before 1920. He was liv. on 14 Apr 1930 with his brother, John B. Abner, Sturgeon, Jackson Co., KY.

Ella Allen, b.11 Jun 1884 Clay Co., KY. She appeared as Head of Household on the census of 20 Jan 1920 Allen, Clay Co., KY. She m2. Brison Mobley 27 Nov 1929 Butler Co., OH. She m3. Larkin Reed 10 Jun 1933 Clay, Webster Co., KY. She d.19 Jul 1955 Clay Co., KY, age 71.
Known children of William D.[6] Abner and Ella Allen:
882   i.   Charles "Charley"[7], b. 15 Dec 1906 Clay Co., KY; m. Dolly Gladys Helton.
      ii.   Martha "Maud", b.27 Jul 1909 KY. She d.26 Jul 1997 Lebanon, Warren Co., OH, at age 87.
883   iii.   Malcolm, b. ca.1911 Clay Co., KY; m. Elva (n.n.).
884   iv.   Lucy, b. 12 Feb 1913 Clay Co., KY; m. Anderson Allen.
      v.   Essie, b.27 Feb 1914 Manchester, Clay Co., KY. She m. Merle Emanuel Graham (b.1909 IN) 31 Aug 1933 Scott Co., IN.

475. Lillie[6] Abner (Esther[5] Bishop, Bryson[4], Mary[3] Abner, Elisha[2] Abney, Abner[1]), b. May 1885 Clay Co., KY. She m. Henry Wood (b.ca.1841 KY) ca.1908. She and Henry Wood appeared on the census of 6 May 1930 Sturgeon, Jackson Co., KY. She d.1969.
Known children of Lillie[6] Abner and Henry Wood all b. KY:
      i.   Hollis[7], b. ca.1909.
      ii.   Edith, b. ca.1912.
      iii.   Ida, b. ca.1914.
      iv.   Bill, b. ca.1917.
      v.   John, b. ca.1924.

476. John B.[6] Abner (Esther[5] Bishop, Bryson[4], Mary[3] Abner, Elisha[2] Abney, Abner[1]), b. Apr 1886 Clay Co., KY. He m. Nannie J. Wood (b. ca.1890 KY) on 9 Jun 1912 Jackson Co., KY. He and Nannie J. Wood appeared on the censuses of 14 Apr 1930 and 25 Apr 1940 Sturgeon, Jackson Co., KY. He d.12 Nov 1959 at age 73.
Known children of John B.[6] Abner and Nannie J. Wood all b. KY:
        i. Green[7], b. ca.1914.
       ii. Shelby, b. ca.1916.
      iii. Fairy, b. ca.1919.
      iv. Maud, b. ca.Aug 1925.
       v. Hollis D., b. ca.Mar 1930.
      vi. Marley B., b. ca.Mar 1930.

477. Daniel P. "Dan"[6] Abner (Esther[5] Bishop, Bryson[4], Mary[3] Abner, Elisha[2] Abney, Abner[1]), b.20 Jun 1889 Clay Co., KY. He m. Lucy Noe on 17 Feb 1910 Clay Co., KY. He and Lucy Noe appeared on the censuses of 18 Apr 1910, 17 Jan 1920 Clay Co., KY and 4 Apr 1930 Clay Co., KY. He d.23 Mar 1938 Allen, Clay Co., KY, at age 48 and was bur. Felty Cem., Clay Co., KY.
    Lucy Noe, b.1893 KY. She d.31 Aug 1937 Leeco, Lee Co., KY.
Known children of Daniel P. "Dan"[6] Abner and Lucy Noe:
        i. Elmer[7], b.23 Nov 1910 Clay Co., KY. He d.13 Dec 1935 Clay Co., KY, at age 25 and was bur. Felty Cem., Clay Co., KY.
       ii. Claude, b. ca.1913 KY.
      iii. Vivian Frances, b.17 Aug 1917 Clark Co., KY; d.10 Jan 1992 Cumberland, Cumberland Co., KY,ae.74. She was cremated.
      iv. June, b.28 Jun 1920 Manchester, Clay Co., KY. She m. Carl Edward Krauss (b.1917) on 11 Jun 1945 Greene Co., OH. She m. Frank Mabin (b.1908) on 11 Aug 1951 Darke Co., OH. She d.22 Jul 1962 Lima, Allen Co., OH, at age 42.
       v. Callie, b.13 Mar 1922 Clay Co., KY. She d.30 Dec 1935 Clay Co., KY, at age 13 and was bur. Felty Cem., Clay Co., KY.
      vi. Robert M., b.4 Mar 1925 Clay Co., KY. He d.30 May 2001 Fayetteville, Cumberland Co., NC, at age 76.
      vii. Henry, b. ca.1928 Clay Co., KY.

478. Shelby[6] Abner (Esther[5] Bishop, Bryson[4], Mary[3] Abner, Elisha[2] Abney, Abner[1]), b.Feb 1891 Clay Co., KY. He m. Eva Bowman (b.1886) on 12 Aug 1911 Clay Co., KY. He and Eva Bowman appeared on the censuses of 8 Jan 1920 Sexton Creek, Clay Co., KY and 8 Apr 1930 Pond Creek, Jackson Co., KY. He d.1936.
Known children of Shelby[6] Abner and Eva Bowman:
        i. Lula[7], b. ca.1913 Clay Co., KY.
       ii. (son) was stillborn1 Dec 1914 Teges, Clay Co., KY.
      iii. Rose Roxanne, b.4 May 1916 Clay Co., KY. She d.2 Oct 1979 Mongomery, Hamilton Co., OH, at age 63.
      iv. Cate, b.29 May 1919 Clay Co., KY. She d.26 Dec 1981 OH at age 62.

479. Ida[6] Abner (Esther[5] Bishop, Bryson[4], Mary[3] Abner, Elisha[2] Abney, Abner[1]), b.22 Jun 1894 Clay Co., KY. She m. Lucian S. Byrd Sr. She d.22 Jan 1962 Richmond, Wayne Co., IN, at age 67 and was bur. Dale Cem., Connersville, Fayette Co., IN.
    Lucian S. Byrd Sr, b.New Year's Eve, 31 Dec 1882 Teges, Clay Co., KY. He d.23 Apr 1955 Hamilton, Butler Co., OH, age 72; bur. Dale Cem.
Known children of Ida[6] Abner and Lucian S. Byrd Sr.:
        i. Earl H.[7], b.1911. He d.1985.
       ii. Preston J, b.1913. He d.1986.
      iii. Jessie, b.1915. She d.2007.
      iv. Lillie, b.1917. She d.1976.
       v. Lucian S., b.1920. He d.2004.

480. James Kelter[6] Johnson Sr. (Mary[5] Smith, Charles[4], Margaret[3] Abner, Elisha[2] Abney, Abner[1]), b.1 Jun 1902 Clark Co.;He m. Katie Clark on 23 Nov 1921 Frankfort, Franklin Co., KY; d.16 May 1976 Midway, Woodford Co., KY, age 73; bur. Midway Cem., Midway, Woodford Co., KY.
    Katie Clark, b.6 Jun 1902 Scott Co., KY. She d.8 Apr 1990 Woodford Co., KY, at age 87 and was bur. on 10 Apr 1990 Midway Cem.
Known child of James Kelter[6] Johnson Sr. and Katie Clark:
    885   i. Marjorie K.[7], b. 27 Jan 1923 Woodford Co., KY; m. PFC Joseph Walter Diamond (USArmy).

481. (numbered in error. See #495 on page 137)

482. Lucy "Catherine"[6] Abner (William[5], Enoch[4], Enoch[3] Abney, Elisha[2], Abner[1]), b.18 Jan 1873 Clay Co., KY. She m. James Henry "Jim" Henson on 21 Jul 1891 Clay Co., KY. She and James Henry "Jim" Henson appeared on the censuses of 26 Jun 1900, 30 Apr 1910 and 24 Jan 1920 Clay Co., KY. She d.11 Mar 1951 Clay Co., KY, at age 78 and was bur. Goose Rock Cem., Goose Rock, Clay Co., KY.
    James Henry "Jim" Henson, b.27 Feb 1863 Clay Co., KY. He d.28 Dec 1952 Garrard, Clay Co., KY, at age 89 and was bur. Goose Rock Cem.
Known children of Lucy "Catherine"[6] Abner and James Henry "Jim" Henson all b. Clay Co., KY:
        i. Mamye "Mamie"[7], b.Apr 1893. She d.1973.
       ii. Martha, b.May 1894.
      iii. Leila, b.Jan 1898.
      iv. Edward, b. ca.1903.
       v. Elizabeth "Lizzie", b.1905. She d.1975.
      vi. William "Bill", b. ca.1907.
      vii. Tollman, b. ca.Feb 1910.
     viii. Dora Mae "Dorie", b.1911. She d.1990.
      ix. Roberta, b.1916. She d.1976.

483. John[6] Abner (William[5], Enoch[4], Enoch[3] Abney, Elisha[2], Abner[1]), b.May 1878 Clay Co., KY. He m. Bettie Lee "Betsie" Harris (b. Oct 1880 KY) on 3 Aug 1895 Clay Co., KY. He and Bettie Lee Harris appeared on the censuses of 6 Jun 1900, 28 Apr 1910, 24 Jan 1920 and of 2 May 1930 Clay Co., KY. He appeared on the census of 26 Apr 1940 Clay Co., KY. He d.1957 and was bur. Paces Creek Cem., Garrard, Clay Co., KY.

Known children of John⁶ Abner and Bettie Lee "Betsie" Harris all b. Clay Co., KY:

    887   i.   Ive H. "IV"⁷, b. 20 Jul 1897; m. Fronia Stacy; m. Alta House.

            ii.   (baby), b. ca.1900; d. before 1910 Clay Co., KY.

    888   iii.   Belle, b. ca.1901; m. Shirley Gray.

            iv.   (baby), b. ca.1903; d. before 1910 Clay Co., KY.

            v.   (baby), b. ca.1905; d. before 1910 Clay Co., KY.

    889   vi.   Daniel, b. ca.1907; m. Rosa Smith.

            vii.   (baby), b. ca.1909; d. before 1910 Clay Co., KY.

    890   viii.   Shiloh Junior, b. 3 Aug 1915; m. Lizzie (n.n.).

    891   ix.   Shirley, b. 8 Dec 1919; m. Dona Mills.

            x.   Troy, b. ca.1924.

484. Alabama⁶ Abner (Richard⁵, Enoch⁴, Enoch³ Abney, Elisha², Abner¹), b.Oct 1891 Clay Co., KY. She m. Martin J. "Mart" Fisher Sr. on 19 Nov 1910 Clay Co., KY. She and Martin J. "Mart" Fisher Sr. appeared on the censuses of 7 Jan 1920 Whites Branch, Clay Co., KY; 18 Apr 1930 Knox Co., KY; and 24 Apr 1940 Clay Co., KY. She d.7 Jun 1948 Knox Hosp., Barbourville, Knox Co., KY, at age 56; bur. Manchester, Clay Co., KY.

    Martin J. "Mart" Fisher Sr, b.1890 KY. He d.7 Sep 1954 KY.

Known children of Alabama⁶ Abner and Martin J. "Mart" Fisher Sr.:

            i.   Willie⁷, b. ca.1912 Clay Co., KY.

            ii.   Virgil, b.23 Dec 1913 Clay Co., KY. He d.16 Feb 1917 of the measles, Barbourville, Knox Co., KY, at age 3 and was bur. White Cem., Goose Rock, Clay Co., KY.

            iii.   Cecil, b.4 Feb 1916 Clay Co., KY; d.4 Feb 1916 Clay Co., KY; bur. Brown Mission Cem., Laurel Creek, Clay Co., KY.

            iv.   Martha, b.3 Mar 1917 Knox Co., KY.

            v.   Georgia, b. ca.Jul 1919 Clay Co., KY.

            vi.   Lewis, b. ca.1923 Knox Co., KY.

            vii.   Myrtle, b.1925 Knox Co., KY.

            viii.   Irene, b. ca.1928. She d.1928 Lower Horse Creek, Clay Co., KY.

            ix.   Martin J. "Mart", b.1932 Clay Co., KY.

485. Theo⁶ Abner (Richard⁵, Enoch⁴, Enoch³ Abney, Elisha², Abner¹), b.26 Dec 1902 Clay Co., KY; m. Artie "Elise" Kinder 13 Sep 1930 Harlan, Harlan Co., KY. He and Artie appeared on the census of 5 Apr 1940 Wallins Creek, Harlan Co., KY. He d.9 Aug 1947 Boyd Co., KY, age 44.

    Artie "Elise" Kinder, b.17 Dec 1908 KY. She d.13 Oct 1991 Harlan, Harlan Co., KY, at age 82.

Known children of Theo⁶ Abner and Artie "Elise" Kinder all b. Harlan Co., KY,:

            i.   Cecil⁷, b. ca.1932.

            ii.   Billy, b. ca.1934.

            iii.   Bobby, b. ca.1938.

            iv.   Thelma M., b. ca.Sep 1939.

486. Sophia "Sofie"⁶ Smith (Mary⁵ Abner, Enoch⁴, Enoch³ Abney, Elisha², Abner¹), b. ca.1869 Clay Co., KY. She m. Pierce Abner, son of James Monroe Abner and Sythia "Almira" McGill, on 5 Feb 1885 KY. She was liv. on 14 Jun 1900 with grandfather, William Smith, Otter Creek, Clay Co., KY. She d.29 Dec 1941 Knox Co., KY.

    Pierce Abner, b.15 May 1861 Clay Co., KY. He m2. Ellen Harvey Roberts on 3 Sep 1891 Clinton, DeWitt Co., IL. He and Ellen Harvey Roberts appeared on the censuses of 2 Jun 1900 Mount Hope, McLean Co., IL; and 16 Apr 1910 Illini, Macon Co., IL. He d.1 Jun 1931 Hammond, Lake Co., IN, at age 70 and was bur. Elmwood Cem., Hammond, Lake Co., IN.

Known child of Sophia "Sofie"⁶ Smith and Pierce Abner:

            i.   Joseph L. "Joe"⁷, b. 22 Jan 1889 KY; m. Rosana Frederick; m. Effie Jane Stewart. (see # 437 on page 128).

487. Dora E.⁶ Abner (Milton⁵, Enoch⁴, Enoch³ Abney, Elisha², Abner¹), b.22 Apr 1882 Clay Co., KY. She m. John C. Lawson on 15 Jun 1919. She and John C. Lawson appeared on the censuses of 3 Feb 1920 Trosper, Knox Co., KY; and 4 Apr 1930 and Clay Co., KY. She, appeared as Head of Household on the census of 8 Apr 1940 Clay Co., KY. She d.5 Apr 1947 Clay Co., KY, at age 64; bur. Abner Cem., Cottongim, Clay Co., KY.

    John C. Lawson, b. ca.1888 KY. He d. before 1940.

Known child of Dora E.⁶ Abner and John C. Lawson:

    892   i.   Sawyers A.⁷, b. ca.1922 KY; m. Tressie Asher.

488. Emma⁶ Abner (Milton⁵, Enoch⁴, Enoch³ Abney, Elisha², Abner¹), b.Sep 1885 Clay Co., KY. She m. Carlo Lyttle Lewis ca.1908. She and Carlo Lyttle Lewis appeared on the censuses of 18 Apr 1910 and 19 Jan 1920 Manchester, Clay Co., KY; and 2 Apr 1930 Lower Horse Creek, Clay Co., KY. She d.1967 and was bur. Gibbs Cem., Manchester, Clay Co., KY.

    Carlo Lyttle Lewis, b.1889 KY. He d.1961 and was bur. Mount Peace Cem., Saint Cloud, Osceola Co., FL.

Known children of Emma⁶ Abner and Carlo Lyttle Lewis:

            i.   Isabella⁷, b. ca.Jan 1910 Clay Co., KY.

            ii.   Cleo, b.1912.

            iii.   Lawrence, b.1914. He d.1994.

            iv.   Ellen, b.1918.

            v.   Ida, b.1920. He d.2014.

489. Taylor⁶ Abner (Milton⁵, Enoch⁴, Enoch³ Abney, Elisha², Abner¹), b.Mar 1890 Clay Co., KY. He m. Minnie Herd ca.1912. He and Minnie Herd appeared on the censuses of 10 Jan 1920, 4 Apr 1930 and 8 Apr 1940 Clay Co., KY. He d.1 Sep 1957 Cottongim, Clay Co., KY, at age 67 and was bur. White-Hubbard Cem., Cottongim, Clay Co., KY.

    Minnie Herd, b.1896 Clay Co., KY. She d.1957 Clay Co., KY and was bur. White-Hubbard Cem., Cottongim, Clay Co., KY.

Known children of Taylor⁶ Abner and Minnie Herd:

    893   i.   Milton "Elijah"⁷, b. 9 Aug 1913 Clay Co., KY; m. Edna Mae Harris.

894   ii.   Edna, b. 25 Oct 1915 Clay Co., KY; m. Beve Smith.

        iii.   Mae, b.11 Mar 1918 Manchester, Clay Co., KY. She m. Pvt. J.L. Sparks (USMC-WWII) in 1942. She d.14 Feb 2010 Richmond, Wayne Co., IN, at age 91 and was bur. Goshen Cem., Richmond, Wayne Co., IN.

                Pvt. J.L. Sparks (USMC-WWII), b.23 Oct 1922 Lancaster, Garrard Co., KY. He d.3 Aug 1984 Richmond, Wayne Co., IN, at age 61 and was bur. Goshen Cem., Richmond, Wayne Co., IN.

        iv.   Mariah Virginia "Jennie" m. (n.n.) Mills. , b.12 Feb 1920. She d.10 Jun 1982 at age 62 and was bur. Highland Cem., Fort Mitchell, Kenton Co., KY.

        v.   Taylor Junior, b.9 Feb 1923 Clay Co., KY; d.10 Feb 1923 Clay Co., KY; bur. Orchard Hill Cem., Urban, Clay Co., KY.

        vi.   John A., b.12 May 1925 Clay Co., KY. He m. Nettie Mae Gabbard. He d.8 Jan 1970 at age 44 and was bur. Brown Mission Cem., Laurel Creek, Clay Co., KY.

                Nettie Mae Gabbard, b.1932. She m2. Raleigh Smith. She d.2007 and was bur. Brown Mission Cem., Laurel Creek.

        vii.   Hannah B., b. ca. Nov 1927 Clay Co., KY.

        viii.   Ida, b. ca. Dec 1929 Clay Co., KY.

895   ix.   Beve "PJ," b. 13 Feb 1932 Clay Co., KY; m. Tressie Asher.

        x.   Ernest, b. ca.1935 Clay Co., KY.

        xi.   Nancy Marie m. Robert Curry. , b.20 Mar 1937 Clay Co., KY. She d.5 Sep 2019 Manchester, Clay Co., KY, at age 82 and was bur. Manchester Mem. Gardens, Manchester, Clay Co., KY.

490. Ollie[6] Abner (Milton[5], Enoch[4], Enoch[3] Abney, Elisha[2], Abner[1]), b.8 Jun 1893 Clay Co., KY. She m. Sawyers R. Smith. She d.29 Jun 1969 at age 76 and was bur. White-Hubbard Cem., Cottongim, Clay Co., KY.

    Sawyers R. Smith, b.25 Mar 1891. He d.25 May 1967 at age 76 and was bur. White-Hubbard Cem., Cottongim, Clay Co., KY.

Known children of Ollie[6] Abner and Sawyers R. Smith:

        i.   Coyd[7], b.1915. He d.1987.

        ii.   Clarence R., b.1917. He d.1992.

        iii.   Tip, b.1919. He d.2002.

        iv.   Otis, b.1921. He d.1997.

        v.   Nettie Mae, b.1923. She d.1992.

491. John "Johnny Beerfield"[6] Abner (Milton[5], Enoch[4], Enoch[3] Abney, Elisha[2], Abner[1]), b.18 Feb 1899 Clay Co., KY. He m. Mallie Bundy ca.1930. He and Mallie Bundy appeared on the census of 8 Apr 1940 Clay Co., KY. He d.1 Nov 1976 at age 77 and was bur. White-Hubbard Cem., Cottongim, Clay Co., KY.

    Mallie Bundy, b.12 Apr 1913. She d.8 Oct 1994 at age 81 and was bur. White-Hubbard Cem., Cottongim, Clay Co., KY.

Known children of John "Johnny Beerfield"[6] Abner and Mallie Bundy all b. Clay Co., KY:

        i.   Tennie[7], b. ca.1931.

        ii.   Dora, b. ca.1933.

        iii.   William, b. ca.1937.

896   iv.   Warner Oland "Big O," b. 22 Aug 1938; m1. Laura Philpot; m2. Shawanna Swafford.

492. Harvey[6] Abner (Milton[5], Enoch[4], Enoch[3] Abney, Elisha[2], Abner[1]), b.3 Mar 1901 Clay Co., KY. He m. Ida "Belle" Herd on 9 Jan 1926. He and Ida Herd appeared on the census of 8 Apr 1930 Cottongim, Clay Co., KY. He d.29 Aug 1972 age 71; bur. Hurd Cem., Sibert, Clay Co., KY.

    Ida "Belle" Herd, b.9 Nov 1901 Clay Co., KY. She d.11 Jul 1982 Whitley Co., KY, at age 80 and was bur. Hurd Cem., Sibert, Clay Co., KY.

Known children of Harvey[6] Abner and Ida "Belle" Herd:

        i.   Curtis "Curt"[7], b.9 Jul 1927. He d.6 Nov 1950 at age 23 and was bur. Hurd Cem., Sibert, Clay Co., KY.

        ii.   Helen, b.17 May 1929. She d.18 Jun 1940 at age 11 and was bur. Hurd Cem., Sibert, Clay Co., KY.

493. Amelia May "Mealie"[6] Abner (Theophilus[5], Enoch[4], Enoch[3] Abney, Elisha[2], Abner[1]), b.May 1883 Clay Co., KY. She m. Dillard "Dill" Smith, son of Daugherty W. Smith and Leanna Wagers, on 22 Jan 1902 Manchester, Clay Co., KY. She and Dillard "Dill" Smith appeared on the census of 20 Jan 1920 Girdler, Knox Co., KY. She d.30 May 1952 Knox Co., KY.

    Dillard "Dill" Smith, b.13 Mar 1881 Knox Co., KY. He appeared on the census of 25 Apr 1910 Girdler, Knox Co., KY. He appeared on the census of 10 Apr 1930 Knox Co., KY. He d.27 Dec 1943 Pineview, Bell Co., KY, at age 62.

Known children of Amelia May "Mealie"[6] Abner and Dillard "Dill" Smith:

        i.   Odie[7], b.1903.

        ii.   James W., b.1904. He d.1976.

        iii.   Edward, b.1906. He d.1989.

        iv.   Theophilus General "Theo", b.1908. He d.1955.

        v.   Matt, b.1913. He d.1914.

        vi.   Samantha, b.1915. She d.1971.

        vii.   Everett, b.1917. He d.1918.

        viii.   Pearl, b. ca.Sep 1919. She d.1955.

        ix.   Hazel Abner, b.1921. She d.2003.

494. Thomas "Tommy"[6] Abner (Theophilus[5], Enoch[4], Enoch[3] Abney, Elisha[2], Abner[1]), b.23 Apr 1885 Clay Co., KY. He m. Isabelle "Belle" Smith on 30 Sep 1908 Manchester, Clay Co., KY. He and Isabelle "Belle" Smith appeared on the censuses of 5 May 1910 and 16 Jan 1920 Whites Branch, Clay Co., KY; 15 Apr 1930 Lincoln, Clay Co., KY; and 6 Apr 1940 Clay Co., KY. He d.8 Apr 1959 Lincoln, Clay Co., KY, at age 73 and was bur. Abner Cem., Lincoln, Clay Co., KY.

    Isabelle "Belle" Smith, b.1890. She d.14 May 1972 and was bur. Abner Cem., Lincoln, Clay Co., KY.

Known children of Thomas "Tommy"[6] Abner and Isabelle "Belle" Smith all b. Clay Co., KY:

897   i.   Ethel[7], b. 27 Jul 1909; m. Pearl B. Fee.

        ii.   Elzie, b.30 Sep 1911. He m. Rachael Sturdivant (b. ca.1915) on 9 Sep 1939 Harlan, Harlan Co., KY. He and Rachael Sturdivant appeared on the census of 16 Apr 1940 Kitts, Harlan Co., KY. He d.30 Sep 1989 at age 78.

iii.   Suda "Sudie", b. ca.Feb 1915.
iv.   Minnie, b. ca.1917. She m. Willie Simpson (b.ca.1913) on 30 Dec 1939 Coldiron, Harlan Co., KY.
v.   Ida, b. ca.Aug 1919.
vi.   Lida, b. ca.1921. She m. M.C. Keen (b.ca.1918) on 23 Oct 1941 Manchester, Clay Co., KY.
vii.   Charlsie, b. ca.1925.
viii.   Chelsie Mae, b. ca.1933. She m. Carlo Mills (b.ca.1917) on 20 Dec 1949 Knox Co., KY.

495. Steven "Steve"[6] Abner (Theophilus[5], Enoch[4], Enoch[3] Abney, Elisha[2], Abner[1]), b.6 Jun 1889 Clay Co., KY. He m. Susan Lewis on 10 Sep 1910. He and Susan Lewis appeared on the censuses of 16 Jan 1920, 12 Apr 1930 and 8 May 1940 Knox Co., KY. He d.22 Jan 1955 Bull Creek, Knox Co., KY, at age 65 and was bur. Abner Family Cem., Woollum, Knox Co., KY.
    Susan Lewis, b.9 May 1892 Knox Co., KY. She d.27 Mar 1981 at age 88 and was bur. Abner Family Cem., Woollum, Knox Co., KY.
Known children of Steven "Steve"[6] Abner and Susan Lewis:
    898   i.   Leonard[7], b. 8 Aug 1911; m. Nannie Cottongim.
    899   ii.   Anna Beatrice, b. 19 Aug 1913; m. Crit Barnes.
    900   iii.   Chester, b. 16 May 1916; m. Lorene Cottongim.
    886   iv.   Theodore "Ted", b.6 Jan 1919. He m. Marie "Polly" Hoskins on 16 Feb 1946 Clay Co., KY. He d.26 Jan 1992 at age 73 and was bur. Abner Family Cem., Woollum, Knox Co., KY. [author's note: he was numbered out of sequence]
        Marie "Polly" Hoskins, b.4 Sep 1930 Clay Co., KY; d. New Year's Eve, 31 Jan 2019 Englewood, Duval Co., FL.
    901   v.   Lucy Katherine, b. 14 Jul 1921 Knox Co., KY; m. Rev. Riley H. Parker.
    902   vi.   General Ralph "Jersey Bull," b. 14 Jun 1924 Knox Co., KY; m. Minnie Pearl "Pearlie" White.
    903   vii.   Malvia L., b. 6 Apr 1927; m. Henry E. Jarvis; m. Homer R. Wolfe.
         viii.   Thelma m. Elbert Spurlock (USArmy-WWII). , b.27 Jan 1930. She d.1 Mar 2011 at age 81 and was bur. in 2012 Irvin Hill Cem., Oneida, Clay Co., KY.
        Elbert Spurlock (USArmy-WWII), b.6 Aug 1925. He d.29 Sep 1975 at age 50 and was bur. Irvin Hill Cem., Oneida.
         ix.   Ishmael, b.18 Jun 1934 Woollum, Knox Co., KY. He d.18 Jun 1934 Woollum, Knox Co., KY and was bur. Abner Family Cem., Woollum, Knox Co., KY.

496. Eva Mae "Evie"[6] Abner (Theophilus[5], Enoch[4], Enoch[3] Abney, Elisha[2], Abner[1]), b.22 Oct 1893 Clay Co., KY. She m. Elbert Sams on 14 Dec 1908 Manchester, Clay Co., KY. She and Elbert Sams appeared on the censuses of 18 Apr 1910 Road Fork, Knox Co., KY; 30 Jan 1920 Barbourville, Knox Co., KY; and 3 Apr 1940 North Corbin, Laurel Co., KY. She d.18 May 1991 at age 97 and was bur. Hopewell Cem., North Corbin, Laurel Co., KY.
    Elbert Sams, b.13 Mar 1883 and was bur. Hopewell Cem., North Corbin, Laurel Co., KY.
Known children of Eva Mae "Evie"[6] Abner and Elbert Sams:
        i.   Bessie[7] m. (n.n.) Mills. , b. ca.1910 KY. She d.4 May 1962 and was bur. Hopewell Cem., Corbin, Whitley Co., KY.
        ii.   Florry, b. ca.1914 KY.
        iii.   Lena, b.1916. She d.1917.
        iv.   Clifford, b.1920. He d.1935.
        v.   Elbert, b.1923. He d.2000.

497. Theophilus "General"[6] Abner Jr. (Theophilus[5], Enoch[4], Enoch[3] Abney, Elisha[2], Abner[1]), b.11 Apr 1904 Clay Co., KY. He m. Hester Broughton. He and Hester appeared on the census of 6 Apr 1940 Blue Hole, Clay Co., KY; d.15 Nov 1975 Bluehole, Clay Co., KY, at age 71.
    Hester Broughton, b.17 Feb 1914 Knox Co., KY. She d.14 Oct 1997 Clay Co., KY, at age 83.
Known children of Theophilus "General"[6] Abner Jr. and Hester Broughton:
        i.   Addie[7], b. ca.1933 Clay Co., KY.
        ii.   Denver, b. New Year's Day, 1 Jan 1937 Manchester, Clay Co., KY. He d. on his 79th birthday, New Year's Day, 1 Jan 2016 Eaton, Preble Co., OH.
        iii.   Mattie, b.15 Apr 1938 Clay Co., KY. She m. James T. Chadwell on 19 Feb 1962. She d.8 Jun 2014 London, Laurel Co., KY, at age 76 and was bur. Smith-Roberts Cem., Sasser, Laurel Co., KY.
        James T. Chadwell, b.19 Oct 1930 Laurel Co., KY. He d.12 Jun 2016 London, Laurel Co., KY, at age 85.
        iv.   Taft, b. ca.Feb 1940 Clay Co., KY.

498. Cora[6] Abner (Theophilus[5], Enoch[4], Enoch[3] Abney, Elisha[2], Abner[1]), b.12 Apr 1906 Clay Co., KY. She m. Lawrence Swafford on New Year's Eve, 31 Dec 1914 Clay Co., KY. She and Lawrence Swafford appeared on the censuses of 16 Jan 1920 Whites Branch, Clay Co., KY; and 8 Apr 1940 Barbourville, Knox Co., KY. She d.13 Feb 1951 at age 44.
    Lawrence Swafford, b.1896. He was liv. on 15 Apr 1930 with father-in-law, Theo Abner, Lincoln, Clay Co., KY. He d.1985.
Known children of Cora[6] Abner and Lawrence Swafford:
        i.   Elmer[7], b.1924. He d.1995.
        ii.   Virgil, b.1932. He d.2000.
        iii.   Earl E, b.1935.

499. Jasper Lafayette[6] Garner Sr. (James[5], Martha[4] Abney, Enoch[3], Elisha[2], Abner[1]) and Bertha Ann Craig . He, b.28 Mar 1903 Clark Co., AR. He m. Bertha Ann Craig on 4 Apr 1923. He d.10 Jul 1982 Clark Co., AR, at age 79.
Known children of Jasper Lafayette[6] Garner Sr. and Bertha Ann Craig:
        i.   Ina Lee[7] and Stephen A. Laucerica -2h. She and James W. Partridge -1h. , b.24 Oct 1925 Clark Co., AR. She m. James W. Partridge on 19 May 1943. She m. Stephen A. Laucerica on 19 Feb 1945.
        ii.   Jasper Lafayette and Emma Jean Patterson . He, b.7 May 1927 Clark Co., AR. He m. Emma Jean Patterson on 31 Jul 1948.
        iii.   Wilma Ruth and James Richard Gonzales . , b.8 Nov 1928. She m. James Richard Gonzales on 19 May 1943.
500. Melford Evans "Meil"[6] McKinney (David[5], Tamar[4] McClenachan, Sarah[3] Abney, John[2], Abner[1]), b.21 Feb 1874 Cave City, Barren Co., KY. He m. Lula Jane Anderson. He d.21 Apr 1934 Hopkinsville, Christian Co., KY, at age 60; bur. Walnut Hill Cem., Park City, Barren Co., KY.

Lula Jane Anderson, b.10 Sep 1885 Posey Co., IN. She d.10 Jan 1966 Glasgow, Barren Co., KY, at age 80 and was bur. Walnut Hill Cem. Known child of Melford Evans "Meil"[6] McKinney and Lula Jane Anderson:

    904   i.   Corinne[7], b. New Year's Eve, 31 Jan 1903; m. Aston Enlo Logsdon.

501. Ada Lee[6] Rhea (William[5], Tamar[4] McClenachan, Sarah[3] Abney, John[2], Abner[1]), b.3 Apr 1880 Little Rock, Saline Co., AR. She m. Aron Samuel "Sam" Barton on 8 Nov 1895. They divorced on 6 Oct 1908. She d.1 Nov 1953 Waco, McLennan Co., TX, at age 73; bur. Waco Mem. Park, Waco, McLennan Co., TX.
    Aron Samuel "Sam" Barton, b.22 Dec 1876 TX. He d.26 Oct 1943 Corsicana, Navarro Co., TX, at age 66 and was bur. Lone Oak Cem., Booming Grove, Navarro Co., TX.
Known children of Ada Lee[6] Rhea and Aron Samuel "Sam" Barton:
            i.   Myrtle Viola[7], b.21 Sep 1899.

502. Finis Ewing[6] Kinsolving (William[5], Mary[4] Abney, William[3], John[2], Abner[1]), b.18 Sep 1859 Lyon Co., KY. He m. Pearl E. Lamb on 26 Aug 1914 Lyon Co., KY. He and Pearl E. Lamb appeared on the censuses of 20 Jan 1920 and 4 Apr 1930 Eddyville, Lyon Co., KY. He d.17 Apr 1938 Lyon Co., KY, at age 78 and was bur. Glenns Chapel Meth. Ch. Cem., Eddyville, Lyon Co., KY.
    Pearl E. Lamb, b.12 Jun 1888 KY. She appeared as Head of Household on the census of 24 Apr 1940 Lyon Co., KY. She d.14 Feb 1970 Caldwell Co., KY, at age 81 and was bur. Glenns Chapel Meth. Ch. Cem., Eddyville, Lyon Co., KY.
Known children of Finis Ewing[6] Kinsolving and Pearl E. Lamb both b. Lyon Co., KY:
            i.   Verona E.[7], b.26 Nov 1915; m. R.B. Tandy. d.10 Feb 1999 Caldwell Co., KY, ae.83; bur. Tandy Cem., Caldwell Co., KY.
                    R.B. Tandy, b.14 Aug 1899. He d.26 Dec 1979 at age 80 and was bur. Tandy Cem., Caldwell Co., KY.
    905   ii.   William Glenn, b. 15 Aug 1918; m. Anda Mae (n.n.); m. Mary E. McClure; m. Cleopartra Frances Moore.

503. Mary Bledsoe "Minnie"[6] Abney (Ulysses[5], William[4], William[3], John[2], Abner[1]), b.29 Jul 1861. She m. Joseph Nelson "Josi" Clarkson on 12 Feb 1885. She d.5 Jul 1893 Nelson Co., VA, at age 31 and was bur. Abney Family Cem., Mint Spring, Augusta Co., VA.
    Joseph Nelson "Josi" Clarkson, b.22 Sep 1861 Nelson Co., VA. He d.12 Apr 1942 City of Staunton, VA, at age 80 and was bur. Thornrose Cem., City of Staunton, VA.
Known child of Mary Bledsoe "Minnie"[6] Abney and Joseph Nelson "Josi" Clarkson both b. Roseland, Nelson Co., VA:
    906   i.   John "Abney"[7], b. 9 Aug 1886; m. Alethia Potter.
            ii.   Charles Nelson Chenoweth, b.3 Jul 1898. He d.13 Jul 1981 City of Staunton, VA, at age 83 and was bur. Thornrose Cem.

504. Shelton Spillsbury[6] Abney II (William[5], Shelton[4], William[3], John[2], Abner[1]), b.5 Dec 1879 (near Versailles), Morgan Co., MO. He m. Virginia Katherine Smith, daughter of Dr. Thomas Adams Smith II and Kate Howard, on 25 Oct 1905 Napton, Saline Co., MO. He and Virginia Katherine Smith appeared on the censuses of 4 May 1910, 16 Jan 1920, 24 Apr 1930 and 27 Apr 1940 Arrow Rock, Saline Co., MO. He d.26 Oct 1951 Fulton, Callaway Co., MO, at age 71 and was bur. Mem. Presbyterian Ch. Cem., Napton, Saline Co., MO.
    Virginia Katherine Smith, b.27 Nov 1881 St. Louis Co., MO; d.20 Jun 1950 Marshall, Saline Co., MO, age 68; bur. Mem. Presby. Ch. Cem.
Known children of Shelton Spillsbury[6] Abney II and Virginia Katherine Smith all b. Napton, Saline Co., MO:
            i.   Mary Katherine "Kack"[7] was Advertising Mgr. , b.18 Aug 1907. She m. Dwight "Goodrich" Gamble (USArmy-WWII) on 28 Mar 1942. She d.27 May 2000 at age 92; bur. Jefferson Barracks National Cem., Lemay, St. Louis Co., MO.
    907   ii.   Virginia Penn "GeeGee," b. 28 Mar 1909; m. John William Bryant.
    908   iii. Thomas Smith "Tom," b. 18 Feb 1911; m. Marie Mildred Ballowe.
            iv.   Charlotte Ann, b.26 Jul 1912. She m. Edgar Louis Metzger on 11 Oct 1952. She was the author of the book, *In Search of Kate* (published 1978). She d.25 Nov 2003 at age 91 and was bur. Hillcrest Abby Crematory and Maus., Saint Louis, MO.
                    Edgar Louis Metzger, b.22 Feb 1903. He d.1 Feb 1990 at age 86 and was bur. Hillcrest Abby Crematory and Maus.
    909   v.   Shelton Spillsbury, b. 16 Jun 1915; m. Nadine Colville Lee.

505. 1st Lt. William Lycurgus "Will"[6] Abney Jr., M.D. (USArmy-WWI) (William[5], Shelton[4], William[3], John[2], Abner[1]), b.26 Sep 1883 Morgan Co., MO. He appeared on the census of 18 Apr 1910 Blackwater, Cooper Co., MO. He m. Mary "Rowena" McMahan, daughter of Jesse Thomas McMahan and Carrie Jennie DeHaven, on 26 Oct 1910 Lamine Township, Cooper Co., MO. He and Mary "Rowena" McMahan appeared on the censuses of 7 Jan 1920 and 14 Apr 1930 Blackwater, Cooper Co., MO; and 30 Apr 1940 Walton, Washington Co., MO. William died on a visit to the Virgin Islands 10 May 1941 Puerto Rico, VI, at age 57 and was bur. Mem. Presbyterian Ch. Cem., Napton, Saline Co., MO.
    Mary "Rowena" McMahan, b.21 Dec 1887 Lamine City, Cooper Co., MO; She d.21 Jan 1939 Booneville, Cooper Co., MO, age 51; bur. Mem. Presbyterian Ch. Cem., Napton, Saline Co., MO.
Known children of 1st Lt. William Lycurgus "Will"[6] Abney Jr., M.D. (USArmy-WWI) and Mary "Rowena" McMahan both b. Blackwater, MO:
            i.   Mary Caroline[7], b.6 Nov 1911. She m. Frank H. Squillace in 1936. She d.20 May 1945 Kirkland, King Co., WA, at age 33 and was bur. Mem. Presbyterian Ch. Cem., Napton, Saline Co., MO.
                    Frank H. Squillace, b.18 Nov 1908 Jersey City, Hudson Co., NJ. He d.1942; bur. Mem. Presbyterian Ch. Cem.
    910   ii.   William Lycurgus "Billy," b. 20 Aug 1915; m. Elizabeth Anne Stillwell.

506. Harry Fox "Hood"[6] Abney (William[5], Shelton[4], William[3], John[2], Abner[1]), b.23 Mar 1890 Morgan Co., MO. He m1. Mary Berry Smith, daughter of Dr. Thomas Adams Smith II and Kate Howard, on 12 Oct 1914 Saline Co., MO. He and Mary Berry Smith appeared on the censuses of 9 Jan 1920, Apr 1930 and 23 May 1940 Marshall, Saline Co., MO. He m2. Elizabeth Rachel Hawkins in 1948. He d.17 Apr 1969 Marshall, Saline Co., MO, at age 79 and was bur. Mem. Presbyterian Ch. Cem., Napton, Saline Co., MO.
    Mary Berry Smith, b.22 Jan 1890 St. Louis Co., MO. She d.28 Mar 1947 Marshall, Saline Co., MO, age 57; bur. Mem. Presbyterian Ch. Cem.
Known children of Harry Fox "Hood"[6] Abney and Mary Berry Smith all b. Napton, Saline Co., MO,:
    911   i.   Kate Howard[7], b. 15 Oct 1915; m2. 2Lt. Otho Pence (USAAF-WWII); m2. Capt. James Arthur Malcolm (BAF-WWII).
    912   ii.   Mary Frances, b. 8 Apr 1919; m. Fred Leroy Hillis (USAAF).
    913   iii. Margaret Hood "Madge," b. 21 May 1921; m1. & div. William L. Bolles; m2. John Dean Swisher.
            iv.   Cynthia Berry, b.25 Apr 1925.
    914   v.   Agnes Berkeley, b. 19 Aug 1926; m. George Peuris Whittington Jr. (USMC-WWII).

Elizabeth Rachel Hawkins, b.30 Nov 1894 Monroe Co., MO. She d.New Year's Eve, 31 Jan 1959 Saline Co., MO, at age 64 and was bur. Mem. Presbyterian Ch. Cem., Napton, Saline Co., MO.
There were no known children of Harry Fox "Hood"[6] Abney and Elizabeth Rachel Hawkins.

507. Josie Adah[6] Abney (James[5], Robert[4], John[3], John[2], Abner[1]), b.27 Sep 1862 LaRue Co., KY. She m. Henry Gardner on 27 Feb 1884 LaRue Co., KY. She and Henry Gardner appeared on the censuses of 2 Jun 1900 and 25 Apr 1910 Magnolia, LaRue Co., KY. She d.26 Jul 1927 at age 64 and was bur. Magnolia Presbyterian Ch. Cem., Magnolia, LaRue Co., KY.
   Henry Gardner, b.26 Oct 1856 LaRue Co., KY; Informant for mother-in-law's death cert. 15 Apr 1914 Magnolia, LaRue Co., KY. He d.1939.
Known children of Josie Adah[6] Abney and Henry Gardner:
               i.   James Allen "Jimmy"[7], b.7 Jan 1885 Magnolia, LaRue Co., KY. He m. Minnie Ragland on 1 Nov 1904 Hodgenville, LaRue Co., KY. He d.26 Feb 1971 LaRue Co., KY, at age 86.
915   ii. Charles W., b. Jun 1890 Magnolia, LaRue Co., KY; m. Mary Lou Jaggers.
               iii. (infant son), b.21 Feb 1902 LaRue Co., KY. He d.21 Feb 1902 LaRue Co., KY; bur. Magnolia Presbyterian Ch. Cem.
               iv. Lura, b. ca.1905 Magnolia, LaRue Co., KY.

508. Charles Milton "Charlie"[6] Abney (James[5], Robert[4], John[3], John[2], Abner[1]), b.2 Aug 1864 LaRue Co., KY. He m1. Lenora "Nora" Beavers on 16 Nov 1885 Hodgenville, LaRue Co., KY. He and Lenora "Nora" Beavers appeared on the census of 2 Jun 1900 Elizabethtown, Hardin Co., KY. He m2. Mary West on 22 Sep 1908 King Co., WA. He and Mary West appeared on the census of 1910 Seattle, King Co., WA. He and Mary West appeared on the censuses of 7 Jan 1920 and 2 Apr 1930 Seattle, King Co., WA. He d.4 Dec 1937 Sedro-Wooley, Skagit Co., WA, at age 73 and was bur. Burlington, Skagit Co., WA.
   Lenora "Nora" Beavers, b.2 Nov 1866 Magnolia, LaRue Co., KY. She d.30 Jun 1906 Spokane, Spokane Co., WA, at age 39 and was bur. Fairmount Mem. Park, Spokane, Spokane Co., WA.
Known children of Charles Milton "Charlie"[6] Abney and Lenora "Nora" Beavers:
               i.   Jessie E.[7], b.5 Nov 1886 Magnolia, LaRue Co., KY. She d.31 Oct 1891 Magnolia, LaRue Co., KY, at age 4 and was bur. Magnolia Presbyterian Ch. Cem., Magnolia, LaRue Co., KY.
916   ii. Burgess Corydon, b. 22 Feb 1889 Louisville, Jefferson Co., KY; m. Leona B. Schneider.
   Mary West, b. ca.1881 Republic of Ireland.
There were no known children of Charles Milton "Charlie"[6] Abney and Mary West.

509. Mildred Antoinette "Nettie"[6] Abney (Milton[5], Robert[4], John[3], John[2], Abner[1]), b.7 Dec 1864 LaRue Co., KY. She m. David S. Lewis on 18 Oct 1882 Hodgenville, LaRue Co., KY. She and David S. Lewis appeared on the censuses of 13 Jun 1900 Hart Co., KY; and 1910 Hammondsville, Hart Co., KY. She d.1 Apr 1956 at age 91 and was bur. Magnolia Presbyterian Ch. Cem., Magnolia, LaRue Co., KY.
   David S. Lewis, b.17 Jul 1858 KY. He d.13 Nov 1918 Pike View, Hart Co., KY, at age 60 and was bur. Magnolia Presbyterian Ch. Cem.
Known children of Mildred Antoinette "Nettie"[6] Abney and David S. Lewis all b. KY:
               i.   Clarence D.[7], b.Apr 1884. He m. Carrie B. Jaggers (b.ca.1888) on 19 Dec 1906 Magnolia, LaRue Co., KY.
               ii. Mary Frances "Fannie", b.Dec 1892. She m. Arthur Preston. d.Feb 1923 at age 30 and was bur. Mount Olivet Cem., Eastwood, Kalamazoo Co., MI.
                   Arthur Preston, b.1884 MI. He d.16 Jan 1927 Kalamazoo, Kalamazoo Co., MI and was bur. Mount Olivet Cem.
917   iii. Neoma Ella "Oma," b. 24 Feb 1896; m. Della Clifton Cruse.
               iv. Willia D., b.28 Jan 1900. She m. Jess L. Gardner. d.27 Sep 1991 at age 91 and was bur. Magnolia Presbyterian Ch. Cem.
                   Jess L. Gardner, b.22 Apr 1893 KY. He d.25 Aug 1985 KY at age 92 and was bur. Magnolia Presbyterian Ch. Cem.

510. Joseph Gillian[6] Abney (Milton[5], Robert[4], John[3], John[2], Abner[1]), b.14 Sep 1866 LaRue Co., KY. He m. Lula "Lulie" Friend on 18 Dec 1888 LaRue Co., KY. He and Lula "Lulie" Friend appeared on the censuses of 6 Jun 1900 Louisville, Jefferson Co., KY; and 5 May 1910, 5 Jan 1920, 9 Apr 1930, and 4 Apr 1940 Pawnee, Sangamon Co., IL. He d.3 Jun 1941 Pawnee, Sangamon Co., IL, at age 74 and was bur. Horse Creek Cem., Pawnee, Sangamon Co., IL.
   Lula "Lulie" Friend, b.16 Nov 1867 KY. She d.31 Aug 1922 Springfield, Sangamon Co., IL, at age 54 and was bur. Horse Creek Cem., Pawnee.
Known children of Joseph Gillian[6] Abney and Lula "Lulie" Friend:
918   i.   Emmett William[7], b. 21 Jan 1890 Magnolia, LaRue Co., KY; m. Olive "Beryl" Davis; m. Dena Hanson.
919   ii. Selia M. "Lela," b. Sep 1891 KY; m. Ross Fishburn.
920   iii. Iva D., b. Nov 1893 KY; m. Ben Sweet.
921   iv. Hettie F., b. Jan 1895 KY; m. Russell White.

511. Ada[6] Abney (Joshua[5], Robert[4], John[3], John[2], Abner[1]), b.20 Dec 1883 LaRue Co., KY. She m. John Thomas Hines on 11 Feb 1912 LaRue Co., KY. She and John Thomas Hines were liv. on 26 Jan 1920 with father-in-law, Joshua M. Abney, Magnolia, LaRue Co., KY. She d.2 Feb 1980 Magnolia, LaRue Co., KY, at age 96 and was bur. Magnolia Presbyterian Ch. Cem., Magnolia, LaRue Co., KY.
   John Thomas Hines, b.4 Jan 1872 KY. He d. New Year's Eve, 31 Jan 1956 Magnolia, LaRue Co., KY, age 84; bur. Magnolia Presb. Ch. Cem.
Known children of Ada[6] Abney and John Thomas Hines:
               i.   Nannie M.[7], b. ca.1913 LaRue Co., KY.
               ii. Hattie F., b.29 Nov 1914 KY. She m. Omer S. Chaney. d.11 May 2008 Horse Cave, Hart Co., KY, at age 93 and was bur. Community Cem., Hart Co., KY.
                   Omer S. Chaney, b.1924. He d.1986 and was bur. Community Cem., Hart Co., KY.
               iii. Lena, b. ca.1917 LaRue Co., KY.
               iv. William B., b. ca.Jul 1918 LaRue Co., KY.

512. Wilhelmina Loretta "Lura"[6] Bayne (Margaret[5] Lasley, Gertrude[4] Abney, John[3], John[2], Abner[1]), b.20 Oct 1858 Centerpoint, LaRue Co., KY. She m. Dr. Charles Zachary Aud on 3 Oct 1876 Cecilia, Hardin Co., KY. She and Dr. Charles Zachary Aud appeared on the censuses of 24 Jun 1880 Elizabethtown, Hardin Co., KY; and of 16 Jan 1920 Louisville, Jefferson Co., KY. She d.13 Mar 1937 Louisville, Jefferson Co., KY, at age 78 and was bur. on 15 Mar 1937 Calvary Cem., Louisville, Jefferson Co., KY.
   Dr. Charles Zachary Aud, b.18 Apr 1846 Knottsville, Daviess Co., KY; d.15 Jul 1924 Louisville, Jefferson Co., KY, ae.78; bur. Calvary Cem.

Known children of Wilhelmina Loretta "Lura"*[6]* Bayne and Dr. Charles Zachary Aud:

     922   i.   Alice "Attie"*[7]*, b. 25 Aug 1877 Cecilia, Hardin Co., KY; m. Dr. Herbert Roberts Nusz.

             ii.   Ann Nancy "Nannie", b.1879 KY. She d.1962.

             iii. Generose, b.1880. She d.1974.

             iv. Charles Althanius, b.1882. He d.1955.

             v.   Mary Ellen, b.1886. She d.1886.

             vi. Francis Guy, b.1887 KY. He d.1959.

             vii. Hillary Joseph, b.1890. He d.1890.

Generation Seven

513. John Thomas*[7]* Crabtree (Polly*[6]* Chancellor, David*[5]*, Rebecca*[4]* Abney, Joshua*[3]*, Elisha*[2]*, Abner*[1]*), b.27 May 1876 Clark Co., IL. He appeared on the census of 5 Jun 1900 Casey Twp., Clark Co., IL. He m. Ica Ellen McFarland ca.1900 IL. He and Ica Ellen McFarland appeared on the censuses of 29 Apr 1910 Rock Twp., Gage City, Ellis Co., OK; 6 Jan 1920 Justice Twp., Ellis Co., OK and 9 Apr 1930 North St., Gage City, Ellis Co., OK. He appeared on the census of 14 May 1940 with his sister, *Eva Closson*, Austin Twp., Ellis Co., OK. He d.23 Nov 1963 Gage, Ellis Co., OK, at age 87 and was bur. Gage Mem. Cem., Gage, Ellis Co., OK.

    Ica Ellen McFarland, b.25 Nov 1875 Clark Co., IL. She d.8 Jan 1911 Gage, Ellis Co., OK, age 35; bur. Gage Mem. Cem., Gage, Ellis Co., OK.

Known children of John Thomas*[7]* Crabtree and Ica Ellen McFarland:

     923   i.   Ted Dean "Teddy"*[8]*, b. 22 Sep 1901 IL; m. Florene L. (n.n.).

     924   ii.   Leo E., b. ca.1904 OK; m. Florence (n.n.).

     925   iii. Cuma C., b. ca.1906 OK; m. Herman Solomon Hoffine.

             iv. Eunice E., b. ca.1909 OK.

514. Effie Iva (Eva's twin)*[7]* Crabtree (Polly*[6]* Chancellor, David*[5]*, Rebecca*[4]* Abney, Joshua*[3]*, Elisha*[2]*, Abner*[1]*), b.7 Oct 1879 Martinsville, Clark Co., IL. She m. William J. "Will" McFarland ca.1898. They were liv. in 1902 OK. She and William J. "Will" McFarland appeared on the censuses of 7 Jun 1900 Casey Twp., Clark Co., IL; 30 Apr 1910 Rock Twp., Ellis Co., OK; and 6 Jan 1920 and 16 Apr 1930 Austin, Ellis Co., OK. She was liv. on 14 May 1940 with her son, L. Wayne McFarland, Austin Twp., Ellis Co., OK. She d.1954 and was bur. Gage Mem. Cem., Gage, Ellis Co., OK.

    William J. "Will" McFarland, b. Nov 1879 IL. He d.1937 and was bur. Gage Mem. Cem., Gage, Ellis Co., OK.

Known children of Effie Iva (Eva's twin)*[7]* Crabtree and William J. "Will" McFarland:

     926   i.   Erma Ellen*[8]*, b. 13 Aug 1899 IL; m. George Claus Toellner.

     927   ii.   Leonard Wayne "Sam," b. 18 Jul 1901 Martinsville, Clark Co., IL; m. Hattie Mae Koons.

     928   iii. Todd A. "Toddy," b. 8 May 1903 IL; m. Myrtle (n.n.).

515. David Floyd*[7]* Griffith (Mary*[6]* Chancellor, David*[5]*, Rebecca*[4]* Abney, Joshua*[3]*, Elisha*[2]*, Abner*[1]*), b.2 Feb 1862 IL. He m1. Lydia C. Weir on 18 Mar 1886 Clark Co., IL. He m2. Roxie Ray in 1890 Clark Co., IL. He appeared on the census of 27 Jun 1900 Crooked Creek Twp., Cumberland Co., IL. He appeared on the census of 22 Apr 1910 Rock Twp., Gage City, Ellis Co., OK. He was liv. 13 Jan 1920 with son-in-law, John H. Ross, Austin Twp., Ellis Co., OK. He d.27 Apr 1921 at age 59 and was bur. Gage Mem. Cem., Gage, Ellis Co., OK.

    Lydia C. Weir, b. ca.1864. She d.7 Apr 1899 and was bur. Saint Paul Cem., Clark Co., IL.

There were no known children of David Floyd*[7]* Griffith and Lydia C. Weir.

    Roxie Ray, b.1867. She d.14 Aug 1898 and was bur. Washington Street Cem., Casey, Clark Co., IL.

Known children of David Floyd*[7]* Griffith and Roxie Ray all b. IL:

             i.   Mary J.*[8]*, b. ca.1892.

     929   ii.   Lula Myrtle, b. 1892; m. John Henry Ross Jr.

             iii. Bruce E., b.6 May 1895. He appeared on the census of 13 Jan 1920 with brother-in-law, John H. Ross, Austin Twp., Ellis Co., OK. He d.5 Apr 1961 at age 65 and was bur. Gage Mem. Cem., Gage, Ellis Co., OK.

     930   iv. Nelie Fern, b. 9 Feb 1897; m. Bert Wallace Sober Sr.

516. Euphame Rachel*[7]* Griffith (Mary*[6]* Chancellor, David*[5]*, Rebecca*[4]* Abney, Joshua*[3]*, Elisha*[2]*, Abner*[1]*), b.25 Feb 1870 IL; m. Charles S. Simmons, son of Anderson Simmons and Sarah Curtis; d.20 Jan 1935 Martinsville, Clark Co., IL, age 64; bur. Baird Cem., Martinsville, Clark Co., IL.

    Charles Solman Simmons, b.15 Jun 1869 Martinsville, Clark Co., IL. He d.7 Oct 1939 Martinsville, Clark Co., IL, at age 70; bur. Baird Cem.

Known children of Euphame Rachel*[7]* Griffith and Charles Solman Simmons:

             i.   Glennie*[8]*, b.20 Apr 1904 Martinsville, Clark Co., IL. She m. Fred Burger on 15 Jun 1938. She d.2 Oct 1994 Terre Haute, Vigo Co., IN, at age 90 and was bur. Ridgelawn Cem., Martinsville, Clark Co., IL.

                 Fred Burger, b.21 Sep 1918 Anderson Twp., Clark Co., IL. He d.4 Oct 1998 Marshall, Clark Co., IL, at age 80.

517. Hezekiah*[7]* Griffith Sr. (Mary*[6]* Chancellor, David*[5]*, Rebecca*[4]* Abney, Joshua*[3]*, Elisha*[2]*, Abner*[1]*), b.8 Oct 1873 Casey, Clark Co., IL. He appeared on the census of 22 Apr 1910 Rock Twp., Gage City, Ellis Co., OK. He m. Cora E. Bryant, daughter of Joshua Bryant and Elizabeth (n.n.), on 23 Apr 1913 Garfield Co., OK. He d.9 Jan 1941 OK at age 67 and was bur. Harmon Cem., Harmon, Ellis Co., OK.

    Cora E. Bryant, b.1886 KS. She d.1959 and was bur. Harmon Cem., Harmon, Ellis Co., OK.

Known children of Hezekiah*[7]* Griffith Sr. and Cora E. Bryant:

             i.   May L.*[8]*, b. est.1816.

             ii.   Leona B., b. est.1818.

             iii. James Newton, b.21 Mar 1914 OK. He d.26 Dec 1961 Los Angeles Co., CA, at age 47 and was bur. Harmon Cem.

             iv. Helen, b. est.1915.

             v.   Albert Nelson, b.31 Jul 1920 OK. He m. Winifred Ailene Aiken on 13 Aug 1976 Clark Co., NV. He d.15 Nov 1983 San Bernardino Co., CA, at age 63 and was bur. Harmon Cem., Harmon, Ellis Co., OK.

     931   vi. Hezekiah "Hezie," b. 14 Mar 1922; m. Beulah "Boots" Fessler.

             vii. Nora G., b. est.1924.

             viii. Gladys, b. est.1926.

             ix. Orpha Jean, b. est.1928.

518. Florence Ann[7] Gillilan (Rebecca[6] Chancellor, David[5], Rebecca[4] Abney, Joshua[3], Elisha[2], Abner[1]), b.24 Mar 1886 Clark Co., IL; m. Jos. Myers, son of James Myers, on 8 Nov 1905 Woodward Co., OK; d.27 Mar 1967 age 81; bur. Chapel Hill Cem., Oklahoma City, Oklahoma Co., OK.
    Joseph Myers, Oklahoma City, Oklahoma Co., OK. He, b.29 Apr 1879 Benedict, KS. He m1. Ada Tarter on 11 Apr 1901 Benedict, KS. He d.7 Jan 1963 at age 83 and was bur. Chapel Hill Cem.
Known children of Florence Ann[7] Gillilan and Joseph Myers :
      i. Laura Leola Pearl[8], b.4 Aug 1907 Arnette, OK; m. Theron Barber. Liv. Ponca City, OK; Liv. in 1995 Ontario, CA.
      ii. James Richard, b.10 Jan 1910 Arnette, OK; m. Neva Cantrell Astoria, MO.
      iii. Donald Paul, b.1 Jun 1912 Manes, Wright Co., MO. He m. Ethel Mae Hayes, Kemlin, OK; Liv. 1995 Covington, OK.
932   iv. Joseph Clair, b. 14 Nov 1914 Chanute, Neosho Co., KS; m. Elma Jean Hopkins.
      v. Belva Mae Vivian, b.20 Nov 1916 Chanute, Neosho Co., KS. She m. Allen Robert Littleton; Lived 1995 Edmond, OK.
      vi. Rita, b.30 Jul 2917 Three Sands, OK; m. Leroy Brown, Mt. Grove, MO; Liv. 1995 Pomme de Terre, Hickory Co., MO.

519. Henry Columbus "Clum"[7] McKay (Mary[6] Chancellor, Ewing[5], Rebecca[4] Abney, Joshua[3], Elisha[2], Abner[1]), b.27 Dec 1859 IN. He m. Sarah M. Palmer. He d.16 Jul 1943 Lawton, Comanche Co., OK, at age 83 and was bur. Pecan Cem., Lawton, Comanche Co., OK.
    Sarah M. Palmer, b.10 Feb 1858. She d.1 Dec 1937 at age 79 and was bur. Pecan Cem., Lawton, Comanche Co., OK.
Known child of Henry Columbus "Clum"[7] McKay and Sarah M. Palmer:
      i. Aubrey A.[8], b.Dec 1882 MO. He d.21 Sep 1900 Dover, Kingfisher Co., OK, at age 17 and was bur. New Home Cem., Dover, Kingfisher Co., OK.

520. Robert Leroy[7] McKay (Mary[6] Chancellor, Ewing[5], Rebecca[4] Abney, Joshua[3], Elisha[2], Abner[1]), b.3 Dec 1862 IL. He m1. Altha Lewis. He m2. Martha "Mattie" Swank, daughter of Martin L. Swank and Eliza C. Palmer. He d.3 Jun 1944 Kirksville, Adair Co., MO, at age 81 and was bur. Humphreys Cem., Humphreys, Sullivan Co., MO.
Known children of Robert Leroy[7] McKay and Altha Lewis:
933   i. Austin Derr "AD"[8], b. 12 Sep 1891 Humphreys, Sullivan Co., MO; m. Lera Elba Justus.
934   ii. Alva Ross, b. 28 Jul 1895; m. Beulah May Justus.
    Martha "Mattie" Swank, b.18 Sep 1868 Livingston Co., MO. She d.30 Aug 1932 Humphreys, Sullivan Co., MO, at age 63.
There were no known children of Robert Leroy[7] McKay and Martha "Mattie" Swank.

521. Arminta Jane[7] McKay (Mary[6] Chancellor, Ewing[5], Rebecca[4] Abney, Joshua[3], Elisha[2], Abner[1]), b.18 May 1865; m. F.L. Pickett.. She d.13 Jul 1920 MO at age 55 and was bur. Humphreys Cem., Humphreys, Sullivan Co., MO.
Known children of Arminta Jane[7] McKay and F.L. Pickett:
      i. Roy[8], b.25 Mar 1885. He d.24 Jun 1904 MO at age 19 and was bur. Humphreys Cem., Humphreys, Sullivan Co., MO.
935   ii. Mary Adelia, b. 17 Aug 1886 Humphreys, Sullivan Co., MO; m. Clyde Willie Lowther.

522. Walter Delbert[7] McKay (Mary[6] Chancellor, Ewing[5], Rebecca[4] Abney, Joshua[3], Elisha[2], Abner[1]), b.19 Jun 1872 Sullivan Co., MO. He m. Hattie Grace Williams, daughter of Robert Everett Williams and Mary Hodge Dunlap, in 1895. He d.8 Mar 1959 Reger, Sullivan Co., MO, at age 86 and was bur. Glaze Cem., Sullivan Co., MO.
    Hattie Grace Williams, b.7 Mar 1875 Humphreys, Sullivan Co., MO. She d.18 Apr 1961 Reger, Sullivan Co., MO, at age 86; bur. Glaze Cem.
Known children of Walter Delbert[7] McKay and Hattie Grace Williams:
936   i. Gilbert Everett[8], b. 11 Mar 1896 Reger, Sullivan Co., MO; m. Velma Pratt.
937   ii. Elgeva Beulah, b. 23 Dec 1896.
938   iii. Mary Isabelle, b. 28 Dec 1901 Reger, Sullivan Co., MO; m. Buel McClaren.
939   iv. Betha Ruby, b. 21 Jun 1904 Sullivan Co., MO; m. Monroe Wilson White.
940   v. Lillie Ruth, b. 21 Jun 1904 Sullivan Co., MO; m. Dewayne Minter Ford.
      vi. Imogene Grace, b.13 Jul 1908 Humphreys, Sullivan Co., MO. She m. Millard Franklin Swank in 1925. She d.18 Sep 1994 Milan, Sullivan Co., MO, at age 86 and was bur. Shatto Cem., Milan, Sullivan Co., MO.
          Millard Franklin Swank, b.2 Aug 1905 Sullivan Co., MO; d.19 Sep 1981 Milan, Sullivan Co., MO; bur. Shatto Cem.
      vii. Ila Lucile, b.7 Feb 1914 Sullivan Co., MO. She d.28 Feb 1914 Sullivan Co., MO; bur. Glaze Cem., Sullivan Co., MO.

523. Henry Columbus[7] Chancellor Jr. (Henry[6], Ewing[5], Rebecca[4] Abney, Joshua[3], Elisha[2], Abner[1]), b.2 Jan 1868 Arcadia, Crawford Co., KS. He m1. Irma C. (n.n.). He m2. Pearl Victoria Freeman, daughter of Richard M. Freeman and Angeline E. Wise. He d.22 Apr 1951 Lamar, Barton Co., MO, at age 83 and was bur. Lake Cem., Lamar Heights, Barton Co., MO.
    Irma C. (n.n.), b.29 Dec 1870. She d.23 May 1891 at age 20 and was bur. Rosebank Cem., Mulberry, Crawford Co., KS.
Known child of Henry Columbus[7] Chancellor Jr. and Irma C. (n.n.):
      i. Albert E.[8], b.4 May 1891.
    Pearl Victoria Freeman, b. New Year's Eve, 31 Jan 1880 Edwardsport, Knox Co., IN. She d.12 Jul 1948 Springfield, Greene Co., MO, at age 68 and was bur. Lake Cem., Lamar Heights, Barton Co., MO.
Known children of Henry Columbus[7] Chancellor Jr. and Pearl Victoria Freeman:
      i. Harold Clayton[8] m. Elsie N. Inglis. He, b.18 Jul 1902 Pittsburg, Crawford Co., KS. He d.Christmas Eve, 24 Dec 1951 Lamar, Barton Co., MO, at age 49 and was bur. Lake Cem., Lamar Heights, Barton Co., MO.
          Elsie N. Inglis, b.9 Jul 1903. She d.27 Oct 1998 at age 95 and was bur. Lake Cem., Lamar Heights, Barton Co., MO.
941   ii. Richard Freeman, b. 3 Nov 1917 Mindenmines, Barton Co., MO; m. Lone Williams.

524. John "William"[7] Chancellor (Henry[6], Ewing[5], Rebecca[4] Abney, Joshua[3], Elisha[2], Abner[1]), b.Feb 1870 KS. He m. Mary (n.n.) ca.1892.
    Mary (n.n.), b.Mar 1873 KS.
Known children of John "William"[7] Chancellor and Mary (n.n.):
      i. John[8], b.Aug 1893 KS.
      ii. Roy, b.Aug 1895 MO.
      iii. Emma, b.Jan 1897 MO.
      iv. Fred, b.Sep 1899 MO.

525. Lottie I.[7] Chancellor (Henry[6], Ewing[5], Rebecca[4] Abney, Joshua[3], Elisha[2], Abner[1]), b.8 Oct 1876 Arcadia, Crawford Co., KS. She m. Adolphos Marion "Dolly" Moore, son of M.S. Moore and Lucinda Hobick. She and Adolphos Marion "Dolly" Moore appeared on the census of 2 Jun 1900 Mindenmines, Barton Co., MO. She d.11 Jan 1952 Mindenmines, Barton Co., MO, at age 75; bur. Rosebank Cem., Mulberry, Crawford Co., KS.
    Adolphos Marion "Dolly" Moore, b.2 Jul 1871 IN. He d.31 May 1953 Mindenmines, Barton Co., MO, at age 81 and was bur. Rosebank Cem.
Known children of Lottie I.[7] Chancellor and Adolphos Marion "Dolly" Moore:
    942   i.   Tressia I.[8], b. 18 Sep 1895 MO; m. Doskey Omega Short.
           ii.   Elsie M., b.Feb 1897 MO. She d.18 Jul 1902 at age 5 and was bur. Rosebank Cem., Mulberry, Crawford Co., KS.
           iii. Verda L., b.Jan 1899 MO.
           iv.   Nettie A., b.22 Jan 1901. She d.1 Dec 1905 at age 4 and was bur. Rosebank Cem., Mulberry, Crawford Co., KS.
    943   v.   Iva Margaret, b. 29 Aug 1904 Mindenmines, Barton Co., MO; m. Almon DeWitt Willis.
           vi.   Thelma I., b.11 Mar 1907; m. Howard Williams; d.11 May 1988 Galena, Cherokee Co., KS, age 81; bur. Rosebank Cem.
                 Howard E. Williams, b.1899 MO. He d.1954 and was bur. Rosebank Cem., Mulberry, Crawford Co., KS.
           vii. John Richard, b.16 Sep 1909. He m. Helen Higganbotham. He d.28 Oct 1987 Mindenmines, Barton Co., MO, at age 78 and was bur. Rosebank Cem., Mulberry, Crawford Co., KS.
                 Helen Higganbotham, b.28 Feb 1917. She d.19 Dec 1994 at age 77 and was bur. Rosebank Cem., Mulberry, Crawford.
    944   viii. Marion S, b. 14 Dec 1911 MO; m. Letha L. Robson.

526. Chester Arthur "Art"[7] Chancellor (WWI) (Henry[6], Ewing[5], Rebecca[4] Abney, Joshua[3], Elisha[2], Abner[1]), b.17 Jul 1891 KS. He m. Alla "Allie" Slate. He d.Sep 1983 at age 92 and was bur. Mount Olive Cem., Pittsburg, Crawford Co., KS.
    Alla "Allie" Slate, b.5 Jul 1887 MO. She d.Dec 1975 Pittsburg, Crawford Co., KS, at age 88 and was bur. Mount Olive Cem., Pittsburg.
Known children of Chester Arthur "Art"[7] Chancellor (WWI) and Alla "Allie" Slate:
           i.   Earl Leroy[8], b.3 Mar 1908 MO. He m. Evelyn Kathryn Burgstrand. He d.Aug 1950 at age 42; bur. Mount Olive Cem.
                 Evelyn K. Burgstrand, b.2 Jan 1910 Nobles Co., MN; d.24 Jan 2003 Kansas City, Platte Co., MO; bur. Mt. Olive Cem.

527. Cora A.[7] Montgomery (Henry[6], Martha[5] Chancellor, Rebecca[4] Abney, Joshua[3], Elisha[2], Abner[1]), b.Oct 1879 IL. She m. William D. Howe. She d.1974 Johnson Twp., Clark Co., IL and was bur. Mount Cem., Johnson Twp., Clark Co., IL.
    William D. Howe, b.1869. He d.1938 and was bur. Mount Cem., Johnson Twp., Clark Co., IL.
Known children of Cora A.[7] Montgomery and William D. Howe:
    945   i.   Ruby Leora[8], b. 17 Jan 1909 Clark Co., IL; m. George Evans Slusser.
           ii.   Russell m. Faye (n.n.).
           iii. Mary m. (n.n.) Hunsaker.
    946   iv.   Mary Velma, b. 12 May 1915 Casey, Clark Co., IL; m. William Carter "Willie" Hunsaker.

528. Norma Agnes[7] Harmeson (Catherine[6] Chancellor, William[5], Rebecca[4] Abney, Joshua[3], Elisha[2], Abner[1]), b.15 Sep 1883. She m. Ivory Albert Burmmett. She d.2 Feb 1965 at age 81 and was bur. Dodge Grove Cem., Mattoon, Coles Co., IL.
    Ivory Albert Burmmett, b.5 Apr 1883. He d.10 Aug 1937 at age 54 and was bur. Dodge Grove Cem., Mattoon, Coles Co., IL.
Known children of Norma Agnes[7] Harmeson and Ivory Albert Burmmett:
    947   i.   Beatrice Mae[8], b. 6 Jun 1905; m. Howard Duane Coverstone.
           ii.   Bonnie Opal m. Dr. Charles Edwin Morgan. , b.9 Sep 1906. She d.29 May 1967 at age 60; bur. Dodge Grove Cem.
                 Dr. Charles Edwin Morgan, b.2 Aug 1869. He d.25 Jan 1952 at age 82 and was bur. Dodge Grove Cem.

529. Nancy Little[7] Abney (John[6], John[5], Paul[4], Joshua[3], Elisha[2], Abner[1]), b.15 Oct 1862 Butler Co., KY. She d.18 Mar 1912 Butler Co., KY, at age 49 and was bur. McHenry, Ohio Co., KY.
    Francis Marion Daugherty, b.2 Jun 1850 Butler Co., KY. He d.23 Feb 1914 Butler Co., KY, at age 63.
Known children of Nancy Little[7] Abney and Francis Marion Daugherty (for some reason, these children went by the mother's surname, *Abney*):
    948   i.   Norton Ville *Abney*[8], b. 20 Jan 1883 Butler Co., KY; m. Effie Mae Beasley.
    949   ii.   Earl *Abney*, b. 28 Sep 1884; m. Harriett Alice "Lillie" Snodgrass.
    950   iii. Laura Belle *Abney*, b. 1 Dec 1885 Butler Co., KY; m. Oscar Sherman Lindsey.
    951   iv.   Beatrice *Abney*, b. 1891; m. Thomas Lafayette Kessinger.
    952   v.   Myrtle *Abney*, b. 30 Sep 1895; m. Carey Hunter.

530. Silavnus[7] Daugherty (Pheoby[6] Abney, John[5], Paul[4], Joshua[3], Elisha[2], Abner[1]), b.29 Jan 1873 Caneyville, Grayson Co., KY. He m. Ruthia Taylor. He d.3 Feb 1951 and was bur. El Reno Cem., El Reno, Canadian Co., OK.
    Ruthia Taylor was also known as Ruthie Taylor 54. , b.26 Mar 1884 Caneyville, Grayson Co., KY. She d.11 Mar 1967 Ok. City, Ok. Co., OK.
Known children of Silavnus[7] Daugherty and Ruthia Taylor:
           i.   Omer[8].
           ii.   Charlie R., b.1906. He d.1979 and was bur. Sierra View Mem. Park, Olivehurst, Yuba Co., CA.
           iii. Jesse Gray, b.22 Nov 1909. He m. Ora Mae Caplinger. He d.3 Aug 1989 at age 79 and was bur. Resthaven Mem. Park, Shawnee, Pottawatomie Co., OK.
                 Ora Mae Caplinger, b.24 Feb 1921. She d.6 May 1978 at age 57 and was bur. Resthaven Mem. Park, Shawnee.
           iv.   Abner Hix, b.31 Aug 1913; m. Dorothy E. (n.n.). He d.29 Jul 1980; bur. Blackburn Cem., Norman, Cleveland Co., OK.
                 Dorothy E. (n.n.), b.16 Jun 1927. She d.10 Jun 1995 at age 67 and was bur. Blackburn Cem., Norman.

531. Samuel J.[7] Daugherty (Pheoby[6] Abney, John[5], Paul[4], Joshua[3], Elisha[2], Abner[1]), b.30 Aug 1878. He m. Pollie Woosley, daughter of Henry Woosley and Sudie Bratcher. He d.2 Jul 1956 at age 77 and was bur. Elder-Anderson Cem., Caneyville, Grayson Co., KY.
    Pollie Woosley, b.8 Mar 1881 Grayson Co., KY. She d.28 Dec 1964 Grayson Co., KY, at age 83 and was bur. Elder-Anderson Cem.
Known child of Samuel J.[7] Daugherty and Pollie Woosley:
           i.   Lovell "Pappy"[8] m. Alma "Jean" (n.n.). He, b.13 Feb 1913 Grayson Co., KY. He d.8 Mar 1990 Caneyville, Grayson Co., KY, at age 77.
                 Alma "Jean" (n.n.), b.31 Jul 1926.

532. Keziah[7] Abney (Jasper[6], John[5], Paul[4], Joshua[3], Elisha[2], Abner[1]), b.23 Jan 1872 Butler Co., KY. She m1. Daniel V. Axton on 2 Jun 1897 Spencer Co., IN. She m2. William Caldwell Perry, son of Randolph F. Perry and Bettie Caldwell, on 18 Aug 1904 Russellville, Logan Co., KY. She d.8 Nov 1959 Evansville, Vanderburgh Co., IN, at age 87 and was bur. Sunset Hill Cem., Rockport, Spencer Co., IN.

Daniel V. Axton , b.18 Jul 1868 IN. He d.13 Apr 1904 Rockport, Spencer Co., IN, at age 35.
Known children of Keziah[7] Abney and Daniel V. Axton :
      i.   Daniel Stratton[8], b.4 Jan 1899. He d.1942.
      ii.   Durant, b. ca.1901 IN.
      iii. Kathleen, b. ca.1902 IN.
  William Caldwell Perry, b.24 Nov 1869 Russellville, Logan Co., KY. He d.5 Apr 1918 Evansville, Vanderburgh Co., IN, at age 48.
Known child of Keziah[7] Abney and William Caldwell Perry:
  953   i.   Laura Belle[8], b. 29 Sep 1905 Russellville, Logan Co., KY; m. Raymond William Knoll .

533. Commodore Perry[7] Abney (Jasper[6], John[5], Paul[4], Joshua[3], Elisha[2], Abner[1]), b.7 Jan 1873 KY. He m. Amelia M. Freschly, daughter of Charles Freschly and Elizabeth "Lizzie" Schumacher, on 16 Jan 1907 Spencer Co., IN. He d.23 Sep 1925 Rockport, Spencer Co., IN, at age 52 and was bur. Sunset Hill Cem., Rockport, Spencer Co., IN.

Amelia M. Freschly, b.20 Oct 1884 Rockport, Spencer Co., IN; d.9 Aug 1944 Evansville, Vanderburgh Co., IN, age 59; bur. Sunset Hill Cem.
Known children of Commodore Perry[7] Abney and Amelia M. Freschly:
      i.   Mary E.[8], b.1907 IN. She m. Pvt. Louis F. Parsley (USArmy-WWI). She d.1992; bur. Shiloh Cem., Reo, Spencer Co., IN.
           Pvt. Louis F. Parsley (USArmy-WWI), b.1894. He m. Bertha Jeffries. He d.1976 and was bur. Shiloh Cem., Reo.
      ii.   Thelma Alice, b.19 Nov 1910 Rockport, Spencer Co., IN. She m. Donald Woolen, son of David Lawrence Woolen and Eva Myrtle Young. She d.14 Dec 2008 Rockport, Spencer Co., IN, at age 98 and was bur. Sunset Hill Cem., Rockport.
           Donald Woolen, b.26 Jan 1914. He d.20 Nov 1993 Spencer, Owen Co., IN, at age 79.
      iii. Margaret, b.14 Mar 1913 Grandview, Spencer Co., IN. She m. William I. "Bill" Ranger. She d.11 Jul 1983 Rockport, Spencer Co., IN, at age 70 and was bur. Sunset Hill Cem., Rockport, Spencer Co., IN.
           William I. "Bill" Ranger, b.29 Sep 1910 Grandview, Spencer Co., IN. He d.9 Apr 1984 Rockport, Spencer Co., IN.

534. Elijah "Dige"[7] Abney (Jasper[6], John[5], Paul[4], Joshua[3], Elisha[2], Abner[1]), b.1 Jul 1882 Rockport, Spencer Co., IN. He m. Francis Carter in 1921. He d.1942 and was bur. Sunset Hill Cem., Rockport, Spencer Co., IN.

Francis Carter, b.25 Jun 1905 IN. She m. William Layman. She d.1 Mar 1986 at age 80; bur. Greenwood Cem., Muscatine, Muscatine Co., IA.
Known children of Elijah "Dige"[7] Abney and Francis Carter:
      i.   Dorothy E.[8], b.6 Dec 1922. She d.4 Nov 1989 at age 66.
      ii.   Glenna Frances, b.31 Jan 1923. She d.New Year's Eve, 31 Dec 1924 at age 1; bur. Sunset Hill Cem..
  954 iii. Charles Perry, b. 1 Feb 1925; m. Betty Lou Motteler.
  955 iv. Delbert Dige, b. 7 Dec 1926 Rockport, Spencer Co., IN; m. Myrle Keener.
      v.   Joe Billy, b.9 Jan 1928. He d.9 Jun 2011 at age 83; bur. Fort Sam Houston National Cem., San Antonio, Bexar Co., TX.
      vi. Betty Joyce, b.10 Mar 1930.
      vii. Eleanor Glenn m. (n.n.) Cortez. , b.26 May 1933 Rockport, Parke Co., IN. She m. John Blanco Cortez, son of Juan Alfonso Cortez and Rosa Blanco, on 1 Apr 1967 Rock Island, Rock Island Co., She d.2 Aug 2006 Davenport, Scott Co., IA, at age 73 and was bur. Calvary Cem., Rock Island, Rock Island Co., IL.
           John Blanco Cortez, b.16 Jul 1915 Durango, México. He d.18 Feb 2003 Davenport, Scott Co., IA, at age 87.
      viii. Shirley "Ray", b.13 Feb 1935.

535. John William[7] Abney (James[6], John[5], Paul[4], Joshua[3], Elisha[2], Abner[1]), b.25 Jul 1868 KY. He m1. Bessie Kizer in 1890. He m2. Mary Sarah Fleenor in 1890. He d.30 Dec 1945 McLean Co., KY, at age 77 and was bur. Mount Vernon Bapt. Church Cem., Calhoun, McLean Co., KY.

Mary Sarah Fleenor, b.1872 Butler Co., KY. She d.17 Apr 1911 McLean Co., KY and was bur. Calhoun Cem., Calhoun, McLean Co., KY.
Known children of John William[7] Abney and Mary Sarah Fleenor:
      i.   John William Robert[8], b.9 Jan 1891 McLean Co., KY. He d.9 Apr 1911 McLean Co., KY, at age 20 and was bur. Mount Liberty Baptist Church Cem., Wyman, McLean Co., KY.
  956 ii.   Gertrude, b. 13 Feb 1892 KY; m. Harold Valentine Moore.
      iii. Millard J., b.23 Feb 1893 McLean Co., KY. He d.1917.
  957 iv. Thurman, b. 1894; m. Eva L. Ward.
  958 v.   Pearl, b. 31 Oct 1894 Butler Co., KY; m. Bennie Evans.
      vi. Olee, b.1898. He d.1923 and was bur. Mount Vernon Baptist Church Cem., Calhoun, McLean Co., KY.
  959 vii. Lula M., b. 17 Jan 1898 Butler Co., KY; m. Columbus N. Mitchell.
  Bessie Kizer, b.1885; d.26 Nov 1936 Evansville, Vanderburgh Co., IN; bur. Park Lawn Cem. and Maus., Evansville, Vanderburgh Co., IN.
Known children of John William[7] Abney and Bessie Kizer:
      i.   Virgil[8] m. Bertha Mae Morgan. He, b.26 Feb 1904 McLean Co., KY. He d.19 Jan 1995 Evansville, Vanderburgh Co., IN, at age 90 and was bur. Park Lawn Cem. and Mausoleum, Evansville, Vanderburgh Co., IN.
           Bertha Mae Morgan, b.28 Mar 1904 Henderson Co., KY. She d.30 Dec 1967 Evansville, Vanderburgh Co., IN, at age 63 and was bur. Rose Hill Cem., Newburgh, Warrick Co., IN.
  960 ii.   Clifton, b. 5 Mar 1908 IN; m. Naomi Marie Waters.
      iii. Audrey, b.1909. She d.1996.
  961 iv. Audrey, b. 14 Dec 1909; m. Gertie Corum.
      v.   Osie May m. (n.n.) Lloyd. , b.19 Jul 1912. She d.17 Jul 1996 at age 83 and was bur. St. John - St. Joseph Catholic Diocesan Cem., Hammond, Lake Co., IN.
      vi. Ruben, b.28 Apr 1913 KY. He d.4 Sep 1994 age 81; bur. Alexander Mem. Park Cem., Evansville, Vanderburgh Co., IN.
      vii. Nora Dell, b.22 Feb 1915 Calhoun, McLean Co., KY. She m. (n.n.) Hayden. She d.26 Jun 2000 Boonville, Warrick Co., IN, at age 85 and was bur. Maple Grove Cem., Boonville, Warrick Co., IN.
      viii. PFC Pascal (USArmy-WWII), b.5 Oct 1916 KY. Killed in Action 8 Feb 1945 Philippines, at age 28.
  962 ix. Margaret M. "Millie," b. 1919 McLean Co., KY; m. Odis C. Meredith.

       x.   Hubert Louis, b.21 Jun 1921 McLean Co., KY. He m. Dorothy VanBibber, daughter of George Milton VanBibber and Ethel Christine Conner. He d.28 Mar 1988 Evansville, Vanderburgh Co., IN, at age 66 and was bur. Park Lawn Cem. and Mausoleum, Evansville, Vanderburgh Co., IN.

                Dorothy VanBibber, b.17 Mar 1922. She d.1 Nov 1987 IN at age 65 and was bur. Park Lawn Cem. and Mausoleum.

963   xi.   Louis John "Red," b. 20 Aug 1928 Calhoun, McLean Co., KY; m. Anna Louise Yunker.

536. Mary Angieline "Angie"[7] Abney (James[6], John[5], Paul[4], Joshua[3], Elisha[2], Abner[1]), b.14 Dec 1871 KY. She m. George Wilson, son of Augustus Alexander Wilson and Delitha Jane Dickens, on 3 Jan 1891 McLean Co., KY. She d.5 Jan 1957 Rumsey, McLean Co., KY, at age 85 and was bur. Calhoun Cem., Calhoun, McLean Co., KY.

    George Wilson, b.3 Mar 1871 McLean Co., KY. He d.25 Mar 1959 McLean Co., KY, at age 88 and was bur. Calhoun Cem., Calhoun.

Known children of Mary Angieline "Angie"[7] Abney and George Wilson:

   964   i.   George Wesley[8], b. 22 Sep 1895 KY; m. Louise Carter.
   965   ii.   Nellie R., b. 16 Oct 1900; m. Jesse "Jess" Garrett.

537. James Wesley[7] Abney (James[6], John[5], Paul[4], Joshua[3], Elisha[2], Abner[1]), b.20 May 1874. He m. Minnie Daugherty ca.1894. He and Minnie appeared on the censuses of 11 May 1910 and Jan 1920 McLean Co., KY. He d.9 Jun 1949 McLean Co., KY, at age 75 and was bur. Mount Vernon Baptist Church Cem., Calhoun, McLean Co., KY.

    Minnie Daugherty, b.14 Oct 1875 KY. She d.15 Sep 1943 McLean Co., KY, at age 67.

Known children of James Wesley[7] Abney and Minnie Daugherty:

   966   i.   Effie[8], b. 15 Sep 1898 McLean Co., KY; m. (n.n.) Austin.
          ii.   Gilbert, b.5 Jul 1901 McLean Co., KY. He d.6 Mar 1983 at age 81; bur. Calhoun Cem., Calhoun, McLean Co., KY.
   967   iii.   Edgar, b. 16 Dec 1903 McLean Co., KY; m. Hallie Ray McClellan; m. Avah Wilson.
          iv.   Flora Ann, b.24 May 1910 McLean Co., KY. She m. Pvt. Charles M. Galloway (USArmy-WWI), son of Sam Galloway and Lydia G. Kennedy. She d.19 May 1992 at age 81 and was bur. Calhoun Cem., Calhoun, McLean Co., KY.

                Pvt. Charles M. Galloway (USArmy-WWI), b.1 Mar 1890. He d.18 Aug 1979 at age 89 and was bur. Calhoun Cem.
          v.   Mary Jane, b.13 Aug 1912 McLean Co., KY. She m. Thomas Abraham Hendricks. She d.26 Sep 1999 at age 87 and was bur. Calhoun Cem., Calhoun, McLean Co., KY.

                Thomas Abraham Hendricks, b.19 Aug 1903. He d.30 Jun 1994 at age 90.
          vi.   Clarence D., b.26 Nov 1914 McLean Co., KY. He d.11 Dec 1914 McLean Co., KY; bur. Mount Vernon Baptist Church Cem., Calhoun, McLean Co., KY.
         vii.   Larance E., b.26 Nov 1914 McLean Co., KY. He d.17 Dec 1914 McLean Co., KY; bur. Mount Vernon Baptist Ch. Cem.
       viii.   Henry S., b.28 May 1918. He d.28 May 1918 and was bur. Mount Vernon Baptist Ch. Cem., Calhoun, McLean Co., KY.
          ix.   Hawden, b. ca.1919 McLean Co., KY.

538. George Washington[7] Abney (James[6], John[5], Paul[4], Joshua[3], Elisha[2], Abner[1]), b.2 Jun 1880 KY. He m. Betty Nolin, daughter of John W. Nolin and (n.n.), on 3 May 1899 McLean Co., KY. He, 29, appeared as Head of Household on the census of 11 May 1910 McLean Co., KY. He d.5 Jan 1968 McLean Co., KY, at age 87.

    Betty Nolin, b.17 Dec 1880. She d.2 Sep 1958 McLean Co., KY, at age 77.

Known children of George Washington[7] Abney and Betty Nolin:

          i.   Mary E.[8], b. ca.1903 McLean Co., KY.
          ii.   Truman, b. ca.1905 McLean Co.
         iii.   Nady, b. ca.1908 McLean Co., KY.

539. William M.[7] Abney (James[6], John[5], Paul[4], Joshua[3], Elisha[2], Abner[1]), b.6 Jun 1882 McLean Co., KY. He m. Lula "Lou" Kessinger on 4 Mar 1901 McLean Co., KY. He and Lula appeared on the census of 11 May 1910 McLean Co., KY. He d.5 Apr 1915 McLean Co., KY, at age 32.

    Lula "Lou" Kessinger, b.3 Apr 1879 Butler Co., KY. She, appeared as Head of Household on the census of 9 Feb 1920 McLean Co., KY. She d.16 Aug 1965 McLean Co., KY, at age 86.

Known children of William M.[7] Abney and Lula "Lou" Kessinger:

          i.   Hallie Bell[8], b.29 Dec 1901 McLean Co., KY. She m. William H. Cook. d.17 Feb 1993 McLean Co., KY, at age 91.

              William H. Cook d.5 Jul 1966 McLean Co., KY.
          ii.   Grey Roosevelt d. before 1910.
         iii.   Orville C., b.6 Apr 1907 Ohio Co., KY. He m. LaBelle Carter (b.1915). He d.6 Feb 1969 McLean Co., KY, at age 61.
         iv.   D. "Woody" m. Lena Hancock. He, b.11 Jul 1911 McLean Co., KY.

              Lena Hancock, b.30 Dec 1912. She d.25 Feb 1980 McLean Co., KY, at age 67.
   968   v.   Roscoe "William," b. 26 Jul 1914 McLean Co., KY; m. Gladys Haynes Howard.

540. Charles Newton "Charlie"[7] Abney (James[6], John[5], Paul[4], Joshua[3], Elisha[2], Abner[1]), b.1883 KY. He m. Agnes (n.n.) ca.1899. He and Agnes appeared on the census of 11 May 1910 McLean Co., KY. He d.1964. (Agnes was b. ca. 1884).

Known children of Charles Newton "Charlie"[7] Abney and Agnes (n.n.) all b. McLean Co., KY:

          i.   Willie[8], b. ca.1900.
          ii.   Tommy, b. ca.1902.
         iii.   (n.n.), b. ca.1904; d. before 1910 McLean Co., KY.
         iv.   Lillian, b. ca.1906.

541. Naoma[7] Daugherty (Mary[6] Abney, John[5], Paul[4], Joshua[3], Elisha[2], Abner[1]), b.3 May 1875 Butler Co., KY. She m. Dr. Elonzo Snodgrass, son of Sanford S. Snodgrass and Susan A. Daugherty, in 1890 Butler Co., KY. She and Dr. Elonzo Snodgrass appeared on the census of 21 Jun 1900 Butler Co., KY. She was liv. on 22 Jan 1920 and 9 Apr 1930 with son-in-law, William Dunn, Hartford, Ohio Co., KY. She d.16 Jul 1935 Hartford, Ohio Co., KY, at age 60 and was bur. Green Brier Cem., Utica, Daviess Co., KY.

    Dr. Elonzo Snodgrass, b.2 Apr 1869 Butler Co., KY. He d. Independence Day, 4 Jul 1917 Gilstrap, Butler Co., KY, at age 48.

Known children of Naoma[7] Daugherty and Dr. Elonzo Snodgrass both b. Butler Co., KY:
    969   i.   Mittie[8], b. 21 Jan 1891; m. John William Felty.
    970   ii.   Mattie Lucille, b. 30 Aug 1899; m. William Hershel Dunn.

542. Fannie Cates[7] Hunter (Martha[6] Abney, John[5], Paul[4], Joshua[3], Elisha[2], Abner[1]), b.29 Apr 1883 KY. She m. Pinkney B. Hart. She d.13 Apr 1961 Beaver Dam, Ohio Co., KY, at age 77 and was bur. Bethel Cem., Horton, Ohio Co., KY.
    Pinkney B. Hart, b.1859 KY. He d.1940 Ohio Co., KY.
Known child of Fannie Cates[7] Hunter and Pinkney B. Hart:
            i.   Jack Palmer[8], b.22 Jun 1915 Grayson Co., KY; m1. Iva Corrine Schroader in 1937. He m2. Hazel Ruby Smith, daughter of Estil Smith and Bettie Wells; d.26 Jul 1973 Ohio Co., KY, age 58; bur. Sunnyside Cem., Beaver Dam, Ohio Co., KY.
                Iva Corrine Schroader, b.24 Jun 1920 Ohio Co., KY. She d.28 Jan 2002 Scott Co., IN, at age 81 and was bur. Walnut Ridge Cem., Jeffersonville, Clark Co., IN.
                Hazel Ruby Smith, b.15 Jun 1915 Hartford, Ohio Co., KY. She d.4 Nov 2002 at age 87 and was bur. Sunnyside Cem..

543. Mollie Tichenor[7] Hunter (Martha[6] Abney, John[5], Paul[4], Joshua[3], Elisha[2], Abner[1]), b.30 Jun 1885. She m. Lee Jones. She d.9 Jun 1983 at age 97 and was bur. Oakwood Cem., Hartford, Ohio Co., KY.
    Lee Jones, b.23 Dec 1880. He d. Mar 1974 at age 93 and was bur. Oakwood Cem., Hartford, Ohio Co., KY.
Known child of Mollie Tichenor[7] Hunter and Lee Jones:
    971   i.   Pauline[8], b. 28 Oct 1909; m. Willis James.

544. Carey[7] Hunter (Martha[6] Abney, John[5], Paul[4], Joshua[3], Elisha[2], Abner[1]), b.7 Nov 1894 McLean Co., KY. He m. Myrtle Abney, daughter of Francis Marion Daugherty and Nancy Little Abney. He d.19 Jun 1942 Ohio Co., KY, at age 47; bur. Sunnyside Cem., Beaver Dam, Ohio Co., KY.
    Myrtle Abney (#952), b.30 Sep 1895. She d.24 May 1990 at age 94 and was bur. Sunnyside Cem., Beaver Dam, Ohio Co., KY.
Known children of Carey[7] Hunter and Myrtle Abney:
    972   i.   Carrie Lee[8], b. 13 Sep 1914; m. Bardwell Ashby.
            ii.   Sue, b.17 May 1918; m. Hoyt Thos. Wilson. d.14 Oct 2001 KY, ae 83; bur. Sunnyside Cem., Beaver Dam, Ohio Co., KY.
                Hoyt Thomas Wilson, b.8 Feb 1907 Ohio Co., KY. He d.11 Nov 1991 Ohio Co., KY, at age 84.
            iii.   Martha Jo, b.20 Apr 1923. She m. Carlyle Thienes on 11 Jul 1942. She d.25 Mar 2011 at age 87; bur. Sunnyside Cem.
                Carlyle Thienes, b.19 May 1922. He d.5 Mar 2012 at age 89.

545. Lucy Jane[7] Abney (Jesse[6], John[5], Paul[4], Joshua[3], Elisha[2], Abner[1]), b.19 Aug 1878. She m1. (n.n.) Bartley. Liv. on 25 Apr 1910 with her mother, Central City, Muhlenberg Co., KY. She m2. (n.n.) Wells. She d.26 Sep 1955 at age 77; bur. Mt Zion Presb. Ch. Cem., Central City, KY.
Known child of Lucy Jane[7] Abney and (n.n.) Bartley:
            i.   Ida[8], b. ca.1902 KY. She was liv. on 30 Jan 1920 with grandmother, Mahala Abney, Central City, Muhlenberg Co., KY.
There were no known children of Lucy Jane[7] Abney and (n.n.) Wells.

546. Walter Green[7] Abney Sr. (Jesse[6], John[5], Paul[4], Joshua[3], Elisha[2], Abner[1]), b.28 Aug 1879 Butler Co., KY. He m. Laura Riggs. He d.2 Oct 1923 at age 44 and was bur. Tomberlin Cem., England, Lonoke Co., AR.
    Laura Riggs, b.1882. She d.1942 and was bur. Tomberlin Cem., England, Lonoke Co., AR.
Known children of Walter Green[7] Abney Sr. and Laura Riggs:
            i.   Jessie Marie[8] m. John James Cappadora. , b.9 Mar 1906. She d.31 May 1995 at age 89 and was bur. St. Michael the Archangel Catholic Cem., Palatine, Cook Co., IL.
                John James Cappadora, b.13 Dec 1902. He d.7 Feb 1956 at age 53; bur. Wunder's Cem., Chicago, Cook Co., IL.
            ii.   Walter Green.
    973   iii.   Loney, b. 1916; m. Ferman Hanger; m. Walter H. Tupman (USN-WWI, Korea).
            iv.   Margaret Odell m. Walter S. Sokarski (USN). , b.13 Aug 1918. She d.14 Jun 1999 at age 80; bur. Wunder's Cem., Chicago.
                Walter S. Sokarski (USN), b.15 Apr 1923. He d.Apr 1992 and was bur. Wunder's Cem., Chicago, Cook Co., IL.

547. Lon J. "Lonnie"[7] Abney (Daniel[6], John[5], Paul[4], Joshua[3], Elisha[2], Abner[1]), b.29 May 1880 Daviess Co., KY. He m. Mittie L. Pinkston. He and Mittie appeared on the census of Jan 1920 McLean Co., KY. He d. Christmas Eve, 24 Dec 1963 McLean Co., KY, at age 83.
    Mittie L. Pinkston, b.15 Oct 1881 McLean Co., KY. She d.8 Feb 1957 McLean Co., KY, at age 75.
Known children of Lon J. "Lonnie"[7] Abney and Mittie L. Pinkston:
            i.   Ellis[8], b.1900. He d.1970.
            ii.   Sudie May, b.1902. She d.1913.
            iii.   Dan T., b.1902. He d.1986.
            iv.   John W., b.1909. He d.1982.
             v.   Alney L., b.1912. He d.2000.
            vi.   Christine, b. ca.1914 McLean Co., KY.
            vii.   Haynes E., b.1917. He d.1982.
            viii.   Lula Corene, b.1921. She d.2009.
            ix.   Alvie, b.1924. He d.1944.

548. Sallie Barbara[7] Abney (Daniel[6], John[5], Paul[4], Joshua[3], Elisha[2], Abner[1]), b.24 Aug 1891. She m. Ernest Deno. She d.10 Nov 1973 at age 82 and was bur. Calhoun Cem., Calhoun, McLean Co., KY.
    Ernest Deno, b.28 Nov 1877 AR. He d.28 Sep 1957 Calhoun, McLean Co., KY, at age 79 and was bur. Calhoun Cem., Calhoun.
Known children of Sallie Barbara[7] Abney and Ernest Deno:
    974   i.   Ira William[8], b. 3 May 1917; m. Mabel Marie Vanover.
    975   ii.   Helen Bernice, b. 23 Aug 1925; m. Rev. Pvt. Charles Monroe Vanover (USArmy-WWII).
            iii.   Edward Eugene "Gene", b.24 Oct 1929 Calhoun, McLean Co., KY. He d.6 Jun 2013 McLean Co., KY, at age 83 and was bur. Nickel Ridge Cem., Panther, Daviess Co., KY.

549. Newell[7] Moore (Calvin[6], Mary[5] Abney, Paul[4], Joshua[3], Elisha[2], Abner[1]), b.12 Feb 1875 KY. He m. Lula E. Taylor, daughter of (n.n.) Taylor and Percilla Ann White. He d.10 Feb 1915 Butler Co., KY, at age 39 and was bur. Mount Vernon Cem., Dexterville, Butler Co., KY.
    Lula E. Taylor, b.25 Feb 1883 Butler Co., KY. She d.16 Aug 1918 Butler Co., KY, at age 35 and was bur. Mount Vernon Cem., Dexterville.
Known children of Newell[7] Moore and Lula E. Taylor all b. Butler Co., KY:
    i.   Oval[8], b.10 Feb 1902. He was liv. on 28 Jan 1920 with uncle, Melvin L. Taylor, Butler Co., KY. He d.28 Mar 1924 Jefferson Co., KY, at age 22 and was bur. Mount Vernon Cem., Dexterville, Butler Co., KY.
    ii. Thelma, b.2 Oct 1904. She was liv. on 28 Jan 1920 with uncle, Melvin L. Taylor, Butler Co., KY. She d.4 Mar 1923 Gilstrap, Butler Co., KY, at age 18 and was bur. Mount Vernon Cem., Dexterville, Butler Co., KY.
    iii. Jay, b. ca.1908. He was liv. on 28 Jan 1920 with uncle, Melvin L. Taylor, Butler Co., KY.
    iv. Toy P, b.22 Apr 1910. He was liv. on 28 Jan 1920 with uncle, Melvin L. Taylor, Butler Co., KY. He was listed as a resident in Pvt. Toy P. Moore's (USArmy) household in the census report on 15 Apr 1930 Fort Eustis, Warwick Co., VA. He d.2 Aug 1933 Butler Co., KY, at age 23 and was bur. Mount Vernon Cem., Dexterville, Butler Co., KY.
    v.   Justus O. "Justie", b.18 Apr 1914. He was liv. on 28 Jan 1920 with uncle, Melvin L. Taylor, Butler Co., KY. He m. Lillie Myrtle Evans. He and Lillie appeared on the census of 17 Apr 1940 Butler Co., KY. He d.8 Sep 1958 Russellville, Logan Co., KY, at age 44 and was bur. Oak Grove Baptist Church Cem., Russellville, Logan Co., KY.
            Lillie Myrtle Evans, b.10 Dec 1916 Butler Co., KY. She d.25 Jul 2001 Russellville, Logan Co., KY, at age 84 and was bur. Oak Grove Baptist Church Cem., Russellville, Logan Co., KY.

550. Lafayette[7] Moore (Calvin[6], Mary[5] Abney, Paul[4], Joshua[3], Elisha[2], Abner[1]), b.8 Feb 1877 Butler Co., KY. He m. Elmeda (n.n.) (b. ca. 1871 KY) ca.1900. He and Elmeda appeared on the census of 3 May 1910 Butler Co., KY. He appeared on the census of New Year's Eve, 31 Jan 1920 Ohio Co., KY. He d.22 Feb 1958 Dawson Springs, Hopkins Co., KY, at age 81 and was bur. Mount Vernon Cem., Dexterville, Butler Co., KY.
Known children of Lafayette[7] Moore and Elmeda (n.n.) all b. Butler Co., KY,:
    i.   Asa "Acy"[8], b. ca.1901. He was (an unknown value) in 1920 Coal Miner.
    ii. Giles, b. ca.1903. He was (an unknown value) in 1920 Coal Miner.
    iii. Isaac "Otto", b. ca.1906.
    iv. Roscoe, b. ca.Mar 1910.

551. John W.[7] Moore (Calvin[6], Mary[5] Abney, Paul[4], Joshua[3], Elisha[2], Abner[1]), b.22 Aug 1879 Butler Co., KY. He m. Etty Roxie Howard ca.1911. He d.25 Feb 1930 Ohio Co., KY, at age 50 and was bur. Mount Vernon Cem., Dexterville, Butler Co., KY.
Known children of John W.[7] Moore and Etty Roxie Howard both b. Butler Co., KY:
    i.   Shady[8], b.28 Feb 1912. He d.27 Feb 1914 Butler Co., KY, age 1; bur. Mount Vernon Cem., Dexterville, Butler Co., KY.
    ii. Leafy, b.24 Jan 1914. She d.24 Feb 1914 Butler Co., KY and was bur. Mount Vernon Cem., Dexterville, Butler Co., KY.

552. Nicey J.[7] Moore (Paul[6], Mary[5] Abney, Paul[4], Joshua[3], Elisha[2], Abner[1]), b.30 Sep 1883. She m. Homer Abner, son of Silas Curtis Abney and Calista "Calesty" Barton, on 1 Feb 1904 Butler Co., KY. She and Homer appeared on censuses of 18 Apr 1910 Central City, Muhlenberg Co., KY; and 18 Apr 1930 and 13 Apr 1940 Centertown, Ohio Co., KY. She d.3 Jan 1970 age 86; bur. Mount Vernon Cem., Dexterville, Butler Co., KY.
    Homer Abner (#271), b.18 Apr 1877 Butler Co., KY. He d.28 Mar 1963 Centertown, Ohio Co., KY, at age 85; bur. Mount Vernon Cem.
Known children of Nicey J.[7] Moore and Homer Abner:
    i.   Carl "Carlie"[8], b. 11 Jun 1906; m. Nellie Irene Barrett. (see # 575 on page 150).
    ii.   Oakie Pearl, b. 20 Apr 1909; m. Robert Elson Hoskins. (see # 576 on page 150).
    iii. Charlie, b. 17 Feb 1913 Ohio Co., KY; m. Cornelia B. Doyal. (see # 577 on page 150).
    iv.   Tom, b. 5 Nov 1914 Butler, Pendleton Co., KY; m. Lois "Lee" Smith. (see # 578 on page 150).
    v.   Hubert B., b. 20 Apr 1917 Butler Co., KY; m. Stella J. Sheffield. (see # 579 on page 150).
    vi.   Troy "Willie," b. 29 Oct 1919 KY; m. Justine Sheffield. (see page 96).
    vii. Jack, b. 4 Oct 1921 KY; m. Wilda Katheryn Patterson. (see page 96).
    viii. (infant son), b. 21 Feb 1926 Centertown, Ohio Co., KY. (see page 96).
    ix.   Everette, b. 18 Apr 1929 KY; m. Ritta Jane Coffman. (see page 96).

553. Veachel Loven[7] Moore (Paul[6], Mary[5] Abney, Paul[4], Joshua[3], Elisha[2], Abner[1]) m. Clodia Phelps. He, b.1 Jul 1885 KY. He d.11 May 1953 Butler Co., KY, at age 67 and was bur. Mount Vernon Cem., Dexterville, Butler Co., KY.
    Clodia Phelps, b.19 May 1898. She d.11 Mar 1967 Butler Co., KY, at age 68 and was bur. Mount Vernon Cem., Dexterville, Butler Co., KY.
Known child of Veachel Loven[7] Moore and Clodia Phelps:
    976   i.   Effie Pearl[8], b. 18 Jan 1920; m. Harlet E. Coots.

554. Finis[7] Moore (Finis[6], Mary[5] Abney, Paul[4], Joshua[3], Elisha[2], Abner[1]), b. ca.1882 Butler Co., KY. He m. Mary (n.n.) (b.ca.1884 KY) ca.1900.
Known children of Finis[7] Moore and Mary (n.n.) all b. KY:
    i.   (n.n.)[8], b.ca. 1902; d. before 1910 KY.
    ii. (n.n.), b. ca. 1904; d. before 1910 KY.
    iii. Mammie, b. ca.1906.

555. Nathan T.[7] Moore (Finis[6], Mary[5] Abney, Paul[4], Joshua[3], Elisha[2], Abner[1]), b.3 Sep 1889. He m1. Paul "Alice" Moore, daughter of Paul Abney (#260) Moore and Katherine Jane Moore, ca.1912. He and *Alice* appeared on the census of 21 Jan 1920 Butler Co., KY. He m2. Lelia Jane Burden ca.1929. He d.3 Dec 1975 at age 86 and was bur. Render Cem., McHenry, Ohio Co., KY.
    Paul "Alice" Moore, b. 20 May 1897 Butler Co., KY. She d.16 Feb 1923 Ohio Co., KY
Known children of Nathan T.[7] Moore and Paul Alice Moore, both b. KY:
          i.   Lucy[8], b. ca.1915.
    977   ii. Lawson, b. 24 Nov 1916; m. Lillian B. Dennison; m. Edna B. Rowe.
    Lelia Jane Burden, b.19 Jan 1904. She d.22 Apr 1996 at age 92 and was bur. Render Cem., McHenry, Ohio Co., KY.
Known children of Nathan T.[7] Moore and Lelia Jane Burden:
    978   i.   Eula Christine[8], b. 27 May 1930; m. PFC Hallie Woodward Renfrow (USArmy-WWII).

  ii. Allison C., b.20 Sep 1934. She d.22 Nov 2006 at age 72 and was bur. Render Cem., McHenry, Ohio Co., KY.

  iii. Ova Mae, b.3 Jun 1936. She m. Bennie F. Burden, son of (n.n.) Burden and Sarah Frances Kessinger. She d.12 Jan 2017 at age 80 and was bur. Render Cem., McHenry, Ohio Co., KY.

    Bennie F. Burden, b.15 Feb 1928. He d.18 Mar 1985 at age 57 and was bur. Render Cem., McHenry, Ohio Co., KY.

  iv. Woodie T., b.10 May 1943. He d.10 May 2014 at age 71 and was bur. Render Cem., McHenry, Ohio Co., KY.

556. Daniel Lee "Dan"[7] Moore (Finis[6], Mary[5] Abney, Paul[4], Joshua[3], Elisha[2], Abner[1]), b.15 May 1896. He m. Delia Ann Burden. He d.8 Apr 1985 at age 88 and was bur. Render Cem., McHenry, Ohio Co., KY.

  Delia Ann Burden, b.7 Apr 1905. She d.23 Sep 1986 at age 81 and was bur. Render Cem., McHenry, Ohio Co., KY.

Known children of Daniel Lee "Dan"[7] Moore and Delia Ann Burden:

  i. Marjorie Oma "Margie"[8], b.5 Jun 1924. She m. Milton Crowe, son of James Harrison Crowe and Janie Wilson. She d.26 Apr 2013 IN at age 88 and was bur. Render Cem., McHenry, Ohio Co., IN.

    Milton Crowe, b.30 Jan 1921. He d.14 Dec 1973 KY at age 52 and was bur. Render Cem., McHenry, Ohio Co., KY.

979 ii. Oscar W., b. 25 Apr 1925; m. Lora Simpson.

  iii. Arthur, b.19 Oct 1928. He d.19 Oct 1928 and was bur. Render Cem., McHenry, Ohio Co., KY.

  iv. Marie Nita, b.25 Feb 1930 Ohio Co., KY. She m1. PFC Birthel "Wig" McClure (USArmy-WWII), s/o of Wm. Hezekiah McClure & Mary Ann Meredith. She m2. Thomas Edmund "Tom" Stofer, s/o James Garland Stofer & Margaret Elizabeth Thomas. She d.26 Dec 2018 Newburgh, Warrick Co., IN, age 88; bur. Green Brier Cem., Utica, Daviess Co., KY.

    PFC Birthel "Wig" McClure (USArmy-WWII), b.24 Jul 1914. He d.14 May 1992 at age 77; bur. Green Brier Cem.

    Thomas Edmund "Tom" Stofer, b.21 Jan 1925 McLean Co., KY. He m1. June Hughart. He m2. Sue Jewell Underwood. He d.17 Oct 2007 Daviess Co., KY, at age 82 and was bur. Oak Hill Cem., Livermore, McLean Co., KY.

  v. L.B, b.14 Sep 1938. He d.24 Jul 1940 at age 1 and was bur. Render Cem., McHenry, Ohio Co., KY.

557. Thomas Shofta "Tom"[7] Moore (USArmy-WWI) (Finis[6], Mary[5] Abney, Paul[4], Joshua[3], Elisha[2], Abner[1]), b.7 Feb 1900 Ohio Co., KY; m. Effie Marie Trail, d/o of John Wm. Trail & Margaret Alice Burton; d.18 Apr 1981 Ohio Co., KY, age 81; bur. Render Cem., McHenry, Ohio Co., KY.

  Effie Marie Trail, b.24 Sep 1902. She d.15 Mar 1961 at age 58 and was bur. Render Cem., McHenry, Ohio Co., KY.

Known children of Thomas Shofta "Tom"[7] Moore (USArmy-WWI) and Effie Marie Trail:

980 i. Ruth[8], b. 4 Mar 1931; m. Robert Lee Eury.

  ii. Everett Eugene, b.20 Jun 1934. He m. Monia J. (n.n.) on 18 Jul 1957. He d.24 Jun 2015 at age 81 and was bur. Fairview Cem., Baizetown, Ohio Co., KY.

    Monia J. (n.n.), b.15 May 1932.

558. Nola Jane[7] Moore (Finis[6], Mary[5] Abney, Paul[4], Joshua[3], Elisha[2], Abner[1]), b.16 Feb 1903 Butler Co., KY. She m. Myrtle Hurt (WWI) on 2 Jan 1920 Ohio Co., KY. She d.20 Jul 1972 Butler Co., KY, at age 69 and was bur. Render Cem., McHenry, Ohio Co., KY.

  Myrtle Hurt (WWI), b.6 Aug 1896 Rosine, Ohio Co., KY. He d.11 Jan 1971 Hartford, Ohio Co., KY, at age 74 and was bur. Render Cem.

Known children of Nola Jane[7] Moore and Myrtle Hurt (WWI):

981 i. Alva C.[8], b. 27 Apr 1921 Ohio Co., KY; m. Mary Catherine Faught.

982 ii. Stella B., b. 25 Aug 1922 McHenry, Ohio Co., KY; m. Cecil Raymond Sr.

  iii. Marvin Russell, b.Sep 1926 Ohio Co., KY. He d.30 Mar 1943 Muhlenberg Co., KY, at age 16; bur. Render Cem.

  iv. Albert Dalton, b.16 Feb 1932 Ohio Co., KY. He d.8 Jun 1981 Ohio Co., KY, at age 49 and was bur. Render Cem.

  v. Bobby Don, b.13 Feb 1938. He m. Freda Sue Growbarger, daughter of Dewey Henry Growbarger and Ella Maureen Decker, in 1962. He d.4 Nov 1998 at age 60 and was bur. Render Cem., McHenry, Ohio Co., KY.

    Freda Sue Growbarger, b.3 Feb 1945; d.17 Dec 1997 age 52; bur. Mt. Olivet Cem., Wheat Ridge, Jefferson Co., CO.

  vi. Jerry Lee, b.22 Sep 1940 Ohio Co., KY. He d.29 Sep 1940 Ohio Co., KY; bur. Render Cem., McHenry, Ohio Co., KY.

  vii. Nancy Jane, b.15 Aug 1946 Ohio Co., KY. She m. Webb Victor Swift on 31 Jul 1964. She d.5 Oct 1988 Owensboro, Daviess Co., KY, at age 42 and was bur. Rosine Cem., Rosine, Ohio Co., KY.

    Webb Victor Swift, b.21 Aug 1944. He d.26 Aug 2008 at age 64 and was bur. Rosine Cem., Rosine, Ohio Co., KY.

559. Bessie[7] Moore (Jessie's twin) (Finis[6], Mary[5] Abney, Paul[4], Joshua[3], Elisha[2], Abner[1]), b.28 May 1909 Butler Co., KY. She m. Audra Embry, son of Robert John Embry and Vicy Green, on 23 Dec 1939. She d.6 Feb 1982 Ohio Co., KY, age 72; bur. Render Cem., McHenry, Ohio Co., KY.

  Audra Embry, b.28 May 1909 Ohio Co., KY. He d.12 Mar 1985 Ohio Co., KY, at age 75 and was bur. Render Cem., McHenry, Ohio Co., KY.

Known children of Bessie[7] Moore (Jessie's twin) and Audra Embry:

  i. Allison Lee[8], b.13 Oct 1940 Ohio Co., KY. He m. Rebecca Ann "Becky" (n.n.) on 8 Sep 2005. He d.2 Sep 2006 KY at age 65 and was bur. Render Cem., McHenry, Ohio Co., KY.

    Rebecca Ann "Becky" (n.n.), b.16 Jul 1954.

  ii. Netta J., b.11 Feb 1943 and was bur. Render Cem., McHenry, Ohio Co., KY.

560. Jessie[7] Moore (Bessie's twin) (Finis[6], Mary[5] Abney, Paul[4], Joshua[3], Elisha[2], Abner[1]), b.28 May 1909. He m. Wilma Lois Bishop, daughter of Jess Harrison Bishop and Verna Ensor. He d.30 Jan 1990 at age 80 and was bur. Render Cem., McHenry, Ohio Co., KY.

  Wilma Lois Bishop, b.15 Jul 1922. She d.14 Jul 1989 at age 67 and was bur. Render Cem., McHenry, Ohio Co., KY.

Known children of Jessie[7] Moore (Bessie's twin) and Wilma Lois Bishop:

  i. Patricia Sue[8], b.1 Feb 1940. She d.Christmas Eve, 24 Dec 1941 at age 1; bur. Render Cem., McHenry, Ohio Co., KY.

  ii. Jessie Carol "Bubby", b.6 Sep 1942. He m. Sandra Lee Smith, daughter of Joseph Smith and Clara Louise White, on 15 Feb 1963. He d.29 Apr 2016 at age 73 and was bur. Echols Cem., Echols, Ohio Co., KKY.

    Sandra Lee Smith, b.15 Aug 1944. She d.10 Mar 1998 at age 53 and was bur. Echols Cem., Echols, Ohio Co., KY.

561. Estella "Stella"[7] Baize (Mary[6] Moore, Mary[5] Abney, Paul[4], Joshua[3], Elisha[2], Abner[1]), b. New Year's Eve, 31 Dec 1892 KY. She m1. Charlie Baker ca.1908. She and Charlie Baker appeared on the census of 29 Apr 1910 Hopkins Co., KY. She m2. Adam B. Fain ca.1911. She and Adam B. Fain appeared on the censuses of 5 Apr 1930 Cleveland, Cuyahoga Co., OH; and 30 Apr 1940 Chester Twp., Geauga Co., OH. She d.21 Jan 1972 Ashtabula Co., OH, at age 79 and was bur. Middlefield Cem., Middlefield, Geauga Co., OH.

Charlie Baker, b. ca.1889 KY.
Known child of Estella "Stella"[7] Baize and Charlie Baker:
      i.   Galleston[8], b. ca.1909 KY.
   Adam B. Fain, b. ca.1874 TN.
Known children of Estella "Stella"[7] Baize and Adam B. Fain:
      i.   Elah[8], b. ca.1912 TN.
     ii. Raymond, b. ca.1914 TN.
983   iii. Lillian Mae, b. 21 Mar 1916 Hohenwald, Lewis Co., TN; m. (n.n.) McHugh.

562. Brankley B.[7] Moore (Thomas[6], Mary[5] Abney, Paul[4], Joshua[3], Elisha[2], Abner[1]), b.13 Apr 1893 Butler Co., KY. He m. Alice L. Embry ca.1924. He and Alice appeared as Head of Household on the censuses of 25 Apr 1930 and 6 Apr 1940 Ohio Co., KY. He d.23 Nov 1952 Ohio Co., KY, at age 59 and was bur. Sunnyside Cem., Beaver Dam, Ohio Co., KY.
   Alice L. Embry, b.10 Feb 1904. She d.19 May 1979 at age 75 and was bur. Sunnyside Cem., Beaver Dam, Ohio Co., KY.
Known children of Brankley B.[7] Moore and Alice L. Embry:
      i.   Estill Doran[8], b.22 Nov 1926 KY. He d.3 Aug 2001 KY at age 74; bur. Sunnyside Cem., Beaver Dam, Ohio Co., KY.
984   ii. Delia "Martine," b. 11 Sep 1928 Ohio Co., KY; m. Stanley Stolarz.
     iii. Maurine, b. ca.1931 KY.
     iv. Janie "Tootsie", b.19 Jun 1931 Ohio Co., KY. She m. S.Sgt. Alva Dupree Decker (USArmy-WWII), son of Alfonzo Decker and Mary Ann Keown. She d.28 Nov 2018 Ohio Co., KY, at age 87 and was bur. Sunnyside Cem., Beaver Dam.
         S.Sgt. Alva Dupree Decker (USArmy-WWII), b.14 Dec 1921 Ohio Co., KY. He m1. Mary Virginia Shoulders. He d.3 Mar 1990 Ohio Co., KY, at age 68.

563. Louella F.[7] Flener (Lucinda[6] Deweese, Nicey[5] Abney, Paul[4], Joshua[3], Elisha[2], Abner[1]), b.8 Apr 1886 Butler Co., KY. She m. Harrison Abner (#268 on page 95), son of Isaac Newton Abney and Sylvia Embry. She and Harrison Abner appeared on the census of 1 May 1940 Butler Co., KY. She d.27 Jul 1958 Bowling Green, Warren Co., KY, at age 72 and was bur. Mount Vernon Cem., Dexterville, Butler Co., KY.
   Harrison Abner, b.10 Jul 1887. He d.13 Oct 1959 at age 72 and was bur. Mount Vernon Cem., Dexterville, Butler Co., KY.
Known children of Louella F.[7] Flener and Harrison Abner:
      i.   Erdie Lee[8], b. 4 Feb 1925; m. Cpl. Paul John Stopka (USAAF-WWII). (see page 95)
     ii. Orvel, b. 11 Jul 1909. (see page 95)
     iii. Ora V., b. 22 Sep 1910; m. James Doolin"Jim" Evans Sr. (see # 567 below and page 149).
     iv. Senora, b. 29 Jun 1912; m. Obie Coots. (see # 568 on page 149).
      v. Louie, b. 26 May 1914 Butler Co., KY; m. Carl Evans. (see # 569 on page 149).
     vi. Lester C., b. 16 May 1915; m. Elsie (n.n.). (see # 570 on page 149).
    vii. Eulalia, b. 2 Sep 1916; m. Waller D. Spencer. (see page 95)
   viii. Lester B., b. 3 Oct 1919; m. Bonnie L. (n.n.). (see page 95)
     ix. Verline T., b. 31 May 1921 Butler Co., KY; m. Roy Lee Hudson. (see # 571 on page 149).
      x. Carolyn Faye, b. 8 Nov 1945 Butler Co., KY; m. Bobby D. Kelley. (see page 95)

564. Perry Hines[7] Flener (Lucinda[6] Deweese, Nicey[5] Abney, Paul[4], Joshua[3], Elisha[2], Abner[1]), b.22 Dec 1887 Flener, Butler Co., KY. He m. Hallie B. Howard, daughter of James "Monroe" Howard and Paulina E. Embry, on 28 Aug 1925 Butler Co., KY. He and Hallie appeared on the census of 1 May 1940 Butler Co., KY. He d.25 Oct 1961 Louisville, Jefferson Co., KY, at age 73; bur. Mount Vernon Cem., Dexterville, Butler Co., KY.
   Hallie B. Howard, b.16 Nov 1899 Butler Co., KY. She m. Elza Daugherty on 22 Sep 1922 Butler Co., KY. She d.17 Feb 1955 Flener, Butler Co., KY, at age 55 and was bur. Mount Vernon Cem., Dexterville, Butler Co., KY.
Known children of Perry Hines[7] Flener and Hallie B. Howard:
985   i.   Osburn Ray[8], b. 14 Jul 1926 Flener, Butler Co., KY; m. Kathryn Jane "Janie" Hill; m. Bettie Day Smith.
     ii. Ivan, b. ca.1934 Butler Co., KY.
     iii. Erlene, b. ca.1938 Butler Co., KY.

565. Dexter[7] De Weese (Elijah[6], Nicey[5] Abney, Paul[4], Joshua[3], Elisha[2], Abner[1]) m. Emma Klumple. He, b.1899 KY. He d.5 Jan 1960 Grand Haven, Ottawa Co., MI and was bur. Lake Forest Cem., Grand Haven, Ottawa Co., MI.
   Emma Klumple, b.5 Apr 1900 Grand Haven, Ottawa Co., MI. She d.10 May 1978 Grand Haven, Ottawa Co., MI, at age 78; Lake Forest Cem.
Known child of Dexter[7] De Weese and Emma Klumple:
      i.   Robert Dexter[8], b.13 Dec 1927 Spring Lake, Ottawa Co., MI. He d.7 Oct 1997 Muskegon, Muskegon Co., MI, at age 69 and was bur. Lake Forest Cem., Grand Haven, Ottawa Co., MI.

566. May[7] Evans (Armedia[6] Daugherty, Hannah[5] Abney, Paul[4], Joshua[3], Elisha[2], Abner[1]), b.19 May 1894 Willow Springs, Howell Co., MO. She m1. William Conn on 31 Jul 1910 Okemah, Okfuskee Co., OK. She m2. Wallice Downes on 8 Jul 1916 Okemah, Okfuskee Co., OK. She m3. Alvin Monroe Whitehead on 8 Jun 1918 Okemah, Okfuskee Co., OK. She m4. William McKinley on 14 Dec 1940 Okemah, Okfuskee Co., OK. She d.19 Aug 1946 Norman, Cleveland Co., OK, at age 52 and was bur. IOFF Mem. Gardens Cem., Norman, Cleveland Co., OK.
Known child of May[7] Evans and William Conn:
986   i.   Pearl[8], b. 6 Jan 1912 Okemah, Okfuskee Co., OK; m. William Marshall "Bill" Jones (USArmy-WWII).
There were no known children of May[7] Evans and Wallice Downes.
There were no known children of May[7] Evans and Alvin Monroe Whitehead.
There were no known children of May[7] Evans and William McKinley.

567. Ora V.[7] Abner (Harrison[6], Isaac[5] Abney, Paul[4], Joshua[3], Elisha[2], Abner[1]), b.22 Sep 1910. She m. James Doolin"Jim" Evans Sr., son of Ancil Evans and Mary Frances Legrand, on 2 Sep 1927. She d.19 Apr 1996 at age 85 and was bur. Mount Vernon Cem., Dexterville, Butler Co., KY.
   James Doolin"Jim" Evans Sr, b.5 Nov 1907 Butler Co., KY. He d.17 Sep 1978 Bowling Green, Warren Co., KY, at age 70; bur. Mount Vernon Cem., Dexterville, Butler Co., KY.

Known children of Ora V.[7] Abner and James Doolin"Jim" Evans Sr.:

    i.   James D.[8], b.12 Jul 1929 Butler Co., KY. He d.21 May 1949 Wooster, Wayne Co., OH, at age 19 and was bur. Mount Vernon Cem., Dexterville, Butler Co., KY.

    ii.   Forest C, b.18 Mar 1931 Butler Co., KY. He m. Linda D. (n.n.) on 5 Nov 1958. He d.20 Apr 2002 Beaver Dam, Ohio Co., KY, at age 71 and was bur. Sunnyside Cem., Beaver Dam, Ohio Co., KY.

             Linda D. (n.n.), b.16 Dec 1938.

    iii.   Elmer Ray, b.4 Apr 1933 Flener, Butler Co., KY. He m. Phyllis Jean Abney, daughter of Carlos E. Abney (USN-WWII) and Opal M. Frizzell, on 23 Feb 1953. He d.11 Dec 2003 Beaver Dam, Ohio Co., KY, at age 70 and was bur. Sunnyside Cem., Beaver Dam, Ohio Co., KY.

             Phyllis Jean Abney, b.25 May 1936 Bowling Green, Warren Co., KY. She d.1 Feb 2016 Ohio Co., KY, at age 79 and was bur. Sunnyside Cem., Beaver Dam, Ohio Co., KY.

    iv.   Emeline, b.14 Jan 1939 Butler Co., KY. She m. Odie B. Embry, son of Owen Embry and Nova Duke. She d.14 Oct 2019 Morgantown, Butler Co., KY, at age 80 and was bur. Isiah Evans Cem., Morgantown, Butler Co., KY.

             Odie B. Embry, b.4 Apr 1927. He d.21 Mar 1998 at age 70; bur. Isiah Evans Cem., Morgantown, Butler Co., KY.

568. Senora[7] Abner (Harrison[6], Isaac[5] Abney, Paul[4], Joshua[3], Elisha[2], Abner[1]), b.29 Jun 1912. She m. Obie Coots, son of Esker Coots and Cordelia Henderson, on 19 Apr 1929. She d.22 Apr 1991 at age 78 and was bur. Mount Vernon Cem., Dexterville, Butler Co., KY.

    Obie Coots, b.3 Aug 1906. He d.11 Sep 1989 at age 83.

Known children of Senora[7] Abner and Obie Coots:

    i.   Glenwood[8], b.11 Apr 1930 Butler Co., KY. He d.12 Apr 1930 Butler Co., KY and was bur. Mount Vernon Cem., Dexterville, Butler Co., KY.

  987   ii.   Earl C, b. 2 Apr 1932; m. Stefanie E. Oszek.

    iii.   Alma, b.24 Feb 1937. She d.27 Feb 1937 and was bur. Mount Vernon Cem., Dexterville, Butler Co., KY.

    iv.   Herman Ray, b.11 Nov 1941 Butler Co., KY. He d.29 Nov 2009 Morgantown, Butler Co., KY, at age 68 and was bur. Aberdeen Baptist Church Cem., Morgantown, Butler Co., KY.

569. Louie[7] Abner (Harrison[6], Isaac[5] Abney, Paul[4], Joshua[3], Elisha[2], Abner[1]), b.26 May 1914 Butler Co., KY. She m. Carl Evans on 10 Nov 1932 KY. She and Carl Evans appeared on the census of 1 May 1940 Butler Co., KY. She d.27 Nov 1998 Butler Co., KY, at age 84 and was bur. Isiah Evans Cem., Morgantown, Butler Co., KY.

    Carl Evans, b.25 Jul 1909 Butler Co., KY. He d.16 Jun 1960 Butler Co., KY, at age 50.

Known children of Louie[7] Abner and Carl Evans all b. Butler Co., KY:

    i.   Deyoide A.[8] m. Novella (n.n.). He, b. ca.1935.

  988   ii.   Kathleen Mae, b. 16 Jun 1937.

    iii.   Irene G., b.1939. She m. (n.n.) Givens.

  989   iv.   Deloide C., b. 28 Nov 1942; m. Linda Sue (n.n.).

    v.   J.C.

570. Lester C.[7] Abner (Harrison[6], Isaac[5] Abney, Paul[4], Joshua[3], Elisha[2], Abner[1]), b.16 May 1915. He m. Elsie (n.n.) on 23 Jun 1934. He d.23 Aug 1993 at age 78 and was bur. Fisher Cem., Heidrick, Knox Co., KY.

    Elsie (n.n.), b.New Year's Eve, 31 Dec 1915. She d.9 Feb 1996 at age 80 and was bur. Fisher Cem., Heidrick, Knox Co., KY.

Known children of Lester C.[7] Abner and Elsie (n.n.):

    i.   David Smallwood[8] m. Karen (n.n.).

    ii.   Doyle m. Patty (n.n.).

    iii.   Dean m. Kim (n.n.).

    iv.   Donna m. Charles Calloway.

    v.   Carol m. (n.n.) Bright.

    vi.   Beverly m. (n.n.) Lamb.

  990   vii.   Joan, b. 3 Dec 1940; m. Clarence Johnson.

571. Verline T.[7] Abner (Harrison[6], Isaac[5] Abney, Paul[4], Joshua[3], Elisha[2], Abner[1]), b.31 May 1921 Butler Co., KY. She m. Roy Lee Hudson. She d.6 Feb 2015 Regis Woods Nursing Home, Louisville, Jefferson Co., KY, at age 93; bur. Mount Vernon Cem., Dexterville, Butler Co., KY.

    Roy Lee Hudson, b.15 Jul 1921 Ohio Co., KY. He d.4 Oct 1996 Louisville, Jefferson Co., KY, at age 75.

Known child of Verline T.[7] Abner and Roy Lee Hudson:

    i.   Janice Lee[8], b.4 Sep 1942. She d.5 Jun 1943 and was bur. Mount Vernon Cem., Dexterville, Butler Co., KY.

572. Flora Inez[7] Goff (Rena[6] Abner, Silas[5] Abney, Paul[4], Joshua[3], Elisha[2], Abner[1]), b.12 Mar 1892 Butler Co., KY. She was liv. on 8 Jun 1900 with grandmother, Clesta Abner, Livermore, McLean Co., KY. She m. Counce Turner on 19 Dec 1906 Hartford, Ohio Co., KY. She d.16 Aug 1975 Indianapolis, Marion Co., IN, at age 83 and was bur. Fairview Cem., Linton, Greene Co., IN.

    Counce Turner, b.10 Jan 1884. He d.1946 and was bur. Fairview Cem., Linton, Greene Co., IN.

Known children of Flora Inez[7] Goff and Counce Turner:

    i.   Elva A.[8], b. ca.1908.

    ii.   Leon, b. ca.1910.

  991   iii.   Arthur, b. 12 Aug 1912 Ohio Co., KY; m. Juanita (n.n.).

573. Aubrey[7] Loyd (Rena[6] Abner, Silas[5] Abney, Paul[4], Joshua[3], Elisha[2], Abner[1]), b.30 Jan 1906 Ohio Co., KY. He m. Catherine Anastasia Marian Soeder, daughter of Albert Herman Kleier and Augusta Soeder, on 26 Jun 1930. He d.24 Jun 1994 Louisville, Jefferson Co., KY, at age 88 and was bur. Resthaven Mem. Cem., Louisville, Jefferson Co., KY.

    Catherine Anastasia Marian Soeder, b.19 May 1911 Louisville, Jefferson Co., KY. She d.11 Feb 2005 Louisville, Jefferson Co., KY, age 93.

Known child of Aubrey[7] Loyd and Catherine Anastasia Marian Soeder:

  992   i.   Mark A.[8], m. Margaret (N.N.).

574. Ray[7] Loyd (Rena[6] Abner, Silas[5] Abney, Paul[4], Joshua[3], Elisha[2], Abner[1]), b.5 Feb 1917 McHenry, Ohio Co., KY. He m. Gertrude "Alene" Gilpin. He d.New Year's Day, 1 Jan 1999 Louisville, Jefferson Co., KY, at age 81.

    Gertrude "Alene" Gilpin, b.21 Dec 1922 Jefferson Co., KY. She d.23 Feb 2013 Jefferson Co., KY, at age 90.
Known children of Ray[7] Loyd and Gertrude "Alene" Gilpin:
                    i.   Patricia "Pat"[8] m. Jim Carman.
        993   ii.   Sharon, b. 12 Jun 1946 Louisville, Jefferson Co., KY; m. Terry Jennette.

575. Carl "Carlie"[7] Abner (Homer[6], Silas[5] Abney, Paul[4], Joshua[3], Elisha[2], Abner[1]), b.11 Jun 1906. He m. Nellie Irene Barrett in 1928. He d.17 May 1970 at age 63 and was bur. Waltons Creek Church Cem., Centertown, Ohio Co., KY.

    Nellie Irene Barrett, b.19 Oct 1909. She d.30 Mar 1995 at age 85 and was bur. Waltons Creek Church Cem., Centertown, Ohio Co., KY.
Known children of Carl "Carlie"[7] Abner and Nellie Irene Barrett:
                    i.   Zola[8], b.10 Sep 1929 Centertown, Ohio Co., KY. She m. Harrison Douglas Willcutts Jr. on 15 Oct 1953. She d.10 Nov 2012 Loveland, Larimer Co., CO, at age 83.
                          Harrison Douglas Willcutts Jr, b.1923. He d.1967.

576. Oakie Pearl[7] Abner (Homer[6], Silas[5] Abney, Paul[4], Joshua[3], Elisha[2], Abner[1]), b.20 Apr 1909. She m. Robert Elson Hoskins, son of Herman Hoskins and Louisa Ellen Barrett, on 20 Apr 1932. She d.11 May 1988 at age 79 and was bur. Centertown Cem., Centertown, Ohio Co., KY.

    Robert Elson Hoskins, b.29 Dec 1906 Ohio Co., KY. He d.8 Aug 2002 Centertown, Ohio Co., KY, at age 95 and was bur. Centertown Cem.
Known children of Oakie Pearl[7] Abner and Robert Elson Hoskins:
                    i.   Raymon[8], b. and d. 14 Apr 1933 Ohio Co., KY and was bur. Waltons Creek Church Cem., Centertown, Ohio Co., KY.
        994   ii.   Thomas T. "Tom," b. 29 Apr 1940 Ohio Co., KY; m. Jonell Osborne; m. Arlene (n.n.).
                  iii.   Reathel "Melvin", b.29 Aug 1945. He m. Sheryl O'Connell, daughter of Boyde O'Connell, on 5 Mar 1966. He d.24 Feb 2009 at age 63 and was bur. Centertown Cem., Centertown, Ohio Co., KY.
                          Cheryl O'Connell, b.13 May 1947 IL. She d.29 Dec 2009 at age 62 and was bur. Centertown Cem., Centertown.

577. Charlie[7] Abner (Homer[6], Silas[5] Abney, Paul[4], Joshua[3], Elisha[2], Abner[1]), b.17 Feb 1913 Ohio Co., KY. He m. Cornelia B. Doyal on 19 Oct 1935. He and Cornelia B. Doyal appeared on the census of 13 Apr 1940 Centertown, Ohio Co., KY. He d.6 Nov 1989 Centertown, Ohio Co., KY, at age 76 and was bur. Waltons Creek Church Cem., Centertown, Ohio Co., KY.

    Cornelia B. Doyal, b.24 Feb 1918. She d.19 Dec 1997 at age 79 and was bur. Waltons Creek Church Cem., Centertown, Ohio Co., KY.
Known children of Charlie[7] Abner and Cornelia B. Doyal both b. Centertown, Ohio Co., KY:
                    i.   Samuel D.[8], b.27 Jul 1936. He d.7 Jul 2009 Ohio Co., KY, at age 72 and was bur. Waltons Creek Church Cem.
                  ii.   Mary A., b. ca.Mar 1940.

578. Tom[7] Abner (Homer[6], Silas[5] Abney, Paul[4], Joshua[3], Elisha[2], Abner[1]), b.5 Nov 1914 Butler, Pendleton Co., KY. He m. Lois "Lee" Smith, daughter of James Smith and Roseanna Phillips, ca.1945. He d.Jun 1986 Lake Co., IN, at age 71 and was bur. Memory Lane Mem. Cem., Schererville, Lake Co., IN.

    Lois "Lee" Smith, b.23 Mar 1924 Centertown, Ohio Co., KY. She d.4 Apr 2019 at age 95.
Known child of Tom[7] Abner and Lois "Lee" Smith:
        995   i.   Michael L.[8], m. Tina Miller.

579. Hubert B.[7] Abner (Homer[6], Silas[5] Abney, Paul[4], Joshua[3], Elisha[2], Abner[1]), b.20 Apr 1917 Butler Co., KY. He m. Stella J. Sheffield, d/o Wm. L. Sheffield and Naomi Hoover. He d.28 Aug 1995 Valparaiso, Porter Co., IN, age 78; bur. Graceland Mem. Park, Valparaiso, Porter Co., IN.

    Stella J. Sheffield, b.5 Jan 1922 Ohio Co., KY. She d.4 Aug 1982 Hobart, Lake Co., IN, at age 60 and was bur. Graceland Mem. Park.
Known child of Hubert B.[7] Abner and Stella J. Sheffield:
                    i.   Bobby R.[8]

580. Sally "Sadie"[7] Abner (George[6], Silas[5] Abney, Paul[4], Joshua[3], Elisha[2], Abner[1]), b.6 Mar 1914 Morgan Co., AL. She m. James Elsworth Sowers in 1934. She d.4 Sep 1994 Morgan Co., AL, at age 80 and was bur. New Friendship Baptist Church Cem., Somerville, Morgan Co., AL.

    James Elsworth Sowers, b.4 Jun 1915. He d.21 Oct 1978 at age 63 and was bur. Bellview Baptist Church Cem., Decatur, Morgan Co., AL.
Known child of Sally "Sadie"[7] Abner and James Elsworth Sowers:
        996   i.   Minnie Lou[8], b. 15 Sep 1935 AL; m. William Henry "Junior" Reeves Jr.

581. Newt[7] Abner Sr. (George[6], Silas[5] Abney, Paul[4], Joshua[3], Elisha[2], Abner[1]), b.16 Apr 1916 TN. He m. Audie Macie Dunaway, daughter of Samuel Marion Dunaway and Elnora E. Grantland, ca.1940. He d.17 Jan 1998 Sparta, Kent Co., MI, at age 81 and was bur. New Friendship Baptist Church Cem., Somerville, Morgan Co., AL.

    Audie Macie Dunaway, b.28 Sep 1900. She m1. James Hubert Taylor on 3 Feb 1919 Morgan Co., AL. They were divorced. She d. New Year's Eve, 31 Dec 1979 at age 79.
Known children of Newt[7] Abner Sr. and Audie Macie Dunaway:
                    i.   Macie Earle[8], b.4 Jan 1941.
        997   ii.   Newt, b. 6 Mar 1943 Somerville, Morgan Co., AL; m. Carol (n.n.).
                  iii.   Patsy Carol "Pat", b.17 Jun 1947 Somerville, Morgan Co., AL. She d.24 May 2007 Ruleville, Sunflower Co., MS, at age 59 and was bur. New Friendship Baptist Church Cem., Somerville, Morgan Co., AL.

582. Bertha Lee "Berthie"[7] Abner (George[6], Silas[5] Abney, Paul[4], Joshua[3], Elisha[2], Abner[1]), b.19 Jan 1919 Priceville, Morgan Co., AL. She m. Claude Aleen Davis, son of John William Davis and Martha K. Bradford, in 1935. She d.6 May 1997 Brandon, Hillsborough Co., FL, at age 78 and was bur. Holly Hill Mem. Park, Middleburg, Clay Co., FL.
Bertha Lee "Berthie"[7] Abner and Claude Aleen Davis had 15 children:
six were stillborn: four boys and two girls; Nine were born alive: Clyde Jr., John Allen, Margie "Marie" [1941-1983; m. (n.n.) Mullen], Tommy, Jerry Truman, James Donald, Faye [m. (n.n.) Capell], Geraldine [m. (n.n.) Yarborough] and Rose Lee [m. (n.n.) Townsell].

583. Arrie[7] Abner (George[6], Silas[5] Abney, Paul[4], Joshua[3], Elisha[2], Abner[1]), b.10 Nov 1921 Morgan Co., AL. He m. Lois "Myrtle" Murphree. He d.17 Sep 1989 at age 67 and was bur. New Friendship Baptist Church Cem., Somerville, Morgan Co., AL.
Known children of Arrie[7] Abner and Lois "Myrtle" Murphree:

	i.	Joan[8] d..
	ii.	Bobby Lee.
998	iii.	Rayburn A., b. 30 Sep 1947 Blount Co., AL; m. Willodean "Monk" (n.n.).
999	iv.	Loyd George, b. 11 Aug 1951 Blount Co., AL; m. (n.n.).
1000	v.	Ellen Irene, b. 21 Jun 1953 Lawrence Co., AL; m. Bill "Billy Joe" Key.
1001	vi.	Mary, b. 17 Jul 1954 Blount Co., AL; m. Perry Lucas.
	vii.	Dwight Thomas.

584. Clistie[7] Abner (George[6], Silas[5] Abney, Paul[4], Joshua[3], Elisha[2], Abner[1]), b.4 Apr 1922 Priceville, Morgan Co., AL. She m. PFC Carl Thomas Bradley (USArmy-WWI, Korea) and was bur. New Friendship Bapt. Church Cem., Somerville, Morgan Co., AL. She d.7 Oct 1993 Huntsville, Madison Co., AL, at age 71.
    PFC Carl Thomas Bradley (USArmy-WWI, Korea), b.27 Oct 1921 Lawrence Co., AL. He d.29 Dec 1986 Birmingham, Jefferson Co., AL, at age 65 and was bur. New Friendship Bapt. Church Cem., Somerville, Morgan Co., AL.
Known children of Clistie[7] Abner and PFC Carl Thomas Bradley (USArmy-WWI, Korea):

	i.	Carl Thomas[8].
	ii.	James "Lee."
	iii.	Ricky L.
	iv.	Charles Russell "Charlie."
	v.	Virginia Gayle.
	vi.	Kathy Ann m. (n.n.) Spry.
	vii.	Teresa Ann m. (n.n.) Bates.
1002	viii.	Katie Mae, b. 9 Oct 1943 Morgan Co., AL; m. Kenneth M. Cockrell.

585. Hobert P.[7] Abner (George[6], Silas[5] Abney, Paul[4], Joshua[3], Elisha[2], Abner[1]), b.15 Feb 1925 Morgan Co., AL. He m1. Flora Elizabeth Anders. He m2. Carol (n.n.). He d.15 Jan 1983 Falkville, Morgan Co., AL, age 57; bur. New Friendship Bapt. Church Cem., Somerville, Morgan Co., AL.
Known children of Hobert P.[7] Abner and Flora Elizabeth Anders:

	i.	Dennis[8].
	ii.	Jimmy.
	iii.	Lowell.
1003	iv.	Joyce Marie, b. 24 Jan 1956; m. Leman "O'Neal" Osborn.

    Carol (n.n.), b.3 Jan 1945.
There were no known children of Hobert P.[7] Abner and Carol (n.n.).

586. James "Owen"[7] Abner Sr. (George[6], Silas[5] Abney, Paul[4], Joshua[3], Elisha[2], Abner[1]), b.30 Jun 1929 Morgan Co., AL. He d.17 Mar 1981 Dundee, Polk Co., FL, at age 51 and was bur. Mount Tabor Cem., Hartselle, Morgan Co., AL.
Known child of James "Owen"[7] Abner Sr.:

	i.	James Owen[8].

587. Maudie[7] Abner (George[6], Silas[5] Abney, Paul[4], Joshua[3], Elisha[2], Abner[1]), b.12 Sep 1932 Morgan Co., AL. She m. James Olan Reeves (USArmy-WWII), son of William Henry Reeves and Willie Lee Segars, in Nov 1946 Morgan Co., AL. She d.30 Sep 1997 Moulton, Lawrence Co., AL, at age 65 and was bur. Johnson Chapel UMC Cem., Danville, Morgan Co., AL.
    James Olan Reeves (USArmy-WWII), b.31 Oct 1921 Hartselle, Morgan Co., AL. He d.5 Feb 1980 Decatur, Morgan Co., AL, at age 58.
Known children of Maudie[7] Abner and James Olan Reeves (USArmy-WWII):

	i.	Gloria[8] m. (n.n.) Cockrell.
	ii.	Jacqueline m. (n.n.) Bates.
	iii.	Janice.
	iv.	Tina.
	v.	Melissa.
	vi.	Betty m. (n.n.) Proctor.
	vii.	Peggy m. (n.n.) Smith.
	viii.	James M.
	ix.	Ronnie.
	x.	Bart.
	xi.	Terry Lynn "Beaver", b.8 Mar 1959 Morgan Co., AL. He d.15 May 1993 Morgan Co., AL, at age 34 and was bur. Johnson Chapel UMC Cem., Danville, Morgan Co., AL.

588. Henry Dale[7] Abner (William[6], Louis[5], William[4] Abney, Joshua[3], Elisha[2], Abner[1]), b.3 May 1928. He m. Ruby Faye Moore, daughter of Charles Moore and Ella (n.n.), in 1946. He d. New Year's Day, 1 Jan 2002 Sedgwick Co., KS, at age 73 and was bur. Resthaven Gardens of Memory, Wichita, Sedgwick Co., KS.
    Ruby Faye Moore, b.16 Nov 1927 Slant, Scott Co., VA. She d.11 Sep 2005 Valley Center, Sedgwick Co., KS, at age 77 and was bur. Resthaven Gardens of Memory, Wichita, Sedgwick Co., KS.
Known children of Henry Dale[7] Abner and Ruby Faye Moore:

	i.	Louise[8], b.10 Jul 1930. She m. Roy L. Howe on 26 Aug 1951. She d. Independence Day, 4 Jul 1991 at age 60 and was bur. Pleasant Ridge Cem., Goddard, Sedgwick Co., KS.
		Roy L. Howe, b.30 Oct 1928.

589. Estalena[7] Dearmore (Mary[6] Abner, Louis[5], William[4] Abney, Joshua[3], Elisha[2], Abner[1]) m. Robert Megee. , b.2 Sep 1929 Gassville, Baxter Co., AR. She d.30 Dec 1994 Burlington, Racine Co., WI, at age 65 and was bur. Chapel Hill Gardens West, Oakbrook Terrace, DuPage Co., IL.
Known children of Estalena[7] Dearmore and Robert Megee:
      i.   Stacey[8] m. (n.n.) Carlson.
      ii. Laura m. Bill Giegenbaum.

590. Ida Irene[7] Wills (Elizabeth[6] Abney, Wilburn[5], Benjamin[4], Hezekiah[3], Elisha[2], Abner[1]), b.2 Oct 1872 Paulding Co., GA. She m. Anselm Abel Ashcraft in 1888. She d.13 Nov 1955 DeLand, Volusia Co., FL, at age 83 and was bur. Methodist Cem., Pierson, Volusia Co., FL.
    Anselm Abel Ashcraft, b.29 Mar 1859 Randolph Co., AL. He d.24 Feb 1959 Volusia Co., FL, at age 99 and was bur. Methodist Cem., Pierson.
Known children of Ida Irene[7] Wills and Anselm Abel Ashcraft:
      i.   Esther[8], b.21 Aug 1891 Coosa Co., AL. She m. (n.n.) Gaston. d.28 Apr 1966 De Leon Springs, Volusia Co., FL, at age 74 and was bur. Methodist Cem., Pierson, Volusia Co., FL.
      ii. Anselm Jackson (USArmy-WWI), b.16 Sep 1894 Coosa Co., AL. He d.17 Dec 1917 Base Hospital, France, at age 23 and was bur. Mount Olive Cem., Mount Olive, Coosa Co., AL.
      iii. Minnie Elizabeth, b.30 Sep 1896 Whitesboro, Grayson Co., TX. She m. Oscar Jerome Camp. d.30 Jun 1967 DeLand, Volusia Co., FL, at age 70 and was bur. Methodist Cem., Pierson, Volusia Co., FL.
             Oscar Jerome Camp, b.5 Jan 1894 AL. He d. New Year's Eve, 31 Jan 1981 Gainsville, Alachua Co., FL, at age 87.
      iv. Ada Amanda, b.21 Jan 1900 Hanover, Coosa Co., AL. She m. Andrew Emanuel "Andy" Anderson. d.1 Feb 1995 Tallahassee, Leon Co., FL, at age 95 and was bur. Methodist Cem., Pierson, Volusia Co., FL.
             Andrew Emanuel "Andy" Anderson, b.28 Mar 1894 Weston, Fairfield Co., CT. He d. Christmas Day, 25 Dec 1956 Palatka, Putnam Co., FL, at age 62.
      v. Oscar Simpson, b.11 Aug 1902 Hanover, Coosa Co., AL. He d.12 Apr 1960 Jacksonville, Duval Co., FL, at age 57 and was bur. Jacksonville Memory Gardens, Orange Park, Clay Co., FL.
      vi. John Washington, b.12 Dec 1904 Coosa Co., AL. He m. Lessie "Dixie" Ladora. He d.3 Jun 1996 Jacksonville, Duval Co., FL, at age 91 and was bur. Valhalla Cem., Midfield, Jefferson Co., AL.
             Lessie "Dixie" Ladora, b.8 Sep 1904. She d.13 Feb 1983 at age 78 and was bur. Valhalla Cem., Midfield.
      vii. Lula "Marion", b.14 Dec 1906 Mount Olive, Coosa Co., AL. She m1. Stanley Carl Adolph Swanson in 1923. She m2. Pvt. Paul Bertel Anderson (USArmy-WWII). She d. New Year's Day, 1 Jan 1996 Melbourne, Brevard Co., FL, at age 89 and was bur. Methodist Cem., Pierson, Volusia Co., FL.
             Stanley Carl Adolph Swanson, b.18 Dec 1890 Galesburg, Knox Co., IL. He d.15 Dec 1972 Seminole Co., FL, at age 81 and was bur. Ebenezer Lutheran Cem., Pierson, Volusia Co., FL.
             Pvt. Paul Bertel Anderson (USArmy-WWII), b.8 Feb 1909. He d.14 Aug 1977 Lakeland, Polk Co., FL, at age 68 and was bur. Methodist Cem., Pierson, Volusia Co., FL.
      viii. Ida "Irene", b.26 Nov 1908 Mount Olive, Coosa Co., AL. She m. William H. "Bill" Fowler (USArmy-WWII) in 1937. She d.23 Jul 1997 Melbourne, Brevard Co., FL, at age 88; bur. Florida Mem. Gardens, Rockledge, Brevard Co., FL.
             William H. "Bill" Fowler (USArmy-WWII), b.18 Sep 1909 Sunnyside, Jefferson Co., AL. He d.1 Feb 1979 Melbourne, Brevard Co., FL, at age 69 and was bur. Florida Mem. Gardens, Rockledge, Brevard Co., FL.
      ix. Mary Dorthula, b.3 Dec 1911 Mount Olive, Coosa Co., AL. She m. Doyle Nathaniel Rouse. d.30 Sep 2006 Clay Co., AL, at age 94 and was bur. Methodist Cem., Pierson, Volusia Co., FL.
             Doyle Nathaniel Rouse, b.24 Jun 1909 Polk Co., FL. He d.10 Sep 1995 Birmingham, Jefferson Co., AL, at age 86 and was bur. Methodist Cem., Pierson, Volusia Co., AL.
      x. Susan "Arline", b.4 Oct 1914 Coosa Co., AL; m. (n.n.) Hughes; d.13 Jun 1999 Naples, Collier Co., FL, age 84. (cremated).

591. Etta[7] Wills (Elizabeth[6] Abney, Wilburn[5], Benjamin[4], Hezekiah[3], Elisha[2], Abner[1]), b.29 Oct 1874. She m. William M. Brock. She d.10 Apr 1904 at age 29 and was bur. Pleasant Valley Bapt. Ch. Cem. #2, Leonard, Cherokee Co., AL.
    William M. Brock, b.1871. He m. Alice L. (n.n.). He d.1934 and was bur. Pleasant Valley Bapt. Ch. Cem. #2, Leonard, Cherokee Co., AL.
Known children of Etta[7] Wills and William M. Brock:
      i.   Eva[8], b.5 Feb 1899. She m. Eugene Hobson Smith. d.4 Jun 1970 at age 71 and was bur. Pleasant Valley Bapt. Ch. Cem. #2, Leonard, Cherokee Co., AL.
             Eugene Hobson Smith, b.1 Jun 1898; d.19 Jun 1964 Cherokee Co., AL, ae 66; bur. Pleasant Valley Bapt.Ch.Cem. #2.

592. Minnie M.[7] Wills (Elizabeth[6] Abney, Wilburn[5], Benjamin[4], Hezekiah[3], Elisha[2], Abner[1]), b.8 Sep 1877. She m. Robert Edward Downs ca.1893. She d.15 Jan 1939 Gadsden, Etowah Co., AL, at age 61 and was bur. Forrest Cem., Gadsden, Etowah Co., AL.
    Robert Edward Downs, b.1 Mar 1870 Etowah Co., AL. He m2. Georgia Maddox. He d.26 Jan 1958 Gadsden, Etowah Co., AL, at age 87 and was bur. Forrest Cem., Gadsden, Etowah Co., AL.
Known children of Minnie M.[7] Wills and Robert Edward Downs:
 1004   i.   Alma Ruth[8], b. 11 Feb 1894 AL; m. Lester M. Calhoun.
       ii. Esther Ellen, b.10 Sep 1899 AL. She m. Joseph William Jones in 1922. She d.13 Mar 1987 Gadsden, Etowah Co., AL, at age 87 and was bur. Forrest Cem., Gadsden, Etowah Co., AL.
             Joseph William Jones, b.23 Nov 1882. He m. Nora Mary Jones in 1898; d.3 Oct 1972 AL age 89; bur. Forrest Cem.
 1005 iii. Naomi Elizabeth, b. 18 Mar 1903 AL; m. Leonard William Short Sr.
 1006 iv. Gresham Gerald, b. 29 Jul 1906 AL; m. Lillian Omega; m. Ruby Luceil Perrine.
 1007 v. Kermit Roosevelt, b. 23 Jul 1912 AL; m. Lillian McClendon.
       vi. Lorene, b.26 Sep 1914 AL. She d.25 Oct 1946 Gadsden, Etowah Co., AL, at age 32 and was bur. Forrest Cem., Gadsden.
       vii. Ione Marie, b.20 Jun 1918. She m. James William Chitwood Sr. She m. Marvin Eugene Stephens. She d.1 Sep 1999 at age 81 and was bur. Crestwood Mem. Cem., East Gadsden, Etowah Co., AL.
             James William Chitwood Sr, b.21 Sep 1910. He d.29 Mar 1964 at age 53 and was bur. Crestwood Mem. Cem., East Gadsden, Etowah Co., AL.
             Marvin Eugene Stephens, b.15 Aug 1900. He d.20 Feb 1984 at age 83 and was bur. Crestwood Mem. Cem., East Gadsden, Etowah Co., L.

593. John Calloway "Uncle John"[7] Abney (Washington[6], Wilburn[5], Benjamin[4], Hezekiah[3], Elisha[2], Abner[1]) He, b.22 Aug 1881 West Armuchee, Walker Co., GA. He was known to everyone as "Uncle John". He m. Grace V. Mize, daughter of Calvin Augustus "Callaway" Mize and Harriette "Elizabeth" Mize. He was liv. on 16 Apr 1930 with sister, Myrtis Edge, LaFayette, Walker Co., GA. He and Grace V. Mize lived in 1935 Walker Co., GA. He and Grace V. Mize appeared on the census of 10 Apr 1940 Summerville, Chattooga Co., GA. He d.15 Nov 1969 GA at age 88 and was bur. LaFayette Cem., LaFayette, Walker Co., GA.

Grace V. Mize, b.26 Jul 1890 GA. She was liv. on 4 Apr 1930 with her father, Augustus Mize, Rome, Floyd Co., GA. She d.25 Feb 1970 at age 79 and was bur. LaFayette Cem., LaFayette, Walker Co., GA.
Known child of John Calloway[7] Abney and Grace V. Mize:
      1008   i.   James Dwight[8], b. 11 May 1916 GA; m. Ella "Elizabeth" King.

594. Grover Cleveland[7] Abney Sr. (Washington[6], Wilburn[5], Benjamin[4], Hezekiah[3], Elisha[2], Abner[1]), b.3 Jul 1885 West Amurchee, Walker Co., GA. He m. Lillian "Lillie" Black on 22 Dec 1910. He and Lillian "Lillie" Black appeared on the censuses of 8 Jan 1920, 2 Apr 1930 and 16 Apr 1940 Ringgold, Catoosa Co., GA. He d.10 Jun 1947 at age 61 and was bur. Nathan Anderson Historic Cem., Ringgold, Catoosa Co., GA.

Lillian "Lillie" Black, b.29 Nov 1892. She d.3 Sep 1981 at age 88 and was bur. Nathan Anderson Historic Cem., Ringgold, Catoosa Co., GA.
Known children of Grover Cleveland[7] Abney Sr. and Lillian "Lillie" Black:
      1009   i.   Raymond Lee[8], b. 27 Dec 1911; m. Martha Louise Elrod.
            ii.   Alton "Woodrow", b.14 Aug 1914 LaFayette, Walker Co., GA. He d.30 Dec 2001 GA at age 87.
      1010 iii.   Grover "Watson," b. 27 Apr 1917 GA; m. Wilma Davis.
      1011 iv.   James Howard, b. 28 Sep 1919 GA; m. Bertie Catherine Cowart.
      1012   v.   Grover Cleveland, b. 15 Oct 1924 GA; m. Anita Greene.
      1013 vi.   Marshall Edwin, b. 20 Aug 1927 GA; m. Vivian A. Beaver.
          vii.   Jesse A., b.23 Nov 1930 GA. He m. Shirley O. (n.n.) in 1955. He d.14 Oct 1991 at age 60 and was bur. Nathan Anderson Historic Cem., Ringgold, Catoosa Co., GA.
                    Shirley O. (n.n.), b.29 Dec 1936. She d.23 Aug 1985 at age 48 and was bur. Nathan Anderson Historic Cem.

595. Mollie[7] Abney (Washington[6], Wilburn[5], Benjamin[4], Hezekiah[3], Elisha[2], Abner[1]), b.15 Apr 1888 West Amurchee, Walker Co., GA. She m. Lloyd Williams in 1908. She d.29 Sep 1927 GA at age 39.
Known children of Mollie[7] Abney and Lloyd Williams:
            i.   Oscar[8]. He was Grocer.
            ii.   Dan.
          iii.   Myrtle m. (n.n.) Spangler.
          iv.   Jessie Bea m. (n.n.) Oliver.
           v.   Lottie Mae m. (n.n.) Maxey.
          vi.   Ruby m. (n.n.) Ledbetter.
         vii.   Lewis. He was Doctor.

596. William Luther "Luke"[7] Abney Sr. (Washington[6], Wilburn[5], Benjamin[4], Hezekiah[3], Elisha[2], Abner[1]), b.10 May 1889 West Amurchee, Walker Co., GA; m. Maude Williams, d/o John Williams and Mary (n.n,) on 29 May 1910. He and Maude Victoria Williams appeared on the censuses of 19 Jan 1920, 9 Apr 1930 and 9 Apr 1940 LaFayette, Walker Co., GA. He d.8 Jul 1941, age 52; bur. LaFayette Cem., LaFayette, Walker Co., GA.

Maude Victoria Williams, b.30 May 1894 GA. She d.9 Jun 1978 LaFayette, Walker Co., GA, age 84; bur. LaFayette Cem., LaFayette.
Known children of William Luther "Luke"[7] Abney Sr. and Maude Victoria Williams:
      1014   i.   Jessie "Blanche"[8], b. 15 Mar 1913 Linwood, Walker Co., GA; m. Daniel William "Bill" Kimbell.
      1015   ii.   Archie "Dennis," b. 14 Dec 1914 GA; m. Thelma Simmons.
      1016 iii.   William "Luther," b. 24 Oct 1916; m. Lillian Jennings.
      1017 iv.   Mary Ella, b. 4 Sep 1918 GA; m. Thurlo G. Smith Sr.
      1018   v.   Ross Louis, b. 5 Jun 1920 LaFayette, GA; m. Charlotte Elizabeth Culpepper.
      1019 vi.   Fredia Roberta, b. 22 Jul 1922 Walker Co., GA; m. Henry "Clyde" Poole (USArmy-WWII).
      1020 vii.   Garnet "Ray," b. 20 Dec 1924 LaFayette, Walker Co., GA; m. Jo Ballard; m. Ernestine Heston.
      1021 viii.   Martha Rebecca, b. 5 May 1929 Walker Co., GA; m. William Marvin "Bill" Fricks (USN-WWII, Korea).
          ix.   Virginia Lee, b.19 Apr 1931. She m. n.n. Ezell.
           x.   Myra Jean, b.2 Apr 1935. She m. Jerry Wilhelm.

597. Stella "Lee"[7] Abney (Washington[6], Wilburn[5], Benjamin[4], Hezekiah[3], Elisha[2], Abner[1]), b.23 Dec 1892 GA. She m. Thomas Andrew Cochran Sr. She d.23 Sep 1973 GA at age 80.
    Thomas Andrew "Tom" Cochran Sr.
Known child of Stella "Lee"[7] Abney and Thomas Andrew Cochran Sr.:
            i.   Thomas Andrew Jr.[8]

598. Luvena "Myrtis"[7] Abney (Washington[6], Wilburn[5], Benjamin[4], Hezekiah[3], Elisha[2], Abner[1]), b.15 Jun 1895 GA. She m. John E. Edge in 1918. She and John E. Edge appeared on the census of 16 Apr 1930 LaFayette, Walker Co., GA.
Known children of Luvena "Myrtis"[7] Abney and John E. Edge both b. GA:
            i.   John Paul[8], b. ca.1922.
            ii.   Betty Jo, b. ca.1926. She m. (n.n.) Summerlin .

599. James Mack "Jim"[7] Abney (Washington[6], Wilburn[5], Benjamin[4], Hezekiah[3], Elisha[2], Abner[1]), b.15 May 1898 GA. He m. Mary Bulah Evitt. He and Mary Bulah Evitt appeared on the censuses of 16 Apr 1930 Albertville, Marshall Co., AL; and 9 Apr 1940 LaFayette, Walker Co., GA. He d.30 Sep 1955 GA at age 57 and was bur. LaFayette Cem., LaFayette, Walker Co., GA.
Known children of James Mack "Jim"[7] Abney and Mary Bulah Evitt both b. GA:
            i.   James "Mack"[8], b.1 Apr 1922. He d.11 Jun 1948 at age 26 and was bur. LaFayette Cem., LaFayette, Walker Co., GA.
            ii.   Bob, b. ca.1924.

600. Jesse Andrew "Jess"[7] Abney (Washington[6], Wilburn[5], Benjamin[4], Hezekiah[3], Elisha[2], Abner[1]), b.27 Oct 1904 West Armuchee, Walker Co., GA. He m. Martha Camp Shaw, daughter of Frank Mercer Shaw and Nannie Suttles Clements, on 1 Feb 1930. He and Martha Camp Shaw appeared on the censuses of 7 Apr 1930 and 18 Apr 1940 LaFayette, Walker Co., GA. He d.24 Sep 1971 Walker Co., GA, at age 66 and was bur. LaFayette Cem., LaFayette, Walker Co., GA.
      Martha Camp Shaw, b.3 Nov 1908 Shaw, Walker Co., GA. She was Teacher; d.8 Dec 1989 at age 81 and was bur. LaFayette Cem., LaFayette.
Known child of Jesse Andrew "Jess"[7] Abney and Martha Camp Shaw:
    1022   i.   William Shaw "Billy"[8], b. 10 Oct 1934 LaFayette, Walker Co., GA; m. Ann Elenora Walker.

601. Nora May[7] Brown (Lula[6] Abney, Wilburn[5], Benjamin[4], Hezekiah[3], Elisha[2], Abner[1]), b.Jul 1888 GA. She m. John "Oscar" Hall ca.1914. She and John appeared on the censuses of 8 Jan 1920 Red Rock, Cobb Co., GA; 11 Apr 1930 Rome, Floyd Co., GA; and 7 Apr 1940 Cobb Co., GA.
      John "Oscar" Hall, b. ca.1889 GA. He lived in 1935 Rome, Floyd Co., GA.
Known child of Nora May[7] Brown and John "Oscar" Hall:
            i.   Ruby "Lena"[8], b.1915 GA.

602. Lillie Mae[7] Abney (Robert[6], Wilburn[5], Benjamin[4], Hezekiah[3], Elisha[2], Abner[1]), b.18 May 1896 Paulding Co., GA. She m1. Henry Charles Pope ca.1913. She and Henry Charles Pope appeared on the censuses of 19 Jan 1920 Graham, DeKalb Co., AL; and 7 Apr 1930 Cedartown, Pollk Co., GA. She was liv. on 13 Apr 1940 lodger with White family, Cedartown, Polk Co., GA. She m2. (n.n.) Camp. She d.11 Sep 1970 at age 74 and was bur. Poplar Springs Cem., Haralson Co., GA.
      Henry Charles Pope, b.23 Jul 1892 Haralson Co., GA. He was a Policeman. He was killed in the line of duty on 3 Sep 1934 at the City Hall, Tallapoosa, Haralson Co., GA at age 42 and was bur. Ebenezer Church Cem., Haralson Co., GA.

"The Cleburne News" (newspaper) Heflin, Cleburne Co., Alabama
Issue of Thursday, SEPTEMBER 6, 1934:

COUPLE SLAIN - OFFICER SHOT

Anniston, Ala., Sept. 3

    Night Policeman Henry C. Pope, age 42, of Tallapoosa, Ga., was in critical condition today at Garner Hospital with a bullet wound in the abdomen as a result of a shooting at the City Hall in Tallapoosa, Ga., where Mr. Clyde (Claude) Ledlow and Mrs. Ledlow are alleged to have been slain by the officer Sunday.
    Acccording to information reaching Anniston, the Ledlows had gone to the city hall about 2 o'clock Sunday morning to bail Mrs. Ledlow's nephew, Kenneth Sewell, out of jail. Sewell, it is said, had been arrested on a charge of drinking. The officer told them Sewell was not sober enough to be released and Mrs. Ledlow is said to have fired on Pope.
    Pope, it was said, drew his own pistol and shot Mrs. Ledlow, causing instant death. Then Mr. Ledlow, it is reported, attempted to shoot the officer, who sent a bullet into the man's head. Ledlow was brought to Anniston but ambulance drivers said he died before they got out.

The Anniston Daily Star (newspaper)
Issue of Thursday, SEPTEMBER 13, 1934

BULLET WOUND PROVES FATAL

Anniston, Ala., [Monday] *Sept. 10th*

Henry C. Pope, age 42, night policeman at Tallapoosa, d. Sunday afternoon at Garner Hospital from an abdominal bullet wound inflicted a week ago at the city hall in Tallapoosa where the officer shot and killed a man and a woman after he was fired on by the woman.
Funeral services were conducted at 2 o'clock Monday afternoon at Ebenezer church near Tallapoosa. The officer said he was shot by Mrs. Clyde Ledlow who came to the city hall to see about posting bond for her nephew who had been arrested on a minor charge. Pope stated that he shot the woman and her husband when the latter tried to get the officer's pistol on 13 Sep 1934.
Known children of Lillie Mae[7] Abney and Henry Charles Pope:
            i.   Lewis James[8] m. Theda B. Allen. He, b.21 Apr 1914 GA. He lived in 1935 Cedartown, Polk Co., GA. He and Theda B. Allen appeared on the census of 12 Apr 1940 Atlanta, Fulton Co., GA. He d.19 Jun 1965 at age 51 and was bur. Poplar Springs Cem., Haralson Co., GA.
                  Theda B. Allen, b.20 Feb 1917. She lived in 1935 Tallapoosa, Haralson Co., GA. She d.29 Mar 1998 Haralson Co., GA, at age 81 and was bur. Poplar Springs Cem., Haralson Co., GA.
           ii.   Evelyn, b. ca.Sep 1916 GA.
         iii.   Lee, b. ca.Nov 1919 GA.
         iv.   Nannie Alline, b.6 Jan 1923 Haralson Co., GA. She d.18 Jan 1923 Buchanan, Haralson Co., GA and was bur. Ebenezer Church Cem., Haralson Co., GA.
          v.   George Fredrick, b.15 Aug 1924 Haralson Co., GA. He m. Edna Mooney ca.1936. He was liv. on 12 Apr 1940 with brother, Lewis Pope, Atlanta, Fulton Co., GA. He d.8 Jun 1990 Durham, Durham Co., NC, at age 65 and was bur. Oakwood Cem., Mebane, Orange Co., NC.
         vi.   Jeanette, b.2 Mar 1932 Cedartown, Polk Co., GA. She d.3 Mar 1932 Cedartown, Polk Co., GA and was bur. Pine Bower Bapt. Ch. Cem., Cedartown, Polk Co., GA.
There were no known children of Lillie Mae[7] Abney and (n.n.) Camp.

603. Minnie L.[7] Abney (Robert[6], Wilburn[5], Benjamin[4], Hezekiah[3], Elisha[2], Abner[1]), b.22 May 1902 Buchanan, Haralson Co., GA. She m. Harvey Jackson "Jack" Perry Sr. ca.1920. She and Harvey appeared on the censuses of 17 Jan 1920 Albertville, Marshall Co., AL; 4 Apr 1930 Cedartown, Polk Co., GA; and 2 May 1940 Haralson Co., GA; d. 31 Oct 1965 Polk Co., GA; bur. Buchanan City Cem., Buchanan, Haralson Co., GA.
      Harvey Jackson "Jack" Perry Sr, b.27 Feb 1895 Buchanan, Haralson Co., GA. He d.28 May 1982 at age 87 and was bur. Buchanan City Cem.

Known children of Minnie L.[7] Abney and Harvey Jackson "Jack" Perry Sr.:
- 1023   i.   William "Leroy"[8], b. 16 Apr 1921 Haralson Co., GA; m. Ruby V. McDowell.
-       ii.   Harvie Jackson "Jack", b.11 Nov 1923 Buchanan, Haralson Co., GA. He d.5 Dec 1992 Fulton Co., GA, at age 69 and was bur. Buchanan City Cem., Buchanan, Haralson Co., GA.
-      iii.   Mary Charlotte m. Henry Warren Champ (USArmy-WWII). , b.18 Sep 1925 Gadsden, Etowah Co., AL. She d.7 Jun 1999 at age 73 and was bur. Buchanan City Cem., Buchanan, Haralson Co., GA.
  - Henry Warren Champ (USArmy-WWII), b.8 Dec 1917. He d.15 Mar 1999 at age 81; Buchanan City Cem., Buchanan.

604. Marvin "Doc"[7] Abney (Robert[6], Wilburn[5], Benjamin[4], Hezekiah[3], Elisha[2], Abner[1]), b.12 Oct 1913 GA; m. Lucille Elizabeth Williams ca.1932. He and Lucille appeared on the census of 29 Apr 1940 Buchanan, Haralson Co., GA. He d.22 May 1957, age 43; bur. Buchanan City Cem.
     Lucille Elizabeth Williams, b.6 Oct 1914. She d.29 May 1997 at age 82 and was bur. Buchanan City Cem., Buchanan, Haralson Co., GA.
Known children of Marvin "Doc"[7] Abney and Lucille Elizabeth Williams:
- 1024   i.   Mary Frances[8], b. 19 Jan 1933; m. Clyde Emanuel "Buddy" Pullen.
- 1025   ii.   James Robert, b. 24 Oct 1935 GA; m. (n.n.).
-      iii.   Henry G., b. ca.1938 GA.
-      iv.   Fannie Louise, b.1946. She d.1946 and was bur. Buchanan City Cem., Buchanan, Haralson Co., GA.
-      v.   (infant), b.1948. He d.1948 and was bur. Buchanan City Cem., Buchanan, Haralson Co., GA.

605. Alice "Mae"[7] Camp (Corrin[6] Abney, Wilburn[5], Benjamin[4], Hezekiah[3], Elisha[2], Abner[1]), b.10 Jan 1899 Paulding Co., GA. She m. Willie Arthur Davis ca.1913. She and Willie Arthur Davis appeared on the censuses of 14 Jan 1920 Lost Mountain, Cobb Co., GA; of 21 Apr 1930 Mineral Bluff, Fannin Co., GA; and 24 Apr 1940 Fulton Co., GA. She d.22 Aug 1959 Cobb Co., GA, at age 60; bur. New Hope Cem., Dallas, Paulding Co., GA.
     Willie Arthur Davis, b.8 Jul 1896 GA. He d.15 Mar 1982 Douglas Co., GA, at age 85 and was bur. New Hope Cem., Dallas.
Known children of Alice "Mae"[7] Camp and Willie Arthur Davis all b. GA:
- 1026   i.   Ruby Lorene[8], b. 2 Aug 1914; m. Pvt. Randolph R. Childs (USArmy-WWII).
-      ii.   James N., b. ca.1917.
-      iii.   Evie "Leone", b.27 Oct 1920. She d.19 Mar 1986 at age 65 and was bur. New Hope Cem., Dallas, Paulding Co., GA.
- 1027   iv.   Carl Lee, b. 16 Mar 1924; m. Frances Louise Rutherford.
-      v.   Junior "Ralph", b.25 Jul 1926. He m. Virginia L. (n.n.) in 1946. He d.22 Oct 1975 at age 49 and was bur. New Hope Cem. Virginia L. (n.n.), b.6 Feb 1925.
-      vi.   William Lamar m. Kathleen Cheatwood. He, b.17 Mar 1940. He d.3 Mar 2015 at age 74 and was bur. Tallapoosa E. Bapt. Ch. Cem., Tallapoosa, Haralson Co., GA.
  - Kathleen Cheatwood, b.3 Mar 1940. She d.21 Apr 2012 at age 72 and was bur. Tallapoosa E. Bapt. Ch. Cem.

606. Emma Lou[7] Camp (Corrin[6] Abney, Wilburn[5], Benjamin[4], Hezekiah[3], Elisha[2], Abner[1]), b.5 Oct 1908 Cobb Co., GA. She m. Pvt. Marcus Pritchett (USArmy) ca.1933. She and Pvt. Marcus Pritchett (USArmy) appeared on the census of 3 Apr 1940 Cobb Co., GA. She d.5 Apr 1983 Hiram, Paulding Co., GA, at age 74 and was bur. Pleasant Hill Bapt. Ch. Cem., Powder Springs, Cobb Co., GA.
     Pvt. Marcus Pritchett (USArmy), b.29 Apr 1896 GA. He d.12 Sep 1974 at age 78.
Known children of Emma Lou[7] Camp and Pvt. Marcus Pritchett (USArmy) both b. GA:
-      i.   Charley A.[8], b. ca.1934.
-      ii.   Hershel F., b.18 May 1935. He m. Edna Earl on 3 May 1954. He d.28 Jan 2010 at age 74 and was bur. Pleasant Hill Bapt. Ch. Cem., Powder Springs, Cobb Co., GA.
  - Edna Earl, b.30 Dec 1935. She d.9 Apr 2009 at age 73 and was bur. Pleasant Hill Bapt. Ch. Cem., Powder Springs.

607. Altha Magdelia[7] Camp (Corrin[6] Abney, Wilburn[5], Benjamin[4], Hezekiah[3], Elisha[2], Abner[1]), b.7 Jan 1913 New Hope, Paulding Co., GA. She m. Raymond Woodrow "Ray" Finch on 7 Aug 1932 Paulding Co., GA. She and Raymond Woodrow "Ray" Finch appeared on the census of 15 Apr 1940 California, Paulding Co., GA. She d.8 Jul 1998 Mableton, Cobb Co., GA, at age 85; bur. New Hope Cem., Dallas, Paulding Co., GA.
     Raymond Woodrow "Ray" Finch, b.9 Mar 1913 Paulding Co., GA. He d.15 Jun 1997 Mableton, Paulding Co., GA, at age 84.
Known children of Altha Magdelia[7] Camp and Raymond Woodrow "Ray" Finch:
-      i.   Carlton[8], b. ca.1935 GA.
-      ii.   Eleanor, b. ca.1936 GA.
- 1028   iii.   Raymond C., b. est.1942; m. Faye Patterson.
-      iv.   Howard Hennaly, b.15 Jun 1944 and was bur. New Hope Cem., Dallas, Paulding Co., GA.

608. Gordon Lee[7] Camp (Corrin[6] Abney, Wilburn[5], Benjamin[4], Hezekiah[3], Elisha[2], Abner[1]), b.17 Oct 1915 GA. He m. Hazel Evelyn Henson ca.1935. He and Hazel Evelyn Henson were living on 1 Apr 1935 Paulding Co., GA. He and Hazel Evelyn Henson appeared on the census of 12 Apr 1940 Irondale, Jefferson Co., AL. He d.20 Jul 1996 at age 80 and was bur. Jefferson Mem. Gardens East, Trussville, Jefferson Co., AL.
     Hazel Evelyn Henson, b.18 May 1913 Dallas, Paulding Co., GA. She d.1 Oct 2001 AL at age 88 and was bur. Jefferson Mem. Gardens East, Trussville, Jefferson Co., AL.
Known children of Gordon Lee[7] Camp and Hazel Evelyn Henson:
-      i.   Evelyn[8], b. ca.1937 GA.
- 1029   ii.   Carolyn, b. 2 Nov 1939 AL; m. Bill Thomason.

609. Mary Frances[7] Abney (George[6], Benjamin[5], Benjamin[4], Hezekiah[3], Elisha[2], Abner[1]), b.4 Feb 1878 AL. She m. John Francis Machen ca.1896. She d. Independence Day, 4 Jul 1954 Gilmer, Upshur Co., TX, at age 76 and was bur. Gilmer City Cem., Gilmer, Upshur Co., TX.
     John Francis Machen, b.8 Apr 1874 AL. He d.21 Feb 1955 Upshur Co., TX, at age 80; bur. Gilmer City Cem., Gilmer, Upshur Co., TX.
Known children of Mary Frances[7] Abney and John Francis Machen both b. AL:
-      i.   Francis Milford[8], b.18 Feb 1897. He d.10 Jun 1901 Marshall Co., AL, at age 4 and was bur. Asbury UMC Cem., Asbury, Marshall Co., AL.
-      ii.   Ernest, b.24 Aug 1898. He d.11 Jun 1901 Marshall Co., AL, at age 2 and was bur. Asbury UMC Cem., Asbury, Marshall Co., AL.

610. Mattie William⁷ Abney (George⁶, Benjamin⁵, Benjamin⁴, Hezekiah³, Elisha², Abner¹), b.5 Sep 1881 AL. She m. James "Martin" Hall on 28 Oct 1900 Marshall Co., AL. She d.5 May 1965 at age 83 and was bur. Gilmer City Cem., Gilmer, Upshur Co., TX.
James "Martin" Hall, b.7 Sep 1877 Marshall Co., AL. He d.25 Jul 1950 Gilmer, Upshur Co., TX, at age 72 and was bur. Gilmer City Cem.
Known children of Mattie William⁷ Abney and James "Martin" Hall:
    1030   i.   George Schiffman⁸, b. 5 Dec 1901; m. Lorine Martin.
    1031   ii. Bowman Christopher, b. 17 Mar 1903 TX; m. Cullie Mae Hill.
            iii. Barney Wilson, b.11 Aug 1909 Upshur Co., TX. He d.14 Mar 1967 Houston, Harris Co., TX, at age 57.

611. Christopher Columbus "CC"⁷ Abney Sr. (George⁶, Benjamin⁵, Benjamin⁴, Hezekiah³, Elisha², Abner¹), b.14 Jul 1884 AL. He m. Mary Josephine "Josie" Aycock in 1910. He and Mary Josephine "Josie" Aycock appeared on the censuses of 28 Jan 1920 and 17 Apr 1930 Upshur Co., TX. He d.26 Feb 1934 Upshur Co., TX, at age 49 and was bur. Gilmer City Cem., Gilmer, Upshur Co., TX.
Mary Josephine "Josie" Aycock, b.15 Dec 1883 Marshall Co., MS. She appeared as Head of Household on the census of 9 Apr 1940 Upshur Co., TX. She d.5 Aug 1958 Gilmer, Upshur Co., TX, at age 74 and was bur. Gilmer City Cem., Gilmer, Upshur Co., TX.
Known child of Christopher Columbus "CC"⁷ Abney Sr. and Mary Josephine "Josie" Aycock:
            i.   Christopher Columbus "Chris" Jr.⁸, b. ca.1914 TX. He m. Charlene (n.n.). He lived on 9 Apr 1940 with mother, Josephine Abney, Upshur Co., TX. [Charlene (n.n.), b. ca.1922 TX.]

612. Perino "Frank"⁷ Abney (George⁶, Benjamin⁵, Benjamin⁴, Hezekiah³, Elisha², Abner¹), b.12 Nov 1889 Marshall Co., AL. He m1. Gladys Susanna Mitchell ca.1912. He m2. Annie Elizabeth Willis in 1929. He and Annie Elizabeth Willis lived on 19 Apr 1930 with his mother, Olivia Abney, Upshur Co., TX. He and Annie Elizabeth Willis appeared on the census of 20 Apr 1940 Upshur Co., TX. He d.17 Oct 1978 at age 88 and was bur. Gilmer City Cem., Gilmer, Upshur Co., TX.
Gladys Susanna Mitchell, b.16 Jun 1891. She d.8 Dec 1918 at age 27 and was bur. LaFayette Cem., LaFayette, Upshur Co., TX.
Known child of Perino "Frank"⁷ Abney and Gladys Susanna Mitchell:
    1032   i.   Cora Bell⁸, b. 27 Jul 1915; m. Ophie L. Collier.
Known child of Perino "Frank"⁷ Abney and (n.n.) Dodd:
            i.   (n.n.)⁸, b. illegitimate est.1918.
Annie Elizabeth Willis, b.9 Sep 1906 TX. She m1. (n.n.) Swanner ca.1926; d. New Year's Eve, 31 Jan 1988, age 81; bur. Gilmer City Cem.
Known child of Perino "Frank"⁷ Abney and Annie Elizabeth Willis:
    1033   i.   Patsy Ruth⁸, b. ca.1931 Upshur Co., TX; m. n.n. Clark; m. Cpl. Chester Robinson Sr. (USArmy-WWII); m. n.n. Dyke.

613. Falecia Roseline Mae "Rossie"⁷ Moore (Mary⁶ Abney, Benjamin⁵, Benjamin⁴, Hezekiah³, Elisha², Abner¹), b.7 Mar 1877. She m. Jasper Ruben Rowan in 1900. She d.4 Jun 1942 at age 65 and was bur. Wynnville Cem., Wynnville, Blount Co., AL.
Jasper Ruben Rowan, b.10 Aug 1873. He d.6 Mar 1941 at age 67 and was bur. Wynnville Cem., Wynnville, Blount Co., AL.
Known child of Falecia Roseline Mae "Rossie"⁷ Moore and Jasper Ruben Rowan:
    1034   i.   Bessie Mae⁸, b. 10 Dec 1905 AL; m. Joseph Quincy Morton.

614. Henry Osborn⁷ Moore (Mary⁶ Abney, Benjamin⁵, Benjamin⁴, Hezekiah³, Elisha², Abner¹), b.18 Dec 1878. He m. Della Lucendie Burt in 1899. He d.18 Sep 1959 at age 80 and was bur. Asbury UMC Cem., Asbury, Marshall Co., AL.
Della Lucendie Burt, b.7 Feb 1883 AL. She d.16 Feb 1969 Albertville, Marshall Co., AL, at age 86 and was bur. Asbury UMC Cem., Asbury.
Known children of Henry Osborn⁷ Moore and Della Lucendie Burt:
            i.   Alma⁸, b.18 Aug 1900 Marshall Co., AL. She d.27 Dec 1985 Albertville, Marshall Co., AL, at age 85 and was bur. Asbury UMC Cem., Asbury, Marshall Co., AL.
    1035   ii. Earl Buford, b. New Year's Eve, 31 Dec 1919; m. Mildred McCulley.

615. Mary Leeoma "Oma"⁷ Moore (Mary⁶ Abney, Benjamin⁵, Benjamin⁴, Hezekiah³, Elisha², Abner¹), b.4 May 1882. She m. Edward Culbert ca.1905. She d.12 Dec 1977 at age 95 and was bur. Woosley Cem., Kirbytown, Marshall Co., AL.
Edward Culbert, b.8 Jun 1878. He d.11 Jun 1935 at age 57 and was bur. Woosley Cem., Kirbytown, Marshall Co., AL.
Known children of Mary Leeoma "Oma"⁷ Moore and Edward Culbert:
    1036   i.   Ena⁸, b. 14 Jan 1906; m. Horace Cromwell Porter.
            ii. Mae, b.12 May 1907. She m. Frank W. Dobbs. d.24 Feb 2002 at age 94 and was bur. Woosley Cem., Kirbytown.
                     Frank W. Dobbs, b.9 Aug 1901. He d.2 Jul 1967 at age 65 and was bur. Geraldine Cem., Geraldine, DeKalb Co., AL.
            iii. Eudessa, b.28 May 1908 Marshall Co., AL. She m. Samuel Randall Higdon (WWI). She d.25 May 2000 at age 91 and was bur. Altoona-Walnut Grove Cem., Altoona, Etowah Co., AL.
                     Samuel Randall Higdon (WWI), b.14 Feb 1893. He d.26 Feb 1972 at age 79; bur. Altoona-Walnut Grove Cem.
    1037   iv. John Luther, b. 5 Mar 1910 Marshall Co., AL; m. Opal Waldrop.
            v.   Cullen, b.5 Feb 1912 Marshall Co., AL. He m. Lillie Mae Davis. He d.18 Mar 1995 Langston, Jackson Co., AL, at age 83 and was bur. Langston Cem., Langston, Jackson Co., AL.
                     Lillie Mae Davis, b.17 Oct 1916. She d.15 May 2003 at age 86 and was bur. Langston Cem., Langston.
            vi. Nellie Ruth, b.27 Mar 1921. She m. Cleburn M. Wilkerson in 1941. She d.17 Jan 1991 at age 69 and was bur. Marshall Mem. Gardens, Albertville, Marshall Co., AL.
                     Cleburn M. Wilkerson, b.22 Feb 1921; d.6 Oct 1995, age 74; bur. Natchez National Cem., Natchez, Adams Co., MS.

616. John Luther⁷ Moore (Mary⁶ Abney, Benjamin⁵, Benjamin⁴, Hezekiah³, Elisha², Abner¹), b.2 Sep 1886. He m. Noma Mae Lee ca.1912. He d.2 Jul 1972 at age 85 and was bur. Asbury UMC Cem., Asbury, Marshall Co., AL.
Noma Mae Lee, b.9 May 1895 AL. She d.14 Oct 1972 Boaz, Marshall Co., AL, at age 77 and was bur. Asbury UMC Cem., Asbury.
Known children of John Luther⁷ Moore and Noma Mae Lee:
    1038   i.   Moody Fosion⁸, b. 21 Sep 1913 AL; m. Audrey Upton.
    1039   ii. Beatrice Alene, b. 30 May 1918; m. Curtis Garrett.
    1040   iii. D.C., b. 27 Feb 1923; m. Mary "Nonee" Andrews.

      iv.   Willene, b.21 Nov 1926 Marshall Co., AL. She m. Claud Henry "Glenn" Mullinax (USN-WWII). d.10 Aug 2007 Albertville, Marshall Co., AL, at age 80 and was bur. New Macedonia Bapt. Ch. Cem., McVille, Marshall Co., AL.
           Claud Henry "Glenn" Mullinax (USN-WWII), b.2 Sep 1924 Corbin, Whitley Co., KY. He d.8 Oct 2007 Albertville, Marshall Co., AL, at age 83.

617. Grover S.[7] Moore Sr. (Mary[6] Abney, Benjamin[5], Benjamin[4], Hezekiah[3], Elisha[2], Abner[1]), b.21 Nov 1890. He m. Eula Hays. He d.8 Oct 1965 at age 74 and was bur. Memory Gardens of Jefferson Co., Nederland, Jefferson Co., TX.
    Eula Hays, b.16 Feb 1899. She d.31 Mar 1979 at age 80 and was bur. Memory Gardens of Jefferson Co., Nederland, Jefferson Co., TX.
Known children of Grover S.[7] Moore Sr. and Eula Hays:
      i.   Grover S.[8].
      ii. (dau.). She m. Norman Meritt.

618. Dewey Hobson "Hob"[7] Moore (Mary[6] Abney, Benjamin[5], Benjamin[4], Hezekiah[3], Elisha[2], Abner[1]), b.12 Dec 1898. He m. Cecile Belle Carter on 31 Mar 1920. He d.24 Apr 1983 at age 84 and was bur. Asbury UMC Cem., Asbury, Marshall Co., AL.
    Cecile Belle Carter, b.1 Sep 1899. She d.9 Dec 1979 at age 80 and was bur. Asbury UMC Cem., Asbury, Marshall Co., AL.
Known children of Dewey Hobson "Hob"[7] Moore and Cecile Belle Carter:
      i.   Dewey Herbert[8] m. Billie S. (n.n.). He, b.11 May 1921. He d.28 Jun 1986 at age 65 and was bur. Mount Carmel Cem., Guntersville, Marshall Co., AL.
           Billie S. (n.n.), b.30 Apr 1929. She d.30 Mar 1999 at age 69 and was bur. Mount Carmel Cem., Guntersville.
1041 ii. John Byron, b. 3 Jul 1925; m. Clara Othell Teal.
1042 iii. Opal Ruth, b. 13 Feb 1929; m. Cpl. Wilbur Lee Thacker (USArmy-Korea).
      iv. Willadean, b.18 Mar 1931 Marshall Co., AL. She d.24 Jul 2014 Round Rock, Williamson Co., TX, at age 83 and was bur. Asbury UMC Cem., Asbury, Marshall Co., AL.

619. Hattie[7] Abney (James[6], Benjamin[5], Benjamin[4], Hezekiah[3], Elisha[2], Abner[1]), b.Mar 1892 AL. She m. Guy Calvin Bateman ca.1917. She and Guy Calvin Bateman appeared on the censuses of 20 Jan 1920 and 3 Apr 1930 Texline, Dallam Co., TX; and 10 Apr 1940 Amarillo, Potter Co., TX. She d.1973 and was bur. Memorial Park Cem., Amarillo, Potter Co., TX.
    Guy Calvin Bateman, b.5 Oct 1889 Joplin, Jasper Co., MO. He d.5 Jul 1967 Amarillo, Potter Co., TX, at age 77; bur. Memorial Park Cem.
Known child of Hattie[7] Abney and Guy Calvin Bateman:
      i.   Cecil G.[8], b. ca.Jul 1918 AZ.

620. Margaret B. "Maggie Bob"[7] Abney (James[6], Benjamin[5], Benjamin[4], Hezekiah[3], Elisha[2], Abner[1]), b. Feb 1896 TX. She m. Robert Fulton Hefley ca.1930. She and Robert Fulton Hefley appeared on the census of 1 May 1940 Texline, Dallam Co., TX. She d.1999; bur. Texline Cem.
    Robert Fulton Hefley, b.1886. He d.1956 and was bur. Texline Cem., Texline, Dallam Co., TX.
Known children of Margaret B. "Maggie Bob"[7] Abney and Robert Fulton Hefley:
1043 i.   Bobbye Lou[8], b. 21 Aug 1931 Clayton, Union Co., NM; m. Don R. Wood.
1044 ii. Richard Franklin "Bud," b. 18 Feb 1933 Clayton, Union Co., NM; m. Kathryn "Kay" Glenn.
      iii. Betty "Sue", b. ca.1935. She m. (n.n.) Persons.

621. Earnestteen[7] Abney (James[6], Benjamin[5], Benjamin[4], Hezekiah[3], Elisha[2], Abner[1]), b. Christmas Eve, 24 Dec 1901 TX. She m. Smith "Edward" Temple ca.1924. She and Smith "Edward" Temple appeared on the censuses of 4 Apr 1930 Wichita Falls, Wichita Co., TX; and 8 Apr 1940 Childress, Childress Co., TX. She d.12 Mar 1985 at age 83 and was bur. Texline Cem., Texline, Dallam Co., TX.
    Smith "Edward" Temple, b.17 Mar 1902 TX. He d.22 Sep 1960 at age 58 and was bur. Texline Cem., Texline, Dallam Co., TX.
Known children of Earnestteen[7] Abney and Smith "Edward" Temple:
      i.   Edward "Curtis"[8], b. ca.1927 TX.
      ii. Juanita W., b. ca.1928 NM.
      iii. Jack H., b. ca.1931 TX.
      iv. Maggie A., b. ca.1936 TX.

622. Temple H. "Tempie"[7] Abney (James[6], Benjamin[5], Benjamin[4], Hezekiah[3], Elisha[2], Abner[1]), b.15 Feb 1904 TX. He m. Pauline Beatty on 27 May 1934 Clayton, Union Co., NM. He and Pauline Beatty appeared on the census of 1 May 1940 Texline, Dallam Co., TX. He d.16 Sep 1978 at age 74 and was bur. Texline Cem., Texline, Dallam Co., TX.
    Pauline Beatty, b.26 Sep 1910 OK. She d.15 Apr 2007 at age 96 and was bur. Texline Cem., Texline, Dallam Co., TX.
Known children of Temple H. "Tempie"[7] Abney and Pauline Beatty:
      i.   Margaret Lynn[8], b. ca.Apr 1939 NM. She m. (n.n.) Detten.
      ii. Temple H. He m. Karen (n.n.).
1045 iii. James Talmage "Jim," b. 8 Jun 1944; m. Paula (n.n.).
      iv. Alicia. She m. (n.n.) Neimeier.

623. Lillie Ann[7] Abney (William[6], Benjamin[5], Benjamin[4], Hezekiah[3], Elisha[2], Abner[1]), b.9 Dec 1881 Marhsall Co., AL. She m. John "Craton" Guest in 1899. She and John "Craton" Guest appeared on the censuses of 9 Jun 1900 Marshall Co., AL; 18 Apr 1910 DeKalb Co., AL; and 12 Jan 1920, 12 Apr 1930 and 12 Apr 1940 Albertville, Marshall Co., AL. She d.9 Sep 1971 at age 89 and was bur. Memory Hill Cem., Albertville.
    John "Craton" Guest, b.Jun 1874 AL. He d.1947 and was bur. Memory Hill Cem., Albertville, Marshall Co., AL.
Known children of Lillie Ann[7] Abney and John "Craton" Guest all b. AL:
1046 i.   Dovie P.[8], b. 7 Dec 1899; m. Ellis M. Grey.
      ii. Gartrell G., b.30 Apr 1901. He lived on 24 Apr 1930 (lodger), Cleveland, Cuyahoga, OH. He d.25 Mar 1932 at age 30 and was bur. Memory Hill Cem., Albertville, Marshall Co., AL.
      iii. Orby L., b.1903. He m1. (n.n.) (she died before 1940). He lived in 1935 Albuquerque, Bernalillo Co., NM. He was liv. on 12 Apr 1940 with parents, Albertville, Marshall Co., AL; m2. Irene F. (n.n.); d.1974; bur. Pompano Beach So. Lawn Cem.
           Irene F. (n.n.), b.1914. She d.1996 and was bur. Pompano Beach So. Lawn Cem., Pompano Beach, Broward Co., FL.

624. Jasper Emmett[7] Abney (William[6], Benjamin[5], Benjamin[4], Hezekiah[3], Elisha[2], Abner[1]), b.26 Feb 1884 Marhsall Co., AL. He m. Ella M. Clements on Christmas Eve, 24 Dec 1908 DeKalb Co., AL. He appeared on the census of 15 Jan 1920 Marshall Co., AL. He lived in 1935 Portland, Multnomah Co., OR. He appeared on the census of 2 Apr 1940 Firgrove, Pierce Co., WA. He d.9 Mar 1957 Puyallup, Pierce Co., WA, at age 73 and was bur. Woodbine Cem., Puyallup, Pierce Co., WA.
    Ella M. Clements, b.Oct 1892 Talladega Co., AL. She d.6 Jul 1917 Anniston, Calhoun Co., AL, at age 24 and was bur. Pine Grove Cem., Anniston, Calhoun Co., AL.
Known children of Jasper Emmett[7] Abney and Ella M. Clements both b. Marhsall Co., AL:
              i.   Luella[8], b. ca.1911.
     1047   ii.   Huston, b. 16 Apr 1912; m1. Leona Agnes Campbell; m2. Clara Margaret Steadman.

625. James G.[7] Abney (USArmy-WWI) (William[6], Benjamin[5], Benjamin[4], Hezekiah[3], Elisha[2], Abner[1]), b.29 Nov 1886 Marhsall Co., AL. He m. Ina Bell Kent in 1919. He and Ina Bell Kent appeared on the censuses of 19 Jan 1920 Albertville, Marshall Co., AL; and 23 Apr 1930 and 24 Apr 1940 Hooper, Marshall Co., AL. He d.9 Nov 1950 at age 63 and was bur. Solitude Bapt. Ch. Cem., Albertville, Marshall Co., AL.
    Ina Bell Kent, b.18 Sep 1896 DeKalb Co., AL. She d.2 Feb 1964 Albertville, Marshall Co., AL, at age 67; bur. Solitude Bapt. Ch. Cem.
Known children of James G.[7] Abney (USArmy-WWI) and Ina Bell Kent:
              i.   Corrine[8] m. (n.n.) Harris.
             ii.   Corinne, b. ca.1921 AL.
            iii.   Vivian, b.12 Dec 1927. She d.16 Nov 2015 at age 87; bur. Solitude Bapt. Ch. Cem., Albertville, Marshall Co., AL.

626. Cora Lee[7] Abney (William[6], Benjamin[5], Benjamin[4], Hezekiah[3], Elisha[2], Abner[1]) m. Amos W. "AW" Chiles. , b.14 Jan 1890 Marhsall Co., AL. She and Amos W. "AW" Chiles appeared on the censuses of 24 Jan 1920 and 9 Apr 1940 Albertville, Marshall Co., AL. She d.29 Dec 1979 at age 89 and was bur. Memory Hill Cem., Albertville, Marshall Co., AL.
    Amos W. "AW" Chiles, b.21 Oct 1886 GA. He d.18 Feb 1968 at age 81 and was bur. Memory Hill Cem., Albertville, Marshall Co., AL.
Known children of Cora Lee[7] Abney and Amos W. "AW" Chiles:
     1048   i.   Audra Ellington "Andy"[8], b. 2 Jul 1915 AL; m. Mary Huddleston.
             ii.   Fred W., b. ca.Sep 1918 AL.
            iii.   Mary Nell m. George Houston Dicus. , b.27 Jul 1922. She d.17 Jul 1974 at age 51 and was bur. Cedar Hill Cem., Scottsboro, Jackson Co., AL.
                    George Houston Dicus m. Elizabeth Holder. He, b.14 Aug 1922. He d.17 Jan 1988 at age 65; bur. Cedar Hill Cem.

627. Homer[7] Abney (William[6], Benjamin[5], Benjamin[4], Hezekiah[3], Elisha[2], Abner[1]), b.8 Sep 1892 Marhsall Co., AL. He m. Sarah Ann Orr ca.1911. He and Sarah Ann Orr appeared on the censuses of 12 Jan 1920 Whiton, DeKalb Co., AL; 18 Apr 1930 Marshall Co., AL and 1 May 1940 DeKalb Co., AL. He d.16 Sep 1974 Boaz, Marshall Co., AL, at age 82; bur. New Harmony Missionary Bapt. Ch. Cem., Geraldine, DeKalb Co., AL.
    Sarah Ann Orr, b.7 Mar 1893. She d.3 Sep 1984 AL at age 91 and was bur. New Harmony Missionary Bapt. Ch. Cem., Geraldine.
Known children of Homer[7] Abney and Sarah Ann Orr:
              i.   Frank[8].
     1049   ii.   Wilma, b. ca.1914 AL; m. n.n. Hammock.
            iii.   Gladys, b. ca.Oct 1915 AL.
             iv.   Fred W., b.27 Nov 1918 AL. He d.7 Jul 1927 at age 8 and was bur. New Harmony Missionary Bapt. Ch. Cem., Geraldine.
              v.   Alice "Inez", b. ca.1923 AL.
     1050   vi.   Hazel Nell, b. 10 Sep 1924; m. Arvil Decker.
            vii.   Carl, b.4 Apr 1926 AL. He m. Rosa L. Hall. He d.26 Oct 2002 at age 76 and was bur. New Harmony Missionary Bapt. Ch. Cem., Geraldine, DeKalb Co., AL.
                    Rosa L. Hall, b.21 Nov 1934. She d.8 Oct 2002 at age 67 and was bur. New Harmony Missionary Bapt. Ch. Cem.
           viii.   Imogene "Jean", b. ca.1930 AL.

628. Joseph "Vernon"[7] Abney (Bunyan's twin) (William[6], Benjamin[5], Benjamin[4], Hezekiah[3], Elisha[2], Abner[1]), b.2 Aug 1894 Marhsall Co., AL. He m. Comilla Pearl Rains in 1912. He and Comilla Pearl Rains appeared on the censuses of 12 Jan 1920 Marshall Co., AL and 18 Apr 1930 Marshall Co., AL. They were still living in 1935 Marshall Co., AL. He and Comilla Pearl Rains appeared on the census of 8 Apr 1940 Gadsden, Etowah Co., AL. He d.2 Apr 1973 at age 78 and was bur. Asbury UMC Cem., Asbury, Marshall Co., AL.
    Comilla Pearl Rains, b.23 May 1897 Asbury, Marshall Co., AL; d.22 Aug 1974 Gadsden, Etowah Co., AL, age 77; bur. Asbury UMC Cem.
Known children of Joseph "Vernon"[7] Abney (Bunyan's twin) and Comilla Pearl Rains all b. AL:
              i.   Thelma Artell[8], b.6 Aug 1913; m. Buford P. Bowen. They lived in 1935 Marshall Co., AL. They appeared on the census of 5 Apr 1940 Gadsden, Etowah Co., AL. She d.1 Aug 1994 age 80; bur. Forrest Cem., Gadsden, Etowah Co., AL.
                    Buford P. Bowen, b. New Year's Day, 1 Jan 1917. Both Buford and his wife, Thelma worked in a Cotton Mill. He was a weaver and she was a spinner in 1940. He d.25 Feb 1969 at age 52 and was bur. Forrest Cem., Gadsden.
             ii.   Delma McKinley, b.1 Mar 1917. He m. Thelma (n.n.) (she was b. ca. 1919 AL). He m. Mae F. (n.n.). He d.3 Feb 1944 Phenix City, Russell Co., AL, at age 26 and was bur. Riverdale Cem., Columbus, Muscogee Co., GA.
     1051   iii.   Lincoln Freeman, b. 20 May 1920; m. Mozelle Pike; m. Edna E. Lantrip.

629. Wilson Gordon[7] Abney Sr. (USArmy-WWI) (William[6], Benjamin[5], Benjamin[4], Hezekiah[3], Elisha[2], Abner[1]), b.20 Dec 1897 Marhsall Co., AL; m1. Marion A. (n.n.). He m2. Violet Gregg on 2 Oct 1938. He d.21 Oct 1994, age 96; bur. Memory Hill Cem., Albertville, Marshall Co., AL.
    Marion A. (n.n.), b.28 Jun 1902. She d.19 Apr 1927 at age 24.
There were no known children of Wilson Gordon[7] Abney Sr. (USArmy-WWI) and Marion A. (n.n.).
Known child of Wilson Gordon[7] Abney Sr. (USArmy-WWI):
              i.   Wilson Gordon[8], b.26 Jul 1929. He m. Joan Esther (n.n.). He d.23 Nov 1996 at age 67 and was bur. Riverside National Cem., Riverside, Riverside Co., CA.
                    Joan Esther (n.n.), b.3 Mar 1931. She d.5 Feb 2015 at age 83 and was bur. Riverside National Cem., Riverside.
    Violet Gregg, b.7 Sep 1915. She d.27 Dec 2008 at age 93 and was bur. Memory Hill Cem., Albertville, Marshall Co., AL.
There were no known children of Wilson Gordon[7] Abney Sr. (USArmy-WWI) and Violet Gregg.

630. Vellie D.[7] Abney (David[6], Benjamin[5], Benjamin[4], Hezekiah[3], Elisha[2], Abner[1]), b.17 Nov 1887 AL. She was liv. on 22 Jun 1900 with grandfather, T.J. King, Marshall Co., AL. She m. Herman Emil Vogel ca.1908. She and Herman Emil Vogel appeared on the censuses of 11 May 1910 Navarro Co., TX; and 15 Jan 1920 Brown Co., TX and 15 Apr 1930 Brown Co., TX. She d.19 Nov 1939 Brownwood, Brown Co., TX, at age 52 and was bur. Winchell Cem., Winchell, Brown Co., TX.

Herman Emil Vogel, b.4 Jun 1874 Hamburg-Mitte, Hamburg, Germany. He appeared on the census of 8 Apr 1940 Brown Co., TX. He d.16 Oct 1954 Brownwood, Brown Co., TX, at age 80 and was bur. Winchell Cem., Winchell, Brown Co., TX.

Known children of Vellie D.[7] Abney and Herman Emil Vogel:

           i.   Birtha[8], b.20 Aug 1908 TX. She d.10 Oct 1909 TX at age 1; bur. Chatfield Cemetery New, Chatfield, Navarro Co., TX.

           ii.   Buddie, b.1 Oct 1909 TX. He d.1 Oct 1909 TX and was bur. Chatfield Cemetery New, Chatfield, Navarro Co., TX.

           iii.   Homer Lee, b.28 Oct 1910. He d.23 Mar 1915 at age 4 and was bur. Winchell Cem., Winchell, Brown Co., TX.

1052   iv.   Grover Ree, b. 11 Jan 1912 TX; m. Exa Mae Virginia Kelly.

1053   v.   Thomas Vernon "Tom," b. 22 Jan 1913 Chatfield, Navarro Co., TX; m. Edlean Johnson.

           vi.   Luther B., b. ca.Oct 1914 TX. He m. Velma (n.n.). He d.2002 and was bur. Eastlawn Mem. Park, Early, Brown Co., TX.
                Velma (n.n.), b.1913. She d.2001 and was bur. Eastlawn Mem. Park, Early, Brown Co., X.

           vii.   Woodie O'Dell "Dell" m. Laura Wanda Merrell. He, b.12 Apr 1915 Winchell, Brown Co., TX. He d.7 Mar 1965 Fort Worth, Tarrant Co., TX, at age 49 and was bur. Winchell Cem., Winchell, Brown Co., TX.
                Laura Wanda Merrell, b.24 Oct 1916 Brownwood, Brown Co., TX. She d.10 Aug 2000 Garnett, Anderson Co., TX, at age 83 and was bur. Greenleaf Cem., Brownwood, Brown Co., TX.

1054   viii.   Velma "Christine," b. 22 Dec 1916 TX; m. Cecil Vance Riordan.

           ix.   William F. "Sandy", b. ca.Jun 1917 TX. He m. Viola Erlean Lewis in 1939. He d.1966; bur. Eastlawn Mem. Park, Early.
                Viola Erlean Lewis, b.27 Aug 1920 and d.18 Jul 2004 Brownwood, Brown Co., TX, ae.83; bur. Eastlawn Mem. Park.

1055   x.   Rubie "Arlene," b. 12 Mar 1919 Winchell, Brown Co., TX; m. Jay Cal Alcorn (USN-WWII).

           xi.   Herman "Earl", b.23 Apr 1922 Winchell, Brown Co., TX. He m. Dorothy Nell Lee on 3 Dec 1948. He d.19 Jan 2005 Fort Worth, Tarrant Co., TX, at age 82 and was bur. Greenleaf Cem., Brownwood, Brown Co., TX.
                Dorothy Nell Lee, b.28 Feb 1917. She d.2 Mar 2004 at age 87 and was bur. Greenleaf Cem., Brownwood.

           xii.   Alice Marie, b. ca.1925 TX. She m. (n.n.) Markham. She d. before 2002.

631. James Holliway "Tiney"[7] Abney (David[6], Benjamin[5], Benjamin[4], Hezekiah[3], Elisha[2], Abner[1]), b.8 Aug 1905. He m. Mary "Lillian" Simmons on 27 Aug 1922. He d.20 May 1979 Martling, Marshall Co., AL, at age 73 and was bur. Martling Community Cem., Martling, Marshall Co., AL.

Mary "Lillian" Simmons, b.11 Jun 1906 and d.21 Feb 1980 Martling, Marshall Co., AL, at age 73; and was bur. Martling Community Cem.

Known children of James Holliway "Tiney"[7] Abney and Mary "Lillian" Simmons both b. Martling, Marshall Co., AL:

1056   i.   James Edward[8], b. 21 Oct 1924; m. Edith Louise Roden.

           ii.   Byron Clay "Corkey", b.20 Jan 1927. He d.13 Sep 2003 Birmingham, Jefferson Co., AL, at age 76 and was bur. Memory Hill Cem., Albertville, Marshall Co., AL.

632. Mary "Lillian"[7] Rooks (Eva[6] Abney, Benjamin[5], Benjamin[4], Hezekiah[3], Elisha[2], Abner[1]), b.10 Apr 1902 AL. She m. James Mathew Huffstutler in Feb 1920 Winston Co., AL. She and James Mathew Huffstutler appeared on the censuses of 22 Apr 1930 and 13 Apr 1940 Walker Co., AL. She d.18 Dec 1968 Walker Co., AL, at age 66 and was bur. New Prospect Bapt. Ch. Cem., Jasper, Walker Co., AL.

James Mathew Huffstutler, b.13 Jan 1895 AL. He d.23 Mar 1979 Walker Co., AL, at age 84.

Known children of Mary "Lillian"[7] Rooks and James Mathew Huffstutler:

1057   i.   Artemis J. "Artie"[8], b. Christmas Eve, 24 Dec 1920 Arley, Winston Co., AL; m. John A. Kratsas (USArmy-WWII).

           ii.   Essie C., b. ca.1923; m. Hubert Berton Hill; d.19 Sep 2019; bur. New Prospect Bapt. Ch. Cem., Jasper, Walker Co., AL.
                Hubert Berton Hill, b.16 Apr 1914 Winston Co., AL; d.14 Apr 1982 Walker Co., AL, age 67; bur. New Prospect.

           iii.   James Troy, b.1 Sep 1924 Walker Co., AL. He d.20 Dec 1928 Walker Co., AL, at age 4 and was bur. New Prospect.

           iv.   Evie Beatrice "Bea" m. Wilson Allen Anderson (USN-WWII). , b.1 Sep 1926 Jasper, Walker Co., AL. She d.9 Jan 2017 Decatur, Morgan Co., AL, at age 90 and was bur. New Prospect Bapt. Ch. Cem., Jasper, Walker Co., AL.
                Wilson Allen Anderson (USN-WWII), b.14 Mar 1926 TN. He d.30 May 2014 TN at age 88; bur. New Prospect.

           v.   *T.Sgt.* Roy F. (USAF-Korea, Nam), b.30 Sep 1928 Walker Co., AL. He m. Winifred E. (n.n.). He d.22 Oct 1987 at age 59 and was bur. Fort Sam Houston National Cem., San Antonio, Bexar Co., TX.
                Winifred E. (n.n.), b.3 Jul 1927. She d.27 Feb 2003 at age 75 and was bur. Fort Sam Houston National Cem..

           vi.   *S.Sgt.* John (USAF-Korea), b.27 Dec 1930 AL. He d.7 Jan 1998 at age 67 and was bur. San Jacinto Mem. Park, Houston.

           vii.   Frances m. (n.n.) Murray. , b. ca.1934 AL.

633. John Richard "Jack"[7] Rooks (Eva[6] Abney, Benjamin[5], Benjamin[4], Hezekiah[3], Elisha[2], Abner[1]), b.20 May 1904 Marshall Co., AL. He m. Minnie Hilda "Nana" Bacon in 1934. He d.2 Nov 1980 Torrance, Los Angeles Co., CA, at age 76 and was bur. Green Hills Mem. Park, Rancho Palos Verdes, Los Angeles Co., CA.

Minnie Hilda "Nana" Bacon, b.15 Feb 1916 Eastport, Tishomingo Co., MS. She d.8 Jan 2005 Torrance, Los Angeles Co., CA, at age 88 and was bur. Green Hills Mem. Park, Rancho Palos Verdes, Los Angeles Co., CA.

Known children of John Richard "Jack"[7] Rooks and Minnie Hilda "Nana" Bacon:

1058   i.   Evelyn "June"[8], b. 30 Sep 1935 Chattanooga, Hamilton Co., TN; m1. Raymond Wahrman (USArmy); m2. Ray Harris Selvidge.

           ii.   Evie J., b. ca.1938 TN.

           iii.   Shirlee Ann m. (n.n.) Fins. , b.5 Dec 1939 Cullman, Cullman Co., AL. She d.20 Jan 2009 Redondo Beach, Los Angeles Co., CA, at age 69 and was bur. Green Hills Mem. Park, Rancho Palos Verdes, Los Angeles Co., CA.

634. Ezey Lee[7] Reeves (Sarah[6] Abney, Andrew[5], Benjamin[4], Hezekiah[3], Elisha[2], Abner[1]), b.21 Dec 1878 AL. She m. John Thomas "Tom" Pettit on 8 Nov 1896 Bell, Grayson Co., TX. She d.14 Jul 1964 Gilmer, Upshur Co., TX, at age 85 and was bur. Morris Cem., Pritchett, Upshur Co., TX.

John Thomas "Tom" Pettit, b.27 Sep 1879 Upshur Co., TX. He d.11 Sep 1946 Bronte, Coke Co., TX, at age 66.

Known children of Ezey Lee[7] Reeves and John Thomas "Tom" Pettit:

1059   i.   Addie Belle[8], b. 4 Apr 1913; m. Cpl. Hardy "Foster" Beaver (USArmy-WWII).

635. Dultsenia Catherine "Seaney"[7] Reeves (Sarah[6] Abney, Andrew[5], Benjamin[4], Hezekiah[3], Elisha[2], Abner[1]), b.21 Feb 1880 GA. She m. William Thomas Foster ca.1898. She d.13 Aug 1964 Pleasanton, Atascosa Co., TX, at age 84 and was bur. Morris Cem., Pritchett, Upshur Co., TX.
    William Thomas Foster, b.7 Jan 1873. He d.21 Mar 1933 Gilmer, Upshur Co., TX, at age 60 and was bur. on 23 Mar 1933 Morris Cem.
Known children of Dultsenia Catherine "Seaney"[7] Reeves and William Thomas Foster:
    1060   i.   Cora Lee[8], b. 26 Oct 1899; m. Grover Cleveland McNair.
            ii.   Amy, b.24 Feb 1908. She m. Wiley C. Gay in 1924. She d.1 May 1993 at age 85 and was bur. Sunset Mem. Park, Gilmer, Upshur Co., TX.
                      Wiley C. Gay, b.5 Aug 1902. He d.14 Nov 1967 at age 65 and was bur. Sunset Mem. Park, Gilmer, Upshur Co., TX.
    1061   iii. Drucilla "Dot," b. 6 Feb 1917 Upshur Co., TX; m. James Warren Gholson.

636. Mary "Erminta"[7] Sargent (Amanda[6] Abney, Andrew[5], Benjamin[4], Hezekiah[3], Elisha[2], Abner[1]), b.30 Jan 1878 AL. She m1. Thomas Sherman Bynum ca.1901. She and Thomas Sherman Bynum appeared on the census of 18 Apr 1910 Titus Co., TX. She m2. Cleo Carson Burton. She and Cleo Carson Burton appeared on the census of 30 Jan 1920 Titus Co., TX. She d.26 Feb 1928 Cookville, Titus Co., TX, at age 50 and was bur. Concord Cem., Omaha, Morris Co., TX.
    Thomas Sherman Bynum, b.10 Sep 1866 TX. He m1. Ruby Roach; d.12 Jan 1912 age 45; bur. Old Cookville Cem., Cookville, Titus Co., TX.
Known children of Mary "Erminta"[7] Sargent and Thomas Sherman Bynum all b. TX:
            i.   (baby)[8], b. ca.1902.
            ii.   James "Ollie" Wayne, b.30 Sep 1904. He m. Beaulah Hunter. He d.23 May 1968 at age 63 and was bur. Liberty Hill Cem., Argo, Titus Co., TX.
                      Beaulah Hunter, b.10 Apr 1907; m2. Charles Henry "Pete" Derrick. She d.26 Feb 1992 age 84; bur. Liberty Hill Cem.
    1062   iii. Bessie O., b. 21 Jul 1907; m. William Ernest Traylor.
    Cleo Carson Burton, b.17 May 1884 KY. He m2. Sarah Jane Sargent (sister of his first wife), daughter of William B. Sargent and Amanda Catherine "Mandy" Abney, ca.1929. He and Sarah Jane Sargent appeared on the census of 17 Apr 1930 Titus Co., TX. He d.5 Feb 1936 Cookville, Titus Co., TX, at age 51 and was bur. Concord Cem., Omaha, Morris Co., TX.
There were no known children of Mary "Erminta"[7] Sargent and Cleo Carson Burton.

637. Sarah Jane[7] Sargent (Amanda[6] Abney, Andrew[5], Benjamin[4], Hezekiah[3], Elisha[2], Abner[1]), b.7 May 1884 AL. She m1. Samuel Wesley "Sam" Van Zandt in 1901. She m2. Samuel Monroe "SM" Stevens in 1923. She m3. Cleo Carson Burton ca.1929. She and Cleo Carson Burton appeared on the census of 17 Apr 1930 Titus Co., TX. She d.10 Oct 1967 Mount Pleasant, Titus Co., TX, at age 83; bur. Center Grove Cem., Titus Co., TX.
    Samuel Wesley "Sam" Van Zandt, b.20 Jan 1882. He d.11 Jul 1920 at age 38 and was bur. Lone Star Cem., Mount Pleasant, Titus Co., TX.
Known children of Sarah Jane[7] Sargent and Samuel Wesley "Sam" Van Zandt:
            i.   Marion Leslie[8], b.26 May 1902 Titus Co., TX. He m. Allie Marie Littleton in 1962. He d.6 Jan 1977 Mount Pleasant, Titus Co., TX, at age 74 and was bur. Lone Star Cem., Mount Pleasant, Titus Co., TX.
                      Allie Marie Littleton, b.7 Jan 1917 and d.17 Sep 1980 Simms, Bowie Co., TX, at age 63 and was bur. Lone Star Cem.
    1063   ii.   William Ernest, b. 23 Jun 1905; m. Ruth Louvenia Brown.
    1064   iii. Erastus "Rasters," b. 13 Jul 1912 TX; m1. Eva Lorie Patrick; m2. Annie L. Hooper; m3. Frances D. Philpot.
    Samuel Monroe "SM" Stevens, b.8 Oct 1884 Mount Pleasant, Titus Co., TX. He d.11 Jan 1942 Huntsville, Walker Co., TX, at age 57 and was bur. Captain Joe Byrd Cem., Huntsville, Walker Co., TX.
Known child of Sarah Jane[7] Sargent and Samuel Monroe "SM" Stevens:
    1065   i.   Jewel Lillian[8], b. 10 Dec 1923 Titus Co., TX; m. SSgt. Morgan Randolph Dunn (USAF-WWII).
    Cleo Carson Burton, b.17 May 1884 KY. He m. Mary "Erminta" Sargent (see #636 above)
There were no known children of Sarah Jane[7] Sargent and Cleo Carson Burton.

638. William Zillman[7] Sargent (Amanda[6] Abney, Andrew[5], Benjamin[4], Hezekiah[3], Elisha[2], Abner[1]), b.27 May 1886 AL. He m1. Mary Missouri Landrum ca.1905. He and Mary Missouri Landrum appeared on the censuses of 16 Apr 1910 and 5 Jan 1920 Titus Co., TX. He m2. Esta Mae (n.n.) ca.1937. He and Esta Mae (n.n.) appeared on the census of 25 Apr 1940 Titus Co., TX. He d.13 Nov 1940 at age 54 and was bur. Center Grove Cem., Titus Co., TX.
    Mary Missouri Landrum, b.7 Oct 1888 TX. She d.6 Sep 1936 at age 47 and was bur. Center Grove Cem., Titus Co., TX.
Known children of William Zillman[7] Sargent and Mary Missouri Landrum:
            i.   Willie Mae[8], b.19 Aug 1907 TX. She d.19 Aug 1907 TX and was bur. Concord Cem., Omaha, Morris Co., TX.
            ii.   Gladys B., b. ca.May 1909 TX.
    1066   iii. Zillman Taylor, b. 11 Oct 1913 TX; m. Helen Catherine Bohanon.
            iv.   Wilma Lee m. J.D. Walker. , b.15 Apr 1918. She d.26 Dec 1996 at age 78; bur. Center Grove Cem., Titus Co., TX.
                      J.D. Walker, b.14 Jun 1911. He d.25 Feb 1995 at age 83 and was bur. Center Grove Cem., Titus Co., TX.
            v.   Vannoy Harold m. Fannie Lou Roper. [According to Linda Leake Amerson (Findagrave.com), Vannoy had siblings: James, Marie, Gladys B., Zillman Taylor and Wilma Lee Sargent Walker. The author has been unable to verify James and Marie.] He, b.12 Dec 1921 Titus Co., TX. He d.9 Jul 1986 at age 64 and was bur. Center Grove Cem., Titus Co., TX.
                      Fannie Lou Roper, b.2 Sep 1923. She d.28 Jan 2011 at age 87 and was bur. Center Grove Cem., Titus Co., TX.
    Esta Mae (n.n.), b. ca.1902 TX.
There were no known children of William Zillman[7] Sargent and Esta Mae (n.n.).

639. John Franklin[7] Sargent (Amanda[6] Abney, Andrew[5], Benjamin[4], Hezekiah[3], Elisha[2], Abner[1]) m. Ocie Mae Lunsford. He, b.9 Dec 1889 TX. He d.4 Aug 1953 at age 63 and was bur. Center Grove Cem., Titus Co., TX.
    Ocie Mae Lunsford, b.Christmas Eve, 24 Dec 1895. She d.13 Apr 1982 at age 86 and was bur. Center Grove Cem., Titus Co., TX.
Known children of John Franklin[7] Sargent and Ocie Mae Lunsford:
    1067   i.   Ocie May[8], b. 1912 Titus Co., TX; m. Marcus Moss.
    1068   ii.   Elvis, b. 25 Sep 1918; m. Dorothy Currey.

640. George Lee[7] Sargent (Amanda[6] Abney, Andrew[5], Benjamin[4], Hezekiah[3], Elisha[2], Abner[1]) m. Ollie May Moore. He, b.9 Feb 1892. He d.13 Sep 1952 at age 60 and was bur. Center Grove Cem., Titus Co., TX.

Ollie May Moore, b.9 Feb 1892. She d.26 Jun 1940 at age 48 and was bur. Center Grove Cem., Titus Co., TX.
Known child of George Lee⁷ Sargent and Ollie May Moore:
    1069   i.   Johnnie Woodrow "Woody"⁸, b. 19 Dec 1918; m. Eunice Clark.

641. Albert Thadous⁷ Sargent (Amanda⁶ Abney, Andrew⁵, Benjamin⁴, Hezekiah³, Elisha², Abner¹) m. Julia Elvia Hardin. He, b.10 Oct 1895 Morris Co., TX. He d.15 Mar 1965 Mount Pleasant, Titus Co., TX, at age 69 and was bur. Center Grove Cem., Titus Co., TX.
    Julia Elvia Hardin, b.14 Feb 1897 AR. She d.7 Dec 1986 TX at age 89 and was bur. Center Grove Cem., Titus Co., TX.
Known children of Albert Thadous⁷ Sargent and Julia Elvia Hardin:
        i.   James Albert⁸, b.29 Oct 1931 Titus Co., TX; m. Millie Elizabeth Elliott; d.31 Aug 1972 TX age 40; Center Grove Cem.
             Millie Elizabeth Elliott, b.7 Mar 1931. She d.12 Apr 1972 at age 41 and was bur. Center Grove Cem., Titus Co., TX.
        ii.   Fannie Jean m. Billy "Bob" Tosh. , b.10 Jun 1933 Cookville, Titus Co., TX. She d.14 Apr 2013 Cookville, Titus Co., TX, at age 79 and was bur. Center Grove Cem., Titus Co., TX.
             Billy "Bob" Tosh, b.25 Mar 1926. He d.19 Apr 2002 at age 76 and was bur. Center Grove Cem., Titus Co., TX.

642. Haze "Anna"⁷ Ellison (Sarah⁶ Abney, Hezekiah⁵, Benjamin⁴, Hezekiah³, Elisha², Abner¹), b.4 May 1878 Acworth, Cobb Co., AR. She m. John Franklin Pelfrey on 8 Sep 1895 Decatur, DeKalb Co., GA. She d.4 Nov 1963 Oklahoma City, Oklahoma Co., OK, at age 85 and was bur. Maysville Cem., Maysville, Garvin Co., OK.
    John Franklin Pelfrey, b.30 May 1874 Pratt City, Jefferson Co., AL. He d.2 Sep 1942 Maysville, Garvin Co., OK, age 68; bur. Maysville Cem.
Known children of Haze "Anna"⁷ Ellison and John Franklin Pelfrey:
    1070   i.   Thomas Franklin⁸, b. 13 Jul 1896 Pratt City, Jefferson Co., AL; m. Avis Jewell McGregor.
    1071   ii.   Vera Ethel, b. 4 Aug 1897 Carbon Hill, Walker Co., AL; m. Marion Albert Matthews Sr.
        iii.   Anna Mae, b.29 Sep 1904 Walker Co., AL. She d.29 Jul 1943 Clinton, Custer Co., OK, at age 38; bur. Maysville Cem.
        iv.   Maudine Ruth, b.8 Jul 1915 Haleyville, Winston Co., AL. She m. John Aaron Flynn in 1933. She d.14 Nov 1942 OK at age 27 and was bur. Maysville Cem., Maysville, Garvin Co., OK.
             John Aaron Flynn, b.22 Mar 1910 Charleston, Franklin Co., AR. He d.11 May 1997 Tulsa, Tulsa Co., OK, at age 87.

643. Richard Lawrence⁷ Ellison (Sarah⁶ Abney, Hezekiah⁵, Benjamin⁴, Hezekiah³, Elisha², Abner¹) m. Alma May Newman. He, b.20 Feb 1887 Cartersville, Bartow Co., GA. He d.27 Jul 1977 San Bernardino Co., CA, at age 90 and was bur. Forest Hill Cem., Birmingham, Jefferson Co., AL.
    Alma May Newman, b.28 Jul 1891. She d.20 Jul 1974 at age 82 and was bur. Forest Hill Cem., Birmingham, Jefferson Co., AL.
Known child of Richard Lawrence⁷ Ellison and Alma May Newman:
        i.   Katherine⁸, b.7 Feb 1918. She d.23 Jun 1943 at age 25 and was bur. Forest Hill Cem., Birmingham, Jefferson Co., AL.

644. DeWitt Talmage "Dee"⁷ Abney (Hezekiah⁶, Hezekiah⁵, Benjamin⁴, Hezekiah³, Elisha², Abner¹) m. Lela Mae Barnes. He, b.18 Nov 1897 Cartersville, Bartow Co., GA. He and Lela Mae Barnes appeared on the census of 4 Apr 1930 Jeter, Choctaw Co., OK. He d.13 Jan 1979 OK at age 81 and was bur. Goodland Cem., Choctaw Co., OK.
    Lela Mae Barnes, b.9 Mar 1906 Lockesburg, Sevier Co., AR. She d.6 Jul 2000 Hugo, Choctaw Co., OK, at age 94; bur. Goodland Cem.
Known children of DeWitt Talmage "Dee"⁷ Abney and Lela Mae Barnes:
    1072   i.   Evalena⁸, b. 7 Jul 1923 Gay, Choctaw Co., OK; m. Fowler Nabors; m. Melvin L. Benton.
        ii.   Dorothy, b. ca.1925 OK; m. (n.n.) Hitchcock.
        iii.   LeRoy, b.21 Sep 1927 OK. He d.21 Jul 1928 OK and was bur. Goodland Cem., Choctaw Co., OK.
        iv.   J.D., b. ca.Aug 1929 OK.
        v.   J.R.
        vi.   James.
        vii.   Leo.
        viii.   Cleo Edward "Ed."
        ix.   J.C.
        x.   Velma Lou. She m. (n.n.) Sangster.
        xi.   Lula Mae "Lou". She m. (n.n.) Hardaway.
        xii.   Janice. She m. (n.n.) Boyd.
    1073   xiii.   Floria "Jean," b. New Year's Day, 1 Jan 1948 Gay, Choctaw Co., OK; m. (n.n.) McDaniel.

645. George Washington⁷ Abney (Hezekiah⁶, Hezekiah⁵, Benjamin⁴, Hezekiah³, Elisha², Abner¹) m. Dovie Lee Kelly. He, b.10 Jul 1899 Bartow Co., GA. He and Dovie Lee Kelly appeared on the census of 12 Apr 1940 Jeter, Choctaw Co., OK. He d.8 May 1988 Victorville, San Bernardino Co., CA, at age 88.
    Dovie Lee Kelly, b. ca.1905 OK.
Known children of George Washington⁷ Abney and Dovie Lee Kelly:
        i.   Nova Katherine "Kate"⁸, b.1924 OK. She d.2003.
        ii.   Junior C. "JC", b.9 Jul 1926 TX. He d.13 Apr 2013, age 86; bur. Riverside National Cem., Riverside, Riverside Co., CA.
        iii.   James Richard, b.1929 TX. He d.2008.

646. William "Grady"⁷ Abney (Hezekiah⁶, Hezekiah⁵, Benjamin⁴, Hezekiah³, Elisha², Abner¹) m. Ora Bell Barnes. He, b.22 Sep 1901 GA. He d.8 Oct 1987 Tulare Co., CA, at age 86 and was bur. Tulare Cem., Tulare, Tulare Co., CA.
    Ora Bell Barnes, b.10 Jun 1909 AR. She d.29 Jan 2000 Tulare, Tulare Co., CA, at age 90 and was bur. Tulare Cem., Tulare, Tulare Co., CA.
Known child of William "Grady"⁷ Abney and Ora Bell Barnes:
        i.   Weldon Glenn⁸, b.29 Mar 1939 OK. He d.16 Jan 1964 Aguila, Maricopa Co., AZ, at age 24 and was bur. Tulare Cem., Tulare, Tulare Co., OK.

647. Paul Leonard⁷ Abney Sr. (Hezekiah⁶, Hezekiah⁵, Benjamin⁴, Hezekiah³, Elisha², Abner¹), b.4 Jan 1904 Choctaw Co., OK. He m1. Orpha Mae Pasley on 25 Nov 1932. He m2. Betty Jean Warren on 27 Nov 1960 Paris, Lamar Co., TX. He d.8 Jan 1993 Lamar Co., TX, at age 89 and was bur. Goodland Cem., Choctaw Co., OK.

Orpha Mae Pasley, b.27 Mar 1914 OK. She d.18 Jun 1979 at age 65 and was bur. Sunset Mem. Park, Albuquerque, Bernalillo Co., NM.
Known children of Paul Leonard[7] Abney Sr. and Orpha Mae Pasley:
       1074   i.   Paul Leonard[8], b. 22 Nov 1933 Hugo, Choctaw Co., OK; m. Bobbie Ray Rice.
               ii. Earline m1. (n.n.) Gibson. She m2. (n.n.) Hodges.
              iii. Nancy m. (n.n.) Duncan.
Betty Jean Warren, b.1927 Udall, Cowley Co., KS. She d.1998 Paris, Lamar Co., TX and was bur. Goodland Cem., Choctaw Co., OK.
There were no known children of Paul Leonard[7] Abney Sr. and Betty Jean Warren.

648. Lucy "Irena"[7] Abney (Hezekiah[6], Hezekiah[5], Benjamin[4], Hezekiah[3], Elisha[2], Abner[1]), b.3 Aug 1908 Marshall Co., AL. She m. George Austin Merrick ca.1934. She and George Austin Merrick appeared on the census of 25 Apr 1940 Causey, Roosevelt Co., NM. She d.28 Jan 1944 Causey, Roosevelt Co., NM, at age 35 and was bur. Causey Cem., Causey, Roosevelt Co., NM.
George Austin Merrick, b.10 Dec 1915 Causey, Roosevelt Co., NM. He m. Ivy Lorine Fouse. He d.27 Mar 1985 Perryton, Ochiltree Co., TX, at age 69 and was bur. Ochiltree Cem., Perryton, Ochiltree Co., TX.
Known children of Lucy "Irena"[7] Abney and George Austin Merrick:
               i.   Austin[8], b. ca.1935 NM.
               ii. Maxine, b.1937. She d.1938 and was bur. Causey Cem., Causey, Roosevelt Co., NM.

649. Ephus Louis[7] Abney (Hezekiah[6], Hezekiah[5], Benjamin[4], Hezekiah[3], Elisha[2], Abner[1]), b.16 Sep 1910 AL. He m. Minnie Delilah Swagger ca.1931. He m. Opal J. Tarrant. He and Minnie Delilah Swagger appeared on the census of 17 Apr 1940 Jeter, Choctaw Co., OK. He d.7 Aug 1985 OK at age 74 and was bur. Goodland Cem., Choctaw Co., OK.
Minnie Delilah Swagger, b.26 Feb 1915 De Queen, Sevier Co., AR. She d.9 May 1975 Lubbock, Lubbock Co., TX, at age 60 and was bur. Resthaven Mem. Park, Lubbock, Lubbock Co., TX.
Known children of Ephus Louis[7] Abney and Minnie Delilah Swagger:
               i.   Betty Jean[8], b.5 Sep 1932 Choctaw Co., OK. She m. Kenneth Pitchford West (USN-WWII) in 1984. She d.15 May 1993 Antlers, Pushmataha Co., OK, at age 60 and was bur. Shoat Springs Cem., Hugo, Choctaw Co., OK.
                     Kenneth Pitchford West (USN-WWII), b.9 Feb 1928 OK and was bur. Restland Cem., Boswell, Choctaw Co., OK. He d.13 Jan 1993 Choctaw Co., OK, at age 64.
               ii. Bessie Lee, b.23 Mar 1935 Gay, Choctaw Co., OK. She m. Clinton J. Hill in 1952. She d.18 Dec 2012 Hugo, Choctaw Co., OK, at age 77 and was bur. Shoat Springs Cem., Hugo, Choctaw Co., OK.
                     Clinton J. Hill, b.31 Mar 1927. He d.30 Jul 2007 at age 80; bur. Shoat Springs Cem., Hugo, Choctaw Co., OK.
              iii. Frances "Louise", b.17 Nov 1937. She m. Butch Mandrell. d.23 Dec 2000 at age 63.
Opal J. Tarrant, b.13 Nov 1918 Reese, Cherokee Co., TX and was bur. Goodland Cem., Choctaw Co., OK. She d.4 Jan 1981 OK at age 62.
Known children of Ephus Louis[7] Abney and Opal J. Tarrant:
               i.   Sheila May[8] m. (n.n.) Gamblin.
               ii. Ann.

650. Hezekiah Karr[7] Abney (USArmy-WWII) (Hezekiah[6], Hezekiah[5], Benjamin[4], Hezekiah[3], Elisha[2], Abner[1]), b.29 Apr 1921. He m. Agnes Johnson in Jan 1966. He d.17 Apr 2002 at age 80 and was bur. Goodland Cem., Choctaw Co., OK.
Agnes Johnson, b.11 Aug 1925 Kent, Choctaw Co., OK; m1. (n.n.) Oakes; d.20 Jan 1998 Paris, Lamar Co., TX, age 72; bur. Goodland Cem.
Known child of Hezekiah Karr[7] Abney (USArmy-WWII) and Agnes Johnson:
               i.   Curtis[8].

651. Georgia Rosina[7] Abney (George[6], Hezekiah[5], Benjamin[4], Hezekiah[3], Elisha[2], Abner[1]), b.12 Dec 1905 Floyd Co., GA. She m. PFC Columbus Alexander Tidwell (USArmy-WWI) ca.1922. She and Columbus appeared on the censuses of 17 Apr 1930 Bartow Co., GA; and 29 Apr 1940 Rome, Floyd Co., GA. She d.8 Apr 1977 Floyd Co., GA, at age 71 and was bur. East View Cem., Rome, Floyd Co., GA.
PFC Columbus Alexander Tidwell (USArmy-WWI), b.11 Jan 1897. He d.24 Jun 1963 at age 66 and was bur. East View Cem., Rome.
Known children Rosina[7] Abney and PFC Columbus Alexander Tidwell (USArmy-WWI):
       1075   i.   Oralee[8], b. 15 Jun 1923; m. Howard Jones.
               ii. Lenton A., b. ca.Apr 1929.

652. Clifton[7] Abney (George[6], Hezekiah[5], Benjamin[4], Hezekiah[3], Elisha[2], Abner[1]), b.2 Nov 1908 Floyd Co., GA. He and his brother, Clarence Abney were liv. on 8 Apr 1930 as boarders with Houwse family, Rome, Floyd Co., GA. He m. Beatrice Tatum ca.1933. He and Beatrice appeared on the census of 11 Apr 1940 Rome, Floyd Co., GA. He d. Christmas Eve, 24 Dec 1950 at age 42; bur. East View Cem., Rome, Floyd Co., GA.
Beatrice Tatum, b.6 Jan 1915 Calhoun, Gordon Co., GA. She m2. Melvin McBurnett in 1953. She d.17 Sep 1980 Floyd Co., GA, at age 65 and was bur. East View Cem., Rome, Floyd Co., GA.
Known child of Clifton[7] Abney and Beatrice Tatum:
       1076   i.   Patsy Jo[8], b. 13 Nov 1934 Rome, Floyd Co., GA; m. Elston Lee Gentry Sr.

653. Samantha Jane "Janie"[7] Abney (George[6], George[5], Benjamin[4], Hezekiah[3], Elisha[2], Abner[1]), b.6 Aug 1887 AL. She m. William Henry Jarvis Sr. ca.1903. She d.12 Apr 1917 at age 29. She d. Friendship UMC Cem., Gardendale, Jefferson Co., AL.
William Henry Jarvis Sr, b. ca.1887 IL. He m2. Gladys B. (n.n.) ca.1918. He and Gladys B. (n.n.) appeared on the census of 21 Jan 1920 Coalburg, Jefferson Co., AL.
Known children of Samantha Jane "Janie"[7] Abney and William Henry Jarvis Sr.:
               i.   Charles[8], b. Friendship UMC Cem., Brookside, Jefferson Co., AL.
               ii. Esther was bur. Friendship UMC Cem., Brookside, Jefferson Co., AL.
              iii. Annie.
       1077   iv. Troy Lee, b. 9 Jun 1910 Jefferson Co., AL; m. Lucille Franklin.
              v. Ralph Jackson, b.18 Mar 1912 Jefferson Co., AL. He and Troy Lee Jarvis were liv. on 4 Apr 1930 with his grandfather, George Abney, Jefferson Co., AL. He d.10 Jan 1985 Brookside, Jefferson Co., AL, at age 72.

654. John W.[7] Abney Sr. (George[6], George[5], Benjamin[4], Hezekiah[3], Elisha[2], Abner[1]), b.5 Oct 1889 AL. He m. Aslie M. (n.n.) ca.1910. He and Aslie appeared on the censuses of 9 Jan 1920 Jefferson Co., AL; and 4 Apr 1930 and 22 Apr 1940 Mineral Springs, Jefferson Co., AL.
    Aslie M. (n.n.), b. ca.1890 AL.
Known children of John W.[7] Abney Sr. and Aslie M. (n.n.) all b. AL:
        i.   Lucille[8], b. ca.1911.
        ii.   Cora M., b. ca.1914.
        iii.   John W. "JW", b. ca.1919.
        iv.   Mildred V., b. ca.1923.

655. King David "Dave"[7] Abney (George[6], George[5], Benjamin[4], Hezekiah[3], Elisha[2], Abner[1]), b.13 Sep 1892 AL. He m. Bessie Vita Sparks ca.1912. He and Bessie Vita Sparks appeared on the censuses of 9 Jan 1920 and 4 Apr 1930 Jefferson Co., AL; and 22 Apr 1940 Mineral Springs, Jefferson Co., AL. He d.10 Apr 1969 Birmingham, Jefferson Co., AL, at age 76 and was bur. Friendship UMC Cem., Gardendale, Jefferson Co., AL.
    Bessie Vita Sparks, b.9 Mar 1894. She d.31 Aug 1977 Birmingham, Jefferson Co., AL, at age 83 and was bur. Friendship UMC Cem.
Known children of King David "Dave"[7] Abney and Bessie Vita Sparks:
1078   i.   Paul Edward[8], b. 9 Jan 1913 Watson, Jefferson Co., AL; m. Ruby Lee Barron.
        ii.   (infant son), b. ca.1915. He d. ca.1915 (at birth), Greenville, Butler Co., AL and was bur. Friendship UMC Cem.
        iii.   Greenville, b. ca.1917. She d. ca.1917 (in infancy), Greenville, Butler Co., AL and was bur. Friendship UMC Cem.
        iv.   Estelle D., b. ca.1919 AL. She was liv. in 1998.
        v.   George David, b.23 Sep 1925. He d.11 Sep 1969 at age 43 and was bur. Friendship UMC Cem.

656. Daisy[7] Abney (George[6], George[5], Benjamin[4], Hezekiah[3], Elisha[2], Abner[1]), b.7 Jun 1904 AL. She m. Fred Cleveland Fuller ca.1919. She and Fred Cleveland Fuller appeared on the censuses of 24 Apr 1930 and 22 Apr 1940 Mineral Springs, Jefferson Co., AL. She d.12 Dec 1995 at age 91 and was bur. Friendship UMC Cem., Gardendale, Jefferson Co., AL.
    Fred Cleveland Fuller, b.15 Sep 1897 AL. He m1. Mary Abney, daughter of John Abney [his parentage is unknown to this author], ca.1913. He d.30 May 1932 Jefferson Co., AL, at age 34 and was bur. Friendship UMC Cem., Gardendale, Jefferson Co., AL. [He and Mary Abney had three sons: (n.n.) Fuller, Pvt. Adron T. Fuller (USArmy), and Angus Fuller.]
Known children of Daisy[7] Abney and Fred Cleveland Fuller both b. AL:
1079   i.   Eugene "David"[8], b. 1928; m. Lucille McCulley Vinston.
1080   ii.   Mary Ellen, b. ca.Oct 1929; m. Cecil Barry Easter (USN-WWII).

657. Elbert "Arnold"[7] Abney (George[6], George[5], Benjamin[4], Hezekiah[3], Elisha[2], Abner[1]), b.1908 AL. He m. Linnie (n.n.) ca.1938. They appeared on the census of 22 Apr 1940 Mineral Springs, Jefferson Co., AL. He d.1983; bur. Jefferson Mem. Gardens East, Trussville, Jefferson Co., AL.
    Linnie (n.n.), b.1914 AL. She d.1996 and was bur. Jefferson Mem. Gardens East, Trussville, Jefferson Co., AL.
Known child of Elbert "Arnold"[7] Abney and Linnie (n.n.):
        i.   Betty Carol[8], b. ca.1939 AL.

658. Homer Garton[7] Abney (John[6], George[5], Benjamin[4], Hezekiah[3], Elisha[2], Abner[1]), b.18 Sep 1890 AL. He m. Lela Mae Gault ca.1914. He and Lela Mae Gault appeared on the censuses of 18 Feb 1920, 10 Apr 1930 and 9 Apr 1940 Dallas Co., TX. He d.13 Sep 1969 Rockwall, Rockwall Co., TX, at age 78 and was bur. Grove Hill Mem. Park, Dallas, Dallas Co., TX.
    Lela Mae Gault, b.16 Jul 1896 TN. She d.8 Jun 1976 Garland, Dallas Co., TX, at age 79.
Known children of Homer Garton[7] Abney and Lela Mae Gault:
1081   i.   Johnny Calvin[8], b. 11 Jun 1915 Dallas, Dallas Co., TX; m. Winona Helen Kilgore; m. Dorothy F. Pruitt.
        ii.   Anna Doris "Annie", b.26 Oct 1918. She m. Haskell Jefferson Spillman on 2 May 1938. They appeared on the census of 10 Apr 1940 Dallas, Dallas Co., TX. She d.14 Jun 2009 at age 90; bur. Grove Hill Mem. Park, Dallas, Dallas Co., TX. Haskell Jefferson Spillman, b.7 Mar 1917. He d.22 Jul 1981 at age 64.
1082   iii.   Elbert Lloyd, b. 1921 Dallas, Dallas Co., TX; m. Teresa H. Harris; m. Annie Jean McCallum.
        iv.   Willie, b.7 Dec 1923; d.10 Jan 1987 Dallas, Dallas Co., TX, age 63; bur. Grove Hill Mem. Park, Dallas, Dallas Co., TX.
        v.   Sgt. Homer Ray (USArmy-Korea), b.22 Aug 1926. He became a Prisoner of War on 30 Nov 1950 POW, near Kunu-ri, North Korea. He d. 22 Jan 1951 in captivity in North Korea, at age 24. His name is inscribed on the *Courts of the Missing* at Honolulu Memorial Honolulu Memorial, Honolulu, Honolulu Co., HI. His name is also inscribed on the National Korean War Veterans Memorial, Washington, DC. More than 7,800 soldiers of the Korean War remain unaccounted for, with over 5,000 believed to be in North Korea.

659. Mattie Bell[7] Abney (John[6], George[5], Benjamin[4], Hezekiah[3], Elisha[2], Abner[1]), b. Jul 1893. She m. Frank Alexander DeMoss ca.1920. She d.5 Jan 1938 at age 44 and was bur. McCree Cem., Dallas, Dallas Co., TX.
    Frank Alexander DeMoss, b.23 Mar 1890. He d.6 Jul 1947 at age 57 and was bur. McCree Cem., Dallas, Dallas Co., TX.
Known child of Mattie Bell[7] Abney and Frank Alexander DeMoss:
1083   i.   Homer Welton "Buddy"[8], b. 21 Jul 1921; m. Stella "Alois" Horton; m. Dortha Nell Dean.

660. Vergia Mae "Vergie"[7] Abney (John[6], George[5], Benjamin[4], Hezekiah[3], Elisha[2], Abner[1]), b.4 Aug 1896 Dallas Co., TX. She m. Benjamin Franklin "Frank" Young Sr. ca.1912. She and Benjamin were liv. on 6 Jan 1920 with his brother, Virgil H. Young, Dallas, Dallas Co., TX. She and Benjamin appeared on the census of 14 Apr 1930 and 9 Apr 1940 Dallas, Dallas Co., TX. She d.5 Feb 1961 Dallas, Dallas Co., TX, at age 64 and was bur. Grove Hill Mem. Park, Dallas, Dallas Co., TX.
    Benjamin Franklin "Frank" Young Sr, b.15 Feb 1891 Parker Co., TX; d.8 Jun 1981 Dallas, Dallas Co., TX, age 90; bur. Grove Hill Mem. Park.
Known children of Vergia Mae "Vergie"[7] Abney and Benjamin Franklin "Frank" Young Sr.:
        i.   Augusta Marie "Gussie"[8] m. Roy E. Ailes. , b.14 Feb 1914 Dallas Co., TX. She d.3 Sep 2004 Mesquite, Dallas Co., TX, at age 90 and was bur. Grove Hill Mem. Park, Dallas, Dallas Co., TX.
           Roy E. Ailes, b.1913. He d.1985 and was bur. Grove Hill Mem. Park, Dallas, Dallas Co., TX.
1084   ii.   Benjamin Frank "Ben," b. ca.Apr 1917 TX; m. Dorothy Lee Haley.

   iii. Maybelle, b.9 May 1920 TX. She m. Morris Claude McGowan in 1943. She d.21 Apr 1983 Dallas, Dallas Co., TX, at age 62 and was bur. Grove Hill Mem. Park, Dallas, Dallas Co., TX.
     Morris Claude McGowan, b.9 Oct 1904 Miller Grove, Hopkins Co., TX. He d.10 Jul 1965 Dallas, Dallas Co., TX, at age 60 and was bur. Grove Hill Mem. Park, Dallas, Dallas Co., TX.
   iv. Wayne Foster, b.14 Jul 1922 Dallas Co., TX. He d.29 Mar 1976 Dallas Co., TX, at age 53 and was bur. Grove Hill Mem. Park, Dallas, Dallas Co., TX.

661. Opal Augusta[7] Abney (John[6], George[5], Benjamin[4], Hezekiah[3], Elisha[2], Abner[1]), b.30 Jun 1906. She m. Fred Gus Bryant ca.1923. She d.22 Feb 1976 at age 69 and was bur. Grove Hill Mem. Park, Dallas, Dallas Co., TX.
  Fred Gus Bryant, b.15 Dec 1898. He d.9 Apr 1985 at age 86 and was bur. Grove Hill Mem. Park, Dallas, Dallas Co., TX.
Known children of Opal Augusta[7] Abney and Fred Gus Bryant:
   i. Opal Faye[8], b.15 Oct 1924. She m. J.M. "Mack" Dorman on 20 Jul 1949. She d.4 Feb 1996 at age 71 and was bur. Grove Hill Mem. Park, Dallas, Dallas Co., TX.
     J.M. "Mack" Dorman, b.7 Dec 1910. He d.2 Jul 1982 at age 71 and was bur. Grove Hill Mem. Park, Dallas.
   ii. Gussie Alene m. James Edward "Sonny" Jasper. , b.14 Dec 1926. She d.22 Aug 2008 TX at age 81 and was bur. Grove Hill Mem. Park, Dallas, Dallas Co., TX.
     James Edward "Sonny" Jasper, b.25 Nov 1926 Dallas Co., TX; d.29 Jun 2002 Eustace, Henderson Co., TX, at age 75 and was bur. Grove Hill Mem. Park, Dallas, Dallas Co., TX.
   iii. Vernon Harvey, b.4 May 1929. He m. Norma Kathleen Bolton on 21 Oct 1950 Forney, Kaufman Co., TX. He d.14 Feb 2019 at age 89 and was bur. Grove Hill Mem. Park, Dallas, Dallas Co., TX.
     Norma Kathleen Bolton, b.14 Jun 1934; d.6 Jan 2019 Greenville, Hunt Co., TX, age 84; bur. Grove Hill Mem. Park.
   iv. Rex Arlon b.26 Feb 1933 Dallas, Dallas Co., TX. He m. Judy G. (n.n.) (she was b.1942). He,d.25 Jun 1993 Mesquite, Dallas Co., TX, at age 60 and was bur. Grove Hill Mem. Park, Dallas, Dallas Co., TX.

662. Mina Faye[7] Abney (John[6], George[5], Benjamin[4], Hezekiah[3], Elisha[2], Abner[1]), b.5 Oct 1913 TX. She m. Howard Ernest Carrigan ca.1930. She and Howard appeared on the census of 23 Apr 1940 Texas City, Galveston Co., TX. She d.29 Dec 1983 at age 70; bur. Grove Hill Mem. Park.
  Howard Ernest Carrigan, b.7 Aug 1906 TX. He d.8 Feb 1970 Dallas, Dallas Co., TX, at age 63.
Known children of Mina Faye[7] Abney and Howard Ernest Carrigan:
   i. Howard Eugene[8], b.13 Jan 1931 TX. He m. Edith Loraine Manning on 12 Aug 1950 Rockwall, Rockwall Co., TX. He d.27 Nov 2005 Dallas Co., TX, at age 74 and was bur. Mount Carmel Cem., Wolfe City, Hunt Co., TX.
   ii. Alma Jo, b.26 May 1932 TX. She m. S.Sgt. W.B. "Dub" Tullos (USArmy-WWII) in 1948. She d.4 Dec 2009 at age 77 and was bur. Grove Hill Mem. Park, Dallas, Dallas Co., TX.
     S.Sgt. W.B. "Dub" Tullos (USArmy-WWII), b.21 Feb 1921. He d.14 Jun 1971 at age 50; bur. Grove Hill Mem. Park.
1085 iii. Wanda Ruth, b. 2 Jul 1935 Parkland Hosp., Dallas, Dallas Co., TX; m. Glen Lancaster (USArmy).
   iv. James Everett, b.7 Nov 1937 TX. He d.7 Apr 2002 at age 64. He was cremated.
   v. Marvin G., b.19 Aug 1943 TX. He d.21 Sep 2000 at age 57 and was bur. Grove Hill Mem. Park, Dallas, Dallas Co., TX.

663. William Houston "Will"[7] Abney (William[6], George[5], Benjamin[4], Hezekiah[3], Elisha[2], Abner[1]), b.13 Nov 1891 AL. He m. Elizabeth "Lizzie" Payne ca.1913. He and Elizabeth "Lizzie" Payne appeared on the census of 27 Jan 1920 McLennan Co., TX. He d.9 Jan 1925 Freestone Co., TX, at age 33 and was bur. China Spring Cem., China Spring, McLennan Co., TX.
  Elizabeth "Lizzie" Payne, b.3 Feb 1889 China Spring, McLennan Co., TX. She m2. Robert Franklin Gibson ca.1929. She and Robert appeared on the census of Apr 1930 McLennan Co., TX. They were divorced before 1940. She appeared as Head of Household on the census of 17 Apr 1940 Waco, McLennan Co., TX. She d.11 Feb 1959 Waco, McLennan Co., TX, at age 70; bur. China Spring Cem., China Spring, McLennan Co., TX.
Known children of William Houston "Will"[7] Abney and Elizabeth "Lizzie" Payne:
1086 i. William Texas[8], b. 1 Dec 1914 China Spring, McLennan Co., TX; m. Mary Evelyn Holt.
   ii. Will was stillborn 19 May 1922 China Spring, McLennan Co., TX.
1087 iii. Billie Jean, b. 27 Jun 1925 Waco, McLennan Co., TX; m. George Blair (USAF).

664. John "Philip"[7] Abney (William[6], George[5], Benjamin[4], Hezekiah[3], Elisha[2], Abner[1]), b.29 Oct 1898 Crawford, McLennan Co., TX. He m. Mable Clara McAdams ca.1923. He and Mable censuses of 16 Apr 1930 and 26 Apr 1940 Dallas Co., TX. He d.26 Oct 1977 Grand Saline, Van Zandt Co., TX, at age 78 and was bur. Grove Hill Mem. Park, Dallas, Dallas Co., TX.
  Mable Clara McAdams, b.28 Dec 1907. She d.8 Jul 2004 Dallas, Dallas Co., TX, at age 96 and was bur. Grove Hill Mem. Park, Dallas.
Known children of John "Philip"[7] Abney and Mable Clara McAdams:
1088 i. Wilma D.[8], b. 23 Jul 1925 Coryell Co., TX; m. Alvin Dorris Choate Sr. (USArmy-WWII).
1089 ii. Randle "David," b. 25 Feb 1928 TX; m. JoAnn Kline.
   iii. Clara May, b.5 Oct 1931 Dallas, Dallas Co., TX. She m1. Travis Avon "Ted" Coker. m2. PFC Lonnie H. Cox (USArmy-WWII). She d.13 Jan 1973 Dallas, Dallas Co., TX, at age 41.
     Travis Avon "Ted" Coker, b.21 May 1927 Hopkins Co., TX. He d.5 Aug 1988 Sulphur Springs, Hopkins Co., TX, at age 61 and was bur. Greenpond Cem., Como, Hopkins Co., TX.
     PFC Lonnie H. Cox (USArmy-WWII), b.30 Dec 1917 Kaufman Co., TX. He d.17 Dec 1970 Dallas, Dallas Co., TX, at age 52 and was bur. Grove Hill Mem. Park, Dallas, Dallas Co., TX.
   iv. Shirley, b. ca.1935 TX.

665. Rosa E.[7] Abney (William[6], George[5], Benjamin[4], Hezekiah[3], Elisha[2], Abner[1]), b.18 Jan 1903 TX. She m. George William "Guy" Griffith ca.1922. She and George appeared on the censuses of 9 Apr 1930 Coryell Co., TX; and 4 Apr 1940 Gatesville, Coryell Co., TX. She d.16 Dec 1980 Houston, Harris Co., TX, at age 77 and was bur. Odd Fellows Cem., Gatesville, Coryell Co., TX.
  George William "Guy" Griffith, b.21 Oct 1902 Clifton, Bosque Co., TX; d.12 Feb 1961 Gatesville, Coryell Co., TX; bur. Odd Fellows Cem.
Known child of Rosa E.[7] Abney and George William "Guy" Griffith:
   i. Margaret "Louise"[8], b. ca.1924 TX.

666. Ann May "Annie"[7] Abney (William[6], George[5], Benjamin[4], Hezekiah[3], Elisha[2], Abner[1]), b. ca.1907 TX. She m. James "Owen" Brashear ca.1927. She and James "Owen" Brashear appeared on the census of 9 Apr 1930 Salem, Doña Ana Co., NM. She and James "Owen" Brashear lived on 1 Apr 1935 Arrey, Sierra Co., NM. She and James "Owen" Brashear appeared on the census of 3 Apr 1940 Bayard, Grant Co., NM.
        James "Owen" Brashear, b. ca.1905 TX.
Known children of Ann May "Annie"[7] Abney and James "Owen" Brashear:
                i.   Ruby Joyce[8], b. ca.Oct 1928 TX.
                ii.   Kathleen M., b. ca.1939 NM.

667. Mammie "Alyce"[7] Abney (William[6], George[5], Benjamin[4], Hezekiah[3], Elisha[2], Abner[1]), b. ca.Oct 1909 TX. She m. Truman Phifer ca.1929. She and Truman Phifer appeared on the censuses of 14 Apr 1930 and 3 Apr 1940 Dallas, Dallas Co., TX.
        Truman Phifer, b. ca.1902 TX.
Known children of Mammie "Alyce"[7] Abney and Truman Phifer all b. TX:
                i.   Katherine[8], b. ca.Mar 1930.
                ii.   Fonscene, b. ca.1932.
                iii. Bobby Earl, b. ca.1934.
                iv.   Jerry L., b. ca.1938.

668. Ludie Mae[7] Abney (Alex[6], George[5], Benjamin[4], Hezekiah[3], Elisha[2], Abner[1]), b.1893. She m1. Frank O. "Foree" Myers in 1914. She and the boys were liv. on 3 Jan 1920 with father, Frank Abney, Jefferson Co., AL. She m2. Robert "Frank" Clowdus on 25 Feb 1922 Birmingham, Jefferson Co., AL. She and Robert "Frank" Clowdus appeared on the census of 8 Apr 1930 Sayreton, Jefferson Co., AL. They were divorced in 1939. She was liv. on 11 Apr 1940 with son, Herman, Sayreton, Jefferson Co., AL. She d.1975; bur. Friendship UMC Cem., Gardendale, Jefferson Co., AL.
        Frank O. "Foree" Myers d. before 1920.
Known children of Ludie Mae[7] Abney and Frank O. "Foree" Myers both b. AL:
        1090   i.   Herman Mancel[8], b. 2 Nov 1915; m1. Eva Mae Beasley; m2. Doris J. Myers.
                ii.   Milton, b. ca.1918.
There were no known children of Ludie Mae[7] Abney and Robert "Frank" Clowdus.

669. Gordon W.[7] Abney Sr. (USArmy-WWI) (Alex[6], George[5], Benjamin[4], Hezekiah[3], Elisha[2], Abner[1]), b.29 Apr 1895 AL. He m. Geneva M. (n.n.) (she was b. ca. 1911 AL) ca.1921. He and Geneva appeared on the censuses of 2 Apr 1930 Jefferson Co., AL; and 26 Apr 1940 Gardendale, Jefferson Co., AL. He d.24 Jan 1982 at age 86 and was bur. Walker Chapel Mem. Gardens, Fultondale, Jefferson Co., AL.
Known children of Gordon W.[7] Abney Sr. (USArmy-WWI) and Geneva M. (n.n.) both b. AL:
                i.   Margie[8], b.15 Mar 1922. She m. (n.n.) Tusa. d.16 Jun 2004 LA at age 82.
        1091   ii.   Gordon W., b. 15 Oct 1924; m. Jewel Dean.

670. James William "Will"[7] Abney (Alex[6], George[5], Benjamin[4], Hezekiah[3], Elisha[2], Abner[1]), b.8 Mar 1898 AL. He m. Agnes Cox ca.1920. He and Agnes Cox appeared on the censuses of 10 Apr 1930 and 22 Apr 1940 Sayreton, Jefferson Co., AL. He d.27 Jan 1964 at age 65 and was bur. Oakwood Mem. Gardens, Gardendale, Jefferson Co., AL.
        Agnes Cox, b.27 Aug 1901 AL. She d.20 Dec 1983 AL at age 82 and was bur. Oakwood Mem. Gardens, Gardendale, Jefferson Co., AL.
Known children of James William "Will"[7] Abney and Agnes Cox all b. AL:
                i.   Phillis C.[8], b. ca.1922.
                ii.   James A., b. ca.1924.
                iii. William, b. ca.1931.
                iv.   Robert, b. ca.1935.

671. Jesse Clinton "Clint"[7] Abney (Alex[6], George[5], Benjamin[4], Hezekiah[3], Elisha[2], Abner[1]), b.7 Nov 1902 AL. He m. Willine Wright ca.1925. He and Willine Wright appeared on the censuses of 8 Apr 1930 Sayreton, Jefferson Co., AL; and 5 Apr 1940 Fairmont, Jefferson Co., AL. He d.17 Aug 1969 at age 66 and was bur. Friendship UMC Cem., Gardendale, Jefferson Co., AL.
        Willine Wright, b.22 Oct 1911 AL. She d.13 Aug 1988 at age 76 and was bur. Friendship UMC Cem., Gardendale, Jefferson Co., AL.
Known children of Jesse Clinton "Clint"[7] Abney and Willine Wright:
                i.   Mildred[8], b.19 Nov 1926 AL; m. Donald Lee Fortenberry; d.27 Jan 1995 at age 68 and was bur. Friendship UMC Cem..
                      Donald Lee Fortenberry, b.15 Jul 1929; d.7 Jul 2008 New Castle, Jefferson Co., AL; bur. Friendship UMC Cem.
                ii.   Donald, b. ca.1931 AL.
                iii. Gloria Faye, b. ca.1933. She m. (n.n.) Caffee.
                iv.   Carolyn. She m. (n.n.) Bailey.
                v.   Linda. She m. (n.n.) Bias.

672. Albert Franklin[7] Abney (Alex[6], George[5], Benjamin[4], Hezekiah[3], Elisha[2], Abner[1]), b.12 Oct 1905 AL. He m. Clara Bell Lamons on 4 Aug 1928. He and Clara appeared on the censuses of 9 Apr 1930 and 13 Apr 1940 Birmingham, Jefferson Co., AL. He d. New Year's Eve, 31 Dec 1952 at age 47 and was bur. Friendship UMC Cem., Gardendale, Jefferson Co., AL.
Known children of Albert Franklin[7] Abney and Clara Bell Lamons all b. AL:
                i.   Albert "Lloyd"[8], b. ca.Aug 1929.
                ii.   Bettie Jean, b. ca.1931.
                iii. Martha Ann, b. ca.1935.

673. John David[7] Abney (Alex[6], George[5], Benjamin[4], Hezekiah[3], Elisha[2], Abner[1]), b.14 Jan 1907 AL. He m. May Belle Peffer ca.1927. He and May Belle Peffer appeared on the censuses of 25 Apr 1930 Walker Co., AL; and 17 Apr 1940 Gardendale, Jefferson Co., AL. He d.27 Oct 1962 at age 55 and was bur. Friendship UMC Cem., Gardendale, Jefferson Co., AL.
Known children of John David[7] Abney and May Belle Peffer:
                i.   John Howard[8], b. ca.Feb 1928 AL. He m. Maureen (n.n.).
                ii.   Peggy Sue, b. ca.1933 AL. She m. Frank Sylvester.

1092   iii.   Tommy Franklin, b. 26 Sep 1934; m. Shirley Jean Harris.
1093   iv.   Waltis Eugene "Gene," b. 4 Apr 1938; m. Brenda (n.n.).
       v.   Jackie, b. AL. She m. Bill Hinson.

674.   Rev. Horace Junior "June"[7] Abney (Alex[6], George[5], Benjamin[4], Hezekiah[3], Elisha[2], Abner[1]), b.8 Jun 1910 AL. He m. Stella Mae Roberts ca.1935. He and Stella Mae Roberts appeared on the census of 4 Apr 1940 Birmingham, Jefferson Co., AL. He d.17 Dec 1968 at age 58 and was bur. Friendship UMC Cem., Gardendale, Jefferson Co., AL.
     Stella Mae Roberts, b.30 Mar 1916. She d.6 May 1977 at age 61 and was bur. Friendship UMC Cem., Gardendale, Jefferson Co., AL.
Known children of Rev. Horace Junior "June"[7] Abney and Stella Mae Roberts:
1094   i.   Nancy "Janine"[8], b. 8 Apr 1936; m. L.G. Graham.
      ii.   Margaret "Lenora" m. Ray "Brother" Simpson. , b. ca.1939 AL.
1095   iii.   Horace "Grover," b. 9 Feb 1942; m. Barbara "Bobbie" (n.n.).

675.   Edith M.[7] Abney (Alex[6], George[5], Benjamin[4], Hezekiah[3], Elisha[2], Abner[1]), b.27 Mar 1918 AL. She m. Joseph Peter Giamportone (USN-WWII) ca.1935. She and Joseph Peter Giamportone (USN-WWII) appeared on the census of 11 Apr 1940 Sayreton, Jefferson Co., AL. She d.1 Jul 1989 at age 71 and was bur. Friendship UMC Cem., Gardendale, Jefferson Co., AL.
     Joseph Peter Giamportone (USN-WWII), b.12 Feb 1910. He m. Rose Mary (n.n.). He d.27 Dec 1986 at age 76 and was bur. Chattanooga National Cem., Chattanooga, Hamilton Co., TN.
Known children of Edith M.[7] Abney and Joseph Peter Giamportone (USN-WWII) both b. AL:
      i.   Ross[8], b. ca.1936.
      ii.   Marie, b. ca.1938.

676.   Isa Belle "Icie"[7] Abney (Marion[6], George[5], Benjamin[4], Hezekiah[3], Elisha[2], Abner[1]), b.13 Oct 1896 AL. She m. R.H. Myers on 18 Sep 1915 Jefferson Co., AL. She m. Charles Curtis Clowdus ca.1921. She and Charles Curtis Clowdus appeared on the census of 3 Apr 1940 Birmingham, Jefferson Co., AL. She d.18 Jun 1960 at age 63 and was bur. Friendship UMC Cem., Gardendale, Jefferson Co., AL.
Known children of Isa Belle "Icie"[7] Abney and R.H. Myers:
      i.   Thelma Loraine[8], b.4 Aug 1917 AL. She m. Aubrey Thomas Smith (USN-WWII) in 1953. She d.23 Jul 1963 VA at age 45 and was bur. Friendship UMC Cem., Gardendale, Jefferson Co., AL.
         Aubrey Thomas Smith (USN-WWII), b.26 Aug 1923 AL. He m. Georgia Ann Smith in 1946. He d.5 Aug 1972 Alexandria, VA, at age 48 and was bur. Cahaba Heights Bapt. Ch. Cem., Vestavia Hills, Jefferson Co., AL.
     Charles Curtis Clowdus, b.16 Aug 1899 Chepultepec, Blount Co., AL. He d.11 Sep 1972 at age 73 and was bur. Friendship UMC Cem.
Known children of Isa Belle "Icie"[7] Abney and Charles Curtis Clowdus:
      i.   Margaret Justina[8] m. Robert H. Amacher (USArmy-WWII). , b.26 Dec 1922 Jefferson Co., AL. She d.29 Apr 1994 at age 71 and was bur. Fairview Cem., Ridgway, Elk Co., PA.
         Robert H. Amacher (USArmy-WWII), b.6 Sep 1921. He d.4 Nov 1987 at age 66 and was bur. Fairview Cem.
      ii.   Charles, b. ca.1926.

677.   George Washington[7] Abney (Peter[6], George[5], Benjamin[4], Hezekiah[3], Elisha[2], Abner[1]), b.4 Aug 1901 AL. He m. Vera Hodges ca.1921. He and Vera Hodges appeared on the censuses of 14 Apr 1930 Fairmont, Jefferson Co., AL; and 22 Apr 1940 Sayreton, Jefferson Co., AL. He d.18 Feb 1967 AL at age 65 and was bur. Walker Chapel Mem. Gardens, Fultondale, Jefferson Co., AL.
     Vera Hodges, b.7 Feb 1897. She d.8 Jul 1988 Jefferson Co., AL, at age 91 and was bur. Walker Chapel Mem. Gardens, Fultondale.
Known children of George Washington[7] Abney and Vera Hodges:
      i.   George Merle[8], b.14 Oct 1922 AL. He d.6 Dec 1928 at age 6 and was bur. Walker Chapel Mem. Gardens, Fultondale.
      ii.   Alice Elizabeth, b.11 Jul 1924 Jefferson Co., AL. She m. Jack P. Dray (USN-WWII) on 8 Sep 1947. She d.4 Feb 1981 Caddo Par., LA, at age 56 and was bur. Mulhearn Mem. Park Cem., Monroe, Ouachita Par., LA.
         Jack P. Dray (USN-WWII), b.27 Aug 1923. He d.4 Feb 1983 Tulsa, OK, at age 59.
      iii.   Lavera, b. ca.Mar 1926 AL; m. (n.n.) Reed.
1096   iv.   Helen, b. ca.Jul 1927; m. Pvt. Harold W. Fromhold (USArmy-WWII).
      v.   Ruth, b. ca.1932 AL.
      vi.   Kenneth, b. ca.1935 AL.
      vii.   Clarence L., b. ca.1936 AL; m. Faye (n.n.).

678.   Julius "Vernie"[7] Abney (Peter[6], George[5], Benjamin[4], Hezekiah[3], Elisha[2], Abner[1]), b.13 Feb 1904 AL. He m. Nancy Lula Brown on Christmas Day, 25 Dec 1926 Birmingham, Jefferson Co., AL. He and Nancy Lula Brown appeared on the censuses of 29 Apr 1930 Fairmont, Jefferson Co., AL; and 20 Apr 1940 Gardendale, Jefferson Co., AL. He d.19 Dec 1963 at age 59; bur. Friendship UMC Cem., Gardendale, Jefferson Co., AL.
     Nancy Lula Brown, b.17 Apr 1907 AL. She d.5 Jan 1961 AL at age 53 and was bur. Friendship UMC Cem., Gardendale, Jefferson Co., AL.
Known child of Julius "Vernie"[7] Abney and Nancy Lula Brown:
      i.   LuVerne[8], b.6 Jan 1936 AL. She d.14 Jul 2003 at age 67; bur. Friendship UMC Cem., Gardendale, Jefferson Co., AL.

679.   Elsie Ruby[7] Abney (Peter[6], George[5], Benjamin[4], Hezekiah[3], Elisha[2], Abner[1]), b.8 Apr 1908. She m. Raymond Daniel Rockett Sr. on 21 Apr 1924 Birmingham, Jefferson Co., AL. She and Raymond appeared on the censuses of 11 Apr 1930 Jefferson Co., AL; and 22 Apr 1940 Sayreton, Jefferson Co., AL. She d.1 Dec 1992 at age 84 and was bur. Friendship UMC Cem., Gardendale, Jefferson Co., AL.
     Raymond Daniel Rockett Sr, b.26 Jul 1903 Lipscomb, Jefferson Co., AL. He d.4 Sep 1960 Birmingham, Jefferson Co., AL, at age 57.
Known children of Elsie Ruby[7] Abney and Raymond Daniel Rockett Sr.:
      i.   Ruby Doris[8], b.1 Mar 1925. She m. Harding Arthur Palmer on Christmas Day, 25 Dec 1943 Jefferson Co., AL. She d.20 Dec 1994 at age 69 and was bur. Friendship UMC Cem., Gardendale, Jefferson Co., AL.
      ii.   Raymond Daniel, b.13 Mar 1927. He d.22 Jan 1973, age 45; bur. Friendship UMC Cem., Gardendale, Jefferson Co., AL.

680.   Hubert[7] Abney Sr. (Peter[6], George[5], Benjamin[4], Hezekiah[3], Elisha[2], Abner[1]), b.16 Jun 1910 AL. He m. Gillian R. (n.n.) (b.ca.1918 AL) ca.1932. They appeared on the census of 3 Apr 1940 Fairmont, Jefferson Co., AL. He d.1 Oct 1983 Kimberly, Jefferson Co., AL, at age 73.

Known children of Hubert[7] Abney Sr. and Gillian R. (n.n.) all b. AL:
    i.   Barbara L.[8], b. ca.1933.
    ii. Hubert, b.10 Sep 1934. He d.29 Jun 1940 at age 5; bur. Walker Chapel Mem. Gardens, Fultondale, Jefferson Co., AL.
    iii. Douglas R., b. ca.1936.

681. Lillie Mae[7] Abney (Peter[6], George[5], Benjamin[4], Hezekiah[3], Elisha[2], Abner[1]), b.9 Jul 1913. She m. Franklin "Floyd" Green on 12 Oct 1929 Jefferson Co., AL. She and Franklin "Floyd" Green appeared on the censuses of 11 Apr 1930 Lewisburg, Jefferson Co., AL; and 5 Apr 1940 Birmingham, Jefferson Co., AL. She d.29 Apr 1981 at age 67 and was bur. Walker Chapel Mem. Gardens, Fultondale, Jefferson Co., AL.
    Franklin "Floyd" Green, b.6 Dec 1899. He d.22 Mar 1972 at age 72; bur. Walker Chapel Mem. Gardens, Fultondale, Jefferson Co., AL.
Known children of Lillie Mae[7] Abney and Franklin "Floyd" Green:
    i.   Floyd Flowers[8], b. ca.1931 AL.
    ii. Glenda Fay, b. ca.1938 AL.
1097 iii. James "Jim," b. 25 Jan 1942; m. Judith "Judy" Townsend.

682. Elizabeth Jane "Lizzie"[7] Abney (James[6], George[5], Benjamin[4], Hezekiah[3], Elisha[2], Abner[1]), b.10 Mar 1914 AL. She m. William Harry Madden ca.1938. She d.14 Jan 1976 at age 61 and was bur. Happy Home Bapt. Ch. Cem., Guntersville, Marshall Co., AL.
    William Harry Madden, b.21 Aug 1914 Rome, Floyd Co., GA; d.26 Oct 1975 Guntersville, Marshall Co., AL, age 61; bur. Happy Home Cem.
Known child of Elizabeth Jane "Lizzie"[7] Abney and William Harry Madden:
1098 i.   Harry Lee[8], b. 1 Sep 1939 AL; m. Evelyn S. (n.n.).

683. Roy[7] Abney (James[6], George[5], Benjamin[4], Hezekiah[3], Elisha[2], Abner[1]), b.13 Aug 1915 AL. He m. Magdalene Gibson. He d.Feb 1986 at age 70 and was bur. Myrtle Hill Mem. Park, Tampa, Hillsborough Co., FL.
    Magdalene Gibson, b.11 Mar 1925 Nauvoo, Walker Co., AL. She d.11 Feb 2007 Lakeland, Polk Co., FL, age 81; bur. Myrtle Hill Mem. Park.
Known children of Roy[7] Abney and Magdalene Gibson:
    i.   Donnie[8].
    ii. Terry.
    iii. Ronald.
    iv. Charlie.
1099 v.   Donald Ray, b. 15 Oct 1945 Jefferson Co., AL; m. Bonnie Sue Criegler.
1100 vi. David Arnold, b. 6 Dec 1947 Jefferson Co., AL; m. (n.n.).
1101 vii. Samuel Robert, b. 11 Jun 1950 Birmingham, Jefferson Co., AL; m. JoAnn Davis.

684. L.Cpl. Raymond Jackson[7] Abney (USMC-WWII) (James[6], George[5], Benjamin[4], Hezekiah[3], Elisha[2], Abner[1]) m. Dorothy E. Little. He, b.13 Sep 1917 AL. He d.5 May 1995 AL at age 77 and was bur. Oakwood Mem. Gardens, Gardendale, Jefferson Co., AL.
    Dorothy E. Little, b.3 May 1924 AL. She d.26 Dec 2004 at age 80 and was bur. Oakwood Mem. Gardens, Gardendale, Jefferson Co., AL.
Known children of L.Cpl. Raymond Jackson[7] Abney (USMC-WWII) and Dorothy E. Little:
    i.   Mike[8].
    ii. Raymond "Thomas", b.2 Feb 1947. He d.25 Mar 2008 at age 61 and was bur. Oakwood Mem. Gardens, Gardendale.
1102 iii. Larry Joe, b. 31 Jul 1949; m. Debra Jo McBrayer.

685. Emma Estelle[7] Abney (James[6], George[5], Benjamin[4], Hezekiah[3], Elisha[2], Abner[1]), b.2 Oct 1924. She m. Edwin Grey Tate on 30 Nov 1944 Jefferson Co., AL. She d.5 May 1964 Bessemer, Jefferson Co., AL, at age 39 and was bur. Friendship UMC Cem., Gardendale, Jefferson Co., AL.
    Edwin Grey Tate, b.26 Dec 1920. He d.9 May 1976 at age 55 and was bur. Friendship UMC Cem., Gardendale, Jefferson Co., AL.
Known children of Emma Estelle[7] Abney and Edwin Grey Tate:
    i.   Raymond Edmond "Ray"[8], b.15 Sep 1945 Birmingham, Jefferson Co., AL. He d.11 Dec 2010 Gardendale, Jefferson Co., AL, at age 65 and was bur. Friendship UMC Cem., Gardendale, Jefferson Co., AL.
    ii. Robert Carson, b.11 Oct 1947; m. Virginia G. "Tiny." He was murdered 20 Jun 1979 age 31; bur. Friendship UMC Cem. Virginia G. "Tiny", b.9 Jan 1937.
    iii. Bertha Jean, b.17 Nov 1957. She d.23 Nov 1957 and was bur. Friendship UMC Cem., Gardendale, Jefferson Co., AL.

686. Thomas Floyd "Tom"[7] Abney (James[6], George[5], Benjamin[4], Hezekiah[3], Elisha[2], Abner[1]), b.14 Jul 1928 Watson, Jefferson Co., AL. He m. Mary Ann "Doll" Arbuckle, daughter of Thomas Crowell Arbuckle and Lillie Mae Turner, on 22 Nov 1962 Montgomery, Montgomery Co., AL. He d.4 Apr 2004 AL at age 75 and was bur. Linns Crossing Cem., Graysville, AL.
    Mary Ann "Doll" Arbuckle, b.20 Sep 1935. She d.23 Oct 1997 at age 62 and was bur. Linns Crossing Cem., Graysville, Jefferson Co., AL.
Known children of Thomas Floyd "Tom"[7] Abney and Mary Ann "Doll" Arbuckle:
    i.   Daniel[8]. He m. Anita (n.n.) (gen.).
          Anita is a family genealogist with whom the author was in contact from 2002 until shortly before her father-in-law passed away. Unfortunately, her contact information was lost in the devastation resulting from Hurricane Katrina. Cousin Anita provided information on the family of James M. Abney (#305) and his father, Pvt. George W. Abney (CSA) (#109)
    ii. James.
    iii. David.
    iv. Nora. She m. Vick Parker.
    v. Avonette. She m. Joe Parker.
    vi. Stacey. She m. (n.n.) Gartrell.

687. Luther E.[7] Abney (Henry[6], William[5], Benjamin[4], Hezekiah[3], Elisha[2], Abner[1]), b. ca.1901 AL. He m. Vanna "Estelle" Kilpatrick ca.1926. He and Vanna appeared on the census of 18 Apr 1930 Howelton, Etowah Co., AL. He was liv. on 23 Apr 1940 with his brother, James Abney, Lawrence Co., TN.
    Vanna "Estelle" Kilpatrick, b.17 Mar 1906 AL. She and her daughter, Margaret Helen Abney were liv. on 3 May 1940 with her mother, Hettie Kilpatrick, Etowah Co., AL. She d.6 Oct 1982 at age 76.

Known children of Luther E.[7] Abney and Vanna "Estelle" Kilpatrick all b. AL:
-     i.   Margaret Helen[8], b. ca.1929. She m. Joe Harold Parker (b. ca.1927) on 6 May 1950 Etowah Co., AL.
-     ii.   Mary Ruth, b.1931; m. George Davis Welsh (1922-2002) on 25 Nov 1952 AL. She d.14 Mar 2001 Cherokee Co., AL.
-     iii.   Trula Faye, b. ca.1938. She m. Belton Jackson Addison (b. ca.1935) on 1 Dec 1956 Alabama City, Etowah Co., AL.

688.   Emma Lee[7] Abney (Henry[6], William[5], Benjamin[4], Hezekiah[3], Elisha[2], Abner[1]), b.3 Dec 1903 AL. She m. Albert Madison Story (1903-1991) on 25 Jan 1925 Lawrence Co., TN. She d.24 Jun 1964 Evansville, Vanderburgh Co., IN, at age 60.
Known children of Emma Lee[7] Abney and Albert Madison Story:
-     i.   Chester Lee[8], b.6 Oct 1926 Lawrence Co., TN. He d.1993 Auburndale, Polk Co., FL.
-     ii.   Lawrence, b.7 Jul 1930 KY.
-     iii.   Shirley Ann, b.13 Jun 1936 Hopkinsville, Christian Co., KY.

689.   Zora "Bell"[7] Abney (William[6], William[5], Benjamin[4], Hezekiah[3], Elisha[2], Abner[1]), b.16 Feb 1904 GA. She m. Pink W. Turley Sr. in 1923. She and Pink W. Turley Sr. appeared on the census of 23 Apr 1930 Cobb Co., GA. She d.16 Nov 1970 Cobb Co., GA, at age 66 and was bur. Milford Cem., Marietta, Cobb Co., GA.
    Pink W. Turley Sr, b.30 Jun 1903 GA. He d.11 Dec 1989 GA at age 86 and was bur. Milford Cem., Marietta, Cobb Co., GA.
Known children of Zora "Bell"[7] Abney and Pink W. Turley Sr.:
-     i.   Pink W. "Junior"[8], b. ca.1924 TN.
-     ii.   Anna M., b. ca.1926 GA.
-     iii.   Hubert, b. ca.1927 GA.
-     iv.   Gene, b.8 Oct 1929 GA. He d.31 Aug 1930 Cobb Co., GA and was bur. Milford Cem., Marietta, Cobb Co., GA.
-     v.   James T., b.8 Oct 1929.
-     vi.   J.W, b.8 Oct 1929 GA.

690.   Elizabeth Ovelle "Lizzie"[7] Abney (William[6], William[5], Benjamin[4], Hezekiah[3], Elisha[2], Abner[1]), b.19 Jan 1908 GA. She m. Paul R. Colbert ca.1932. She and Paul R. Colbert were liv. on 24 Apr 1940 with cousin, Bob B. Howell, Dallas, Paulding Co., GA. She d.23 Jul 1982 Fulton Co., GA, at age 74 and was bur. Mount Olivet Bapt. Ch. Cem. #1, Dallas, Paulding Co., GA.
    Paul R. Colbert, b.1905. He d.1961 and was bur. Mount Olivet Bapt. Ch. Cem. #1, Dallas, Paulding Co., GA.
Known children of Elizabeth Ovelle "Lizzie"[7] Abney and Paul R. Colbert:
-     i.   (infant dau.)[8], b. and d.24 Jan 1933 and was bur. Mount Olivet Bapt. Ch. Cem. #1, Dallas, Paulding Co., GA.
-     ii.   Mary "Joan", b.16 Aug 1936. She m. Jimmy Gazaway. She d. Leap Day, 29 Feb 2008 at age 71 and was bur. Paulding Mem. Gardens, Hiram, Paulding Co., GA.
  -          Jimmy Gazaway, b.24 Apr 1937. He d.3 Sep 2014 at age 77 and was bur. Paulding Mem. Gardens, Hiram.

691.   Paul Revere[7] Abney (USArmy-WWII) (William[6], William[5], Benjamin[4], Hezekiah[3], Elisha[2], Abner[1]), b.19 Dec 1910 GA. He m. Bessie "Granny" Adair ca.1936. He and Bessie appeared on the census of 10 Apr 1940 Red Rock, Cobb Co., GA. He d.20 May 1969 Naples, Collier Co., FL, at age 58 and was bur. County Line Cem., Acworth Beach, Cobb Co., GA.
    Bessie "Granny" Adair, b.24 Apr 1912 Cobb Co., GA. She d.5 Apr 2007 Kennesaw, Cobb Co., GA, at age 94 and was bur. Mountain View Park Cem., Marietta, Cobb Co., GA.
Known children of Paul Revere[7] Abney (USArmy-WWII) and Bessie "Granny" Adair:
-     i.   James O.[8], b. ca.1937 GA; m. Claudell (n.n.)
-     ii.   William Joe "Bob", b.19 Aug 1937 GA. He m. Lula Mae (n.n.). He d.1 Nov 2007 age 70; bur. Mountain View Park Cem.
-     iii.   Glenn Paul, b.27 Feb 1939 GA. He d.16 Oct 2001 Marietta, Cobb Co., GA, at age 62; bur. Mountain View Park Cem.
-     iv.   Melba, b. GA; m. (n.n.) Blackwood.
- 1103   v.   Donald Ray, b. 9 Jan 1944; m. (n.n.).
-     vi.   Martha b. GA; m. Gene Trotter.
-     vii.   Linda, b.1946. She m. Dale Williamson. She d.2007 and was bur. Mountain View Park Cem., Marietta, Cobb Co., GA.

692.   Joe Wheeler[7] Abney (USArmy) (William[6], William[5], Benjamin[4], Hezekiah[3], Elisha[2], Abner[1]), b.11 Nov 1917 Cobb Co., GA; m. Sophiann Anntoinette Stagliano in 1947; d.21 Feb 2011 Riverside, Riverside Co., CA, age 93; bur. Riverside National Cem., Riverside, Riverside Co., CA.
    Sophiann Anntoinette Stagliano, b.17 Aug 1928 Portland, Multnomah Co., OR. She d.17 Jan 2017 Riverside, Riverside Co., CA, at age 88 and was bur. Riverside National Cem., Riverside, Riverside Co., CA.
Known children of Joe Wheeler[7] Abney (USArmy) and Sophiann Anntoinette Stagliano:
-     i.   David[8].
- 1104   ii.   Carol, m. Jerry Hensel.

693.   Emil "Newton"[7] Lorren (Leticia[6] Abney, Eli[5], Benjamin[4], Hezekiah[3], Elisha[2], Abner[1]), b.2 Nov 1894 AL. He m. Ruby Florence Warmack ca.1931. He and Ruby Florence Warmack appeared on the census of 6 May 1940 Neuse River, Wake Co., NC. He d.15 Aug 1985 NC at age 90.
    Ruby Florence Warmack, b.25 Nov 1905. She d.25 Nov 1996 on her birthday, Raleigh, Wake Co., NC, at age 91.
Known children of Emil "Newton"[7] Lorren and Ruby Florence Warmack:
-     i.   Charlotte[8], b. ca.1932 NC.
-     ii.   Clarice, b. ca.1934 Wake Co., NC.
-     iii.   Shirley, b.19 Sep 1936 Wake Co., NC. She d.3 Feb 1956 Raleigh, Wake Co., NC, at age 19.
-     iv.   Ruby M., b. ca.1939 Wake Co., NC.

694.   John Luther[7] Lorren (Leticia[6] Abney, Eli[5], Benjamin[4], Hezekiah[3], Elisha[2], Abner[1]), b.6 Jul 1896 Cleburne Co., AL. He m. Mary Anna "May" Gilley ca.1913. He and Mary appeared on the census of 3 Apr 1930 Raleigh, Wake Co., NC. He d.10 May 1939 Raleigh, Wake Co., NC, at age 42 and was bur. New Bethel Cem., Borden Springs, Cleburne Co., AL.
    Mary Anna "May" Gilley, b.3 Jun 1892 Blount Co., AL. She d.15 Apr 1970 Raleigh, Wake Co., NC, at age 77 and was bur. Raleigh Mem. Park, Raleigh, Wake Co., NC.

Known children of John Luther[7] Lorren and Mary Anna "May" Gilley:

       i.   John "Harlson"[8], b.20 Jul 1915 Cleburne Co., AL. He d.17 Jul 1993 Raleigh, Wake Co., NC, at age 77 and was bur. Raleigh Mem. Park, Raleigh, Wake Co., NC.

1105   ii.   Kathleen Frances, b. 17 Jul 1924 Raleigh, Wake Co., NC; m. (n.n.) Thomas.

1106   iii. Claude Ealton, b. 19 Feb 1927 Raleigh, Wake Co., NC; m. Angeline Ferrant.

       iv. Ruby Mae m. Henry H. Bryant. , b.13 May 1929 Raleigh, Wake Co., NC. She d.16 Apr 1968 Raleigh, Wake Co., NC, at age 38 and was bur. Raleigh Mem. Park, Raleigh, Wake Co., NC.

695. Theresa B. "Lizzie"[7] Lorren (Leticia[6] Abney, Eli[5], Benjamin[4], Hezekiah[3], Elisha[2], Abner[1]), b.19 Jul 1904 Cleburne, AL; m. Robert C. Dyer ca.1931. They appeared on the census of 10 Apr 1940 Borden Springs, Cleburne Co., AL. She d.22 Nov 1980 Raleigh, Wake Co., NC, age 76.

    Robert C. Dyer, b. ca.1912 AL.

Known children of Theresa B. "Lizzie"[7] Lorren and Robert C. Dyer both b. AL:

       i.   Billie Dove[8], b. ca.1932.

       ii.   Emil Robert, b. ca.1938.

696. Agee Virgil[7] Lorren (Leticia[6] Abney, Eli[5], Benjamin[4], Hezekiah[3], Elisha[2], Abner[1]), b. ca.1906 Cleburne, AL. He m. Alma M. (n.n.) ca.1929. He and Alma appeared on the censuses of 11 Apr 1930 and 10 Apr 1940 Gadsden, Etowah Co., AL. He d.17 Dec 1964 Gadsden, Etowah Co., AL.

    Alma M. (n.n.), b. ca.1908 AL.

Known child of Agee Virgil[7] Lorren and Alma M. (n.n.):

       i.   Willis E.[8], b. ca.Feb 1930 Etowah Co., AL.

697. Pearl Lena[7] Lorren (Leticia[6] Abney, Eli[5], Benjamin[4], Hezekiah[3], Elisha[2], Abner[1]), b.16 Apr 1908 Cleburne Co., AL. She m. Floyd William Baswell in 1929. She and Floyd William Baswell appeared on the census of 9 Apr 1940 Borden Springs, Cleburne Co., AL. She d.25 Jan 1968 Rome, Floyd Co., GA, at age 59 and was bur. Piedmont Memory Gardens, Piedmont, Calhoun Co., AL.

    Floyd William Baswell, b.6 Jan 1908 Collinsville, DeKalb Co., AL. He d.15 Jan 1981 AL at age 73 and was bur. Piedmont Memory Gardens.

Known children of Pearl Lena[7] Lorren and Floyd William Baswell:

       i.   Lona Ree[8], b. ca.1932 AL. m. (n.n.) Hunt.

       ii.   Casey Noble, b. ca.1933 AL.

       iii. Loney Carolyn, b. ca.1934 AL.

1107   iv. William "Herbert," b. 17 Sep 1935 Cleburne Co., AL; m. Linda S. Motes.

       v.   Pearl R., b. ca.1937 AL.

       vi. Toni, b. AL. m. (n.n.) Tierce.

698. Jessie Carrmon[7] Lorren (Leticia[6] Abney, Eli[5], Benjamin[4], Hezekiah[3], Elisha[2], Abner[1]) m. Annette (n.n.). He, b.14 Jul 1910 Cleburne, AL. He and Annette appeared on the census of 10 Apr 1940 Borden Springs, Cleburne Co., AL. He d.18 Aug 1996 Gadsden, Etowah Co., AL, at age 86.

    Annette (n.n.), b. ca.1912 AL.

Known children of Jessie Carrmon[7] Lorren and Annette (n.n.) both b. AL:

       i.   Mary Jannett[8], b. ca.1934.

       ii.   Kennith R, b. ca.1939.

699. John "Wesley"[7] Abney (Eli[6], Eli[5], Benjamin[4], Hezekiah[3], Elisha[2], Abner[1]), b.28 Feb 1900 AL. He m. Myrtle Lucille Roberts ca.1919. They appeared on the census of 10 Jan 1920 with his father, Eli F. Abney, Oak Level, Cleburne Co., AL. John moved his family to Cedartown, Polk Co., GA in 1920; to Etowah Co., AL in 1923; to Piedmont, Calhoun Co., AL in 1926; and to Etowah Co., AL in 1927. He and Myrtle appeared on the census of 8 Apr 1930 Gadsden, Etowah Co., AL. By 1 Apr 1935 they lived in 1935 Rainsville, DeKalb Co., AL. They appeared on the census of 7 May 1940 DeKalb Co., AL. He d.17 Sep 1995 DeKalb Co., AL, at age 95; bur. Mountain View Memory Gardens, Fort Payne, DeKalb Co., AL.

    Myrtle Lucille Roberts, b.22 Sep 1901 AL. She d.7 Oct 1977 DeKalb Co., AL, at age 76 and was bur. Mountain View Memory Gardens.

Known children of John "Wesley"[7] Abney and Myrtle Lucille Roberts:

       i.   *S.Sgt.* Howard "Luster" (USAF-WWII)[8], b.23 May 1921 Polk Co., GA. He was wounded in action on 19 Aug 1943. He m. Edith Virginia Sterling ca.1944; d.20 Aug 2002 age 81; bur. Crestwood Mem. Cem., East Gadsden, Etowah Co., AL.

               Edith Virginia Sterling, b.18 Jan 1922. She d.29 Mar 2014 at age 92 and was bur. Crestwood Mem. Cem.

       ii.   Dorothy, b. ca.1924 AL; m. (n.n.) Bishop.

       iii. Edward, b. ca.Feb 1926 AL; m. Mary (n.n.).

1108   iv. Ola Mae, b. 28 May 1928 AL; m. Clarence Peter "Pete" Hill Sr.

1109   v.   Betty Lorine, b. 24 Aug 1931 Gadsden, Etowah Co., AL; m. Norman S. Ross (USArmy-WWII).

       vi. Margaret "Bittie", b. ca.1932 AL; m. Pete Ballew.

       vii. Billy, b. ca.1935 AL; m. Charlotte (n.n.).

       viii. Illa "Faye", b. ca.1938 AL; m. Gene Frizzell.

       ix. Josephine, b. ca.Mar 1940 AL m. Wendell McDonald.

700. William McKinley "Mac"[7] Abney (Posey[6], Eli[5], Benjamin[4], Hezekiah[3], Elisha[2], Abner[1]), b.16 Sep 1902 AL. He m. Ruby Mae Smith ca.1927. He and Ruby Mae Smith appeared on the censuses of 14 Apr 1930 Alabama City, Etowah Co., AL; and 4 Apr 1940 Gadsden, Etowah Co., AL. He d.10 Apr 1993 East Gadsden, Etowah Co., AL, at age 90.

    Ruby Mae Smith, b.18 Nov 1909. She d.6 Jan 1984 at age 74 and was bur. Crestwood Mem. Cem., East Gadsden, Etowah Co., AL.

Known children of William McKinley "Mac"[7] Abney and Ruby Mae Smith:

1110   i.   James Hugh[8], b. 3 May 1929; m. Nila Jean Elrod.

       ii.   Martha, b. ca.1933 AL. m. (n.n.) Elrod.

1111   iii. Sarah Ann, b. 30 Dec 1934 Etowah Co., AL; m. Donald Boone "Don" House.

       iv. Hoyt Lamar, b.17 Nov 1939. He m. Glenna M. Whorton (b.8 Sep 1942) in Mar 1961 Cleburne Co., AL. He d.23 Jun 1992 Ashville, Buncombe Co., NC, at age 52 and was bur. Katy Moragne Hughes Cem., Gadsden, Etowah Co., AL.

       v.   Betty, b. est.1941 AL; m. Ronny Johnson.

701. Jessie "Pauline"[7] Abney (Posey[6], Eli[5], Benjamin[4], Hezekiah[3], Elisha[2], Abner[1]), b.23 Mar 1917 AL. She was liv. on 14 Apr 1930 with brother, Mac Abney, Alabama City, Etowah Co., AL. She m. Lamar Brock Overstreet. She and Lamar Brock Overstreet appeared on the census of 9 Apr 1940 Attalla, Etowah Co., AL. She d.8 Jul 1973 Gadsden, Etowah Co., AL, at age 56 and was bur. Oak Hill Cem., Attalla, Etowah Co., AL.
  Lamar Brock Overstreet, b.16 Dec 1918. He d.7 Jun 1998 at age 79 and was bur. Oak Hill Cem., Attalla, Etowah Co., AL.
Known child of Jessie "Pauline"[7] Abney and Lamar Brock Overstreet:
    1112   i.   Patricia Ann[8], b. 3 Nov 1947; m. (n.n.) Maroney.

702. Martin Luther[7] Crawford (Rosa[6] Abney, Eli[5], Benjamin[4], Hezekiah[3], Elisha[2], Abner[1]), b.1902. He m. Dallie Harris (1904-1991). He d.1956.
Known children of Martin Luther[7] Crawford and Dallie Harris:
    i.   Alton Harold[8], b.1925. He d.1995.
    ii.   Herbert Welton, b.1925. He d.2008.

703. Jessie P.[7] McWhorter (Sarah[6] Abney, Eli[5], Benjamin[4], Hezekiah[3], Elisha[2], Abner[1]), b.24 Oct 1909. He m. Mary Lee Champion on 27 Aug 1938. He d.18 Jul 1980 at age 70 and was bur. Mount Tabor Meth. Ch. Cem., Westover, Shelby Co., AL.
  Mary Lee Champion, b.15 May 1919 Shelby Co., AL. She d.13 Feb 1997 Shelby Co., AL, at age 77.
Known children of Jessie P.[7] McWhorter and Mary Lee Champion:
    i.   Billy F.[8], b.26 Jul 1941. He m. Patricia Nicholson. He d.4 Mar 2014 at age 72 and was bur. Green Hill Mem. Gardens, Childersburg, Talladega Co., AL.
        Patricia Nicholson, b.28 Jun 1948; d.18 May 2002 Sylacauga, Talladega Co., AL; bur. Green Hill Mem. Gardens.
    ii.   Donald Wayne, b.30 Oct 1948 AL. He d.19 Mar 1997 AL at age 48 and was bur. Mount Tabor Meth. Ch. Cem., Westover.

704. Grace N.[7] McWhorter (Sarah[6] Abney, Eli[5], Benjamin[4], Hezekiah[3], Elisha[2], Abner[1]), b.16 Oct 1913. She m. Thomas C. Cochran. They lived on 1 Apr 1935 Piedmont, Calhoun Co., AL. She and Thomas C. Cochran appeared on the census of 12 Apr 1940 Central City, Muhlenberg Co., KY. She d.16 Feb 1998 at age 84 and was bur. Ozark Mem. Park Cem., Joplin, Jasper Co., MO.
  Thomas C. Cochran, b.6 Sep 1903 MO. He d.17 May 1995 at age 91 and was bur. Ozark Mem. Park Cem., Joplin, Jasper Co., MO.
Known child of Grace N.[7] McWhorter and Thomas C. Cochran:
    i.   Betty Jane[8], b. ca.1936 KY.

705. Johnnie[7] McWhorter (Sarah[6] Abney, Eli[5], Benjamin[4], Hezekiah[3], Elisha[2], Abner[1]), b.12 Aug 1918. She m1. PFC Willie C. Flemons (USArmy-WWII) in 1941. She m2. Calvin Edmund Hanks. She d.1 Apr 2008 AL at age 89; bur. Forestlawn Gardens and Maus., Anniston, Calhoun Co., AL.
  PFC Willie C. Flemons (USArmy-WWII), b.11 Oct 1915. He d.10 Jan 1995 at age 79.
There were no known children of Johnnie[7] McWhorter and PFC Willie C. Flemons (USArmy-WWII).
  Calvin Edmund Hanks, b.21 Dec 1923 Gadsden, Etowah Co., AL. He d.21 Feb 2002 Anniston, Calhoun Co., AL, at age 78.
Known child of Johnnie[7] McWhorter and Calvin Edmund Hanks:
    i.   Ginger Gail[8], b.6 Oct 1959. She m. (n.n.) Sprayberry. d.23 Nov 2009 at age 50 and was bur. Forestlawn Gardens and Maus., Anniston, Calhoun Co., AL.

706. Ruby Lee[7] Abney (John[6], Eli[5], Benjamin[4], Hezekiah[3], Elisha[2], Abner[1]), b.15 Nov 1920 Carroll Co., GA. She m. Sgt. Arthur "Austin" Payne (USN-WWII) ca.1939. She and Arthur appeared on the census of 20 Apr 1940 Cullman Co., AL. She d.10 Sep 1988 Cullman, Cullman Co., AL, at age 67 and was bur. Simcoe United Methodist Cem., Simcoe, Cullman Co., AL.
  Sgt. Arthur "Austin" Payne (USN-WWII), b.9 May 1911 GA. He m1. Lillie Estell Gates. He d.4 Jun 1986 Cullman Co., AL, at age 75 and was bur. Simcoe United Methodist Cem., Simcoe, Cullman Co., AL.
Known children of Ruby Lee[7] Abney and Sgt. Arthur "Austin" Payne (USN-WWII):
    i.   (dau.)[8].
    ii.   Brian m. and had issue, 3 known children.
    iii. Jada m. and had issue, 1 known child.

707. Carl Horace[7] Abney (USN-WWII) (John[6], Eli[5], Benjamin[4], Hezekiah[3], Elisha[2], Abner[1]) m. Nellie Znobia Frost. He m. Margie Sue Caldwell. He, b.2 Apr 1923 Cullman, Cullman Co., AL. He d.27 Dec 1991 Ft. Walton Beach, Okaloosa Co., FL, at age 68 and was bur. Simcoe United Methodist Cem., Simcoe, Cullman Co., AL.
  Nellie Znobia Frost m2. Pvt. Charles B. Brown (USArmy-WWII). , b.10 May 1938. She d.9 Mar 2008 at age 69.
There were no known children of Carl Horace[7] Abney (USN-WWII) and Nellie Znobia Frost.
  Margie Sue Caldwell, b.19 Jul 1929.
Known children of Carl Horace[7] Abney (USN-WWII) and Margie Sue Caldwell:
    1115   i.   Michael Harlan "Mike"[8], b. 26 Jan 1952 Cullman, Cullman Co., AL; m. Barbara Kristen Bailey (gen.).
    1116   ii.   Carol Annette, b. 31 Oct 1954 Cullman, Cullman Co., AL; m. Carl Davis.
    1117   iii. Suzanne, b. ca.1963; m. Curtis Swartz.

708. Mazelle[7] Abney (John[6], Eli[5], Benjamin[4], Hezekiah[3], Elisha[2], Abner[1]) m. Rev. Pless "Ivon" Echols (USArmy-WWII). , b.27 Jul 1925 AL. She d.14 Sep 2007 Cullman, Cullman Co., AL, at age 82 and was bur. Simcoe United Methodist Cem., Simcoe, Cullman Co., AL.
  Rev. Pless "Ivon" Echols (USArmy-WWII), b.21 Mar 1922 Jones Chapel, Cullman Co., AL. He d.16 Mar 1990 at age 67 and was bur. Simcoe United Methodist Cem., Simcoe, Cullman Co., AL.
Known children of Mazelle[7] Abney and Rev. Pless "Ivon" Echols (USArmy-WWII):
    1118   i.   Charles[8].
    1119   ii.   Cynthia.

709. Bobbie Dean[7] Abney (John[6], Eli[5], Benjamin[4], Hezekiah[3], Elisha[2], Abner[1]), b.3 Jul 1930. She m. Cecil "Ray" Adams on 11 Jun 1959. She d.21 Nov 2003 Cullman, Cullman Co., AL, at age 73 and was bur. Simcoe United Methodist Cem., Simcoe, Cullman Co., AL.
  Cecil "Ray" Adams, b.28 Oct 1935 Cullman Co., AL. He d.11 May 2007 Cullman, Cullman Co., AL, at age 71 and was bur. Simcoe United Methodist Cem., Simcoe, Cullman Co., AL.

Known children of Bobbie Dean⁷ Abney and Cecil "Ray" Adams:
>   i.   Scott⁸.
> 1120 ii. Brett John, b. 27 Dec 1966 Cullman, Cullman Co., AL; m. (n.n.).

710. James Edward "Jim"⁷ Abney (John⁶, Eli⁵, Benjamin⁴, Hezekiah³, Elisha², Abner¹) m. Arnita Oaks. He, b.5 Aug 1933 AL. He d.30 Mar 2017 Raleigh, Wake Co., NC, at age 83 and was bur. Ephesus Bapt. Ch. Cem., Raleigh, Wake Co., NC.
Known children of James Edward "Jim"⁷ Abney and Arnita Oaks:
> 1121 i.   David⁸, m. Marsha (n.n.).
> 1122 ii. Amy, m. Chase Tew.

711. Adele⁷ Burkhalter (Martha⁶ Abney, James⁵, Benjamin⁴, Hezekiah³, Elisha², Abner¹) m. Walter J. Garrard. , b.17 Aug 1895. She d.29 Jan 1995 at age 99 and was bur. Powder Springs City Cem., Powder Springs, Cobb Co., GA.
Walter J. Garrard, b.7 Nov 1886. He d.29 Apr 1970 at age 83 and was bur. Powder Springs City Cem., Powder Springs, Cobb Co., GA.
Known children of Adele⁷ Burkhalter and Walter J. Garrard:
>   i.   James W.⁸, b.29 Dec 1919. He m. Mary E. (n.n.). He d.21 Feb 2012 Powder Springs, Cobb Co., GA, at age 92 and was bur. Powder Springs City Cem., Powder Springs, Cobb Co., GA.
>   Mary E. (n.n.), b.5 Nov 1917. She d.6 Oct 1999 at age 81 and was bur. Powder Springs City Cem., Powder Springs.

712. James Othel⁷ Burkhalter (Martha⁶ Abney, James⁵, Benjamin⁴, Hezekiah³, Elisha², Abner¹) m. Elsie Hollis. He, b.26 Jul 1897. He d.2 Feb 1961 at age 63 and was bur. Pleasant Hope Cem., Rome, Floyd Co., GA.
Elsie Hollis, b.20 Jun 1906. She d.15 Apr 1967 at age 60 and was bur. Pleasant Hope Cem., Rome, Floyd Co., GA.
Known children of James Othel⁷ Burkhalter and Elsie Hollis:
>   i.   Rodney⁸.
>   ii. Patty Juanita, b.19 Dec 1932 Floyd Co., GA. She d.9 Mar 1995 Rome, Floyd Co., GA, at age 62 and was bur. Pleasant Hope Cem., Rome, Floyd Co., GA.

713. Early Prentice⁷ Burkhalter (Martha⁶ Abney, James⁵, Benjamin⁴, Hezekiah³, Elisha², Abner¹), b.14 Sep 1908 Floyd Co., GA. He m. Mary Evelyn Wilkerson (b.1911). He d.29 Nov 1980 Floyd Co., GA at age 72 and was bur. Greenwood Cem., Cedartown, Polk Co., GA.
Known children of Early Prentice⁷ Burkhalter and Mary Evelyn Wilkerson:
>   i.   W.E.⁸.
>   ii. (dau.) m. Charles Brock.
>   iii. (dau.) m. Kermit Bussey.

714. Mary Jane⁷ Burkhalter (Martha⁶ Abney, James⁵, Benjamin⁴, Hezekiah³, Elisha², Abner¹) m. Edward Bennie Weaver Sr. , b.3 Oct 1911 Cedartown, Polk Co., GA. She d.5 Jan 2005 AL at age 93 and was bur. Forrest Cem., Gadsden, Etowah Co., AL.
Edward Bennie Weaver Sr, b.9 Jul 1904 Cedartown, Polk Co., GA. He d.12 Apr 1982 Gadsden, Etowah Co., AL, at age 77; bur. Forrest Cem.
Known children of Mary Jane⁷ Burkhalter and Edward Bennie Weaver Sr. both b. Cedartown, Polk Co., GA:
>   i.   Edward Benny⁸, b.10 Dec 1933. He d.25 Sep 2014 Gadsden, Etowah Co., AL, at age 80. He was cremated.
> 1123 ii. Roy Leonard, b. 23 Dec 1935; m. (n.n.).

715. PFC James "Everett"⁷ Abney (USArmy-WWI) (Marion⁶, James⁵, Benjamin⁴, Hezekiah³, Elisha², Abner¹), b.25 Jul 1892 Floyd Co., GA. He m. Bessie Jewell Chafin. He d.19 Jun 1981 Rome, Floyd Co., GA, at age 88.
Bessie Jewell Chafin, b.5 Jan 1903 Floyd Co., GA. She d.26 Feb 1992 Rome, Floyd Co., GA, at age 89; bur. Flint Hill Cem., Floyd Co., GA.
Known children of PFC James "Everett"⁷ Abney (USArmy-WWI) and Bessie Jewell Chafin:
>   i.   Jewell⁸, b. and d.30 Nov 1922 Floyd Co., GA; bur. Pleasant Hope Cem., Rome, Floyd Co., GA.
>   ii. James Howard, b.30 Nov 1922. He d.10 Mar 1980 at age 57 and was bur. Flint Hill Cem., Floyd Co., GA.
>   iii. Doris Margaret, b.16 Apr 1929. She m. Harold Lamar Perry. d.10 Nov 2015 Rome, Floyd Co., GA, at age 86 and was bur. Oaknoll Mem. Gardens Cem., Rome, Floyd Co., GA.
>   Harold Lamar Perry, b.20 Jul 1922. He d.15 Nov 1968 at age 46 and was bur. Oaknoll Mem. Gardens Cem., Rome.

716. Henry "Curtis"⁷ Abney (USArmy-WWI) (Marion⁶, James⁵, Benjamin⁴, Hezekiah³, Elisha², Abner¹), b.22 Jan 1896. He appeared on the census of 20 Jan 1920 Floyd Co., GA. He m. Connie Mae Compton ca.1922. He and Connie appeared on the censuses of 2 Apr 1930 Floyd Co., GA; and 24 Apr 1940 Howell, Floyd Co., GA. He d.27 Nov 1962 at age 66 and was bur. East View Cem., Rome, Floyd Co., GA.
Connie Mae Compton, b.8 Apr 1903 Polk Co., GA. She d.27 Feb 1980 Floyd Co., GA, at age 76 and was bur. East View Cem., Rome.
Known children of Henry "Curtis"⁷ Abney (USArmy-WWI) and Connie Mae Compton:
> 1124 i.   Hazel Katherine⁸, b. 17 Feb 1923; m. Sgt. James Livingston Farrer (USArmy-WWII).
> 1125 ii. Margie Louise, b. 11 Sep 1924 Floyd Co., GA; m. Emmett Coleman Akins.

717. William "Bryant"⁷ Abney (Marion⁶, James⁵, Benjamin⁴, Hezekiah³, Elisha², Abner¹), b.25 Apr 1900 AL. He m. Julia "Alice" Mathis ca.1918. They appeared on the censuses of 20 Jan 1920 Floyd Co., GA and 3 Apr 1930 Floyd Co., GA; and 27 Apr 1940 Chulio, Floyd Co., GA. He d.2 Sep 1963 at age 63 and was bur. Pleasant Hope Cem., Rome, Floyd Co., GA.
Julia "Alice" Mathis, b.20 Feb 1898. She d.28 Apr 1952 at age 54 and was bur. Pleasant Hope Cem., Rome, Floyd Co., GA.
Known children of William "Bryant"⁷ Abney and Julia "Alice" Mathis:
> 1126 i.   William "Gwinnett"⁸, b. 16 Jun 1919 Rome, Floyd Co., GA; m. Katherine Mildred Byrd.
>   ii. Raiden Mathis, b.31 Aug 1920 Rome, Floyd Co., GA. He m. Minnie "Frances" Gilstrap. He d.8 May 1987 Winterville, Clarke Co., GA, at age 66 and was bur. Corinth Cem., Oconee Co., GA.
>   Minnie "Frances" Gilstrap, b.30 Mar 1921 Rome, Floyd Co., GA. She d.10 Feb 2006 Winterville, Clarke Co., GA, at age 84 and was bur. Corinth Cem., Oconee Co., GA.
> 1127 iii. James Marion Chaney "Jimmy," b. 30 Apr 1922; m. Viola Victoria Gilstrap.
> 1128 iv. Ralph "Syndnor," b. 29 Sep 1924 Rome, Floyd Co., GA; m. Josephine Teresa "Jay" Puleo; m. Dorothy (n.n.).

       v.   Mildred Sue, b.13 Jan 1926 Floyd Co., GA. She m. William Hubert Lumpkin. She d.16 Jun 2013 Cumming, Forsyth Co., GA, at age 87 and was bur. Floyd Memory Gardens, Rome, Floyd Co., GA.

              William Hubert Lumpkin, b.9 Dec 1923 Floyd Co., GA. He m. Ira Joan Avans. He d.9 Sep 2004 Rome, Floyd Co., GA, at age 80 and was bur. Floyd Memory Gardens, Rome, Floyd Co., GA.

1129   vi.   Robert Bryant "Bobby," b. 3 Sep 1927 Lindale, Floyd Co., GA; m. Annie Jo George.

1130 vii. Billy John, b. 10 Jul 1929; m. Ruby N. Erwin.

      viii. Joseph Luther "Joe", b.4 Apr 1939; d.2 Mar 2002 age 62; bur. Gwinnett Mem. Park, Lawrenceville, Gwinnett Co., GA.

718. **Myrtle Beatrice[7] Abney** (Marion[6], James[5], Benjamin[4], Hezekiah[3], Elisha[2], Abner[1]), b.6 Jun 1906. She m. Nolan Smith on Christmas Eve, 24 Dec 1931. She d.5 May 2008 Silver Creek, Floyd Co., GA, at age 101 and was bur. Pleasant Hope Cem., Rome, Floyd Co., GA.
    Nolan Smith, b.31 Aug 1898 Carroll Co., GA. He d.27 Aug 1953 Rome, Floyd Co., GA, at age 54 and was bur. Pleasant Hope Cem., Rome.
Known children of Myrtle Beatrice[7] Abney and Nolan Smith:
       i.   Benjamin Marion "BM"[8], b.4 Mar 1940 Rome, Floyd Co., GA. He d.1 Sep 2016 Floyd Co., GA, at age 76 and was bur. Rome Mem. Park South, Rome, Floyd Co., GA.

719. **Gordon Lee "Joe"[7] Abney** (Marion[6], James[5], Benjamin[4], Hezekiah[3], Elisha[2], Abner[1]), b.10 Jul 1908 Floyd Co., GA. was owner of *Abney Grocery*. He m. Lucile Carney ca.1926. They appeared on the censuses of 2 Apr 1930 Floyd Co., GA; and 3 Apr 1940 Lindale, Floyd Co., GA. He d.19 Jun 1962 at age 53 and was bur. East View Cem., Rome, Floyd Co., GA.
    Lucile Carney, b.30 Aug 1908 Floyd Co., GA. She d.2 Oct 1984 at age 76 and was bur. East View Cem., Rome, Floyd Co., GA.
Known child of Gordon Lee "Joe"[7] Abney and Lucile Carney:
       i.   William Hubert[8], b.17 Feb 1928. He d.28 Mar 1958 at age 30 and was bur. East View Cem., Rome, Floyd Co., GA.

720. **Lenora "Mae Bell"[7] Burkhalter** (Melissa[6] Abney, James[5], Benjamin[4], Hezekiah[3], Elisha[2], Abner[1]) m. (n.n.) Washington. , b.24 May 1891 Floyd Co., GA. She d.1 Nov 1969 Rome, Floyd Co., GA, at age 78 and was bur. New Bethel Cem., Floyd Co., GA.
    Known child of Lenora "Mae Bell"[7] Burkhalter and (n.n.) Washington:
1131   i.   Allen David[8], b. 4 May 1909; m. Lizzie Lucile "Cil" Wallace.

721. **Dallas Grady[7] Burkhalter** (Melissa[6] Abney, James[5], Benjamin[4], Hezekiah[3], Elisha[2], Abner[1]) m. Cora Myrtle Bruce. He, b.30 Jan 1893 GA. He d.6 Nov 1959 DeKalb Co., GA, at age 66 and was bur. New Bethel Cem., Floyd Co., GA.
    Cora Myrtle Bruce, b.New Year's Day, 1 Jan 1894 TN; d.3 Apr 1977 Rome, Floyd Co., GA, age 83; bur. New Bethel Cem., Floyd Co., GA.
Known children of Dallas Grady[7] Burkhalter and Cora Myrtle Bruce:
       i.   James Earl[8], b.30 Jan 1918 Floyd Co., GA. He d.25 Feb 1918 Floyd Co., GA and was bur. New Bethel Cem.
      ii.   Edna, b.4 Mar 1920. She m. Robert Lee "Bob" Gilbert Jr. d.17 Nov 1984 at age 64; bur. Oaknoll Mem. Gardens Cem.
             Robt Lee "Bob" Gilbert Jr (28 May 1919-d.30 Jan 1981); bur. Oaknoll Mem. Gardens Cem., Rome, Floyd Co., GA.
     iii.   Milburn Austin, b.27 Nov 1922 Floyd Co., GA; d.8 Jan 1923 Floyd Co., GA; bur. Oaknoll Mem. Gardens Cem.
     iv.   Dallas "Grady", b.5 Aug 1924 Floyd Co., GA; d.5 Aug 1924 Floyd Co., GA; bur. New Bethel Cem., Floyd Co., GA.
      v.   Grady Houston, b.19 Nov 1926 Lindale, Floyd Co., GA. He d.14 Apr 2016 Rome, Floyd Co., GA, at age 89.
     vi.   Sarah, b.28 Jul 1929. She m. Louis Calvin Neblett. She d.9 Jan 1998 at age 68 and was bur. Holy Innocents Cem., Lake Village, Chicot Co., AR.
             Louis Calvin Neblett, b.11 Apr 1928 Helena, Phillips Co., AR. He m2. Thelma Matthews. He d.21 Dec 2001 Lake Village, Chicot Co., AR, at age 73.
    vii.   Roger Paul "Rod" m. Jonnie Maxwell. He, b.19 Jul 1932 Lindale, Floyd Co., GA. He d.8 Dec 2011 Aragon, Polk Co., GA, at age 79 and was bur. Kennesaw Mem. Park, Marietta, Cobb Co., GA.
             Jonnie Maxwell, b.6 Apr 1923. She d.23 Mar 2002 Acworth, Cobb Co., GA, at age 78.

722. **Erma Gertrude[7] Burkhalter** (Melissa[6] Abney, James[5], Benjamin[4], Hezekiah[3], Elisha[2], Abner[1]) m. John Ellis Caldwell. , b.11 Sep 1895. She d.23 Mar 1970 at age 74 and was bur. New Bethel Cem., Floyd Co., GA.
    John Ellis Caldwell, b.8 Feb 1888 Polk Co., GA. He d.11 Nov 1973 Rome, Floyd Co., GA, at age 85 and was bur. New Bethel Cem.
Known children of Erma Gertrude[7] Burkhalter and John Ellis Caldwell:
       i.   Gertrude "Sis"[8], b. Christmas Day, 25 Dec 1913 Polk Co., GA. She m. Arnold Emory Bennett. She d.3 Jan 1972 Rome, Floyd Co., GA, at age 58 and was bur. New Bethel Cem., Floyd Co., GA.
             Arnold Emory Bennett, b.23 Feb 1913 Pickens Co., GA. He m. Pansy Louise Hardeman in 1975. He d.17 Apr 1995 Rome, Floyd Co., GA, at age 82 and was bur. New Bethel Cem., Floyd Co., GA.
      ii.   Hershell, b.27 Dec 1915. He m. Christine M. (n.n.). He d.25 Apr 1985 at age 69 and was bur. New Bethel Cem.
             Christine M. (n.n.), b.6 Jun 1916 and was bur. New Bethel Cem., Floyd Co., GA. She d.18 May 1994 at age 77.
     iii.   Jewell, b.8 Mar 1918. She d.22 Jul 1919 at age 1 and was bur. New Bethel Cem., Floyd Co., GA.
     iv.   Shireald David, b.14 May 1921 Polk Co., GA. He m. Lillian Bernice Crider on 23 Dec 1943. He d.Christmas Day, 25 Dec 1990 Rome, Floyd Co., GA, at age 69 and was bur. New Bethel Cem., Floyd Co., GA.
             Lillian Bernice Crider, b.21 Jun 1920 Cherokee Co., AL. She d.1 Apr 2005 Rome, Floyd Co., GA, at age 84 and was bur. New Bethel Cem., Floyd Co., GA.
      v.   Thomas Noah, b.11 Oct 1922. He m. Frances G. (n.n.). He d.24 Sep 1995 at age 72; bur. Oaknoll Mem. Gardens Cem.
     vi.   Cordelia, b.4 Sep 1930. She m. Edward David Smith. d.22 Jun 2009 at age 78 and was bur. Rome Mem. Park South, Rome, Floyd Co., GA.
             Edward David Smith, b.18 Dec 1930 TN. He d.12 Aug 2012 Tupelo, Lee Co., MS, at age 81.

723. **John Austin[7] Burkhalter** (Melissa[6] Abney, James[5], Benjamin[4], Hezekiah[3], Elisha[2], Abner[1]) m. Minnie Lee Winkle. He, b.15 Dec 1897 GA. He d.24 Nov 1970 Floyd Co., GA, at age 72 and was bur. New Bethel Cem., Floyd Co., GA.
    Minnie Lee Winkle, b.8 May 1902. She d.11 May 1987 Floyd Co., GA, at age 85 and was bur. New Bethel Cem., Floyd Co., GA.

Known children of John Austin[7] Burkhalter and Minnie Lee Winkle:
  i. Lyndell[8], b.26 Oct 1922; m. Robt. Madden Sr.; 2 Aug 2010 Floyd Co., GA, ae.87; bur. New Bethel Cem., Floyd Co., GA.
    Robert Bennie Madden Sr, b.13 Jun 1922; d.10 Jan 1998 Cedartown, Polk Co., GA, at age 75; bur. New Bethel Cem.
  ii. Zylpha Louise, b.10 Jul 1924 Floyd Co., GA. She d.11 Nov 1953 Floyd Co., GA, at age 29; bur. New Bethel Cem.
  iii. Arvil A., b.1 Dec 1926. He m. Flora Virginia Perry. He d.5 Dec 1981 at age 55 and was bur. Oaknoll Mem. Gardens Cem.
    Flora Virginia Perry, b.20 Mar 1930 Floyd Co., GA. She d.6 Jan 2014 Silver Creek, Floyd Co., GA, at age 83 and was bur. Oaknoll Mem. Gardens Cem., Rome, Floyd Co., GA.
  iv. John Winston, b.3 Oct 1933 Floyd Co., GA. He d.3 Oct 1933 Floyd Co., GA and was bur. New Bethel Cem.

724. William Garvin[7] Burkhalter Sr. (Melissa[6] Abney, James[5], Benjamin[4], Hezekiah[3], Elisha[2], Abner[1]) m. Opal Lemming. He, b.5 Jun 1900. He d.27 Oct 1981 Floyd Co., GA, at age 81 and was bur. New Bethel Cem., Floyd Co., GA.
  Opal Lemming, b.29 Jul 1905 Floyd Co., GA. She d.28 Jul 1967 Floyd Co., GA, at age 61 and was bur. New Bethel Cem.
Known children of William Garvin[7] Burkhalter Sr. and Opal Lemming:
  i. Nolan G.[8], b.15 Aug 1922 Floyd Co., GA. He d.13 Oct 1925 Floyd Co., GA, at age 3 and was bur. New Bethel Cem.
  ii. Howard Varnell (US Military), b. Christmas Eve, 24 Dec 1924 Lindale, Floyd Co., GA. He d.20 Jan 1982 at age 57 and was bur. Arlington National Cem., Arlington, Arlington Co., VA.
  iii. Betty Avanell m. David Austin Barrett. , b.18 Jun 1927. She d.25 Oct 1977 GA at age 50; bur. New Bethel Cem.
    David Austin Barrett, b.8 Nov 1924 Floyd Co., GA; d.28 Jul 1974 Rome, Floyd Co., GA, age 49; bur. New Bethel Cem.
1132 iv. William Garvin, b. 2 May 1929 Floyd Co., GA; m. Margaret Catherine Griffin.
  v. Lionel, b.15 Sep 1931. He d.3 Sep 1990 at age 58 and was bur. New Bethel Cem., Floyd Co., GA.
1133 vi. Jimmy Allen, b. 28 Jan 1935; m. Frances Irine Lingerfelt.

725. Ethel Elvada[7] Burkhalter (Melissa[6] Abney, James[5], Benjamin[4], Hezekiah[3], Elisha[2], Abner[1]), b.24 Nov 1902 Floyd Co., GA. She m. Homer Lee Brackett in 1923. She d.4 Dec 1932 Rome, Floyd Co., GA, at age 30 and was bur. Oaknoll Mem. Gardens Cem., Floyd Co., GA.
  Homer Lee Brackett, b.1 Oct 1900. He m. Mary Viola Ledford. He d.20 Dec 1978 at age 78.
Known children of Ethel Elvada[7] Burkhalter and Homer Lee Brackett:
  i. Ruth Marcelene "Margie"[8] m. William Robert Tuck Sr. (USN-WWII). , b.30 Jan 1932. She d.27 Dec 1989 at age 57 and was bur. Oaknoll Mem. Gardens Cem., Rome, Floyd Co., GA.
    William Robert Tuck Sr. (USN-WWII), b.14 Jul 1926 Polk Co., GA. He d.21 Sep 1979 Rome, Floyd Co., GA, at age 53 and was bur. Oaknoll Mem. Gardens Cem., Rome, Floyd Co., GA.

726. Malory David[7] Burkhalter (Melissa[6] Abney, James[5], Benjamin[4], Hezekiah[3], Elisha[2], Abner[1]) m. Ruby Wallace. He, b.9 Sep 1905. He d.13 Jul 1971 GA at age 65 and was bur. New Bethel Cem., Floyd Co., GA.
  Ruby Wallace, b.26 Dec 1909 Cleburne Co., AL. She d.4 Dec 1996 Rome, Floyd Co., GA, at age 86 and was bur. New Bethel Cem.
Known children of Malory David[7] Burkhalter and Ruby Wallace:
  i. Billy David[8], b.24 Jul 1931 GA. He m. Betty R. Clark in 1973. He d.6 Aug 1997 Rome, Floyd Co., GA, at age 66 and was bur. East View Cem., Rome, Floyd Co., GA.
    Betty R. Clark, b.31 Aug 1933 GA. She m1. Warren Edward Tucker in 1948. She d.6 Oct 2002 Rome, Floyd Co., GA, at age 69 and was bur. East View Cem., Rome, Floyd Co., GA.
1134 ii. Roy Percy, b. 12 Aug 1934 Floyd Co., GA; m. Glaydean Collum.
1135 iii. Ida Vaunita, b. 18 Jul 1936 Silver Creek, Floyd Co., GA; m. Billy Ray Spears.
  iv. Charles Eugene, b.24 Jul 1938. He m. Mary G. (n.n.). He d.25 Jan 2000 at age 61; bur. Rome Mem. Park South, Rome, Floyd Co., GA.
  v. Melba Jean, b.4 Dec 1940 Rome, Floyd Co., GA. She m1. Glenn E. Rampley in 1960. She m2. Delmas Howard Franklin Sr. in 1979. She d.19 Jul 2017 Rome, Floyd Co., GA, at age 76 and was bur. New Bethel Cem., Floyd Co., GA.
    Glenn E. Rampley, b.15 Jul 1935 GA. He d.17 Jan 1979 Floyd Co., GA, at age 43 and was bur. New Bethel Cem.
    Delmas Howard Franklin Sr, b.2 Mar 1930 Page, Fayette Co., WV. He m. Eva Gillette Lewis in 1950. He d.14 Jan 2006 at age 75 and was bur. East View Cem., Floyd Co., GA.
  vi. Donna Lynn, b.21 Dec 1954 Floyd Co., GA. She d.24 Jan 2008 Rome, Floyd Co., GA, at age 53; bur. New Bethel Cem.

727. Elsie Cloe[7] Burkhalter (Melissa[6] Abney, James[5], Benjamin[4], Hezekiah[3], Elisha[2], Abner[1]), b.27 Dec 1907. She m. James Gus Cargle on 14 Nov 1926. She d.14 Jan 1987 at age 79 and was bur. New Bethel Cem., Floyd Co., GA.
  James Gus Cargle, b.1 Apr 1905. He d.21 Oct 1986 at age 81 and was bur. New Bethel Cem., Floyd Co., GA.
Known children of Elsie Cloe[7] Burkhalter and James Gus Cargle:
  i. Marcelle[8], b.17 Oct 1927. She m. Robert D. Wood on 11 Nov 1982. She d.13 Jun 1997 at age 69; bur. New Bethel Cem.
  ii. Bobbie Nell m. Charles Daniel "Sarge" Comes (USN, USArmy-WWII, Korea, Nam). , b.4 Jun 1930. She d.3 Nov 2012 at age 82 and was bur. New Bethel Cem., Floyd Co., GA.
    Charles Daniel "Sarge" Comes (USN, USArmy-WWII, Korea, Nam), b.20 Apr 1928 Irvington, Essex Co., NJ. He d.25 Feb 2018 Rome, Floyd Co., GA, at age 89 and was bur. New Bethel Cem., Floyd Co., GA.
  iii. Ted Winford m. Mae Nell (n.n.). He, b.6 Jul 1933. He d.23 Nov 1964 at age 31; bur. New Bethel Cem., Floyd Co., GA.
    Mae Nell (n.n.), b.11 Mar 1938.
1136 iv. Morris Clayton, b. 20 May 1942 Rome, Floyd Co., GA; m. Mary Alice Tidwell.

728. Dovie Mae[7] Miller (Geretie[6] Abney, James[5], Benjamin[4], Hezekiah[3], Elisha[2], Abner[1]) m. Jesse Lee Cox. , b.Christmas Eve, 24 Dec 1893. She d.27 May 1969 Wax, Floyd Co., GA, at age 75.
  Jesse Lee Cox, b.7 Sep 1889 Chattooga Co., GA. He d.30 May 1959 Rome, Floyd Co., GA, at age 69 and was bur. Pleasant Hope Cem., Rome.
Known children of Dovie Mae[7] Miller and Jesse Lee Cox:
  i. Pauline[8] m. Thurman Joe Burkhalter (USN-WWII). , b.30 Nov 1909. She d.19 Jun 1986 at age 76 and was bur. Pleasant Hope Cem., Rome, Floyd Co., GA.
    Thurman Joe Burkhalter (USN-WWII), b.8 Jul 1909; d.17 Apr 1982 Floyd Co., GA, age 72; bur. Pleasant Hope Cem.

           ii.   Howard, b.22 Jun 1911. He d.6 Sep 1912 GA at age 1 and was bur. Pleasant Hope Cem., Rome, Floyd Co., GA.

1137   iii.   Bertha Estelle, b. 17 Feb 1913; m. Truman Clyde Newberry.

1138   iv.   Margaret Hazel, b. 24 Jul 1915 Polk Co., GA; m. Rayford Lewis Fricks.

1139   v.   Harold Lee, b. 1 May 1917 Polk Co., GA; m. Kinnie Bee Bynum; m. Hallie Clair Partee.

1140   vi.   Ella Mae, b. 2 Apr 1919; m. Ray Franklin Waters.

1141   vii.   Mary Magdeline, b. 19 Jan 1921; m. Stilman Posey Sisson.

           viii. Herman James, b.29 Nov 1922 Floyd Co., GA. He m. Grace Gilmore on Christmas Eve, 24 Dec 1942. He d.6 Jan 2006 Floyd Co., GA, at age 83 and was bur. Pleasant Hope Cem., Rome, Floyd Co., GA.

                  Grace Gilmore, b.23 Aug 1925 Floyd Co., GA. She d.20 Dec 2010 Floyd Co., GA, at age 85.

           ix.   Blanche, b.21 Jul 1925 Floyd Co., GA. She m. James Howared Lemaster Sr. on 1 Jul 1950. She d.21 Jan 2006 Silver Creek, Floyd Co., GA, at age 80 and was bur. Pleasant Hope Cem., Rome, Floyd Co., GA.

                  James Howared Lemaster Sr, b.13 Jul 1928. He d.4 Oct 2002 at age 74.

1142   x.   Patsy Ruth, b. 26 May 1932 Silver Creek, Floyd Co., GA; m. PFC Belton Palmer Sheffield Jr. (USArmy-WWII).

729. Gertrude[7] Miller (Geretie[6] Abney, James[5], Benjamin[4], Hezekiah[3], Elisha[2], Abner[1]) m. Othel Blair Scoggins. , b.28 Jun 1897. She d.10 Mar 1944 at age 46 and was bur. Pleasant Hope Cem., Rome, Floyd Co., GA.

    Othel Blair Scoggins, b.26 Jan 1893. He d.16 Mar 1978 at age 85 and was bur. Pleasant Hope Cem., Rome, Floyd Co., GA.

Known children of Gertrude[7] Miller and Othel Blair Scoggins:

           i.   Othel Varnell[8], b.23 Feb 1919. He m. Minnie Dean Melvin in 1938. He d.10 Oct 1963 at age 44; bur. Pleasant Hope Cem.

                  Minnie Dean Melvin, b.2 May 1920 Fitzgerald, Ben Hill Co., GA. She m2. Harry Cleveland Broach in 1978. She d.15 Mar 1999 Rome, Floyd Co., GA, at age 78.

730. Emma Viola[7] Abney (William[6], James[5], Benjamin[4], Hezekiah[3], Elisha[2], Abner[1]), b.21 Nov 1905 Polk Co., GA. She m. Amos Gentry ca.1939. She d.10 Jul 1987 Floyd Co., GA, at age 81 and was bur. Oakland Cem., Rome, Floyd Co., GA.

    Amos Gentry, b.10 Feb 1916 Rome, Floyd Co., GA. He d.7 Jun 1980 Rome, Floyd Co., GA, at age 64 and was bur. Oakland Cem., Rome.

Known children of Emma Viola[7] Abney and Amos Gentry:

           i.   Frances Ruth[8], b.5 Aug 1940. She m. (n.n.) Brown. d.23 Aug 1973 at age 33 and was bur. Oakland Cem., Rome.

1143   ii.   Violet Patricia "Pat," b. 9 Jul 1945; m. Larry Dale McCullough Sr.

731. Gertha Estelle[7] Reynolds (Lillie[6] Abney, James[5], Benjamin[4], Hezekiah[3], Elisha[2], Abner[1]), b.15 Jul 1902 Floyd Co., GA. She m. Thomas Preston Mull in 1919. She d.11 Mar 1988 Rome, Floyd Co., GA, at age 85 and was bur. East View Cem., Rome, Floyd Co., GA.

    Thomas Preston Mull, b.1 Apr 1902 GA. He d.19 Nov 1980 Rome, Floyd Co., GA, at age 78 and was bur. East View Cem., Rome.

Known children of Gertha Estelle[7] Reynolds and Thomas Preston Mull:

           i.   Doyal Preston[8], b.2 Sep 1923 Floyd Co., GA. He d.4 May 2003 Floyd Co., GA, at age 79 and was bur. East View Cem., Rome, Floyd Co., GA.

           ii.   Dorothy Imogene, b.4 Sep 1928. She d.28 Oct 1983 at age 55 and was bur. East View Cem., Rome, Floyd Co., GA.

732. Bernice Irene[7] Reynolds (Lillie[6] Abney, James[5], Benjamin[4], Hezekiah[3], Elisha[2], Abner[1]) m. George W. Manis. , b.26 Apr 1906 GA. She d.18 Feb 1998 Dalton, Whitfield Co., GA, at age 91 and was bur. Varnell Cem., Varnell, Whitfield Co., GA.

    George W. Manis, b.16 Sep 1901. He d.13 Aug 1968 at age 66 and was bur. Varnell Cem., Varnell, Whitfield Co., GA.

Known child of Bernice Irene[7] Reynolds and George W. Manis:

1144   i.   Betty June[8], b. 8 Nov 1930 Athens, McMinn Co., TN; m. Loyd Edward Stinson (USN-WWII).

733. Frances Marion[7] Abney (Sylvester[6], James[5], Benjamin[4], Hezekiah[3], Elisha[2], Abner[1]) m. PFC Harry O. Stone (USArmy). , b.4 Aug 1918 Floyd Co., GA. She d.12 Sep 2012 Rome, Floyd Co., GA, at age 94 and was bur. East View Cem., Rome, Floyd Co., GA.

    PFC Harry O. Stone (USArmy), b.25 Jan 1911. He d.22 Jun 1979 at age 68 and was bur. West Hill Cem., Dalton, Whitfield Co., GA.

Known child of Frances Marion[7] Abney and PFC Harry O. Stone (USArmy):

           i.   Michael Lee[8], b.21 Nov 1950. He d.23 Apr 1988 at age 37 and was bur. East View Cem., Rome, Floyd Co., GA.

734. PFC Calvin Vester[7] Abney (USArmy-WWII) (Sylvester[6], James[5], Benjamin[4], Hezekiah[3], Elisha[2], Abner[1]), b.15 Dec 1925. He m. Doris Juanita Bell on 31 Aug 1949. He d.23 Feb 2006 at age 80 and was bur. East View Cem., Rome, Floyd Co., GA.

    Doris Juanita Bell, b.29 Oct 1930. She d.21 Jul 1984 at age 53 and was bur. East View Cem., Rome, Floyd Co., GA.

Known children of PFC Calvin Vester[7] Abney (USArmy-WWII) and Doris Juanita Bell:

           i.   Sheron[8] m. (n.n.) Grady.

           ii.   Mitchell.

           iii.   Phillip.

           iv.   Teresa "Diane", b.16 Jan 1953 Rome, Floyd Co., GA. She m1. (n.n.) Payne. She m2. Wayne Christian. She d.8 Mar 2014 Rome, Floyd Co., GA, at age 61 and was bur. East View Cem., Rome, Floyd Co., GA.

735. Pvt. Rayford Martin[7] Abney (USArmy) (Sylvester[6], James[5], Benjamin[4], Hezekiah[3], Elisha[2], Abner[1]) m. Dorothy Fay "Dot" Moore. He, b.30 Mar 1928. He d.16 Feb 1995 at age 66 and was bur. East View Cem., Rome, Floyd Co., GA.

    Dorothy Fay "Dot" Moore, b.16 Aug 1935 Polk Co., GA. She d.23 Nov 2012 Rome, Floyd Co., GA, at age 77 and was bur. East View Cem.

Known children of Pvt. Rayford Martin[7] Abney (USArmy) and Dorothy Fay "Dot" Moore:

1145   i.   Susan[8], m. Dean Oswalt.

1146   ii.   Keith, m. Melanie (n.n.).

736. Eunice Josephine[7] Abney (Robert[6], Joseph[5], Benjamin[4], Hezekiah[3], Elisha[2], Abner[1]), b.13 Oct 1904 Paulding Co., GA; m. Homer E. Hunt on 5 Oct 1917. They appeared on the censuses of 19 Jan 1920 Roxana, Paulding Co., GA; of 8 Apr 1930 Moultrie, Colquitt Co., GA; and 17 Apr 1940 Autreyville, Colquitt Co., GA; d.26 Oct 1986 Coolidge, Thomas Co., GA, age 82; bur. Big Creek Bapt. Ch. Cem., Coolidge, Thomas Co., GA.

    Homer Edward Hunt, b.13 Apr 1895 Paulding Co., GA. He d.24 Nov 1977 Thomas Co., GA, at age 82 and was bur. Big Creek Bapt. Ch. Cem.

Known children of Eunice Josephine[7] Abney and Homer Edward Hunt:
      i.   Christine[8], b. ca.1918.
      ii. C.L., b. ca.Jan 1920 Paulding Co., A. He d. before 1930.
      iii. James Edward, b.15 Dec 1921. He d.20 Jun 1973 at age 51 and was bur. Greenwood Cem., Cairo, Grady Co., GA.
      iv. Terrell, b. ca.1923 GA.
      v. Lewell "Wasul", b. ca.Dec 1925 GA.
      vi. Nellie Nadrine, b. ca.1931 GA.
      vii. Bobbie Hazel, b.20 Oct 1932 Colquitt Co., GA. She m. Ed Edwin White on 24 May 1954. She d.1 Aug 2020 Colquitt Co., GA, at age 87 and was bur. Big Creek Bapt. Ch. Cem., Coolidge, Thomas Co., GA.
           Ed Edwin White, b.23 Jun 1934. He d.28 Aug 2001 at age 67 and was bur. Big Creek Bapt. Ch. Cem., Coolidge.
      viii. Teddy "Ray", b. ca.1936 GA.
      ix. Ronald "Jack", b.10 Apr 1939 Thomas Co., GA. He m. (n.n.) on 12 Aug 1960. He d.19 Jul 2004 Thomas Co., GA, at age 65 and was bur. Laurel Hill Cem., Thomasville, Thomas Co., GA.
  1147 x. Billy Joe, b. ca.1942 GA; m. Betty Marie Bozeman.
      xi. Opal Diane, b. ca.1944 GA.

737. Grace Pauline "Gracie"[7] Abney (Robert[6], Joseph[5], Benjamin[4], Hezekiah[3], Elisha[2], Abner[1]), b.20 Jul 1910. She m1. W. Hosey McMichen ca.1924. She and W. Hosey McMichen appeared on the census of 8 Apr 1930 Acorntree Dist., Paulding Co., GA. She m2. Charlie Martin Culpepper. She d.8 Apr 1982 at age 71 and was bur. Riverdale Cem., Columbus, Muscogee Co., GA.
    W. Hosey McMichen, b. ca.1875 GA.
Known child of Grace Pauline "Gracie"[7] Abney and W. Hosey McMichen:
      i.   Virginia[8], b. ca.1926 GA.
    Charlie Martin Culpepper, b.3 Mar 1907 Russell Co., AL. He d.27 Mar 1954 Muscogee Co., GA, at age 47 and was bur. Riverdale Cem.
There were no known children of Grace Pauline "Gracie"[7] Abney and Charlie Martin Culpepper.

738. Roberta Etta[7] Abney (Robert[6], Joseph[5], Benjamin[4], Hezekiah[3], Elisha[2], Abner[1]), b.15 Nov 1923 Muscogee Co., GA. She m. Ralph Thomas Murray (USNR-WWII) in 1940. She d.18 Oct 1963 Muscogee Co., GA, at age 39 and was bur. Riverdale Cem., Columbus, Muscogee Co., GA.
    Ralph Thomas Murray (USNR-WWII), b.21 Oct 1919 Columbus, Muscogee Co., GA; d.18 Oct 1963 Muscogee Co., GA; bur. Riverdale Cem.
Known children of Roberta Etta[7] Abney and Ralph Thomas Murray (USNR-WWII):
      i.   Tommie Sue[8], b.27 Jun 1941 Muscogee Co., GA. She d.21 Sep 1958 Telfair Co., GA, at age 17 and was bur. Riverdale Cem., Columbus, Muscogee Co., GA.
      ii. Janice Darnell m. SFC Harland E. Smith (USArmy-Nam). , b.21 Mar 1944 Columbus, Muscogee Co., GA. She d. Christmas Eve, 24 Dec 2014 SC at age 70 and was bur. Fort Jackson National Cem., Columbia, Richland Co., SC.
           SFC Harland E. Smith (USArmy-Nam), b.6 Jun 1941. He d.10 Jan 2012 at age 70; bur. Fort Jackson National Cem.

739. Alpha[7] Prewett (Minnie[6] Abney, Joseph[5], Benjamin[4], Hezekiah[3], Elisha[2], Abner[1]), b.18 Nov 1900. She m. Homer Carnes. She d.7 Dec 1978 at age 78 and was bur. Town Creek Bapt. Ch. Cem., Chavies, DeKalb Co., AL.
    Homer Carnes, b.20 Apr 1898. He d.2 May 1983 at age 85 and was bur. Town Creek Bapt. Ch. Cem., Chavies, DeKalb Co., AL.
Known children of Alpha[7] Prewett and Homer Carnes:
  1148 i.   Edith Inez[8], b. 27 Jun 1918 DeKalb Co., AL; m. Gladston Paul Bryant (USN-WWII).
  1149 ii. Vera Mae, b. 20 Nov 1920; m. Franklin Eugene "Gene" Kean.
      iii. Opal Vestelle m. (n.n.) Wilson. , b.18 Jul 1926. She d.15 Apr 2010 at age 83 and was bur. Town Creek Bapt. Ch. Cem., Chavies, DeKalb Co., AL.
      iv. Ray M., b.16 Oct 1931 Sylvania, DeKalb Co., AL. He d.18 Feb 2002 Hixson, Hamilton Co., TN, at age 70 and was bur. Hamilton Mem. Gardens, Hixson, Hamilton Co., TN.

740. Howell Herman[7] Abney Sr. (Alonzo[6], Joseph[5], Benjamin[4], Hezekiah[3], Elisha[2], Abner[1]), b.1922 GA. He m. Katherine Louise Duncan. He d.1990 and was bur. Mount Harmony Mem. Gardens Cem., Mableton, Cobb Co., GA.
    Katherine Louise Duncan, b.1922. She d.2002 and was bur. Mount Harmony Mem. Gardens Cem., Mableton, Cobb Co., GA.
Known children of Howell Herman[7] Abney Sr. and Katherine Louise Duncan:
      i.   Debi[8] m. (n.n.) Haynie.
      ii. Howell Herman, b.20 Sep 1949. He d.28 Dec 1998 at age 49 and was bur. Mount Harmony Mem. Gardens Cem., Mableton, Cobb Co., GA.

741. William "Robert"[7] Abney (John[6], Charles[5], Benjamin[4], Hezekiah[3], Elisha[2], Abner[1]) m. Verna J. Latham. He, b.15 May 1931 Edwardsville, Cleburne Co., AL. He d.29 Nov 2004 Fruithurst, Cleburne Co., AL, at age 73 and was bur. Upper Cane Creek Cem., Fruithurst, Cleburne Co., AL.
    Verna J. Latham, b.17 Sep 1933 Delta, Clay Co., AL. She d.16 Mar 2013 AL at age 79.
Known children of William "Robert"[7] Abney and Verna J. Latham:
  1150 i.   Jeff[8]. He m. Martie (n.n.).

742. Rev. Jessie "Allen"[7] Abney Sr. (John[6], Charles[5], Benjamin[4], Hezekiah[3], Elisha[2], Abner[1]), b.17 May 1935 Edwardsville, Cleburne Co., AL. He m1. Ruth Vertell Connell on 30 Aug 1957 Upper Creek Meth. Ch., Fruithurst, Cleburne Co., AL. He m2. Joy (n.n.) on 15 Jun 1979. He d.6 Jun 2009 Fruithurst, Cleburne Co., AL, at age 74 and was bur. Upper Cane Creek Cem., Fruithurst, Cleburne Co., AL.
Known children of Rev. Jessie "Allen"[7] Abney Sr. and Ruth Vertell Connell:
      i.   Kathy[8] m. Greg Blair.
      ii. Carol m. Dave Fasick.
      iii. Keith m. Michelle (n.n.).
      iv. John m. Jincy (n.n.).
Known children of Rev. Jessie "Allen"[7] Abney Sr. and Joy (n.n.):
      i.   Jonathan[8] m. Amanda (n.n.).
      ii. Jessie Allen.

743. Rev. Benjamin Franklin "Benny"⁷ Abney (John⁶, Charles⁵, Benjamin⁴, Hezekiah³, Elisha², Abner¹), b.21 Oct 1938 Fruithurst, Cleburne Co., AL. He m. Connie Lenell Hulsey on 21 Jun 1957. He d.27 Mar 2020 Fruithurst, Cleburne Co., AL, at age 81 and was bur. Upper Creek Meth. Ch., Fruithurst, Cleburne Co., AL.
   Connie Lenell Hulsey, b.8 Dec 1939 Cleburne Co., AL. She d.25 Jun 2019 AL at age 79.
Known children of Rev. Benjamin Franklin "Benny"⁷ Abney and Connie Lenell Hulsey:
            i.   Susan⁸. She m. Jerry Miller.
    1151   ii. Philip. He m. Tracey (n.n.).

744. Rachel Edna⁷ Abney (William⁶, Charles⁵, Benjamin⁴, Hezekiah³, Elisha², Abner¹) m. James Hurshel Furgerson. , b.27 Feb 1929 Cleburne Co., AL. She d.27 Sep 2000 Chickamauga, Walker Co., GA, at age 71 and was bur. LaFayette Memory Gardens, LaFayette, Walker Co., GA.
   James Hurshel Furgerson, b.6 Jun 1921 Cleburne Co., AL; d.17 Feb 2012 Chickamauga, Walker Co., GA; bur. LaFayette Memory Gardens.
Known child of Rachel Edna⁷ Abney and James Hurshel Furgerson:
            i.   (dau.)⁸.

745. Fannie "Ethel"⁷ Dobbins (Laura⁶ Abney, Pinkney⁵, Wiley⁴, Hezekiah³, Elisha², Abner¹), b.31 Aug 1885 TN. She m. Charles Sylvester "Charley" McMackin Sr. in 1901. She and Charles Sylvester "Charley" McMackin Sr. appeared on the censuses of 10 May 1910, 15 Jan 1920 and 3 Apr 1930 Greene Co., TN. She d.27 Jan 1968 at age 82 and was bur. Milburnton UMC Cem., Greene Co., TN.
   Charles Sylvester "Charley" McMackin Sr, b.6 Jun 1883 Greene Co., TN. He d.24 Nov 1944 Sullivan Co., TN, at age 61.
Known children of Fannie "Ethel"⁷ Dobbins and Charles Sylvester "Charley" McMackin Sr. all b. TN:
    1152   i.   John D.⁸, b. 19 Sep 1902; m. Ethel Evans.
            ii. Rita, b. ca.1911.
            iii. Halbert, b. ca.1915.
            iv. Carl, b. ca.Oct 1919.
            v.   Charles Sylvester, b. ca.1925.

746. Thomas "Buford"⁷ Dobbins (Laura⁶ Abney, Pinkney⁵, Wiley⁴, Hezekiah³, Elisha², Abner¹), b. Jun 1891 TN. He m. Mary A. (n.n.) (b. ca.1886 TN). He and Mary A. appeared on the censuses of 5 Feb 1920, 22 Apr 1930 and 7 May 1940 Greeneville, Greene Co., TN.
Known children of Thomas "Buford"⁷ Dobbins and Mary A. (n.n.) both b. TN:
            i.   Kathleen⁸, b. ca.1912.
            ii. Alice "Olivia", b. ca.1914.

747. Ethel Winaforde⁷ Abney (John⁶, Pinkney⁵, Wiley⁴, Hezekiah³, Elisha², Abner¹), b.1892 VA. She m. John L. Marcum, son of Caleb Marcum and Ellen Fugate, in 1910. She and John L. Marcum appeared on the census of 29 Apr 1910 Rose Hill, Lee Co., VA. She appeared as Head of Household on the census of 6 May 1940 Rose Hill, Lee Co., VA. She d.1966 and was bur. Abney Cem., Lee Co., VA.
   John L. Marcum, b.23 Nov 1886. He d.7 Jan 1953 at age 66 and was bur. Hobbs Cem., Rose Hill, Lee Co., VA.
Known children of Ethel Winaforde⁷ Abney and John L. Marcum:
            i.   Hubert⁸, b. ca.1916 VA.
            ii. Mae Kathleen m. Dr. James Roy Olinger. , b.11 May 1918 Rose Hill, Lee Co., VA. She d.26 Feb 1999 Rose Hill, Lee Co., VA, at age 80 and was bur. Morgan Cem., Rose Hill, Lee Co., VA.
                     Dr. James Roy Olinger, b.18 May 1896. He d.1954 and was bur. Olinger Fam. Cem. #318, Olinger, Lee Co., VA.
            iii. Nora, b. ca.1921 VA.
    1153   iv. Georgia I. "Georgie," b. 22 Mar 1922 Rose Hill, Lee Co., VA; m. Thomas Patton "Pat" Short.
            v.   Mable, b. ca.1924 VA.
    1154   vi. Paul Cale, b. 4 Jun 1926 Rose Hill, Lee Co., VA; m. (n.n.).
            vii. Glen, b. ca.1929 VA.
            viii. Devers "Red", b.1930 VA. He d.2012 and was bur. Ewing-McClure Cem., Jonesville, Lee Co., VA.
            ix. Mary E, b. ca.1932 VA.
            x.   Alma, b. ca.1934 VA.

748. Elizabeth E. "Lizzy"⁷ Abney (John⁶, Pinkney⁵, Wiley⁴, Hezekiah³, Elisha², Abner¹), b.27 Jul 1902 VA. She m. Dennis J. Evans ca.1925. She and Dennis J. Evans appeared on the census of 10 Apr 1930 Greene Co., TN. She was liv. on 9 May 1940 with her mother, Sarah Abney, Rose Hill, Lee Co., VA. She d.20 Apr 1978 at age 75 and was bur. Campbell Cem., Rose Hill, Lee Co., VA.
   Dennis J. Evans, b. ca.1906 TN.
Known children of Elizabeth E. "Lizzy"⁷ Abney and Dennis J. Evans:
            i.   Dennis R.⁸, b.14 Dec 1926 VA. He d.5 Jan 2007 at age 80 and was bur. Campbell Cem., Rose Hill, Lee Co., VA.
            ii. Kenneth R., b. ca.1929 TN.
            iii. William, b. ca.1931 TN.

749. John "Floyd"⁷ Abney (John⁶, Pinkney⁵, Wiley⁴, Hezekiah³, Elisha², Abner¹), b.15 Feb 1904 Rose Hill, Lee Co., VA. He m1. Martha Ann "Annie" Farris on 23 Dec 1926 Claiborne Co., TN. He and Martha were liv. on 18 Apr 1930 with his mother, Sarah Abney, Rose Hill Dist., Lee Co., VA. He and the children were liv. on 6 May 1940 with his mother, Sarah Abney, Rose Hill, Lee Co., AL. He m2. Sarah Delilah McCurry, daughter of William "Bill" McCurry and Cynthia Virginia Thomas, on 25 Nov 1950 Montgomery Co., MD. He d.2 Jun 1988 MD at age 84 and was bur. Glenwood Baptist Church Cem., Glenwood, Howard Co., MD.
   Martha Ann "Annie" Farris, b.24 Feb 1905 Hancock Co., TN. She m. Fin Luther Winzenrith in 1940. She d.23 Nov 1972 at age 67 and was bur. Luce Creek Cem., Annapolis, Anne Arundel Co., MD.
Known children of John "Floyd"⁷ Abney and Martha Ann "Annie" Farris:
            i.   Delores Lee "Lois"⁸, b.27 Apr 1928 Hancock Co., TN. She m. (n.n.) Rank. d.1 Oct 2009 Winchester, Frederick Co., VA.
            ii. Joy, b. ca.1930 VA.
            iii. Dora, b. ca.1933 VA.
    1155   iv. Margaret "Marie," b. 28 Dec 1934 Rose Hill, Lee Co., VA; m1. Glenn Rice Lyerly; m2. Rev. Eugene Albert "Gene" Dixon

v.   John "Roscoe", b.30 Nov 1936. He d.28 Jul 1937 and was bur. Abney Cem., Lee Co., VA.

1156   vi.   Morgan Floyd (gen., originator, contributor), b. 1937 Rose Hill, Lee Co., VA; m1. Nellie J. Williams; m2. Janet M. Kiser. Sarah Delilah McCurry, b.27 Nov 1909. She d.16 Nov 1984 at age 74; bur. Glenwood Baptist Church Cem., Glenwood, Howard Co., MD. There were no known children of John "Floyd"[7] Abney and Sarah Delilah McCurry.

750.   Carrie Olivia[7] Abney (John[6], Pinkney[5], Wiley[4], Hezekiah[3], Elisha[2], Abner[1]), b.1896 VA. She lived on 13 May 1910 with Unc. Frank Dobbins, Greene Co., TN. She m. Lincoln L. "Link" Marcum, son of George M. Marcum and Maranda M. Stone, ca.1917. She and Lincoln L. "Link" Marcum appeared on the censuses of 22 Jan 1920 and 11 Apr 1930 Hancock Co., TN. She d.1974 and was bur. Marcum Cem., Rose Hill, Lee Co., VA.
   Lincoln L. "Link" Marcum, b.28 Nov 1889 Rose Hill, Lee Co., VA. He d.6 Jan 1954 Rose Hill, Lee Co., VA, at age 64.
Known children of Carrie Olivia[7] Abney and Lincoln L. "Link" Marcum:
   i.   Chester E.[8], b.10 Aug 1918 TN. He d.9 Aug 1980 at age 61 and was bur. Marcum Cem., Rose Hill, Lee Co., VA.
   ii.   Louis, b. ca.1924 Hancock Co., TN.
   iii.   Hoover, b. ca.Jan 1930 Hancock Co., TN.

751.   Benjamin Parker[7] Abney Sr. (John[6], James[5], Wiley[4], Hezekiah[3], Elisha[2], Abner[1]), b.27 Aug 1912; m. Nora D. Davis 121. He d.21 Feb 1982.
Known children of Benjamin Parker[7] Abney Sr. and Nora D. Davis:
   1157   i.   Faye[8], b. 11 Sep 1932.
   1158   ii.   Benjamin Parker, b. 21 Nov 1938.
   1159   iii.   John Wesley, b. 21 Apr 1950.

752.   Jesse Brooks[7] Abney Jr. (Jesse[6], James[5], Andrew[4], Hezekiah[3], Elisha[2], Abner[1]), b.18 Aug 1897 AL. He m1. Ola Estelle Gillespie ca.1920. He m2. Inga Kamrud. He d.10 Jan 1979 Sonoma Co., CA, at age 81 and was bur. Greenwood Cem., Greenwood, Whatcom Co., WA.
   Ola Estelle Gillespie, b.1901. She d.1988.
Known children of Jesse Brooks[7] Abney Jr. and Ola Estelle Gillespie:
   i.   Dorothy "Estelle"[8] m. S.Sgt. Robert John Watson Jr. (USArmy-WWII). , b.27 Oct 1921. She d.4 Dec 1992 at age 71 and was bur. Jefferson Mem. Gardens East, Trussville, Jefferson Co., AL.
      S.Sgt. Robert John Watson Jr. (USArmy-WWII), b.3 Mar 1923; d.19 Nov 2007; bur. Jefferson Mem. Gardens East.
   ii.   Jack E., b.1923. He d.1981 and was bur. Jefferson Mem. Gardens East, Trussville, Jefferson Co., AL.
Known child of Jesse Brooks[7] Abney Jr. and Inga Kamrud:
   i.   Shirley Jayne[8], b.24 Sep 1943; m. Kenneth Wayne Maloy; d.26 Aug 1,995; bur. Allen Cem., Allen, Pontotoc Co., OK.
      Kenneth Wayne Maloy, b.5 Jul 1946. He d.7 Feb 1982 at age 35 and was bur. Allen Cem., Allen, Pontotoc Co., OK.

753.   Lotice[7] Abner (Wyatt[6], William[5], James[4] Abney, Hezekiah[3], Elisha[2], Abner[1]), b.21 May 1901. She m. Pvt. John A. Pike (USArmy-WWI). d.4 Aug 1971 at age 70 and was bur. Franklin City Cem., Franklin, Heard Co., GA.
   Pvt. John A. Pike (USArmy-WWI), b.23 Mar 1891. He d.3 Dec 1949 at age 58 and was bur. Franklin City Cem., Franklin, Heard Co., GA.
Known children of Lotice[7] Abner and Pvt. John A. Pike (USArmy-WWI):
   i.   Dawson[8], b.24 May 1920. He d.29 Jan 1932 at age 11 and was bur. Franklin City Cem., Franklin, Heard Co., GA.
   ii.   Bonnie M., b.15 Sep 1934 Franklin, Heard Co., GA. He m. Juanita C. (n.n.). He d.18 Jun 2013 Griffin, Spalding Co., GA, at age 78 and was bur. Franklin City Cem., Franklin, Heard Co., GA.
      Juanita C. (n.n.), b.14 Jun 1936. She d.10 Dec 1991 at age 55; bur. Franklin City Cem., Franklin, Heard Co., GA.
   iii.   Eloise, b.11 May 1938. She d.11 May 1938 and was bur. Franklin City Cem., Franklin, Heard Co., GA.

754.   Richard Lee[7] Abner (Wyatt[6], William[5], James[4] Abney, Hezekiah[3], Elisha[2], Abner[1]), b.18 Mar 1905. He m. Annie Mae Abner, daughter of Wiley "Frank" Abner and Odessa Bell "Dessie" White, in 1929. He and Annie Mae Abner appeared on the census of 22 Apr 1930 Franklin, Heard Co., GA. He d.7 Jul 1941 at age 36 and was bur. Franklin City Cem., Franklin, Heard Co., GA.
   Annie Mae Abner, b.20 Feb 1913 Heard Co., GA. She m2. (n.n.) Rogers. She d.25 Oct 1999 Newnan, Coweta Co., GA, at age 86 and was bur. Oak Hill Cem., Newnan, Coweta Co., GA.
Known child of Richard Lee[7] Abner and Annie Mae Abner:
   i.   Raymond L.[8], b. ca.Apr 1927 GA. He was liv. on 2 Apr 1940 with grandfather, Heflin Abner, Heard Co., GA.

755.   Luda G. "Ludie"[7] Abner (Wyatt[6], William[5], James[4] Abney, Hezekiah[3], Elisha[2], Abner[1]), b.14 Nov 1906 Spalding Co., GA; m. John Fletcher "Fletch" Eady 24 Oct 1926 Heard Co., GA. They appeared on the census of 21 Apr 1930 Franklin, Heard Co., GA; d.10 Mar 1972 Heard Co., GA.
   John Fletcher "Fletch" Eady, b.6 May 1878 Heard Co., GA. He d.1 Mar 1942 Heard Co., GA, at age 63.
Known children of Ludie G.[7] Abner and John Fletcher Eady all b. Heard Co., GA:
   i.   Dewey Oliver[8], b.13 Jun 1927. He d.17 Jul 2008 Spalding Co., GA, at age 81.
   ii.   Rufus Robert, b.15 May 1931. He d.2 Jul 1977 Spalding Co., GA, at age 46.
   iii.   Johnny Frank, b.9 Feb 1936. He d.2 May 1996 Spalding Co., GA, at age 60.
   iv.   Alfred, b.11 Dec 1938. He d.5 May 2004 Spalding Co., GA, at age 65.

756.   Samuel B. "Sam"[7] Abner (Wyatt[6], William[5], James[4] Abney, Hezekiah[3], Elisha[2], Abner[1]), b.30 Aug 1908 GA. He m. Myrtice Costley. He d.25 May 1996 Coweta Co., GA, at age 87 and was bur. Franklin City Cem., Franklin, Heard Co., GA.
   Myrtice Costley, b.9 Aug 1910 Greece. She d.3 Jul 1994 Heard Co., GA, at age 83 and was bur. Franklin City Cem., Franklin, Heard Co., GA.
Known children of Samuel B. "Sam"[7] Abner and Myrtice Costley:
   i.   Bennie S.[8], b.16 Jun 1935. He m. Opal Fuller on 3 Jul 1954 Heard Co., GA. He m. Faye I. (n.n.) (She was b. 6 Oct 1941). He d.27 Aug 1987 at age 52 and was bur. Franklin City Cem., Franklin, Heard Co., GA.

757.   Mildred Woodall[7] Abner (Millard's twin) (Wyatt[6], William[5], James[4] Abney, Hezekiah[3], Elisha[2], Abner[1]), b.9 Sep 1913 Heard Co., GA. She m. James A. Strickland; d.6 Aug 2004 Luthersville, Meriwether Co., GA, age 90; bur. Luthersville City Cem., Luthersville, Meriwether Co., GA.
   James Archer Strickland, b.21 Dec 1910. He d.19 Jul 1984 at age 73 and was bur. Luthersville City Cem., Luthersville, Meriwether Co., GA.

Known children of Mildred Woodall[7] Abner (Millard's twin) and James Archer Strickland:

        i.   Eloise[8], b.20 May 1947 Meriwether Co., GA. She m. Rev. Harry T. Gann. d.6 Feb 2015 Coweta Co., GA, at age 67 and was bur. Luthersville City Cem., Luthersville, Meriwether Co., GA.
                Rev. Harry T. Gann, b.21 Jun 1943.

       ii.   James E, b.30 Jan 1950 Luthersville, Meriwether Co., GA. He m. Ellen (Whitman?) (b. 30 Oct in the 1950's) on 11 Oct 1968. He d.24 Mar 2015 GA at age 65 and was bur. Luthersville City Cem., Luthersville, Meriwether Co., GA.

758. Lizzie Lou[7] Abner (Wyatt[6], William[5], James[4] Abney, Hezekiah[3], Elisha[2], Abner[1]), b.26 Mar 1915. She m1. George Bluford Pike ca.1933. She m2. Robert Lee Hickey. She d.23 Aug 2012 at age 97 and was bur. Franklin City Cem., Franklin, Heard Co., GA.
    George Bluford Pike, b.30 Apr 1912. He d.7 Nov 1942 at age 30 and was bur. Wesley Chapel Cem., Heard Co., GA.
Known children of Lizzie Lou[7] Abner and George Bluford Pike:

        i.   Mary Hautense[8], b.14 Feb 1934 LaGrange, Troup Co., GA. She m. James Austin Buchanan. She d.8 May 2002 LaGrange, Troup Co., GA, at age 68 and was bur. Franklin City Cem., Franklin, Heard Co., GA.
                James Austin Buchanan, b.30 Apr 1933 Roopville, Carroll Co., GA. He d.13 Jul 1992 Coweta Co., GA, at age 59 and was bur. Franklin City Cem., Franklin, Heard Co., GA.

       ii.   Lizzie Ruth, b.15 May 1942 Troup Co., GA. She m. Randall Quillian Buchanan in 1958. She d.3 Jun 1972 Coweta Co., GA, at age 30 and was bur. Franklin City Cem., Franklin, Heard Co., GA.
                Randall Quillian Buchanan, b.21 Oct 1934 Roopville, Carroll Co., GA. He d.26 Jan 2012 Franklin, Heard Co., GA, at age 77 and was bur. Franklin City Cem., Franklin, Heard Co., GA.
    Robert Lee Hickey, b.10 Jan 1926. He d.26 May 2005 at age 79 and was bur. Franklin City Cem., Franklin, Heard Co., GA.
There were no known children of Lizzie Lou[7] Abner and Robert Lee Hickey.

759. Luta[7] Abner (Rufus[6], William[5], James[4] Abney, Hezekiah[3], Elisha[2], Abner[1]), b.21 Dec 1906 GA. She m. Pierce Oliver Davis on 22 Aug 1924 in Chambers Co., AL. She d.10 Apr 1996 in Fulton Co., GA.
    Pierce Oliver Davis, b. 21 Sep 1902 Randolph Co., AL; d.25 Mar 1970 Coweta Co., GA.
Known children of Luta[7] Abner and Pierce Oliver Davis:

        i.   Sybil Virginia[8], b. 1925 Heard Co., GA; d.27 Apr 2012
       ii.   Leonard Bruce, b. 27 Jun 1927 Heard Co., GA; d.3 Jan 1992 Newnan, Coweta Co., GA

760. Rufus B.[7] Daniel Sr. (Carrie[6] Abner, William[5], James[4] Abney, Hezekiah[3], Elisha[2], Abner[1]) m. Edna Francis Bass. He, b.11 Aug 1911. He d.8 Jul 1958 at age 46 and was bur. Shadowlawn Cem., LaGrange, Troup Co., GA.
    Edna Francis Bass, b.8 Nov 1913. She d.25 Aug 1954 at age 40 and was bur. Hillview East Cem., LaGrange, Troup Co., GA.
Known children of Rufus B.[7] Daniel Sr. and Edna Francis Bass:

        i.   Raymond Bryant[8], b.17 Dec 1931 LaGrange, Troup Co., GA. He d.22 Feb 1997 Reidsville, Rockingham Co., NC, at age 65 and was bur. Reidlawn Cem., Reidsville, Rockingham Co., NC.
       ii.   Rufus B., b.1935 LaGrange, Troup Co., GA. He d.28 Jan 1963 LaGrange, Troup Co., GA and was bur. Cross Point Church Cem., Louise, Troup Co., GA.
      iii.   Shirley Jean m. Roy L. Hopkins. , b.23 Feb 1937 LaGrange, Troup Co., GA. She d.19 Dec 1998 Eden, Rockingham Co., NC, at age 61 and was bur. Mountain View Cem., Ridgeway, Henry Co., VA.
                Roy L. Hopkins, b.31 May 1932. He d.12 May 2000 at age 67 and was bur. Mountain View Cem., Ridgeway.
       iv.   Edward Floyd, b.24 Mar 1940 LaGrange, Troup Co., GA; d.21 Mar 1992 San Bernardino Co., CA. He was cremated.
        v.   Erlene, b.1 Aug 1942 LaGrange, Troup Co., GA; m. (n.n.) Anger. d.25 Mar 2015 Myrtle Beach, Horry Co., SC. (cremated)
       vi.   Donald Lee, b.24 Sep 1945. He d.10 Apr 2006 at age 60; bur. Restlawn Memory Gardens, LaGrange, Troup Co., GA.
      vii.   Kenneth L. "Ken", b.23 Jun 1947 LaGrange, Troup Co., GA. He m. Patricia "Pat" Turner in 1969. He d.18 Sep 2018 LaGrange, Troup Co., GA, at age 71 and was bur. Meadoway Gardens Cem., LaGrange, Troup Co., GA.
                Patricia "Pat" Turner, b.25 Oct 1948 and d.18 Jul 2017 LaGrange, Troup Co., GA; bur. Meadoway Gardens Cem.
     viii.   Michael Joe "Mike", b.7 Oct 1950 LaGrange, Troup Co., GA. He m. Carolyn (n.n.). He d.16 Dec 2015 Luthersville, Meriwether Co., GA, at age 65. He was cremated.

761. Annie Mae[7] Abner (Wiley[6], William[5], James[4] Abney, Hezekiah[3], Elisha[2], Abner[1]), She m1. Richard Lee Abner (see #754 on page 177); she m2. (n.n.) Rogers. There were no known children of Annie Mae[7] Abner and (n.n.) Rogers.

762. Ruby Inez[7] Abner (Wiley[6], William[5], James[4] Abney, Hezekiah[3], Elisha[2], Abner[1]), b.23 May 1916. She m. Rufus Lance Arrington Sr. She d.3 Jan 2006 at age 89 and was bur. Franklin City Cem., Franklin, Heard Co., GA.
    Rufus Lance Arrington Sr, b.22 May 1913. He d.26 Jan 1993 at age 79 and was bur. Franklin City Cem., Franklin, Heard Co., GA.
Known child of Ruby Inez[7] Abner and Rufus Lance Arrington Sr.:

        i.   Irene[8], b.6 Nov 1942. She d.9 Jan 2003 at age 60 and was bur. Franklin City Cem., Franklin, Heard Co., GA.

763. Frank "Amos"[7] Abner (USArmy-WWII) (Wiley[6], William[5], James[4] Abney, Hezekiah[3], Elisha[2], Abner[1]) m. Grace Inez Pike. He, b.16 Apr 1922. He d.8 Nov 1993 at age 71 and was bur. Franklin City Cem., Franklin, Heard Co., GA.
    Grace Inez Pike, b.21 May 1925. She d.29 Oct 2011 at age 86 and was bur. Franklin City Cem., Franklin, Heard Co., GA.
Known child of Frank "Amos"[7] Abner (USArmy-WWII) and Grace Inez Pike:

        i.   Ronald[8] m. Sharon (n.n.).

764. Lula[7] Abna (Robert[6], James[5], James[4] Abney, Hezekiah[3], Elisha[2], Abner[1]) m. Terrell Jackson. , b.2 Jun 1902 Franklin, Heard Co., GA. She d.31 May 1987 Hallettsville, Lavaca Co., TX, at age 84 and was bur. Starrville Cem., Starrville, Smith Co., TX.
    Terrell Jackson, b.18 Apr 1891 Smith Co., TX. He d.8 Aug 1975 TX at age 84 and was bur. Starrville Cem., Starrville, Smith Co., TX.
Known children of Lula[7] Abna and Terrell Jackson:

        i.   Martha R.[8], b.13 Oct 1924 Smith Co., TX. She d.24 Apr 1998 Smith Co., TX, at age 73 and was bur. Starrville Cem.
       ii.   Roger Earl, b.8 Jul 1937 Smith Co., TX; m. Ada Soderstrom; d.13 Sep 1995 Tyler, Smith Co., TX, bur. Starrville Cem.

Ada Soderstrom, b.17 Jun 1944.
  iii.   Donald Leamon, b.16 Jul 1945 Gladewater, Gregg Co., TX. He d.21 Nov 1973 Gonzales Co., TX; bur. Starrville Cem.

765. Eula Mae^7 Abna (Robert^6, James^5, James^4 Abney, Hezekiah^3, Elisha^2, Abner^1) m. Benjamin Franklin "Ben" Hewitt. , b.12 Mar 1904 GA. She d.23 Apr 1987 Gladewater, Smith Co., TX, at age 83 and was bur. Friendship Cem., Friendship (Starrville), Smith Co., TX.
    Benjamin Franklin "Ben" Hewitt, b.4 Jun 1900. He d.22 Apr 1955 Smith Co., TX, at age 54 and was bur. Friendship Cem.
Known children of Eula Mae^7 Abna and Benjamin Franklin "Ben" Hewitt:
      i.   Bryan Barry (USN-WWII)^8, b.11 May 1924 Winona, Smith Co., TX. He m. Iris Ferchaud. He d.30 Dec 1985 at age 61 and was bur. Houston National Cem., Houston, Harris Co., TX.
            Iris Ferchaud, b.19 Jan 1920 New Orleans, Orleans Par., LA. She d.13 Jul 2000 at age 80; bur. Houston Nat'l Cem.
  1160   ii.   B.F., b. 13 Sep 1932 Starrville, Smith Co., TX; m. Tiffy (n.n.).
      iii.   Royce, b.6 Mar 1947 Gregg Co., TX. He d.7 Mar 1947 Gregg Co., TX and was bur. Friendship Cem.

766. Alice^7 Abna (Robert^6, James^5, James^4 Abney, Hezekiah^3, Elisha^2, Abner^1), b.25 Mar 1906 Judson, Gregg Co., TX. She m. Walter Rex Smallwood Sr. ca.1925. She and Walter Rex Smallwood Sr. appeared on the census of 16 Apr 1930 Gregg Co., TX. She d.29 Jul 1991 Smith Co., TX, at age 85 and was bur. Starrville Cem., Starrville, Smith Co., TX.
    Walter Rex Smallwood Sr, b.21 Jun 1908 TX. He m. Mildred Leona Buck on 22 Dec 1937. He d.7 Nov 1981 at age 73.
Known children of Alice^7 Abna and Walter Rex Smallwood Sr.:
      i.   Walter Rex^8, b.19 Aug 1926 and d.20 Aug 1926 Gregg Co., TX; bur. Rock Springs Cem., Gladewater, Gregg Co., TX.
      ii.   Robert Elmer, b.15 Nov 1927 Gladewater, Gregg Co., TX.
      iii.   Billy Ray, b.23 Dec 1931 Gladewater, Gregg Co., TX.
      iv.   Frances Vernell, b.29 Jun 1933 and d.27 Nov 1995 Gregg Co., TX; m. (n.n.) Noell; bur. Rock Springs Cem., Gladewater.

767. Cpl. Joseph Elmer "Joe"^{7} Abna (USAAC-WWII) (Robert^6, James^5, James^4 Abney, Hezekiah^3, Elisha^2, Abner^1), b.11 Aug 1910 Coleman, Perry Co., AL. He m1. Dessie Mae Nolan in 1933. He m2. Willie Frances Griffin ca.1938. He d.Jun 1946 in an automobile accident, Gregg Co., TX, at age 35 and was bur. Starrville Cem., Starrville, Smith Co., TX.
    Dessie Mae Nolan, b.19 Jan 1908 Tyler, Smith Co., TX; d.23 Dec 1933 Tyler, Smith Co., TX, age 25; bur. Center Cem., Tyler, Smith Co., TX.
Known child of Cpl. Joseph Elmer "Joe"^{7} Abna (USAAC-WWII) and Dessie Mae Nolan:
  1161   i.   Nellie Jo^8, b. 16 Dec 1933 Starrville, Smith Co., TX; m. Oscar McKay Capps.
    Willie Frances Griffin, b.30 Dec 1916 Lufkin, Angelina Co., TX. She d.29 Jul 1994 Denton, Denton Co., TX, at age 77 and was bur. Bullard Cem., Bullard, Smith Co., TX.
Known children of Cpl. Joseph Elmer "Joe"^{7} Abna (USAAC-WWII) and Willie Frances Griffin:
      i.   Jocie^8 m. (n.n.) Lewis.
      ii.   Pat Eugene, b. New Year's Day, 1 Jan 1939 Dallas, Dallas Co., TX. He d.24 Apr 1995 Denton, Denton Co., TX, at age 56 and was bur. Starrville Cem., Starrville, Smith Co., TX.
  1162   iii.   George Michael "Mike," b. 24 Jul 1943 Bullard, Smith Co., TX; m. (n.n.).
  1163   iv.   Richard Wayne, b. 4 Dec 1945 Amarillo, Potter Co., TX; m. Linda (n.n.).

768. Bernice^7 Abna (Robert^6, James^5, James^4 Abney, Hezekiah^3, Elisha^2, Abner^1), b.20 Mar 1916 Fisher Farm, Winona, Smith Co., TX. She m. Marvin Royce Roberts on 20 Jul 1944 Gilmer, Upshur Co., TX. She d.22 Aug 2006 Fisher Farm, Winona, Smith Co., TX, at age 90 and was bur. Starville Cem., Starrville, Smith Co., TX.
    Marvin Royce Roberts, b.30 Mar 1910 Winona, Smith Co., TX. He d.1 May 1981 Longview, Gregg Co., TX, at age 71; bur. Starrville Cem.
Known children of Bernice^7 Abna and Marvin Royce Roberts:
  1164   i.   Sarilee^8, b. 21 Jun 1941 Gladewater, Gregg Co., TX; m. James "Jimmy" Brewer.
  1165   ii.   Ronald Royce, b. 3 Feb 1946 Gladewater, Gregg Co., TX.
      iii.   Mary Alice, b.1 Dec 1947 Longview, Gregg Co., TX. She m. Danny Johnson.

769. William James^7 Abna (Ales^6, James^5, James^4 Abney, Hezekiah^3, Elisha^2, Abner^1), b.28 Mar 1927 Eagan, East Point, Fulton Co., GA. He m. Tommie Lee Mitchell. He d.6 Nov 1991 Fulton Co., GA, at age 64 and was bur. College Park Cem., College Park, Fulton Co., GA.
    Tommie Lee Mitchell, b.14 May 1931 Jonesboro, Clayton Co., GA. She d.9 Mar 2013 Jackson, Butts Co., GA, at age 81 and was bur. Jackson City Cem., Jackson, Butts Co., GA.
Known children of William James^7 Abna and Tommie Lee Mitchell:
      i.   Tommy James^8, b.1952. He d.1999 and was bur. College Park Cem., College Park, Fulton Co., GA.
      ii.   Denny Ray, b.1958. He d.2 Feb 1975 Hall Co., GA and was bur. College Park Cem., College Park, Fulton Co., GA.
  1166   iii.   Pamela K., b. 2 Aug 1962 Atlanta, Fulton Co., GA; m. (n.n.) Scarborough.

770. Sgt. Donald Eugene^7 Abna (USAF-Korea) (Ales^6, James^5, James^4 Abney, Hezekiah^3, Elisha^2, Abner^1) m. Mary Ann Smith. He, b.2 Sep 1928 Eagan, East Point, Fulton Co., GA. He d.31 Oct 2002 Fayetteville, Fayette Co., GA, at age 74 and was bur. Westminster Mem. Gardens, Peachtree City, Fayette Co., GA.
    Mary Ann Smith, b.23 Jan 1933 Chattanooga, Hamilton Co., TN. She d.22 Mar 2003 Fayetteville, Fayette Co., GA, at age 70 and was bur. Westminster Mem. Gardens, Peachtree City, Fayette Co., GA.
Known children of Sgt. Donald Eugene^7 Abna (USAF-Korea) and Mary Ann Smith:
      i.   Joel^8.
      ii.   Melissa.
  1167   iii.   Beth. She m. Rev. David Paul.

771. Jack Allen^7 Bailey (Viola^6 Johnson, Sarah^5 Abney, Joel^4, Hezekiah^3, Elisha^2, Abner^1) m. Gracie Magdalena Cheatwood. He, b.31 Oct 1909 Jackson Co., AL. He d.21 Nov 1970 Harris Co., TX, at age 61 and was bur. Colonial Gardens, Marshall, Harrison Co., TX.
    Gracie Magdalena Cheatwood, b.7 Mar 1912 Panola, Panola Co., TX; d.11 Jan 1993 Marshall, Harrison Co., TX; bur. Colonial Gardens.

Known children of Jack Allen⁷ Bailey and Gracie Magdalena Cheatwood:
       i. Doris Ann⁸, b.18 May 1935 Panola Co., TX. She m. PFC Billy Don McMahan (USArmy) in 1968. She d.27 Jun 2017 Shreveport, Caddo Par., LA, at age 82 and was bur. Yates Mem. Cem., Scottsville, Harrison Co., TX.
           PFC Billy Don McMahan (USArmy), b.13 Jun 1928 Columbia Co., AR; d.13 Nov 2014 Waskom, Harrison Co., TX.

772. Lonie Mae⁷ Hightower (Levia⁶ Johnson, Sarah⁵ Abney, Joel⁴, Hezekiah³, Elisha², Abner¹), b.20 Sep 1900 Jackson Co., AL. She m. George Washington Brincefield, son of John William Brincefield and Maggie Evelena Vandever. d.7 Jul 1942 Coalgate, Coal Co., OK, at age 41 and was bur. Lehigh Cem., Lehigh, Coal Co., OK.
    George Washington Brincefield, b.18 Sep 1897 Huntsville, Madison Co., AL. He m2. Virginia Iona "Virgie" Baughman. He d.19 Jul 1966 Yakima, Yakima Co., WA, at age 68 and was bur. Evergreen Mem. Park, East Wenatchee, Douglas Co., WA.
Known children of Lonie Mae⁷ Hightower and George Washington Brincefield:
   1168   i. William Howard⁸, b. 6 May 1919 Newalla, Oklahoma Co., OK; m. Virginia Eileen Brockmiller; m. Audra Lavon Earney.
   1169 ii. Lillie Mae, b. 2 Nov 1920 McLoud, Pottawatomie Co., OK; m1. Henry Otis Fink; m2. Pvt. Lowell H. Walker (USArmy-WWII); m. Berthel Ernest Sweeten.
   1170 iii. Lloyd Albert, b. 16 Apr 1922 Cairo, Coal Co., OK; m. Mildred "Marie" Garrison.
   1171 iv. George Edward, b. 28 Jan 1923 Cairo, Coal Co., OK; m. Margaret Mae "Marge" Brockmiller.
   1172 v. Margaret Louise, b. 28 Jun 1927 Stonewall, Pontotoc Co., OK; m. Willie Hubert "Bill" Nanney.
       vi. Clarence Glen, b.19 Apr 1929 Anadarko, Caddo Co., OK. He m1. Marjorie Ann Ripperger in 1955. He m2. Lois Lucill Bowdre in 1986. He d.19 Jan 2017 Rock Island, Douglas Co., WA, at age 87. He was cremated.
           Marjorie Ann Ripperger, b.15 Jul 1932 Ackworth, Warren Co., IA. She d.5 Feb 1976 Wenatchee, Chelan Co., WA, at age 43 and was bur. Evergreen Mem. Park, East Wenatchee, Douglas Co., WA.
           Lois Lucill Bowdre, b.6 Feb 1927 Roundup, Musselshell Co., MT. She d.31 Mar 2003 East Wenatchee, Douglas Co., WA, at age 76. She was cremated.
      vii. Effie Fern, b.16 Nov 1933 Lehigh, Coal Co., OK. She m1. William Ellis Hill (USArmy-WWII) in 1949. She m2. Howard Eldon Carlson in 1971. She d.19 Dec 2013 East Wenatchee, Douglas Co., WA, at age 80. She was cremated.
           William Ellis Hill (USArmy-WWII), b.13 Mar 1927 San Jose, Santa Clara Co., CA. He d.31 May 2002 Snohomish, Snohomish Co., WA, at age 75 and was bur. Evergreen Mem. Park, East Wenatchee, Douglas Co., WA.
           Howard Eldon Carlson, b.8 Jul 1934 Machias, Snohomish Co., WA; d.18 Apr 2018 Rock Island, Douglas Co., WA.
     viii. Ernest Lee, b.Nov 1935 and d.19 Dec 1937 Lehigh, Coal Co., WA, at age 2; bur. Lehigh Cem., Lehigh, Coal Co., WA.
       ix. Joyce Gean, b.8 Apr 1939 Lehigh, Coal Co., WA. She m1. Rex Fredrick Searles. She m2. Alvie Lee Grice Sr. d.13 May 2011 Rock Island, Douglas Co., WA, at age 72. She was cremated.
           Rex Fredrick Searles, b.26 Sep 1931 Port Angeles, Clallam Co., WA. He d.25 Jul 1998 Wenatchee, Chelan Co., WA, at age 66. He was cremated.
           Alvie Lee Grice Sr, b.5 May 1934 AR. He d.29 Aug 2001 Judsonia, White Co., AR, at age 67 and was bur. Velvet Ridge Cem., Bald Knob, White Co., AR.
       x. Arvard B., b.5 Mar 1942 Lehigh, Coal Co., OK. He d.5 Mar 1942 Lehigh, Coal Co., OK; bur. Lehigh Cem., Lehigh.

773. Delos Harrison⁷ Pittman (Lou⁶ Johnson, Sarah⁵ Abney, Joel⁴, Hezekiah³, Elisha², Abner¹), b.6 May 1910 Scottsboro, Jackson Co., AL. He m. Daisy Lee Curry in 1928. He d.15 Jun 1982 Kilgore, Gregg Co., TX, at age 72 and was bur. Langley Cem., Beckville, Panola Co., TX.
    Daisy Lee Curry, b.17 Aug 1911 Rayville, Richland Par., LA. She d.29 Oct 2003 Longview, Gregg Co., TX, at age 92 and was bur. Langley Cem., Beckville, Panola Co., TX.
Known children of Delos Harrison⁷ Pittman and Daisy Lee Curry:
   1173   i. Edna Wynell⁸, b. 30 Oct 1929 Beckville, Panola Co., TX; m. Thurman "Cotton" McIntosh.
       ii. Sonny, b.18 Jul 1933. He d.18 Jul 1933 and was bur. Langley Cem., Beckville, Panola Co., TX.
      iii. Etta Louise, b.3 May 1937. She d.3 May 1937 and was bur. Langley Cem., Beckville, Panola Co., TX.
      iv. Charlsie Fay, b.17 Dec 1942. She d.17 Dec 1942 and was bur. Langley Cem., Beckville, Panola Co., TX.

774. Zoda Lewis⁷ Johnson (George⁶, Sarah⁵ Abney, Joel⁴, Hezekiah³, Elisha², Abner¹) m. Gladys Ovelle Holt. He, b.5 May 1908 Scottsboro, Jackson Co., AL. He d.26 Apr 1977 Longview, Gregg Co., TX, at age 68 and was bur. Youngblood Cem., Beckville, Panola Co., TX.
    Gladys Ovelle Holt, b.28 Mar 1909 Ennis, Ellis Co., TX; d.16 Sep 1979 Nacogdoches, Nocogdoches Co., TN, age 70; bur. Youngblood Cem.
Known children of Zoda Lewis⁷ Johnson and Gladys Ovelle Holt:
       i. (infant son)⁸, b.8 Mar 1910 Panola Co., TX. He d.8 Mar 1910 Panola Co., TX and was bur. Youngblood Cem..
       ii. Dydemer, b.1912 Panola Co., TX. He d.27 Jun 1912 Panola Co., TX and was bur. Youngblood Cem.
      iii. David Kenneth "DK", b.16 Feb 1939 Gregg Co., TX. He m. Delores Faye Ingram on 8 Jun 1958. He d.10 Jul 2019 Tyler, Smith Co., TX, at age 80 and was bur. Fairview Church Cem., Nacogdoches, Nocogdoches Co., TX.
           Delores Faye Ingram, b.12 Mar 1940 Longview, Gregg Co., TX. She d.27 Jun 2005 Nacogdoches, Nocogdoches Co., TX, at age 65 and was bur. Fairview Church Cem., Nacogdoches, Nocogdoches Co., TX.

775. Nellie Faye⁷ Wininger (Minnie⁶ Abney, John⁵, Joel⁴, Hezekiah³, Elisha², Abner¹) m. Francis "Marion" R. Liles. , b.18 Jul 1908 Hytop, Jackson Co., AL. She d.15 Jan 1984 Albertville, Marshall Co., AL, at age 75 and was bur. Marshall Mem. Gardens, Albertville, Marshall Co., AL.
    Francis "Marion" R. Liles, b.2 Jul 1907 Malone, Randolph Co., AL; d.4 Mar 1969 Albertville, Marshall Co., AL; bur. Marshall Mem. Gardens.
Known children of Nellie Faye⁷ Wininger and Francis "Marion" R. Liles all b. Pisgah, Jackson Co., AL:
   1174   i. Marion Kenneth⁸, b. 22 Mar 1930; m. Dorotha Mae "Dot" George.
       ii. William Sanford "Bill", b.8 Jun 1937. He m. Tommie Sue White on 4 Jun 1956 Alabama City, Etowah Co., AL. He d.1 Jul 2020 Guntersville, Marshall Co., AL, at age 83 and was bur. Green Haven Mem. Gardens, Central, Jackson Co., AL.
           Tommie Sue White, b.22 Feb 1937 Central, Jackson Co., AL; d.16 Jun 2020 Huntsville, Madison Co., AL, age 83.
      iii. Donald Earl, b.17 Mar 1944. He m. Shirley Faye Ferguson. He d.5 Sep 2009 Estill Springs, Franklin Co., TN, at age 65 and was bur. Paynes Cem., Estill Springs, Franklin Co., TN.
           Shirley Faye Ferguson, b.28 Apr 1943 Pisgah, Jackson Co., AL. She d.22 Dec 2000 GA at age 57 and was bur. Pisgah Cem., Pisgah, Jackson Co., AL.

776. Lucinda Katherine "Katie"[7] Wininger (Minnie[6] Abney, John[5], Joel[4], Hezekiah[3], Elisha[2], Abner[1]), b.18 Aug 1909 Hytop, Jackson Co., AL. She m. Doris Sanford Hodnett on 5 Jan 1930 Pisgah, Jackson Co., AL. She lived in 1998. She d.6 Oct 2005 Chattanooga, Hamilton Co., TN, at age 96 and was bur. Lakewood Memory Gardens West, Tiftonia, Hamilton Co., TN.

    Doris Sanford Hodnett, b.19 Nov 1909 Ashland, Clay Co., AL. He d.11 Jan 1990 Chattanooga, Hamilton Co., TN, at age 80 and was bur. Lakewood Memory Gardens West, Tiftonia, Hamilton Co., TN.

Known children of Lucinda Katherine "Katie"[7] Wininger and Doris Sanford Hodnett:

1175	i.	Helen Margaret[8], b. 10 Jan 1932; m. Ernest Dale Coady.
	ii.	Hester Aline, b.22 Jan 1934. She d.12 Jun 1935 at age 1 and was bur. Pisgah Cem., Pisgah, Jackson Co., AL.
1176	iii.	Sarah Wyndol, b. 27 Nov 1935 Pisgah, Jackson Co., AL; m. Earl Miller Jr. (USAF); m. Arthur Clark Griffith.
1177	iv.	Carlton Leroy, b. 16 Feb 1937 Pisgah, Jackson Co., AL; m. Zeobia Joetta "Jodie" Henry.
1178	v.	Daris Kay, b. 11 Mar 1939 Pisgah, Jackson Co., AL; m. Bobby Reese Walton.
	vi.	Tobitha Dean, b.24 Sep 1940 Pisgah, Jackson Co., AL. He d.8 Jul 1990 unm., Chattanooga, Hamilton Co., TN, at age 49 and was bur. Lakewood Memory Gardens West, Tiftonia, Hamilton Co., TN.

777. Nathan Allen[7] Wininger (Minnie[6] Abney, John[5], Joel[4], Hezekiah[3], Elisha[2], Abner[1]), b.30 Mar 1911 Jackson Co., AL. He m. Judy E. Metcalf on 19 Oct 1930 Dutton, Jackson Co., AL. He lived ca.1936 Mount Pleasant, Titus Co., TX. He d.6 Apr 1986 Rainsville, DeKalb Co., AL, at age 75 and was bur. Pisgah Cem., Pisgah, Jackson Co., AL.

    Judy E. Metcalf, b.19 Nov 1914. She m. Robert G. Grant.

Known children of Nathan Allen[7] Wininger and Judy E. Metcalf both b. Jackson Co., AL:

	i.	Geraldine[8].
	ii.	Bettie Joe, b.13 Oct 1935. She d.17 Jul 1938 Mount Pleasant, Titus Co., TX, at age 2 and was bur. Damascus Cem., Mount Pleasant, Titus Co., TX.

778. Oscar Dan[7] Wininger (Minnie[6] Abney, John[5], Joel[4], Hezekiah[3], Elisha[2], Abner[1]), b.15 Aug 1915. He m1. Maureen Owen. He m2. Grace Mertz 218. He d.16 Aug 1989 at age 74 and was bur. West Hill Cem., Dalton, Whitfield Co., GA.

Known child of Oscar Dan[7] Wininger and Maureen Owen:

1179	i.	William R. "Billy"[8], b. 22 Jun 1944; m. Etta (n.n.).

There are no known children of Oscar Dan Wininger and Grace Mertz

779. Elsie May[7] Wininger (Minnie[6] Abney, John[5], Joel[4], Hezekiah[3], Elisha[2], Abner[1]), b.20 Mar 1919. She m. James Sanford DeBerry, son of John Alfred DeBerry and Samantha Caldonia Hodnett, in 1936. She d.9 Dec 1994 Chattanooga, Hamilton Co., TN, at age 75 and was bur. Lakewood Memory Gardens East, Chattanooga, Hamilton Co., TN.

    James Sanford DeBerry, b.14 Nov 1913. He d.1 Nov 1984 at age 70 and was bur. Lakewood Memory Gardens East, Chattanooga.

Known children of Elsie May[7] Wininger and James Sanford DeBerry:

	i.	James Boyd[8] was bur. Lakewood Memory Gardens South, Lakeview, Catoosa Co., GA. He, b.27 Apr 1938. He m. Myrna Winifred Priddy ca.1959. He d.7 May 2016 Fort Oglethorpe, Catoosa Co., GA, at age 78.
		Myrna Winifred Priddy, b.19 Mar 1938. She d.24 Jun 2015 Fort Oglethorpe, Catoosa Co., GA, at age 77 and was bur. Lakewood Memory Gardens South, Lakeview, Catoosa Co., GA.
	ii.	Gene Paul, b.10 Apr 1940 Pisgah, Jackson Co., AL. He m. DeAnn (n.n.) ca.1964. He d.28 Jan 2019 at age 78 and was bur. Tennessee Georgia Mem. Park, Rossville, Walker Co., GA.

780. Eva M. "Evie"[7] Bean (Essie[6] Abney, John[5], Joel[4], Hezekiah[3], Elisha[2], Abner[1]), b. ca.Mar 1909 Jackson Co., AL. She m. (n.n.) Penny ca.1925. She appeared on the census of 16 Apr 1930 Lupton City, Hamilton Co., TN.

    Known children of Eva M. "Evie"[7] Bean and (n.n.) Penny both b. TN:

	i.	Levern "Lester"[8], b. ca.1927. He and Learn "Leroy" Penny were liv. on 3 Apr 1940 with their grandfather, William Bean, Lupton City, Hamilton Co., TN.
	ii.	Learn "Leroy", b. ca.1928. He and Levern "Lester" Penny were liv. on 3 Apr 1940 with their grandfather, William Bean, Lupton City, Hamilton Co., TN.

781. Grace Julie "Gracie"[7] Bean (Essie[6] Abney, John[5], Joel[4], Hezekiah[3], Elisha[2], Abner[1]) m. (n.n.) Smith. , b.28 Apr 1917 Maxwell, Jackson Co., AL. She d.19 May 1995 Chattanooga, Hamilton Co., TN, at age 78.

Known child of Grace Julie "Gracie"[7] Bean and (n.n.) Smith:

	i.	Patsy[8], b. ca.1936 TN.

782. William "Harvey"[7] Abney (William[6], John[5], Joel[4], Hezekiah[3], Elisha[2], Abner[1]), b.4 Jun 1913 Jackson Co., AL. He m. Johnnie Cross ca.1939. He and Johnnie Cross appeared on the census of 16 Apr 1940 Jackson Co., AL. He d.29 May 2008 Stevenson, Jackson Co., AL, at age 94 and was bur. Stevenson City Cem., Stevenson, Jackson Co., AL.

    Johnnie Cross, b.14 Feb 1917. She d.13 Mar 1993 at age 76 and was bur. Stevenson City Cem., Stevenson, Jackson Co., AL.

Known child of William "Harvey"[7] Abney and Johnnie Cross:

	i.	David H.[8], b.6 Oct 1944. He d.24 Jan 1960 at age 15 and was bur. Cross Cem. #04, Stevenson, Jackson Co., AL.

783. John[7] Abney (William[6], John[5], Joel[4], Hezekiah[3], Elisha[2], Abner[1]), b.16 Jun 1927 Stevenson, Jackson Co., AL. He m. Mary Lee Owens ca.1946. He d.23 Nov 2018 Stevenson, Jackson Co., AL, at age 91 and was bur. Bonaventure Cem., Bridgeport, Jackson Co., AL.

    Mary Lee Owens, b.8 Feb 1930. She d.1 Dec 2008 at age 78 and was bur. Bonaventure Cem., Bridgeport, Jackson Co., AL.

Known children of John[7] Abney and Mary Lee Owens:

	i.	Michael[8] m. Sissy (n.n.).
	ii.	Peggy m. Robert Brizendine.
	iii.	Donny.
1180	iv.	James Clyde, b. 31 Jul 1948; m. Frankie Jean Wallace.

784. Ethel[7] Abney (Louis[6], John[5], Joel[4], Hezekiah[3], Elisha[2], Abner[1]) m. Leonard Levee Rainey. , b.10 Jun 1914. She d.26 Dec 1988 at age 74 and was bur. Oglethorpe Mem. Gardens, Saint Simons Island, Glynn Co., GA.
      Leonard Levee Rainey, b.21 Jul 1913 Paulding Co., GA. He d.14 Jan 1977 Temple, Carroll Co., GA, at age 63 and was bur. Center Point UMC Cem., Temple, Carroll Co., A.
Known children of Ethel[7] Abney and Leonard Levee Rainey:
          i.   Bennett Levee[8], b.26 Jan 1933 Dallas, Paulding Co., GA; d.21 Feb 2017 Brunswick, Glynn Co., GA, at age 84. (cremated)
          ii.   Clarence Edgar, b.30 Oct 1937. He d.19 Feb 2016 at age 78. He was cremated.

785. Alvin Ray[7] Abney (Alonzo[6], John[5], Joel[4], Hezekiah[3], Elisha[2], Abner[1]) m. Joyce (n.n.). He, b.4 Dec 1932 Hixson, Hamilton Co., TN. He d.10 Apr 1967 Chicago, Cook Co., IL, at age 34.
Known child of Alvin Ray[7] Abney and Joyce (n.n.):
   1181   i.   Marty Ray[8], b. 13 May 1959.

786. Lee Alvin[7] Waddle (Lelius[6], Rebecca[5] Abney, Joel[4], Hezekiah[3], Elisha[2], Abner[1]) m. Versie Ree Wooten. He, b.17 Dec 1920. He d.10 Mar 2002 Jacksonville, Duval Co., FL, at age 81 and was bur. Gethsemane Mem. Gardens, Jacksonville, Duval Co., FL.
      Versie Ree Wooten, b.20 Sep 1927. She d.26 Mar 1991 at age 63 and was bur. Gethsemane Mem. Gardens, Jacksonville, Duval Co., FL.
Known child of Lee Alvin[7] Waddle and Versie Ree Wooten:
          i.   Lelius Franklin[8], b.18 Sep 1947 Jacksonville, Duval Co., FL. He d.4 Jun 2010 at age 62; bur. Gethsemane Mem. Gardens.

787. Gladys Rebecca[7] Walden (Elsie[6] Waddle, Rebecca[5] Abney, Joel[4], Hezekiah[3], Elisha[2], Abner[1]) m. Albert Wright. , b.2 Sep 1923 Wellington, Calhoun Co., AL. She d.4 Sep 2014 Jacksonville, Duval Co., FL, at age 91 and was bur. Long Branch Cem., Clay Co., FL.
      Albert Wright, b.29 Apr 1918 FL. He d.14 Jul 1962 Jacksonville, Duval Co., FL, at age 44 and was bur. Long Branch Cem., Clay Co., FL.
Known children of Gladys Rebecca[7] Walden and Albert Wright:
          i.   (infant son)[8], b.21 Apr 1942. He d.21 Apr 1942 and was bur. Long Branch Cem., Clay Co., FL.
          ii.   (infant daughter), b.12 Sep 1943. She d.21 Sep 1943 and was bur. Long Branch Cem., Clay Co., FL.

788. Grovene[7] Walden (Elsie[6] Waddle, Rebecca[5] Abney, Joel[4], Hezekiah[3], Elisha[2], Abner[1]), b.12 Feb 1926 Calhoun Co., AL. She m. Ephrain Thomas in 1945. She d.3 Jul 2008 Jacksonville, Duval Co., FL, at age 82 and was bur. Riverside Mem. Park, Jacksonville, Duval Co., FL.
      Ephrain Thomas, b.11 Nov 1924. He d.8 Jan 1992 at age 67 and was bur. Riverside Mem. Park, Jacksonville, Duval Co., FL.
Known children of Grovene[7] Walden and Ephrain Thomas both b. Jacksonville, Duval Co., FL:
          i.   Roy[8], b.23 Nov 1947. He m. Joe Louise Crawford. He d.23 Mar 2020 Jacksonville, Duval Co., FL, at age 72 and was bur. Evergreen Cem., Jacksonville, Duval Co., FL.
          ii.   Joe, b.4 Apr 1951. He m. Carol K. (n.n.) (she was b.26 Jul 1947) on Independence Day, 4 Jul 1981. He d.3 Jan 2016 Decatur, Macon Co., IL, at age 64 and was bur. Boiling Springs Cem., Decatur, Macon Co., IL.

789. CMSgt. James Edward[7] Walden (USAF-Korea, Nam) (Elsie[6] Waddle, Rebecca[5] Abney, Joel[4], Hezekiah[3], Elisha[2], Abner[1]), b.25 Jul 1929 Rock Springs, Blount Co., AL. He m. Janie (n.n.) ca.1951. He d.7 Feb 2010 Jacksonville, Duval Co., FL, at age 80 and was bur. Jacksonville National Cem., Jacksonville, Duval Co., FL.
Known children of CMSgt. James Edward[7] Walden (USAF-Korea, Nam) and Janie (n.n.):
          i.   Cindy[8].
          ii.   Lynn.
          iii. Debbie.
          iv.   Craig.

790. Sarah Bluford "Blufie"[7] Abney (Nancy[6] Allen, Susan[5] Abner, William[4], Elisha[3], Elisha[2] Abney, Abner[1]), b.3 Apr 1872. She m. J.E. McGuire. She d.20 Apr 1930 at age 58 and was bur. Davis-Witt Cem., Rockcastle Co., KY.
      J.E. McGuire, b.29 Mar 1866. He d.27 Dec 1955 at age 89 and was bur. Davis-Witt Cem., Rockcastle Co., KY.
Known children of Sarah Bluford "Blufie"[7] Abney and J.E. McGuire:
          i.   Ann[8], b.1891; m1. Robert O. Bowman; m2. William Thomas Linville; d.1978; bur. Berea Cem., Berea, Madison Co., KY.
                      Robert O. Bowman, b.1888. He d.1947.
                      William Thomas Linville, b.1884. He d.1916.

791. Martha Jane[7] Abney (Nancy[6] Allen, Susan[5] Abner, William[4], Elisha[3], Elisha[2] Abney, Abner[1]), b.Jan 1874 Rockcastle Co., KY. She m. Olmstead Mitchell Payne ca.1890. She d.26 Feb 1949 Rockcastle Co., KY, at age 75 and was bur. A.T. Abney Mem. Garden, Rockcastle Co., KY.
      Olmstead Mitchell Payne, b.Jul 1864 Rockcastle Co., KY. He d.22 Jan 1951 Rockcastle Co., KY, at age 86; bur. A.T. Abney Mem. Garden.
Known children of Martha Jane[7] Abney and Olmstead Mitchell Payne:
          i.   George T.[8], b.1891. He d.1949.
          ii.   Virgie, b.1893. She d.1979.
          iii. William Stanley, b.1896. He d.1973.
          iv.   Ruth Mae, b.1898. She d.1992.
          v.   Angie, b.1900. She d.1980.
          vi.   Howard G., b.1903. He d.1978.
          vii. John Burgess, b.1905. He d.1971.
          viii. Nathan Bluford, b.1907. He d.1993.
          ix.   Hilda, b.1910. She d.1998.
          x.   Edna, b.1914. She d.1941.
          xi.   Cleveland E., b.1917. He d.1997.

792. Ollie Jane[7] Abney (Nancy[6] Allen, Susan[5] Abner, William[4], Elisha[3], Elisha[2] Abney, Abner[1]) m. Thomas Clinton Holt. , b.25 Apr 1879 Rockcastle Co., KY. She d.30 Sep 1960 KY at age 81 and was bur. A.T. Abney Mem. Garden, Rockcastle Co., KY.

Thomas Clinton Holt, b.27 Oct 1877. He d.9 Apr 1957 at age 79 and was bur. Davis-Witt Cem., Rockcastle Co., KY.
Known children of Ollie Jane[7] Abney and Thomas Clinton Holt:
    i.   Curfew F.[8], b.1905. He d.1983.
    ii.   Neureul, b.1908. She d.1995.
    iii.   Verolya, b.1911. She d.1952.

793. Robert T.[7] Abney Sr. (Nancy[6] Allen, Susan[5] Abner, William[4], Elisha[3], Elisha[2] Abney, Abner[1]), b.6 Nov 1890 Rockcastle Co., KY. He m. Bess M. "Bessie" McWhorter on 26 Dec 1913 Madison Co., KY. He and Bess M. "Bessie" McWhorter appeared on the censuses of 14 Jan 1920 Scaffold Cane, Rockcastle Co., KY; and 8 Apr 1930 and 4 Apr 1940 Coyle, Jackson Co., KY. He d.8 Dec 1963 at age 73 and was bur. A.T. Abney Mem. Garden, Rockcastle Co., KY.
Bess M. "Bessie" McWhorter, b.10 Sep 1888. She d.2 Aug 1959 at age 70 and was bur. A.T. Abney Mem. Garden, Rockcastle Co., KY.
Known children of Robert T.[7] Abney Sr. and Bess M. "Bessie" McWhorter:
    i.   Stella Burnam[8], b. ca.Jun 1918 KY.
1182   ii.   Nancy E., b. 16 Jul 1920; m. Cecil Morris.
    iii.   David, b.4 Aug 1922. He d.4 Aug 1922 and was bur. A.T. Abney Mem. Garden, Rockcastle Co., KY.
    iv.   Reuben C., b.21 Jan 1926. He d.21 Aug 1960 at age 34 and was bur. A.T. Abney Mem. Garden, Rockcastle Co., KY.
    v.   Geneva "Jenna", b.21 Jun 1928 Madison Co., KY; m. Robert A. Jones; d.27 Dec 2010 Middlesboro, Bell Co., KY, ae. 82. Robert A. Jones, b.1818. He d.2002.
    vi.   Robert T., b.7 Jul 1932 Rockcastle Co., KY. He d.13 Feb 2005 Chaves Co., NM, at age 72 and was bur. Madison Co. Mem. Gardens, Terrill, Madison Co., KY.

794. Reuben J.[7] Abney (Nancy[6] Allen, Susan[5] Abner, William[4], Elisha[3], Elisha[2] Abney, Abner[1]), b.2 Jul 1894 Rockcastle Co., KY. He m. Edith Ann Linville on 23 Dec 1914 Rockcastle Co., KY. He and Edith appeared on the censuses of 6 Jan 1920 and 9 Apr 1930 Berea, Madison Co., KY; and 2 Apr 1940 Madison Co., KY. [author's note: On the 1940 census there is a 14-year old "daughter" named "Juanita," born in Ohio. She is not listed in the 1930 census. Is she their "daughter-in-law", adopted daughter, a natural daughter who was simply missed in the 1930 census?] He d.30 May 1968 Madison Co., KY, at age 73 and was bur. Berea Cem., Berea, Madison Co., KY.
Edith Ann Linville, b.2 Jul 1897 Rockcastle Co., KY. She d.16 Feb 1968 at age 70 and was bur. Berea Cem., Berea, Madison Co., KY.
Known children of Reuben J.[7] Abney and Edith Ann Linville both b. KY:
    i.   Reuben "Leonard"[8], b.8 Nov 1915; m. Alma Louise Cox. He and Alma Louise Cox appeared on the census of 9 Apr 1940 Pineville, Bell Co., KY. He d.31 May 1980 KY at age 64; bur. Madison Co. Mem. Gardens, Terrill, Madison Co., KY.
       Alma Louise Cox, b.26 Mar 1921 Wayne Co., KY. She d.8 Apr 1965 Berea, Madison Co., KY, at age 44 and was bur. Madison Co. Mem. Gardens, Berea, Madison Co., KY.
    ii.   James Robert "Bob", b.15 Jan 1917. He d.8 Mar 2000 at age 83 and was bur. Berea Cem., Berea, Madison Co., Y.

795. Gilbert Taylor[7] Abner (William[6], David[5], William[4], Elisha[3], Elisha[2] Abney, Abner[1]), b.31 Jul 1890 KY. He m. Eva Davis in 1912. He d.22 Feb 1972 Lancaster, Garrard Co., KY, at age 81 and was bur. Lancaster Cem., Lancaster, Garrard Co., KY.
Eva Davis, b.Mar 1892 IN. She d.6 Aug 1953 Lancaster, Garrard Co., KY, at age 61.
Known children of Gilbert Taylor[7] Abner and Eva Davis:
1183   i.   Margaret Neva[8], b. 22 Apr 1915 Campbellsville, Taylor Co., KY; m. PFC Coy Hudson Arnold Sr. (USArmy-WWII).
1184   ii.   John "Ralph," b. 24 Apr 1917 IA; m. Tommy Lou Adams.

796. Armilda "Mildred"[7] Allen (Sarah[6], Easter[5] Abner, William[4], Elisha[3], Elisha[2] Abney, Abner[1]), b. illegitimate on 4 Mar 1896 KY. She m. Anderson Eversole on 21 Nov 1913 Clay Co., KY. She d.10 Jan 1946 at age 49 and was bur. Stipps Hill Cem., Franklin Co., IN.
Anderson Eversole, b.5 Sep 1894. He d.15 Apr 1955 at age 61 and was bur. Stipps Hill Cem., Franklin Co., IN.
Known children of Armilda "Mildred"[7] Allen and Anderson Eversole:
    i.   Preston[8], b.1916 Clay Co., KY. He d.1993.
    ii.   Viola, b.1918 Clay Co., KY. She d.1994.
    iii.   Ruth, b.1923 Butler Co., KY. She d.2004.
    iv.   Thelma, b.1 Mar 1934 Posey, Franklin Co., IN. She d.18 Mar 1934 Posey, Franklin Co., IN.
1185   v.   Geraldine. She m1. (n.n.) Whitaker; m2. (n.n.) Bachelor.

797. David Francis[7] Abner (Shelby[6], Lewis[5], William[4], Elisha[3], Elisha[2] Abney, Abner[1]), b.31 Jan 1925 Teges, Clay Co., KY. He m. Rozella Marie Littlefield on 13 Jan 1945. He d.11 Mar 2013 Morehead, Rowan Co., KY, at age 88.
Rozella Marie Littlefield, b.6 Dec 1921 Cherokee Co., OK. She d.25 Aug 2014 Morehead, Rowan Co., KY, at age 92.
Known child of David Francis[7] Abner and Rozella Marie Littlefield:
    i.   Michael Glenn[8], b.28 Nov 1952. He d.Jun 2000 at age 47.

798. Walter Clyde[7] Abner (George[6], Lewis[5], William[4], Elisha[3], Elisha[2] Abney, Abner[1]), b.29 Mar 1912 Clay Co., KY. He m. Chloe Sizemore on 13 Feb 1932. He d.6 Mar 1974 Connersville, Fayette Co., IN, at age 61; bur. Laurel North Cem., Laurel, Franklin Co., IN.
Chloe Sizemore, b.28 Feb 1911 Owsley Co., KY. She d.11 Jan 1998 Muncie, Delaware Co., IN, at age 86; bur. Laurel North Cem., Laurel.
Known children of Walter Clyde[7] Abner and Chloe Sizemore:
1186   i.   Vivian D. "Vickie"[8], b. 9 Feb 1933 Manchester, Clay Co., KY; m. Halford F. "Pete" Gerrian (USArmy-Korea); m. Lelan Clyde "Lee" Haynes.
1187   ii.   D.F, b. 12 Oct 1934 Clay Co., KY; m. Norita Clara McFarland.
    iii.   Walter Ray, b.8 May 1944 Clay Co., KY. He d.10 Apr 2013 Indianapolis, Marion Co., IN, age 68; bur. Laurel North Cem.

799. Ethel Mae[7] Abner (Charles[6], Robert[5], William[4], Elisha[3], Elisha[2] Abney, Abner[1]), b.28 May 1899 Clay Co., KY; m1. Herbert Baker in 1923; m2. Howard Kenneth Crawley in 1937; d.27 Jun 1972 Clarksville, Montgomery Co., TN, age 73; bur. Millville Cem., Millville, Butler Co., OH.
Herbert Baker, b.5 Apr 1899 KY. He d.14 Apr 1937 Posey, Franklin Co., IN, at age 38.

Known children of Ethel Mae[7] Abner and Herbert Baker:
       i.   Evelyn[8], b.11 Sep 1926 Hamilton, Butler Co., OH. She m. Ruford Marcum in 1947. She d.8 Jan 2010 Richmond, Wayne Co., IN, at age 83 and was bur. Union Cem., Lyonsville, Fayette Co., IN.
           Ruford Marcum, b.1 Mar 1921 Clay Co., KY; d.10 Jul 1997 Indianapolis, Marion Co., IN, age 76; bur. Union Cem.
      ii.   PFC Jack D. (USAAC-WWII), b.28 Sep 1927 Cincinnati, Hamilton Co., OH. He d.10 Nov 1946 Griesheim, Landkreis Darmstadt-Dieburg, Hessen, Germany, at age 19 and was bur. Greenwood Cem., Hamilton, Butler Co., OH.
      iii. Kathryn, b.1930. She m. Cpl. Emmett Delano Hamblin (USAAC-WWII) in 1946. She d.1968 and was bur. Millville Cem.
           Cpl. Emmett Delano Hamblin (USAAC-WWII), b.13 Nov 1924 OH. He d.10 Oct 1989 Hamilton, Butler Co., OH, at age 64 and was bur. Millville Cem., Hamilton, Butler Co., OH.
      iv. Clinton G., b.28 Apr 1931 Laurel, Franklin Co., IN; m. Suzanne Abercrombie; d.22 Apr 1999 Connersville, IN, at age 67.
           Suzanne Abercrombie, b.6 Jan 1937 Laurel, Franklin Co., IN; d.26 Feb 2000 Richmond, Wayne Co., IN; bur. Dale Cem.
   Howard Kenneth Crawley, b.1910. He d.1983.
There were no known children of Ethel Mae[7] Abner and Howard Kenneth Crawley.

800. Cpl. Daniel "Dan"[7] Abner (USArmy-WWII) (Charles[6], Robert[5], William[4], Elisha[3], Elisha[2] Abney, Abner[1]) m. Beryle R. Kelly. He, b.17 Aug 1917 Franklin Co., IN. He d.26 Jul 1995 at age 77 and was bur. Millville Cem., Millville, Butler Co., OH.
   Beryle R. Kelly, b.29 Jun 1925 NJ. She d.19 May 1982 Hamilton, Butler Co., OH, at age 56.
Known children of Cpl. Daniel "Dan"[7] Abner (USArmy-WWII) and Beryle R. Kelly:
       i.   Dan[8] m. Ginny (n.n.).
   1188   ii.   Michael Edward, b. 24 Nov 1951; m. (n.n.).

801. Herbert[7] Abner (USN-WWII) (Charles[6], Robert[5], William[4], Elisha[3], Elisha[2] Abney, Abner[1]), b.11 Jun 1926 Hamilton, Butler Co., OH. He served in the U.S. Navy from 11 Feb 1944 to 28 Apr 1946. He m. Goldie Clark on 5 Jun 1947 Goshen. He d.15 Jul 1967 Hamilton, Butler Co., OH, at age 41 and was bur. Millville Cem., Millville, Butler Co., OH.
Known children of Herbert[7] Abner (USN-WWII) and Goldie Clark:
       i.   Kenneth[8].
      ii.   Geraldine.
      iii. Karen.
      iv. Sheila.
      v.   Willa.
      vi. Brenda.

802. Elizabeth "Lizzie"[7] Abner (Jack[6], Robert[5], William[4], Elisha[3], Elisha[2] Abney, Abner[1]), b.23 Sep 1904 Clay Co., KY; m1. Ezra Kelton ca.1921; m2. Robert Hay in 1934 Clark Co., IN; m3. Charles L. Ashton. She d.12 Mar 1980 age 75; bur. Walnut Ridge Cem., Jefferson, Clark Co., IN.
   Ezra Kelton, b.29 Jul 1891 KY. He d.11 Jan 1931 Corbin, Knox Co., KY, at age 39.
Known children of Elizabeth "Lizzie"[7] Abner and Ezra Kelton:
       i.   Ralph R.[8], b.1922. He d.2008.
      ii.   Joyce, b.1925. She d.2009.
      iii. Thomas W, b.1928. He d.2000.
   Robert Hay, b.6 Feb 1896 Leitchfield, Grayson Co., KY.
There were no known children of Elizabeth "Lizzie"[7] Abner and Robert Hay.
   Charles L. Ashton, b.16 Sep 1894. He d.18 Oct 1965 at age 71 and was bur. Walnut Ridge Cem., Jefferson, Clark Co., KY.
There were no known children of Elizabeth "Lizzie"[7] Abner and Charles L. Ashton.

803. Preston Innominatus[7] Abner (Jack[6], Robert[5], William[4], Elisha[3], Elisha[2] Abney, Abner[1]), b.10 Apr 1910 Clay Co., KY. He m. Thelma L. Henderson in 1935 Wayne Co., IN. He and Thelma L. Henderson were liv. on 20 May 1940 with his mother-in-law, Fannie Henderson, Middletown, Butler Co., OH. He d.19 Jan 1982 at age 71 and was bur. Woodside Cem., Middletown, Butler Co., KY.
   Thelma L. Henderson, b.1917. She d.1984 and was bur. Woodside Cem., Middletown, Butler Co., KY.
Known children of Preston Innominatus[7] Abner and Thelma L. Henderson all b. OH:
       i.   Robert[8], b. ca.1936.
   1189   ii.   Jack D. "Jackie," b. 23 Apr 1938; m. Phyllis J. Duff.
      iii. Gerald, b. est.1941.

804. Mary[7] Abner (Jack[6], Robert[5], William[4], Elisha[3], Elisha[2] Abney, Abner[1]) m. William Edward Allen. , b.Christmas Day, 25 Dec 1911. She d.20 Jul 1972 at age 60 and was bur. Maxaline Baker Cem., Oneida, Clay Co., KY.
   William Edward Allen, b.15 Nov 1903. He d.Christmas Day, 25 Dec 1969 at age 66; bur. Maxaline Baker Cem., Oneida, Clay Co., KY.
Known children of Mary[7] Abner and William Edward Allen:
       i.   Marvin Edward[8], b.1929. He d.1979.
      ii.   Colleen, b.1931. She d.1986.
      iii. Ethel Marie, b.1933. She d.1996.
      iv. Leo, b.1935. He d.2002.
      v.   Paul Jennings, b.1939. He d.2014.
      vi. Wilbur, b.1941. He d.2012.

805. Zetta Pearl[7] Abner (Daniel[6], Robert[5], William[4], Elisha[3], Elisha[2] Abney, Abner[1]) m. John A. Russo. , b.6 Dec 1923 Hamilton, Butler Co., OH. She d.9 Jun 1980 Hamilton, Butler Co., OH, at age 56 and was bur. Rose Hill Burial Park, Hamilton, Butler Co., OH.
   John A. Russo, b.5 Jul 1914 OH. He d.16 Mar 1984 Hamilton, Butler Co., OH, at age 69.
Known children of Zetta Pearl[7] Abner and John A. Russo:
       i.   Carol Jean[8], b.7 Jul 1937 Hamilton, Butler Co., OH. She m. Orville Jess "Bud" Baxter. d.11 Aug 2010 Hamilton, Butler Co., OH, at age 73 and was bur. Rose Hill Burial Park, Hamilton, Butler Co., OH.

Orville Jess "Bud" Baxter, b.29 May 1934 Monroe, Butler Co., OH. He d.9 Aug 2003 Hamilton, Butler Co., OH, at age 69 and was bur. Rose Hill Burial Park, Hamilton, Butler Co., OH.

806. Harold D.[7] Abner (Daniel[6], Robert[5], William[4], Elisha[3], Elisha[2] Abney, Abner[1]), b.12 Nov 1931 Hamilton, Butler Co., OH. He m. Jewel Dean South on 15 Nov 1951 Hamilton, Butler Co., OH. He d.6 Feb 2002 Hamilton, Butler Co., OH, at age 70 and was bur. Rose Hill Burial Park, Hamilton, Butler Co., OH.

Jewel Dean South, b.23 Sep 1934 Hamilton, Butler Co., OH. She d.15 Dec 2014 Hamilton, Butler Co., OH, age 80; bur. Rose Hill Burial Park.
Known children of Harold D.[7] Abner and Jewel Dean South:
 i. Peggy[8] m. Eric Scott.
 ii. Karen m. Thomas Couch.
 iii. Brian m. Julie (n.n.).
 iv. Linda Sue, b.22 Sep 1953 Hamilton, Butler Co., OH. She m. (n.n.) Davis. d.29 Jun 1996 Hamilton, Butler Co., OH, at age 42 and was bur. Rose Hill Burial Park, Hamilton, Butler Co., OH.

807. Emaline[7] Abner (Wiley[6], John[5], Lacy[4], Elisha[3], Elisha[2] Abney, Abner[1]), b.3 Mar 1896 Owsley Co., KY. She m. Jacob Carmack Jr. ca.1914. She and Jacob Carmack Jr. appeared on the census of 12 Feb 1920 Bullskin, Clay Co., KY. She d.2 Jan 1989 Laurel Co., KY, at age 92.

Jacob Carmack Jr, b.12 Aug 1889 Owsley Co., KY. He d.Jul 1969 KY at age 79.
Known children of Emaline[7] Abner and Jacob Carmack Jr.:
 i. Eunice[8], b. ca.Nov 1915 Clay Co., KY.
 ii. Dolly, b. ca.Jul 1917 Clay Co., KY.
 iii. Isaac, b.1920 Clay Co., KY.
 iv. Mary, b. ca.1921.

808. Isabelle[7] Abner (Wiley[6], John[5], Lacy[4], Elisha[3], Elisha[2] Abney, Abner[1]), b. ca.1903 Owsley Co., KY; m. William Fugate (b.1900) 21 Oct 1920 Clay Co., KY. She and William Fugate appeared on the census of 14 Apr 1930 Hazard, Perry Co., KY. She d.2 Jan 1989 Lily, Laurel Co., KY.
Known children of Isabelle[7] Abner and William Fugate all b. KY:
 i. Martha[8], b. ca.1923.
 ii. Andrw, b. ca.1924.
 iii. Anna, b. ca.1927.
 iv. Barbara, b.Mar 1930.

809. John "Johnny"[7] Abner (Wiley[6], John[5], Lacy[4], Elisha[3], Elisha[2] Abney, Abner[1]), b.3 Jun 1905 Owsley Co., KY. He m1. Eva Cornett (b.1907) on 7 Aug 1924 Clay Co., KY. He m2. Frances Barger on 25 Jul 1927 Clay Co., KY. He and Frances Barger appeared on the census of 8 Apr 1930 Panco, Clay Co., KY. He d.1 Apr 1983 Bullskin, Clay Co., KY, at age 77 and was bur. Fairview Cem., Panco, Clay Co., KY.
There were no known children of John "Johnny"[7] Abner and Eva Cornett.

Frances Barger, b.15 Jan 1905 Leslie Co., KY. She d.2 Apr 1986 Barcreek, Clay Co., KY, age 81; bur. Fairview Cem., Panco, Clay Co., KY.
Known children of John "Johnny"[7] Abner and Frances Barger:
 i. Lee[8].
 ii. Mary Ethel m. (n.n.) Hollen.
 iii. Sadie m. (n.n.) Young.
 iv. Edgar.
 v. Margie, b.22 Jul 1928. She m. Charlie Collins on 23 Mar 1946 London, Laurel Co., KY. She d.9 Nov 2017 Louisville, Jefferson Co., KY, at age 89 and was bur. Warsaw Cem., Warsaw, Gallatin Co., KY.
  Charlie Collins, b.27 Oct 1928. He d.24 Feb 2007 at age 78 and was bur. Warsaw Cem., Warsaw, Gallatin Co., KY.
1190 vi. Sam, b. Christmas Day, 25 Dec 1929 KY; m. Pauline Young.
 vii. Ada, b.20 Jan 1933 Clay Co., KY. She d.14 Apr 1935 Clay Co., KY, age 2; bur. Hensley Cem., Big Creek, Clay Co., KY.
1191 viii. Granville Wiley "GW," b. 14 Jan 1935 KY; m. Audrey Davidson.
 ix. Astor, b.1937.

810. Mattie[7] Abner (Wiley[6], John[5], Lacy[4], Elisha[3], Elisha[2] Abney, Abner[1]), b. ca.Jul 1916 Clay Co., KY. She m. Ray Barger (b. ca.1915) on 27 Jun 1936 Clay Co., KY. She and Ray Barger appeared on the census of 1 May 1940 Clay Co., KY.
Known children of Mattie[7] Abner and Ray Barger both b. Clay Co., KY,:
 i. Imogene[8], b. ca.1938.
 ii. Anna Marie, b. ca.Mar 1939.

811. Robert "Pearl"[7] Abner (USArmy-WWII) (James[6], Harvey[5], Lacy[4], Elisha[3], Elisha[2] Abney, Abner[1]), b.7 Oct 1923 Clay Co., KY; m. Mary Childs (b.ca.1930) 29 Jan 1949 Clay Co., KY; d.10 Jul 2013 Cincinnati, Hamilton Co., OH, at age 89; bur. Rest Haven Mem. Park, Evendale, Hamilton Co., OH.
Known children of Robert "Pearl"[7] Abner (USArmy-WWII) and Mary Childs:
 i. Marlene[8] m. (n.n.) Kroger.
 ii. Mike m. Carolina (n.n.).
 iii. Shirley m. Charlie Eifert.
 iv. Sue.

812. Billy Gene[7] Abner Sr. (James[6], Harvey[5], Lacy[4], Elisha[3], Elisha[2] Abney, Abner[1]) m. Ruby L. Huggins. He, b.19 May 1937 Clay Co., KY. He d.10 Nov 2012 London, Laurel Co., KY, at age 75 and was bur. A.R. Dyche Mem. Park, London, Laurel Co., KY.

Ruby L. Huggins, b.14 Jan 1937. She d.26 Sep 1997 at age 60 and was bur. A.R. Dyche Mem. Park, London, Laurel Co., KY.
Known children of Billy Gene[7] Abner Sr. and Ruby L. Huggins:
 i. Debbie[8] m. (n.n.) Helton.
 ii. Sandra m. Dave Whipper.

        iii.   Billy Gene m. Christina (n.n.).

        iv.   Anna.

813. Raleigh Alben⁷ Abner (USN) (James⁶, Harvey⁵, Lacy⁴, Elisha³, Elisha² Abney, Abner¹) m. (n.n.). He, b.19 Oct 1939 Clay Co., KY. He d.10 Jan 2017 FL at age 77 and was bur. Lauderdale Mem. Park, Fort Lauderdale, Broward Co., FL.
Known children of Raleigh Alben⁷ Abner (USN):

        i.   Kimberly⁸.

        ii.   Rhonda.

        iii.   Sheila.

        iv.   Richie.

814. Preston⁷ Abner (Bryson⁶, Harvey⁵, Lacy⁴, Elisha³, Elisha² Abney, Abner¹), b.14 Apr 1923 Clay Co., KY. He m. Bernice (n.n.). He d.16 Apr 1997 Dayton, Montgomery Co., OH, at age 74 and was bur. Woodland Cem. and Arboretum, Dayton, Montgomery Co., OH.
Known children of Preston⁷ Abner and Bernice (n.n.):

        i.   Betty L.⁸, b.2 Jan 1962. She m. Lyle Seebeck. She m. Andrew R. Horstman. d.21 Feb 2019 at age 57 and was bur. Woodland Cem. and Arboretum, Dayton, Montgomery Co., OH.
             Lyle Seebeck d.2019.
             Andrew R. Horstman, b.19 Mar 1987 Dayton, Montgomery Co., OH. He d.30 May 2020 Dayton, Montgomery Co., OH, at age 33 and was bur. Woodland Cem. and Arboretum, Dayton, Montgomery Co., OH.

        ii.   Leslie.

815. Isaac⁷ Abner (John⁶, Samuel⁵, Lacy⁴, Elisha³, Elisha² Abney, Abner¹) m. Myrtle Gabbard. He, b.28 Feb 1914 Owsley Co., KY. He d.21 Feb 1990 at age 75 and was bur. Esau-Gabbard Cem., Ricetown, Owsley Co., KY.
    Myrtle Gabbard, b.10 Jan 1908 Owsley Co., KY. She d.27 Nov 1994 Dillsboro, Dearb. Co., IN, at age 86 and was bur. Esau-Gabbard Cem.
Known children of Isaac⁷ Abner and Myrtle Gabbard:

        i.   Ruth⁸ d.8 Oct 1940 and was bur. Esau-Gabbard Cem., Ricetown, Owsley Co., KY.

        ii.   Pete Gabbard.

        iii.   Lucy m. Bob Belew.

        iv.   Barb m. Don Waller.

        v.   Alice m. Tom Burns.

        vi.   Geraldine m. (n.n.) Dobbins.

        vii.   Paul.

  1192 viii.   Archie Brown, b. 21 Nov 1936 Booneville, Owsley Co., KY; m. Wanda (n.n.).

816. Elizabeth⁷ Riley (Isabel⁶ Sandlin, James⁵, Nancy⁴ Abner, Elisha³, Elisha² Abney, Abner¹), b.9 Jun 1903 Perry Co., KY. m. Nathan Ellington Greear Sr. 11 Nov 1920 Perry Co., KY She d.14 Dec 1983 Scottsburg, Scott Co., IN; bur. Scottsburg Cem., Scottsburg, Scott Co., IN.
    Nathan Ellington Greear Sr, b.31 Jul 1898 Grassy Creek, Morgan Co., KY; d.20 Sep 1988 Scottsburg, Scott Co., IN; bur. Scottsburg Cem.
Known child of Elizabeth⁷ Riley and Nathan Ellington Greear Sr.:

  1193 i.   Nathan Ellington⁸, b.9 Aug 1921; m. Euphemia Joan Puccini.

817. Emma⁷ Baker (Bryson⁶, Eliza⁵ Abner, Willis⁴, Elisha³, Elisha² Abney, Abner¹), b.1 Jul 1909 Breathitt Co., KY; m. Owens Brewer on 23 Jul 1928 Lebanon, Warren Co., OH; d.29 May 1996 Seymour, Jackson Co., IN, at age 86 and was bur. Vallonia Cem., Vallonia, Jackson Co., IN.
    Owens Brewer, b.25 May 1908 Clay Co., KY. He d.2 Jun 1965 Seymour, Jackson Co., IN, at age 57 and was bur. Vallonia Cem., Vallonia.
Known children of Emma⁷ Baker and Owens Brewer:

        i.   Grover⁸.

        ii.   Harold B.

        iii.   Beulah m. (n.n.) Hamilton.

818. PFC Rosco⁷ Baker (USArmy-WWII) (Bryson⁶, Eliza⁵ Abner, Willis⁴, Elisha³, Elisha² Abney, Abner¹) m. Edna (n.n.). He, b.17 Jul 1912. He m. Edna (n.n.). He d.5 Jun 1952 at age 39 and was bur. Grays Knob Cem., Grays Knob, Harlan Co., KY.
    Known child of PFC Rosco⁷ Baker (USArmy-WWII) and Edna (n.n.):

        i.   Floyd Dwayne⁸, b.11 Sep 1946. He d.2 Sep 1998 at age 51 and was bur. Resthaven Cem., Keith, Harlan Co., KY.

819. Mamie⁷ Abner (Robert⁶, William⁵, Willis⁴, Elisha³, Elisha² Abney, Abner¹), b.11 Nov 1905 KY. She m. Clarence Barger Sr., son of Benjamin Franklin Barger and Rosa B. Gay, in 1923. She d.13 Feb 1997 OH at age 91 and was bur. Laurel Cem., Laurel, Clermont Co., OH.
    Clarence Barger Sr, b.22 Apr 1901 KY. He d.20 Feb 1974 at age 72 and was bur. Laurel Cem., Laurel, Clermont Co., OH.
Known children of Mamie⁷ Abner and Clarence Barger Sr.:

  1194 i.   Clarence⁸, b. 28 Jun 1924; m. Nellie (n.n.).

        ii.   Claudius, b.12 Nov 1930. He m. Betty Jean (n.n.) on 5 Aug 1950. He d.11 Sep 1994 at age 63 and was bur. Laurel Cem., Laurel, Clermont Co., OH. [Betty Jean (n.n.), b.16 Jul 1935.]

820. Elbert⁷ Abner (Robert⁶, William⁵, Willis⁴, Elisha³, Elisha² Abney, Abner¹) m. Maude Combs, daughter of Norma Jewell Meadow. He, b.26 Feb 1907 KY. He d.9 Nov 1974 Clermont Co., OH, at age 67 and was bur. Laurel Cem., Laurel, Clermont Co., OH.
    Maude Combs, b.29 Nov 1910 Perry Co., KY. She d.10 Aug 1990 Clermont Co., OH, at age 79 and was bur. Laurel Cem., Laurel.
Known children of Elbert⁷ Abner and Maude Combs:

  1195 i.   David Jerald⁸, b. 25 Apr 1937 Bethel, Clermont Co., OH; m. Norma Jewell Meadow.

  1196 ii.   Nancy Carol, b. 25 Sep 1939; m. Terry Alan Kidd.

  1197 iii.   John R., b. 14 Nov 1942; m. Joyce A. Perry.

        iv.   Jim.

  1198 v.   Steven E., b. 10 Mar 1945 Moscow, Clermont Co., OH; m. Glenda Brewer.

821. Willis[7] Abner (USArmy-WWII) (Robert[6], William[5], Willis[4], Elisha[3], Elisha[2] Abney, Abner[1]), b.8 May 1917. He m. Betty M. McClaskie ca.1937. He m. Marcella "Marty" Decknadel. He d.1 Dec 2004 at age 87 and was bur. Graceland Mem. Gardens, Milford, Clermont Co., OH.
   Betty M. McClaskie, b.4 Sep 1921. She m. (n.n.) Tooker. She d.30 Jul 1997 at age 75; bur. Kirkwood Cem., London, Madison Co., OH.
Known children of Willis[7] Abner (USArmy-WWII) and Betty M. McClaskie:
   i.   Barbara A. "Barb"[8], b.5 Dec 1938. She m. John Wesley Mason Jr. (USN-Nam). She d.13 Dec 2016 at age 78 and was bur. Kirkwood Cem., London, Madison Co., OH.
            John Wesley Mason Jr. (USN-Nam), b.1941. He d.1991 and was bur. Kirkwood Cem., London, Madison Co., OH.
   ii. Richard L., b.24 Aug 1940. He m. Darlene (n.n.) (she was b.7 Dec 1941). He d.29 Jun 2007 at age 66 and was bur. Kirkwood Cem., London, Madison Co., OH.
   1199 iii. Peggy, b. 4 Feb 1943 Clermont Co., OH; m. George McLaughlin.
   Marcella "Marty" Decknadel, b.1937. She d.2011 and was bur. Graceland Mem. Gardens, Milford, Clermont Co., OH.
There were no known children of Willis[7] Abner (USArmy-WWII) and Marcella "Marty" Decknadel.

822. SSgt Homer[7] Abner (USMC-WWII) (Robert[6], William[5], Willis[4], Elisha[3], Elisha[2] Abney, Abner[1]), b.24 Jan 1921. He m. Lena Combs. He d.4 Feb 2006 at age 85 and was bur. Laurel Cem., Laurel, Clermont Co., OH.
   Lena Combs, b.1 Sep 1924. She d.15 Mar 2014 Clermont Co., OH, at age 89 and was bur. Laurel Cem., Laurel, Clermont Co., OH.
Known child of SSgt Homer[7] Abner (USMC-WWII) and Lena Combs:
   i.   Gary Keith[8], b.25 Aug 1947 OH. He d.2 Oct 1976 Cincinnati, Hamilton Co., OH, at age 29 and was bur. Laurel Cem., Laurel, Clermont Co., OH.

823. Florence "Flossie"[7] Napier (Mary[6] Abner, William[5], Willis[4], Elisha[3], Elisha[2] Abney, Abner[1]), b.20 Apr 1906. She m. Jessie Bowling. d.15 Jul 1988 at age 82.
Known child of Florence "Flossie"[7] Napier and Jessie Bowling:
   1200 i. Wade[8], b. 12 Apr 1940 Buckhorn, Perry Co., KY; m. Pat (n.n.).

824. Eldren[7] Napier Sr. (Hannah[6] Abner, William[5], Willis[4], Elisha[3], Elisha[2] Abney, Abner[1]), b.23 Apr 1914 Perry Co., KY. He m. Orpha Julie Gross, daughter of Sam Gross and Delora Gay, on 16 Dec 1934. He and Orpha appeared on the census of 26 Apr 1940 Owsley Co., KY. He d.7 Oct 1976 Austin, Scott Co., IN, at age 62 and was bur. Wesley Chapel Cem., Austin, Scott Co., IN.
   Orpha Julie Gross, b.28 Jan 1919 Perry Co., KY. She d.2 Dec 1989 Austin, Scott Co., IN, at age 70 and was bur. Wesley Chapel Cem., Austin.
Known children of Eldren[7] Napier Sr. and Orpha Julie Gross (birth order unknown):
   i.   JoAnn[8]. She m. (n.n.) Soloe.
   ii.   Mary. She m. (n.n.) Manley.
   iii. Betty. She m. (n.n.) Bard.
   iv.   Linda. She m. (n.n.) Sweany.
   v.   Maxine. She m. (n.n.) St. Clair.
   vi.   Charles.
   vii. Eldren.
   viii. Jack.
   ix.   Norma J., b. ca.1935 Owsley Co., KY. She m. (n.n.) England.
   1201 x. Billie Franklin, b. 9 Apr 1937; m. Phyllis J. (n.n.).
   xi.   Conley B., b.11 Apr 1939. He d.19 Jul 2009 at age 70 and was bur. Wesley Chapel Cem., Austin, Scott Co., IN.

825. Nancy Ann[7] Bowling (Elizabeth[6] Abner, William[5], Willis[4], Elisha[3], Elisha[2] Abney, Abner[1]) m. PFC Letcher Smith (USArmy-WWII). , b.9 Jan 1926 Bowlington, Perry Co., KY. She d.18 Sep 1976 Austin, Scott Co., IN, at age 50 and was bur. Johnston Cem., Buckhorn, Perry Co., KY.
   PFC Letcher Smith (USArmy-WWII), b.14 Dec 1921 Perry Co., KY. He d.10 Jun 1991 Scottsburg, Scott Co., IN, age 69; bur. Johnston Cem.
Known child of Nancy Ann[7] Bowling and PFC Letcher Smith (USArmy-WWII):
   1202 i. Billy Dean[8], b. 4 Apr 1954 Hamilton, Butler Co., OH; m. Donna Marie Haney.

826. Bill[7] Bowling (Elizabeth[6] Abner, William[5], Willis[4], Elisha[3], Elisha[2] Abney, Abner[1]), b.20 Sep 1927 Bowlington, Perry Co., KY. He m. Tilda Marie (n.n.). He d.6 Feb 2008 Indianapolis, Marion Co., IN, age 80 and was bur. New Crown Cem. & Mausoleum, Indianapolis, Marion Co., IN.
   Tilda Marie (n.n.), b.3 Mar 1933. She d.3 Sep 2006 at age 73 and was bur. New Crown Cem. & Mausoleum, Indianapolis, Marion Co., IN.
Known children of Bill[7] Bowling and Tilda Marie (n.n.) (birth order unknown):
   i.   Dennis[8]. He m. Penny (n.n.).
   ii.   Andrew.
   iii. Robert. He m. Tammy (n.n.).
   iv.   Jimmy.
   v.   Randell. He m. Gail (n.n.).
   vi.   Ronald.
   vii. Mary. She m. (n.n.) Davis.
   viii. Darrell.

827. Elmira[7] Bowling (Elizabeth[6] Abner, William[5], Willis[4], Elisha[3], Elisha[2] Abney, Abner[1]), b.6 Nov 1934 Louisville, Jefferson Co., KY. She m. Herbert "Gerald" Payne. d.7 Nov 2017 Louisville, Jefferson Co., KY, at age 83 and was bur. Evergreen Cem., Louisville, Jefferson Co., KY.
   Herbert "Gerald" Payne, b.19 Jan 1927. He d.4 Dec 2004 at age 77 and was bur. Saint Theresa Cem., Rhodelia, Meade Co., KY.
Known children of Elmira[7] Bowling and Herbert "Gerald" Payne:
   i.   Gerald Edward[8].
   ii.   Gary L.
   1203 iii. Michael Ray.
   1204 iv. Wanda June, m. Robert Lee Stafford Sr.

828. Pearl[7] Abner (Willis[6], William[5], Willis[4], Elisha[3], Elisha[2] Abney, Abner[1]), b.20 Feb 1931 Hamilton, Butler Co., OH; m. Donald Retherford on 11 Mar 1950. She d.10 Jan 2005 Hamilton, Butler Co., OH, at age 73; bur. Rose Hill Burial Park, Hamilton, Butler Co., OH.
    Donald Retherford, b.4 Sep 1931 Hamilton, Butler Co., OH. He d.6 Feb 2013 Okeana, Butler Co., OH, at age 81; bur. Rose Hill Burial Park.
Known children of Pearl[7] Abner and Donald Retherford (birth order unknown):
   i. Jennifer[8]. He m. Paul McCollum.
   ii. Donald "Woody". He m. Diana (n.n.).
   iii. Holly. She m. Dennis Jones.
   iv. Rebecca. She m. (n.n.) Scott.
   v. Jeffrey.

829. Adolph[7] Abner (Anderson[6], William[5], Willis[4], Elisha[3], Elisha[2] Abney, Abner[1]), b.5 Mar 1927. He m. Lavonne Rosalean "Bonnie" Rickard. He d.31 Jul 1991 Indianapolis, Marion Co., IN, at age 64 and was bur. Crown Hill Cem., Indianapolis, Marion Co., IN.
    Lavonne Rosalean "Bonnie" Rickard, b.26 Oct 1932 Indianapolis, Marion Co., IL. She d.13 Dec 2017 at age 85 and was bur. Crown Hill Cem.
Known children of Adolph[7] Abner and Lavonne Rosalean "Bonnie" Rickard (birth order unknown):
   i. Winona[8]. She m. Frank Wilson.
   ii. Neal. He m. Patty (n.n.).
   iii. Michael.
   iv. Sandra. She m. Lonnie Groenenboom.
   v. Marguerite. She m. (n.n.) Collins.
   vi. Carol. She m. (n.n.) Brickart.
   vii. Joseph Scott, b.13 May 1955 Indianapolis, Marion Co., IN. He d.13 May 1955 Indianapolis, Marion Co., IN and was bur. New Crown Cem. & Mausoleum, Indianapolis, Marion Co., IN.
   viii. Anderson Lee "Andy", b.9 May 1966 Indianapolis, Marion Co., IN. He d.30 Sep 1996 Indianapolis, Marion Co., IN, at age 30 and was bur. Crown Hill Cem., Indianapolis, Marion Co., IN.

830. Elizabeth[7] Abner (Edward[6], Elisha[5], Willis[4], Elisha[3], Elisha[2] Abney, Abner[1]), b.30 Apr 1920 Perry Co., KY. She m. PFC Hargis Oliver Sr. (USArmy-WWII) on 18 Jul 1942. She d.30 Sep 2009 Connersville, Fayette Co., IN, at age 89; bur. Dale Cem., Connersville, Fayette Co., IN.
    PFC Hargis Oliver Sr. (USArmy-WWII), b.23 Oct 1920 Hazard, Perry Co., KY; d.9 Sep 2003 Connersville, Fayette Co., IN; bur. Dale Cem.
Known children of Elizabeth[7] Abner and PFC Hargis Oliver Sr. (USArmy-WWII):
   i. Hargis[8] m. Loreda (n.n.).
1205 ii. Ola "Faye," b. 2 Sep 1946 Perry Co., KY; m. James Sanders.
   iii. Dorothy, b.9 Jan 1948 Connersville, Fayette Co., IN. She m. Ross Clark Hinesman on 7 Jul 1976 Jacksboro, Campbell Co., TN. She d.5 Jan 2017 IN at age 68 and was bur. Columbia Cem., Connersville, Fayette Co., IN.
     Ross Clark Hinesman, b.20 May 1945 Napoleon, Henry Co., OH. He d.25 Apr 2010 Connersville, Fayette Co., IN, at age 64 and was bur. Columbia Cem., Connersville, Fayette Co., IN.
   iv. Letha "Toots", b.25 Jul 1949. She m. Stephen Ray Lykins, son of Ova Vernon Lykins and Rosetta Chasteen. She d.7 Jan 2000 at age 50. , b. Columbia Cem., Connersville, Fayette Co., IN.
     Stephen Ray Lykins, b.21 Sep 1957. He d.13 Jul 2000 at age 42 and was bur. Columbia Cem., Connersville.
   v. David Edward, b. New Year's Day, 1 Jan 1952 Connersville, Fayette Co., IN. He d.4 Feb 1954 IN at age 2 and was bur. West Point Cem., Liberty, Union Co., IN.
   vi. Mark, b.2 Jun 1953. He m. Mary Elizabeth Clifton, daughter of James Clifton and Beatrice Bales. He d.13 Oct 2006 at age 53 and was bur. Hopewell Cem., Richland, Rush Co., IN.
     Mary Elizabeth Clifton, b.18 Jun 1954 VA; d.13 Feb 2018, Richmond, Wayne Co., IN, age 63; bur. Hopewell Cem.
   vii. Denise m. Billy Legere Sr.
1206 viii. Deborah "Debbie," b. 2 Mar 1957 Connersville, Fayette Co., IN; m1. Daniel Sylvester Koontz; m2. Edward L. Wilson.
   ix. Charlie. He m. Teresa (n.n.).
1207 x. Melita Kay, b. 20 Mar 1961 Connersville, Fayette Co., IN; m. (n.n.) Collins.

831. Daniel B. "Dan"[7] Abner (USArmy-WWII) (Edward[6], Elisha[5], Willis[4], Elisha[3], Elisha[2] Abney, Abner[1]), b.20 Jan 1922 Buckhorn, Perry Co., KY. He m. Ruby Daniel. He d.20 Apr 1977 Lexington, Fayette Co., KY, at age 55 and was bur. Buckhorn Cem., Buckhorn, Perry Co., KY.
Known children of Daniel B. "Dan"[7] Abner (USArmy-WWII) and Ruby Daniel (birth order unknown):
   i. Regina[8] m. (n.n.) Light.
   ii. Nadina m. (n.n.) Ott.
   iii. Wanda Sue m. (n.n.) Maupin.
   iv. Rickie.
   v. Darlene m. (n.n.) Stamper.
1208 vi. Washington Edward "Dickie," b. 22 May 1947 Owsley Co., KY; m. Helen Rice.
   vii. Joseph Casey, b.12 Sep 1961 Oneida, Clay Co., KY. He d.30 Aug 2011 Fayette Co., KY, at age 49 and was bur. Buckhorn Cem., Buckhorn, Perry Co., KY.

832. Sgt. Taulbee[7] Abner Sr. (USArmy-WWII) (Edward[6], Elisha[5], Willis[4], Elisha[3], Elisha[2] Abney, Abner[1]), b.16 Aug 1925 Hazard, Perry Co., KY. He m. Dorothy M. Stroud. He d.22 Sep 1982 Indianapolis, Marion Co., IN, at age 57 and was bur. Crown Hill Cem., Indianapolis, Marion Co., IN.
    Dorothy M. Stroud, b.24 Nov 1925. She d.25 Jan 2003 at age 77 and was bur. Crown Hill Cem., Indianapolis, Marion Co., IN.
Known children of Sgt. Taulbee[7] Abner Sr. (USArmy-WWII) and Dorothy M. Stroud (birth order unknown):
   i. Janet[8].
   ii. Ronald.
   iii. William.
   iv. Jimmie.
   v. Judith Ann, b.1944. She d.1944 and was bur. West Point Cem., Liberty, Union Co., IN.
   vi. Taulbee, b.25 Aug 1946 Connersville, Fayette Co., IN; d.3 Sep 1946 Connersville, Fayette Co., IN; bur. West Point Cem.

833. Edward "Ed"*7* Abner (Edward*6*, Elisha*5*, Willis*4*, Elisha*3*, Elisha*2* Abney, Abner*1*), b.19 May 1929 Perry Co., KY. He m. Jeanette McKnight, daughter of Walter McKnight Sr, in 1950. He d.26 Feb 2000 Preble Co., OH, at age 70; bur. Sugar Grove Cem., West Alexandria, Preble Co., OH.
       Jeanette McKnight, b.18 Apr 1935 Perry Co., KY. She d.23 Jul 1988, Dayton, Montgomery Co., OH, at age 53; bur. Sugar Grove Cem.
Known children of Edward "Ed"*7* Abner and Jeanette McKnight (birth order unknown):
      i.   Joseph A. "Joe"*8*.
      ii.   Franklin J. "Frank."
      iii. David Michael "Mickey", b.30 Oct 1956 Dayton, Montgomery Co., OH. He d.16 Feb 1976 Cincinnati, Hamilton Co., OH, at age 19 and was bur. Sugar Grove Cem., West Alexandria, Preble Co., OH.

834. Charlie*7* Abner (Edward*6*, Elisha*5*, Willis*4*, Elisha*3*, Elisha*2* Abney, Abner*1*), b.23 Oct 1933 Perry Co., KY. He m. Hazel Susan Rice on 21 Nov 1955. He d.31 Jul 1984 Perry Co., KY, at age 50 and was bur. Abner Family Cem., Buckhorn, Perry Co., KY.
       Hazel Susan Rice, b.6 Aug 1940 Perry Co., KY. She d.24 Aug 1997 Harlan Co., KY, at age 57 and was bur. Abner Family Cem., Buckhorn.
Known children of Charlie*7* Abner and Hazel Susan Rice (birth order unknown):
      i.   Benny*8*.
      ii.   Robert.
      iii. Geraldine.
      iv.   Anne m. (n.n.) Collins.
      v.   Glenda m. (n.n.) Smith.
      vi.   Marlene m. (n.n.) Stokely.
      vii. Nancy m. (n.n.) Baker.
      viii. Elisha.
      ix.   William.
      x.   Tolbert.
      xi.   Culley.
1209 xii. Dennis Charles "Goat," b. 21 Jul 1962 Perry Co., KY; m. Pouleine Roberts.
      xiii. John Wayne, b.4 Oct 1964 Perry Co., KY. He d.30 Oct 1977 Perry Co., KY, at age 13 and was bur. Abner Family Cem., Buckhorn, Perry Co., KY.

835. Dorothy*7* Abner (Edward*6*, Elisha*5*, Willis*4*, Elisha*3*, Elisha*2* Abney, Abner*1*), b.11 Nov 1935 Buckhorn, Perry Co., KY. She m. Green Berry Adams in 1954. She d.7 May 1994 Hazard, Perry Co., KY, at age 58 and was bur. Abner Family Cem., Buckhorn, Perry Co., KY.
       Green Berry Adams, b.19 May 1919 Morris Fork, Breathitt Co., KY; d.13 Dec 2007 Brooksville, Bracken Co., KY; bur. Abner Family Cem.
Known children of Dorothy*7* Abner and Green Berry Adams (birth order unknown):
      i.   Jerry*8* m. Beatrice (n.n.).
      ii.   Eugene m. Pam (n.n.).
      iii. Patsy m. Mart Herald.
      iv.   Elmer Ray m. Donna (n.n.).
      v.   Vernon.
      vi.   Darrell m. Crystal (n.n.).
1210 vii. Samuel "Howard," b. 17 Aug 1961 Buckhorn, Perry Co., KY.
1211 viii. Harold, b. 13 Feb 1970 Hyden, Leslie Co., KY.

836. Willis*7* Abner (Edward*6*, Elisha*5*, Willis*4*, Elisha*3*, Elisha*2* Abney, Abner*1*) m. Janice Kay Brooks. He, b.27 Dec 1938 Buckhorn, Perry Co., KY. He d.6 Nov 2015 Garrett, Floyd Co., KY, at age 76 and was bur. Chaffins Cem., Mousie, Knott Co., KY.
Known children of Willis*7* Abner and Janice Kay Brooks (birth order unknown):
      i.   Terry Randall*8*.
      ii.   Tony Marvin m. Mary (n.n.).
      iii. Tommy.
      iv.   Jonathon.
      v.   Kathy Marilyn m. (n.n.) McQueen.
      vi.   Vickie Evelyn m. Jeff Sandlin.
      vii. Heather m. Tracy McQueen.

837. Hugh*7* Terry (Brownlow*6*, Mary*5* Abner, Willis*4*, Elisha*3*, Elisha*2* Abney, Abner*1*) m. Laura Barrett. He, b.8 Jan 1912 Athol, Lee Co., KY. He d.18 Oct 1944 Kings Mills, Warren Co., OH, at age 32 and was bur. Hugh Bryant Cem., Copebranch, Breathitt Co., KY.
       Laura Barrett, b.24 Apr 1914 KY. She d.8 Oct 1987 Austin, Scott Co., IN, at age 73 and was bur. Spurgeon Mem. Park, Austin, Scott Co., IN.
Known children of Hugh*7* Terry and Laura Barrett:
1212 i.   Sterlin*8*, b. 25 Oct 1932; m. Samantha Gilbert.
      ii.   Mable, b.25 Sep 1934 Athol, Lee Co., KY. She m. James S. Smith on 6 Mar 1955. She d.7 Apr 2018 Austin, Scott Co., IN, at age 83 and was bur. Spurgeon Mem. Park, Austin, Scott Co., IN.
              James S. Smith, b.11 Aug 1930 Breathitt Co., KY. He d.29 Apr 2019 Scottsburg, Scott Co., IN, at age 88 and was bur. Spurgeon Mem. Park, Austin, Scott Co., IN.
1213 iii. Tom Junior, b. 8 Jan 1937; m. Shelby Jean Wooten.
      iv.   Juanita, b.11 Apr 1942 Lerose, Owsley Co., KY. She d.28 Mar 2000 Scottsburg, Scott Co., IN, at age 57 and was bur. Spurgeon Mem. Park, Austin, Scott Co., IN.

838. Gracie E.*7* Woods (Mattie*6* Terry, Mary*5* Abner, Willis*4*, Elisha*3*, Elisha*2* Abney, Abner*1*) m. Wesley Durbin. , b.25 Sep 1913 Breathitt Co., KY. She d.16 May 2004 Beattyville, Lee Co., KY, at age 90 and was bur. White Ash Cem., Beattyville, Lee Co., KY.
       Wesley Durbin, b.23 Jun 1912. He d.20 Dec 1990 at age 78 and was bur. White Ash Cem., Beattyville, Lee Co., KY.

Known children of Gracie E.⁷ Woods and Wesley Durbin:
      i.   Myra Lee⁸, b.7 Jun 1938 Beattyville, Lee Co., KY; Marvin Warner; d.13 Jan 2017 Vandalia, Montgomery Co., OH, at age 78 and was bur. White Ash Cem., Beattyville, Lee Co., KY.
          Marvin Warner, b.18 Jul 1936 and d.6 Nov 1995 Beattyville, Lee Co., KY, at age 59 and was bur. White Ash Cem.
      ii. Mary Louise, b.28 Apr 1951 Lee Co., KY. She d.25 Feb 2016 Beattyville, Lee Co., KY, at age 64; bur. White Ash Cem.

839. Albert⁷ Willoughby (Lillie⁶ Abner, John⁵, Willis⁴, Elisha³, Elisha² Abney, Abner¹) m. Clarene McCarty. He, b.12 Apr 1927 Mount Sterling, Montgomery Co., KY. He d.11 Sep 1972 Lexington, Fayette Co., KY, at age 45 and was bur. Lexington Cem., Lexington, Fayette Co., KY.
    Clarene McCarty, b.22 Oct 1929 Owingsville, Bath Co., KY. She d.3 Apr 2009 Lexington, Fayette Co., KY, at age 79; bur. Lexington Cem.
Known child of Albert⁷ Willoughby and Clarene McCarty:
      i.   Cindy Lane⁸, b.27 Sep 1958 Bath Co., KY. She d.17 Mar 2006 Fayette Co., KY, at age 47 and was bur. Lexington Cem.

840. Beulah Lenora⁷ Abner (Elisha⁶, Daniel⁵, Willis⁴, Elisha³, Elisha² Abney, Abner¹) m. Clyde Keeton. , b.9 Aug 1919 KY. She d.Christmas Day, 25 Dec 2000 Phoenix, Maricopa Co., AZ, at age 81 and was bur. Glendale Mem. Park, Glendale, Maricopa Co., AZ.
    Clyde Keeton, b.8 Jan 1919 Morgan Co., KY. He d.3 Oct 1997 Maricopa Co., AZ, at age 78.
Known child of Beulah Lenora⁷ Abner and Clyde Keeton:
      i.   Judith⁸, b.23 Aug 1941 Ashland Co., OH. She d.14 May 1998 Maricopa Co., AZ, at age 56; bur. Glendale Mem. Park.

841. Bernice M.⁷ Abner (Elisha⁶, Daniel⁵, Willis⁴, Elisha³, Elisha² Abney, Abner¹), b.14 Jan 1922. She m. Pvt. Emmett A. Curry Jr. (USArmy-WWIi) in 1940. She d.24 Sep 1987 at age 65 and was bur. Rose Hill Burial Park and Maus., Ashland, Boyd Co., KY.
    Pvt. Emmett A. Curry Jr. (USArmy-WWIi), b.29 Mar 1922. He d.12 Nov 1991 at age 69 and was bur. Ashland Cem., Ashland, Boyd Co., KY.
Known child of Bernice M.⁷ Abner and Pvt. Emmett A. Curry Jr. (USArmy-WWIi):
      i.   Lorna D.⁸, b.1941. She d.1993 and was bur. Rose Hill Burial Park and Maus., Ashland, Boyd Co., KY.

842. Naomi Faye⁷ Abner (Elisha⁶, Daniel⁵, Willis⁴, Elisha³, Elisha² Abney, Abner¹) m. Ivor Roberts. , b.27 Oct 1930 Ashland, Boyd Co., KY. She d.11 Jul 2000 Middletown, Butler Co., OH, at age 69 and was bur. Woodside Cem., Middletown, Butler Co., OH.
    Ivor Roberts, b.4 Oct 1929 Hyden, Leslie Co., KY. He d.4 Feb 2015 Butler Co., OH, at age 85 and was bur. Woodside Cem., Middletown.
Known children of Naomi Faye⁷ Abner and Ivor Roberts:
      i.   Deborah K.⁸, b.28 Feb 1956 Middletown, Butler Co., OH. She d.25 Oct 2015 Middletown, Butler Co., OH, at age 59 and was bur. Woodside Cem., Middletown, Butler Co., OH.
      ii. Timothy, b.25 Jun 1959. He m. Karen (n.n.) (she was b.11 Aug 1957) on 12 Jul 1980. He d.13 Jun 2011 at age 51 and was bur. Woodside Cem., Middletown, Butler Co., OH.

843. James Larry⁷ Abner Sr. (Elisha⁶, Daniel⁵, Willis⁴, Elisha³, Elisha² Abney, Abner¹) m. Carolyn R. Taylor. He, b.21 Oct 1936 Ashland, Boyd Co., KY. He d.15 Aug 1985 Middleton, Butler Co., OH, at age 48 and was bur. Woodside Cem., Middleton, Butler Co., OH.
    Carolyn R. Taylor, b.21 Mar 1939. She d.4 Nov 2008 at age 69 and was bur. Woodside Cem., Middleton, Butler Co., OH.
Known children of James Larry⁷ Abner Sr. and Carolyn R. Taylor:
      i.   Julie⁸.
      ii. James Larry.

844. Gary Wayne⁷ Abner (Elisha⁶, Daniel⁵, Willis⁴, Elisha³, Elisha² Abney, Abner¹) m. Mable E. Dean. He, b.18 Sep 1939 Ashland, Boyd Co., KY. He d.22 Apr 2018 Middleton, Butler Co., OH, at age 78 and was bur. Butler County Mem. Park, Trenton, Butler Co., OH.
Known children of Gary Wayne⁷ Abner and Mable E. Dean:
      i.   Kathy⁸ m. Richard France.
  1214 ii. David Wayne, b. 2 Dec 1960 Middleton, Butler Co. OH; m. Julie A.

845. Dan B. "Bo"⁷ Abner (Jerry⁶, Daniel⁵, Willis⁴, Elisha³, Elisha² Abney, Abner¹), b.26 Mar 1928 Middleton, Butler Co., OH. He m. Juanita Lovely on 19 Jun 1957. He d.20 Feb 2012 Clifton, Hamilton Co., OH, at age 83 and was bur. Butler County Mem. Park, Trenton, Butler Co., OH.
    Juanita Lovely, b.27 Jul 1932.
Known children of Dan B. "Bo"⁷ Abner and Juanita Lovely:
  1215 i.   Jerry B.⁸.
      ii. Linda K.
      iii. Dan Martin, b.22 Feb 1961. He d.23 Dec 1977 at age 16 and was bur. Butler County Mem. Park, Trenton, Butler Co., OH.

846. William Cleveland "Bill"⁷ Abner (John⁶, Andrew⁵, Enoch⁴, Elisha³, Elisha² Abney, Abner¹), b.21 Jun 1914 Madison Co., AR. He m1. Geneva Cornett, daughter of Boyd Cornett and Golda Wimer, on 22 Dec 1935. He m2. Lewise Miles. He m3. Nora Bethel Moore. He d.13 Aug 2010 at age 96 and was bur. Gracelawn Cem., Van Buren, Crawford Co., AR.
    Geneva Cornett, b.3 Sep 1918 St. Paul, Madison Co., AR. She d.28 May 1984 Fort Smith, Sebastian Co., AR, at age 65; bur. Gracelawn Cem.
Known children of William Cleveland "Bill"⁷ Abner and Geneva Cornett:
  1216 i.   Willeta Fay⁸, b. 21 Nov 1937 Santa Maria, CA; m. Robert G. Keeter.
  1217 ii. LaVeda Mae, b. 30 Dec 1939 Orange, CA; m. Bill Fraley.
There were no known children of William Cleveland "Bill"⁷ Abner and Lewise Miles.
    Nora Bethel Moore, b.21 Nov 1917 Lincoln, Washington Co., AR. She d.27 Sep 2013 Fort Smith, Sebastian Co., AR, at age 95 and was bur. Fort Smith National Cem., Fort Smith, Sebastian Co., AR.
There were no known children of William Cleveland "Bill"⁷ Abner and Nora Bethel Moore.

847. Emily "Mavis"⁷ Abner (Jefferson⁶, Andrew⁵, Enoch⁴, Elisha³, Elisha² Abney, Abner¹), b.28 Mar 1934 St. Paul, Madison Co., AR. She m. Waldon Dewey Powell. She m. William Clifford Long. She d.Independence Day, 4 Jul 1979 Fayetteville, Washington Co., AR, at age 45 and was bur. Walnut Grove Cem., Crosses, Madison Co., AR.

Waldon Dewey Powell, b.12 Dec 1932 Madison Co., AR. He d.20 Feb 1984 Madison Co., AR, at age 51 and was bur. Bohannan Mountain Cem., Huntsville, Madison Co., AR.
Known children of Emily "Mavis"[7] Abner and Waldon Dewey Powell:
        i.   Charlotte[8], b. ca.1953 Madison Co., AR; m. (n.n.) Rankin.
       ii.   Walda Jean, b.14 Nov 1955. She d.6 Jun 1956 auto accident, Madison Co., AR and was bur. Bohannan Mountain Cem., Huntsville, Madison Co., AR.
     iii.   Gary, b. Madison Co., AR.
     iv.   Larry, b. Madison Co., AR.
There were no known children of Emily "Mavis"[7] Abner and William Clifford Long.

848. Loraine[7] Abner (Jefferson[6], Andrew[5], Enoch[4], Elisha[3], Elisha[2] Abney, Abner[1]) m. Floyd Leon Hull. , b.2 Nov 1936 AR. She d.26 Nov 2009 East Wenatchee, Douglas Co., WA, at age 73 and was bur. Methow Cem., Methow, Okanogan Co., WA.
    Floyd Leon Hull, b.3 Mar 1927 Madison Co., AR. He d.10 Jan 1985 Methow, Okonogan Co., WA, at age 57.
Known child of Loraine[7] Abner and Floyd Leon Hull:
        i.   Mary Cathryn[8], b.4 Jan 1967. She d.10 Feb 2007 at age 40.

849. Bert Hollis[7] Abner (Roscoe[6], John[5], James[4], Menan[3], Elisha[2] Abney, Abner[1]), b.21 Nov 1900 Liberty, Union Co., IN. He m1. Dorothy May Stalnaker (b. Jan 2012) on 19 Aug 1922 Butler Co., OH. He m2. Rowena Evelyn Hinds ca.1925. He and Rowena Evelyn Hinds appeared on the census of 8 Apr 1930 Indianapolis, Marion Co., IN. He m. Eva Mary Hopper in 1943. He d.23 Dec 1969 Indianapolis, Marion Co., IN, at age 69 and was bur. Brownsburg Cem., Brownsburg, Hendricks Co., IN.
Known child of Bert Hollis[7] Abner and Dorothy May Stalnaker:
        i.   Billy Switzer[8], b.11 Jun 1923 Indianapolis, Marion Co., IN. He m. Letus Fowler. He d.20 Oct 1988 Chiefland, Levy Co., FL, at age 65 and was bur. Chiefland Cem., Chiefland, Levy Co., FL.
              Letus Fowler, b.22 Oct 1913 Day, Lafayette Co., FL; d.29 Aug 1992 Suwannee, Dixie Co., FL; bur. Chiefland Cem.
    Rowena Evelyn Hinds, b.18 Jan 1908 Frankford, Clinton Co., IN. She d.18 Aug 1982 at age 74 and was bur. Bunnell Cem., Frankfort.
There were no known children of Bert Hollis[7] Abner and Rowena Evelyn Hinds.
    Eva Mary Hopper, b.17 Oct 1909 Montgomery Co., TN. She d.10 Jun 1976 Indianapolis, Marion Co., IN, at age 66; bur. Brownsburg Cem.
There were no known children of Bert Hollis[7] Abner and Eva Mary Hopper.

850. Harold Merle[7] Abner Sr. (Roscoe[6], John[5], James[4], Menan[3], Elisha[2] Abney, Abner[1]), b.19 Aug 1906 IN. He m. Ruth Louise Zahrt ca.1929. He and Ruth Louise Zahrt appeared on the census of 9 Apr 1940 La Porte, La Porte Co., IN. He d.22 Sep 1972 La Porte, La Porte Co., IN, at age 66 and was bur. Pine Lake Cem., La Porte, La Porte Co., IN.
    Ruth Louise Zahrt, b.22 May 1912 IN. She d.7 Apr 1986 Fort Myers, Lee Co., FL, at age 73.
Known children of Harold Merle[7] Abner Sr. and Ruth Louise Zahrt:
        i.   Louise Marie[8], b.7 Apr 1930 La Porte Co., IN. She m. Walter Ernest Gangwer on 18 Sep 1965 La Porte, La Porte Co., IN. She d.13 Aug 1976 South Bend, St. Joseph Co., IN, at age 46 and was bur. Pine Lake Cem., La Porte, La Porte Co., IN.
              Walter Ernest Gangwer, b.20 Dec 1918. He d.Mar 1979 at age 60 and was bur. Pine Lake Cem., La Porte.
       ii.   Harold Merle, b.23 Feb 1933 La Porte, La Porte Co., IN. He m. Marilee Lou Johnson (1935-2018). He d.9 Apr 1989 Fort Myers, Lee Co., FL, at age 56.

851. Florence May[7] Abner (Roscoe[6], John[5], James[4], Menan[3], Elisha[2] Abney, Abner[1]) m. Clarence Verle Creamer. , b.17 Nov 1917 Union Co., IN. She d.29 Apr 1980 Indianapolis, Marion Co., IN, at age 62 and was bur. Anderson Mem. Park, Anderson, Madison Co., IN.
    Clarence Verle Creamer, b.20 Feb 1916 Summitville, Madison Co., IN; d.23 Oct 1995 Plainfield, Hendricks Co., IN, age 79. He was cremated.
Known children of Florence May[7] Abner and Clarence Verle Creamer:
        i.   Clarence William[8], b.28 Apr 1935 Elwood, Madison Co., IN. He d.25 Mar 2002 Indianapolis, Marion Co., IN, at age 66 and was bur. New Palestine Cem., New Palestine, Hancock Co., IN.
       ii.   Ralph Raymond, b.27 Jul 1940 IN. He m. Phyllis (n.n.). He d.23 Aug 1969 Anderson, Madison Co., IN, at age 29 and was bur. Anderson Mem. Park, Anderson, Madison Co., IN.
     iii.   Carolyn Rose, b.25 Feb 1949 Elwood, Madison Co., IN. She m. Larry C. Badgley in 1966. She d.7 Nov 2019 IN at age 70 and was bur. Forest Lawn Memory Gardens, Greenwood, Johnson Co., IN.
              Larry C. Badgley, b.11 May 1945. He d.24 Feb 2017 at age 71 and was bur. Forest Lawn Memory Gardens.

852. Esther Leotta[7] Abner (Smith[6], John[5], James[4], Menan[3], Elisha[2] Abney, Abner[1]) m. Robert Clifford Worster. , b.6 Oct 1901 Liberty, Union Co., IN. She d.6 Jan 1984 Connersville, Fayette Co., IN, at age 82 and was bur. Everton Cem., Everton, Fayette Co., IN.
    Robert Clifford Worster, b.9 May 1893 Columbia, Fayette Co., IN. He d.18 Jul 1958 Connersville, Fayette Co., IN, age 65; bur. Everton Cem.
Known child of Esther Leotta[7] Abner and Robert Clifford Worster:
        i.   Glenn David[8], b.1926. He d.1940.

853. Mary E.[7] Abner (Smith[6], John[5], James[4], Menan[3], Elisha[2] Abney, Abner[1]) m. Herbert Riley Eastin. , b.10 May 1907 Union Co., IN. She m. Lloyd Russell Behymer in 1925. She d.29 Dec 1992 Richmond, Wayne Co., IN, at age 85 and was bur. Earlham Cem., Richmond, Wayne Co., IN.
    Herbert Riley Eastin, b.11 Aug 1905 OH. He d.25 Jul 1986 Richmond, Wayne Co., IN, at age 80 and was bur. Earlham Cem., Richmond.
There were no known children of Mary E.[7] Abner and Herbert Riley Eastin.
    Lloyd Russell Behymer, b.28 Jul 1902 Hancock Co., OH. He d.11 Nov 1980 Los Angeles Co., CA, at age 78 and was bur. Rose Hills Mem. Park, Whittier, Los Angeles Co., CA.
Known children of Mary E.[7] Abner and Lloyd Russell Behymer:
        i.   Roy Leon[8], b.1927. He d.1998.
       ii.   Harold Leslie, b.1928. He d.1998.

854. Sophie[7] Abner (Joseph[6], Pierce[5], James[4], Menan[3], Elisha[2] Abney, Abner[1]), b.29 Jan 1915 Clay Co., KY. She m. Thomas "Tommy" Smith on 19 Jul 1933 Knox Co., KY. She d.Apr 1994 KY at age 79.

Thomas "Tommy" Smith, b.1908. He d.1970.
Known children of Sophie⁷ Abner and Thomas "Tommy" Smith:
       i.   Earl⁸, b.1937. He d.1991.
      ii. Flossie, b.1943. She d.2004.
     iii. Elmer, b.1949. He d.2016.

855. Thea⁷ Abner (Joseph⁶, Pierce⁵, James⁴, Menan³, Elisha² Abney, Abner¹), b.6 Jul 1934 Knox Co., KY. He m. Wanda Gibson (b.1 Mar 1935) on 9 Oct 1954. He d.9 Jun 2015 Pineville, Bell Co., KY, at age 80 and was bur. Calvin Jordan Cem., Woollum, Knox Co., KY.
Known children of Thea⁷ Abner and Wanda Gibson (birth order unknown):
       i.   Charles⁸ m. Christine (n.n.).
      ii. Kenneth.
     iii. Gerald Wayne.
1218   iv. Joseph "Joe," b. 14 Jul 1958 Bell Co., KY; m. Brenda (n.n.).

856. Boone⁷ Abner (Joseph⁶, Pierce⁵, James⁴, Menan³, Elisha² Abney, Abner¹) m. (n.n.). He Birth year is wrong on FaG! He was younger than Thea...AND only 3 years old on the 1930 census. He, b.19 Jun 1936 Hammond, Knox Co., KY. He d.30 Jan 2018 Cincinnati, Hamilton Co., OH, at age 81 and was bur. Calvin Jordan Cem., Woollum, Knox Co., KY.
Known children of Boone⁷ Abner (birth order unknown):
       i.   Charlotte⁸.
      ii. Timmy.
     iii. Penny m. (n.n.) Johnson.
     iv. Lisa m. (n.n.) Reynolds.
      v. Mary m. (n.n.) White.
     vi. Stacy.

857. John N.⁷ Abner (USN) (Joseph⁶, Pierce⁵, James⁴, Menan³, Elisha² Abney, Abner¹) m. Lydia Ann Smith. He, b.22 Feb 1940 Knox Co., KY. He d.26 Oct 1988 Flat Lick, Knox Co., KY, at age 48 and was bur. Calvin Jordan Cem., Woollum, Knox Co., KY.
Known children of John N.⁷ Abner (USN) and Lydia Ann Smith:
       i.   (n.n.)⁸.
      ii. (n.n.).

858. Wilson Taylor⁷ Abner (Taylor⁶, Daniel⁵, James⁴, Menan³, Elisha² Abney, Abner¹), b.5 Sep 1915 Richmond, Wayne Co., IN. He m. Zola Ethel Bane (ca.1918-2005) on 7 Aug 1937 Wayne Co., IN. He and Zola Ethel Bane appeared on the census of 18 Apr 1940 Richmond, Wayne Co., IN. He d.1 Feb 1996 Richmond, Wayne Co., IN, at age 80.
Known child of Wilson Taylor⁷ Abner and Zola Ethel Bane:
       i.   Patricia⁸, b. ca.1939 Richmond, Wayne Co., IN.

859. James Monroe⁷ Abner Jr. (James⁶, Daniel⁵, James⁴, Menan³, Elisha² Abney, Abner¹), b.28 May 1929 Greensfork, Randolph Co., IN. He m. Glenna Mae Skinner (1929-2016) on 7 Apr 1950 Wayne Co., IN. He d.18 Jan 2003 Beech Grove, Marion Co., IN, at age 73.
Known children of James Monroe⁷ Abner Jr. and Glenna Mae Skinner:
       i.   Douglas Monroe⁸, b. New Year's Eve, 31 Dec 1950 Wayne Co., IN; d.21 Aug 2011 Yellow Springs, Greene Co., OH.
      ii. Mari Lynn, b.22 Dec 1955 Richmond, Wayne Co., IN. She d.13 Jul 1994 Richmond, Wayne Co., IN, at age 38.

860. Jennie Nancy "Nannie"⁷ Abner (Robert⁶, James⁵, Richard⁴, Menan³, Elisha² Abney, Abner¹), b.11 Dec 1906 Knox Co., KY. She m1. Huram Clyde "Hutie" Delph on 5 Nov 1923 IN. She m2. James H. Martin ca.1926. She m3. William "Darald" Aldridge in 1934. She m4. George Dewey Mitchell. She d.7 Dec 1993 Clinton, Vermillion Co., IN, at age 86 and was bur. Walnut Grove Cem., Clinton, Vermillion Co., IN.
   Huram Clyde "Hutie" Delph, b.7 Nov 1904 London, Laurel Co., KY. He d.3 Feb 1973 Connersville, Fayette Co., IN, at age 68.
Known child of Jennie Nancy "Nannie"⁷ Abner and Huram Clyde "Hutie" Delph:
1219   i.   Martha "Gloria"⁸, b. 24 Jan 1924 Clinton, Vermillion Co., IN; m. James Van Horn; div. James Van Horn.
   James H. Martin, b.28 Feb 1893 Anderson Co., TN. He d.16 Aug 1932 Terre Haute, Vigo Co., IN; bur. Shepherds Cem., Shepherdsville, IN.
Known child of Jennie Nancy "Nannie"⁷ Abner and James H. Martin:
1220   i.   Wilma "Ruth"⁸, b. 12 Oct 1927 Vermillion Co., IN; m. Raymond F. Rigsby.
   William "Darald" Aldridge, b.10 May 1912 Alberta, BC, Canada; d.28 Aug 1937 Crown Point, Lake Co., IN, age 25; bur. Walnut Grove Cem.
Known child of Jennie Nancy "Nannie"⁷ Abner and William "Darald" Aldridge:
1221   i.   Robert Charles⁸, b. 8 Jun 1935; m. Delores "Lorrie" Topete.
   George Dewey Mitchell, b.1900. He d.1966 and was bur. Walnut Grove Cem., Clinton, Vermillion Co., IN.
There were no known children of Jennie Nancy "Nannie"⁷ Abner and George Dewey Mitchell.

861. PFC Ulis Ambrose "Tad"⁷ Abner (USArmy-WWII) (Robert⁶, James⁵, Richard⁴, Menan³, Elisha² Abney, Abner¹), b.5 Apr 1918 Clinton, Vermillion Co., IN; m. Goldie Ione Payton, d/o William Clifford Payton and Catherine Sutton, on 22 Jul 1945 Clinton, Vermillion Co., IN. He and Goldie were divorced in 1959. He d.29 Sep 1975 Clinton, Vermillion Co., IN, age 57; bur. Walnut Grove Cem., Clinton, Vermillion Co., IN.
   Goldie Ione Payton, b.22 Jun 1924 Clinton, Vermillion Co., IN; d.16 Apr 1995 Clinton, Vermillion Co., IN, age 70; bur. Walnut Grove Cem.
Known children of PFC Ulis Ambrose "Tad"⁷ Abner (USArmy-WWII) and Goldie Ione Payton both b. Clinton, Vermillion Co., IN,:
1222   i.   Sandrea Kay "Sandy"⁸, b. 29 May 1946; m. Fred Dale Cook (USANG).
      ii. Betty Jean "BJ", b.14 Aug 1947.

862. Joseph Homer "Chip"⁷ Abner (Robert⁶, James⁵, Richard⁴, Menan³, Elisha² Abney, Abner¹), b.20 May 1920 Clinton, Vermillion Co., IN. He and his brother, Arnold Thomas Abner were liv. on 10 Apr 1940 lodgers with William Aldridge family, North, Lake Co., IN. He m. Mary Frances D'Angelo on 4 Mar 1952. He d.2 Mar 1966 South Bend, St. Joseph Co., IN, at age 45.
   Mary Frances D'Angelo, b.2 Jan 1929 East Chicago, Lake Co., IN.

Known children of Joseph Homer "Chip"[7] Abner and Mary Frances D'Angelo:
  1223 i. Mary Jo[8], b. 7 Dec 1955 Hammond, Lake Co., IN; m. Patrick K. Dennis; div. Patrick K. Dennis.
     ii. Susan Marie, b.1963 LaPorte, LaPorte Co., IN. She d.1963 LaPorte, LaPorte Co., IN.

863. James "Elmer"[7] Abner (Robert[6], James[5], Richard[4], Menan[3], Elisha[2] Abney, Abner[1]), b.4 Nov 1922 Clinton, Vermillion Co., IN. He m. Betty R. Gray on 5 Oct 1946. They were divorced. He d.11 Jun 1964 Clinton, Vermillion Co., IN, at age 41.
  Betty R. Gray, b.23 Jun 1927 Vermillion Co., IN. She d.7 Jun 2013 Clinton, Vermillion Co., IN, at age 85.
Known children of James "Elmer"[7] Abner and Betty R. Gray both b. Clinton, Vermillion Co., IN:
  1224 i. John Paul[8], b. 9 Jun 1947; m. Carolyn "Jean" Smith.
  1225 ii. Nancy Kay, b. 2 Jul 1950; m. Robert Ferris; div. Robert Ferris.

864. Beulah Irene "Boots"[7] Abner (Robert[6], James[5], Richard[4], Menan[3], Elisha[2] Abney, Abner[1]), b.1 May 1926 Clinton, Vermillion Co., IN. She m. Earl Leon Guinn on 22 Apr 1946. She d.16 Jul 2016 Clinton, Vermillion Co., IN, at age 90.
  Earl Leon Guinn, b.24 Jan 1926 Clinton, Vermillion Co., IN. He d.16 Jul 2000 Terre Haute, Vigo Co., IN, at age 74.
Known children of Beulah Irene "Boots"[7] Abner and Earl Leon Guinn both b. Clinton, Vermillion Co., IN:
  1226 i. Michael Leon[8], b. 3 Dec 1946; m. Martha Louise Steely; m. Darla K. Carrell; div. Darla K. Carrell.
  1227 ii. Tony Lee, b. 2 May 1957; m. Cindy Lynnett Seaton.

865. Verna Bruce[7] Abner (Lloyd[6], Elisha[5], Richard[4], Menan[3], Elisha[2] Abney, Abner[1]), b.18 Jul 1926 Knox Co., KY. She m1. S.Sgt. Leon Arthur Pittman. She m2. (n.n.) Wyatt. d.2 May 2011 at age 84 and was bur. Roseberry Cem., Mascot, Knox Co., TN.
  S.Sgt. Leon Arthur Pittman, b.25 Jun 1906. He d.20 Oct 1973 at age 67 and was bur. Roseberry Cem., Mascot, Knox Co., TN.
There were no known children of Verna Bruce[7] Abner and S.Sgt. Leon Arthur Pittman.
Known children of Verna Bruce[7] Abner and (n.n.) Wyatt:
     i. Garry Lloyd[8], b.24 Feb 1947 London, Laurel Co., KY. He d.Dec 1990 Houston, Harris Co., TX, at age 43 and was bur. Forest Park Cem., Houston, Harris Co., TX.

866. Cholista Maxine[7] Abner (Lloyd[6], Elisha[5], Richard[4], Menan[3], Elisha[2] Abney, Abner[1]), b.12 Jun 1929 Knox Co., KY. She m. George R. Ledford (USN-WWII). d.15 Aug 2007 Corbin, Knox Co., KY, at age 78 and was bur. Rest Haven Cem., Corbin, Knox Co., KY.
  George R. Ledford (USN-WWII), b.4 Feb 1927 Knox Co., KY. He d.11 Nov 1992 Corbin, Knox Co., KY, at age 65; bur. Rest Haven Cem.
Known children of Cholista Maxine[7] Abner and George R. Ledford (USN-WWII):
     i. Lorna Rayleen[8], b.9 Jul 1952 Whitley Co., KY. She d.14 Nov 2015 Corbin, Knox Co., KY, at age 63 and was bur. Rest Haven Cem., Corbin, Knox Co., KY.

867. Glenna Ester[7] Abner (Lloyd[6], Elisha[5], Richard[4], Menan[3], Elisha[2] Abney, Abner[1]), b.31 Mar 1932 Knox Co., KY. She m1. Eugene Smith. She m2. (n.n.) Morgan. d.13 Dec 1986 Cincinnati, Hamilton Co., OH, at age 54; bur. Arlington Mem. Gardens, Mount Healthy, Hamilton Co., OH.
There were no known children of Glenna Ester[7] Abner and Eugene Smith.
Known children of Glenna Ester[7] Abner and (n.n.) Morgan (birth order unknown):
     i. Julie Anne[8] m. (n.n.) Woods.
     ii. Douglas.
     iii. Bradley.
     iv. John Allan, b.15 Nov 1948. He died in an automobile accident on 4 Nov 1977, Lexington, Fayette Co., KY, at age 28 and was bur. Arlington Mem. Gardens, Mount Healthy, Hamilton Co., OH.

868. Walter[7] Abner (Gilbert[6], Charles[5], Richard[4], Menan[3], Elisha[2] Abney, Abner[1]), b.30 Jan 1912 Knox Co., KY. He m. Axie Grubb on 23 Jan 1934. He d.3 Aug 1994 KY at age 82 and was bur. Nan Riley Cem., Woollum, Knox Co., KY.
  Axie Grubb, b.28 Mar 1916 KY. She d.29 Sep 2000 Danville, Boyle Co., KY, at age 84 and was bur. Nan Riley Cem., Woollum.
Known children of Walter[7] Abner and Axie Grubb:
     i. Jean[8], b.13 Dec 1934. She m. Samson Smith. d.6 Mar 2015 at age 80 and was bur. Danville Mem. Gardens, Danville, Boyle Co., KY.
  1228 ii. Andrew "Cotton," b. 23 Aug 1936 Knox Co., KY; m. Annia Cheek; m. Elva Jean Smith; m. Oda Mae Asher.

869. Tommy[7] Abner (Robert[6], Charles[5], Richard[4], Menan[3], Elisha[2] Abney, Abner[1]) m. Hilda Fisher. He, b.9 Sep 1912. He d.19 Sep 1989 at age 77 and was bur. Fisher Cem., Heidrick, Knox Co., KY.
  Hilda Fisher, b.14 Dec 1908. She d.10 Aug 1996 at age 87 and was bur. Fisher Cem., Heidrick, Knox Co., KY.
Known children of Tommy[7] Abner and Hilda Fisher:
     i. Sandra[8], b.27 Jun 1946. She m. Jerry Bowman. d.12 Nov 2014 Gray, Knox Co., KY, at age 68 and was bur. Fisher Cem., Heidrick, Knox Co., KY.

870. PFC John "David"[7] Abner (USArmy-WWII) (Finley[6], Charles[5], Richard[4], Menan[3], Elisha[2] Abney, Abner[1]), b.22 Aug 1924. He m. Beaulah Jackson on 1 Nov 1949. He m. Myrtle Henson in 1995. He d.18 May 2004 at age 79 and was bur. Fisher Cem., Heidrick, Knox Co., KY.
Known children of PFC John "David"[7] Abner (USArmy-WWII) and Beaulah Jackson (birth order unknown):
     i. Carly J.[8] m. Shirley (n.n.).
     ii. John Stephen m. Denise (n.n.).
     iii. Mark D. m. Rhonda (n.n.).
     iv. Brenda Ruth m. Ronnie Corey.
     v. Rebecca L. m. Larry Cain.
  Myrtle Henson, b.14 May 1934 Clay Co., KY. She m. Leonard Smith in 1955. She d.13 Nov 2005 Knox Co., KY, at age 71 and was bur. Goose Rock Cem., Goose Rock, Clay Co., KY.
There were no known children of PFC John "David"[7] Abner (USArmy-WWII) and Myrtle Henson.

871. Charles Franklin[7] Abner (USArmy) (Finley[6], Charles[5], Richard[4], Menan[3], Elisha[2] Abney, Abner[1]), b.21 Jan 1937 KY. He m. Judith Mina Daley. He d.4 Apr 1999 Dayton, Montgomery Co., OH, at age 62 and was bur. Polk Grove Cem., Montgomery Co., OH.
Known children of Charles Franklin[7] Abner (USArmy) and Judith Mina Daley:
      i.   Tammy[8] m. Mitchell Gibson.
      ii. Bonita Jane.

872. George Arthur[7] Abner (USN-WWII) (Theodore[6], Joseph[5], Richard[4], Menan[3], Elisha[2] Abney, Abner[1]), b.26 Jan 1925. He m. Rose Marie "Rosie" Lax in 1946. He d.25 Mar 1991 at age 66 and was bur. Valhalla Mem. Park and Maus., Godfrey, Madison Co., IL.
   Rose Marie "Rosie" Lax, b.23 Apr 1928 IL. She m. John C. Westphal. She d.26 Sep 2014 Alton, Madison Co., IL, at age 86.
Known children of George Arthur[7] Abner (USN-WWII) and Rose Marie "Rosie" Lax:
1229   i.   Ronald Max[8], b. 2 Jul 1947 Calvert City, Marshall Co., KY; m. (n.n.).
        ii. Dianne m. (n.n.) Mortimer. , b.12 Jul 1952. She d.13 Apr 2005 at age 52 and was bur. Valhalla Mem. Park and Maus., Godfrey, Madison Co., IL.

873. Carmel[7] Abner (Lewis[6], James[5], John[4], Menan[3], Elisha[2] Abney, Abner[1]), b.25 Jan 1942 Jackson Co., KY. He m. Norma Whicker ca.1968. He d.24 Aug 2020 Richmond, Wayne Co., IN, at age 78 and was bur. Crown Hill Cem., Centerville, Wayne Co., IN.
Known child of Carmel[7] Abner and Norma Whicker:
1230   i.   Terry[8], m. Christi (n.n.).

874. Airis "Victor"[7] Abnee Jr. (Airis[6], William[5], Lincoln[4], John[3] Abney, Elisha[2], Abner[1]), b.1923 KY. He m. Doris Heuck. He d.2017 and was bur. Edgewood Cem., Cedarville, Mackinac Co., MI.
   Doris Heuck, b.1923. She d.1997 and was bur. Edgewood Cem., Cedarville, Mackinac Co., MI.
Known children of Airis "Victor"[7] Abnee Jr. and Doris Heuck:
      i.   Airis Victor "Trip"[8], b.1952. He d.2008 and was bur. Edgewood Cem., Cedarville, Mackinac Co., MI.

875. Wanda Claudia "C"[7] Abnee (Claude[6], Clarence[5], Lincoln[4], John[3] Abney, Elisha[2], Abner[1]), b.6 Sep 1939 Nicholas Co., KY. She m. Gerald Richard Jefferson. d.11 Sep 2008 Sadieville, Scott Co., KY, at age 69.
Known children of Wanda Claudia "C"[7] Abnee and Gerald Richard Jefferson:
      i.   Terry W.[8], b.1957 Nicholas Co., KY.
1231   ii. Jerome Gantry, b. 1961 Nicholas Co., KY; m. (n.n.).
        iii. Tyrone Gregory, b.1961 Nicholas Co., KY.
        iv. Kimberly Gail, b.1968 Franklin Co, KY.
        v. Chandi Nicole, b.1973 Fayette Co., KY.

876. Dorothy Belle[7] Abnee (Claude[6], Clarence[5], Lincoln[4], John[3] Abney, Elisha[2], Abner[1]), b.10 Nov 1940 Carlisle, Nicholas Co., KY. She m. William Lee "Bill" Earlywine (b.14 Jun 1936). She d.23 Jul 2016 St. Joseph Hospice Care Center, Lexington, Fayette Co., KY, at age 75 and was bur. Evergreen Memory Gardens, Paris, Bourbon Co., KY.
Known children of Dorothy Belle[7] Abnee and William Lee "Bill" Earlywine:
1232   i.   Laura[8], m. (n.n.) Clark.
        ii. Jessica Renee, b.27 Mar 1979 Fayette Co., KY.

877. Jerry Wayne[7] Abnee (Claude[6], Clarence[5], Lincoln[4], John[3] Abney, Elisha[2], Abner[1]) m. Lydia Vice. He, b.24 Jul 1947 Carlisle, Nicholas Co., KY. He d.2 Jul 2018 Lexington, Fayette Co., KY, at age 70 and was bur. Carlisle Cem., Carlisle, Nicholas Co., KY.
Known children of Jerry Wayne[7] Abnee and Lydia Vice (birth order unknown):
      i.   Zoe R.[8].
      ii. Jeffrey.

878. William Conley "Conn"[7] Abnee (Shy[6], Clarence[5], Lincoln[4], John[3] Abney, Elisha[2], Abner[1]), He m. Barbara (n.n.). He was Executive Director of *National Steel Bridge Alliance*, Mount Olivet, Robertson Co., KY. He was Executive Director of *Geothermal Heat Pump Consortium*.
Known children of William Conley "Conn"[7] Abnee and Barbara (birth order unknown):
      i.   Leslie[8] m. (n.n.) Thornton.
      ii. Amanda. She m. Mark Gumbert. In 2018, she was an Extension Water Quality Specialist, Lexington, Fayette Co., KY.. From *Water in Kentucky: Natural History, Communities, and Conservation*:
          AMANDA ABNEE GUMBERT is an extension specialist for water quality at the University. Her area of emphasis is agricultural water--quality issues, with special interests in riparian areas and watershed management. Her work focuses on education and outreach efforts to protect Kentucky's -water resources. She received BS and MS degrees in Plant and Soil Science and a PhD in Soil Science from the University. Gumbert grew up on a farm in rural northeastern Kentucky, to which she attributes her appreciation of the land and natural resources. She currently lives in Lexington, Kentucky.
1233   iii. Justin, m. Jennifer Beaty.

879. Estella Rodella "Stella"[7] Kelley (Matilda[6] Murray, Malinda[5] Hunt, Nancy[4] Abner, John[3] Abney, Elisha[2], Abner[1]), b.2 Feb 1887 Seligman, Barry Co., MO. She m1. Olin Toliver Lewis Sr. on 2 Nov 1903 Dawson, Tulsa Co., Indian Territory. She m2. Clarence Edward Watts in Jul 1937 Pawhuska, Osage Co., OK. She d.21 Feb 1981 Tulsa, Tulsa Co., OK, at age 94 and was bur. Rose Hill Mem. Park, Tulsa, Tulsa Co., OK.
   Olin Toliver Lewis Sr, b.7 Apr 1880 Abilene, Taylor Co., TX; d.18 Aug 1932 Pawhuska, Osage Co., OK; bur. Oaklawn Cem., Tulsa, OK.
Known children of Estella Rodella "Stella"[7] Kelley and Olin Toliver Lewis Sr.:
      i.   Teece[8], b.1907 Dawson, Tulsa Co., OK.
1234   ii. Olin Toliver, b. 11 Nov 1918 Pawhuska, Osage Co., OK; m. Marjory May "Peggy" Starbuck; m. Florine Rosa Colburn.
   Clarence Edward Watts, b.21 Apr 1906 Webster Co., MO. He d.23 Jul 1970 Tulsa, Tulsa Co., OK, at age 64; bur. Rose Hill Mem. Park, Tulsa.
There were no known children of Estella Rodella "Stella"[7] Kelley and Clarence Edward Watts.

880. Walter I.[7] Bishop Sr. (USN) (James[6], David[5], Abraham[4], Mary[3] Abner, Elisha[2] Abney, Abner[1]), b.30 Aug 1900 KY. He m1. Mollie Gay on 4 Sep 1925 Owsley Co., KY. He m2. Dora Carmack on 20 Oct 1934. He and Dora Carmack appeared on the census of 20 Apr 1940 Owsley Co., KY. He d.10 Apr 1986 at age 85 and was bur. Deerfield Cem., South Lebanon, Warren Co., OH.
    Mollie Gay, b.2 Apr 1904 Owsley Co., KY. She d.4 Sep 1929 Owsley Co., KY, at age 25.
Known children of Walter I.[7] Bishop Sr. (USN) and Mollie Gay both b. Owsley Co., KY,:
>   i.   Albert[8], b.1 Nov 1926.
>   ii. Elsie M., b.1928.
    Dora Carmack, b.29 Mar 1911. She d.14 Oct 2000 at age 89 and was bur. Deerfield Cem., South Lebanon, Warren Co., OH.
Known children of Walter I.[7] Bishop Sr. (USN) and Dora Carmack:
>   i.   Vera Gleennita[8], b.30 Jul 1935. She d.2016.
>   ii. Walter I. Jr., b.1936. He d.1992.
>   iii. James Pershing, b.1942. He d.2005.
>   iv. Janie (gen.), b. KY. She m. (n.n.) Campbell. The author worked with Cousin Janie in the mid-1990's. The author is grateful for the information she provided on the line of Samuel "Sam" Bishop and Mary "Polly" Abner (#10). She shared her information abundantly to further the research on her line. She is to be recognized for her wonderful work.
>   v.   Bruce W., b.1950. He d.1996.

881. Rosa Belle[7] Bishop (Robert[6], John[5], Abraham[4], Mary[3] Abner, Elisha[2] Abney, Abner[1]), b.27 Jun 1918 KY. She m. Oakie Johnson on 16 Apr 1936 Felty, Clay Co., KY. She and Oakie Johnson appeared on the census of 24 Apr 1940 Clay Co., KY. She d.18 Jun 1976 at age 57 and was bur. Deerfield Cem., South Lebanon, Warren Co., OH.
    Oakie Johnson, b.25 Jul 1911 Clay Co., KY. He d.8 Aug 2001 South Lebanon, Warren Co., OH, at age 90 and was bur. Deerfield Cem.
Known children of Rosa Belle[7] Bishop and Oakie Johnson:
> 1235 i.   Orvas[8], b. ca.1938 KY; m. Laura E. Metcalf (gen.).
>   ii. Rondal, b.1944. He d.2009.
>   iii. Della Jean, b.1945. She d.2015.
>   iv. Phillip, b.1953. He d.2017.

882. Charles "Charley"[7] Abner (William[6], Esther[5] Bishop, Bryson[4], Mary[3] Abner, Elisha[2] Abney, Abner[1]), b.15 Dec 1906 Clay Co., KY; m. Dolly Gladys Helton 1928 Barboursville, Knox Co., KY. They appeared on the census of 18 Apr 1940 Vienna, Scott Co., IN. He d.19 Aug 1992 age 85.
    Dolly Gladys Helton, b.25 Jan 1908 Woodbine, Knox Co., KY. She d.New Year's Eve, 31 Dec 1991 at age 83.
Known children of Charles "Charley"[7] Abner and Dolly Gladys Helton:
>   i.   Robert[8], b. ca.1932.
>   ii. Donald, b. ca.1934.
>   iii. McKinley, b. ca.1936.
>   iv. Leona J., b. ca.1940.

883. Malcolm[7] Abner (William[6], Esther[5] Bishop, Bryson[4], Mary[3] Abner, Elisha[2] Abney, Abner[1]), b. ca.1911 Clay Co., KY. He m. Elva (n.n.) (b. ca.1918 KY). They appeared on the census of 4 Apr 1940 Clay Co., KY. Known children of Malcolm[7] Abner and Elva (n.n.) both b. KY:
>   i.   Alvie[8], b. ca.1936.
>   ii. Basel, b. ca.1939.

884. Lucy[7] Abner (William[6], Esther[5] Bishop, Bryson[4], Mary[3] Abner, Elisha[2] Abney, Abner[1]), b.12 Feb 1913 Clay Co., KY. She m. Anderson Allen. d.16 Mar 1985 Independence, Kenton Co., KY, at age 72 and was bur. Maxaline Baker Cem., Oneida, Clay Co., KY.
    Anderson Allen, b.10 Sep 1900. He d.19 Aug 1970 at age 69 and was bur. Maxaline Baker Cem., Oneida, Clay Co., KY.
Known children of Lucy[7] Abner and Anderson Allen:
>   i.   Van[8], b.1934. He d.2008.
>   ii. Shirley, b.1936. She d.2016.

885. Marjorie K.[7] Johnson (gen.) (James[6], Mary[5] Smith, Charles[4], Margaret[3] Abner, Elisha[2] Abney, Abner[1]), b.27 Jan 1923 Woodford Co., KY. She m. PFC Joseph Walter Diamond (USArmy). Cousin Marjorie Johnson Diamond is one of the Abney family researchers of the *Greatest Generation* (see page viii). The author began working with her in 1996 when she lived in Midway, Woodford Co., KY; and continued working with her until contact was lost during Hurricane Katrina (2005). Cousin Marjorie was a great pleasure to work with, and instrumental in forming the author's knowledge of Margaret Larken Abner (see pages xvii, 1, 19, 22, 25, 36 and #11 in this chapter on pages 41, 43-44). Cousin Marjorie loved her family history and was always willing to share and expand her knowledge. She was a blessing to this author and to the descendants of Margaret Larken Abner m. Isham O. Smith. Cousin Marjorie d.19 Jan 2011 at age 87 and was bur. Midway Cem., Midway, Woodford Co., KY.
    PFC Joseph Walter Diamond (USArmy), b.10 Dec 1918 Franklin Co., KY. He d. Christmas Day, 25 Dec 1983 Fayette Co., KY, at age 65 and was bur. Midway Cem., Midway, Woodford Co., KY.
Known child of Marjorie K.[7] Johnson (gen.) and PFC Joseph Walter Diamond (USArmy):
>   i.   James Walter[8], b.19 Apr 1941 Versailles, Woodford Co., KY. He d.20 Aug 2018 Georgetown, Scott Co., KY, at age 77.

886. Theodore "Ted"[7] Abner (Steve[6], Theodore[5], Enoch[4], Enoch[3] Abney, Elisha[2], Abner[1]), b.6 Jan 1919 Woodlawn, Campbell Co., KY. He m. Marie Hoskins on 12 Dec 1946. [author's note: Theodore was misnumbered. He should have been #901. Do not be confused.]
Known children of Theodore[7] Abner and Marie Hoskins:
>   i.   Steve Tyson (gen.)[8], b.3 Oct 1948 South Lyon, Oakland Co., MI. He m./div. & had a dau. Steve worked with John Hensell, as he appears in Hensell's books. The author began working with Steve in 2019. Steve graciously sent information on his family to the author. His data corrects several typographical errors in Hensell's book.
>   ii. Fred Tyson, b.16 Apr 1947 South Lyon, MI. He m. Julie Ann Stevens on 2 Jul 1966.
>   iii. Jack. He married, divorced and remarried. He and n.n. (w/o Jack Abner) . He, b.6 Jun 1950 KY.
>   iv. Ted, b.6 Sep 1952. He d.13 Mar 1971 at age 18.

887. Ive H. "IV"[7] Abner (John[6], William[5], Enoch[4], Enoch[3] Abney, Elisha[2], Abner[1]), b.20 Jul 1897 Clay Co., KY. He m1. Fronia Stacy on 20 Apr 1922 Manchester, Clay Co., KY. He and Fronia Stacy appeared on the censuses of 4 Apr 1930 Clay Co., KY; and 6 Apr 1940 Manchester, Clay Co., KY. He m2. Alta House on 20 Oct 1940 Manchester, Clay Co., KY. He d.24 Mar 1955 at age 57.

   Fronia Stacy, b.24 Jan 1906 KY. She d.12 Jun 1938 at age 32 and was bur. Paces Creek Cem., Garrard, Clay Co., KY.
Known children of Ive H. "IV"[7] Abner and Fronia Stacy all b. Clay Co., KY:
     i.   Clarence Ricketts[8], b. ca.1923. He m1. Abert Griffith (b.28 Jan 1924 WV) on 10 Nov 1956 Maumee, Lucas Co., OH. He m2. Theresa Marie Costa (b. ca.1940) on 5 Oct 1959 NH.
     ii.   Bernice, b. ca.1924. She m. Irvin Mader (b. ca.1912) on 30 Oct 1942 Sandusky, Erie Co., OH.
     iii.   Doris, b. ca. Mar 1928. She m1. Herbert Gray (b. ca.1924) on 31 Jul 1943 Manchester, Clay Co., KY. She m2. George T. Curry (b. ca.1923) on 6 Sep 1947 Manchester, Clay Co., KY. She d.2000.
     iv.   Ralph, b. ca.Mar 1930.
     v.   Lois Faye "Flossie", b. ca.1935. She d.2003.
   Alta House, b. ca.1903. She m1. (n.n.) Hyde.
There were no known children of Ive H. "IV"[7] Abner and Alta House.

888. Belle[7] Abner (John[6], William[5], Enoch[4], Enoch[3] Abney, Elisha[2], Abner[1]), b. ca.1901 Clay Co., KY. She m. Shirley Gray (1894-1974) on 21 Dec 1920 Clay Co., KY.
Known children of Belle[7] Abner and Shirley Gray:
     i.   Cecil G.[8], b.1921. He d.1923.
     ii.   Cleo, b.1921. She d.1965.
     iii.   Beulah, b.1924. She d.1941.
     iv.   Shirley, b.1928. He d.2002.
     v.   Edward, b.1930. He d.2009.
     vi.   Charles, b.1930. He d.2009.
     vii.   Hobert M., b.1933. He d.2001.
     viii.   Evelyne, b.1935. She d.2006.
     ix.   Bernice, b.1937. She d.2015.

889. Daniel[7] Abner (John[6], William[5], Enoch[4], Enoch[3] Abney, Elisha[2], Abner[1]), b. ca.1907 Clay Co., KY; m. Rosa Smith (b. ca.1914)
Known child of Daniel[7] Abner and Rosa Smith:
     i.   Clyde[8], b. New Year's Eve, 31 Jan 1931 Manchester, Clay Co., KY. He d.7 Apr 1997 Clay Co., KY, at age 66.

890. Shiloh Junior[7] Abner (John[6], William[5], Enoch[4], Enoch[3] Abney, Elisha[2], Abner[1]), b.3 Aug 1915 Clay Co., KY. He m. Lizzie (n.n.) (b. ca.1878 KY). He and Lizzie appeared on the census of 26 Apr 1940 Clay Co., KY. He d.1 May 1956 Pineville, Bell Co., KY, at age 40.
Known child of Shiloh Junior[7] Abner and Lizzie (n.n.):
     i.   Clarence[8], b. ca.1923 Clay Co., KY.

891. Shirley[7] Abner (John[6], William[5], Enoch[4], Enoch[3] Abney, Elisha[2], Abner[1]), b.8 Dec 1919 Clay Co., KY. He m. Dona Mills (1919-2004). He d.6 Jun 1991 Manchester, Clay Co., KY, at age 71.
Known child of Shirley[7] Abner and Dona Mills:
     i.   Wanda[8], b.1958. She d.1960.

892. Sawyers A.[7] Lawson (Dora[6] Abner, Milton[5], Enoch[4], Enoch[3] Abney, Elisha[2], Abner[1]), b. ca.1922 KY; m. Tressie Asher.
   Tressie Asher, b.7 Nov 1925 Clay Co., KY. She m1. (#895) Beve "PJ" Abner (USAF-Korea), son of Taylor Abner and Minnie Herd and had issue. d.15 Aug 2020 Burning Springs, Clay Co., KY, at age 94 and was bur. Asher Cem., Cottongim, Clay Co., KY.
Known child of Sawyers A.[7] Lawson and Tressie Asher:
     i.   John[8].

893. Milton "Elijah"[7] Abner (Taylor[6], Milton[5], Enoch[4], Enoch[3] Abney, Elisha[2], Abner[1]), b.9 Aug 1913 Clay Co., KY; m. Edna Mae Harris. He and Edna Mae Harris appeared on the census of 8 Apr 1940 Clay Co., KY. He d.30 Aug 1973 at age 60 and was bur. Hurd Cem., Sibert, Clay Co., KY.
   Edna Mae Harris, b.24 Jun 1917.
Known children of Milton "Elijah"[7] Abner and Edna Mae Harris:
     i.   Ella "Flora"[8], b.1935. She d.1966 and was bur. White-Hubbard Cem., Cottongim, Clay Co., KY.
     ii.   Junior, b.1 Jun 1943 Clay Co., KY. He d.2 Jul 1943 Clay Co., KY.

894. Edna[7] Abner (Taylor[6], Milton[5], Enoch[4], Enoch[3] Abney, Elisha[2], Abner[1]), b.25 Oct 1915 Clay Co., KY. She m. Beve Smith. She d.27 Aug 1965 at age 49 and was bur. Hampton Cem., Girdler, Knox Co., KY.
   Beve Smith, b.17 Jan 1912. He d.26 Sep 1969 at age 57 and was bur. Hampton Cem., Girdler, Knox Co., KY.
Known children of Edna[7] Abner and Beve Smith:
     i.   Belve Gene[8], b.3 Sep 1946. He d.18 Jul 2007 Knox Co., KY, at age 60; bur. Hampton Cem., Girdler, Knox Co., KY.

895. Beve "PJ"[7] Abner (USAF-Korea) (Taylor[6], Milton[5], Enoch[4], Enoch[3] Abney, Elisha[2], Abner[1]), b.13 Feb 1932 Clay Co., KY. He m. Tressie Asher. He d.28 Nov 2000 Clay Co., KY, at age 68 and was bur. Asher Cem., Cottongim, Clay Co., KY.
   Tressie Asher, b.7 Nov 1925 Clay Co., KY. She m2. Beve's 1st cousin, (#892) Sawyers A. Lawson, son of John C. Lawson and Dora E. Abner. d.15 Aug 2020 Burning Springs, Clay Co., KY, at age 94 and was bur. Asher Cem., Cottongim, Clay Co., KY.
Known children of Beve "PJ"[7] Abner (USAF-Korea) and Tressie Asher:
     i.   Paul[8].
     ii.   Leon.

896. Warner Oland "Big O"[7] Abner (John[6], Milton[5], Enoch[4], Enoch[3] Abney, Elisha[2], Abner[1]), b.22 Aug 1938 Clay Co., KY. He m1. Laura Philpot. He m2. Shawanna Swafford. He d.7 May 2016 Lexington, Fayette Co., KY, at age 77 and was bur. Engine Cem., Bluehole, Clay Co., KY. Known children of Warner Oland "Big O"[7] Abner and Laura Philpot:

    i.   Lisa[8] m. (n.n.) Edwards.
    ii. David "Tiny."
    iii. Gene.
    iv. Rebecca m. (n.n.) Ferrell.

There were no known children of Warner Oland "Big O"[7] Abner and Shawanna Swafford.

897. Ethel[7] Abner (Thomas[6], Theophilus[5], Enoch[4], Enoch[3] Abney, Elisha[2], Abner[1]), b.27 Jul 1909 Clay Co., KY. She m. Pearl B. Fee on 21 Apr 1928 Harlan, Harlan Co., KY. She and Pearl B. Fee appeared on the census of 22 Apr 1930 Harlan Co., KY. She and Pearl B. Fee appeared on the census of 16 Apr 1940 Kitts, Harlan Co., KY. She d.27 Nov 1978 Laurel Co., KY, at age 69 and was bur. C.D. Ward Cem., Laurel Co., KY.
    Pearl B. Fee, b.1904 VA. He d.1979 and was bur. C.D. Ward Cem., Laurel Co., KY.
Known children of Ethel[7] Abner and Pearl B. Fee:

    i.   Kenneth Eugene[8], b. ca.Nov 1929 Harlan Co., KY.
    ii. Curtis "Marvin", b.1931. He d.1989.
    iii. William "Carl", b.1934.
    iv. Pearl "Earl", b.1936. She d.2000.
    v. Wilma Jean, b. ca.Aug 1939 Harlan Co., KY.
    vi. Donald Ray, b.1941. He d.1962.

898. Leonard[7] Abner (Steven[6], Theophilus[5], Enoch[4], Enoch[3] Abney, Elisha[2], Abner[1]), b.8 Aug 1911. He m. Nannie Cottongim on Christmas Eve, 24 Dec 1929. He and Nannie Cottongim were liv. on 12 Apr 1930 with father, Stephen Abner, Woollum, Knox Co., KY. He and Nannie Cottongim appeared on the census of 24 Apr 1940 Clay Co., KY. He d.9 Aug 1996 at age 85 and was bur. Bundy-Delph Cem., Cottongim, Clay Co., KY.
    Nannie Cottongim, b.6 Apr 1912. She d.2 Oct 1990 at age 78 and was bur. Bundy-Delph Cem., Cottongim, Clay Co., KY.
Known children of Leonard[7] Abner and Nannie Cottongim both b. KY:

    i.   Amanda[8], b. ca.1931.
    ii. Harvie G., b. ca.1934.

899. Anna Beatrice[7] Abner (Steven[6], Theophilus[5], Enoch[4], Enoch[3] Abney, Elisha[2], Abner[1]), b.19 Aug 1913. She m. Crit Barnes (b.1913) on 1 Jul 1936 Knox Co., KY. She d.1 Aug 1988 Butler Co., OH, at age 74 and was bur. Millville Cem., Millville, Butler Co., OH.
Known children of Anna Beatrice[7] Abner and Crit Barnes:

    i.   Byrl Carson[8], b.1938.
    ii. Jennetta, b.1940.

900. Chester[7] Abner (USArmy-WWII) (Steven[6], Theophilus[5], Enoch[4], Enoch[3] Abney, Elisha[2], Abner[1]), b.16 May 1916. He m. Lorene Cottongim on 7 Jan 1947 Manchester, Clay Co., KY. He d.13 Nov 1994 at age 78 and was bur. Cottongim Cem., Cottongim, Clay Co., KY.
    Lorene Cottongim, b.3 Feb 1931 Cottongim, Clay Co., KY. She d.18 Oct 2015 Lexington, Fayette Co., KY, at age 84.
Known children of Chester[7] Abner (USArmy-WWII) and Lorene Cottongim:

    i.   Wilma[8] m. (n.n.) Hatfield.
    ii. Eugene.
    iii. Ronnie Joe m. Yvonne (n.n.).
    iv. Wanda m. John Tye.
    v. Lisa m. (n.n.) Ellis.

901. Lucy Katherine[7] Abner (Steven[6], Theophilus[5], Enoch[4], Enoch[3] Abney, Elisha[2], Abner[1]), b.14 Jul 1921 Knox Co., KY. She m. Rev. Riley H. Parker on 21 Oct 1939. She d.26 Feb 2006 Oxford, Butler Co., OH, at age 84 and was bur. Millville Cem., Millville, Butler Co., OH.
    Rev. Riley H. Parker, b.10 Feb 1923 Manchester, Clay Co., KY. He d.7 Jun 2015 at age 92 and was bur. Millville Cem., Millville.
Known children of Lucy Katherine[7] Abner and Rev. Riley H. Parker:

    i.   Glen Dale[8], b.1941. He d.2003.
    ii. Gaston Bowling, b.1960. He d.2000.

902. General Ralph "Jersey Bull"[7] Abner (Steven[6], Theophilus[5], Enoch[4], Enoch[3] Abney, Elisha[2], Abner[1]), b.14 Jun 1924 Knox Co., KY. He m. Minnie Pearl "Pearlie" White on 24 May 1947 Manchester, Clay Co., KY. He d.2 Dec 1992 Knox Co., KY, at age 68 and was bur. Abner Family Cem., Woollum, Knox Co., KY.
    Minnie Pearl "Pearlie" White, b.10 Sep 1926. She d.17 Mar 1998 at age 71 and was bur. Abner Family Cem., Woollum, Knox Co., KY.
Known children of General Ralph "Jersey Bull"[7] Abner and Minnie Pearl "Pearlie" White:

  1236 i.   Lucy Thelma[8], b. 11 Feb 1952 Clay Co., KY; m. Robert E. Gabbard.
         ii. Michael, b.27 Apr 1956 Knox Co., KY. He d.31 Oct 1977 Barbourville, Knox Co., KY, age 21; bur. Abner Family Cem.
         iii. Charles, b. KY.

903. Malvia L.[7] Abner (Steven[6], Theophilus[5], Enoch[4], Enoch[3] Abney, Elisha[2], Abner[1]), b.6 Apr 1927. She m1. Henry E. Jarvis in 1942. She m2. Homer R. Wolfe in 1977. She d.2 Feb 1985 at age 57 and was bur. James Reid Cem., Manchester, Clay Co., KY.
    Henry E. Jarvis, b.6 Nov 1924 Manchester, Clay Co., KY. He d.15 Jan 1963 Manchester, Clay Co., KY, at age 38.
Known children of Malvia L.[7] Abner and Henry E. Jarvis:

    i.   Everett[8], b.1942. He d.1986.
    ii. Malvia, b.1944. She d.1944.

    Homer R. Wolfe, b.8 Aug 1920 Clay Co., KY. He d.2 Sep 2014 Hazard, Perry Co., KY, at age 94 and was bur. James Reid Cem., Manchester. There were no known children of Malvia L.[7] Abner and Homer R. Wolfe.

904. Corinne[7] McKinney (Melford[6], David[5], Tamar[4] McClenachan, Sarah[3] Abney, John[2], Abner[1]), b.31 Jan 1903. She m. Aston Enlo Logsdon in 1923. She d.Christmas Eve, 24 Dec 1992 at age 89 and was bur. Resthaven Mem. Cem., Louisville, Jefferson Co., KY.
     Aston Enlo Logsdon, b.25 Feb 1901 KY. He d.2 Oct 1969 Shelbyville, Shelby Co., KY, at age 68.
Known children of Corinne[7] McKinney and Aston Enlo Logsdon:
       i.   Loretta[8], b.1924. She d.1948.
      ii.   Mildred, b.1926. She d.2004.
     iii. Lawrence Alex, b.1928. He d.1979.

905. William Glenn[7] Kinsolving Sr. (Finis[6], William[5], Mary[4] Abney, William[3], John[2], Abner[1]), b.15 Aug 1918 Lyon Co., KY. He m1. Anda Mae (n.n.) ca.1939 Lyon Co., KY. He and Anda Mae were liv. on 24 Apr 1940 with his mother, *Pearl Kinsolving*, Lyon Co., KY. He m2. Mary E. McClure. He m3. Cleopartra Frances Moore. He d.1 Jul 2000 Evansville, Vanderburgh Co., IN, at age 81 and was bur. Rosedale Cem., Dawson Springs, Hopkins Co., KY.
Known children of William Glenn[7] Kinsolving Sr. (unsure which wife mothered these children):
       i.   Regina[8] m. (n.n.) Garrison.
      ii.   Tony.
Known child of William Glenn[7] Kinsolving Sr. and Anda Mae (n.n.):
       i.   Janet Yvonne[8], b. ca.Feb 1940 Lyon Co., KY; m. (n.n.) Madden.
Known child of William Glenn[7] Kinsolving Sr. and Mary E. McClure:
  1237   i.   William Glenn "Billy" Jr. (gen.)[8], m1. (n.n.); m2. (n.n.); m3. Dawn Marie McCuiston.
     Cleopartra Frances Moore, b.16 Mar 1922. She d.17 Nov 1998 at age 76 and was bur. Rosedale Cem., Dawson Springs, Hopkins Co., KY.
There were no known children of William Glenn[7] Kinsolving Sr. and Cleopartra Frances Moore.

906. John "Abney"[7] Clarkson (Mary[6] Abney, Ulysses[5], William[4], William[3], John[2], Abner[1]), b.9 Aug 1886 Roseland, Nelson Co., VA. He was liv. on 2 May 1910 with uncle, William G. Abney, South River, Augusta Co., VA. He m. Alethia Potter in 1913. He d.29 Sep 1939 Baltimore, MD, at age 53 and was bur. Thornrose Cem., City of Staunton, VA.
     Alethia Potter, b.18 Aug 1880 Washington, DC. She d.5 Jun 1962 City of Staunton, VA, at age 81 and was bur. Thornrose Cem.
Known children of John "Abney"[7] Clarkson and Alethia Potter both b. Augusta Co., VA:
       i.   Mary Abney[8], b.20 Mar 1914. She m. Charles Robert Smith. d.1 Aug 1997 City of Staunton, VA, at age 83 and was bur. Thornrose Cem., City of Staunton, VA.
               Charles Robert Smith, b.14 Jul 1904. He d.26 Oct 1940 at age 36 and was bur. Thornrose Cem.
      ii.   Alethia Potter, b.5 Jun 1916. She d.17 Dec 1977 Augusta Co., VA, at age 61 and was bur. Thornrose Cem.

907. Virginia Penn "GeeGee"[7] Abney (Shelton[6], William[5], Shelton[4], William[3], John[2], Abner[1]) was School Teacher. , b.28 Mar 1909 Napton, Saline Co., MO. She m. John William Bryant, son of Henry Pryor Bryant and Mabel Florence Garrison, on 14 Nov 1936 Napton, Saline Co., MO. She d.4 Jan 2006 GA at age 96 and was bur. Mem. Presbyterian Ch. Cem., Napton, Saline Co., MO.
     John William Bryant, b.18 Apr 1909 Marshall, Saline Co., MO. He d.2000 and was bur. in 2001 Mem. Presbyterian Ch. Cem., Napton.
Known children Penn "GeeGee"[7] Abney and John William Bryant:
  1238   i.   Sheila Louise[8], b. 28 Sep 1937 Jefferson City, MO; m. Leroy Charles Weissinger; div. Leroy Charles Weissinger.
  1239   ii.   John Michael "Mike," b. 22 Dec 1945 Evanston, IL; m. Margaret Louise Hanning.

908. Thomas Smith "Tom"[7] Abney (Shelton[6], William[5], Shelton[4], William[3], John[2], Abner[1]) was Farmer. He, b.18 Feb 1911 Napton, Saline Co., MO. He m. Marie Mildred Ballowe, daughter of LeRobie Ballowe and Alpha Edna Miles, on 26 Dec 1942 Marshall, Saline Co., MO. He d.21 Jun 1986 Marshall, Saline Co., MO, at age 75 and was bur. Mem. Presbyterian Ch. Cem., Napton, Saline Co., MO.
     Marie Mildred Ballowe, b.2 Jun 1920 New Frankfort, Saline Co., MO. She m. (n.n.).
Known children of Thomas Smith "Tom"[7] Abney and Marie Mildred Ballowe all b. Marshall, Saline Co., MO,:
  1240   i.   Robert Dale[8], b. 31 Jul 1937; m. Delores Cohron; div. Delores Cohron; m. Bonnie Leslie MacLean.
  1241   ii.   Donald Wayne, b. 16 Oct 1940; m1. and div. Willie Dean Moore; m2. and div. Sharon Jean Rollins; m3. Lee Ann Morgan.
  1242 iii. Thomas Shelton, b. 10 Mar 1944; m. Terry Harlene Ross.
      iv. Alpha "Pat", b.16 Mar 1949; m. Sharon E. Compton, d/o Burwin Rex Compton and Aurie Belle Eubanks, on 16 Mar 1975.

909. 2nd Lt. Shelton Spillsbury[7] Abney Jr. (USArmy-WWII) (Shelton[6], William[5], Shelton[4], William[3], John[2], Abner[1]), b.16 Jun 1915 Napton, Saline Co., MO. He was a Missouri State Highway Patrolman. He was liv. on 8 Apr 1940 Bethany, Harrison Co., MO. He m. Nadine Colville Lee on 18 May 1940. He d.27 Jan 1965 Harrisonville, Cass Co., MO, at age 49 and was bur. Sunset Hill Cem., Warrensburg, Johnson Co., MO.
     Nadine Colville Lee, b.4 May 1914. She d.6 Sep 1993 at age 79 and was bur. Sunset Hill Cem., Warrensburg, Johnson Co., MO.
Known child of 2nd Lt. Shelton Spillsbury[7] Abney Jr. (USArmy-WWII) and Nadine Colville Lee both b. MO:
  1243   i.   Nancy Ann[8], m. Robert Reynold Bahl.
      ii.   Edwin Lee.

910. William Lycurgus "Billy"[7] Abney III (USAAC-Korea) (William[6], William[5], Shelton[4], William[3], John[2], Abner[1]), b.20 Aug 1915 Blackwater, Cooper Co., MO. He m. Elizabeth Anne Stillwell on 2 May 1943 Tucson, Pima Co., AZ. He d.5 Dec 1998 Denver, Denver Co., CO, at age 83.
     Elizabeth Anne Stillwell also went by the name of Betty . , b.25 Feb 1919 Waukon, Allamakee Co., IA. She d.13 Apr 1992 AZ at age 73.
Known children of William Lycurgus "Billy"[7] Abney III (USAAC-Korea) and Elizabeth Anne Stillwell:
       i.   William Lycurgus[8], b.10 Dec 1946. He m. Jean Ann Larson on 21 May 1977.
      ii.   Lewis Brent, b.29 Jul 1950.

911. Kate Howard[7] Abney (Harry[6], William[5], Shelton[4], William[3], John[2], Abner[1]), b.15 Oct 1915 Napton, Saline Co., MO. She m1. 2nd Lt. Otho Pence (USAAF-WWII) in 1942. She worked with the American Red Cross. She m2. Capt. James Arthur "Jim" Malcolm (BAF), son of William Douglas Finch-Malcolm and Annie Frances Prodger, on 19 Oct 1947 Brantford, Brant Co., ON, Canada.
     2nd Lt. Otho Pence (USAAF-WWII), b.1915 MO. He d. New Year's Day, 1 Jan 1943 in battle (North Africa), Tunis, Tunisia and was bur. Jefferson Barracks National Cem., Lemay, St. Louis Co., MO.

There were no known children of Kate Howard[7] Abney and 2nd Lt. Otho Pence (USAAF-WWII).

Capt. James Arthur "Jim" Malcolm (BAF-WWII), b.2 Dec 1919 Sydenham, County Kent, England, UK; James was a captain in the Royal Warwickshire Regiment of the British Army.

Known children of Kate Howard[7] Abney and Capt. James Arthur "Jim" Malcolm (BAF-WWII):

 i. Douglas William[8], b.16 Dec 1948 Brantford, ON, Canada. He m. Carol Jordan on 5 Jun 1971 Stratford, ON, Canada.
 ii. Victoria Mary, b.24 Apr 1950 Brantford, ON, Canada. She lived in 1978 London, England, UK.
 iii. Keith Howard, b.20 Jun 1952 Toronto, ON, Canada. He m. Mary Anne Lindecker on 18 Jun 1977 Monroe, Monroe Co., MI. He lived in 1978 Toronto, ON, Canada.
    Mary Anne Lindecker, b. Toledo, Lucas Co., OH.
 iv. Nancy Elizabeth, b.5 Feb 1955 Toronto, ON, Canada. She lived in 1978 St. Catherines, ON, Canada.

912. Mary Frances[7] Abney (Harry[6], William[5], Shelton[4], William[3], John[2], Abner[1]), b.8 Apr 1919 Napton, Saline Co., MO. She m. Fred Leroy Hillis (USAAF), son of Sam Hillis and Hattie Franklin, on 10 Nov 1942 San Antonio, Bexas Co., TX.

Fred Leroy Hillis (USAAF), b.6 Aug 1917 Broseley, Butler Co., MO. He d.28 Feb 1972 at age 54 and was bur. on 2 Mar 1972 Dallas, TX.
Known children of Mary Frances[7] Abney and Fred Leroy Hillis (USAAF):

 1244 i. Cynthia Ann[8], b. 9 Sep 1943 Eglin Field, FL; m. William Ray Harper Sr; div. William Ray Harper Sr; m. Robert McBride.
 ii. Frederic Lawrence, b.2 Mar 1947 Columbia, MO.
 iii. Mary Frances, b.30 Jan 1950 St. Louis, MO. She m. Miles Edwin Johnson on 30 May 1970 St. Louis, MO, but no issue. She and Miles Edwin Johnson were divorced in 1973.
 1245 iv. Valerie Hood, b. 7 Jul 1955 Dallas, TX; m. Ray Brayn Sizemore Jr.
 v. Virginia Lynn, b.15 Jul 1957 Houston, TX.

913. Margaret Hood "Madge"[7] Abney (Harry[6], William[5], Shelton[4], William[3], John[2], Abner[1]), b.21 May 1921 Napton, Saline Co., MO. She m1. William L. Bolles, son of Laurence Hartmann Bolles I and Mary Malloy, on 26 Jun 1943. She and William L. Bolles were divorced in 1971. She m2. John Dean Swisher in 1976.

William L. Bolles, b.19 Jul 1919 St. Louis, MO.
Known children of Margaret Hood "Madge"[7] Abney and William L. Bolles:

 1246 i. Gloria Howard[8], b. 13 Dec 1945 Dallas, TX; m. Bradford Leon "Brad" Watkins.
 ii. Lawrence Hartmann, b.8 Mar 1949. He m. Bonnie Mae Wesp on 5 Nov 1971. He and Bonnie Mae Wesp were divorced in 1975.

There were no known children of Margaret Hood "Madge"[7] Abney and John Dean Swisher.

914. Agnes Berkeley[7] Abney (Harry[6], William[5], Shelton[4], William[3], John[2], Abner[1]), b.19 Aug 1926 Napton, Saline Co., MO. She m. George Peuris Whittington Jr. (USMC-WWII), son of George Peuris Whittington Sr. and Susan Bullitt Dixon Burbank, on 6 Dec 1947. She was liv. in 1978 Henderson, Henderson Co., KY.

George Peuris Whittington Jr. (USMC-WWII)., b.5 Oct 1913 Hot Springs, Garland Co., AR. George served in the Marines with duty in China during the SinoJapanese War. He entered D-Day in the Rangers Battlion. He received DSC, Silver Star, Bronze Star, Purple Heart - Korea - Maj. Reg. Comb. Team. George's military service was 3.5 years. He was liv. in 1978 Henderson, Henderson Co., KY.
Known children of Agnes Berkeley[7] Abney and George Peuris Whittington Jr. (USMC-WWII):

 i. Charles Hood[8], b.16 Sep 1948 Columbus, GA. He lived in 1978 near Lexington, KY.
 ii. Janet Louise, b.23 Feb 1952 Jefferson City, MO. She lived in 1978 NY.
 iii. Richard Burbank, b.13 Feb 1956 Henderson, Henderson Co., KY.
 iv. Elizabeth, b.2 May 1959 Evansville, Vanderburgh Co., IN.

915. Charles W.[7] Gardner (Josie[6] Abney, James[5], Robert[4], John[3], John[2], Abner[1]) m. Mary Lou Jaggers. He, b.Jun 1890 Magnolia, LaRue Co., KY.
Known child of Charles W.[7] Gardner and Mary Lou Jaggers:

 i. Ilma Generose[8], b.1911. She d.1914.

916. Burgess Corydon[7] Abney (Charles[6], James[5], Robert[4], John[3], John[2], Abner[1]), b.22 Feb 1889 Louisville, Jefferson Co., KY. He m. Leona B. Schneider on 12 Aug 1907 Spokane, Spokane Co., WA. He and Leona appeared on the censuses of 22 Apr 1910, 6 Jan 1920 and 3 Apr 1930 Seattle, King Co., WA. He d.16 Oct 1937 Phoenix, Maricopa Co., AZ, at age 48 and was bur. Fairmont Mem. Park, Spokane, Spokane Co., WA.

Leona B. Schneider, b.10 Jan 1888 IL; m2. Earl Forney. She d.6 Feb 1960 Apache Junction, Pinal Co., AZ, age 72; bur. Fairmont Mem. Park.
Known children of Burgess Corydon[7] Abney and Leona B. Schneider:

 i. Charles Henry[8], b.21 Nov 1907 Seattle, King Co., WA. He m. Rose Alice Maring on 11 Jun 1932 Duwamish, King Co., WA. He and Rose appeared on the census of 15 Apr 1940 Seattle, King Co., WA. He d.21 Jul 1945 Doctors Hospital, Seattle, King Co., WA, at age 37 and was bur. Acadia Mem. Park & Funeral Home, Lake Forest Park, King Co., WA.
    Rose Alice Maring, b.6 Mar 1914 Sandpoint, Bonner Co., ID. She m2. John George Stewart in 1946. She d.25 Mar 1951 Portland, Multnomah Co., OR, at age 37.

917. Neoma Ella "Oma"[7] Lewis (Mildred[6] Abney, Milton[5], Robert[4], John[3], John[2], Abner[1]), b.24 Feb 1896 KY. She m. Della Clifton Cruse. d.4 Oct 1972 at age 76 and was bur. Red Hill Cem., Hodgenville, LaRue Co., KY.

Della Clifton Cruse, b.20 Feb 1895. He d.29 Nov 1982 at age 87.
Known child of Neoma Ella "Oma"[7] Lewis and Della Clifton Cruse:

 1247 i. Lucille[8], m. Harry Bowling.

918. Emmett William[7] Abney (Joseph[6], Milton[5], Robert[4], John[3], John[2], Abner[1]), b.21 Jan 1890 Magnolia, LaRue Co., KY. He m1. Olive "Beryl" Davis ca.1917. He and Olive "Beryl" Davis appeared on the censuses of 5 Jan 1920, 7 Apr 1930 and 4 Apr 1940 Clow, Kittson Co., IL. He m2. Dena Hanson on 15 Nov 1958 Kittson Co., MN. He d.Jan 1963 MN and was bur. Greenwood Cem., Hallock, Kittson Co., MN.

Olive "Beryl" Davis, b.5 Mar 1893. She d.6 Apr 1955 at age 62 and was bur. Greenwood Cem., Hallock, Kittson Co., MN.

Known children of Emmett William⁷ Abney and Olive "Beryl" Davis:
>   i.   Bessie A.⁸, b.11 Feb 1918 Orleans, Kittson Co., MN. She m. Edwin Swenson. d.31 Mar 2009 Warroad, Roseau Co., MN,
>   at age 91 and was bur. Greenwood Cem., Hallock, Kittson Co., MN.
>   Edwin Swenson, b.1911. He d.1987 and was bur. Greenwood Cem., Hallock, Kittson Co., MN.
> 1248 ii.   Charles J, b. Dec 1919 Kittson Co., MN; m. Elaine (n.n.).
>   iii.   Lela B, b. ca.1922 IL.
>   iv.   Shirley P, b. ca.Feb 1930 Kittson Co., IL.

Dena Hanson, b. ca.1893.
There were no known children of Emmett William⁷ Abney and Dena Hanson.

919. Selia M. "Lela"⁷ Abney (Joseph⁶, Milton⁵, Robert⁴, John³, John², Abner¹), b.Sep 1891 KY. She m. Ross Fishburn ca.1913. She and Ross Fishburn appeared on the censuses of 30 Jan 1920 and 8 Apr 1930 Pawnee, Sangamon Co., IL.
      Ross Fishburn, b. ca.1885 OH. He appeared on the census of 23 Apr 1940 Pawnee, Sangamon Co., IL.
Known child of Selia M. "Lela"⁷ Abney and Ross Fishburn:
>   i.   Howard A.⁸, b. ca.1929 IL.

920. Iva D.⁷ Abney (Joseph⁶, Milton⁵, Robert⁴, John³, John², Abner¹), b.Nov 1893 KY. She m. Ben Sweet ca.1926. They div. before 1930. She and her son, Earl Wayne Sweet were liv. on 9 Apr 1930 with her, Joseph G. Abney, Pawnee, Sangamon Co., IL. She was liv. on 4 Apr 1940 with father, Joseph G. Abney, Pawnee, Sangamon Co., IL.
Known children of Iva D.⁷ Abney and Ben Sweet:
>   i.   Earl Wayne⁸, b.8 Nov 1926 Springfield, Sangamon Co., IL. He m. Beverly Jean Dunlap in 1944. He d.30 Jan 2016 Virden,
>   Macoupin Co., IL, at age 89.
>   Beverly Jean Dunlap, b.1926 IL. She d.11 Oct 2018.

921. Hettie F.⁷ Abney (Joseph⁶, Milton⁵, Robert⁴, John³, John², Abner¹), b. Jan 1895 KY. She m. Russell White (b.1895 IL).
Known children of Hettie F.⁷ Abney and Russell White:
>   i.   Marjorie H.⁸, b.1918.
>   ii.   Doris F., b.1920.
>   iii.   Harold R., b.1922.
>   iv.   Lucille, b.1924. She m. Ray Ottis Deihl (1920-2007). d.2009.

922. Alice "Attie"⁷ Aud (Wilhelmina⁶ Bayne, Margaret⁵ Lasley, Gertrude⁴ Abney, John³, John², Abner¹), b.25 Aug 1877 Cecilia, Hardin Co., KY. She m. Dr. Herbert Roberts Nusz on 1 Nov 1898 Cecilia, Hardin Co., KY. They appeared on the census of 7 Jan 1920 Cecilia, Hardin Co., KY. She d.2 Sep 1955 Elizabethtown, Hardin Co., KY, at age 78 and was bur. on 4 Sep 1955 St. James Cem., Elizabethtown, Hardin Co., KY.
      Dr. Herbert Roberts Nusz, b.3 Apr 1875 Louisville, Jefferson Co., KY; d.1 Apr 1962 Elizabethtown, Hardin Co., KY; bur. St. James Cem.
Known children of Alice "Attie"⁷ Aud and Dr. Herbert Roberts Nusz:
>   i.   Generose⁸, b. ca.1900 Cecilia, Hardin Co., KY.
>   ii.   Zach, b. ca.1901 Cecilia, Hardin Co., KY.
> 1249 iii.   Helen Dorothy, b. 6 Jul 1903 Cecilia, Hardin Co., KY; m. James "Ray" Jenkins Sr.
>   iv.   Herberts Roberts, b.1911. He d.1911.
>   v.   William Keith "Billy", b.1915 Cecilia, Hardin Co., KY. He d.1989.

Generation Eight

923. Ted Dean "Teddy"⁸ Crabtree (John⁷, Polly⁶ Chancellor, David⁵, Rebecca⁴ Abney, Joshua³, Elisha², Abner¹), b.22 Sep 1901 IL. He m. Florene L. (n.n.) ca.1920 OK. He and Florene appeared on the censuses of 17 Apr 1930 and 5 Apr 1940 Rock Twp., Gage City, Ellis Co., OK. He d.9 Jan 1979 at age 77 and was bur. Gage Mem. Cem., Gage, Ellis Co., OK.
      Florene L. (n.n.), b.8 Jun 1900 AR. She was a Public School Teacher. She d.13 Jan 1990 at age 89 and was bur. Gage Mem. Cem., Gage.
Known children of Ted Dean "Teddy"⁸ Crabtree and Florene L. (n.n.):
>   i.   Catherine Louise⁹, b.29 Apr 1921 Ellis Co., OK. She m. Rev. Leslie Arthur Farrell. d.24 Apr 1999 Ada, Pontotoc Co.,
>   OK, at age 77 and was bur. Gage Mem. Cem., Gage, Ellis Co., OK.
>   Rev. Leslie Arthur Farrell, b.1 Sep 1917. He d.23 May 2001 AR at age 83 and was bur. Gage Mem. Cem., Gage.
>   ii.   Barbara E., b. ca.1932 OK.

924. Leo E.⁸ Crabtree (John⁷, Polly⁶ Chancellor, David⁵, Rebecca⁴ Abney, Joshua³, Elisha², Abner¹), b. ca.1904 OK. He m. Florence (n.n.) (b. ca.1908 OK). They appeared on the censuses of 16 Apr 1930 Austin Twp., Ellis Co., OK; and 5 Apr 1940 Rock Twp., Gage City, Ellis Co., OK.
Known children of Leo E.⁸ Crabtree and Florence (n.n.) all b. OK:
>   i.   Bonnie Lee⁹, b. ca.1924.
>   ii.   Billy Jean, b. ca.1925.
>   iii.   Lois Arlene, b.1927. She d.26 Apr 1935 and was bur. Gage Mem. Cem., Gage, Ellis Co., OK.
>   iv.   Johnny N., b. ca.1931.
>   v.   Leo Carvell, b.Jul 1939.

925. Cuma C.⁸ Crabtree (John⁷, Polly⁶ Chancellor, David⁵, Rebecca⁴ Abney, Joshua³, Elisha², Abner¹), b. ca.1906 OK. She m. Herman Solomon Hoffine, son of Jim Hoffine and Margrete (n.n.), ca.1925. She and Herman appeared on the censuses of 16 Apr 1930 Austin Twp., Ellis Co., OK; and 12 Apr 1940 Wichita, Sedgwick Co., KS. She d.30 Mar 1963 and was bur. Cypress Lawn Mem. Park, Colma, San Mateo Co., CA.
      Herman Solomon Hoffine, b. ca.1903 NE. He d.17 May 1981 and was bur. on 17 May 1981 Cypress Lawn Mem. Park, Colma.
Known children of Cuma C.⁸ Crabtree and Herman Solomon Hoffine:
> 1250 i.   Robert Dean "Bobby"⁹, b. 11 Jul 1926 Pretty Prairie, Reno Co., KS; m. Wilma Charlotte Hauser.
>   ii.   Thelda Y., b.Oct 1927 OK. She m. Roy Sawtell.

926. Erma Ellen⁸ McFarland (Effie⁷ Crabtree, Polly⁶ Chancellor, David⁵, Rebecca⁴ Abney, Joshua³, Elisha², Abner¹), b.13 Aug 1899 IL. She m. George Claus Toellner, son of John Herman Toellner and Geshen (n.n.), on 21 Dec 1915 Ellis Co., OK. She and George appeared on the censuses of 12 Jan 1920, 16 Apr 1930 and 13 May 1940 Austin Twp., Ellis Co., OK. She d.15 Mar 1974 Gage, Ellis Co., OK, at age 74 and was bur. Gage Mem. Cem., Gage, Ellis Co., OK.

    George Claus Toellner, b.14 Dec 1888 Nebraska City, Otoe Co., NE; d.27 Jul 1961 Gage, Ellis Co., OK, at age 72; bur. Gage Mem. Cem.

Known children of Erma Ellen⁸ McFarland and George Claus Toellner:

       i.   John "Raymond"⁹, b.19 Dec 1916 Ellis Co., OK. He d.Nov 1985 Gage, Ellis Co., OK, at age 68; bur. Gage Mem. Cem.

      ii. Viola Tawanda "Toots", b.15 Feb 1918 OK. She m. Alfred C. "Al" Molloy, son of Nova E. Molloy and Mary J. (n.n.). She and Alfred appeared on the census of 13 May 1940 Austin Twp., Ellis Co., OK. She d.25 Feb 1999 Gage, Ellis Co., OK, at age 81 and was bur. Gage Mem. Cem., Gage, Ellis Co., OK.

           Alfred C. "Al" Molloy, b.19 Apr 1913. He d.14 Oct 1980 at age 67 and was bur. on 16 Oct 1980 Gage Mem. Cem.

     iii. Neva Eileen, b.Leap Day, 29 Feb 1924. She m. Jim Raymond Luthi, son of Adolphus Luthi and Rose Mary Yenney, on 24 Feb 1959. She d.29 Aug 2006 Woodward Regional Med. Ctr., Woodward Co., OK, at age 82; bur. Gage Mem. Cem.

           Jim Raymond Luthi, b.27 Sep 1905 Gage, Ellis Co., OK. He m. Helen Irvin on Christmas Eve, 24 Dec 1929. He d.2 Dec 1992 Woodward Co., OK, at age 87.

927. Leonard Wayne "Sam"⁸ McFarland (Effie⁷ Crabtree, Polly⁶ Chancellor, David⁵, Rebecca⁴ Abney, Joshua³, Elisha², Abner¹), b.18 Jul 1901 Martinsville, Clark Co., IL. He was liv. on 16 Apr 1930 with father, William McFarland, Austin Twp., Ellis Co., OK. He m. Hattie Mae Koons, daughter of Charles Koons and Eliza Jane Gibson, on 10 May 1932. He and Hattie appeared on the census of 14 May 1940 Austin Twp., Ellis Co., OK. He d.28 Aug 1989 Woodward Nursing Center, Woodward, Woodward Co., OK, at age 88; bur. Gage Mem. Cem., Gage, Ellis Co., OK.

    Hattie Mae Koons, b.19 Jul 1910 Ellis Co., OK. She d.8 Apr 1987 Ellis Co., OK, at age 76.

Known children of Leonard Wayne "Sam"⁸ McFarland and Hattie Mae Koons:

       i.   Duane⁹.

      ii. Dennis.

928. Todd A. "Toddy"⁸ McFarland (Effie⁷ Crabtree, Polly⁶ Chancellor, David⁵, Rebecca⁴ Abney, Joshua³, Elisha², Abner¹), b.8 May 1903 IL. He m. Myrtle (n.n.) (b. ca.1907 KS). He and Myrtle were liv. on 16 Apr 1930 with his father, Will McFarland, Austin, Ellis Co., OK. He d.23 Jan 1936 at age 32 and was bur. Gage Mem. Cem., Gage, Ellis Co., OK.

Known children of Todd A. "Toddy"⁸ McFarland and Myrtle (n.n.) both b. OK:

       i.   Ruby May⁹, b. ca.1925.

      ii. Jack Ray, b. ca.1928.

929. Lula Myrtle⁸ Griffith (David⁷, Mary⁶ Chancellor, David⁵, Rebecca⁴ Abney, Joshua³, Elisha², Abner¹), b.1892 IL. She m. John Henry Ross Jr., son of John Henry Ross Sr. and Frances Elvina Dain, on 22 Jan 1912 Ellis Co., OK. She and John appeared on the census of 13 Jan 1920 Austin Twp., Ellis Co., OK. She d.30 Jan 1962 and was bur. Harmon Cem., Harmon, Ellis Co., OK.

    John Henry Ross Jr, b.14 Jan 1887 NE. He d.25 Nov 1950 OK at age 63.

Known children of Lula Myrtle⁸ Griffith and John Henry Ross Jr.:

       i.   Charles W.⁹, b.17 Nov 1913. He d.23 Jan 1914 and was bur. Harmon Cem., Harmon, Ellis Co., OK.

      ii. George Oliver, b.3 Feb 1915. He d.12 Mar 1915 and was bur. Harmon Cem., Harmon, Ellis Co., OK.

     iii. Orville Ellis m. Jacqueline D. Sheldon, daughter of Carl H. Sheldon and Marguerite L. Saggau. He, b.24 Sep 1917 OK. He d.15 Nov 1992 Wichita, Sedgwick Co., KS, at age 75 and was bur. Marion Cem., Marion, Marion Co., KS.

           Jacqueline D. Sheldon, b. New Year's Day, 1 Jan 1917; d. Dec 1995 Wichita, Sedgwick Co., KS; bur. Marion Cem.

      iv. Dorothy Eileen, b.3 Aug 1922. She m. John Stanley McClung in 1947. She d.29 Jun 1996 at age 73; bur. Harmon Cem.

           John Stanley McClung, b.23 Mar 1911 Oklahoma City, Oklahoma Co., OK. He d.11 Nov 2001 Woodward, Woodward Co., OK, at age 90 and was bur. Harmon Cem., Harmon, Ellis Co., OK.

       v.   Mary E., b.21 May 1925. She m. (n.n.) Koch. d.11 Dec 1988 at age 63; bur. Shattuck Cem., Shattuck, Ellis Co., OK.

      vi. Anna Bell, b.11 Feb 1927. She d.12 Feb 1927 and was bur. Harmon Cem., Harmon, Ellis Co., OK.

     vii. Zella E., b. est.1929.

    viii. Leroy E., b.21 Apr 1931. He m. A. Louise (n.n.) (b.1940). He d.20 Feb 1998 Wichita, Sedgwick Co., KS, at age 66 and was bur. Resthaven Gardens of Memory, Wichita, Sedgwick Co., KS.

930. Nelie Fern⁸ Griffith (David⁷, Mary⁶ Chancellor, David⁵, Rebecca⁴ Abney, Joshua³, Elisha², Abner¹), b.9 Feb 1897 IL; m. Bert Wallace Sober Sr., son of August Sober and Katherine Seymour. She d. Christmas Day, 25 Dec 1935, age 38; bur. Odd Fellows Cem., Ponca City, Kay Co., OK.

    Bert Wallace Sober Sr, b.21 Jun 1890. He d.8 Mar 1952 at age 61 and was bur. Odd Fellows Cem., Ponca City, Kay Co., OK.

Known children of Nelie Fern⁸ Griffith & Bert Wallace Sober Sr. all b. in OK (unsure birth order for youngest three: Gary, Jimmy and Billy Jean):

       i.   Grace, b. ca.1913

      ii. Rolla Eugene⁹, b.1915. m. Naomi Irene Ivie (1918-1993) 10 Oct 1936 Kay Co., OK; d.2005

     iii. Everett, b. ca.1917

      iv. Marie "Dolly," b.1920; m. (n.n.) Burdick

1251   v.   Gerald Ray, b. 14 Sep 1922 Shidler, Osage Co., OK; m. Dorothy Carter; m. *PM2* Nancy Hope Smith (USN).

      vi. Reva, b.1925; m. (n.n.) Butcher.

     vii. Bert Wallace Jr., b.1927.

    viii. Betty Darlene, b.1929; m. (n.n.) Pigg; d.2009.

1252   ix. Zelma "Earlene," b. 26 Apr 1931 Ponca City, Kay Co., OK; m1. PFC Roy Neal Corey (USAF); m2. John Elwood Martin; m3. Ivy Arthur Nelson (US Mil.).

       x.   Bobby Lee, b. ca.1937

      xi. Kenneth, b. ca.1938

     xii. Gary.

    xiii. Jimmy.

    xiv. Billy Jean. m. (n.n.) Horton

931. Hezekiah "Hezie"[8] Griffith Jr. (USArmy WWII) (Hezekiah[7], Mary[6] Chancellor, David[5], Rebecca[4] Abney, Joshua[3], Elisha[2], Abner[1]), b.14 Mar 1922. He m. Beulah "Boots" Fessler on 28 Feb 1946 Ellis Co., OK. He d.28 May 2004 Tulsa, Tulsa Co., OK, at age 82 and was bur. Gage Mem. Cem., Gage, Ellis Co., OK.
    Beulah "Boots" Fessler, b.12 May 1925. She d.15 Dec 1997 at age 72.
Known children of Hezekiah "Hezie"[8] Griffith Jr. (USArmy WWII) and Beulah "Boots" Fessler:
                    i.   Edris[9].

932. Joseph Clair[8] Myers Sr. (Florence[7] Gillilan, Rebecca[6] Chancellor, David[5], Rebecca[4] Abney, Joshua[3], Elisha[2], Abner[1]), b.14 Nov 1914 Chanute, Neosho Co., KS. He m. Elma Jean Hopkins. He lived in 1995 Yucaipa, CA. He died 09 Apr 2004 in San Bernadino Co., CA.
    Elma Jean Hopkins, b.30 Jul 1918 Rayborn, Wright Co., MO; d.29 Jun 1981 Alhambra, Los Angeles Co., CA.
Known children of Joseph Clair[8] Myers and Elma Jean Hopkins:
                    i.   Joseph Clair Jr. (gen.)[9], b.13 Aug 1940 Los Angeles, CA. He m. Christine Luis. The author worked on the family history with Cousin Joe for a decade, beginning in 1995. His father passed away in the year before Hurricane Katrina. Cousin Joe sent a large package of wonderful information just before the author lost contact with him. Cousin Joe is credited for the author's knowledge on the Chancellor family (#19). It was truly a pleasure working with such a nice, family-loving man.
    1253   ii.   Norman Robert, b. 1944.

933. Austin Derr "AD"[8] McKay (Robert[7], Mary[6] Chancellor, Ewing[5], Rebecca[4] Abney, Joshua[3], Elisha[2], Abner[1]), b.12 Sep 1891 Humphreys, Sullivan Co., MO. He m. Lera Elba Justus. He d.16 Nov 1966 Kirksville, Adair Co., MO, at age 75.
    Lera Elba Justus, b.1889. She d.1976 MO and was bur. Humphreys Cem., Humphreys, Sullivan Co., MO.
Known children of Austin Derr "AD"[8] McKay and Lera Elba Justus:
    1254   i.   Elnor Vernetta[9], b. 18 Apr 1914 Novinger, Adair Co., MO; m. Raymond Franklin Wolter.
                    ii.   Austin Junior, b.Jul 1917 Novinger, Adair Co., MO. He d.17 Mar 1919 Pattonsburg, Daviess Co., MO, at age 1 and was bur. Humphreys Cem., Humphreys, Sullivan Co., MO.
                    iii. Velma K., b.1919. She m. Paul C. Yardley on 12 Jul 1943. She d.21 Mar 2010 Saint Joseph, Buchanan Co., MO and was bur. Saint Joseph Memorial Park, Saint Joseph, Buchanan Co., MO.
    1255   iv.   Eva Lee, b. 26 Sep 1921 Knox Co., MO; m. Kenneth Dale Lewis Sr.

934. Alva Ross[8] McKay (Robert[7], Mary[6] Chancellor, Ewing[5], Rebecca[4] Abney, Joshua[3], Elisha[2], Abner[1]), b.28 Jul 1895. He m. Beulah May Justus. He d.2 Dec 1969 at age 74 and was bur. Odd Fellows Cem., Trenton, Grundy Co., MO.
    Beulah May Justus, b.23 May 1897. She d.27 May 1966 at age 69 and was bur. Odd Fellows Cem., Trenton, Grundy Co., MO.
Known children of Alva Ross[8] McKay and Beulah May Justus:
    1256   i.   Harry E.[9], b. 10 Apr 1916 Brimson, Grundy Co., MO; m. Anna Gertrude Snyder.
                    ii.   Donald Floyd, b.23 Nov 1921 MO. He m. Geraldine Woosley. He d.4 Sep 1983 Houston, Harris Co., TX, at age 61 and was bur. Memorial Oaks Cem., Houston, Harris Co., TX.
                          Geraldine Woosley, b.14 Jun 1923. She d.14 Oct 2011 at age 88 and was bur. Memorial Oaks Cem., Houston.

935. Mary Adelia[8] Pickett (Arminta[7] McKay, Mary[6] Chancellor, Ewing[5], Rebecca[4] Abney, Joshua[3], Elisha[2], Abner[1]), b.17 Aug 1886 Humphreys, Sullivan Co., MO. She m. Clyde Willie Lowther, son of William Thomas Lowther and Matilda Snyder, on 28 Dec 1908. She d.8 Jan 1980 Spickard, Grundy Co., MO, at age 93 and was bur. Humphreys Cem., Humphreys, Sullivan Co., MO.
    Clyde Willie Lowther, b.5 Jul 1882 WV. He d.27 Dec 1967 Spickard, Grundy Co., MO, at age 85.
Known children of Mary Adelia[8] Pickett and Clyde Willie Lowther:
    1257   i.   Forest[9], b. 1913 Humphreys, Sullivan Co., MO; m. Lois McKinney.
                    ii.   Dean.
    1258   iii. Pauline M, b. 17 Apr 1921 MO; m. Jacob O. "Jake" Cooper.
    1259   iv.   Paul Martin, b. 17 Apr 1921 Humphreys, Sullivan Co., MO; m. Mary Josephine "Jo" Van Dyke.
                    v.   Bobbie Eugene "Bob", b.2 Aug 1924. He d.12 Oct 2003 at age 79 and was bur. Humphreys Cem., Humphreys.

936. Gilbert Everett[8] McKay (Walter[7], Mary[6] Chancellor, Ewing[5], Rebecca[4] Abney, Joshua[3], Elisha[2], Abner[1]), b.11 Mar 1896 Reger, Sullivan Co., MO. He m. Velma Pratt, daughter of Samuel Arthur Pratt and Perisa Jane Wade, in 1919. He d.5 Jan 1980 Milan, Sullivan Co., MO, at age 83 and was bur. Humphreys Cem., Humphreys, Sullivan Co., MO.
    Velma Pratt, b.12 Apr 1900 MO. She d.30 Oct 1987 Trenton, Grundy Co., MO, at age 87 and was bur. Humphreys Cem., Humphreys.
Known children of Gilbert Everett[8] McKay and Velma Pratt:
                    i.   Clarence Glen[9], b.19 Nov 1926. He m. Helen Ruth Glidewell in 1947. He d.6 Jun 1990 at age 63 and was bur. Humphreys Cem., Humphreys, Sullivan Co., MO.
                          Helen Ruth Glidewell, b.16 Aug 1928. She d.28 Feb 2018 at age 89 and was bur. Humphreys Cem., Humphreys.

937. Elgeva Beulah[8] McKay (Walter[7], Mary[6] Chancellor, Ewing[5], Rebecca[4] Abney, Joshua[3], Elisha[2], Abner[1]), b.23 Dec 1896. She m. Vern Seckington, son of Anthony Seckington and Georgia Ann Ames, in 1917. She d.30 Jul 1970 at age 73 and was bur. Glaze Cem., Sullivan Co., MO.
    Vern Seckington, b.25 Apr 1897 Maryville, Nodaway Co., MO. He d.13 Jul 1972 Milan, Sullivan Co., MO, at age 75 and was bur. Glaze Cem.
Known children of Elgeva Beulah[8] McKay and Vern Seckington:
    1260   i.   Gerald Vernon "Vern"[9], b. 5 Dec 1918 Sullivan Co., MO; m. Reva Elaine Knifong.
                    ii.   Harold D., b.19 Mar 1920. He m. Thelma M. (n.n.). He d.New Year's Eve, 31 Jan 1988 at age 67; bur. Glaze Cem.
                          Thelma M. (n.n.), b.Christmas Eve, 24 Dec 1928. She d.29 Nov 1993 at age 64.
                    iii. Margaret.

938. Mary Isabelle[8] McKay (Walter[7], Mary[6] Chancellor, Ewing[5], Rebecca[4] Abney, Joshua[3], Elisha[2], Abner[1]), b.28 Dec 1901 Reger, Sullivan Co., MO. She m. Buel McClaren, son of John Wesley McClaren and Matilda C. Norman, on 10 Nov 1920. She d.24 Jul 1994 Milan, Sullivan Co., MO, at age 92 and was bur. Glaze Cem., Sullivan Co., MO.
    Buel McClaren, b.16 Jan 1901 Reger, Sullivan Co., MO. He d.11 Aug 1976 Milan, Sullivan Co., MO, at age 75 and was bur. Glaze Cem.

Known children of Mary Isabelle[8] McKay and Buel McClaren both b. Reger, Sullivan Co., MO:

    1261   i.   Ila Lee[9], b. 25 Sep 1921; m. Robert Rex "Bob" Stephenson.

    1262   ii.   Dorothy Evelyn "Dot," b. 9 Nov 1925; m. Raymond "Jay" Wattenbarger.

939. Betha Ruby[8] McKay (Lillie's twin) (Walter[7], Mary[6] Chancellor, Ewing[5], Rebecca[4] Abney, Joshua[3], Elisha[2], Abner[1]), b.21 Jun 1904 Sullivan Co., MO. She m. Monroe Wilson White, son of Everett Monta White and Celia A. (N.N.), in 1930. She d.28 Jun 1961 Davenport, Scott Co., IA, at age 57 and was bur. Oakwood Cem., Milan, Sullivan Co., MO.

    Monroe Wilson White, b.16 Apr 1913 Milan, Sullivan Co., MO. He m2. El Verna Mary Ann Riessen in 1979. He d.26 Aug 1984 Wilton, Muscatine Co., IA, at age 71.

Known children of Betha Ruby[8] McKay (Lillie's twin) and Monroe Wilson White:

    i.   Alfred M.[9], b.17 Sep 1931. He d.16 Oct 2002 at age 71 and was bur. Walcott Cem., Walcott, Scott Co., IA.

940. Lillie Ruth[8] McKay (Betha's twin) (Walter[7], Mary[6] Chancellor, Ewing[5], Rebecca[4] Abney, Joshua[3], Elisha[2], Abner[1]), b.21 Jun 1904 Sullivan Co., MO. She m. Dewayne Minter Ford, son of George Thomas Ford and Mary Orlene Melinda Tipton, in 1928. She d.4 Mar 1999 Milan, Sullivan Co., MO, at age 94 and was bur. Schrock Cem., Reger, Sullivan Co., MO.

    Dewayne Minter Ford, b.4 Dec 1903 Reger, Sullivan Co., MO. He d.6 Dec 1979 Reger, Sullivan Co., MO, age 76 and was bur. Schrock Cem.

Known children of Lillie Ruth[8] McKay (Betha's twin) and Dewayne Minter Ford:

    i.   Ruby J.[9] m. Gerald Williams.

    ii.   Chester F. m. Teresa A. Moore.

    iii.   Charles Earl, b.12 Dec 1932 Osgood, Sullivan Co., MO. He d.3 Dec 1970 Iowa City, Johnson Co., IA, at age 37.

    iv.   Dale L., b. est.1934. He m. Carolyn S. Heitman.

    v.   Jerry Max, b.12 Mar 1938 Reger, Sullivan Co., MO. He d.26 Aug 1953 Reger, Sullivan Co., MO, at age 15 and was bur. Schrock Cem., Reger, Sullivan Co., MO.

    vi.   Jackie Rex, b.12 Mar 1938 Reger, Sullivan Co., MO. She d.28 Dec 1949 Reger, Sullivan Co., MO, at age 11 and was bur. Schrock Cem., Reger, Sullivan Co., MO.

    vii.   Lois Orlene, b.21 Feb 1941 Sullivan Co., MO. She d.16 May 1945 Sullivan Co., MO, at age 4 and was bur. Schrock Cem., Reger, Sullivan Co., MO.

    1263   viii.   David Russel, b. 21 Jul 1943; m. Carolyn Sue Clark.

    ix.   Mary F. m. Orville Aaron McNear.

941. Richard Freeman[8] Chancellor (Henry[7], Henry[6], Ewing[5], Rebecca[4] Abney, Joshua[3], Elisha[2], Abner[1]), b.3 Nov 1917 Mindenmines, Barton Co., MO. He m. Hazel "Lone" Williams. He d.17 May 2000 Joplin, Jasper Co., MO, age 82 and was bur. Lake Cem., Lamar Heights, Barton Co., MO. Hazel "Lone" Williams, b.18 Jan 1926 Marceline, Linn Co., MO; d.17 Jun 2020 Joplin, Jasper Co., MO; bur. Lake Cem., Lamar Heights.

Known children of Richard Freeman[8] Chancellor and Hazel "Lone" Williams:

    i.   Victoria Lynn[9], b.22 Aug 1948; m. Thomas Allen Stansberry; d.17 Feb 1969 age 20, bur. Lake Cem., Lamar Heights.

    ii.   Brad.

    iii.   Henry Clay, b.20 Dec 1952 and d.16 Sep 2008 Lamar, Barton Co., MO, at age 55 and was bur. Lake Cem., Lamar Heights.

    iv.   Eric.

942. Tressia I.[8] Moore (Lottie[7] Chancellor, Henry[6], Ewing[5], Rebecca[4] Abney, Joshua[3], Elisha[2], Abner[1]), b.18 Sep 1895 MO. She m. Doskey Omega Short, son of James M. Short and Emma F. Alexander. d.27 Aug 1990 at age 94 and was bur. Rosebank Cem., Mulberry, Crawford Co., KS.

    Doskey Omega Short, b.29 Aug 1891 Appleton City, St. Clair Co., MO. He d.19 Jan 1985 at age 93 and was bur. Rosebank Cem., Mulberry.

Known children of Tressia I.[8] Moore and Doskey Omega Short:

    i.   Retha L.[9], b.1914. She d.1935 and was bur. Rosebank Cem., Mulberry, Crawford Co., KS.

    ii.   Carroll L, b.1917. He d.1933 and was bur. Rosebank Cem., Mulberry, Crawford Co., KS.

943. Iva Margaret[8] Moore (Lottie[7] Chancellor, Henry[6], Ewing[5], Rebecca[4] Abney, Joshua[3], Elisha[2], Abner[1]), b.29 Aug 1904 Mindenmines, Barton Co., MO. She m. Almon DeWitt Willis, son of William Almon Willis and Winnie E. Harris, ca.1925. She and Almon DeWitt Willis appeared on the censuses of 21 Apr 1930 and 16 Apr 1940 Galena, Cherokee Co., KS. She d.22 Apr 1997 Galena, Cherokee Co., KS, at age 92 and was bur. Rosebank Cem., Mulberry, Crawford Co., KS.

    Mayor Almon DeWitt Willis, b.12 Dec 1904 Frontenac, Crawford Co., KS. He was Mayor of Galena, KS (1954-1955). He d.30 Dec 1967 Joplin, Jasper Co., MO, at age 63 and was bur. Rosebank Cem., Mulberry, Crawford Co., KS.

Known children of Iva Margaret[8] Moore and Almon DeWitt Willis:

    1264   i.   William Almon "Bill"[9], b. 23 Mar 1927 MO; m. Pauline Ruth "Polly" Allen.

    ii.   Willa June, b. ca.1935 KS; m. (n.n.) Murray.

    iii.   Wilma Jean, b. ca.1938 KS; m. (n.n.) Holstrom.

    iv.   Richard "Butch."

944. Marion S.[8] Moore (Lottie[7] Chancellor, Henry[6], Ewing[5], Rebecca[4] Abney, Joshua[3], Elisha[2], Abner[1]), b.14 Dec 1911 MO. He m. Letha L. Robson, daughter of Joseph Robson and Alice Mae Hodgson. He d.22 Sep 2008 Pittsburg, Crawford Co., KS, at age 96 and was bur. Rosebank Cem., Mulberry, Crawford Co., KS.

    Letha L. Robson, b.16 Jul 1916. She d.1 May 1983 Mindenmines, Barton Co., MO, at age 66.

Known children of Marion S.[8] Moore and Letha L. Robson:

    1265   i.   Marilyn Joann[9], b. 19 Aug 1935 Mindenmines, Barton Co., MO; m. Keith Beaver.

    ii.   Larry.

945. Ruby Leora[8] Howe (Cora[7] Montgomery, Henry[6], Martha[5] Chancellor, Rebecca[4] Abney, Joshua[3], Elisha[2], Abner[1]), b.17 Jan 1909 Clark Co., IL. She m. George Evans Slusser, son of Everett Ernest Slusser and Anna Catherine Spraker, on 22 Feb 1930. She d.12 Feb 1980 Martinsville, Clark Co., IL, at age 71 and was bur. Wesley Chapel Cem., Marshall, Clark Co., IL.

    George Evans Slusser, b.22 Feb 1909 Clark Co., IL. He d.27 Jul 1969 Clark Co., IL, at age 60 and was bur. Wesley Chapel Cem., Marshall.

Known child of Ruby Leora[8] Howe and George Evans Slusser:
   i. James[9].

946. Mary Velma[8] Howe (Cora[7] Montgomery, Henry[6], Martha[5] Chancellor, Rebecca[4] Abney, Joshua[3], Elisha[2], Abner[1]), b.12 May 1915 Casey, Clark Co., IL. She m. William Carter "Willie" Hunsaker, son of Charles Thurman Hunsaker and Lucille Elizabeth Yelton. She d.28 Oct 2014 El Paso, Woodford Co., IL, at age 99 and was bur. Hazel Dell South Cem., Hazel Dell, Cumberland Co., IL.
  William Carter "Willie" Hunsaker, b.10 Oct 1911 Hildago, Jasper Co., IL. He d.16 May 1985 El Paso, Woodford Co., IL, at age 73 and was bur. Hazel Dell South Cem., Hazel Dell, Cumberland Co., IL.
Known child of Mary Velma[8] Howe and William Carter "Willie" Hunsaker:
   i. (infant son)[9] d.5 Dec 1935 IL and was bur. Hazel Dell South Cem., Hazel Dell, Cumberland Co., IL.

947. Beatrice Mae[8] Burmmett (Norma[7] Harmeson, Catherine[6] Chancellor, William[5], Rebecca[4] Abney, Joshua[3], Elisha[2], Abner[1]), b.6 Jun 1905. She m. Howard Duane Coverstone in 1925. She d.6 Sep 1928 Mattoon, Coles Co., IL, age 23; bur. Dodge Grove Cem., Mattoon, Coles Co., IL.
  Howard Duane Coverstone, b.26 May 1903 IL. He m. Isabelle May on 27 Sep 1933. He d.25 Sep 1981 Mattoon, Coles Co., IL, at age 78.
Known child of Beatrice Mae[8] Burmmett and Howard Duane Coverstone:
 1266 i. Jack Dean[9], b. 17 Dec 1925; m. Norma Louise Richards.

948. Norton Ville[8] Abney (WWI) (Nancy[7], John[6], John[5], Paul[4], Joshua[3], Elisha[2], Abner[1]), b.20 Jan 1883 Butler Co., KY. He m. Effie Mae Beasley, daughter of (n.n.) Beasley and Martha Arzena Daugherty, on 17 Oct 1908. He d.18 Jul 1959 Ohio Co., KY, at age 76 and was bur. Sunnyside Cem., Beaver Dam, Ohio Co., KY.
  Effie Mae Beasley, b.12 May 1888 Butler Co., KY. She d.24 Aug 1967 Beaver Dam, Ohio Co., KY, at age 79 and was bur. Sunnyside Cem.
Known children of Norton Ville[8] Abney (WWI) and Effie Mae Beasley:
 1267 i. Carlos E.[9], b. 2 Feb 1910 Ohio Co., KY; m. Opal M. Frizzell.
 1268 ii. Hallie, b. 17 Jul 1912 Ohio Co., KY; m. Lee Frizzell.
   iii. Helen, b.1917. She m. Richard Thomas Garrison, son of Henry Richard Garrison and Mable Bailey McDaniel, on 22 Aug 1938. She d.4 Oct 1998 KY and was bur. Sunnyside Cem., Beaver Dam, Ohio Co., KY.
    Richard Thomas Garrison, b.27 May 1917. He d.3 Jun 1962 KY at age 45 and was bur. Sunnyside Cem.
   iv. Charles D., b.9 Dec 1919 Ohio Co., KY. He d.23 Dec 2010 Wooster, Wayne Co., OH, at age 91 and was bur. Sherwood Mem. Gardens, Wooster, Wayne Co., OH.
   v. Mary Loretta, b.23 May 1922 Ohio Co., KY. She d.8 Nov 2000 Ohio Co., KY, at age 78 and was bur. Sunnyside Cem.
 1269 vi. Leonis M., b. 24 Mar 1925 Ohio Co., KY; m. Jean Stone; m. Anna Young.
 1270 vii. Leon, b. 24 Mar 1925; m. (n.n.).

949. Earl[8] Abney (Nancy[7], John[6], John[5], Paul[4], Joshua[3], Elisha[2], Abner[1]), b.28 Sep 1884. He m. Harriett Alice "Lillie" Snodgrass. He d.9 Mar 1920 at age 35 and was bur. Mount Vernon Cem., Dexterville, Butler Co., KY.
  Harriett Alice "Lillie" Snodgrass, b.28 Sep 1884. She d.18 Sep 1964 at age 79 and was bur. Mount Vernon Cem., Dexterville, Butler Co., KY.
Known children of Earl[8] Abney and Harriett Alice "Lillie" Snodgrass:
   i. Guy A.[9], b.27 May 1907 Butler Co., KY. He m. Stella Phelps. He d.20 Apr 1974 Owensboro, Daviess Co., KY, at age 66 and was bur. Rosehill Elmwood Cem., Owensboro, Daviess Co., KY.
    Stella Phelps, b.8 May 1906 Butler Co., KY; d.13 Aug 1989 Jefferson Co., KY, age 83; bur. Rosehill Elmwood Cem.

950. Laura Belle[8] Abney (Nancy[7], John[6], John[5], Paul[4], Joshua[3], Elisha[2], Abner[1]), b.1 Dec 1885 Butler Co., KY;.m. Oscar Sherman Lindsey, s/o James Alfred Lindsey & Martha J. Pharris, in 1907; d.28 Apr 1936 Ohio Co., KY, age 50; bur. Taylor Mines Cem., Beaver Dam, Ohio Co., KY.
  Oscar Sherman Lindsey, b.27 Oct 1882 Butler Co., KY. He d.7 Dec 1925 Ohio Co., KY, at age 43 and was bur. Taylor Mines Cem.
Known child of Laura Belle[8] Abney and Oscar Sherman Lindsey:
 1271 i. Oliver "Cyrus"[9], b. 4 Apr 1911 Ohio Co., KY; m. Leona Elsie Maddox.

951. Beatrice[8] Abney (Nancy[7], John[6], John[5], Paul[4], Joshua[3], Elisha[2], Abner[1]), b.1891. She m. Thomas Lafayette Kessinger, son of (n.n.) Kessinger and Mary J. (n.n.), in 1910. She and Thomas Lafayette Kessinger appeared on the censuses of 16 Apr 1910 Butler Co., KY; 18 Apr 1930 Ohio Co., KY and 6 Apr 1940 McHenry, Ohio Co., KY. She d.17 Apr 1969 and was bur. Oakwood Cem., Hartford, Ohio Co., KY.
  Thomas Lafayette Kessinger, b.13 Oct 1881. He d.18 Aug 1946 at age 64.
Known children of Beatrice[8] Abney and Thomas Lafayette Kessinger all b. Ohio Co., KY:
   i. Earl M.[9], b. ca.1912.
   ii. Edward L., b.8 Jun 1914. He d.Christmas Eve, 24 Dec 1946 at age 32; bur. Oakwood Cem., Hartford, Ohio Co., KY.
   iii. Everett T., b. ca.1923.
   iv. Nannie Lee, b. ca.1927.
   v. Annie Belle, b. ca.1928.
   vi. Fred, b.26 Mar 1930. He d.26 Mar 1930 Ohio Co., KY and was bur. Taylor Mines Cem., Beaver Dam, Ohio Co., KY.
   vii. Carl, b.26 Mar 1930. He m. Alma Modean Moseley, daughter of Rufus Harrison Moseley and Mary Jane Decker. He d.17 Nov 2006 Owensboro, Daviess Co., KY, at age 76 and was bur. Pond Run Cem., Echols, Ohio Co., KY.
    Alma Modean Moseley, b.5 Jun 1933 Ohio Co., KY; d.26 Jul 2001 Daviess Co., KY, age 68; bur. Pond Run Cem.

952. Myrtle[8] Abney (Nancy[7], John[6], John[5], Paul[4], Joshua[3], Elisha[2], Abner[1]), b.30 Sep 1895. She m. Carey Hunter, son of Joseph P. Hunter and Martha Barbara "Patsy" Abney. She d.24 May 1990 at age 94 and was bur. Sunnyside Cem., Beaver Dam, Ohio Co., KY.
  Carey Hunter (#544), b.7 Nov 1894 McLean Co., KY. He d.19 Jun 1942 Ohio Co., KY, at age 47 and was bur. Sunnyside Cem., Beaver Dam.
Known children of Myrtle[8] Abney and Carey Hunter:
   i. Carrie Lee[9], b. 13 Sep 1914; m. Bardwell Ashby. (see # 972 on page 207).
   ii. Sue, b. 17 May 1918; m. Hoyt Thomas Wilson. (see page 145).
   iii. Martha Jo, b. 20 Apr 1923; m. Carlyle Thienes. (see page 145).

953. Laura Belle^8 Perry (Keziah^7 Abney, Jasper^6, John^5, Paul^4, Joshua^3, Elisha^2, Abner^1), b.29 Sep 1905 Russellville, Logan Co., KY. She m. Raymond William Knoll , son of William J. Knoll and Magdalena Wurth, on 30 Mar 1931 Evansville, Vanderburgh Co., IN. She d.11 Sep 1999 at age 93 and was bur. Centenary UMC Cem., Evansville, Vanderburgh Co., IN.

    Raymond William Knoll , b.12 Apr 1906 and d.7 Feb 1994 Evansville, Vanderburgh Co., IN, age 87; bur. Centenary UMC Cem., Evansville.
Known child of Laura Belle^8 Perry and Raymond William Knoll :
      1272   i.   Raymond Perry^9, b. 17 Jun 1932 Evansville, Vanderburgh Co., IN; m. Betty Jean West.

954. Charles Perry^8 Abney (USN-WWII) (Elijah^7, Jasper^6, John^5, Paul^4, Joshua^3, Elisha^2, Abner^1) m. Betty Lou Motteler, daughter of Otto Motteler and Orlena (n.n.). He, b.1 Feb 1925. He d.19 Mar 2005 at age 80 and was bur. Abraham Lincoln National Cem., Elwood, Will Co., IL.

    Betty Lou Motteler, b.26 Oct 1928. She d.31 Oct 2011 Bolingbrook, Will Co., IL, at age 83 and was bur. Abraham Lincoln National Cem.
Known children of Charles Perry^8 Abney (USN-WWII) and Betty Lou Motteler:
         i.   Sharon^9 m. Terry Gunty.
        ii.   Sandra m. Donald Wolz.
      iii.   Carol m. (n.n.) Carver.
      iv.   Kathie m. Louis Ignatowicz.
       v.   Chuck m. Chris (n.n.).
      vi.   Dan m. Erika (n.n.).
     vii.   Mike m. Barb (n.n.).
    viii.   Ron m. Pam (n.n.).

955. Delbert Dige^8 Abney (USArmy-WWII) (Elijah^7, Jasper^6, John^5, Paul^4, Joshua^3, Elisha^2, Abner^1), b.7 Dec 1926 Rockport, Spencer Co., IN. He m. Myrle Keener on 7 Dec 1963 Davenport, Scott Co., IA. He d.29 Sep 2002 Muscatine, Muscatine Co., IA, at age 75 and was bur. Greenwood Cem., Muscatine, Muscatine Co., IA.

    Myrle Keener m1. (n.n.) Shaner and had issue: Richard L, Jeffery, Teresa and Carolyn.
Known children of Delbert Dige^8 Abney (USArmy-WWII) and Myrle Keener:
         i.   Doug^9 m. Peggy (n.n.).
        ii.   Darren.

956. Gertrude^8 Abney (John^7, James^6, John^5, Paul^4, Joshua^3, Elisha^2, Abner^1), b.13 Feb 1892 KY. She m. Harold Valentine Moore, son of (n.n.) Moore and Margaret Ann Hampton, ca.1920. She and Harold Valentine Moore appeared on the census of 14 Apr 1930 Butler Co., KY. She appeared as Head of Household on the census of 2 May 1940 Butler Co., KY. She d.1 Oct 1967 Butler Co., KY, at age 75 and was bur. Mount Vernon Cem., Dexterville, Butler Co., KY.

    Harold Valentine Moore, b.15 May 1893 Butler Co., KY. He d.21 Jun 1934 Butler Co., KY, at age 41 and was bur. Mount Vernon Cem.
Known children of Gertrude^8 Abney and Harold Valentine Moore:
      1273   i.   Erdine Vaye^9, b. 15 May 1921.
           ii.   Thomas S., b.13 Aug 1924 Butler Co., KY. He d.22 Jan 2009 Butler Co., KY, at age 84 and was bur. Mount Vernon Cem.
      1274   iii.   Kenneth, b. 7 Jul 1926 Butler Co., KY; m. Vida (n.n.).
           iv.   Thurman, b. ca.1929 Butler Co., KY.
            v.   Vernon Valentine, b.18 Jun 1930 Butler Co., KY. He d.17 Mar 2011 Butler Co., KY, at age 80; bur. Mount Vernon Cem.
           vi.   Dimple "Morene", b. ca.1933 Butler Co., KY; m. (n.n.) Daugherty.

957. Thurman^8 Abney (John^7, James^6, John^5, Paul^4, Joshua^3, Elisha^2, Abner^1), b.1894. He m. Eva L. Ward. He appeared as Head of Household on the census of 23 Apr 1940 Pigeon Twp., Evansville, Vanderburgh Co., IN. He d.1987 and was bur. Park Lawn Cem. and Mausoleum, Evansville, Vanderburgh Co., IN.

    Eva L. Ward, b.1894. She d.1978 and was bur. Park Lawn Cem. and Mausoleum, Evansville, Vanderburgh Co., IN.
Known children of Thurman^8 Abney and Eva L. Ward:
         i.   Raymond^9.
        ii.   Bonnie Ree, b.1914. She d.1966 and was bur. Park Lawn Cem. and Mausoleum, Evansville, Vanderburgh Co., IN.
      iii.   Chester, b.1916. He d.1917 and was bur. Mount Vernon Baptist Church Cem., Calhoun, McLean Co., KY.
      iv.   Lester L., b.10 Nov 1917. He m. Estelene A. (n.n.) He d.3 Jul 1993 at age 75 and was bur. Sunset Mem. Gardens Cem.
           Estelene A. (n.n.), b.30 Apr 1920; d.9 Jul 2008;bur. Sunset Mem. Gardens Cem., Evansville, Vanderburgh Co., IN.
       v.   Irene, b.1919. She d.1921 and was bur. Mount Vernon Baptist Church Cem., Calhoun, McLean Co., KY.
      vi.   Rena Myrl, b.25 Nov 1921 McLean Co., KY. She m. Robert G. Underwood (USArmy-WWII) ca.1944. She d.5 Apr 2006 IN at age 84 and was bur. Park Lawn Cem. and Mausoleum, Evansville, Vanderburgh Co., IN.
           Robert G. Underwood (USArmy-WWII), b.18 Apr 1924. He d.16 Nov 2001 at age 77 and was bur. Park Lawn Cem.
      1275   vii.   Louis W., b. 5 Dec 1924 IN; m. Thelma L. (n.n.); m. Nora "Elizabeth" Bland.
      1276   viii.   Robert "Bob," b. Christmas Day, 25 Dec 1926 Evansville, Vanderburgh Co., IN; m. (n.n.).
      1277   ix.   Mary Kathryn, b. 1930 IN; m. Merle Edward Downen.
           x.   Raymond, b. ca.1933 IN.
           xi.   Delores M., b.26 May 1938 and d.26 May 1938 Evansville, Vanderburgh Co., IN and was bur. Park Lawn Cem.

958. Pearl^8 Abney (John^7, James^6, John^5, Paul^4, Joshua^3, Elisha^2, Abner^1), b.31 Oct 1894 Butler Co., KY. She m. Bennie Evans, son of James Melvin Evans and Viola F. Haven, on 5 Feb 1910. She d.23 Feb 1984 Morgantown, Butler Co., KY, at age 89 and was bur. Mount Liberty Church Cem., Morgantown, Butler Co., KY.

    Bennie Evans, b.22 Feb 1894 Ohio Co., KY. He d.24 Jan 1995 Morgantown, Butler Co., KY, at age 100.
Known child of Pearl^8 Abney and Bennie Evans:
         i.   Dorothy^9, b.19 Nov 1913 Butler Co., KY. She m. Rufus Bunyan Taylor in 1941 Butler Co., KY. She d.23 Jul 1992 Morgantown, Butler Co., KY, at age 78 and was bur. Mount Vernon Cem., Dexterville, Butler Co., KY.
           Rufus Bunyan Taylor, b.23 Aug 1894 Casey, Butler Co., KY. He d.10 Apr 1974 Banock, Butler Co., KY, at age 79 and was bur. Mount Vernon Cem., Dexterville, Butler Co., KY.

959. Lula M.^{8} Abney (John^7, James^6, John^5, Paul^4, Joshua^3, Elisha^2, Abner^1), b.17 Jan 1898 Butler Co., KY. She m. Columbus N. Mitchell on 27 Feb 1917. She d.22 Sep 1981 Jefferson Co., KY, at age 83 and was bur. Mount Vernon Cem., Dexterville, Butler Co., KY.
    Columbus N. Mitchell, b.21 Jan 1885 Butler Co., KY. He d.25 Apr 1956 Jefferson Co., KY, at age 71 and was bur. Mount Vernon Cem.
Known children of Lula M.^{8} Abney and Columbus N. Mitchell:
> i.   Gusta^9, b.16 Jul 1917 Monford, Butler Co., KY. He d.16 Jul 1917 Monford, Butler Co., KY; bur. Mount Vernon Cem.
> ii.   Jessie, b.8 Feb 1918 Monford, Butler Co., KY. She d.8 Feb 1918 Monford, Butler Co., KY; bur. Mount Vernon Cem.
> 1278   iii. Erlene, b. 21 Nov 1923 Morgantown, Butler Co., KY; m. Cody Overt Goodall (USArmy-WWII).
> iv.   Raymond m. Ruby LaVaughn Brooks, daughter of Jasper Brooks and Myrtle Embry. He, b.25 Aug 1926 Butler Co., KY. He d.12 Aug 1999 Louisville, Jefferson Co., KY, age 72; bur. Chapel Union Church Cem., Morgantown, Butler Co., KY.
>> Ruby LaVaughn Brooks, b.14 Aug 1933. She d.24 Sep 2014 at age 81 and was bur. Chapel Union Church Cem.
> 1279   v.   Arllis C., b. 9 Apr 1934; m. (n.n.).

960. Clifton^8 Abney (John^7, James^6, John^5, Paul^4, Joshua^3, Elisha^2, Abner^1), b.5 Mar 1908 IN. He m. Naomi Marie Waters. He d.14 Feb 1974 Saint Wendel, Vanderburgh Co., IN, at age 65 and was bur. Park Lawn Cem. and Mausoleum, Evansville, Vanderburgh Co., IN.
    Naomi Marie Waters, b.6 May 1912 McLean Co., KY. She d.3 Jan 1974 Vanderburgh Co., IN, at age 61.
Known child of Clifton^8 Abney and Naomi Marie Waters:
> i.   Robert Eugene^9, b.18 Nov 1941 IN. He d.11 Jun 1946 Evansville, Vanderburgh Co., IN, at age 4; bur. Park Lawn Cem.

961. Audrey^8 Abney (John^7, James^6, John^5, Paul^4, Joshua^3, Elisha^2, Abner^1), b.14 Dec 1909. She m. Gertie Corum, son of John R. Corum and Lydia E. Tucker, in 1927. She and Gertie Corum appeared on the census of 11 Apr 1930 McLean Co., KY. She d.11 Dec 1996 at age 86 and was bur. Calhoun Cem., Calhoun, McLean Co., KY.
    Gertie Corum, b.12 Dec 1906. He appeared on the census of 16 Apr 1940 McLean Co., KY. He d.24 Sep 1990 at age 83; bur. Calhoun Cem.
Known children of Audrey^8 Abney and Gertie Corum both b. KY:
> i.   Thomas Lindy^9, b.7 Jan 1928. He m. Dorothy Lee Jennings, daughter of Frederick D. Jennings and Corine Wills. He d.16 Oct 1996 at age 68 and was bur. Calhoun Cem., Calhoun, McLean Co., KY.
>> Dorothy Lee Jennings, b.16 Oct 1927.
> ii.   Robert, b. ca.1934.

962. Margaret M. "Millie"^{8} Abney (John^7, James^6, John^5, Paul^4, Joshua^3, Elisha^2, Abner^1), b.1919 McLean Co., KY. She m. Odis C. Meredith. She d.20 Oct 2000 and was bur. Park Lawn Cem. and Mausoleum, Evansville, Vanderburgh Co., IN.
    Odis C. Meredith, b.1917. He d.26 Apr 1966 and was bur. Park Lawn Cem. and Mausoleum, Evansville, Vanderburgh Co., IN.
Known child of Margaret M. "Millie"^{8} Abney and Odis C. Meredith:
> 1280   i.   Odis Carl^9, b. 18 Dec 1943.

963. S.Sgt. Louis John "Red"^{8} Abney (USAF-Korea) (John^7, James^6, John^5, Paul^4, Joshua^3, Elisha^2, Abner^1), b.20 Aug 1928 Calhoun, McLean Co., KY. He m. Anna Louise Yunker, daughter of John Jake Yunker and Katherine Werne, ca.1953. He d.New Year's Day, 1 Jan 2009 at age 80 and was bur. Tupman Cem., Evansville, Vanderburgh Co., KY.
    Anna Louise Yunker, b.Independence Day, 4 Jul 1926.
Known children of S.Sgt. Louis John "Red"^{8} Abney (USAF-Korea) and Anna Louise Yunker:
> 1281   i.   Alan^9, m. Brenda (n.n.).
> 1282   ii.   Susan "Sue," m. Jerry Skinner.
> 1283   iii. Dan Louis, m. Tonya (n.n.).

964. George Wesley^8 Wilson (Mary^7 Abney, James^6, John^5, Paul^4, Joshua^3, Elisha^2, Abner^1), b.22 Sep 1895 KY. He m. Louise Carter. He d.22 May 1958 Owensvoro, Daviess Co., KY, at age 62 and was bur. Calhoun Cem., Calhoun, McLean Co., KY.
    Louise Carter, b.1916. She d.Dec 1945 and was bur. New Cypress Cem., Rumsey, McLean Co., KY.
Known child of George Wesley^8 Wilson and Louise Carter:
> 1284   i.   Mary Frances^9, b. 23 May 1939 Metcalfe Co., KY; m. Thomas Dale Sutherland; m. McArthur DeWitt.

965. Nellie R.^{8} Wilson (Mary^7 Abney, James^6, John^5, Paul^4, Joshua^3, Elisha^2, Abner^1), b.16 Oct 1900. She m. Jesse "Jess" Garrett KY. They appeared on the census of 9 Feb 1920 McLean Co., KY. She d.1 May 1979 at age 78 and was bur. New Cypress Cem., Rumsey, McLean Co., KY.
    Jesse "Jess" Garrett, b.23 Oct 1883. He m1. Nannie Lee Davis. He appeared on the census of 21 Apr 1910 Daviess Co., KY. He d.30 Nov 1964 at age 81 and was bur. New Cypress Cem., Rumsey, McLean Co., KY.
Known children of Nellie R.^{8} Wilson and Jesse "Jess" Garrett:
> i.   Manuel^9, b. ca.1912 KY.
> ii.   Ethel, b. Jan 1920 KY.
> iii. Josephine, b.12 Oct 1921 KY. She m. Basil Leo Rickard in 1940. She d.4 Apr 2003 Madisonville, Hopkins Co., KY, at age 81 and was bur. Odd Fellows Cem., Madisonville, Hopkins Co., KY.
>> Basil Leo Rickard, b.23 Apr 1912 McLean Co., KY; d.20 Jul 1993 Madisonville, Hopkins Co., KY, bur. Odd Fellows.
> 1285   iv. Jesse Ray, b. 20 Feb 1923 KY; m. Judy Brown.
> 1286   v.   James Luther, b. 4 Mar 1925; m. Mary F. (n.n.).
> vi.   Elmer E., b.23 Nov 1934 McLean Co., KY. He d.14 Jul 1956 at age 21; bur. Maple Hill Cem., Fairfield, Wayne Co., IL.
> vii. Delmar A., b.28 Sep 1936 McLean Co., KY. He d.17 Oct 2000 Madisonville, Hopkins Co., KY, at age 64 and was bur. New Salem Church Cem., Nortonville, Hopkins Co., KY.
> 1287 viii. Patricia Nell, b. 22 Feb 1941 McLean Co., KY; m. William Perkins.

966. Effie^8 Abney (James^7, James^6, John^5, Paul^4, Joshua^3, Elisha^2, Abner^1), b.15 Sep 1898 McLean Co., KY. She m. (n.n.) Austin. She d.27 Jan 1985 at age 86 and was bur. Calhoun Cem., Calhoun, McLean Co., KY.
Known child of Effie^8 Abney and (n.n.) Austin:
> i.   Oswald^9, b.6 Jul 1925. He d.18 Apr 2001 at age 75 and was bur. Calhoun Cem., Calhoun, McLean Co., KY.

967. Edgar[8] Abney (James[7], James[6], John[5], Paul[4], Joshua[3], Elisha[2], Abner[1]), b.16 Dec 1903 McLean Co., KY. He m1. Hallie Ray McClellan. He on the census of 10 Apr 1940 McLean Co., KY. He m2. Avah Wilson, daughter of Rayburn W. Wilson and Ida E. Coomes. He d.26 Aug 1975 at age 71 and was bur. Mount Vernon Baptist Church Cem., Calhoun, McLean Co., KY.

Hallie Ray McClellan, b.23 May 1898 KY. She d.29 Apr 1949 at age 50 and was bur. Mount Vernon Baptist Church Cem., Calhoun.
Known children of Edgar[8] Abney and Hallie Ray McClellan:

　　　　　i.　James F. "Jimmy"[9], b.15 Jan 1933 KY and was bur. Mount Vernon Baptist Church Cem., Calhoun, McLean Co., KY. He
　　　　　　　m. Janet E. (n.n.) on 14 Apr 1951. He d.17 Oct 2007 at age 74. (Janet E. (n.n.), b.27 Apr 1934.)

Avah Wilson, b.29 Oct 1908. She m1. Hermon Pinkston. She d.6 Sep 2000 at age 91 and was bur. Calhoun Cem., Calhoun, McLean Co., KY.
There were no known children of Edgar[8] Abney and Avah Wilson.

968. Roscoe "William"[8] Abney (William[7], James[6], John[5], Paul[4], Joshua[3], Elisha[2], Abner[1]), b.26 Jul 1914 McLean Co., KY. He m. Gladys Haynes Howard on 13 Aug 1936 McLean Co., KY. He d.31 Aug 1994 McLean Co., KY, at age 80.

Gladys Haynes Howard, b.17 May 1919 McLean Co., KY. She was liv. in 1998 Calhoun, McLean Co., KY.
Known children of Roscoe "William"[8] Abney and Gladys Haynes Howard:

1288　　i.　Charles[9], b. 10 Feb 1937 McLean Co., KY; m. Lee Morris.
1289　　ii.　Jerry Roberts, b. 14 Dec 1938 McLean Co., KY; m. Earlene Clements.
1290　　iii.　Betty, b. 7 Aug 1941 McLean Co., KY; m. Gerald Iglehart; m. Louard Gray.
1291　　iv.　Darrell, b. 28 Mar 1945 McLean Co., KY; m. Kay Hargarett.
1292　　v.　Terry, b. 1 Jun 1947 McLean Co., KY; m. Shelia Brown.
1293　　vi.　Russell, b. 19 Mar 1951 McLean Co., KY; m. Pam Brush.
1294　　vii.　Norman, b. 19 Apr 1954 McLean Co., KY; m. Candy Bidwell.
1295　　viii.　Deborah "Debby," b. 20 Jul 1957 Owensboro, Daviess Co., KY; m. Alan Blus.
1296　　ix.　Judy, b. 28 May 1959 Owensboro, Daviess Co., KY; m. Johnny McCart.

969. Mittie[8] Snodgrass (Naoma[7] Daugherty, Mary[6] Abney, John[5], Paul[4], Joshua[3], Elisha[2], Abner[1]) m. John William Felty, son of Nickolas C. "Nickles" Felty and Polly Evelyn Embry. , b.21 Jan 1891 Butler Co., KY. She d.24 Jun 1951 Hartford, Ohio Co., KY, at age 60 and was bur. Oakwood Cem., Hartford, Ohio Co., KY.

John William Felty, b.23 Apr 1883. He d.2 Dec 1965 at age 82 and was bur. Oakwood Cem., Hartford, Ohio Co., KY.
Known children of Mittie[8] Snodgrass and John William Felty:

1297　　i.　Lucille[9], b. 4 Oct 1909; m. Arrel Rowe Himes Sr.
1298　　ii.　Faye, b. 28 Mar 1912; m. Joseph Duke Carson Sr.
1299　　iii.　Ruby Grey, b. 23 Sep 1913 Butler Co., KY; m. Everett J. Patton.
　　　　　iv.　Mabel, b.9 Sep 1915 Butler Co., KY. She m. Ray Brawner (USN-WWII), son of (n.n.) Brawner and Lula Hudson. She
　　　　　　　d.1 Dec 1990 Hartford, Ohio Co., KY, at age 75 and was bur. Oakwood Cem., Hartford, Ohio Co., KY.
　　　　　　　　Ray Brawner (USN-WWII), b.26 Jul 1908 OH. He d.18 Oct 1973 at age 65 and was bur. Oakwood Cem., Hartford.
　　　　　v.　Era Mae, b.26 May 1917. She m. Ellis Luther King, son of Samuel Luther King and Margaret Melvin, after 1940. She
　　　　　　　d.31 May 1984 at age 67 and was bur. Oakwood Cem., Hartford, Ohio Co., KY.
　　　　　　　　Ellis Luther King, b.Christmas Eve, 24 Dec 1902. He d.21 Feb 1993 at age 90 and was bur. Oakwood Cem., Hartford.
1300　　vi.　Claudia, b. 27 Oct 1919; m. Maj. Irvin Krone White (USMC-WWII, Korea).
　　　　　vii.　Clifty J., b.29 Dec 1921. She m. W.J. Murphy. d.13 Nov 1999 at age 77 and was bur. Oakwood Cem., Hartford.
　　　　　　　W.J. Murphy, b.16 Nov 1929.
　　　　　viii.　Edna C., b.9 May 1924 Butler Co., KY. She d.22 Aug 1964 Daviess Co., KY, at age 40 and was bur. Oakwood Cem.
　　　　　ix.　Leonard Edward, b.3 Jul 1926. He d.4 Nov 1952 at age 26 and was bur. Oakwood Cem., Hartford, Ohio Co., KY.
1301　　x.　John Snodgrass, b. 29 Oct 1934.

970. Mattie Lucille[8] Snodgrass (Naoma[7] Daugherty, Mary[6] Abney, John[5], Paul[4], Joshua[3], Elisha[2], Abner[1]), b.30 Aug 1899 Butler Co., KY. She m. William Hershel Dunn, son of Joshua M. Dunn and Lillian Bailey. They appeared on the censuses of 22 Jan 1920 Butler Co., KY; and 9 Apr 1930 and 1 Apr 1940 Hartford, Ohio Co., KY. She d.3 May 1976 Hartford, Ohio Co., KY, at age 76; bur. Oakwood Cem., Hartford, Ohio Co., KY.

William Hershel Dunn, b. New Year's Eve, 31 Dec 1894 Chalybeate, Edmonson Co., KY. He d.12 Dec 1982 Mobile, Mobile Co., AL, at age 87 and was bur. Oakwood Cem., Hartford, Ohio Co., KY.
Known children of Mattie Lucille[8] Snodgrass and William Hershel Dunn:

1302　　i.　Bennie[9], b. 24 Jan 1916 Butler Co., KY; m. John Edd Thompson Sr.
1303　　ii.　Hershel "Ray," b. 3 Apr 1919; m. Hannah H. Barrass.
　　　　　iii.　Jeanne d.infancy.
1304　　iv.　Lennie Grey, b. 11 Feb 1924 Ohio Co., KY; m. S. Sgt. William Elliott Johnson Sr. (USArmy-WWII).
　　　　　v.　William "Malcolm" m. Sue (n.n.). He, b. ca.Mar 1940 Hartford, Ohio Co., KY.

971. Pauline[8] Jones (Mollie[7] Hunter, Martha[6] Abney, John[5], Paul[4], Joshua[3], Elisha[2], Abner[1]), b.28 Oct 1909. She m. Willis James. She d.10 Aug 1989 at age 79 and was bur. Oakwood Cem., Hartford, Ohio Co., KY.

Willis James, b.1904. He d.12 Dec 1972 and was bur. Oakwood Cem., Hartford, Ohio Co., KY.
Known children of Pauline[8] Jones and Willis James:

　　　　　i.　Barbara Deane[9], b.23 Jul 1940. She d.19 Jan 1943 at age 2 and was bur. Oakwood Cem., Hartford, Ohio Co., KY.
　　　　　ii.　Kenneth Ray "Kenny", b.6 Mar 1946. He m. Mary I. Tinnell (b.21 Jan 1953) on 17 May 1974. He d.30 Aug 2008 at age
　　　　　　　62 and was bur. Nickel Ridge Cem., Panther, Daviess Co., KY.

972. Carrie Lee[8] Hunter (Carey[7], Martha[6] Abney, John[5], Paul[4], Joshua[3], Elisha[2], Abner[1]) m. Bardwell Ashby. , b.13 Sep 1914. She d.29 Mar 2003 at age 88 and was bur. Sunnyside Cem., Beaver Dam, Ohio Co., KY.

Bardwell Ashby, b.29 Jun 1913. He d.19 Sep 2002 at age 89 and was bur. Sunnyside Cem., Beaver Dam, Ohio Co., KY.
Known child of Carrie Lee[8] Hunter and Bardwell Ashby:

　　　　　i.　Charles Bardwell[9], b.10 Sep 1939. He d.25 Feb 1960 Rio de Janeiro, Brazil, at age 20 and was bur. Sunnyside Cem.

973. Loney⁸ Abney (Walter⁷, Jesse⁶, John⁵, Paul⁴, Joshua³, Elisha², Abner¹), b.1916. She m1. Ferman Hanger and had issue. She m2. Walter H. Tupman (USN-WWI, Korea) (1923-1995), but no issue. She d.2005 and was bur. Cedar Grove Cem., Salem, Dent Co., MO.
    Ferman Hanger, b.1907. He d.1982.
Known child of Loney⁸ Abney and Ferman Hanger:
        i.   Arlene D.⁹, b.27 Feb 1934. She d.1 Mar 1934 and was bur. Empire Cem., Gladden, Dent Co., MO.

974. Ira William⁸ Deno (WWII) (Sallie⁷ Abney, Daniel⁶, John⁵, Paul⁴, Joshua³, Elisha², Abner¹), b.3 May 1917. He m. Mabel Marie Vanover, daughter of Harrison Owen Vanover and Josephine Wilson, ca.1937. He and Mabel Marie Vanover appeared on the census of 2 Apr 1940 McLean Co., KY. He d.21 Nov 1976 at age 59 and was bur. Calhoun Cem., Calhoun, McLean Co., KY.
    Mabel Marie Vanover, b.New Year's Eve, 31 Dec 1919 KY. She d.26 Mar 1995 at age 75 and was bur. Calhoun Cem., Calhoun.
Known children of Ira William⁸ Deno (WWII) and Mabel Marie Vanover:
    1305   i.   Robert William "Bobby"⁹, b. 6 Dec 1938 McLean Co., KY; m. Norma J. Welch.
           ii. Ernest H., b. ca.Mar 1940 McLean Co., KY.
           iii. Larry W., b.5 Feb 1942. He d.23 Feb 2002 at age 60 and was bur. Cox Cem., Dubois Co., IN.
           iv. Hugh Noble, b.29 Jun 1943. He d.2 Sep 1999 at age 56 and was bur. Calhoun Cem., Calhoun, McLean Co., KY.
           v.   Myrtle Marie, b.29 Jun 1945 Calhoun, McLean Co., KY. She m. Pvt. Willard Gray Crowe (USArmy-Nam), son of Elivs C. Crowe and Vertie Lee Finley, ca.1965. She d.Christmas Day, 25 Dec 2005 Owensboro, Daviess Co., KY, at age 60 and was bur. Mount Carmel Cem., Buford, Ohio Co., KY.
                    Pvt. Willard Gray Crowe (USArmy-Nam), b.31 Mar 1943 Daviess Co., KY. He d.2 May 2001 Owensboro, Daviess Co., KY, at age 58.
           vi. Edith Myrtle, b.13 Oct 1952. She d.23 Mar 1955 at age 2 and was bur. Calhoun Cem., Calhoun, McLean Co., KY.
           vii. Betty Rosalene "Be Be" m. (n.n.) Galloway. , b.27 Feb 1956 Daviess Co., KY. She d.14 Jul 2006 Owensboro, Daviess Co., KY, at age 50 and was bur. Rosehill Elmwood Cem., Owensboro, Daviess Co., KY.

975. Helen Bernice⁸ Deno (Sallie⁷ Abney, Daniel⁶, John⁵, Paul⁴, Joshua³, Elisha², Abner¹), b.23 Aug 1925; m. Rev. Pvt. Charles Monroe Vanover (USArmy-WWII), son of Harrison Owen Vanover and Josephine Wilson. d.29 Jun 2006 at age 80; bur. Calhoun Cem., Calhoun, McLean Co., KY.
    Rev. Pvt. Charles Monroe Vanover (USArmy-WWII), b.16 May 1918 McLean Co., KY; d.21 Apr 1992 Owensboro, Daviess Co., KY, age 73.
Known children of Helen Bernice⁸ Deno and Rev. Pvt. Charles Monroe Vanover (USArmy-WWII):
        i.   James O.⁹ m. Erlinda (n.n.).
        ii. Neal m. Faye (n.n.).
        iii. Ann m. L.B. Cox.
        iv. John m. Margaret (n.n.).
        v.   Brenda m. Billy Ford.
        vi. Ruth m. Jackie Horn.
        vii. Thelma m. (n.n.) Anderson.
    1306 viii. Charles Edward, b. 25 Mar 1941 McLean Co., KY; m. (n.n.).
        ix. Martha Jean, b.11 Nov 1951. She d.30 Dec 1951 and was bur. Calhoun Cem., Calhoun, McLean Co., KY.
        x.   Danny, b.14 Nov 1952 Daviess Co., KY. He d.19 Apr 2019 Owensboro, Daviess Co., KY, at age 66; bur. Calhoun Cem.
        xi. Nancy C., b.17 Apr 1954. She m. (n.n.) Dowell. d.12 Mar 2005 at age 50 and was bur. Calhoun Cem.

976. Effie Pearl⁸ Moore (Veachel⁷, Paul⁶, Mary⁵ Abney, Paul⁴, Joshua³, Elisha², Abner¹), b.18 Jan 1920. She m. Harlet E. Coots. d.19 Apr 1993 at age 73 and was bur. Sunnyside Cem., Beaver Dam, Ohio Co., KY.
    Harlet E. Coots, b.26 Oct 1914. He d.12 Sep 1983 at age 68 and was bur. Sunnyside Cem., Beaver Dam, Ohio Co., KY.
Known children of Effie Pearl⁸ Moore and Harlet E. Coots:
        i.   Lemmie D.⁹, b.3 May 1936. He m. LuSandra Stenberg. He d.7 Oct 2016 at age 80. He was cremated.
                LuSandra Stenberg, b.30 Mar 1938 KY. She d.28 Oct 2018 Ohio Co., KY, at age 80.
        ii. Jerry Lloyd, b.9 Oct 1944 Ohio Co., KY. He d.13 Dec 2009 Owensboro, Daviess Co., KY, at age 65 and was bur. Liberty Cem., Beaver Dam, Ohio Co., KY.

977. Lawson⁸ Moore (Nathan⁷, Finis⁶, Mary⁵ Abney, Paul⁴, Joshua³, Elisha², Abner¹), b.24 Nov 1916 KY. He m. Lillian B. Dennison, daughter of Simon Dennison and Effie Myrtle Gatchel, ca.1942. He m. Edna B. Rowe. He d.9 Jul 1983 Cincinnati, Hamilton Co., OH, at age 66.
    Lillian B. Dennison, b.16 Aug 1916 McHenry, Ohio Co., KY. She d.8 Aug 1970 Chicago, Cook Co., IL, at age 53 and was bur. Concordia Cem., Forest Park, Cook Co., IL.
Known child of Lawson⁸ Moore and Lillian B. Dennison:
    1307   i.   Helen Christine "Chris"⁹, b. 26 Jun 1943 Cincinnati, Hamilton Co., OH.
    Edna B. Rowe, b.7 Jul 1913 KY; d.8 Sep 1973 Cincinnati, Hamilton Co., OH, at age 60 and was bur. Spring Grove Cem., Cincinnati, OH.
There were no known children of Lawson⁸ Moore and Edna B. Rowe.

978. Eula Christine⁸ Moore (Nathan⁷, Finis⁶, Mary⁵ Abney, Paul⁴, Joshua³, Elisha², Abner¹), b.27 May 1930. She m. PFC Hallie Woodward Renfrow (USArmy-WWII), son of Leonard Washington Renfrow and Ruby Opal Baize. She d.8 Jan 2006 at age 75 and was bur. Bell's Run Cem., Bell's Run, Ohio Co., KY.
    PFC Hallie Woodward Renfrow (USArmy-WWII), b.3 Aug 1926. He d.26 Aug 1983 at age 57 and was bur. Bell's Run Cem., Bell's Run.
Known children of Eula Christine⁸ Moore and PFC Hallie Woodward Renfrow (USArmy-WWII) both b. Ohio Co., KY:
    1308   i.   William Denton⁹, b. 3 Apr 1949; m. (n.n.).
        ii. Sherry Elaine, b.19 Nov 1958. She m. (n.n.) Bryant. d.24 Sep 2009 Owensboro, Daviess Co., KY, at age 50 and was bur. Cedar Grove Cem., Midland, Muhlenberg Co., KY.

979. Oscar W.⁸ Moore (Daniel⁷, Finis⁶, Mary⁵ Abney, Paul⁴, Joshua³, Elisha², Abner¹) m. Lora Simpson, daughter of Eura Simpson and Minnie Jane Kessinger. He, b.25 Apr 1925. He d.14 Apr 1988 at age 62 and was bur. Render Cem., McHenry, Ohio Co., KY.
    Lora Simpson, b.29 Oct 1923. She d.13 Oct 2011 at age 87 and was bur. Render Cem., McHenry, Ohio Co., KY.

Known child of Oscar W.[8] Moore and Lora Simpson:
>   i.   Stephen Eugene[9], b.28 Nov 1952. He d.21 Feb 2013 at age 60 and was bur. Render Cem., McHenry, Ohio Co., KY.

980. Ruth[8] Moore (Thomas[7], Finis[6], Mary[5] Abney, Paul[4], Joshua[3], Elisha[2], Abner[1]), b.4 Mar 1931. She m. Robert Lee Eury, son of James Henderson Eury and Mary Ann Forrest. She d.12 Apr 1984 at age 53 and was bur. Bethel UMC Cem., New London, Stanly Co., NC.
>   Robert Lee Eury, b.6 Mar 1917. He d.24 Jan 1984 at age 66 and was bur. Bethel UMC Cem., New London, Stanly Co., NC.
Known child of Ruth[8] Moore and Robert Lee Eury:
>   i.   Robert Michael[9], b.6 Sep 1957; d.20 Nov 2004, age 47 and was bur. Norview Gardens Cem., Norwood, Stanly Co., NC.

981. Sgt. Alva C.[8] Hert (USArmy-WWII) (Nola[7] Moore, Finis[6], Mary[5] Abney, Paul[4], Joshua[3], Elisha[2], Abner[1]), b.27 Apr 1921 Ohio Co., KY. He m. Mary Catherine Faught on 10 Dec 1941 Ohio Co., KY. He d.25 Jul 1975 Marion, Williamson Co., IL, at age 54 and was bur. Render Cem., McHenry, Ohio Co., KY.
Known child of Sgt. Alva C.[8] Hert (USArmy-WWII) and Mary Catherine Faught:
> 1309 i.   Diana Sue[9], b. 7 Jul 1946 McHenry, Ohio Co., KY; m. (n.n.) Darnell.

982. Stella B.[8] Hurt (Nola[7] Moore, Finis[6], Mary[5] Abney, Paul[4], Joshua[3], Elisha[2], Abner[1]), b.25 Aug 1922 McHenry, Ohio Co., KY. She m. Cecil Raymond Sr., son of Jake Raymond and Stella Brown. She d.3 Jan 2011 at age 88 and was bur. Alexander Mem. Park Cem., Evansville, Vanderburgh Co., IN.
>   Cecil Raymond Sr, b.22 Feb 1915 McHenry, Ohio Co., KY. He d.17 Jul 1992 Evansville, Vanderburgh Co., IN, at age 77.
Known child of Stella B.[8] Hurt and Cecil Raymond Sr.:
> 1310 i.   Cecil[9], b. 1 Nov 1942 McHenry, Ohio Co., KY; m. Patrice Toney.

983. Lillian Mae[8] Fain (Estella[7] Baize, Mary[6] Moore, Mary[5] Abney, Paul[4], Joshua[3], Elisha[2], Abner[1]), b.21 Mar 1916 Hohenwald, Lewis Co., TN. She m. (n.n.) McHugh. d.1 Oct 1994 Geauga Co., OH, at age 78 and was bur. Middlefield Cem., Middlefield, Geauga Co., OH.
>   Known child of Lillian Mae[8] Fain and (n.n.) McHugh:
>   i.   Warren Richard[9], b.23 May 1936 Cleveland, Cuyahoga Co., OH. He d.18 Dec 2000 Youngstown, Mahoning Co., OH, at age 64 and was bur. Middlefield Cem., Middlefield, Geauga Co., OH.

984. Delia "Martine"[8] Moore (Brankley[7], Thomas[6], Mary[5] Abney, Paul[4], Joshua[3], Elisha[2], Abner[1]), b.11 Sep 1928 Ohio Co., KY. She m. Stanley Stolarz (d.1984). d.7 Nov 2018 Las Vegas, Clark Co., NV, at age 90 and was bur. Holy Cross Cem. and Mausoleums, Calumet City, Cook Co., IL.
Known children of Delia "Martine"[8] Moore and Stanley Stolarz:
>   i.   Debbie[9] m. Robert Coffee.
>   ii. Reisha m. Bob Beck Mihalso.

985. Osburn Ray[8] Flener (WWII) (Perry[7], Lucinda[6] Deweese, Nicey[5] Abney, Paul[4], Joshua[3], Elisha[2], Abner[1]), b.14 Jul 1926 Flener, Butler Co., KY. He m. Kathryn Jane "Janie" Hill, daughter of Robert Bruce Hill and Georgia Hill, on 22 Dec 1945. He m. Bettie Day Smith (1929-2017), but no issue. He d.25 Oct 2014 Bowling Green, Warren Co., KY, at age 88 and was bur. Fairview Cem., Bowling Green, Warren Co., KY.
>   Kathryn Jane "Janie" Hill, b.8 Oct 1927 Morgantown, Butler Co., KY. She d.17 Nov 1979 Bowling Green, Warren Co., KY, at age 52.
Known children of Osburn Ray[8] Flener (WWII) and Kathryn Jane "Janie" Hill:
>   i.   Danny Ray[9], b.30 Jun 1948 Bowling Green, Warren Co., KY. He d.30 Jun 1948 Bowling Green, Warren Co., KY and was bur. Old Riverview Cem., Morgantown, Butler Co., KY.
>   ii. Penny Jane.
>   iii. Lou Ann.
>   iv. Mark Hill.
>   v.   Samuel Ray.

986. Pearl[8] Conn (May[7] Evans, Armedia[6] Daugherty, Hannah[5] Abney, Paul[4], Joshua[3], Elisha[2], Abner[1]), b.6 Jan 1912 Okemah, Okfuskee Co., OK. She m. William Marshall "Bill" Jones (USArmy-WWII), son of William Jones and Alice Harper. d.2 Aug 1932 University Hosp., Oklahoma City, Oklahoma Co., OK, at age 20 and was bur. Sunny Lane Cem., Del City, Oklahoma Co., OK.
>   William Marshall "Bill" Jones (USArmy-WWII), b.13 Sep 1906 OK. He d.20 Oct 1975 Stillwater, Payne Co., OK, at age 69.
Known children of Pearl[8] Conn and William Marshall "Bill" Jones (USArmy-WWII) both b. Okemah, Okfuskee Co., OK:
>   i.   Pearl Vilice "Pearly"[9], b.30 Dec 1929. She m. PFC Joseph Jackson Harber (USArmy-WWII), son of Joseph R. Harber and Dona Faye Bramlett. She d.31 Aug 2012 Oklahoma City, Oklahoma Co., OK, at age 82 and was bur. Resurrection Mem. Cem., Oklahoma City, Oklahoma Co., OK.
>   PFC Joseph Jackson Harber (USArmy-WWII), b.25 Jul 1927 Calico Rock, Izard Co., AR. He d.22 Aug 1994 Oklahoma City, Oklahoma Co., OK, at age 67.
>   ii. William "Billy", b.1931. He d.2 Aug 1932 University Hosp., Oklahoma City, Oklahoma Co., OK and was bur. Sunny Lane Cem., Del City, Okfuskee Co., OK.

987. Earl C.[8] Coots (USArmy) (Senora[7] Abner, Harrison[6], Isaac[5] Abney, Paul[4], Joshua[3], Elisha[2], Abner[1]), b.2 Apr 1932. He m. Stefanie E. Oszek. He d.5 Aug 1992 at age 60 and was bur. Chapel Union Church Cem., Morgantown, Butler Co., KY.
>   Stefanie E. Oszek, b.21 Jun 1930. She d.12 Apr 2015 at age 84.
Known children of Earl C.[8] Coots (USArmy) and Stefanie E. Oszek all b. KY:
>   i.   Connie[9] m. William Moss.
>   ii. Johnny.
> 1311 iii. Steven Lee "Steve," b. 14 Dec 1961; m. Violet P. Johnson.
>   iv. Mary Ann.

988. Kathleen Mae[8] Evans (Louie[7] Abner, Harrison[6], Isaac[5] Abney, Paul[4], Joshua[3], Elisha[2], Abner[1]), b.16 Jun 1937 Butler Co., KY. She d.12 Dec 2015 Bowling Green, Warren Co., KY, at age 78 and was bur. on 14 Dec 2015 New Liberty Cem., Warren Co., KY.

Known child of Kathleen Mae[8] Evans:
       i.   Jerry Lee *Evans*[9] d. before 2015.

989. Deloide C.[8] Evans (Louie[7] Abner, Harrison[6], Isaac[5] Abney, Paul[4], Joshua[3], Elisha[2], Abner[1]), b.28 Nov 1942 Butler Co., KY. He m. Linda Sue (n.n.) (b.15 Mar 1946) on 11 Jun 1962. He d.25 Nov 2014 Morgantown, Butler Co., KY, age 71 and was bur. New Liberty Cem., Butler Co., KY.
Known children of Deloide C.[8] Evans and Linda Sue (n.n.):
       i.   Melissa[9] m. Steve Cook.
      ii.   Steven.

990. Joan[8] Abner (Lester[7], Harrison[6], Isaac[5] Abney, Paul[4], Joshua[3], Elisha[2], Abner[1]), b.3 Dec 1940. She m. Clarence Johnson. d.12 Mar 2016 OH at age 75 and was bur. Fisher Cem., Heidrick, Knox Co., KY.
Known children of Joan[8] Abner and Clarence Johnson:
   1312   i.   Michael Dean[9], m. Alexis (n.n.).
   1313 ii.   Melissa Carol, m. Jim Nugent.

991. Arthur[8] Turner (Flora[7] Goff, Rena[6] Abner, Silas[5] Abney, Paul[4], Joshua[3], Elisha[2], Abner[1]), b.12 Aug 1912 Ohio Co., KY. He m. Juanita (n.n.) on 11 Sep 1935. He d.16 Nov 1991 Bloomfield, Greene Co., IN, at age 79 and was bur. Fairview Cem., Linton, Greene Co., IN.
    Juanita (n.n.), b.1919. She d.1999 and was bur. Fairview Cem., Linton, Greene Co., IN.
Known children of Arthur[8] Turner and Juanita (n.n.):
   1314   i.   Shirley Ann[9], b. 7 Sep 1936 Linton, Greene Co., IN; m. Gary Jackson.
          ii.   Norman "Buddy", b.13 Jul 1938. He d.12 Jan 1983 at age 44 and was bur. Fairview Cem., Linton, Greene Co., IN.

992. Mark A.[8] Loyd Sr. (Aubrey[7], Rena[6] Abner, Silas[5] Abney, Paul[4], Joshua[3], Elisha[2], Abner[1]) m. Margaret (N.N.).
Known children of Mark A.[8] Loyd Sr. and Margaret (N.N.):
       i.   Mark A.[9].
      ii.   Matt.
     iii.   James.
     iv.   Jessica m. Curt Isakson.

993. Sharon[8] Loyd (Ray[7], Rena[6] Abner, Silas[5] Abney, Paul[4], Joshua[3], Elisha[2], Abner[1]), b.12 Jun 1946 Louisville, Jefferson Co., KY. She m. Terry Jennette in 1964. She d.19 Dec 2018 Louisville, Jefferson Co., KY, at age 72 and was bur. Resthaven Mem. Cem., Louisville, Jefferson Co., KY.
Known children of Sharon[8] Loyd and Terry Jennette:
       i.   Todd[9] m. Geralyn (N.N.).
      ii.   Kimberly m. Chris Meeks.
     iii.   Tiffany m. Darryl Love.

994. Thomas T. "Tom"[8] Hoskins (USAF-Nam) (Oakie[7] Abner, Homer[6], Silas[5] Abney, Paul[4], Joshua[3], Elisha[2], Abner[1]), b.29 Apr 1940 Ohio Co., KY. He m1. Jonell Osborne, daughter of James William Osborne and Bernice Baughn. He m2. Arlene (n.n.), but no issue. He d.26 Dec 2014 Owensboro, Daviess Co., KY, at age 74 and was bur. Waltons Creek Church Cem., Centertown, Ohio Co., KY.
    Jonell Osborne, b.20 Mar 1959 Evansville, Vanderburgh Co., IN. She d.15 May 1993 Indianapolis, Marion Co., IN, at age 34.
Known children of Thomas T. "Tom"[8] Hoskins (USAF-Nam) and Jonell Osborne:
       i.   Nathan[9].
      ii.   Harold Kerr.
     iii.   Vickie m. Jerry Noble.

995. Michael L.[8] Abner (Tom[7], Homer[6], Silas[5] Abney, Paul[4], Joshua[3], Elisha[2], Abner[1]) m. Tina Miller.
Known children of Michael L.[8] Abner and Tina Miller:
       i.   Kim[9].
      ii.   Michael A.

996. Minnie Lou[8] Sowers (Sally[7] Abner, George[6], Silas[5] Abney, Paul[4], Joshua[3], Elisha[2], Abner[1]), b.15 Sep 1935 AL. She m. William Henry "Junior" Reeves Jr. d.25 Jul 2016 Decatur, Morgan Co., AL, at age 80.
    William Henry "Junior" Reeves Jr, b.24 Sep 1928 AL. He, b.11 Jan 2016 Moulton, Lawrence Co., AL and was bur. East Lawrence Mem. Gardens, Moulton, Lawrence Co., AL.
Known children of Minnie Lou[8] Sowers and William Henry "Junior" Reeves Jr.:
       i.   William Donald "Pete"[9], b.8 Jan 1953. He d.26 Jan 2019 at age 66; bur. Union Hill Cem., Moulton, Lawrence Co., AL.
      ii.   Wanda Kay, b.26 May 1959. She m. (n.n.) Parker. She d.29 Jun 2004 at age 45 and was bur. East Lawrence Mem. Gardens.

997. Newt[8] Abner Jr. (Newt[7], George[6], Silas[5] Abney, Paul[4], Joshua[3], Elisha[2], Abner[1]), b.6 Mar 1943 Somerville, Morgan Co., AL. He m. Carol (n.n.). He d.7 Apr 1998 OH at age 55 and was bur. Greenlawn Mem. Park, Akron, Summit Co., OH.
Known children of Newt[8] Abner Jr. and Carol (n.n.):
       i.   Craig[9] m. Tammy (n.n.).
      ii.   Greg.
     iii.   Dwight.

998. Rayburn A.[8] Abner (Arrie[7], George[6], Silas[5] Abney, Paul[4], Joshua[3], Elisha[2], Abner[1]) m. Willodean "Monk" (n.n.). He, b.30 Sep 1947 Blount Co., AL. He d.3 Aug 2003 Cullman Co., AL, at age 55 and was bur. Roswell Creek Cem., Strawberry, Blount Co., AL.
Known children of Rayburn A.[8] Abner and Willodean "Monk" (n.n.):
       i.   Charlie[9].
      ii.   Kala.

999. Loyd George[8] Abner (Arrie[7], George[6], Silas[5] Abney, Paul[4], Joshua[3], Elisha[2], Abner[1]) m. (n.n.). He, b.11 Aug 1951 Blount Co., AL. He d.18 Aug 2010 TN at age 59 and was bur. Roswell Creek Cem., Strawberry, Blount Co., AL.
Known children of Loyd George[8] Abner and (n.n.):
     i.   Jamie Jordan[9].
     ii.   Belinda.

1000. Ellen Irene[8] Abner (Arrie[7], George[6], Silas[5] Abney, Paul[4], Joshua[3], Elisha[2], Abner[1]), b.21 Jun 1953 Lawrence Co., AL. She m. Bill "Billy Joe" Key ca.1968. She d.13 Mar 2011 Grant, Marshall Co., AL, at age 57 and was bur. Roswell Creek Cem., Strawberry, Blount Co., AL.
Known children of Ellen Irene[8] Abner and Bill "Billy Joe" Key:
     i.   James Callahan[9].
     ii.   Billy Joe m. Betty (n.n.).
     iii. John m. Erin (n.n.).
     iv. Jim m. Janet (n.n.).

1001. Mary[8] Abner (Arrie[7], George[6], Silas[5] Abney, Paul[4], Joshua[3], Elisha[2], Abner[1]), b.17 Jul 1954 Blount Co., AL. She m. Perry Lucas. d.3 Feb 2016 Birmingham, Jefferson Co., AL, at age 61 and was bur. Roswell Creek Cem., Strawberry, Blount Co., AL.
Known child of Mary[8] Abner and Perry Lucas:
     i.   David[9] m. Jennifer (n.n.).

1002. Katie Mae[8] Bradley (Clistie[7] Abner, George[6], Silas[5] Abney, Paul[4], Joshua[3], Elisha[2], Abner[1]), b.9 Oct 1943 Morgan Co., AL. She m. Kenneth M. Cockrell, son of Lacy Cockrell and Bula O. (n.n.). d.3 Mar 2011 Decatur, Morgan Co., AL, at age 67 and was bur. New Friendship Bapt. Church Cem., Somerville, Morgan Co., AL.
    Kenneth M. Cockrell m. Dorothy Mills. He was (an unknown value) farmer & painter. He, b.1 May 1942 AL. He d.5 Sep 2006 Decatur, Morgan Co., AL, at age 64 and was bur. Chapel Hill Cem., Decatur, Morgan Co., AL.
Known children of Katie Mae[8] Bradley and Kenneth M. Cockrell:
     i.   James Edward[9].
     ii.   Jody m. Linda (n.n.).
     iii. Ed Bradley.

1003. Joyce Marie[8] Abner (Hobert[7], George[6], Silas[5] Abney, Paul[4], Joshua[3], Elisha[2], Abner[1]) m. Leman "O'Neal" Osborn, son of Claudie Osborn and Lillie Mae (n.n.). , b.24 Jan 1956. She d.Leap Day, 29 Feb 2004 at age 48 and was bur. Center Cem., Lawrence Co., AL.
    Leman "O'Neal" Osborn, b.3 Nov 1944 and was bur. Center Cem., Lawrence Co., AL. He d.8 Aug 2017 at age 72.
Known children of Joyce Marie[8] Abner and Leman "O'Neal" Osborn (birth order unknown): Leman "Bubba", Marshall m. Lisa(n.n.), Richard m. Mary (n.n.), Marvin, Robert m. Lagina (n.n.), Randy m. Cindy (n.n.), Tina m. Mike Grimes, Flora, Angie m. Allen Lee, Joyce m. Gary Porter, Holly m1. (n.n.) Strickland; m2. Jonathan Davis, Lisa Rene m. Jimmy White, Amanda Bell, and April m. Michael Burgett.

1004. Alma Ruth[8] Downs (Minnie[7] Wills, Elizabeth[6] Abney, Wilburn[5], Benjamin[4], Hezekiah[3], Elisha[2], Abner[1]) m. Lester M. Calhoun. , b.11 Feb 1894 AL. She d.20 Jul 1984 Lake Worth, Palm Beach Co., FL, at age 90; bur. Old Harmony Bapt. Ch. Cem., Rainbow City, Etowah Co., AL.
    Lester M. Calhoun, b.15 Jan 1898 St. Clair Co., AL; d.1 Mar 1980 Rainbow City, Etowah Co., AL, age 82; bur. Old Harmony Bapt. Ch. Cem.
Known children of Alma Ruth[8] Downs and Lester M. Calhoun:
     i.   Woodrow R.[9] m. Donna B. (n.n.). He, b.3 Jun 1919. He d.3 Jul 2001 at age 82.
     ii.   James Ted, b.16 Oct 1920 AL. He d.27 Aug 2012 Rainbow City, Etowah Co., AL, at age 91 and was bur. Crestwood Mem. Cem., East Gadsden, Etowah Co., AL.

1005. Naomi Elizabeth[8] Downs (Minnie[7] Wills, Elizabeth[6] Abney, Wilburn[5], Benjamin[4], Hezekiah[3], Elisha[2], Abner[1]) m. Leonard William Short Sr. , b.18 Mar 1903 AL. She d.30 Jul 1994 at age 91 and was bur. Greenwood Cem., Montgomery, Montgomery Co., AL.
    Leonard William Short Sr, b.30 Jul 1894 Elmore Co., AL. He d.12 Jun 1957 at age 62 and was bur. Greenwood Cem., Montgomery.
Known child of Naomi Elizabeth[8] Downs and Leonard William Short Sr.:
     i.   Leonard William Jr. (USN-WWII, Korea, Nam)[9], b.28 Feb 1926 Montgomery Co., AL. He d.16 Aug 1990 at age 64 and was bur. Barrancas National Cem., Pensacola, Escambia Co., FL.

1006. Gresham Gerald[8] Downs (Minnie[7] Wills, Elizabeth[6] Abney, Wilburn[5], Benjamin[4], Hezekiah[3], Elisha[2], Abner[1]), b.29 Jul 1906 AL. He m1. Lillian Omega. He m2. Ruby Luceil Perrine. He d.4 Jun 1965 Gadsden, Etowah Co., AL, at age 58; bur. Forrest Cem., Gadsden, Etowah Co., AL.
    Lillian Omega m2. Jack Hasty. , b.15 Mar 1906. She d.16 Sep 1976 at age 70 and was bur. Elmwood Cem., Birmingham, Jefferson Co., AL. There were no known children of Gresham Gerald[8] Downs and Lillian Omega.
    Ruby Luceil Perrine, b.26 Mar 1924 Etowah Co., AL; d.10 Feb 2009 Etowah Co., AL, age 84; bur. Tillison Cem., Gadsden, Etowah Co., AL.
Known child of Gresham Gerald[8] Downs and Ruby Luceil Perrine:
     i.   Donna Ruth[9], b.11 Jul 1950; m. (n.n.) Calhoun. d.14 Jun 2020 Gadsden, Etowah Co., AL, age 69; bur. Unity Baptist Ch. Cem., Etowah Co., AL.

1007. Pvt. Kermit Roosevelt[8] Downs (USArmy-WWII) (Minnie[7] Wills, Elizabeth[6] Abney, Wilburn[5], Benjamin[4], Hezekiah[3], Elisha[2], Abner[1]) m. Lillian McClendon. He, b.23 Jul 1912 AL. He d.14 Apr 1967 Gadsden, Etowah Co., AL, at age 54; bur. Forrest Cem., Gadsden, Etowah Co., AL.
    Lillian McClendon, b.31 Oct 1916 Whitney Junction, St. Clair Co., AL; d.15 Feb 2006 Gadsden, Etowah Co., AL, age 89; bur. Forrest Cem.
Known children of Pvt. Kermit Roosevelt[8] Downs (USArmy-WWII) and Lillian McClendon:
     i.   Mack[9].
     ii.   Don.

1008. S.Sgt. James Dwight[8] Abney (USArmy-WWII) (John[7], Washington[6], Wilburn[5], Benjamin[4], Hezekiah[3], Elisha[2], Abner[1]), b.11 May 1916 GA. He m. Ella "Elizabeth" King. He d.28 Jan 1985 at age 68 and was bur. Summerville Cem., Summerville, Chattooga Co., GA.
    Ella "Elizabeth" King, b.15 Oct 1920 Menlo, Chattooga Co., GA. She d.26 Sep 2013 Rome, Floyd Co., GA, at age 92; bur. Summerville Cem.

Known child of S.Sgt. James Dwight[8] Abney (USArmy-WWII) and Ella "Elizabeth" King:
        1315   i.   James King[9], m. Charlene (n.n.).

1009. Raymond Lee[8] Abney Sr. (Grover[7], Washington[6], Wilburn[5], Benjamin[4], Hezekiah[3], Elisha[2], Abner[1]), b.27 Dec 1911. He owned *Abney's Chrysler, Dodge & Plymouth*, LaFayette, Walker Co., GA. He m. Martha Louise Elrod ca.1936. He was also owner of *Abney's Chrysler, Dodge & Plymouth*, Ringgold, Catoosa Co., GA. He d.19 Jan 1983 at age 71 and was bur. Anderson Mem. Gardens, Ringgold, Catoosa Co., GA.
      Martha Louise Elrod, b.6 Sep 1915. She d.24 Jun 2009 at age 93 and was bur. Anderson Mem. Gardens, Ringgold, Catoosa Co., GA.
Known children of Raymond Lee[8] Abney Sr. and Martha Louise Elrod:
        1316   i.   Raymond Lee[9], b. 4 Oct 1937; m. Charlotte Jeanette Crawford.
        1317   ii.   Kenneth Julian "Ken," b. 26 Jun 1941; m. Elizabeth "Faye" Crawford.

1010. Grover "Watson"[8] Abney (Grover[7], Washington[6], Wilburn[5], Benjamin[4], Hezekiah[3], Elisha[2], Abner[1]) m. Wilma Davis. He, b.27 Apr 1917 GA. He and Wilma Davis appeared on the census of 5 Apr 1940 Ringgold, Catoosa Co., GA. He d.6 Mar 1999 at age 81 and was bur. Nathan Anderson Historic Cem., Ringgold, Catoosa Co., GA.
      Wilma Davis, b.26 Oct 1918 GA. She d.25 Feb 1999 at age 80 and was bur. Nathan Anderson Historic Cem., Ringgold, Catoosa Co., GA.
Known child of Grover "Watson"[8] Abney and Wilma Davis:
               i.   Carole Jacqueline[9], b.23 Dec 1939. She d.18 Jan 2019 Catoosa Co., GA, at age 79; bur. Nathan Anderson Historic Cem.

1011. James Howard[8] Abney Sr. (USN-WWII) (Grover[7], Washington[6], Wilburn[5], Benjamin[4], Hezekiah[3], Elisha[2], Abner[1]) m. Bertie Catherine Cowart. He, b.28 Sep 1919 GA. He, b.1 May 1975 and was bur. Nathan Anderson Historic Cem., Ringgold, Catoosa Co., GA.
      Bertie Catherine Cowart, b.21 Aug 1920 and d.16 Mar 2011 Ringgold, Catoosa Co., GA, at age 90; bur. Nathan Anderson Historic Cem.
Known child of James Howard[8] Abney Sr. (USN-WWII) and Bertie Catherine Cowart:
               i.   James Howard[9], b.14 Jul 1942. He d.8 Mar 2007 Ringgold, Catoosa Co., GA, at age 64 and was bur. Nathan Anderson Historic Cem., Ringgold, Catoosa Co., GA.

1012. PFC Grover Cleveland[8] Abney Jr. (USArmy-WWII) (Grover[7], Washington[6], Wilburn[5], Benjamin[4], Hezekiah[3], Elisha[2], Abner[1]), b.15 Oct 1924 GA. He m. Anita Greene. He d.2 Feb 1989 at age 64 and was bur. Nathan Anderson Historic Cem., Ringgold, Catoosa Co., GA.
      Anita Greene, b.5 Sep 1930. She d.30 Apr 2011 at age 80 and was bur. Nathan Anderson Historic Cem., Ringgold, Catoosa Co., GA.
Known children of PFC Grover Cleveland[8] Abney Jr. (USArmy-WWII) and Anita Greene:
               i.   William Michael "Mike"[9], b.26 Feb 1950. He d.4 Feb 2018 at age 67 and was bur. Chattanooga National Cem., Chattanooga, Hamilton Co., TN.
               ii.   Patti m. John Thomas.

1013. Marshall Edwin[8] Abney (Grover[7], Washington[6], Wilburn[5], Benjamin[4], Hezekiah[3], Elisha[2], Abner[1]), b.20 Aug 1927 GA. He m. Vivian A. Beaver ca.1947. He d.6 Oct 2011 Ringgold, Catoosa Co., GA, at age 84 and was bur. Nathan Anderson Historic Cem., Ringgold, Catoosa Co., GA.
      Vivian A. Beaver, b.19 Jul 1927 Saint Augustine, St. Johns Co., FL. She d.12 Dec 2008 GA at age 81; bur. Nathan Anderson Historic Cem.
Known children of Marshall Edwin[8] Abney and Vivian A. Beaver:
        1318   i.   Lamar[9], m. (n.n.).
        1319   ii.   Jackie, m. (n.n.) Wofford.

1014. Jessie "Blanche"[8] Abney (William[7], Washington[6], Wilburn[5], Benjamin[4], Hezekiah[3], Elisha[2], Abner[1]), b.15 Mar 1913 Linwood, Walker Co., GA. She m. Daniel William "Bill" Kimbell on 9 Jul 1933. She and Daniel William "Bill" Kimbell appeared on the census of 11 Apr 1940 Trion, Chattooga Co., GA. She d.7 Jul 2000 at age 87 and was bur. LaFayette Cem., LaFayette, Walker Co., GA.
      Daniel William "Bill" Kimbell, b.20 Jan 1911. He d.9 Apr 1987 at age 76 and was bur. LaFayette Cem., LaFayette, Walker Co., GA.
Known children of Jessie "Blanche"[8] Abney and Daniel William "Bill" Kimbell both b. Trion, Chattooga Co., GA,:
               i.   Daniel Luther "Dan"[9], b. ca.1935.
               ii.   Maudine Anne, b. ca.1939.

1015. Archie "Dennis"[8] Abney (William[7], Washington[6], Wilburn[5], Benjamin[4], Hezekiah[3], Elisha[2], Abner[1]), b.14 Dec 1914 GA; m. Thelma Simmons on 27 Jul 1935. They appeared on the census of 15 Apr 1940 Lyerly, Chattooga Co., GA. They also lived in Jackson, TN, Bennettsville, SC and in 1984 in 1984 LaFayette, Chattooga Co., GA. He d.4 Nov 1987 age 72; bur. LaFayette Cem., LaFayette, Walker Co., GA.
      Thelma Simmons, b.4 Dec 1915 GA. She d.24 Nov 1991 at age 75 and was bur. LaFayette Cem., LaFayette, Walker Co., A.
Known children of Archie "Dennis"[8] Abney and Thelma Simmons both b. LaFayette, GA,:
        1320   i.   Denny[9], b. 17 Mar 1945; m. Rozanne Clements.
        1321   ii.   Carol, b. 18 Jan 1949; m. n.n.

1016. William "Luther"[8] Abney Jr. (USArmy-WWII) (William[7], Washington[6], Wilburn[5], Benjamin[4], Hezekiah[3], Elisha[2], Abner[1]), b.24 Oct 1916. He also went by "Bill" and "WL". He was a lawyer and a judge. He m. Lillian Jennings, daughter of Enoch Wesley Jennings and Ninna Dye, on 17 Aug 1940. He d.15 Jun 1997 at age 80 and was bur. LaFayette Cem., LaFayette, Walker Co., GA.
      Lillian Jennings, b.3 Jul 1918 Chattanooga, Hamilton Co., TN. She d.22 Dec 2003 at age 85 and was bur. LaFayette Cem., LaFayette.
Known children of William "Luther"[8] Abney Jr. (USArmy-WWII) and Lillian Jennings:
        1322   i.   Chris[9], b. 2 Mar 1944; m. David Zeigler.
        1323   ii.   Vicki Lynn, b. 7 Sep 1947; m. J. Gaut Ragsdale.
               iii. Billie Ann, b.7 Feb 1955. She was a tennis coach.

1017. Mary Ella[8] Abney (William[7], Washington[6], Wilburn[5], Benjamin[4], Hezekiah[3], Elisha[2], Abner[1]), b.4 Sep 1918 GA. She m. Thurlo G. Smith Sr. She lived in 1984 LaFayette, GA. She d.20 Jan 2008 at age 89 and was bur. LaFayette Cem., LaFayette, Walker Co., GA.
      Thurlo G. Smith Sr, b.12 Apr 1915. He d.27 Jan 1977 at age 61 and was bur. LaFayette Cem., LaFayette, Walker Co., GA.
Known child of Mary Ella[8] Abney and Thurlo G. Smith Sr.:
               i.   Thurlo "Grady"[9], b.17 Oct 1946 GA; m. Micki Shields on 1 Sep 1967; d.4 May 2016 age 69 and was bur. LaFayette Cem.

1018. Ross Louis[8] Abney Sr. (William[7], Washington[6], Wilburn[5], Benjamin[4], Hezekiah[3], Elisha[2], Abner[1]), b.5 Jun 1920 LaFayette, GA. He owned *Abney's Department Store*. He m. Charlotte Elizabeth Culpepper ca.1942 GA; d.04 Jul 1985; bur. LaFayette Cem., LaFayette, Walker Co., GA.

Charlotte Elizabeth Culpepper, b.26 Dec 1921 Barney, Brooks Co., GA; d.26 Mar 2010 LaFayette, Walker Co., GA, bur. LaFayette Cem.
Known children of Ross Louis[8] Abney Sr. and Charlotte Elizabeth Culpepper:
          i.   Ross Louis[9], b.21 Dec 1943 GA. He d.21 Dec 1943 GA and was bur. LaFayette Cem., LaFayette, Walker Co., GA.
1324 ii. Wallace Randall "Randy," b. 29 Mar 1946 Walker Co., GA; m. Carolyn "Carol" Bennett.
1325 iii. Andy, b. GA; m. Gail (Leslie) Thompson.
1326 iv. Sandy, b. GA; m. John Shadden.

1019. Fredia Roberta[8] Abney (William[7], Washington[6], Wilburn[5], Benjamin[4], Hezekiah[3], Elisha[2], Abner[1]), b.22 Jul 1922 Walker Co., GA. She was a teacher. She m. Henry "Clyde" Poole (USArmy-WWII) on Christmas Day, 25 Dec 1950. She lived in 1984 Treutlen Co., GA. She d.9 May 2009 GA at age 86 and was bur. Holton Chapel Cem., Soperton, Treutlen Co., GA.

Henry "Clyde" Poole (USArmy-WWII), b.24 Sep 1924 Treutlen Co., GA. He lived in 1984 Treutlen Co., GA. He d.14 Jul 2001 Fairview Park Hospital, Dublin, Laurens Co., GA, at age 76 and was bur. Holton Chapel Cem., Soperton, Treutlen Co., GA.
Known children of Fredia Roberta[8] Abney and Henry "Clyde" Poole (USArmy-WWII):
    i. Suzanne[9] m. (n.n.) Bankston.
    ii. Suzanne Abney, b.1956.

1020. Garnet "Ray"[8] Abney (William[7], Washington[6], Wilburn[5], Benjamin[4], Hezekiah[3], Elisha[2], Abner[1]), b.20 Dec 1924 LaFayette, Walker Co., GA. He m1. Jo Ballard in 1946. He m2. Ernestine Heston (b.9 Mar 1941), but no issue on 25 Nov 1977. He d.9 May 2009 LaFayette, Walker Co., GA, at age 84 and was bur. LaFayette Cem., LaFayette, Walker Co., GA.
Known children of Garnet "Ray"[8] Abney and Jo Ballard:
1327 i. LaRaye[9], b. GA; m1. Buddy Ely; m2. Bob Holcomb.
1328 ii. Dale, m1. Harvey Hinkle; m2. Bill Young.
1329 iii. Terry, m. Sandra Helms.
1330 iv. Jill, m1. Steve Marlin; m2. Gary Browers.

1021. Martha Rebecca[8] Abney (William[7], Washington[6], Wilburn[5], Benjamin[4], Hezekiah[3], Elisha[2], Abner[1]), b.5 May 1929 Walker Co., GA. She m. William Marvin "Bill" Fricks (USN-WWII, Korea) on 23 Jul 1949. She d.17 Feb 2012 Floyd Co., GA, at age 82 and was bur. Georgia National Cem., Canton, Cherokee Co., GA.

William Marvin "Bill" Fricks (USN-WWII, Korea), b.8 Mar 1925 Rome, Floyd Co., GA. In Jun 1967 he owned *Bill Fricks Furniture*. He was Mayor of Rome (Floyd Co., GA) 2000 and 2001. He d.20 Jan 2017 at age 91 and was bur. Georgia National Cem., Canton, Cherokee Co., GA.
Known children of Martha Rebecca[8] Abney and William Marvin "Bill" Fricks (USN-WWII, Korea):
1331 i. Greg[9], m. Ramona (n.n.).
1332 ii. Rob, m. Tami (n.n.).
1333 iii. Marsha.

1022. *Judge* William Shaw "Billy"[8] Abney (Jesse[7], Washington[6], Wilburn[5], Benjamin[4], Hezekiah[3], Elisha[2], Abner[1]), b.10 Oct 1934 LaFayette, Walker Co., GA. He m. Ann Elenora Walker, daughter of James Edward Walker and Carolyn Graham Smith, on 19 Aug 1961 Hamilton Co., TN. He was a judge. He d.18 Nov 2002 at age 68 and was bur. LaFayette Cem., LaFayette, Walker Co., GA.

Ann Elenora Walker, b.9 Aug 1936 Hamilton Co., TN.
Known children of Judge William Shaw "Billy"[8] Abney and Ann Elenora Walker both b. Walker Co., GA,:
    i. Shaw Walker[9], b.14 Aug 1968.
    ii. Anna Louise, b.13 Mar 1973.

1023. William "Leroy"[8] Perry (USArmy-WWII) (Minnie[7] Abney, Robert[6], Wilburn[5], Benjamin[4], Hezekiah[3], Elisha[2], Abner[1]), b.16 Apr 1921 Haralson Co., GA. He m. Ruby V. McDowell ca.1939. He and Ruby V. McDowell were liv. on 2 May 1940 with his father, Harvey Perry, Haralson Co., GA. He d.27 Dec 1983 at age 62 and was bur. Buchanan City Cem., Buchanan, Haralson Co., GA.

Ruby V. McDowell, b.24 Jun 1924 Haralson Co., GA. She d.3 Nov 2009 at age 85.
Known children of William "Leroy"[8] Perry (USArmy-WWII) and Ruby V. McDowell:
    i. Judy[9] m. Steve Weber.
    ii. Donna m. Creig Holcombe.
    iii. Terri Lee m. Mark Blumen.

1024. Mary Frances[8] Abney (Marvin[7], Robert[6], Wilburn[5], Benjamin[4], Hezekiah[3], Elisha[2], Abner[1]), b.19 Jan 1933. She m. Clyde Emanuel "Buddy" Pullen. d.21 Oct 1996 at age 63 and was bur. New Bethel Cem., Floyd Co., GA.

Clyde Emanuel "Buddy" Pullen, b.19 Mar 1932 Polk Co., GA. He d.26 Jan 1983 Rome, Floyd Co., GA, at age 50; bur. New Bethel Cem.
Known children of Mary Frances[8] Abney and Clyde Emanuel "Buddy" Pullen:
    i. Duane Lovvorn "Bubba"[9], b.5 Nov 1965 Cedartown, Polk Co., GA. He d.3 Mar 1991 Cedartown, Polk Co., GA, at age 25 and was bur. New Bethel Cem., Floyd Co., GA.

1025. James Robert[8] Abney (USAF) (Marvin[7], Robert[6], Wilburn[5], Benjamin[4], Hezekiah[3], Elisha[2], Abner[1]) m. (n.n.). He, b.24 Oct 1935 GA. He d.14 Oct 1996 at age 60 and was bur. Buchanan City Cem., Buchanan, Haralson Co., GA.
Known child of James Robert[8] Abney (USAF) and (n.n.):
    i. (n.n.)[9].

1026. Ruby Lorene[8] Davis (Alice[7] Camp, Corrin[6] Abney, Wilburn[5], Benjamin[4], Hezekiah[3], Elisha[2], Abner[1]), b.2 Aug 1914 GA. She m. Pvt. Randolph R. Childs (USArmy-WWII). She d.5 Mar 1938 Atlanta, Fulton Co., GA, at age 23; bur. Beersheeba Bapt. Ch. Cem., Henry Co., GA.

Pvt. Randolph R. Childs (USArmy-WWII), b.23 Jun 1908. He d.2 Sep 1986 at age 78 and was bur. Beersheeba Bapt. Ch. Cem.

Known children of Ruby Lorene[8] Davis and Pvt. Randolph R. Childs (USArmy-WWII):
    i.   (Infant Son)[9] was bur. Beersheeba Bapt. Ch. Cem., Henry Co., GA.
    ii.   Jerry Dean, b.13 Sep 1936. He d.4 Mar 1938 at age 1 and was bur. Beersheeba Bapt. Ch. Cem., Henry Co., GA.

1027. Pvt. Carl Lee[8] Davis Sr. (USArmy) (Alice[7] Camp, Corrin[6] Abney, Wilburn[5], Benjamin[4], Hezekiah[3], Elisha[2], Abner[1]) m. Frances Louise Rutherford. He, b.16 Mar 1924 GA. He d.10 Jul 1999 GA at age 75 and was bur. Georgia Mem. Park, Marietta, Cobb Co., GA.
    Frances Louise Rutherford, b.28 Aug 1927. She d.13 Jan 1997 at age 69 and was bur. Georgia Mem. Park, Marietta, Cobb Co., GA.
Known child of Pvt. Carl Lee[8] Davis Sr. (USArmy) and Frances Louise Rutherford: Carl Lee[9].

1028. Raymond C.[8] Finch (Altha[7] Camp, Corrin[6] Abney, Wilburn[5], Benjamin[4], Hezekiah[3], Elisha[2], Abner[1]), b. est.1942. He m. Faye Patterson.
Known child of Raymond C.[8] Finch and Faye Patterson:
    i.   Martin C. (gen.)[9] lived in 1999 Woodstock, Cherokee Co., GA when the author began working with him. He is largely responsible and to be thanked for the Camp line from Corrin Frances Abney (#284).

1029. Carolyn[8] Camp (Gordon[7], Corrin[6] Abney, Wilburn[5], Benjamin[4], Hezekiah[3], Elisha[2], Abner[1]), b.2 Nov 1939 AL. She m. Bill Thomason ca.1959. She d.21 Jun 2017 at age 77 and was bur. Jefferson Mem. Gardens South, Hoover, Jefferson Co., AL.
Known children of Carolyn[8] Camp and Bill Thomason:
    i.   Maria[9] m. (n.n.) McClung.
    ii.   Judy m. Jeff Sanders.
    iii. Gary.

1030. George Schiffman[8] Hall (Mattie[7] Abney, George[6], Benjamin[5], Benjamin[4], Hezekiah[3], Elisha[2], Abner[1]), b.5 Dec 1901. He m. Lorine Martin. He d.24 Jan 1978 at age 76 and was bur. Gilmer City Cem., Gilmer, Upshur Co., TX.
    Lorine Martin, b.7 Dec 1905. She d.25 Aug 2004 at age 98 and was bur. Gilmer City Cem., Gilmer, Upshur Co., TX.
Known child of George Schiffman[8] Hall and Lorine Martin:
  1334   i.   James Edwin[9], b. 8 Dec 1928 Henderson, Rusk Co., TX; m. Annie Louis Robinson.

1031. Bowman Christopher[8] Hall (Mattie[7] Abney, George[6], Benjamin[5], Benjamin[4], Hezekiah[3], Elisha[2], Abner[1]), b.17 Mar 1903 TX. He m. Cullie Mae Hill in 1923. He d.2 Sep 1997 TX at age 94.
    Cullie Mae Hill, b.16 Apr 1903 TX. She d.26 Dec 1979 Gilmer, Upshur Co., TX, at age 76.
Known children of Bowman Christopher[8] Hall and Cullie Mae Hill:
    i.   Bonnie Jean[9], b.2 Oct 1925 Gilmer, Upshur Co., TX. She m. John Edward Hall. d.10 Jun 2003 Palestine, Anderson Co., TX, at age 77 and was bur. Stonewall Cem., Stonewall, DeSoto Par., LA.
         John Edward Hall, b. Christmas Eve, 24 Dec 1931 Stonewall, DeSoto Par., LA. He d.3 Jun 2008 Tyler, Smith Co., TX, at age 76 and was bur. Stonewall Cem., Stonewall, DeSoto Par., LA.

1032. Cora Bell[8] Abney (Perino[7], George[6], Benjamin[5], Benjamin[4], Hezekiah[3], Elisha[2], Abner[1]), b.27 Jul 1915; m. Ophie L. Collier ca.1932. They appeared on the census of 12 Apr 1940 Upshur Co., TX. She d.8 Apr 2002 at age 86; bur. Gilmer City Cem., Gilmer, Upshur Co., TX.
    Ophie L. Collier, b.2 Feb 1911. He d.2 Jul 2004 at age 93 and was bur. Gilmer City Cem., Gilmer, Upshur Co., TX.
Known children of Cora Bell[8] Abney and Ophie L. Collier all b. TX:
    i.   Perino Frank[9], b. ca.1933.
    ii.   James Sidney, b. ca.1935.
    iii. Leslie Oneal, b. ca.1939.

1033. Patsy Ruth[8] Abney (gen.) (Perino[7], George[6], Benjamin[5], Benjamin[4], Hezekiah[3], Elisha[2], Abner[1]), b. ca.1931 Upshur Co., TX. She m1. (n.n.) Clark. She m2. Cpl. Chester Robinson Sr. (USArmy-WWII) ca.1952. She m3. (n.n.) Dyke, but no issue. She lived in 1998 Upshur Co., TX when she was introduced to the author by her granddaughter, Ruth (#1335i) They provided extensive knowledge of the Benjamin Hezekiah Abney line.
Known child of Patsy Ruth[8] Abney (gen.) and (n.n.) Clark:
    i.   Linda[9] m. (n.n.) Bagley.
    Cpl. Chester Robinson Sr. (USArmy-WWII), b.25 Aug 1922. He d.18 Mar 1977, age 54; bur. Lone Mountain Cem., Gilmer, Upshur Co., TX.
Known child of Patsy Ruth[8] Abney (gen.) and Cpl. Chester Robinson Sr. (USArmy-WWII):
  1335   i.   Chester[9], b. 12 May 1953; m. Mattie Godwin.

1034. Bessie Mae[8] Rowan (Falecia[7] Moore, Mary[6] Abney, Benjamin[5], Benjamin[4], Hezekiah[3], Elisha[2], Abner[1]), b.10 Dec 1905 AL. She m. Joseph Quincy Morton ca.1935. She d.15 Nov 1990 at age 84 and was bur. Pleasant Grove Cem., Snead, Blount Co., AL.
    Joseph Quincy Morton, b.10 Dec 1910. He d.7 Nov 1980 at age 69 and was bur. Pleasant Grove Cem., Snead, Blount Co., AL.
Known child of Bessie Mae[8] Rowan and Joseph Quincy Morton:
  1336   i.   Rossie "Jamay"[9], b. 6 Dec 1936 Blount Co., AL; m. Daniel Coy "DC" Williams.

1035. Earl Buford[8] Moore (Henry[7], Mary[6] Abney, Benjamin[5], Benjamin[4], Hezekiah[3], Elisha[2], Abner[1]), b. New Year's Eve, 31 Dec 1919. He m. Mildred McCulley. He d.17 Oct 1982 at age 62 and was bur. Pleasant Ridge Bapt. Ch. Cem., Hueytown, Jefferson Co., AL.
    Mildred McCulley, b.12 Aug 1924. She d.31 Aug 2001 at age 77 and was bur. Pleasant Ridge Bapt. Ch. Cem., Hueytown, Jefferson Co., AL.
Known children of Earl Buford[8] Moore and Mildred McCulley:
    i.   Eddie[9].
    ii.   Linda m. (n.n.) Stoves.
  1337   iii. Michael Earl, b. 1948 Jefferson Co., AL; m. Janice (n.n.).

1036. Ena[8] Culbert (Mary[7] Moore, Mary[6] Abney, Benjamin[5], Benjamin[4], Hezekiah[3], Elisha[2], Abner[1]), b.14 Jan 1906. She m. Horace Cromwell Porter in 1932. She d.24 Sep 1952 at age 46 and was bur. Geraldine Cem., Geraldine, DeKalb Co., AL.
    Horace Cromwell Porter, b.23 Dec 1901. He m. Jewell Iris Wigley in 1953. He d.28 Feb 1988 at age 86 and was bur. Geraldine Cem., Geraldine.

Known children of Ena[8] Culbert and Horace Cromwell Porter:
       i.   Frances Wilma[9], b.13 Apr 1936; m. William Lesser Kuykendall Jr. (USArmy). She was bur. Fairview Methodist Ch. Cem., Dawson, DeKalb Co., AL.
               William Lesser Kuykendall Jr. (USArmy), b.26 Mar 1936; d.11 Jan 1998, age 61; bur. Fairview Methodist Ch. Cem.

1037. John Luther[8] Culbert (USArmy-WWII) (Mary[7] Moore, Mary[6] Abney, Benjamin[5], Benjamin[4], Hezekiah[3], Elisha[2], Abner[1]), b.5 Mar 1910 Marshall Co., AL. He m. Opal Waldrop. He d.12 Sep 1986 Northport, Tuscaloosa Co., AL, at age 76 and was bur. Williamson Cem., Northport, Tuscaloosa Co., AL.
    Opal Waldrop, b.2 Feb 1913 AL. She d.4 Mar 1986 Northport, Tuscaloosa Co., AL, at age 73 and was bur. Williamson Cem., Northport, Tuscaloosa Co., AL.
Known children of John Luther[8] Culbert (USArmy-WWII) and Opal Waldrop:
    1338   i.   Walter O'Neal[9], b. 30 Apr 1938 AL; m. Linda D. (n.n.).

1038. Moody Fosion[8] Moore (John[7], Mary[6] Abney, Benjamin[5], Benjamin[4], Hezekiah[3], Elisha[2], Abner[1]) m. Audrey Upton. He, b.21 Sep 1913 AL. He d.8 Apr 1974 Birmingham, Jefferson Co., AL, at age 60 and was bur. Asbury UMC Cem., Asbury, Marshall Co., AL.
    Audrey Upton, b.23 Dec 1922. She d.7 Apr 1993 at age 70 and was bur. Asbury UMC Cem., Asbury, Marshall Co., AL.
Known children of Moody Fosion[8] Moore and Audrey Upton:
    1339   i.   Barbara Ann[9], b. 18 May 1940 Albertville, Marshall Co., AL; m. Gus Tom DeMoes.

1039. Beatrice Alene[8] Moore (John[7], Mary[6] Abney, Benjamin[5], Benjamin[4], Hezekiah[3], Elisha[2], Abner[1]) m. Curtis Garrett. , b.30 May 1918. She d.6 Jun 2004 at age 86 and was bur. Asbury UMC Cem., Asbury, Marshall Co., AL.
    Curtis Garrett, b.2 Apr 1915. He d.25 Sep 1995 at age 80 and was bur. Asbury UMC Cem., Asbury, Marshall Co., AL.
Known children of Beatrice Alene[8] Moore and Curtis Garrett:
    1340   i.   Jerry Wayne[9], b. 21 Jul 1937; m. Myra "Lynda" Strange.

1040. Cpl. D.C.[8] Moore (USArmy-WWII) (John[7], Mary[6] Abney, Benjamin[5], Benjamin[4], Hezekiah[3], Elisha[2], Abner[1]) m. Mary "Nonee" Andrews. He, b.27 Feb 1923. He d.7 Jun 1996 AL at age 73 and was bur. Buffalo Presbyterian Ch. Cem., Greensboro, Guilford Co., NC.
    Mary "Nonee" Andrews, b.21 Jan 1920 Greensboro, Guilford Co., NC. She d.18 Feb 2012 at age 92 and was bur. Buffalo Presbyterian Ch. Cem., Greensboro, Guilford Co., NC.
Known children of Cpl. D.C.[8] Moore (USArmy-WWII) and Mary "Nonee" Andrews:
       i.   Jan[9] m. (n.n.) Davis.
    1341   ii.   Cynthia, b. 23 Sep 1948 Greensboro, Guilford Co., NC; m. Edwin Cleveland "Pete" Brackett Jr.

1041. John Byron[8] Moore (Dewey[7], Mary[6] Abney, Benjamin[5], Benjamin[4], Hezekiah[3], Elisha[2], Abner[1]), b.3 Jul 1925. He m. Clara Othell Teal on 12 Oct 1944. He d.10 Aug 1977 at age 52 and was bur. Martling Community Cem., Martling, Marshall Co., AL.
    Clara Othell Teal, b.2 Jan 1926. She d.30 Nov 1992 at age 66 and was bur. Martling Community Cem., Martling, Marshall Co., AL.
Known children of John Byron[8] Moore and Clara Othell Teal:
       i.   Valanda Diane[9], b.7 Jul 1950. She d.16 Jan 1951 and was bur. Martling Community Cem., Martling, Marshall Co., AL.

1042. Opal Ruth[8] Moore (Dewey[7], Mary[6] Abney, Benjamin[5], Benjamin[4], Hezekiah[3], Elisha[2], Abner[1]), b.13 Feb 1929. She associated with (n.n.) and had issue. She m. Cpl. Wilbur Lee Thacker (USArmy-Korea) on 18 Apr 1961 Walker Co., GA. She d.13 Jan 2007 at age 77 and was bur. Lakewood Memory Gardens South, Lakeview, Catoosa Co., GA.
Known children of Opal Ruth[8] Moore and (n.n.):
       i.   John Alan *Moore*[9], b.25 Sep 1953. He m. Brenda (n.n.). He d.18 Dec 2016 Rossville, Walker Co., GA, at age 63. He was cremated.
    Cpl. Wilbur Lee Thacker (USArmy-Korea), b.17 Mar 1932 Fyffe, DeKalb Co., AL. He m. Juanita Lee Stone on 7 Aug 1948 DeKalb Co., AL. He d.13 Feb 1997 Rossville, Walker Co., GA, at age 64 and was bur. Chattanooga National Cem., Chattanooga, Hamilton Co., TN.
Known children of Opal Ruth[8] Moore and Cpl. Wilbur Lee Thacker (USArmy-Korea):
       i.   Terri Lynn[9] m. (n.n.) Lofty.

1043. Bobbye Lou[8] Hefley (Margaret[7] Abney, James[6], Benjamin[5], Benjamin[4], Hezekiah[3], Elisha[2], Abner[1]), b.21 Aug 1931 Clayton, Union Co., NM. She m. Don R. Wood on 18 Mar 1951. She d.20 Jan 2013 Oro Valley, Pima Co., AZ, at age 81.
Known children of Bobbye Lou[8] Hefley and Don R. Wood:
       i.   Donna[9] m. (n.n.) Winter.
       ii.   Deana m. (n.n.) Chillion.

1044. Richard Franklin "Bud"[8] Hefley (Margaret[7] Abney, James[6], Benjamin[5], Benjamin[4], Hezekiah[3], Elisha[2], Abner[1]), b.18 Feb 1933 Clayton, Union Co., NM. He m. Kathryn "Kay" Glenn on 7 Jun 1959 Texline, Dallam Co., TX. He d.1 May 2013 Dalhart, Hartley Co., TX, at age 80 and was bur. Texline Cem., Texline, Dallam Co., TX.
Known children of Richard Franklin "Bud"[8] Hefley and Kathryn "Kay" Glenn:
    1342   i.   Gay[9], m. Gerald Wilhelm.
    1343   ii.   Joy, m. Alan Ritchie.
    1344   iii.   Bob, m. Lewetta (n.n.).

1045. James Talmage "Jim"[8] Abney (USTANG) (Temple[7], James[6], Benjamin[5], Benjamin[4], Hezekiah[3], Elisha[2], Abner[1]) m. Paula (n.n.). He, b.8 Jun 1944. He d.5 Dec 1944.
Known children of James Talmage "Jim"[8] Abney (USTANG) and Paula (n.n.):
    1345   i.   Sam[9], m. Kathryn (n.n.).

1046. Dovie P.[8] Guest (Lillie[7] Abney, William[6], Benjamin[5], Benjamin[4], Hezekiah[3], Elisha[2], Abner[1]), b.7 Dec 1899 AL. She m. Ellis M. Grey ca.1921 AL. They appeared on the censuses of 11 Apr 1930 Birmingham, Jefferson Co., AL and 8 Apr 1940 Albertville, Marshall Co., AL. She d.15 Nov 1996 at age 96 and was bur. Memory Hill Cem., Albertville, Marshall Co., AL.
    Ellis M. Grey, b.29 Dec 1898 AL. He d.7 May 1989 at age 90 and was bur. Memory Hill Cem., Albertville, Marshall Co., AL.
Known children of Dovie P.[8] Guest and Ellis M. Grey both b. AL:
            i.   Mary E.[9], b. ca.1923.
            ii. Nancy A., b. ca.1932.

1047. Huston[8] Abney (USArmy) (Jasper[7], William[6], Benjamin[5], Benjamin[4], Hezekiah[3], Elisha[2], Abner[1]), b.16 Apr 1912 Marhsall Co., AL. He appeared on the census of 9 Apr 1930 in the Alabama Boys Industrial School, Jefferson Co., AL. He m1. Leona Agnes Campbell in 1935. He m2. Clara Margaret Steadman in 1946. He d.11 Mar 1997 Puyallup, Pierce Co., WA, at age 84; bur. Woodbine Cem., Puyallup, Pierce Co., WA.
    Leona Agnes Campbell, b.15 May 1920 Grays Harbor Co., WA. She was liv. in 1935 Puyallup, Pierce Co., WA. She was liv. on 11 Apr 1940 with her mother, Eva Campbell, Puyallup, Pierce Co., WA. She d.14 Mar 1984 Pierce Co., WA, at age 63.
Known children of Huston[8] Abney (USArmy) and Leona Agnes Campbell:
    1346   i.   Huston "Earl" (gen.)[9], b. 22 Jul 1937 Tacoma, Pierce Co., WA; m. Mary Louise Kendall (gen.).
            ii. Bernice, b. ca.1938 WA.
            iii. Faith.
Known child of Huston[8] Abney (USArmy):
            i.   Bob[9], b. illegitimate in 1942.
    Clara Margaret Steadman, b.20 Oct 1928. She m. John R. Beers in 1999. She d.20 Mar 2011 at age 82.
Known children of Huston[8] Abney (USArmy) and Clara Margaret Steadman:
            i.   Baby Girl[9], b.9 Apr 1948 and d.10 Apr 1948 Tacoma, Pierce Co., WA; bur. Woodbine Cem., Puyallup, Pierce Co., WA.
            ii. Pauline m. (n.n.) Foister.
            iii. Susan.

1048. Audra Ellington "Andy"[8] Chiles (Cora[7] Abney, William[6], Benjamin[5], Benjamin[4], Hezekiah[3], Elisha[2], Abner[1]), b.2 Jul 1915 AL. He m. Mary Huddleston. He d.28 Jul 2005 at age 90 and was bur. Memory Hill Cem., Albertville, Marshall Co., AL.
    Mary Huddleston, b.28 Oct 1918 Birmingham, Jefferson Co., AL. She d.28 Apr 2012 Birmingham, Jefferson Co., AL, at age 93.
Known children of Audra Ellington "Andy"[8] Chiles and Mary Huddleston:
    1347   i.   John[9], m. (n.n.).
            ii. Nancy Lee, b.11 Dec 1947 Albertville, Marshall Co., AL. She d.11 Sep 2009 Birmingham, Jefferson Co., AL, at age 61 and was bur. Memory Hill Cem., Albertville, Marshall Co., AL.

1049. Wilma[8] Abney (Homer[7], William[6], Benjamin[5], Benjamin[4], Hezekiah[3], Elisha[2], Abner[1]), b. ca.1914 AL; m. (n.n.) Hammock.
Known child of Wilma[8] Abney and (n.n.) Hammock:
            i.   Tony (gen.)[9] The author began working with Cousin Tony in 2002. He is responsible for the line of Homer Abney (#627).

1050. Hazel Nell[8] Abney (Homer[7], William[6], Benjamin[5], Benjamin[4], Hezekiah[3], Elisha[2], Abner[1]), b.10 Sep 1924. She m. Arvil Decker. She d.10 Feb 2016 Chattanooga, Hamilton Co., TN, at age 91 and was bur. Whiton UMC Cem., Whiton, DeKalb Co., AL.
    Arvil Decker, b.11 Aug 1923. He d.4 Sep 1996 at age 73 and was bur. Whiton UMC Cem., Whiton, DeKalb Co., AL.
Known child of Hazel Nell[8] Abney and Arvil Decker:
            i.   Nancy Nell[9], b.10 Aug 1950 and She d. New Year's Eve, 31 Jan 1967 Marshall Co., AL, age 16; bur. Whiton UMC Cem.

1051. Lincoln Freeman[8] Abney (Joseph[7], William[6], Benjamin[5], Benjamin[4], Hezekiah[3], Elisha[2], Abner[1]), b.20 May 1920 AL. He m1. Mozelle Pike in 1937. He and Mozelle Pike appeared on the census of 4 Apr 1940 DeKalb Co., AL. He m2. Edna E. Lantrip in 1988. He d.3 Dec 1994 Bessemer, Jefferson Co., AL, at age 74 and was bur. Forest Grove Mem. Gardens, Pleasant Grove, Jefferson Co., AL.
    Mozelle Pike, b.18 Jan 1920. She d.3 Jun 2001 at age 81 and was bur. Hopewell Bapt. Ch. Cem., Hopewell, DeKalb Co., AL.
Known children of Lincoln Freeman[8] Abney and Mozelle Pike:
            i.   (baby)[9] was stillborn1938
            ii. Durrell Phillip, b.19 Nov 1941 DeKalb Co., AL. He d.31 May 2004 DeKalb Co., AL, at age 62 and was bur. Hopewell Bapt. Ch. Cem., Hopewell, DeKalb Co., AL.
            iii. (dau).
            iv. (dau).
            v.   (dau).
    Edna E. Lantrip, b.24 Oct 1919. She d.25 Sep 1998 at age 78 and was bur. Forest Grove Mem. Gardens, Pleasant Grove, Jefferson Co., AL.
There were no known children of Lincoln Freeman[8] Abney and Edna E. Lantrip.

1052. Grover Ree[8] Vogel (Vellie[7] Abney, David[6], Benjamin[5], Benjamin[4], Hezekiah[3], Elisha[2], Abner[1]), b.11 Jan 1912 TX. He m. Exa Mae Virginia Kelly. He d.30 Nov 1991 TX at age 79 and was bur. Winchell Cem., Winchell, Brown Co., TX.
    Exa Mae Virginia Kelly, b.6 May 1917 Bangs, Brown Co., TX. She d.22 Aug 2001 San Saba Co., TX, at age 84 and was bur. Winchell Cem.
Known children of Grover Ree[8] Vogel and Exa Mae Virginia Kelly:
    1348   i.   Herman Ree[9], b. 1935; m. Barbara Jean Brown.
            ii. Norman Wayne, b.21 Feb 1937 Brown Co., TX. He d.5 May 1957 TX at age 20 and was bur. Winchell Cem., Winchell.
    1349   iii. Billy Kyle "Wild Bill," b. 23 Jul 1941; m. Kathy Jean "Katie" Moody.
            iv. Velma m. (n.n.) Gauny.

1053. Thomas Vernon "Tom"[8] Vogel (Vellie[7] Abney, David[6], Benjamin[5], Benjamin[4], Hezekiah[3], Elisha[2], Abner[1]), b.22 Jan 1913 Chatfield, Navarro Co., TX; m. Edlean Johnson on 22 Feb 1936 McGregor, TX; d.6 Apr 1974 Mesquite, Dallas Co., TX, age 61; bur. Grove Hill Mem. Park, Dallas, Dallas Co., TX.
    Edlean Johnson, b.11 Aug 1917 Austin, Travis Co., TX. She d.11 Nov 2009, Dallas, Dallas Co., TX, at age 92; bur. Grove Hill Mem. Park.

Known children of Thomas Vernon "Tom"[8] Vogel and Edlean Johnson:

        i.   Patricia[9] m. (n.n.) Lancaster.

       ii.   Jerry m. Janie (n.n.).

1350   iii.   Vernon Kenneth, b. 11 May 1937 Waco, McLennan Co., TX; m. Teddie Irene Pairsh.

1054. Velma "Christine"[8] Vogel (Vellie[7] Abney, David[6], Benjamin[5], Benjamin[4], Hezekiah[3], Elisha[2], Abner[1]), b.22 Dec 1916 TX. She m. Cecil Vance Riordan. She d.1 Mar 2001 at age 84 and was bur. Mount Olive Cem., Big Spring, Howard Co., TX.

    Cecil Vance Riordan, b.11 Oct 1910. He d.21 May 2003 at age 92 and was bur. Mount Olive Cem., Big Spring, Howard Co., TX.

Known children of Velma "Christine"[8] Vogel and Cecil Vance Riordan:

        i.   Priscilla[9] m. Tad Corbet.

       ii.   Beverly m. Tip Miller.

      iii.   Stephen Paul "Steve", b.4 Apr 1950 Breckenridge, Stephens Co., TX; d.20 May 2016 Midland, Midland Co., TX, age 66.

1055. Rubie "Arlene"[8] Vogel (Vellie[7] Abney, David[6], Benjamin[5], Benjamin[4], Hezekiah[3], Elisha[2], Abner[1]), b.12 Mar 1919 Winchell, Brown Co., TX; m. Jay Cal Alcorn (USN-WWII) 4 Dec 1941; d.1 Feb 2002 Odessa, Ector Co., TX, age 82; bur. Sunset Mem. Gardens, Odessa, Ector Co., TX.

    Jay Cal Alcorn (USN-WWII), b.23 Aug 1907. He d.14 Jun 1988 Odessa, Ector Co., TX, at age 80 and was bur. Sunset Mem. Gardens, Odessa.

Known children of Rubie "Arlene"[8] Vogel and Jay Cal Alcorn (USN-WWII):

        i.   Michael C.[9].

       ii.   Joe Abney m. (n.n.) Tali.

1056. James Edward[8] Abney (James[7], David[6], Benjamin[5], Benjamin[4], Hezekiah[3], Elisha[2], Abner[1]), b.21 Oct 1924 Martling, Marshall Co., AL. He m. Edith Louise Roden. He d.13 Mar 2010 Martling, Marshall Co., AL, at age 85; bur. Martling Community Cem., Martling, Marshall Co., AL.

    Edith Louise Roden, b.10 Feb 1925. She d.9 Nov 2013 at age 88 and was bur. Marshall Mem. Gardens, Albertville, Marshall Co., AL.

Known child of James Edward[8] Abney and Edith Louise Roden:

        i.   Gilda Ann[9] m. (n.n.) Denney. , b.21 Jun 1947 and d.16 Jun 1969 Marshall Co., AL, age 21; bur. Marshall Mem. Gardens.

1057. Artemis J. "Artie"[8] Huffstutler (Mary[7] Rooks, Eva[6] Abney, Benjamin[5], Benjamin[4], Hezekiah[3], Elisha[2], Abner[1]), b. Christmas Eve, 24 Dec 1920 Arley, Winston Co., AL; m. John A. Kratsas (USArmy-WWII). d.18 Mar 2011 Wrightsville, York Co., PA, at age 90; bur. Mount Rose Cem.

    John A. Kratsas (USArmy-WWII), b.7 May 1916. He d.27 Sep 2015 at age 99 and was bur. Mount Rose Cem., York, York Co., PA.

Known children of Artemis J. "Artie"[8] Huffstutler and John A. Kratsas (USArmy-WWII):

        i.   Aristotle[9] m. Carol (n.n.).

       ii.   James m. Celeine (n.n.).

      iii.   Alexandria m. Anthony Condemi.

      iv.   Maria m. (n.n.) Carrieri.

1058. Evelyn "June"[8] Rooks (John[7], Eva[6] Abney, Benjamin[5], Benjamin[4], Hezekiah[3], Elisha[2], Abner[1]), b.30 Sep 1935 Chattanooga, Hamilton Co., TN. She m. Raymond Wahrman (USArmy). She m. Ray Harris Selvidge in 1956. She d.22 Apr 1985 Lakewood, Los Angeles Co., CA, at age 49 and was bur. Green Hills Mem. Park, Rancho Palos Verdes, Los Angeles Co., CA.

Known child of Evelyn "June"[8] Rooks and Raymond Wahrman (USArmy):

1351   i.   Yvonne Catherine "Vonnie"[9], b. 22 Jun 1954 France; m. Arthur Santellano; m. Ted Jolly.

    Ray Harris Selvidge, b.7 Jun 1935 Columbus, Muscogee Co., GA. He d.15 Mar 2008 Santa Barbara Co., CA, at age 72. He was cremated. There were no known children of Evelyn "June"[8] Rooks and Ray Harris Selvidge.

1059. Addie Belle[8] Pettit (Ezey[7] Reeves, Sarah[6] Abney, Andrew[5], Benjamin[4], Hezekiah[3], Elisha[2], Abner[1]), b.4 Apr 1913. She m. Cpl. Hardy "Foster" Beaver (USArmy-WWII) in 1946. She d.8 Dec 2006 at age 93 and was bur. Sunset Mem. Park, Gilmer, Upshur Co., TX.

    Cpl. Hardy "Foster" Beaver (USArmy-WWII), b.20 Jul 1913 Mings Chapel Community, Upshur Co., TX. He d.11 Sep 1987 at age 74 and was bur. Sunset Mem. Park, Gilmer, Upshur Co., TX.

Known child of Addie Belle[8] Pettit and Cpl. Hardy "Foster" Beaver (USArmy-WWII):

        i.   Thomas Wilson[9], b.7 Nov 1948. He d.28 Jul 2004 at age 55 and was bur. Sunset Mem. Park, Gilmer, Upshur Co., TX.

1060. Cora Lee[8] Foster (Dultsenia[7] Reeves, Sarah[6] Abney, Andrew[5], Benjamin[4], Hezekiah[3], Elisha[2], Abner[1]) m. Grover Cleveland McNair. , b.26 Oct 1899. She d.3 Feb 1995 at age 95 and was bur. Sunset Mem. Park, Gilmer, Upshur Co., TX.

    Grover Cleveland McNair, b.23 May 1891 TX. He d.22 Dec 1982 Gilmer, Upshur Co., TX, at age 91 and was bur. Sunset Mem. Park, Gilmer.

Known children of Cora Lee[8] Foster and Grover Cleveland McNair:

        i.   Wacil D.[9], b.5 Aug 1920. He m. Margaret C. McNair. He d.23 Oct 1995 at age 75 and was bur. Sunset Mem. Park, Gilmer.

           Margaret C. McNair, b.2 Nov 1919. She d.9 Mar 2001 at age 81 and was bur. Sunset Mem. Park, Gilmer.

1352   ii.   Sherwyn Lane, b. 13 Apr 1923 Pritchett, Upshur Co., TX; m. Lesta "Chere" Livingston.

      iii.   Dalmon Moody, b.4 Oct 1926 Pritchett, Upshur Co., TX. He m. Edna Ann Carothers. He d.31 Mar 1994 Boerne, Kendall Co., TX, at age 67 and was bur. Boerne Cem., Boerne, Kendall Co., TX.

           Edna Ann Carothers, b.7 Dec 1929 Rochester, Haskell Co., TX. She d.30 Nov 2017 Boerne, Kendall Co., TX, at age 87 and was bur. Boerne Cem., Boerne, Kendall Co., TX.

1061. Drucilla "Dot"[8] Foster (Dultsenia[7] Reeves, Sarah[6] Abney, Andrew[5], Benjamin[4], Hezekiah[3], Elisha[2], Abner[1]), b.6 Feb 1917 Upshur Co., TX. She m. James Warren Gholson. d.18 Feb 1968 Vivian, Caddo Par., LA, at age 51 and was bur. Vivian Cem., Vivian, Caddo Par., LA.

    James Warren Gholson m. Josephine Boyter. He, b.19 Sep 1911. He d.20 Jun 1994 at age 82; bur. Vivian Cem., Vivian, Caddo Par., LA.

Known child of Drucilla "Dot"[8] Foster and James Warren Gholson:

        i.   James Warren "Jim"[9], b.20 May 1945 Vivian, Caddo Par., LA. He m. Evelyn Lynn Riegel ca.1978. He d.21 Jan 2015 Loma Rica, Yuba Co., CA, at age 69 and was bur. Hillcrest Mem. Pk. & Maus., Red Chute, Bossier Par., LA.

           Evelyn Lynn Riegel, b.18 Sep 1942 San Antonio, Bexar Co., TX. She d.11 Apr 2018 Marysville, Yuba Co., CA, at age 75.

1062. Bessie O.[8] Bynum (Mary[7] Sargent, Amanda[6] Abney, Andrew[5], Benjamin[4], Hezekiah[3], Elisha[2], Abner[1]), b.21 Jul 1907 TX. She m. William Ernest Traylor. d.3 Jan 1983 Titus Co., TX, at age 75 and was bur. Center Grove Cem., Titus Co., TX.

William Ernest Traylor, b.10 Feb 1902 Titus Co., TX. He d.19 Mar 1941 Cookville, Titus Co., TX, at age 39 and was bur. Center Grove Cem.
Known children of Bessie O.[8] Bynum and William Ernest Traylor:
- i. Sherrill William[9], b.22 Mar 1929 Cookville, Titus Co., TX. He m. Mary Katherine Smelser on 21 Feb 1969. He d.19 Aug 1995 Titus Co., TX, at age 66 and was bur. Center Grove Cem., Titus Co., TX.
- ii. Betty Jane, b.17 Aug 1933. She d.1 Apr 2011 at age 77 and was bur. Center Grove Cem., Titus Co., TX.

1063. William Ernest[8] Van Zandt (Sarah[7] Sargent, Amanda[6] Abney, Andrew[5], Benjamin[4], Hezekiah[3], Elisha[2], Abner[1]), b.23 Jun 1905; m. Ruth Louvenia Brown. They appeared on the census of 16 Apr 1930 Titus Co., TX; d.4 Dec 1979; bur. Edwards Cem., Mount Pleasant, Titus Co., TX.

Ruth Louvenia Brown, b.23 Jun 1911. She and her daughter, Charlene Van Zandt were liv. on 22 Apr 1940 with Ruth's father, Albert Brown, Titus Co., TX. She d.19 Oct 2007 at age 96 and was bur. Lakeview Mem. Gardens, Longview, Gregg Co., TX.
Known children of William Ernest[8] Van Zandt and Ruth Louvenia Brown:
- i. Carol Dean[9].
- ii. Charlene, b.21 Jan 1936 Titus Co., TX. She m. Walter Louis "Tiny" Rains in 1953. She d.20 Jan 1997 Smith Co., TX, at age 60 and was bur. Bascom Cem., Bascom, Smith Co., TX.
  - Walter Louis "Tiny" Rains, b.25 Jul 1926. He d.19 Dec 2010 Tyler, Smith Co., TX, at age 84; bur. Bascom Cem.

1064. Erastus "Rasters"[8] Van Zandt (Sarah[7] Sargent, Amanda[6] Abney, Andrew[5], Benjamin[4], Hezekiah[3], Elisha[2], Abner[1]), b.13 Jul 1912 TX. He m1. Eva Lorie Patrick. He m2. Annie L. Hooper in 1982 Morris Co., TX, but no issue. He m3. Frances D. Philpot in 1986 Morris Co., TX, but no issue. He d.15 Nov 1988 Titus Co., TX, at age 76 and was bur. Center Grove Cem., Titus Co., TX.

Eva Lorie Patrick, b.24 Sep 1919 TX. She d.20 Mar 1981 Mount Pleasant, Titus Co., TX, at age 61 and was bur. Center Grove Cem.
Known child of Erastus "Rasters"[8] Van Zandt and Eva Lorie Patrick:
- i. Gary Wayne[9], b.27 Oct 1944 Pittsburg, Camp Co., TX. He m. Sybil Fay (n.n.) (b.26 Aug 1940) on 26 Aug 1966. He d.5 Jul 1993 at age 48 and was bur. Center Grove Cem., Titus Co., TX.

1065. Jewel Lillian[8] Stevens (Sarah[7] Sargent, Amanda[6] Abney, Andrew[5], Benjamin[4], Hezekiah[3], Elisha[2], Abner[1]), b.10 Dec 1923 Titus Co., TX. She m. SSgt. Morgan Randolph Dunn (USAF-WWII) in 1942. She d.9 Jan 2014 Mount Pleasant, Titus Co., TX, at age 90; bur. Edwards Cem.

SSgt. Morgan Randolph Dunn (USAF-WWII), b.19 Apr 1921 Mount Pleasant, Titus Co., TX. He d.14 Oct 2003 Mount Pleasant, Titus Co., TX, at age 82 and was bur. Edwards Cem., Mount Pleasant, Titus Co., TX.
Known child of Jewel Lillian[8] Stevens and SSgt. Morgan Randolph Dunn (USAF-WWII):
- 1353 i. Sheila[9], b. 12 Aug 1946 Mount Pleasant, Titus Co., TX; m. Jackie Ray Barrett Sr.

1066. Zillman Taylor[8] Sargent (William[7], Amanda[6] Abney, Andrew[5], Benjamin[4], Hezekiah[3], Elisha[2], Abner[1]), b.11 Oct 1913 TX. He m. Helen Catherine Bohanon on 16 Sep 1931. He d.8 May 1995 at age 81 and was bur. Concord Cem., Omaha, Morris Co., TX.

Helen Catherine Bohanon, b.21 Mar 1916 AZ. She d.10 Apr 2007 at age 91.
Known children of Zillman Taylor[8] Sargent and Helen Catherine Bohanon:
- i. Juanita[9] m. (n.n.) Hare. , b.4 Nov 1934 Mount Pleasant, Titus Co., TX. She d.29 Jan 2013 Dallas, Dallas Co., TX, at age 78 and was bur. Concord Cem., Omaha, Morris Co., TX.
- ii. Mary J., b. ca.1939 TX.
- iii. Jerry W., b. ca.1939 TX.

1067. Ocie May[8] Sargent (John[7], Amanda[6] Abney, Andrew[5], Benjamin[4], Hezekiah[3], Elisha[2], Abner[1]) m. Marcus Moss. , b.1912 Titus Co., TX. She d.12 Sep 1998 and was bur. Center Grove Cem., Titus Co., TX.

Marcus Moss, b.4 May 1914. He d.27 Apr 1970 at age 55 and was bur. Center Grove Cem., Titus Co., TX.
Known children of Ocie May[8] Sargent and Marcus Moss:
- 1354 i. Neal[9], b. 3 Jan 1934 Cookville, Titus Co., TX; m. Johnnie Jean Parker.
- ii. Wayne.
- iii. Larry Dean, b.24 Jan 1940. He d.23 May 1969 at age 29 and was bur. Center Grove Cem., Titus Co., TX.

1068. Elvis[8] Sargent (John[7], Amanda[6] Abney, Andrew[5], Benjamin[4], Hezekiah[3], Elisha[2], Abner[1]), b.25 Sep 1918. He m. Dorothy Currey on 21 Mar 1936. He d.24 Jul 1998 at age 79 and was bur. Center Grove Cem., Titus Co., TX.

Dorothy Currey, b.26 Sep 1916. She d.7 Jul 2006 at age 89.
Known child of Elvis[8] Sargent and Dorothy Currey:
- i. Suzanne[9], b.15 Feb 1944 Pittsburg, Camp Co., TX; m. Wayne Charlton. d.9 Mar 2016 Mt. Pleasant, Titus Co., TX, ae.72.

1069. Johnnie Woodrow "Woody"[8] Sargent (George[7], Amanda[6] Abney, Andrew[5], Benjamin[4], Hezekiah[3], Elisha[2], Abner[1]) m. Eunice Clark. He, b.19 Dec 1918. He d.17 Jul 1998 at age 79 and was bur. Nevills Chapel Cem., Mount Pleasant, Titus Co., TX.
Known children of Johnnie Woodrow "Woody"[8] Sargent and Eunice Clark:
- 1355 i. Charles Lee "Nebo"[9], b. 9 Sep 1941 Mount Pleasant, Titus Co., TX; m. Teresa (n.n.).
- ii. Jerry Dean, b.20 Apr 1945. He d.2 Mar 2008 at age 62 and was bur. Mount Moriah Cem., Morris Co., TX.
- 1356 iii. Randolph "Randy," b. 9 Oct 1948 Mount Pleasant, Titus Co., TX; m. Sherry Poole.

1070. Thomas Franklin[8] Pelfrey (Haze[7] Ellison, Sarah[6] Abney, Hezekiah[5], Benjamin[4], Hezekiah[3], Elisha[2], Abner[1]), b.13 Jul 1896 Pratt City, Jefferson Co., AL. He m. Avis Jewell McGregor on 26 Jul 1931 Stratford, Garvin Co., OK. He d.24 Jul 1978 Pauls Valley, Garvin Co., OK, at age 82 and was bur. Mount Olivet Cem., Pauls Valley, Garvin Co., OK.

Avis Jewell McGregor, b.12 Jan 1907 Pontotoc, Pontotoc Co., MS; d.14 Jun 2001 Wynnewood, Garvin Co., OK, age 94; bur. Mt. Olivet Cem.
Known children of Thomas Franklin[8] Pelfrey and Avis Jewell McGregor:
- 1357 i. Jewel[9], b. 1 Dec 1932 Maysville, Garvin Co., OK; m. Jesse H. "Whiff" Palmertree Sr. (USN-WWII).
- ii. John Thomas, b.14 Dec 1938. He d.22 May 1963 at age 24; bur. Mount Olivet Cem., Pauls Valley, Garvin Co., OK.

1071. Vera Ethel[8] Pelfrey (Haze[7] Ellison, Sarah[6] Abney, Hezekiah[5], Benjamin[4], Hezekiah[3], Elisha[2], Abner[1]), b.4 Aug 1897 Carbon Hill, Walker Co., AL. She m. Marion Albert Matthews Sr. on 30 Sep 1917 Elmore City, Garvin Co., OK. She d.23 Jul 1968 Norman, Cleveland Co., OK, at age 70 and was bur. Maysville Cem., Maysville, Garvin Co., OK.
    Marion Albert Matthews Sr, b.16 Jan 1885 Graham, Young Co., TX; d.1 May 1944 Oklahoma City, Oklahoma Co., OK; bur. Maysville Cem.
Known child of Vera Ethel[8] Pelfrey and Marion Albert Matthews Sr.:
    1358   i.   Emmett Lewis[9], b. 8 Feb 1920 Stratford, Garvin Co., OK; m. Betty Kathryn McGee.

1072. Evalena[8] Abney (DeWitt[7], Hezekiah[6], Hezekiah[5], Benjamin[4], Hezekiah[3], Elisha[2], Abner[1]), b.7 Jul 1923 Gay, Choctaw Co., OK. She m1. Fowler Nabors on 25 Jul 1945 Hugo, Choctaw Co., OK. She m2. Melvin L. Benton on 12 Jun 1997. She d.14 Jun 2009 Hugo, Choctaw Co., OK, at age 85 and was bur. Springs Chapel Cem., Hugo, Choctaw Co., OK.
    Fowler Nabors, b.11 Dec 1910. He d.12 Jan 1989 at age 78.
Known children of Evalena[8] Abney and Fowler Nabors:
        i.   Mary Ann[9] m. (n.n.) Ward.
    Melvin L. Benton, b.4 Feb 1931 Floyd, White Co., AR. He d.27 Feb 2012 OK at age 81 and was bur. Springs Chapel Cem., Hugo.
There were no known children of Evalena[8] Abney and Melvin L. Benton.

1073. Floria "Jean"[8] Abney (DeWitt[7], Hezekiah[6], Hezekiah[5], Benjamin[4], Hezekiah[3], Elisha[2], Abner[1]), b. New Year's Day, 1 Jan 1948 Gay, Choctaw Co., OK. She m. (n.n.) McDaniel. d.25 Oct 2019 OK at age 71. She was cremated.
    Known children of Floria "Jean"[8] Abney and (n.n.) McDaniel:
        i.   Earl[9] m. Amber (n.n.).
        ii.   Stacey.
        iii. Melissa m. (n.n.) Cash.

1074. Paul Leonard[8] Abney Jr. (USArmy) (Paul[7], Hezekiah[6], Hezekiah[5], Benjamin[4], Hezekiah[3], Elisha[2], Abner[1]), m. Bobbie Ray Rice. He, b.22 Nov 1933 Hugo, Choctaw Co., OK. He d.24 Jun 2004 Pine Bluff, Jefferson Co., AR, age 70; bur. Pinewood Mem. Park, Crossett, Ashley Co., AR.
    Bobbie Ray Rice, b.1 Apr 1937 Crossett, Ashley Co., AR. She d.26 Nov 2009 Crossett, Ashley Co., AR, at age 72; bur. Pinewood Mem. Park.
Known children of Paul Leonard[8] Abney Jr. (USArmy) and Bobbie Ray Rice:
        i.   Tim[9] m. Pam (n.n.).
        ii.   Jon m. Dana (n.n.).
        iii. Paula m. (n.n.) Beard.

1075. Oralee[8] Tidwell (Georgia[7] Abney, George[6], Hezekiah[5], Benjamin[4], Hezekiah[3], Elisha[2], Abner[1]), b.15 Jun 1923. She m. Howard Jones (b. ca.1921 GA) ca.1939. She d.13 Feb 2001 at age 77 and was bur. East View Cem., Rome, Floyd Co., GA.
Known child of Oralee[8] Tidwell and Howard Jones:
        i.   Randall Bradford "Red"[9], b.5 Sep 1940 Floyd Co., GA. He m. Glenda Ferrell Williamson on 1 Jul 1967. He d.18 Sep 2016 Lindale, Floyd Co., GA, at age 76 and was bur. Rome Mem. Park S., Rome, Floyd Co., GA.
                Glenda Ferrell Williamson, b.17 Jun 1942. She d.19 Sep 2016 at age 74 and was bur. Rome Mem. Park S., Rome.

1076. Patsy Jo[8] Abney (Clifton[7], George[6], Hezekiah[5], Benjamin[4], Hezekiah[3], Elisha[2], Abner[1]), b.13 Nov 1934 Rome, Floyd Co., GA. She m. Elston Lee Gentry Sr. on 15 Dec 1951. She d.27 Jun 2011 Rome, Floyd Co., GA, at age 76; bur. Oaknoll Mem. Gardens Cem., Rome, Floyd Co., GA.
    Elston Lee Gentry Sr, b.7 May 1932 Taylorsville, Bartow Co., GA. He d.26 Apr 2018 Rome, Floyd Co., GA, at age 85.
Known children of Patsy Jo[8] Abney and Elston Lee Gentry Sr.:
        i.   Diane[9] d.1994.
    1359   ii.   Elston Lee "Chuck," b. 14 Dec 1954 Rome, Floyd Co., GA; m. Kecia (n.n.).
    1360   iii. Laura, m. Donny Key.
    1361   iv.   James "Jimmy," m. Darlene (n.n.).

1077. Troy Lee[8] Jarvis (Samantha[7] Abney, George[6], George[5], Benjamin[4], Hezekiah[3], Elisha[2], Abner[1]), b.9 Jun 1910 Jefferson Co., AL. He and his brother, Ralph Jackson Jarvis were liv. on 4 Apr 1930 with their grandfather, George Abney, Jefferson Co., AL. He m. Lucille Franklin ca.1932. He and Lucille Franklin appeared on the census of 26 Apr 1940 Republic, Jefferson Co., AL. He d.14 Jul 1967 Birmingham, Jefferson Co., AL, at age 57 and was bur. Bivens Chapel Cem., Brookside, Jefferson Co., AL.
    Lucille Franklin, b.18 Sep 1912 Jefferson Co., AL. She d.12 Apr 1999 Watson, Jefferson Co., AL, at age 86 and was bur. Bivens Chapel Cem.
Known children of Troy Lee[8] Jarvis and Lucille Franklin:
        i.   William Eugene "Billy"[9], b.4 Oct 1933 Jefferson Co., AL; d.1953 Republic, Jefferson Co., AL; bur. Bivens Chapel Cem.
        ii.   Janice Virginia m. (n.n.) Johnson. , b. est.1937.
    1362   iii. Starlin Jackson "Jack," b. 19 Sep 1941 Jefferson Co., AL; m. (n.n.).

1078. Paul Edward[8] Abney (King[7], George[6], George[5], Benjamin[4], Hezekiah[3], Elisha[2], Abner[1]), b.9 Jan 1913 Watson, Jefferson Co., AL. He m. Ruby Lee Barron ca.1948. He was liv. in 1998. He d.21 Jan 2005 at age 92 and was bur. Friendship UMC Cem., Gardendale, Jefferson Co., AL.
    Ruby Lee Barron, b.4 Nov 1819 El Dorado (now Fieldstown), Jefferson Co., AL. She d.23 Dec 2004 at age 185; bur. Friendship UMC Cem.
Known children of Paul Edward[8] Abney and Ruby Lee Barron:
    1363   i.   Jerrell Wayne (gen.)[9], b. 2 Oct 1949 Birmingham, Jefferson Co., AL; m. Kathy Marie Mayo; div. Kathy Marie Mayo.

1079. Eugene "David"[8] Fuller (Daisy[7] Abney, George[6], George[5], Benjamin[4], Hezekiah[3], Elisha[2], Abner[1]), b.1928 AL. He m. Lucille McCulley Vinston on 22 Apr 1949 Jefferson Co., AL. He d.27 Sep 2009 AL and was bur. Friendship UMC Cem., Gardendale, Jefferson Co., AL.
    Lucille McCulley Vinston, b.3 Jun 1928. She d.19 Jun 2016 AL at age 88 and was bur. Friendship UMC Cem., Gardendale, Jefferson Co., AL.
Known children of Eugene "David"[8] Fuller and Lucille McCulley Vinston:
        i.   Dale Allen[9], b.13 Feb 1955 Jefferson Co., AL. He d.9 Apr 1956 at age 1 and was bur. Friendship UMC Cem.

1080. Mary Ellen[8] Fuller (Daisy[7] Abney, George[6], George[5], Benjamin[4], Hezekiah[3], Elisha[2], Abner[1]), b. ca.Oct 1929 AL. She m. Cecil Barry Easter (USN-WWII) on 25 Nov 1948 Jefferson Co., AL.
    Cecil Barry Easter (USN-WWII), b.11 Oct 1925 Birmingham, Jefferson Co., AL. He d.8 Jul 2017 Birmingham, Jefferson Co., AL, at age 91 and was bur. Elmwood Cem., Birmingham, Jefferson Co., AL.
Known children of Mary Ellen[8] Fuller and Cecil Barry Easter (USN-WWII):
        1364   i.   Carolyn Ruth[9], m. Reid Lamphere.
        1365   ii.   Cynthia Ellen, m. (n.n.) Rogers.

1081. Johnny Calvin[8] Abney (Homer[7], John[6], George[5], Benjamin[4], Hezekiah[3], Elisha[2], Abner[1]), b.11 Jun 1915 Dallas, Dallas Co., TX. He m1. Winona Helen Kilgore in 1937. He and Winona Helen Kilgore appeared on the census of 21 May 1940 Dallas, Dallas Co., TX. He m2. Dorothy F. Pruitt. He d.17 Mar 1978 Dallas, Dallas Co., TX, at age 62 and was bur. Grove Hill Mem. Park, Dallas, Dallas Co., TX.
    Winona Helen Kilgore, b.5 Jan 1922 Van Zandt Co., TX. She m. Robert E. Pruitt in 1951. She m2. Harold Thomas Higley in 1966. She d.7 Jun 1990 Dallas, Dallas Co., TX, at age 68 and was bur. Laurel Oaks Mem. Park, Mesquite, Dallas Co., TX.
Known children of Johnny Calvin[8] Abney and Winona Helen Kilgore both b. TX:
        1366   i.   Mildred Faye[9], b. 3 Feb 1938; m. Gerald Franklin Shaw.
               ii.   Patricia Sue m. Sonny Holmes. , b. ca.Apr 1940. She and Sonny Holmes lived in 2018 Galveston, Galveston Co., TX.
    Dorothy F. Pruitt, b.2 Jun 1923. She d.23 Jul 1988 at age 65 and was bur. Grove Hill Mem. Park, Dallas, Dallas Co., TX.
There were no known children of Johnny Calvin[8] Abney and Dorothy F. Pruitt.

1082. Elbert Lloyd[8] Abney (Homer[7], John[6], George[5], Benjamin[4], Hezekiah[3], Elisha[2], Abner[1]), b.1921 Dallas, Dallas Co., TX. He m1. Teresa H. Harris. He m2. Annie Jean McCallum in 1961 but no issue. He d.1968 Dallas, Dallas Co., TX; bur. Grove Hill Mem. Park, Dallas, Dallas Co., TX.
    Teresa H. Harris, b.1925. She d.19 Oct 1977 and was bur. Restland Mem. Park, Dallas, Dallas Co., TX.
Known child of Elbert Lloyd[8] Abney and Teresa H. Harris:
               i.   Gregory H.[9], b.1956. He d.1984 and was bur. Restland Mem. Park, Dallas, Dallas Co., TX.
    Annie Jean McCallum, b.1 Aug 1928 Parkland Hosp., Dallas, Dallas Co., TX. She m. Billy Mac Cline (USN-WWII) in 1945. She m2. Sgt. Paul Gene Hawkins (USAAC-WWI) in 1969. She d.17 Sep 2015 Corsicana, Navarro Co., TX, at age 87.

1083. Homer Welton "Buddy"[8] DeMoss (Mattie[7] Abney, John[6], George[5], Benjamin[4], Hezekiah[3], Elisha[2], Abner[1]), b.21 Jul 1921. He was liv. on 9 Apr 1940 with his uncle, Frank Young, Dallas, Dallas Co., TX. He m1. Stella "Alois" Horton on 4 Aug 1940. He m2. Dortha Nell Dean in 1984 but no issue. He d.18 Aug 1994 at age 73 and was bur. Laurel Oaks Mem. Park, Mesquite, Dallas Co., TX.
    Stella "Alois" Horton, b.31 Aug 1922. She d.23 Apr 1983 at age 60 and was bur. Laurel Oaks Mem. Park, Mesquite, Dallas Co., TX.
Known child of Homer Welton "Buddy"[8] DeMoss and Stella "Alois" Horton:
               i.   Welton Owen[9], b.20 Sep 1945. He d.11 Jan 1960 at age 14; bur. Laurel Oaks Mem. Park, Mesquite, Dallas Co., TX.
    Dortha Nell Dean, b.16 Sep 1925 Wolfe City, Hunt Co., TX. She d.14 Nov 1999 Dallas, TX and was bur. Restland Mem. Park, Dallas, , TX.

1084. Benjamin Frank "Ben"[8] Young Jr. (Vergia[7] Abney, John[6], George[5], Benjamin[4], Hezekiah[3], Elisha[2], Abner[1]), b. ca.Apr 1917 TX. He m. Dorothy Lee Haley ca.1937. He and Dorothy Lee Haley appeared on the census of 16 Apr 1940 Dallas, Dallas Co., TX. He d.18 Nov 1988 Dallas Co., TX and was bur. Grove Hill Mem. Park, Dallas, Dallas Co., TX.
    Dorothy Lee Haley, b.13 Jan 1918. She d.16 May 1998 Dallas Co., TX, at age 80 and was bur. Grove Hill Mem. Park, Dallas, Dallas Co., TX.
Known child of Benjamin Frank "Ben"[8] Young Jr. and Dorothy Lee Haley:
               i.   Ronald F.[9], b.11 Jun 1938 TX. He d.25 Sep 1991 at age 53 and was bur. Grove Hill Mem. Park, Dallas, Dallas Co., TX.

1085. Wanda Ruth[8] Carrigan (Mina[7] Abney, John[6], George[5], Benjamin[4], Hezekiah[3], Elisha[2], Abner[1]), b.2 Jul 1935 Parkland Hosp., Dallas, Dallas Co., TX. She m. Glen Lancaster (USArmy) on 7 May 1955. She d.2 Jan 2018 at age 82 and was bur. Restland Mem. Park, Dallas, Dallas Co., TX.
    Glen Lancaster (USArmy), b.20 Apr 1928 Holland, Bell Co., TX. He d.21 Feb 2010 TX at age 81 and was bur. Restland Mem. Park, Dallas.
Known child of Wanda Ruth[8] Carrigan and Glen Lancaster (USArmy):
        1367   i.   Sandra[9], m. Brad Zastrow.

1086. William Texas[8] Abney Sr. (USArmy-WWII) (William[7], William[6], George[5], Benjamin[4], Hezekiah[3], Elisha[2], Abner[1]) b.1 Dec 1914 China Spring, McLennan Co., TX; m. Mary E. Holt; d.26 Jan 1993 Waco, McLennan Co.; bur. China Spring Cem., China Spring, McLennan Co., TX.
    Mary Evelyn Holt, b.18 Oct 1918. She m. James William Mast. She d.5 Nov 2004 at age 86 and was bur. Forest Lawn Cem., Dallas.
Known children of William Texas[8] Abney Sr. (USArmy-WWII) and Mary Evelyn Holt (birth order unknown):
               i.   Gerald Wayne[9].
              ii.   Dena.
            iii.   Tina.
            iv.   Jean Yvonne m. (n.n.) Kelley.
              v.   William Texas.
            vi.   Steven.
           vii.   Mark.
          viii.   Elizabeth Ann, b.30 May 1954 and d.31 May 1954 Waco, McLennan Co., TX and was bur. China Spring Cem.

1087. Billie Jean[8] Abney (William[7], William[6], George[5], Benjamin[4], Hezekiah[3], Elisha[2], Abner[1]) m. George Blair (USAF). , b.27 Jun 1925 Waco, McLennan Co., TX. She d.2 Apr 2011 Madison, Dane Co., WI, at age 85.
Known children of Billie Jean[8] Abney and George Blair (USAF) (birth order unknown):
               i.   Linda[9] m. Steve Sundberg.
              ii.   Jim m. Pat (n.n.).
            iii.   Ron.
            iv.   Ed m. JoAnn (n.n.).
             v.   David.
            vi.   Paul m. Debbie (n.n.).

1088. Wilma D.[8] Abney (John[7], William[6], George[5], Benjamin[4], Hezekiah[3], Elisha[2], Abner[1]), b.23 Jul 1925 Coryell Co., TX. She m. Alvin Dorris Choate Sr. (USArmy-WWII). She d.1 Jul 2012 Dallas, Dallas Co., TX, at age 86 and was bur. Grove Hill Mem. Park, Dallas, Dallas Co., TX.
    Alvin Dorris Choate Sr. (USArmy-WWII), b.1916. He d.1981.
Known child of Wilma D.[8] Abney and Alvin Dorris Choate Sr. (USArmy-WWII):
      i.   Alvin Dorris Jr.[9]

1089. Randle "David"[8] Abney (John[7], William[6], George[5], Benjamin[4], Hezekiah[3], Elisha[2], Abner[1]), b.25 Feb 1928 TX. He m. JoAnn Kline. He d.11 Jun 2002 at age 74. He was cremated.
    JoAnn Kline, b.20 Jan 1933 Dallas, Dallas Co., TX. She d.7 Jan 2011 at age 77 and was bur. Oakland Cem., Dallas, Dallas Co., TX.
Known children of Randle "David"[8] Abney and JoAnn Kline (birth order unknown):
      i.   John Conner[9] m. Karla (n.n.).
     ii.   Joe Clifton.
    iii.   Connie m. Bill Oliver.
    iv.   Jana m. Steve Risinger.
     v.   Traci m. Greg Walls.

1090. Herman Mancel[8] Myers (Ludie[7] Abney, Alex[6], George[5], Benjamin[4], Hezekiah[3], Elisha[2], Abner[1]), b.2 Nov 1915 AL. He appeared on the census of 11 Apr 1940 Sayreton, Jefferson Co., AL. He m1. Eva Mae Beasley ca.1940. He m2. Doris J. Myers in 1979 but no issue. He d.6 Jan 1987 at age 71 and was bur. Friendship UMC Cem., Gardendale, Jefferson Co., AL.
    Eva Mae Beasley, b.26 May 1922 AL. She d.30 Jan 1961 AL at age 38.
Known children of Herman Mancel[8] Myers and Eva Mae Beasley:
      i.   Tommie Mancel[9], b.6 Aug 1941 AL. He d.6 Aug 1941 AL; bur. Friendship UMC Cem., Gardendale, Jefferson Co., AL.
  1368 ii.   Patricia Ann, b. 8 Dec 1946; m. Louie Edward Talley.
    iii.   Sandra Elaine, b.17 Sep 1948 Jefferson Co., AL. She d.25 Oct 1955 WV at age 7 and was bur. Friendship UMC Cem.
    iv.   Gwendolyn Sue m. Robert Leroy Tidwell. , b.13 Jul 1952 AL. She d.15 Apr 2019 at age 66; bur. Friendship UMC Cem.
           Robert Leroy Tidwell, b.19 Sep 1945. He d.26 Oct 1973 at age 28 and was bur. Friendship UMC Cem.
    Doris J. Myers, b.13 Jun 1921. She d.18 Sep 1991 at age 70.

1091. Gordon W.[8] Abney Jr. (USN-WWII) (Gordon[7], Alex[6], George[5], Benjamin[4], Hezekiah[3], Elisha[2], Abner[1]), b.15 Oct 1924 AL. He m. Jewel Dean. He d.29 Jan 2012 at age 87 and was bur. Walker Chapel Mem. Gardens, Fultondale, Jefferson Co., AL.
    Jewel Dean, b.7 Jun 1946. She d.20 Jun 1999 at age 53.
Known children of Gordon W.[8] Abney Jr. (USN-WWII) and Jewel Dean (birth order unknown):
      i.   Michael Gordon[9].
     ii.   Chelita m. (n.n.) Freeman.
    iii.   Woodrow Wayne.
    iv.   Mary Diana m. (n.n.) Davis.
     v.   Melinda Sue m. (n.n.) Bailey.
    vi.   Marion Jo m. (n.n.) Brantley.

1092. Tommy Franklin[8] Abney Sr. (John[7], Alex[6], George[5], Benjamin[4], Hezekiah[3], Elisha[2], Abner[1]), b.26 Sep 1934. He m. Shirley Jean Harris ca.1960. He d.6 Dec 2018 at age 84 and was bur. Oakwood Mem. Gardens, Gardendale, Jefferson Co., AL.
    Shirley Jean Harris, b.29 Aug 1940 Alexander City, Tallapoosa Co., AL. She d.24 Nov 2016 AL at age 76; bur. Oakwood Mem. Gardens.
Known children of Tommy Franklin[8] Abney Sr. and Shirley Jean Harris (birth order unknown):
      i.   Tommy Franklin[9].
  1369 ii.   Thomas Ashley, m. Angela (n.n.).
  1370 iii.   Susan Denise, m. (n.n.) Tracy.
  1371 iv.   Christi Jean, m. David Widener.

1093. Waltis Eugene "Gene"[8] Abney (John[7], Alex[6], George[5], Benjamin[4], Hezekiah[3], Elisha[2], Abner[1]), b.4 Apr 1938. He m. Brenda (n.n.). He d.27 Oct 2016 AL at age 78. He was cremated.
Known children of Waltis Eugene "Gene"[8] Abney and Brenda (birth order unknown):
      i.   Shannon Lea[9].
     ii.   John David.
    iii.   Christopher Ray.

1094. Nancy "Janine"[8] Abney (Horace[7], Alex[6], George[5], Benjamin[4], Hezekiah[3], Elisha[2], Abner[1]), b.8 Apr 1936. She m. L.G. Graham. d.15 Apr 2015 at age 79 and was bur. Friendship UMC Cem., Gardendale, Jefferson Co., AL.
    L.G. Graham, b.31 Jan 1930. He d.12 Nov 1971 at age 41.
Known children of Nancy "Janine"[8] Abney and L.G. Graham:
      i.   Terry Daniel[9], b.4 Nov 1961. He d.11 Feb 1962 and was bur. Friendship UMC Cem., Gardendale, Jefferson Co., AL.

1095. Horace "Grover"[8] Abney Sr. (Horace[7], Alex[6], George[5], Benjamin[4], Hezekiah[3], Elisha[2], Abner[1]), b.9 Feb 1942. He m. Barbara "Bobbie" (n.n.) ca.1959. He d.23 Dec 2005 at age 63 and was bur. Friendship UMC Cem., Gardendale, Jefferson Co., AL.
    Barbara "Bobbie" (n.n.), b.12 Jan 1943.
Known children of Horace "Grover"[8] Abney Sr. and Barbara "Bobbie" (birth order unknown):
      i.   Peanut[9] m. Teresa (n.n.).
     ii.   Jeffery.
    iii.   Barbara "Rena", b.6 Nov 1960 Jefferson Co., AL. She m. Jeff Marsh. She d.27 Mar 2010 Jefferson Co., AL, at age 49 and was bur. Friendship UMC Cem., Gardendale, Jefferson Co., AL.

1096. Helen[8] Abney (George[7], Peter[6], George[5], Benjamin[4], Hezekiah[3], Elisha[2], Abner[1]), b. ca. Jul 1927. She m. Pvt. Harold W. Fromhold (USArmy-WWII). She d.30 May 2012 Fultondale, Jefferson Co., AL and was bur. Walker Chapel Mem. Gardens, Fultondale, Jefferson Co., AL.
      Pvt. Harold W. Fromhold (USArmy-WWII) He was a POW in WWII POW in WWII. He, b.17 Feb 1925. He d.27 Nov 2009 at age 84.
Known children of Helen[8] Abney and Pvt. Harold W. Fromhold (USArmy-WWII) (birth order unknown):
            i.   Ronald W.[9].
   1372   ii.   Debra, m. (n.n.) Aaron.
            iii. Danny Harold.

1097. James "Jim"[8] Green (Lillie[7] Abney, Peter[6], George[5], Benjamin[4], Hezekiah[3], Elisha[2], Abner[1]), b.25 Jan 1942. He m. Judith "Judy" Townsend. He d.8 Feb 2015 at age 73. He was cremated.
Known children of James "Jim"[8] Green and Judith "Judy" Townsend (birth order unknown):
            i.   David[9].
            ii.   Brenda m. (n.n.) Hill.

1098. Harry Lee[8] Madden (Elizabeth[7] Abney, James[6], George[5], Benjamin[4], Hezekiah[3], Elisha[2], Abner[1]), b.1 Sep 1939 AL. He m. Evelyn S. (n.n.) ca.1959. He d.26 Jan 2014 Augusta, Richmond Co., GA, at age 74 and was bur. Hillcrest Mem. Park Cem., Augusta, Richmond Co., GA.
Known children of Harry Lee[8] Madden and Evelyn S. (birth order unknown):
            i.   Kathy M.[9] m. Terry Ellenberg.
            ii.   Connie M. m. Larry Lariscey.
   1373   iii. Rhonda Michelle, b. 27 Mar 1966; m. Thomas D. "McFee" McPherson.

1099. Donald Ray[8] Abney (Roy[7], James[6], George[5], Benjamin[4], Hezekiah[3], Elisha[2], Abner[1]), b.15 Oct 1945 Jefferson Co., AL. He m. Bonnie Sue Criegler in 1963. He d.22 Sep 2012 Ocala, Marion Co., FL, at age 66 and was bur. Fort McCoy Cem., Fort McCoy, Marion Co., FL.
      Bonnie Sue Criegler, b.4 Mar 1945. She d.16 Jan 2000 at age 54 and was bur. Fort McCoy Cem., Fort McCoy, Marion Co., FL.
Known children of Donald Ray[8] Abney and Bonnie Sue Criegler (birth order unknown):
            i.   Dina[9].
            ii.   Kenny.
            iii. Dennis Ray, b.19 Jun 1968 Tampa, Hillsborough Co., FL. A race car driver, he d.14 Oct 1989 in a race car accident at Lakeland Interstate Raceway, Lakeland, Polk Co., FL, age 21; bur. Myrtle Hill Mem. Park, Tampa, Hillsborough Co., FL. (See: https://en.wikipedia.org/wiki/List_of_driver_deaths_in_motorsport#A)

1100. David Arnold[8] Abney (Roy[7], James[6], George[5], Benjamin[4], Hezekiah[3], Elisha[2], Abner[1]), b.6 Dec 1947 Jefferson Co., AL. He m. (n.n.). He d.20 May 2008 Fort McCoy, Marion Co., FL, at age 60 and was bur. Myrtle Hill Mem. Park, Tampa, Hillsborough Co., FL.
Known children of David Arnold[8] Abney (birth order unknown):
            i.   Mark[9].
            ii.   Darrell.
            iii. Lisa m. (n.n.) Yaun.
            iv. Debra m. (n.n.) Allan.

1101. Samuel Robert[8] Abney Sr. (Roy[7], James[6], George[5], Benjamin[4], Hezekiah[3], Elisha[2], Abner[1]), b.11 Jun 1950 Birmingham, Jefferson Co., AL. He m. JoAnn Davis. He d.12 Feb 1994 Fort McCoy, Marion Co., FL, at age 43 and was bur. Fort McCoy Cem., Fort McCoy, Marion Co., FL.
Known children of Samuel Robert[8] Abney Sr. and JoAnn Davis (birth order unknown):
            i.   Samuel Robert[9].
            ii.   Brenda Elaine.

1102. Larry Joe[8] Abney (Raymond[7], James[6], George[5], Benjamin[4], Hezekiah[3], Elisha[2], Abner[1]), b.31 Jul 1949. He m. Debra Jo McBrayer. He d.11 May 2005 at age 55 and was bur. Oakwood Mem. Gardens, Gardendale, Jefferson Co., AL.
      Debra Jo McBrayer, b.27 Sep 1950. She d.18 Sep 2014 at age 63 and was bur. Oakwood Mem. Gardens, Gardendale, Jefferson Co., AL.
Known child of Larry Joe[8] Abney and Debra Jo McBrayer:
            i.   Larry Lee[9] m. Wendy (n.n.).

1103. Donald Ray[8] Abney (Paul[7], William[6], William[5], Benjamin[4], Hezekiah[3], Elisha[2], Abner[1]), b.9 Jan 1944. He m. (n.n.). He d.12 May 2018 at age 74 and was bur. Mountain View Park Cem., Marietta, Cobb Co., GA.
Known children of Donald Ray[8] Abney (birth order unknown):
            i.   Tim[9] m. Michelle (n.n.).
            ii.   Vickie m. Paul Oswalt.
            iii. Brian.

1104. Carol[8] Abney (Joe[7], William[6], William[5], Benjamin[4], Hezekiah[3], Elisha[2], Abner[1]) m. Jerry Hensel.
Known children of Carol[8] Abney and Jerry Hensel (birth order unknown):
   1374   i.   Mark[9], m. Lauren (n.n.).
            ii.   Peter.

1105. Kathleen Frances[8] Lorren (John[7], Leticia[6] Abney, Eli[5], Benjamin[4], Hezekiah[3], Elisha[2], Abner[1]), b.17 Jul 1924 Raleigh, Wake Co., NC. She m. (n.n.) Thomas. d.14 Oct 2000 Raleigh, Wake Co., NC, at age 76 and was bur. Raleigh Mem. Park, Raleigh, Wake Co., NC.
Known children of Kathleen Frances[8] Lorren and (n.n.) Thomas (birth order unknown):
            i.   Dell[9] m. (n.n.) Hilliard.
            ii.   Natasha m. (n.n.) Longanecker.
            iii. Sherin m. (n.n.) Smetana.

1106. Claude Ealton[8] Lorren (USN-WWII) (John[7], Leticia[6] Abney, Eli[5], Benjamin[4], Hezekiah[3], Elisha[2], Abner[1]), b.19 Feb 1927 Raleigh, Wake Co., NC. He m. Angeline Ferrant. He d.17 Jun 1986 Wake Co., NC, at age 59 and was bur. Raleigh Mem. Park, Raleigh, Wake Co., NC.
Known children of Claude Ealton[8] Lorren (USN-WWII) and Angeline Ferrant (birth order unknown):
        i.   Stanley S.[9].
        ii. John C.
        iii. Claudia m. Pollander.
        iv. Christina m. (n.n.) Anderson.
        v.   Marie A.

1107. William "Herbert"[8] Baswell (Pearl[7] Lorren, Leticia[6] Abney, Eli[5], Benjamin[4], Hezekiah[3], Elisha[2], Abner[1]), b.17 Sep 1935 Cleburne Co., AL. He m. Linda S. Motes ca.1960. He d.26 Jan 2015 Gadsden, Etowah Co., AL, age 79; bur. Piedmont Memory Gardens, Piedmont, Calhoun Co., AL.
Linda S. Motes, b.22 May 1944 Calhoun Co., AL. She d.15 Aug 2012 Gadsden, Etowah Co., AL, at age 68; bur. Piedmont Memory Gardens.
Known children of William "Herbert"[8] Baswell and Linda S. Motes (birth order unknown):
1375   i.   Sandra[9], m. (n.n.) Holmes.
1376   ii. Shirley, m. Jackie Black.
        iii. Carley.

1108. Ola Mae[8] Abney (John[7], Eli[6], Eli[5], Benjamin[4], Hezekiah[3], Elisha[2], Abner[1]), b.28 May 1928 AL. She m. Clarence Peter "Pete" Hill Sr. d.27 Dec 2013 Anniston, Calhoun Co., AL, at age 85 and was bur. Anniston Mem. Gardens, Anniston, Calhoun Co., AL.
Known children of Ola Mae[8] Abney and Clarence Peter "Pete" Hill Sr. (birth order unknown):
        i.   Cynthia[9] m. Bob Perkinson.
        ii. Clarence Peter.

1109. Betty Lorine[8] Abney (John[7], Eli[6], Eli[5], Benjamin[4], Hezekiah[3], Elisha[2], Abner[1]), b.24 Aug 1931 Gadsden, Etowah Co., AL; m. Norman S. Ross (USArmy-WWII) ca.1950; d.27 Mar 2015 Rossville, Walker Co., GA, ae.83; bur. Tennessee Georgia Mem. Park, Rossville, Walker Co., GA.
Norman S. Ross (USArmy-WWII), b.13 Feb 1924. He d.25 May 2010 Rossville, Walker Co., GA, age 86; bur. Tennessee Georgia Mem. Park.
Known children of Betty Lorine[8] Abney and Norman S. Ross (USArmy-WWII) (birth order unknown):
1377   i.   Nancy[9], m. (n.n.) Plemons.
        ii. Sharon m. Doug Mazza.
        iii. Doris m. (n.n.) Hillibrand.
1378   iv. Norman Christopher "Chris," b. 1 Oct 1965; m. (n.n.).

1110. James Hugh[8] Abney (USArmy) (William[7], Posey[6], Eli[5], Benjamin[4], Hezekiah[3], Elisha[2], Abner[1]) m. Nila Jean Elrod. He, b.3 May 1929. He d.27 Oct 2000 at age 71 and was bur. Chana Creek PBC Cem., Kent, Elmore Co., AL.
Nila Jean Elrod, b.17 Apr 1929. She d.6 Dec 2011 at age 82 and was bur. Crestwood Mem. Cem., East Gadsden, Etowah Co., AL.
Known children of James Hugh[8] Abney (USArmy) and Nila Jean Elrod (birth order unknown):
1379   i.   Mike[9], m. (n.n.).
1380   ii. Ginger, m. Kennon Wilson.

1111. Sarah Ann[8] Abney (William[7], Posey[6], Eli[5], Benjamin[4], Hezekiah[3], Elisha[2], Abner[1]) m. Donald Boone "Don" House. , b.30 Dec 1934 Etowah Co., AL. She d.3 Oct 2006 Jefferson Co., AL, at age 71.
Donald Boone "Don" House, b.9 Feb 1033 Cullman Co., AL. He d.15 Oct 1989 Jefferson Co., AL, at age 956.
Known children of Sarah Ann[8] Abney and Donald Boone "Don" House (birth order unknown):
        i.   Bart[9].
        ii. Kellie m. Pat Hopkins.

1112. Patricia Ann[8] Overstreet (Jessie[7] Abney, Posey[6], Eli[5], Benjamin[4], Hezekiah[3], Elisha[2], Abner[1]), b.3 Nov 1947. She m. (n.n.) Maroney. d.20 Feb 2017 at age 69 and was bur. Oak Hill Cem., Attalla, Etowah Co., AL.
Known child of Patricia Ann[8] Overstreet and (n.n.) Maroney:
        i.   Jeffery Lamar[9], b.30 Jun 1979. He d.16 Nov 1979 and was bur. Oak Hill Cem., Attalla, Etowah Co., AL.

1115. Michael Harlan "Mike"[8] Abney (Carl[7], John[6], Eli[5], Benjamin[4], Hezekiah[3], Elisha[2], Abner[1]), b.26 Jan 1952 Cullman, Cullman Co., AL. He m. Barbara Kristen Bailey (gen.), daughter of (n.n.) Bailey and Barbara (n.n.) (gen.). They were all living in Paris, TN in 1998.
Barbara Kristen "Kris" Bailey (gen.). , b.26 Apr 1955 Port Clinton, Ottawa Co., OH. The author began working with Barbara Bailey (Kris's mother) in 1996 and the daughter shortly thereafter. Barbara and Kris were both pleasant and joyful ladies and truly a pleasure to work with. Due to their diligent work, the entire line of Eli Newton "Bish" Abney has been connected to its rightful place in Benjamin Hezekiah Abney's family.
Known children of Michael Harlan "Mike"[8] Abney and Barbara Kristen Bailey (gen.):
        i.   Charlotte Amalie[9], b.8 Jun 1982 Columbus, OH.
        ii. Kevin Joseph, b.4 Nov 1986 Gallatin, Sumner Co., TN.

1116. Carol Annette[8] Abney (Carl[7], John[6], Eli[5], Benjamin[4], Hezekiah[3], Elisha[2], Abner[1]), b.31 Oct 1954 Cullman, Cullman Co., AL. m. Carl Davis.
Known children of Carol Annette[8] Abney and Carl Davis both b. Ft. Walton Beach, Okaloosa Co., FL,:
        i.   John William[9] m. Leslie (n.n.) He, b.29 Jul 1974.
        ii. Matthew Leeland, b.20 Nov 1978.

1117. Suzanne[8] Abney (Carl[7], John[6], Eli[5], Benjamin[4], Hezekiah[3], Elisha[2], Abner[1]), b. ca.1963. She m. Curtis Swartz.
Known children of Suzanne[8] Abney and Curtis Swartz:
        i.   Phillip Michael[9].
        ii. Tabitha Faye.
        iii. Joseph.

1118. Charles[8] Echols (Mazelle[7] Abney, John[6], Eli[5], Benjamin[4], Hezekiah[3], Elisha[2], Abner[1]). He m. Victoria (n.n.) and had issue:
      i.   John Austin[9], b.Oct 1981 Birmingham, Jefferson Co., AL.

1119. Cynthia[8] Echols (Mazelle[7] Abney, John[6], Eli[5], Benjamin[4], Hezekiah[3], Elisha[2], Abner[1]). She m. (n.n.) and had issue:
    1381   i.   Jessica[9].

1120. Brett John[8] Adams (Bobbie[7] Abney, John[6], Eli[5], Benjamin[4], Hezekiah[3], Elisha[2], Abner[1]), b.27 Dec 1966 Cullman, Cullman Co., AL. He m. (n.n.). He d.13 Sep 2012 Cullman, Cullman Co., AL, at age 45 and was bur. Simcoe United Methodist Cem., Simcoe, Cullman Co., AL. Known children of Brett John[8] Adams:
      i.   Baylor[9].
      ii. Parker.

1121. David[8] Abney (James[7], John[6], Eli[5], Benjamin[4], Hezekiah[3], Elisha[2], Abner[1]) m. Marsha (n.n.) and had issue: Karlye[9].

1122. Amy[8] Abney (James[7], John[6], Eli[5], Benjamin[4], Hezekiah[3], Elisha[2], Abner[1]) m. Chase Tew and had issue:
      i.   Cooper[9].
      ii. Addison.

1123. Roy Leonard[8] Weaver Sr. (Mary[7] Burkhalter, Martha[6] Abney, James[5], Benjamin[4], Hezekiah[3], Elisha[2], Abner[1]), b.23 Dec 1935 Cedartown, Polk Co., GA. He m. (n.n.). He d.14 Dec 1983 Gadsden, Etowah Co., AL, at age 47 and was bur. Forrest Cem., Gadsden, Etowah Co., AL. Known children of Roy Leonard[8] Weaver Sr. and (n.n.):
      i.   Roy L.[9].
      ii. Samuel.

1124. Hazel Katherine[8] Abney (Henry[7], Marion[6], James[5], Benjamin[4], Hezekiah[3], Elisha[2], Abner[1]), b.17 Feb 1923. She m. Sgt. James Livingston Farrer (USArmy-WWII) on 19 Oct 1952. She d.27 Mar 2012 at age 89 and was bur. East View Cem., Rome, Floyd Co., GA. Sgt. James Livingston Farrer (USArmy-WWII), b.12 May 1915 Floyd Co., GA. He d.18 Dec 2004 Floyd Co., GA, at age 89; bur. East View Cem. Known children of Hazel Katherine[8] Abney and Sgt. James Livingston Farrer (USArmy-WWII):
    1382   i.   Amy[9], m. (n.n.) Drummond.
           ii. James C. "Jimmy."

1125. Margie Louise[8] Abney (Henry[7], Marion[6], James[5], Benjamin[4], Hezekiah[3], Elisha[2], Abner[1]), b.11 Sep 1924 Floyd Co., GA. She m. Emmett Coleman Akins on 16 Jun 1952. She d.6 Dec 2016 Calhoun, Gordon Co., GA, at age 92 and was bur. East View Cem., Rome, Floyd Co., GA.
    Emmett Coleman Akins, b.16 Sep 1912 Lindale, Floyd Co., GA. He d.13 Jul 1986 Lindale, Floyd Co., GA, at age 73; bur. East View Cem. Known child of Margie Louise[8] Abney and Emmett Coleman Akins: Donna[9] (she m. John Wilson).

1126. Rev. William "Gwinnett"[8] Abney Sr. (William[7], Marion[6], James[5], Benjamin[4], Hezekiah[3], Elisha[2], Abner[1]), b.16 Jun 1919 Rome, Floyd Co., GA. He m. Katherine Mildred Byrd ca.1937. He and Katherine Mildred Byrd appeared on the census of 9 Apr 1940 Lindale, Floyd Co., GA. He d.13 Apr 2010 Gwinnett Co., GA, at age 90 and was bur. Peachtree Mem. Park, Norcross, Gwinnett Co., GA.
    Katherine Mildred Byrd, b.9 Aug 1920 Floyd Co., GA. She d.9 Mar 2009 at age 88 and was bur. Peachtree Mem. Park, Norcross. Known children of Rev. William "Gwinnett"[8] Abney Sr. and Katherine Mildred Byrd:
      i.   William Gwinnett "Bill"[9] m. Angie (n.n.). He, b. ca.1938 GA.
      ii. Norma m. (n.n.) Wilson. , b. ca.Nov 1939 GA.
      iii. Jerry m. Ibis (n.n.).
      iv. Nancy m. (n.n.) Crane.

1127. James Marion Chaney "Jimmy"[8] Abney (USN-WWII) (gen.) (William[7], Marion[6], James[5], Benjamin[4], Hezekiah[3], Elisha[2], Abner[1]), b.30 Apr 1922. He m. Viola Victoria Gilstrap on 5 Apr 1942. He d.25 Aug 1998 at age 76 and was bur. Rome Mem. Park South, Rome, Floyd Co., GA. Cousin Jimmy was a genealogist of the Greatest Generation who worked on the family history with his son, William. They are credited with providing much of the information in this book, on the descendants of James Alfred "Alf" Abney (#112).
    Viola Victoria Gilstrap, b.18 Sep 1923 Floyd Co., GA. She d.10 Aug 2019 Rome, Floyd Co., GA, at age 95; bur. Rome Mem. Park South. Known children of James Marion Chaney "Jimmy"[8] Abney (USN-WWII) (gen.) and Viola Victoria Gilstrap:
      i.   Charles[9] m. Betty (n.n.).
      ii. Mike m. Carole (n.n.).
      iii. Brenda m. Gene Hughes.
      iv. Omar "William" (gen.), b.1948. He worked with the author in 2002 and provided much information on his family.
      v. James Robert "Roddy", b.28 Aug 1951. He d.27 Jan 2010 at age 58 and was bur. Rome Mem. Park South, Rome.

1128. Ralph "Syndnor"[8] Abney (USN-WWII) (William[7], Marion[6], James[5], Benjamin[4], Hezekiah[3], Elisha[2], Abner[1]), b.29 Sep 1924 Rome, Floyd Co., GA. He m1. Josephine Teresa "Jay" Puleo on 9 Jan 1943 New York City, NY. He m2. Dorothy (n.n.) but no issue. He d.23 Sep 1991 Albuquerque, Bernalillo Co., NM, at age 66 and was bur. Pleasant Hope Cem., Rome, Floyd Co., GA.
    Josephine Teresa "Jay" Puleo, b.15 Jun 1918 Boston, Suffolk Co., MA. She d.11 Dec 1992 Albuquerque, Bernalillo Co., NM, at age 74 and was bur. Calvary Catholic Cem., Enid, Garfield Co., OK. Known children of Ralph "Syndnor"[8] Abney (USN-WWII) and Josephine Teresa "Jay" Puleo:
      i.   J. Harrison[9].
      ii. Ralph Syndnor.
      iii. Jae Annette, b.21 Jun 1945; m. William D. "Wild Bill Jr." Harrison; d.31 May 1996, age 50; bur. Calvary Catholic Cem. William D. "Wild Bill Jr." Harrison, b.20 Jun 1945.
      iv. Linda Sue, b.14 Aug 1947 NY; m. Richard J. Faulkner Sr. 29 Nov 1964; d.4 Nov 2016, ae.69; bur. Calvary Catholic Cem. Richard J. Faulkner Sr, b.17 Jan 1943.

1129. Robert Bryant "Bobby"[8] Abney Sr. (USAF-WWII) (William[7], Marion[6], James[5], Benjamin[4], Hezekiah[3], Elisha[2], Abner[1]), b.3 Sep 1927 Lindale, Floyd Co., GA. He m. Annie Jo George on 8 Apr 1950. He d.2 Nov 2019 Rome, Floyd Co., GA, at age 92. He was cremated.

    Annie Jo George, b.27 Mar 1927 Alabama City, Etowah Co., AL. She d.1 Dec 2014 Rome, Floyd Co., GA, at age 87.

Known children of Robert Bryant "Bobby"[8] Abney Sr. (USAF-WWII) and Annie Jo George (birth order unknown):

        i.   Mark J.[9].

        ii. Annette m. James Willkie.

        iii. Edward W.

1383   iv. Robert Bryant "Bob," b. 23 Feb 1957; m. Ingeborg (n.n.); div. Ingeborg (n.n.).

1130. Rev. Billy John[8] Abney Sr. (William[7], Marion[6], James[5], Benjamin[4], Hezekiah[3], Elisha[2], Abner[1]), b.10 Jul 1929; m. Ruby N. Erwin.

    Ruby N. Erwin, b.7 Dec 1928. She d.27 Feb 1998 at age 69 and was bur. Macon Mem. Park, Macon, Bibb Co., GA.

Known children of Rev. Billy John[8] Abney Sr. and Ruby N. Erwin:

        i.   Billy John[9], b.14 Nov 1950. He d.28 Jun 1982 at age 31 and was bur. Macon Mem. Park, Macon, Bibb Co., GA.

        ii. Sara Virginia, b.2 May 1954. She d.1 Jul 1993 GA at age 39 and was bur. Macon Mem. Park, Macon, Bibb Co., GA.

1384   iii. Luther Dale, b. 16 Feb 1958; m. Penny Ann Thistlewood.

1131. Allen David[8] Washington (Lenora[7] Burkhalter, Melissa[6] Abney, James[5], Benjamin[4], Hezekiah[3], Elisha[2], Abner[1]) m. Lizzie Lucile "Cil" Wallace. He, b.4 May 1909. He d.3 Dec 1991 Floyd Co., GA, at age 82 and was bur. New Bethel Cem., Floyd Co., GA.

    Lizzie Lucile "Cil" Wallace, b.18 Feb 1912. She d.26 Mar 2008 Floyd Co., GA, at age 96 and was bur. New Bethel Cem., Floyd Co., GA.

Known child of Allen David[8] Washington and Lizzie Lucile "Cil" Wallace:

        i.   Bobby Allen[9], b.29 Jan 1932. He d.15 Feb 1932 and was bur. New Bethel Cem., Floyd Co., GA.

1132. William Garvin[8] Burkhalter Jr. (William[7], Melissa[6] Abney, James[5], Benjamin[4], Hezekiah[3], Elisha[2], Abner[1]) m. Margaret Catherine Griffin. He, b.2 May 1929 Floyd Co., GA. He d.8 Mar 2015 Floyd Co., GA, at age 85 and was bur. New Bethel Cem., Floyd Co., GA.

    Margaret Catherine Griffin, b.20 Jan 1930 Floyd Co., GA. She d.19 Aug 2012 Silver Creek, Floyd Co., GA, at age 82; bur. New Bethel Cem.

Known child of William Garvin[8] Burkhalter Jr. and Margaret Catherine Griffin:

        i.   David Leon[9], b.16 Dec 1956 GA. He d.30 Dec 2009 Floyd Co., GA, at age 53 and was bur. New Bethel Cem.

1133. PFC Jimmy Allen[8] Burkhalter (USArmy) (William[7], Melissa[6] Abney, James[5], Benjamin[4], Hezekiah[3], Elisha[2], Abner[1]), b.28 Jan 1935. He m. Frances Irine Lingerfelt on 14 Apr 1962. He d.5 Jul 1990 at age 55 and was bur. Oaknoll Mem. Gardens Cem., Rome, Floyd Co., GA.

Known children of PFC Jimmy Allen[8] Burkhalter (USArmy) and Frances Irine Lingerfelt (birth order unknown):

        i.   Susan[9] m. (n.n.) Holmes.

        ii. Gary.

1134. Roy Percy[8] Burkhalter (Malory[7], Melissa[6] Abney, James[5], Benjamin[4], Hezekiah[3], Elisha[2], Abner[1]), b.12 Aug 1934 Floyd Co., GA. He m. Glaydean Collum. He d.2 Mar 2005 Silver Creek, Floyd Co., GA, at age 70 and was bur. New Bethel Cem., Floyd Co., GA.

    Glaydean Collum, b.30 Jan 1937. She d.29 Jul 2006 Floyd Co., GA, at age 69 and was bur. New Bethel Cem., Floyd Co., GA.

Known child of Roy Percy[8] Burkhalter and Glaydean Collum:

        i.   Wanda Faye[9], b.27 May 1957 Rome, Floyd Co., GA; d.20 Jun 2020 Rome, Floyd Co., GA, age 63; bur. New Bethel Cem.

1135. Ida Vaunita[8] Burkhalter (Malory[7], Melissa[6] Abney, James[5], Benjamin[4], Hezekiah[3], Elisha[2], Abner[1]), b.18 Jul 1936 Silver Creek, Floyd Co., GA; m. Billy Ray Spears on 31 Oct 1953. She d.2 Feb 2018 Rome, Floyd Co., GA, at age 81; bur. Floyd Memory Gardens, Rome, Floyd Co., GA.

Known children of Ida Vaunita[8] Burkhalter and Billy Ray Spears (birth order unknown):

        i.   Tammy[9] m. Michael Moore.

        ii. Michael Ray.

        iii. Anthony Lee m. Marsha (n.n.).

1136. Rev. Morris Clayton[8] Cargle (Elsie[7] Burkhalter, Melissa[6] Abney, James[5], Benjamin[4], Hezekiah[3], Elisha[2], Abner[1]), b.20 May 1942 Rome, Floyd Co., GA; m. Mary Alice Tidwell on 7 Dec 1962. He was co-owner *Cargle Bros. Construction*; d.16 Jul 2020 Rome, Floyd Co., GA, age 78.

Known children of Rev. Morris Clayton[8] Cargle and Mary Alice Tidwell (birth order unknown):

        i.   Kenneth[9] m. Diana (n.n.).

        ii. Kristi Lynn m. (n.n.) Womack.

1137. Bertha Estelle[8] Cox (Dovie[7] Miller, Geretie[6] Abney, James[5], Benjamin[4], Hezekiah[3], Elisha[2], Abner[1]), b.17 Feb 1913. She m. Truman Clyde Newberry on 14 Apr 1937. She d.28 Aug 1979 at age 66 and was bur. Pleasant Hope Cem., Rome, Floyd Co., GA.

    Truman Clyde Newberry, b.14 Sep 1916. He d.8 Aug 1981 at age 64.

Known children of Bertha Estelle[8] Cox and Truman Clyde Newberry:

        i.   Doris Hazel[9], b.2 Jun 1928 Floyd Co., GA. She m1. (n.n.) Wright. She m2. (n.n.) Murdock. d.24 Aug 2020 Rome, Floyd Co., GA, at age 92 and was bur. Pleasant Hope Cem., Rome, Floyd Co., GA.

        ii. Billy James, b.12 Apr 1937 Floyd Co., GA. He d.16 Jul 1987 Rome, Floyd Co., GA, at age 50; bur. Pleasant Hope Cem.

1385   iii. Jerry Lee, b. 17 Mar 1938 Floyd Co., GA; m. Gloria Faye Ingram.

        iv. Earl Junior m. Charlotte Joyce Jones. He, b.11 May 1940 Floyd Co., GA. He d.27 Apr 2012 Rome, Floyd Co., GA, at age 71 and was bur. Rome Mem. Park South, Rome, Floyd Co., GA.

              Charlotte Joyce Jones, b.18 Jun 1942. She d.19 Jan 2007 at age 64 and was bur. Rome Mem. Park South.

        v.   Glenda M., b.9 May 1943. She m. Thomas Lamar "Tommy" Pate. d.26 Feb 2009 at age 65 and was bur. Floyd Memory Gardens, Rome, Floyd Co., GA

              Thomas Lamar "Tommy" Pate, b.30 May 1943 Rome, Floyd Co., GA. He d.10 Dec 2019 Silver Creek, Floyd Co., GA, at age 76 and was bur. Floyd Memory Gardens, Rome, Floyd Co., GA.

1386   vi. Travis Darrell, b. 18 Feb 1948; m. Joann (n.n.).

        vii. Michael Stanley, b.8 Feb 1950 Floyd Co., GA. He d.3 Jan 2010 Rome, Floyd Co., GA, age 59; bur. Pleasant Hope Cem.

1138. Margaret Hazel[8] Cox (Dovie[7] Miller, Geretie[6] Abney, James[5], Benjamin[4], Hezekiah[3], Elisha[2], Abner[1]) m. Rayford Lewis Fricks. , b.24 Jul 1915 Polk Co., GA. She d.31 Jul 1981 Rome, Floyd Co., GA, at age 66 and was bur. Pleasant Hope Cem., Rome, Floyd Co., GA.
     Rayford Lewis Fricks, b. Christmas Day, 25 Dec 1911 GA. He d.19 May 1978 Rome, Floyd Co., GA, at age 66.
Known child of Margaret Hazel[8] Cox and Rayford Lewis Fricks:
        i.   Barbara Jean[9], b.19 Nov 1936 Riverside, Floyd Co., GA. She m. Donald Howard "Baltimore" Smith. d.16 Feb 1993 Lindale, Floyd Co., GA, at age 56 and was bur. Floyd Memory Gardens, Rome, Floyd Co., GA.
              Donald Howard "Baltimore" Smith, b.1 Dec 1933 GA. He d.2 May 2003 Rome, Floyd Co., GA, at age 69 and was bur. Floyd Memory Gardens, Rome, Floyd Co., GA.

1139. PFC Harold Lee[8] Cox (USArmy-WWII) (Dovie[7] Miller, Geretie[6] Abney, James[5], Benjamin[4], Hezekiah[3], Elisha[2], Abner[1]), b.1 May 1917 Polk Co., GA. He m1. Kinnie Bee Bynum ca.1936. He m2. Hallie Clair Partee in 1946. He d.17 May 1984 Rome, Floyd Co., GA, at age 67 and was bur. Pleasant Hope Cem., Rome, Floyd Co., GA.
     Kinnie Bee Bynum, b.24 Feb 1914; m2. James Tommy Brock. She d.4 Oct 1991, age 77; bur. Pisgah Bapt. Ch. Cem., Rome, Floyd Co., GA.
Known children of PFC Harold Lee[8] Cox (USArmy-WWII) and Kinnie Bee Bynum:
        i.   Melba Sue[9], b.15 Jan 1937 Floyd Co., GA; d.26 May 2007 Lindale, Floyd Co., GA, age 70; bur. Pisgah Bapt. Ch. Cem.
       ii.   Dorothy Lee "Dot", b.31 Jan 1939. She m. (n.n.) Owens. d.20 Mar 2007 at age 68 and was bur. Pisgah Bapt. Ch. Cem.
      iii.   Hazel Mae, b.14 Jul 1942. She d.15 Jul 1942 and was bur. Pleasant Hope Cem., Rome, Floyd Co., GA.
     Hallie Clair Partee, b.19 May 1925. She d.4 Feb 2011 at age 85 and was bur. Pleasant Hope Cem., Rome, Floyd Co., GA.
Known child of PFC Harold Lee[8] Cox (USArmy-WWII) and Hallie Clair Partee:
        i.   David Harold[9], b.16 Feb 1947. He d.31 Oct 2008 at age 61 and was bur. Pleasant Hope Cem., Rome, Floyd Co., GA.

1140. Ella Mae[8] Cox (Dovie[7] Miller, Geretie[6] Abney, James[5], Benjamin[4], Hezekiah[3], Elisha[2], Abner[1]), b.2 Apr 1919. She m. Ray Franklin Waters. d.2 Jul 1960 at age 41 and was bur. Pleasant Hope Cem., Rome, Floyd Co., GA.
     Ray Franklin Waters, b.25 Aug 1915. He d.11 Dec 1996 at age 81 and was bur. Pleasant Hope Cem., Rome, Floyd Co., GA.
Known children of Ella Mae[8] Cox and Ray Franklin Waters:
        i.   James R.[9], b.15 Oct 1939 GA. He d.16 Oct 1939 GA and was bur. Pleasant Hope Cem., Rome, Floyd Co., GA.
       ii.   Ronald Franklin, b.28 Jul 1948 Floyd Co., GA. He d.28 Aug 1948 Floyd Co., GA and was bur. Pleasant Hope Cem.
      iii.   Wanda Kay, b.11 Dec 1950. She m. (n.n.) Jones. d.9 Oct 2007 at age 56; bur. Rome Mem. Park South, Rome, GA.

1141. Mary Magdeline[8] Cox (Dovie[7] Miller, Geretie[6] Abney, James[5], Benjamin[4], Hezekiah[3], Elisha[2], Abner[1]), b.19 Jan 1921. She m. Stilman Posey Sisson. d.15 May 1998 at age 77 and was bur. Damascus Cem., Floyd Co., GA.
     Stilman Posey Sisson, b.9 Jul 1916. He d.16 Aug 1970 at age 54 and was bur. Damascus Cem., Floyd Co., GA.
Known children of Mary Magdeline[8] Cox and Stilman Posey Sisson:
        i.   Juanita[9], b.21 Sep 1936 Floyd Co., GA. She m. S.Sgt. George Burnes Hughes (USArmy-WWII). d.8 Oct 2011 Rome, Floyd Co., GA, at age 75 and was bur. Cross Roads Church Cem., Tallapoosa, Haralson Co., GA.
              S.Sgt. George Burnes Hughes (USArmy-WWII), b.30 Jun 1922. He d.6 Feb 1994 age 71; bur. Cross Roads Ch. Cem.

1142. Patsy Ruth[8] Cox (Dovie[7] Miller, Geretie[6] Abney, James[5], Benjamin[4], Hezekiah[3], Elisha[2], Abner[1]) m. PFC Belton Palmer Sheffield Jr. (USArmy-WWII). , b.26 May 1932 Silver Creek, Floyd Co., GA. She d.5 Feb 2011 Silver Creek, Floyd Co., GA, age 78; bur. Pleasant Hope Cem.
     PFC Belton Palmer Sheffield Jr. (USArmy-WWII), b.1 Nov 1921 Polk Co., GA; d.23 Oct 2002 Rome, GA; bur. Pleasant Hope Cem., Rome.
Known child of Patsy Ruth[8] Cox and PFC Belton Palmer Sheffield Jr. (USArmy-WWII):
        i.   Russell Lamar[9], b.19 Oct 1951 Rome, Floyd Co., GA. He m. Cherry Milam. He d.20 May 2020 Rome, Floyd Co., GA, at age 68 and was bur. Pleasant Hope Cem., Rome, Floyd Co., GA.

1143. Violet Patricia "Pat"[8] Gentry (Emma[7] Abney, William[6], James[5], Benjamin[4], Hezekiah[3], Elisha[2], Abner[1]), b.9 Jul 1945. She m. Larry Dale McCullough Sr. d.6 Aug 1985 at age 40.
     Larry Dale McCullough Sr, b.29 Nov 1944 Chattooga Co., GA. He d.13 Apr 2001 at age 56 and was bur. Rome Mem. Park South, Rome.
Known children of Violet Patricia "Pat"[8] Gentry and Larry Dale McCullough Sr.:
        i.   Larry Dale[9].
       ii.   Debbie Gail, b.29 Sep 1964 Floyd Co., GA. She m. (n.n.) Gazerro. d.12 Aug 2015 Aragon, Polk Co., GA, at age 50 and was bur. Oakland Cem., Rome, Floyd Co., GA.

1144. Betty June[8] Manis (Bernice[7] Reynolds, Lillie[6] Abney, James[5], Benjamin[4], Hezekiah[3], Elisha[2], Abner[1]), b.8 Nov 1930 Athens, McMinn Co., TN; m. Loyd Stinson (USN-WWII); d.1 May 2012 Cohutta, Whitfield Co., GA, ae.81; bur. United Mem. Gardens, Beaverdale, Whitfield Co., GA.
     Loyd Edward Stinson (USN-WWII), b.23 Dec 1924 GA. He d.30 Aug 1996 Dalton, Whitfield Co., GA, at age 71; bur. United Mem. Gardens.
Known child of Betty June[8] Manis and Loyd Edward Stinson (USN-WWII):
        i.   PFC Loyd Michael "Mike" (USArmy-Nam)[9], b.5 Jun 1948 Dalton, Whitfield Co., GA. He d.25 Nov 2016 Dalton, Whitfield Co., GA, at age 68 and was bur. Chattanooga National Cem., Chattanooga, Hamilton Co., TN.

1145. Susan[8] Abney (Rayford[7], Sylvester[6], James[5], Benjamin[4], Hezekiah[3], Elisha[2], Abner[1]) m. Dean Oswalt and had issue:
        i.   Sarah Danielle[9].

1146. Keith[8] Abney (Rayford[7], Sylvester[6], James[5], Benjamin[4], Hezekiah[3], Elisha[2], Abner[1]) m. Melanie (n.n.) and had issue:
        i.   Taylor Elizabeth[9].
       ii.   Cody Keith.

1147. Billy Joe[8] Hunt (Eunice[7] Abney, Robert[6], Joseph[5], Benjamin[4], Hezekiah[3], Elisha[2], Abner[1]), b. ca.1942 GA. He m. Betty Marie Bozeman.
Known child of Billy Joe[8] Hunt and Betty Marie Bozeman:
        i.   Billy "Christopher" (gen.)[9], b.1970. The author began working with Christopher in 1998. Thanks to Christopher for much information supplied on Joseph Calloway Abney (#113) and the descendants of his son, Robert Andrew Abney (#325).

1148. Edith Inez[8] Carnes (Alpha[7] Prewett, Minnie[6] Abney, Joseph[5], Benjamin[4], Hezekiah[3], Elisha[2], Abner[1]), b.27 Jun 1918 DeKalb Co., AL; m. Gladston Bryant (USN-WWII). d.30 Apr 1993 Fort Payne, DeKalb Co., AL, age 74; bur. Town Creek Bapt. Ch. Cem., Chavies, DeKalb Co., AL.
   Gladston Paul Bryant (USN-WWII), b.1918. He d.1987 and was bur. Town Creek Bapt. Ch. Cem., Chavies, DeKalb Co., AL.
Known child of Edith Inez[8] Carnes and Gladston Paul Bryant (USN-WWII):
       i.   Doris Elaine[9], b.28 Feb 1946 DeKalb Co., AL. She m. Royce Floyd Burnett (USArmy). d.16 Sep 2016 Lebanon, Wilson Co., TN, at age 70 and was bur. Allen Mem. Bapt. Ch. Cem., Fort Payne, DeKalb Co., AL.
           Royce Floyd Burnett (USArmy), b.30 Jan 1943 DeKalb Co., AL. He d.29 Oct 2017 Lebanon, Wilson Co., TN, at age 74 and was bur. Allen Mem. Bapt. Ch. Cem., Fort Payne, DeKalb Co., AL.

1149. Vera Mae[8] Carnes (Alpha[7] Prewett, Minnie[6] Abney, Joseph[5], Benjamin[4], Hezekiah[3], Elisha[2], Abner[1]), b.20 Nov 1920. She m. Franklin Eugene "Gene" Kean. d.25 Oct 1981 at age 60 and was bur. Lakewood Memory Gardens West, Tiftonia, Hamilton Co., TN.
   Franklin Eugene "Gene" Kean, b.6 Jun 1920. He d.25 Jan 1990 at age 69 and was bur. Lakewood Memory Gardens West, Tiftonia.
Known child of Vera Mae[8] Carnes and Franklin Eugene "Gene" Kean:
       i.   Carol Ann[9], b.27 Sep 1940. She m. Ernest M. Kirchmeyer. d.14 Apr 2019 Chattanooga, Hamilton Co., TN, at age 78 and was bur. Hooker Cem., Wildwood, Dade Co., GA.
           Ernest M. Kirchmeyer, b.17 Feb 1940. He d.29 Mar 2009 at age 69; bur. Hooker Cem., Wildwood, Dade Co., GA.

1150. Jeff[8] Abney (William[7], John[6], Charles[5], Benjamin[4], Hezekiah[3], Elisha[2], Abner[1]) m. Martie (n.n.) and had issue: Samuel[9]; Ellen; Peter.

1151. Philip[8] Abney (Benjamin[7], John[6], Charles[5], Benjamin[4], Hezekiah[3], Elisha[2], Abner[1]) m. Tracey (n.n.) and had issue:
   1387   i.   Michael[9], m. Andrea (n.n.).
   1388   ii.   Kristen, m. Cameron Dupree.

1152. John D.[8] McMackin (Fannie[7] Dobbins, Laura[6] Abney, Pinkney[5], Wiley[4], Hezekiah[3], Elisha[2], Abner[1]), b.19 Sep 1902 TN. He m. Ethel Evans on 23 Mar 1924 Greene Co., TN. He and Ethel Evans appeared on the censuses of 11 Apr 1930 Akron, Summit Co., OH; and 29 May 1940 Springfield, Summit Co., OH. He d.27 Jul 1954 at age 51 and was bur. Pleasant Hill Cem., Greene Co., TN.
   Ethel Evans, b.3 May 1900. She d.15 Jul 1992 at age 92 and was bur. Pleasant Hill Cem., Greene Co., TN.
Known children of John D.[8] McMackin and Ethel Evans:
       i.   Helen[9], b. ca.1925 OH.
      ii.   John T, b. ca. Nov 1926 OH.
    iii.   Clyde A. (?), b.8 Feb 1927; m. Mary Katherine Bolton. He d.15 Dec 1996, age 69; Pleasant Hill Cem., Greene Co., TN.
           Mary Katherine Bolton, b.1 Sep 1937 Greene Co., TN. She d.27 Apr 2018 at age 80 and was bur. Pleasant Hill Cem.

1153. Georgia I. "Georgie"[8] Marcum (Ethel[7] Abney, John[6], Pinkney[5], Wiley[4], Hezekiah[3], Elisha[2], Abner[1]), b.22 Mar 1922 Rose Hill, Lee Co., VA. She m. Thomas Patton "Pat" Short. d.7 Jul 2001 Rose Hill, Lee Co., VA, at age 79 and was bur. Lee Memorial Gardens, Woodway, Lee Co., VA.
   Thomas Patton "Pat" Short d. Apr 1991 and was bur. Lee Memorial Gardens, Woodway, Lee Co., VA.
Known children I. "Georgie"[8] Marcum and Thomas Patton "Pat" Short:
   1389   i.   Patty L.[9], b. 10 Jun 1948 Middlesboro, Bell Co., KY; m. Jim Cox.
      ii.   Curtis Ray, b.27 Aug 1954. He d.8 May 2020 at age 65 and was bur. Powell Valley Cem., Dryden, Lee Co., VA.

1154. Paul Cale[8] Marcum (Ethel[7] Abney, John[6], Pinkney[5], Wiley[4], Hezekiah[3], Elisha[2], Abner[1]) m. (n.n.). He, b.4 Jun 1926 Rose Hill, Lee Co., VA. He d.19 Feb 2009 Pennington Gap, Lee Co., VA, at age 82 and was bur. on 21 Feb 2009 Old Campbell Cem., Rose Hill, Lee Co., VA.
Known children of Paul Cale[8] Marcum (birth order unknown):
       i.   Sue[9] m. Thomas Earl Lakins.
   1390   ii.   Ken, m. Lucretia (n.n.).
   1391   iii.   Louise, m. Larry Hartley.
   1392   iv.   Brenda, m. Bob Walker.
   1393   v.   Loretta, b. 6 Feb 1963; m. Charlie Rouse.

1155. Margaret "Marie"[8] Abney (John[7], John[6], Pinkney[5], Wiley[4], Hezekiah[3], Elisha[2], Abner[1]), b.28 Dec 1934 Rose Hill, Lee Co., VA. She m1. Glenn Rice Lyerly (29 Mar 1922-3 Mar 1956), son of Walter Lee Lyerly and Beulah Correll, on 27 Nov 1954 Frederick Co., MD, but no issue. She m2. Rev. Eugene Albert "Gene" Dixon (USN-Korea, Nam), son of Robert Leander Dixon and Nellie Ethel Hayter, on 17 Jan 1957 South Norfolk, VA, but no issue. She d.11 Nov 1990 Wallowa, Wallowa Co., OR, at age 55 and was bur. Wallowa Cem., Wallowa, Wallowa Co., OR.
Known children of Margaret "Marie"[8] Abney:
       i.   Robert E. Dixon[9], b.23 Feb 1956 and was bur. Wallowa Cem., Wallowa, Wallowa Co., OR. He m. Melodee (n.n.). He d.3 Oct 1978 Enterprise, Wallowa Co., OR, at age 22.
   1394   ii.   Delores Darlene Dixon (gen.), b. 1957; m1. (n.n.) Irwin; m2. Edward Nove "Eddie" Renfroe (gen.).
    Rev. Eugene Albert "Gene" Dixon (USN-Korea, Nam), b.24 May 1933 La Grande, Union Co., OR. He d.9 Apr 1991 Wallowa, Wallowa Co., OR, at age 57 and was bur. Wallowa Cem., Wallowa, Wallowa Co., OR.

1156. Morgan Floyd[8] Abney (gen., originator, contributor, USMC, USArmy-Korea, Nam) (John[7], John[6], Pinkney[5], Wiley[4], Hezekiah[3], Elisha[2], Abner[1]), b.1937 Rose Hill, Lee Co., VA. He m. Nellie J. Williams (b.1933). He m. Janet M. Kiser (b.1955) on 17 Apr 2010 but no issue. Having served his country honorably in the Marine Corps (1950-1955) and Army (1955-1980), he retired in 1980 and opened *Morgan's Automotive*. He lives in 2019 Georgetown, TX. Cousin Morgan is the originator of the idea for the writing of this book. After the author published the ***Abney Family History Series, Vol. I***, Cousin Morgan requested volume II cover the descendants of Abner Abney. And the rest is history! Read more about Cousin Morgan on page xi, *About the Contributors*. The author donated to Cousin Morgan the very first ***Abney, Abner, Abna, Abnee*** book ever printed. It was an honor to work with this great patriot.
Known children of Morgan Floyd[8] Abney (gen.) and Nellie J. Williams:
       i.   Gary Wayne[9], b.1959 Middlesboro, Bell Co., KY. He lived in 2019 Killeen, TX.

1157. Faye[8] Abney (Benjamin[7], John[6], James[5], Wiley[4], Hezekiah[3], Elisha[2], Abner[1]), b.11 Sep 1932; m. Jack H. Williamson and had issue:
    i.   Sandra[9], b.8 Aug 1952.
    ii. Linda, b.21 Mar 1955.
    iii. Becky, b.5 Apr 1958.
    iv. Jennifer, b.23 Jan 1972.

1158. Benjamin Parker[8] Abney Jr. (Benjamin[7], John[6], James[5], Wiley[4], Hezekiah[3], Elisha[2], Abner[1]), b.21 Nov 1938; m. Carolyn Jones & had issue:
    i.   Tyron Allen[9], b.16 Jun 1969.

1159. John Wesley[8] Abney Sr. (Benjamin[7], John[6], James[5], Wiley[4], Hezekiah[3], Elisha[2], Abner[1]) and Connie Underhill 121. He, b.21 Apr 1950. He lived in Okeechobee, FL when the author made contact with him on 24 Mar 1998. He was such a pleasure to chat with, and, although not a genealogist, graciously provided much information on the descendants of James Allen Abney (#120), grandson of Wiley Abney (#27). Cousin John's kindness and generosity are appreciated by the author. His contribution all those years ago have made this a better book.
    Known children of John Wesley[8] Abney Sr. and Connie Underhill:
    i.   John Wesley[9], b.20 Feb 1972. He lived in 1998 Okeechobee, FL.
    ii. Kyle Mitchell, b.24 Aug 1975.

1160. B.F.[8] Hewitt (Eula[7] Abna, Robert[6], James[5], James[4] Abney, Hezekiah[3], Elisha[2], Abner[1]), b.13 Sep 1932 Starrville, Smith Co., TX. He m. Tiffy (n.n.). He was owner of *B.F. Hewitt Antique Clock Repair*. He d.6 Sep 2011 Liberty, Liberty Co., TX, at age 78 and was bur. Friendship Cem., Friendship (Starrville), Smith Co., TX.
Known children of B.F.[8] Hewitt and Tiffy (n.n.):
    i.   Rhonda[9].
    ii. Debra.

1161. Nellie Jo[8] Abna (Joseph[7], Robert[6], James[5], James[4] Abney, Hezekiah[3], Elisha[2], Abner[1]) m. Oscar McKay Capps. , b.16 Dec 1933 Starrville, Smith Co., TX. She d.15 Nov 2006 Tyler, Smith Co., TX, at age 72 and was bur. Center Cem., Tyler, Smith Co., TX.
    Oscar McKay Capps, b.5 Dec 1927 Tatum, Rusk Co., TX. He d.28 Apr 1998 Tyler, Smith Co., TX, at age 70 and was bur. Center Cem., Tyler.
Known children of Nellie Jo[8] Abna and Oscar McKay Capps:
    i.   Teresa[9].
    ii. Susan.
    iii. Lana.

1162. Sgt. George Michael "Mike"[8] Abna (USAF-Nam) (Joseph[7], Robert[6], James[5], James[4] Abney, Hezekiah[3], Elisha[2], Abner[1]) m. (n.n.). He, b.24 Jul 1943 Bullard, Smith Co., TX. He d.4 Oct 2009 at age 66 and was bur. Bullard Cem., Bullard, Smith Co., TX.
Known children of Sgt. George Michael "Mike"[8] Abna (USAF-Nam):
    i.   Michael Brandon[9].
    ii. Cassandra m. (n.n.) Splawn.
    iii. Tonya m. (n.n.) Slatt.

1163. Richard Wayne[8] Abna (Joseph[7], Robert[6], James[5], James[4] Abney, Hezekiah[3], Elisha[2], Abner[1]), b.4 Dec 1945 Amarillo, Potter Co., TX. He m. Linda (n.n.) ca.1965. He d.11 Jan 2017 Tyler, Smith Co., TX, at age 71 and was bur. Bullard Cem., Bullard, Smith Co., TX.
Known children of Richard Wayne[8] Abna and Linda:
    i.   Joey[9] m. Gwen (n.n.).
    ii. Jennifer m. Roland Fernandez.
    iii. Alicia m. (n.n.) Whetsell.

1164. Sarilee[8] Roberts (Bernice[7] Abna, Robert[6], James[5], James[4] Abney, Hezekiah[3], Elisha[2], Abner[1]), b.21 Jun 1941 Gladewater, Gregg Co., TX. She m. James "Jimmy" Brewer on 9 Sep 1960 Greggton, Gregg Co., TX.
    James "Jimmy" Brewer, b.9 Nov 1941 Tyler, Smith Co., TX; d.21 Nov 1994 Longview, Gregg Co., TX, ae.53; bur. Grace Hill Cem., Longview.
Known children of Sarilee[8] Roberts and James "Jimmy" Brewer both b. Longview, Gregg Co., TX,:
  1395 i.   Penny (gen.)[9], b. 22 Oct 1961; m. Timothy Andrew Daniel; m. Dale Wade Blankinship.
  1396 ii. James David, b. 13 Oct 1964; m. Kayce Lynn May.

1165. Ronald Royce[8] Roberts (Bernice[7] Abna, Robert[6], James[5], James[4] Abney, Hezekiah[3], Elisha[2], Abner[1]), b.3 Feb 1946 Gladewater, Gregg Co., TX; m. Linda Dell Harris and had issue:
    i.   Stephanie Camille[9].

1166. Pamela K.[8] Abna (William[7], Ales[6], James[5], James[4] Abney, Hezekiah[3], Elisha[2], Abner[1]), b.2 Aug 1962 Atlanta, Fulton Co., GA. She m. (n.n.) Scarborough. d.15 Jan 2014 at age 51 and was bur. Jackson City Cem., Jackson, Butts Co., GA.
Known children of Pamela K.[8] Abna and (n.n.) Scarborough:
  1397 i.   Ashley P.[9], b. 20 Apr 1982.

1167. Beth[8] Abna (Donald[7], Ales[6], James[5], James[4] Abney, Hezekiah[3], Elisha[2], Abner[1]) m. Rev. David Paul and had issue:
    i.   Darryl[9].
    ii. Hannah.

1168. PFC William Howard[8] Brincefield (USArmy-WWII) (Lonie[7] Hightower, Levia[6] Johnson, Sarah[5] Abney, Joel[4], Hezekiah[3], Elisha[2], Abner[1]), b.6 May 1919 Newalla, Oklahoma Co., OK. He m1. Virginia Eileen Brockmiller in 1946. He m2. Audra Lavon Earney. He d.22 Aug 2002 Wenatchee, Chelan Co., WA, at age 83 and was bur. Evergreen Mem. Park, East Wenatchee, Douglas Co., WA.
    Virginia Eileen Brockmiller, b.7 Nov 1931 Malaga, Chelan Co., WA; d.31 May 2004 Portland, Multnomah Co., OR, age 72. She was cremated.

Known child of PFC William Howard[8] Brincefield (USArmy-WWII) and Virginia Eileen Brockmiller:
        i.   Russell Lee[9], b.15 Dec 1954 Wenatchee, Chelan Co., WA; d.25 Apr 2010 East Wenatchee, Douglas Co., WA (cremated)
    Audra Lavon Earney, b.11 Dec 1934 Springfield, Greene Co., MO. She d.19 May 2011 Malaga, Chelan Co., WA, at age 76 and was bur.
Wenatchee City Cem., Wenatchee, Chelan Co., WA.
Known child of PFC William Howard[8] Brincefield (USArmy-WWII) and Audra Lavon Earney:
    1398   i.   Dewana Rene[9], b. 30 May 1967 Wenatchee, Chelan Co., WA; m. Scott Browne.

1169. Lillie Mae[8] Brincefield (Lonie[7] Hightower, Levia[6] Johnson, Sarah[5] Abney, Joel[4], Hezekiah[3], Elisha[2], Abner[1]), b.2 Nov 1920 McLoud,
Pottawatomie Co., OK. She m1. Henry Otis Fink, but no issue; m2. Pvt. Lowell H. Walker (USArmy-WWII) in 1938. She m3. Berthel Ernest
Sweeten in 1945, but no issue. She d.12 Aug 1992 Lehigh, Coal Co., OK, at age 71 and was bur. Lehigh Cem., Lehigh, Coal Co., OK.
    Henry Otis Fink, b.23 Jan 1900 Logan Co., AR. He d.Oct 1977 Atoka, Atoka Co., OK, age 77; bur. Lehigh Cem., Lehigh, Coal Co., OK.
    Pvt. Lowell H. Walker (USArmy-WWII), b.17 Aug 1918 Lehigh, Coal Co., OK. He d.24 Feb 1971 Lehigh, Coal Co., OK, at age 52.
Known child of Lillie Mae[8] Brincefield and Pvt. Lowell H. Walker (USArmy-WWII):
        i.   Charley Hayes[9], b.30 Dec 1939 Lehigh, Coal Co., OK. He d.Jul 1940 Lehigh, Coal Co., OK; bur. Lehigh Cem., Lehigh.
    Berthel Ernest Sweeten, b.6 Nov 1914. He d.17 Feb 1997 at age 82 and was bur. Lehigh Cem., Lehigh, Coal Co., OK.

1170. Lloyd Albert[8] Brincefield (Lonie[7] Hightower, Levia[6] Johnson, Sarah[5] Abney, Joel[4], Hezekiah[3], Elisha[2], Abner[1]), b.16 Apr 1922 Cairo, Coal
Co., OK; m. Mildred Garrison; d.29 May 1981 Wenatchee, Chelan Co., WA, ae.59; bur. Evergreen Mem. Park, East Wenatchee, Douglas Co., WA.
    Mildred "Marie" Garrison, b.22 Feb 1918 Rose, Mayes Co., OK; d.10 Mar 2009 Wenatchee, Chelan Co., WA; bur. Evergreen Mem. Pk.
Known child of Lloyd Albert[8] Brincefield and Mildred "Marie" Garrison:
        i.   Tommy Lloyd[9], b.19 Aug 1951 Wenatchee, Chelan Co., WA. He d.10 Dec 1977 Rock Island, Douglas Co., WA, at age
            26 and was bur. Evergreen Mem. Park, East Wenatchee, Douglas Co., WA.

1171. George Edward[8] Brincefield (Lonie[7] Hightower, Levia[6] Johnson, Sarah[5] Abney, Joel[4], Hezekiah[3], Elisha[2], Abner[1]), b.28 Jan 1923 Cairo,
Coal Co., OK. He m. Margaret Mae "Marge" Brockmiller in 1946. He d.24 Mar 2017 Wenatchee, Douglas Co., WA, at age 94.
    Margaret Mae "Marge" Brockmiller, b.16 Nov 1928 Odessa, Lincoln Co., WA. She d.16 Mar 1996 Wenatchee, Douglas Co., WA, at age 67
and was bur. Evergreen Mem. Park, East Wenatchee, Douglas Co., WA.
Known child of George Edward[8] Brincefield and Margaret Mae "Marge" Brockmiller:
    1399   i.   Ronald Dean "Ron"[9], b. 14 Aug 1945 Wenatchee, Chelan Co., WA.

1172. Margaret Louise[8] Brincefield (Lonie[7] Hightower, Levia[6] Johnson, Sarah[5] Abney, Joel[4], Hezekiah[3], Elisha[2], Abner[1]), b.28 Jun 1927 Stonewall,
Pontotoc Co., OK; m. Willie Nanney 1943; d.18 Jan 2017 Chickasha, Grady Co., OK, ae.89; bur. Mill Creek Cem., Mill Creek, Johnston Co., OK.
    Willie Hubert "Bill" Nanney, b.3 Dec 1925 Wilson, Atoka Co., OK; d.23 Dec 1998 Pauls Valley, Garvin Co., OK, ae.73; bur. Mill Creek Cem.
Known child of Margaret Louise[8] Brincefield and Willie Hubert "Bill" Nanney:
        i.   Willie Harold[9], b.10 Feb 1946 Wapanucka, Johnston Co., OK. He d.1 Aug 2005 Oklahoma City, Oklahoma Co., OK, at
            age 59 and was bur. Mill Creek Cem., Mill Creek, Johnston Co., OK.

1173. Edna Wynell[8] Pittman (Delos[7], Lou[6] Johnson, Sarah[5] Abney, Joel[4], Hezekiah[3], Elisha[2], Abner[1]), b.30 Oct 1929 Beckville, Panola Co., TX.
She m. Thurman "Cotton" McIntosh. d.27 Jul 2019 Longview, Gregg Co., TX, age 89; bur. Lakeview Mem. Gardens, Longview, Gregg Co., TX.
    Thurman "Cotton" McIntosh, b.28 Sep 1923 Pritchett, Upshur Co., TX. He d.18 Apr 2011 Longview, Gregg Co., TX, at age 87 and was bur.
Lakeview Mem. Gardens, Longview, Gregg Co., TX.
Known child of Edna Wynell[8] Pittman and Thurman "Cotton" McIntosh:
        i.   Tommy Neal[9], b.12 May 1956 and d.21 Jun 1973 Gregg Co., TX, at age 17 and was bur. Lakeview Mem. Gardens.

1174. Marion Kenneth[8] Liles (Nellie[7] Wininger, Minnie[6] Abney, John[5], Joel[4], Hezekiah[3], Elisha[2], Abner[1]), b.22 Mar 1930 Pisgah, Jackson Co.,
AL. He m. Dorotha Mae "Dot" George on 6 Mar 1950 Marshall Co., AL. He d.7 Oct 2013 Albertville, Marshall Co., AL, at age 83 and was bur.
Marshall Mem. Gardens, Albertville, Marshall Co., AL.
    Dorotha Mae "Dot" George, b.5 Mar 1931 Guntersville, Marshall Co., AL.
Known child of Marion Kenneth[8] Liles and Dorotha Mae "Dot" George:
        i.   William Michael[9], b.21 Oct 1951. He d.2 Jul 2020 at age 68 and was bur. Marshall Mem. Gardens, Albertville.

1175. Helen Margaret[8] Hodnett (Lucinda[7] Wininger, Minnie[6] Abney, John[5], Joel[4], Hezekiah[3], Elisha[2], Abner[1]), b.10 Jan 1932; m. Ernest Dale
Coady Chattanooga, Hamilton Co., TN and had issue:
        i.   Pamela Margaret[9], b.1952; m. William Frazier Mathis.
        ii.   Cheryl Andra, b.1958; m. Charles Ray Vaughn.

1176. Sarah Wyndol[8] Hodnett (Lucinda[7] Wininger, Minnie[6] Abney, John[5], Joel[4], Hezekiah[3], Elisha[2], Abner[1]), b.27 Nov 1935 Pisgah, Jackson Co.,
AL. She m1. Earl Miller Jr. (USAF). She m2. Arthur Clark Griffith, but no issue.
    Earl Miller Jr. (USAF), b.11 Apr 1932 Clifford, Bartholomew Co., IN.
Known children of Sarah Wyndol[8] Hodnett and Earl Miller Jr. (USAF):
    1400   i.   Janice Katherine "Jan"[9], b. 30 Oct 1954 Potter Air Force Base, Amarillo, Potter Co., TX; m. William Burt Elliott.
    1401   ii.   Dana Earl, b. 1 Sep 1955 Chattanooga, Hamilton Co., TN; m. Julie Ann Inkster.
    1402   iii. Jeffrey Allen, b. 10 Jul 1960 Chattanooga, Hamilton Co., TN; m. Sharon Morgan; div. Sharon Morgan.

1177. Carlton Leroy[8] Hodnett (Lucinda[7] Wininger, Minnie[6] Abney, John[5], Joel[4], Hezekiah[3], Elisha[2], Abner[1]), b.16 Feb 1937 Pisgah, Jackson Co.,
AL. He m. Zeobia Joetta "Jodie" Henry (b.1935) and had issue:
Known children of Carlton Leroy[8] Hodnett and Zeobia Joetta "Jodie" Henry:
        i.   Christopher Leroy[9] d.infancy.
        ii.   Timothy Scott, b.1960.
        iii. Jane Elizabeth, b.1966. She d.1974.

1178. Daris Kay[8] Hodnett (Lucinda[7] Wininger, Minnie[6] Abney, John[5], Joel[4], Hezekiah[3], Elisha[2], Abner[1]), b.11 Mar 1939 Pisgah, Jackson Co., AL; m. Bobby Reese Walton and had issue:
      i.   Regina[9], b.5 Jul 1960. She m. Joseph Randall Drummer.
      ii. Michael Lynn, b.3 Feb 1968.
      iii. Corey Layne, b.19 Jul 1969. He m. Amy Ruth King.

1179. William R. "Billy"[8] Wininger (USAF-Nam) (Oscar[7], Minnie[6] Abney, John[5], Joel[4], Hezekiah[3], Elisha[2], Abner[1]), b.22 Jun 1944. He m. Etta (n.n.). He d.9 Feb 2014 Dalton, Whitfield Co., GA, at age 69 and was bur. United Mem. Gardens, Beaverdale, Whitfield Co., GA.
Known children of William R. "Billy"[8] Wininger (USAF-Nam) and Etta (n.n.):
      i.   Renee[9] m. Matt Jones.
      ii. William Danny, b.8 Nov 1979. He d.15 Nov 2007 at age 28.

1180. James Clyde[8] Abney (John[7], William[6], John[5], Joel[4], Hezekiah[3], Elisha[2], Abner[1]), b.31 Jul 1948. He m. Frankie Jean Wallace. He d.27 May 2016 Stevenson, Jackson Co., AL, at age 67 and was bur. Bonaventure Cem., Bridgeport, Jackson Co., AL.
Known children of James Clyde[8] Abney and Frankie Jean Wallace (birth order unknown):
      i.   Connie[9] m. Leon Wilson.
  1403 ii. Cindy, m. Steven North Sr.

1181. Marty Ray[8] Abney (USArmy) (Alvin[7], Alonzo[6], John[5], Joel[4], Hezekiah[3], Elisha[2], Abner[1]), b.13 May 1959. He d.16 Aug 2015 at age 56 and was bur. Abraham Lincoln National Cem., Elwood, Will Co., IL.
Known children of Marty Ray[8] Abney (USArmy) (birth order unknown):
      i.   Jason Ray[9].
      ii. Tiffany m. Dave Edwards.
      iii. Kimberlee.

1182. Nancy E.[8] Abney (Robert[7], Nancy[6] Allen, Susan[5] Abner, William[4], Elisha[3], Elisha[2] Abney, Abner[1]), b.16 Jul 1920. She m. Cecil Morris. She d.7 Jun 1984 at age 63 and was bur. McKee Cem., McKee, Jackson Co., KY.
    Cecil Morris, b.18 Sep 1915. He d.25 Jan 2000 at age 84 and was bur. McKee Cem., McKee, Jackson Co., KY.
Known child of Nancy E.[8] Abney and Cecil Morris:
      i.   Edward Dale[9], b.1939. He d.2007.

1183. Margaret Neva[8] Abner (Gilbert[7], William[6], David[5], William[4], Elisha[3], Elisha[2] Abney, Abner[1]), b.22 Apr 1915 Campbellsville, Taylor Co., KY; m. PFC Coy Arnold (USArmy-WWII). d.15 Aug 1981 Lancaster, Garrard Co., KY, age 66; bur. Lancaster Cem., Lancaster, Garrard Co., KY.
    PFC Coy Hudson Arnold Sr. (USArmy-WWII), b.9 Mar 1915 and d.29 May 2006 Garrard Co., KY, at age 91 and was bur. Lancaster Cem.
Known child of Margaret Neva[8] Abner and PFC Coy Hudson Arnold Sr. (USArmy-WWII):
      i.   Margaret Ann[9], b.15 May 1934. She d.15 May 1934 and was bur. Lancaster Cem., Lancaster, Garrard Co., KY.

1184. T.Sgt. John "Ralph"[8] Abner Sr. (USArmy-WWII) (Gilbert[7], William[6], David[5], William[4], Elisha[3], Elisha[2] Abney, Abner[1]), b.24 Apr 1917 IA. He m. Tommy Lou Adams on 12 Jan 1947. He was owner of *Abner's Shoes*, Lebanon, Marion Co., KY. He d.7 Mar 1966 Lebanon, Marion Co., KY, at age 48 and was bur. Lancaster Cem., Lancaster, Garrard Co., KY.
    Tommy Lou Adams, b.12 Dec 1924 Wagoner, Wagoner Co., OK. She d.2 Dec 2011 Muskogee, Muskogee Co., OK, at age 86 and was bur. Elmwood Cem., Wagoner, Wagoner Co., OK.
Known children of T.Sgt. John "Ralph"[8] Abner Sr. (USArmy-WWII) and Tommy Lou Adams:
      i.   Libby Lou[9], b.10 Jul 1952 Lebanon, Marion Co., KY.
      ii. John Ralph "Johnny", b.21 May 1956.

1185. Geraldine[8] Eversole (Armilda[7] Allen, Sarah[6], Easter[5] Abner, William[4], Elisha[3], Elisha[2] Abney, Abner[1]) m1. (n.n.) Whitaker. She m2. (n.n.) Bachelor, but no issue.
Known child of Geraldine[8] Eversole and (n.n.) Whitaker:
      i.   Penny (gen.)[9]. She m. (n.n.) Brown. The author only recently began working with Cousin Penny to clear up some misconceptions on the Abner family. The author is grateful that she provided her line from Sarah Jane Allen (#376).

1186. Vivian D. "Vickie"[8] Abner (Walter[7], George[6], Lewis[5], William[4], Elisha[3], Elisha[2] Abney, Abner[1]), b.9 Feb 1933 Manchester, Clay Co., KY. She m1. Halford F. "Pete" Gerrian (USArmy-Korea) on 17 May 1952. She m2. Lelan Clyde "Lee" Haynes ca.1970 but no issue. She d.5 May 2015 IN at age 82 and was bur. Elm Ridge Mem. Park, Muncie, Delaware Co., IN.
    Halford F. "Pete" Gerrian (USArmy-Korea), b.13 Feb 1929 Felicity, Clermont Co., OH. He d.25 Jun 1966 Laurel, Franklin Co., IN, at age 37.
Known children of Vivian D. "Vickie"[8] Abner and Halford F. "Pete" Gerrian (USArmy-Korea) (birth order unknown):
      i.   David[9].
      ii. Floyd.
      iii. Muichell.
    Lelan Clyde "Lee" Haynes, b.2 Dec 1943 Stearns, McCreary Co., KY. He d.3 Mar 2012 Muncie, Delaware Co., IN, at age 68.

1187. D.F.[8] Abner (Walter[7], George[6], Lewis[5], William[4], Elisha[3], Elisha[2] Abney, Abner[1]) m. Norita Clara McFarland. He, b.12 Oct 1934 Clay Co., KY. He d.31 Mar 2012 Brookville, Franklin Co., IN, at age 77 and was bur. Laurel North Cem., Laurel, Franklin Co., IN.
    Norita Clara McFarland, b.2 Sep 1937 Laurel, Franklin Co., IN; d.2 Aug 1980 Connersville, Fayette Co., IN, age 42; bur. Laurel North Cem.
Known child of D.F.[8] Abner and Norita Clara McFarland:
      i.   Teresa[9] m. Mike Ford.

1188. Cpl. Michael Edward[8] Abner (USMC-Nam) (Daniel[7], Charles[6], Robert[5], William[4], Elisha[3], Elisha[2] Abney, Abner[1]), b.24 Nov 1951. He m. (n.n.). He d.29 Jun 2007 at home, Cedar Grove, Franklin Co., IN, at age 55 and was bur. Millville Cem., Millville, Butler Co., OH.

Known children of Cpl. Michael Edward^8 Abner (USMC-Nam) (birth order unknown):
- i.   Michael Shane^9 m. Amy (n.n.).
- ii. Dawn Marie m. Andy Goble.
- iii. Leslie m. Randy Closson.

1189. Jack D. "Jackie"^{8} Abner Sr. (Preston^7, Jack^6, Robert^5, William^4, Elisha^3, Elisha^2 Abney, Abner^1), b.23 Apr 1938 OH. He m. Phyllis J. Duff. He d.29 Dec 2013 at age 75 and was bur. Woodside Cem., Middletown, Butler Co., OH.
Known children of Jack D. "Jackie"^{8} Abner Sr. and Phyllis J. Duff (birth order unknown):
- i.   Jack D.^{9}.
- ii. Jeff m. Tina (n.n.).

1190. Sam^8 Abner (John^7, Wiley^6, John^5, Lacy^4, Elisha^3, Elisha^2 Abney, Abner^1), b. Christmas Day, 25 Dec 1929 KY. He m. Pauline Young. He d.16 Mar 2018 East Bernstadt, Laurel Co., KY, at age 88 and was bur. Sam Abner Cem., East Bernstadt, Laurel Co., KY.
    Pauline Young, b.19 Apr 1937 Leslie Co., KY. She d.24 Nov 2013 Richmond, Madison Co., KY, at age 76 and was bur. Sam Abner Cem., East Bernstadt, Laurel Co., KY.
Known children of Sam^8 Abner and Pauline Young (birth order unknown):
- i.   George^9 m. Lois Jean (n.n.).
- ii.   Terry m. Teresa (n.n.).
- iii. Johnny m. Sherry (n.n.).
- iv.   Loretta m. Astor Gross.
- v.   Thelma m. (n.n.) Eads.
- vi.   Rosa Lee m. Allen Ray Reeves.
- vii. Donna Jean m. (n.n.) Davidson.
- viii. Virginia m. Ronald Blackburn.
- ix.   Saul.

1191. Granville Wiley "GW"^{8} Abner (John^7, Wiley^6, John^5, Lacy^4, Elisha^3, Elisha^2 Abney, Abner^1) m. Audrey Davidson. He, b.14 Jan 1935 KY. He d.24 Apr 2009 at age 74 and was bur. Fairview Cem., Panco, Clay Co., KY.
    Audrey Davidson, b.13 Nov 1933 Clay Co., KY. She d.8 Jan 2016 Manchester, Clay Co., KY, at age 82 and was bur. Fairview Cem., Panco.
Known children of Granville Wiley "GW"^{8} Abner and Audrey Davidson (birth order unknown):
- i.   Jimmy^9 m. Joann (n.n.). He m. Geneva (n.n.).
- ii. Billy.
- iii. Rebecca m. Darrell Rice.
- iv. Rosie Marie, b.24 May 1964 Leslie Co., KY. She d.16 Oct 1986 Clay Co., KY, at age 22 and was bur. Fairview Cem., Panco, Clay Co., KY.

1192. Archie Brown^8 Abner (USArmy-Korea) (Isaac^7, John^6, Samuel^5, Lacy^4, Elisha^3, Elisha^2 Abney, Abner^1) m. Wanda (n.n.). He, b.21 Nov 1936 Booneville, Owsley Co., KY. He d.28 Nov 2018 Aurora, Dearb. Co., IN, at age 82 and was bur. Greendale Cem., Greendale, Dearb. Co., IN.
Known children of Archie Brown^8 Abner (USArmy-Korea) and Wanda (birth order unknown):
- i.   Randy^9 m. Nina (n.n.).
- ii. Perry.
- iii. Vivian m. Jim Beckmeyer.
- iv. Cindy m. Dean Loos.
- v.   Jodie m. Bob Ogles.

1193. Sgt. Nathan Ellington^8 Greear Jr. (USAAF-WWII) (Elizabeth^7 Riley, Isabel^6 Sandlin, James^5, Nancy^4 Abner, Elisha^3, Elisha^2 Abney, Abner^1), b.9 Aug 1921 in Bonny Blue, Lee Co., VA. He m. Euphemia Joan Puccini 17 Jan 1947 Scott Co., IN. He d.10 Aug 1952 in Jeffersonville, Clark Co., IN and was bur. Scottsburg Cem., Scottsburg, Scott Co., IN.
    Euphemia Joan Puccini, b.1923. She was liv. in 1996.
Known children of Sgt. Nathan Ellington^8 Greear Jr. (USAAF-WWII) and Euphemia Joan Puccini:
- i.   Mary Elizabeth (gen.)^9, b.1949. She m. Noah Milton South Jr. (b.1949). The author began working with Mary on the Abner family in 1996. A descendant of Elisha Abner Jr. (#7), her great-grandmother, Isabel Gross Sandlin (#399) was 2nd cousin to *Congressional Medal of Honor* recipient, Sgt. Willie Sandlin (#420). In 1998, Mary lived in MI. She deserves much credit for information on the descendants of Elisha Abner Jr. (#7) as well as the family of *Red Jim* Sandlin (#54).

1194. Clarence^8 Barger Jr. (Mamie^7 Abner, Robert^6, William^5, Willis^4, Elisha^3, Elisha^2 Abney, Abner^1), b.28 Jun 1924. He m. Nellie (n.n.). He d.1 Sep 1974 at age 50 and was bur. Laurel Cem., Laurel, Clermont Co., OH.
    Nellie (n.n.) d.8 Sep 2008 and was bur. Laurel Cem., Laurel, Clermont Co., OH.
Known children of Clarence^8 Barger Jr. and Nellie (birth order unknown):
- i.   Mary^9 m. (n.n.) Hasler.
- ii. Beverly m. (n.n.) Rich.
- iii. Geraldine m. (n.n.) Shaw.
- 1404 iv. Robert Taylor, b. 1 Feb 1948; m. Bonnie Morgan.

1195. David Jerald^8 Abner (Elbert^7, Robert^6, William^5, Willis^4, Elisha^3, Elisha^2 Abney, Abner^1) m. Norma Jewell Meadow. He, b.25 Apr 1937 Bethel, Clermont Co., OH. He d.26 May 1991 Cincinnati, Hamilton Co., OH, at age 54 and was bur. Laurel Cem., Laurel, Clermont Co., OH.
    Norma Jewell Meadow, b.2 Jul 1938. She d.10 Feb 2018 at age 79 and was bur. Laurel Cem., Laurel, Clermont Co., OH.
Known children of David Jerald^8 Abner and Norma Jewell Meadow:
- 1405 i. John Lee^9, m. Debbie (n.n.).

1196. Nancy Carol⁸ Abner (Elbert⁷, Robert⁶, William⁵, Willis⁴, Elisha³, Elisha² Abney, Abner¹), b.25 Sep 1939. She m. Terry Alan Kidd (b.7 Oct 1939) on 7 Jul 1956. She d.5 Nov 2015 at age 76 and was bur. Lebanon Cem., Lebanon, Warren Co., OH.
Known children of Nancy Carol⁸ Abner and Terry Alan Kidd (birth order unknown):
        i.   Kathy⁹ m. Mark Mahan.
        ii. Victor.
        iii. Kelly m. Jim Johnson.
        iv. Kevin m. Donna (n.n.).
        v. Terry Alan m. Melissa (n.n.).

1197. John R.⁸ Abner (Elbert⁷, Robert⁶, William⁵, Willis⁴, Elisha³, Elisha² Abney, Abner¹), b.14 Nov 1942. He m. Joyce A. Perry (b.23 Aug 1945). He d.24 Apr 2013 at age 70 and was bur. Laurel Cem., Laurel, Clermont Co., OH.
Known children of John R.⁸ Abner and Joyce A. Perry:
        i.   Richard D.⁹, b.8 Oct 1958 OH. He d.4 Apr 2015 OH at age 56 and was bur. Laurel Cem., Laurel, Clermont Co., OH.
        ii. Sherry m. Rick Day.

1198. Steven E.⁸ Abner (Elbert⁷, Robert⁶, William⁵, Willis⁴, Elisha³, Elisha² Abney, Abner¹), b.10 Mar 1945 Moscow, Clermont Co., OH. He m. Glenda Brewer (she m2. Ernie Barger). He d.26 Jun 2018 OH at age 73 and was bur. Laurel Cem., Laurel, Clermont Co., OH.
Known children of Steven E.⁸ Abner and Glenda Brewer:
        i.   Michelle D.⁹ m. Steve Jones.
        ii. Robert A. "Rob" m. Dana R. (n.n.).
        iii. Eric S. m. Teka (n.n.).
 1406   iv. Mark Steven, b. 28 Apr 1972; m. Roxanne Lambert.

1199. Peggy⁸ Abner (Willis⁷, Robert⁶, William⁵, Willis⁴, Elisha³, Elisha² Abney, Abner¹), b.4 Feb 1943 Clermont Co., OH. She m. George McLaughlin. d.11 Jul 2007 at age 64. She was cremated.
Known children of Peggy⁸ Abner and George McLaughlin:
        i.   Betty⁹ m. James Hosler.
        ii. Mary m. David Bender.

1200. Wade⁸ Bowling (Florence⁷ Napier, Mary⁶ Abner, William⁵, Willis⁴, Elisha³, Elisha² Abney, Abner¹), b.12 Apr 1940 Buckhorn, Perry Co., KY. He m. Pat (n.n.). He d.25 Sep 2015 Butler Co., OH, at age 75 and was bur. Moberly Graveyard, Estill Co., KY.
Known children of Wade⁸ Bowling and Pat:
        i.   Randy⁹.
        ii. Anthony Wade "Tony", b.27 May 1963. He d.15 Dec 1981 at age 18.
        iii. Charlene m. Gary Scott.

1201. Billie Franklin⁸ Napier (USArmy) (Eldren⁷, Hannah⁶ Abner, William⁵, Willis⁴, Elisha³, Elisha² Abney, Abner¹), b.9 Apr 1937. He m. Phyllis J. (n.n.) (b.1940). He d.10 Aug 2012 Memphis, Shelby Co., TN, age 75; bur. Memphis Funeral Home & Mem. Gardens, Bartlett, Shelby Co., TN.
Known children of Billie Franklin⁸ Napier (USArmy) and Phyllis J:
 1407   i.   Anna⁹, m. (n.n.) Barlish.
 1408   ii. Sherry, m. Jimmie Bruhn.

1202. Billy Dean⁸ Smith (Nancy⁷ Bowling, Elizabeth⁶ Abner, William⁵, Willis⁴, Elisha³, Elisha² Abney, Abner¹), b.4 Apr 1954 Hamilton, Butler Co., OH. He d.11 Sep 2017 Ridgeland, Jasper Co., SC, at age 63 and was bur. Johnston Cem., Buckhorn, Perry Co., KY.
    Donna Marie Haney, b.18 Oct 1960 Scott Co., IN. She d.31 Oct 2007 Kissimmee, Osceola Co., FL, at age 47. She was cremated.
Known child of Billy Dean⁸ Smith and Donna Marie Haney:
        i.   Tammy⁹.

1203. Michael Ray⁸ Payne Sr. (Elmira⁷ Bowling, Elizabeth⁶ Abner, William⁵, Willis⁴, Elisha³, Elisha² Abney, Abner¹). He sired:
        i.   Michael Ray⁹.

1204. Wanda June⁸ Payne (Elmira⁷ Bowling, Elizabeth⁶ Abner, William⁵, Willis⁴, Elisha³, Elisha² Abney, Abner¹) m. Robert Lee Stafford Sr.
Known children of Wanda June⁸ Payne and Robert Lee Stafford Sr.:
        i.   Robert Lee⁹.

1205. Ola "Faye"⁸ Oliver (Elizabeth⁷ Abner, Edward⁶, Elisha⁵, Willis⁴, Elisha³, Elisha² Abney, Abner¹), b.2 Sep 1946 Perry Co., KY; She m. James Sanders, s/o Elmer Sanders and Lottie Saylor; d.16 Jul 2018 Connersville, Fayette Co., IN, age 71; bur. Dale Cem., Connersville, Fayette Co., IN.
    James Sanders, b.28 Feb 1935 Arjay, Bell Co., KY. He m1. Juanita Horner. He d.3 Apr 1999 Greenwood, Johnson Co., KY, at age 64 and was bur. Dale Cem., Connersville, Fayette Co., IN.
Known children of Ola "Faye"⁸ Oliver and James Sanders:
        i.   Tammy⁹ m. Greg Trevino-Dent.
        ii. James.
        iii. Herbert "Herb."
        iv. Edna m. Ed Simmons.
 1409   v. Steven James, b. 21 Jan 1975; m. (n.n.).

1206. Deborah "Debbie"⁸ Oliver (Elizabeth⁷ Abner, Edward⁶, Elisha⁵, Willis⁴, Elisha³, Elisha² Abney, Abner¹), b.2 Mar 1957 Connersville, Fayette Co., IN. She m1. Daniel Sylvester "Danny" Koontz, son of James Edward Koontz and Margaret Marie Kidd, in 1974. She m2. Edward L. Wilson, but no issue. She d.14 Jan 1993 Connersville, Fayette Co., IN, at age 35 and was bur. West Point Cem., Liberty, Union Co., IN.
    Daniel Sylvester "Danny" Koontz, b.27 Jan 1957 Madison, Jefferson Co., IN. He d.12 Mar 2007 Madison, Jefferson Co., IN, at age 50.

Known child of Deborah "Debbie"*8* Oliver and Daniel Sylvester "Danny" Koontz:
    1410   i.   Jeremiah Dan*9*, b. 27 Jan 1982 Madison, Jefferson Co., IN.

1207. Melita Kay*8* Oliver (Elizabeth*7* Abner, Edward*6*, Elisha*5*, Willis*4*, Elisha*3*, Elisha*2* Abney, Abner*1*) m. (n.n.) Collins. , b.20 Mar 1961 Connersville, Fayette Co., IN. She d.9 Jan 2018 Desert Valley Hospital, Victorville, San Bernardino Co., CA, at age 56. She was cremated.
Known children of Melita Kay*8* Oliver and (n.n.) Collins (birth order unknown):
        i.   Wanda*9* m. (n.n.) Norman.
        ii.   Chrystal.
    1411   iii.   William, m. Ashley (n.n.).

1208. Washington Edward "Dickie"*8* Abner (USArmy-Nam) (Daniel*7*, Edward*6*, Elisha*5*, Willis*4*, Elisha*3*, Elisha*2* Abney, Abner*1*), b.22 May 1947 Owsley Co., KY. He m. Helen Rice ca.1981. He d.30 Oct 2009 Owsley Co., KY, at age 62; bur. Buckhorn Cem., Buckhorn, Perry Co., KY.
Known children of Washington Edward "Dickie"*8* Abner (USArmy-Nam) and Helen Rice (birth order unknown):
        i.   Jerry Edward*9*.
        ii.   Claude Wayne.
        iii.   Dickie Lee.
        iv.   Sharon Evelyn m. (n.n.) Noble.
        v.   Regina m. (n.n.) Hurley.

1209. Dennis Charles "Goat"*8* Abner (Charlie*7*, Edward*6*, Elisha*5*, Willis*4*, Elisha*3*, Elisha*2* Abney, Abner*1*), b.21 Jul 1962 Perry Co., KY. He m. Pouleine Roberts. He d.21 Dec 2019 Frankfort, Franklin Co., KY, at age 57 and was bur. Abner Family Cem., Buckhorn, Perry Co., KY.
Known children of Dennis Charles "Goat"*8* Abner and Pouleine Roberts (birth order unknown):
        i.   Jeremy Charles*9*.
        ii.   Jessica Susanna.
        iii.   Jennifer Evelyn m. (n.n.) Lonaker.

1210. Samuel "Howard"*8* Adams (Dorothy*7* Abner, Edward*6*, Elisha*5*, Willis*4*, Elisha*3*, Elisha*2* Abney, Abner*1*), b.17 Aug 1961 Buckhorn, Perry Co., KY. He d.2 May 2018 Smiths Grove, Warren Co., KY, at age 56 and was bur. Abner Family Cem., Buckhorn, Perry Co., KY.
Known child of Samuel "Howard"*8* Adams and Mary Marquez:
        i.   James*9*.

1211. Harold*8* Adams (Dorothy*7* Abner, Edward*6*, Elisha*5*, Willis*4*, Elisha*3*, Elisha*2* Abney, Abner*1*), b.13 Feb 1970 Hyden, Leslie Co., KY. He d.12 Apr 2017 Booneville, Owsley Co., KY, at age 47 and was bur. Abner Family Cem., Buckhorn, Perry Co., KY.
Known child of Harold*8* Adams:
        i.   Aiden*9*.

1212. Sterlin*8* Terry (Hugh*7*, Brownlow*6*, Mary*5* Abner, Willis*4*, Elisha*3*, Elisha*2* Abney, Abner*1*) m. Samantha Gilbert. He, b.25 Oct 1932. He d.27 Nov 1995 at age 63 and was bur. Spurgeon Mem. Park, Austin, Scott Co., IN.
    Samantha Gilbert, b.26 Apr 1936. She d.29 Nov 2006 at age 70 and was bur. Spurgeon Mem. Park, Austin, Scott Co., IN.
Known child of Sterlin*8* Terry and Samantha Gilbert:
        i.   Sterling*9*, b.29 Jul 1955 Scottsburg, Scott Co., IN. He d.27 Jul 2016 New Albany, Floyd Co., IN, at age 60 and was bur. Spurgeon Mem. Park, Austin, Scott Co., IN.

1213. Tom Junior*8* Terry (Hugh*7*, Brownlow*6*, Mary*5* Abner, Willis*4*, Elisha*3*, Elisha*2* Abney, Abner*1*), b.8 Jan 1937. He m. Shelby Jean Wooten. He d. New Year's Day, 1 Jan 2013 Jeffersonville, Clark Co., IN, at age 75 and was bur. Spurgeon Mem. Park, Austin, Scott Co., IN.
    Shelby Jean Wooten, b.4 Aug 1936. She d.11 May 1974 at age 37 and was bur. Spurgeon Mem. Park, Austin, Scott Co., IN.
Known children of Tom Junior*8* Terry and Shelby Jean Wooten:
        i.   Ira "Peewee"*9*, b.9 Sep 1956 Chicago, Cook Co., IL. He d.30 Aug 2006 Scottsburg, Scott Co., IN, at age 49 and was bur. Spurgeon Mem. Park, Austin, Scott Co., IN.
        ii.   Michael Wayne, b.6 Oct 1958 Seymour, Jackson Co., IN. He d.13 Apr 2016 Austin, Scott Co., IN, at age 57 and was bur. Spurgeon Mem. Park, Austin, Scott Co., IN.
        iii.   David, b.23 Jun 1962 Chicago, Cook Co., IL. He d.16 Jul 2012 Jeffersonville, Clark Co., IN, at age 50 and was bur. Spurgeon Mem. Park, Austin, Scott Co., IN.
        iv.   Burlin, b.24 Mar 1967 Chicago, Cook Co., IL. He d.1 Jul 2015 Jeffersonville, Clark Co., IN, at age 48 and was bur. Spurgeon Mem. Park, Austin, Scott Co., IN.
        v.   Jeffery Lee, b.25 May 1968 Chicago, Cook Co., IL. He d.20 Oct 2017 Seymour, Jackson Co., IN, at age 49 and was bur. Spurgeon Mem. Park, Austin, Scott Co., IN.

1214. David Wayne*8* Abner (Gary*7*, Elisha*6*, Daniel*5*, Willis*4*, Elisha*3*, Elisha*2* Abney, Abner*1*), b.2 Dec 1960 Middleton, Butler Co., OH. He m. Julie A. (b.1955). He d.28 Dec 2007 Hamilton, Butler Co., OH, at age 47 and was bur. Butler County Mem. Park, Trenton, Butler Co., OH.
Known children of David Wayne*8* Abner and Julie A. (birth order unknown):
        i.   Robert James*9*.
        ii.   Elisha Wayne "Eli."
        iii.   Kayla Anne.

1215. Jerry B.*8* Abner (Dan*7*, Jerry*6*, Daniel*5*, Willis*4*, Elisha*3*, Elisha*2* Abney, Abner*1*).
Known children of Jerry B.*8* Abner:
        i.   Jeffery Daniel*9*.

1216. Willeta Fay*8* Abner (William*7*, John*6*, Andrew*5*, Enoch*4*, Elisha*3*, Elisha*2* Abney, Abner*1*), b.21 Nov 1937 Santa Maria, CA; m. Robert Keeter.

Known children of Willeta Fay[8] Abner and Robert G. Keeter:
       i.   William Floyd[9], b.15 Nov 1955.
      ii.   Bradley Robert, b.21 Nov 1957.
     iii. Nick Anthony, b.12 Dec 1962.
     iv. Kimberly Cornett, b.3 Sep 1967.

1217. LaVeda Mae[8] Abner (William[7], John[6], Andrew[5], Enoch[4], Elisha[3], Elisha[2] Abney, Abner[1]), b.30 Dec 1939 Orange, CA; m. Bill Fraley. Issue:
       i.   Frankie "Jeanine" (gen.)[9], b.25 Sep 1957. She m. n.n. Wiley. Cousin Jeanine lived in Arkansas in 1998 when she and the author began working together. She is to be thanked for the line of Andrew Jackson "Jack" Abner (#164).
      ii.   Kellie Lynn, b.21 Sep 1960.
     iii. Michael William, b.27 Aug 1962.

1218. Joseph "Joe"[8] Abner (Thea[7], Joseph[6], Pierce[5], James[4], Menan[3], Elisha[2] Abney, Abner[1]) m. Brenda (n.n.). He, b.14 Jul 1958 Bell Co., KY. He d.9 Apr 2018 Pineville, Bell Co., KY, at age 59 and was bur. Calvin Jordan Cem., Pineville, Bell Co., KY.
Known children of Joseph "Joe"[8] Abner and Brenda (n.n.):
       i.   Diana Kay[9] m. Michael Brown.
      ii.   Collean m. Chris Masingo.
     iii. Rochelle.
     iv. Elizabeth m. (n.n.) Hanes.
      v.   Geneva m. Joe Messer.

1219. Martha "Gloria"[8] Delph (Jennie[7] Abner, Robert[6], James[5], Richard[4], Menan[3], Elisha[2] Abney, Abner[1]), b.24 Jan 1924 Clinton, Vermillion Co., IN. She was liv. on 14 Apr 1930 and 15 Apr 1940 with grandfather, Robert B. Abner, Clinton, Vermillion Co., IN. She m. James Van Horn on 9 Oct 1943. They were divorced. She d.15 Dec 1991 Vermillion Co., IN, age 67; bur. Walnut Grove Cem., Clinton, Vermillion Co., IN.
Known children of Martha "Gloria"[8] Delph and James Van Horn:
  1412   i.   James "Jimmy"[9], b. 2 Sep 1844; m. Patricia Kay Parks; div. Patricia Kay Parks.
  1413   ii.   Carole, b. 1948; m. Larry Edmonson.

1220. Wilma "Ruth"[8] Martin (Jennie[7] Abner, Robert[6], James[5], Richard[4], Menan[3], Elisha[2] Abney, Abner[1]), b.12 Oct 1927 Vermillion Co., IN. She m. Raymond F. Rigsby (1925-2005) on 22 Apr 1946. She d.30 Oct 2001 Clinton, Vermillion Co., IN, at age 74 and was bur. Walnut Grove Cem.
Known children of Wilma "Ruth"[8] Martin and Raymond F. Rigsby:
  1414   i.   Thomas Ray "Tommy"[9], b. 20 Oct 1949; m1. & div. Billie M. Kelsheimer; m2. & div. Donna L. Kyle; m3. Patsy N. Wray.
  1415   ii.   Robert Franklin, b. 2 Oct 1952; m. Elizabeth Trantham; div. Elizabeth Trantham.

1221. Robert Charles[8] Aldridge (Jennie[7] Abner, Robert[6], James[5], Richard[4], Menan[3], Elisha[2] Abney, Abner[1]), b.8 Jun 1935. He m. Delores "Lorrie" Topete in 1961 and had issue:
  1416   i.   William Darald[9], b. 5 Jan 1962; m. Susan Motkowski.

1222. Sandrea Kay "Sandy"[8] Abner (gen., contributor) (Ulis[7], Robert[6], James[5], Richard[4], Menan[3], Elisha[2] Abney, Abner[1]), b.29 May 1946 Clinton, Vermillion Co., IN. She m. Fred Dale Cook (USANG) on 27 Nov 1965 Clinton, Vermillion Co., IN. The author only recently began working with Cousin Sandy (2018). She was generous enough to send the marriage licenses for Menan Abner, which proved beyond the shadow of a doubt that there was no Monroe Abner. Cousin Sandy truly loves her family and graciously accepted her role as *contributor* when it was firmly decided to write this book. She picked up the mantle from Cousin Judy Vietri and worked diligently to properly place her Richard Abner into his proper family. Cousin Sandy continued to be very helpful as a researcher and has been able to contribute much information to this book. It has truly been a pleasure working with Cousin Sandy to clear up the many misconceptions on the line of Menan Abner (#8). (also see *About the Contributors* on page xi)
    Fred Dale Cook (USANG), b.3 Nov 1943 Terre Haute, Virgo Co., IN.
Known children of Sandrea Kay "Sandy"[8] Abner (gen.) and Fred Dale Cook (USANG):
  1417   i.   Aaron Thomas[9], b. 6 Jan 1969 Terre Haute, Virgo Co., IN; m1. & div. Marie "Annette" Myers; m2. Vicki J. Flynn.
  1418   ii.   Brent Richard, b. 8 Jul 1970 Terre Haute, Vigo Co., IN; m. & div. Tannya James.
  1419 iii. Craig Allen, b. 3 Mar 1975 Vincennes, Knox Co., IN; m. Dawn R. Hautsch.

1223. Mary Jo[8] Abner (Joseph[7], Robert[6], James[5], Richard[4], Menan[3], Elisha[2] Abney, Abner[1]), b.7 Dec 1955 Hammond, Lake Co., IN. She m. Patrick K. Dennis on 5 Aug 1983. They were divorced.
Known children of Mary Jo[8] Abner and Patrick K. Dennis all b. LaPorte, LaPorte Co., IN:
  1420   i.   Joseph Kirk[9], b. 14 Oct 1985.
      ii.   Kathleen Marie, b.7 Aug 1990. She m. Nathanial E. James.
             Nathanial E. James, b.15 Sep 2015.
  1421 iii. Susan Kristine, b. 6 Mar 1992; m. Joseph Hefner; div. Joseph Hefner.

1224. John Paul[8] Abner (James[7], Robert[6], James[5], Richard[4], Menan[3], Elisha[2] Abney, Abner[1]), b.9 Jun 1947 Clinton, Vermillion Co., IN. He m. Carolyn "Jean" Smith on 9 Jun 1968. He d.26 Feb 2018 Clinton, Vermillion Co., IN, at age 70.
    Carolyn "Jean" Smith, b.26 Mar 1950 Clinton, Vermillion Co., IN.
Known children of John Paul[8] Abner and Carolyn "Jean" Smith both b. Clinton, Vermillion Co., IN,:
       i.   John Joseph[9], b.3 Jan 1971. He m. Kendra Wessling. He and Kendra Wessling were divorced.
  1422   ii.   Daniel Bryan, b. 4 Oct 1975; m. Billie Edwards; div. Billie Edwards.

1225. Nancy Kay[8] Abner (James[7], Robert[6], James[5], Richard[4], Menan[3], Elisha[2] Abney, Abner[1]), b.2 Jul 1950 Clinton, Vermillion Co., IN. She m. Robert Ferris in Jan 1971. They were divorced.
Known child of Nancy Kay[8] Abner and Robert Ferris:
       i.   Eric Allen[9], b.Sep 1975.

1226.   Michael Leon⁸ Guinn (Beulah⁷ Abner, Robert⁶, James⁵, Richard⁴, Menan³, Elisha² Abney, Abner¹), b.3 Dec 1946 Clinton, Vermillion Co., IN. He m1. Martha Louise Steely (27 Aug 1942 AL-29 Nov 2016 Harriman, Roane Co., TN), but no issue. He m2. Darla K. Carrell on 18 Sep 1965 Clinton, Vermillion Co., IN. He and Darla K. Carrell were divorced in 1984 Vermillion Co., IN. He d.20 Jul 2020 at age 73.

    Darla K. Carrell, b.27 Sep 1946 Clinton, Vermillion Co., IN. She d.7 Jan 2007 Clinton, Vermillion Co., IN, at age 60.

Known children of Michael Leon⁸ Guinn and Darla K. Carrell both b. Terre Haute, Vigo Co., IN,:

    1423   i.   Michael Joseph⁹, b. 21 Jul 1970; m. Carmen Rebecca Smith.

    1424   ii.   Jeffrey Allen, b. 6 Oct 1976; m. Kimberly "Renee" White; m. Jennifer Wells.

1227.   Tony Lee⁸ Guinn (Beulah⁷ Abner, Robert⁶, James⁵, Richard⁴, Menan³, Elisha² Abney, Abner¹), b.2 May 1957 Clinton, Vermillion Co., IN. He m. Cindy Lynnett Seaton on 14 Oct 1978 Clinton, Vermillion Co., IN.

    Cindy Lynnett Seaton, b.22 Jun 1959 Paris, Edgar Co., IL.

Known children of Tony Lee⁸ Guinn and Cindy Lynnett Seaton:

    1425   i.   Andrew Joseph⁹, b. 18 Oct 1981; m. Trisha Lee Crow.

    1426   ii.   Stephanie Nicole, b. 4 Jan 1988; m. Tim J. Hastings; div. Tim J. Hastings.

1228.   Andrew "Cotton"⁸ Abner (Walter⁷, Gilbert⁶, Charles⁵, Richard⁴, Menan³, Elisha² Abney, Abner¹), b.23 Aug 1936 Knox Co., KY; m1. Annia Cheek, but no issue; m2. Elva Jean Smith; m3. Oda Mae Asher (17 Dec 1946 Knox Co., KY-1 Nov 1998 Knox Co., KY) in 1985, but no issue. He d.6 Jun 2012 Knox Co., KY, at age 75; bur. Asher Cem., Cottongim, Clay Co., KY.

    Elva Jean Smith, b.10 Jun 1954 Knox Co., KY. She d.3 May 2014 Somerset, Pulaski Co., KY, at age 59.

Known children of Andrew "Cotton"⁸ Abner and Elva Jean Smith (birth order unknown):

    i.   Marty⁹ m. Maranda (n.n.).

    ii.   Angela K.

    iii.   Tony.

1229.   Ronald Max⁸ Abner (George⁷, Theodore⁶, Joseph⁵, Richard⁴, Menan³, Elisha² Abney, Abner¹) m. (n.n.). He, b.2 Jul 1947 Calvert City, Marshall Co., KY. He d.1 Jul 1996 Richmond, Madison Co., KY, at age 48 and was bur. Lee-Dodds Cem., Lyon Co., KY.

Known children of Ronald Max⁸ Abner (birth order unknown):

    i.   Ronald⁹.

    ii.   Michael m. Linda (n.n.).

    iii.   Christina.

    iv.   Tabatha.

    v.   Rhonda m. Mike Young.

    vi.   Carol m. Danny Smock.

1230.   Terry⁸ Abner (Carmel⁷, Lewis⁶, James⁵, John⁴, Menan³, Elisha² Abney, Abner¹) m. Christi (n.n.) and had issue: Tony⁹.

1231.   Jerome Gantry⁸ Jefferson Sr. (Wanda⁷ Abnee, Claude⁶, Clarence⁵, Lincoln⁴, John³ Abney, Elisha², Abner¹), b.1961 Nicholas Co., KY. m. (n.n.) and had issue: Jerome Gantry⁹.

1232.   Laura⁸ Earlywine (Dorothy⁷ Abnee, Claude⁶, Clarence⁵, Lincoln⁴, John³ Abney, Elisha², Abner¹) m. (n.n.) Clark and had issue:

    i.   Danielle⁹.

    ii.   Jamal.

    iii.   Kyesha.

1233.   Justin⁸ Abnee (William⁷, Shy⁶, Clarence⁵, Lincoln⁴, John³ Abney, Elisha², Abner¹) m. Jennifer Beaty. He was a teacher at North Bullitt High School, Hebron Estates, Bullitt Co., KY.

Known children of Justin⁸ Abnee and Jennifer Beaty (birth order unknown):

    i.   Jacob⁹.

    ii.   Conner Abnee. He was a quarterback for North Bullitt High School (Shepherdsville), Hebron Estates, Bullitt Co., KY. He was ranked #44 of the top 50 passing leaders in the state on 17 Dec 2018 North Bullitt High School

    iii.   Jackson.

1234.   Olin Toliver⁸ Lewis Jr. (USN-WWII) (Estella⁷ Kelley, Matilda⁶ Murray, Malinda⁵ Hunt, Nancy⁴ Abner, John³ Abney, Elisha², Abner¹), b.11 Nov 1918 Pawhuska, Osage Co., OK. He m1. Marjory May "Peggy" Starbuck on 2 Jun 1937 Siloam Springs, Benton Co., AR. He m2. Florine Rosa Colburn on 12 Feb 2000 God is Alive Wedding Chapel, Tulsa, Tulsa Co., OK, but no issue. He d.6 Mar 2010 Tulsa, Tulsa Co., OK, at age 91 and was bur. Rose Hill Mem. Park, Tulsa, Tulsa Co., OK.

    Marjory May "Peggy" Starbuck, b.27 Jul 1919 Preston, Okmulgee Co., OK. She d.24 Jan 1999 Collinsville, Tulsa Co., OK, at age 79 and was bur. Rose Hill Mem. Park, Tulsa, Tulsa Co., OK.

Known children of Olin Toliver⁸ Lewis Jr. (USN-WWII) and Marjory May "Peggy" Starbuck all b. Tulsa, Tulsa Co., OK:

    i.   Judy May⁹, b.22 Jul 1939. She m. Joseph Gabriel Vietri Jr. on 1 Nov 1957 Dawson, Tulsa Co., OK.

        Joseph Gabriel Vietri Jr, b.3 Aug 1936 Brooklyn, Kings Co., NY.

    ii.   Phillip Mack, b.12 Dec 1942. He d.16 Feb 1946 Tulsa, Tulsa Co., OK, at age 3 and was bur. Rose Hill Mem. Park, Tulsa.

    iii.   Linda Sue, b.19 Oct 1946. She m. Gerald "Duane" Cantrell on 29 Jan 1966. She d.13 Nov 2010 Collinsville, Tulsa Co., OK, at age 64 and was bur. Rose Hill Mem. Park, Tulsa, Tulsa Co., OK.

        Gerald "Duane" Cantrell, b.11 May 1936 Robinson Ranch, Rogers Co., OK. He d.5 Oct 2016 at age 80 and was bur. Rose Hill Mem. Park, Tulsa.

    iv.   Patricia Ann, b.27 Oct 1954. She m. Jeffrey Namm on 28 Mar 1985 New York, NY.

    Florine Rosa Colburn, b.8 Feb 1920. She d.21 May 2006 Wagoner, Wagoner Co., OK, at age 86.

1235. Orvas[8] Johnson (Rosa[7] Bishop, Robert[6], John[5], Abraham[4], Mary[3] Abner, Elisha[2] Abney, Abner[1]), b. ca.1938 KY. He m. Laura E. Metcalf (gen.), daughter of Bleve Metcalf and Geneva Abney.
    Laura E. Metcalf (gen.) lived on 17 Jun 1996 Oneida, Clay Co., KY. The author began working with Cousin Laura and her daughter, Kimberly in June 1996. Cousin Laura actually descends from the Paul Abney (bapt.1699) branch of the Abney family. At the time, the author did not realize that Cousin Laura's husband, Orvas Johnson, descends from Paul's brother, Abner Abney, the subject of this book. Cousin John Hensell was confused on the husband of Mary Abner (gen.3) calling him both William and Samuel Bishop. Cousin Laura and her daughter, Kimberly had gotten Orvas Johnson's ancestor back to John Bishop (UA). We are now able to connect John Bishop to his grandfather, Samuel "Sam" Bishop through his father, Abraham "Abel" Bishop. So completes the connection. Cousin Laura's line is as follows: Dannett Abney Sr. (colonial ancestor); Paul Abney (bapt.1699); John Abney "the Lost Son"; John Abney [Jr.]; Tucker Abney; Clement Abney; Sanford Abney; Edgar Abney; Geneva Abney m. Bleve Metcalf. Sharing information with Cousins Laura and Kimberly was a wonderful way to expand on both Abney family branches, and discover her connection to Paul Abney through "the Lost Son". The author will ever be grateful to this mother/daughter team of Laura and Kimberly.
Known child of Orvas[8] Johnson and Laura E. Metcalf (gen.):
    i.   Kimberly (gen.)[9] lived on 27 Jun 1996 Oneida, Clay Co., KY. It has now been learned that Cousin Kimberly descends from two Abney brothers, to wit: Paul Abney (bapt.1699) on her mother's side; and Abner Abney (subject of this book) on her father's side. She is a wonderful genealogist and compliment to the mother/daughter team.

1236. Lucy Thelma[8] Abner (General[7], Steven[6], Theophilus[5], Enoch[4], Enoch[3] Abney, Elisha[2], Abner[1]), b.11 Feb 1952 Clay Co., KY. She m. Robert E. Gabbard in 1969. She d.28 Feb 2014 Camden, Preble Co., OH, at age 62 and was bur. Fairmont Cem., Camden, Preble Co., OH.
Known children of Lucy Thelma[8] Abner and Robert E. Gabbard:
    i.   Julie[9] m. Mike Adamson.
    ii. Rebecca m. James Jones.
    iii. Tim m. Roxanne (n.n.).

1237. William Glenn "Billy"[8] Kinsolving Jr. (gen.) (William[7], Finis[6], William[5], Mary[4] Abney, William[3], John[2], Abner[1]), m1. (n.n.), but no issue; m2. (n.n.), but no issue; m3. Dawn Marie McCuiston and had issue: Jesse Orion[9]. The author began working with Cousin Billy in 1998 through the *Centralized Abney Archives*. Since the author was well aware of the Kinsolving family connection to the Abney family (Hensell's *Abney* [1974]; *Abney Supplement* [1988] and Metzger's *In Search of Kate* [1978]), it was truly a pleasure meeting a descendant thereof and correcting and expounding on the work of Cousin John Hensell and confirming and expounding on the work of Cousin Charlotte Abney Metzger. Cousin Billy was truly a pleasure to work with. His knowledge of the *Rev.* William Abney Kinsolving (#221) family has enhanced the information in this book.

1238. Sheila Louise[8] Bryant (Virginia[7] Abney, Shelton[6], William[5], Shelton[4], William[3], John[2], Abner[1]) was Regional Manager. , b.28 Sep 1937 Jefferson City, MO. She m. Leroy Charles "Roy" Weissinger on 28 Apr 1961. She and Leroy Charles Weissinger were divorced.
Known children of Sheila Louise[8] Bryant and Leroy Charles Weissinger both b. Tallahassee, FL:
    i.   Eric John[9], b.14 Jun 1963.
    ii. Christopher Eugene, b.6 Aug 1967.

1239. John Michael "Mike"[8] Bryant (Virginia[7] Abney, Shelton[6], William[5], Shelton[4], William[3], John[2], Abner[1]), b.22 Dec 1945 Evanston, IL. He m. Margaret Louise Hanning, daughter of Charles Askey Hanning and Margaret Agnes Hughes, on 14 Feb 1970 Spartanburg, Spartanburg Co., SC.
    Margaret Louise Hanning, b.14 Dec 1948 Atlantic City, Atlantic Co., NJ. She was christened on 10 Apr 1949 Kelton, SC.
Known children of John Michael "Mike"[8] Bryant and Margaret Louise Hanning both b. Ft. Lauderdale, FL:
    i.   Kary Elizabeth[9], b.8 May 1974.
    ii. Bradley Yale, b.24 Feb 1976.

1240. Robert Dale[8] Abney (Thomas[7], Shelton[6], William[5], Shelton[4], William[3], John[2], Abner[1]), b.31 Jul 1937 Marshall, Saline Co., MO. Robert and his brother, Donald were adopted by Marie's second husband, Tom Abney. He m1. Delores Cohron in Sep 1958. He and Delores Cohron were divorced in 1965. He m2. Bonnie Leslie MacLean (b.14 May 1940 Juneau, AK), daughter of Andrew Kenyon MacLean and Cornelia Marie Birkland, on 14 Dec 1971 San Mateo, San Mateo Co., CA, but no issue.
Known children of Robert Dale[8] Abney and Delores Cohron:
    i.   Robin Del[9], b.18 Apr 1959 Tustin, Orange Co., CA.
    ii. Thomas Smith, b.1 Dec 1962 Kingsville, Kleberg Co., TX.

1241. Donald Wayne[8] Abney (Thomas[7], Shelton[6], William[5], Shelton[4], William[3], John[2], Abner[1]), b.16 Oct 1940 Marshall, Saline Co., MO. Donald and his brother, Robert were adopted by Marie's second husband, Tom Abney. He m1. Willie Dean Moore in May 1958. He and Willie Dean Moore were divorced in 1960. He m2. Sharon Jean Rollins on 15 Jun 1962. He and Sharon Jean Rollins were divorced on 13 Feb 1975. He m3. Lee Ann Morgan on 13 Dec 1976, but no issue.
Known child of Donald Wayne[8] Abney and Willie Dean Moore:
    i.   Donald Wayne[9], b.Apr 1959.
Known children of Donald Wayne[8] Abney and Sharon Jean Rollins:
    i.   Sherri Jean[9], b.25 Oct 1963.
    ii. Shelly Jo, b.25 Oct 1963.

1242. Thomas Shelton[8] Abney (Thomas[7], Shelton[6], William[5], Shelton[4], William[3], John[2], Abner[1]), b.10 Mar 1944 Marshall, Saline Co., MO. He m. Terry Harlene Ross (b.4 Mar 1949 Marshall, MO), daughter of Harland Ross and Dorothy King, on 11 Jun 1966 Marshall, Saline Co., MO.
Known child of Thomas Shelton[8] Abney and Terry Harlene Ross:
    i.   Kimberly Anjanette[9], b.30 Mar 1972 Tampa, FL.

1243. Nancy Ann[8] Abney (Shelton[7], Shelton[6], William[5], Shelton[4], William[3], John[2], Abner[1]), b. MO. She m. Robert Reynold Bahl and had issue:
    i.   Robert Shelton[9].
    ii. Roger Reynold.
    iii. Rorald Lee.

1244. Cynthia Ann "Cookie"[8] Hillis (gen.) (Mary[7] Abney, Harry[6], William[5], Shelton[4], William[3], John[2], Abner[1]), b.9 Sep 1943 Eglin Field, FL. She m1. William Ray Harper Sr. (b.1943), son of Winifred O. Harper and Juanita B. Taylor, on 14 Apr 1963. She was a KLM Ground Host. She and William Ray Harper Sr. were divorced in 1971. She m2. Robert McBride in Jun 1975, but no issue. She lived in 2001 Spicewood, TX.
Known child of Cynthia Ann "Cookie"[8] Hillis (gen.):
      i.   Lisa Butterworth[9], b. before 1963.
Known children of Cynthia Ann "Cookie"[8] Hillis (gen.) and William Ray Harper Sr.:
      i.   Charlotte Ann[9], b.20 Nov 1963 Houston, TX. She lived in 2001.
      ii. William Ray, b.1 Jun 1968. He lived in 2001.

1245. Valerie Hood[8] Hillis (Mary[7] Abney, Harry[6], William[5], Shelton[4], William[3], John[2], Abner[1]), b.7 Jul 1955 Dallas, TX. She m. Ray Brayn Sizemore Jr. (b.1952) on New Year's Day, 1 Jan 1974.
Known child of Valerie Hood[8] Hillis and Ray Brayn Sizemore Jr.:
      i.   Brooke Harmony[9], b.1974 Houston, TX.

1246. Gloria Howard[8] Bolles (Margaret[7] Abney, Harry[6], William[5], Shelton[4], William[3], John[2], Abner[1]), b.13 Dec 1945 Dallas, TX. She m. Bradford Leon "Brad" Watkins, son of Everett Leon Watkins and Roberta Alice Brown, on 17 Aug 1968. She was a teacher, living 1978 in Wichita, KS.
Known child of Gloria Howard[8] Bolles and Bradford Leon "Brad" Watkins:
      i.   Kevin Mark[9], b.22 Aug 1975.

1247. Lucille[8] Cruse (Neoma[7] Lewis, Mildred[6] Abney, Milton[5], Robert[4], John[3], John[2], Abner[1]) m. Harry Bowling and had issue (birth order unk.):
      i.   Laura Ann[9] m. R.M. Bowles.
      ii. Bob.
      iii. John.
      iv. Mary Lou.
      v.   Steve.

1248. Charles J.[8] Abney (Emmett[7], Joseph[6], Milton[5], Robert[4], John[3], John[2], Abner[1]), b.Dec 1919 Kittson Co., MN. He m. Elaine (n.n.) (b. ca.1918 MN) ca.1938 MN. They appeared on the census of 4 Apr 1940 Orleans, Kittson Co., MN.
Known child of Charles J.[8] Abney and Elaine (n.n.):
      i.   Diana[9], b. ca.1939 Kittson Co., MN.

1249. Helen Dorothy[8] Nusz (Alice[7] Aud, Wilhelmina[6] Bayne, Margaret[5] Lasley, Gertrude[4] Abney, John[3], John[2], Abner[1]), b.6 Jul 1903 Cecilia, Hardin Co., KY. She m. James "Ray" Jenkins Sr. on 17 Oct 1925 Cecilia, Hardin Co., KY. They appeared on the censuses of 14 Apr 1930 and 18 Apr 1940 Elizabethtown, Hardin Co., KY. She d.11 Nov 1987 Louisville, Jefferson Co., KY, at age 84 and was bur. on 14 Nov 1987 Hardin Mem. Park, Elizabethtown, Hardin Co., KY.
   James "Ray" Jenkins Sr, b.22 Mar 1903 and d.12 Nov 1977 Elizabethtown, Hardin Co., KY, at age 74 and was bur. Hardin Mem. Park.
Known children of Helen Dorothy[8] Nusz and James "Ray" Jenkins Sr. all b. Elizabethtown, Hardin Co., KY,:
      i.   James "Ray"[9], b. ca.Sep 1929.
  1427 ii. Herbert Neff, b. 14 Oct 1936; m. Wilhelmina Milton.
      iii. Dorothy, b. ca.Sep 1939.

Generation Nine

1250. Robert Dean "Bobby"[9] Hoffine (USAAC WWII) (Cuma[8] Crabtree, John[7], Polly[6] Chancellor, David[5], Rebecca[4] Abney, Joshua[3], Elisha[2], Abner[1]), b.11 Jul 1926 Pretty Prairie, Reno Co., KS. He owned *Hoffine Printing*. He m. Wilma Charlotte Hauser, daughter of William F. Hauser and Mary Kahle, on 7 Dec 1952 Oklahoma City, Oklahoma Co., OK. He d.14 Nov 2005 Boulder City, Clark Co., NV, at age 79 and was bur. Redwood Mem. Cem., West Jordan, Salt Lake Co., UT.
   Wilma Charlotte Hauser, b.23 Feb 1924 KS. She d.1 Jun 2000 Salt Lake City, Salt Lake Co., UT, at age 76.
Known children of Robert Dean "Bobby"[9] Hoffine (USAAC WWII) and Wilma Charlotte Hauser (birth order unknown):
      i.   Diane[10] m. Steve Cross.
      ii. Jenny m. Russell Okerlund.
      iii. Robert m. Rhonda (n.n.).
      iv. Kathy m. Greg Wheeler.
      v.   Kent.

1251. Gerald Ray[9] Sober (USN-WWII) (Nelie[8] Griffith, David[7], Mary[6] Chancellor, David[5], Rebecca[4] Abney, Joshua[3], Elisha[2], Abner[1]), b.14 Sep 1922 Shidler, Osage Co., OK; m1. Dorothy Carter in Apr 1942; m2. Nancy Hope Smith (USN), daughter of Tom Smith and Mai M. Carter, on 12 Aug 1974 Tulsa, Tulsa Co., OK, but no issue; d.9 Aug 2007 Ponca City, Kay Co., OK, age 84; bur. Odd Fellows Cem., Ponca City, Kay Co., OK.
Known children of Gerald Ray[9] Sober (USN-WWII) and Dorothy Carter:
      i.   Nancy Ruth[10] m. Don Keathly.
      ii. Kay m. (n.n.) Zang.
      iii. Richard "Dick" m. Janice (n.n.).
      iv. Tom m. Pam (n.n.).
   Nancy Hope Smith (USN) was a member of the *Daughters of the Confederacy* as well as the *Daughters of the American Revolution*. She was a pilot and an author. She was (an unknown value) DAR. , b.4 Jan 1925 OK. She d.5 Nov 2008 OK at age 83.

1252. Zelma "Earlene"[9] Sober (Nelie[8] Griffith, David[7], Mary[6] Chancellor, David[5], Rebecca[4] Abney, Joshua[3], Elisha[2], Abner[1]), b.26 Apr 1931 Ponca City, Kay Co., OK. She m1. PFC Roy Neal Corey (USAF) on 18 Aug 1951, but no issue. She m2. John Elwood Martin on 20 Jun 1955 and had issue. She m3. Ivy Arthur Nelson (US Mil.) in 1967 but no issue. She d.27 Mar 1998 Southwest Med. Ctr., Oklahoma City, Oklahoma Co., OK, at age 66 and was bur. Longwood Cem., Ponca City, Kay Co., OK.

PFC Roy Neal Corey (USAF), b.6 Sep 1929. He d.9 Nov 1992 at age 63.
John Elwood Martin, b.30 Nov 1918 Newkirk, Kay Co., OK. He d.20 Aug 1966 Ponca City, Kay Co., OK, at age 47.
Known children of Zelma "Earlene"[9] Sober and John Elwood Martin:
      i.   Beverly Faye[10] m. (n.n.) Bouchard.
      ii.   Mary Lynn m. (n.n.) Baxter.
   Ivy Arthur Nelson (US Mil.), b.1 May 1914. He d.20 Sep 1993 at age 79 and was bur. Mount Vernon Cem., Lamont, Grant Co., OK.

1253. Norman Robert[9] Myers (Joseph[8], Florence[7] Gillilan, Rebecca[6] Chancellor, David[5], Rebecca[4] Abney, Joshua[3], Elisha[2], Abner[1]), b.1944. He m. Sue (n.n.). They lived in 1998 Walnut, CA.
Known children of Norman Robert[9] Myers and Sue:
      i.   Ryan Robert[10].
      ii.   Melanie.

1254. Elnor Vernetta[9] McKay (Austin[8], Robert[7], Mary[6] Chancellor, Ewing[5], Rebecca[4] Abney, Joshua[3], Elisha[2], Abner[1]), b.18 Apr 1914 Novinger, Adair Co., MO. She m. Raymond Franklin Wolter, son of Frank Essics Wolter and Norma Laura Shotton. She d.22 Feb 1947 Quincy, Adams Co., IL, at age 32 and was bur. Knox City Cem., Knox City, Knox Co., MO.
   Raymond Franklin Wolter, b.18 Jun 1913 and d.3 Oct 1997 Knox City, Knox Co., MO, at age 84 and was bur. Knox City Cem.
Known child of Elnor Vernetta[9] McKay and Raymond Franklin Wolter:
      i.   Jerry Ray[10], b.12 Oct 1941 Quincy, Adams Co., IL. He d.19 Jun 2010 La Belle, Lewis Co., MO, at age 68.

1255. Eva Lee[9] McKay (Austin[8], Robert[7], Mary[6] Chancellor, Ewing[5], Rebecca[4] Abney, Joshua[3], Elisha[2], Abner[1]), b.26 Sep 1921 Knox Co., MO. She m. Kenneth Dale Lewis Sr., son of Clifford Eugene "Cliff" Lewis and Mary Jane Tully, on 25 Apr 1943 Canton, Lewis Co., MO. She d.16 Mar 2003 Kirksville, Adair Co., MO, at age 81 and bur. IOFF Cem., Hurdland, Knox Co., MO.
   Kenneth Dale Lewis Sr, b.17 Apr 1917 Knox Co., MO. He d.3 Aug 2000 Kirksville, Adair Co., MO, at age 83 and was bur. IOOF Cem.
Known children of Eva Lee[9] McKay and Kenneth Dale Lewis Sr. (birth order unknown):
      i.   Kenneth Dale[10] d..
      ii.   Linda L. m. Robert Fleak.
      iii. Vickey L. m. John F. Habben.
      iv. Paul McKay.

1256. Harry E.[9] McKay (Alva[8], Robert[7], Mary[6] Chancellor, Ewing[5], Rebecca[4] Abney, Joshua[3], Elisha[2], Abner[1]), b.10 Apr 1916 Brimson, Grundy Co., MO. He m. Anna Gertrude Snyder, daughter of James R. Snyder and Phoebe J. Jumper, on 28 May 1939 Galt, Grundy Co., MO. He d.18 Mar 1996 at age 79 and was bur. Resthaven Mem. Gardens, Trenton, Grundy Co., MO.
   Anna Gertrude Snyder, b.22 Feb 1922 Princeton, Mercer Co., MO. She d.7 Sep 2011 Trenton, Grundy Co., MO; bur. Resthaven Mem. Gardens.
Known children of Harry E.[9] McKay and Anna Gertrude Snyder:
      i.   James Ross[10], b.1 Jul 1941. He d.27 Sep 1965 at age 24.
      ii.   Annette m. (n.n.) Brodie.
      iii. Ray.
      iv. Bill.

1257. Forest[9] Lowther (Mary[8] Pickett, Arminta[7] McKay, Mary[6] Chancellor, Ewing[5], Rebecca[4] Abney, Joshua[3], Elisha[2], Abner[1]), b.1913 Humphreys, Sullivan Co., MO. He m. Lois McKinney; d.Aug 1969 Long Beach, Los Angeles Co., CA; bur. Long Beach, Los Angeles Co., CA.
Known children of Forest[9] Lowther and Lois McKinney:
      i.   Joyce[10].
      ii.   Ardis.

1258. Pauline M.[9] Lowther (Paul's twin) (Mary[8] Pickett, Arminta[7] McKay, Mary[6] Chancellor, Ewing[5], Rebecca[4] Abney, Joshua[3], Elisha[2], Abner[1]), b.17 Apr 1921 MO. She m. Jacob O. "Jake" Cooper on Christmas Day, 25 Dec 1943. She d.17 Nov 2011 Hiwatha, Linn Co., IA, at age 90 and was bur. Lafayette Cem., Alburnett, Linn Co., IA.
   Jacob O. "Jake" Cooper, b.5 Oct 1907 Half Rock, Mercer Co., MO; m1. Alice V. (n.n.). He d.29 Jan 1989 IA at age 81; bur. Lafayette Cem.
Known children of Pauline M.[9] Lowther and Jacob O. "Jake" Cooper:
      i.   Mary Sue[10] m. Charlie Rozek.
      ii.   Alan m. Becky (n.n.).

1259. Paul Martin[9] Lowther (USAAC) (Pauline's twin) (Mary[8] Pickett, Arminta[7] McKay, Mary[6] Chancellor, Ewing[5], Rebecca[4] Abney, Joshua[3], Elisha[2], Abner[1]), b.17 Apr 1921 Humphreys, Sullivan Co., MO. He m. Mary Josephine "Jo" Van Dyke (d.1993). He d.28 Jun 2010 Warsaw, Benton Co., MO, at age 89 and was bur. Humphreys Cem., Humphreys, Sullivan Co., MO.
Known children of Paul Martin[9] Lowther (USAAC) and Mary Josephine "Jo" Van Dyke:
  1428   i.   Paula[10], m. Jim Shannon.
      ii.   Pamela m. Mike Fennewald.

1260. Gerald Vernon "Vern"[9] Seckington (Elgeva[8] McKay, Walter[7], Mary[6] Chancellor, Ewing[5], Rebecca[4] Abney, Joshua[3], Elisha[2], Abner[1]), b.5 Dec 1918 Sullivan Co., MO. He m. Reva Elaine Knifong, daughter of William Bryan Knifong and Bessie Emoline Jones, on 17 Apr 1940. He d.21 Dec 1985 Marshall, Saline Co., MO, at age 67 and was bur. White Oak Cem., Milan, Sullivan Co., MO.
   Reva Elaine Knifong, b.16 Oct 1919 Sullivan Co., MO. She d.5 Jun 2015 Marshall, Saline Co., MO, at age 95 and was bur. White Oak Cem.
Known children of Gerald Vernon "Vern"[9] Seckington and Reva Elaine Knifong:
      i.   Jeanett[10], b. ca.1942 MO.
      ii.   Linda Sue, b.21 Aug 1944. She d.9 Nov 1944 and was bur. White Oak Cem., Milan, Sullivan Co., MO.

1261. Ila Lee[9] McClaren (Mary[8] McKay, Walter[7], Mary[6] Chancellor, Ewing[5], Rebecca[4] Abney, Joshua[3], Elisha[2], Abner[1]), b.25 Sep 1921 Reger, Sullivan Co., MO. She m. Robert Rex "Bob" Stephenson on 26 Nov 1939. She d.1 Oct 2012 Milan, Sullivan Co., MO, at age 91; bur. Glaze Cem., Sullivan Co., MO.

Robert Rex "Bob" Stephenson, b.31 Jan 1921 Cora, Sullivan Co., MO. He d.6 Jul 2003 Milan, Sullivan Co., MO, at age 82; bur. Glaze Cem.
Known children of Ila Lee[9] McClaren and Robert Rex "Bob" Stephenson:
　　　　i.　Robert "Keith"[10] m. Barbara Ford.
　　　　ii.　David Eugene m. Nedra Carter.
　　　　iii.　Charles Lindley m. Rosa Smith. He m. Dianna Jones.

1262. Dorothy Evelyn "Dot"[9] McClaren (Mary[8] McKay, Walter[7], Mary[6] Chancellor, Ewing[5], Rebecca[4] Abney, Joshua[3], Elisha[2], Abner[1]), b.9 Nov 1925 Reger, Sullivan Co., MO. She m. Raymond "Jay" Wattenbarger, son of Raymond Paul Wattenbarger and Nellie Elizabeth Lumsden, on 17 Jun 1946. She d.9 Sep 1996 Columbia, Boone Co., MO, at age 70 and was bur. Parklawn Memory Gardens Cem., Brookfield, Linn Co., MO.

Raymond "Jay" Wattenbarger, b.6 May 1926 Browning, Linn Co., MO. He d.13 Jun 2002 Kirksville, Adair Co., MO, at age 76.
Known children of Dorothy Evelyn "Dot"[9] McClaren and Raymond "Jay" Wattenbarger:
　　　　i.　Larry Max[10] m. Donna Lulf.
　　　　ii.　Darrell Jay m. Barbara Wayland.
　　　　iii.　Janice Elaine m. Richard Abeln. She m. Danny Burris. She m. William DuVall.

1263. David Russel[9] Ford Sr. (Lillie[8] McKay, Walter[7], Mary[6] Chancellor, Ewing[5], Rebecca[4] Abney, Joshua[3], Elisha[2], Abner[1]), b.21 Jul 1943. He m. Carolyn Sue Clark on 12 Apr 1969. He d.29 Mar 1999 at age 55 and was bur. Dunlap Cem., Rose Hill, Butler Co., KS.

Carolyn Sue Clark, b.3 Jul 1948 Trenton, Grundy Co., MO. She d.11 Dec 2010 Wichita, Sedgwick Co., KS, at age 62.
Known children of David Russel[9] Ford Sr. and Carolyn Sue Clark:
　　　　i.　David Russel[10], b.2 Jun 1970.
　　　　ii.　Carol Denise.

1264. William Almon "Bill"[9] Willis (USArmy) (Iva[8] Moore, Lottie[7] Chancellor, Henry[6], Ewing[5], Rebecca[4] Abney, Joshua[3], Elisha[2], Abner[1]), b.23 Mar 1927 MO. He m. Pauline Ruth "Polly" Allen on 29 Dec 1946 Galena, Cherokee Co., KS. He d.9 Nov 2016 Ardmore, Carter Co., OK, at age 89 and was bur. Hewitt Cem., Wilson, Carter Co., OK.

Pauline Ruth "Polly" Allen, b.1927. She d.1992 and was bur. Hewitt Cem., Wilson, Carter Co., OK.
Known child of William Almon "Bill"[9] Willis (USArmy) and Pauline Ruth "Polly" Allen:
　　　　i.　William Allen "Junior"[10], b.7 Dec 1947. He d.13 Mar 1983 at age 35 and was bur. Hewitt Cem., Wilson, Carter Co., OK.

1265. Marilyn Joann[9] Moore (Marion[8], Lottie[7] Chancellor, Henry[6], Ewing[5], Rebecca[4] Abney, Joshua[3], Elisha[2], Abner[1]), b.19 Aug 1935 Mindenmines, Barton Co., MO. She m. Keith Beaver on 15 Dec 1953 Mindenmines, Crawford Co., MO. She d.18 Mar 2017 Pittsburg, Crawford Co., KS, at age 81 and was bur. Crocker Cem., Pleasant View Twp., Cherokee Co., KS.

Known children of Marilyn Joann[9] Moore and Keith Beaver:
　　1429　i.　Sherry[10], m. Jim Chapman.
　　　　ii.　Michael.
　　　　iii.　Mark m. Dianne (n.n.).

1266. Jack Dean[9] Coverstone (Beatrice[8] Burmmett, Norma[7] Harmeson, Catherine[6] Chancellor, William[5], Rebecca[4] Abney, Joshua[3], Elisha[2], Abner[1]), b.17 Dec 1925. He m. Norma Louise Richards, daughter of Orva Richards and Elsie (n.n.), on 7 Mar 1947. He d.29 Jan 1992 Kingman, Mohave Co., AZ, at age 66 and was bur. Mound Cem., Charleston, Coles Co., IL.

Norma Louise Richards, b.27 Apr 1922 Charleston, Coles Co., IL. She d.3 Jan 2008 Mattoon, Coles Co., IL, at age 85; bur. Mound Cem.
Known children of Jack Dean[9] Coverstone and Norma Louise Richards:
　　1430　i.　Larry[10], m. Kay (n.n.).
　　1431　ii.　Bea, m. Dan Conley.
　　　　iii.　Patty m. (n.n.) Lewis.

1267. Carlos E.[9] Abney (USN-WWII) (Norton[8], Nancy[7], John[6], John[5], Paul[4], Joshua[3], Elisha[2], Abner[1]), b.2 Feb 1910 Ohio Co., KY. He m. Opal M. Frizzell, daughter of Benjamin Harrison Frizzell and Lydia Ray Snodgrass, on 19 Jan 1928. He d.20 Nov 1977 Beaver Dam, Ohio Co., KY, at age 67 and was bur. Sunnyside Cem., Beaver Dam, Ohio Co., KY.

Opal M. Frizzell, b.15 Nov 1909 Beaver Dam, Ohio Co., KY. She d.23 Jul 1998 Owensboro, Daviess Co., KY, at age 88; bur. Sunnyside Cem.
Known children of Carlos E.[9] Abney (USN-WWII) and Opal M. Frizzell:
　　　　i.　Carlos E.[10], b.1 Aug 1930 KY; d.1 Oct 1931 Ohio Co., KY, age 1; bur. Taylor Mines Cem., Beaver Dam, Ohio Co., KY.
　　　　ii.　Pauline, b.1 Oct 1932 KY; d.28 Mar 1934 KY, age 1; bur. Taylor Mines Cem., Beaver Dam, Ohio Co., KY.
　　　　iii.　Phyllis Jean, b.25 May 1936 Bowling Green, Warren Co., KY. She m. Elmer Ray Evans (USArmy-Korea), son of James Doolin"Jim" Evans Sr. and Ora V. Abner, on 23 Feb 1953. She d.1 Feb 2016 Ohio Co., KY, at age 79 and was bur. Sunnyside Cem., Beaver Dam, Ohio Co., KY.
　　　　　　　Elmer Ray Evans (USArmy-Korea), b.4 Apr 1933 Flener, Butler Co., KY. He d.11 Dec 2003 Beaver Dam, Ohio Co., KY, at age 70 and was bur. Sunnyside Cem., Beaver Dam, Ohio Co., KY.

1268. Hallie[9] Abney (Norton[8], Nancy[7], John[6], John[5], Paul[4], Joshua[3], Elisha[2], Abner[1]), b.17 Jul 1912 Ohio Co., KY. She m. Lee Frizzell, son of Benjamin Harrison Frizzell and Lydia Ray Snodgrass. She d.2 Jan 2007 KY at age 94 and was bur. Sunnyside Cem., Beaver Dam, Ohio Co., KY.

Lee Frizzell, b.7 Jul 1913. He d.3 Feb 1978 at age 64 and was bur. Sunnyside Cem., Beaver Dam, Ohio Co., KY.
Known child of Hallie[9] Abney and Lee Frizzell:
　　　　i.　Harold Dean[10], b.10 Sep 1933. He d.25 Nov 2008 at age 75 and was bur. Sunnyside Cem., Beaver Dam, Ohio Co., KY.

1269. Leonis M.[9] Abney (Norton[8], Nancy[7], John[6], John[5], Paul[4], Joshua[3], Elisha[2], Abner[1]), b.24 Mar 1925 Ohio Co., KY; m1. Jean Stone on 4 Jun 1945, but no issue; m2. Anna Young on 13 Dec 1947. He d.7 May 1984 Ohio Co., KY, age 59; bur. Sunnyside Cem., Beaver Dam, Ohio Co., KY.

Anna Young, b.31 Jan 1930.
Known child of Leonis M.[9] Abney and Anna Young:
      i.   Anita Joann[10], b.14 Oct 1954. She d.7 Sep 2007 at age 52 and was bur. Sunnyside Cem., Beaver Dam, Ohio Co., KY.

1270. Leon[9] Abney (USArmy-WWII) (Norton[8], Nancy[7], John[6], John[5], Paul[4], Joshua[3], Elisha[2], Abner[1]) m. (n.n.). He, b.24 Mar 1925. He d.8 Jan 2015 at age 89 and was bur. Sunnyside Cem., Beaver Dam, Ohio Co., KY.
Known child of Leon[9] Abney (USArmy-WWII) and (n.n.):
      i.   Michael Leon[10], b.8 Mar 1950. He d.19 Mar 2016 at age 66. He was cremated.

1271. Oliver "Cyrus"[9] Lindsey (Laura[8] Abney, Nancy[7], John[6], John[5], Paul[4], Joshua[3], Elisha[2], Abner[1]), b.4 Apr 1911 Ohio Co., KY. He m. Leona Elsie Maddox, daughter of Estill Thomas Maddox and Leona Howard, in 1928. He d.12 Jun 1937 Daviess Co., KY, at age 26 and was bur. Taylor Mines Cem., Beaver Dam, Ohio Co., KY.
    Leona Elsie Maddox, b.27 Jan 1911 McHenry, Ohio Co., KY. She m. George J. Fromm on 10 Apr 1941 Palmyra, Marion Co., MO. She d.29 Oct 1994 Peoria, Peoria Co., IL, at age 83 and was bur. Springdale Cem. and Mausoleum, Peoria, Peoria Co., IL.
Known children of Oliver "Cyrus"[9] Lindsey and Leona Elsie Maddox:
      i.   Edgar Ray[10], b.8 Dec 1929 Ohio Co., KY. He d.5 Jul 1939 Ohio Co., KY, at age 9 and was bur. Taylor Mines Cem.
      ii. Darrell S m. Judith L. Kircher. He was (an unknown value) Salesman. He, b.24 Jul 1933 McHenry, Ohio Co., KY. He d.12 Jun 1990 La Grange, Cook Co., IL, at age 56 and was bur. Springdale Cem. and Mausoleum, Peoria, Peoria Co., IL. Judith L. Kircher, b.5 Jan 1936.

1272. Raymond Perry[9] Knoll (Laura[8] Perry, Keziah[7] Abney, Jasper[6], John[5], Paul[4], Joshua[3], Elisha[2], Abner[1]), b.17 Jun 1932 Evansville, Vanderburgh Co., IN; m. Betty Jean West, daughter of John Thomas West and Flossie Elizabeth Hougland, on 27 Nov 1957 Evansville, Vanderburgh Co., IN; d.3 Jun 2013 Evansville, Vanderburgh Co., IN, age 80; bur. Centenary UMC Cem., Evansville, Vanderburgh Co., IN.
    Betty Jean West, b.10 Mar 1933 Central City, Muhlenberg Co., KY. She d.31 Jul 1992 Evansville, Vanderburgh Co., IN, at age 59.
Known child of Raymond Perry[9] Knoll and Betty Jean West:
      i.   Laura Marie (gen.)[10], b.14 Jan 1965 Evansville, Vanderburgh Co., IN. She m. Aaron Brent Lamb on 3 Jul 1993 Evansville, Vanderburgh Co., IN. She lived in 1997 Evansville, Vanderburgh Co., IN when the author began working with her on the Abney family history. Descending from Rev. Paul Colby Abney, Cousin Laura is responsible for much of the author's knowledge on his descendants (confirmed by Cousin Debby Blus, #1295). The author found Cousin Laura very nice to work with, extremely munificent with her work, and deserving of recognition for her service to the Abney family history. Aaron Brent Lamb , b.25 Feb 1965 Evansville, Vanderburgh Co., IN.

1273. Erdine Vaye[9] Moore (Gertrude[8] Abney, John[7], James[6], John[5], Paul[4], Joshua[3], Elisha[2], Abner[1]), b.15 May 1921. She d.12 Dec 2003 Dexterville, Butler Co., KY, at age 82 and was bur. Mount Vernon Cem., Dexterville, Butler Co., KY. Known child of Erdine Vaye[9] Moore:
      i.   Lecia Gayle (gen.)[10] m. (n.n.) House. Cousin Lecia and the author made contact around 1998 from the now defunct *Abney GenForum*. She provided information on the very large family of John William Abney (#535) and Mary Sarah Fleenor.

1274. Kenneth[9] Moore (USArmy-WWII) (Gertrude[8] Abney, John[7], James[6], John[5], Paul[4], Joshua[3], Elisha[2], Abner[1]) m. Vida (n.n.). He, b.7 Jul 1926 Butler Co., KY. He d.22 Oct 2016 Morgantown, Butler Co., KY, at age 90 and was bur. Chapel Union Church Cem., Morgantown, Butler Co., KY.
Known children of Kenneth[9] Moore (USArmy-WWII) and Vida:
      i.   Dwight[10].
      ii. Bobby.
      iii. Pamela m. Donnie Hester.

1275. Louis W.[9] Abney (USArmy-WWII) (Thurman[8], John[7], James[6], John[5], Paul[4], Joshua[3], Elisha[2], Abner[1]), b.5 Dec 1924 IN. He m1. Thelma L. (n.n.). He m2. Nora "Elizabeth" Bland, daughter of Leamon Washington Bland and Ollie M. Smith, but no issue. He d.23 Dec 2001 Deaconess Hospital, Evansville, Vanderburgh Co., IN, at age 77 and was bur. Sunset Mem. Gardens Cem., Evansville, Vanderburgh Co., IN.
    Thelma L. (n.n.), b.1920. She d.16 Nov 1999 and was bur. Sunset Mem. Gardens Cem., Evansville, Vanderburgh Co., IN.
Known children of Louis W.[9] Abney (USArmy-WWII) and Thelma L.:
      i.   Brenda[10] m. (n.n.) Paul.
      ii. Raymond Michael.
    Nora "Elizabeth" Bland, b.6 Jul 1931 Cadiz, Trigg Co., KY. She d.28 Dec 2014 Newburgh, Warrick Co., IN, at age 83.

1276. Robert "Bob"[9] Abney (USArmy-WWII) (Thurman[8], John[7], James[6], John[5], Paul[4], Joshua[3], Elisha[2], Abner[1]), b.Christmas Day, 25 Dec 1926 Evansville, Vanderburgh Co., IN. He m. (n.n.) ca.1945. He d.2 May 2011 Newburgh, Warrick Co., IN, at age 84 and was bur. Park Lawn Cem. and Mausoleum, Evansville, Vanderburgh Co., IN. Robert "Bob"[9] Abney (USArmy-WWII) sired three sons (n.n.)

1277. Mary Kathryn[9] Abney (Thurman[8], John[7], James[6], John[5], Paul[4], Joshua[3], Elisha[2], Abner[1]), b.1930 IN. She m. Merle Edward Downen, son of Earl Downen and Viola Mohr, in 1946. She d.2007 and was bur. Alexander Mem. Park Cem., Evansville, Vanderburgh Co., IN.
    Merle Edward Downen, b.22 Jul 1928 and d.5 Nov 2013 Evansville, Vanderburgh Co., IN, at age 85 and was bur. Alexander Mem. Park Cem.
Known children of Mary Kathryn[9] Abney and Merle Edward Downen:
      i.   Jo Anna Merle[10] m. (n.n.) Eskew.
      ii. Larry Wayne.
      iii. Debra Ann m. (n.n.) Niles.
      iv. Timothy Scott.

1278. Erlene[9] Mitchell (Lula[8] Abney, John[7], James[6], John[5], Paul[4], Joshua[3], Elisha[2], Abner[1]) m. Cody Overt Goodall (USArmy-WWII). , b.21 Nov 1923 Morgantown, Butler Co., KY and was bur. Louisville Mem. Gardens, Louisville, Jefferson Co., KY. She d.21 May 2005 Louisville, Jefferson Co., KY, at age 81. Erlene and Cody had issue: 2 daughters (n.n.)
    Cody Overt Goodall (USArmy-WWII), b.23 May 1924 Butler Co., KY. He d.16 Dec 2002 Louisville, Jefferson Co., KY, at age 78.

1279. Arllis C.^{9} Mitchell (Lula^8 Abney, John^7, James^6, John^5, Paul^4, Joshua^3, Elisha^2, Abner^1) m. (n.n.). He, b.9 Apr 1934. He d.8 Feb 2008 Louisville, Jefferson Co., KY, at age 73. He was cremated. Arllis sired a son (n.n.).

1280. Odis Carl^9 Meredith Sr. (USArmy) (Margaret^8 Abney, John^7, James^6, John^5, Paul^4, Joshua^3, Elisha^2, Abner^1), b.18 Dec 1943; d.22 Oct 2013 Evansville, Vanderburgh Co., IN, age 69; bur. Park Lawn Cem. and Mausoleum, Evansville, Vanderburgh Co., IN. He sired a son: Odis Carl^{10}.

1281. Alan^9 Lane (Louis^8 Abney, John^7, James^6, John^5, Paul^4, Joshua^3, Elisha^2, Abner^1), d.15 Apr 2008. He m. Brenda (n.n.) and had issue:
  i.   Christopher^{10}.
  ii. Gregory.

1282. Susan "Sue"^{9} Abney (Louis^8, John^7, James^6, John^5, Paul^4, Joshua^3, Elisha^2, Abner^1) m. Jerry Skinner and had issue: John A.^{10}.

1283. Dan Louis^9 Abney (Louis^8, John^7, James^6, John^5, Paul^4, Joshua^3, Elisha^2, Abner^1) m. Tonya (n.n.) and had issue:
  i.   Shauna^{10} m. Mark Bassmeier.
  ii. Cody.

1284. Mary Frances^9 Wilson (George^8, Mary^7 Abney, James^6, John^5, Paul^4, Joshua^3, Elisha^2, Abner^1), b.23 May 1939 Metcalfe Co., KY. She m. Thomas Dale Sutherland. She m. McArthur DeWitt, son of Levy DeWitt and Bessie E. Richardson, but no issue. She d.30 Aug 1998 Daviess Co., KY, at age 59 and was bur. Calhoun Cem., Calhoun, McLean Co., KY.
    Thomas Dale Sutherland, b.10 Feb 1948 Pleasant Ridge, Daviess Co., KY; d.25 Jan 2018 Owensboro, Daviess Co., KY; bur. Cates Cem. Known child of Mary Frances^9 Wilson and Thomas Dale Sutherland: Thomas Ray^{10}, b.1961. He d.30 Jan 2016. He was cremated.
    McArthur DeWitt, b.25 Jun 1914 Lawrenceburg, Anderson Co., KY. He d.14 Dec 1991 Calhoun, McLean Co., KY, at age 77.

1285. Jesse Ray^9 Garrett (Nellie^8 Wilson, Mary^7 Abney, James^6, John^5, Paul^4, Joshua^3, Elisha^2, Abner^1), b.20 Feb 1923 KY; m. Judy Brown on 11 Jan 1969; d.8 Aug 2014 Baptist Health Hosp., Paducah, McCracken Co., KY, at age 91; bur. Pleasant Valley Cem., Providence, Webster Co., KY.
    Judy Brown, b.17 Oct 1941.
Known children of Jesse Ray^9 Garrett and Judy Brown: Donald^{10} m. Joyce (n.n.), and Carolyn.

1286. James Luther^9 Garrett (Nellie^8 Wilson, Mary^7 Abney, James^6, John^5, Paul^4, Joshua^3, Elisha^2, Abner^1), b.4 Mar 1925. He m. Mary F. (n.n.) on 20 May 1946. He d.27 Apr 1998 at age 73 and was bur. Kossuth Cem., Mediapolis, Des Moines Co., IA.
    Mary F. (n.n.), b.17 Aug 1926. She d.18 Apr 1990 at age 63.
Known children of James Luther^9 Garrett and Mary F. (n.n.): Fred^{10}, Warren, Lisa and Scott.

1287. Patricia Nell^9 Garrett (Nellie^8 Wilson, Mary^7 Abney, James^6, John^5, Paul^4, Joshua^3, Elisha^2, Abner^1) m. William Perkins. , b.22 Feb 1941 McLean Co., KY. She d.20 Jun 2015 Greenville, Muhlenberg Co., KY, at age 74 and was bur. Rose Hill Cem., Central City, Muhlenberg Co., KY.
Known children of Patricia Nell^9 Garrett and William Perkins:
  i.   Bill^{10} m. Renee (n.n.).
  ii. Karen m. Larry Raley.

1288. Charles^9 Abney Sr. (Roscoe^8, William^7, James^6, John^5, Paul^4, Joshua^3, Elisha^2, Abner^1), b.10 Feb 1937 McLean Co., KY. He m. Lee Morris on 20 May 1960 Cincinnati, Hamilton Co., OH and had issue: Charles^{10}, b.7 Mar 1969.

1289. Jerry Roberts^9 Abney (Roscoe^8, William^7, James^6, John^5, Paul^4, Joshua^3, Elisha^2, Abner^1), b.14 Dec 1938 McLean Co., KY. He m. Earlene Clements (b.8 Dec 1940 Davis Co., KY) on 22 Aug 1959 Browns Valley, Daviess Co., KY.
Known children of Jerry Roberts^9 Abney and Earlene Clements:
  1432 i.   Cathy Lynn^{10}, b. 9 May 1962 Davis Co., KY; m. Todd Burden.
  1433 ii.   Jerry Roberts, b. 2 Jul 1963 Davis Co., KY; m. Kathryn Moon.
  1434 iii. Lee Ann, b. 5 Nov 1964 TN; m. Scott Starkey.
        iv.   Joseph Gregory "Greg", b.31 Mar 1967 Davis Co., KY.
        v.   Nicholas "Nick", b.18 Jan 1979 Davis Co., KY.

1290. Betty^9 Abney (Roscoe^8, William^7, James^6, John^5, Paul^4, Joshua^3, Elisha^2, Abner^1), b.7 Aug 1941 McLean Co., KY. She m1. Gerald Iglehart (b. McLean Co., KY) on 17 Aug 1962 McLean Co., KY. She m2. Louard Gray (b.25 Oct 1932) on 30 Jun 1990 Princeton, Caldwell Co., KY, but no issue. Known children of Betty^9 Abney and Gerald Iglehart:
  1435 i.   Peggy Denice^{10}, b. 27 May 1965 KY; m. Dana Hartigan.
        ii. Kerry Michael, b.24 Sep 1968.

1291. Darrell^9 Abney Sr. (Roscoe^8, William^7, James^6, John^5, Paul^4, Joshua^3, Elisha^2, Abner^1), b.28 Mar 1945 McLean Co., KY. He m. Kay Hargarett (b.4 Feb 1944) on 3 Jul 1971 Maysville, Mason Co., KY.
Known children of Darrell^9 Abney Sr. and Kay Hargarett:
  i.   Kathryn^{10}, b.22 Apr 1973.
  ii.   Betsy, b.8 Oct 1976.
  iii. Darrell, b.17 Dec 1978.

1292. Terry^9 Abney (Roscoe^8, William^7, James^6, John^5, Paul^4, Joshua^3, Elisha^2, Abner^1), b.1 Jun 1947 McLean Co., KY. He m. Shelia Brown (b. McLean Co., KY) on 12 Sep 1968 McLean Co., KY.
Known children of Terry^9 Abney and Shelia Brown:
  i.   Jason^{10}, b.9 Jan 1974.
  ii. Trisha, b.18 Jul 1978.

1293. Russell[9] Abney (Roscoe[8], William[7], James[6], John[5], Paul[4], Joshua[3], Elisha[2], Abner[1]), b.19 Mar 1951 McLean Co., KY. He m. Pam Brush on 31 May 1980 FL and had issue:
          i.   Alexis[10], b.29 Jun 1981.
          ii.   Rebecca, b.21 Jan 1983.
          iii. William, b.4 May 1990.

1294. Norman[9] Abney (Roscoe[8], William[7], James[6], John[5], Paul[4], Joshua[3], Elisha[2], Abner[1]) and Candy Bidwell 135. He, b.19 Apr 1954 McLean Co., KY. He m. Candy Bidwell (b.4 Mar 1959) on 27 Apr 1990 Charleston, SC and had issue:
Known children of Norman[9] Abney and Candy Bidwell:
          i.   Carly[10], b.24 Aug 1993.
          ii.   Paul, b.21 Dec 1996.

1295. Deborah "Debby"[9] Abney (gen.) (Roscoe[8], William[7], James[6], John[5], Paul[4], Joshua[3], Elisha[2], Abner[1]), b.20 Jul 1957 Owensboro, Daviess Co., KY. She m. Alan Blus on 5 May 1984 Cincinnati, Hamilton Co., OH. She is a graduate of Western Kentucky University (*Go Hilltoppers*). The author began working with Cousin Debby in 1998. Another descendant of Rev. Paul Colby Abney, Cousin Debby was wonderfully generous with her research. Her work confirmed and agreed with Cousin Laura Knoll Lamb's work (see #1272i, pg.240). The author appreciates the work of Cousin Debby and is pleased to give credit where credit is due. Although they haven't worked on the family history together in recent years, the author remains in contact with Cousin Debby via Facebook to this day.
    Alan Blus, b.11 Feb 1960 Toledo, Lucas Co., OH. He was liv. in 1998.
Known children of Deborah "Debby"[9] Abney (gen.) and Alan Blus:
          i.   Joseph Alan[10], b.28 Nov 1985 Cincinnati, Hamilton Co., OH.
          ii.   Jessica, b.16 Sep 1987.

1296. Judy[9] Abney (Roscoe[8], William[7], James[6], John[5], Paul[4], Joshua[3], Elisha[2], Abner[1]), b.28 May 1959 Owensboro, Daviess Co., KY. She m. Johnny McCart (b.5 Jul 1960) on 31 Mar 1990 Lauerenciville, GA and had issue:
          i.   Amanda[10], b.3 Mar 1993.
          ii.   Nathaniel, b.28 Feb 1995.

1297. Lucille[9] Felty (Mittie[8] Snodgrass, Naoma[7] Daugherty, Mary[6] Abney, John[5], Paul[4], Joshua[3], Elisha[2], Abner[1]), b.4 Oct 1909. She m. Arrel Rowe Himes Sr., son of John R. Himes and Lottie H. Hamlet. She d.15 Apr 1978 at age 68 and was bur. Oakwood Cem., Hartford, Ohio Co., KY.
    Arrel Rowe Himes Sr, b.9 Oct 1906. He d.2 Nov 1989 at age 83.
Known children of Lucille[9] Felty and Arrel Rowe Himes Sr.:
          i.   Arrel Rowe[10], b.18 Jun 1929. He m. (n.n.). He m. Ina Waltrude Tichenor on 6 Sep 1964. He d.16 May 2018 at age 88 and was bur. Beula Cumberland Presbyterian Ch. Cem., Beda, Ohio Co., KY.
               Ina Waltrude Tichenor, b.4 Nov 1922. She m. John Everett Mickel Jr. on New Year's Eve, 31 Dec 1941. She d.7 Feb 2008 KY at age 85.
          ii.   Lucille Carrol, b.22 Nov 1939 Hartford, Ohio Co., KY. She m. Billy Joe Hoagland, son of J.T. Hoagland and Lizzie Ford. She d.7 Jul 2019 Bowling Green, Warren Co., KY, at age 79 and was bur. Oakwood Cem., Hartford, Ohio Co., KY.
               Billy Joe Hoagland, b.30 Mar 1937 Hartford, Ohio Co., KY. He d.27 Jul 2007 Warren Co., KY, at age 70 and was bur. Oakwood Cem., Hartford, Ohio Co., KY.
          iii. Elaine Grey Headstone shows birthdate of 18 Aug 1945. Kentucky Birth Index gives 18 Sep 1945. , b.18 Sep 1945. She m. Robert H. Crea on 28 Mar 1964. She d.11 May 2004 at age 58 and was bur. Oakwood Cem., Hartford, Ohio Co., KY.
               Robert H. Crea, b.30 Aug 1944.

1298. Faye[9] Felty (Mittie[8] Snodgrass, Naoma[7] Daugherty, Mary[6] Abney, John[5], Paul[4], Joshua[3], Elisha[2], Abner[1]), b.28 Mar 1912; m. Joseph Duke Carson Sr., son of Ulysses Simpson Carson and Edessa Gabriel Duke. She d.24 Feb 1987 age 74; bur. Oakwood Cem., Hartford, Ohio Co., KY.
    Joseph Duke Carson Sr, b.9 Jul 1907. He d.25 Jun 1980 at age 72 and was bur. Oakwood Cem., Hartford, Ohio Co., KY.
Known children of Faye[9] Felty and Joseph Duke Carson Sr.:
          i.   Virginia Faye[10], b.2 Dec 1928. She m. Cpl. Arthur Earl Statom (USArmy-WWII) and was bur. Pleasant Grove Baptist Ch. Cem., Sorgho, Daviess Co., KY. She d.7 Mar 2004 at age 75.
               Cpl. Arthur Earl Statom (USArmy-WWII), b.18 Jul 1922. He d. Christmas Eve, 24 Dec 2002 at age 80 and was bur. Pleasant Grove Baptist Ch. Cem., Sorgho, Daviess Co., KY.
          ii.   (infant son), b.20 Nov 1930. He d.8 Feb 1931 and was bur. Oakwood Cem., Hartford, Ohio Co., KY.
          iii. Joseph Duke, b.5 Aug 1938. He d.1 Sep 1995 at age 57 and was bur. Oakwood Cem., Hartford, Ohio Co., KY.
          iv. James Gabriel, b.27 Oct 1941. He d.21 Feb 2015 at age 73 and was bur. Oakwood Cem., Hartford, Ohio Co., KY.
          v.   Mittie Anna, b.21 Nov 1949. She d.10 Sep 2014 at age 64 and was bur. Oakwood Cem., Hartford, Ohio Co., KY.

1299. Ruby Grey[9] Felty (Mittie[8] Snodgrass, Naoma[7] Daugherty, Mary[6] Abney, John[5], Paul[4], Joshua[3], Elisha[2], Abner[1]), b.23 Sep 1913 Butler Co., KY. She m. Everett J. Patton, son of Ernest J. Patton and Lula Whittaker. She d.27 Apr 1985 Danville, Hendricks Co., IN, at age 71 and was bur. Barnett's Creek Baptist Church Cem., Bells Run, Ohio Co., KY.
    Everett J. Patton, b.19 Jan 1910 Ohio Co., KY. He d.17 Nov 1979 Owensboro, Daviess Co., KY, at age 69.
Known child of Ruby Grey[9] Felty and Everett J. Patton:
          i.   Jackie Lou[10], b. ca.1939 KY.

1300. Claudia[9] Felty (Mittie[8] Snodgrass, Naoma[7] Daugherty, Mary[6] Abney, John[5], Paul[4], Joshua[3], Elisha[2], Abner[1]), b.27 Oct 1919. She m. Maj. Irvin Krone White (USMC-WWII, Korea) on 26 Sep 1939. She d.6 Jan 2001 at age 81 and was bur. Oakwood Cem., Hartford, Ohio Co., KY.
    Maj. Irvin Krone White (USMC-WWII, Korea), b.19 Mar 1911 Ohio Co., KY. He d.25 Sep 2005 Ohio Co., KY, age 94; bur. Oakwood Cem.
Known child of Claudia[9] Felty and Maj. Irvin Krone White (USMC-WWII, Korea):
          i.   Lydia Robin[10], b.9 Sep 1955. She d.9 Sep 1955 and was bur. Oakwood Cem., Hartford, Ohio Co., KY.

1301. John Snodgrass[9] Felty (Mittie[8] Snodgrass, Naoma[7] Daugherty, Mary[6] Abney, John[5], Paul[4], Joshua[3], Elisha[2], Abner[1]), b.29 Oct 1934. He d.6 Dec 1992 Oldham Co., KY, at age 58 and was bur. Oakwood Cem., Hartford, Ohio Co., KY.
Known children of John Snodgrass[9] Felty:
        i.   Julia Ann[10] m. (n.n.) Johnson. , b.29 Aug 1959. She d.28 Mar 2016 at age 56. She was cremated.
        ii. Melinda Sue, b.10 Jul 1963; m. David D. Carpenter. d.1 Mar 2006 age 42; bur. Oakwood Cem., Hartford, Ohio Co., KY.
             David D. Carpenter, b.19 Mar 1960.

1302. Bennie[9] Dunn (Mattie[8] Snodgrass, Naoma[7] Daugherty, Mary[6] Abney, John[5], Paul[4], Joshua[3], Elisha[2], Abner[1]), b.24 Jan 1916 Butler Co., KY; m. John Thompson, s/o George Lee Thompson and Olive Edna Carson. She d.11 Jun 2009, age 93; bur. Pine Crest Cem., Mobile, Mobile Co., AL.
    John Edd Thompson Sr, b.13 Jun 1913. He d.12 Jan 1970 at age 56 and was bur. Pine Crest Cem., Mobile, Mobile Co., AL.
Known children of Bennie[9] Dunn and John Edd Thompson Sr.:
        i.   John Edd[10].
        ii. William Lee "Bill."
        iii. Jean m. (n.n.) Schemensky.

1303. Dr. Hershel "Ray"[9] Dunn (USAA-WWII) (Mattie[8] Snodgrass, Naoma[7] Daugherty, Mary[6] Abney, John[5], Paul[4], Joshua[3], Elisha[2], Abner[1]), b.3 Apr 1919. He m. Hannah H. Barrass. He graduated in 1952 from the University of Louisville School of Dentistry. He d.28 Feb 2008 Hanson, Hopkins Co., KY, at age 88 and was bur. Christian Church Cem., Providence, Webster Co., KY.
    Hannah H. Barrass, b.10 Nov 1922.
Known children of Dr. Hershel "Ray"[9] Dunn (USAA-WWII) and Hannah H. Barrass:
        i.   Pat[10] m. Bobby Eddings.
        ii. Candy m. Paul Marshall.
        iii. Jon m. Betty (n.n.).
  1436 iv. Steve, b. 26 Dec 1953 Daviess Co., KY; m. Linda (n.n.); m. Linda Turley.

1304. Lennie Grey[9] Dunn (Mattie[8] Snodgrass, Naoma[7] Daugherty, Mary[6] Abney, John[5], Paul[4], Joshua[3], Elisha[2], Abner[1]), b.11 Feb 1924 Ohio Co., KY. She m. S. Sgt. William Elliott Johnson Sr. (USArmy-WWII), son of Arthur Edward Johnson and Iris Moiser Elliott, ca.1946. She d.13 Feb 2014 Mobile, Mobile Co., AL, at age 90 and was bur. Pine Crest Cem., Mobile, Mobile Co., AL.
    S.Sgt. William Elliott Johnson Sr. (USArmy-WWII), b.17 Feb 1921. He, b.25 Sep 2006; bur. Pine Crest Cem., Mobile, Mobile Co., AL.
Known child of Lennie Grey[9] Dunn and S. Sgt. William Elliott Johnson Sr. (USArmy-WWII):
  1437   i.   William Elliott[10], m. Debby (n.n.).

1305. Robert William "Bobby"[9] Deno (Ira[8], Sallie[7] Abney, Daniel[6], John[5], Paul[4], Joshua[3], Elisha[2], Abner[1]), b.6 Dec 1938 McLean Co., KY. He m. Norma J. Welch. He d.15 Jan 2013 Owensboro, Daviess Co., KY, at age 74 and was bur. Utica Baptist Church Cem., Utica, Daviess Co., KY.
    Norma J. Welch, b.1 Aug 1962. She d.3 Oct 2011 at age 49.
Known child of Robert William "Bobby"[9] Deno and Norma J. Welch:
        i.   Rebecca Ann[10] m. Ronnie Ray "Spanky" Kirk, son of Vernon Kirk Jr. , b.9 Mar 1963. She d.16 Feb 2011 at age 47 and was bur. Rosehill Elmwood Cem., Owensboro, Daviess Co., KY.
             Ronnie Ray "Spanky" Kirk, b.5 May 1965. He d.3 Jan 2005 at age 39 and was bur. Rosehill Elmwood Cem.

1306. Charles Edward[9] Vanover Sr. (Helen[8] Deno, Sallie[7] Abney, Daniel[6], John[5], Paul[4], Joshua[3], Elisha[2], Abner[1]), b.25 Mar 1941 McLean Co., KY. He m. (n.n.). He d.22 Nov 2013 Owensboro, Daviess Co., KY, at age 72 and was bur. Calhoun Cem., Calhoun, McLean Co., KY.
Known children of Charles Edward[9] Vanover Sr. (birth order unknown):
        i.   Agnes Elizabeth[10] m. (n.n.) Gilmore.
        ii. Sheila m. (n.n.) Speed.
        iii. Mary m. David Rue.
        iv. Charles Edward.
        v.   Juanita m. (n.n.) Turner.
        vi. Christopher Thomas.

1307. Helen Christine "Chris"[9] Moore (Lawson[8], Nathan[7], Finis[6], Mary[5] Abney, Paul[4], Joshua[3], Elisha[2], Abner[1]), b.26 Jun 1943 Cincinnati, Hamilton Co., OH. She d.14 Oct 2017 Arcola, Douglas Co., IL, at age 74.
Known child of Helen Christine "Chris"[9] Moore:
        i.   Jeffrey Lee *Jones*[10] He was stillborn 16 Aug 1971 East Lawn Cem., Urbana, Champaign Co., IL and was bur. East Lawn Cem., Urbana, Champaign Co., IL.

1308. William Denton[9] Renfrow (Eula[8] Moore, Nathan[7], Finis[6], Mary[5] Abney, Paul[4], Joshua[3], Elisha[2], Abner[1]), b.3 Apr 1949 Ohio Co., KY. He m. (n.n.). He d.30 Oct 2015 Owensboro, Daviess Co., KY, at age 66 and was bur. Bell's Run Cem., Bell's Run, Ohio Co., KY.
Known children of William Denton[9] Renfrow:
        i.   Charlotte Evonne[10], b.15 May 1968 Huntingburg, Dubois Co., IN. She d.16 Jan 2018 at age 49 and was bur. Bell's Run Cem., Bell's Run, Ohio Co., KY.
        ii. Geraldine Michelle, b.11 Nov 1971. She m. (n.n.) Basham. d.1 Dec 2016 at age 45. She was cremated.

1309. Diana Sue[9] Hert (Alva[8], Nola[7] Moore, Finis[6], Mary[5] Abney, Paul[4], Joshua[3], Elisha[2], Abner[1]) m. (n.n.) Darnell. , b.7 Jul 1946 McHenry, Ohio Co., KY. She d.14 Feb 2017 Boaz, Graves Co., KY, at age 70. She was cremated.
Known children of Diana Sue[9] Hert and (n.n.) Darnell (birth order unknown):
        i.   (infant son)[10].
        ii. Catherine m1. (n.n.) Silkwood. She m2. (n.n.) Gordon. She m3. (n.n.) English.
        iii. Teresa.
        iv. Kimberly.

1310. Cecil⁹ Raymond Jr. (Stella⁸ Hurt, Nola⁷ Moore, Finis⁶, Mary⁵ Abney, Paul⁴, Joshua³, Elisha², Abner¹), b.1 Nov 1942 McHenry, Ohio Co., KY. He m. Patrice Toney ca.1968. He d.24 Aug 2019 Evansville, Vanderburgh Co., IN, age 76; bur. Rose Hill Cem., Newburgh, Warrick Co., IN.
Known children of Cecil⁹ Raymond Jr. and Patrice Toney:
    1438   i.   Allison¹⁰, m. Dave Novak.
    1439   ii.   Andrea, m. Ryan McKinney.
    1440   iii.   Alisa, m. (n.n.) Knapp.

1311. Steven Lee "Steve"⁹ Coots (Earl⁸, Senora⁷ Abner, Harrison⁶, Isaac⁵ Abney, Paul⁴, Joshua³, Elisha², Abner¹), b.14 Dec 1961 KY; m. Violet Johnson 15 Jun 1985; d.9 Jun 2017 Bowling Green, Warren Co., KY, ae.55; bur. Bowling Green Gardens Cem., Bowling Green, Warren Co., KY.
    Violet P. Johnson, b.19 Nov 1963.
Known children of Steven Lee "Steve"⁹ Coots and Violet P. Johnson both b. KY:
    1441   i.   Christopher¹⁰, m. Jennilee (n.n.).
         ii.   Tyler.

1312. Michael Dean⁹ Johnson Sr. (Joan⁸ Abner, Lester⁷, Harrison⁶, Isaac⁵ Abney, Paul⁴, Joshua³, Elisha², Abner¹) m. Alexis (n.n.) and had issue:
         i.   Victoria Nicole¹⁰.
         ii.   Michael Dean.

1313. Melissa Carol⁹ Johnson (Joan⁸ Abner, Lester⁷, Harrison⁶, Isaac⁵ Abney, Paul⁴, Joshua³, Elisha², Abner¹) m. Jim Nugent and had issue:
         i.   Mary¹⁰.
         ii.   Jimmie.

1314. Shirley Ann⁹ Turner (Arthur⁸, Flora⁷ Goff, Rena⁶ Abner, Silas⁵ Abney, Paul⁴, Joshua³, Elisha², Abner¹), b.7 Sep 1936 Linton, Greene Co., IN. She m. Gary Jackson. She d.6 Nov 2019 Plainfield, Hendricks Co., IN, at age 83; bur. West Ridge Park Cem., Indianapolis, Marion Co., IN.
    Gary Jackson, b.1937. He d.2006 and was bur. West Ridge Park Cem., Indianapolis, Marion Co., IN.
Known children of Shirley Ann⁹ Turner and Gary Jackson (birth order unknown):
         i.   Mark¹⁰.
         ii.   Kim m. Mike Stidham.
         iii.   Sherry m. Jim Weaver.
         iv.   Dana m. John Turner.

1315. James King⁹ Abney (James⁸, John⁷, Washington⁶, Wilburn⁵, Benjamin⁴, Hezekiah³, Elisha², Abner¹) m. Charlene (n.n.) and had issue:
         i.   Robert Kelly¹⁰.
         ii.   Jesse Aaron.

1316. Raymond Lee⁹ Abney Jr. (Raymond⁸, Grover⁷, Washington⁶, Wilburn⁵, Benjamin⁴, Hezekiah³, Elisha², Abner¹), b.4 Oct 1937; m. Charlotte Crawford ca.1961. He owned *Abney Pharmacy*, Ringgold, Catoosa Co., GA; d.29 Dec 2019 Ringgold, Catoosa Co., GA, age 82. He was cremated.
    Charlotte Jeanette Crawford, b.7 Mar 1941 Ringgold, Catoosa Co., GA. She d.20 Nov 2014 Ringgold, Catoosa Co., GA, at age 73.
Known children of Raymond Lee⁹ Abney Jr. and Charlotte Jeanette Crawford:
    1442   i.   Raymond Lee¹⁰, b. ca.1963; m. (n.n.).
         ii.   Andrew Crawford "Andy", b.4 Jun 1966; d.28 Nov 2001; bur. Anderson Mem. Gardens, Ringgold, Catoosa Co., GA.

1317. Kenneth Julian "Ken"⁹ Abney (USArmy) (Raymond⁸, Grover⁷, Washington⁶, Wilburn⁵, Benjamin⁴, Hezekiah³, Elisha², Abner¹), b.26 Jun 1941. He m. Elizabeth "Faye" Crawford. He owned *Abney Tire and Lube*. He d.10 Dec 2005 at age 64 and was bur. Anderson Mem. Gardens, Ringgold, Catoosa Co., GA.
    Elizabeth "Faye" Crawford, b.21 Oct 1943 GA. She d.24 Aug 2017 GA at age 73 and was bur. Anderson Mem. Gardens, Ringgold.
Known children of Kenneth Julian "Ken"⁹ Abney (USArmy) and Elizabeth "Faye" Crawford: Paige¹⁰ m. (n.n.) McBryar; and Keith

1318. Lamar⁹ Abney (Marshall⁸, Grover⁷, Washington⁶, Wilburn⁵, Benjamin⁴, Hezekiah³, Elisha², Abner¹) m. (n.n.) and had issue:
         i.   Austin¹⁰.
         ii.   Jacqueline.

1319. Jackie⁹ Abney (Marshall⁸, Grover⁷, Washington⁶, Wilburn⁵, Benjamin⁴, Hezekiah³, Elisha², Abner¹) m. (n.n.) Wofford and had issue: Cam¹⁰.

1320. Denny⁹ Abney (Archie⁸, William⁷, Washington⁶, Wilburn⁵, Benjamin⁴, Hezekiah³, Elisha², Abner¹), b.17 Mar 1945 LaFayette, GA. He m. Rozanne "Rozy" Clements on 6 Aug 1966 and had issue:
         i.   Lucy¹⁰, b.4 Mar 1968.
         ii.   Pat, b. ca.1970.
         iii.   Noelle, b. ca.1976.
         iv.   Bo, b.27 Jul 1980.

1321. Carol⁹ Abney (Archie⁸, William⁷, Washington⁶, Wilburn⁵, Benjamin⁴, Hezekiah³, Elisha², Abner¹), b.18 Jan 1949 LaFayette, GA. She m. (n.n.) on Independence Day, 4 Jul 1967 and had issue:
         i.   Angie¹⁰, b. ca.1971.
         ii.   Kevin, b. ca.1974.

1322. Chris⁹ Abney (William⁸, William⁷, Washington⁶, Wilburn⁵, Benjamin⁴, Hezekiah³, Elisha², Abner¹), b.2 Mar 1944. She was a corporate executive director. She m. David Zeigler on 11 Sep 1966 and had issue:
         i.   Travis Alexander¹⁰, b.26 May 1974.

1323. Vicki Lynn[9] Abney (William[8], William[7], Washington[6], Wilburn[5], Benjamin[4], Hezekiah[3], Elisha[2], Abner[1]), b.7 Sep 1947. She m. J. Gaut Ragsdale on 24 Jun 1978. She lived in 1984 Baton Rouge, East Baton Rouge Par., LA.
Known child of Vicki Lynn[9] Abney and J. Gaut Ragsdale:
      i. Mary Lillian[10], b.10 Nov 1983.

1324. Wallace Randall "Randy"[9] Abney (Ross[8], William[7], Washington[6], Wilburn[5], Benjamin[4], Hezekiah[3], Elisha[2], Abner[1]), b.29 Mar 1946 Walker Co., GA. He m. Carolyn "Carol" Bennett, daughter of John Henry Bennett and Evelyn Nelms Bennett, on New Year's Day, 1 Jan 1967 Atlanta, Fulton Co., GA. He lived in 1984 LaFayette, GA.
    Carolyn "Carol" Bennett, b.29 Nov 1946 Madison Co., GA. She lived in 1984 LaFayette, GA.
Known children of Wallace Randall "Randy"[9] Abney and Carolyn "Carol" Bennett both b. Memorial Hospital, Chattanooga, TN,:
      i. Laura[10], b.20 Mar 1969. She m. (n.n.) Wilhoite. lived in 1984 LaFayette, GA.
     ii. Renee, b.6 Mar 1973. She m. (n.n.) Musick. lived in 1984 LaFayette, GA.

1325. Andy[9] Abney (Ross[8], William[7], Washington[6], Wilburn[5], Benjamin[4], Hezekiah[3], Elisha[2], Abner[1]), b. GA; m. Gail (Leslie) Thompson; issue:
      i. Adam[10], b. ca.1977.
     ii. Brandon, b. ca.1980.

1326. Sandy[9] Abney (Ross[8], William[7], Washington[6], Wilburn[5], Benjamin[4], Hezekiah[3], Elisha[2], Abner[1]), b. GA; m. John Shadden and had issue:
      i. Nicholas[10].
     ii. Catie.

1327. LaRaye[9] Abney (Garnet[8], William[7], Washington[6], Wilburn[5], Benjamin[4], Hezekiah[3], Elisha[2], Abner[1]), b. GA. She m1. Buddy Ely and had issue. She m2. Bob Holcomb, but no issue.
Known children of LaRaye[9] Abney and Buddy Ely:
      i. Tiffany[10].
     ii. Heather.

1328. Dale[9] Abney (Garnet[8], William[7], Washington[6], Wilburn[5], Benjamin[4], Hezekiah[3], Elisha[2], Abner[1]) m1. Harvey Hinkle. She m2. Bill Young.
Known child of Dale[9] Abney and Harvey Hinkle:
      i. Heath[10].

1329. Terry[9] Abney (Garnet[8], William[7], Washington[6], Wilburn[5], Benjamin[4], Hezekiah[3], Elisha[2], Abner[1]) m. Sandra Helms and had issue:
      i. Shannon[10].
     ii. Telly.
    iii. Ben.

1330. Jill[9] Abney (Garnet[8], William[7], Washington[6], Wilburn[5], Benjamin[4], Hezekiah[3], Elisha[2], Abner[1]) m1. Steve Marlin. She m2. Gary Browers.
Known child of Jill[9] Abney and Steve Marlin:
      i. Bret[10].

1331. Greg[9] Fricks (Martha[8] Abney, William[7], Washington[6], Wilburn[5], Benjamin[4], Hezekiah[3], Elisha[2], Abner[1]) m. Ramona (n.n.) and had issue:
   1443   i. Rie Rie[10], m. Michael Rubadue.
   1444   ii. Will, m. Karen (n.n.).
          iii. Grier m. Derek (n.n.).
          iv. Garret.

1332. Rob[9] Fricks (Martha[8] Abney, William[7], Washington[6], Wilburn[5], Benjamin[4], Hezekiah[3], Elisha[2], Abner[1]) m. Tami (n.n.) and had issue:
      i. Robert "Bo"[10].
     ii. Abney.
    iii. Mathis.

1333. Marsha[9] Fricks (Martha[8] Abney, William[7], Washington[6], Wilburn[5], Benjamin[4], Hezekiah[3], Elisha[2], Abner[1]). She had issue:
      i. Ashley[10].
     ii. Trey.

1334. James Edwin[9] Hall (USN) (George[8], Mattie[7] Abney, George[6], Benjamin[5], Benjamin[4], Hezekiah[3], Elisha[2], Abner[1]), b.8 Dec 1928 Henderson, Rusk Co., TX. He m. Annie Louis Robinson on 6 Sep 1950. He d.20 Sep 2018 Gilmer, Upshur Co., TX, at age 89.
Known children of James Edwin[9] Hall (USN) and Annie Louis Robinson:
      i. James Michael[10].
     ii. Cassie m. (n.n.) Nelson.
    iii. Deborah m. John Owen Stanley.

1335. Chester[9] Robinson Jr. (Patsy[8] Abney, Perino[7], George[6], Benjamin[5], Benjamin[4], Hezekiah[3], Elisha[2], Abner[1]), b.12 May 1953. He m. Mattie Godwin ca.1971. He d.4 Sep 1995 at age 42.
Known children of Chester[9] Robinson Jr. and Mattie Godwin:
      i. Ruth Ann (gen.)[10], b.6 Jun 1972. She m. Eric Ruesing. She lived in 1998 Gwinn, MI when she contacted the author through the *Centralized Abney Archives* website. She is a granddaughter of genealogist, Patsy Ruth Abney Robinson (#1033) and introduced the later to the author. They provided extensive research on the Benjamin Hezekiah Abney family.
          Eric Ruesing lived in 1998 Gwinn, MI.
     ii. Amanda Leigh, b.31 Aug 1976. She lived in 1998 Gilmer, Upshur Co., TX.

1336. Rossie "Jamay"[9] Morton (Bessie[8] Rowan, Falecia[7] Moore, Mary[6] Abney, Benjamin[5], Benjamin[4], Hezekiah[3], Elisha[2], Abner[1]), b.6 Dec 1936 Blount Co., AL. She m. Daniel Coy "DC" Williams ca.1956. She d.23 May 2020 at age 83; bur. Pleasant Grove Cem., Snead, Blount Co., AL.
    Daniel Coy "DC" Williams, b.21 Jan 1936. He d.25 Aug 2020 at age 84.
Known children of Rossie "Jamay"[9] Morton and Daniel Coy "DC" Williams:
        i.   Anita Kay[10] m. Bill Prickett.
       ii.   Amy Rochelle.

1337. Michael Earl[9] Moore (Earl[8], Henry[7], Mary[6] Abney, Benjamin[5], Benjamin[4], Hezekiah[3], Elisha[2], Abner[1]), b.1948 Jefferson Co., AL. He m. Janice (n.n.). He d.15 Jul 2019 Jefferson Co., AL and was bur. Highland Mem. Gardens, Bessemer, Jefferson Co., AL.
Known children of Michael Earl[9] Moore and Janice (n.n.):
        i.   Jason[10] m. Tammy (n.n.).
       ii.   Jerry.
      iii.   Allison m. Jason Tanner.

1338. Walter O'Neal[9] Culbert (John[8], Mary[7] Moore, Mary[6] Abney, Benjamin[5], Benjamin[4], Hezekiah[3], Elisha[2], Abner[1]), b.30 Apr 1938 AL. He m. Linda D. (n.n.). He d.18 Mar 2005 Tuscaloosa Co., AL, at age 66.
Known child of Walter O'Neal[9] Culbert and Linda D. (n.n.):
        i.   John[10].

1339. Barbara Ann[9] Moore (Moody[8], John[7], Mary[6] Abney, Benjamin[5], Benjamin[4], Hezekiah[3], Elisha[2], Abner[1]), b.18 May 1940 Albertville, Marshall Co., AL. She m. Gus Tom DeMoes in 1960. She d.6 Jul 2014 Houston, Harris Co., TX, at age 74 and was bur. Elmwood Cem.
    Gus Tom DeMoes, b.20 Jul 1939 Greece. He immigrated in 1947 to U.S.A., from Greece. He d.19 Jun 2012 Houston, Harris Co., TX, at age 72 and was bur. Elmwood Cem., Birmingham, Jefferson Co., AL.
Known child of Barbara Ann[9] Moore and Gus Tom DeMoes: i.   (son)[10].

1340. Jerry Wayne[9] Garrett (Beatrice[8] Moore, John[7], Mary[6] Abney, Benjamin[5], Benjamin[4], Hezekiah[3], Elisha[2], Abner[1]), b.21 Jul 1937. He m. Myra "Lynda" Strange ca.1959. He d.8 Nov 2014 at age 77 and was bur. Asbury UMC Cem., Asbury, Marshall Co., AL.
    Myra "Lynda" Strange, b.4 Aug 1943.
Known children of Jerry Wayne[9] Garrett and Myra "Lynda" Strange:
        i.   Jeff[10] m. Lisa (n.n.).
       ii.   Red m. Beth (n.n.).

1341. Cynthia[9] Moore (D.C.[8], John[7], Mary[6] Abney, Benjamin[5], Benjamin[4], Hezekiah[3], Elisha[2], Abner[1]) m. Edwin Cleveland "Pete" Brackett Jr. , b.23 Sep 1948 Greensboro, Guilford Co., NC. She d.18 Jan 2007 Concord, Cabarrus Co., NC, at age 58. She was cremated.
    Edwin Cleveland "Pete" Brackett Jr, b.27 Oct 1946 Mooresville, Iredell Co., NC; d.26 Nov 2004 North Myrtle Beach, Horry Co., SC, age 58.
Known children of Cynthia[9] Moore and Edwin Cleveland "Pete" Brackett Jr.:
        i.   Coleen[10] m. (n.n.) Keller.
       ii.   Allyson m. Mark Seymour.
      iii.   Mary Geneva.
   1445   iv.   Robin Braelli, m. Russell Juhl.
       v.   Candace MacIvey.

1342. Gay[9] Hefley (Richard[8], Margaret[7] Abney, James[6], Benjamin[5], Benjamin[4], Hezekiah[3], Elisha[2], Abner[1]) m. Gerald Wilhelm and had issue:
        i.   Brent[10].
       ii.   Lynnsey.

1343. Joy[9] Hefley (Richard[8], Margaret[7] Abney, James[6], Benjamin[5], Benjamin[4], Hezekiah[3], Elisha[2], Abner[1]) m. Alan Ritchie and had issue:
        i.   Jordan[10].
       ii.   Garrison.

1344. Bob[9] Hefley (Richard[8], Margaret[7] Abney, James[6], Benjamin[5], Benjamin[4], Hezekiah[3], Elisha[2], Abner[1]) m. Lewetta (n.n.) and had issue:
        i.   Marie[10].
       ii.   Glenn.
      iii.   Morgan.

1345. Sam[9] Abney (James[8], Temple[7], James[6], Benjamin[5], Benjamin[4], Hezekiah[3], Elisha[2], Abner[1]) m. Kathryn (n.n.) and had issue:
        i.   Shields[10].
       ii.   Porter.
      iii.   Heyward.

1346. Huston "Earl"[9] Abney (gen.) (Huston[8], Jasper[7], William[6], Benjamin[5], Benjamin[4], Hezekiah[3], Elisha[2], Abner[1]), b.22 Jul 1937 Tacoma, Pierce Co., WA. He m. Mary Louise Kendall (gen.), daughter of Jessie James Kendall and Bethel (n.n.). He lived in 1998 Puyallup, WA when the author began working with his wife, Mary on the Abney family history. Eventually, the author also made contact with Earl and their son, Jeff, both of whom were family genealogists. More recently, the author has enjoyed a close relationship with their other son, Mark Kendall Abney. Huston "Earl" Abney lived on 23 Jan 2017 St. George, UT. He d.28 Dec 2019 Saint George, Washington Co., UT, at age 82 and was bur. Sumner Cem.
    Mary Louise Kendall (gen.), b.25 Apr 1939 Tacoma, Pierce Co., WA; She lived in 1998 Puyallup, WA when the author began working with her on the Abney family. She was introduced to the author by genealogist, Sherry Combs (a descendant of Paul Abney [bapt.1699] who had contacted the author through the *Centralized Abney Archives* website). Mary was a wonderful, pleasant lady to work with. The majority of the information on the descendants of William "Henry" Abney (#289) came from Cousin Mary. She d.18 Aug 2003 WA and was buried in Sumner Cem., Sumner, Pierce Co., WA. Although an Abney by marriage only, her passing left a void in Abney family research and in the Abney family.

Known children of Huston "Earl"⁹ Abney (gen.) and Mary Louise Kendall (gen.):

    i.   Cynthia Louise "Cindy"¹⁰ m. Ken Cnossen and had issue: Sara; Jared.

    ii. Jeffery Earl "Jeff" (gen.) m. Mercedes Manalong and had issue: Francesca; Kayla. He lived in 1998 Round Rock, TX.

    iii. Mark Kendall, b.1962. He m1. Cynthia Marie Williford and had issue: Garrett Ashley (b.6 Aug 1984); Brittany Marie (b.18 Aug 1985); Alyssa Noel (b.24 Jun 1987); Christopher Ryan (b.27 Sep 1987). Mark m2. (n.n.) and had issue: Hallie Kendall Danielle; Addison Nicole; Mark m3. Terece Rossilyn Daines on 9 Aug 2008. Cousin Mark is one of the author's closest friends on social media. The author appreciates his straight-forward posts and often unique insight.

1347. John⁹ Chiles (Audra⁸, Cora⁷ Abney, William⁶, Benjamin⁵, Benjamin⁴, Hezekiah³, Elisha², Abner¹) was an attorney; m. (n.n.) and had issue (birth order unknown): Mary¹⁰; Anna; and Robert.

1348. Herman Ree⁹ Vogel (Grover⁸, Vellie⁷ Abney, David⁶, Benjamin⁵, Benjamin⁴, Hezekiah³, Elisha², Abner¹), b.1935. He m. Barbara Jean Brown on 18 Jul 1959. He d.2007 and was bur. Eastlawn Mem. Park, Early, Brown Co., Tx.
    Barbara Jean Brown, b.29 Jul 1940. She d.15 Sep 2017 at age 77 and was bur. Eastlawn Mem. Park, Early, Brown Co., Tx.
Known children of Herman Ree⁹ Vogel and Barbara Jean Brown:

    i.   Gregory Wayne¹⁰, b.6 May 1961. He d.9 Nov 1990 at age 29 and was bur. Eastlawn Mem. Park, Early, Brown Co., Tx.

    ii. Donna.

1349. Billy Kyle "Wild Bill"⁹ Vogel Sr. (Grover⁸, Vellie⁷ Abney, David⁶, Benjamin⁵, Benjamin⁴, Hezekiah³, Elisha², Abner¹), b.23 Jul 1941. He m. Kathy Jean "Katie" Moody in 1961 Monahans, Ward Co., TX. He d.20 Oct 1999 at age 58 and was bur. Bangs Cem., Bangs, Brown Co., TX.
    Kathy Jean "Katie" Moody, b.8 Mar 1946. She d.21 Jan 2017 at age 70 and was bur. Bangs Cem., Bangs, Brown Co., TX.
Known children of Billy Kyle "Wild Bill"⁹ Vogel Sr. and Kathy Jean "Katie" Moody (unsure of birth order): Billy Kyle¹⁰; Karen m. (n.n.) Taylor; Bobby Joe; Jerry Powell; Tammy; Sharon m. (n.n.) Petty; Missie m. (n.n.) Lawson; Angela; Grover "Wayne" (b.7 Sep 1967. He d.27 Feb 2011 at age 43 and was bur. Bangs Cem., Bangs, Brown Co., TX).

1350. Vernon Kenneth⁹ Vogel (Thomas⁸, Vellie⁷ Abney, David⁶, Benjamin⁵, Benjamin⁴, Hezekiah³, Elisha², Abner¹), b.11 May 1937 Waco, McLennan Co., TX. He m. Teddie Irene Pairsh (b.9 Jul 1939 Webb Co., TX) on 22 Jun 1957. He d.25 Aug 2013 Irving, Dallas Co., TX, at age 76 and was bur. Oak Branch Cem., Waxahachie, Ellis Co., TX.
Known children of Vernon Kenneth⁹ Vogel and Teddie Irene Pairsh (unsure of birth order): Vikki¹⁰; Kregg; and Valli m. Kevin (n.n.).

1351. Yvonne Catherine "Vonnie"⁹ Wahrman (Evelyn⁸ Rooks, John⁷, Eva⁶ Abney, Benjamin⁵, Benjamin⁴, Hezekiah³, Elisha², Abner¹), b.22 Jun 1954 France. She m1. Arthur Santellano and had issue. She m2. Ted Jolly but no issue. She d.24 Apr 2000 Mission Viejo, Orange Co., CA, at age 45 and was bur. Green Hills Mem. Park, Rancho Palos Verdes, Los Angeles Co., CA.
Known children of Yvonne Catherine "Vonnie"⁹ Wahrman and Arthur Santellano: Katrina¹⁰; Anita.

1352. Sherwyn Lane⁹ McNair (USN-WWII) (Cora⁸ Foster, Dultsenia⁷ Reeves, Sarah⁶ Abney, Andrew⁵, Benjamin⁴, Hezekiah³, Elisha², Abner¹), b.13 Apr 1923 Pritchett, Upshur Co., TX. He m. Lesta "Chere" Livingston on 15 Jun 1952 at the family home, Marfa, Presidio Co., TX. He d.30 Nov 2016 at age 93 and was bur. Texas St. Vets. Cem., Abilene, Jones Co., TX.
    Lesta "Chere" Livingston, b.9 Jul 1930 Marfa, Presidio Co., TX. She d.30 Aug 2018 at age 88 and was bur. Texas St. Vets. Cem., Abilene.
Known children of Sherwyn Lane⁹ McNair (USN-WWII) and Lesta "Chere" Livingston: Nancy¹⁰ m. Jim Jones; Melinda m. Frank Rausch.

1353. Sheila⁹ Dunn (Jewel⁸ Stevens, Sarah⁷ Sargent, Amanda⁶ Abney, Andrew⁵, Benjamin⁴, Hezekiah³, Elisha², Abner¹), b.12 Aug 1946 Mount Pleasant, Titus Co., TX; m. Jackie Barrett in 1974; d.3 Feb 2001 White Settlement, Tarrant Co., TX, age 54; bur. Jesse Cem., Jesse, OK.
    Jackie Ray Barrett Sr, b.26 Sep 1937 Stonewall, Pontotoc Co., OK. He m1. Linda Kay Ireland in 1957. He d.9 Mar 2002 Fort Worth, Tarrant Co., TX, at age 64 and was bur. Jesse Cem., Jesse, Pontotoc Co., OK. Known child of Sheila⁹ Dunn and Jackie Ray Barrett Sr.: Shamra¹⁰.

1354. Neal⁹ Moss (Ocie⁸ Sargent, John⁷, Amanda⁶ Abney, Andrew⁵, Benjamin⁴, Hezekiah³, Elisha², Abner¹), b.3 Jan 1934 Cookville, Titus Co., TX. He m. Johnnie Jean Parker in 1955. He d.13 Feb 2016 at age 82 and was bur. Smithfield Cem., North Richland Hills, Tarrant Co., TX.
    Johnnie Jean Parker, b.10 Aug 1938. She d.10 Dec 2004 at age 66; bur. Smithfield Cem., North Richland Hills, Tarrant Co., TX. Known children of Neal⁹ Moss and Johnnie Jean Parker: Rick¹⁰ m. Kolleen (n.n.); David m. Rhonda (n.n.); Kathy m. (n.n.) Jones; Sherry m. Steve Hampton.

1355. Charles Lee "Nebo"⁹ Sargent (Johnnie⁸, George⁷, Amanda⁶ Abney, Andrew⁵, Benjamin⁴, Hezekiah³, Elisha², Abner¹) m. Teresa (n.n.). He, b.9 Sep 1941 Mount Pleasant, Titus Co., TX. He d.20 Jul 2011 Mount Pleasant, Titus Co., TX, at age 69. Known children of Charles Lee "Nebo"⁹ Sargent and Teresa (n.n.): Johnnie Roper¹⁰; Jeff m. Michelle (n.n.); Gaylon m. Gary Straka; Pattie m. (n.n.) Stinson.

1356. Randolph "Randy"⁹ Sargent (Johnnie⁸, George⁷, Amanda⁶ Abney, Andrew⁵, Benjamin⁴, Hezekiah³, Elisha², Abner¹) m. Sherry Poole. He, b.9 Oct 1948 Mount Pleasant, Titus Co., TX. He d.14 Apr 2015 at age 66 and was bur. Maple Springs Cem., Newsome, Camp Co., TX.
Known child of Randolph "Randy"⁹ Sargent and Sherry Poole:

    i.   Randy Aaron "Stallings"¹⁰, b.2 Jul 1982 Waco, McLennan Co., TX. He d.24 Oct 2010 Wood Co., TX, at age 28 and was bur. Maple Springs Cem., Newsome, Camp Co., TX.

1357. Jewel⁹ Pelfrey (Thomas⁸, Haze⁷ Ellison, Sarah⁶ Abney, Hezekiah⁵, Benjamin⁴, Hezekiah³, Elisha², Abner¹), b.1 Dec 1932 Maysville, Garvin Co., OK. She m. Jesse H. "Whiff" Palmertree Sr. (USN-WWII). She d.22 Sep 2016 Wynnewood, Garvin Co., OK, at age 83 and was bur. Oaklawn Cem., Wynnewood, Garvin Co., OK.
    Jesse H. "Whiff" Palmertree Sr. (USN-WWII), b.30 Jul 1921. He d.13 Nov 1986 at age 65.
Known children of Jewel⁹ Pelfrey and Jesse H. "Whiff" Palmertree Sr. (USN-WWII):

    i.   Nancy¹⁰.

    ii. Yvonna.

    iii. Phyllis.

    iv. Jesse H. "Jay", b.10 Sep 1954. He d.12 May 2011 at age 56 and was bur. Oaklawn Cem., Wynnewood, Garvin Co., OK.

1358. CMSgt. Emmett Lewis[9] Matthews (USAF-WWII) (Vera[8] Pelfrey, Haze[7] Ellison, Sarah[6] Abney, Hezekiah[5], Benjamin[4], Hezekiah[3], Elisha[2], Abner[1]), b.8 Feb 1920 Stratford, Garvin Co., OK. He m. Betty Kathryn McGee on 5 Nov 1949 Fort Worth, Tarrant Co., TX. He d.15 Sep 2012 Pauls Valley, Garvin Co., OK, at age 92.
> Betty Kathryn McGee, b. Independence Day, 4 Jul 1927 Pauls Valley, Garvin Co., OK. She d.20 Jul 2007 Paoli, Garvin Co., OK, at age 80 and was bur. Mount Olivet Cem., Pauls Valley, Garvin Co., OK.
Known child of CMSgt. Emmett Lewis[9] Matthews (USAF-WWII) and Betty Kathryn McGee:
> 1446   i.   Emmett "Butch"[10], m. Jo Ann (n.n.).

1359. Elston Lee "Chuck"[9] Gentry Jr. (Patsy[8] Abney, Clifton[7], George[6], Hezekiah[5], Benjamin[4], Hezekiah[3], Elisha[2], Abner[1]) m. Kecia (n.n.). He, b.14 Dec 1954 Rome, Floyd Co., GA. He d.19 Dec 2010 Rome, Floyd Co., GA, age 56; bur. Oaknoll Mem. Gardens Cem., Rome, Floyd Co., GA.
Known child of Elston Lee "Chuck"[9] Gentry Jr. and Kecia (n.n.):
> i.   Randy[10].

1360. Laura[9] Gentry (Patsy[8] Abney, Clifton[7], George[6], Hezekiah[5], Benjamin[4], Hezekiah[3], Elisha[2], Abner[1]) m. Donny Key and had issue: Andy[10].

1361. James "Jimmy"[9] Gentry (Patsy[8] Abney, Clifton[7], George[6], Hezekiah[5], Benjamin[4], Hezekiah[3], Elisha[2], Abner[1]) m. Darlene (n.n.) and had issue: Randy[10].

1362. Starlin Jackson "Jack"[9] Jarvis Sr (Troy[8], Samantha[7] Abney, George[6], George[5], Benjamin[4], Hezekiah[3], Elisha[2], Abner[1]), b.19 Sep 1941 Jefferson Co., AL. He m. (n.n.). He d.6 Mar 2015 Cumming, Forsyth Co., GA, at age 73; bur. Bivens Chapel Cem., Brookside, Jefferson Co., GA.
Known child of Starlin Jackson "Jack"[9] Jarvis Sr and (n.n.):
> i.   Starlin Jackson[10].

1363. Jerrell Wayne[9] Abney (gen.) (Paul[8], King[7], George[6], George[5], Benjamin[4], Hezekiah[3], Elisha[2], Abner[1]), b.2 Oct 1949 Birmingham, Jefferson Co., AL. He m. Kathy Marie Mayo ca.1982. He and Kathy Marie Mayo were divorced in 1986. Cousin Jerrell lived in 1998 Birmingham, Jefferson Co., AL when he made contact with the author through the old *Centralized Abney Archives*. Much of the information on the line of Pvt. George Washington Abney Sr. (CSA) (#109) came as a result of the author working with Cousin Jerrell (who proved to be very generous with his research).
Known child of Jerrell Wayne[9] Abney (gen.) and Kathy Marie Mayo:
> i.   Katie Marye[10], b.30 Nov 1983 Birmingham, Jefferson Co., AL.

1364. Carolyn Ruth[9] Easter (Mary[8] Fuller, Daisy[7] Abney, George[6], George[5], Benjamin[4], Hezekiah[3], Elisha[2], Abner[1]) m. Reid Lamphere; had issue:
> i.   Tiffany[10].
> 1447   ii.   Jeremiah, m. (n.n.) Shalome.

1365. Cynthia Ellen[9] Easter (Mary[8] Fuller, Daisy[7] Abney, George[6], George[5], Benjamin[4], Hezekiah[3], Elisha[2], Abner[1]) m. (n.n.) Rogers & had issue:
> i.   Lindsey[10].
> ii.   Grant.

1366. Mildred Faye[9] Abney (Johnny[8], Homer[7], John[6], George[5], Benjamin[4], Hezekiah[3], Elisha[2], Abner[1]), b.3 Feb 1938 TX. She m. Gerald Franklin Shaw in 1958. She d.10 Apr 2018 at age 80 and was bur. High Cem., Canton, Van Zandt Co., TX.
> Gerald Franklin Shaw, b.17 Jul 1936 Wallace, Van Zandt Co., TX. He d.9 Oct 2014 Canton, Van Zandt Co., TX, at age 78; bur. High Cem.
Known child of Mildred Faye[9] Abney and Gerald Franklin Shaw:
> i.   Robert[10], b. TX.

1367. Sandra[9] Lancaster (Wanda[8] Carrigan, Mina[7] Abney, John[6], George[5], Benjamin[4], Hezekiah[3], Elisha[2], Abner[1]) m. Brad Zastrow and had issue:
> i.   Lauren[10].
> ii.   Blake.

1368. Patricia Ann[9] Myers (Herman[8], Ludie[7] Abney, Alex[6], George[5], Benjamin[4], Hezekiah[3], Elisha[2], Abner[1]), b.8 Dec 1946. She m. Louie Edward Talley in 1971.
> Louie Edward Talley, b.4 Feb 1941. He d.21 Feb 1999 at age 58 and was bur. Walker Chapel Mem. Gardens, Fultondale, Jefferson Co., AL.
Known child of Patricia Ann[9] Myers and Louie Edward Talley:
> i.   Jeanne Kay[10], b.17 Feb 1966. She m. Patrick Weinreich (b.3 Jan 1964). d.14 Sep 2012 Trafford, Jefferson Co., AL, at age 46 and was bur. Mount Zion Meth. Ch. Cem., Cullman, Cullman Co., AL.

1369. Thomas Ashley[9] Abney (Tommy[8], John[7], Alex[6], George[5], Benjamin[4], Hezekiah[3], Elisha[2], Abner[1]) m. Angela (n.n.) and had issue:
> i.   Ashlyn Danielle[10].
> ii.   Austin.
> iii. Ashton "Gage."

1370. Susan Denise[9] Abney (Tommy[8], John[7], Alex[6], George[5], Benjamin[4], Hezekiah[3], Elisha[2], Abner[1]) m. (n.n.) Tracy and had issue:
> 1448   i.   Joseph David[10], m. Tiffani (n.n.).

1371. Christi Jean[9] Abney (Tommy[8], John[7], Alex[6], George[5], Benjamin[4], Hezekiah[3], Elisha[2], Abner[1]) m. David Widener and had issue:
> i.   Stephen Harris[10].
> ii.   Nicholas Glen m. Kelsie (n.n.).

1372. Debra[9] Fromhold (Helen[8] Abney, George[7], Peter[6], George[5], Benjamin[4], Hezekiah[3], Elisha[2], Abner[1]) m. (n.n.) Aaron and had issue:
> i.   Kimberly[10] m. David McGee.

1373. Rhonda Michelle^9 Madden (Harry^8, Elizabeth^7 Abney, James^6, George^5, Benjamin^4, Hezekiah^3, Elisha^2, Abner^1), b.27 Mar 1966. She m. Thomas D. "McFee" McPherson. d.1 Dec 2016 Augusta, Richmond Co., GA, at age 50.
    Thomas D. "McFee" McPherson, b.24 Jul 1956. He d.18 Mar 2007 at age 50 and was bur. Westover Mem. Park, Augusta, Richmond Co., GA. Known children of Rhonda Michelle^9 Madden and Thomas D. "McFee" McPherson:
        i.   Ben^{10}.
        ii. Jake.
        iii. Caroline.

1374. Mark^9 Hensel (Carol^8 Abney, Joe^7, William^6, William^5, Benjamin^4, Hezekiah^3, Elisha^2, Abner^1) m. Lauren (n.n.) and had issue: Ruby^{10}.

1375. Sandra^9 Baswell (William^8, Pearl^7 Lorren, Leticia^6 Abney, Eli^5, Benjamin^4, Hezekiah^3, Elisha^2, Abner^1) m. (n.n.) Holmes; had issue: Hillery^{10}.

1376. Shirley^9 Baswell (William^8, Pearl^7 Lorren, Leticia^6 Abney, Eli^5, Benjamin^4, Hezekiah^3, Elisha^2, Abner^1) m. Jackie Black and had issue:
        i.   Ethan^{10}.
        ii. Jacob.

1377. Nancy^9 Ross (Betty^8 Abney, John^7, Eli^6, Eli^5, Benjamin^4, Hezekiah^3, Elisha^2, Abner^1) m. (n.n.) Plemons and had issue:
        i.   Shannon^{10}.
        ii. Bryan.

1378. Norman Christopher "Chris"^{9} Ross (Betty^8 Abney, John^7, Eli^6, Eli^5, Benjamin^4, Hezekiah^3, Elisha^2, Abner^1), b.1 Oct 1965. He m. (n.n.). He d.14 Jul 2014 Rossville, Walker Co., GA, at age 48. He was cremated.
Known children of Norman Christopher "Chris"^{9} Ross and (n.n.):
        i.   Blake Christopher^{10}.
        ii. Christian "Elizabeth" m. (n.n.) Andrews.

1379. Mike^9 Abney (James^8, William^7, Posey^6, Eli^5, Benjamin^4, Hezekiah^3, Elisha^2, Abner^1) m. (n.n.) and had issue: Cody^{10}; Callie.

1380. Ginger^9 Abney (James^8, William^7, Posey^6, Eli^5, Benjamin^4, Hezekiah^3, Elisha^2, Abner^1) m. Kennon Wilson and had issue: Vaughn^{10}.

1381. Jessica^9 (n.n.) (Cynthia^8 Echols, Mazelle^7 Abney, John^6, Eli^5, Benjamin^4, Hezekiah^3, Elisha^2, Abner^1). She had a daughter.

1382. Amy^9 Farrer (Hazel^8 Abney, Henry^7, Marion^6, James^5, Benjamin^4, Hezekiah^3, Elisha^2, Abner^1) m. (n.n.) Drummond and had issue: Katie^{10}.

1383. MSgt. Robert Bryant "Bob"^{9} Abney Jr. (USAF-Persian Gulf) (Robert^8, William^7, Marion^6, James^5, Benjamin^4, Hezekiah^3, Elisha^2, Abner^1), b.23 Feb 1957. He m. Ingeborg (n.n.). They div. 2000. He d.28 Mar 2016 at age 59; bur. Tallahassee National Cem., Tallahassee, Leon Co., FL.
Known child of MSgt. Robert Bryant "Bob"^{9} Abney Jr. (USAF-Persian Gulf) and Ingeborg (n.n.):
        i.   Megan Nicole^{10}, b.19 Sep 1987 Bitburg, Rhineland-Palatinate, Germany. She d.30 Aug 2010 at age 22 in an auto accident. She was bur. Tallahassee National Cem., Tallahassee, Leon Co., FL.

1384. Luther Dale^9 Abney Sr. (Billy^8, William^7, Marion^6, James^5, Benjamin^4, Hezekiah^3, Elisha^2, Abner^1), b.16 Feb 1958. He m. Penny Ann Thistlewood, but no issue. He d.5 Jun 2006 at age 48 and was bur. Ramah Bapt. Ch. Cem., Gordon, Wilkinson Co., GA.
    Penny Ann Thistlewood, b.23 Dec 1968. She d.24 Oct 2013 at age 44 and was bur. Ramah Bapt. Ch. Cem., Gordon, Wilkinson Co., GA.
Known child of Luther Dale^9 Abney Sr. and (n.n.):
        i.   Luther Dale Jr.^{10}.

1385. Jerry Lee^9 Newberry (Bertha^8 Cox, Dovie^7 Miller, Geretie^6 Abney, James^5, Benjamin^4, Hezekiah^3, Elisha^2, Abner^1), b.17 Mar 1938 Floyd Co., GA. He m. Gloria Faye Ingram. He d.21 Jan 1973 Rome, Floyd Co., GA, at age 34 and was bur. Pleasant Hope Cem., Rome, Floyd Co., GA.
    Gloria Faye Ingram, b.22 Jul 1940. She d.24 Jul 1993 at age 53 and was bur. Pleasant Hope Cem., Rome, Floyd Co., GA.
Known child of Jerry Lee^9 Newberry and Gloria Faye Ingram:
        i.   Anita Jo^{10}, b.23 Dec 1960 Rome, Floyd Co., GA; d.3 May 2018 Rome, Floyd Co., GA, age 57; bur. Pleasant Hope Cem.

1386. Travis Darrell^9 Newberry Sr. (Bertha^8 Cox, Dovie^7 Miller, Geretie^6 Abney, James^5, Benjamin^4, Hezekiah^3, Elisha^2, Abner^1), b.18 Feb 1948. He m. Joann (n.n.). He d.21 Jan 2013 at age 64 and was bur. Lindale Cem., Lindale, Floyd Co., GA.
Known children of Travis Darrell^9 Newberry Sr. and Joann (n.n.) (birth order unknown):
        i.   Robin^{10} m. Enrique Cordova.
        ii. Travis Darrell.
        iii. Ted Lamar.
        iv. Jason m. Jessica (n.n.).

1387. Michael^9 Abney (Philip^8, Benjamin^7, John^6, Charles^5, Benjamin^4, Hezekiah^3, Elisha^2, Abner^1) m. Andrea (n.n.) & had issue: Amelia^{10}; Liam.

1388. Kristen^9 Abney (Philip^8, Benjamin^7, John^6, Charles^5, Benjamin^4, Hezekiah^3, Elisha^2, Abner^1) m. Cameron Dupree and had issue: Kolie^{10}.

1389. Patty L.^{9} Short (Georgia^8 Marcum, Ethel^7 Abney, John^6, Pinkney^5, Wiley^4, Hezekiah^3, Elisha^2, Abner^1), b.10 Jun 1948 Middlesboro, Bell Co., KY. She m. Jim Cox ca.1968; d.21 Nov 2008 Pennington Gap, Lee Co., VA, age 60; bur. Lee Memorial Gardens, Woodway, Lee Co., VA.
Known children of Patty L.^{9} Short and Jim Cox:
        i.   Dena^{10} m. Jerome Dean.
        ii. Chad.
  1450   iii. Benjamin Lee "Ben," b. 27 Dec 1973 Middlesboro, Bell Co., KY; m. Rebecca (n.n.).

1390. Ken^9 Marcum (Paul^8, Ethel^7 Abney, John^6, Pinkney^5, Wiley^4, Hezekiah^3, Elisha^2, Abner^1) m. Lucretia (n.n.) and had issue:
       i.   Zach^{10}.
       ii.   Nick m. Erin (n.n.).

1391. Louise^9 Marcum (Paul^8, Ethel^7 Abney, John^6, Pinkney^5, Wiley^4, Hezekiah^3, Elisha^2, Abner^1) m. Larry Hartley and had issue: Traci^{10}.

1392. Brenda^9 Marcum (Paul^8, Ethel^7 Abney, John^6, Pinkney^5, Wiley^4, Hezekiah^3, Elisha^2, Abner^1) m. Bob Walker and had issue: Shane^{10}.

1393. Loretta^9 Marcum (Paul^8, Ethel^7 Abney, John^6, Pinkney^5, Wiley^4, Hezekiah^3, Elisha^2, Abner^1), b.6 Feb 1963. She m. Charlie Rouse (b.28 Dec 1965) on 20 Jun 1986. She d.14 Jul 2004 at age 41 and was bur. Old Campbell Cem., Rose Hill, Lee Co., VA.
Known child of Loretta^9 Marcum and Charlie Rouse:
      1451   i.   Chad^{10}, m. Marie (n.n.).

1394. Delores Darlene^9 Dixon (gen.) (Margaret^8 Abney, John^7, John^6, Pinkney^5, Wiley^4, Hezekiah^3, Elisha^2, Abner^1), b.1957. She m1. (n.n.) Irwin but no issue. She m2. Edward Nove "Eddie" Renfroe (gen.) on 1 Oct 1972 Wallowa, Wallowa Co., OR. The author only recently "met" Cousins Delores and Eddie over social media. They have been found to be wonderful patriots and lovers of their family. They generously provided the information on the family of Margaret "Marie" Abney (#1155). The author plans to keep this communication going for years to come.
Known children of Delores Darlene^9 Dixon (gen.) and Edward Nove "Eddie" Renfroe (gen.):
       i.   Rose Ethel^{10}, b.18 Apr 1973 Enterprise, Wallowa Co., OR.
       ii.   Angelique Ranea, b.21 Aug 1974 Cottage Grove, Lane Co., OR.
       iii.   Edward Albert "Eddie", b.24 Jan 1979 Enterprise, Wallowa Co., OR.

1395. Penny^9 Brewer (gen.) (Sarilee^8 Roberts, Bernice^7 Abna, Robert^6, James^5, James^4 Abney, Hezekiah^3, Elisha^2, Abner^1), b.22 Oct 1961 Longview, Gregg Co., TX. She m1. Timothy Andrew Daniel in Longview, Gregg Co., TX. She m2. Dale Wade Blankinship on 8 Jun 1991 Fort Worth, Tarrant Co., TX. She lived in 1998 TX when she contacted the author via the *Centralized Abney Archives* website. She was the author's first introduction to the *Abna* family of Georgia; and is the informant for most of the information on the *Abna* descendants. She was a great blessing to this author. Her work eventually, and unknowingly, added an additional surname to the title of this book, *Abney, Abner, **Abna**, Abnee*.
     Timothy Andrew Daniel, b.22 May 1951 El Paso, El Paso Co., TX.
Known child of Penny^9 Brewer (gen.) and Timothy Andrew Daniel:
       i.   Grant Royce^{10}, b.17 Jul 1986 Longview, Gregg Co., TX. He was bapt.17 Jul 1994.
     Dale Wade Blankinship, b.8 Apr 1957 Fort Worth, Tarrant Co., TX.
Known child of Penny^9 Brewer (gen.) and Dale Wade Blankinship:
       i.   Morgan Eliza^{10}, b.6 Jul 1993 Fort Worth, Tarrant Co., TX.

1396. James David^9 Brewer (Sarilee^8 Roberts, Bernice^7 Abna, Robert^6, James^5, James^4 Abney, Hezekiah^3, Elisha^2, Abner^1), b.13 Oct 1964 Longview, Gregg Co., TX. He m. Kayce Lynn May on 7 Jul 1991 Temple, Bell Co., TX.
     Kayce Lynn May, b.3 Oct 1966 Fort Worth, Tarrant Co., TX.
Known child of James David^9 Brewer and Kayce Lynn May:
       i.   Samantha Leighann^{10}, b.23 Mar 1997 Dallas, Dallas Co., TX.

1397. Ashley P.^{9} Scarborough (Pamela^8 Abna, William^7, Ales^6, James^5, James^4 Abney, Hezekiah^3, Elisha^2, Abner^1), b.20 Apr 1982. She d.24 Aug 2007 at age 25 and was bur. Jackson City Cem., Jackson, Butts Co., GA.
Known child of Ashley P.^{9} Scarborough: i.   Gracie^{10}.

1398. Dewana Rene^9 Brincefield (William^8, Lonie^7 Hightower, Levia^6 Johnson, Sarah^5 Abney, Joel^4, Hezekiah^3, Elisha^2, Abner^1), b.30 May 1967 Wenatchee, Chelan Co., WA; m. Scott Browne on 8 Aug 1998; d.29 Jan 2011, age 43; bur. Greenacres Mem. Park, Ferndale, Whatcom Co., WA.
Known children of Dewana Rene^9 Brincefield and Scott Browne:
       i.   Logan^{10}, b. ca.2001.
       ii.   Blakely, b. ca.2004.

1399. Ronald Dean "Ron"^{9} Brincefield (George^8, Lonie^7 Hightower, Levia^6 Johnson, Sarah^5 Abney, Joel^4, Hezekiah^3, Elisha^2, Abner^1), b.14 Aug 1945 and d.7 Aug 1995 Wenatchee, Chelan Co., WA, age 49; bur. Evergreen Mem. Park, East Wenatchee, Douglas Co., WA.
Known child of Ronald Dean "Ron"^{9} Brincefield:
       i.   Jeffery Troy^{10}, b.31 Mar 1969 Wenatchee, Chelan Co., WA. He d.2 Dec 2007 truck accident, (near) Naches, Yakima Co., WA, at age 38. He was cremated.

1400. Janice Katherine "Jan"^{9} Miller (gen.) (Sarah^8 Hodnett, Lucinda^7 Wininger, Minnie^6 Abney, John^5, Joel^4, Hezekiah^3, Elisha^2, Abner^1), b.30 Oct 1954 Potter Air Force Base, Amarillo, Potter Co., TX. She m. William Burt Elliott on 24 Mar 1979 Ringgold, Catoosa Co., GA. They lived in 1998 Chattanooga, Hamilton Co., TN. The very amicable Cousin Jan contacted the author in 1998 through the now defunct *Abney GenForum*. She is the primary source for the descendants of Joel Jonathan Abney (#31), son of Hezekiah Abney (#1). The information provided by Cousin Jan, printed here, will certainly be a great aid to those descended Joel J. Abney. Her gracious sharing of her information will never be forgotten.
     William Burt Elliott, b.19 Sep 1953 Chattanooga, Hamilton Co., TN.
Known children of Janice Katherine "Jan"^{9} Miller (gen.) and William Burt Elliott both b. Chattanooga, Hamilton Co., TN,:
       i.   Brett Patterson^{10}, b.27 Sep 1980. He lived in 1998 Chattanooga, Hamilton Co., TN.
       ii.   Megan Suzanne, b.28 Jan 1984. She lived in 1998 Chattanooga, Hamilton Co., TN.

1401. Dana Earl^9 Miller (Sarah^8 Hodnett, Lucinda^7 Wininger, Minnie^6 Abney, John^5, Joel^4, Hezekiah^3, Elisha^2, Abner^1), b.1 Sep 1955 Chattanooga, Hamilton Co., TN. He m. Julie Ann Inkster in 1978 Chattanooga, Hamilton Co., TN.
Known child of Dana Earl^9 Miller and Julie Ann Inkster:
       i.   Danielle Elise^{10}, b.1978. She m. Jimmy Elliott in 1997 Lenexa, Johnson Co., KS.

1402. Jeffrey Allen⁹ Miller (Sarah⁸ Hodnett, Lucinda⁷ Wininger, Minnie⁶ Abney, John⁵, Joel⁴, Hezekiah³, Elisha², Abner¹), b.10 Jul 1960 Chattanooga, Hamilton Co., TN. He m. Sharon Morgan. They were divorced.
Known children of Jeffrey Allen⁹ Miller and Sharon Morgan:
    i. Jennifer Nicole¹⁰, b.1984.
    ii. Jeremy Nicholas, b.1986.

1403. Cindy⁹ Abney (James⁸, John⁷, William⁶, John⁵, Joel⁴, Hezekiah³, Elisha², Abner¹) m. Steven North Sr.
Known children of Cindy⁹ Abney and Steven North Sr.:
    i. Steven¹⁰.
    ii. Matthew.
    iii. Joshua.

1404. Robert Taylor⁹ Barger (Clarence⁸, Mamie⁷ Abner, Robert⁶, William⁵, Willis⁴, Elisha³, Elisha² Abney, Abner¹), b.1 Feb 1948. He m. Bonnie Morgan. He d.5 Dec 2003 at age 55 and was bur. Laurel Cem., Laurel, Clermont Co., OH.
  Bonnie Morgan, b.10 Jan 1948. She m2. Edward Moore on 8 Jul 1978. She d.5 Sep 2007 at age 59 and was bur. Pierce Township Cem., Pierce Township, Clermont Co., OH.
Known children of Robert Taylor⁹ Barger and Bonnie Morgan:
    i. Robert¹⁰ m. Angela (n.n.).
  1452 ii. Byron W., b. 8 Jun 1971; m. Misty Humphries.

1405. John Lee⁹ Abner Sr. (David⁸, Elbert⁷, Robert⁶, William⁵, Willis⁴, Elisha³, Elisha² Abney, Abner¹) m. Debbie (n.n.) and had issue:
  1453 i. John Lee "Johnny"¹⁰, m. (n.n.).
    ii. Christopher (gen.). The author only began working with Cousin Christopher in 2019, when he began working on this book. Cousin Christopher was kind enough to share his knowledge of his Abner line for inclusion in this volume. For this, the author is very grateful.
    iii. Matthew.

1406. Mark Steven⁹ Abner (Steven⁸, Elbert⁷, Robert⁶, William⁵, Willis⁴, Elisha³, Elisha² Abney, Abner¹), b.28 Apr 1972. He m. Roxanne Lambert. He d.17 Jul 2004 at age 32 and was bur. Laurel Cem., Laurel, Clermont Co., OH.
Known children of Mark Steven⁹ Abner and Roxanne Lambert:
    i. Robert¹⁰.
    ii. Saraya.

1407. Anna⁹ Napier (Billie⁸, Eldren⁷, Hannah⁶ Abner, William⁵, Willis⁴, Elisha³, Elisha² Abney, Abner¹) m. (n.n.) Barlish and had issue:
    i. Lindsey¹⁰.

1408. Sherry⁹ Napier (Billie⁸, Eldren⁷, Hannah⁶ Abner, William⁵, Willis⁴, Elisha³, Elisha² Abney, Abner¹) m. Jimmie Bruhn and had issue:
    i. Kaleigh¹⁰.
    ii. Andrew.

1409. Steven James⁹ Sanders (Ola⁸ Oliver, Elizabeth⁷ Abner, Edward⁶, Elisha⁵, Willis⁴, Elisha³, Elisha² Abney, Abner¹), b.21 Jan 1975; m. (n.n.); d.29 Oct 2013 Fayette Regional Health Sys. ER, Connersville, Fayette Co., IN, at age 38 and was bur. Dale Cem., Connersville, Fayette Co., IN.
Known children of Steven James⁹ Sanders and (n.n.): two daughters and one son.

1410. Jeremiah Dan⁹ Koontz (Deborah⁸ Oliver, Elizabeth⁷ Abner, Edward⁶, Elisha⁵, Willis⁴, Elisha³, Elisha² Abney, Abner¹), b.27 Jan 1982 Madison, Jefferson Co., IN. He d.10 Aug 2012 Madison, Jefferson Co., IN, at age 30 and was bur. Springdale Cem., Madison, Jefferson Co., IN.
Known child of Jeremiah Dan⁹ Koontz:
    i. James A.¹⁰.

1411. William⁹ Collins (Melita⁸ Oliver, Elizabeth⁷ Abner, Edward⁶, Elisha⁵, Willis⁴, Elisha³, Elisha² Abney, Abner¹) m. Ashley (n.n.) & had issue:
    i. Alexis¹⁰.
    ii. Aubriana.
    iii. Carión.

1412. James "Jimmy"⁹ Van Horn (Martha⁸ Delph, Jennie⁷ Abner, Robert⁶, James⁵, Richard⁴, Menan³, Elisha² Abney, Abner¹), b.2 Sep 1844. He m. Patricia Kay Parks. He and Patricia Kay Parks were divorced. He d.13 Sep 1975 at age 131.
Known child of James "Jimmy"⁹ Van Horn and Patricia Kay Parks:
    i. James Boyd¹⁰.

1413. Carole⁹ Van Horn (Martha⁸ Delph, Jennie⁷ Abner, Robert⁶, James⁵, Richard⁴, Menan³, Elisha² Abney, Abner¹), b.1948. She m. Larry Edmonson and had issue:
    i. Gina¹⁰.
    ii. Abby.

1414. Thomas Ray "Tommy"⁹ Rigsby (Wilma⁸ Martin, Jennie⁷ Abner, Robert⁶, James⁵, Richard⁴, Menan³, Elisha² Abney, Abner¹), b.20 Oct 1949. He m1. Billie Marie Kelsheimer on 3 Apr 1970. They were divorced. He m2. Donna L. Kyle on 30 Sep 1976 but no issue. They were divorced. He m3. Patsy N. Wray on 21 Apr 1988 but no issue. He d.14 Mar 2016 IN at age 66.
Known child of Thomas Ray "Tommy"⁹ Rigsby and Billie Marie Kelsheimer:
    i. Amanda Ray¹⁰.

1415. Robert Franklin⁹ Rigsby (Wilma⁸ Martin, Jennie⁷ Abner, Robert⁶, James⁵, Richard⁴, Menan³, Elisha² Abney, Abner¹), b.2 Oct 1952. He m. Elizabeth Trantham on 21 Apr 1978. He and Elizabeth Trantham were divorced. He d.1 May 2014 Greene Co., OH, at age 61.
Known children of Robert Franklin⁹ Rigsby and Elizabeth Trantham:
        i.   Raymond Todd¹⁰.
       ii.   Bobi J.

1416. William Darald⁹ Aldridge (Robert⁸, Jennie⁷ Abner, Robert⁶, James⁵, Richard⁴, Menan³, Elisha² Abney, Abner¹), b.5 Jan 1962. He m. Susan Motkowski on 23 Oct 1982.
Known children of William Darald⁹ Aldridge and Susan Motkowski:
        i.   Amanda¹⁰, b.1984.
       ii.   Rachel Lynn, b.1987.
      iii.   William Boyd, b.1988.
      iv.   Victoria, b.1991.

1417. Aaron Thomas⁹ Cook (USAF) (Sandrea⁸ Abner, Ulis⁷, Robert⁶, James⁵, Richard⁴, Menan³, Elisha² Abney, Abner¹), b.6 Jan 1969 Terre Haute, Virgo Co., IN. He joined the USAF in 1987. He m1. Marie "Annette" Myers in 1994 Gatlinburg, Sevier Co., TN. They were divorced. He m2. Vicki J. Flynn on 3 Jul 1998 Jekyll Island, Glynn Co., GA. After serving his country honorably, he retired from the USAF in 2001.
Known child of Aaron Thomas⁹ Cook (USAF) and Marie "Annette" Myers:
1454   i.   Erin Elizabeth¹⁰, b. 9 Sep 1994 Evansville, Vanderburgh Co., IN.
    Vicki J. Flynn, b.15 Mar 1972 Bedford, Lawrence Co., IN.
Known child of Aaron Thomas⁹ Cook (USAF) and Vicki J. Flynn:
        i.   Emma Lucille¹⁰, b.6 Mar 2000 Huntington, Cabell Co., WV.

1418. Brent Richard⁹ Cook (Sandrea⁸ Abner, Ulis⁷, Robert⁶, James⁵, Richard⁴, Menan³, Elisha² Abney, Abner¹), b.8 Jul 1970 Terre Haute, Vigo Co., IN. He m. Tannya James in 2005. He and Tannya James were divorced.
Known child of Brent Richard⁹ Cook and Tannya James:
        i.   Bradyn Quinten¹⁰, b.10 Jul 2005 Huntingburg, Dubois Co., IN.

1419. Craig Allen⁹ Cook (Sandrea⁸ Abner, Ulis⁷, Robert⁶, James⁵, Richard⁴, Menan³, Elisha² Abney, Abner¹), b.3 Mar 1975 Vincennes, Knox Co., IN. He m. Dawn R. Hautsch on 27 Mar 2004 Jasper, Dubois Co., IN.
    Dawn R. Hautsch, b.5 Oct 1976 Jasper, Dubois Co., IN. She m. Nolan Miller.
Known children of Craig Allen⁹ Cook and Dawn R. Hautsch:
        i.   Katie Shane¹⁰, b.8 Feb 2005 Huntingburg, Dubois Co., IN.
       ii.   Janie Mae, b.11 Jan 2011 Lee's Summit, Lawrence Co., MO.

1420. Joseph Kirk⁹ Dennis (Mary⁸ Abner, Joseph⁷, Robert⁶, James⁵, Richard⁴, Menan³, Elisha² Abney, Abner¹), b.14 Oct 1985 LaPorte, LaPorte Co., IN. Known children of Joseph Kirk⁹ Dennis:
        i.   William Joseph Benjamin¹⁰, b.27 Jun 2014 LaPorte, LaPorte Co., IN.

1421. Susan Kristine⁹ Dennis (Mary⁸ Abner, Joseph⁷, Robert⁶, James⁵, Richard⁴, Menan³, Elisha² Abney, Abner¹), b.6 Mar 1992 LaPorte, LaPorte Co., IN. She m. Joseph Hefner on 15 Apr 2011. She and Joseph Hefner were divorced on 2 Apr 2013.
Known child of Susan Kristine⁹ Dennis:
        i.   Victoria Marie¹⁰, b.New Year's Eve, 31 Dec 2012 LaPorte, LaPorte Co., IN.
Known child of Susan Kristine⁹ Dennis and Joseph Hefner:
        i.   Dominic Joseph¹⁰, b.24 Jun 2011 LaPorte, LaPorte Co., IN.

1422. Daniel Bryan⁹ Abner (John⁸, James⁷, Robert⁶, James⁵, Richard⁴, Menan³, Elisha² Abney, Abner¹), b.4 Oct 1975 Clinton, Vermillion Co., IN. He m. Billie Edwards on 9 Aug 1997. He and Billie Edwards were divorced in Feb 2007.
Known children of Daniel Bryan⁹ Abner and Billie Edwards all b. Indianapolis, Marion Co., IN,:
        i.   Daniel Joseph¹⁰, b.19 Jan 2003.
       ii.   Samuel Thomas, b.19 Jan 2003.
      iii.   Lane McPherson, b.19 Jan 2003.

1423. Michael Joseph⁹ Guinn (Michael⁸, Beulah⁷ Abner, Robert⁶, James⁵, Richard⁴, Menan³, Elisha² Abney, Abner¹), b.21 Jul 1970 Terre Haute, Vigo Co., IN. He m. Carmen Rebecca Smith on 14 Apr 2000 Gatlinburg, Sevier Co., TN.
Known child of Michael Joseph⁹ Guinn and Carmen Rebecca Smith:
        i.   Matthew Drake¹⁰, b.2 Nov 2002 Knoxville, Knox Co., TN.

1424. Jeffrey Allen⁹ Guinn (Michael⁸, Beulah⁷ Abner, Robert⁶, James⁵, Richard⁴, Menan³, Elisha² Abney, Abner¹), b.6 Oct 1976 Terre Haute, Vigo Co., IN. He m1. Kimberly "Renee" White on 16 Apr 2001 TN. They were divorced in 2016 Roane Co., TN. He m2. Jennifer Wells on 19 Apr 2016 Savannnah, Chatham Co., GA, but no issue.
Known children of Jeffrey Allen⁹ Guinn and Kimberly "Renee" White both b. Knoxville, Knox Co., TN,:
        i.   Kylee Renee¹⁰, b.21 Aug 2006.
       ii.   Karoline Irene, b.16 Dec 2014.

1425. Andrew Joseph⁹ Guinn (Tony⁸, Beulah⁷ Abner, Robert⁶, James⁵, Richard⁴, Menan³, Elisha² Abney, Abner¹), b.18 Oct 1981. He m. Trisha Lee Crow on 5 Oct 2005 Terre Haute, Vigo Co., IN.
    Trisha Lee Crow, b.13 Mar 1983.
Known children of Andrew Joseph⁹ Guinn and Trisha Lee Crow:
        i.   Alicia Jolee¹⁰, b.22 Oct 2008.

1426. Stephanie Nicole[9] Guinn (Tony[8], Beulah[7] Abner, Robert[6], James[5], Richard[4], Menan[3], Elisha[2] Abney, Abner[1]), b.4 Jan 1988. She m. Tim J. Hastings on 8 Sep 2007. She and Tim J. Hastings were divorced.
Known child of Stephanie Nicole[9] Guinn and Tim J. Hastings:
      i.   Jaiden Nicole[10], b.2 Jun 2007.

1427. Herbert Neff[9] Jenkins (Helen[8] Nusz, Alice[7] Aud, Wilhelmina[6] Bayne, Margaret[5] Lasley, Gertrude[4] Abney, John[3], John[2], Abner[1]), b.14 Oct 1936 Elizabethtown, Hardin Co., KY. He m. Wilhelmina Milton on 12 Jul 1958 Waycross, Ware Co., GA.
    Wilhelmina Milton, b.3 Sep 1936 Macon, Bibb Co., GA.
Known children of Herbert Neff[9] Jenkins and Wilhelmina Milton both b. Elizabethtown, Hardin Co., KY:
1455   i.   Robert Gregory[10], b. 15 Feb 1960; m. Hedda Susan Schmidthuber.
      ii.   Kirk Christopher (gen.), b.20 Oct 1961. He was bapt.19 Nov 1961 Elizabethtown, Hardin Co., KY. He m. Susan Ann Murtha on 2 Nov 1991 Cathedral of St. Matthew the Apostle, Washington, DC. He was a lawyer who lived in 1996 Pacifica, San Mateo Co., CA. In August 1996, Cousin Kirk contacted the author and they began working on the Abney family together. He was one of the earliest descendants of John Key Abney (#17) who worked with the author. Much of information on the descendants of John Key Abney in this book came from Cousin Kirk. His generosity with his time and work are greatly appreciated.
           Susan Ann Murtha, b.21 Feb 1956 Dobbs Ferry, Westchester Co., NY. She was bapt.25 Mar 1956 Dobbs Ferry, Westchester Co., NY. She lived in 1996 Pacifica, CA.

Generation Ten

1428. Paula[10] Lowther (Paul[9], Mary[8] Pickett, Arminta[7] McKay, Mary[6] Chancellor, Ewing[5], Rebecca[4] Abney, Joshua[3], Elisha[2], Abner[1]) m. Jim Shannon and had issue:
      i.   Ryan[11] d.1981.
      ii.   Mitch m. Kristen (n.n.).

1429. Sherry[10] Beaver (Marilyn[9] Moore, Marion[8], Lottie[7] Chancellor, Henry[6], Ewing[5], Rebecca[4] Abney, Joshua[3], Elisha[2], Abner[1]) m. Jim Chapman and had issue: Nathan "Nonny"[11].

1430. Larry[10] Coverstone (Jack[9], Beatrice[8] Burmmett, Norma[7] Harmeson, Catherine[6] Chancellor, William[5], Rebecca[4] Abney, Joshua[3], Elisha[2], Abner[1]) m. Kay (n.n.) and had issue: Justin[11].

1431. Bea[10] Coverstone (Jack[9], Beatrice[8] Burmmett, Norma[7] Harmeson, Catherine[6] Chancellor, William[5], Rebecca[4] Abney, Joshua[3], Elisha[2], Abner[1]) m. Dan Conley and had issue: Troy[11].

1432. Cathy Lynn[10] Abney (gen.) (Jerry[9], Roscoe[8], William[7], James[6], John[5], Paul[4], Joshua[3], Elisha[2], Abner[1]), b.9 May 1962 Davis Co., KY. She m. Todd Burden on 14 Jun 1985 Livermore, McLean Co., KY. Cousin Cathy contacted the author in 1998 through the *Centralized Abney Archives* website. The information on the descendants of Roscoe "William" Abney (#968) was kindly shared by Cousin Cathy with the author. It was truly a pleasure working with Cousin Cathy.
    Todd Burden, b.10 Feb 1962 Davis Co., KY.
Known children of Cathy Lynn[10] Abney (gen.) and Todd Burden:
      i.   Emily[11], b.27 Jul 1988.
      ii.   Samuel, b.22 Jul 1994.

1433. Jerry Roberts[10] Abney Sr. (Jerry[9], Roscoe[8], William[7], James[6], John[5], Paul[4], Joshua[3], Elisha[2], Abner[1]), b.2 Jul 1963 Davis Co., KY. He m. Kathryn Moon (b.4 Mar 1963) on 17 Aug 1985 WV and had issue:
Known children of Jerry Roberts[10] Abney Sr. and Kathryn Moon:
      i.   Joseph Roberts[11], b.5 Sep 1988.
      ii.   Jennifer, b.18 Dec 1991.
      iii.   Mary M., b.25 Jan 1995.

1434. Lee Ann[10] Abney (Jerry[9], Roscoe[8], William[7], James[6], John[5], Paul[4], Joshua[3], Elisha[2], Abner[1]), b.5 Nov 1964 TN. She m. Scott Starkey (b.19 May 1964) on 20 Dec 1987 Calhoun, McLean Co., KY and had issue:
Known child of Lee Ann[10] Abney and Scott Starkey:
      i.   Elijah Scott[11], b.7 Sep 1996.

1435. Peggy Denice[10] Iglehart (Betty[9] Abney, Roscoe[8], William[7], James[6], John[5], Paul[4], Joshua[3], Elisha[2], Abner[1]) m. Dana Hartigan (b.26 Jul 19671 KY) in Princeton, Caldwell Co., KY. , b.27 May 1965 KY.
Known children of Peggy Denice[10] Iglehart and Dana Hartigan:
      i.   Heather[11], b.21 Jan 1986.
      ii.   Holly, b.2 Mar 1989.

1436. Steve[10] Dunn (Hershel[9], Mattie[8] Snodgrass, Naoma[7] Daugherty, Mary[6] Abney, John[5], Paul[4], Joshua[3], Elisha[2], Abner[1]), b.26 Dec 1953 Daviess Co., KY; m. Linda Turley. He d.5 Jun 2013 Providence, Webster Co., KY, at age 59; bur. Christian Church Cem., Providence, Webster Co., KY.
Known children of Steve[10] Dunn and Linda Turley:
      i.   Stephen Warren[11].
      ii.   Elizabeth Marie m. (n.n.) Brown.
      iii.   Tiffany Cole m. (n.n.) Hall.

1437. William Elliott¹⁰ Johnson Jr. (Lennie⁹ Dunn, Mattie⁸ Snodgrass, Naoma⁷ Daugherty, Mary⁶ Abney, John⁵, Paul⁴, Joshua³, Elisha², Abner¹) m. Debby (n.n.). and had issue:
      i.   Elizabeth Blair¹¹ m. Jason Glass.
      ii. Lacy Grey m. Rob Sweet.

1438. Allison¹⁰ Raymond (Cecil⁹, Stella⁸ Hurt, Nola⁷ Moore, Finis⁶, Mary⁵ Abney, Paul⁴, Joshua³, Elisha², Abner¹) m. Dave Novak and had issue:
      i.   Brenna¹¹.
      ii. Abby.

1439. Andrea¹⁰ Raymond (Cecil⁹, Stella⁸ Hurt, Nola⁷ Moore, Finis⁶, Mary⁵ Abney, Paul⁴, Joshua³, Elisha², Abner¹) m. Ryan McKinney; had issue:
      i.   Avery¹¹.
      ii. Cade.
      iii. Trey.

1440. Alisa¹⁰ Raymond (Cecil⁹, Stella⁸ Hurt, Nola⁷ Moore, Finis⁶, Mary⁵ Abney, Paul⁴, Joshua³, Elisha², Abner¹) m. (n.n.) Knapp and had issue:
      i.   Cecilia¹¹.
      ii. Callie.

1441. Christopher¹⁰ Coots (Steven⁹, Earl⁸, Senora⁷ Abner, Harrison⁶, Isaac⁵ Abney, Paul⁴, Joshua³, Elisha², Abner¹), b. KY. He m. Jennilee (n.n.) and had issue: i.   Paislee¹¹, b. ca.2017.

1442. Raymond Lee¹⁰ Abney III (Raymond⁹, Raymond⁸, Grover⁷, Washington⁶, Wilburn⁵, Benjamin⁴, Hezekiah³, Elisha², Abner¹), b. ca.1963. Known children of Raymond Lee¹⁰ Abney III and (n.n.):
      i.   Raymond Lee¹¹.
      ii. Charlotte Gabriella.

1443. Rie Rie¹⁰ Fricks (Greg⁹, Martha⁸ Abney, William⁷, Washington⁶, Wilburn⁵, Benjamin⁴, Hezekiah³, Elisha², Abner¹) m. Michael Rubadue and had issue: i.   Ross¹¹.
      ii. Anna.

1444. Will¹⁰ Fricks (Greg⁹, Martha⁸ Abney, William⁷, Washington⁶, Wilburn⁵, Benjamin⁴, Hezekiah³, Elisha², Abner¹) m. Karen (n.n.) & had issue:
      i.   Aria¹¹.

1445. Robin Braelli¹⁰ Brackett (Cynthia⁹ Moore, D.C.⁸, John⁷, Mary⁶ Abney, Benjamin⁵, Benjamin⁴, Hezekiah³, Elisha², Abner¹) m. Russell Juhl and had issue: i.   Reilee Nicole¹¹.

1446. Emmett "Butch"¹⁰ Matthews (Emmett⁹, Vera⁸ Pelfrey, Haze⁷ Ellison, Sarah⁶ Abney, Hezekiah⁵, Benjamin⁴, Hezekiah³, Elisha², Abner¹) m. Jo Ann (n.n.) and had issue:
      i.   Kristina¹¹.

1447. Jeremiah¹⁰ Lamphere (Carolyn⁹ Easter, Mary⁸ Fuller, Daisy⁷ Abney, George⁶, George⁵, Benjamin⁴, Hezekiah³, Elisha², Abner¹) m. (n.n.) Shalome and had issue:
      i.   Judah¹¹.

1448. Joseph David¹⁰ Tracy (Susan⁹ Abney, Tommy⁸, John⁷, Alex⁶, George⁵, Benjamin⁴, Hezekiah³, Elisha², Abner¹) m. Tiffani (n.n.) & had issue:
      i.   Bryleigh Grace¹¹.

1449. Katie¹⁰ Drummond (Amy⁹ Farrer, Hazel⁸ Abney, Henry⁷, Marion⁶, James⁵, Benjamin⁴, Hezekiah³, Elisha², Abner¹) had issue:
      i.   Emma¹¹.

1450. Benjamin Lee "Ben"¹⁰ Cox (Patty⁹ Short, Georgia⁸ Marcum, Ethel⁷ Abney, John⁶, Pinkney⁵, Wiley⁴, Hezekiah³, Elisha², Abner¹), b.27 Dec 1973 Middlesboro, Bell Co., KY. He m. Rebecca (n.n.). He d.23 Oct 2011 Pennington Gap, Lee Co., VA, at age 37 and was bur. Lee Mem. Gardens, Woodway, Lee Co., VA.
Known children of Benjamin Lee "Ben"¹⁰ Cox and Rebecca (n.n.):
      i.   Courtney¹¹.
      ii. Caitlyn.

1451. Chad¹⁰ Rouse (Loretta⁹ Marcum, Paul⁸, Ethel⁷ Abney, John⁶, Pinkney⁵, Wiley⁴, Hezekiah³, Elisha², Abner¹) m. Marie (n.n.) and had issue:
      i.   Morgan¹¹.

1452. Byron W.¹⁰ Barger (Robert⁹, Clarence⁸, Mamie⁷ Abner, Robert⁶, William⁵, Willis⁴, Elisha³, Elisha² Abney, Abner¹) m. Misty Humphries. He, b.8 Jun 1971. He d.7 May 2009 at age 37 and was bur. Laurel Cem., Laurel, Clermont Co., OH.
Known children of Byron W.¹⁰ Barger and Misty Humphries:
      i.   Taylor¹¹.
      ii. Morgan.
      iii. Lane.
      iv. Dalton.

1453. John Lee "Johnny"¹⁰ Abner Jr. (John⁹, David⁸, Elbert⁷, Robert⁶, William⁵, Willis⁴, Elisha³, Elisha² Abney, Abner¹) m. (n.n.) and had issue:
      i.   John Lee "Johnny"¹¹.

1454. Erin Elizabeth[10] Cook (Aaron[9], Sandrea[8] Abner, Ulis[7], Robert[6], James[5], Richard[4], Menan[3], Elisha[2] Abney, Abner[1]), b.9 Sep 1994 Evansville, Vanderburgh Co., IN. She m. Corey R. Mathias in May 2016 Charleston, SC.

Corey R. Mathias, b.26 Oct 1992 Huntingburg, Dubois Co., IN.

Known children of Erin Elizabeth[10] Cook and Corey R. Mathias all b. Charleston, Charleston Co., SC,:

    i.   Quinn Caroline[11], b.11 Jun 2015.

    ii. Harper Grace, b.4 Oct 2017.

    iii. Rowan Dale, b.16 Jun 2020.

1455. Robert Gregory[10] Jenkins (Herbert[9], Helen[8] Nusz, Alice[7] Aud, Wilhelmina[6] Bayne, Margaret[5] Lasley, Gertrude[4] Abney, John[3], John[2], Abner[1]), b.15 Feb 1960 Elizabethtown, Hardin Co., KY. He m. Hedda Susan Schmidthuber on 24 Jun 1983 St. James, Elizabethtown, Hardin Co., KY. He lived in 1996 Cordova, TN.

Hedda Susan Schmidthuber, b.26 May 1960 Fort Riley, KS. She lived in 1996 Cordova, TN.

Known children of Robert Gregory[10] Jenkins and Hedda Susan Schmidthuber:

    i.   Zachary Neff[11], b.1 Feb 1988 San Antonio, TX. He lived in 1996 Cordova, TN.

    ii. Benjamin Bayne, b.19 Dec 1991 Memphis, TN. He lived in 1996 Cordova, TN.

    iii. William Bond, b.6 Dec 1994 Elizabethtown, Hardin Co., KY. He lived in 1996 Cordova, TN.

Appendix A
Abney, Abner, Abna, Abnee
Etymology

Although the misspelling of the name, *Abney* occurred in other branches (specifically in some branches of Paul Abney [bapt.1699]), the family of Elisha Abney Sr. gave us an amazing variety of surname spellings. There is no doubt Elisha knew his name was *Abney*. So, what happened to his children and grandchildren? It actually seems to have begun early in the history of the Elisha Abner Sr. family. The 1787 tax list of Wilkes County, North Carolina, the 1790 census of Greenville County, Ninety-Six District, South Carolina, tax records of Carter County, Tennessee and the census records Clay County, Kentucky all show *Abner*. However, the corruption from *Abney* to *Abner* was as much an error of the records-keepers as it was pronunciation. Proof of this bears out in deeds, court records and the fact that some of his descendants used the correct spelling, *Abney* and/or correct pronunciation (as in *Abnee*). When Elisha *Abney* Sr. purchased 150 acres of land on August 9, 1796 in Carter County, Tennessee, his name is recorded as *Elisha Abner*. When he sold 150 acres in Carter County on October 4, 1805, although the deed reads Elisha *Abner* to Isaac Lincoln, it is signed Elisha *Abney*. Even Carter County tax records differ. In 1796, 1797 and 1799, his surname is recorded as *Abner*. However, in 1800 we read Elisha *Abney*. When, in Carter County, one Joseph Fisher is appointed overseer of a public road, Elisha *Abney* and Abner *Abney* are both on the road crew. From the time the family arrived in Clay County, the surname *Abner* was firmly attached to his name, albeit, as the author has shown, in spelling only. In the census records of 1810 and 1820 Clay County, Kentucky, his name is spelled *Abner*. To make matters worse, there are only two people in his household in 1820. The author has firmly identified these two people as Elisha Abney Sr. and his son, Enoch Abney. There is no doubt the census-taker was quite confused, as he named the head of household *Enoch Abner Sr*. The author theorizes that Elisha's son, Enoch (age 17 at the time) was the informant. The record should have read *Elisha Abney Sr*.

The name, written as *Abner* became prominent, yea dominant, in Clay County, Kentucky. However, the surname *Abner* was also used in Georgia by the William Duncan Abner family. He was a grandson of Hezekiah Abney.

In the author's opinion, the oddest surname spelling in use is *Abnee* (obviously a phonetic spelling of Abney) used by the Lincoln Abnee (originally of Clay Co., KY) family, presently and prominently of Nicholas Co., KY. While the most vulgar spelling is *Abna* (obviously a more relaxed phonetic spelling of *Abner*) used by the James Andrew (originally of Heard Co., GA) Abna family, presently of Fulton Co., GA.

Now, the author presents a quick etymology of the various *Abney* surnames, and the reason this book is so titled: *Abney, Abner, Abna, & Abnee*. The following chart shows the etymology of the surnames Abney, Abner, Abna and Abnee and the first marriage year of the user.

Descendants of Elisha Abney Sr. (est.1741-aft.1820) and their Surnames										
Joshua ABNEY m.1795	*Pvt.* Abner ABNEY m.1803	Hezekiah ABNEY m.est.1801			Elisha, Jr. ABNER m.ca.1806	Menan ABNER m1.1813	John, Sr. ABNEY m1.ca.1825		Enoch, Sr. ABNEY m1.1822	
ABNEY family	ABNEY family	James M. ABNEY m.ca.1876		others ABNEY	ABNER families	ABNER families	Lincoln ABNEE m.1851	(others) ABNER	Enoch, Jr. ABNER m.1842	Andrew ABNEY m.1857
		William D. ABNER m.ca.1870	James A. ABNA m.ca.1876	ABNEY families			ABNEE family	ABNER families	ABNER family	ABNEY families
		ABNER family	ABNA family							

Using Elisha Abney Sr. as the first generation, by the fourth generation we have established all the surnames in use in the Abney family today (and the title of this volume), to wit: Abney, Abner, Abna and Abnee.

Although there are other odd variations (Abaney, etc.) these are rare, usually occurring only once and not carried on in subsequent generations. Indexers are seen making even funnier mistakes (Abuscy, etc.).

When Renia Abney (daughter of Silas Curtis Abney and Calista Barton) married Robert Weekley Goff, her name was written (in the marriage license) as Renia *Abnier*. Silas, her father, who could neither read nor write, signed with his "x" mark. His surname is also given as *Abnier*. This shows for certain the pronunciation (*Abni*) of the surname ABNEY was certainly known, but the records keeper was confused by the Kentucky accent and added the "r".

Appendix B
When and Where Were the Children of Elisha Abney Sr. Born?

It is truly amazing how a family can be properly constructed using the limited data available in census and tax records. Adding the marriage records and military service confirms this family group. Therefore, examining the available evidence (1787 Tax List and Federal Census Records from 1790-1860, individual marriage records and military records), the author has been able to create a table showing how he constructed the family of Elisha Abney/Abner Sr., including their nearly perfect years of birth and places.

Name	Year	1787 tax list		census→ 1790		1800		1810	
		age	yr. span	age	yr. span	age	yr. span	age	yr. span
Elisha Sr	e.1741 VA	**21-60**	1727-1766	**16+**	before 1775			**45+**	before 1765
(wife)	?	no age given	female	no age given	female			45+	before 1765
Joshua	c.1771 VA	<21	after 1766	16+	before 1775	m.1795 KY			
Jerusha (?)	e.1773 VA	no age given	female	no age given	female				
Ann (?)	e.1775 VA	no age given	female	no age given	female				
(dau) (?)	e.1777 VA	no age given	female	no age given	female				
Abner	c.1779 VA	<21	after 1766	<16	1775-1790	m.1803 TN			
Hezekiah	c.1781 VA	<21	after 1766	<16	1775-1890	m.c.1801 KY?			
Dorcas	c.1784 VA	no age given	female	no age given	female	m.1808 KY			
Elisha Jr	c.1787 NC			<16	1775-1790	m.1806 KY		**16-25**	1785-1794
Menan	c.1790 NC			<16	1775-1790			<u>16-25</u>	1785-1794
John Sr	c.1794 SW Terr							<u>10-15</u>	1795-1800
Mary "Polly"	c.1795 SW Terr							<u>10-15</u>	1795-1800
Margaret Larken	1798 TN							<u><10</u>	1801-1810
Enoch Sr	c.1803 TN							<u><10</u>	1801-1810

(continued on the page 260)

For the tables in appendix B:

a white box means the information therein agrees with the given birth year either perfectly or within one year.

a dark grey box means the individual has not been located in the census for that year.

a light grey box with white font means the information in the census is off by more than one year.

a black box means the individual was not alive at this time (either not born yet, nor already deceased).

Appendix B

(continued from page 259)

Name	Year	1820		1830		1840		1850	1860
		age	yr. span	age	yr. span	age	yr. span	age	age
Elisha Sr	e.1741 VA	45+	before 1775	d.bef. 1830?					
(wife)	?	d.bef. 1820?							
Joshua	c.1771 VA	45+	before 1775	50<60	1771-1780	70-80	1761-1770	d.1845	
Jerusha (?)	e.1773 VA								
Ann (?)	e.1775 VA								
(dau.) (?)	e.1777 VA								
Abner	c.1779 VA								
Hezekiah	c.1781 VA			40<50	1781-1790	50<60	1781-1790		80/SC
Dorcas	c.1784 VA			40<50	1781-1790	50<60	1781-1790	66/TN c.1784	
Elisha Jr	c.1787 NC	26<45	1776-1794	40<50	1781-1790	50<60 m2.1838	1781-1790	67/VA c.1783	d.c.1855
Menan	c.1790 NC	26<45 m1.1813	1776-1794	30<40 m2.1829	1791-1800	m3.1836 KY		60/NC c.1790	d.c.1853
John Sr	c.1794 SW Terr	m1. ca. 1825 KY	m.1829 KY	30<40	1791-1800	50<60	1781-1790	56/TN c.1794	
Mary "Polly"	c.1795 SW Terr	26<45 m.1811	1776-1794	30<40	1791-1800	40<50	1791-1800	75/TN 1775	
Margaret Larken	1798 TN	16<26 m.1819	1795-1804	30<40	1791-1800	40<50	1791-1800	52/VA	67/VA
Enoch Sr	c.1803 TN	16<26	1795-1804	30<40 m1.1822	1791-1800	40<50 m2.1838	1791-1800	47/TN	d.1854

For the tables in appendix B:
a white box means the information therein agrees with the given birth year either perfectly or within one year.
a dark grey box means the individual has not been located in the census for that year.
a light grey box with white font means the information in the census is off by more than one year.
a black box means the individual was not alive at this time (either not born yet, nor already deceased).

The tables in Appendix B are based on a full-color report created by the author entitled, "When Did These Abney/Abner's Think They Were Born" © 2020 R. Robert Abney Jr. in which the author was able to properly reconstruct the family of Elisha Abney Sr.

Appendix C
Timeline of Events of Interest to the Abner Abney family

So many people have written to the author claiming he was incorrect about a certain birth place. The author was forced to explain to these well-meaning family researchers that a person cannot be born <u>in</u> a place which did NOT exist when they were born. During the research for this book, how often did the author encounter a person alleged born in, for example, Cobb County, Georgia in 1804. The problem is Cobb County wasn't in existence in 1804. Cobb County was created in **1832**. Before that it was the Cherokee Nation. It is highly doubtful Hezekiah Abney's children were born in the Cherokee Nation and impossible that they were born in Cobb County. Likewise, in many of the Abner families, people were allegedly found in Clay or Owsley Counties before they were created. Since Elisha Abney Sr. sold his land in Carter County, Tennessee in 1805, it is likely he arrived in Kentucky in 1805-1806…but NOT in Clay County (which didn't exist until **1807**). Since the Abner's seemed to populate (primarily) the northern part of Clay County, they likely arrived in Madison County, Kentucky ca.1805-1806; And their homes fell into Clay County in 1807. With this in mind, the author has assembled the following timeline so the reader can know if a place was in existence at a particular date in time.

Date/Year	Event	Other Information
1702	King William Co., VA	
1721	formation of Spotsylvania Co., VA	from parts of Essex, King & Queen, & King Wm. Cos., VA
1728	formation of Goochland Co., VA	from Henrico Shire
1738	formation of Augusta Co., VA	from Orange Co., VA
1744	formation of Albemarle Co., VA	from western part of Goochland Co., VA
1761	formation of Amherst Co., VA	from part of southwestern Albemarle Co., VA
1769-1776	The Watauga Association	
1776-1777	Washington Dist., NC	
1777	formation of Fluvanna Co., VA	from Albemarle Co., VA
1777-1784	*informal* Washington Dist.	
20 Apr 1778	formation of Wilkes Co., NC	from parts of Surry Co. & Wash. Dist., NC
1784-1788	extra-legal State of Franklin	
1784-1789	Wayne Co., State of Franklin	
02 Jan 1788	State of Georgia Statehood	
22 May 1786	formation of Greenville Co., SC	in old Ninety-Six District, SC
1790-1796	Southwest Territory	from extra-legal State of Franklin
1790-1796	Washington Co., Southwest Territory	(Formerly Washington Dist., NC)
01 Jun 1792	Commonwealth of Kentucky Statehood	
20 Dec 1792	formation of Green Co., KY	from parts of Lincoln & Nelson Cos., KY
11 Feb 1796	formation of Jackson Co., GA	from part of Franklin Co., GA
01 Jun 1796	State of Tennessee Statehood	
1796	formation of Carter Co., TN	from Washington Co., SW Terr. Courthouse fire 1933
20 Dec 1798	formation of Barren Co., KY	from parts of Warren and Green Counties, KY
1810	formation of Butler Co., KY	from portions of Logan & Ohio Cos., KY. Courthouse burned 1872
1807	formation of Clay Co., KY	from part of Floyd, Knox & Madison Cos., KY. Courthouse burned 20 Jan 1936
1832	formation of Cobb Co., GA	carved out of the Cherokee Nation
1843	formation of Owsley Co., KY	from pts. of Clay, Breathitt & Estill Cos., KY. Courthouse burned Jan. 1929 all documents lost
1902	Staunton, VA	separated from Augusta Co., VA

𝔅𝔦𝔟𝔩𝔦𝔬𝔤𝔯𝔞𝔭𝔥𝔶
Some Sources Used in this Book

The following is not an exhaustive list...

- Public Records (Census, Deeds, Marriage, Military, Vital Records, Grave, Obituaries, etc.) of the various states, counties and cities
- Family Bible Records
- Abney Family History Series, Vol. I: Abney – Ancestors and Descendants of Dr. Abraham Abney of Virginia (for Chapt. I pedigrees)
- Abney by John R. Hensell (1974)
- Abney Supplement by John R. Hensell (1988)
- Abstracts of Early Kentucky Wills, by J. Estelle King (2003)
- Abstracts of Virginia Land Patents and Grants, by Nell Marion Nugent (1934)
- Albemarle County, Virginia Deeds and Will Abstracts 1748-1752 (1990) by Ruth and Sam Sparacio
- Albemarle County in Virginia, by Rev. Edgar Woods (1978)
- Amherst County, Virginia, Courthouse Miniatures – Abstracts...Deed Bk. C. (1963), by Bailey Fulton Davis
- Amherst County, Virginia, Courthouse Miniatures – Abstracts...Deed Bk. P. (1966), by Bailey Fulton Davis
- Augusta County Marriages 1748-1850 by John Vogt and T. William Kethley Jr. (1986)
- Bernard Grandparents (1976) by Ted Bernard
- Bourbon News, the (Paris, KY)
- Carter County, Tennessee 1836 Tennessee Civil Districts and Tax Lists by James L. Douthat (1993)
- Casey Family History (http://www.rcasey.net/master/winelijj.htm)
- Cavaliers & Pioneers – Abstracts of Virginia Land Patents and Grants, Vol. II (1666-1695), by Nell Marion Nugent (1977)
- Cavaliers & Pioneers – Abstracts of Virginia Land Patents and Grants, Vol. III (1695-1732), by Nell Marion Nugent (1979)
- Cavaliers & Pioneers – Abstracts of Virginia Land Patents and Grants, Vol. IV (1732-1741), by Nell Marion Nugent (1994)
- Chronicles of the Scotch-Irish Settlement in Virginia (in three volumes) by Lyman Chalkley
- Daughters of the American Revolution Lineage Books (various)
- Deeds of Amherst Co., Virginia 1761-1807 & Albemarle Co. 1748-1763 (1979), by Rev. Bailey F. Davis
- Descendants of John Abner, Sr. by Judy Vietri (pub. in Three Forks of the Kentucky River Historical Association)
- Early Alabama Marriages 1813-1850, &c., by Family Adventures (1991)
- Executive Journals of the Council of Colonial Virginia (Vols. I-V), H.R. McIlwaine, editor
- FamilySearch.org (an excellent source for census records, marriage records and many other scanned documents)
- Findagrave.com (an excellent source for headstone pictures, and sometimes obituaries and photographs, but some erroneous data)
- First Marriage Records of Augusta County, Virginia 1785-1813, by the Col. Thomas Hughart Chapter DAR (1962)
- Fredericksville Parish Vestry Book 1742-1787, by Edith Rosalie Davis (1981)
- Genealogical Abstracts from 18th Century Virginia Newspapers, by Robert K. Headley Jr. (1987)
- Genealogy Report for James Kennedy (2011)
- Georgia Black Book, by Robert Scott Davis Jr. (1982)
- Greenville County, South Carolina – Deed Books Index 1787-1802, by Robertalee Lent (1966)
- Harrison County Courier
- History of Bourbon, Scott, Harrison and Nicholas Counties, Kentucky by Dr. Robert Peter (1882)
- In Search of Kate, by C.A. Abney Metzger (1978)
- James M. Swofford & Descendants by Melanie Easterly (from Families of the Ozarks: http://familiesoftheozarks.org/swofford-family/james-m-swofford-decendants/
- Kentucky: A History of the State, by W.H. Perrin, J.H. Battle and G.C. Kniffin (1887)
- Kentucky Births and Christenings, 1839-1960
- Kentucky County Marriages, 1797-1954
- Kentucky High School Athletic Association
- Latter Day Saints (see FamilySearch.org)
- Marriage Bonds and Other Marriage Records of Amherst County, Virginia, by William Montgomery Sweeny (1980)
- Marriages of Albemarle County and Charlottesville, Virginina 1781-1929, by William L. Norford (1956)
- Missouri History (Missouri Sec. of State) https://www.sos.mo.gov/archives/history/historicallistings/molega
- Missouri Marriages: 1826-1850, by Liahona Research, Inc. (1993)
- Paper of Miami County (IN)
- Political Graveyard (http://politicalgraveyard.com/geo/MO/ofc/sthse1940s.html)
- Time and date calculator: https://www.timeanddate.com/date/weekday.html
- United States Federal Census Records (provided by Familysearch.org)
- Upper Part of Greenville Co., S.C., by Mann Batson
- Vestry Book and Accounts of the Churchwardens of St. Mary's Leicester 1652-1729 (1912) by Henry Hartopp
- Virginia Colonial Soldiers (1988), by Lloyd D. Bockstruck
- Virginia County Court Records – Deed Book 3 (12 Feb 1761-09 Aug 1764), by Ruth & Sam Sparacio (1988)
- Virginia County Court Records – Deed Book 4 (09 Aug 1764-12 Aug 1768), , by Ruth & Sam Sparacio (1989)

- Virginia County Court Records – Deed Abstracts of Albemarle County, Virginia (1772-1776), by Ruth & Sam Sparacio (1990)
- Virginia County Court Records – Deed Abstracts of Albemarle County, Virginia (1748-1776), by Ruth & Sam Sparacio (1992)
- Virginia County Records (Spotsylvania County 1721-1800) (1905), by William Armstrong Crozier
- Virginia Revolutionary Publick Claims – Vol. II (1992), by J. & R. Slatten Abercrombie
- Virginia Vital Records [from various publications], Judith McGhan, editor (1984)
- Virginia Wills and Administrations 1632-1800, by Clayton Torrence (1965)
- Virginia Wills Before 1799 (1924) by William Montgomery Clemens
- Walker County Georgia Heritage 1833-1983 (pub. 1984, Walker County Historical Society)
- Water in Kentucky: Natural History, Communities, and Conservation (Ed. Brian D. Lee, Daniel I. Carey & Alice L. Jones)
- Weekday Calculator: https://www.timeanddate.com/date/weekday.html
- Wills of Amherst Co., Virginia 1761-1865 (1985), by Bailey Fulton Davis
- Wininger Family History by Robert Casey & Harold Casey (pub.2003)
- https://sparkplaza.wpengine.com/wp-content/uploads/2016/06/State_of_Franklin_map.jpg

Addenda

primum addendum:

Mary Unity Calloway

This addendum should begin: **Who was the wife of Elisha Abney Sr. (#2)?**

There is much on the Internet as concerns the alleged name of his wife. For decades, many genealogists believed there was a *Calloway* family involved with the Abney family, due to the fact that Benjamin Hezekiah Abney (grandson of Elisha Abney Sr.) named a son William *Callaway* Abney. Most genealogists believed Benjamin Hezekiah Abney's wife was a Calloway. Some even gave her the name Frances Anne Calloway.

However, it is now believed that Benjamin Hezekiah Abney's <u>mother</u> was the Calloway (i.e. wife of Elisha Abney Sr.). Still, the author was presented no proof nor documentation showing this possibility… until now.

What the author is calling "the DNA Community" has come up with some information which is of great interest to this book and the readers thereof.

Before delving into that information, let the author make his position clear on this family:

- Firstly, the author will, once again as before, voice the opinion that Elisha Abney Sr. never "personally" used the surname variation *Abner*. This has been shown in every document in which he signed. Only the recorders and census-takers wrote his surname as *Abner*.
- Secondly, the author firmly denounces the use of any middle name for Elisha Abney Sr. (including Enoch). In the 1820 census, for some reason, his household was erroneously listed as *Enoch Abner Sr.* Since he and his youngest child, Enoch were the only two people living in the household, it appears obvious to this author that the census taker was confused as to which name was that of the Head of Household. This generation (of the Abney family) simply did not use middle names. That practice began in the next generation (and usually used the middle name to honor a member of the distaff family (such as one's mother or wife; or the father of one's wife). Examples of this practice in the Abney family are: Paul Collins Abney (son of Lucy Collins), John Key Abney (grandson of Anne Key), Dannett Abney Witt (grandson of Dannett Abney Jr.), Samuel Meredith Spraggins (grandson of Mary Meredith Abney), John Spragins Gorman (grandson of Martha Abney Spraggins), &c. Many people, when they see someone referred to by two names, automatically (and often correctly) assume one of the names is the middle name. In this case, however, the author believes it was simply an census-taker accident. Besides, why wasn't Elisha Abner Jr. ever referred to by *Elisha Enoch* (since Elisha was a "junior")?
- Thirdly, the author herewith admits he has not researched the alleged families (*Calloway* and *Anderson*) which will be discussed here.

The disclaimer out of the way, following is information received from Cousin D. Rachael Bishop (descendant of Leonard Jasper Abney Sr.) is from "the DNA Community":

According to DNA information (received from Cousin D. Rachael Bishop):
Mary Unity CALLAWAY (1741-1827) m1. Jacob ANDERSON (1731-1822) and had issue:
1.   Mary Jane Anderson (with whom Cousin Rachael has matched DNA on 3 of her descendants!)

Mary Unity CALLAWAY m2. Elisha ABNEY Sr. & had issue, as reported in this book (with whom Cousin Rachael has matched DNA (as of this writing) on the following: 2 on Joshua Abney [whom they refer to as Joshua Abner], 4 on Dorcas Abner; 1 on Menan Abner; and 2 on Mary Abner [whom they refer to as Mary Sarah Abner]). [note: there are many more matches now.]

It has become increasingly obvious that Cousin Rachael is from Elisha's line (matching DNA over 32 times) to both him and his unknown wife). For this and other reasons, the author believes that her ancestor, Leonard Jasper ABNEY Sr. was a son of Pvt. Abner ABNEY (son of Elisha ABNEY Sr.). Hopefully her DNA comparisons with the RUSSELL family will give us more information, which, as of this printing shows very significant matches to the RUSSELL Family of Carter County, Tennessee.

That, however, is NOT our problem in this addendum. Our problem is with the alleged Mary Unity CALLAWAY. If, as reported to me, she truly was a CALLOWAY (it seems the DNA bears this out), then:
1.   Why was she married to Elisha whilst Jacob ANDERSON was still alive? Divorce was rare in early Tennessee. If it was divorce…
2.   Why is Mary Unity CALLAWAY given the death date of 1827? She is not accounted for on the 1820 census of *Enoch Abner Sr.*

After additional research, it is reported that Mary CALLAWAY had about 10 children with ANDERSON from 1760-1784. If that is the fact, then it is absolutely impossible that this alleged Mary Unity CALLAWAY was Elisha's wife (as Elisha sired 13 children from ca.1771-1803). In other words, she could not have had children simultaneously with both men. Therefore, the wife of Elisha Abney Sr. is still in abeyance. However, it is probable she was of the Calloway family. The author believes it possible that "Mary Unity Calloway" was actually two different people, perhaps sisters, Mary Calloway and Unity Calloway. However, this is purely conjectural.

secundo addendum:

Possible Descendants of Pvt. Abner Abney of Virginia

Generation Three of Abner Abney (ca.1711-ca.1751)

1. Pvt. Abner³ Abney (War of 1812) (Elisha², Abner¹), b.1779 Amherst Co., VA. He married Alyda Russell on 26 Aug 1803 Carter Co., TN. (see pages xvii, xix, 1, 19-20, 22-23, 25, 33, 41, 257, 259-260). Work is still in progress on Pvt. Abner Abney, but much information is coming to light. Possible/probable child of Pvt. Abner³ Abney (War of 1812) and Alyda Russell:
    2   i.   Leonard Jasper⁴, b. 15 May 1806 TN; m1. Ellen "Gincy" Crenshaw; m2. Nancy Barlow.

Generation Four

2. Leonard Jasper⁴ Abney Sr. (Abner³, Elisha², Abner¹), b. 15 May 1806 TN. He m1. Ellen "Gincy" Crenshaw ca.1825. He appeared on the census of 1830 Hancock Co., IL. He was living on 26 Dec 1834 Des Moines Co., IA Terr. He appeared on the Iowa Territory Census of 1836. He appeared as Head of Household on the census of 1840 Des Moines Co., IA Terr. He and Ellen "Gincy" Crenshaw appeared on the census of 3 Oct 1850 Flint River, Des Moines Co., IA. He appeared on the Iowa State Census of 1852, 1854 and 1856 (Flint River, Des Moines Co., IA). He appeared on the census of 1860 Flint River, Des Moines, Polk Co., IA. He m2. Nancy Barlow on 1 Apr 1863, but no issue. Leonard d.19 Jul 1864 Lima, Adams Co., IL, at age 58. Bur. Ridge Park Cem., Marshall, Saline Co., MO.

     There is strong evidence that Leonard Jasper Abney Sr. was a son of Pvt. Abner Abney and Alyda Russell (see Chapter III, page 25). Through the work of this author; Cousin Carolyn Berry Bishop and her daughter, Cousin D. Rachael Bishop (descendants of Leonard Jasper Abney Sr.); Cousin Morgan Floyd Abney (contributor and originator of this work); and Cousin John Michael Abney (contributor and proofreader of this work), proof that Leonard Jasper Abney Sr. was a son of Pvt. Abner Abney is coming closer. The dates and places (and a name or two) match perfectly. But the best proof lies in DNA. Cousin Rachael Bishop has three mentions of matches with the DNA of the descendants of *Elisha Enoch Abner Sr.* (more correctly: Elisha Abney Sr.). [Author's note: These lines are so named for DNA purposes. There is no proof that Elisha Abney Sr. was named Elisha Enoch Abner, nor that his wife's name was Mary Unity Calloway, although there is little doubt she is a Calloway due to DNA matches.] In one of those mentions she has 32 matches and 22 in another. Showing a match with Joshua Abney (but not his wife) is a good indication that she is of the Elisha Abney Sr. line…but NOT from any of the known sons (heretofore discovered, until the recent discovery of Pvt. Abner Abney). She also has three matches with the Mary Anderson Line [apparently a daughter of Mary Unity Calloway (1741-1827) and her first husband Jacob Anderson]. As Cousin Rachael noted, "Matching on the Anderson descendants is a good way to triangulate that we have the right mother!" As of this writing, Cousin Rachael is presently corresponding with the Russell descendants of Carter Co., TN and hopes to have DNA with that family will prove her descent from Alyda Russell, therefore Pvt. Abner Abney. A match with the Russell descendants of Carter County, Tennessee would be proof enough. She would match the (heretofore known) children of Elisha Abney Sr., but not their spouses; the wife of Elisha Abney Sr.; then the wife of Pvt. Abner Abney and that will be it! The report on the Russell DNA is very promising.

     Ellen "Gincy" Crenshaw, b.4 Apr 1806 TN; d.3 Jun 1860 Middletown, Des Moines Co., IA, at age 54; bur. Leuins Point Cem.
Known children of Leonard Jasper⁴ Abney Sr. and Ellen "Gincy" Crenshaw:
    3   i.   Lydia Ellen⁵, b.22 Dec 1826 Burlington, Des Moines Co., IA; m. James Madison Crawford.
          ii.   Celetha Ann, b.13 Nov 1828 Hancock Co., IL; m. David Jacob Hammer; d.18 Dec 1852 Des Moines Co., IA, age 24.
         iii.   Cynthia, b.ca.1829 IL; m. John Henderson in 1953.
          iv.   L. Frances, b. 27 Oct 1830 Hancock Co., IL. D.29 Dec 1842 Des Moines Co., IA, age 12; bur. Leuins Point Cem.
           v.   Mary N., b. 9 Nov 1834 and d. aft.1850 Des Moines Co., IA. bur. Leuins Point Cem., Middletown, Des Moines Co., IA.
          vi.   Elizabeth, b. 27 Jun 1837 Des Moines Co., IA; d.11 Dec 1856 Des Moines Co., IA, at age 19. bur. Leuins Point Cem.
         vii.   Franklin M., b. 30 Mar 1840 and d. 30 Jul 1858 Des Moines Co., IA, age 18. bur. Leuins Point Cem., Middletown.
    4   viii.   Leonard Jasper "Leon," b. 19 Dec 1842 IA; m1. Emeline Merimon Perry; m2. Rebecca Louisiana "Lou" Ennis.
          ix.   Gincy "Virginia", b. 22 Aug 1846 and d.12 Mar 1857 Des Moines Co., IA, at age 10; bur. Leuins Point Cem.

Generation Five

3. Lydia Ellen⁵ Abney (Leonard⁴, Abner³, Elisha², Abner¹)), b.22 Dec 1826 Burlington, Des Moines Co., IA. She m. James Madison Crawford on 9 Apr 1845 Burlington, Des Moines Co., IA; d.16 Sep 1858 Henry Co., IA, at age 31; bur. Leuins Point Cem., Middletown, Des Moines Co., IA.
     James Madison Crawford, b. 7 Apr 1825 Howard Co., MO. He m2. Julia Ann Lee in 1860; He d.13 Jan 1909 New London, Henry Co., IA, at age 83; bur. Burge Cem., New London, Henry Co., IA.
Known children of Lydia Ellen⁵ Abney and James Madison Crawford:
           i.   Leonard Jasper⁶, b. 5 Aug 1846 IA. He died on 21 Sep 1846 IA. bur. Leuins Point Cem., Middletown.
          ii.   Mary Jane, b. 12 Feb 1848 New London, Henry Co., IA. d.6 Aug 1914 Henry Co., IA, at age 66; bur. Burge Cem., New London, Henry Co., IA.
         iii.   Maylizbeth Iowa Belle "May", b. 2 May 1855 IA. D.5 Dec 1874 IA, age 19; was buried Burge Cem.

4. Leonard Jasper "Leon"⁵ Abney Jr. (UA) (Leonard⁴, Abner³, Elisha², Abner¹), b. 19 Dec 1842 IA. He m1. Emeline Merimon Perry on 16 Sep 1862 Adams Co., IL. He and Emeline Merimon Perry appeared on the census of 23 Jun 1870 Blackwater, Saline Co., MO. He m2. Rebecca Louisiana "Lou" Ennis on 2 Mar 1880 Saline Co., MO, but no issue. He and Rebecca Louisiana "Lou" Ennis appeared on the censuses of 26 Jun 1880 and 12 Jun 1900 Marshall, Saline Co., MO. He was living on 15 Apr 1910 with son-in-law, George Harrison, Marshall, Saline Co., MO. He died on 31 May 1913 Marshall, Saline Co., MO, at age 70. Bur. Ridge Park Cem., Marshall, Saline Co., MO.
     Emeline Merimon Perry, b. 1 Oct 1843 IA; d.15 Sep 1878, age 34; bur. Mount Olive Cem., Marshall, Saline Co., MO.

Known children of Leonard Jasper "Leon"*[5]* Abney Jr. (UA) and Emeline Merimon Perry:

     5   i.   Diton H.*[6]*, b. 9 Jul 1863 IL; m. Sallie Roe.

     6   ii.   Hattie Florence, b. 17 Oct 1865 IL; m. George Benjamin McClelland "Clell" Harrison.

           iii.   Claude Russell, b. 12 May 1871 MO. He m1. Elizabeth "Bessie" (n.n.) in 1893. They appeared on the census of 19 Apr 1910 Marshall, Saline Co., MO. He m2. Alma M. Murry. He and Alma appeared on the census of 2 Apr 1940 Kansas City, Jackson Co., MO. He d.12 Feb 1943 Kansas City, Jackson Co., MO, at age 71; bur. Ridge Park Cem., Marshall.

                 Elizabeth "Bessie" (n.n.), b. 25 Dec 1865 Scotland, UK; d.4 Jul 1923 Saint Joseph, Buchanan Co., MO, at age 57. She was bur. Ridge Park Cem., Marshall, Saline Co., MO.

                 Alma M. Murry, b. 23 Feb 1885 Springfield, Greene Co., MO; d.30 Dec 1963 Kansas City, Jackson Co., MO, at age 78; bur. Ridge Park Cem., Marshall, Saline Co., MO.

           iv.   Valora "Zina", b.1Apr 1878 Marshall, Saline Co., MO; m.8 Oct 1902 Robert Wallace Campbell. d.25 Jul 1949. in 1900 Saline Co., MO. Valora and Robert had issue: Sara Louise (1904-1986) and Robert Wallace Jr. (1908-1997).

Rebecca Louisiana "Lou" Ennis, b. 5 Apr 1834 MO. She m1. Benjamin Franklin Coffey in 1855; d.13 Jan 1908; bur. Ridge Park Cem.

Generation Six

5. Diton H.*[6]* Abney (Leonard*[5]*, Leonard*[4]*, Abner*[3]*, Elisha*[2]*, Abner*[1]*) m. Sallie Roe. He, b. 9 Jul 1863 IL. He died on 20 Sep 1937 Kansas City, Jackson Co., MO, at age 74; bur. Ridge Park Cem., Marshall, Saline Co., MO.

Sallie Roe, born on 21 Dec 1868 Pilot Grove, Cooper Co., MO; d.18 Jan 1956 Little Blue, Jackson Co., MO, age 87; bur. Ridge Park Cem.
Known children of Diton H.*[6]* Abney and Sallie Roe:

           i.   Herbert M.*[7]*, b.25 Dec 1888 MO. He died on 2 Nov 1918 Kansas City, Jackson Co., MO, age 29; bur. Ridge Park Cem.

6. Hattie Florence*[6]* Abney (Leonard*[5]*, Leonard*[4]*, Abner*[3]*, Elisha*[2]*, Abner*[1]*) was b. on 17 Oct 1865 IL. She m. George Benjamin McClelland "Clell" Harrison ca.1891. She and George Benjamin McClelland "Clell" Harrison appeared on the censuses of 13 Jun 1900, 15 Apr 1910 and 7 Jan 1920 Marshall, Saline Co., MO. D.19 Jul 1942 Marshall, Saline Co., MO, at age 76. Bur. Ridge Park Cem., Marshall, Saline Co., MO.

George Benjamin McClelland "Clell" Harrison was b. on 8 Jul 1862 OH. He died on 9 Oct 1959 at age 97. Bur. Ridge Park Cem., Marshall.
Known children of Hattie Florence*[6]* Abney and George Benjamin McClelland "Clell" Harrison:

           i.   Leonard V.*[7]* was b. in Sep 1891 MO.

           ii.   Abney. He died young, ca.1904-1905, at age 2.

     7   iii.   Florence Valora, b.1902 MO; m. Charles Thomas Berry.

Generation Seven

7. Florence Valora*[7]* Harrison (Hattie*[6]* Abney, Leonard*[5]*, Leonard*[4]*, Abner*[3]*, Elisha*[2]*, Abner*[1]*), b.in 1902 MO. She m. Charles Thomas Berry ca.1928 MO. She and Charles Thomas Berry appeared on the censuses of 5 Apr 1930 and 26 Apr 1940 Sweet Springs, Saline Co., MO. She died in 1989.

Charles Thomas Berry, b.in 1900 MO. He died in 1979.
Known children of Florence Valora*[7]* Harrison and Charles Thomas Berry all born MO:

     8   i.   Carolyn (gen.)*[8]*, b.1930; m1. Benjamin Bishop; m2. Robert Eugene Becker.

           ii.   Marjorie, b.1932 Sweet Springs, MO. m. (n.n.) and had issue.

           iii.   (n.n.), b.ca.1935. He died before 1940 MO.

Generation Eight

8. Carolyn*[8]* Berry (gen.) (Florence*[7]* Harrison, Hattie*[6]* Abney, Leonard*[5]*, Leonard*[4]*, Abner*[3]*, Elisha*[2]*, Abner*[1]*), b.27 Jun 1930 Sweet Springs, MO. She m1. Benjamin Bishop, son of Isak Fybisovitch of Russia (ca.1882-1961) and Esther Leitess of Belarus (1890-1926) [Note: Benjamin was not kin to the Kentucky Bishops]. She m2. Robert Eugene Becker (b.23 Feb 1924 Paonia, Delta Co., CO; d.17 Oct 2013 Monterey, CA), but no issue. She d.22 Dec 2015. Cousin Carolyn began working on her family history in the 1970's, and worked with the author for many years, even prior to his forming the *Centralized Abney Archives*. She was one of the author's inspirations for *the Abney Family Researcher* newsletter. The author posted her problem (Problem #3) in the very first issue of *the Abney Family Researcher* newsletter, attempting to discover the parentage of her ancestor, Leonard Jasper Abney Sr. Unfortunately, she and the author were unable to discover the connection in her lifetime. But working with her daughter, Rachael Bishop (below), the author was able to make breakthroughs in 2018 (locating the probable birthplace [Carter Co., TN] of her ancestor) and 2020 (locating the prime subject believed to be her ancestor, Pvt. Abner Abney). Cousin Carolyn was an excellent genealogist, working at a time when it was more difficult to find information, pre-computers. Much of the research materials of Cousin Carolyn were donated to the author by her daughter, Cousin Rachael. Studying Cousin Carolyn's notes, one can easily see that she was very organized and meticulous in her work. Cousin Carolyn deserves recognition as one of the finest examples of Abney family researchers and deserves her place of honor on page viii of this book.

Benjamin Bishop, b.10 Feb 1923 Bronx, NY; d.9 Mar 1994 Kingston, NY. [His father, Isak Fybisovitch was a painting contractor, who changed his surname to Bishop to make it easier to find him in the White Pages. Isak was b. ca. 1882 in Starodub, Bryansk Oblast, Russia; d.1961 NY]
Known children of Carolyn*[8]* Berry (gen.) and Benjamin Bishop:

     9   i.   Deborah "Rachael" (gen.)*[9]*, b.15 Dec 1959 Carmel, CA; m. & div. Matthew John Thomas "Matt" Kelly (b.13 Aug 1955 Bennington, VT) on 22 Apr 1994 in Hoosick Falls, NY.

           ii.   (dau.). She m. (n.n.) and had issue.

Generation Nine

9. Deborah "Rachael"*[9]* Bishop (gen.) (Carolyn*[8]* Berry, Florence*[7]* Harrison, Hattie*[6]* Abney, Leonard*[5]*, Leonard*[4]*, Abner*[3]*, Elisha*[2]*, Abner*[1]*), b.in 1959. She m. Matthew J.T. Kelly, but later divorced. Cousin Rachael, the daughter of a genealogist, picked up her mother's mantle on Abney family research in 2015. She attempted to contact the author on 13 Jan 2016 (to donate her mother's research materials to him), but her email went to Robert Hal Abney (Contributor to Vol. I) instead. R.H. Abney forwarded the email to the author on the same day, but the author didn't get around to reading it until over a year later and replied on 25 Feb 2017. They spoke on the telephone and via email. She began working with the author immediately and did, indeed, send him much of her mother's research materials. After many emails and telephone calls, the author, on 3 Jan 2018 while writing the ***Abney Family History Series, Vol. I***, he realized the connection between Leonard Jasper Abney Sr. and his father was probably

in Carter County, TN. Due to earlier information that Isaac Abney m. Dicy Russell in Carter County, TN (*Abney Supplement* by Hensell), the author mistakenly assigned Isaac as Leonard's father. Contributor of this current volume, John Michael Abney notified the author that Isaac's wife's surname was unknown; And furthermore, Isaac was never in Carter County. This sent the author back to the drawing board, at which time he realized Abner Abney (who m. Alyda Russell in 1803) was indeed a prime candidate. In the meantime, Cousin Rachael Bishop had taken another approach, namely DNA. Through her communications with, what the author calls "the DNA Community", she has proved she descends from Elisha Abney Sr. Interestingly, she matched the sons but not the wives. The author believes this is because she should match the DNA of the Russell family. As of this writing, she is waiting for additional information from the Russell DNA. The breakthrough that Cousin Carolyn (her mother) and the author strove for may finally be coming to fruition. Cousin Rachael should be an example for all genealogists to follow. She is sharing, empathetic, meticulous (like her mother) and tenacious. She continues to be a great pleasure with whom to work!

Children of Deborah "Rachael"[9] Bishop (gen-440) and Matthew John Thomas "Matt" Kelly:

  i.   Liam Benjamin Boone[10], b.19 Apr 1999 Charlottesville, VA
  ii. Ronan Isaac Morgan, b.20 May 2003 Charlottesville, VA

tertio addendum:

Descendants of Willis E. Abner (USArmy)

Generation Six of Abner Abney (ca.1711-ca.1751)

411.   Willis E.[6] Abner (USArmy; Elizabeth's twin) (William[5], Willis[4], Elisha[3], Elisha[2] Abney, Abner[1]), b.21 Oct 1890 Lillian, Perry Co., KY. He appeared in the census of 3 May 1910 Bowling, Perry Co., KY as *brother-in-law* liv. with Robert Bowling. He associated with (but never married) Elizabeth Bowling, d/o of Elisha Bowling and Ann Napier. He m. Sattie Barger, d/o of Henry D. Barger and Newark "Arkey" Gilbert, on 3 Jun 1918 Perry Co., KY. Willis d.7 Jun 1971 Hamilton, Butler Co., OH, age 80; bur. Rose Hill Burial Park, Hamilton, OH. (see page 123).

Elizabeth Bowling, b.30 Mar 1890 KY. She m. Justice Tucker Begley circa 1916. She d.2 May 1983 Cincinnati, Hamilton Co., OH, at age 93. She was bur. Spring Grove Cem., Cincinnati, Hamilton Co., OH.

Known child of Willis E.[6] Abner (USArmy) and Elizabeth Bowling:

2   i.   Gordon Willis[7], b. 13 Apr 1918 Bowlington, Perry Co., KY.

Sattie Barger, b. Jun 1893 Perry Co., KY. She d. on 12 Sep 1959 Hamilton Co., OH, at age 66; bur. Rose Hill Burial Park, Hamilton.

Known children of Willis E.[6] Abner (USArmy) and Sattie Barger:

  i.   Denver[7] was born on 6 Oct 1921. He died on 6 Sep 1983 at age 61. He was buried Rose Hill Burial Park, Hamilton.
  ii. Billie, b.5 Dec 1927 OH; He married Mattie Velma Callahan, daughter of David John Callahan and Hazel Dell Allen, in 1948.d. in Still, Dept. du Bas-Rhin, Alsace, France. He was buried Rose Hill Burial Park, Hamilton, Butler Co., OH.
       Mattie Velma Callahan was born on 8 May 1924. She died on 10 Oct 2008 at age 84. She was buried Desert View Mem. Park, Victorville, San Bernardino Co., CA.
3   iii. Pearl, b. 20 Feb 1931 Hamilton, Butler Co., OH; m. Donald Retherford.
  iv. Merlie was born in 1935. She died in 1971.
  v.   Rufus, b.17 Apr 1938 Butler Co., OH; d.17 Oct 1968 El Paso, El Paso Co., TN, age 30; bur. Rose Hill Burial Park.

Generation Seven

2.   Cpl. Gordon Willis[7]Abner (USArmy-WWII) (Willis[6], William[5], Willis[4], Elisha[3], Elisha[2] Abney, Abner[1]), b.13 Apr 1918 Bowlington, Perry Co., KY as Gordon Willis *Bishop*. At some point, he took his father's surname, *Abner*. He fought in the Pacific Theater in World War II. After the war, he m. Pauline Helen Becknell and had issue. He died on 24 Apr 1972 Cincinnati, Hamilton Co., OH, age 54; bur. Spring Grove Cem.

Known child of Cpl. Gordon Willis[2] Abner (USArmy-WWII) and Pauline Helen Becknell:

4   i.   Gordon Carlton[3], b. 11 Jan 1956 KY.

3.   Pearl[2] Abner (Willis[6], William[5], Willis[4], Elisha[3], Elisha[2] Abney, Abner[1]), b.20 Feb 1931 Hamilton, Butler Co., OH; m. Donald Retherford, s/o Emery Retherford and Florence Cope, on 11 Mar 1950; d.10 Jan 2005 Hamilton, Butler Co., OH, age 73; bur. Rose Hill Burial Park, Hamilton.

Donald Retherford, b.4 Sep 1931 Hamilton, Butler Co., OH; d.6 Feb 2013 Okeana, Butler Co., OH, age 81; bur. Rose Hill Burial Park.

Known children of Pearl[2] Abner and Donald Retherford are as follows:

  i.   Jennifer[3] married Paul McCollum.
  ii. Donald "Woody" married Diana (n.n.).
  iii. Holly married Dennis Jones.
  iv. Rebecca married (n.n.) Scott.
  v.   Jeffrey.

Generation Eight

4.   Gordon Carlton[3] Abner (Gordon[2], Willis[6], William[5], Willis[4], Elisha[3], Elisha[2] Abney, Abner[1]), b.11 Jan 1956 KY; Associated with C.A. Howard.

Known child of Gordon Carlton[3] Abner and Constance Anne Howard:

5   i.   Jerimy Sean (gen.)[4], b. 17 Dec 1976 Hamilton Co., OH; m. (n.n.).

Generation Nine

5.   Jerimy Sean[4] Abner (gen.) (Gordon[3], Gordon[2], Willis[1]), b.17 Dec 1976 Hamilton Co., OH. Cousin Jerimy began working with the author when the latter began writing this volume. He is active in what the author refers to as "the DNA Community" and has utilized DNA to discover his own ancestry. He is an active member of https://www.wikitree.com, where he holds badges: *DNA Project Member*, *Pre-1700 Certified*, and *Volunteer*. It has been a pleasure working with Cousin Jerimy to correct and expand the knowledge of his ancestry. He m. (n.n.) and had issue:

  i.   Eisel Carlton[5] was born on 15 Jan 2014.
  ii. Sophia Celeste was born on 23 Mar 2018.

quarto addendum:

Descendants of William Squire Abner

Generation Five of Abner Abney (ca.1711-ca.1751)

205. William Squire[5] Abner (Enoch[4], Enoch[3] Abney, Elisha[2], Abner[1]), b.4 Dec 1842 Clay Co., KY. He m. Julia Elizabeth Cottongim on New Year's Day, 1 Jan 1870. He and Julia Elizabeth Cottongim appeared on the censuses of 11 Jun 1880 and 6 Jun 1900 Clay Co., KY. He d.7 Feb 1917 Clay Co., KY, at age 74 and was bur. Paces Creek Cem., Garrard, Clay Co., KY. (see Chapter V, page 83.)

Julia Elizabeth Cottongim, b.7 Feb 1855 Clay Co., KY. She d.12 Jul 1932 Clay Co., KY, at age 77. Some say "Elizabeth" was her first name. But marriage license and headstone both read Julia as her first name.

Known children of William Squire[5] Abner and Julia Elizabeth Cottongim all b. Clay Co., KY (see Quarto Addendum for more issue):

	i.	Mary Jane "Jenny"[6], b. ca.1870 m. William Gray and had issue.
482	ii.	Lucy "Catherine," b. 18 Jan 1873; m. James Henry "Jim" Henson. (see Chapter V, page 134)
	iii.	Nancy Ann, b.10 Aug 1876. She d.3 Jan 1953 at age 76 and was bur. Paces Creek Cem., Garrard, Clay Co., KY. She had issue: George *Abner* who m. Chelsea Hooker and had issue.
483	iv.	John, b. May 1878; m. Bettie Lee "Betsie" Harris. (see Chapter V, pages 134-135)
	v.	Sarah Elizabeth, (1880-1971) m. William Gray and had issue.
	vi.	Martha, (1886-1975) m. Dan Harris and had issue.
1	vii.	Gilbert Garrard, (1887-1981) m. Vicie Gibson (1893-1971), which see below.
	viii.	Daughtery "Daw", (1890-1971) m. Mattie J. Turner and had issue.
	ix.	Emma, (1892-1967) m. Scott Loughran and had issue.
	x.	William Lawrence, (1900-1989) m. Ollie Estep (1910-1986) and had issue.
	xi.	Lillie N., (1904-1978) m. William M. Spurlock (1902-1983)

Generation Six

1. Gilbert Garrard[6] Abner (William[5], Enoch[4], Enoch[3] Abney, Elisha[2], Abner[1]), b.9 May 1887. He m. Vicie Gibson. He d.9 Jan 1981, age 93 and was bur. Manchester Mem. Gardens, Manchester, Clay Co., KY.

Vicie Gibson, b.2 Mar 1893; d.5 Mar 1971; bur. Manchester Mem. Gardens.

Known children of Gilbert Garrard[6] Abner and Vicie Gibson:

	i.	Georgia[7], (1912-2002)
2	ii.	Minnie, (1915-1980) m. Cloyd Smith (1909-1991), which see below.
	iii.	William G. "Bill", (1918-1987) m. Buena Brumley and had issue.
	iv.	Eva Belle, (1921-2005)
	v.	Chelsea, (1923-2008)

Generation Seven

2. Minnie[7] Abner (Gilbert[6], William[5], Enoch[4], Enoch[3] Abney, Elisha[2], Abner[1]), b.7 Jun 1915. She m. Cloyd Smith. She d.29 May 1980 and was bur. Manchester Mem. Gardens, Manchester, Clay Co., KY

Cloyd Smith, b.15 Dec 1909; d.14 Aug 1991; bur. Manchester Mem. Gardens.

Known children of Minnie[7] Abner and Cloyd Smith:

3	i.	1st Lt. Calvin Coolidge (USArmy)[8], (1932-1987) m. Janie Ruth Coffey (1930-2003), which see below.
	ii.	Joyce Katherine, b.7 Mar 1935. m. Seldon Webb (29 Nov 1934-10 May 2008) and had issue.
	iii.	Frances Yvonne, (8 Jun 1937-28 Dec 2011) m. Chester "Teddy" Webb (12 Nov 1935-26 Jun 1989) and had issue.

Generation Eight

3. 1st Lt. Calvin Coolidge[8] Smith (USArmy) (Minnie[7] Abner, Gilbert[6], William[5], Enoch[4], Enoch[3] Abney, Elisha[2], Abner[1]), b.14 Jun 1932 Clay Co., KY; He served in the U.S. Army ROTC (1950-1954), on Active Duty (1954-1956) and in the Reserves (1956-1959). He d.15 Nov 1987 Lincoln Co., KY; bur. Buffalo Springs Cem., Stanford, Lincoln Co., KY

Janie Ruth Coffey, b.27 Nov 1930 Rockcastle Co., KY; d.2 Dec 2003 Lexington, Fayette Co., KY; bur. Buffalo Springs Cem.

Known children of Minnie[7] Abner and Cloyd Smith (birth order unknown):

	i.	David Lee[9], b.28 Oct 1955; m1. Bertha Florence Fletcher (b.31 Mar 1953) and had issue: Richard Dale (b. Sep 1981); David m2. Candella Sue "Candy" Holmes (b.23 Oct 1967) and had issue: Matthew Aaron (b.1 Nov 1994), Logan Tyler (b.16 Apr 1996) and Solomon Lee (b.27 May 1999)
	ii.	Calvin Lynn, b.23 Oct 1953. He m1. Cathy Sue Yates and had issue: Jason Whitney (b.24 Nov 1977) and Amanda Lynn (b.10 Jan 1980; m. Brown and had issue); Calvin m2. Jan Hanley; He m3. Leticia Kay Brogle.
	iii.	Phillip Layne, b.1 Jan 1959; m. Connie Sue Beldon (b.1 Feb 1960) and had issue: Bradley Shane (b.7 Jan 1980; m. Lee Ann Kelley and had issue: Jackson Brady and Brayden Lucas). Phillip m2. Jaime Marie Parkey (b.25 Jan 1979 and had issue: Caleb Isaiah (b.16 Jun 2010).
	iv.	Jonathan Logan (gen.). He m. Delores (n.n.) which see on page 270.
	v.	Joseph Lanier, b.23 Aug 1968; m1. Gweneth Moore (d.29 May 1999) and had issue: Ashley Cheyenne (b.12 Mar 1993) and Robert Casey (b.11 Nov 1994). Joseph m2. Pamela Kay Rhoades (b.6 Apr 1968)
	vi.	Amy Lu, b. 28 Jul 1970; m. James Nicholas "Jim" Bastin (b.14 Jun 1974) and had issue: Tobias Michael (b.22 May 1999), Tyler Cal (b.5 Sep 2000) and Tinsley Brooke (b.24 Sep 2003).

Generation Nine

3. Jonathan Logan^9 Smith (Calvin^8 Smith, Minnie^7 Abner, Gilbert^6, William^5, Enoch^4, Enoch^3 Abney, Elisha^2, Abner^1), b.14 Oct 1965; He m. Dolores Martha Warburg (b.5 Mar 1965) and had issue. Cousin Jonathan made contact with the author just in time to add his family to this Addenda. He was kind enough to supply the information on his family line back to William Squire Abner. The author looks forward to working with Cousin Jonathan in the future.

Known children of Jonathan Logan^9 Smith and Dolores Martha Warburg:

     i.   Calvin Coolidge II^{10}, b.4 Aug 1990
     i.   Carson Franklin, b.4 May 1993
     i.   Clayton Abner, b.22 Dec 1994
     i.   Cassidy Logan, b.14 Nov 1997

Index to the Names, Titles, Books, Businesses, Organizations, &c.

To create an exhaustive index to this book would take another book. There are literally thousands of names and multiple names in these pages. The author, therefore presents herewith, an abbreviated index. Hopefully the reader will desire to delve more deeply and read this book cover-to-cover. For the sake of brevity, the pedigrees are not indexed. See the Table of the Pedigrees (page xxii). The plates (pictures of maps and documents) are near the center of this book (beginning with page A [after page 38], and indexed as pages A-L). Finally, if you are unable to find the name you seek, try searching for the parents' name(s), spouse's name, grandparents' name(s) or children's name(s). Moreover, search the *nomen nescio* at the end of the index. These are a few persons which the author did not know the surname. Happy hunting and *bonne chance!*

A

Abel
Wilhelmina...109
Abercrombie
Agnes...111
Abna
Ales Ridley "Abe" Jr...112
Ales Ridley "Abe" Sr...112
Alice...179
Alicia...228
Bernice...179
Beth...179, 228
Callie Eugenia...111
Cassandra...228
Denny Ray...179
Detie "Annie"...69
Sgt. Donald Eugene...179
Dorothy Belle...194
Emily Ophelia...111
Eula Mae...179
Sgt. George Michael (USAF-Nam)...179, 228
Harry Vernon...112
James Andrew "Jim"...69, 257
Jeffrey...194
Jennifer...228
Jerry Wayne...194
Jocie...179
Joel...179
Joey...228
Cpl. Joseph Elmer (USAAC-WWII)...179
Katie Dell...111
Lina...111
Lois Grace Dell (gen.)...111 (also see Duckett)
Lula...178
Mary Alice...179
Melissa...179
Michael Brandon...228
Minnie Elizabeth...111-112
Molly Lee...111
Nellie Jo...179, 228
Oline...111
Pamela K...228
Pat Eugene...179
Richard Wayne...179, 228
Robert James...111
Ronald Royce...179
Sarilee...179
Tommy James...179
Tonya...228
William James...179
Abna Family...250, 257
Abnee
Airis Victor "Trip"...194
Airis "Victor" Jr...131, 194
Airis "Victor" Sr...80, 131
Amanda...194
Amanda "Mandy"...74
Amanda Jane...73
Arch...74
Bessie...79, 131
Charles R. "Charlie"...53, 79
Clarence Thomas...53, 80
Claude...80, 132
Connor...235
Dorothy Belle...132
Edward "Eddie"...80
Effie D...53, 80
Ennis...79
Fannie...53
Herman...79
Homer...79
Jacob...235

Jackson...235
James C...53
Jerry Wayne...132
John Lincoln...80
John "Milton"...53
Justin...194, 235
Lee...53
Leslie...194
Lincoln "Link"...52-53, 257
Malcolm...80
Mary Frances...53
Mary J. "Tootsie"...132
Milton...53
Myrtle...132
Nona...79
Opal...80
Ora Lee...80
Robert S...53, 79
Rowena H...80
Russell...79
Serilda...79
Shy Conley...80, 132
Wanda Claudia "C"...132, 194
William Conley "Conn"...132, 194
William Henry...80
Zoe R...194
Abnee and Mussinon Company...53
Abner
Addie...118
Adolph...188
Alabama...52
Alabama (s/o Richard)...135
Alcy E...54
Allie C...109
Almira...75
Alphonsas...77
Amanda...85
Ambros...110
Amelia May...136
Anderson...123
Andrew "Cotton"...235
Andrew Jackson "Jack"...76
Anna Beatrice...197
Annie Mae...177-178
Archie Brown...231
Arrie...151
Arthur "Doc"...82
Arthur G...81
Arthur Thomas "Tom"...133
Arthur Vaughn...82
Arvilla...97
Asbury...118
Belle...196
Benjamin Heflin Hill...110
Bernice...81
Bernice M...190
Bert Hollis...191
Bertha...150
Bessie P...127
Beulah Irene "Boots"...193
Beulah Lenora...190
Beve "PJ"...196
Beverly "Beve"...85
Beverly P...72
Billie...123, 268
Billy Gene Sr...185
Boone...192
Breckinridge "Breck"...54
Bryson...120
Callie...54
Calvin Daniel...77
Carl...150
Carmel...194
Carolyn Faye...95

Carrie (gen.)...xiii (also see Ford)
Carrie Dell...110
Catherine......50
Cecil H...109
Charles Benjamin...118
Charles Kenneth...82
Charles Madison...78
Charlie...150
Charlie (s/o Edward)...189
Charles "Charley"...195
Charlie Frank...110
Charles Franklin...194
Charlie M...109
Chester...197
Chester Garfield...129
Cholista Maxine...193
Christopher (gen.)...xiii, 251
Churchill Cornelius...82
Clara E...75
Clara Eva...128
Clarence...118
Cleveland Robert...119
Clistie...151
Clyde...117
Colby...73
Cora...137
Cyntha...73
D.F....230
Dan B. "Bo"...190
Daniel...196
Cpl. Daniel (USArmy-WWII)...184
Daniel B. (USArmy-WWII)...188
Daniel Boone...76
Daniel Boone (USArmy-WWII)...119
Daniel Bryan...252
Daniel Isaac...77
Daniel P...117
Daniel P. "Dan"...134
David...72
David Francis...183
David Wayne...233
Della...119
Della "Dellie"...131
Dennis Charles "Goat"...233
Denver...123, 268
Docie...117
Dora E...135
Dora Lee...125
Dora Mae...129
Dorothy...189
Dory...83
Dory (d/o Robert)...116
Dow...131
Easter...72
Edna...196
Edward "Ed"...189
Edward "Ned"...123-124
Eisel Carlton...268
Elbert...186
Electer I...109
Eli Cleveland...76
Elisha (s/o Menan)...42
Elisha (s/o James)...128
Pvt. Elisha (UA, s/o John Abney Sr.)...43
Elisha (s/o John A.)...50
Elisha (s/o Richard)...78
Elisha Jr....xvii, 1, 19-20, 22-24, 26, 33, 35, 42, 257, 259-260, 265
Elisha B...51
Elisha B. (s/o Willis)...75
Elisha Morris...125
Eliza (d/o Willis)...74
Eliza J...73
Eliza Jane...74

Please send documented additions and corrections to: R.R. Abney Jr.   email:
1213 Indiana St.   rrabneyjr@hotmail.com
Chalmette, LA 70043-5401

The First Edition of this book was completed on November 14, 2020
and published on November 22nd, 2020
birthday of the author's beloved grandfather,
Robert "Ralph" Abney
(22 Nov 1889-15 Apr 1964)

Computer programs used in the creation of this book:
The Master Genealogist v.8.09 Gold Edition ®   ThumbsPlus Pro v.7 ®
Microsoft Word (M.S. Office 2019) ®   Paint (MicroSoft Windows 10 ®)
combinepdf.com   Scanning for Kodak Verite 55 Plus ®
doPDF 10 ® by Softland

℘ostscript ⚜ Special Thanks

I, the author, R.R. Abney Jr., wish to extend a special note of thanks to the following Abney family members:

First and foremost, my biggest thanks and undying love to my loving wife:

Mary Grace Lazo Mercader Abney

…for the patience you have displayed as I spent many hours, days, weeks and months writing this book. I also appreciate your kind assistance in editing, copying, scanning, research, and most of all, your support. I know how difficult it was for you, as I seemingly ignored you. You shared in my sacrifice in order to get this book published, and I recognize you for that. You are appreciated and loved more than you know.

A special thanks to contributor and originator of the idea of this book, *Cousin*:

Morgan Floyd Abney

…at whose suggestion this book came to fruition. If not for you, Cousin Morgan, this book would not exist. Your love of family has inspired me. Your love of country has delighted me. Thank you for your military service! I am proud to call you cousin! You have my respect and my love. I extend my special thanks to you; And, I am certain, the thanks of all the descendants of Abner Abney of Virginia are extended to you, as well.

Thanks to my graphics artist, *Cousin-in-law*:

Stacie Kyomi Arai Abney

…my graphics artist extraordinaire for the beautiful work on the covers of both volumes of the Abney Family History Series (Vol. I, Abney: Ancestry and Genealogy of Dr. Abraham Abney of Virginia, 2nd Edition; and Vol. II, Abney, Abner, Abna, Abnee: Ancestry and Genealogy of Abner Abney of Virginia. Your work is now, as always, appreciated.

Thanks to contributor and proofreader, *Cousin*:

John Michael Abney

…for his relentless research, unselfish sharing and most of all…Proofreading! For those of you who do not realize it, proofreading is an invaluable (and difficult) part of publishing a book. Cousin John also has a knack for finding lost sources! Thank you, Cousin John for the hours you spent helping the Abney, Abner, Abna and Abnee family have a more accurate account of their family history.

Thanks to contributor, *Cousin*:

Judy Lewis Vietri

…for her many years of excellent work on the sons of Elisha Abney Sr., especially on Menan Abner. Very few have taken on the burden of unraveling this difficult line. You have succeeded brilliantly where few have attempted to tread. The descendants of Menan Abner and all the other Elisha Abney Sr. lines appreciate you.

Thanks to contributor, *Cousin*:

Sandrea Kay "Sandy" Abner Cook

…for continuing and expanding the research begun by Cousin Judy Vietri. Cousin Sandy has discovered some wonderful information which shows, in this author's opinion, by greater weight or preponderance of the evidence, that Richard Abner was a son of Menan Abner and Agnes Bowling. Thanks, Sandy, for sharing all your wonderful work and documentation.

Thanks to contributor, *Cousin*:

Grace Lynette Crouch Prater

…for being a wonderful cousin and genealogist. I began working with Cousin Grace at the turn of the century, and it has been my pleasure and my privilege. Thank you for all your input into this book.

Thanks to:

Sherry Lynn Baker

Founder and first president of the Owsley County Historical Society and founder and past president of the Owsley County History and Genealogy Society. Thank you for your wonderful knowledge of Owsley County history (which has been important to correctly reporting many of the lines in this book), and more specifically for your interesting and factual stories about the Abner families, Baker families, and Woods families.

Finally, a special thanks to:

Deborah "Rachael" Bishop

…for being tenacious, methodic, and willing to share. Cousin Rachael, you are a "chip off the ole block." I enjoyed working with your darling mother, who was amongst those who inspired the *Abney Family Researcher* newsletter. When I work with you, I feel as though your mother is still with us, at least in spirit. You are so much like her. Thank you for your wonderful research. Surely you have made your mother proud!

THANKS, EVERYONE!

Raymond Robert "Bobby" Abney Jr.

is pleased to present volume II of the Abney Family History Series:

Abney, Abner, Abna, Abnee

Ancestry and Genealogy of
Abner Abney of Virginia

By: Raymond Robert "Bobby" Abney Jr.
including independent research of contributors
Morgan F. Abney, John M. Abney, Sandy Abner Cook, Judy L. Vietri, Grace C. Prater

The *Abney Guru* has done it again! With the success of the two editions of the first volume of the **Abney Family History Series** (*Abney: Ancestry and Genealogy of Dr. Abraham Abney of Virginia*) the author, Raymond Robert Abney Jr., also known as Robert, Bobby, and RR, was requested by Cousin Morgan Abney to write the second Abney volume on the family of Abner Abney (youngest brother of Dr. Abraham Abney). Much has changed in the way this family was first reported, and this book reflects these changes, including many corrections and thousands of additions to all previously published works. This book is a must-have for every Abney, Abner, Abna and Abnee descendent and Abney library.

The author now presents the most complete, documented and factual account of the Abner Abney branch of the Abney Family (Abney, Abner, Abna and Abnee surname variations) from its humble roots in the 18th century British Colony of Virginia to today's Abney families spread from Virginia and Kentucky throughout the United States.

Abney, Abner, Abna, Abnee subtitled: *Ancestry and Genealogy of Abner Abney of Virginia* (first edition)
Pricing: $60.00   price includes handling/packaging/shipping (book rate) [Suggested Retail Price: $85]

(note: Vol. I of the Abney Family History, which includes Abner Abney's ancestry, can also be ordered on this form.)

Please copy order form. Do not remove from book. Thanks!

Please type or print clearly

Order Form:

Name: _____

Address: _____

City: _____

State & Zip Code: _____

Tel: (_____)_____

Email: _____

[] Check if you are purchasing this book for someone else.

Mail to (if different from purchaser):

Name: _____

Address: _____

City: _____

State & Zip Code: _____

Volume II:

_____ **copies of the current** *Abney, Abner, Abna, Abnee* **book (Vol. II), ($60 each) in Case Bound (hard cover)**

Volume I:

_____ copies of the *Abney* book (**Vol. I**), beautiful second edition (sale price $48 each) in **Case Bound** (hard cover)

_____ copies of the *Abney* book (**Vol. I**) first (collector's) edition (sale price $35 each) in **Perfect Bound** (soft cover)

Payment Options:

Check or Money Order (payable to R.R. Abney Jr.)	PayPal.com
Enclosed is a [] check or [] money order for: $_____	[] paid @ paypal.com – rrabneyjr@hotmail.com $_____
send order form to: Abney, Abner, Abna, Abnee Book – A 1213 Indiana St. Chalmette, LA 70043-5401	After paying through PayPal, send order form to: rrabneyjr@hotmail.com with the subject line as: Abney Book Order ← (Or mail to the address on the right.)

www.ingramcontent.com/pod-product-compliance
Lightning Source LLC
Chambersburg PA
CBHW080801300326
41914CB00055B/992